THE OFFICIAL®
PRICE GUIDE TO
ANTIQUES and COLLECTIBLES

THE OFFICIAL®
PRICE GUIDE TO
ANTIQUES AND COLLECTIBLES

FIFTEENTH EDITION

ERIC ALBERTA
AND ART MAIER

HOUSE OF COLLECTIBLES • NEW YORK

Copyright © 1997 by Eric Alberta and Art Maier

All rights reserved under International and Pan-American Conventions.

HC This is a registered trademark of Random House, Inc.

Published by House of Collectibles
201 East 50th Street
New York, NY 10022

Distributed by Ballantine Books, a division of Random House, Inc., New York, and simultaneously in Canada by Random House of Canada Limited, Toronto.

http://www.randomhouse.com

Manufactured in the United States of America

ISSN: 1050-6144

ISBN: 0-876-37960-9

Cover design by Min Choi

Top left to right: Pair of Mandarin and Panther Lamps, painted plaster, mkd. *Continental Art*, 1950, ht. 33", $200–$300; Countertop Butter Churn, c. 1915, $70–110; Columbia Family Scale, c. 1910, $18–28; Eggbeater, c. 1900, $25–35; New Space Station, Horikawa, c. 1965, $700–$1000.

Bottom left to right: *Annette and the Mystery at Smugglers' Cove*, Whitman TV Book, $12–$14; *A Day in the Jungle*, Little Golden Book, without dust jacket, $18–25; *Monkees Who's Got the Button?* Whitman TV Book, $18–$22; Country Quilt, $200–$300; Oak Spindleback Chair with bent wood arms, c. 1910, $70–$110.

Cover photography © George Kerrigan.

Fifteenth Edition: March 1997

10 9 8 7 6 5 4 3 2 1

To Neil and Pauline Alberta,
Frederick and Ruth Maier

Contents

Introduction

Collectors will remember 1996 as the year of the Jackie O. sale. Everyone wanted part of the $34,000,000 estate offered at Sotheby's. But those prices are not part of the world that the rest of us inhabit. It will be a long time before another Tiffany's tape measure will sell for $50,000.

We think the biggest news of the year is the Internet. More and more collectors and dealers are posting their wants and offerings on various electronic bulletin boards. Listings at America Online include Homer Laughlin china, cookie jars, Depression glass, Hummels, pens, and Swatch watches. The Internet is not just for buying and selling. The give and take of queries and answers posted by diverse members of the collecting community provide an excellent pooling of knowledge.

The 1970s are back in fashion. It's not just the clothes we see modeled by the superstars and the music we hear on the radio. The toys and memorabilia of that era are now more sought after and more available, as more and more baby boomers search the attics of mainstream America for plastic gold.

Ten "hot spots" in the market are:
- Fire King Jadeite restaurant glassware
- Architectural still banks
- Rock 'N' Roll record albums
- Early automobiles
- Transportation memorabilia
- Figural doorstops
- Schoenhut animals
- Advertising character items
- Space toys
- Early Americana

Most prices we monitored are not blowing through the roof. Collecting in the nineties remains a hobby, not an investment portfolio. The majority of low-end items—under $100—have hardly moved at all. High-end items—over $2000—have reflected their increasing scarcity with better performances.

TIPS FOR COLLECTING

• In most areas, condition is everything. The difference between perfect and almost perfect can be the difference between $100 and $1000 or more! If an item needs restoration, know what that will cost before you buy. Also remember that a restored antique is generally worth much less than an unrestored piece in pristine condition.

• Just because something is rare, doesn't mean that it is valuable.

• Do your homework! The information age has created an explosion of material on all subjects and topics. Taking advantage of a public library's book search service is well worth the time. Books are often expensive, but a $50 book can often save you from many $100 mistakes.

• Pay attention to fakes and average pieces. Learning the ordinary teaches about the extraordinary.

• What goes up often comes down. Amazing prices are often reported, but a market that is slowly ebbing away will rarely be reported in the press.

• Always be sure whether or not the seller is providing a guarantee of authenticity. If he or she is, get it in writing; if not, know what you're buying!

TIPS FOR BUYING AT AUCTION

• Always thoroughly examine every piece before you bid on it. If you haven't examined it, DON'T BID.

• Always set your limit for yourself before you start bidding. Don't let auction frenzy drive your bidding.

• Make sure the auctioneer can see your bid. If you bid with just the nod of a head, the auctioneer may be selling to the woman in front of you.

• And yes, if your nose itches, you can scratch it without buying a fifteen-foot chandelier; just don't stare the auctioneer in the eye while you're doing it.

SELLING

A dealer must make his profit to stay in business and many businesses are expensive to run. The difference between a dealer's buying price and his selling price must cover the rent, the car, and everything else. Hence, the selling price of an item may be only a fraction of the price tagged in the window (or quoted in this guide!), especially for inexpensive items.

TIPS FOR SELLING AT AUCTION

• Choose your auction house by the service they offer, not the estimate they quote. You can't deposit an estimate in the bank.

• Don't be greedy. An item with a high estimate and reserve scares away many potential buyers. And once an item has failed to sell (or "bought in"), it is harder to sell the next time.

• Understand your contract:
  - What is the commission?
  - Who pays for photographs?
  - Who pays for insurance?
  - What is the reserve (or minimum price) set at?
  - Is there a "buy-in" fee for items that fail to sell?
  - When is payment made?

PRICES

Collecting is not the same as investing. If the value of your collection increases with time and rising markets, consider it a bonus. Most collections do not make money, they absorb it.

The prices in this book represent the average price that an informed buyer will pay a knowledgeable and specialized dealer for these items.

The antiques and collectibles market is not the stock market. Prices do not tick up and down on a daily basis.

FAKES

The ever increasing availability of cheap labor and expensive machines has

resulted in the production of countless fakes in all fields. Most dealers are honest, but many honest dealers get fooled. We advise:
 • Learn to recognize tool marks and which tools were used when.
 • Learn to use a black light. (*The Black Light Book* is available from *Antique & Collectors Reproduction News* - see our list of publications)
 • Visit museum gift shops and other places where high quality reproductions are sold.
 • Learn the styles of the times. Many fakes give themselves away because they just don't "feel right."
 • Subscribe to *Antique & Collectors Reproduction News* (see our list of publications). It's a great monthly report on fakes and reproductions that have appeared in the collectibles market.
 • If it's too good to be true, it's probably not true.

USING THIS GUIDE
Sections are laid out by category.
Abbreviations are used throughout. Some that appear most often are:

Amer.-American	len.-length
attrib.-attributed	mah.-mahogany
bkgd.-background	mtd.-mounted
c.-circa	orig.-original
cent.-century	pr.-pair
dec.-decoration	pt.-pint
dia.-diameter	ptd.-painted
dr.-drawer	qt.-quart
ea.-each	rect.-rectangular
Eng.-English	sq.-square
'-feet (linear)	uph.-upholstered
ftd.-footed	w.-width or wide
ht.-height or high	w/-with
kt.-karat	WWI, WWII-World War II and II
"-inches	

We have often abbreviated States of the Union by their two-letter postal code (e.g. Maine-ME, Massachusetts-MA, etc.). The term "sight" preceding a measurement refers to visible image.

COLLECTING RELATED PUBLICATIONS
Hundreds of periodicals on antiques and collectibles exist, some for very specialized areas. Here are some of our favorite general news publications:

A B Bookman's Weekly
70 Outwater Lane
Garfield, NJ 07026
(201) 772-4282

Antiques & The Arts Weekly
("Newtown Bee")
Box 5503
Newtown, CT 06470
(203) 426-3141

Antique & Collectors
Reproduction News
Box 71174
Des Moines, IA 50325
(800) 227-5531.

Antique Toy World
Publisher and editor Dale Kelley
P.O. Box 34509
Chicago, IL 60364
(312) 725-0633

Comic Buyer's Guide
700 East State Street
Iola, WI 54990

Dolls The Collector's Magazine
P.O. Box 1972
Marion, OH 43305

Doll Reader
Hobby House Press
900 Frederick Street
Cumberland MD, 21502

Goldmine Magazine
700 East State Street
Iola, WI 54990

Maine Antique Digest (MAD)
911 Main Street
Box 645
Waldoboro, ME 04572
(207) 832-7534

Today's Collector
700 East State Street
Iola, WI 54990

Toy Collector and Price Guide
700 East State Street
Iola, WI 54990

Toy Shop
Circulation Dept. AUE
700 East State Street
Iola, WI. 54990
(800) 258-0929

Unravel the Gavel
PO Box 171
Ctr. Barnstead, NH 03225
(newspaper covering New
England's country auctions)

Advertising Memorabilia

Successful advertising draws people to a store or a product. Artists who design advertisements compete with thousands of other images that bombard consumers. Advertisements must get attention, inform, and allure. Advertising often reflects the views and desires of society at a given time. Antique advertising has been an active collecting area for years. Andy Warhol and others blurred the boundry between commercial art and fine art. People recognized that dynamic advertising is good art. In 1990 a Campbell's Soup sign depicting the American flag sold for over $90,000 (no connection to Warhol). Although similar examples have since sold for less, it focused attention on the field and attracted a larger audience.

The diversity of advertising is astounding. Collectors can concentrate on eras, products, companies, signs, tins, trade cards, watches, premiums, dolls, figural displays, toys, etc. In recent years interest has increased in post-World War II advertising. Adding these collectors to the pre-war collectors creates a huge and growing market. The prices listed below are for items in excellent or better condition. Although some wear is expected on older items it should not be substantial or interfere with the visual appeal of the item. Condition for newer items are near mint. The other section in this book that contains advertising and promotional material is Toys and Playthings. For further reading see *Hake's Guide to Advertising Collectibles*, Ted Hake, Wallace Homestead, Radnor, PA, 1992; *Advertising Character Collectibles*, Warren Dotz, Collector Books, Paducah, KY, 1993; and *Huxford's Collecting Advertising*, Sharon and Bob Huxford, Collector Books, Paducah, KY, 1993.

Texaco Standee, c. 1950, $150-$200. —Item courtesy of Jim Glaab's Collector's Showcase. Eveready Battery Counter Top Display, c. 1935, $250-$500. —Photo courtesy of Phillips Auctioneers.

	LOW	HIGH
Alka Seltzer Calendar, 1942	$ 45	$ 65
Ambassador Scotch Pitcher, white, 1960s	9	12
American Agriculturist Sign, embossed tin, 1920s, 6.5" x 13"	30	40
Armstrong Tire Ashtray, clear, round, red decal, 1950s, dia. 5.75"	12	16

	LOW	HIGH
Arrow Trailer Rentals Sign, embossed U.S. map, 1940s, 14" x 18"	$ 65	$ 95
Aunt Jemima and Chef Potholder Hangers, 1948, ht. 11"	32	42
Aunt Jemima Breakfast Club Mirror, round, 1935	45	70
Aunt Jemima Plastic Syrup Pitcher, 1950s, ht. 5"	45	65
Axelrod the Basset Hound Plastic Bank, 1960s, ht. 8"	30	40
Ayers' Cherry Pectoral Trade Card, girl on front, ailments on back	4	6
Ayers' Sarsaparilla Trade Card, 2 women w/ children and dog on front	4	6
Bacardi Rum Ashtray, white china, 1960s, dia. 4.5"	8	12
Baranger Studios Automaton, The Seven Dwarfs, 1940s, ht. 18"	2000	3000
Barnum's Animal Crackers Sign, commemorative tin, 1979, dia. 4"	6	8
Bear Brand Hosiery Cardboard Box, 1915, 5" x 7"	70	90
Beck's Brewing Tray, picture of a buffalo, 1950s, dia. 13"	50	70
Beefeater Gin Figural Composition Display, 1960s	80	100
Bell Plastic Telephone, 1950s, len. 7"	40	50
Bert and Harry Piel Metal Statue, 1955, ht. 9"	50	80
Bert and Harry Piel Vinyl Store Display, 1965, ht. 11.5"	40	60
Bert Parkes Spiedel Watch Band Animated Display, 1950s, ht. 21"	800	1100
Bickmore Shaving Cream Die-Cut Cardboard Sign, man shaving, 1940s	80	140
Big Boy Nodder, 1965, ht. 8"	100	150
Blatz Beer Bar Display, 3 baseball players, 1960s, ht. 16"	150	200
Blatz Beer Display, 3 baseball players, 1968, ht. 11"	100	150
Borden's Milk Truck, 1940s, len. 9"	300	500
Bromo Seltzer Tip Tray, 1930s	60	90
Bud Man Ceramic Beer Stein, 1989, ht. 8.5"	20	30
Budweiser Ashtray, glass, round, 1950s, dia. 5"	8	10
Budweiser Beer Booklet, 20 pp., 1965, 5" x 7"	7	9
Budweiser Sign, plastic w/ light-up bottle, 1960s, 5" x 12"	45	75
Buffalo Pitts Calendar, Indian and Buffalo, 1911	320	430
Bull Dog Malt Liquor Decal, 1940s, sq. 7"	8	10
Bull Durham Bullfighters Sign, cardboard, 1920s, 14" x 22"	500	800
Bunny Bread Sign, red and white embossed tin, 1940s, 3.5" x 28"	60	90
Burma Shave, set of 3 wooden signs, 1930s, 10" x 3.5"	300	530
C.I. Heed and Co. Trade Card, telephone series, testimonials on reverse	6	10
Calumet Baking Powder Thermometer, can and child, 1920s, ht. 21"	300	500
Camel Cigarettes Ashtray, round tin, logo in center, 1950s, dia. 3.5"	8	12
Camel Cigarettes Booklet "Know Your Nerves," 1934, 3" x 4"	10	17
Camel Cigarettes Calendar, 1963	18	22
Campbell Kid Silverware, 3-piece set, 1940s	35	45
Campbell Kids Chef Rubber Squeeze Doll, 1950, ht. 7"	60	90
Canadian Club Sign, for a ceiling fan, round, 1930s, dia. 7"	30	45
Carnation Milk Tip Tray, 1930s	45	75
Ceresota Flour Match Safe, boy slicing bread, 1915, ht. 5.5"	200	300
Charlie the Tuna Telephone, 1980s, ht. 10"	60	80
Charlie the Tuna Vinyl Squeeze Doll, 1975, ht. 7.5"	40	50
Cherry Smash Porcelain Syrup Dispenser, 1910, ht. 16"	800	1400
Chesterfield Cigarette Tin, 1940s	15	22
Chevrolet Motor Cars Calendar, 1920, ht. 14.5"	300	500
Chivas Regal Ashtray, Wade china, triangular, 1950s, len. 11.5"	8	12
City Club Crushed Cubes Tobacco Upright Pocket Tin, 1935, ht. 4.5"	175	225
Clanky Chocolate Syrup Container, 1965, ht. 10"	25	35
Colonel Sanders Plastic Bank, 1965, ht. 12.5"	30	50

	LOW	HIGH
Colonel Sanders Plastic Nodder, 1965, ht. 7"	$50	$ 70
Columbia Bicycles Trade Card, cyclists at night, 1910	15	25
Corbys Stir Container, plastic, 1950s, ht. 6"	20	25
Coronet Waiter VSQ Brandy Store Display, 1955, ht. 19"	125	175
Crackle Puppet, 1984, ht. 4"	8	12
Cream of Kentucky Heart-Shaped Thermometer, plastic, 1950s, ht. 10.5"	50	70
Crest Sparkle Telephone, 1980s, ht. 11"	20	30
Dandy Bread Door Handle, metal, loaf and slices, 1940s, 3" x 13"	50	70
De Laval Cream Separator Figural Match Holder, 1915, ht. 6.5"	120	180
De Soto Auto Banner, red, gold, and black fringed silk, 1951, 38" x 66"	500	900
Diamond Dyes Tin and Wood Case, children, girl w/ camera, 1910, ht. 30"	700	1300
Dino the Dinosaur Green Plastic Bank (Sinclair), 1965, len. 4"	18	22
Dino the Dinosaur Inflatable Toy, 1965, ht. 12"	20	30
Dino the Dinosaur Soap, in original box, 1964, len. 3 1/2"	8	12
Dobbins' Soap, 6 Trade Cards, Shakespeare's "Six Ages of Man"	20	25
Dr. Jayne's Expectorant Poster, 1895, 13.5" x 29"	500	800
Dr. Mile's Remedies Calendar, girl and boy, 1908	300	500
Dr. Pepper Bottle Opener, cast iron, 1930s	20	30
Dr. Pepper Calendar, 1950	25	45
Dr. Pepper Thermometer, bottle and clock, "10, 2 and 4," 1930s, ht. 17"	220	340
Dr. Pepper Tin Sign, red and white, 1950s, 6" x 18"	60	80
Dutch Boy Cardboard Sign, "wet paint" picture of boy, 1930s, 6" x 9"	80	140
Dutch Boy Figural String Holder w/ Bucket, 1915, 13" x 30"	2000	2500
E. Robinson's and Sons Beer Tray, factory scene, 1895, dia. 13.5"	400	600
E.R. Durkee and Co. Spices Wooden Box, elephants and India, 1895, 12" x 7"	60	90
Elsie the Cow China Mug (Borden), 1940, ht. 2.75"	35	45
Elsie the Cow Lighted Dial Electric Clock, 1948, dia. 14"	300	400
Elsie the Cow Vinyl Bank, 1970s, ht. 9"	60	80
Equitable Life Insurance Calendar, 1904	100	150
Ernie the Keebler Elf Vinyl Squeeze Doll, 1975, ht. 7"	12	15
Esky *Esquire Magazine* Cardboard Display, 1960s	100	150
Esso Glass Bank, 1940s, ht. 5"	30	40

Below left to right: Cunard Lines Travel Agency sign, $1200-$2000. Hamilton Watch Animated Store Display, c. 1950, $1200-$2200.
—Photo courtesy of Phillips Auctioneers.

	LOW	HIGH
Esso Oildrop Red Plastic Bank, 1960s, ht. 7"	$ 70	$ 90
Esso Tiger Pitcher and 6 Glasses, 1950s	50	75
Esso Tiger Plastic Bank, 1960s, ht. 8.5"	30	40
Eveready Safety Razor Clock, man shaving dial, 1915, ht. 28"	2000	3000
Eveready Cat Plastic Bank, 1972, ht. 6"	25	35
Falstaff Beer Pocket Protector, 1960s	4	6
Falstaff Beer Tray, Sir Falstaff holding bottle and tray, 1940s, dia. 12"	60	80
Firestone Tire Ashtray, Texas Central Expo, 1936	20	30
Florida Orange Bird Plastic Bank, 1972, ht. 5"	18	22
Florida Orange Bird Plastic Nodder, 1972, ht. 7"	20	30
Ford Gramophone/Postcard, Car, Santa, and R. Clooney, 1956	10	15
Ford Tractor Sign, masonite, 1940s, 11" x 21"	30	50
Fred Fossil Resin Statue Store Display	75	125
Freese's Cementing Glue Trade Card, 1 vertical ill., 1885	6	10
Funny Face Walkers, 1970, ht. 3"	60	80
General Electric Radio Wooden Jointed Drum Major Figure, 1935, ht. 18"	1000	1500
General Electric Refrigerator-Form Clock, 1930s, ht. 9"	100	150
Glenfiddich Pitcher, black, 1970s	8	12
Gold Dust Die-Cut Double-Sided Hanging Banner, 1900, len. 15.5"	5000	7500
Grape Nuts Tin Sign, girl and Saint Bernard, 1910, 20" x 30"	1000	1500
Hall's Vegetable Sicilian Hair Renewer Trade Card, testimonials on reverse, portrait of girl on front	7	9
Hamm's Bear Ceramic Bank, 1980, ht. 11"	15	20
Hammer's Ice Cream Tray, 1920s	50	70
Happy Foot Composition Store Display, 1950, ht. 12"	300	500
Harry Hood (Milk and Juice) Vinyl Figure, 1970s	60	80
Hazard Smokeless Powder Calendar, boy and dog, 1910, 17" x 17"	180	230
Heinekin Dutch Boy w/ Bottle Figural Display, 1960s, ht. 15"	80	120
Heinz Vinegar Sign, bottle and salad, 1910, 12" x 22"	160	220
Helping Hand Clock, 1985, ht. 6"	25	35
Hines Cognac Bottle Store Display, 1940s, ht. 20"	25	35
Hires Root Beer *Magic Story* Booklet, 1934	10	15
Hires Root Beer Mug, boy w/ mug, "Join Health and Cheer," 1900	150	250
Hires Root Beer Syrup Dispenser, hourglass shape, 1912, ht. 14"	400	600
Hires Root Beer Thermometer, bottle shape, 1930s, ht. 7"	100	160
Hires Root Beer Tin Chalkboard, 1940s, 10" x 20"	180	220
Hires Root Beer Tray, 1910	200	500
His Man Figural Cologne Bottle, 1960, ht. 6"	40	60
Hody's Peanut Butter Tin Pail, kids on peanut seesaw, 1925, ht. 3.5"	150	200
Honey Moon Tobacco Upright Pocket Tin, 1935, ht. 4.5"	200	250
Horseford's Self-Rising Bread Preparation Trade Card, 1900	3	5
Hotpoint Wooden Jointed Figure, 1938, ht. 15"	800	1300
Hoyt's Cologne Trade Card, picturing large frog, 1883	3	5
Hoyt's German Cologne Paper Sign, boy and girl writing on wall, 1895, 20" x 29"	1000	1500
Hush Puppy Dog Bank, 1970s, ht. 8"	25	35
Icee Bear Vinyl Bank, 1970s, ht. 8"	25	45
Iron Fireman Metal Figural Ashtray, 1940s, ht. 5"	70	90
Ivory Soap Cardboard Sign, little girl washing dolls' clothes, 1915, 17" x 24"	800	1000
Jersey Cream Blotter, children, 1920s, 4" x 9"	20	30
Jersey Cream Tray, 1915, dia. 12"	150	200

Left to right: B-1 Lemon-Lime Store Display, c. 1960, $100-$150; Columbia Ring Animated Display, c. 1950, $140-$220; Mohawk Carpet Animated Display, c. 1948, $300-$500. —Photo courtesy of Phillips Auctioneers.

	LOW	HIGH
Johnnie Pfeiffer Plaster Store Display, 1955, ht. 8"	$ 60	$ 80
Johnny Walker, Man in Top Hat Store Display, 1950s, ht. 16"	100	150
Jolly Green Giant Sprout Vinyl Squeeze Doll, 1975, ht. 6.5"	20	30
Jolly Green Giant Vinyl Squeeze Doll, 1975, ht. 9.5"	35	45
Jumbo Trade Card, P.T. Barnum's circus elephant	6	10
Kellogg's *Funny Jungleland Moving Pictures Book*, 1930s, 6" x 8"	35	55
Ken-L-Ration Cat and Sugar and Creamer, plastic, 1955, ht. 3"	25	35
Kool-Aid Dancing Pitcher Man, 1990, ht. 9"	20	30
Kool-Aid Pitcher Man Mechanical Bank, 1970, ht. 7"	40	60
Labatt's Figural Vinyl Display, 1960s	50	75
Lamb Knit Figural Store Display, 1930s, ht. 15"	400	600
Latest Novelty Trade Card, Secret Motto Ring, engravings of ring in corners, 1870s	15	20
Little Sprout Talking Stuffed Doll, 1970s	40	60
Lovell and Covel Candies Tin Pail, house, 1925, ht. 3"	120	200
Lovell and Covel Candies Tin Pail, Little Red Riding Hood, 1925, ht. 3"	90	150
Lovell and Covel Candies Tin Pail, Peter Rabbit, 1925, ht. 3"	180	220
Lucky Strike Cardboard Sign, 1935, 13.5" x 18"	100	150
Lucky Strike Cigarette Tin, 1930s	25	35
Mack Bulldog Hood Ornament, 1965, ht. 3"	20	30
Mammoth Brand Peanuts, 10-lb. can, 1925, ht. 11"	250	350
Maryland Club Mixture Upright Pocket Tobacco Tin, building in circle, 1918, ht. 4"	300	400
McCormick Paper Calendar, 1911, 13" x 20"	150	250
Menehune of Hawaii Plastic Bank, 1972, ht. 9.5"	40	60
Menita Bread Tin Sign, The Lone Ranger, 1948, 24" x 36"	400	600
Michelin Man (Bibendum) Plastic Ashtray, 1935, ht. 4.5"	100	150
Michelin Man (Bibendum) Vinyl Statue, 1980, ht. 14"	30	40
Miller High Life Tip Tray, 1940s, len. 4"	30	40
Miss Curity Plastic Store Display Figure, 1955, ht. 19"	100	150
Mobil Double-Sided Pegasus Gas Globe, 1920s, dia. 18"	300	400
Moxie Horse/Rider Wheeled Vehicle, 1920s, 6" x 9.5"	1200	1800
Mr. Bubble Plastic Figural Bank, 1970s, ht. 7"	35	45

	LOW	HIGH
Mr. Clean Plastic Figural Bottle, 1960s, ht. 12"	$ 80	$ 100
Mr. Clean Vinyl Doll, 1960s, ht. 8"	150	200
Mr. Peanut Peanut Butter Maker, 1970s, ht. 12.5"	35	45
Mr. Peanut Store Display, plastic head, top hat lid, 1970s, ht. 12.5"	50	75
Mr. Peanut Wooden Jointed Doll, 1930s, ht. 9"	300	400
Mr. Tomato Talking Alarm Clock (Heinz), 1980s, ht. 9.5"	200	250
Mr. Wiggle Rubber Hand Puppet (Jello), 1965, ht. 6"	70	90
Nature's Remedy-Vegetine The Blood Purifier Trade Card, girl	4	6
Neco Wafers Paper Sign, 1925, 12" x 20"	200	400
Old Angus Scotch Whiskey Figural Display, 1960s, ht. 14"	80	100
Old Crowe Plastic Store Display, 1965, ht. 5.5"	20	30
Old Dutch Cleanser Booklet, 1930s, 3" x 6"	9	12
Old Milwaukee Beer Sign, plastic, woman in Victorian clothing, 1960s, 15" x 22"	25	45
Opia Cigar Tip Tray, woman in veil, 1910, dia. 4.25"	150	250
Orange Crush Cardboard Sign, pinup girl, 1950s, 12" x 15"	45	65
Orange Crush Sign, 1940s	70	90
Orange Crush Tray, oval w/ Diana and stags, 1930	100	150
Pabst Blue Ribbon Beer Tray, "Finest Beer Served Anywhere," 1940s, dia. 13"	30	40
Pabst Blue Ribbon Store Display, motorist in horseless carriage, 1950s	70	90
Page's Glue Trade Card, humorous, men stuck to bench w/ maker's product, printed by Bufford, 1890	10	15
Palmolive Soap Mirror, Dionne Quintuplets and doctor	30	60
Patton's Ice Cream Tray, oval logo, glass and dish of ice cream, 1920s, sq. 13.5" .	90	140
Pepsi-Cola Bottle Opener, cast iron, 1930s	12	18
Pepsi-Cola Can Bank, 75-year commemorative, 1973	8	12
Pepsi-Cola Embossed Tin Sign, "Here's Health," 1920, 28" x 20"	300	500
Pepsi-Cola Tin Sign, "America's Biggest Nickel's Worth," 1930, 10" x 30" ..	300	500
Pepsi-Cola Tip Tray, Pepsi Lady, blue, 1908, 4" x 6"	600	900
Philco Transistor Man Figure, 1960s, ht. 5"	60	80
Pizza Hut Pete Plastic Bank, 1970s, ht. 7.5"	25	40
Planters Peanut Jar, raised peanuts on sides, 1910, ht. 13"	300	400

Left to right: Slinky Animated Store Display, c. 1956, $700-$1200. Marilyn Monroe Playing Cards Store Display, c. 1955, $300-$500; cards sealed in the pack $100-$150 per pack. —Photo courtesy of Phillips Auctioneers.

	LOW	HIGH
Ponds Extract Co. Trade Card, cures on reverse, 1900	$ 3	$ 5
Pop Puppet, 1984, ht. 4"	8	12
Poppin' Fresh Telephone, 1985, ht. 14"	70	90
Poppin' Fresh Vinyl Squeeze Doll, 1975, ht. 6.5"	8	10
Prince Albert Tobacco Upright Pocket Tin, 1960s, ht. 4.5"	8	10
Punchy Hawaiian Punch Plastic Telephone, 1980, ht. 11"	80	120
Putnam Dyes Tin Cabinet, horses and riders, 1920s, 19" x 15"	120	180
Quaker Oats Figural Plastic Mug, 1970s, ht. 4"	18	22
Quik Bunny Plastic Mug, 1980s, ht. 4.5"	7	9
R.C.A. Nipper Dog Store Display, 1920s, ht. 36"	800	1200
R.C.A. Radiotron Wooden Jointed Doll (M. Parrish design), 1935, ht. 16"	900	1400
Raid Bug Clock Radio, 1980s, ht. 7"	100	150
Raid Bug Plastic Telephone, 1980s, ht. 9"	100	150
Raid Bug Remote Control Robot, 1980s, ht. 12"	150	250
Raid Bug Wind-Up Walking Toy, 1980s, ht. 4"	35	45
Rainer Beer Tray, woman in ruffled hat, 1903, dia. 13"	300	500
Red Goose Plaster Statue, 1945, ht. 5"	30	40
Red Goose Shoes Figural String Holder, 1920s, ht. 28"	2000	2500
Reddy Kilowatt Lightning Bolt Plastic Statue, 1950s, ht. 6"	180	230
Reddy Kilowatt Wooden Jointed Figure, 1950s, ht. 12"	380	480
Rheingold Metal Stir Container, 1950s, ht. 8"	25	35
Rising Sun Stove Polish Trade Card, delivery boy stealing kiss from house-wife, 1890s	6	10
Riverside Tires, owl and tire plaster statue, 1960s, ht. 5"	75	95
Ronald McDonald Cloth Doll, 1970s, ht. 16"	18	22
Ronald McDonald Plastic Telephone, 1985, ht. 10"	60	80
Rough on Rats Trade Card, E.R. Wells, "A Box Will Keep Your House Free"	8	12
Royal Baking Powder Booklet, "Making Biscuits," 1927	10	15
Royal Baking Powder Booklet, "Comical Cruises of Captain Cooky," 1926	25	35
Rumford Baking Powder Booklet, 1920s	8	12
Scrubbing Bubble Toy Brush, 1990, ht. 3"	4	6
Seagrams Figural 7 (Seven Crown) Lamp, plastic, 1950s	25	35
Seagrams Seven Crown Bottle Store Display, 1940s, ht. 18.5"	30	40
Sears and Roebuck Tip Tray, lady and city scene, 1920s	60	80
Shakey Pizza Chef Ceramic Bank, 1970s, ht. 6"	30	40
Sinclair Motor Oils Paper Sign, dinosaur, 1940s, 28" x 42"	200	350
Sir Walter Raleigh Smoking Tobacco Canister, 1950s	12	18
666 Liquid Medicine Fan, 2 children on horse, 1935	25	35
Smokey the Bear Plastic Bank, 1970s, ht. 8"	25	35
Snap Puppet, 1980s, ht. 4"	8	12
Sparkle Plastic Telephone, 1980s, ht. 11"	30	40
Speedy Alka-Seltzer Button, 1960s, dia. 1.25"	30	40
Speedy Alka-Seltzer Figural Display, 1970s, ht. 8"	300	450
Speedy Alka-Seltzer Vinyl Squeeze Toy, 1960s, ht. 5.5"	175	225
Spuds MacKenzie Plastic Lamp, 1980s, ht. 15"	70	120
Squires Pig Tin Sign, 1920s, 20" x 24"	600	900
Squirt Bottle Opener, cast iron, 1930s	20	25
Squirt Ceramic Bank, 1950s, ht. 8"	150	200
Squirt Composition Store Display, 1950s, ht. 13"	400	5000
Stork Club Wooden Display Vase, 1950s, ht. 7.5"	150	250
Stroh's Bohemian Cardboard Sign, top-hatted man, 1910, 15" x 32"	200	250

	LOW	HIGH
Sunoco Blue Gas Globe, 1935, dia. 16"	$ 200	$ 300
Sure Shot Tobacco Counter Tin, Indian w/ bow, 1915, 10" x 15"	400	600
Tagament Tommy Figure, 1985, ht. 5"	20	30
Tappan Chef Painted Plaster Figure, 1955, ht. 8"	50	75
Tarrant's Seltzer Aperient Trade Card, little girl and sewing basket, cures on reverse	3	5
Texaco Fire Chief Helmet, plastic, 1960s	70	90
Texaco Oil Can Bank, 1 qt., 1970s	15	20
Tiger Brand Chewing Tobacco Counter Cannister, 1900, ht. 12"	200	300
Times Square Tobacco Upright Pocket Tin, 1935, ht. 4.5"	250	350
Tony the Tiger Vinyl Squeeze Doll, 1975, ht. 7.5"	35	45
Trix Rabbit Vinyl Squeeze Doll, 1977, ht. 9"	30	40
Trout-Line Burley Cut Tobacco Upright Pocket Tin, 1925, ht. 3.75"	300	400
Tydol Oil Man License Plate Holder, 1935, ht. 7"	40	50
Union Metallic Cartridge Co. Calendar, boy w/ shotgun, 1901, 13" x 26"	800	1300
Uniroyal Naugahyde Nauga Stuffed Doll, 1960s, ht. 10"	25	35
Utica Club Tray, lady's hand holding a glass of U.C., 1940s, dia. 12"	50	70
Wards Vivovim Bread Thermometer, smiling toddler, 1915, ht. 21"	200	300
Waterbury Watch Co. Trade Card, multi-panel cartoon story, 1884	20	25
Weiner Mobile, pop-up Oscar, 1955, ht. 4.5"	150	200
Weiner Mobile, no pop-up Oscar, 1980, ht. 4.5"	12	17
Westinghouse Tuff Guy Plaster Statue, 1950s, ht. 4.5"	75	100
Whistle Soda Tin Blackboard, adorned w/ gnomes, 1915, 20" x 27"	250	350
White Horse Whiskey Ashtray, figural horse head, 1930s	70	110
White Rock Mineral Water Sign, tin, 1910, 4" x 12"	180	220
White Rock Tip Tray, 1920s	60	90
Wiedmann Brewing Rookwood Stein, raised eagle design, 1930s, ht. 5"	200	400
Wieland's Lager Tin Tray, Indian princess, 1900, dia. 13"	500	700
Willie the Kool Penguin Plaster Statue, 1955, ht. 4.5"	90	130
Willimantic Thread Trade Card, pictures Brooklyn Bridge, Forbes Lith. Co.	10	12
Worcester Salt Trade Card, in the form of eyeglasses w/ eye holes at center, 1885	15	20
World's Largest Fruithouse Trade Card, tall building, 1885	10	15
Wrigley's Gum Streetcar Sign, Wrigley arrow boy, 1920s, 10" x 20"	100	150
Yeast Foam Poster, little girl, tin-rimmed, 1920s, 10" x 14"	100	150
Yuengling Brewery Calendar, 1903, 20" x 27"	700	900

Left to right: Hohner Harmonica Illuminated Display, c. 1935, $600-$900. —Photo courtesy of Phillips Auctioneers. Valvoline Cup Grease Tin, c. 1920, $80-$100.—Item courtesy of Jim Glaab's Collector's Showcase.

African American Memorabilia

For the past century, the depiction of African Americans has been a reflection of this country's fitful growth as a free nation. Although many of the images are derogatory and degrading, both black and white collectors have found them historically interesting. A nation learning from its mistakes will find endless education here.

	LOW	AVG.	HIGH
Advertising Photograph, life-size cutout, Magic Johnson .... $ 60		$ 75	$ 90
Advertising Photograph, life-size cutout, Michael Jordan 50		. 60	70
Aunt Jemima Doll Bell, polka-dot dress and bandanna w/cotton apron marked "Nashville, Tenn.," ht. 4.25" 110		135	160
Aunt Jemima Syrup Pitcher, wearing red dress and bandanna, ht. 5.25" 60		78	90
Bandanna, leaders of Haiti, cotton,1890, 26" x 28" 1200		1500	1800
Bisque Figurine, 2 children sharing potty seat, black child on left, white child on right, c. 1890, ht. 4" 100		120	140
Black Cloth Rag doll, blue overall-style pants with red and white checkered shirt, yarn hair, button eyes, ht. 20" 270		340	410
Black Cloth Rag Doll, wearing black overalls, gray felt hat, ht. 14" 100		130	160
Blackface Cast-Iron Pencil Sharpener, insert pencil on side of face and shavings discharge through lips, ht. 1.5" 120		145	170
Black Panther Magazine, May 19, 1963, Malcolm X issue 140		180	220
Book, Cab Calloway, hi de ho 140		175	210
Book, Garrison, William Lloyd, personal copy of *Juvenile Poems For the Use of Free American Children of Every Complexion* 3000		4000	5000
Book, Harris, Joel Chandler, first edition copy of *Uncle Remus, His Songs and His Sayings* 680		850	1020
Cakewalk poster, from Danbury Opera House, 1866 620		775	930
Chad Valley Bank, smiling black gentleman on front of round bank, wearing brown checkered jacket, ht. 5" 250		310	370
Cream of Wheat Chef Cookie Jar, black man in chef's outfit, Japan, 1940s, ht. 10" 1600		2000	2400
Face Spoon, silver, handle is black man's face, inscribed "Sunny South," Jacksonville, Fla., marked sterling, bears Shiebler emblem, len. 4" 90		110	130
Gold Dust Advertising Postcard, depicts black children cleaning large globe 40		50.	60
Harlem Globetrotters Coca Cola sign, 1952 880		1100	1320
"How Ink is Made" figurine, black child sitting in tub of black ink, by Shelley China, ht. 3.5" 70		190	110
Josephine Baker Playbill 30		40	50
"Mammy" Pin Cushion Tape Measure Doll, original box, Japan, ht. 5.5" 90		110	130
Mammy Still Bank, dressed in red dress w/ white apron and kerchief, ht. 5" 90		117	140
Martin Luther King Memorial Fan, paperboard on wooden stick, ht. 12" 30		34	40
Trixy Molasses Pin, black person w/ red bow tie and braids w/ yellow ribbon, dia. 3.5" 40		50	60

Autographs

The personal mark of the famous and revered has always attracted collectors. The following abbreviations are used: *ALS* -Autograph Letter Signed (a letter hand-written by the person who signed it), *LS* -Letter Signed (a letter typed or written out by another person), *DS* -Document Signed (a signed document), *PhS* -Photo Signed, *Cut Sig.* -Cut Signature (a signature cut from a letter, autograph book, or other source).

We have divided this section into Artists, Authors, Civil War Figures, Entertainmers, and Presidents.

Artists

	ALS		Cut Sig.	
	Low	High	Low	High
Benson, Frank W.	$ 36	$ 150	$ 8	$ 12
Ceilini, Benvenuto	7500	20,000	700	900
Cezanne, Paul	800	5000	60	80
Chagall, Marc	340	400	44	56
Church, Frederick S.	220	280	24	30
Corot, Camille	170	500	34	44
Crulkshank, George	50	300	24	34
DaVinci, Leonardo	70,000	120,000	3500	4500
Degas, Edgar	750	5000	120	150
Eastlake, Sir Charles L.	50	200	16	20
Forain, Jean	24	350	6	8
Forrester, Alfred Henry	56	68	6	8
Gauguin, Paul	1300	10,000	44	56
Gibson, Charles Dana	50	250	14	20
Gifford, R. Swain	16	150	4	8
Landseer, Sir Edwin	44	300	6	10
Lawrence, Sir Thomas	240	300	12	16
Lear, Edward	350	5000	24	28
Leslie, C.R.	80	100	8	12
Matisse, Henri	280	5000	40	60
Michelangelo, Buonarroti	30,000	100,000	2500	3200
Modigilani, Amedee	1400	5000	140	200
Monet, Claude	500	5000	24	30
Pissarro, Camille	300	2000	50	66
Raphael, Sanzlo	70,000	300,000	3500	5000
Rembrant van Riyn	50,000	300,000	8000	12,000
Remington, Frederick	300	2500	60	100
Renoir, Pierre A.	700	5000	120	170
Rossetti, Dante G.	200	2500	60	80
Rouault, George S.	300	1000	50	70
Rubens, Peter Paul	18,000	50,000	1400	2000
Sargent, J.S.	220	3000	24	30
Sully, Thomas	220	2000	24	30
West, Benjamin	340	5000	24	30
Whistler, James A.M.	240	5000	34	44
Wyeth, N.C.	140	1000	14	20

Marc Chagall

Authors

Authors' letters have always been a favorite of collectors. But just like the novels and poems they wrote, content counts! A letter refusing a dinner invitation is worth a fraction of a letter discussing alternative endings of a play.

Examples: Alger, Melville, Wolfe, Lowell, Eliot, and Hemingway.

	LS		ALS	
	Low	High	Low	High
Alcott, Louisa May	$ 500	$ 700	$ 1000	$ 1400
Alger, Horatio	60	80	400	550
Bryant, William C.	150	190	300	380
Burnett, Frances H.	34	44	60	70
Burroughs, John	70	100	100	500
Curtis, George W.	28	36	32	40
Dana, R.H., Jr.	84	106	200	300
Davis, Richard H.	16	20	28	36
Fiske, John	20	28	24	30
Hale, Edward E.	28	36	44	56
Harris, Joel C.	200	300	600	5000
Hawthorne, Nathaniel	300	4000	1000	10,000
Hemingway, Ernest	500	5000	1000	10,000
Hubbard, Elbert	36	46	70	80
Irving, Washington	100	2000	1000	10,000
Kilmer, Joyce	350	450	800	1000
Longfellow, H.W.	100	500	150	3000
Lowell, James R.	50	150	100	500
Melville, Herman	3000	15,000	5000	20,000
Mencken, H.L.	50	250	100	500
O'Neill, Eugene	200	5000	1000	5000
Pierpont, John	60	80	120	160
Porter, W.S. (O. Henry)	1600	2000	1600	2000
Sikes, William W.	24	44	60	70
Stockton, Frank	80	100	170	220
Stoddard, R.H.	60	80	120	160
Stowe, H.B.	100	500	500	5000
Tarkington, Booth	350	450	500	700
Taylor, Bayard	80	100	160	200
Thoreau, Henry D.	3000	5000	5000	10,000
Thorpe, Thomas B.	80	100	160	200
Wolfe, Thomas	500	1500	1000	5000

Civil War

Not everyone recognizes the officers and heroes of the Civil War. But a sharp eye can still pluck these nuggets from the piles of old letters and documents that still turn up in attics. Condition, content, and date can drive the value above (or below) the ranges noted here.

	ALS		DS		Cut Sig.	
	Low	High	Low	High	Low	High
Ammen, Rear Adm. Daniel . $ 35	$ 42	$ 18	$ 23	$ 4	$ 6
Anderson, James P. 36	43	18	23	5	6
Anderson, Brig. Gen. Robert .. 60	75	25	33	7	11
Andrew, John A. 18	23	8	10	3	4
Augur, Christopher C. 14	16	4	7	1	2
Badeau, Adam 14	16	4	7	1	2
Banks, Nathaniel P. 50	65	18	23	8	11
Beauregard, G.T. 275	350	90	110	14	19
Benton, James G. 10	12	8	9	2	3
Berdan, Hiram 43	50	14	18	4	6
Bernard, John G. 18	22	8	10	3	5
Bocock, Thomas S. 20	26	8	10	2	3
Bonham, M.L. 14	18	8	10	2	3
Bragg, Braxton 42	50	18	23	8	11
Buchanan, Thomas M. 125	175	38	50	20	27
Burnside, A.E. 90	120	33	45	12	18
Butterfield, Daniel 20	28	10	15	4	7
Cleburne, Patrick R. 240	300	100	140	35	55
Corse, Brig. Gen. John M. 14	20	8	11	3	5
Cosby, George B. 20	28	10	15	5	7
Crittenden, Thomas 20	28	10	15	5	7
Custer, George A. 850	875	250	330	60	90
Dahlgren, Rear Adm. J. 33	40	20	28	5	7
Davis, Jefferson 1100	2000	325	475	50	80
Dix, Gen. John A. 45	60	20	28	5	7
Early, Jubal A. 90	130	50	70	8	3
Farragut, Adm. D.G. 275	350	125	200	15	22
Floyd, John B. 20	29	8	13	3	5
Forney, Maj. Gen. J.H. 20	29	8	13	3	5
Foster, John G. 17	23	8	12	3	5
Fremont,Gen. J.C. 35	43	10	15	6	9
French, Samuel G. 40	56	10	15	6	9
Gardner, Franklin 25	35	8	13	3	5
Garnett, Robert S. 32	43	11	18	3	5
Gilmore, Gen. Quincy A. 25	34	8	11	3	5
Gladden, Adley H. 70	95	21	30	10	15
Gordon, John B. 32	42	10	14	3	5
Gorgas, Josiah 32	42	10	14	3	5
Halleck, H.W. 45	60	22	29	5	8
Hancock, W.S. 35	43	15	20	3	5
Heintzelman, S.P. 22	28	10	14	3	5
Hooker, Gen. Joseph 34	42	12	19	5	8
Humphries, A.K. 34	42	12	19	5	8
Ingraham, Duncan N. 40	58	15	20	5	8

	ALS		DS		Cut Sig.	
	Low	High	Low	High	Low	High
Iverson, Alfred .... $ 35	$ 45	$ 15	$ 20	$ 3	$ 5
Jackson, "Stonewall" 2800	4500	700	1200	150	200
Jackson, W.H. 36	47	15	20	6	9
Johnston, Joseph E. 45	60	20	32	6	9
Jones, David R. 95	130	45	70	15	22
Kearny, Philip 200	275	70	95	20	28
Lee, FitzHugh 32	45	15	20	3	5
Lee, Robert E. 500	900	200	325	80	110
Logan, Maj. Gen. John A. 26	35	15	10	4	7
Longstreet, James 26	35	10	15	4	7
Luce, Adm. Stephen 33	40	10	15	4	7
Lyon, Gen. Nathaniel 110	150	45	70	20	28
Mahone, William 33	40	10	15	4	7
McArthur, John 40	50	15	22	4	7
McClellan, Geo. B. 58	75	22	32	6	9
Mason, James M. 275	350	80	120	20	29
Meade, George G. 45	58	18	26	6	10
Meagher, Thomas F. 26	36	10	15	4	7
Mosby, John S. 26	36	10	15	4	7
Pickett, George E. 300	415	115	170	18	25
Porter, Adm. David 110	170	50	75	8	12
Porter, FitzJohn 45	65	15	23	5	8
Porter, Horace 33	42	15	23	3	5
Price, Sterling 40	60	20	29	5	8
Pryor, Roger A. 47	75	20	29	5	8
Ransom, Robert, Jr. 80	100	22	30	5	8
Reagan, John H. 33	47	15	22	4	7
Richardson, J.B. 33	47	15	22	4	7
Ripley, R.S. 38	50	15	22	4	7
Rosecrans, W.S. 80	110	22	28	8	12
Scott, Winfield 200	300	80	130	15	20
Seddon, James A. 110	150	35	50	7	12
Seward, William H. 150	210	47	65	10	15
Sherman, William T. 220	300	70	100	15	22
Sigel, Franz 37	50	15	22	4	7
Sneed, John L.T. 40	62	22	28	5	8
Stanton, Edwin M. 130	220	45	85	10	15
Stephens, Alexander H. 80	110	23	32	5	8
Sumner, Charles 80	110	23	32	5	8
Taylor, Richard 100	140	35	50	8	11
Thomas, Maj. Gen. G.H. 150	200	47	62	11	15
Thompson, M.J. 110	140	35	50	8	11
Toombs, Robert 90	110	22	28	5	9
Twiggs, David E. 40	65	15	22	4	7
Waterhouse, Richard 50	75	15	22	5	8
Welles, Gideon 75	110	22	28	5	8
Wheeler, Gen. Joseph 50	75	22	28	5	8
Winslow, Adm. John A. 75	110	30	39	5	8
Wool, John E. 50	75	22	28	3	5

Entertainers

Who signed that photo? As big stars received more requests for signed photos than they could supply themselves, they (or their studios) hired secretaries to sign photos for them. In the case of Jean Harlow, her mother signed most of the photos picturing this star.

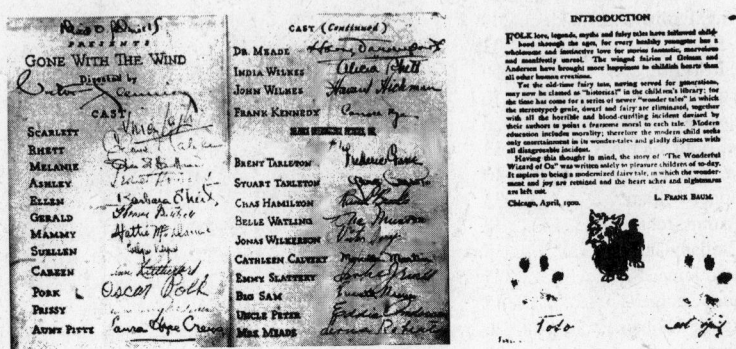

Left: Autographed "Gone With the Wind" script with signatures of the entire movie cast sold for $13,200 at auction; Right: "The New Wizard of Oz Book" with the paw prints of Toto on the introduction, sold for $20,900 at auction. One-of-a-kind rarities of cultural icons are worth vastly more than the sum total of the signatures involved. — Photos courtesy of Christie's East.

| | PhS | | Plain Sig. | |
	Low	High	Low	High
Alda, Alan	$ 14.00	$ 22.00	$ 3.00	$ 4.50
Allen, Gracie	70.00	100.00	8.00	11.00
Allen, Steve	2.30	3.70	1.00	1.50
Allen, Woody	7.50	12.00	2.00	4.00
Allyson, June	4.80	6.60	1.00	1.40
Altman, Robert	8.00	11.00	1.60	2.00
Ameche, Don	4.30	6.00	1.00	1.50
Andress, Ursula	5.80	10.00	1.00	1.50
Andrews, Julie	2.90	4.50	1.00	1.40
Arden, Eve	4.60	5.80	1.00	1.50
Arkin, Alan	5.70	9.00	1.00	1.50
Arness, James	2.90	4.40	1.00	1.50
Arthur, Beatrice	4.50	6.00	1.00	1.60
Arthur, Jean	4.60	6.00	1.00	1.60
Astin, John	2.00	3.80	1.00	1.50
Bacall, Lauren	13.00	21.00	2.30	4.00
Backus, Jim	3.00	4.50	1.00	1.50

	PhS		Plain Sig.	
	Low	High	Low	High
Ball, Lucille	$ 9.40	$ 13.60	$ 1.00	$ 1.40
Ballard, Kaye	3.60	5.00	1.00	1.60
Balsam, Martin	3.00	4.60	1.00	1.60
Bancroft, Anne	6.00	9.00	1.00	1.40
Bardot, Brigitte	23.80	31.00	3.00	4.30
Barr, Roseanne	9.00	12.00	2.00	3.00
Barry, Gene	4.50	6.00	1.00	1.50
Barrymore, Drew	6.00	9.00	1.00	1.50
Bartholomew, Freddie	6.00	9.00	1.00	1.50
Bates, Alan	6.00	8.00	1.00	1.60
Bates, Kathy	4.00	7.00	1.00	1.50
Baxter, Anne	2.90	4.70	1.00	1.50
Bean, Orson	2.90	4.00	1.00	1.50
Beatty, Warren	7.40	10.00	1.60	2.00
Bel Geddes, Barbara	3.00	4.40	1.00	1.50
Bellamy, Ralph	4.70	6.00	1.00	1.60
Belushi, Jim	5.00	8.00	1.00	1.50
Belushi, John	270.00	350.00	40.00	50.00
Benny, Jack	50.00	75.00	7.00	11.00
Bergen, Candice	6.00	9.00	1.00	1.50
Bergman, Ingmar	14.40	22.50	1.60	2.30
Bergman, Ingrid	80.00	120.00	9.00	13.00
Berle, Milton	7.50	11.50	1.60	2.00
Bernardi, Hershel	3.00	4.40	1.00	1.60
Bill Cosby	12.00	15.00	3.00	5.00
Bishop, Joey	3.00	4.40	1.00	1.60
Bisset, Jacqueline	4.50	6.00	1.00	1.50
Bixby, Bill	4.50	6.30	1.00	1.40
Black, Karen	2.80	4.50	1.00	1.60
Blair, Linda	7.00	12.00	1.50	2.50
Blondell, Joan	3.00	4.40	1.00	1.50
Bloom, Claire	8.50	13.40	1.60	2.00
Blyth, Ann	2.80	4.30	1.00	1.60
Bogarde, Dirk	4.50	6.00	1.00	1.60
Bogart, Humphrey	180.00	250.00	18.00	26.00
Bogdanovich, Peter	14.40	21.30	1.60	2.30
Boone, Richard	15.70	22.00	1.60	2.30
Booth, Shirley	7.00	10.00	1.50	2.40
Borge, Victor	4.40	6.00	1.00	1.50
Borgnine, Ernest	4.40	6.00	1.00	1.50
Bosley, Tom	3.00	4.50	1.00	1.50
Boyer, Charles	14.00	22.00	1.60	2.70
Boyle, Peter	4.50	6.00	1.00	1.60
Branagh, Kenneth	5.00	8.00	1.00	1.50
Brando, Marlon	30.00	47.40	4.00	7.50
Brazzi, Rossano	3.00	4.30	1.00	1.50
Brenner, David	3.00	4.50	1.00	1.50
Bridges, Beau	3.00	4.50	1.00	1.40
Brolin, James	2.50	4.00	1.00	1.50
Bronson, Charles	6.30	9.00	1.00	1.50

	PhS		Plain Sig.	
	Low	High	Low	High
Brooks, Mel	$ 7.00	$ 11.00	$ 1.00	$ 1.40
Brynner, Yul	4.50	5.70	1.00	1.50
Bujold, Genevieve	4.40	6.00	1.00	1.60
Burnett, Carol	4.00	6.00	1.00	1.40
Burr, Raymond	4.50	6.00	1.00	1.50
Burstyn, Ellen	5.00	8.00	1.00	1.50
Burton, Richard	65.00	100.00	7.00	12.00
Buttons, Red	3.00	4.70	1.00	1.50
Buzzi, Ruth	3.00	4.40	1.00	1.50
Caan, James	7.40	10.00	1.50	2.00
Cabot, Sebastian	5.30	9.00	1.00	1.50
Caesar, Sid	4.50	6.00	1.00	1.40
Cagney, James	25.00	35.00	4.70	7.00
Caine, Michael	4.40	5.80	1.00	1.50
Calhoun, Rory	2.90	4.70	1.00	1.50
Cantor, Eddie	60.00	85.00	12.00	15.00
Cardinale, Claudia	9.00	12.00	1.50	2.30
Carlisle, Kitty	7.80	3.70	1.00	1.50
Carney, Art	4.50	6.00	1.00	1.50
Caron, Leslie	6.00	9.00	1.00	1.60
Carradine, David	10.00	15.00	1.50	2.00
Carradine, John	4.70	5.70	1.00	1.50
Carrey, Jim	12.00	15.00	3.00	5.00
Carson, Joanna	10.00	14.00	1.40	2.30
Carson, Johnny	5.00	9.00	1.50	2.00
Caruso, Enrico	300.00	375.00	25.00	50.00
Cassavetes, John	3.00	4.50	1.00	1.60
Cavett, Dick	3.00	4.60	1.00	1.60
Chamberlain, Richard	6.00	9.00	1.00	1.50
Chaney, Lon	85.00	125.00	15.00	20.00
Chaplin, Charles	110.00	150.00	8.00	14.00
Charisse, Cyd	6.00	8.00	1.00	1.50
Chase, Chevy	4.00	6.00	1.00	1.50
Christie, Julie	7.00	10.00	1.50	2.00
Clapton, Eric	11.00	13.00	2.00	4.00
Close, Glenn	5.00	8.00	1.00	1.50
Cobain, Kurt	200.00	275.00	40.00	50.00
Coburn, James	4.00	6.00	1.00	1.40
Coca, Imogene	7.00	10.00	1.00	1.40
Coco, James	2.50	4.00	1.00	1.60
Cohan, George M.	70.00	100.00	14.00	20.00
Colbert, Claudette	14.00	22.00	3.00	4.00
Collins, Joan	3.00	4.40	1.00	1.50
Collins, Phil	4.00	6.00	1.00	1.50
Connery, Sean	4.80	6.30	1.00	1.50
Connors, Chuck	4.70	6.00	1.00	1.40
Connors, Michael	3.00	4.70	1.00	1.50
Conrad, Michael	3.00	4.50	1.00	1.50
Conrad, Robert	3.90	5.50	1.00	1.50
Conway, Tim	2.00	3.80	1.00	1.50

	PhS		Plain Sig.	
	Low	High	Low	High
Coogan, Jackie	$ 6.00	$ 8.70	$ 1.00	$ 1.60
Cook, Barbara	3.00	4.50	1.00	1.60
Cooper, Gary	60.00	90.00	4.30	7.00
Cooper, Jackie	4.50	5.70	1.00	1.60
Copperfield, David	6.00	8.00	1.00	1.50
Cosby, Bill	3.00	4.40	1.00	1.50
Crabbe, Buster	23.00	38.00	3.00	5.00
Crane, Bob	2.90	4.80	1.00	1.40
Crawford, Cindy	6.00	8.00	1.00	1.50
Crawford, Joan	118.00	165.00	18.00	26.00
Crenna, Richard	3.00	4.50	1.00	1.40
Cronyn, Hume	4.70	6.00	1.00	1.40
Culp, Robert	2.90	4.40	1.00	1.50
Curtis, Jamie Lee	4.00	6.00	1.00	1.50
Curtis, Ken	3.00	4.40	1.00	1.50
Cusack, John	3.00	5.00	1.00	1.50
Cushing, Peter	4.70	5.70	1.00	1.40
Daltry, Roger	9.00	12.00	2.00	4.00
Dangerfield, Rodney	3.00	4.70	1.00	1.50
Danner, Blythe	4.70	5.80	1.00	1.60
Darby, Kim	3.00	4.50	1.00	1.60
Darren, James	4.30	6.00	1.00	1.40
Davis, Bette	20.00	30.00	4.40	7.00
Davis, Ossie	4.50	6.30	1.00	1.50
Day-Lewis, Daniel	6.00	8.00	1.00	1.50
Dean, James	250.00	350.00	30.00	40.00
Dee, Sandra	4.50	5.70	1.00	1.50
DeHaviland, Olivia	14.50	23.40	2.30	3.00
Delon, Alain	6.30	9.00	1.00	1.40
DeLuise, Dom	2.80	4.70	1.00	1.60
Deneuve, Catherine	6.00	9.00	1.00	1.40
De Niro, Robert	10.00	15.00	1.40	2.30
Dennis, Sandy	7.50	10.00	1.00	1.60
Denver, Bob	4.50	6.00	1.00	1.50
Depp, Johnny	7.00	10.00	1.00	1.50
Derek, Bo	15.00	25.00	3.00	4.70
Derek, John	7.80	10.00	1.60	2.30
Dewhurst, Colleen	7.50	10.00	1.00	1.60
Dey, Susan	3.00	4.50	1.00	1.50
Dickinson, Angie	4.50	5.80	1.00	1.40
Dietrich, Marlene	25.00	45.00	5.80	10.00
Diller, Phyllis	3.00	4.60	1.00	1.50
Donahue, Troy	4.30	6.30	1.00	1.60
Douglas, Kirk	4.40	5.80	1.00	1.60
Douglas, Mike	6.00	8.50	1.00	1.50
Downs, Hugh	3.00	4.50	1.00	1.50
Dreyfuss, Richard	7.00	10.00	1.00	1.50
Duke, Patty	4.80	5.70	1.00	1.50
Dunaway, Faye	7.00	10.00	1.50	2.00
Duncan, Sandy	3.00	4.70	1.00	1.50

	PhS		Plain Sig.	
	Low	High	Low	High
Dunne, Irene	$ 6.30	$ 9.00	$ 1.00	$ 1.40
Durante, Jimmy	13.00	19.80	2.00	4.50
Durbin, Deanna	11.70	14.90	2.00	3.60
Duvall, Robert	10.00	15.70	1.50	2.30
Eastwood, Clint	15.00	21.40	1.50	2.30
Ebsen, Buddy	3.00	4.50	1.00	1.40
Eden, Barbara	4.40	6.00	1.00	1.40
Falk, Peter	6.00	9.00	1.00	1.50
Farrow, Mia	10.00	14.40	1.50	2.00
Fawcett, Farrah	12.40	19.00	2.00	3.80
Faye, Alice	3.00	4.50	1.00	1.50
Feldman, Marty	10.00	15.70	1.60	2.30
Feldon, Barbara	3.00	4.50	1.00	1.60
Fellini, Federico	14.50	24.00	3.00	5.40
Ferrer, Jose	4.50	6.00	1.00	1.40
Ferrer, Mel	4.50	5.50	1.00	1.50
Ferris, Barbara	7.00	10.00	1.00	1.50
Field, Sally	2.30	3.50	1.00	1.50
Fiennes, Ralph	3.00	5.00	1.00	1.50
Finney, Albert	4.30	6.00	1.00	1.50
Fisher, Carrie	9.30	12.30	1.00	1.40
Fitzgerald, Geraldine	6.00	9.00	1.00	1.50
Fonda, Bridget	4.00	6.00	1.00	1.50
Fonda, Henry	40.00	50.00	3.00	4.50
Fonda, Jane	10.00	16.00	1.50	2.00
Fonda, Peter	7.50	10.00	1.00	1.60
Fontaine, Frank	3.00	4.50	1.00	1.40
Fontaine, Joan	7.00	10.00	1.00	1.40
Fontanne, Lynn	20.00	30.00	3.90	6.00
Forsythe, John	2.90	4.40	1.00	1.50
Fosse, Bob	3.00	4.30	1.00	1.50
Foster, Jodi	5.00	7.00	1.00	1.50
Foxx, Redd	3.50	6.00	1.00	1.40
Franciosa, Tony	2.90	4.30	1.00	1.60
Francis, Arlene	2.90	4.40	1.00	1.50
Franciscus, James	3.00	4.50	1.00	1.40
Freeman, Morgan	10.00	15.00	2.00	4.00
Frost, David	3.00	4.30	1.00	1.50
Funt, Allen	2.00	3.50	1.00	1.50
Gable, Clark	400.00	500.00	125.00	190.00
Gabor, Eva	4.50	5.80	1.00	1.50
Gabor, Zsa Zsa	4.30	6.30	1.00	1.50
Garbo, Greta	700.00	1000.00	275.00	350.00
Gardenia, Vincent	2.90	4.40	1.00	1.60
Gardner, Ava	12.40	15.80	1.50	2.40
Garner, James	3.50	5.80	1.00	1.50
Garson, Greer	9.00	11.90	1.40	2.30
Gaynor, Janet	11.00	15.40	1.60	2.30
Gaynor, Mitzi	3.00	4.30	1.00	1.40
Gazzara, Ben	2.90	4.80	1.00	1.60

Photo of Jean Harlow signed by her mother,
"Mama Jean" Harlow.

	PhS		Plain Sig.	
	Low	High	Low	High
Gentry, Bobbie	$ 6.00	$ 9.00	$ 1.00	$ 1.40
Gere, Richard	10.00	15.00	1.50	2.00
Gingold, Hermione	4.40	5.70	1.00	1.50
Gleason, Jackie	4.00	5.70	1.00	1.40
Gobel, George	5.80	9.50	1.00	1.60
Goddard, Paulette	9.00	12.00	1.60	2.40
Godfrey, Arthur	15.00	25.00	3.00	4.60
Goodman, John	8.00	10.00	1.00	1.50
Gordon, Gale	3.00	4.70	1.00	1.60
Gordon, Ruth	6.00	9.40	1.00	1.50
Gould, Elliott	4.30	6.00	1.00	1.50
Goulding, Ray	2.00	3.50	1.00	1.50
Graham, Martha	15.00	25.00	1.50	2.30
Granger, Farley	3.00	4.70	1.00	1.40
Granger, Stewart	3.00	4.40	1.00	1.40
Grant, Cary	15.50	22.70	2.30	3.80
Grant, Hugh	7.00	9.00	1.00	1.50
Grant, Lee	3.00	4.40	1.00	1.50
Graves, Peter	3.00	4.50	1.00	1.60
Greene, Lorne	4.50	5.70	1.00	1.50

	PhS		Plain Sig.	
	Low	High	Low	High
Grey, Joel	$ 4.50	$ 6.00	$ 1.00	$ 1.50
Griffin, Merv	5.80	9.00	1.00	1.50
Griffith, Andy	4.70	6.00	1.00	1.60
Guardino, Harry	3.00	4.40	1.00	1.50
Guinness, Alec	14.50	21.00	3.00	4.40
Hackett, Buddy	3.00	4.50	1.00	1.60
Hackett, Joan	3.00	4.00	1.00	1.60
Hackman, Gene	3.00	4.70	1.00	1.50
Hagen, Uta	4.40	6.00	1.00	1.50
Hagman, Larry	13.30	18.80	1.50	2.50
Hale, Barbara	3.00	4.50	1.00	1.50
Hall, Arsenio	2.00	4.00	1.00	1.50
Hall, Monty	2.00	3.50	1.00	1.40
Hanks, Tom	10.00	15.00	2.00	4.00
Harlow, Jean	500.00	600.00	50.00	75.00
Harris, Julie	8.00	10.00	1.00	1.50
Harris, Richard	7.00	10.00	1.00	1.50
Harrison, George	170.00	250.00	40.00	60.00
Harrison, Rex	4.50	6.00	1.00	1.50
Hartman, David	3.00	4.50	1.00	1.50
Hawke, Ethan	8.00	10.00	1.00	1.50
Hawn, Goldie	6.00	9.30	1.00	1.50
Hayes, Helen	8.00	10.00	1.60	2.30
Hayworth, Rita	15.00	22.30	3.00	4.50
Heatherton, Joey	4.50	5.70	1.00	1.50
Henderson, Florence	2.80	4.30	1.00	1.40
Hendrix, Jimi	250.00	350.00	30.00	50.00
Hepburn, Audrey	4.50	5.80	1.00	1.50
Hepburn, Katharine	20.00	40.00	3.00	5.80
Heston, Charlton	9.50	12.50	1.40	2.30
Hitchcock, Alfred	25.00	35.00	1.50	2.70
Hoffman, Dustin	7.40	10.00	1.00	1.40
Holbrook, Hal	4.30	6.00	1.00	1.40
Holden, William	45.00	60.00	1.00	1.40
Holder, Geoffrey	3.00	4.30	1.00	1.60
Holliman, Earl	2.80	4.40	1.00	1.40
Holly, Buddy	200.00	300.00	30.00	45.00
Holm, Celeste	4.50	6.30	1.00	1.50
Hope, Bob	6.30	9.00	1.50	2.30
Hopkins, Anthony	8.00	10.00	1.00	1.40
Hopper, Dennis	7.00	10.00	1.00	1.50
Howard, Trevor	4.50	6.30	1.00	1.60
Hudson, Rock	7.00	10.00	1.00	1.50
Hunt, Linda	2.90	4.50	1.00	1.50
Hunter, Holly	6.00	8.00	1.00	1.50
Hunter, Kim	4.70	5.80	1.00	1.50
Hurt, William	4.00	6.00	1.00	1.50
Huston, John	12.00	15.00	1.50	2.30
Huston, Walter	30.00	50.00	4.60	7.80
Hutton, Betty	6.30	8.80	1.00	1.60

	PhS		Plain Sig.	
	Low	High	Low	High
Hutton, Lauren	$ 3.00	$ 4.30	$ 1.00	$ 1.60
Hynde, Chrissie	10.00	15.00	2.00	4.00
Ireland, John	3.00	4.50	1.00	1.40
Jackson, Glenda	7.00	10.00	1.00	1.50
Jackson, Kate	4.50	6.00	1.00	1.60
Janssen, David	23.00	28.50	3.00	4.30
Jeffreys, Anne	3.00	4.40	1.00	1.40
Jessel, George	15.00	23.50	1.50	2.70
John, Elton	10.00	15.00	2.00	4.00
Johns, Glynis	3.00	4.40	1.00	1.60
Johnson, Van	4.50	5.80	1.00	1.50
Jolson, Al	100.00	125.00	15.00	22.00
Jones, Dean	3.00	4.50	1.00	1.60
Jones, Shirley	4.70	6.00	1.00	1.40
Jones, Tommy Lee	8.00	10.00	1.00	1.50
Joplin, Janis	175.00	250.00	30.00	45.00
Kahn, Madeline	9.40	12.50	1.60	2.30
Kaplan, Gabe	4.50	5.80	1.00	1.50
Kaye, Danny	13.00	9.00	1.50	2.30
Kazan, Elia	12.00	15.30	2.30	3.70
Keach, Stacy	6.00	9.00	1.00	1.50
Keaton, Diane	7.00	10.00	1.00	1.40
Keaton, Michael	7.00	9.00	1.00	1.50
Keeler, Ruby	11.00	14.00	1.60	2.00
Keitel, Harvey	5.00	7.00	1.00	1.50
Keith, Brian	4.40	5.80	1.00	1.40
Kellerman, Sally	7.70	10.00	1.00	1.50
Kelly, Grace	200.00	350.00	7.80	11.40
Kennedy, George	3.00	4.50	1.00	1.40
Kerr, Deborah	6.00	9.30	1.00	1.50
Keyes, Evelyn	2.90	4.30	1.00	1.50
Kiley, Richard	4.50	6.30	1.00	1.40
King, Alan	3.00	4.50	1.00	1.60
Klugman, Jack	6.00	9.00	1.00	1.50
Knots, Don	3.00	4.50	1.00	1.60
Korman, Harvey	2.90	4.50	1.00	1.50
Kramer, Stanley	10.00	13.40	1.50	2.30
Kristofferson, Kris	8.00	12.00	1.00	1.50
Kubrick, Stanley	15.00	22.00	1.40	2.00
Lamarr, Hedy	45.00	75.00	6.00	10.00
Lamas, Fernando	14.00	17.50	1.40	2.90
Lancaster, Burt	12.30	15.70	1.50	2.00
Lanchester, Elsa	6.00	9.50	1.00	1.50
Landau, Martin	4.50	6.00	1.00	1.60
Landon, Michael	4.30	6.00	1.00	1.50
Lang, k.d.	6.00	8.00	1.00	1.50
Lange, Hope	2.90	4.30	1.00	1.50
Lange, Jessica	5.00	7.00	1.00	1.50
Langella, Frank	6.00	8.50	1.00	1.40
Lansbury, Angela	3.00	4.70	1.00	1.60

	PhS		Plain Sig.	
	Low	High	Low	High
Lasser, Louise	$ 8.00	$ 11.00	$ 1.00	$ 1.60
Laurie, Piper	3.00	4.00	1.00	1.60
Lavin, Linda	6.00	7.50	1.00	1.50
Lawford, Peter	6.00	8.50	1.00	1.50
Lawrence, Vicki	3.00	4.30	1.00	1.60
Leachman, Cloris	4.40	6.30	1.00	1.60
Learned, Michael	4.40	6.00	1.00	1.50
Lee, Bruce	115.00	150.00	40.00	60.00
Lee, Christopher	4.70	5.70	1.00	1.40
Leigh, Janet	6.00	9.30	1.00	1.60
Leigh, Jennifer Jason	6.00	8.00	1.00	1.50
Lemmon, Jack	9.30	12.00	1.50	2.30
Lennon, John	350.00	500.00	50.00	75.00
Leno, Jay	4.00	5.00	1.00	1.50
Letterman, David	4.00	5.00	1.00	1.50
Lewis, Jerry	2.90	4.50	1.00	1.50
Lewis, Shari	4.40	6.00	1.00	1.50
Liberace	11.50	16.50	1.50	3.00
Linden, Hal	4.50	6.30	1.00	1.50
Linkletter, Art	3.00	4.40	1.00	1.40
Lipton, Peggy	3.00	4.50	1.00	1.50
Little, Richard	3.00	4.70	1.00	1.50
Lockhart, June	2.90	4.30	1.00	1.50
Lollobrigida, Gina	15.50	21.40	1.50	2.00
Lombard, Carole	150.00	225.00	14.00	22.00
Longet, Claudine	12.00	14.70	1.50	2.00
Loren, Sophia	25.00	34.00	2.90	4.70
Louise, Tina	2.90	4.70	1.00	1.60
Love, Courtney	12.00	15.00	1.00	1.50
Lovett, Lyle	5.00	7.00	1.00	1.50
Loy, Myrna	14.00	23.50	1.60	2.00
Lucas, George	8.00	10.00	1.00	1.50
Lunt, Alfred	18.40	30.00	3.00	6.00
Lupino, Ida	5.70	8.80	1.00	1.40
MacGraw, Ali	12.00	14.80	1.60	2.00
MacLaine, Shirley	14.00	21.50	1.40	2.30
MacMurray, Fred	12.40	14.70	1.40	2.40
Madonna	75.00	100.00	5.00	10.00
Majors, Lee	7.30	10.00	1.00	1.50
Malden, Karl	2.90	4.80	1.00	1.50
Malkovich, John	4.00	6.00	1.00	1.50
Marceau, Marcel	22.50	29.80	3.00	4.30
Margolin, Janet	2.90	4.50	1.00	1.40
Marshall, E. G.	4.70	6.30	1.00	1.40
Martin, Dick	3.00	4.30	1.00	1.50
Martin, Ross	3.00	4.50	1.00	1.50
Marvin, Lee	6.30	9.50	1.00	1.50
Marx, Groucho	70.00	100.00	7.40	12.70
Mason, Jackie	3.00	4.70	1.00	1.40
Mason, James	4.70	6.00	1.00	1.50

	PhS		Plain Sig.	
	Low	High	Low	High
Mason, Pamela	$ 2.90	$ 4.60	$ 1.00	$ 1.50
Massey, Raymond	6.00	8.50	1.00	1.50
Matthau, Walter	6.00	9.50	1.00	1.50
Mayo, Virginia	3.00	4.40	1.00	1.50
McCartney, Paul	250.00	350.00	35.00	50.00
McCrea, Joel	7.40	12.00	1.50	2.90
McDowall, Roddy	4.00	6.00	1.00	1.50
McGavin, Darren	3.00	4.40	1.00	1.50
McGoohan, Patrick	6.00	8.50	1.00	1.50
McMahon, Ed	2.30	3.50	1.00	1.50
McQueen, Steve	38.00	50.00	7.40	11.70
Meadows, Audrey	2.90	4.70	1.00	1.50
Meadows, Jayne	3.00	4.30	1.00	1.50
Meara, Anne	3.00	4.50	1.00	1.50
Mercouri, Melina	7.30	10.00	1.60	2.00
Meredith, Burgess	7.50	10.00	1.50	2.00
Merrill, Dina	6.00	8.70	1.00	1.50
Midler, Bette	10.00	14.00	1.60	2.40
Milland, Ray	5.70	9.00	1.00	1.40
Mitchum, Robert	5.50	9.00	1.00	1.60
Monroe, Marilyn	600.00	900.00	50.00	100.00
Montalban, Ricardo	3.00	4.50	1.00	1.40
Montand, Yves	4.50	6.00	1.00	1.50
Montgomery, Elizabeth	2.90	4.50	1.00	1.40
Montgomery, George	3.00	4.70	1.00	1.50
Montgomery, Robert	2.80	4.70	1.00	1.40
Moore, Demi	4.00	6.00	1.00	1.50
Moore, Mary Tyler	4.50	6.40	1.00	1.40
Moore, Roger	8.00	10.00	1.50	2.30
Moreau, Jeanne	4.50	6.00	1.00	1.50
Moreno, Rita	4.50	6.00	1.00	1.50
Morgan, Henry	4.50	6.00	1.00	1.50
Morley, Robert	3.00	4.30	1.00	1.40
Morrow, Vic	3.00	4.30	1.00	1.50
Morse, Robert	3.00	4.40	1.00	1.60
Mostel, Zero	18.00	24.50	2.40	3.70
Murphy, Eddie	5.00	7.00	1.00	1.50
Murphy, George	18.40	26.50	3.00	4.70
Murray, Anne	4.50	6.00	1.00	1.50
Murray, Arthur	7.50	10.00	1.00	1.40
Nabors, Jim	2.90	4.40	1.00	1.50
Neal, Patricia	11.70	15.50	1.50	2.00
Neeson, Liam	4.00	6.00	1.00	1.50
Neill, Sam	3.00	5.00	1.00	1.50
Newhart, Bob	2.90	4.70	1.00	1.50
Newman, Paul	15.40	22.00	1.40	2.40
Newmar, Julie	7.50	12.70	1.00	1.50
Nichols, Mike	12.40	14.40	1.50	2.00
Nicholson, Jack	10.00	13.50	1.50	2.00
Nimoy, Leonard	15.00	23.50	2.30	3.90

	PhS		Plain Sig.	
	Low	High	Low	High
Niven, David	$ 28.40	$ 47.00	$ 4.50	$ 7.50
Nolan, Lloyd	4.50	6.30	1.00	1.50
Nolte, Nick	3.00	4.50	1.00	1.60
Novak, Kim	7.70	10.00	1.50	2.00
O'Brian, Hugh	2.90	4.70	1.00	1.40
O'Brien, Edmund	3.00	4.70	1.00	1.50
O'Brien, Margaret	4.50	6.00	1.00	1.50
O'Connell, Helen	4.30	6.00	1.00	1.60
O'Connor, Carroll	5.70	9.00	1.00	1.50
O'Hara, Jill	2.90	4.50	1.00	1.40
O'Hara, Maureen	4.30	6.30	1.00	1.50
O'Neal, Patrick	3.00	4.70	1.00	1.40
O'Neal, Ryan	6.30	7.00	1.00	1.50
O'Neal, Tatum	9.40	12.00	1.00	1.40
O'Sullivan, Maureen	4.30	6.30	1.00	1.40
O'Toole, Peter	7.80	10.00	1.00	1.50
Oakie, Jack	6.30	9.00	1.00	1.50
Oberon, Merle	9.00	11.40	1.00	1.60
Olivier, Laurence	17.00	28.00	3.00	4.40
Osmond, Donny	3.00	4.00	1.00	1.50
Osmond, Marie	4.50	7.00	1.00	1.60
Paar, Jack	2.80	4.30	1.00	1.50
Pacino, Al	10.00	13.40	1.50	2.00
Page, Geraldine	4.30	6.00	1.00	1.50
Palance, Jack	4.40	6.00	1.00	1.40
Papp, Joseph	7.50	10.00	1.00	1.50
Parker, Eleanor	7.70	10.00	1.00	1.40
Parker, Fess	6.00	9.30	1.00	1.50
Parker, Suzy	2.90	4.40	1.00	1.50
Parks, Bert	2.90	4.40	1.00	1.50
Parsons, Estelle	4.50	5.70	1.00	1.60
Parton, Dolly	12.40	16.00	1.60	2.70
Pearl, Minnie	6.30	9.00	1.00	1.50
Peck, Gregory	12.40	17.00	1.40	2.40
Peppard, George	4.70	6.00	1.00	1.50
Perkins, Anthony	2.80	4.50	1.00	1.50
Perrine, Valerie	7.30	11.00	1.00	1.50
Pfeiffer, Michelle	10.00	14.00	1.50	2.00
Pickford, Mary	22.00	30.00	3.00	4.30
Pidgeon, Walter	4.70	6.00	1.00	1.50
Pitt, Brad	6.00	9.00	1.00	1.50
Pleasance, Donald	7.80	10.00	1.00	1.40
Pleshette, Suzanne	4.40	5.80	1.00	1.50
Plimpton, George	4.40	6.30	1.00	1.50
Plowright, Joan	3.00	4.40	1.00	1.60
Plummer, Christopher	7.30	10.00	1.00	1.60
Poitier, Sidney	7.00	10.00	1.40	2.30
Polanski, Roman	15.00	22.50	2.30	3.80
Ponti, Carlo	15.00	25.00	1.00	1.60
Powell, Jane	3.00	4.40	1.00	1.50

	PhS		Plain Sig.	
	Low	High	Low	High
Powell, William	$ 15.00	$ 23.50	$ 1.50	$ 2.40
Powers, Stephanie	2.80	4.70	1.00	1.40
Preminger, Otto	11.80	14.80	1.40	3.00
Prentiss, Paula	4.30	5.80	1.00	1.50
Presley, Elvis	500.00	800.00	75.00	150.00
Preston, Robert	4.40	6.00	1.00	1.60
Prinz, Freddie	74.90	104.80	12.00	17.00
Provine, Dorothy	3.00	4.50	1.00	1.50
Prowse, Juliet	4.60	6.30	1.00	1.60
Pryor, Richard	15.50	22.30	1.50	2.50
Quinn, Anthony	9.40	12.00	1.40	2.30
Raft, George	12.30	15.30	1.40	3.00
Raitt, Bonnie	8.00	10.00	1.00	1.50
Raitt, John	4.40	6.00	1.00	1.50
Randall, Tony	2.90	4.40	1.00	1.40
Ray, Aldo	3.00	4.30	1.00	1.50
Raye, Martha	8.50	12.40	1.50	2.30
Redford, Robert	9.00	12.50	1.50	2.40
Redgrave, Lynn	7.70	10.00	1.00	1.50
Redgrave, Michael	8.70	11.30	1.50	2.00
Redgrave, Vanessa	14.30	21.50	3.00	4.30
Reed, Donna	3.00	4.70	1.00	1.40
Reed, Rex	2.40	3.70	1.00	1.50
Reilly, Charles Nelson	3.00	4.50	1.00	1.50
Reiner, Carl	4.30	6.00	1.00	1.50
Reiner, Rob	5.70	8.00	1.00	1.60
Remick, Lee	4.40	6.30	1.00	1.50
Reynolds, Burt	14.00	22.00	3.00	5.00
Richardson, Natasha	4.00	6.00	1.00	1.50
Rickles, Don	2.90	4.30	1.00	1.40
Rigg, Diana	8.50	12.50	1.00	1.50
Rivera, Chita	3.00	4.70	1.00	1.50
Robards, Jason Jr.	7.50	10.00	1.00	1.50
Robbins, Tim	7.00	10.00	1.00	1.50
Roberts, Julia	5.00	7.00	1.00	1.50
Robertson, Cliff	3.00	4.50	1.00	1.40
Rogers, Ginger	11.80	14.00	1.50	2.30
Romero, Cesar	2.80	4.50	1.00	1.50
Rooney, Mickey	4.30	6.00	1.00	1.50
Ross, Katharine	2.90	4.40	1.00	1.60
Roundtree, Richard	3.00	4.70	1.00	1.40
Rowan, Dan	4.50	6.30	1.00	1.50
Rowlands, Gena	3.00	4.00	1.00	1.50
Rule, Janice	3.00	4.70	1.00	1.50
Rush, Barbara	4.50	5.70	1.00	1.50
Russell, Jane	7.80	11.00	1.00	1.50
Russell, Ken	8.00	11.00	1.00	1.40
Ryder, Winona	6.00	8.00	1.00	1.50
Sahl, Mort	3.00	4.50	1.00	1.50
Saint, Eva Marie	5.80	8.70	1.00	1.50
Sainte Marie, Buffy	9.00	13.00	1.00	1.50

	PhS		Plain Sig.	
	Low	High	Low	High
Sales, Soupy	$ 3.00	$ 4.30	$ 1.00	$ 1.40
Sarandon, Susan	6.00	8.00	1.00	1.50
Sarrazin, Michael	9.00	12.00	1.00	1.50
Savalas, Telly	7.80	10.00	1.00	1.50
Saxon, John	2.80	4.50	1.00	1.40
Schell, Maria	4.30	6.00	1.00	1.40
Schiffer, Claudia	7.00	10.00	1.00	1.50
Schwarzenegger, Arnold	17.00	25.00	2.00	3.50
Scott, George C.	15.00	25.00	1.60	2.30
Scott, Randolph	5.80	9.00	1.00	1.50
Seberg, Jean	3.00	4.70	1.00	1.50
Segal, George	4.50	5.70	1.00	1.60
Sellers, Peter	23.70	30.00	4.00	7.70
Sharif, Omar	9.00	12.00	1.00	1.60
Shatner, William	4.30	5.70	1.00	1.40
Shaw, Robert	3.00	4.50	1.00	1.60
Shearer, Norma	12.50	15.00	1.50	2.30
Shepard, Sam	4.00	6.00	1.00	1.50
Shepherd, Cybill	12.00	15.00	1.00	1.60
Shields, Brooke	30.00	47.00	7.40	12.00
Shriver, Maria	2.00	4.00	1.00	1.50
Signoret, Simone	4.40	6.40	1.00	1.50
Silvers, Phil	4.50	6.00	1.00	1.60
Simmons, Jean	2.90	4.50	1.00	1.60
Simon, Carly	6.00	8.00	1.00	1.50
Skelton, Red	5.80	8.70	1.00	1.50
Snipes, Wesley	6.00	8.00	1.00	1.50
Sommer, Elke	12.00	14.40	1.40	2.30
Sorvino, Paul	9.50	11.90	1.00	1.60
Sothern, Ann	4.50	5.80	1.00	1.50
Spacek, Sissy	2.90	4.50	1.00	1.50
Spielberg, Stephen	8.00	10.00	1.00	1.50
St. James, Susan	3.00	4.50	1.00	1.60
St. John, Jill	4.50	5.80	1.00	1.40
Stack, Robert	4.70	6.00	1.00	1.50
Stallone, Sylvester	17.00	25.70	2.30	3.80
Stamp, Terence	4.70	6.00	1.00	1.50
Stanwyck, Barbara	8.00	10.00	1.00	1.50
Stapleton, Maureen	4.50	6.30	1.00	1.60
Starr, Ringo	150.00	200.00	25.00	35.00
Steiger, Rod	7.00	10.00	1.00	1.50
Stevens, Connie	3.00	4.70	1.00	1.50
Stewart, James	10.00	14.00	1.40	2.30
Stockwell, Dean	3.00	4.30	1.00	1.60
Stone, Milburn	6.40	10.00	1.50	2.70
Storch, Larry	3.00	4.40	1.00	1.50
Strasberg, Lee	20.00	30.00	3.00	4.30
Strasberg, Susan	4.50	6.00	1.00	1.50
Streisand, Barbra	15.00	20.00	2.00	3.50
Stritch, Elaine	2.90	4.40	1.00	1.50

	PhS		Plain Sig.	
	Low	High	Low	High
Struthers, Sally	$ 8.70	$ 12.30	$ 1.50	$ 2.30
Sullivan, Barry	2.90	4.50	1.00	1.50
Sutherland, Donald	8.70	12.30	1.50	2.00
Swanson, Gloria	25.00	45.00	4.50	8.00
Swit, Loretta	13.00	21.90	2.00	4.00
Tandy, Jessica	6.00	7.70	1.00	1.50
Tate, Sharon	150.00	250.00	14.00	22.00
Taylor, Elizabeth	35.00	50.00	4.30	7.50
Taylor, Kent	3.00	4.30	1.00	1.50
Taylor, Rod	3.00	4.50	1.00	1.60
Temple, Shirley	15.00	20.00	2.00	3.50
Thomas, Danny	4.30	6.00	1.00	1.50
Thomas, Marlo	6.30	7.30	1.00	1.40
Thomas, Richard	4.70	5.80	1.00	1.50
Thompson, Emma	5.00	7.00	1.00	1.50
Thurman, Uma	6.00	8.00	1.00	1.50
Tierney, Gene	5.80	7.50	1.00	1.50
Tilly, Jennifer	3.00	5.00	1.00	1.50
Todd, Richard	2.90	4.50	1.00	1.60
Tomlin, Lily	4.30	6.00	1.00	1.60
Torn, Rip	2.90	4.50	1.00	1.50
Townsend, Pete	9.00	12.00	2.00	4.00
Travolta, John	17.00	24.00	3.00	4.70
Trevor, Claire	4.40	6.40	1.00	1.50
Tucker, Forrest	3.00	4.70	1.00	1.40
Turner, Lana	15.00	20.00	2.00	3.50
Twiggy	40.00	60.00	6.00	9.00
Tyson, Cicely	4.50	6.30	1.00	1.50
Uggams, Leslie	2.50	4.50	1.00	1.50
Ullman, Liv	11.00	15.00	1.50	2.00
Ustinov, Peter	4.70	6.00	1.00	1.60
Vaccaro, Brenda	3.00	4.80	1.00	1.50
Valentino, Rudolph	400.00	500.00	35.00	50.00
Van Cleef, Lee	9.00	12.00	1.00	1.50
Van Doren, Mamie	4.30	6.00	1.00	1.50
Van Dyke, Dick	6.00	8.70	1.00	1.40
Van Peebles, Mario	3.00	5.00	1.00	1.50
Vance, Vivian	6.00	7.00	1.00	1.50
Vandervere, Trish	4.70	6.00	1.00	1.50
Vaughn, Robert	4.40	5.70	1.00	1.60
Vereen, Ben	2.90	4.70	1.00	1.60
Vigoda, Abe	3.00	4.70	1.00	1.60
Voight, Jon	8.00	11.00	1.00	1.50
Von Sydow, Max	4.40	6.00	1.00	1.50
Waggoner, Lyle	3.00	4.50	1.00	1.40
Wagner, Lindsay	3.00	4.50	1.00	1.50
Wagner, Robert	8.80	14.50	1.50	2.30
Walker, Clint	2.90	4.50	1.00	1.50
Wallach, Eli	6.00	9.40	1.00	1.40
Walston, Ray	4.30	6.00	1.00	1.50

	PhS		Plain Sig.	
	Low	High	Low	High
Warden, Jack	$ 2.90	$ 4.30	$ 1.00	$ 1.50
Warner, David	4.40	6.00	1.00	1.40
Waters, Ethel	6.00	9.00	1.00	1.50
Waterston, Sam	3.00	5.00	1.00	1.50
Wayans, Damon	5.00	7.00	1.00	1.50
Wayne, David	3.00	4.50	1.00	1.50
Wayne, John	50.00	75.00	6.00	9.00
Weaver, Dennis	3.00	4.30	1.00	1.60
Webb, Jack	3.00	4.30	1.00	1.50
Weissmuller, Johnny	12.00	18.00	2.00	4.40
Welch, Raquel	11.70	15.80	1.60	2.00
Weld, Tuesday	3.00	4.50	1.00	1.60
Welk, Lawrence	2.80	4.40	1.00	1.50
Welles, Orson	12.00	14.00	1.60	2.30
West, Adam	4.50	5.80	1.00	1.50
West, Mae	44.50	59.70	4.50	7.00
White, Betty	2.90	4.40	1.00	1.50
Whitman, Stuart	2.90	4.50	1.00	1.60
Whitmore, James	4.50	6.00	1.00	1.50
Widmark, Richard	3.00	4.40	1.00	1.50
Wiest, Dianne	4.00	6.00	1.00	1.50
Wilde, Cornel	4.50	6.00	1.00	1.60
Wilder, Billy	7.00	10.00	1.00	1.50
Williams, Cindy	4.30	5.80	1.00	1.50
Williams, Esther	2.80	4.50	1.00	1.50
Williams, Robin	8.00	10.00	1.00	1.50
Willis, Bruce	6.00	8.00	1.00	1.50
Wilson, Flip	3.00	4.30	1.00	1.60
Winfrey, Oprah	4.00	6.00	1.00	1.50
Winkler, Henry	14.00	22.00	2.80	4.60
Winters, Jonathan	3.00	4.50	1.00	1.50
Winters, Shelley	4.50	6.00	1.00	1.60

*Cut signatures of Curly Howard and Larry Fine of "Three Stooges"
fame brought $1870 at auction. — Photo courtesy of Christie's East.*

	PhS		Plain Sig.	
	Low	High	Low	High
Withers, Jane	$ 3.00	$ 4.40	$ 1.00	$ 1.50
Wood, Natalie	50.00	70.00	7.50	12.50
Woodward, Joanne	4.50	6.00	1.00	1.60
Worley, Jo Anne	2.90	4.30	1.00	1.50
Wray, Fay	9.00	11.00	1.00	1.40
Wyatt, Jane	3.00	4.30	1.00	1.40
Wyler, William	4.40	6.00	1.00	1.50
Wyman, Jane	8.50	14.00	1.50	2.50
Wynn, Ed	35.00	50.00	4.50	7.50
Wynn, Kennan	2.90	4.50	1.00	1.60
Wynter, Dana	3.00	4.50	1.00	1.50
York, Dick	2.90	4.40	1.00	1.50
York, Michael	7.50	10.00	1.00	1.50
York, Susannah	5.70	9.50	1.00	1.40
Young, Alan	4.30	6.00	1.00	1.50
Young, Gig	8.00	12.00	1.50	2.00
Young, Loretta	6.00	7.50	1.00	1.50
Young, Robert	4.00	6.30	1.00	1.40
Youngman, Henny	4.70	6.00	1.00	1.50
Zanuck, Daryl	12.50	14.00	1.50	2.40
Zimbalist, Efrem, Jr.	4.75	5.50	1.00	1.50

Presidents

Presidential letters and autographs are among the most valuable. George Washington, like many men of his era, was a prolific writer. His autograph letters are often offered at auction (notably Swann Galleries in New York City). Dwight Eisenhower, however, rarely took a pen to hand for more than a signature. An Eisenhower ALS is often worth more than a Washington ALS! Also beware of auto-pen. This automatic signing device became entrenched in the White House in the early 1960s. It has signed a vast majority of letters coming from the presidents since that time.

ALS and LS

	ALS		LS	
	Low	High	Low	High
Washington, George	$10,000	$150,000	$5000	$100,000
Adams, John	8000	40,000	4000	15,000
Jefferson, Thomas	10,000	50,000	5000	25,000
Madison, James	2000	10,000	1000	5000
Monroe, James	1000	10,000	1000	5000
Adams, John Q.	1000	10,000	500	3000
Jackson, Andrew	1500	10,000	500	5000
Van Buren, Martin	500	2000	300	2000
Harrison, William H.	500	5000	300	3000
Tyler, John	500	4000	300	2000
Polk, James K.	500	5000	300	2000
Taylor, Zachary	500	5000	300	3000
Fillmore, Millard	500	3000	300	3000
Pierce, Franklin	500	2500	200	2000
Buchanan, James	300	2500	250	1000
Lincoln, Abraham	7500	50,000	5000	20,000
Johnson, Andrew	1000	5000	500	2500
Grant, U.S.	500	25,000	300	10,000
Hayes, R.B.	200	1000	100	500
Garfield, James	200	1500	500	2500
Arthur, Chester A.	400	1500	300	2500
Cleveland, Grover	200	5000	200	2500
Harrison, Benjamin	200	2000	150	2500
McKinley, William	200	2000	100	750
Roosevelt, Theodore	500	7500	150	3000
Taft, William H.	200	1000	100	500
Wilson, Woodrow	500	5000	100	500
Harding, Warren G.	500	2000	200	500
Coolidge, Calvin	1000	5000	100	500
Hoover, Herbert	2000	5000	100	400
Roosevelt, Franklin	1000	5000	150	2500
Truman, Harry	1000	3000	150	500
Eisenhower, Dwight	1000	5000	150	500
Kennedy, John F.	1000	10,000	3000	4000
Johnson, Lyndon	1000	5000	150	500
Nixon, Richard M.	1000	10,000	150	1000
Ford, Gerald	1000	3000	150	500
Carter, Jimmy	1000	3000	150	500
Reagan, Ronald	1000	5000	150	1000
Bush, George	500	2500	100	500
Clinton, Bill	1000	2500	100	500

Richard Nixon
actual signature.

Richard Nixon
auto-pen signature.

DS, PhS, and Cut Sig.

	DS		PhS		Cut Sig.	
	Low	High	Low	High	Low	High
Washington, George	$ 8000	$ 16,000	—	—	$ 2000	$ 5000
Adams, John	2000	6000	—	—	1600	2400
Jefferson, Thomas	4000	8000	—	—	2000	4000
Madison, James	1000	1600	—	—	600	1000
Monroe, James	800	1200	—	—	600	1000
Adams, John Q.	600	1000	—	—	200	400
Jackson, Andrew	800	1400	—	—	600	1000
Van Buren, Martin	600	1000	—	—	300	500
Harrison, William H.	1000	1600	—	—	200	400
Tyler, John	800	1200	—	—	160	240
Polk, James K.	800	1400	—	—	200	400
Taylor, Zachary	1000	1600	—	—	300	500
Fillmore, Millard	300	500	—	—	200	400
Pierce, Franklin	800	1200	—	—	200	400
Buchanan, James	400	800	—	—	300	500
Lincoln, Abraham	4000	8000	$ 15,000	$ 50,000	1000	3500
Johnson, Andrew	800	1600	3000	5000	400	800
Grant, U.S.	800	1400	1000	1600	500	700
Hayes, R.B.	400	600	600	1000	300	500
Garfield, James	400	800	2000	3000	200	400
Arthur, Chester A.	600	1000	1200	1800	300	600
Cleveland, Grover	300	500	600	900	200	300
Harrison, Benjamin	400	600	2000	3000	300	500
McKinley, William	300	500	1200	1800	200	300
Roosevelt, Theodore	600	1000	800	1200	300	500
Taft, William H.	300	500	800	1200	200	300
Wilson, Woodrow	600	1000	800	1200	300	500
Harding, Warren G.	200	400	400	800	200	300
Coolidge, Calvin	200	400	300	500	100	300
Hoover, Herbert	200	400	200	400	100	300
Roosevelt, Franklin	300	500	600	1000	200	400
Truman, Harry	200	400	400	800	200	400
Eisenhower, Dwight	200	400	400	800	300	500
Kennedy, John F.	300	1500	300	750	200	500
Johnson, Lyndon	200	300	200	600	200	400
Nixon, Richard M.	200	300	200	400	100	200
Ford, Gerald	200	300	200	400	100	200
Carter, Jimmy	200	300	100	300	100	300
Reagan, Ronald	1000	1400	300	500	200	400
Bush, George	200	300	200	300	100	300
Clinton, Bill	200	300	200	300	100	200

John Adams *J. Q. Adams.*

Above left: John Adams. Above right: John Quincy Adams.
Below left: Chester A. Arthur. Below right: Grover Cleveland.

Above left: Bill Clinton —autopen. Above right: Dwight Eisenhower.
Below left: Gerald Ford. Below right: Ulysses S. Grant.

Above left: Warren G. Harding. Above right: Benjamin Harrison.
Below left: William Henry Harrison. Below right: Rutherford B. Hayes.

Above left: Herbert Hoover. Above right: Andrew Jackson.

Above left: Thomas Jefferson. Above right: Andrew Johnson.
Below left: Lyndon B. Johnson. Below right: John Kennedy.

Above left: Abraham Lincoln. Above right: James Madison.
Below left: William McKinley. Below right: James Monroe.

Above left: Ronald Reagan. Above right: Franklin Roosevelt.
Below left: Theodore Roosevelt. Below right: Zachery Taylor.

Above left: Harry Truman. Above right: John Tyler.
Below left: George Washington. Below right: Woodrow Wilson.

Baskets

There are several types of basket construction. Wickerwork, the most common and widely used technique, is an over-and-under pattern. Twining is similar; two strands are twisted as they are woven over and under, producing a finer weave. Plaiting gives a checkerboard effect in either a tight weave or left with open spaces. Twill work is similar, but with a diagonal effect achieved by changing the number of strands over which the weaver passes. Coiling is the most desirable weave for the collector. This technique has been refined since its conception around 7000 BC. Fibers are wrapped around and stitched together to form the basket's shape. Most of these pieces were either used for ceremonial purposes or for holding liquids, since these tightly woven containers were leak proof.

Baskets are easy to care for but a few basic rules must be followed: Never wash an Indian basket, especially baskets made of pine needles, straw, grass or leaves. Dust them gently using a soft sable artist's brush. Willow, oak, hickory, and rattan baskets may be washed in a mild solution of Murphy's Oil Soap and dried briefly in a sunny location. Baskets continuously exposed to the sun will fade.

Pima large coiled tray, dia. 20",
$3000 at auction.

	AUCTION	RETAIL Low	High
Aleutian Lidded Basket, w/ colored yarn	$ 1000	$ 1950	$ 350
Apache Coiled Storage Basket, geometric motifs, ht. 12"	700	1300	2500
Birch Bark Basket, 8.5"	40	70	130
Burden Basket, miniature, 6.5"	190	350	620
California Basket, tightly woven, diamond motif, dia. 5.5"	200	370	650
Cedar Bark and Spruce Root Lidded Basket, 4.5"	45	80	150
Chilcotin Basket, fully imbricated, sq., 4"	150	280	500
Chilcotin Burden Basket, 11"	210	400	700
Chilcotin Burden Basket, 16.5"	240	450	850
Chilcotin Coiled Lidded Basket, 5"	130	240	420
Chilcotin Coiled Pedestal Basket, w/ gallery, 10.5"	300	560	1000
Chilcotin Coiled Trinket Basket, 7"	225	420	750
Chilcotin Lidded Basket w/ tree design, 7"	250	470	820
Chilcotin Round Coiled Basket, w/ gallery, 6.5"	210	390	680
Clothes, round w/ 2 handles	150	280	500
Coiled Lilooet Burden Basket, c.1900, 15"	1750	3250	5700
Coiled Pomo Basket, w/ arrowhead design	200	370	650
Drying, New England, 30" x 48", shallow rim, c. 1850	300	560	1000
Field Basket, oak splint, c. 1885	190	350	620

	AUCTION	RETAIL Low	High
Fraser River Burden Basket, 15"	$ 275	$ 510	$ 900
Haida Cedar Bark Basket, 13"	275	510	900
Haida Spruce Root Basket	55	100	180
Hopi Coiled Plaque Caught in Basket Dance, 1991, 9"	55	100	180
Japanese, tightly woven circular, dia. 9"	200	370	650
Kilkitatl Salish Basket, 8"	250	470	820
Knitting Basket, fully imbricated, 4.5"	170	320	550
Knob Top Coiled Thompson River Basket, 5.5"	335	620	1200
Knob Top Thompson River Basket w/ tree design, 8.5"	255	470	830
Laundry, oak splint, 1910	70	130	230
Lidded Salish Basket, w/ butterfly design, c.1920, 18"	2250	4190	7500
Lidded Salish Basket, w/ double handles, 28"	475	880	1550
Lilooet Coiled Burden Basket, maker's prov., c.1905, 13"	1300	2500	4500
Mission Tray, dia. 12"	300	560	1000
Nantucket Lightship, 5" x 10"	600	1120	2000
Nootka Basket, 11"	75	140	240
Nootka Basketry Covered Bottle, 5"	105	200	340
Nootka Basketry Covered Bottle, c.1920	100	190	330
Nootka Basketry Covered Cobalt Blue Bottle w/ thunderbird	120	220	400
Nootka Basketry Covered Jar, w/ zoomorphic design	525	1000	1750
Nootka Lidded Basket, 3.5"	55	100	180
Nootka Lidded Basket, 4"	75	140	240
Nootka Lidded Basket, w/ canoe and bird design, 10"	180	330	600
Nootka Lidded Basket, w/ duck and reindeer design	85	160	280
Nootka Lidded Basket, w/ wolf design, 3"	65	120	200
Nootka Oval Basket, w/ salal berry dye	210	390	680
Nootka Oval Basket, w/ whaling design, 4.5"	475	880	1550
Nootka Round Basket, w/ whale and canoe design, 4.5"	180	330	600
Nootka Round Lidded Basket, 3.5"	60	110	200
Nootka Shell-Covered Basket, w/ animal design	380	700	1240
Nootka Woven Cedar Bark Basket, 12"	130	240	420
Pima Coiled, flaring body, human figures, dia. 10"	400	740	1300
Salish Basket, 10"	70	130	230
Salish Basket, 11"	25	50	80
Salish Basket, 15"	90	170	300
Salish Basket, fully imbricated, lidded, 6"	275	510	900
Salish Basket, w/ leather handles, c.1920	150	280	500
Salish Basket, zig zag design, 16.5"	275	510	900
Salish Basketry Tray, 18"	80	150	260
Salish Basketry Trunk, 23"	350	650	1140
Salish Boat Shape Basket, w/ gallery, 16.75"	150	280	490
Salish Cradle Basket, 24"	170	320	550
Salish Female Papoose Cradle Basket, 27.5"	200	370	650
Salish Fishing Creel/Pipe Bag Basket, 12"	450	840	1470
Salish Imbricated Basket, w/ handles, 11.5"	200	370	650
Salish Papoose Cradle Basket, 30"	200	370	650
Salish Rectangular Basket, 13.5"	95	180	310
Salish Rectangular Basket Purse, 7"	75	140	240
Salish Rectangular Lidded Basket, w/ diamond design, 15.5"	225	420	730
Salish Round Lidded Basket, 8.5"	175	330	570

	AUCTION	RETAIL Low	High
Salish Snake Track Basket, fully imbricated, lidded, c.1890, 9"	$ 425	$ 800	$ 1500
Salish Wool Knitting Basket, 10.5"	250	470	820
Sewing, wicker	40	70	130
Shaker, cheese, round, dia. 12"	340	630	1110
Splint, collecting, tightly woven, 8" x 9"	40	70	130
Splint, hickory, open handles	50	90	160
Splint, oval, wooded handles	80	150	260
Split, oak, buttocks	90	170	300
Thompson River Basket, 7.5"	40	70	130
Thompson River Basket, fully imbricated, lidded, 8.75"	1400	2600	4500
Thompson River Burden Basket, w/ handles, 22"	200	370	650
Thompson River Coiled Basket, w/ line imbrication, 12"	210	390	680
Thompson River Coiled Basket, w/ snake design, 8.25"	475	880	1550
Thompson River Coiled Imbricated Trinket Basket, c.1900, 7.75"	350	650	1140
Thompson River Lidded Basket, w/ beaded imbrication, 10"	300	560	1000
Thompson River Pedestal Basket, 10"	50	90	160
Tlingit Knob Top Spruce Root Basket, 19th c., 5.75"	500	930	1600
Ucluelet Nootka Basket, 4.5"	100	190	330
Woodlands Birch Bark Basket, w/ moosehair and quill	250	470	850
Yurok Basket, 6"	270	500	900

Right: Nantucket lightship basket, 5" x 10", $ 700- $ 900.

Left: High quality baskets from Asian tribal groups are often the best value for money: Thai carrying basket, ht. 10", $50-$100.

Beer-Related Memorabilia
Beer Cans

Beer cans are a relatively new phenomena. Krueger Brewing Company in Richmond, Virginia introduced them in 1935. Called flat tops because of the shape of the can top, a beer can opener and instructions on its use were initially given to purchasers free of charge. America learned quickly. Cone tops or crowntainers appeared shortly afterward from the Jos. Schlitz Co. The advantage of the cone top was that small breweries could produce them on a bottling production line and avoid investing in expensive equipment. They were not as popular with consumers and by the 1960s they were virtually extinct. The next innovation—pull tabs or tab tops—eliminated the need for openers.

There are a variety of ways to collect beer cans. Hobbyists collect full cans or empties. Collectors can concentrate on specific themes such as brand, state, region, or tops.

The following prices are for mint examples opened or unopened. Rust, dents, and scratches decrease the value of a beer can. Each entry below begins with the name brand and a description, followed by the type of top, the number of ounces, and the brewery name. Many colors are abbreviated throughout, such as wt. for white, bl. for blue, blk. for black, and met. for metallic. Other abbreviations used are: CT cone top, FT flat top, and TT tab top.

Many firms produced the same product in other states or licensed others to produce it. This leads to confusion. For detailed information see *The Official Price Guide to Beer Cans,* Bill Mugrage, House of Collectibles, Random House, NY, 1993. He is listed in the back of this book. The guide suggests to check older, full cans periodically to make sure they are not leaking and, if you want to drain a full can, open it from the bottom where it can't be seen. Mr. Mugrage also dispels the myth about the value of Billy Beer. He states that any of the five different versions of Billy Beer are worth $2-$3 each, not hundreds of dollars as rumored. The collector's club is The Beer Can Collectors of America, 747 Mercus Court, Fenton, MO 83026.

	LOW	HIGH
Altes Lager, silver and blk. crowntainer, CT, 12 oz., Tivoli	$ 80	$ 100
American, red, wt., bl., and gold, name/ bl. script, CT, 12 oz., Am.	90	140
Atlantic Beer, depicts antebellum scene w/ carriage and mansion, FT, 12 oz., Atlantic	600	650
B and B Beer, blue can w/ yellow beer glass, FT, 12 oz., Southern	500	550
Banner Extra Dry, wt. and red, "Prem. Beer" in bl., FT, 12 oz., Cumberland	15	20
Bantam Ale, squat, wt. and lt. grn., FT, 8 oz., Gobel	30	40
Bartels Pure, wt. and red, man w/ beard, FT, 12 oz., Lion	70	90
Bavarian Jay Vee, bl. and wt., FT, 12 oz., Grace	90	120
Bavarian's Old Style, wt., gold, and red, name/ gold lettering, CT, 12 oz., Bav.	80	100
Bay State Ale, green w/ fisherman at the wheel, FT, 12 oz., Commonwealth	600	650
Becker's Best, silver w/ blk. lettering, FT, 12 oz., Becker	90	110
Becker's Uinta Club, silver, bl., and red, bronco, CT, 12 oz., Bker	120	160
Ben Brew, yellow and gold, "100% Grain Beer," CT, 12 oz., Franklin	90	120
Beverwyck Ale, shamrock, CT, 12 oz., Beverwyck	75	85
Blackhawk, Native American profile, CT, 12 oz., Blackhawk	125	150
Blk. Dallas Malt Liq., bl. and blk., evening skyline, TT, 12 oz., Walter	70	90
Bond Hill Beer, bl., gold and red, FT, 12 oz., Gretz	600	650
Boston Light Ale, blk., wt. and red, lighthouse, CT, 12 oz., Boston	850	950
Brown Derby Beer, brown and green w/ derby and cane, FT, 12 oz., Humboldt	250	350
Buccaneer Beer, gold, wt., pirate, FT, 12 oz., Gulf	400	600
Budweiser Malt Liquor, TT, 16 oz., Anh.-Busch	50	70
Budweiser, "Tab Top," TT, 16 oz., Anh.-Busch	4	6

LOW HIGH

Buffalo Brew, orange house, FT, 12 oz., Cold Spring .... $ 2 $ 3
Burger, wt. and dark red, no outline name, FT, 12 oz., Burger 12   18
Burgermeister Prem., cream, red, and gold, gold bands, FT, 12 oz., Warsaw 5   9
Cab Cream Ale, copper color w/ horse and buggy, FT, 12 oz., Wehle 850   950
Cascade, "King Size" near top, TT, 16 oz., Blitz Weinhard 12   15
Cee Bee, red and wt., TT, 12 oz., Colonial 12   18
Champagne Velvet Beer, gold can, eagle logo, CT, 12 oz., Terre Haute
    Brewing Co. 350   450
Coal Cracker Beer, multi-color, TT, 12 oz., Yuengling 3   5
Condon's Beer, red and wt., script w/ leaf surround, CT, 12 oz., Condon 650   750
Country Club, wt., red, and gold, FT, 12 oz., Goetz 20   30
Croft Cream Ale, green can, yellow lettering, 3 heads, CT, 32 oz., Boston ... 400   450
Drewry's Malt Liq., red, green, and wt., "A Man's Drink," FT, 12 oz., Drewry .. 700   900
Frisco Beer, brown, blk. and wt. cartouche of San Francisco skyline,
    FT, 12 oz., General 600   650
Gerst 77 Beer, met., gold, red, wt., CT, 12 oz., Gerst 500   600
Glory B. Beer, red, wt. and bl., FT, 12 oz., Pacific Coast Grocery 1000   1200
Gretz Ale, yellow oval, red lettering, CT, 12 oz., Gretz 1000   1200
Highlander Prem., red and wt., revised ver., FT, 12 oz., Missoula 12   18
Hillman's Superb, bl. and gold, FT, 12 oz., Empire 60   80
Hof-Brau, red and wt., name/ gray, bl. lettering, TT, 12 oz., Maier 8   12
Hofbrau, cream wt. and red, German inn, FT, 12 oz., Hofbrau 18   22
Hoffman House, wt., brn. and red, FT, 12 oz., Walter 4   7
Holiday Special, wt. and brn. w/ bl. bands top and bottom., FT, 12 oz., Potosi .. 12   18
Horton Beer, orange can, block lettering, CT, 12 oz., Horton 400   450
Kingsbury Real Draft, wt., brn. and red, wood grain, TT, 12 oz., Kingsbury 8   10
Knickerbocker Nat., wt. w/ red and bl. ribbons, bl. lettering, TT, 7 oz.,
    Ruppert 10   15
Koehler, dk. bl. and wt., orange trim name, TT, 12 oz., Erie 3   5
Koenig Brau, gold and wt., TT, 12 oz., Koenig Brau 8   10
Krueger, yel., red, and wt., "Lt. Lager" in blk., FT, 12 oz., Krueger 40   60
Little Dutch Beer, oval w/ Dutch boy and windmills, CT, 32 oz., Wacker .. 1000   1200
London Lobby Beer, red, blk. and wht. parchment design w/ yellow
    highlights, CT, 12 oz., Miami Valley 750   850
Lucky Lager, pale bl. and gold, name curved, TT, 12 oz., Lucky Lager 5   7
Lucky Malt Liquor, TT, 16 oz., Lucky Lager 30   40
M.C. Beer, yellow can, bl. circle, CT, 12 oz., Mt. Carbon 600   650
Maier Select, red, wt., and bl., bl. leaf near top, TT, 12 oz., Maier 40   60
Malt Duck, purple and wt., TT, 12 oz., National 40   60
Manheim, red and wt., TT, 12 oz., Reading 9   12
Meister Brau, wt., gold, and red, red band at top, FT, 12 oz., Peter Hand 8   12
Mile Hi, red, wt., and bl., Colorado mountains, FT, 12 oz., Tivoli 40   60
Miller Select, red, wt., and bl.,1/4 moon in bl. medallion, FT, 12 oz., Miller .. 50   60
Milwaukee Prem., wt.,, red, and gold, FT, 12 oz., Waukee 15   20
Milwaukee's Best, bl. and wt., stein, FT, 12 oz., Gettelman 18   22
Mitchell's Prem., red, wt. and bl., FT, 12 oz., Mitchell 100   150
National Ale, green U.S. map, CT, 12 oz., National 500   550
National Beer, red U.S. map, CT, 12 oz., National 1000   1200
North Star XXX Beer, bl., wt., silver star, FT, 12 oz., Schmidt 25   35
Old Dutch Beer, brown and orange label w/ windmill, CT, 12 oz., Old
    Dutch 650   750

	LOW	HIGH
Old Milwaukee, red and wt., dk. printing on shield, FT, 12 oz., Schlitz	$ 5	$ 7
P.O.C. Pilsner Beer, maroon, gold label, CT, 12 oz., Pilsner	90	110
Pabst Bl. Ribbon, gold, wt., and bl., slogan above gold band., FT, 12 oz., Pabst	8	12
Pabst Bl. Ribbon, red, wt., and bl., FT, 12 oz., Pabst	8	10
Pacific Beer, bl. can, wt. lettering, CT, 12 oz., Rainier	300	500
Pearl Beer, wt., bl, TT, 12 oz., Pearl	8	12
Penguin Extra Dry, wt., bl., FT, 12 oz., Horlacher	12	18
Pfeiffer's, gold, wt., and red, horizon. striping, FT, 12 oz., Pfeiffer	8	12
Pickwick Ale, gold, blk., and wt., FT, 12 oz., Haffenreffer	100	150
Piel's, gold, silver, and blk., name/ wt., FT, 12 oz., Piel's	10	15
Primo Hawaiian, met. gold, wt., map, TT, 12 oz., Jos. Schlitz	18	22
Prinz Brau Beer, "Anniversary Offer," TT, 12 oz., Prinz Brau	20	30
Rainer Ale, green., gold label, TT, 12 oz., Rainer	12	18
Red Fox Beer, red can w/ dressed fox, CT, 12 oz., Largay	850	950
Senate Beer, red, brown trim, FT, 12 oz., C. Heurich	200	250
Sick's Select Beer, met. maroon, yellow, 6 globe, FT, 12 oz., Sick's	100	125
Silver State Beer, bl. and wt. can w/ script lettering, Schneider	1200	1400
Stag, "Half Quart" large wt. letters near top, TT, 16 oz., Carling	5	7
Stallion XII, gold, wt., and red. illus. of horse, TT, 12 oz., Gold Medal	80	100
Standard Cream Ale, green, wt., and gold, TT, 12 oz., Std. Rochester	15	20
Standard Dry Ale, bl., wt., and gold, TT, 12 oz., Eastern	5	7
Stegmaier Bock, brown and wt., "Truly Brewed," TT, 12 oz., Stegmaier	2	3
Stegmaier Gold Medal, gold and wt., TT, 12 oz., Stegmaier	2	3
Sunshine Vitamin D, brn. and wt., CT, 12 oz., Schlitz	60	80
Topaz (crowntainer), silver, red stripes near bottom, CT, 12 oz., Koller	100	150
Topper Draught (gal.), CT, 64 oz., Standard	40	50
Tropical Beer, brown and wt., CT, 12 oz., Florida	500	550
Tropical Prem., brn. and wt. "Taste Tells," CT, 12 oz., Florida	350	450
Tru-Blue Ale, bl., green, yellow, and wt., 10-star decoration, CT, 12 oz., North Hampton	350	400
Valley Forge Beer, yellow lettering in red shield w/ cannons and crest, FT, 32 oz., Adam Scheidt	400	450
Viking Draft Beer, brown, blk., FT, 12 oz., Spearman	380	420
Wagner's Gambrinus, gold and multi, CT, 12 oz., Wagner	120	160
Wiedemann (crowntainer), CT, 12 oz., Wiedemann	80	120

Left to right: Ballantine, $16-$20; Horlacher, $8-$12; Schaefer, $25-$35. —Items Courtesy Jim Glaab's Collector's Showcase.

Beer Trays

Are they a work of art? Or are they just a bit of nostalgia? Beer trays should have no rust and a minimum of scratches. Valuable trays, like some of the early Anheuser-Busch trays, are now reproduced in large quantities.

Left to right: Anheuser-Busch tray, c. 1900, $2000-$3000; E. Robinson's & Sons tray, c. 1895, $400-$600. —Photos courtesy of James D. Julia, Inc.

	LOW	HIGH
Ambassador, G. Krueger, Newark, NJ; shield-form logo in blue, gold, red, "Ambassador Export Brewed Beer," white bkgd., ca. 1950, 11"	$ 40	$ 70
Ballantine, P. Ballantine & Sons, Newark, NJ; 3-ring logo in white, blue bkgd., yellow lettering, ca. 1950, 11"	20	30
Beverwyck, Beverwyck, Albany, NY; shield w/ 4 "B"s above "Famous Beverwyck Beer," green bkgd., gold center, ca. 1940, 11"	80	130
Beverwyck, Beverwyck, Albany, NY; "Beverwyck Brand Irish Cream Ale" on green cloverleaf, ca. 1940, 12"	80	130
Blatz, Blatz, Milwaukee, WC; oval script logo, blue bkgd., red center, white lettering, ca. 1950, 11"	15	20
Blatz, Blatz, Milwaukee, WC; 3 figures in forms of bottle, can and barrel, white bkgd., ca. 1950, 12"	50	80
Budweiser, Anheuser-Busch, St. Louis, MO; beer bottle and tall glass, red bkgd. w/ wheat and hops, ca. 1940, 11"	35	50
Budweiser, Anheuser-Busch, St. Louis, MO; eagle logo above red, yellow, and green geometric shapes, white bkgd., ca. 1950, 11"	20	30
Busch, Anheuser-Busch, St. Louis, MO; "Busch Bavarian" on polychrome mountain scene, ca. 1960, 12"	20	25
Clipper, Harvard, Lowell, MA; polychrome clipper ship, ca. 1940, 12"	200	350
Croft, Croft, Boston, MA; 3 head drinking above yellow block lettering, green bkgd., ca. 1940, 12"	90	160
Dawson's, Dawson, New Bedford, MA; polychrome dinner scene, ca. 1940, 11"	110	190
Dobler, Dobler, "Dobler Beer and Ale," white bkgd. w/ green stripes, ca. 1950, 11"	50	80
Fort Schuyler, Utica, Utica. NY; "Fort Schuyler Ales and Lager" surrounding polychrome fort, black bkgd., ca. 1950, 11"	80	130

	LOW	HIGH

Gretz, William Gretz, Phila., PA; man w/ white mustache and ca. 1900
   clothes above "Gretz Beer," blue bkgd., yellow lettering, ca. 1950, 11" ... $ 70 $ 120

Hampden, Hampden, Willimansett, MA; polychrome man standing on
   barrel, yellow bkgd., green edge, ca. 1940, 12" 60   110

Harvard, Harvard, Lowell, MA; flag logo above "Harvard • Ale, • Beer, •
   Porter," gray bkgd., red lettering, ca. 1940, 12" 50   90

Hedrick, Hedrick, Albany, NY; "Still the Best, Hedrick Ale and Lager,"
   gold lettering on wood-grain bkgd., ca. 1950, 12" 50   90

Hull's, Hull, New Haven, CT; depicts can and bottle on wood-grain bkgd.,
   ca. 1940, 11" 110   190

Hull's, Hull, New Haven, CT; polychrome woman w/ beer glass, blue
   bkgd., ca. 1940, 11" 125   175

Hull's, Hull, New Haven, CT; polychrome mug and white center on wood-
   grain bkgd., ca. 1950, 12" 60   110

Iroquois, Iroquois Beverage, Buffalo, NY; Indian chief w/ feathered bonnet
   in profile in gold and brown, ca. 1960, 12" 40   60

Knickerbocker, Jacob Ruppert, New York, NY; colonial man holding beer
   mug, wood-grain bkgd., ca. 1960, 11" 30   50

Koch's, Fred Koch Brewery, Dunkirk, NY; "Go All the Way...Drink Koch's
   Beer-Ale," red diamond, gray bkgd., ca. 1960, 12" 40   60

Krueger, G. Krueger, Newark, NJ; K/man logo above Krueger Beer-Ale, red
   bkgd., ca. 1950, 11" 40   60

Krueger, G. Krueger, Cranston, RI; gold and gray shield, lion logo, white
   bkgd., ca. 1960, 11" 30   50

Leinenkugel's, Jacob Leinenkugel, Chippewa Falls, WC; Indian woman
   profile logo above "Leinenkugel's Beer," lettering on lip, white bkgd.,
   ca. 1960, 11" 25   35

Lone Star, Lone Star, San Antonio, TX; star topped shield on gold and white
   bkgd., "makes the most nature's best," ca. 1960, 12" 30   50

Miller, Miller, Milwaukee, WC; white seal above "100 Years in America"
   above Miller High Life logo, gold bkgd., ca. 1950, 11" 25   35

Narragansett, Narragansett, Cranston, RI; logo above "The Famous Old
   Narragansett Ale," red bkgd., ca. 1940, 12" 80   130

Old Ranger, Hornell, Hornell, NY; "Old Ranger" above man in coonskin
   cap, white (top) and red (bottom) bkgd., ca. 1950, 11" 60   110

Old Stock, Phila., Phila., PA; "Drink Old Stock/Finest Beer in Town," red
   bkgd., white lettering, ca. 1940, 11" 100   125

Old Style, G. Heilemann, LaCrosse, WC; polychrome Bavarian village
   scene, white bkgd., ca. 1970, 11" 7   9

Olympia, Olympia, Olympia, WA; "Hale Export Olympia Beer" above
   horseshoe and "It's the Water," white bkgd., ca. 1970, 12" 4   6

Pabst, Pabst, Milwaukee, WC; "What'll you have?" above blue ribbon logo,
   white bkgd., ca. 1950, 11" 10   15

Point, Stevens Point, Stevens Pt., WC; American Eagle logo above "Point
   Bicentennial Beer," white bkgd., ca. 1970, 12" 10   15

Prior, Adam Scheidt, Norristown, PA; rampant lion and unicorn flanking
   "Tasty Prior Lager/Beer" on striped gold bkgd., ca. 1950, 11" 40   70

R & H, Rubsam & Horrmann, New York, NY; "R & H Beer-Ale," centered
   by five yellow circles, lettering on lip, yellow bkgd., ca. 1950, 12" 50   80

Schaefer, F.M. Schaefer, Brooklyn, NY; Schaefer logo, white lettering, red
   bkgd., ca. 1950, 11" 15   20

	LOW	HIGH
Schlitz, Jos. Schlitz, Milwaukee, WC; 5 small polychrome scenes surrounding Schlitz logo, white and blue bkgd., ca. 1960, 12"	$ 15	$ 20
Schlitz, Jos. Schlitz, Milwaukee, WC; ten globe designs surrounding Schlitz logo, white bkgd., ca. 1960, 12"	15	20
Schlitz Light, Jos. Schlitz, Milwaukee, WC; globe above "Schlitz Light Beer" over stylized sun, white bkgd., ca. 1970, 12"	8	12
Schmidt's, C. Schmidt & Sons, Phila., PA; crest above "Schmidt's of Philadelphia Beer and Ale," gold bkgd., ca. 1960, 12"	20	40
Stanton, Stanton, Troy, NY; "Absolutely the Best Ever Brewed" above "Stanton Beer," white bkgd., ca. 1940, 11"	80	130
Star, Star, Boston, MA; polychrome colonial tavern scene, ca. 1940, 11"	170	290
Stoney's, Jones, Smithton, PA; "Enjoy Yourself W/ Stoney's," 2 cartoon figures, red bkgd., ca. 1960, 12"	60	110
Utica Club, West End, Utica, NY; polychrome hand and beer glass under "Utica Club Pilsner Beer-Cream Ale," white bkgd., ca. 1960, 12"	20	30
Utica Club, West End, Utica, NY; polychrome factory building "The Famous Utica Beer," ca. 1950, 11"	50	90

Scheidt's Ram's Head Ale, ca. 1948, $25-$40.

Boxes

During the 18th and 19th centuries, Americans used boxes as utilitarian items. They made specialized boxes for a wide variety of purposes, from containers for food to storage of wedding dresses. Small boxes, for trinkets, matches or cigarettes, are some of the most collectible.

Late 18th/early 19th century boxes, clockwise from top left: New England bird's eye maple box, length 12"; $2800, New England inlaid tea caddy, length 11", $650; Pennsylvania Chippendale walnut work box, length 14", $2200; New England Chippendale sewing box, length 13", $1100. — *Photo courtesy of Northeast Auctions.*

	AUCTION	RETAIL Low	High
Apple-Form Box, early 19th cent., ht. 5"	$ 400	$ 700	$ 1100
Battersea Box, enamel bird form, late 18th cent., len. 3"	700	1230	1930
Battersea Enamel Necessaire, len. 3"	450	790	1240
Bible Box, carved elm wood of oblong form, front carved "I.W. 1787," len. 25"	400	700	1100
Bible Box, Pa. wal. w/ inlaid monogram "MG," Chester County; interior fitted w/ till and 2 secret drawers, raised on ball feet, ht. 10", w. 20.5", d. 14"	3000	5250	8250
Casket-Form Box, Eng. regency rosewood grained, len. 15".	200	350	550
Cutlery Box, late 19th cent., len. 3", on mah. stand, len. 17"	400	700	1100
Decanter Case, French brass inlaid burl wal., fitted w/ crystal bottles and wines, len. 13"	1600	2800	4400
Hatbox, "A Peep at Moon," early 19th cent., blue wallpaper, len. 19"	850	1490	2340
Hatbox, early 19th cent., oval blue ground, "A Peep at Moon," len. 17"	600	1050	1650
Hatbox, early 19th cent., w/ parrot and lighthouse decoration	800	1400	2200
Hatbox, early 19th cent., yellow ground, chariots, len. 17"	150	260	410
Hatbox, early 19th cent., yellow ground, w/ hunters, len. 20"	200	350	550
Hatbox, Hannah Davis, early 19th cent., blue ground, floral, dec., labeled	850	1490	2340

	AUCTION	RETAIL	
		Low	High
Hatbox, yellow ground, early 19th cent., depicting lute player, len. 16"	$ 350	$ 610	$ 960
Hatbox, yellow ground, early 19th cent., Erie Canal, len. 16"	300	530	830
Hatbox, yellow ground, early 19th cent., w/ classical views, len. 17"	350	610	960
Hatbox, yellow ground, early 19th cent., w/ giraffe design, len. 19"	400	700	1100
Hatboxes, early 19th cent., 2 nested blue ground hatboxes w/ classical landscapes, len. of largest 19".	1500	2630	4130
Horseman's Riding Box, Amer. red-painted and decorated, front lid decorated w/ running horse, ends and back w/ horse motifs, top w/ carrying handle, len. 22"	1600	2800	4400
Humidor, Eng. inlaid burl wal. dome top w/ oval inlay, fitted on stand w/ drawer on sq. legs, ht. 41", len. 25"	3600	6300	9900
Knife Box, diminutive Shagreen w/ brass fittings, ht. 8"	450	790	1240
Knife Boxes, pr., Hpwt. mah. of serpentine form, w/ elaborate inlaid shell, silver mount monogrammed "CJEJ," ht. 14"	6500	11,300	17,800
Knife Boxes, pr., inlaid mah. serpentine form, ht. 15"	550	960	1510
Lap Desk, brass-bound mah.	200	350	550
Mechanical Jewelry Box, continental w/ faux-tortoise finish and brass inlay, len. 13"	1000	1750	2750
Pantry Box, N.E. painted, lid decorated w/ double star motif, side w/ pr. of shields, dia. 6.5"	2300	4000	6000
Pipe Box, Amer. Chippendale carved mah., late 18th cent., ht. 16"	1100	1800	3000
Pipe Box w/ heart cut-out in green paint, ht. 20"	225	390	620
Sewing Box, Eng. penwork, early 19th cent., len. 6"	500	880	1380
Sewing Box, late 19th cent., red leather w/ brass hardware	350	610	960
Snuff Box, risqué papier-mâché, mid-19th cent.	450	790	1240
Snuff Box, w/ ivory miniature of George Washington, dia. 3.5".	1300	2280	3580
Spice Box, Eng. oak w/ molded panel door, ht. 13"	800	1400	2200
Spice Cabinet, Eng. W. & M., fruitwood w/ drawer, ht. 27"	1000	1750	2750
Storage Box, N.E. painted and decorated pine of dovetailed construction, w/ swirling blue-green putty decorations and side handles, len. 24"	800	1400	2200
Tea Caddy, bird's-eye maple and mah., len. 8"	275	480	760
Tea Caddy, Eng., early 19th cent., bowfront mah. w/ paterae inlay, len. 8"	425	740	1170
Tea Caddy, Eng., early 19th cent., inlaid mah. w/ paterae and quarter-fan spandrels	400	700	1100
Tea Caddy, Eng. inlaid burl-walnut rect. w/ canted corners, len. 12"	600	1050	1650
Tea Caddy, Eng. mah. coffin-form, len. 7"	200	350	550
Tea Caddy, Eng. penwork, early 19th cent., len. 9"	900	1580	2480
Tea Caddy, Hexagonal Quill-work, late 18th cent., len. 13"	1300	2280	3580
Tea Caddy, Regency-style faux-tortoiseshell, len. 12"	1150	2010	3160
Tea Caddy, Chippendale inlaid mah. bombe form, len. 11"	750	1310	2060
Work Box, N.E. painted and decorated	200	350	550
Work Box, India-trade zebra wood w/ elaborate fitted interior, len. 14"	500	880	1380

Cameras

Louis Daguerre invented the first commercial camera in 1839. For the next 30 years nearly all cameras were for professional studios. During the 1870s amateur photography bloomed. The cameras of the late 19th century were generally large and bulky box cameras and bellows cameras. But strange and sometimes bizarre novelty cameras also appeared, including cameras designed in the forms of pocket watches, canes, and even neckties. In 1888 the Eastman Dry Plate and Film Company introduced the first commercially available roll film camera, the Kodak. It followed with the No. 1 Kodak the next year. Soon the Eastman Kodak Company came to dominate the American market. The hundreds of various cameras produced under the Kodak name outstrip any other maker's production record.

Collectors want cameras that are complete and in working order. Some allowance is made for the fragility of leather bellows and rubber parts. For further information see *The Official Price Guide to Collectible Cameras* and *Camera Collecting*, by Jason Schneider.

Assorted

	LOW	HIGH		LOW	HIGH
Adams Minex	$ 340	$ 430	Ansco Shur-Flash	$ 10	$ 15
Adams Yale No. 2	310	400	Ansco Vest Pocket No. 2	60	70
Adox Blitz	20	25	Ansco Viking	20	30
Adox Golf	40	50	Ansco Viking Readyset	20	30
Agfa Ambi-Silette	280	350	Anscoflex	20	25
Agfa Captain	20	25	Anthony Ascot Cycle No. 1	110	140
Agfa Clipper PD-16	10	15	Apollo	50	60
Agfa Clipper Special	20	25	Argoflex	20	30
Agfa Isolette Super	30	40	Argus A2B	40	50
Agfa Isomat	10	15	Argus A3	40	50
Agfa Karat 36	70	90	Argus Argoflash (AA)	60	70
Agfa Memo	120	150	Argus Argoflex	20	30
Agfa Readyset 1A	40	50	Argus Argoflex Model E	20	30
Agfa Shur-Shot	20	25	Argus Argoflex Model EM	20	30
Agfa Silette	60	70	Argus Autronic 35	60	70
Agfa Super Silette	60	70	Argus Autronic C 3	60	70
Agfa Ventura Deluxe	10	15	Argus C2	100	125
Agfa View	140	170	Argus C3 Match-Matic	50	60
Aires 35 IIIL	70	90	Argus C44R	100	125
Aires 35 V	110	140	Argus C4R	100	125
Aires Airesflex	100	125	Argus FA	50	60
Aires Penta 35	110	140	Arrow	20	30
Aires Viscount	60	80	ASR Foto-Disc	920	1150
Altissa	60	80	Astraflex	320	400
Altix	80	100	Autoflex (Kiyabashi)	70	90
Altura	110	140	Automatica (Durst)	230	290
Ansco Anscoflex	20	25	Baby Brownie	10	15
Ansco Automatic Reflex	230	290	Baida Baldina Super	100	120
Ansco (Box)	20	25	Balda Baldax	60	80
Ansco Clipper Flash	20	25	Balda Baldina	60	80
Ansco Folding No. 7	60	70	Balda Poka	20	30
Ansco Readyset No. 1A	20	30	Balda Rollbox 120	25	30
Ansco Regent	60	80	Balda Super Pontura	110	140
Ansco Semi-Automatic	320	400	Baldaxette	80	100

	LOW	HIGH
Baldessa	$ 70	$ 90
Baldi	100	120
Bantam f5.6	60	70
Bantam RF f3.9	60	70
Bauer	50	60
Beier Beira	320	400
Beier Precisa	70	90
Beier Rifax	60	70
Beira	320	400
Beirax	50	60
Belca Belfoca	60	70
Belca Belplasca	690	860
Belca Beltica	60	70
Belfoca	60	70
Bellieni Jumelle Stereo	370	460
Belplasca	690	860
Benson Street	320	400
Berning Robot I	210	260
Billy (Agfa)	20	30
Billy Record (Agfa)	20	30
Bioflex	20	30
Blair Kamaret	830	1000
Blair Lucidograph No. 1	1350	1750
Blair View	370	460
Bolsey B	50	60
Bolsey Bolseyflex	40	50
Bolsey Expiorer	70	90
Bolsey Reflex	650	800
Boyer Altessa	230	290
Braun Paxette Automatic III	60	80
Braun Paxette Super	60	80
Braun Paxina II	40	50
Bullard (Magazine)	550	690
Bulls-Eye (Boston)	110	140
Bulls-Eye Folding No. 2	230	290
Bulls-Eye No. 2	60	70
Bulls-Eye No. 4 Special	140	180
Burke & James Grover	170	210
Burke & James Rexo 3	30	40
Burke & James Rexo Junior 1A	30	40
Burke & James Rexo Junior 3	30	40
Butcher Carbine Reflex	220	280
Butcher Midg No. 00	60	80
Cam-O	140	170
Camera- Lite	460	580
Camera Radio (Tom Thumb)	230	290
Candid Perfex Forty-Four	60	80
Candid Perfex One-O-Two	60	80
Canon 7-S	460	580

	LOW	HIGH
Canon Demi	$ 100	$ 125
Canon Dial-35	100	125
Canon II-F	230	290
Canon IV-F	260	320
Canonet	100	125
Carpentier Photo-Jumelle	420	520
Century Universal View	320	400
Certo Certonet	60	70
Certo Dolly	100	125
Certo Dolly Supersport	100	125
Certo Doppel Box	60	80
Certonet	60	70
Certotrop	80	100
Chevron	320	400
Chiyodo Konan Automat 16	230	290
Chiyoko	100	120
Ciro Ciro-flex Model C	50	60
Ciro-flex	50	60
Citoskop (Contessa)	600	750
Close & Cone Quad	230	290
Color Camera (Fotochrome)	60	70
Compass	1500	1850
Conley Kewpie No. 3	30	40
Conley Kewpie No. 3A	50	60
Conley Stereo Box	690	860
Conley View	230	290
Contessa Cocarette	70	90
Contessa Ergo	2120	2650
Contessa Nic 63	60	70
Coronet Vogue	140	180
Cosmic 35	60	70
Dallmeyer Speed	600	750
Dangelmaier Decora l	40	50
Daydark Photo Postcard	280	350
Daydark Tintype	180	230
Deckrullo-Nettel (Contessa)	740	925
Decora (Dangelmaier)	40	50
Dehel	40	50
Dejur Reflex	70	90
Delta Stereo	110	140
Detrola 400	550	700
Detrola Modet GW	30	40
Devry QRS Kamra	100	125
Diplomat	20	30
Dollina (Certo)	130	160
Doppel Box (Certo)	60	80
Doris	40	50
Dossert Detective	1750	2225
Duaflex IV	10	15
Duchessa (Contessa)	280	350
Duex	20	30

	LOW	HIGH
Duo Six-20	$ 110	$ 140
Duo Six-20 Series II	100	120
Durst Duca	210	260
Ebner	460	580
Elaner	50	60
Emson	40	50
Ernemann Heag I	60	80
Ernemann Heag II-Series II	60	80
Ernemann Heag VII	70	90
Ernemann Klapp	280	350
Ernemann Two-Shuttered	420	520
Eulitz Grisette	100	120
Eureka Junior No. 2	140	170
Exco	230	290
Expo Easy-Load	140	170
Expo Police	420	520
Expo Watch	180	230
Fed-Flash	20	25
Fed No. 1	140	170
Feinoptische Astraflex II	370	460
Feinwrek Mec 16 SB	110	140
Felica	20	25
Fiesta (Brownie)	10	15
Film Plate Premo	80	100
Finette	50	60
Firstflex	50	60
Flektar	60	80
Foitzik Trier Unca	60	70
Folding Rainbow Hawkeye	30	40
Foth Derby Model II	80	100
Foth Derby Model 1	80	100
Fotochrome Color Camera	60	70
Franke & Heidecke Rollei 16	110	140
Galter Hopalong Cassidy	50	60
Gamma	920	1150
Gaumont Spido Stereo	410	510
Gemflex	600	750
Genie	1020	1270
Gennert Montauk Folding	140	170
Gevabox	20	30
Gilles-Faller Studio Camera	650	810
Goerz Ango	230	290
Goerz Tengor	60	80
Goldeck-16	280	350
Goldi	110	140
Goltz & Breutmann Mentorett	320	400
Graflex Auto	230	290
Graflex Auto R.B.	280	350
Graflex Fingerprint	200	250
Graflex R.B. Series D	200	250
Graflex Stereo Auto	$ 2760	$ 3450
Gray	370	460
Guthe & Thorsch Kawee	110	140
Guthe & Throsch Praktiflex	100	120
Haking Halina	20	30
Hamco	20	30
Haneel Tri-Vision Stereo	70	90
Hare Stereo	2750	3450
Harmony	20	30
Hit	20	30
Hit Stereo	140	180
Hoei Ebony 35	20	25
Hofert Eho Stereo Box	180	220
Home Portrait Graflex	460	580
Homer 16	50	60
Houghton Ensign Popular Reflex	230	290
Houghton Ensign Reflex	230	290
Houghton Klito Folding	100	120
Houghton May Fair	30	40
Houghton Midget	100	120
Hüttig Atom	370	460
Hüttig Ideal Stereo	310	390
Hüttig Stereolette	460	580
Ica Atom Vertical Format	320	400
Ica Cupido	60	80
Ica Halloh 505	70	90
Ica Icarette C	70	90
Ica Juwel Universal	500	630
Ica Nelson 225	80	100
Ica Toska	60	70
Ihagee Exa II a	70	90
Ihagee Exakta C	370	460
Ihagee Exakta II	140	170
Ihagee Ultrix Auto	100	120
Inspectograph (Graflex)	200	250
Iso Duplex	280	350
Japy Pascal	1380	1730
Jumelle (Gallus)	370	460
Kenflex	50	60
Kent	20	30
Keystone Street Camera	320	400
Kiev	110	140
King Regula	50	60
King Regula B	50	60
King Regula IIID	50	60
Kiyabashi Autoflex	70	90
Kodet Folding No. 4	740	920
Konan (Chiyodo)	230	290
Konishiroku Konica II	100	120
Krauss Eka	2210	2760

	LOW	HIGH
Krauss Polyscop	$ 370	$ 460
Kullenberg Field	420	520
Laack Padie	60	80
Lancaster Ladies Camera	2210	2760
Lancaster Merveilleux	280	350
Le Reve	370	460
Leitz Leica I c	420	520
Leitz Leica I g	1290	1610
Leitz Leica II c	320	400
Leitz Leica II (D) Black	320	400
Leitz Leica III 9	1020	1270
Leitz Leica III b (G)	420	520
Leitz Leica III c	230	290
Leitz Leica III c K-Model	1200	1500
Leitz Leica III (F) Chrome	250	310
Leitz Ur-Leica (Replica)	1380	1730
Leullier Summum Special	370	460
LevyRoth Minigraph	2390	2990
Linhof Silar	230	290
Linhof Stereo Panorama	550	690
Linhof Technika l	970	1210
Lizars Challenge	320	400
Lumiere Eljy	140	170
Lumiere Lumix F	50	60
Lumiere Sinox	50	60
Lumiere Sterelux	370	460
Mamiya 6	100	130
Manhattan Wizard A	500	630
Manhattan Wizard Senior	140	180
Manufok Tenax	100	120
Marion Soho Reflex	650	810
Medalist I	230	290
Meisupi-Half	20	30
Meopta Flexaret	100	120
Meopta Mikroma	180	230
Midget (Coronet)	130	160
Mikut Color Camera	5520	6900
Mimosa I	420	520
Mimosa II	370	460
Minetta	20	25
Minolta 16	50	60
Minolta 35	170	210
Minolta A2	60	70
Minolta Semi-Minolta	100	130
Minox A	140	170
Minox III Gold Plated	3310	4140
Minox III-S	130	160
Minox (made in USSR)	1380	1730
Miranda G	160	200
Mitsukoshi Picny	180	230
Moller Cambinox	1380	1730

	LOW	HIGH
Monroe Model 7	$ 230	$ 290
Montanus Montiflex	180	230
Montgomery Ward Model B	110	140
Monti Monte-35	40	50
Moscow-4	230	290
Motormatic 35	70	90
Motormatic (Eastman)	70	90
Multiplying View (Wing)	10,000	12,500
Murer Express	230	290
Murer Reflex	230	290
National Graflex	260	330
Naturalist's Graflex	5150	6440
Negel 18 (Recomar)	140	170
Nettel Argus	2300	2880
Nettel Deckrullo	320	400
Nettel (Folding Plate)	110	140
Nikkorex	140	180
Nikon S2	370	460
Nikon S3	740	920
Nikon SP	920	1150
Nishida Westar	60	80
Olympus Olympus 35	70	90
Olympus Pen F	200	250
Olympus Pen FT	280	350
Ontobloc (Cornu)	100	120
Opema	460	580
Owla Stereo	280	350
Papigny Jumelle Stereo	420	520
PDQ (Chicago Ferrotype)	180	230
Peerflekta	50	60
Pentacon Penti	100	120

Jem Flash, $20-$30.

	LOW	HIGH
Penti	$ 100	$ 120
Periflex (Corfield)	320	400
Perka	320	400
Petri	60	80
Photo-Porst Hapo 35	50	60
Pipon (Magazine)	180	230
Pipon Self-Worker	460	580
Plate Camera No. 4 Series D	170	210
Plaubel (Folding Plate)	70	90
Plaubel Makina II	310	390
Plaubel Makina III	310	390
Plaubel Makina Stereo	2300	2880
Polaroid Model 180	410	510
Polaroid Model 80 B	20	25
Polaroid Model 800	20	30
Polaroid Model 900	20	30
Popular Pressman (SLR)	210	260
Pouva Start	40	50
Premium (Plate Box)	370	460
Pygmee (Carmen)	280	350
Raaco	200	250
Ray Ray Jr.	110	140
Ray Ray No. 1	110	140
RB Auto Graflex	280	350
Recomar No. 18	120	150
Reflex Camera Co. Reflex	300	380
Regal Miniature	20	25
Regent (Japan)	20	30
Rex Kayson	80	100
Ricoh-35	50	60
Ricohflex	50	60
Riken Steky	100	120
Riken Steky II	80	100
Riken Steky IIIb	80	100
Robra	60	80
Royer Savoyflex	140	170
Ruthine	50	60
Saint Louis	320	400
Schleissner Bower X	20	30
Scovill Mascot	830	1040
Secam Stereophot	1200	1500
Seneca Busy Bee	120	150
Seneca Chautauqua	100	120
Sept (Debrie)	320	400
Shalco	20	30
Shew Eclipse	460	580
Sida Extra	110	140
Simmon Omega 120	420	520
Sinclair Una	460	580
Singlo	100	120
Solida (Franka)	50	60

	LOW	HIGH
Spartus 120	$ 25	$ 20
Spartus 35	20	25
Spartus Spartaflex	20	25
Speed Candid Perfex	110	140
Starlet (Brownie)	20	25
Steroco (Contessa)	460	580
Stöckig Union	180	230
Sunart Folding View	230	290
Suter Detective Magazine	1100	1380
Suter Muro Stereo	740	920
Taisei Koki Welmy 35	50	60
Takahashi Gelto D III	140	170
Tanaka Tanack IV-S	230	290
Thornward Dandy	110	140
Tintype Camera (New York Ferrotype)	370	460
Tivoli	420	520
Tone	180	230
Tropical Clarissa	2210	2760
Twin 20 (Brownie)	10	15
Ultra Fex	40	50
Universal Corsair I	40	50
Universal Roamer II	30	40
Universal Twinflex	60	80
Universal Univex Model A	20	30
Utility Cariton	20	25
Utility Press Flash	20	25
Vest Pocket Jiffy	20	30
Vigilant Six-16	50	60
Vive M.P. C.	110	140
Vive No. 1	170	210
Vive Tourist	160	200
Voigtländer Avus	70	90
Voigtländer Bessa l	100	120
Voigtländer Vito B	60	80
Voigtländer Vito II	60	80
Walz-Wide	70	90
Welta Perle	80	100
Welta Superflekta	830	1040
Welta Welti	60	80
Welta Weltur	230	290
Western Cyclone Sr.	70	90
Windsor Stereo	180	230
Wirgin Edinex	60	80
Wirgin Gewirette	120	150
Zeh Zeca	60	80
Zeiss Baldur Box	60	80
Zeiss Contax I	1100	1380
Zeiss Contax IIa	280	350
Zeiss Piccolette	280	350
Zeiss Trix	80	100

Eastman Kodak

	LOW	HIGH
Anniversary Camera	$ 17	$ 32
Automatic 35	37	50
Baby Brownie	8	12
Bantam f3.9 RF	35	50
Bantam Flash	45	65
Bantam RF f3.9	35	50
Beau Brownie	65	100
Brownie Baby	8	12
Brownie (box) No. 0	22	45
Brownie (box) No. 1 Improved	55	80
Brownie (box) No. 1 (orig.)	750	1100
Brownie (box) No. 2	12	18
Brownie (box) No. 2A	10	14
Brownie (box) No. 2C	10	15
Brownie (box) No. 3	10	16
Brownie Folding No. 2	28	40
Brownie Holiday	6	9
Bullet No. 2	60	90
Bullet No. 4	100	150
Bulls-Eye No. 2	30	60
Cirkut No. 10	2750	3750
Cirkut No. 5	800	1200
Cirkut Outfit No. 6	850	1550
Daylight Kodak A	1250	1850
Daylight Kodak B	600	1000
Ektra	650	1100
Eureka No. 2	80	140
Falcon No. 2	75	120
Flexo No. 2	40	60
Flush Back Kodak No. 3	65	115
Folding Kodak No. 4A	70	110
Gift Kodak	85	133
Girl Scout Kodak	120	200
Hawkette No. 2	20	50
Hawkeye Cartridge No. 2	10	16
Hawkeye Film Pack No. 2	15	25
Hawkeye Vest Pocket	25	50
Jiffy Kodak Six-16	19	30
Jiffy Kodak Vest Pocket	16	20
Kodak 35	20	36
Kodak 35 Rangefinder	25	40
Kodak Automatic 35	36	50
Kodak Junior No. 1	20	35
Kodak No. 1	1100	1600
Kodak No. 2	500	700
Kodak No. 3	500	800
Kodak (orig. model)	3500	5000
Kodak Reflex Model I	50	75
Kodak Senior Six-16	40	60

	LOW	HIGH
Kodak Six-16 Special	$ 50	$ 80
Kodak Six-20	40	70
Kodak Super Six-20	1300	1900
Kodet Folding No. 4	550	850
Kodet No. 4	300	500
Medalist I	150	250
Monitor Six-16	30	50
Motormatic 35	50	75
Nagel Junior	26	40
Petite	150	200
Pony II	10	30
Pony IV	15	25
Premo Cartridge No. 00	50	70
Premo Cartridge No. 2	15	25
Premo No. 12	40	60
Premo Senior	100	150
Premoette No. 1	43	60
Recomar No. 18	80	120
Regent	300	500
Retina Automatic I	150	200
Retina I	74	135
Retina III C	160	270
Retina Reflex	100	150
Retina Reflex III	120	175
Retina Reflex IV	160	260
Retinette IA	50	80
Signet 30	35	50
Special Kodak No. 1A	50	70
Speed Kodak No. 1A	220	300
Star Premo	60	100
Super Kodak Six-20	1300	1900
Tourist	14	20
Tourist II	14	20
Vanity Kodak	100	150
Vanity Kodak Ensemble	1100	1600
Zenith Kodak No. 3	210	310

Kodak Brownie.

Canes

Canes are either simple walking sticks or "gadget" canes that conceal a sword, pistol, musical instrument, or other device. The stylish canes of Europe came into vogue in the 17th and 18th centuries, while the 19th century saw gadget canes reaching their peak of popularity. When buying a cane or walking stick, examine it closely for indications of hidden compartments. Many devices go undiscovered for years.

Carved folk art canes are judged by their style and the skill of the carver. Many of the most desirable ones date from the mid-19th century. We've seen many of varying quality in the auctions of New England.

"Good" examples are undamaged with simple carving or simple forming. "Best" examples have superior carving or forming and (if wood or metal) a fine patina.

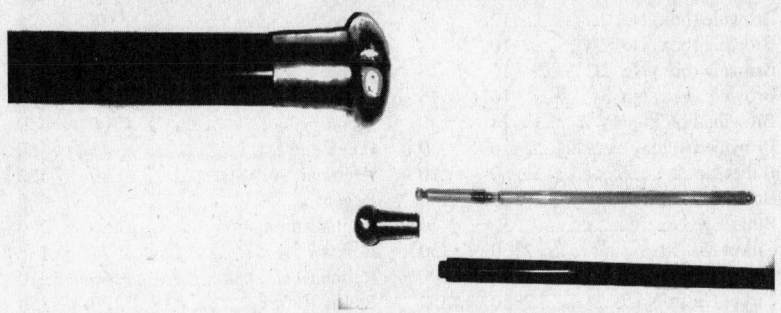

Ordinary canes can contain some surprises. The silver handled cane, above left, opens to reveal a thin glass bottle, above right.

	GOOD	BETTER	BEST
Bamboo, curved handle, c. 1920	$ 17	$ 25	$ 45
Bone Handled Cane, geometric carving	100	150	200
Bottle Cane, glass liner holds liquor, 36"	150	200	400
Bucolic Nude, bronze	3500	3750	4000
Cactus Wood Cane, owned by General Patton	—	—	1200
Civil War Motifs, carved, signed, c. 1863	1200	1600	2000
Clenched Hand, ivory, c. 1870	180	300	500
Dog's Head, carved and painted, late 19th century	300	350	400
Dog's Head, wood w/ brown eyes, c. 1900	40	65	125
Eagle Head, Tiffany silver	2500	3000	3500
Fist Holding Key, ivory	2500	2750	3000
Glass, green, hand-blown	85	100	225
Gun Cane, late 19th century	1200	1500	1700
Hound's Head, ivory, c. 1890	70	125	235
Monkey, hand-carved	95	132	275
Mother-of-Pearl, gold, c. 1900	65	100	200
Narwhal Cane, in leather case	—	—	6000
Parade Cane, china clown head	40	55	115

	GOOD	BETTER	BEST
Phrenology Head	—	—	$ 5000
Reproduction Oak Cane, horse	$ 7	$ 18	30
Reproduction Oak Cane, eagle	7	18	30
Reproduction Oak Cane, duck	7	18	30
Snake Carved Walking Stick, late 19th century	100	150	200
Staghorn, carved with face, mid-19th century	300	350	400
Swiss Watch, in silver mount	500	1600	3500
Umbrella Cane, wood case, 34"	90	135	265
Victorian Lady's Leg, ivory	300	1000	4000
Walking Stick, gold head	110	145	300
Walking Stick, sterling head	50	65	140
Wildcat Fighting a Snake, ivory	800	1200	1600
Woolly Mammoth Ivory Cane, w/ carved animal	600	1000	2000

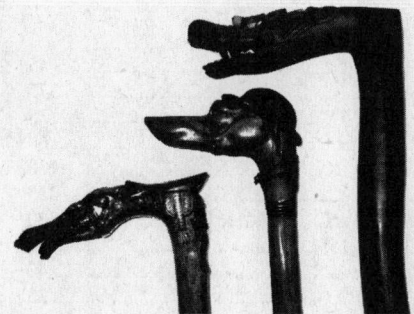

Left to right: Finely carved European horse head cane, $75-$120; polychrome decorated carved English hound head cane, $100-$150; modern carved Asian dragon cane, $20-$30.

Chalkware

Plaster of Paris figurines painted in bright colors are called chalkware. Originally produced as a cheap imitation of Staffordshire and Bennington wares during the middle and late 1800s, American companies later manufactured examples as carnival prizes during the first half of the 20th century. Animals with nodding heads are especially rare. Few were produced and even fewer have survived through the years. They are sometimes found in the Midwest.

Check closely for condition. Because of their fragility, many pieces are restored. Measurements refer to largest dimension. Prices are for perfect (P), minor paint loss (M), and restored (R).

Left: Floral pocket watch holder, 13", c. 1840, $1000; right: love birds, 8", c. 1850, $700.

	P	M	R
Apple, w/ red cheeks, bank, 5" c. 1900s	$ 45	$ 25	$ 17
Bird, nesting, 7", c. 1800s	375	240	175
Black Child, w/ watermelon, 4", c. 1900s	35	20	15
Bookends, pirates, c. 1900s, pr.	60	35	25
Boy, reading books, c. 1900s, 10.5"	130	80	55
Cat, c. 1800s, 4.5"	225	145	110
Cat, c. 1800s, 10.5"	300	175	125
Charley McCarthy, c. 1900s, 15"	33	20	14
Dancing Lady, c. 1900s, 14"	40	18	13
Dawrf, German, c. 1930s, 11"	35	20	14
Dog, c. 1900s, 8.5"	180	120	85
Dove, c. 1900s, green w/ blue wings, 12"	275	185	130
Dove, c. 1800s, green w/ yellow wings, 6"	365	230	165
Duck, c. 1900s, 5"	80	40	25
Eagle, c. 1800s, spread, 9.5"	400	260	180
Fruit Basket, 8", c. 1800s	425	275	200
Horn of Plenty, c. 1900s, 14"	38	15	13
Indian, Cigar Store, reclining, 23"	350	200	135
Lamb, c. 1800s, 8.5"	365	230	165
Lamb, c. 1900, 6.5"	75	50	35
Owl, c. 1900, 12"	248	165	110
Parrot, c. 1800s, 10.5"	1500	1000	650
Pigeon, c. 1900, 10"	180	120	85
Poodles, c. 1800, 7.75"	280	175	125
Rabbit, c. 1900, 8"	125	90	60
Rooster, c. 1800s, 6"	450	300	200
Santa Claus, c. 1900, 24"	225	140	100
Sheep, mother w/ babies, c. 1900, 7"	130	75	50
Shepherd, German, c. 1900, 17.5"	124	75	50
Squirrel, c. 1800s, 10"	248	165	110
Stag, c. 1800s, 9.5"	600	450	275

Clocks

The types of clocks listed in the selection below include swing clocks in which the clock mechanism itself is imbedded in the pendulum held by a statue. Banjo clocks have a round face, a tapering neck and a square pendulum base. Calendar clocks show the date as well as the time. Carriage clocks are small, intricate clocks generally about four to five inches high, usually with glass sides. Regulator clocks are precise clocks generally with long pendulums but no bells. Statue clocks combine a clock with a bronze or gilt figure. Kitchen clocks are designed for a shelf and are generally upright with ornate decoration from its edges. Ogee clocks are tall, rectangular clocks framed by a convex and concave molding. Novelty clocks are usually small, inexpensive and in whimsical shapes.

The clocks in this section represent the collectible clocks of the late nineteenth and early twentieth centuries. These represent the first factory produced clocks of the United States which are still frequently seen at auctions and flea markets.

When buying a clock at auction, always factor in the cost of repair. Even if the clock was working during exhibition, by the time it has been moved from display to storage to you, it is often not. Be sure to check for all parts (pendulum, weights, etc.) both before you bid and when you pick it up. Buying from a dealer may cost more money, but can often save on headaches.

Handmade Clocks

	LOW	AVG.	HIGH
Banjo Clock, MA Fed. mah., dial inscribed "A. Willard, Jr., Boston," the front plate w/ inscription "cleaned by E. Taber." ht. 32"	$ 1800	$ 3150	$ 4950
Banjo Clock, MA gilt-front presentation w/ eglomisé of naval battle, throat glass w/ eagle and shield, ht. 41"	1000	1750	2750
Banjo Clock, MA giltwood and eglomisé lyre form, dial inscribed "Sawin and Dyer, Boston," the eglomise panels in red, gold and white, ht. 39"	2200	3850	6050
Banjo Clock, MA giltwood w/ eglomisé panel of naval battle, ht. 33"	800	1400	2200
Banjo Clock, MA, mah. and eglomisé, dial inscribed "Howard, Davis & Dennison, Roxbury." ht. 29"	700	1230	1925
Banjo Clock, MA mah. and eglomisé, lower panel depicting naval battle, ht. 39"	1000	1750	2750
Banjo Clock, MA mah. front and eglomisé, circular dial above eglomisé panels in red, blue, and gold, depicting Aurora in chariot, ht. 33"	1000	1750	2750
Banjo Clock, NH Fed. giltwood and eglomisé by James Cross of Rochester, throat glass w/ Amer. eagle and shield, depicting naval battle, ht. 40"	1300	2280	3575
Dwarf-Case Clock, PA. Fed. cherry. W. Hough, Bridgeport, scrolled pediment above an arched glazed, white painted enamel dial, on waisted case w/ plinth base and French feet, ht. 53"	36,000	63,000	100,000
Girandole Clock, MA giltwood and eglomisé, dial inscribed "L. Curtis, Concord," surmounted by metal eagle, bezel w/ 2 spherules above throat glass inscribed "Patent," lower glass depicting Aurora, within gilt spherules, ht. 47"	9500	16,630	26,000

Left to right: E. Howard & Co. Boston, mahogany regulator, height 30", $2800 at auction; Ithaca walnut and mahogany calender clock, height 20", $2700 at auction. — Photo courtesy of Northeast Auctions.

	LOW	AVG.	HIGH
Pillar and Scroll Shelf Clock, by E. Terry & Sons, CT Fed. mah. and eglomisé, ht. 34"	$ 900	$ 1580	$ 2475
Pillar and Scroll Shelf Clock, labeled Wadsworths & Turners, Litchfield, CT, eglomisé plate of riverscape view	650	1140	1788
Tall-Case Clock, CT Chip. cherry, by Philip Malls, scrolled bonnet-top w/ flame finials above arched door opening to brass dial, w/ waisted case and plinth base on ogee bracket feet, ht. 93"	8000	14,000	22,000
Tall-Case Clock, Eng. japanned chinoiserie decorated, by Thomas Baker-Malling, bonnet w/ arched top and brass dial, w/ waisted case on bracket feet, ht. 83"	2200	3850	6050
Tall-Case Clock, MA Chip. cherry, by Benjamin Willard, Grafton, bonnet w/ arched and glazed door opening to white enamel dial above waisted case on plinth base w/ scalloped banding, w/ ogee bracket feet, ht. 92"	22,500	39,380	61,875
Tall-Case Clock, NH Chip. inlaid cherry, bonnet w/ pierced fret above arched door opening to white enamel dial, waisted case w/ inlaid oval and fluted columns, on plinth base, ht. 85"	11,000	19,250	30,250
Tall-Case Clock, NH Country Fed., painted and dec. w/ brass works inscribed "Elisha Smith, Sanbornton," hood w/ scalloped fretwork and brass finials above glazed door opening to fancy painted metal dial w/ inscription, over waisted case w/ graining and rope-twist quarter-columns on scalloped box base, ht. 78"	6000	10,500	16,500

Above, left to right: Acorn clocks are a rare form, $4000-$8000.
— Photo courtesy of Northeast Auctions. Kitchen clocks are easier to find, $200-$400. — Photo courtesy of George Kerrigan Photography.

Factory Made Clocks

	LOW	AVG.	HIGH
Acme China, c. 1900, Ansonia	$ 60	$ 75	$ 90
Acme Crystal Regulator, c. 1910, Ansonia	280	340	400
Actor Kitchen, c. 1890, E.N. Welsh	260	315	370
Africa Kitchen, c. 1890, Ansonia	200	240	280
Alarm, c. 1900, Jerome	140	160	180
Alarm, c. 1960, Lux & Keebler	10	15	20
Alaska Kitchen, c. 1890, Ansonia	240	270	300
Albatross Cabinet, c. 1900, New Haven	260	320	380
Alpine Kitchen, c. 1890, W.L. Gilbert	210	260	310
Angel Swing No. 2, c. 1875, F. Kroeber	1300	1600	1900
Animated Alarm, c. 1890, F. Kroeber	440	535	630
Animated Alarm, c. 1940, Lux & Keebler	240	305	370
Animated Novelty, c. 1910, Mueller & Son	1460	1650	1840
Ansonia Lever, c. 1900, Ansonia	250	280	310
Arab Cabinet, c. 1900, New Haven	310	375	440
Arab Connecticut Shelf, c. 1890, Ansonia	170	210	250
Arcadian Connecticut Shelf, c. 1890, Ansonia	190	235	280
Archer Statue, c. 1910, W.L. Gilbert	440	500	560
Art Nouveau, c. 1910, Seth Thomas	110	140	170
Art Nouveau Novelty, c. 1910, Ansonia	140	175	210
Astronomical No. 74 Mercury Pendulum, c. 1915, E. Howard	25,000	30,000	35,000
Astronomical Regulator, c. 1890, F. Kroeber	20,000	24,000	28,000
Astronomical Regulator, c. 1900, Ansonia	10,000	13,000	16,000
Astronomical Regulator No. 22, c. 1900, E. Howard	15,000	17,500	20,000
Astronomical Regulator No. 47, c. 1900, E. Howard	19,000	23,000	27,000
Astronomical Standing, c. 1900, E. Howard	22,000	24,000	26,000
Attila Statue, c. 1890, Ansonia	690	840	990
Austria Kitchen, c. 1890, Ansonia	240	280	320
Austrian Calendar, c. 1900, New Haven	800	1015	1230
Automobile, c. 1920, New Haven	70	85	100

Custom-built clocks command high prices. This custom-built Chelsea ship's bell brought $5500 at auction. — Photo courtesy of Northeast Auctions.

	LOW	AVG.	HIGH
Avon Kitchen, c. 1900, New Haven	$ 230	$ 295	$ 360
Aztec Mission, c. 1910, Seth Thomas	490	590	690
Baghdad Regulator, c. 1900, Ansonia	1100	1300	1600
Banjo, c. 1880, E. Howard	3000	3500	4000
Banjo, c. 1890, Waltham	2000	2400	2800
Banjo, c. 1920, E. Ingraham	240	285	330
Bank Regulator, c. 1880, Ithaca Calendar	5300	6720	8140
Banker's Inkstand, c. 1880, Ansonia	410	495	580
Barbara Wall Regulator, c. 1890, New Haven	800	960	1120
Baronet Crystal Regulator, c. 1910, Ansonia	540	635	730
Baseball, c.1890, F. Kroeber	510	630	750
Baseball Pendulum, c. 1940, Lux & Keebler	260	310	360
Bee Drum Alarm, c. 1890, Ansonia	70	80	90
Beehive Shelf, c. 1880, E.N. Welsh	180	215	250
Beehive Shelf, c. 1880, Jerome	220	280	340
Beehive Shelf, c. 1900, New Haven	100	120	140
Bisque Novelty, c. 1890, Ansonia	140	160	180
Black Cat Pendulum, c. 1940, Lux & Keebler	280	345	410
Black Mantle, c. 1890, E.N. Welsh	140	160	180
Black Wood Mantle, c. 1900, E. Ingraham	150	185	220
Black Wood Mantle, c. 1900, New Haven	150	165	180
Blackbird Kitchen, c. 1890, Ansonia	300	355	410
Boar Hunter Statue, c. 1890, Ansonia	540	665	790
Bouquet Novelty, c. 1900, New Haven	190	250	310
Brass Mantle, c. 1890, F. Kroeber	510	620	730
Brass Novelty, c. 1890, Ansonia	140	160	180
Brass Novelty, c. 1890, F. Kroeber	340	415	490
Brass Plaque, c. 1890, F. Kroeber	260	330	400
Brest Crystal Regulator, c. 1910, Waterbury	220	250	280
Bronze and Iron, c. 1900, Mueller & Son	190	245	300
Bronze Mantle, c. 1900, Ansonia	540	640	740
Brooklyn Figure Eight Regulator, c. 1910, Ansonia	2300	3000	3700
Bullfight Alarm, c. 1900, New Haven	290	340	390
Cabinet, c. 1880, F. Kroeber	390	505	620
Cabinet, c. 1890, E.N. Welsh	130	155	180

	LOW	AVG.	HIGH
Cabinet, c. 1890, Seth Thomas	$ 260	$ 335	$ 410
Cabinet, c. 1890, Waterbury	230	275	320
Cabinet, c. 1900, E. Ingraham	180	195	210
Cabinet, c. 1900, W.L. Gilbert	240	285	330
Cabinet, w/ mirrored sides, c. 1880, F. Kroeber	380	465	550
Calais Crystal Regulator, c. 1910, Waterbury	600	750	900
Calendar Alarm, c. 1900, Waterbury	130	155	180
Calendar, c. 1880, F. Kroeber	350	400	450
Calendar, c. 1900, Jerome	2200	2500	2800
Calendar, double dial, c. 1890, Waterbury	1000	1250	1500
Calendar Eclipse Regulator, c. 1900, E.N. Welsh	700	790	880
Canada Kitchen, c. 1890, Ansonia	220	255	290
Capital Kitchen, c. 1910, Seth Thomas	290	345	400
Capital Regulator, c. 1900, Ansonia	1100	1400	1700
Captain Kitchen, c. 1900, New Haven	300	335	370
Carlos Calendar, c. 1890, Ansonia	400	500	600
Carpenter Iron Novelty, c. 1890, Ansonia	220	265	310
Carriage, c. 1890, F. Kroeber	260	335	410
Carriage, c. 1890, Seth Thomas	140	165	190
Carriage, c. 1890, Waterbury	190	225	260
Carriage, c. 1900, E.N. Welsh	100	120	140
Carriage, c. 1900, New Haven	240	285	330
Carriage, c. 1900, W.L. Gilbert	200	250	300
Cast Iron Character, c. 1900, Mueller & Son	300	330	360
Cavalier Statue, c. 1900, Waterbury	270	330	390
Character, c. 1900, Mueller & Son	260	315	370
Checkmate Carriage, c. 1890, F. Kroeber	360	400	440
Chicago Kitchen, c. 1890, Ansonia	280	335	390
China, 13", c. 1900, New Haven	300	355	410
China, 6", c. 1900, New Haven	100	115	130
China Novelty, c. 1890, Ansonia	100	120	140
China Novelty, c. 1900, Seth Thomas	100	120	140
Christine Kitchen, c. 1900, New Haven	250	295	340
Cinderella Kitchen, c. 1900, New Haven	260	290	320
Clifton Regulator, c. 1910, Ansonia	350	435	520
Colby Crystal Regulator, c. 1910, Ansonia	340	400	460
College Kitchen, c. 1910, Seth Thomas	260	305	350
Colorado Kitchen, c. 1890, Ansonia	290	330	370
Comet Carriage, c. 1910, Ansonia	270	315	360
Connecticut Shelf, c. 1875, W.L. Gilbert	300	360	420
Connecticut Shelf, c. 1890, F. Kroeber	220	245	270
Connecticut Shelf, c. 1890, Seth Thomas	190	225	260
Connecticut Shelf, c. 1900, New Haven	260	310	360
Connecticut Shelf Round Top, c. 1880, E. Ingraham	220	250	280
Connecticut Shelf Split Top, c. 1880, E. Ingraham	170	215	260
Connecticut Split Top Shelf, c. 1890, Ansonia	240	275	310
Conroy Kitchen, c. 1900, New Haven	300	340	380
Cottage Connecticut Shelf, c. 1890, Ansonia	130	160	190
Cottage Shelf, c. 1875, W.L. Gilbert	210	255	300
Cottage Shelf, c. 1880, E.N. Welsh	130	160	190
Cottage Shelf, c. 1880, Jerome	200	240	280

	LOW	AVG.	HIGH
Cottage Shelf, c. 1890, F. Kroeber	$ 190	$ 230	$ 270
Cottage Shelf, c. 1900, E. Ingraham	180	220	260
Cottage Shelf, c. 1900, New Haven	100	125	150
Crystal Palace, c. 1890, Ansonia	800	900	1000
Crystal Regulator, c. 1900, New Haven	690	795	900
Crystal Regulator, c. 1900, W.L. Gilbert	590	670	750
Crystal Regulator, c. 1910, Waterbury	420	520	620
Crystal Regulator, c. 1920, New Haven	440	510	580
Crystal Regulator, c. 1920, Seth Thomas	500	630	760
Cuckoo, c. 1945, Lux & Keebler	220	265	310
Cuckoo Mantle, c. 1890, F. Kroeber	540	680	820
Cuckoo Wall, c. 1890, F. Kroeber	400	480	560
Dauntless Alarm, c. 1880, Ansonia	260	315	370
Diplomat Crystal Regulator, c. 1910, Ansonia	740	890	1040
Dog House Pendulum, c. 1940, Lux & Keebler	220	245	270
Domestic Alarm, c. 1880, Ansonia	200	240	280
Don Juan Statue, c. 1890, Ansonia	410	495	580
Don Juan Statue, c. 1900, New Haven	420	485	550
Dora Carriage, c. 1880, Ansonia	180	215	250
Double Dial Calendar, c. 1890, New Haven	1500	1750	2000
Drum Alarm, c. 1890, E.N. Welsh	70	85	100
Drum Alarm, c. 1890, F. Kroeber	110	125	140
Drum Alarm, c. 1890, New Haven	70	85	100
Drum Alarm, c. 1900, W.L. Gilbert	100	125	150
Drum Alarm, c. 1900, Waterbury	100	125	150
Drum Alarm, c. 1920, E. Ingraham	60	80	100
Drum Form Alarm, c. 1890, Seth Thomas	100	110	120
Duchess Crystal Regulator, c. 1910, Ansonia	500	585	670
Ebony Kitchen Hanging, c. 1910, Ansonia	610	730	850
Echo Alarm, c. 1880, Ansonia	300	335	370
Electric, c. 1960, Lux & Keebler	10	20	30
Elfrida Calendar, c. 1890, New Haven	1400	1600	1800
Empire Crystal Regulator, c. 1920, Seth Thomas	500	635	770
Empire Shelf, c. 1875, Seth Thomas	730	810	890
Empire Shelf, c. 1880, E.N. Welsh	420	505	590
Enamel Mantle, c. 1890, Ansonia	580	695	810
English Long Drop Regulator, c. 1910, Ansonia	570	695	820
Etruscan, c. 1900, Mueller & Son	220	285	350
Exposition Kitchen, c. 1900, Seth Thomas	270	340	410
Fancy Alarm, c. 1890, F. Kroeber	130	155	180
Fancy Alarm, c. 1900, W.L. Gilbert	140	175	210
Figure Eight, c. 1880, E. Howard	6500	7500	8500
Figure Eight Calendar, c. 1880, New Haven	1450	1600	1750
Figure Eight Calendar, c. 1890, F. Kroeber	1390	1575	1760
Figure Eight Regulator, c. 1890, Waterbury	380	470	560
Figure Eight Regulator, c. 1900, Ansonia	420	500	580
Figure Eight Regulator, c. 1900, E. Ingraham	570	635	700
Figure Eight Regulator, c. 1900, New Haven	520	580	640
Fleet Kitchen, c. 1910, Seth Thomas	290	340	390
Flora China, c. 1900, Ansonia	60	75	90
Floral, c. 1900, Mueller & Son	220	260	300

	LOW	AVG.	HIGH
Floral Painted, c. 1900, Mueller & Son	$ 200	$ 235	$ 270
Flute Player Statue, c. 1900, New Haven	200	240	280
Fulton, c. 1890, Ansonia	260	330	400
Gallery Brass Lever, c. 1875, W.L. Gilbert	140	170	200
Gallery, c. 1880, E. Ingraham	280	330	380
Gallery, c. 1880, E.N. Welsh	150	175	200
Gallery, c. 1880, Seth Thomas	240	280	320
Gallery, c. 1890, F. Kroeber	670	805	940
Gallery, c. 1890, Jerome	360	420	480
Gallery, c. 1890, Waterbury	170	215	260
Gallery, c. 1900, New Haven	170	200	230
Gem Ink Calendar, c. 1890, Ansonia	380	465	550
Gilt Metal Novelty, c. 1900, Ansonia	110	125	140
Gilt Metal Novelty, c. 1910, W.L. Gilbert	130	155	180
Good Luck Alarm, c. 1880, Ansonia	100	120	140
Gothic Connecticut Shelf, c. 1890, Ansonia	260	295	330
Gothic Iron, c. 1890, Mueller & Son	260	315	370
Gothic Shelf, c. 1875, W.L. Gilbert	260	305	350
Gothic Shelf, c. 1900, New Haven	200	240	280
Grandfather, c. 1880, E. Howard	15,000	16,500	18,000
Grandfather, c. 1890, Seth Thomas	3000	3300	3600
Grandfather, c. 1900, New Haven	4000	4500	5000
Grandfather, c. 1910, Ansonia	7000	8500	10,000
Grandfather, c. 1910, Waterbury	3000	4000	5000
Grandfather No. 83, c. 1900, E. Howard	4000	5125	6250
Grecian Mantle, c. 1880, E. Ingraham	320	420	520
Greek Kitchen, c. 1900, Ansonia	270	345	420
Gypsy Kettle, c. 1890, F. Kroeber	290	330	370
Hampshire, c. 1890, Ansonia	290	350	410
Hanging Cottage, c. 1890, Ithaca Calendar	1250	1500	1750
Hanging Kitchen, c. 1900, W.L. Gilbert	420	480	540
Hanging Regulator No. 14, c. 1900, E. Howard	4000	5000	6000
Harlequin Cabinet, c. 1900, New Haven	300	350	400
Hawk Oak Kitchen, c. 1900, W.L. Gilbert	300	325	350
Heartbeat, c. 1930, Lux & Keebler	140	170	200
Helena China, c. 1900, Ansonia	70	80	90
Herald Kitchen, c. 1890, Ansonia	240	295	350
Hunter and Dog Statue, c. 1900, New Haven	600	800	1000
Huron Mantle, c. 1905 , E. Ingraham	330	400	470
Imitation Walnut Kitchen, c. 1900, New Haven	130	165	200
Inca Cabinet, c. 1910, Ansonia	180	210	240
Inkstand Brass, c. 1900, Ansonia	170	205	240
Inkwell Calendar, c. 1880, F. Kroeber	410	515	620
Ipswich Cabinet, c. 1910, Ansonia	180	200	220
Iron Case, c. 1890, Ithaca Calendar	4000	5500	7000
Iron Figural Mantle, c. 1880, F. Kroeber	260	325	390
Iron Mantle, c. 1890, Ansonia	210	250	290
Iron Mantle, c. 1890, E.N. Welsh	200	245	290
Iron Mantle, c. 1890, F. Kroeber	220	240	260
Iron Mantle, c. 1900, New Haven	170	205	240
Iron Novelty, c. 1880, E.N. Welsh	140	170	200

	LOW	AVG.	HIGH
Iron Novelty, c. 1890, Ansonia	$ 100	$ 120	$ 140
Iron Novelty, c. 1900, Seth Thomas	100	125	150
Ivanhoe Statue, c. 1900, New Haven	190	230	270
Japan Kitchen, c. 1890, Ansonia	220	245	270
Kentucky, c. 1890, Ansonia	270	330	390
Kitchen, c. 1890, E.N. Welsh	260	295	330
Kitchen, c. 1890, F. Kroeber	430	485	540
Kitchen, c. 1890, Seth Thomas	240	295	350
Kitchen, c. 1890, Waterbury	190	245	300
Kitchen, c. 1900, E. Ingraham	300	325	350
Kitchen, c. 1900, New Haven	240	280	320
Kitchen, c. 1900, W.L. Gilbert	210	245	280
Kitchen Hanging, c. 1900, New Haven	360	420	480
Kitchen Wall, c. 1890, Waterbury	390	470	550
Kitchen, w/ mirrored sides, c. 1890, F. Kroeber	560	675	790
La Cette China, c. 1890, Ansonia	400	510	620
La Cruz China, c. 1910, Ansonia	370	420	470
La Nord China, c. 1910, Ansonia	430	485	540
La Sedan China, c. 1910, Ansonia	350	435	520
La Tosca China, c. 1910, Ansonia	430	495	560
Leeds Cabinet, c. 1880, Ansonia	220	255	290
Library, c. 1920, Waltham	210	240	270
Lighthouse, c. 1900, New Haven	420	475	530
Lima, c. 1890, Ansonia	260	335	410
Little Dorrit Alarm, c. 1880, Ansonia	230	290	350
Locomotive Iron Novelty, c. 1890, Ansonia	240	290	340
Lodi Kitchen, c. 1890, Waterbury	170	205	240
Lusitania Novelty, c. 1900, Seth Thomas	270	330	390
Lux Art, c. 1930, Lux & Keebler	140	160	180
Mahogany Mantle, c. 1910, New Haven	70	80	90
Mahogany Mantle, c. 1910, Seth Thomas	130	170	210
Mahogany Mantle, c. 1920, Ansonia	110	130	150
Mahogany Mantle, c. 1920, E. Ingraham	100	115	130
Major Kitchen, c. 1890, New Haven	260	295	330
Mandolin Alarm, c. 1900, New Haven	270	325	380
Mantle Lever, c. 1900, Jerome	300	340	380
Mantle, w/ mirrored sides, c. 1890, New Haven	460	520	580
Mantle, w/ mirrored sides, c. 1900, E. Ingraham	390	480	570
Marble Dial Wall, c. 1900, E. Howard	2600	3200	3800
Marble Gallery, c. 1910, New Haven	390	495	600
Marble Mantle, c. 1900, Ansonia	220	285	350
Marquis Crystal Regulator, c. 1910, Ansonia	1000	1200	1400
Maryland, c. 1890, Ansonia	230	285	340
Mayflower Kitchen, c. 1900, New Haven	240	290	340
Mechanical Bird, c. 1880, F. Kroeber	3700	4150	4600
Mechanical Ship, c. 1880, F. Kroeber	3600	4000	4400
Metropolis Kitchen, c. 1890, Ansonia	280	320	360
Mission, c. 1910, Waterbury	370	425	480
Mission Cabinet, c. 1910, New Haven	270	340	410
Mission Kitchen, c. 1910, New Haven	220	250	280
Mission Kitchen Hanging, c. 1910, New Haven	510	615	720

	LOW	AVG.	HIGH
Mission Novelty, c. 1910, New Haven	$ 210	$ 255	$ 300
Mission Octagon Short Drop, c. 1910, New Haven	350	410	470
Mosel Kitchen, c. 1890, Ansonia	240	300	360
Musical Mantle, c. 1890, F. Kroeber	750	1000	1250
Nautical Chronometer, c. 1910, Waltham	600	700	800
Nectar Kitchen, c. 1900, New Haven	250	275	300
Nightingale Alarm, c. 1880, Ansonia	140	160	180
Novelty, c. 1900, Waterbury	170	210	250
Nymph Statue, c. 1910, Seth Thomas	140	160	180
Octagon Gallery, c. 1890, Jerome	250	280	310
Octagon Gallery, c. 1900, F. Kroeber	220	250	280
Octagon Long Drop Regulator, c. 1900, W.L. Gilbert	410	490	570
Octagon Peep-o-Day, c. 1890, Ansonia	50	60	70
Octagon Princess Alarm, c. 1890, Ansonia	50	65	80
Octagon Regulator Short Drop, c. 1900, W.L. Gilbert	320	395	470
Octagon Short Drop, c. 1890, Jerome	330	395	460
Octagon Short Drop Calendar, c. 1900, Seth Thomas	560	645	730
Octagon Short Drop Regulator, c. 1890, F. Kroeber	470	585	700
Octagon Top Calendar, c. 1880, Ansonia	410	480	550
Octagon Top Calendar, c. 1890, W.L. Gilbert	400	485	570
Octagon Top Long Drop, c. 1900, E. Ingraham	340	395	450
Octagon Top Long Drop Calendar, c. 1910, E. Ingraham	500	610	720
Octagon Top Long Drop Regulator, c. 1890, Seth Thomas	530	640	750
Octagon Top Long Drop Regulator, c. 1900, E. Ingraham	500	610	720
Octagon Top Long Drop Regulator, c. 1900, E.N. Welsh	480	580	680
Octagon Top Long Drop Regulator, c. 1900, New Haven	340	415	490
Octagon Top Long Drop Regulator, c. 1910, Waterbury	520	675	830
Octagon Top Regulator, c. 1890, Ansonia	430	525	620
Octagon Top Shelf, c. 1875, W.L. Gilbert	170	215	260
Octagon Top Shelf, c. 1880, E. Ingraham	180	220	260
Octagon Top Short Drop, c. 1900, E. Ingraham	270	320	370
Octagon Top Short Drop Calendar, c. 1900, New Haven	410	475	540
Octagon Top Short Drop Calendar, c. 1910, E. Ingraham	380	490	600
Octagon Top Short Drop Regulator, c. 1890, Seth Thomas	490	585	680
Octagon Top Short Drop Regulator, c. 1900, E. Ingraham	320	370	420
Octagon Top Short Drop Regulator, c. 1900, E.N. Welsh	350	425	500
Octagon Top Short Drop Regulator, c. 1910, Waterbury	400	445	490
Office Calendar, c. 1900, Seth Thomas	3000	4000	5000
Office Ink, c. 1900, New Haven	280	330	380
Ogee Connecticut Shelf, c. 1875, W.L. Gilbert	240	290	340
Ogee Connecticut Shelf, c. 1890, Ansonia	260	320	380
Ogee Shelf, c. 1870, Jerome	280	325	370
Ogee Shelf, c. 1880, E.N. Welsh	300	345	390
Ogee Shelf, c. 1890, E. Ingraham	250	295	340
Ogee Shelf, c. 1890, Seth Thomas	290	320	350
Ogee Shelf, c. 1890, Waterbury	270	320	370
Olympia Statue, c. 1890, Ansonia	700	850	1000
Onyx Mantle, c. 1900, Ansonia	360	440	520
Onyx Mantle, c. 1900, New Haven	250	315	380
Onyx Mantle, c. 1910, W.L. Gilbert	320	400	480
Open Swinging Regulator, c. 1910, Waterbury	1070	1245	1420

	LOW	AVG.	HIGH
Oriole Carriage, c. 1890, Ansonia	$ 170	$ 195	$ 220
Orpheus Statue, c. 1900, New Haven	220	250	280
Papier-Mâché Shelf, c. 1890, Jerome	270	315	360
Parlor Calendar, c. 1900, Seth Thomas	1280	1590	1900
Parlor Iron, c. 1890, Mueller & Son	160	205	250
Parlor Shelf Regulator, c. 1900, Seth Thomas	540	620	700
Parlor Wall Regulator, c. 1890, F. Kroeber	1000	1200	1400
Parlor Wall Regulator, c. 1890, Seth Thomas	1370	1620	1870
Parlor Wall Regulator, c. 1890, Waterbury	830	1025	1220
Parlor Wall Regulator, c. 1900, Ansonia	640	840	1040
Parlor Wall Regulator, c. 1900, E. Ingraham	880	1120	1360
Parlor Wall Regulator, c. 1900, New Haven	790	985	1180
Parlor Wall Regulator, c. 1900, W.L. Gilbert	1000	1200	1400
Parlor Wall Regulator, c. 1910, Seth Thomas	1100	1300	1500
Pearl Carriage, c. 1900, Ansonia	120	145	170
Pearl Inlaid Papier-Mâché, c. 1890, Jerome	280	360	440
Pendulum, c. 1930, Lux & Keebler	110	125	140
Pet Alarm, c. 1900, New Haven	280	335	390
Philospher Statue, c. 1890, Ansonia	270	335	400
Pillar and Scroll Shelf, c. 1870, Jerome	560	645	730
Pillar and Scroll Shelf, c. 1880, E.N. Welsh	210	245	280
Pillar and Scroll Shelf, c. 1880, Seth Thomas	270	315	360
Pillar and Scroll Shelf, c. 1900, Seth Thomas	220	260	300
Planet Calendar Alarm, c. 1900, Ansonia	160	190	220
Planet Drum Alarm, c. 1880, Ansonia	180	205	230
Plush Novelty, c. 1890, F. Kroeber	250	305	360
Plymouth Cabinet, c. 1880, Ansonia	200	250	300
Porcelain, c. 1900, F. Kroeber	360	405	450
Porcelain Regulator, c. 1910, Ansonia	1900	2315	2730
Porcelain Statue, c. 1910, W.L. Gilbert	350	400	450
Precision Regulator, c. 1890, Seth Thomas	14,000	16,000	18,000
Prince Crystal Regulator, c. 1910, Ansonia	900	1100	1300
Princess Drum Alarm, c. 1880, Ansonia	70	80	90
Racket Drum Alarm, c. 1900, Ansonia	80	90	100
Rebecca at the Well Statue, c. 1910, Seth Thomas	250	325	400
Reflector, c. 1910, Ansonia	830	980	1130
Regulator No. 11, c. 1900, Seth Thomas	2000	2500	3000
Regulator No. 19, c. 1910, Seth Thomas	1800	2400	3000
Regulator, small second hand, c. 1890, Seth Thomas	1250	1500	1750
Regulator, small second hand, c. 1900, New Haven	1100	1400	1700
Regulator, w/ small second, c. 1890, Waterbury	1400	1650	2000
Renaissance Crystal Regulator, c. 1910, Ansonia	1120	1280	1440
Rio Parlor Wall Regulator, c. 1880, Ansonia	1050	1155	1260
Riverdale Cabinet, c. 1910, Ansonia	210	260	310
Rockwood Cabinet, c. 1910, Ansonia	200	245	290
Roman Statue, c. 1900, New Haven	260	335	410
Rome Parlor Shelf, c. 1920, Seth Thomas	260	305	350
Rotary, c. 1890, F. Kroeber	2700	3450	4200
Round Head Regulator, c. 1900, E.N. Welsh	2400	2995	3590
Round Top Connecticut Shelf, c. 1880, W.L. Gilbert	170	200	230
Round Top Long Drop Regulator, c. 1880, W.L. Gilbert	1200	1500	1800

	LOW	AVG.	HIGH
Round Top Long Drop Regulator, c. 1890, F. Kroeber	$ 700	$ 850	$ 1000
Round Top Long Drop Regulator, c. 1890, Waterbury	1250	1500	1750
Round Top Mantle, c. 1900, E. Ingraham	200	235	270
Round Top Shelf, c. 1880, Seth Thomas	160	205	250
Round Top Shelf, c. 1900, New Haven	100	115	130
Round Top Short Drop Regulator, c. 1900, E. Ingraham	320	385	450
Russia Cabinet, c. 1900, New Haven	260	305	350
Saratoga Wall Regulator, c. 1900, W.L. Gilbert	650	780	910
Satellite Carriage, c. 1910, Ansonia	340	415	490
Saxon Statue, c. 1900, New Haven	290	340	390
Senator Kitchen, c. 1900, New Haven	210	245	280
Shannon Kitchen, c. 1900, New Haven	150	185	220
Shaver Alarm, c. 1900, New Haven	290	330	370
Shelf Regulator, c. 1880, Ithaca Calendar	3000	4000	5000
Sled, c. 1890, F. Kroeber	300	400	500
Spring Chronometer, c. 1890, Ithaca Calendar	2000	2400	2800
Spring Statue, c. 1890, Ansonia	800	900	1000
Square Top Regulator, c. 1910, Seth Thomas	1000	1200	1400
Square Top Regulator No. 39, c. 1900, E. Howard	5500	6750	8000
Square Top Short Drop Regulator, c. 1900, New Haven	400	500	600
Square Top Short Drop Regulator, c. 1905, E. Ingraham	250	305	360
Standard Connecticut Round Top, c. 1890, Ansonia	210	245	280
Statue, c. 1890, F. Kroeber	390	460	530
Statue, c. 1900, Mueller & Son	220	260	300
Steeple Connecticut Shelf, c. 1890, Ansonia	200	235	270
Steeple Shelf, c. 1870, F. Kroeber	220	270	320
Steeple Shelf, c. 1870, W.L. Gilbert	220	260	300
Steeple Shelf, c. 1875, Jerome	280	335	390
Steeple Shelf, c. 1880, E.N. Welsh	170	205	240
Steeple Shelf, c. 1890, Seth Thomas	140	165	190
Steeple Shelf, c. 1900, New Haven	160	185	210
Stirrup Novelty, c. 1900, New Haven	280	320	360
Store Regulator, c. 1900, E. Ingraham	500	565	630
Store Regulator, c. 1910, Seth Thomas	460	560	660
Summit Cabinet, c. 1880, Ansonia	230	270	310
Sunlight Alarm, c. 1900, W.L. Gilbert	220	260	300
Sweep Second Regulator "A," c. 1890, E.N. Welsh	4000	5500	7000
Sweep Second Regulator, c. 1890, E.N. Welsh	2000	2500	3000
Sweep Second Regulator, c. 1890, F. Kroeber	6000	8000	10,000
Sweep Second Regulator, c. 1890, Seth Thomas	3000	4500	6000
Sweep Second Regulator, c. 1890, W.L. Gilbert	5000	5500	6000
Sweep Second Regulator, c. 1890, Waterbury	5500	6500	7500
Sweep Second Regulator, c. 1900, New Haven	3800	4600	5400
Sweep Second Regulator, c. 1910, Ansonia	7000	9000	11,000
Swing Arm, c. 1890, Ansonia	3500	4000	4500
Symbol Crystal Regulator, c. 1910, Ansonia	750	1000	1250
Tally Ho Carriage, c. 1880, Ansonia	470	540	610
Teardrop, c. 1890, F. Kroeber	440	555	670
Teardrop Kitchen, c. 1890, Ansonia	430	505	580
Teardrop Kitchen, c. 1890, Seth Thomas	240	280	320
Telephone Pendulum, c. 1940, Lux & Keebler	100	125	150

	LOW	AVG.	HIGH
Tivoli Cabinet, c. 1880, Ansonia	$ 250	$ 290	$ 330
Tomahawk Kitchen, c. 1900, New Haven	250	305	360
Toronto Cabinet, c. 1880, Ansonia	250	285	320
Tourist Carriage, c. 1910, Ansonia	210	250	290
Triumph, c. 1890, Ansonia	450	590	730
Tudor Beehive Shelf, c. 1890, Ansonia	250	295	340
Tunis Cabinet, c. 1890, Ansonia	140	175	210
Turkey Cabinet, c. 1880, Ansonia	200	250	300
Verdi Crystal Regulator, c. 1910, W.L. Gilbert	1100	1250	1400
Victorian Kitchen Barometer/Thermometer, c. 1890, Ansonia	230	285	340
Victory Statue, c. 1900, Seth Thomas	220	245	270
Watch Form. c. 1900, New Haven	200	255	310
Watchmaker's Standing Regulator, c. 1880, E. Howard	5000	6000	7000
Watchman's Wall Regulator, c. 1890, E. Howard	5000	6000	7000
Westminister Chime, c. 1900, New Haven	330	395	460
Westminister Chimes, c. 1910, Seth Thomas	320	410	500
Wheat Sheaf, c. 1900, New Haven	360	430	500
Wood Lever Octagon, c. 1900, New Haven	250	305	360
Woodbine Alarm, c. 1880, Ansonia	180	235	290
Zuni Mission, c. 1910, Seth Thomas	410	480	550

Blinking eye clock by Bradley and Hubbard. Introduced in 1857, these clocks were called winkers. $2200-$3800. —Photo courtesy of Phillips Auctioneers.

Clothing and Accessories
Buttons

Buttons are something we use every day but rarely think about. To the collector, however, buttons are tiny treasures full of history, made of wonderful materials and endless variety. Beautiful, small, and for the most part reasonably priced, buttons make an ideal collectible.

Though buttons date back many centuries, button collecting began in this country in the 1930s. In 1938 the National Button Society was formed. Its members wrote many excellent books in the 1940s and '50s.

Collectors look for a wide range of buttons, from 18th-century porcelains, hand-painted enamels and carved ivory, to mother-of-pearl, black glass, and intricate metals. Most buttons available today are 19th or 20th century. They range in price from as little as 25¢ each to several hundred dollars for some of the rarest varieties. Among the more recent buttons attracting attention are Bakelite, Art Deco, and plastic "realistics." Materials include horn, tin, brass, glass, plastic, ivory, porcelain, bone, shell, and sterling. They may be plain or highly decorated. There are many good examples of military buttons from the Civil War and earlier. Picture buttons may depict historical or biblical scenes, heads of famous people, and animals. As with all collectibles, condition is a major factor in the price. Chips, rust or other damage generally make a button uncollectible.

Our consultant for this area is Adam G. Perl, owner of Pastimes Antiques in Ithaca, NY. He is listed at the back of this book.

	LOW	AVG.	HIGH
Asian, fan design, multi-colored, scalloped border	$ 30	$ 35	$ 40
Asian, floral motif, enameled	35	40	45
Black Glass, animal figure	7	9	10
Black Glass, cameo head	12	15	18
Black Glass, faceted ball, beaded gilt edge	35	40	45
Black Glass, shape of a slipper	10	13	15
Black Onyx, gold-filled, ball-shaped, 19th century	20	25	30
Black Onyx, w/ 14K gold, ball-shaped, 19th century	60	65	70
Brass, 2 children fighting, stamped brass	20	25	30
Brass, Aesop's Fable, stork and vase	35	40	45
Brass, bridge and river scene, black and white, disc.	75	90	105
Brass, cherubs w/ cornucopia and goat	6	8	10
Brass, children playing game, late 19th century	20	25	30
Brass, gypsy girl dancing w/ goat	45	55	65
Brass, mad rooster	10	13	15
Brass, mother feeding child, high relief	20	25	30
Brass, rooster standing on wheat shaft	15	20	25
Celluloid, angel head, gold background, gilt rims	35	40	45
Celluloid, Count Fersen, floral brass frame	20	25	30
Celluloid, Duchess of Devonshire, pastel colors	42	48	55
Celluloid, Marie Antoinette	20	25	30
Ceramic, bird, black and white	25	30	35
Ceramic, bird w/ branch in beak, scalloped border	35	40	45
Ceramic, Cupid, scroll design on edge	45	50	55
Cloisonné, birds flying, brass, black and white w/ red background	80	90	100
Enamel, lady riding bicycle, cut steel border	60	65	70
Enamel, lighthouse w/ boat scene	45	50	55
Enamel, maiden, blue and white, diamond paste border	50	55	60
Enamel, portrait of lady, black background, 18th century	60	68	75
Enamel, rose color scene on white, emb. scroll border	200	220	240

	LOW	AVG.	HIGH
Enamel, shepherdess, light purple, diamond paste border	$ 45	$ 50	$ 55
Enamel, star shape decorated w/ cut steels	16	21	25
Enamel, w/ pearls and 14K gold, ladybug design, 19th century	550	650	750
Enamel, woman at fountain	55	65	75
Glass, black liberty cap and flag, silver frame, 18th century	75	95	125
Glass, French Revolution motif, copper rim	70	79	88
Glass, molded opaque, brown bird design	25	33	41
Gold, 14K, ball shape w/ ribbing, 19th century	60	65	70
Gold, 14K, button set w/ chain, 19th century	50	60	70
Gold, 14K, engraved collar button, 19th century	30	35	40
Gold, 14K, pearl shape, 19th century	60	70	80
Gold, 14K, scrolled edge design, 19th century	60	65	70
Gold, woven hair under swirls, cartwheel design, scalloped edge, 19th century	130	140	150
Gold-filled, ball shape w/ ribbing, 19th century	20	23	26
Gold-plated, dragon	15	20	25
Ivory, cut-out girl and bird, blue background	150	165	180
Ivory, painted child w/ butterflies	85	95	105
Ivory, painted cherub in chariot drawn by 2 horses	90	100	110
Ivory, painted lady and dog, silver rim	40	50	60
Ivory, painted Oriental head	35	40	45
Ivory, Royal Salamander, carved	30	35	40
Mother-of-pearl, 14K gold, simple button, 19th century	75	80	85
Pewter, owl's head	10	15	20
Pierced Brass, Little Red Riding Hood	25	30	35
Porcelain, cherub catching butterflies, pink and white	20	25	30
Porcelain, Cupid, scroll design on edge	45	55	65
Porcelain, flowers and butterfly, 18th century	15	20	25
Porcelain, pasture scene w/ children	30	35	40
Porcelain, w/ gold, painted angels, 19th century	500	530	560
Silver, Bacchus, God of Wine, etched design	30	35	45
Steel, floral design	4	6	8
Turquoise, w/ 14K gold, button set w/ chain, 19th century	95	100	105
Victorian Figure, black glass disc	8	10	12
Wedgwood, classical fig., white on royal blue, gilt rim, 18th century	225	250	275
Wedgwood, classical fig., white relief on blue cut steel border, 18th century	250	270	290
Wedgwood, classical figures, white relief on light blue	50	60	70
Wedgwood, floral design, diamond paste border, silver frame	200	225	250
Wedgwood, warrior, copper border, white relief on royal blue	225	250	275

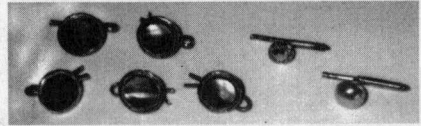  

From left to right: Set of five mother-of-pearl vest buttons, ca. 1940, $30-$50; 14k gold shirt stud, ca. 1910, $10-$15; imitation pearl shirt stud, ca. 1950, $8-$12; celluloid castle button, $35-$45; floral enamel button, $30-$40. — Items courtesy of Pastimes.

Clothing

Vintage clothing is collected by those who wish to add it to their wardrobes as well as by collectors who wish only to display it. Currently, most market activity is in clothes from the 1920s, 1930s, and 1940s. Alterations and construction details are factors in determining price, while skilled workmanship or handmade trims often increase value. Clothing with beadwork is also a good investment.

Vintage clothing requires careful handling. Textiles are perishable: light, humidity, dust, and body oil are potentially harmful. The acids in wood, cardboard, and tissue paper can also hurt clothing. When storing pieces, it is best to wrap items in white sheets and use mothballs. Hang lightweight clothing on padded hangers, and store heavy clothing laid flat.

For further information, contact The Costume Society of America, c/o The Costume Institute, The Metropolitan Museum of Art, New York, NY 10028.

Vintage Fashion

	LOW	HIGH
Adrian, lavender and peach silk evening dress	$ 12,500	$ 20,000
Arnold Scaasi, brown satin coat	530	840
Balenciaga Cocktail Dress, black lace, size 4	700	1100
Balenciaga, navy shantung suit, c. 1940	5000	8500
Bruno Magli, black satin evening pumps, 1950s	60	100
Charles James Cocktail Dress, navy silk faille, 1940s	30,000	45,000
Christian Dior Evening Dress, velvet	650	1000
Emilio Pucci, beaded top, 1960s	1400	2250
Gres Evening Dress, c. 1963	900	1430
Jacques Fath, black dress, 1950s	400	633
Judith Leiber, brown alligator purse, 1960s	1500	2371
Lilly Dache, black velvet hat, 1950s	150	240
Louis Vuitton, travel case	1200	1800
Mainbocher Cocktail Dress, black lace, size 6	530	825
Mainbocher Evening Gown, navy floral lace	2200	3479
Norman Norell, black wool crepe, 1965	800	1265
Rudi Gernreich Kabuki dress, c. 1963	7600	12,000
Saks Fifth Avenue, black alligator purse, 1950s	400	633
Schiaparelli, black satin hat, 1950s	150	240
Silver Mesh Purse, Viennese, c. 1925	1600	2530
Suede Purse, champagne shaped, labeled "Anne Marie"	1800	2800
Valentino Evening Dress, strapless, red silk satin	2400	3750

Hats

Black Wool Hat, D.E. Bishop, Bloomingdale's	40	55
Chesterfield	5	15
Derby, black felt, Dobbs Fifth Avenue	80	124
Fedora, felt	5	15
Madeline-Style Straw Hat, w/ribbon	110	180
Pillbox, edged in black velvet trim w/ rhinestone flowers and butterflies, Norman Durand	60	90
Plumed Hat, Grace Emmy	60	95
Straw Hat, black, fine weave w/ flowers, Flo-Raye	60	95
Straw Hat, pink, Frank Olive	80	125
Straw Hat, w/daisies, Alabert	40	65
Straw Hat, w/navy underbrim and white flower, Frank Olive	40	65

Jeans and Corduroy

	LOW	HIGH
Army and Workmen Shirts	$ 100	$ 170
Corduroy Blazers	200	350
Fashion Denim Jackets	100	170
Flannel Shirts	70	120
Lee and Wrangler Jean Jacket	300	520
Lee Zipper Jeans	100	170
Levi Jean Jackets	400	700
Levi Zipper Jeans	100	170
Levis 501 Button Front Jeans	300	520
Levis 500 Series Zipper Jeans	200	350
Wrangler Zipper Jeans	100	170

Left to right: Lace and printed silk crepe evening gown from the 1930s, $200-$300; Egyptian shawl from the 1920s, unusually large textile made of small silver plates on black mesh, $1000-$2000.

Jewelry, Bakelite

Bakelite is the trade name of the plastic marketed by the Bakelite corporation. Leo Hendrik Baekeland invented this form of phenol formaldehyde in 1909. Since then, it has been used for everything from telephones to jewelry to the heat shield on NASA's Jupiter space probe.

The selection listed below is jewelry whose popularity and prices have soared within recent years.

	GOOD	BETTER	BEST
Bangles			
Half Inch	$ 50	$ 100	$ 225
One Inch	75	150	350
Two Inches	100	200	450
Bracelet Figural Motif			
Bangles	200	300	475
Hinged	225	325	500
Cuff	225	325	500
Bracelet Floral			
Bangle	100	150	350
Hinged	125	175	375
Link	125	175	375
Stretch	75	125	200
Bracelet Geometric			
Bangle	125	200	400
Hinged	150	200	350
Link	75	125	250
Stretch	100	150	400
Bracelet Solid Color			
Bangle	30	60	100
Hinged	40	70	110
Link	40	70	110
Stretch	30	75	125
Bracelet Polychrome			
Bangle	90	130	450
Hinged	125	250	1000
Link	75	125	250
Stretch	100	150	400
Other Bracelets			
Charm	100	200	450
Metal decorated	100	200	500
Rhinestone	50	150	350
Wooden decorated	50	150	250
Necklaces			
Geometric Beads	125	250	500

	GOOD	BETTER	BEST
Polychrome Beads	$ 200	$ 300	$ 500
Solid Color Beads	50	100	250
Trinket	175	275	750

Pins

Figural, etc.	100	200	500
Geometric	100	150	375
Polychrome	80	120	300
Solid Color	35	75	100

Miscellaneous

Buckles	50	100	150
Buttons	35	60	150
Earrings	100	150	200
Rings	50	75	150

Coca-Cola Collectibles

The first batch of Coca-Cola was created by John Pemberton, an Atlanta pharmacist in 1886. Mr. Pemberton was trying to create a tonic rather than a soft drink. The syrup was soon marketed to Willis Venable, an Atlanta soda fountain manager. As legend has it, a clerk mixed the syrup with soda and an empire was born. In 1894 Joseph Biedenhorn started bottling and distributing Coca-Cola in Vicksburg, MS. Coke became the world's favorite soft drink. With over 100 years of advertisements and promotional material Coke collectors have an incredible breadth of material to draw from. The firm has done a great job in promoting its product. One reason collectors love this material is that by viewing it you can draw a time line of our last 100 years. It begins with the Victorian elegance of the 1890s and travels through two World Wars, the Great Depression, Rock 'n' Roll, the country's struggle with the Vietnam War ("I'd Like to Teach the World to Sing"), to today's sports stars' endorsements. Coke ads are usually very appealing and reflective of their time. Since Coca-Cola is now a global entity, the material grows daily, and there are even Coke boutiques specializing in marketing new Coke clothing and products.

The only cautionary note is that there are also many reproductions and items that are done in the style of an earlier era. Such material is often offered as old with prices far beyond its value. Do your homework and deal with knowledgeable people that stand behind their product. The prices below are based on items in excellent or mint condition.

For further information see *Petretti's Coca-Cola Collectibles Price Guide*, Allan Petretti, Nostalgia Publications, Hackensack, NJ, and *Price Guide to Coca-Cola Collectibles*, Deborah Goldstein Hill, Wallace Homestead, Radnor, PA, 1991. You may also wish to contact The Coca-Cola Collectors Club International, P.O. Box 49166, Atlanta, GA 30359.

Left to right: Tray, serving, oval, "Juanita," 1906, $1800-$2200; thermometer, c. 1941, $300-$400; sign, paper, c. 1928, $200-$300.
— Photo courtesy of James D. Julia, Inc.

	LOW	AVG.	HIGH
Ashtray, aluminum, round logo in center, c. 1955	$ 18	$ 20	$ 22
Ashtray and Figural Bottle Match Holder, c. 1940	600	750	900
Ashtray, metal, round, "Things Go Better" on rim, c. 1963	8	9	10
Ashtray, Mexican, painted aluminum, c. 1970	3	4	5
Bank, cap form, c. 1972	14	17	20
Bank, plastic vending machine	80	100	120

Clockwise from above left: Tray, serving, "Topless," sold at auction in 1994 for $12,000. —Photo courtesy of James D. Julia, Inc., Driver's uniform with pants, 1960s, $100-$150; Coca-Cola sunglasses c. 1970s, $18-$22. —Items courtesy of Jim Glaab's Collector's Showcase.

	LOW	AVG.	HIGH
Bank, tin, bat.-operated dispenser, c. 1955	$ 300	$ 400	$ 500
Bingo Card, c. 1940	15	18	20
Blotter, "Delicious and Refreshing," Atlanta Litho., c. 1904	250	305	360
Blotter, "Delicious and Refreshing," Edwards, Deutsch & Heitman, c. 1904	80	90	100
Blotter, "Duster Girl" in auto, c. 1904	400	475	540
Blotter, icy style "Cold" Refreshment, c. 1937	15	18	20
Blotter, "Restores Energy and Strengthens Nerves," c. 1906	80	95	110
Blotter, sprite w/ bottle top hat, c. 1953	5	6	7
Blotter, sprite w/ bottle top hat (Canada), c. 1956	15	19	23
Book Cover, "Always Be Careful," c. 1951	5	6	7
Book Cover, baseball player, c. 1939	10	13	15
Bookmark, celluloid Valentine, 2" x 2.25", c. 1899	300	400	500
Bookmark, Coke can, c. 1960	4	5	6
Bookmark, Hilda Clark, c. 1900	300	350	400
Bookmark, Lillian Nordica, 2" x 6", c. 1904	400	450	500
Bookmark, little girl w/ bird house, c. 1904	400	500	600
Bookmark, owl on perch, celluloid, 1.5" x 3.125", c. 1906	500	600	700
Bottle, "Best by a Dam Site," c. 1910	70	80	90

	LOW	AVG.	HIGH
Bottle, Biedenhorn Candy, straight side w/ label, c. 1910	$ 100	$ 125	$ 150
Bottle, display, red or clear, ht. 20", c. 1923	250	300	350
Bottle, Donald Duck, 7 oz., ptd., c. 1948	15	20	25
Bottle Holder Protector, 6-bottle type, c. 1933	30	35	40
Calendar, boy w/ fishing pole, 12" x 24", c. 1937	300	375	450
Calendar, Garden Girl, 12" x 32", c. 1920	1200	1400	1600
Calendar, girl w/ glass and bottle, 12" x 24", c. 1939	200	250	300
Cigarette Lighter, Coke bottle logo, c. 1965	18	20	22
Cigarette Lighter, Coke bottle shape, c. 1940	20	25	30
Cigarette Lighter, miniature Coke can, c. 1960	15	20	25
Cigarette Lighter, musical, c. 1960	80	100	120
Clock, Bakelite, red "Drink Coca-Cola," dia. 17", c. 1960	80	100	120
Clock, brass mantle type, c. 1954	200	250	300
Clock, dome style, 3" x 5", c. 1950	400	600	800
Clock, leather, 3.25" x 3.25", c. 1919	500	650	800
Clock, regulator style, Gilbert, c. 1930	600	775	950
Clock, re-issue of Betty, c. 1974	30	40	50
Cooler, picnic style, c. 1950	60	70	80
Cutouts, Toonerville Trolley, uncut, c. 1932	250	300	350
Cutouts, Uncle Remus, uncut, c. 1930	300	325	350
Door Pull, bottle shape, c. 1950	100	125	150
Flashlight, bottle-shaped plastic, c. 1968	20	25	30
Glass, 5¢ w/ arrow, c. 1905	300	375	450
Glass, flair type, c. 1925	60	75	90
Glass, flair type, c. 1905	250	300	350
Glass, home type, red/white diamond	5	6	7
Glass, pewter, c. 1930	300	350	400
Ice Pick and Opener, c. 1940	12	14	15
Key Chain, 50th Anniversary Celebration, c. 1936	8	9	10
Key Chain, amber replica bottle w/ brass chain, c. 1964	15	18	20
Key Chain, car key style, c. 1950	12	14	15
Key Chain, red w/ gold bottle, c. 1955	18	20	22
Knife, pocket, 1 blade and opener, Coke bottle design, c. 1910	200	250	300
Knife, pocket, celluloid key, c. 1940	70	80	90
Knife, pocket, Chicago World's Fair, len. 3.5", 1933	30	35	40
Knife, pocket, "Enjoy Coca-Cola," c. 1970	7	8	9
Menu Board, tin, profile of a woman, c. 1940	200	240	280
Mirror, pocket, "Bathing Beauty," c. 1917	900	1100	1300
Mirror, pocket, Coca-Cola Girl, in floral hat turned right, "Drink Delicious Coca-Cola," c. 1914	200	225	250
Mirror, pocket, Coca-Cola Girl, in floral hat turned left, "Drink Coca-Cola," c. 1909	200	250	300
Mirror, pocket, "Drink Coca-Cola 5¢," c. 1914	300	400	500
Mirror, pocket, "Elaine" girl w/ bottle turned right, c. 1917	300	325	350
Mirror, pocket, "Enjoy Thirst," c. 1930	150	175	200
Mirror, pocket, "Garden Girl," c. 1920	300	400	500
Mirror, pocket, Juanita w/ pendant and glass, c. 1909	400	450	500
Mirror, pocket-size, "Relieves Fatigue," c. 1906	400	450	500
Mirror, pocket-size, "St. Louis Exposition," c. 1904	300	350	400
Music Box, cooler, c. 1951	100	125	150
Notebook, brown leather, embossed, c. 1903	160	175	190

	LOW	AVG.	HIGH
Notepad, celluloid-covered, 2.5" x 5", c. 1902	$ 300	$ 350	$ 400
Opener, bone handle knife, c. 1908	150	175	200
Opener, Nashville Anniversary, c. 1952	30	35	40
Opener, skate key style, c. 1935	12	14	15
Opener, "Starr X," c. 1930	8	9	10
Paperweight, Coca-Cola gum, c. 1916	100	125	150
Paperweight, "Coke is Coca-Cola," c. 1948	30	35	40
Pen, ballpoint w/ telephone dialer	8	9	10
Pen, baseball bat, c. 1940	20	25	30
Pencil Box, 10-piece set, c. 1930	25	32	40
Pencil Holder, celluloid, c. 1910	80	90	100
Pencil Sharpener, plastic, c. 1960	6	7	8
Pencil Sharpener, red metal, c. 1933	18	20	22
Plate, glass and Coke bottle motif, dia. 7.25", c. 1930	200	250	300
Plate, "Vienna Art Nude" in orig. frame, c. 1905	600	700	800
Playing Cards, Airplane Spotter (deck), c. 1943	50	60	70
Playing Cards, Girl w/ bottle (deck), c. 1909	800	850	900
Pocket Secretary, leather-bound, c. 1920	80	100	120
Postcard, "All Over the World," c. 1913	300	350	400
Postcard, "Duster Girl" driving car, c. 1906	300	400	500
Postcard, girl w/ clown hat, c. 1909	300	350	400
Postcard, horse and delivery wagon (photo), c. 1900	100	125	150
Postcard, men in speedboat, c. 1913	300	350	400
Postcard, photo of bottling plant, c. 1905	100	125	150
Postcard, school teacher at blackboard, c. 1913	300	350	400
Postcard, truck carrying cases of Coke (photo), c. 1913	100	125	150
Postcards, set of 4 Dick Tracy, orig. package, c. 1942	70	80	90
Record, 45, "I'd Like to Teach the World to Sing," Canada, picture sleeve, c. 1970	18	20	22
Sign, cardboard cutout, couple on bicycle, len. 36", c. 1948	300	400	500
Sign, "Cold Drinks," w/ cups and snowbursts, 14" x 20", c. 1960	25	30	35
Sign, round, metal w/ bottle, dia. 36", 1955	250	300	350
Toy, Cokebot Robot in orig. box, c. 1980	80	100	120
Toy, fountain dispenser, Chilton, 1965	50	55	60
Toy, Matchbox Lorry, 1960	40	55	70
Tray, change, Betty, girl in bonnet, oval, len. 6", c. 1914	250	275	300
Tray, "Hilda Clark," round, dia. 9.75", c. 1903	3000	4250	5500
Tray, serving, "Olympic Games," 15" x 11", c. 1976	20	25	30
Tray, serving, replica of "Duster Girl," c. 1972	10	13	15
Tray, serving, "Sailor Girl," c. 1940	150	190	230
Tray, serving, "Saint Louis Fair," oval, 10.75", c. 1909	1800	2000	2200
Tray, serving, "Santa Claus," 15" x 11", c. 1973	12	14	15
Tray, serving, "Soda Fountain Clerk," c. 1927	300	425	550
Tray, serving, "Springboard Girl," c. 1939	150	185	220
Tray, serving, "Summer Girl," c. 1921	500	650	800
Tray, serving, "Topless," dia. 12.5", c. 1908	*Sold at auction in 1994 for $12,000*		
Tray, TV, candle design, c. 1972	20	25	30
Tray, TV, Thanksgiving motif, c. 1961	30	35	40
Tray, "Two Girls at Car," c. 1942	150	195	240
Wallet, Coca-Cola script, c. 1922	30	35	40
Wallet, Coke bottle emblem, c. 1915	50	60	70
Wallet, embossed coin purse, c. 1906	60	75	90

Coins

American coins are a classic collectible. Some collections that started with some loose change from father's pocket are now built into million dollar obsessions. Beware of altered coins. Some skilled fakers are able to change the date on an otherwise common coin to imitate a rare and valuable example. We have also seen totally fake coins coming from Asia. Some are poor castings whose ill-formed shape gives them away, but others are high quality pieces.

The following ratings are from the American Numismatic Association grading system. For more detailed descriptions, see *The Official A.N.A Grading Standards for United States Coins*, Western Publishing Co., Racine, WI.

Proof—Refers to method of manufacture, distinguished by sharpness of detail and usually with brilliant mirror surface. Proof coins are in perfect mint state.

Uncirculated (MS-60)—No trace of wear but may show some contact marks; surface may be spotted or lack some luster.

About Uncirculated (AU-50)—Traces of light wear on many of the high points. At least half of mint luster is still present.

Extremely Fine (EF-40)—Design is lightly worn throughout, but all features are sharp and well defined. Traces of luster may show.

Very Fine (VF-20)—Shows wear on high points of design. All major details are clear.

Fine (F-12)— Moderate even wear; entire design is bold with pleasing appearance.

Very Good (VG-8)—Well worn; main features clear and bold but rather flat.

Good (G-4)—Heavily worn; design visible but faint in areas. Many details flat.

About Good (AG-3)—Very heavily worn with parts of lettering and date worn smooth.

For further information see *The Handbook of United States Coins* by R.S. Yeoman for wholesale and auction (selling) values, and *A Guide Book of United States Coins* by R.S. Yeoman for retail (buying) values.

Virginia Colony Coinage

Half Penny

	AG-3	G-4	VG-8	F-12	VF-20	EF-40
1773	$ 15.00	$ 25.00	$ 35.00	$ 55.00	$ 80.00	—

Massachusetts State Coinage

Half Cent

	AG-3	G-4	VG-8	F-12	VF-20	EF-40
1787	$ 25.00	$ 40.00	$ 55.00	$ 90.00	$ 175.00	$ 425.00
1788	30.00	45.00	60.00	95.00	200.00	475.00

Half Cents

Liberty Cap Type

	AG-3	G-4	VG-8	F-12	VF-20	EF-40
1794-97	$ 80.00	$ 200.00	$ 325.00	$ 550.00	$ 1000.00	$ 2000.00

Draped Bust Type 1800-08

	AG-3	G-4	VG-8	F-12	VF-20	EF-40
1800	$ 25.00	$ 45.00	$ 60.00	$ 90.00	$ 250.00	—
1803-08	20.00	30.00	40.00	80.00	200.00	—

Classic Head Type 1809-36

	G-4	VG-8	F-12	VF-20	EF-40
1825-35	$ 25.00	$ 35.00	$ 60.00	$ 80.00	$ 300.00

Coronet Type 1840-57

	G-4	VG-8	F-12	VF-20	EF-40
1849-57	$ 35.00	$ 45.00	$ 55.00	$ 75.00	$ 200.00

Large Cents 1796-1807

Draped Bust Type

	G-4	VG-8	F-12	VF-20	EF-40	MS-60
1796-1807	$ 24.00	$ 35.00	$ 60.00	$ 100.00	$ 300.00	$ 650.00

Classic Head Type 1808-14

	G-4	VG-8	F-12	VF-20	EF-40	MS-60
1808-14	$ 30.00	$ 60.00	$ 110.00	$ 350.00	$ 400.00	$ 800.00

Coronet Type 1816-57

	G-4	VG-8	F-12	VF-20	EF-40	MS-60
1816-57	$ 10.00	$ 12.00	$ 15.00	$ 20.00	$ 55.00	$ 250.00

Small Cents

Flying Eagle Type 1856-58

	G-4	VG-8	F-12	VF-20	EF-40	MS-60
1856	$ 2100.00	$ 2500.00	$ 3000.00	$ 3200.00	$ 3400.00	$ 5000.00
1857-58	13.00	15.00	18.00	32.00	67.00	250.00

Indian Head Type 1859-1909

	G-4	VG-8	F-12	VF-20	EF-40	MS-60
1860-64	$ 5.00	$ 7.00	$ 15.00	$ 25.00	$ 30.00	$ 100.00
1865	4.00	5.00	7.00	16.00	24.00	60.00.00
1866-72	20.00	25.00	30.00	60.00	80.00	200.00
1873-76	12.00	15.00	21.00	34.00	55.00	125.00.00
1877	190.00	250.00	360.00	550.00	800.00	2000.00

	G-4	VG-8	F-12	VF-20	EF-40	MS-60
1878	$ 16.00	$ 24.00	$ 30.00	$ 40.00	$ 50.00	$ 140.00
1879	3.00	4.00	6.00	12.00	21.00	52.00
1880-84	2.00	2.50	3.50	6.00	14.00	40.00
1885	3.00	4.50	9.00	15.00	26.00	60.00
1886-1908	1.00	1.25	1.50	3.50	8.00	28.00

Lincoln Type (Wheat Sheaves) 1909-58

	G-4	VG-8	F-12	VF-20	EF-40	MS-60
1909 v.d.b.	$ 1.00	$ 1.50	$ 2.00	$ 2.50	$ 3.00	$ 30.00
1909S v.d.b. ...	280.00	300.00	320.00	350.00	400.00	500.00
1909	.50	.60	.75	1.00	2.00	15.00
1916-39	.15	.25	.35	.50	1.00	4.00
1940-42	.10	.15	.25	.40	.60	1.50
1943 (steel)	.20	.25	.40	.75	2.00	4.00
1944-58	.10	.15	.20	.30	.40	2.00
Exceptions						
1913S	7.00	7.50	9.00	11.00	26.00	95.00
1914D	70.00	80.00	100.00	165.00	390.00	750.00
1914S	8.00	10.00	11.00	19.00	36.00	165.00
1915S	7.00	8.00	9.00	12.00	24.00	100.00
1922D	5.00	6.00	7.00	10.00	19.00	80.00
1922 (plain) ...	165.00	270.00	300.00	500.00	2200.00	4500.00
1924D	9.00	11.00	13.00	20.00	50.00	225.00
1926S	2.00	3.00	4.00	5.00	11.00	100.00
1931D	2.00	2.50	3.50	4.50	7.50	50.00
1931S	32.00	35.00	37.00	40.00	45.00	65.00
1932	1.50	1.75	2.00	2.50	3.00	—
1932D	.70	.90	1.20	1.75	2.50	15.00
1933	.75	.90	1.25	1.50	2.75	16.00
1933D	1.75	2.00	2.25	3.00	4.00	20.00
1944D (stamped over S)	—		140.00	170.00	750.00	
1955 (double die)—		—	400.00	500.00	1500.00	

Two-Cent Pieces

1864-73

	G-4	VG-8	F-12	VF-20	EF-40	MS-60
1864 (sm. motto)	$ 50.00	$ 65.00	$ 85.00	$ 150.00	$ 225.00	$ 550.00
1864-71	5.00	7.00	9.00	18.00	30.00	110.00
1872	75.00	100.00	120.00	220.00	325.00	750.00

Silver Three-Cent Pieces

1851-73

	G-4	VG-8	F-12	VF-20	EF-40	MS-60
1851-62	$ 10.00	$ 14.00	$ 18.00	$ 27.00	$ 50.00	$ 160.00

Nickel Three-Cent Pieces

1865-89

	G-4	VG-8	F-12	VF-20	EF-40	MS-60
1865-74	$ 6.00	$ 6.50	$ 7.50	$ 10.00	$ 17.00	$ 80.00
1875-76	7.00	9.00	11.00	17.00	28.00	130.00
1879-80	50.00	75.00	77.00	80.00	100.00	240.00
1881	5.00	6.00	7.00	12.00	18.00	90.00
1882	55.00	65.00	75.00	85.00	110.00	210.00
1883-87	100.00	150.00	185.00	250.00	350.00	600.00
1888-89	40.00	50.00	60.00	80.00	100.00	230.00

Nickel Five-Cent Pieces

Shield Type 1866-83

	G-4	VG-8	F-12	VF-20	EF-40	MS-60
1866	$ 12.00	$ 16.00	$ 20.00	$ 45.00	$ 80.00	$ 200.00
1867-76	8.00	9.00	11.00	18.00	30.00	100.00
1879-80	220.00	260.00	340.00	400.00	500.00	600.00
1881	150.00	175.00	200.00	260.00	350.00	500.00
1882-83	8.00	9.00	11.00	16.00	26.00	100.00

Liberty Head Type 1883-1913

	G-4	VG-8	F-12	VF-20	EF-40	MS-60
1883-84	$ 6.00	$ 8.00	$ 13.00	$ 22.00	$ 35.00	$ 115.00
1885	160.00	220.00	310.00	400.00	600.00	950.00
1886	40.00	60.00	100.00	155.00	215.00	450.00
1887-96	4.00	5.00	13.00	17.00	32.00	100.00
1897-1912	.55	1.50	4.00	6.00	20.00	75.00
1912D	1.10	2.00	5.00	10.00	45.00	200.00
1912S	35.00	45.00	60.00	225.00	360.00	500.00
1913 (five known)—	—	—	—	—	—	365,000.00

Buffalo Type 1913-38

	G-4	VG-8	F-12	VF-20	EF-40	MS-60
1914D	$ 25.00	$ 35.00	$ 50.00	$ 70.00	$ 100.00	$ 300.00
1914	5.00	6.00	7.00	9.00	16.00	50.00
1915	2.50	3.00	5.00	7.00	13.00	50.00
1915D	6.00	8.00	17.00	35.00	50.00	200.00
1915S	12.00	16.00	30.00	65.00	125.00	500.00
1916	1.00	1.25	1.75	3.00	7.00	50.00
1916 (double die) ..	1100.00	2500.00	4000.00	6000.00	8000.00	14,000.00
1921S	12.00	20.00	40.00	250.00	600.00	1000.00
1923-30	.75	1.00	1.50	2.00	6.00	40.00
1923S-26S	.75	.85	1.00	2.00	5.00	40.00
1931S	3.00	4.00	6.00	7.00	10.00	50.00
1934-38	.35	.45	.65	1.20	3.75	15.00
1937D (3 legs) ..	100.00	155.00	200.00	245.00	310.00	1100.00

Jefferson Type 1938- date

	G-4	VG-8	F-12	VF-20	EF-40	MS-60
1938-42	$ .15	$ .18	$ .20	$ .25	$ .45	$ 2.50
1939D	1.50	2.00	4.00	5.00	7.00	40.00
1939S	.50	.60	.75	1.25	2.50	20.00
1942-45 (silver) ...	.25	.30	.45	.50	1.10	5.00
1946-52	.05	.10	.15	.20	.30	.75

Half Dimes

Flowing Hair Type 1794-95

	AG-3	G-4	VG-8	F-12	VF-20	EF-40
1794-95	$ 300.00	$ 700.00	$ 900.00	$ 1000.00	$ 1200.00	$ 2000.00

Draped Bust Type, Small Eagle

	AG-3	G-4	VG-8	F-12	VF-20	EF-40
1796-97	$ 350.00	$ 750.00	$ 850.00	$ 1100.00	$ 1600.00	$ 2000.00

Draped Bust Type, Heraldic Eagle 1800-05

	AG-3	G-4	VG-8	F-12	VF-20	EF-40
1800-05	$ 200.00	$ 500.00	$ 600.00	$ 900.00	$ 1400.00	$ 2000.00
1802	4000.00	9000.00	15,000.00	21,000.00	30,000.00	50,000.00

Capped Bust Type

	G-4	VG-8	F-12	VF-20	EF-40	MS-60
1829-37	$ 12.00	$ 16.00	$ 25.00	$ 50.00	$ 110.00	$ 400.00
1837 (small 5c)	20.00	30.00	40.00	90.00	150.00	1800.00

Seated Liberty Type 1837-73

	G-4	VG-8	F-12	VF-20	EF-40	MS-60
1837	$ 25.00	$ 35.00	$ 50.00	$ 100.00	$ 210.00	$ 700.00
1838O (no stars)	95.00	100.00	200.00	350.00	700.00	3100.00
1838-73	6.00	7.00	9.00	20.00	43.00	210.00
1844O	60.00	100.00	200.00	350.00	900.00	—
1846	160.00	225.00	350.00	600.00	1200.00	—
1849O	25.00	40.00	75.00	250.00	500.00	—
1852O	20.00	35.00	60.00	150.00	300.00	—
1863	120.00	175.00	225.00	300.00	400.00	750.00
1864	190.00	300.00	350.00	450.00	600.00	1200.00
1864S	25.00	35.00	60.00	100.00	300.00	750.00
1865	200.00	250.00	300.00	350.00	500.00	900.00
1866	125.00	200.00	275.00	350.00	450.00	800.00
1867	250.00	350.00	450.00	550.00	750.00	1250.00
1868	30.00	45.00	70.00	100.00	200.00	400.00

Dimes

Draped Bust Type, Small Eagle

	AG-3	G-4	VG-8	F-12	VF-20	EF-40
1796-97	$ 400.00	$ 900.00	$ 1200.00	$ 1700.00	$ 2500.00	$ 4000.00

Draped Bust Type, Heraldic Eagle

	AG-3	G-4	VG-8	F-12	VF-20	EF-40
1798-1807	$ 250.00	$ 450.00	$ 650.00	$ 750.00	$ 1200.00	$ 1800.00
1804	450.00	1000.00	1500.00	2500.00	3500.00	7000.00

Capped Bust Type 1809-37

	G-4	VG-8	F-12	VF-20	EF-40	MS-60
1809	$ 85.00	$ 140.00	$ 275.00	$ 450.00	$ 800.00	$ 4000.00
1814	25.00	30.00	50.00	150.00	350.00	1500.00
1820-27	15.00	20.00	35.00	90.00	300.00	900.00
1822	250.00	450.00	750.00	1200.00	2000.00	7000.00
1829-37	12.00	15.00	20.00	50.00	175.00	600.00

Seated Liberty Type 1837-91

	G-4	VG-8	F-12	VF-20	EF-40	MS-60
1837	$ 25.00	$ 40.00	$ 65.00	$ 220.00	$ 450.00	$ 1000.00
1838O	30.00	50.00	90.00	275.00	500.00	2400.00
1838-40	6.00	8.00	12.00	25.00	60.00	350.00
1841-52	5.00	8.00	11.00	20.00	45.00	300.00
1841O	7.00	10.00	15.00	35.00	65.00	1000.00
1843O	35.00	70.00	100.00	200.00	550.00	—
1844	30.00	65.00	90.00	200.00	500.00	2000.00
1845O	15.00	25.00	50.00	200.00	500.00	—

1846 .... $ 75.00	$ 100.00	$ 140.00	$ 300.00	$ 750.00	—
1849O 10.00	20.00	30.00	100.00	300.00	—
1851O 10.00	15.00	25.00	70.00	170.00	$ 1500.00
1853-73 .... 6.00	7.00	8.00	16.00	40.00	300.00
1875-91 .... 5.00	6.00	7.00	12.00	25.00	175.00
1856S 65.00	100.00	150.00	300.00	600.00	—
1858S 60.00	90.00	125.00	250.00	450.00	—
1859S 65.00	100.00	150.00	300.00	650.00	2500.00
1860O 300.00	500.00	700.00	1200.00	2500.00	—
1861S 25.00	40.00	55.00	125.00	250.00	1200.00
1863 .... 175.00	250.00	350.00	450.00	550.00	1100.00
1863S 20.00	30.00	45.00	75.00	200.00	900.00
1864 .... 160.00	225.00	325.00	450.00	500.00	1000.00
1865 .... 175.00	250.00	350.00	450.00	600.00	1200.00
1866 .... 175.00	250.00	350.00	500.00	650.00	1200.00
1867 .... 250.00	400.00	500.00	650.00	850.00	1500.00
1868S 12.00	17.00	25.00	60.00	150.00	350.00
1870S 150.00	200.00	250.00	350.00	500.00	1500.00
1871CC 500.00	700.00	900.00	1500.00	2500.00	—
1872CC 250.00	400.00	650.00	1200.00	2500.00	—
1873CC 500.00	800.00	1200.00	2000.00	3500.00	—
1873S 15.00	22.00	30.00	60.00	140.00	900.00
1874CC 1200.00	2000.00	3000.00	3500.00	7000.00	—
1878CC 35.00	50.00	80.00	125.00	250.00	700.00
1879 .... 125.00	180.00	225.00	275.00	400.00	700.00
1880 .... 80.00	120.00	160.00	200.00	350.00	500.00
1881 .... 100.00	175.00	190.00	250.00	350.00	550.00
1884S 12.00	18.00	24.00	45.00	65.00	450.00
1885S 250.00	400.00	500.00	750.00	1000.00	3500.00
1886S 20.00	30.00	40.00	60.00	100.00	600.00
1889S 10.00	15.00	20.00	40.00	75.00	400.00

Barber or Liberty Head Type 1892-1916

	G-4	VG-8	F-12	VF-20	EF-40	MS-60
1892 .... $ 2.20	$ 5.00	$ 9.00	$ 12.00	$ 25.00	$ 115.00
1892O 6.00	9.00	16.00	20.00	30.00	175.00
1892S 25.00	35.00	75.00	125.00	150.00	325.00
1893O 15.00	20.00	50.00	75.00	100.00	250.00
1893S 7.00	12.00	20.00	30.00	50.00	225.00
1894 .... 8.00	14.00	50.00	80.00	100.00	250.00
1894O 30.00	50.00	125.00	175.00	300.00	1000.00
1894S .... —	—	—	—	—	275,000.00
1895 .... 60.00	80.00	200.00	300.00	350.00	600.00
1895O 200.00	300.00	450.00	800.00	1200.00	2100.00
1895S 20.00	35.00	75.00	100.00	120.00	350.00

1896O .... $ 42.00	$ 65.00	$ 175.00	$ 200.00	$ 300.00	$ 600.00
1896S 40.00	60.00	150.00	200.00	300.00	600.00
1897-1916 .... 1.50	2.00	4.00	7.00	20.00	100.00
1897O 30.00	50.00	150.00	200.00	300.00	650.00
1897S 8.00	15.00	50.00	75.00	100.00	300.00
1900O 5.00	15.00	50.00	75.00	150.00	500.00
1901S 30.00	50.00	175.00	275.00	350.00	700.00
1902S 3.00	7.00	25.00	40.00	100.00	300.00
1903S 15.00	20.00	50.00	90.00	200.00	375.00
1904S 10.00	14.00	20.00	36.00	65.00	300.00
1909D 3.00	10.00	35.00	60.00	90.00	350.00
1909S 4.00	10.00	40.00	60.00	125.00	400.00
1913S 8.00	15.00	50.00	90.00	175.00	425.00

Mercury Type 1916-45

	G-4	VG-8	F-12	VF-20	EF-40	MS-60
1916-31 .... $ 1.10	$ 1.70	$ 2.50	$ 4.50	$ 7.00	$ 65.00
1916D 350.00	550.00	1000.00	1400.00	2200.00	4000.00
1921 .... 20.00	40.00	70.00	150.00	350.00	1000.00
1921D 30.00	50.00	90.00	175.00	400.00	1200.00
1925D 3.00	4.00	10.00	30.00	100.00	450.00
1926S 5.00	7.00	15.00	35.00	200.00	1200.00
1927D 3.00	4.00	5.00	15.00	40.00	350.00
1928D 3.00	5.00	7.00	15.00	40.00	300.00
1930S 2.50	3.00	5.00	6.00	15.00	75.00
1931D 4.50	6.25	10.00	20.00	30.00	75.00
1931S 3.00	4.00	5.00	7.00	15.00	60.00
1934-45 .... .55	.65	.80	1.10	1.90	9.00

Roosevelt Type 1946-date

	G-4	VG-8	F-12	VF-20	EF-40	MS-60
1946-64 .... $ .20	$ .25	$ .30	$ .35	$ .55	$ 1.00

Twenty-Cent Pieces

1875-78

	G-4	VG-8	F-12	VF-20	EF-40	MS-60
1875-76 .... $ 50.00	$ 60.00	$ 80.00	$ 110.00	$ 200.00	$ 700.00
1877-78 .... —	—	—	—	—	(very rare)

Quarter Dollars

Draped Bust, Small Eagle

	AG-3	G-4	VG-8	F-12	VF-20	EF-40
1796	$ 1500.00	$ 3000.00	$ 5000.00	$ 7500.00	$ 10,000.00	$ 15,000.00

Draped Bust, Heraldic Eagle 1804-07

	AG-3	G-4	VG-8	F-12	VF-20	EF-40
1804	$ 500.00	$ 800.00	$ 1100.00	$ 2200.00	$ 4000.00	$ 7000.00
1805-07	100.00	200.00	300.00	450.00	850.00	2000.00

Capped Bust Type 1815-38

	AG-3	G-4	VG-8	F-12	VF-20	EF-40
1815-28	$ 25.00	$ 45.00	$ 65.00	$ 95.00	$ 250.00	$ 600.00
1831-38 (sm.) ..	15.00	35.00	40.00	50.00	100.00	200.00

Seated Liberty Type 1838-91

	G-4	VG-8	F-12	VF-20	EF-40	MS-60
1838-42	$ 10.00	$ 15.00	$ 25.00	$ 60.00	$ 200.00	$ 1000.00
1843-47	12.00	16.00	20.00	35.00	75.00	600.00
1843O	15.00	25.00	40.00	70.00	200.00	1000.00
1848-53	20.00	35.00	55.00	75.00	150.00	1000.00
1851O	150.00	250.00	400.00	650.00	1000.00	2000.00
1852O	175.00	250.00	400.00	600.00	1200.00	3500.00
1854-55	8.00	11.00	20.00	30.00	90.00	500.00
1855O	35.00	50.00	100.00	200.00	350.00	2000.00
1855S	35.00	50.00	75.00	150.00	275.00	1500.00
1856-65	8.00	10.00	20.00	27.00	55.00	300.00
1856S	30.00	45.00	75.00	150.00	350.00	1400.00
1857S	50.00	80.00	150.00	300.00	500.00	2000.00
1858S	40.00	60.00	100.00	200.00	400.00	—
1859S	75.00	115.00	175.00	275.00	700.00	—
1859O	15.00	25.00	40.00	75.00	100.00	1000.00
1860S	100.00	150.00	300.00	550.00	1500.00	5000.00
1861S	50.00	75.00	150.00	250.00	450.00	2500.00
1862S	40.00	60.00	100.00	250.00	400.00	2000.00
1864S	150.00	250.00	400.00	750.00	1500.00	—
1864	45.00	65.00	90.00	125.00	250.00	900.00
1865S	65.00	90.00	130.00	275.00	500.00	2500.00
1867-69	100.00	150.00	200.00	300.00	500.00	2000.00
1866	200.00	250.00	350.00	450.00	650.00	2000.00
1870-73	20.00	30.00	50.00	80.00	150.00	850.00
1870CC	1200.00	2000.00	4000.00	6000.00	8000.00	—
1872CC	300.00	450.00	800.00	1500.00	3000.00	7500.00
1872S	250.00	400.00	650.00	1000.00	2000.00	5000.00
1873-74	12.00	16.00	30.00	60.00	200.00	850.00
1873CC	800.00	1200.00	2000.00	3500.00	6500.00	15,000.00
1875-91	8.00	10.00	20.00	25.00	50.00	300.00
1875CC	50.00	75.00	120.00	200.00	400.00	1500.00
1878S	60.00	120.00	175.00	250.00	400.00	1500.00
1879-88	100.00	115.00	150.00	180.00	250.00	650.00

Barber or Liberty Head Type 1892-1916

	G-4	VG-8	F-12	VF-20	EF-40	MS-60
1892	3.50	5.00	15.00	25.00	50.00	200.00
1892O	4.00	8.00	18.00	32.00	65.00	250.00
1892S	15.00	25.00	40.00	60.00	120.00	400.00
1893-96	4.00	6.00	18.00	35.00	70.00	300.00
1896O	5.00	10.00	45.00	150.00	300.00	750.00
1896S	150.00	250.00	500.00	850.00	1200.00	3000.00
1897-1916	3.00	4.00	15.00	25.00	60.00	200.00
1899S	8.00	15.00	20.00	35.00	75.00	300.00
1901O	15.00	30.00	60.00	140.00	300.00	700.00
1901S	1000.00	2000.00	3000.00	4500.00	6000.00	10,000.00
1909O	8.00	15.00	40.00	100.00	200.00	600.00
1913	10.00	20.00	50.00	150.00	400.00	1000.00
1913S	300.00	500.00	1000.00	2000.00	3000.00	4500.00

Standing Liberty Type 1916-30

	G-4	VG-8	F-12	VF-20	EF-40	MS-60
1917-24	$ 11.00	$ 15.00	$ 18.00	$ 30.00	$ 40.00	$ 200.00
1916	800.00	1200.00	1600.00	2000.00	2500.00	4000.00
1918D	20.00	25.00	35.00	50.00	80.00	450.00
1919D	40.00	70.00	100.00	150.00	250.00	800.00
1919S	40.00	60.00	100.00	150.00	300.00	1000.00
1921	50.00	80.00	120.00	175.00	250.00	700.00
1923S	100.00	140.00	180.00	250.00	350.00	750.00
1925-30	3.00	4.00	7.00	15.00	30.00	150.00
1927S	9.00	12.00	50.00	150.00	900.00	3300.00

Washington Type 1932-date

	G-4	VG-8	F-12	VF-20	EF-40	MS-63
1932	$ 3.00	$ 3.50	$ 4.00	$ 6.00	$ 8.00	$ 30.00
1932D	31.00	35.00	45.00	60.00	125.00	400.00
1932S	20.00	30.00	35.00	45.00	65.00	250.00
1934-38	1.00	1.50	2.00	5.00	10.00	50.00
1936D	2.00	5.00	7.00	14.00	35.00	300.00
1937S	1.00	2.50	5.00	10.00	18.00	90.00
1939S	1.00	2.00	4.00	6.00	10.00	50.00
1940D	1.00	2.00	4.00	6.00	12.00	55.00
1941-46	.50	.75	1.00	1.50	1.75	5.00
1947-55	.50	.75	1.00	1.50	1.75	2.00
1949	.50	.75	1.00	1.50	1.75	18.00
1956-64	.50	.50	1.00	1.50	1.75	2.00

Half Dollars

Flowing Hair Type 1794-95

	AG-3	G-4	VG-8	F-12	VF-20	EF-40
1794	$ 500.00	$ 900.00	$ 1500.00	$ 2800.00	$ 4000.00	$ 8000.00
1795	250.00	400.00	500.00	800.00	1550.00	3500.00

Draped Bust, Small Eagle

	AG-3	G-4	VG-8	F-12	VF-20	EF-40
1796-97	$ 7000.00	$ 9000.00	$ 12,000.00	$ 15,000.00	$ 25,000.00	$ 45,000.00

Draped Bust, Heraldic Eagle 1801-07

	AG-3	G-4	VG-8	F-12	VF-20	EF-40
1801-02	$ 100.00	$ 200.00	$ 300.00	$ 500.00	$ 900.00	$ 1800.00
1803-07	45.00	100.00	125.00	200.00	350.00	600.00

Capped Bust Type 1807-36

	G-4	VG-8	F-12	VF-20	EF-40	MS-60
1807-08	$ 40.00	$ 85.00	$ 150.00	$ 300.00	$ 750.00	$ 1500.00
1809-36	30.00	45.00	85.00	175.00	400.00	100.00
1836 "50 CENTS"	600.00	750.00	1000.00	1200.00	2000.00	7000.00
1837-38	30.00	40.00	50.00	75.00	200.00	900.00
1838O	—	—	—	—	—	50,000.00
1839O	120.00	160.00	250.00	400.00	650.00	3000.00

Seated Liberty Type 1839-91

	G-4	VG-8	F-12	VF-20	EF-40	MS-60
1839-65	$ 15.00	$ 20.00	$ 35.00	$ 45.00	$ 75.00	$ 450.00
1866-78	13.00	18.00	30.00	40.00	60.00	450.00
1842O (small date)	500.00	750.00	1000.00	2000.00	4000.00	—
1848	30.00	40.00	60.00	90.00	150.00	850.00
1850	75.00	100.00	150.00	250.00	450.00	1200.00
1851	75.00	120.00	175.00	300.00	500.00	1500.00
1852	100.00	150.00	250.00	400.00	700.00	1600.00
1852O	40.00	60.00	100.00	150.00	300.00	1000.00
1855S	300.00	400.00	700.00	1200.00	3000.00	—
1857S	25.00	35.00	45.00	100.00	300.00	1300.00
1858S	20.00	25.00	35.00	65.00	140.00	850.00
1862	22.00	30.00	40.00	70.00	100.00	650.00
1870CC	450.00	750.00	1500.00	2500.00	4000.00	—
1871CC	100.00	150.00	250.00	400.00	900.00	4000.00
1872CC	50.00	80.00	150.00	275.00	500.00	2500.00
1873CC	75.00	125.00	200.00	350.00	800.00	4000.00
1874CC	150.00	250.00	400.00	700.00	1200.00	5000.00
1874S	30.00	40.00	60.00	150.00	300.00	1300.00
1878CC	200.00	300.00	450.00	750.00	1500.00	4500.00
1878S	5000.00	6500.00	9000.00	13,000.00	18,000.00	30,000.00
1879-90	110.00	140.00	180.00	240.00	350.00	750.00
1891	20.00	30.00	40.00	60.00	100.00	500.00

Barber or Liberty Head Type 1892-1915

	G-4	VG-8	F-12	VF-20	EF-40	MS-60
1892	$ 13.00	$ 25.00	$ 40.00	$ 75.00	$ 200.00	$ 400.00
1892O	75.00	120.00	170.00	250.00	400.00	800.00
1893S	50.00	75.00	120.00	250.00	350.00	900.00
1893-96	6.00	12.00	40.00	70.00	180.00	450.00
1897-1915	5.00	8.00	25.00	50.00	150.00	400.00
1896S	50.00	75.00	100.00	200.00	350.00	1000.00
1897O	50.00	80.00	200.00	400.00	700.00	1400.00
1897S	70.00	100.00	200.00	350.00	550.00	100.00
1898O	15.00	25.00	70.00	150.00	300.00	650.00
1901S	12.00	20.00	75.00	175.00	450.00	1300.00
1901O	7.00	15.00	40.00	100.00	300.00	1100.00
1904S	10.00	20.00	80.00	200.00	400.00	1200.00
1904O	10.00	15.00	50.00	100.00	300.00	1000.00
1913	15.00	25.00	60.00	175.00	300.00	800.00
1914	18.00	35.00	150.00	275.00	450.00	700.00
1915	16.00	25.00	75.00	200.00	350.00	900.00

Liberty Walking Type 1916-47

	G-4	VG-8	F-12	VF-20	EF-40	MS-60
1916	$ 20.00	$ 30.00	$ 50.00	$ 100.00	$ 150.00	$ 250.00
1916D	12.00	17.00	30.00	65.00	120.00	250.00
1916S	40.00	50.00	100.00	250.00	450.00	800.00
1917-18	5.00	8.00	12.00	25.00	35.00	120.00
1919	12.00	17.00	35.00	120.00	375.00	850.00
1919D	10.00	13.00	30.00	120.00	450.00	2000.00
1919S	10.00	12.00	25.00	100.00	500.00	1700.00
1920-33	6.00	7.00	11.00	20.00	70.00	500.00
1921	50.00	75.00	160.00	450.00	1200.00	2500.00
1921D	65.00	100.00	200.00	550.00	1500.00	2200.00
1921S	15.00	20.00	50.00	400.00	3000.00	7500.00
1934-47	3.00	3.25	3.50	4.00	6.00	29.00
1934S	3.00	3.50	4.50	6.00	25.00	200.00
1938D	15.00	20.00	25.00	50.00	100.00	320.00
1941S	2.50	3.50	3.75	4.00	7.00	78.00

Franklin Type 1948-63

	VG-8	F-12	VF-20	EF-40	MS-60
1948	$ 1.75	$ 3.00	$ 3.00	$ 6.00	$ 16.00
1948D	1.50	1.75	2.50	4.50	11.00
1949	1.50	1.75	2.50	4.50	35.00
1950	1.75	5.00	8.00	12.00	70.00
1951	1.50	1.75	2.50	3.50	11.00
1951D	1.50	1.75	2.50	3.50	30.00
1951S	1.50	1.75	2.50	3.50	30.00
1952-63	1.50	1.60	2.25	3.00	5.00
1952S	1.50	1.75	2.50	3.50	30.00
1953	1.50	1.75	3.00	6.00	24.00
1953S	1.50	1.60	2.50	4.00	12.00

Silver Dollars

Flowing Hair Type 1794-95

	AG-3	G-4	VG-8	F-12	VF-20	EF-40
1794	$ 3500.00	$ 8000.00	$ 11,000.00	$ 17,000.00	$ 25,000.00	$ 42,000.00
1795	400.00	700.00	900.00	1200.00	2000.00	4000.00

Draped Bust, Small Eagle

	AG-3	G-4	VG-8	F-12	VF-20	EF-40
1794-98	$ 300.00	$ 600.00	$ 800.00	$ 1000.00	$ 2000.00	$ 3500.00

Draped Bust, Heraldic Eagle

	G-4	VG-8	F-12	VF-20	EF-40	MS-60
1798-1804 ...	$ 300.00	$ 350.00	$ 450.00	$ 700.00	$ 1300.00	$ 8000.00

Seated Liberty Type 1840-73

	VG-8	F-12	VF-20	EF-40	MS-60
1840-73 ....| —	$ 200.00	$ 300.00	$ 350.00	$ 500.00	$ 2000.00
1846O ....| —	200.00	250.00	325.00	650.00	4000.00
1850 ....| —	400.00	550.00	800.00	1200.00	4500.00
1851 ....| —	3000.00	7000.00	8000.00	10,000.00	14,000.00
1852 ....| —	1500.00	7000.00	8000.00	10,000.00	17,000.00
1858 ....| —	2500.00	3500.00	5000.00	5500.00	—
1870CC ....| —	325.00	450.00	650.00	1000.00	4500.00
1870S ....| —	—	50,000.00	70,000.00	90,000.00	—
1871CC ....| —	2200.00	3500.00	4500.00	7500.00	20,000.00
1872CC ....| —	1000.00	1500.00	2500.00	3500.00	15,000.00
1872S ....| —	300.00	400.00	600.00	900.00	7000.00
1873CC ....| —	3000.00	4500.00	7500.00	12,000.00	27,000.00

Trade Dollars 1873-85

	VG-8	F-12	VF-20	EF-40	MS-60
1873-78	$ 65.00	$ 85.00	$ 110.00	$ 150.00	$ 500.00
1879-83 (proof only)	—	—	—	—	1200.00
1884-85 (proof only)	—	—	—	—	very rare

Liberty Head or Morgan Type 1878-1921

	F-12	VF-20	EF-40	AU-50
1878-1921	$ 10.00	$ 12.00	$ 17.00	$ 20.00
1879CC	36.00	100.00	170.00	1000.00

1880CC	$ 45.00	$ 70.00	$ 100.00	$ 130.00
1880O	9.00	12.00	22.00	45.00
1881CC	100.00	120.00	130.00	160.00
1882CC	30.00	45.00	50.00	65.00
1883CC	30.00	45.00	55.00	65.00
1883S	13.00	20.00	90.00	350.00
1884S	15.00	35.00	250.00	4000.00
1886O	13.00	18.00	45.00	220.00
1886S	20.00	35.00	50.00	120.00
1889CC	300.00	650.00	2500.00	6500.00
1889S	20.00	30.00	45.00	90.00
1890CC	30.00	45.00	75.00	200.00
1892CC	50.00	80.00	170.00	300.00
1892S	40.00	100.00	750.00	8000.00
1893	50.00	70.00	140.00	300.00
1893CC	115.00	400.00	700.00	1000.00
1893O	85.00	170.00	350.00	1000.00
1893S	1200.00	2700.00	10,000.00	23,000.00
1894	225.00	350.00	500.00	800.00
1894O	20.00	35.00	125.00	550.00
1895O	100.00	200.00	800.00	8000.00
1895S	175.00	350.00	600.00	1000.00
1896O	12.00	16.00	100.00	650.00
1897O	13.00	17.00	75.00	500.00
1901	25.00	40.00	200.00	1200.00
1903S	55.00	200.00	700.00	2000.00
1904S	35.00	125.00	450.00	850.00

Peace Type 1921-35

	VF-20	EF-40	AU-50	MS-60
1921	$ 30.00	$ 40.00	$ 70.00	$ 140.00
1922-35	8.00	10.00	12.00	25.00
1924S	14.00	20.00	45.00	130.00
1925S	11.00	15.00	25.00	50.00
1926D	10.00	13.00	27.00	45.00
1927	16.00	22.00	35.00	60.00
1927D	14.00	20.00	55.00	120.00
1927S	13.00	18.00	50.00	85.00
1928	100.00	120.00	140.00	175.00

1928S	$ 15.00	$ 18.00	$ 40.00	$ 65.00
1934D	15.00	18.00	40.00	80.00
1934S	40.00	150.00	400.00	1000.00
1935S	12.00	16.00	60.00	100.00

Gold Half Eagle

Classic Head Type

	VG-8	F-12	VF-20	EF-40	AU-50
1834-38	$ 225.00	$ 300.00	$ 500.00	$ 850.00	$ 3000.00

Coronet Type

	F-12	VF-20	EF-40	AU-50
1839-66	$ 400.00	$ 1000.00	$ 2000.00	$ 6000.00
1873	170.00	225.00	500.00	1800.00
1867-77	500.00	1300.00	4000.00	7000.00
1878-1908	130.00	150.00	175.00	200.00

Indian Head Type

	F-12	VF-20	EF-40	AU-50
1908-29 (most)	$ 200.00	$ 225.00	$ 250.00	$ 325.00

Civil War Tokens

	VG-8	F-12	VF-20	EF-40
Copper or Brass	$ 6.00	$ 7.00	$ 9.00	$ 25.00
Nickel or German Silver	22.00	35.00	45.00	75.00
White Metal	27.00	40.00	55.00	85.00
Copper Nickel	35.00	50.00	65.00	100.00
Silver	100.00	150.00	200.00	400.00

Decoys

Decoys most often represent waterfowl, but frog, fish, owl, and crow decoys are not uncommon. Decoys can be solid, hollow, or slat-bodied. They can be either of the floating variety or the "stick-up" variety, which is driven into the ground.

Decoys produced after the mid-19th century are most popular among collectors. Famous decoy carvers include Ira Hudson, Charles Wheeler, Albert Laing, and Mark Whipple. Enthusiasts usually collect decoys by carver, species, or fly-way (path of migration). Decoys made for actual use are more favored by collectors than those intended only for show. Original paint is extremely important to many collectors.

Canada Goose by Nathan "Romley" Horner, West Creek, New Jersey, $8000-$1200.

	AUCTION	RETAIL Low	High
A.E. Crowell, lesser yellowlegs, decorative	$ 7700	$ 12,500	$ 18,000
A.E. Crowell Miniature Golden-Eye Duck, rect. impressed mark, ht. 3"	550	880	1350
A.E. Crowell Miniature Hooded Merganser Duck, rect. impressed mark, ht. 3"	550	880	1350
A.E. Crowell, ruffed grouse, decorative	10,450	16,500	25,000
A. Elmer Crowell, black-bellied plover	4400	7000	10,000
A. Elmer Crowell, sandpiper	21,000	33,000	50,000
Alfred Gardiner, attrib., sickle-billed curlew	100	160	250
Ben Smith, attrib., goldeneye	10,450	16,500	25,000
Black-Bellied Plover Working Decoy	100	160	250
Calvert Tolley, preening brant	1870	3000	4500
Canada Goose Decoy, Long Island, canvas over frame	600	950	1450
Canada Goose Decoy, Long Island, solid body	600	950	1450
Canvasback Drake Decoy, Maryland	50	80	120
Chauncey Wheeler, brant	1155	90	130
Chief Cuffee, sickle-billed curlew, len. 15"	475	750	1150
Connecticut HC Preening Hutchins Goose, repaint	9900	15,000	24,000

	AUCTION	RETAIL	
		Low	High
Corb Reed, HC canvasback	$ 1100	$ 1760	$ 2700
Dave "Umbrella" Watson, HC Canada goose	11,000	17,600	26,000
Dodge Factory Decoy of Canada Goose, WMI owner's brand	900	1440	2200
E. Lee Dudley, bluebill, some repaint and bill repair	9350	15,000	23,000
Ed Parsons, canvasback	1705	2730	4000
English/Dawson, black duck	22,000	35,200	50,000
English/Dawson, lowhcad wigeon hen	29,700	47,500	72,500
English/Dawson, lowhead wigeon	27,500	44,000	67,500
English/Dawson, pintail	143,000	225,000	350,000
English/Dawson, red-breasted merganser hen	66,000	100,000	160,000
Fred Nichols, feeding yellowlegs	25,850	41,000	63,000
George Boyd, yellowlegs	1540	2500	3750
George O'Neal (NC), brant	3190	5000	7500
George Warin (ON), Canada goose	21,450	34,000	52,500
George Warin (ONT), HC Canada goose	7700	12,500	18,500
Gus Moak, canvasback	2750	4400	6750
Gus Wilson, preening white-winged scoter, repaint	8,800	14,000	21,500
Gus Wilson, red-breasted merganser	55,000	88,000	134,000
Gus Wilson, surf scoter with mussel	28,600	45,000	70,000
Harry Jobes, sleeping pintail	80	130	200
Harry M. Shourds, pair goldeneyes	25,000	41,000	63,000
Harry V. Shourds, buffehead	22,000	35,200	53,900
Harry V. Shourds, HC Canada goose	7700	12,500	18,000
Harry V. Shourds, HC red-breasted merganser hen	13,200	21,000	32,000
Harry V. Shourds, hissing Canada goose	200,000	325,000	500,000
Harry V. Shourds, merganser hen	21,500	34,320	52,550
Harry V. Shourds, redhead	27,500	44,000	67,000
Harry V. Shourds, swimming Canada goose	104,500	167,200	250,000
Hays Blue-Winged Teal Drake Decoy	150	240	370
Henry H. Ackerman, canvasback	80	130	200
Henry H. Ackerman, redhead	80	130	200
Joe King, pintail	41,800	66,880	100,000
Joe Lincoln, Canada goose	9350	15,000	23,000
Joe Lincoln, wood duck	165,000	264,000	400,000
John Dilley, red knot	9900	15,840	24,000
John Dilley, ruddy turnstone	10,450	16,720	25,000
John Tax, standing mallard	20,900	33,440	51,000
Johrl Blair, HC pintail	19,800	31,000	48,500
Lloyd Parker, pair red-breasted mergansers	132,000	170,000	250,000
Lothrop Holmes, black-bellied plover	11,550	18,000	28,000
Mallard Decoy, decorative, half-model form, in flight, len. 19"	200	320	500
Merganser Drake Decoy	700	1150	1750
Nathan Cobb, curlew	77,000	125,000	185,000
Nathan Cobb, Sr., curlew, replaced bill	8,250	13,500	20,000
Nathan Rowlcy Horner, mallard	60,500	95,000	145,000
Nathan Rowley Horner, mallard hen	82,500	132,000	200,000
Obediah Verity, oversized curlew	30,000	50,000	75,000
Obediah Verity, pair red-breasted mergansers, repaint	7700	12,500	18,500
Obediah Verity, running red-backed sandpiper	14,850	23,500	36,000
Pintail Drake Decoy, Long Island	175	280	430

	AUCTION	RETAIL	
		Low	High
Plover Shore Bird Working Decoy	$ 60	$ 100	$ 150
Robert Elliston, HC bluebill	9075	14,500	22,000
Robert McGaw, canvasback	1430	2290	3500
Roothead Heron Decoy, on stand, len. 19"	100	160	250
Running Yellowlegs Shore Bird Decoy	200	300	500
Shang Wheeler, bluebill	9350	15,000	23,000
Shang Wheeler, Canada goose	18,700	30,000	45,000
Sink Box Cast-Iron Duck Decoys	200	300	500
Stevens Factory, mallard	9075	14,500	22,000
Thomas Langan, contemporary golden plover after William Bowman	100	160	250
Thomas Langan, sanderling peep shore bird	45	70	110
Thomas Langan, yellowlegs shore bird	45	70	110
Vidacovich Family, mallard	1540	2400	3770
Ward Bros., bookends, mallards	1650	2600	4000
Ward Bros., goldeneye, c. 1940s	1650	2600	4000
Ward Bros., mallard hen, dated 1966	2640	4200	6400
Ward Bros., pintail, dated 1930	1045	1600	2500
Ward Bros., pintail hen, dated 1940	1100	1750	2700
William Bowman, HC brant	1265	2000	3100
William Bowrnan, dowitcher	10,175	16,000	25,000
William Quinn, gadwall	19,800	31,000	48,500
William Quinn, lowhead wigeon	17,600	28,000	43,000
Working Shore Bird Decoy	60	100	150

Two A.E. Crowell miniature duck carvings, ht. 3", $1100 at auction. — Photo courtesy of Northeast Auctions.

Doorstops

Figural doorstops are practical sculptures. Designed to keep doors open to aid ventilation, most of the doorstops below were produced in the first half of the 20th century. Unless otherwise indicated, examples are made of cast iron. Prices are given for items in excellent condition with minimal paint wear. Beware of doorstops with sloppy workmanship and grainy finish; they are probably reproductions. Examine items carefully to detect cracks and repaints.

Our consultant for this area is Jeanne Bertoia, author of *Doorstops, Identification & Values*, Collector Books, Paducah, KY, 1993 (she is listed in the back of this book).

A selection of lady doorstops, prices range from $200 to $500.
—Photo courtesy of Bill Bertoia Auctions.

	LOW	AVG.	HIGH
Ally Sloper, 11.13" x 6.25"	$ 380	$ 410	$ 480
Aunt Jemima, 13.25" x 8"	325	370	415
Basket of Kittens, 10" x 7"	350	400	450
Bathing Beauties, Hubley, signed "Fish," 10.88" x 5.25"	550	600	700
Bear w/ Honey, full-figure, rare, 15" x 6.5"	1400+		
Bear w/ Tree, 7.75" x 4.38"	250	275	300
Bellhop, 8.88" x 4.63"	250	275	300
Bird of Paradise, 13.38" x 7"	325	365	405
Bloodhound, wedge, 13.75" x 7"	300	340	380
Bloodhound, wedge, 15.25" x 4.75"	200	238	275
Bobby Blake, Hubley, designed by Grace Drayton, 9.5" x 5.25"	400	438	475

	LOW	AVG.	HIGH
Boston Terrier, Bradley & Hubbard, 9.63" x 11.75"	$ 275	$ 312	$ 350
Boston Terrier Puppy, 7.75" x 8.5"	200	225	250
Boy w/ Hands in Pockets, full-figure, 10.5" x 3.63"	300	335	370
Butler, rare, 12.5", 6"	375	405	435
Cat, full-figure, 11.5" x 7"	325	350	375
Cat on Base, 12.5" x 7.5"	150	188	225
Cat, wedge, Hubley, 6" x 3"	350	375	400
Clipper Ship, 11" x 13"	50	62	75
Clipper Ship, 12.75" x 13"	40	55	70
Clipper Ship, wedge, 11.63" x 11.63"	45	60	75
Clown, rare, 11.5" x 5.5"	375	400	425
Cockatoo, full-figure, 14" x 4.5"	175	212	250
Cocker Spaniel, wedge, VA Metalcrafters, 9" x 7"	100	125	150
Colonial Woman, Littco Products, 10.25" x 6"	150	188	225
Conestoga Wagon, 8" x 11"	100	138	175
Dachshund, marked "No. 8 Taylor Cook 1930 C.," 5.5" x 7.25"	350	388	425
Deco Hunchback Cat, 2-sided, wedge, 11.75" x 9.13"	300	325	350
Dog and Duck, marked "copyright 1925 by A.M. Greenblatt, Boston, Mass.," 10" x 8.75"	600	650	700
Dolly, Hubley, designed by Grace Drayton, 9.5" x 5.5"	400	438	475
Drum Major, full-figure, solid, 13.5" x 6.5"	350	400	450
Duck, 11" x 6.5"	350	375	400
Ducks, Hubley, 8.25" x 6.25"	300	340	380
Dutch Girl w/ Big Shoes, 9.75" x 9.25"	325	362	400
Elephant, 7.25" x 7.13"	50	75	100
Elephant, Bradley & Hubbard, 10" x 11.75"	200	225	250
English Bulldog, full-figure, 5.75" x 8.5"	125	150	175
Fantail Fish, Hubley, 9.75" x 5.88"	100	138	175
Fawn, marked "No. 6 C. 1930 Taylor Cook," 10" x 6"	175	212	250
Fisherman at Wheel, 6.25" x 6"	125	150	175
Fox Terrier, 10.38" x 10.5"	225	250	275
French Bulldog, Hubley, full-figure, 7.63" x 6.75"	125	150	175
French Girl, Hubley, 9.25" x 5.5"	225	255	285
Geese, Hubley, designed by Fred Everett, 8" x 8"	350	400	450
German Shepherd, full-figure, 9.75" x 13"	125	150	175
Giraffe, Hubley, full-figure, 12.5" x 9"	1000+		
Giraffe, wedge, 13.5" x 5.25"	250	262	275
Girl Holding Bouquet, full-figure, 7.63" x 4.75"	175	200	225
Girl Holding Dress, Bradley & Hubbard, 13" x 6.75"	500	550	600
Girl in Canoe, 4.38" x 10"	500	538	575
Girl Kicking Flower, rare, 9.88" x 7.25"	600	650	700
Guitar Player, 11.88" x 7.13"	475	512	550
Horse, full-figure, Hubley, 10" x 12"	100	125	150
Horse Jumping Fence, Eastern Specialty Co., 7.88" x 11.75"	325	375	425
Huckleberry Finn, Littco Products, 12.5" x 9.5"	500	550	600
Hunchback Cat, 10.63" x 7.5"	100	125	150
Imp, 5.25" x 3"	100	125	150
Judy, 11" x 8.88"	450	488	525
Koala, marked "No. 5 Taylor Cook 1930 C.," 9.25" x 5.5"	400	425	450
Large Frog, full-figure, rare, 14" x 7"	1000+		
Large Mammy, green dress, Hubley, full-figure, 12" x 6"	400	440	480

	LOW	AVG.	HIGH
Large Old Salt, 14.5" x 6.5"	$ 325	$ 350	$ 375
Large Old Salt at Rudder, 14" x 6.75"	400	425	450
Large Putting Golf, Spencer, 2-sided, 16.63" x 5.63"	500	538	575
Lil Red Riding Hood, Hubley, Grace Drayton design, 9.5" x 5"	400	438	475
Little Boy w/ Bear, full-figure, solid, 5.25" x 3.5"	150	175	200
Little Girl, full-figure, solid, 4.88" x 3.75"	150	175	200
Little Girl by Wall, full-figure, solid, 5.25" x 3.25"	150	175	200
Little Heiskell Soldier, emb. "Little Heiskell, Hagerstown, MD, 1769," 10.75" x 6"	325	362	400
Little Jester Girl, full-figure, solid, 5.63" x 3.38"	150	175	200
Mary Quite Contrary, Littco Products, 11.38" x 9.63"	650	725	800
Messenger Boy, Hubley, signed "Fish," 10" x 5.38"	450	488	525
Monkey, wedge, 13.5" x 5.63"	300	338	375
Monkey on Barrel, "No. 3 C. 1930 Taylor Cook," 8.38" x 4.88"	350	388	425
Old Woman, Bradley & Hubbard, 11" x 7"	475	500	525
Olive Picker, Hubley, rare, 7.75" x 8.75"	550	600	650
Ostrich, wedge, 8.5" x 9"	225	250	275
Owl on Books, 9.25" x 6.5"	475	512	550
Pan and Nymph, very rare, 9.25" x 14"	650	700	750
Parlor Maid, Hubley, signed "Fish," 9.25" x 3.5"	780+		
Parrot, marked "No. 4 C. 1930 Taylor Cook," 10.5" x 4.88"	350	388	425
Parrot in Ring, 8" x 7"	100	138	175
Parrot on Ball, 12.13" x 5.5"	125	150	175
Peacock, 5.63" x 8.25"	150	162	175
Peacock, 6.25" x 6.25"	150	175	200
Peasant Girl, Hubley, 8.75" x 5"	175	200	225
Penguin, full-figure, 10.5" x 5"	275	312	350
Penguin, marked "No. 1 C. 1930 Taylor Cook," 9.5" x 5.25"	500	550	600
Penguin w/ Top Hat, Hubley, full-figure, 10.5" x 3.75"	275	312	350
Peter Rabbit, Hubley, designed by Grace Drayton, 9.5" x 4.75"	375	400	425
Pheasant, Hubley, designed by Fred Everett, 8.5" x 7.5"	250	285	320
Pilgrim Boy, double-sided casting, 8.75" x 5.38"	325	362	400
Pirate Girl, marked "Pirate Girl," 13.88" x 7.25"	250	275	300
Pirate w/ Sack, rare, 11.88" x 9.63"	475	500	525
Pirate w/ Sword, 12" x 5.75"	450	488	525
Police Boy, 10.63" x 7.25"	375	425	475
Policeman, marked "LeMur Light Co., pat. pending," 7.88" x 4"	200	250	300
Polly, Hubley, 8.13" x 5.25"	100	125	150
Punch, 12" x 9"	450	500	550
Puppies in Basket, 7" x 7.38"	325	362	400
Quail, Hubley, designed by Fred Everett, 7.25" x 6.25"	300	338	375
Rabbit, wedge, 2-sided, Spencer, 11.5" x 8.75"	425	470	515
Rabbit by Fence, Albany Foundry Co., 6.88" x 8.13"	325	375	400
Rabbit w/ Tophat, 9.88" x 4.75"	375	412	450
Rhumba Dancer, 11.13" x 6.63"	475	505	545
Rooster, 13" x 8.5"	325	350	375
Rooster, 7" x 5.5"	125	150	175
Rooster, Spencer, 2-sided, 13.25" x 11"	500	540	580
Safety First Policeman, rare, emb.d "safety first," 9.5" x 5.63"	625	662	700
Sailor, 11.38" x 5"	425	450	475
Scottie, Wilton Products Inc., 7.75" x 4.5"	75	100	125

	LOW	AVG.	HIGH
Senorita, 11.25" x 7"	$ 275	$ 300	$ 325
Shorebird, 9.75" x 5.13"	275	312	350
Silhouette Girl, Albany Foundry, 11.25" x 10.25"	475	525	575
Sitting Boston Terrier, full-figure, 6.75" x 6.63"	125	150	175
Sitting Bulldog, full-figure, 6.75" x 7"	150	188	225
Skier, full-figure, 12.5" x 5"	400	438	475
Small Halloween Cat, wedge, 5" x 4"	125	150	175
Small Mammy, Hubley, full-figure, green dress, 8.5" x 4.5"	175	200	225
Small Mammy, Hubley, full-figure, red dress, 8.5" x 4.5"	150	188	225
Southern Belle, 11.25" x 6"	150	175	200
Spanish Girl, Hubley, 9" x 5"	175	220	265
Spotted Dog, marked "C. 1930 Taylor Cook," 7.75" x 7.88"	450	475	500
Spotted Dog Sitting, full-figure, solid, 5.5" x 6.5"	175	200	225
Spotted Dog Standing, full-figure, solid, 5.5" x 7"	175	200	225
Springer Spaniel, 6.75" x 7"	125	150	175
Squirrel on Log, 11" x 9.5"	225	262	300
Squirrel w/ Nut, Hubley, 8.5" x 7"	275	312	350
St. Bernard, 8" x 10.5"	125	155	185
St. Bernard, full-figure, 6.75" x 10.38"	250	285	320
Stagecoach, Hubley, 11.25" x 5.88"	125	162	200
Star of Texas, 10.5" x 10.25"	275	300	325
Stork, 13.75" x 8.88"	300	338	375
Stork, full-figure, Hubley, 2.25" x 7"	325	375	425
Swallows, Hubley, 8.5" x 7.5"	300	338	375
Swan, Spencer, 2-sided, 7.88" x 13.5"	500	550	600
Terrier w/ Bushes, marked "copt. 1929 PAL," 8" x 7"	150	162	175
The Constitution, A.M. Greenblatt Studios, c. 1924, 11.75" x 8.5"	100	130	160
The Patrol, full-figure, 8.75" x 3.75"	200	225	250
The Snooper, 2-sided, 13.25" x 4.5"	400	440	480
Tin Soldier, very rare, 11.75" x 4.5"	350	388	425
Topsy, wedge, Hubley, 6" x 4"	250	275	300
Tropical Woman, 12" x 6.25"	150	185	220
Turkeys, 6.38" x 5.75"	225	250	275
Whippet, 6.75" x 7.5"	125	138	150
Whistling Jim, Bradley & Hubbard, very rare, 16.25" x 5.5"	1800+		
White Cockatoo, 11.25" x 9.5"	275	312	365
Wineman, rare, 9.5" x 7"	550	615	680
Wolfhound, wedge, Spencer, 6.5" x 3"	175	200	225
Woman w/ Hatbox, 6.75" x 5.25"	100	125	150
Yawning Child, full-figure, 9" x 5"	150	175	200

Fans

Folding fans were fashionable accessories for women during the 18th, 19th, and even into the early 20th centuries. They used fans not only to show one's social position and wealth, but for coquetry or flirting. In Asia men as well as women utilized them, from the scented fans of the elderly to the black and red implements of the military. A popular export item (particularly the delicate ivory fans, carved under water and much sought after as wedding gifts), fans served many functions in Asian society.

Craftsmen constructed fans in several ways. The most common method was the insertion of sticks into a pleated piece of material called a "leaf." Leaves were made of silk lace, paper, or even vellum (very thin goatskin). Another type of folding fan was called a "brise." The brise fan was made of wide, overlapping sticks, joined by a ribbon. Nearly all fans of both types have scenes or designs painted on them. Another type, considered quite stylish from the 1870s until about 1910, was the feather fan. Usually made of ostrich feathers, this type is quite perishable.

Beautifully drawn, painted, or inscribed, Asian fans fell into two main structural categories. Women's fans usually did not fold, consisting of a piece of paper glued to a flat bamboo handle. Folding fans, used more extensively in ritual ceremonies, or by high born citizens, were made of paper or silk, with wooden, bamboo, ivory, or mother-of-pearl ribs.

Hand painted silk and mother-of-pearl fan, early 20th century, $80-$120. — Photo courtesy of Northeast Auctions.

	LOW	AVG.	HIGH
Advertising, Hires Root Beer, 6.5", c. 1930	$ 20	$ 25	$ 30
Advertising, Homer's 5¢ Cigar, 7", c. 1910	20	25	30
Black Net, with sequins	40	55	70
Bride's, lace, hand-painted	40	55	70
Bride's, lace, sequins, ivory sticks	70	85	100
Brise, Regency, painted vase of flowers	70	100	130
Celluloid, carved flower	70	95	120
Celluloid, miniature	80	100	120

	LOW	AVG.	HIGH
Celluloid, Oriental design	$ 40	$ 50	$ 60
Celluloid, sequins, chiffon	80	95	110
Feather, celluloid sticks	90	105	120
Feather, ivory sticks	190	240	290
Feather, painted, c. 1870	190	220	250
Feather, signed Duvelleroy, c. 1865	900	1100	1300
Feather, small, c. 1890	220	250	280
Feather, tortoiseshell sticks	200	215	230
French, painted, carved, signed	150	160	170
French, painted, ivory sticks	310	355	400
French, painted, signed Jolivet, c. 1870	900	1225	1550
French, painted, tortoise sticks, sequins	300	165	30
Garrett Snuff, advertising, paper, c. 1928	30	35	40
George Washington and Cherry Smash, lithographed	40	55	70
Gold Edge, pink silk, ebony ribs	50	60	70
Hand-painted, floral design, wood	40	50	60
Horn, carved, painted pansies, blue ribbon	180	230	280
Lacquered, black, silver flower	130	145	160
Lacquered, white, silver handle	110	125	140
Marabou Feathers, satin, hand-painted, 20"	250	280	310
Oriental, landscape, 7" x 22", c. 1720-1795, by Fang Shishu	1620	2425	3230
Oriental, magnolia, 6" x 18", c. 1910-1930, by Shao'ang	4000	5000	6000
Oriental, mountain scene, 8" x 22", by Juru Bao	800	1050	1300
Oriental, poem, 7" x 22", c. 1620-1665, by Shu Vouzhang	1100	1200	1300
Oriental, poem, 8" x 21", c. 1820-1870, artist unknown	840	1060	1280
Oriental, poem in character, 7" x 20", c. 1620-1685, by Jiang Jie	1400	1700	2000
Oriental, riverscape, 6" x 20", by Shu Youzhang	1000	1500	2000
Oriental, rocks and bamboo, 7" x 21", c. 1890-1910	700	850	1000
Ostrich Plume, tortoise-shell sticks	80	100	120
Pearl Sticks, sequin design, 8"	70	80	90
Puzzle, 4 scones, two-way opening	275	325	375
Satin Flower Center, carved, ivory sticks	300	335	370
Silk, embroidered, ivory sticks	130	155	180
Silk, hand-painted animal figure and books	40	55	70
Silk, hand-painted figures and floral designs, original box	130	150	170
Silk, Oriental design, ivory and bamboo	80	95	110
Souvenir Centennial, historical buildings, 12"	175	200	225
Wedding, ivory sticks, lace	120	135	150

Figurines

Artisan modeled figurines in pottery and porcelain are a mainstay of the collecting market. Often, the most valuable pieces are not those produced as "limited editions." Quality of design and craft are the most important factors, but condition, rarity and size are also important.

The listings here are by title, followed by maker.

	LOW	AVG.	HIGH
Abigail, Florence Ceramics Co.	$ 90	$ 100	$ 110
Accordion Boy, Ceramic Arts Studio	70	80	90
Adeline, Florence Ceramics Co.	100	110	120
Adonis and Aphrodite, Ceramic Arts Studio	290	325	360
Alden, John, Florence Ceramics Co.	70	80	90
Alice and White Rabbit, Ceramic Arts Studio	60	65	70
Amelia, Florence Ceramics Co.	100	115	130
Amelia in Brocade, Florence Ceramics Co.	340	380	420
Angel, Florence Ceramics Co.	40	45	50
Angels, Kay Finch Ceramics	15	20	25
Anita in Brocade, Florence Ceramics Co.	340	380	420
Ann, Florence Ceramics Co.	50	55	60
Annabel, Florence Ceramics Co.	140	155	170
Arabesque, Ceramic Arts Studio	30	35	40
Archibald the Dragon, Ceramic Arts Studio	70	80	90
Arthur, Brayton Pottery	30	35	40
Asian, Shawnee Pottery	2	5	10
Attitude, Ceramic Arts Studio	30	35	40
Autumn Andy, Ceramic Arts Studio	20	25	30
Baby Black Pegasus, Vernon Kilns	210	235	260
Bald Eagle, 8.5", Cliftwood Potteries	90	100	110
Bali Gong, Ceramic Arts Studio	30	35	40
Bali Hai, Ceramic Arts Studio	30	35	40
Bali Kris, Ceramic Arts Studio	30	35	40
Bali Lao, Ceramic Arts Studio	30	35	40
Balinese Dance Boy and Girl, Ceramic Arts Studio	100	110	120
Ballerina, Florence Ceramics Co.	140	160	180
Ballerina Child, Florence Ceramics Co.	80	90	100
Ballet En Pose, Ceramic Arts Studio	30	35	40
Ballet En Repose, Ceramic Arts Studio	30	35	40
Banjo Girl, Ceramic Arts Studio	40	50	60
Bass Viola Boy, Ceramic Arts Studio	40	50	60
Bear, 2", Morton Pottery Co.	5	10	15
Bedtime Boy and Girl, Ceramic Arts Studio	30	35	40
Berty, Ceramic Arts Studio	80	90	100
Beth, Florence Ceramics Co.	60	65	70
Betsy, Florence Ceramics Co.	80	90	100
Billikin Doll, 11", Cliftwood Potteries	100	110	120
Billikin Doll, 7.5", Cliftwood Potteries	60	65	70
Birthday Girl, Florence Ceramics Co.	120	135	150
Black Girl, Brayton Pottery	220	250	280
Black Girls, Brayton Pottery	150	170	190
Blackamoor, Brayton Pottery	30	35	40

	LOW	AVG.	HIGH
Blackamoor, 7.5", Abingdon Potteries, Inc.	$ 40	$ 45	$ 50
Blossom Girl, Florence Ceramics Co.	60	65	70
Blue Bird, 4.5", Midwest Pottery Co.	15	20	25
Blue Boy, Florence Ceramics Co.	140	160	180
Blue Heron, 11", Midwest Pottery Co.	40	50	60
Blue Jay, 6.5", Midwest Pottery Co.	15	20	25
Bluejay, 2.5", Morton Pottery Co.	5	10	15
Bluejay, 4", Morton Pottery Co.	5	10	15
Blynken, Florence Ceramics Co.	60	65	70
Blythe and Pensive, Ceramic Arts Studio	100	110	120
Bo Peep, Ceramic Arts Studio	30	35	40
Bo Peep's Sheep, Ceramic Arts Studio	20	25	30
Boy, in tuxedo, Florence Ceramics Co.	80	90	100
Boy, w/ fiddle, Florence Ceramics Co.	90	100	110
Boy, w/ Dog, Ceramic Arts Studio	40	45	50
Boy and Tiger, Ceramic Arts Studio	40	45	50
Boy Blue, Ceramic Arts Studio	15	20	25
Bride, Florence Ceramics Co.	340	380	420
Bride and Groom, Ceramic Arts Studio	60	65	70
Buffalo, 10", Cliftwood Potteries	240	265	290
Bull Dog, 11", Cliftwood Potteries	90	100	110
Bust, Florence Ceramics Co.	80	90	100
Camel, 2.5", Midwest Pottery Co.	5	10	15
Camel, 8.5", Midwest Pottery Co.	20	25	30
Camille, Florence Ceramics Co.	80	90	100
Canaries, 4.5", Midwest Pottery Co.	30	35	40
Carol, Florence Ceramics Co.	200	220	240
Caroline in Brocade, Florence Ceramics Co.	340	380	420
Cat, 1.5", Cliftwood Potteries	90	100	110
Cat, 5.75", Cliftwood Potteries	40	45	50
Cat, 6", Cliftwood Potteries	40	45	50
Cat, 6", Morton Pottery Co.	10	15	20
Cat, 8.5", Cliftwood Potteries	40	45	50
Cat, angry, 10.25", Kay Finch Ceramics	80	90	100
Cat, contented, 6", Kay Finch Ceramics	40	50	60
Cat, Persian, 10.75", Kay Finch Ceramics	80	90	100
Cat, playful, 8.5", Kay Finch Ceramics	60	65	70
Catherine, Florence Ceramics Co.	140	160	180
Centaur, Vernon Kilns	660	735	810
Centaurette, Vernon Kilns	370	410	450
Chanticleer, 10.5", Kay Finch Ceramics	100	110	120
Charles, Florence Ceramics Co.	90	100	110
Charmaine, Florence Ceramics Co.	70	80	90
Cherub Head, 2.75", Kay Finch Ceramics	5	10	15
Chicken, Biddy, 8.25", Kay Finch Ceramics	30	35	40
Chicken, Butch, 8.25", Kay Finch Ceramics	30	35	40
Chinese Boy, Florence Ceramics Co.	40	45	50
Chinese Boy, 7.5", Kay Finch Ceramics	20	25	30
Chinese Boy and Girl, Ceramic Arts Studio	30	35	40
Chinese Couple, Ceramic Arts Studio	15	20	25
Chinese Girl, Florence Ceramics Co.	40	45	50

	LOW	AVG.	HIGH
Chinese Girl, 7.5", Kay Finch Ceramics	$ 20	$ 25	$ 30
Chinese Sitting Girl and Boy, Ceramic Arts Studio	15	20	25
Chipmunk, Ceramic Arts Studio	20	25	30
Choir Boy, Florence Ceramics Co.	50	55	60
Cinderella and Prince, Ceramic Arts Studio	40	45	50
Cindy, Florence Ceramics Co.	50	55	60
Circus Bear, Shawnee Pottery	20	25	30
Clarissa, Florence Ceramics Co.	60	65	70
Claudia, Florence Ceramics Co.	90	100	110
Cocker Dog, 11.75", Kay Finch Ceramics	80	90	100
Coleen, Florence Ceramics Co.	60	65	70
Colonial Boy and Girl, Ceramic Arts Studio	40	45	50
Colonial Lady and Man, Ceramic Arts Studio	40	45	50
Comedy and Tragedy, Ceramic Arts Studio	90	100	110
Court Lady, 10.5", Kay Finch Ceramics	30	35	40
Cowboy, Frankoma Potteries	200	220	240
Cowboy on Bronco, 7.5", Midwest Pottery Co.	30	35	40
Cowgirl and Cowboy, Ceramic Arts Studio	50	55	60
Crane, 6", Midwest Pottery Co.	15	20	25
Cuban Child, Ceramic Arts Studio	20	25	30
Cuban Woman, Ceramic Arts Studio	30	35	40
Cynthia, Florence Ceramics Co.	200	220	240
Dancing Dutch Boy and Girl, Ceramic Arts Studio	80	85	90
Dancing Woman, 8.5", Midwest Pottery Co.	20	25	30
David, Florence Ceramics Co.	60	65	70
Deer, 12", Midwest Pottery Co.	30	35	40
Deer, 4.5", Morton Pottery Co.	5	10	15
Deer, 8", Midwest Pottery Co.	15	20	25
Delia, Florence Ceramics Co.	70	75	80
Denise, Florence Ceramics Co.	170	190	210
Diane, Florence Ceramics Co.	90	100	110
Dolores, Florence Ceramics Co.	100	110	120
Donkey, 2", Morton Pottery Co.	30	35	40
Donkey Unicorn, Vernon Kilns	320	355	390
Douglas, Florence Ceramics Co.	70	75	80
Drummer Girl, Ceramic Arts Studio	40	50	60
Duck, 4", Kay Finch Ceramics	5	10	15
Dumbo, Vernon Kilns	120	130	140
Dutch Boy and Girl, Ceramic Arts Studio	15	20	25
Dutch Boy and Girl, sitting, Ceramic Arts Studio	20	25	30
Dutch Love Boy and Girl, Ceramic Arts Studio	30	35	40
Edith, Florence Ceramics Co.	60	65	70
Edward, Florence Ceramics Co.	120	135	150
Elaine, Florence Ceramics Co.	40	45	50
Elephant, Vernon Kilns	320	355	390
Elephant, 17", Kay Finch Ceramics	340	380	420
Elephant, 2.5", Morton Pottery Co.	5	10	15
Elephant, 5", Kay Finch Ceramics	20	25	30
Elephant, 6", Cliftwood Potteries	40	50	60
Elephant, 6.75", Kay Finch Ceramics	40	50	60
Elephant, 7", Cliftwood Potteries	30	35	40

	LOW	AVG.	HIGH
Elephant, 8", Cliftwood Potteries	$ 70	$ 80	$ 90
Elephant, 9", Cliftwood Potteries	40	45	50
Elephant, "GOP/candidate," Morton Pottery Co.	10	15	20
Elisha, Florence Ceramics Co.	90	100	110
Elizabeth, Florence Ceramics Co.	140	155	170
Ellen, Florence Ceramics Co.	70	75	80
Emily, Brayton Pottery	30	35	40
Ethel, Florence Ceramics Co.	60	65	70
Eugenia, Florence Ceramics Co.	170	190	210
Evangeline, Florence Ceramics Co.	50	55	60
Fair Lady, Florence Ceramics Co.	290	325	360
Fall, Florence Ceramics Co.	40	45	50
Fan Dancer, Frankoma Potteries	140	160	180
Fawn, 2.5", Morton Pottery Co.	5	10	15
Female Bust, Midwest Pottery Co.	70	75	80
Female Nude, 11.5", Midwest Pottery Co.	110	125	140
Female Torso, abstract, 10.5", Brayton Pottery	70	75	80
Figaro (Disney), Brayton Pottery	100	110	120
Fighting Cock, 6.5", Midwest Pottery Co.	15	20	25
Fire Couple, Ceramic Arts Studio	180	205	230
Fishing Boy and Farmer Girl, Ceramic Arts Studio	30	35	40
Flame Couple, Ceramic Arts Studio	180	205	230
Flower Girl, Frankoma Potteries	70	80	90
Flute Girl, Ceramic Arts Studio	40	50	60
Frances, Brayton Pottery	30	35	40
Frog, 1", Midwest Pottery Co.	5	10	15
Fruit Girl, 10", Abingdon Potteries, Inc.	90	100	110
Gardener Boy, Frankoma Potteries	90	100	110
Gardener Girl, Frankoma Potteries	70	80	90
Gary, Florence Ceramics Co.	70	80	90
Gay 90s Lady and Man, Ceramic Arts Studio	40	45	50
Gazelle, Shawnee Pottery	40	45	50
Genevieve, Florence Ceramics Co.	100	110	120
Georgia in Brocade, Florence Ceramics Co.	340	380	420
Geppetto (Disney), Brayton Pottery	220	250	280
Geppetto, w/ Pinocchio (Disney), Brayton Pottery	300	335	370
Girl w/ Cat, Ceramic Arts Studio	40	45	50
Girl w/ pail, Florence Ceramics Co.	100	110	120
Godey Lady, 7.5", Kay Finch Ceramics	30	35	40
Godey Lady, 9.5", Kay Finch Ceramics	30	35	40
Godey Man, 7.5", Kay Finch Ceramics	30	35	40
Godey Man, 9.5", Kay Finch Ceramics	30	35	40
Goose, 2", Midwest Pottery Co.	5	10	15
Goose, 2.25", Midwest Pottery Co.	5	10	15
Grace, Florence Ceramics Co.	60	65	70
Grandmother and I, Florence Ceramics Co.	280	310	340
Grandpa Pig, 10.5" x 16", Kay Finch Ceramics	70	80	90
Grumpy Pig, 6", Kay Finch Ceramics	30	35	40
Guitar Boy, Ceramic Arts Studio	40	50	60
Gypsy Girl and Boy, Ceramic Arts Studio	130	145	160
Hansel and Gretel, Ceramic Arts Studio	50	55	60

	LOW	AVG.	HIGH
Hare, Florence Ceramics Co.	$ 90	$ 100	$ 110
Harlem Hoofer, Frankoma Potteries	470	525	580
Harlequin Boy and Girl, Ceramic Arts Studio	140	160	180
Harmonica Boy, Ceramic Arts Studio	40	50	60
Hen, 2.25", Midwest Pottery Co.	5	10	15
Her Majesty, Florence Ceramics Co.	70	75	80
Hiawatha, Ceramic Arts Studio	20	25	30
Hindu Boys, Ceramic Arts Studio	40	45	50
Hippo, Vernon Kilns	320	355	390
Hippo in Tutu, Vernon Kilns	320	355	390
Horse, 2.75", Morton Pottery Co.	5	10	15
Indian Bowl Maker, Frankoma Potteries	90	100	110
Indian Chief, Frankoma Potteries	90	100	110
Irene, Florence Ceramics Co.	50	55	60
Jeanette, Florence Ceramics Co.	70	75	80
Jennifer, Florence Ceramics Co.	130	145	160
Jim, Florence Ceramics Co.	50	55	60
John Kennedy, Jr., Morton Pottery Co.	30	35	40
Jon, Brayton Pottery	30	35	40
Josephine, Florence Ceramics Co.	70	75	80
Joy, Florence Ceramics Co.	50	55	60
Joyce, Florence Ceramics Co.	190	215	240
Julie, Florence Ceramics Co.	70	75	80
Kangaroo, 2.75", Morton Pottery Co.	5	10	15
Kay, Florence Ceramics Co.	60	65	70
King's Jester and Musicians, Ceramic Arts Studio	200	225	250
Kissing Girl and Boy, Ceramic Arts Studio	40	45	50
Kitten, 3.25", Kay Finch Ceramics	5	10	15
Kiu, Florence Ceramics Co.	40	45	50
Kneeling Nude, 7", Abingdon Potteries, Inc.	170	190	210
Lady Diana, Florence Ceramics Co.	140	160	180
Lady Rowena, Ceramic Arts Studio	70	80	90
Lamb, 2.5", Morton Pottery Co.	5	10	15
Lamb, 2.75", Kay Finch Ceramics	5	10	15
Lantern Boy, Florence Ceramics Co.	40	45	50
Laura, Florence Ceramics Co.	100	110	120
Leading Man, Florence Ceramics Co.	140	160	180
Lillian, Florence Ceramics Co.	90	100	110
Lillian Russell, Florence Ceramics Co.	340	380	420
Linda Lou, Florence Ceramics Co.	70	75	80
Lion, 14", Cliftwood Potteries	60	70	80
Lioness, 12", Cliftwood Potteries	60	65	70
Lisa, Florence Ceramics Co.	90	100	110
Little Jack Horner, Ceramic Arts Studio	15	20	25
Lorry, Florence Ceramics Co.	120	135	150
Louis XV, Florence Ceramics Co.	200	220	240
Louis XVI, Florence Ceramics Co.	140	160	180
Louise, Florence Ceramics Co.	100	110	120
Madame Pompadour, Florence Ceramics Co.	200	220	240
Madonna Plain, Florence Ceramics Co.	50	55	60
Madonna w/ Child, Florence Ceramics Co.	70	75	80

	LOW	AVG.	HIGH
Male, abstract, Brayton Pottery	$ 250	$ 280	$ 310
Man in Knickers, 7.5", Morton Pottery Co.	10	15	20
Margot, Florence Ceramics Co.	190	215	240
Marie Antoinette, Florence Ceramics Co.	140	160	180
Marleen in Brocade, Florence Ceramics Co.	340	380	420
Marsie, Florence Ceramics Co.	70	75	80
Martin, Florence Ceramics Co.	170	190	210
Mary and Little Lamb, Ceramic Arts Studio	30	35	40
Matilda, Florence Ceramics Co.	100	110	120
Melanie, Florence Ceramics Co.	70	75	80
Merrymaid, Florence Ceramics Co.	90	105	120
Mexican Boy and Girl, Ceramic Arts Studio	60	65	70
Mikado, Florence Ceramics Co.	140	160	180
Mike, Florence Ceramics Co.	50	55	60
Minnehaha, Ceramic Arts Studio	20	25	30
Miranda, 6.5", Brayton Pottery	30	35	40
Miss Muffet, Ceramic Arts Studio	15	20	25
Modern Dance Woman, Ceramic Arts Studio	60	65	70
Monk, Frankoma Potteries	120	130	140
Mr. Bird, 4.5", Kay Finch Ceramics	15	20	25
Mr. Crow, Vernon Kilns	760	850	940
Mr. Stork, Vernon Kilns	760	850	940
Mrs. Bird, 3", Kay Finch Ceramics	15	20	25
Musette, Florence Ceramics Co.	100	110	120
Nancy, Florence Ceramics Co.	50	55	60
Nita, Florence Ceramics Co.	70	75	80
Nubian Centaurette, Vernon Kilns	370	410	450
Ostrich, Vernon Kilns	680	760	840
Ostrich Ballerina, Vernon Kilns	680	760	840
Our Lady of Grace, Florence Ceramics Co.	50	55	60
Owl, 8.75", Kay Finch Ceramics	30	35	40
Owl, 3.75", Kay Finch Ceramics	15	20	25
Oxen, 3.25", Morton Pottery Co.	30	35	40
Pamela, Florence Ceramics Co.	70	75	80
Parakeet, Florence Ceramics Co.	60	70	80
Parasol, Florence Ceramics Co.	190	215	240
Patricia, Florence Ceramics Co.	90	100	110
Peasant Boy, 6.75", Kay Finch Ceramics	30	35	40
Peasant Girl, Florence Ceramics Co.	60	65	70
Peasant Girl, 6.75", Kay Finch Ceramics	30	35	40
Peasant Woman, Brayton Pottery	30	35	40
Pegasus, Vernon Kilns	370	410	450
Pekinese, 14", Kay Finch Ceramics	80	90	100
Pekingese, Shawnee Pottery	20	25	30
Peter Pan, Ceramic Arts Studio	50	55	60
Pheasant, Florence Ceramics Co.	70	75	80
Pied Piper, Ceramic Arts Studio	30	35	40
Pied Piper Child, Ceramic Arts Studio	20	25	30
Pierrene and Pierrott, Ceramic Arts Studio	80	90	100
Pigeon, Florence Ceramics Co.	70	75	80
Pinkie, Florence Ceramics Co.	140	160	180

	LOW	AVG.	HIGH
Pinocchio (Disney), Brayton Pottery	$ 220	$ 250	$ 280
Pioneer Sam and Susie, Ceramic Arts Studio	40	45	50
Polar Bear, 1.75", Midwest Pottery Co.	5	10	15
Polar Bear, 8.5" x 12", Midwest Pottery Co.	30	35	40
Police Dog, 12", Cliftwood Potteries	80	90	100
Police Dog, 8.5", Cliftwood Potteries	140	160	180
Police Dog, 9", Cliftwood Potteries	40	45	50
Polish Boy and Girl, Ceramic Arts Studio	30	35	40
Pomeranian Dog, 10", Kay Finch Ceramics	80	90	100
Pony, 3.5" x 4.5", Midwest Pottery Co.	5	10	15
Prima Donna, Florence Ceramics Co.	250	280	310
Princess, Florence Ceramics Co.	170	190	210
Priscilla, Florence Ceramics Co.	60	65	70
Puppy, Shawnee Pottery	20	25	30
Rabbit, Ceramic Arts Studio	20	25	30
Rabbit, Shawnee Pottery	20	25	30
Rabbit, 2.5", Midwest Pottery Co.	5	10	15
Rabbit, 3", Morton Pottery Co.	5	10	15
Rabbits, 2.5", Midwest Pottery Co.	20	25	30
Race Horse, 7.25", Midwest Pottery Co.	60	65	70
Rearing Unicorn, Vernon Kilns	320	355	390
Rebecca, Florence Ceramics Co.	100	110	120
Reclining Sprite, Vernon Kilns	150	165	180
Rhett, Florence Ceramics Co.	80	90	100
Road Runner, 8", Midwest Pottery Co.	10	15	20
Roberta, Florence Ceramics Co.	90	100	110
Rooster, 2.25", Midwest Pottery Co.	5	10	15
Rosalie, Florence Ceramics Co.	90	100	110
Rose Marie, Florence Ceramics Co.	90	105	120
Russian Boy and Girl, Ceramic Arts Studio	60	65	70
Sailing Ship, 2", Midwest Pottery Co.	5	10	15
Sally, Brayton Pottery	20	25	30
Sally, Florence Ceramics Co.	60	65	70
Samoan Girl, Gladding, McBean	40	45	50
Samoan Mother and Child, Gladding, McBean	60	65	70
Santa Claus and Evergreen Tree, Ceramic Arts Studio	20	25	30
Sarah, Florence Ceramics Co.	60	65	70
Sarah Bernhardt, Florence Ceramics Co.	390	440	490
Sassy Pig, 3.5", Kay Finch Ceramics	20	25	30
Satyr, Vernon Kilns	140	160	180
Saxophone Boy, Ceramic Arts Studio	40	50	60
Scandie Boy, 5.25", Kay Finch Ceramics	20	25	30
Scandie Girl, 5.25", Kay Finch Ceramics	20	25	30
Scarf Dancer, 13", Abingdon Potteries, Inc.	170	190	210
Scarlett, Florence Ceramics Co.	140	160	180
Seagull, Ceramic Arts Studio	20	25	30
Shen, Florence Ceramics Co.	110	125	140
Shepherdess and Faun, 11.5", Abingdon Potteries, Inc.	90	100	110
Sherri, Florence Ceramics Co.	140	160	180
Shirley, Florence Ceramics Co.	120	135	150
Sitting Girl and Boy, Ceramic Arts Studio	40	45	50

	LOW	AVG.	HIGH
Sitting Unicorn, Vernon Kilns	$ 320	$ 355	$ 390
Sleeping Kitten, 3.25", Kay Finch Ceramics	5	10	15
Smiley Pig, 6.75", Kay Finch Ceramics	30	35	40
Southern Belle and Gentleman, Ceramic Arts Studio	40	45	50
Spaniel, 6", Midwest Pottery Co.	40	45	50
Spanish Dance Couple, Ceramic Arts Studio	90	100	110
Spring Sue, Ceramic Arts Studio	20	25	30
Sprite, Vernon Kilns	150	165	180
Square Dance Boy and Girl, Ceramic Arts Studio	40	45	50
Squirrel, 2", Midwest Pottery Co.	5	10	15
Squirrel, 2.25", Morton Pottery Co.	5	10	15
St. Francis, Ceramic Arts Studio	80	90	100
St. George, Ceramic Arts Studio	90	100	110
Stallion, 10.75", Midwest Pottery Co.	30	30	30
Stallion, 6", Midwest Pottery Co.	10	15	20
Standing Boy and Girl, Ceramic Arts Studio	40	45	50
Standing Fawn, Ceramic Arts Studio	20	25	30
Stork, 4", Morton Pottery Co.	5	10	15
Stork, 7.5", Morton Pottery Co.	15	20	25
Story Hour, Florence Ceramics Co.	220	250	280
Sue, Florence Ceramics Co.	50	55	60
Sue Ellen, Florence Ceramics Co.	80	85	90
Sultan and Harem, Ceramic Arts Studio	70	75	80
Summer Sally, Ceramic Arts Studio	20	25	30
Susan, Florence Ceramics Co.	200	225	250
Swan, 2", Midwest Pottery Co.	5	10	15
Swordfish, 4", Morton Pottery Co.	5	10	15
Taka, Florence Ceramics Co.	120	135	150
Teddy Bear, Shawnee Pottery	20	25	30
Temple Dancer, Ceramic Arts Studio	170	190	210
Tiger, 12", Midwest Pottery Co.	50	55	60
Timothy Mouse, Vernon Kilns	200	220	240
Tom Tom the Piper's Son, Ceramic Arts Studio	40	50	60
Torch Singer, Frankoma Potteries	450	500	550
Turkey, 2.5", Morton Pottery Co.	5	10	15
Turtle, 1", Midwest Pottery Co.	5	10	15
Unicorn, Vernon Kilns	320	355	390
Victor, Florence Ceramics Co.	110	125	140
Victoria, Florence Ceramics Co.	200	220	240
Victorian Lady and Man, Ceramic Arts Studio	40	45	50
Virginia in Brocade, Florence Ceramics Co.	340	380	420
Vivian, Florence Ceramics Co.	120	135	150
Wee Chinese, Ceramic Arts Studio	20	25	30
Wee Dutch, Ceramic Arts Studio	20	25	30
Wee Eskimos, Ceramic Arts Studio	20	25	30
Wee French, Ceramic Arts Studio	20	25	30
Wee Indian Boy, Ceramic Arts Studio	10	15	20
Wee Indian Girl, Ceramic Arts Studio	10	15	20
Wee Indians, Ceramic Arts Studio	20	25	30
Wee Scotch, Ceramic Arts Studio	20	25	30
Wee Swedish, Ceramic Arts Studio	20	25	30

	LOW	AVG.	HIGH
Wild Horse, 2.5", Morton Pottery Co.	$ 5	$ 10	$ 15
Wild Turkey, 11.5", Midwest Pottery Co.	40	45	50
Willy, Ceramic Arts Studio	70	80	90
Winged Sprite, Vernon Kilns	150	165	180
Winkie Pig, 3.75", Kay Finch Ceramics	20	25	30
Winney, Ceramic Arts Studio	70	80	90
Winter Willy, Ceramic Arts Studio	20	25	30
Woman in Bonnet, 7.75", Morton Pottery Co.	15	20	25
Woman and Wolfhound, 11", Midwest Pottery Co.	130	145	160
Woodland Fantasy, Ceramic Arts Studio	15	20	25
Wynken, Florence Ceramics Co.	60	65	70
Yorkshire Terrier, 11", Kay Finch Ceramics	80	90	100
Yorky, 5.5", Kay Finch Ceramics	20	25	30
Zulu Couple, Ceramic Arts Studio	100	110	120

Firefighting Memorabilia

Firefighting collectibles run from the leather buckets kept in homes for fire emergencies, to full hook and ladder trucks. Much equipment used by firemen received heavy use, so today many early items are scarce. This accounts for price variations and the high price often placed on small items.

Top row, left to right: Silver plated fire trumpet, $850, silver plated presentation fire trumpet, $1600; fire helmet with eagle ornament, $200, fire lantern $900, chief's leather fire helmet, $500, brass fire trumpet, $500. —Photo courtesy of Northeast Auctions.

	LOW	AVG.	HIGH
Alarm Box, Gamewell keyless fire alarm telegraph station, cast iron	$ 110	$ 190	$ 300
Alarm Box, oval, Gamewell Grand Central Station, cast iron	220	390	610
Alarm Gong, weight driven, panelled wood case by Charles Chester, New York, with 15" bell	2750	4810	7560
Axe, len. 43", c. 1870	400	600	800
Bell, engine, dia. 10"	385	670	1060
Belt, parade belt, leather	190	250	310
Bucket, leather, decorated with helmet and hatchet	525	675	825
Bucket, leather, painted	475	650	775
Bucket, leather with red design	850	1000	1150
Bucket, tin, painted	100	125	150
Bucket, with owner's name inscribed, c. 1875	2200	5400	8600
Bucket, wooden, iron banding, leather strap handle, ht. 13"	50	75	100
Buckle, "1811," brass with fire engine, engraved, c. 1870	185	235	290
Cap, formal, with badge, c. 1900	200	250	300
Drawing, pumpers, fire, c. 1865	850	1250	1650
Extinguisher, brass, c. 1915	85	120	155
Extinguisher, bulb shape	30	45	60
Extinguisher, glass	140	175	210
Extinguisher, tin	40	55	70
Fire Bell, nickel-plated bronze, outside mechanism, mounted on board	400	600	800

	LOW	AVG.	HIGH
Fire Engine, American LaFrance, 6 cyl., pumper, c. 1948	$ 6500	$ 8500	$ 11,000
Fire Engine, American LaFrance, 6 cyl., type 40 pumper, c. 1917	41,000	52,000	63,000
Fire Engine, American LaFrance, 6 cyl., type 75 pumper, c. 1924	7000	9000	11,000
Fire Engine, American LaFrance, Auburn V.12 engine, ladders, siren, bell, c. 1944	5000	7500	10,000
Fire Engine, Chevrolet, 4 cyl., one ton, fully restored, c. 1927 .	12,000	14,500	17,000
Fire Engine, Ford, 8 cyl., restored, c. 1941	7000	9000	11,000
Fire Engine, Ford, F-6, V-8, equipped. c. 1948	5000	6500	8000
Fire Engine, Ford, unrestored, c. 1947	3500	4000	4500
Fire Engine, Seagrave, Model "A," 4 cyl., restored, c. 1928 ...	45,000	55,000	65,000
Fire Mark, cast iron, c. 1860	650	760	870
Fire Mark, hands clasped, Germantown National Fire, c. 1843	400	460	520
Fire Mark, hydrant, F.A., brass plaque, c. 1843	270	310	350
Fire Mark, hydrant, F.A., brass plaque, c. 1817	570	660	750
Fire Mark, Insurance Co. of Florida, c. 1841	700	800	900
Fire Mark, Mutual Assurance Co., iron plaque	350	425	500
Fire Mark, Twentieth Century	100	135	170
Gong, Gamewell indicator with swan-neck pediment, glazed door, and 15" brass bell, ht. 50"	5225	9000	14,000
Gong, Moses Crane style, gingerbread pediment, ht. 22"	1320	2300	3600
Helmet, aluminum with eagle finial	150	190	230
Helmet, brass with eagle finial	600	700	800
Helmet, hand-painted shield, c. 1880	1200	1500	1800
Helmet, leather, 6-seam, front shield	170	220	270
Helmet, leather, black embossed with brass eagle, c. 1889	260	315	370
Helmet, leather, ornamental parade helmet, 18th century	1700	2000	2300
Helmet, leather, white with eagle, c. 1890	280	355	430
Helmet, leather with trumpet finial	340	405	470
Helmet, spike top, used for parades	360	440	520
Helmet, three cornered, c. 1870	3550	4175	4800
Hose Nozzle, brass, #12	180	215	250
Hose Nozzle, brass, #15	210	260	310
Hose Nozzle, copper, #25	240	290	340
Lamp, Engine, by DeVoursney Bros., New York, silver plated, with 4 etched colored glass windows	990	1750	2750
Lantern, nickel plated	170	240	310
Lantern, wagon style with brass font	430	510	590
Parade Banner, len. 39", c. 1890	350	375	400
Parade Belt, leather with black, white, and red trim, shield on buckle	120	160	200
Spotlight, nickel-plated brass	200	300	400
Tickets, fireman's benefit, c. 1860	20	25	30
Trumpet, brass, engraved	800	1000	1200
Trumpet, nickel plated	410	475	540
Trumpet, silver plated with red tassel	830	890	950
Trumpet, silver presentation, 1867	1815	3180	5000

Fishing Tackle

Rods, reels, flies, and lures comprise the majority of collectible fishing tackle. The manufacture of fishing tackle did not begin in the United States until around 1810.

Reels made by J.F. and B.F. Meeks, B. Milam and Pfleuger are favored, as are rods made by Hiram Leonard. Flies—fake bait made by tying feathers, fur, or other materials around the shaft of a hook—are also popular. There are over 5,000 patterns and sizes of flies, each with its own name. The manufacturer, or tier, of individual flies is very difficult to discern, unless the fly is in its original marked container.

Lures

	LOW	AVG.	HIGH
Creek Chub Husky Musky, #600	$ 192	$ 310	$ 470
Creek Chub Injured Minnow	15	20	40
Ding Bat	25	40	60
F.C. Woods, round body expert wooden minnow, 3.75"	218	350	530
Frank Miller Underwater Minnow, circa 1912	275	440	670
Heddon #200	192	310	470
Heddon #300	357	570	870
Heddon #302, surface minnow	1465	2340	3590
Heddon #700	825	1320	2020
Heddon #850 Swimming Minnow, 4"	300	480	740
Heddon Prowler, prototype	525	840	1290
Hosmer Mechanical Frog, 5.25", circa 1928	2420	3870	5930
Jack Harmon Diver	83	130	200
Lane's Wagtail Minnow	152	240	370
North Channel Minnow, painted, 3.5", circa 1900	330	530	810
Pepper, Yankee aero bass bait	330	530	810
Pikie Minnow	18	30	40
Shakespeare Floating Wooden Minnow #42, 4"	209	330	510
Shakespeare Kazoo Wobbler	152	240	370
Shakespeare Midget Sea Witch, rainbow paint, glass eyes, 2 treble hooks, 2.5"	150	240	370
Shure-Strike Jumbo Mini Mouse Lure, 2.25"	65	100	160

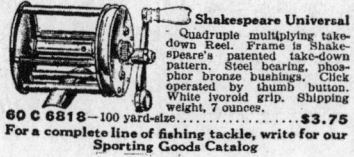

Shakespeare Universal
Quadruple multiplying take-down Reel. Frame is Shake-speare's patented take-down pattern. Steel bearing, phosphor bronze bushings. Click operated by thumb button. White ivoroid grip. Shipping weight, 7 ounces.
60 C 6818—100 yard-size...............**$3.75**
For a complete line of fishing tackle, write for our Sporting Goods Catalog

Shakespeare's Level Winding Reel
Multiplies 3½ times. Nickel plated and phosphor bronze bushings. Sliding click and balanced handle. Spooling device operates on the same principle as the Marhoff level winding reel. An especially high grade reel that will add more pleasure to fishing because of its level winding feature. Length of pillar, 1⅜ inches. Diameter of spool, 1½ inches. Shipping weight, 8½ ounces.
60 C 6791—100-yard size.................... **$7.95**

During the 1920s many suppliers began selling their products through mail order catalogs to meet the growing demand.

Reels

	LOW	AVG.	HIGH
Edward Vom Hofe, #520 Wahoo reel	$ 770	$ 1230	$ 1890
Edward Vom Hofe, model 511	220	350	540
Fin-Nor, 9/0 size big game casting reel	121	190	300
Hardy LRH, lightweight reel	140	220	340
Hardy Zane Gray, big game reel, 14/0 size	2970	4750	7280
J.A. Coxe, 12/0 size, big game reel	825	1320	2020
Julius Vom Hofe, #1 casting reel	182	290	450
Julius Vom Hofe, Abbey and Imbrie	360	580	880
Julius Vom Hofe, Leonard trout reel	1045	1670	2560
Kalamazoo Tackle, Alford Meter reel	80	130	200
L.A. Kiefer, German silver	1100	1760	2700
Pflueger Alpine Model Reel	38	60	90
Pflueger Altipac #1660, 6/0 size	385	620	940
Pflueger Buckeye Reel	115	180	280
Pflueger Portage Cascade Reel	133	210	330
Stan Bogdan, baby trout reel, half inch spool	1430	2290	3500
Stan Bogdan, size 50 single-action salmon reel	1430	2290	3500
Stan Bogdan, size100 multiplying salmon reel	1485	2380	3640
Stan Bogdan, standard reel	1925	3080	4720
Unmarked, 1860s, 1.75" dia. brass casting reel	225	360	550

Rods

	LOW	AVG.	HIGH
Abercrombie and Fitch, 6'6" trout rod	1018	1630	2490
Abercrombie and Fitch, 7'6" trout rod	2970	4750	7280
Art Weiler, 6'9" "heritage rod," #193	467	750	1140
E.F. Payne, 6' trout rod	4400	7700	11,000
H.L. Leonard, 9', 4 piece	363	580	890
Heddon, 9', #125 "expert"	300	480	740
Kaufman and Benson, 4'6" steel rod with reel	91	150	220
Leonard, model 50-Hunt, 8'6"	825	1320	2020
Orvis, 6'6", 2-piece rod	412	660	1010
Orvis, 9', 2-piece rod	137	220	340
Orvis, HLS Graphite, 8'6" fly rod with case	176	280	430
Otto Zwarg, 4/0 size, model 300	1100	1760	2700
Payne, model 208, 9' fly rod	800	1280	1960
Payne, model 308, 9' fly rod	825	1320	2020
Phillipson Deluxe Spinning Rod, model #P64S	168	270	410
Swedish Bamboo Rod, 46"	42	70	100
Unlabelled 6'6" trout rod	50	80	120

Folk Art

American folk art of the 19th and early 20th centuries has become a sophisticated field. Carvers such as Wilhelm Schimmel and John Bellamy have seen extremely high prices. But beware! Only pieces of the highest quality command the prices listed below. We have included listings for damaged pieces to show how steeply the values can fall. Many pieces are restored. Check closely for condition.

Measurements refer to largest dimension. Prices are for auction (A), damaged (D), and retail (R).

	A	D	R
Apple-Form Sign, wood and metal, metal arrow, len. 45.5" ..	$ 1000	$ 1750	$ 2750
Barber Pole, turned and ptd. in red, white and blue, ht. 38"	700	1250	2000
Bust of a Chinaman, mid-19th cent., carved and ptd., ht. 8"	850	1500	2300
Concrete Nurse, by Willie Tarver, ptd. concrete, contemporary	715	1250	2000
Frakturs, pr., of PA German watercolor and ink, one w/ heart and angel motif, the other w/ flower, dated 1810, 8" x 10.5"	1100	1930	3000
Lobster Claw, ptd. depicting Abraham Lincoln w/ Liberty Cap, ht. 11"	2100	3650	5750
Mermaid, by Popeye Reed, carved wood, contemporary	880	1500	2500
Powderhorn of John Ruble, 1793, engraved Amer. flag and eagle decoration and overall genre and figural motifs, w/ inscription, len. 14"	3400	6000	9000
Rooster Figure, PA carved and ptd. in red, gray and black, on sq. plinth, ht. 27"	4000	7000	11,000
Saluting Patriotic Turtle, by Gray Eagle, hard hat and ptd. wood, contemporary	83	150	250
Sign, "The Ancient Mariner"	350	600	950
Skeleton in Coffin, Son Thomas, clay and ptd. wood, contemporary, len. 17"	385	650	1000
Tin Sign, "Live Bait For Sale"	225	400	650
Twig Snake, green and yellow paint	275	500	750
Village Scene in Springtime, watercolor, pen and ink drawing in ptd. and grained frame. 9.75" x 14.5"	2000	3500	5500
Watercolor Portrait Titled "Mary," w/ concentric floral motif and gentleman in colorful costume, labeled on reverse "drawn by Mary Newcomer," 7.5" x 8"	2200	3850	6000
Watercolor Theorem on Velvet, depicting openwork basket of fruit on grassy mound, 15.5" x 19"	600	1000	1650
Woman in a Peach Dress, S.L. Jones, carved polychrome dec. wood, contemporary, ht. 19"	5775	10,000	15,000
Work Stand, inlaid w/ contrasting woods, sq. top dec. w/ stars, diamonds and hearts centering horse, w/ 4 modified cabriole legs, decorated overall w/ similar motifs, w. 15" sq.	1800	3000	5000
Zeppelin Bird House, blue, red and gray, mounted on pedal of bicycle, 40"	850	1500	2350

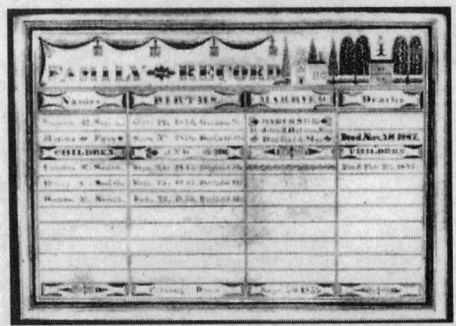

Above: Family record of the Foss-Smith Family, Dixfield, Maine, watercolor and ink, 10" x 14", 1852, $1600 at auction. —Photo courtesy of Northeast Auctions.

Left: Half length carved and painted figurehead, height 50", $3600 at auction. —Photo courtesy of Northeast Auctions.

Furniture

Antique

Antique furniture is a tricky field. The collector needs to be a connoisseur of proportions and alterations. Before the middle of the 19th century, cabinetmakers (not carpenters) made furniture by hand. Each piece was unique. The skill of the craftsman and the success of his design are important factors in evaluating furniture. To learn about the proportions and the aesthetics of American antique furniture, see *The Fine Points of Furniture* by Albert Sack.

Alterations can reduce the value of a piece by over 75%. No collector will sweat over a piece of chipped veneer, but a replaced leg, no matter how skillfully executed, will kill the value of a piece. Also remember that American furniture of the 18th century is more valuable than an otherwise identical English piece.

Abbreviations used in this section: *Q.A.*-Queen Anne, c. 1720-60, *Chip.*-Chippendale, c. 1750-90, *W. & M.*-William and Mary, c. 1690-1740, *Fed.* -Federal, c. 1780-1820, *Eng.*-English, *Amer.*-American, *Min.*-Miniature, *Mah.* -Mahogany, *CT* -Connecticut, *MA* -Massachusetts, *NE*-New England, *PA* -Pennsylvania, *NH*-New Hampshire, *Hpwt.*-Hepplewhite. Note that "style" implies a reproduction made at a later date.

Not all knee-hole desks are equal. The kneehole desk on the right from the Goddard-Townsend workshop carved with three shells is worth over half a million dollars. The ordinary kneehole desk on the left is worth less than one tenth as much. —Photo courtesy of Northeast Auctions.

	AUCTION	RETAIL	
		Low	High
Armchair, Asia trade w/ caned back and seat on turned legs ..	$ 450	$ 790	$ 1238
Armchair, black painted banister-back	250	440	688
Armchair, classical-style mah. curule-form w/ reeded details			
and pierced splat	1500	2630	4000
Armchair, CT cherry and mah.; serpentine crest above pierced			
splat and outward scrolling arms over slip-seat w/ frontal			
cabriole legs on ball and claw feet	3500	6130	9625

	AUCTION	RETAIL	
		Low	High
Armchair, Eng. Chip. mah., pierced ladderback .... $ 600		$ 1050	$ 1650
Armchair, Geo. III mah., open w/ shepherd crook arms, on sq. tapered legs 450		790	1238
Armchair, NE Chip. birch; serpentine crest w/ shell carving and cross-eyed owl splat flanked by molded shaped armrests, above trapezoidal rush seat, on sq. legs w/ box stretcher 600		1000	1800
Armchair, NE W. & M. banister-back, w/ splint seat and sausage turnings 500		880	1375
Armchair, PA Chip. carved wal; serpentine crest w/ carved shell above solid vase splat flanked by stiles joining serpentine-shaped arms above down-swept arm supports, slip-seat over cabriole legs on trifid feet 5000		8750	13,750
Armchair, PA ladderback in old brown paint, w/ arched slats and bulbous frontal stretcher 1000		1750	2750
Armchairs, Flemish, pr., wal. barley-twist open w/ berry and vine needlepoint fabric 3600		6300	10,000
Armchairs, pr., red-painted country ladderback w/ button feet ... 1000		1750	2750
Armchairs, set of 6 Russian carved mah., each w/ splat of twin torches centering an openwork 8-point star above sunburst, on turned swelled legs 6000		10,000	16,500
Armoire, Amer. late Fed. ormolu-mounted cherry, Louisiana, cove molding above 2 long doors on turned feet w/ gilded balls, ht. 71", w. 47" 3750		6560	10,000
Bachelor's Chest, Eng. Chip. mah; case w/ dressing slide above 4 long graduated drawers on bracket feet, w. 30" 2800		5000	7700
Bachelor's Chest, Eng. Chip. mah.; oblong top w/ applied molded edge above case w/ dressing slide and 4 long graduated drawers on molded base w/ bracket feet, w. 29.5" 3500		6000	9500
Banister-back Armchair, NE W. & M., w/ splint seat and sausage turnings 500		880	1375
Bed, French Directoire-style fruitwood 250		440	650
Bed, NE Fed. maple; footposts w/ spiral turnings, tapered headposts joining shaped headboard, w. 54.5", len. 78" 1700		2980	4675
Bedstead, NE Sher. tiger maple, w/ scrolled headboard and turned posts, ht. 78", len. 82", w. 52" 3750		6500	10,000
Bible-Box, NE Pilgrim-century pine w/ pinwheel and lunette designs, len. 23" 1300		2250	3500
Blackamoor, Venetian polychrome painted pedestal w/ gondola base, ht. 43.5" 1700		3000	4500
Blackamoors, pr., Venetian carved, painted and gilded on drapery covered pedestals, ht. 77" 1200		2100	3300
Blanket Chest, PA Chip. wal., dovetailed construction, on high bracket feet, len. 47" 1500		2630	4000
Bookcase, Eng. Chip.-style mah., in 2 parts: upper section w/ geometric glazed doors; lower w/ long drawer over twin doors, ht. 88", len. 52" 2750		4500	7500
Bookcase, Eng. Geo. III mah., in 2 parts: upper section w/ broken arch cornice above Gothic glazed doors; lower case w/ paneled doors on molded base w/ ogee bracket			

The left hand Federal candlestand, c. 1800, is much less desirable than the one on the right, which has interesting inlay and finely formed legs. — Photo courtesy of Northeast Auctions.

	AUCTION	RETAIL Low	High
feet, ht. 92", w. 49"	$ 8000	$ 14,000	$ 22,000
Bookcase, Victorian rosewood low w/ center glazed doors, ht. 40", len. 57"	900	1580	2475
Bookcase on Stand, Asia trade carved hardwood; upper section w/ twin carved and glazed doors; lower on spiral-turned legs, ht. 64", w. 39"	950	1660	2613
Bowfront Chest, NE late Sher. mah; oblong top w/ outset corners over case w/ 4 long drawers w/ flanking reeded columns continuing to turned legs, w. 46"	1100	1900	3000
Breakfast Table, NE Q.A. mah.; oblong top w/ oval drop leaves above shaped apron and cabriole legs on pad feet, len. 42"	1000	1750	2750
Breakfast Table, NY State cherry drop-leaf, len. 40"	300	530	825
Butler's Tray, mah. w/ brass hinges and folding stand	900	1580	2500
Cabinet on Stand, German baroque-style; cabinet w/ panels depicting classical scenes, base w/ griffin and scroll supports, branded "G. Bauer," ht. 63", w. 45"	3000	5250	8250
Candlestand, Amer. black painted dishtop, on modified urn standard w/ tripod cabriole legs and pad feet, ht. 28.5", dia. 21.75"	500	880	1375
Candlestand, Amer. black painted w/ cabriole legs	450	790	1250
Candlestand, CT Fed. cherry dishtop, Norwich area; molded top w/ scalloped lower edge above turned standard and tripod cabriole legs w/ platform pad feet, ht. 28", dia. 14"	5000	8750	13,750
Candlestand, CT inlaid cherry; sq. top w/ applied beaded edge and paterae inlay over baluster-turned standard joining cabriole legs, ht. 26", len. 15"	750	1310	2063
Candlestand, CT Q.A. red-painted; circular top above suppressed ball-turned standard on tripod cabriole legs w/ slipper feet, ht. 27.5", dia. 16"	2800	4900	7700
Candlestand, NE cherry w/ circular top and tripod base	400	700	1100
Candlestand, NE country Hpwt. inlaid cherry; sq. top w/ pat-			

	AUCTION	RETAIL	
		Low	High

erae and quarter-fan inlay, on sq. tapering legs w/ stringing, ht. 26.5", top 22" sq. .... $ 800 $ 1400 $ 2200

Candlestand, NE Fed. birch tip-top; octagonal tilting top above an urn-turned standard joining spider legs on spade feet, ht. 28", len. 21" 800 1400 2200

Candlestand, NE Hpwt. tilt-top; octagonal top above an urn-turned standard joining spider legs, on spade feet, ht. 28", len. 21" 400 700 1100

Candlestand, NE maple w/ octagonal top and tripod cabriole legs, ht. 25" 600 1000 1650

Candlestand, PA Q.A. cherry birdcage; tilting top above an urn standard joining cabriole legs, dia. 20" 1700 3000 4500

Candlestand, PA Q.A. wal. birdcage; circular dishtop above vase-turned standard joining cabriole legs on snake feet, ht. 29", dia. 20.5" 3750 6560 10,000

Canterbury, Eng. Victorian burl wal. w/ pierced fret sides, len. 24" 1600 2800 4400

Card Table, Amer. inlaid mah. demilune, w/ line inlaid apron on 5 sq. tapered legs, len. 36" 400 700 1100

Card Table, Asia trade Sher.-style hardwood w/ long drawer, len. 35" 600 1050 1650

Card Table, Geo. III inlaid mah. demilune; hinged top above an apron joining sq. tapered legs w/ oak-leaf and bell-flower inlay, 36" x 29.75" 4750 8310 13,000

Card Table, Geo. III mah. blockfront; hinged top w/ baize lining above conforming apron w/ single drawer on sq. chamfered legs, ht. 29.5", len. 33" 1100 1930 3000

Card Table, MA Hpwt. inlaid mah.; hinged top w/ bowed front and serpentine sides above an elaborate inlaid apron w/ central oval and flanking rect. panels joining sq. double tapered legs, len. 36" 10,000 17,500 27,500

Card Table, MA Sher. inlaid mah. serpentine-front; apron w/ flame birch panels joining turned and reeded legs, len. 35" 4000 7000 11,000

Card Table, MA Sher. mah. serpentine-front w/ turned and reeded legs, len. 36" 1000 1750 2750

Card Table, NE Hpwt. cherry; oblong top w/ ovolu corners and inlaid shell above conforming apron on sq. tapered legs w/ icicle inlay, len. 35" 3000 5250 8250

Card Table, NE Hpwt. inlaid mah. w/ ovolu corners; hinged top w/ inlaid edge above an apron w/ oval inlay on sq. tapering legs w/ lily-of-the-valley inlay and cuffs, w. 36" .. 2700 4750 7500

Card Table, NE Sher. inlaid mah. serpentine front, probably Portsmouth; hinged top w/ inlaid edge above an apron w/ center inlaid oval panel on ring turned legs, len. 36" 2250 3940 6000

Card Table, NE Sher. inlaid mah. serpentine front, top w/ outset corners and inlaid edge above crossbanded apron joining turned and reeded legs, len. 38" 700 1250 1900

Card Table, NH country Chip. cherry; oblong hinged lid above an apron w/ drawer on sq. legs w/ beaded edge, len. 36" 600 1000 1650

Highly figured woods, such as bird's-eye maple, greatly increase the value of a piece. — Photo courtesy of Northeast Auctions.

	AUCTION	RETAIL Low	High
Card Table, NH Sher. mah. and tiger maple serpentine front; tiger maple hinged top above flame birch apron and turned and reeded legs, w. 34"	$ 2750	$ 4500	$ 7500
Card Table, NY Classical mah. eagle carved; hinged top w/ canted corners and brass inlay above apron and turned acanthus carved columns on plinth base w/ gilded water-leaf and verte antique legs, each foot in form of an eagle head, len. 36"	6000	10,500	16,500
Card Tables, pr., bowfront, NE Fed. mah. and flame birch, Portsmouth, w/ hinged tops above an elaborate flame birch aprons centering rect. panel on ring-turned vase standards continuing to plinth base w/ sabre legs on scrolled toes, len. 36"	7000	12,250	19,000
Cellarette on Stand, Geo. III brass-bound mah. octagonal, fitted w/ lead lining, ht. 27", d. 17"	3250	5750	9000
Center Table, Amer. Classical Revival mah. small w/ specimen marble top; base w/ 3 scrolled and reeded legs continuing to triangular plinth raised on ball feet, ht. 28", dia. 21"	4750	8310	13,000
Center Table, Empire marble-top mah., Philadelphia, circular top above an apron w/ carved edge on 3 turned alabaster and mah. legs on shaped plinth base, ht. 31", dia. 30"	5000	8750	13,750
Chair Table, early Amer. circular; tilting top above shelf w/ drawer below and sq. legs, dia. 48"	1000	1750	2750
Chairs, set of 4 Asia trade carved hardwood, each w/ a shaped back w/ central carved monogram and a cane seat w/ turned and reeded legs	1200	2100	3300

	AUCTION	RETAIL Low	High

Cheese Tray on Stand, rare diminutive figured-mah., branded
"B. Melville, Leuchars," len. 12" .... $ 1000 $ 1750 $ 2750

Chest, Chip. mah. 4-drawer w/ bracket feet, w. 30" 1300   2250   3500

Chest, MA Sher. mah. bowfront; top w/ outset corners above
turned posts and legs, w. 44" 1300   2280   3500

Chest of Drawers, Amer. Hpwt. inlaid mah. w/ 2 short and
3 long drawers, above shaped apron and French feet,
len. 37" 2900   5000   8000

Chest of Drawers, Boston Classical-Revival mah., on melon
feet, w. 48" 1500   2600   4125

Chest of Drawers, CT carved cherry block-and-shell; rect.
top w/ molded edge projecting above case w/ 4 graduated
long drawers, upper one w/ applied convex shells centering
concave carved shell, others w/ conforming blocking on
base molding w/ gadrooning, on ogee bracket feet, ht. 37",
w. 35.5", d. 17.75" 8000   14,000   22,000

Chest of Drawers, CT Chip. cherry, reverse-serpentine-front,
top w/ molded edge above case of 4 long graduated drawers
on molded base w/ ogee bracket feet, ht. 32", case w. 36" .. 9000   15,750   24,750

Chest of Drawers, Amer. Classical carved mah. and bird's-
eye maple, Vermont or Canada, ht. 55", w. 46" 1200   2100   3300

Chest of Drawers, Geo. III carved mah. serpentine-front;
top w/ molded edge over 4 long graduated drawers
flanked by carved and pierced scroll columns, on molded
base w/ incised carved bracket feet, ht. 36", top 47" x 23" .. 11,500   20,000   31,000

Chest of Drawers, Geo. III mah. serpentine-front; top w/
molded edge over dressing slide and 4 long graduated
drawers flanked by stop-fluted free-standing columns,
raised on molded base w/ ogee bracket feet, ht. 36", top
42" x 22" 18,000   31,500   49,500

Chest of Drawers, MA carved mah. oxbow; oblong top w/
molded edge above case w/ 4 long graduated drawers w/
blocked ends, on molded base w/ cabriole legs and ball
and claw feet, w. 33" 13,500   23,000   37,000

Chest of Drawers, MA Chip. mah.; rect. top w/ molded edge
projecting above case w/ 4 graduated long drawers, on
bracket feet, ht. 32.5", w. 40.5" 3250   5690   9000

Chest of Drawers, NE Q.A. red-painted pine, tall, CT/RI
coastal area; rect. top w/ applied molded edge above
case w/ 2 short drawers over 4 long drawers and base
molding on cabriole legs w/ pointy pad feet, ht. 48", w.
38" 7250   12,600   20,000

Chest of Drawers, NE tiger maple 5-drawer, w. 36" 2500   4380   6500

Chest of Drawers, NH Hpwt. inlaid mah. and birch bowfront; top w/ inlaid edge above 4 line inlaid drawers and
an apron w/ drop panel, on flaring French feet, w. 40" 2100   3680   5750

Chest of Drawers, NH Hpwt. inlaid mah; top w/ line inlaid
edge above case w/ 4 drawers over drop-panel apron on
French feet, len. 38" 2000   3500   5500

A double pedestal dining table is more valuable without a frieze or apron. Plain wood and poorly formed legs also lower the value of the lower example.— Photos courtesy of Northeast Auctions.

	AUCTION	RETAIL Low	High
Chest of Drawers, NH Sher. mah. and birch bowfront w/ drop panel, w. 40"	$ 900	$ 1580	$ 2475
Chest of Drawers, PA Hpwt. figured maple and cherry bow front; oblong top above case w/ 4 bowed long drawers over shaped skirt on modified French feet, ht. 38", w. 41"	3500	6000	9000
Chest-on-Stand, W. & M. marquetry inlaid; rect. top w/ elaborate floral inlay over 2 short and 4 long graduated drawers on base w/ single drawer and scroll legs joined by H-stretcher, on ball feet, ht. 57", w. 41"	25,000	43,750	68,750
Chest on Stand, Eng., W. & M. Burl wal.; upper section w/ 2 short over 3 long graduated drawers; lower part w/ single drawer over spiral-turned legs, ht. 51", w. 42"	5250	9000	14,400
Chest on Stand, Eng, W. & M. Min., ht. 14", w. 12", prov: Dimmocks, London	2600	4550	7150
Chest-on-Chest, W. & M. black and gold japanned double-domed, upper section w/ twin doors w/ chinoiserie decoration, opening to an interior w/ japanned drawer; lower case w/ 4 long graduated drawers on molded base w/ ball feet, ht. 78", w. 40"	16,500	28,000	45,000
Chest-on-Frame, NH carved maple; upper section w/ cove molding above case w/ 5 graduated drawers, top one w/ shell carving, on base w/ salamander scrolls and cabriole legs w/ pad feet, ht. 58", case w. 37"	5000	8750	13,750

Centennial pieces closely resemble the eighteenth-century examples, especially after 100 years have improved the patina. Although they are not worth as much as the 200-year-old pieces, there is a real value and a growing market for this furniture. — Photos courtesy of Doyle Auctioneers.

	AUCTION	RETAIL Low	High
Chest w/ Dressing Glass and Deck, N.E. pillar and scroll mah; deck w/ 3 short drawers, projecting case w/ sectional drawer and 2 long drawers, on paw feet. overall ht. 63", w. 39"	$ 1100	$ 1930	$ 3000
Cheval Mirror, faux bamboo-turned maple; beveled mirror plate pivoting within bamboo-turned supports, ht. 78", w. 29"	2200	3850	6000
Child's Chest, Amer. W. & M.; red-stained maple and pine 3-drawer; rect. top w/ applied molded edge above 3 long drawers, on base molding and bun feet, engraved diamond-shaped brasses w/ teardrop pulls, ht. 29", w. 29", d. 18.5"	3000	5250	8250
Child's Highchair in old red paint	50	100	300
Chimney Glass, Q.A. wal. and parcel-gilt; rect. frame w/ carved edge and mirror slip surrounding 3-part beveled plate, fitted w/ brass sockets and lead-crystal candle arms, ht. 20", len. 60"	6750	11,000	18,500
Comb-Back Rocker, NE painted and decorated; w/stenciled floral sprig motif; together w/NE bowback w/9 spindles	475	830	1300
Commode, Continental harewood 2-drawer w/ gray marble op, on turned legs, len. 49"	7750	13,500	21,000
Commode, French Louis XIV ormolu-mounted diminutive 3-drawer, w. 25.5"	3500	6000	9000
Console Table., Geo. II large mah., Irish; rect. purple and white veneered marble top above frieze w/ central shell and flanking gadrooning on cabriole legs w/ leaf-carved knees and ball-and-claw feet, ht. 32", top 52" x 30"	37,000	64,750	100,000
Corner Cupboard, PA Chip. green-painted; projecting molded cornice above paneled door opening to scalloped shelves over similar door, on molded base, doors w/ wrought-iron butterfly hinges, ht. 72.75", w. 28.75", d. 15.75"	7000	12,500	19,000

Slender legs, a more delicate form and striking inlay give the Federal card table on the left a superior value to the one pictured on the right. — Photos courtesy of Northeast Auctions.

	AUCTION	RETAIL	
		Low	High
Counting-House Cupboard, NY State painted and decorated pine, w/ projecting cornice above case w/ folding paneled doors opening to fitted interior w/ dividers and drawers, each w/ alphabetic or numeric designations; over 2 banks of deep drawers centering an opening fitted w/ safe, on bracket feet, w/ overall grain-painted decoration, green trim and yellow lettering, including name "F.L. Cole" and dates 1828-31, w. 65"	$ 16,000	$ 28,000	$ 44,000
Cupboard, small Italian carved wal., w/ 2 short drawers over 2 cupboard doors, ht. 33", len. 33"	3600	6300	9900
Davenport Desk, Eng. wal., w. 23"	1700	2980	4500
Desk on Stand, Geo. I inlaid wal.; hinged slant-lid opening to fitted interior over case w/ 2 short and one long drawer, base w/ drawer raised on turned legs w/ pad feet, ht. 38", w. 17.5"	12,500	21,880	34,000
Dining Chairs, set of 4 Chip. mah. Phila., w/ serpentine crests w/ central leaf-carved motif above pierced lattice-work splats, slip-seats over sq. legs joined by an H-stretcher	4250	7440	11,000
Dining Chairs, set of 5 Chip.-style mah. incl. armchair	1100	1930	3000
Dining Chairs, set of 8 Chip.-style carved mah. pierced ladderback, fitted w/ needlepoint slip-seats; includes 2 armchairs	5200	9000	14,300
Dining Chairs, set of 8 Eng. Chip. mah., each w/ serpentine crest above pierced splat and slip-seat on cabriole legs w/ ball and claw feet	10,000	17,500	27,500
Dining Table, accordion-action, important Amer. Fed. mah., New York; 2 D-form end sections each w/ double-hinged leaf extension, above reeded edge, on twin scrolled supports w/ curved reeded legs w/ acanthus-carved knees and brass paw feet, on rollers, w/ 5 leaves, ht. 28", w. 59.5", len. 130"	115,000	200,000	315,000

	AUCTION	RETAIL Low	High
Dining Table, Amer. Fed.-style inlaid mah., 3-part; center section w/ drop-leaves and end sections w/ canted corners, all on sq. tapered legs elaborately inlaid w/ fans and bellflowers, ht. 29", w. 48", len. 112", extended ..	$ 4500	$ 7750	$ 12,375
Dining Table, Eng. Regency-style 3-pedestal; top w/ banded edge above an urn-turned standard w/ reeded sabre legs on brass paw feet, w. 48", len. 120", includes 2 leaves	3750	6560	10,000
Dining Table, Fed.-style mah. double-pedestal; top w/ cross-banded edge above vase turned pedestals on sabre legs, 44" x 72"; together w/ 2 24" leaves	3500	6130	9625
Dining Table, NE country Sher. cherry drop-leaf; rect. top on plain skirt w/ cylindrical ring-turned legs, 41" x 58", open	500	880	1375
Dining Table, NE Q.A. maple drop-leaf; oblong top w/ rounded leaves above shaped apron on cabriole legs w/ pad feet, len. 41"	1600	2800	4400
Dining Table, PA Chip. wal. drop-leaf on ball and claw feet; rect. leaves w/ rounded corners above an arcade apron w/ beaded detail, ht. 28", w. 42", 48" open	2200	3850	6000
Dining Table, PA Q.A. drop-leaf w/ cabriole legs on pad feet, len. 48"	1300	2400	3500
Dome-Top Trunk, red leather w/ chinoiserie designs in gilt, w/ brass tacks, iron straps and carrying handles, on matching Q.A.-style frame, len. of stand 37.5"	1300	2400	3500
Dressing Mirror, Eng. Geo. III mah., bowfront w/ ivory urn finials, ht. 24"	550	960	1500
Dressing Stand, Eng. Q.A. wal.; shaped mirror w/-carved and gilded slip over 3 short and one long drawer on bracket feet, ht. 27", len. 16"	1000	1750	2750
Dressing Table, NE rosewood grained and decorated, len. 33"	2000	3500	5500
Dressing Table, NY Classical Revival mah., School of Duncan Phyfe; rect. top fitted w/ lyre supports and mirror plate above case of 3 short and one long drawer on reeded curule base, w. 36"	8000	14,000	22,000
Drop-Leaf Dining Table, Amer. Hpwt. mah. in old finish; base w/ 6 tapered legs w/ beaded edge, len. 44"	550	960	1500
Drop-Leaf Table, Amer. Hpwt. wal. w/ bellflower-inlaid sq. tapered legs, len. 48"	900	1580	2475
Drop-Leaf Table, Irish Q.A. mah. single w/ opposing drawer, on cabriole legs w/ scrolled returns and slipper feet, ht. 28", len. 33"	1100	1930	3000
Fancy Chairs, pr., Regency painted and decorated, w/ arched floral painted crests and bamboo turnings	300	530	825
Fancy Chairs, pr., Regency painted and decorated w/ arched crests and feather motif splats	350	600	950
Fancy Chairs, set of 6 rosewood grained, w/ sabre legs	550	960	1500
Farm Table, PA Q.A. wal; oblong top above an apron w/ short and long drawer on turned legs w/ pad feet, ht. 31", top 53" x 30"	1700	3000	4600

The complex block-front form of the slant front desk of the left, together with the well carved claw and ball feet give it a value of about ten times the value of the desk on the right.— Photos courtesy of Northeast Auctions.

	AUCTION	RETAIL Low	High
Field Bed, Amer. carved mah. w/ canopy frame; 4 posts w/ reeded urn turnings and tasseled swags, on rollers, ht. of posts 64"	$ 1900	$ 3300	$ 5400
Fire Grate, Eng. Adam-style w/ urn finials and Greek key openwork apron, ht. 32", len. 35"	300	530	825
Fire Screen, French mah. and giltwood; peaked top w/ ormolu handle and shell motif above winged caryatids raised on scrolled supports w/ gilt anthemion decoration, labeled, ht. 43"	2500	4350	6800
Footstools, pr., early Amer. bird's-eye maple turned splay-leg w/ circular hooked seats	700	1230	1900
Games Table, Regency rosewood brass inlaid and mounted; rect. top w/ partial brass gallery and central adjustable writing surface opening to backgammon board, raised on shaped trestle base w/ sabre legs, ht. 30", len. 36"	8000	14,000	22,000
Gateleg Wall Table, W. & M.; oblong hinged top w/ banded inlay above an arched apron w/ faux front drawers w/ 2 working side drawers, on trumpet-turned legs w/ sq. stretcher and ball feet, ht. 30", len. 36"	17,500	30,000	48,000
Hadley Chest, Pilgrim-century carved oak and pine, mono-grammed "LS," Hadley-Hatfield area of MA; rect. top w/ molded edge and cotter pin hinges lifting above case, front w/ tripartite tulip and foliate-carved recessed panels w/ stippled ground, outer panels w/ monogram, over long drawer, case sides w/ recessed panels, stiles continuing to molded legs, ht. 36", len. 51", d. 20"	65,000	113,750	175,000
Hanging Corner Cupboard, Eng. mah.; dental molding above Gothic glazed door, ht. 44"	700	1230	2000

	AUCTION	RETAIL	
		Low	High

Hanging Corner Cupboard, PA wal., w/ secret compart-
ment below paneled cupboard door, ht. 28" .... $ 2200 $ 3850 $ 6000
Hanging Shelf, mah. w/ shaped sides, 37.5" x 29" 450   790   1200
Hanging Shelf, Sher. mah. bowfront 400   700   1100
Highboy, NE carved maple; upper w/ 5 long graduated
drawers, top one molded as 3, w/ central leaf carving;
lower section w/ long drawer over 3 short drawers,
center one leaf-carved, above heart-motif pierced and
carved apron on cabriole legs w/ pad feet, ht. 76", w. 39" 5250   9000   14,000
Highboy, NE Q.A. maple and pine; case w/ molding and
torus drawer above 2 short and 3 long drawers; lower
section w/ 5 short drawers above an apron w/ drop
pendants joining cabriole legs on pad feet, ht. 72",
w. 38" 6750   11,000   18,500
Highchair, grain-painted Windsor bamboo-turned w/ gilt
highlights 600   1000   1650
Hired Man's Rope Bedstead, w/ red finish; chamfered
headposts w/ vase-turned finials centering peaked head-
board, w/ side rails, w. 54" 900   1500   2475
Hutch Table, early Amer. pine shoe foot w/ oval top, w. 33",
d. 40" 800   1400   2200
Hutch Table, NE maple and pine on shoe-foot base; circular
top pivoting above base fitted as till, w/ remnants of old
paint, dia. 50" 4250   7400   11,000
Kneehole Desk, Geo. I burl wal.; rect. quarter-veneered
top above long drawer over 2 banks of 3 short drawers
on molded base w/ bracket feet, ht. 31.5", top 30" x
19.5" 13,500   23,630   37,000
Lift-Top Desk, NJ country Hpwt. on high tapered legs;
underside of lid w/ compass star motif and marked "
John S. Schen....desk, New Jersey, County of Monmouth,"
w. 28" 800   1400   2200
Linen Press, Amer. Sher. mah., in 2 parts: cornice above twin
panel doors opening to slide-out shelves; lower case
projecting and fitted w/ 4 long graduated drawers, on
turned feet, ht. 7', w. 58" 1600   2800   4400
Looking Glass, MA giltwood and eglomisé; broken cornice
hung w/ spherules above tablet depicting children
dancing over mirror plate, w/ flanking rope turnings,
ht. 37" 1600   2800   4400
Looking Glass, NE Fed. giltwood and eglomisé w/ cornice
hung w/ spherules; frame w/ rope-twist details, ht. 36" 1600   2800   4400
Lowboy, PA Q.A. wal.; oblong top w/ molded edge and
notched corners above case of 2 over 2 short drawers
above shaped apron w/ drop pendant and angular
cabriole legs on Spanish feet, ht. 30", w. 21", d. 34" 14,500   25,000   40,000
Mantel, Salem Fed. w/ center-carved eagle; carving
attributed to Samuel McIntire, ht. 52", len. 6' 5250   9000   14,000
Min. Blanket Chest, pine 3-drawer; scrolled backplate w/
hinged top and 3 drawers above scrolled skirt, ht. 25" 450   800   1250

	AUCTION	RETAIL	
		Low	High

Mirror, Amer. carved and gilded convex w/ spread eagle crest, foliate motifs, Phila.; circular frame w/ reeded and ebonized slip and shell-form pendant drop, ht. 50" ... $ 8000 $ 14,000 $ 22,000

Mirror, Amer. Chip. mah. w/ carved and gilded phoenix, ht. 36" 450   800   1250

Mirror, Amer. Chip. mah. w/ Prince-of-Wales feathers, ht. 28" 400   700   1100

Mirror, Amer. Classical carved giltwood w/ twin fruit-filled cornucopia crest, w/ applied pierced shell above an elliptical mirror plate and foliate pendant drop, ht. 38", w. 30" 5000   8750   13,750

Mirror, Amer. Fed. giltwood w/ eglomisé panel of harbor scene, ht. 31" 250   440   650

Mirror, Amer. Fed. giltwood w/ eglomisé tablet of colonial building, ht. 33" 550   960   1500

Mirror, Chip. carved mah., w/ deep crest w/ flanking ears above rect. plate and matching pendant drop, ht. 35" 650   1140   1750

Mirror, Chip. mah. and parcel-gilt; phoenix crest flanked by leaf scrolling above beveled mirror plate w/ flanking leaf-carved and floral fillets w/ shaped drop pendant, ht. 48" 4000   7000   11,000

Mirror, Chip. mah. scroll-frame w/ giltwood phoenix, ht. 43" 2200   3850   6000

Mirror, Chip. Scrolled crest w/ painted eagle on branch, ht. 42" 500   880   1375

Mirror, Chip. wal. scroll-form w/ pierced and gilded shell, ht. 39" 800   1400   2200

Mirror, Geo. II giltwood broken arched pediment w/ central shell above rect. beveled mirror plate w/ leaf and flower-carved slip above pendant drop w/ shell, ht. 54", w. 37" 6000   10,000   16,500

Mirror, Geo. II giltwood; broken arch pediment w/ central Prince-of-Wales plume above beveled plate w/ leaf-carved slip and apron w/ flowerhead and twin brass candle arms, ht. 42", w. 22.5" 5500   9000   15,000

Mirror, Geo. II wal. and parcel-gilt, possibly Continental; broken arched pediment w/ central rocaille cartouche over mirror plate flanked by gilded fillets and complementary apron, ht. 61", w. 33.5" 4250   7440   11,000

Mirror, Geo. III carved giltwood; pagoda-form top above cartouche-form crest over double mirror plates within an elaborate floral and scroll frame, ht. 77", w. 36" 8500   14,500   23,000

Mirror, Georgian mah. and giltwood; broken scroll pediment centering foliate shield device above rect. frame w/ flanking drapery swags over shaped pendant drop. 60" x 30" 2100   3600   5775

Mirror, MA Fed. giltwood and eglomisé 550   950   1500

Mirror, NE carved Chip., w/ scroll-carved crest and pendant, painted white, ht. 19" 350   610   950

Mirror, Q.A. wal. veneer and parcel-gilt; crest w/ gilded shell above gilded slip w/ mirror plate, ht. 30" 850   1490   2300

Proper proportions are crucial in a valuable highboy. The example on the left has poor proportions and none of the "extras" shown on the right. The bonnet top, the matched carving and the finely formed legs all add to the fine proportions creating a very desirable piece.

	AUCTION	RETAIL	
		Low	High
Mirror, small black-painted Q.A. w/ shaped crest, ht. 23"	$ 1800	$ 3200	$ 5000
Mirror, small Chip., w/ gilt eagle	100	180	350
Mirrors, pr., Continental giltwood Italian or south German, each w/ cartouche-shaped rocaille crest above slip-carved w/ flowerheads and trailing vines, ht. 44", w. 26"	2750	4750	7500
Mirrors, pr., Geo. III-style oval giltwood, style of Thomas Chippendale w/ elaborate leaf and floral carving, ht. 55" ...	4000	7000	11,000
Parlor Suite of Louis XVI, ebonized furniture upholstered in colfax and fowler fabric, comprising settee, pair of open armchairs, and 4 side chairs	2000	3500	5500
Peat Bucket, Geo. III mah. navette-form w/ floral inlay, ht. 15", len. 14"	900	1580	2475
Pembroke Table, Amer. Hpwt. inlaid wal.; oblong top w/ shaped leaves above an apron w/ drawer on sq. tapering legs w/ diamond inlay and stringing, len. 36"	650	1140	1750
Pembroke Table, Amer. Hpwt. mah. w/ bellflower inlay, len. 36"	5000	8750	13,750
Pembroke Table, Eng. Hpwt. mah. drop-leaf, len. 30"	800	1400	2200
Pembroke Table, NE Hpwt. mah. w/ drawer on sq. tapered legs w/ X-stretcher	600	1050	1650
Pembroke Table, NE Sher. mah. w/ turned and reeded legs, len. 33"	900	1500	2475
Pier Mirror, Amer. Classical giltwood w/ gilt shell, ht. 62"	1000	1750	2750
Pier Table, Amer. Classical carved mah. marble top; black marble top above an apron w/ drawer above scrolled legs on plinth base, ht. 37", top 18" x 42"	4500	7500	12,500
Piesafe, Amer. green-painted and pierced sheet metal, w/			

	AUCTION	RETAIL	
		Low	High

molded cornice above cabinet w/ 2 3-panel star-and-
circle design cupboard doors and matching sides, over
drawer on sq. molded legs, ht. 59.5", w. 40.5" .... $ 950 ... $ 1650 ... $ 2600

Porter's Chair, Eng. oak hall; hooded back joining shaped
wings and outscrolling arms above turned stiles, ht. 59" ...... 350 ... 610 ... 963

Prie-Dieu, Italian carved wal., carved w/ panel door and
paw feet, ht. 37", w. 25" .... 2250 ... 4000 ... 6000

Reading Stand, Geo. III rosewood marquetry; hinged top w/
floral inlay above an apron w/ drawer on sq. tapered legs,
ht. 28", len. 22" .... 2500 ... 4380 ... 6875

Rent Table, Eng. Regency mah. octagonal w/ red tooled-
leather top; conforming apron fitted w/ drawers, on turned
pedestal w/ reeded sabre legs on brass toes, ht. 29", w.
40.5" .... 8000 ... 14,000 ... 22,000

Screen, Continental 5-fold canvas w/ landscape panels, in
brown and blue, ht. 71" .... 650 ... 1100 ... 1750

Scroll Mirror, Amer. Chip., ht. 25" .... 300 ... 530 ... 825

Scroll Mirror, Amer. mah. Chip., small, ht. 20" .... 250 ... 440 ... 650

Secretaire Abattant, French Directoire; rect. top w/ cut
corners above long drawer and fall-front writing surface
opening to fitted interior above case w/ 2 long drawers
on shaped apron w/ shaped feet, ht. 56", w. 34" .... 2000 ... 3500 ... 5500

Secretary Bookcase, important MA Fed. inlaid cherry; projecting cornice w/ barber pole inlay above 3 inlaid oval
pinwheels; upper case w/ twin doors, each w/ elaborate

*Better proportions, a more interesting design and brass candle-holders
make the cheval mirror on the left a more valuable piece than the
example on the right.*

	AUCTION	RETAIL Low	High

vase and vine inlay, opening to shelves; lower case w/
slant-lid opening to fitted interior w/ diamond and
pinwheel inlaid prospect door, 4 serpentine graduated
long drawers each w/ checkered inlay centering floral
vase, chamfered concave case corners w/ similar floral
inlay, on base molding w/ ogee feet, similarly inlaid,
ht. 80", w. 43" $100,000 $185,000 $285,000

Secretary, Hpwt.-style inlaid mah. w/ glazed doors above
tambour slides and a writing flap over a case w/ 2
drawers, on sq. tapered legs, ht. 81", w. 40" 2200 3850 6000

Secretary, NE Fed. cherry and inlaid bird's-eye maple; w/
shaped pediment above geometric glazed doors and 2
short drawers; lower part w/ butler's drawer w/ column
inlaid prospect door; French feet, ht. 84", w. 39" 4000 7000 11,000

Secretary, NE late Fed. inlaid mah., in 2 parts: upper w/
cornice w/ geometric contrasting line inlay and brass
rosette terminals centering urn finials above case w/
twin doors opening to fitted interior over twin drawers,
each w/ similar inlay and ivory escutcheons; lower w/
hinged writing flap above long drawer and 2 recessed
cupboard drawers flanked by 2 sham doors and rope
twist columns continuing to tapering reeded legs, doors
and drawers w/ similar inlay and escutcheons, ht. 77",
w. 40.5", d. 20" 2000 3500 5500

Secretary, NH Fed. mah. glazed door. in 2 parts: upper w/
diamond glazed doors; lower section w/ slant-lid over
case w/ 4 graduated long drawers and shaped apron w/
French feet, ht. 80", w. 41" 4000 7000 11,000

Settee, PA painted and decorated triple chairback w/ floral
decoration, len. 71" 500 880 1375

Shaving Mirror, NE mah. w/ 2 drawers 225 390 600

Side Chair, Amer. ladderback in green paint w/ bulbous-
turned stretcher 3500 6000 9000

Side Chair, Eng. Chip. mah., w/ Gothic splat 550 960 1500

Side Chair, MA Chip. carved mah.; serpentine crest w/
central shell above cross-eyed owl splat w/ carved
volutes over slip-seat on cabriole legs w/ pad feet 3200 5600 9000

Side Chair, MA Q.A. wal., yoke crest above vasiform splat
and leather overupholstered trapezoidal seat on cabriole
legs w/ pad feet and recessed block-and-vase-turned
stretcher 1400 2450 3850

Side Chair, MA transitional wal.; serpentine crest w/ carved
ears above pierced splat and slip-seat on cabriole legs
joined by block-and-vase-turned H-stretcher, on
platform pad feet 1400 2500 3850

Side Chair, NE bowback brace-back Windsor w/ vase-
turned legs 450 800 1250

Side Chair, NE country Q.A., w/ oxbow crest and Spanish
feet 550 960 1500

Side Chair, NY country Q.A. yoke-back w/ bulbous stretcher
and pad feet 1100 1900 3000

	AUCTION	RETAIL	
		Low	High
Side Chair, PA Q.A. maple, Savery School; serpentine crest rail above vase splat, rush seat and cabriole legs on drake feet, joined by simple turned stretchers	$ 4750	$ 8000	$ 13,000
Side Chair, RI Fed. mah. w/ pierced splat enclosing an urn; slip-seat above sq. molded legs joined by recessed H-stretcher	450	790	1250
Side Chair, Salem Hpwt. mah. shield-back, School of Samuel McIntire; back w/ foliate carvings and sunburst over serpentine seat on sq. tapered legs	1100	1800	3000
Side Chair, Spanish wal. and tooled leather	700	1230	2000
Side Chair, PA Q.A. wal.; w/ oxbow crest above a vase splat and slip-seat, stretcher of serpentine form	1400	2400	3700
Side Chair, NE country Q.A., w/ oxbow crest above vase splat and rush seat on block and turned legs on Spanish feet	300	500	820
Side Chairs, important set of 3 Q.A. Phila. carved wal., w/ spooned backs, shell-carved crests and vasiform splats; compass slip-seats over shell-carved cabriole legs and trifid feet	90,000	150,000	250,000
Side Chairs, pr., Amer. Chip. mah., each w/ pierced splat above slip-seat on sq. molded legs joined by recessed box stretcher	3500	6000	9600
Side Chairs, pr. of bird's-eye maple fiddleback	375	660	1000
Side Chairs, pr., carved oak and cane Flemish-style	400	700	1100
Side Chairs, pr., Eng.-Flemish carved beech and cane	900	1500	2500
Side Chairs, pr., Eng. Geo. III carved mah.; w/ serpentine crest rails w/ leaf-carved ears above ribbon-carved pierced splats, on slip-seat and cabriole legs w/ leaf-and cabochon-carved knees and ball-and-claw feet	3000	5250	8250

Ormalu mounts, a more dynamic form involving canted corners and deep curves, make the Empire pier table on the left the far superior example.

	AUCTION	RETAIL	
		Low	High

Side Chairs, pr., MA Chip; w/ serpentine crests w/ central
leaf carving on star-punched ground above volute-
carved cross-eyed owl splats, over frontal cabriole legs
on pad feet. .... $ 22,000 $ 38,500 $ 60,000

Side Chairs, pr., NE Chip. mah., Portsmouth; w/ step-
down crests and upturned pointy ears above tapering
pierced splats and trapezoidal slip-seats on sq. legs 1300   2280   3500

Side Chairs, pr., NE country Q.A., each w/ an ox-bow crest
above vase splat and upholstered seat, on block-and-
vase-turned legs w/ Spanish feet 600   1050   1650

Side Chairs, pr., NY Classical figured maple w/ sabre legs 500   880   1350

Side Chairs, set of 4 Amer. Classical Revival, each w/ tablet
crest rail and reeded stiles continuing to reeded sabre
legs, fitted w/ slip seats 1700   3000   4500

Side Chairs, set of 6 Chip. carved mah., Phila., each w/
serpentine crest rail w/ central leaf-carved motif above
pierced Gothic splat, slip-seats over sq. legs w/ molded
edge joined by an H-stretcher 12,500   21,000   34,000

Side Table, primitive heart-form, on triangular apron w/ 3
tapering legs, back an openwork triangle, overall ht.
55", len. 30" 200   350   550

Side Table, Regency mah. ebonized and rosewood banded
2-drawer, ht. 29.5", len. 12.5" closed, d. 17.75" 3250   5500   9000

Sideboard, Amer. Hpwt. inlaid mah. D-front; top w/ line
inlaid edge above central drawer and twin cupboard
doors flanked by bowed cupboard doors, on sq. tapered
legs w/ satinwood inlay, ht. 38", len. 6', d. 27" 8000   14,000   22,000

Sideboard, Amer. Hpwt. inlaid mah. serpentine-front; case
w/ central bowed drawer above pair of cupboard doors
flanked by concave cupboard doors, on sq. tapered legs,
ht. 39", len. 70", d. 27" 4000   7000   11,000

Sideboard, Amer. Sher. mah. and tiger maple bowfront;
shaped backboard above rect. hinged top flanked by
sloping hinged lift-top ends over projecting case w/
bowed paneled cupboard doors opening to shelves and
flanked by recessed panels, case sides each w/ pair of
paneled cupboard doors opening to compartmented
interior, on turned feet, ht. 17.25", len. 24", d. 10" 6250   10,000   17,000

Sideboard, Amer. Sher.-style mah. kidney shape; oblong-
shaped top above case of drawers and doors, on turned
reeded legs, len. 72", w. 28.5" 800   1400   2200

Sideboard, Boston Sher. inlaid mah., School of John and
Thomas Seymour; oblong top w/ outset corners above
case w/ an arrangement of crossbanded drawers and
cupboard doors, on turned and reeded legs, ht. 42", len.
73", d. 25" 5000   8750   13,750

Sideboard, diminutive NE Hpwt. inlaid mah.; oblong
serpentine top above conforming case w/ 3 line-inlaid
drawers over fan-inlaid cupboard doors on line-inlaid
sq. tapered legs, ht. 39.5", len. 58", d. 25" 21,000   36,000   57,000

	AUCTION	RETAIL Low	High

Sideboard, Eng. Hpwt. inlaid mah., demilune case w/ an
rrangement of drawers on sq. tapered legs, ht. 36", len.
72", d. 28" .... $ 5000 $ 8750 $ 13,750

Sideboard, Eng. Hpwt. inlaid mah.; rect. top w/ projecting
center above long drawer and flanking deep drawers,
each w/ contrasting crossbanding, arcade skirt w/ shell
inlay on sq. tapering legs w/ spade feet, ht. 36", len. 60",
d. 27" 4200   7350   11,500

Sideboard, Geo. III mah. serpentine-front; shaped top
above central drawer flanked by bottle and cupboard
doors, on sq. tapered legs w/ spade feet, ht. 37.5", len.
63", d. 25" 17,000   30,000   45,000

Sideboard, NY Hpwt. mah.; oblong top w/ bowed front
above an arrangement of doors, drawers and bottle
drawers on sq. tapered legs, ht. 45", len. 77", d. 23" 1200   2100   3300

Sideboard, small Boston Sher. inlaid mah., Seymour School;
rect. top w/ outset corners above case of 3 short drawers
over pair of cupboard doors w/ flanking inlaid columns
and bottle drawers, on turned tapered legs, ht. 39", len.
58", d. 22" 13,000   22,750   35,000

Silver Table, Geo. III mah; rect. top over blind fret-carved
apron w/ sq. chamfered legs w/ pierced brackets, ht. 28",
top 20" x 30" 4000   7000   11,000

Silver Table, Eng. Chip. mah.; rect. top w/ pierced gallery
above blind fret frieze w/ candle slides on sq. tapering
legs w/ Marlborough feet, ht. 27", w. 20", d. 32" 18,500   32,000   50,000

Slant-Lid Desk, CT Chip. inlaid cherry, opening to an
interior w/ an eagle-decorated prospect door; case w/
fluted quarter-columns and 4 graduated drawers, each
cockbeaded and w/ stringing, on base molding w/
diamond motif and ogee bracket feet, w. 40" 6000   10,000   16,500

Slant-Lid Desk, MA Chip. mah. serpentine-front; lid opening to fitted interior above case w/ 4 long drawers on
molded base w/ center drop and frontal ball-and-claw
feet, w. 42" 3000   5000   8250

Slant-Lid Desk, MA Chip. mah. serpentine-front; oblong
thumbmolded lid opening to fitted interior above case
w/ 4 long graduated drawers w/ blocked ends, on molded
base w/ bold ball-and-claw feet and center drop, w. 42" 6000   10,000   16,500

Slant-Lid Desk, NE Q.A. wal.; oblong thumbmolded lid
opening to an elaborate interior w/ serpentine drawers
below valanced pigeonholes centering pilastered document drawers; case w/ 4 long graduated drawers on
bracket feet, w. 36" 3750   6500   10,000

Slant-Lid Desk, NH Q.A. maple; oblong thumbmolded lid
opening to stepped interior of valanced pigeonholes,
short drawers and document drawers, above case of 4
long graduated drawers on molded base w/ bandy
cabriole legs on pad feet, w. 37" 5250   9000   14,000

Slant-Lid Desk, Phila. Chip. wal.; oblong lid opening to an

The strong tiger maple grain of the wood used in the left hand
Chippendale chest of drawers make it worth over double the value of
the example on the right.

	AUCTION	RETAIL	
		Low	High
interior w/ 2 banks of stepped short drawers centering valanced pigeonholes and document drawers and prospect door opening to 5 shaped drawers, case w/ flanking fluted columns and 4 graduated long drawers, on molded base w/ shaped bracket feet, ht. 42.5", w. 36.75"	$ 12,500	$ 21,500	$ 34,000
Sofa, Amer. Classical Revival mah. w/ scrolled arms, on sabre legs w/ brass casters, len. 84.5"	1000	1750	2750
Sofa, Amer. Fed. mah. arched crest rail above down-swept arms, on turned legs, len. 86"	1000	1750	2750
Sofa, Amer. red-painted country w/ blue and white coverlet fabric, len. 75"	550	960	1500
Sofa, Baltimore Fed. inlaid mah.; arched and bowed back flanked by down-curved arms, overupholstered serpentine seat on sq. tapering legs w/ stringing and oval inlaid dies above bellflowers, on brass cups w/ rollers, len. 66"	14,000	24,500	38,500
Sofa, Eng. Chip. mah. camelback, w/ outscrolled arms and Marlborough legs, len. 81"	2000	3500	5500
Sofa, MA Fed. mah. bowback, len. 78"	3400	6000	9000
Sofa, NE Sher. mah. and flame birch small, possibly Portsmouth, len. 54"	4750	8300	13,000
Sofa, NY Classical carved mah; scrolled armrests above carved and scrolled fruit-filled cornucopia feet on rollers, len. 7'	750	1310	2063
Step-Back Cupboard, PA Chip. wal., in 2 parts: upper section w/ cove molding above twin glazed doors; lower w/ 5 hort drawers over paneled doors, raised on bracket feet, ht. 82", w. 65"	7500	13,000	20,000
Stool, Classical mah. curule-form	800	1400	2200
Stool, W. & M. on trumpet-turned legs w/ H-stretcher, len. 17"	3200	5600	8800
Stools, pr., Geo. III carved mah., each w/ saddle seat above S-shaped carved legs joined by pierced serpentine-carved stretcher, on scroll feet, ht. 18", len. 23"	29,000	50,000	79,000

	AUCTION	RETAIL Low	High
Tall Chest, Clarke County PA Chip. wal.; cornice molding w/ notched cove above case w/ inset fluted quarter-columns and 3 short over 2 short and 4 long graduated drawers, on ogee feet, ht. 62", case w. 37.5"	$ 2500	$ 4300	$ 6500
Tall Chest, NE Chip. 5-drawer, w. 36"	1200	2100	3300
Tall Chest, NE Chip. maple; cove molding above case w/ 5 long drawers on molded base w/ bracket feet, ht. 50", case w. 36"	3100	5400	8500
Tall Chest, RI Chip. tiger maple, w/ molded cornice enclosing recessed tray top above case fitted w/ 2 short over 5 long graduated drawers, each thumbmolded, on base molding w/ bracket feet, retains original brasses, ht. 53", case w. 35.5"	9500	16,000	26,000
Tall-Post Bed, NE Sher. cherry; posts turned and reeded, headposts joined by shaped headboard, ht. 74", w. 58", len. 76"	4750	8000	13,000
Tall-Post Bedstead, NE Fed. turned tiger maple, ht. 85", len. 81", w. 52"	1800	3000	5000
Tap Table, early Amer. w/ breadboard top; apron w/ single drawer joining turned legs w/ elongated button feet, ht. 27", top 26" x 39"	2500	4000	6500
Tavern Table, Pa, W. & M. wal.; rect. top above an apron w/ frieze of long and short drawer, on vase-and-ring-turned legs joined by plain box stretcher, ht. 28.5", w. 28" d. 20.5"	10,000	17,500	27,500
Tea Table, Amer. Q.A. maple rect. top w/ cut corners above an apron and turned legs on pad feet, ht. 27", top 35" x 26"	3000	5250	8250
Tea Table, CT Chapin School cherry tilt-top; pedestal w/ suppressed ball and high cabriole legs, w. 34"	1000	1750	2750
Tea Table, Geo. III carved mah. tilt-top; octagonal top w/ pierced gallery above spiral-turned urn standard joining cabriole legs w/ leaf carving and scrolled feet, ht. 29", dia. 23"	2600	4550	7150
Tea Table, Geo. III mah. diminutive, pie-crust edge tilt-top; top w/ birdcage support above carved standard joining pierced cabriole legs w/ leaf-carved knees and scroll feet, ht. 25", dia. 22"	3600	6300	9900
Tea Table, NE cherry tray-top, rect. top above shaped apron joining cabriole legs on pad feet, ht. 26", top 19" x 30", ill. in Connecticut Historical Society's *Frederick K. and Margaret R. Barbour's Furniture Collection*, p. 24	7000	12,250	20,000
Tea Table, NE Chip. carved mah. tilt-top; sq. serpentine top w/ molded edge above spiral-twist urn-turned column joining tripod cabriole legs w/ leaf-carved knees and ball-and-claw feet, block branded "C. Willis," ht. 29", len. 29"	2400	4200	6600
Tea Table, NE maple porringer-top, w/ turned legs on pad feet, len. 34"	1600	2800	4400
Tea Table, PA Chip. mah. birdcage; circular dish top above			

	AUCTION	RETAIL Low	High

suppressed ball turned standard joining cabriole legs on ball-and-claw feet, ht. 28", dia. 34" .... $ 6250 $ 10,000 $ 17,000

Tea Table, PA wal. dish top; circular top on birdcage support continuing to ball-turned standard joining tripod cabriole legs on pad feet, dia. 32" 3800 6650 10,000

Terrestrial Globe, Amer. Fed. painted and decorated on maple-turned standard w/ cabriole legs, ht. 40" 1600 2800 4400

Tester Bed, Amer. Classical Revival carved mah.; posts elaborately carved w/ pineapples and acanthus leaves, ht. 87", len. 85", w. 66" 8000 14,000 22,000

Trunk, Salem brass-studded red leather, small, w/ label of John Bott 200 350 550

Trunk, tooled-leather covered, Spanish or Italian, w/ slightly domed lid and iron straps and handles, len. 19" 900 1500 2475

Urn Stand, Geo. III carved mah.; shaped sq. top w/ pierced gallery above pierced apron joining cluster-column legs w/ pierced X-form stretcher, ht. 28.5", len. 17" 1700 3000 4500

Urn Stand, Geo. III satinwood; oval form w/ serpentine gallery, apron w/ slide, on sq. tapered legs, ht. 22", len. 15" 850 1500 2400

Urn Stands, pr., Geo. III carved mah., each w/ octagonal top w/ gallery on spiral-twist standard w/ pierced cabriole legs on scroll feet, ht. 27", dia. 12" 6000 10,000 16,500

Wall Table, Amer. late Sher. mah.; oblong hinged top w/ reeded edge above long drawer on turned and reeded legs, len. 40" 600 1050 1650

Wall Table, Regency-style ebonized and giltwood; rect. top over frieze w/ diamond motif on fluted circular legs joined w/ lower shelf, ht. 36", top 18" x 58" 5500 9630 15,000

Window Bench, Geo. III carved mah.; upholstered serpentine seat flanked by outward scrolling arms, frame w/ gadrooning and cabriole legs w/ acanthus and cabochon-carved knees and scroll feet, len. 5', d. 24" 19,000 33,000 52,000

Windsor Armchair, Amer. comb-back; serpentine crest w/ scroll-carved ears above circular arm w/ shaped hand-holds over plank seat and turned legs joined by stretchers . 1100 1930 3025

Windsor Armchair, bowback, w/ shaped handhold above plank seat and turned legs joined by stretchers 850 1490 2338

Windsor Armchair, comb-back; serpentine crest w/ scroll-carved ears above spindle back joining circular arm w/ shaped handholds above plank seat on turned legs 2800 4900 7700

Windsor Armchair, continuous arm, w/ flat armrests and baluster-turned supports and legs joined by similar turned H-stretcher 1000 1750 2750

Windsor Armchairs, pr., black-painted low-back w/ gilt embellishments 1500 2600 4000

Windsor Armchairs, set of 6 PA bowback, each w/ hoop back mortised w/ scrolled arms above plank seat and bamboo-turned legs 4250 7500 11,500

Windsor Bench, Amer. w/ bamboo turnings, w/ paneled crest

	AUCTION	RETAIL	
		Low	High
and olive-green paint, len. 80"	$ 4500	$ 7500	$ 12,500
Windsor Writing Arm, Colonial style	1000	1750	2750
Windsor Settee, Amer. bowback w/ scrolled arms and bulbous-turned legs, len. 6'	3500	6000	9000
Windsor Side Chairs, pr. of bamboo-turned step-down	300	530	825
Wine Stand, Eng. mah; pie-crust edge above baluster standard w/ cabriole legs on ball-and-claw feet, ht. 24", dia. 24"	1100	1900	3000
Wing Chair, Chip. mah. barrel-back, w/ sq. molded legs	4750	8000	13,000
Wing Chair, Chip. mah.; serpentine crested back w/ outward scrolling arms on sq. legs joined by recessed stretcher	3250	5690	9000
Wing Chair, Eng. Q.A. wal.; serpentine crested back w/ shaped wings and outscrolled arms above cabriole legs on pad feet w/ early H-form stretcher	2400	4200	6600
Wing Chair, NE Q.A. carved mah., Newport or Boston; arched upholstered back flanked by ogival wings and tapering conical arms, w/ bowed seat and frontal cabriole legs w/ shell-carved knees and pad feet joined by block-and-vase-turned stretcher	10,000	18,000	28,000
Wing Chair, NY Chip. carved mah.; arched upholstered back flanked by ogival wings over vertical rolled arm-rests above an overupholstered seat cushion and cabriole front legs w/ circular returns on ball-and-claw feet	8000	14,000	220,00
Work Stand, NE painted and decorated country Sher., single drawer in ochre and black, top 19" x 18.5"	900	1580	2475
Work Table, Amer. Sher.; twin leaves centering stack of 2 drawers and bag drawer, on octagonal-turned legs on brass rollers, ht. 29", w. 17", closed	600	1050	1650
Work Table, Boston Empire mah.; oblong top w/ drop leaves above case w/ 2 drawers, on columnar legs w/ plinth base and scroll feet, len. 21"	4200	7350	11,500
Work Table, NE Sher. figured maple 2-drawer; rect. top w/ drop leaves w/ rounded corners above case w/ 2 drawers on baluster-and-ring-turned legs on rollers	1400	2450	3850
Work Table, NY Classical carved mah., w/ rect. top and 3 drawers on pedestal w/ 4 reeded sabre legs w/ acanthus-carved knees, on brass toes w/ rollers	1200	2100	3300
Work Table, Regency brass-mounted kingwood, ht. 29", top 15" x 11"	8000	14,000	22,000

Mission

The name of Stickley dominates the field of Mission furniture. Those items produced by Gustav Stickley with the "Als ich kann" (As I can) label are generally the most valuable of the "commercial" makers. Unlike much Early American furniture, makers often labeled Mission pieces. Such labels increase value. However, Mission pieces designed by Frank Lloyd Wright, which command exceptional value, are not labeled as such. Original (usually dark) finish is an important point in valuing Mission furniture.

Dover Publications and Turn of the Century Editions have reprinted various catalogs of Mission furniture. For further information see also Bruce Johnson's *Arts and Crafts*, published by House of Collectibles, Random House, NY.

Items are listed under their maker. Prices are given for Refinished and Original Finish. Under each catagory are values for labled (L) and unmarked (UM) pieces. Gallery is abbreviated gal.

Marks of Gustav Stickley.

Gustav Stickley

	REFINISHED		ORIG. FIN.	
	L	UM	L	UM
Armchair, 3 splats, orig. upholstered seat, ht. 39.5", w. 24"	$ 400	$ 300	$ 500	$ 400
Armchair, 4 splats, leather seat, ht. 40", w. 24.5"	800	600	1200	1000
Armchair, peaked crest rail over 2 slats, ht. 36.5", w. 27"	400	300	500	400
Armchair, spindled high back, through tenons, ht. 48.5", w. 27.5"	6000	5000	10,000	7000
Armchair, V-back crest rail over 5 splats, exposed leg posts, ht. 37.5", w. 26"	500	400	600	450
Armchair, V-back rail over 5 splats, corbels for arms, through tenons, ht. 36", w. 24.5"	400	300	500	400
Armchair, high back, 20 spindles, corbels for arms, through tenons, ht. 49.5"	9000	7000	12,000	10,000
Armchair, spindled high back, spindles for each arm, through tenons, ht. 48.5", w. 27.5"	9000	7000	12,000	10,000
Armchair, high back, sq. cutouts, continuous arms, box base, w/cutouts, ht. 42.75", w. 32"	5000	4000	7000	6000
Bed, double, maple, inverted V head and footboards, arched apron, w. 54", len. 75"	4000	3000	6000	5000
Bed, single, inverted V-rail over 3 wide slats, canted legs, tapered tops, ht. 43", w. 39"	800	600	1200	1000
Bookcase, 1-door, 16 glass panes, gal. top, ht. 56", w. 36"	4000	3000	5000	4000
Bookcase, 1-door, 16 panes, through tenons, slab sides, gal. top, ht. 56"	3000	2000	3500	2500

	REFINISHED		ORIG. FIN.	
	L	UM	L	UM
Bookcase, 2-door, 8 panes/door, gal. top, ht. 56", w. 48"	$ 4000	$ 3000	$ 5000	$ 4000
Bookcase, 2-door, 12 panes/door, gal. top, ht. 56", w. 54"	3000	2000	3500	2500
Bookcase, 2-door, 8 panes/door, gal. top, ht. 56", w. 35"	3000	2000	3500	2500
Bookcase, 2-door, 6 panes/door, through and key, tenons gal. top, ht. 44", w. 36"	3000	2000	3500	2500
Bookcase, 2-door, 8 panes/door, gal. top, ht. 55.5", w. 47"	3000	2000	3500	2500
Bookcase, 2-door, exposed tenons, 8 panes per door, gal. top, ht. 56", w. 43"	3000	2000	3500	2500
Bookcase, 2-door, keyed tenons, 6 panes per door, gal. top, ht. 44", w. 36"	3000	2000	3500	2500
Bookcase, open, 4 shelves, through tenons, gal. top, ht. 56", w. 36"	3000	2000	3500	2500
Cellaret, flip top, copper tray under, ht. 43", w. 24"	2000	1500	2500	2000
Chair, cube, wide splat on each side, caned seat	5000	4000	7000	6000
Chair, office, leather back and seat, flat arms, swivel base, orig. leather, w. 21"	2000	1500	2500	2000
Chair, office, revolving base, leather seat, ht. 35", w. 18"	800	600	1200	1000
Chair, office, 11 spindles, flat arms, pedestal base, ht. 40", w. 25.5"	5000	4000	7000	6000
Chair, rabbit ear, keyed-through tenons, black leather inset seat w/brass tacks	800	600	1200	1000
Chair, side, 3 splats, leather seat, 1 front and back rail, orig. leather, ht. 38", w. 17.5"	400	300	500	400
Chair, side, plank seat, 3 graduated slats, beveled top front leg posts, ht. 37.5", w. 18.5"	300	200	400	300
Chairs, 4 ladderback, each w/ 3 slats, leather seat w/ tacks, orig. leather, ht. 37.5"	2500	2000	3500	3000
Chairs, 4 side, each w/ 4 slats, arched lower rail, leather cushion seat, ht. 37"	2500	2000	3500	3000
Chest, 2 dr. over 4 dr., chamfered sides, inverted V backsplash, through tenons, ht. 53.5", w. 33"	5000	4000	7000	6000
Chest, 2 dr. over 4 dr., paneled sides, brass pulls, ht. 48", w. 40"	6000	5000	10,000	7000
Chest, 9 dr., maple, arched apron, wooden pulls, backsplash, ht. 50.5"	5000	4000	7000	6000
China Cabinet, 1-door, 20 panes, paneled back, gal. top, ht. 66.5", w. 35.5"	9000	7000	15,000	12,000
China Cabinet, 1-door, glass sides, through tenons, gal. top, ht. 57.5", w. 35"	5000	4000	7000	6000
China Cabinet, 1-door, 9 panes, trapezoidal, butterfly joints, inverted V apron, ht. 65", w. 37"	10,000	7000	20,000	15,000
China Cabinet, 2-door, 2 dr., paneled sides, lower shelf, keyed tenon, ht. 36"	10,000	7000	20,000	15,000
China Cabinet, 2-door, through tenons, 6 panes per door, glass sides, gal. top, ht. 56", w. 51.5"	5000	4000	7000	6000
China Cabinet, 2-door, 8 panes per door and sides, through tenons, V pulls, gal. top, ht. 64", w. 42"	5000	4000	7000	6000

	REFINISHED		ORIG. FIN.	
	L	UM	L	UM
China Cabinet, 4-door, paneled sides, sloped over-hanging top, exposed tenons, ht. 69", w. 42.5" $10,000		$7000	$20,000	$15,000
Costumer, double, 2 tapered legs, posts, copper hardware 1000		800	1500	1000
Costumer, single, tapering post, iron hardware, ht. 68" 500		400	600	450
Day Bed, 5 splats each side, through tenons, ht. 29", w. 31" 2500		2000	3500	3000
Desk, 2 dr. over shaped lower shelf, wrought-iron V-pulls, ht. 30", w. 40" 800		600	1200	1000
Desk, 2 dr., letter trays, 2 dr. w/copper pulls, lower shelf, ht. 36", w. 40" 2000		1500	2500	2000
Desk, double pedestal, 9 dr., keyed tenons, 4 corner posts, orig. leather top, ht. 30.5", w. 47" 4000		3000	6000	5000
Desk, slant front, 1 dr. w/copper pulls, lower shelf, ht. 39", w. 30" 1000		800	1500	1000
Desk, slant front, fitted interior, 1 dr., platform base, ht. 43.5", w. 30" 1000		800	1500	1000
Desk, 1 dr. over kneehole shelf, flanked by 4 dr., copper pulls, exposed tenons, ht. 29", w. 42" 1000		800	1500	1000
Dining Chairs, 5, each w/ 3 slats, short corbels, tapered front legs, ht. 37.5", w. 17" 1500		1000	2000	1500
Dining Chairs, 6, each w/ 3 horizontal back slats, double side stretchers 2000		1500	2500	2000
Dining Chairs, 6, each w/ 3 vert. back slats, arched front and side aprons 4000		3000	6000	5000
Dining Chairs, 9, 1 arm, 8 side, each w/ 3 slats, rush seats 2500		2000	3500	3000
Dresser, 2 over 2 dr., maple, arched apron, tapering standards, mirror, w. 48" 2500		2000	3500	3000
Dresser, 4 dr., mirror, butterfly joints, bowed case, copper V-pulls, ht. 66", w. 48" 4000		3000	6000	5000
Dresser, 5 dr., mirror, butterfly joints, 2 over 3 dr., mortise and tenon, ht. 33", w. 46" 6000		5000	10,000	7000
Dresser, 6 dr., reverse V splashboard, paneled sides, wooden pulls, ht. 52.5" 6000		5000	10,000	7000
Dresser, 4 dr., mirror, butterfly joints, ht. 66", w. 48" 2500		2000	3500	3000
Footstool, flared legs extend above leather top, orig. leather, ht. 4.5", sq. 11.75" 500		400	600	450
Footstool, leather top, sq. faceted nails, sq. flared legs, orig. leather, ht. 4.5", w. 12 sq." 500		400	600	450
Footstool, rush top, arched stretchers, sq. form, orig. upholstery, ht. 18", w. 18.5" 1500		1000	2000	1500
Footstool, upholstered, arched seat rail, exposed tenons, ht. 15.25", w. 20" 500		400	600	450
Gout Stool, flared legs, leather top, ht. 4.5" 500		400	600	450
Mirror, cheval, maple, arched stretcher, inverted V top, ht. 70", w. 34" 1500		1000	2000	1500
Mirror, 3 sections, 4 iron hooks, w. 48" 1500		1000	2000	1500
Morris Chair, 5 slats for each arm, corbels, side stretcher tenons, shaped top rail, ht. 44", w. 31" 3500		2500	4500	3500
Morris Chair, wide flat arm over 5 splats, caned seat,				

	REFINISHED		ORIG. FIN.	
	L	UM	L	UM
ht. 38.5" $4000		$3000	$6000	$5000
Morris Chair, bent arm, 18 spindles for each arm, through tenons, ht. 36", w. 24" 9000		7000	12,000	10,000
Morris Chair, bent arm, 5 splat arms, straight apron, through tenons, ht. 40", w. 33" 6000		5000	10,000	7000
Morris Chair, bent arm, corbels, and 5 splats for each arm, through tenons, ht. 40", w. 23" 5000		4000	7000	6000
Morris Chair, spindled, adjust. back, spring cushion seat, ht. 38.5", w. 27.5" 6000		5000	10,000	7000
Morris Chair, spindled, ladies flat arm, 7 spindles each side, ht. 38" 4000		3000	6000	5000
Rocker, 3 splats, ht. 38", w. 26" 400		300	500	400
Rocker, 4 slats, ht. 33", w. 18.5" 300		200	400	300
Rocker, 5 splats, corbels for arms, through tenons, ht. 38", w. 28" 400		300	500	400
Rocker, concave crest over 2 slats, ht. 33.25", w. 26" 500		400	600	450
Rocker, V-back, 5 vert. back slats, painted cream color, ht. 37", w. 25" 400		300	500	400
Rocker, V-back w/ 5 slats, through arm posts, corbels for front arm 500		400	600	450
Rocker, V-top crest rail, 5 vert slats, corbels 400		300	500	400
Rocker, arm, curved crest over 3 splats, flat arms, orig. leather and tacks, ht. 38.5" 400		300	500	400
Rocker, arm, child's, 3 slats, ht. 25", w. 18" 300		200	400	300
Rocker, sewing, 4 slats, leather seat fits into side stretcher, wide seat rail, ht. 33" 400		300	500	400
Rocker, spindled, 11 spindles in back, open arms w/ corbels under, upholstered seat, ht. 36", w. 26" 2000		1500	2500	2000
Vanity, maple, 2 dr. w/mirror, arched apron, w. 36" 4000		3000	6000	5000

L. & J.G. Stickley

Armchair, 4 splats, long corbels, exposed front tenons, ht. 44", w. 27" 300		200	400	300
Armchair, fixed back, short splat back, extended front posts, ht. 32", w. 26.5" 6000		5000	10,000	7000

Quartered Oak
Plank Top $16⁸⁵

Solid Oak
Top 45 x 28 In. $10⁹⁵

Mission styles were widely copied. Although pieces of furniture may resemble the important makers, their prices do not. The above illustrations came from a Montgomery Ward catalog.

	REFINISHED		ORIG. FIN.	
	L	UM	L	UM
Bookcase, 1-door, 16 panes, V-board back, keyed tenons, gal. top, ht. 55", w. 30" $4000		$3000	$6000	$5000
Bookcase, 1-door, 16 panes, keyed tenons, gal. top, ht. 55", w. 30" 4000		3000	6000	5000
Bookcase, 1-door, 16 panes, keyed tenons, gal. top, ht. 55", w. 30" 4000		3000	6000	5000
Bookcase, 2-door, 12 panes per door, exposed tenons, gal. top, ht. 56.75", w. 50" 6000		5000	10,000	7000
Bookcase, 2-door, 12 panes per door, keyed through tenons, gal. top, ht. 56.5", w. 49" 6000		5000	10,000	7000
Cellaret, copper slide-out tray, 2-doors w/ copper strap work, ht. 35.5", w. 32" 6000		5000	10,000	7000
Chair, side, 5 splats, arched side rail, leather seat, extended posts, ht. 36", w. 19.5" 500		400	600	450
Chair, arm, 6 splats and 6 for each arm, corbels, cane seat insert, ht. 39.5", w. 28" 400		300	500	400
Chest, 2 dr. over 3 graduated dr., arched backsplash and apron, panel sides, ht. 40", (top) w. 38" 1500		1000	2000	1500
Chiffonier, arched backsplash, 2-doors over 4 graduated dr., splay ft, panel sides, ht. 50" (top) w. 36" 1500		1000	2000	1500
Day Bed, canted posts, 4 splats, ht. 27.75", w. 30" 1500		1000	2000	1500
Desk, 1 dr., keyed tenons on lower shelf 800		600	1200	800
Desk, 1 dr., slatted bookshelf sides, ht. 29", w. 44" 800		600	1200	800
Desk, slant front, fitted interior, 2 dr. over 2 dr., gal. top, ht. 42", w. 42" 800		600	1200	800
Desk, writing, 1 dr., letter slots, ... 800		600	1200	800
Dining Chairs, 4, each w/ 3 slats, extended posts, 2 side stretchers, 1 front and back, ht. 35", w. 16.5" 3000		2000	3500	2500
Dining Chairs, 4, each w/ 3 splats, arched front and back stretchers, rush seats, ht. 36" 2500		2000	3500	3000
Dining Chairs, 6, each w/ 3 splats, upholstered seats, double side stretcher, ht. 36" 3000		2000	3500	2500
Footstool, box stretcher, ht. 16", w. 14" 400		300	500	400
Footstool, leather top, stretchers, extended posts, orig. leather, ht. 18", w. 19" 500		400	600	450
Footstool, legs extend above tacked orig. leather top, arched apron, 7 spindle sides, ht. 17", w. 18" 3000		2000	3500	2500
Footstool, tacked leather top, arched apron, 7 spindle sides, extended posts, ht. 16", w. 18" 1500		1000	2000	1500
Footstool, upholstered, arched rail, ht. 16", w. 19.25" 400		300	500	400
Morris Chair, 2 slats for arms, corbels for arms, leather back and seat 1500		1000	2000	1500
Morris Chair, 5 slats on each side, long corbels, exposed tenons, ht. 40", w. 34" 4000		3000	6000	5000
Morris Chair, 5 slats for each arm, long corbels w/ through tenons, spring seat, ht. 39", w. 34" 1500		1000	2000	1500
Morris Chair, flat arm over 6 slats, wide seat rail, ht. 41", w. 26" 1500		1000	2000	1500
Morris Chair, flat arms, through tenons, leather back and seat, ht. 42", w. 29.5" 1500		1000	2000	1500

	REFINISHED		ORIG. FIN.	
	L	UM	L	UM
Morris Chair, adjust. back, flat arm over 16 spindles, leather seat, ht. 39", w. 36"	$2000	$1500	$2500	$2000
Rocker, V-shaped top crest, 5 splats, arched front, side aprons	300	200	400	300
Rocker, cube, 4 back and side slats, slightly higher back, ht. 30", w. 28"	1000	800	1500	1000
Rocker, Morris, flat arm over 6 splats, wide seat rail, ht. 39", w. 25.75"	2000	1500	2500	2000
Rocker, reclining, open arms, through tenons, leather back and seat, ht. 40", w. 24"	800	600	1200	800
Rocker, sewing, 3 slats, leather seat, ht. 30.5", w. 16.5" ...	300	200	400	300

Life Time stamp.

Life Time

	REFINISHED		ORIG. FIN.	
Bookcase, 3 dr. over 2 doors, through tenons, ht. 55", w. 48"	1000	800	1500	1000
Chair, cube, ht. 32", w. 28"	800	600	1200	800
Desk, 1 dr., 2 shelves on each side, round pulls, ht. 29", w. 49"	1000	800	1500	1000
Desk, slant front, extended posts, 1 dr. over 2 doors, arched aprons, through tenons	400	300	500	400
Dining Chairs, 5, each w/ 3 splats	800	600	1200	800
Morris Chair, corbels, post tenons, ht. 41", w. 28"	800	600	1200	1000

Limbert

	REFINISHED		ORIG. FIN.	
Armchair, high back, 2 crest rails over 4 splats, exposed faceted leg tenons, ht. 40", w. 26"	400	300	500	400
Bed, #470	2000	1500	2500	2000
Bookcase, open sided, 1-door, 8 panes, 4 open shelves per side w/ cutouts on top, ht. 47.5", w. 33"	6000	5000	10,000	7000
Bureau, #487.5, w/ mirror and 5 drawers	2200	1700	2750	2250
Cabinet, liquor, amethyst glass-lined tray. 1 dr., 2 doors, full gal., ht. 39", w. 31"	2000	1500	2500	2000
China Cabinet, 1-door, 2 panes over 1, arched aprons, plate rack, copper hardware, ht. 60", w. 25"	3000	2000	3500	2500
Desk, 3 dr., wood pulls, arched corbels, shelf w/ through tenons, ht. 29.5", w. 60"	3000	2000	3500	2500
Dining Chairs, 6, each w/ splat cutouts in top rail, arched apron, ht. 37", w. 18"	3000	2000	3500	2500
Footstool, leather top, extended posts, arched apron	700	500	900	700
Footstool, w/ dr., extended posts, leather top w/ tacks, arched aprons, ht. 12.5", w. 18"	500	400	600	450

	REFINISHED		ORIG. FIN.	
	L	UM	L	UM
Hall Chair, #81, tall cutout back, rare form $4000		$3000	$5000	$4000
Hall Chair, #79, leather and tacks 650		500	1000	700
Hall Chair, keyed tenon, ht. 42", w. 19" 2500		2000	3500	3000
Magazine Stand, #304, inverted V stretchers, 2 slats per side 800		600	1200	800
Settle, drop arm, #649, spade-form cutouts, 14-slat back, w. 78" 1500		1000	2000	1500
Table, drop-leaf oval, #1144 1650		1200	2300	1700
Table, round occasional, #142, cutout legs, dia. 27" 2000		1500	2500	2000
Vanity, arched mirror, 1 dr. over arched apron, through tenons, wood pulls 1500		1000	2000	1500

Roycroft

Bookshelf, vert. slats on back and sides, 4 shelves, ht. 38.5" 3000		2000	3500	2500
Bridal Chest, serpentine sides, keyed tenons centering lift top, copper strapware, ht. 26", w. 36.5" 6000		5000	10,000	7000
Footstool, upholstered, rect., extended posts, ht. 15", w. 17.75" 500		400	600	450
Mirror, iron chains from support bar, sq. mirror, ht. 33", w. 29" 1500		1000	2000	1500
Rocker, 4 splats, rounded arms, ht. 37", w. 31" 2000		1500	2500	2000
Side Chair, #30 1200		900	1500	1200

Shop of the Crafters

Liquor Cabinet, 2 glazed cupboard doors 500		300	500	450
Settle, even arm, inlaid 12,000		8000	17,000	14,000

Stickley Brothers

Armchair, high back, 4 splats, tapering ft. ht. 44", w. 27" 400		300	500	400
China Cabinet, 1-door, 3 over 2 panes, arched apron, through tenons, copper pulls, ht. 56.5", w. 49" 2000		1500	2500	2000

Mission furniture is simple and sparse, as this desk and clock. —Photos courtesy of Northeast Auctions.

	REFINISHED		ORIG. FIN.	
	L	UM	L	UM
China Cabinet, 2 doors, 2 panes over 1 per door, arched stretcher, gal. top, ht. 54," w. 40"	$3000	$2000	$3500	$2500
Desk, bookshelf sides, 1 dr., nickel-washed hardware, ht. 30", w. 38.5"	500	400	600	450
Dining Chairs, set of 12, leather backs and seats	3750	2500	5000	4000
Dining Table, pedestal, w. 60"	5775	4500	7000	6000
Footstool, gout, leather drop in top, 4 legs w/ through tenons, orig. leather, w. 12", d. 19"	400	300	500	400
Footstool, spindled, 7 spindles per side, ht. 15", w. 20.5"	3000	2000	3500	2500
Library Table, mortised lower shelf, w. 60"	1800	1400	2300	1900

Wharton Esherick

	REFINISHED		ORIG. FIN.	
Bench, red painted, 87" x 16.5"	8000	6000	10,000	8000
Chair, hammer handle	4000	3000	5000	4000
Corner Shelf, 157" x 61", 1962	8000	6000	10,000	8000
Dining Table, 77"	15,000	10,000	20,000	16,000
End Table, Cubist, walnut and plywood, 1957	8000	6000	10,000	8000
Hanging Lighting Fixture	15,000	10,000	20,000	16,000
Library Steps, 1965, 35" x 17"	18,000	12,000	25,000	20,000
Library Steps, spiral, 1966, ht. 47"	18,000	12,000	25,000	20,000
Radiator Cover, 105" x 27" x 27"	6000	4000	8000	6000
Sofa, curved straight back	18,000	12,000	24,000	19,000
Tea Cart, 1953	8000	6000	8500	6500

Wallace Nutting

Wallace Nutting's legacy to collectors includes photographs, ironwares, furniture, and an increased public awareness of American antiques. The reproductions of Early American furniture are now seriously collected in their own right, occasionally rising to values over and above some examples of the 18th-century originals that they copy.

Nutting's catalog numbers are given in parentheses. When more than one number is given, they refer to two different, but very similar, items with similar values.

Pilgrim Side Chair (393); Windsor Brace-Back Sidechairs (301)

	AUCTION	RETAIL Low	High
Banister-Back Armchair, carved crest and rush seat above Spanish feet (480)	$ 500	$ 1100	$ 1600
Banister-Back Chair, carved crest and rush seat above Spanish feet (380)	200	500	700
Bed, low urn post (809)	570	1000	2000
Bed, Sheraton, 4-post (846)	2000	4200	7000
Block Front Chest, Massachusetts style	1500	3000	5000
Brewster Chair (411)	1440	3000	5000
Butterfly Drop-Leaf Table, w/ drawer (624)	400	1000	1500
Butterfly Table (624)	990	2000	3500
Candlestand, cross base, turned standard (22), ht. 25", dia. 14"	300	700	1000
Candlestand, Federal (644)	1100	2000	3500
Candlestand, Windsor legs (17), ht. 25", dia. 14"	300	700	1000
Chest (909, 913, 918, 931)	2500	6000	10,000
Chest, Block and Shell (979)	7000	13,000	27,000
Chippendale Giltwood Looking Glass, ht. 53"	1000	1800	3200
Chippendale Highboy, broken swan's neck pediment (989), ht. 85.5", w. 39.5"	4000	7000	12,000
Chippendale Piecrust Tip-Top Tea Table (693-B), ht. 27.5", dia. 33"	1800	3500	6000
Chippendale Ribbon-Back Armchair (459-B)	500	1100	1600
Chippendale Ribbon-Back Side Chair (359-B)	300	700	900
Chippendale Straight-Back Sofa (525)	1500	3000	5000
Corner Chair (430)	650	1400	2000
Cupboard, Bookcase (927)	2000	4200	6000
Day Bed (828)	2160	4500	7600
Desk, Chip. slant front (701, 729)	4500	8000	14,000
Federal Armchair (438)	940	2000	3000
Gateleg Table (621)	1250	2300	3400

	AUCTION	RETAIL	
		Low	High
Gottard Townsend Style 3-Shell Block Front Chest (979), ht. 34.75", w. 39.5"	$ 3000	$ 5500	$ 10,000
Hat Rack (40)	400	700	1400
Ladderback Armchair (490)	400	700	1400
Ladderback Chair (390)	200	500	900
Ladderback Armchair (490, 492)	900	2000	3250
Ladderback Side Chair (374, 390, 392)	330	700	1100
Library Table (637)	1060	2300	4100
Pilgrim Armchair, (480, 493)	1000	2100	3700
Pilgrim Side Chair (393)	200	500	900
Queen Anne Shell-Carved Side Chair (399)	700	1500	2200
Refractory Table (601)	980	2300	3300
Secretary, Chippendale (729)	9000	15,000	27,000
Settee, lowback, Windsor turned legs (533), len. 87"	700	1500	2200
Settle, pine (416)	540	1200	2000
Side Chair, Dutch (361)	690	1400	2800
Side Chair, Federal (338)	600	1200	2700
Side Chair, Spanish foot (380)	670	1300	2300
Slant-Front Desk, w/ 3-shell interior (729), ht. 49", w. 36"	1800	3500	6000
Spoon Rack (903)	310	700	1100
Spoon Rack, chip carved (903), ht. 25"	300	700	1100
Stand, Federal (608)	700	1500	2600
Stand, Windsor candlestand (17)	960	2200	3200
Stool (101, 102, 110)	200	500	770
Stool, Gothic (292)	220	550	850
Stool, Joined (165)	930	2200	3400
Stool, William & Mary (166, 169)	350	800	1400
Table, William & Mary (653)	920	2200	3500
Tavern Table (613, 660)	1200	2500	4600
Tavern Table, ball-turned (613), ht. 30", w. 36"	800	1500	2500
Tavern Table, block-and-ring-turned (660), ht. 27", w. 36"	1200	2500	5000
Tester Bed, Federal (832)	2850	6000	10,000
Tester Bed, Marlborough feet (832-B), ht. 82"	1200	2500	4600
Tester Bed, w/ arched tester and turned feet (846-B), ht. 68"	1200	2500	4600
Treen Dish (27, 30)	150	350	550
Trestle Table (610, 615)	1200	2700	5500
Trestle Table, block-and-ring-turned (615), ht. 30", w. 50"	600	1400	2500
Tuckaway Table (616)	400	900	1300
Wainscot Settle, 3-panel w/ scroll arms (589), len. 57"	400	900	1300
Welsh Dresser (922)	2700	6000	9000
Windsor Bow-Back Armchair (408)	1000	2200	3500
Windsor Brace-Back Side Chair (301)	400	900	1300
Windsor Brace-Back Swivel Chair (329)	400	900	1300
Windsor Comb-Back Armchair (415)	1200	2500	3400
Windsor Comb/Brace-Back Side Chair (333)	800	1500	2500
Windsor Continuous Armchair (401)	1100	2500	4200
Windsor Knuckle Armchair (408)	790	1800	2800
Windsor Slipper Chair (349)	660	1450	2500
Windsor Writing Armchair (451)	1940	4000	7000
Wing Chair, Chippendale (466)	2500	5500	8000
Wing Chair, claw-and-ball feet	2500	5500	8000

Wicker

Wicker is the general term for pieces made of woven rattan, cane, dried grasses, willow, reed, or related material. The wicker heyday in the United States was from about 1860 to 1930. Cyrus Wakefield and the Heywood Brothers were the best known wicker manufacturers. They later joined to become the Heywood-Wakefield Company. Other companies include American Rattan Company and Paine's Manufacturing Company.

While 19th-century wicker is more valuable, pieces from the 1920s and 1930s are also desirable and easier to find. Natural finish wicker is preferred to painted pieces. For more information on wicker, see *The Official Price Guide to Wicker*, published by The House of Collectibles, Random House, NY

Values quoted are for mid-19th century (M-19), painted mid-19th century (PM-19), late 19th-century (L-19), painted late 19th century (PL-19), early 20th century (E-20), painted early 20th century (PE-20), machine-made (M), and painted machine-made (PM). Pieces described as ornate have features such as spooling, rolled arms and backs, unusual shapes, weaving between legs, etc. ("Upholstered" is abbreviated as "uph.")

	M-19	PM-19	L-19	P-19	E-20	PE-20	M	PM
Armchair, ornate	$600	$350	$550	$350	$450	$350	—	—
Armchair, plain	360	210	350	250	270	200	$200	$150
Baby Carriage	770	460	670	440	520	410	460	400
Bassinet, all-wicker	—	—	350	230	300	200	—	—
Birdcage	—	—	250	160	200	125	80	50
Boudoir Chair, w/ cushion	300	180	275	180	—	—	—	—
Bread Basket, open top	250	150	200	125	130	100	70	60
Buffet, all-wicker, plain	1000	800	800	500	600	400	—	—
Buffet, ornate	1310	750	1100	750	—	—	—	—
Bustle Bench	600	350	580	380	—	—	—	—
Chair, spider caning	830	500	700	450	—	—	—	—
Chaise Lounge, ornate	1100	700	900	600	—	—	—	—
Chaise Lounge, plain	800	500	600	500	500	450	380	320
Chandelier	330	190	400	200	250	150	—	—
Coffee Table, glass top	—	—	—	—	230	180	150	130
Coffee Table, oak top	—	—	440	300	300	220	190	160
Corner Chair, ornate	1430	850	1300	750	—	—	—	—
Corner Chair, plain	1100	700	1000	600	—	—	—	—
Cornucopia	—	—	—	—	40	40	20	20
Crib	850	550	850	550	570	450	—	—
Crib, swinging frame	—	—	1000	680	850	650	—	—
Desk (2 or more drawers)	1100	850	1000	750	900	700	600	450
Desk, all-wicker	950	600	700	500	560	440	460	400
Desk, oak top	860	510	750	500	600	450	—	—
Desk, w/ shelves	1100	760	950	700	780	610	500	400
Desk Accessories Stand	—	—	60	40	60	40	—	—
Desk Chair	150	90	120	80	100	75	—	—
Dining Chair	—	—	150	100	130	100	90	70
Dining Table	—	—	1250	900	730	570	—	—
Doll Carriage	300	180	300	190	210	160	90	70
Dresser	3400	2000	3000	2500	2600	2000	700	500
Dresser, w/ mirror	4000	2400	3700	2400	3000	2300	—	—
Easel, ornate	470	300	280	200	—	—	—	—
Easel, plain	220	150	200	130	—	—	—	—

	M-19	PM-19	L-19	P-19	E-20	PE-20	M	PM
End Table, ornate	$770	$460	$500	$400	$300	$230	—	—
End Table, plain	550	300	450	250	230	180	—	—
Etagere, 4 shelves	350	230	280	220	170	130	$160	$140
Field Basket	150	90	130	90	120	80	90	60
Firewood Holder	270	160	220	135	80	60	—	—
Flower Basket	150	80	120	80	90	70	60	50
Folding Stand	—	—	300	190	260	200	50	30
Footstool, uph.	—	—	200	130	160	120	50	30
Hamper	—	—	—	—	125	75	70	60
Highchair	510	300	530	340	310	240	230	190
Hourglass Chair	—	—	380	250	230	180	150	120
Knitting Basket	100	90	100	75	100	75	50	40
Lamp, Floor, no shade	200	160	180	120	—	—	—	—
Lamp, Floor, plain shade	340	240	300	200	—	—	—	—
Lamp, Floor, ornate shade	720	550	650	500	420	300	400	200
Lamp, Table, no shade	360	200	300	200	170	90	50	40
Lamp, Table, plain shade	300	220	370	240	300	240	150	130
Lamp, Table, ornate shade	450	350	425	325	300	200	180	90
Library Table, all-wicker	1000	800	850	600	520	400	270	220
Library Table, oak top	900	750	800	550	400	380	—	—
Lounge Chair	—	—	550	300	340	260	—	—
Loveseat, ornate	950	560	1170	760	800	600	—	—
Loveseat, plain	800	500	900	600	680	500	430	360
Loveseat, uph. seat	1000	700	1000	680	—	—	—	—
Magazine Rack	—	—	440	300	300	250	—	—
Magazine Stand	300	220	270	200	170	100	75	50
Music Cabinet	270	160	—	—	—	—	—	—
Music Stand	190	110	—	—	380	300	—	—
Ottoman	—	—	200	130	180	140	—	—
Photographer's Chair	1400	850	1300	700	—	—	—	—
Picnic Basket, hinged lid	190	110	180	100	140	100	70	40
Picture Frame, h. 30"	210	120	190	100	150	80	—	—
Plant Stand	330	190	300	150	220	170	90	55
Plant Table, ornate	550	320	500	300	310	240	—	—
Plant Table, plain	360	210	300	200	160	120	—	—
Rocker	710	420	790	500	270	210	200	160
Rocker, Child's	420	250	370	240	260	200	150	130
Rocker, Child's, uph.	420	250	350	230	—	—	—	—
Rocker, ornate	740	500	750	500	500	300	180	150
Rocker, plain	310	180	310	200	230	180	—	—
Rocker, Platform, ornate	500	300	550	350	400	300	—	—
Rocker, Platform, plain	450	260	380	250	340	260	—	—
Rocker, uph., w/ pouch	450	260	450	300	360	280	—	—
Settee, ornate	1000	680	1000	680	700	400	—	—
Settee, plain	710	420	820	530	520	400	450	300
Sewing Basket, ornate	270	240	250	200	200	150	—	—
Sewing Basket, plain	190	120	170	100	140	100	—	—
Side Chair, ornate	890	530	800	500	400	200	—	—
Side Chair, plain	600	350	410	270	160	120	110	100
Slipper Chair	510	300	500	320	—	—	—	—
Smoking Stand, ornate	420	250	500	300	300	175	—	—

	M-19	PM-19	L-19	P-19	E-20	PE-20	M	PM
Smoking Stand, plain	$300	$180	$350	$250	$200	$100	—	—
Sofa, ornate	800	650	800	600	550	430	—	—
Sofa, plain	—	—	640	420	440	340	$360	$300
Stool, 3-leg	—	—	90	60	60	50	—	—
Stroller	—	—	580	380	500	300	—	—
Swing	—	—	730	480	470	360	—	—
Table, tilt-top	650	400	750	500	—	—	—	—
Teacart	—	—	580	380	550	430	—	—
Tete-a-Tete Chair	1670	990	1640	1000	1000	700	—	—
Tray, all-wicker	100	60	90	50	75	60	45	30
Tray, glass bottom	—	—	—	—	60	50	30	20
Tray, oak bottom	—	—	90	60	60	50	40	20
Umbrella Stand	270	160	250	150	170	130	—	—
Vanity Bench	270	160	220	120	150	100	—	—
Victrola	—	—	—	—	1560	1220	—	—
Wheelchair	—	—	2000	1300	1500	1000	—	—
Wine Rack	—	—	—	—	60	50	50	40

Wicker rockers, c. 1920s.

Glass
Art Glass

Art Glass developed to satisfy middle class Victorians' love for trinkets. In the late 19th century more Americans had more money to spend on beautifying the home. The decades surrounding the turn of the century produced much of the finest glass. Many of the firms famous then are still in business today. Some still manufacture designs of 60 years ago.

For all practical purposes, glass cannot be restored. A chip may be ground down, but this alters the shape and thus the value. A crack cannot be painted the way a skilled porcelain restorer can hide a small defect in pottery or porcelain. Glass can be damaged by water if it is allowed to sit in a vase or bowl for weeks on end.

For further information see *The Official Price Guide to Glassware*, by Mark Pickvet, House of Collectibles, Random House, NY.

Amberina

	LOW	HIGH
Bowl, swirl, deep fluted, cranberry to amber, gold foliate dec., 7.5" x 10.5"	$ 400	$ 600
Bowl, swirl, fluted, rich red to amber, iridescent finish, ht. 4", dia. 8"	200	300
Butter Pat, daisy and button pattern, dia. 2.75"	175	250
Ewer, Mt. Washington, cranberry to amber, ht. 7"	400	600
Fingerbowl, red, ht. 2.5"	70	120
Fingerbowl and Underplate, red and fuchsia, ht. 2.5", sgn. "LIBBEY," 1917	750	1150
Footed Toothpick Holder, daisy and button pattern, ht. 3"	350	520
Mug, bulbous, amber handle, ht. 4"	225	340
Nappy, hobnailed pattern w/ ruffled edge, ht. 2.75", dia. 4.5"	300	450
Pitcher, bulbous, amber to cranberry, enamel floral dec., ht. 8"	375	560
Pitcher, diamond quilted, applied handle, red shaded to amber, ht. 7", dia. 4.5"	500	750
Salt Shaker, baby thumbprint, pewter top	225	340
Toothpick Holder, tri-cornered top edge in diamond pattern, ht. 2.25"	500	750
Tumbler, cranberry to amber, ht. 5.5"	125	190
Tumbler, dark cranberry to amberina quilted design, ht. 3"	100	150
Tumbler, fuchsia in diamond pattern, ht. 3.75"	125	190
Tumbler, whiskey, diamond quilted, deep red shaded to amber, belltone, ht. 2.5", dia. 2"	300	450
Vase, cylindrical, white enamel dec. of boy carrying a shotgun w/ bird, ht. 6.5"	250	380
Vase, flower petal top, applied spiral trim, cranberry to amber, ht. 10", dia. 5.5"	250	380
Vase, Libbey, deep cranberry vase tapers to amber stem, ht. 11.5"	600	900
Vase, 6.5", sq. opening	170	
Vase, swirl, fan-form top, cranberry to amber, wishbone feet, ht. 8.5", dia. 6.5"	200	300
Wine Glass, ht. 6"	300	450

Argy-Rousseau

	LOW	HIGH
Bowl, pate-de-verre, red background, molded fruit and foliate design in black and red, sgn., 4.5" dia., c. 1925	1800	2700
Bowl, pate-de-verre, expanding cylinder, mottled lavender and green background, molds w/ roses, sgn., 2.5" ht., c. 1925	1500	2250

	LOW	HIGH

Covered Box, circular, light amber, orange, and gray, molded leaves,
strapwork and stars, red mask on lid, sgn., 6" dia., c. 1925 .... $ 4000 $ 6000

Bohemian

Bowl, cobalt overlay, cut hobstars and fans, tapered sides, round, 3.5" ht.,
12" dia. 150   220
Cake Plate, amethyst overlay, cut wave design, hobstars and diamonds,
notched and scalloped rim, 11.5" dia. 100   150
Cologne Bottle, ruby red, frosting at center, medallion w/ etched scene of
deer, w/ stopper, 7.5" ht., 2.5" dia. 350   520
Compote, green overlay, triangles w/ caning, thumbprints and sunburst design,
notched and paneled shafts, 6" ht., 7.5" dia. 75   110
Decanter, cobalt w/ bullseye and fan cuts, paneled neck, clear stopper, 12.5" ht. 125   190
Dish, green overlay w/ 3 cut fans, footed, round, 3.5" ht., 8" dia. 100   150
Vase, amethyst overlay, graduated cut panels, 10" ht. 65   100
Vase, cobalt overlay, trumpet form, graduated cut panels, 7" ht. 80   120

Bristol

Cologne Bottle, green satin finish, gilt reeded handles, 9.5" ht., 3.5" dia. 130   200
Jar, of pink overlay, silver-plated lid, handle and base rim, white interior,
floral dec. of blue and white and enameled duck in flight, 5" ht. 120   180
Lustres, gilt blue glossy and satin fin., each w/ 8 crystal prisms, 10.5" ht.,
5" dia. 320   480
Vase, flattened oval, enamel bird and flowers, bug dec., 2.5" ht., 4.5" dia. . 200   300
Vase, of pink overlay, scalloped cut top w/ gold trim, dec. in blue, white,
and orange enameled flowers, white heron in blue dot pattern, 15" ht. .. 200   300

Burgun & Schverer

Bowl, inverted bell form, brownish-yellow streaked w/ green background,
cut w/ wild animals and flowers, 5.5" dia., c. 1895 3000   4500
Bowl, sawtooth rim, light green streaked w/ red, enamel
floral dec., overlaid and carved in clear, gilt, 7" dia., c. 1895 4000   6000
Vase, bulbous body, sawtooth lip, pale yellow, floral enameled in blue and
green, clear overlay, applied foliage on neck, gilt, 5.5" ht., c. 1895 2000   3000
Vase, bulbous body, long neck, gray shading to lavender, clear overlay,
flora carved, sawtooth neck, gilt, 5.5" ht., c. 1895 2000   3000
Vase, cabinet, baluster, yellow, clear overlay, floral carved, gilt, 5.5" ht.,
c. 1895 3000   4500
Vase, cabinet, spherical, flaring lip, 3 feet, lavender overlay, cut w/ bleeding
hearts and leaves, gilt highlights, 3.5" ht., c. 1895 600   900

Burmese

Bowl, diamond quilted pattern w/ ruffled edge, satin fin., 2.25", dia. 4.5" 300   450
Bowl, fluted edge, satin fin., 3", dia. 6" 450   680
Creamer, applied handle and pedestal base, satin fin., 4" ht. 350   520
Cruet, Mt. Washington, acid fin., melon ribbed, undec., 6.5" ht. 1200   1800
Cruet, Mt. Washington, acid fin., ribbed, w/ stopper, yellow handle, 7" ht. .. 1400   2100
Cup and Saucer, applied handle, satin fin., dia. (cup) 3", (saucer) 5" 500   750
Cylindrical Footed Vase, satin fin., 9" 700   1050
Fairy Lamp, acid fin., deep salmon pink to creamy yellow, rare pressed
Burmese base, clear inside cup, base marked "Clarke," 5" ht., 7" dia. ... 600   900

	LOW	HIGH
Jack-in-the-Pulpit Vase, crimped edge, acid fin., 9.75"	$ 700	$ 1050
Lemonade Glass, w/ applied handle, satin fin., 5"	400	600
Mt. Washington Bowl, diamond quilted pattern w/ folded edge, pinched to basket shape, glossy fin., paper label, 2.75", len. 6.5"	450	680
Mt. Washington Creamer, diamond quilted pattern, glossy fin., 4.25"	450	680
Mt. Washington Trumpet Vase, acid fin., 8"	450	680
Muffineer, Mt. Washington, acid fin., white and colored dots form blossoms, attrib. Timothy Canty, 4.5" ht.	1000	1500
Perfume Bottle, branches and pinecones, satin fin., silver cap w/ monogram, 5"	1200	1800
Rose Bowl, scalloped edge and 3 applied feet, satin fin., 3.5"	325	490
Stick Vase, dec. w/ leaves and blueberries, gold accent stripe, acid fin., 10"	1400	2100
Sugar and Creamer Set, Mt. Washington, acid fin., no dec., ht. 3.5" creamer ..	750	1120
Toothpick Holder, acid fin., bulbous w/ sq. top, dec. w/ brown leaves, white and blue enameled flowers, 3" ht., 2.5" dia.	300	450
Toothpick Holder, acid fin., sq. top, 2.5" ht., 2.5" dia.	200	300
Toothpick Holder and Undertray, tri-cornered shape, quilted design, satin finish, 2.25" dia. (of undertray) 3.5"	400	600
Tumbler, acid fin., 3.75"	130	200
Tumbler, dec. w/ ivy leaves, gold rim, satin fin., 3.75"	400	600
Vase, acid fin., ribbed, scalloped top, 3.5" ht., 2.5" dia.	225	340
Vase, acid fin., undec., 3.5" ht., 5.5" dia.	350	520
Vase, Mt. Washington, enameled polychrome stylized blossoms and foliage, applied handles, 10.5" ht.	1500	2250
Vase, Mt. Washington, bottle, acid fin., salmon pink to yellow, white enameled mums and green foliage, 6.5" ht., 3.5" dia.	350	520
Vase, Mt. Washington, bulbous base, long neck, dec. w/ sacred ibis, oasis scene in raised gold, 12" ht., 7" dia.	3000	4500
Vase, Mt. Washington, egg form, acid fin., dec. w/ daisies and foliage in 3 shades of gold enamel, designs outlined in raised gold, 9" ht., 4.5" dia.	1000	1500
Vase, Mt. Washington, Jack-in-pulpit, acid fin., crimped top, 12.5" ht., 5" dia.	1000	1500
Vase, Mt. Washington, teardrop form, elaborate polychrome and gold floral dec., 10.5" ht., 5.5" dia.	2000	3000
Vase, pinched top, 3 applied feet and berry pontil, satin fin., 7.25"	1000	1500
Vase, shiny fin., ruffled top, 3.5" ht., 3" dia.	220	340
Whiskey Tumbler, Mt. Washington, acid fin., diamond quilted, yellow edge, 2.5" ht.	250	380

Cameo

Bowl, Eng., ribbed, pink on white, acid-cut fish-scales, dec. w/ morning glory vine and butterfly in gold enamel, 7.5" dia., sgn. in enamel	1200	1800
Perfume Bottle, Eng., round, blue ground, dec. w/ carved white blossoms, foliage and butterfly, silver lid, 7.5" ht.	3000	4500
Vase, 4 layers, white to red to clear to green, depicts raspberries and foliage, 7" ht., 4.5" dia., unsgn.	3000	5000
Vase, sgn. by Michel Paris, translucent, frosted ground, brown cut to yellow, sailing scene, 3 acid cuttings, 8.5 ht., 3.5" dia.	1200	1800

Cameo Glass labeled with "Daum, Nancy" or "Webb" is highly valued. But beware of reproductions with a recut label. — Photo courtesy of Northeast Auctions.

Cased

	LOW	HIGH
Bowl, amethyst, w/ painted butterfly, 7.5" dia.	$ 200	$ 300
Lustres, white, cranberry banding, circular medallions, ptd. flowers, pedestal bases, prisms, 12" ht.	200	300
Perfume Bottle, dec. yellow, gilt clear ball stopper, applied jewels, 5.5" ht., 2.5" dia.	200	300
Rose Bowl, amethyst, applied flower and leaves, 3.5" ht., 4" dia.	300	450

Coraline

Pitcher, orange glass, amber applied handle, water lilies of white and green leaves in coraline beading dec., 8.5" ht., 4" dia.	225	340
Lamp Base, satin glass, fern leaf sprays, beaded coraline of yellow, brass burner, 7.5" ht., 3" dia.	150	220
Vase, 4"	170	
Vase, seaweed decoration on pale blue diamond quilted mother-of-pearl, coraline blossoms, applied jewel center, 7" ht.	450	680
Vase, seaweed, pink decoration on gold diamond quilted mother-of-pearl, 6.5" ht.	500	750

Cranberry

Crackle Glass Vase, applied glass base and appointments	50	75
Handled Cup, Mary Gregory, ht. 3.25"	75	100
Herringbone Satin Glass Vase, 6"	140	200
Miniature Threaded Glass Lamps, pr., 12.5"	1000	1500
Sugar Shaker, diamond cut, 5.75"	90	130
Sugar Shaker, sq. 5.75"	90	130
Sugar Shaker, 12 sided, 5.5"	90	130
Vase, Mary Gregory, ht. 5.5"	75	100

Crown Milano

	LOW	HIGH
Bowl, Mt. Washington, white body, gold blossoms and jewels covered w/ gold enamel, 12.5" ht., sgn.	$ 800	$ 1200
Decanter, dec. w/ enamel roses and gold scrolls on neck and stopper, 10" ht., rare early Albertine Crown Milano sign.	1000	1500
Ewer, Mt. Washington, applied handle, color geometric dec., 13" ht., unsgn.	1600	2400
Ewer, Mt. Washington, pastoral dec., 10.5" ht.	2500	3750
Jam Jar, white body, dec. w/ blue and white forget-me-nots, silver-plated lid sgn. Santa Co., sgn. jar, 4" ht.,	350	520
Plate, rose and fired gold scrolling, enameled dots on 3 reserves, 11" dia.	120	180
Rose Bowl, Mt. Washington, all-over dec. of roses, buds, leaves, gold trim, purple numbered pontil	350	520
Salt Shaker, cockle shell, Mt. Washington, white satin body, enamel blossoms, silver-plated top shaped like seashell	375	560
Tray, Mt. Washington, shiny fin., rolled and serrated edges, enamel thistle and foliage dec., outlined w/ raised gold, 9.5" long, 7" w., sgn.	825	1240
Urn, w/ rare crown-shaped lid, raised gold blossom and foliage dec., 16.5" ht., 8" w., 5.5" d., sgn.	2800	4200
Vase, Mt. Washington, bulbous, cream-colored body w/ slender neck, gold blossoms and jewels covered w/ gold enamel, 12.5" ht., sgn.	800	1200
Vase, Mt. Washington, cone-shaped, enamel floral bouquet dec., 8" ht., sgn.	850	1280
Vase, sq.-shaped, rounded corners, 2 delicate applied handles, dec. w/ pastel enamels in tiny free-form geometric patterns, 8" ht., unsgn.	750	1000
Vase, Mt. Washington, sq. w/ rounded corners, applied scroll handles, cream ground, enamel oak leaves and gold acorns, paper label, 8.5" ht.	950	1420

D'argenthal

Bowl, swollen spherical, undulated rim scalloped, yellow background, overlaid in maroon, cut w/ roses, sgn., 6" dia., c. 1900	600	900
Box, covered, shallow circular shape, dark yellow background, overlaid in brown and umber, cut w/ wildflowers, sgn., 3.5" dia., c. 1915	400	600
Vase, baluster shape, light yellow background splashed w/ red, overlaid in red, cut landscape of lake, arched bridge, and trees, sgn., 13.5" ht., c. 1910	2000	3000
Vase, baluster shape, turquoise background, overlaid in dark blue, cut w/ flowers and leaves, sgn., 7" ht., c. 1900	400	600
Vase, cameo, pastoral scene w/ house, trees and chateau in background, sgn., 6.5" ht., 4.5" dia.	480	720
Vase, cameo, dark brown floral pattern, sgn., 14" ht., 6" dia.	650	1000
Vase, cylindrical, orange-yellow background, red overlay, floral cut, sgn., 11.5" ht., c. 1900	700	1100

Desire Christian

Bowl, red shading to amber, green overlay, carved flowers and dragonfly, sgn., 7" dia., c. 1895	1400	2000
Bowl, green shading to turquoise, green overlay, carved lily pads, blossoms, and flying dragonfly, sgn., 6" dia., c. 1895	1200	1800
Vase, bud, compressed sphere, brown shading to olive green, lavender overlay, carved w/ milkweeds, leaves, and grass, sgn., 12" ht., c. 1895	3000	4500
Vase, cylinder expanding to neck, spreading foot, gray w/ red background, carved w/ 2 orchids and leaves, sgn., 14.5" ht., c. 1895	2000	3000

De Vez

	LOW	HIGH
Vase, acid fin. background, dark green shaded to rose landscape scene in 3 acid cuttings, sgn., 9.5" ht., 2" dia.	$ 620	$ 930
Vase, acid fin. background of blue w/ mountain landscape scenes on 3 detailed acid cuttings, sgn., 11.5" ht., 3.5" dia.	700	1100
Vase, acid fin. background of shell pink w/ navy blue shaded to yellow shaded to pink in 3 acid cuttings, mountain scene, sgn., 6.5 ht., 2.5" dia.	630	940
Vase, bulbous body, long cylinder neck, light pink background, overlaid in yellow and blue, cut scene w/ squirrels and mountains, sgn., 13" ht., c. 1900	1100	1650
Vase, cylinder w/ flaring rim and foot, yellow background splashed w/ orange and green, cut river scene, sgn., 5.5" ht., c. 1910	700	1050
Vase, cylinder shape tapering toward the neck, overlaid in lavender shading to pink, cut cartouches enclosing river landscape, sgn., 9.5" ht., c. 1900	800	1200
Vase, elongated pear shape, short cylinder neck, yellow background overlaid in dark blue, cut w/ river scene, sgn., 5.5" ht., c. 1910	700	1050
Vase, pear shape, cylinder neck, flared rim, yellow background, overlaid in orange and blue, cut river scene, sgn., 6" ht., c. 1910	700	1000

Durand

Plate, flashed ruby w/ engraving by Charles Link, 8" dia.	325	500
Vase, bulbous shape, iridescent blue, wide flared neck, 8.5" ht.	225	340
Vase, compressed bulbous, flattened shoulders, waisted and lobed neck, flaring rim, blue iridescence, sgn., 8.5" dia., 1905-30	500	750
Vase, compressed sphere base, cylinder neck expanding into trumpet shape, green background, undulating bands in amber iridescence, sgn., 12" ht., 1905-30	1800	2700
Vase, compressed spherical body, lobed neck, blue, 8.5, ht.	500	750
Vase, compressed spherical, trumpetlike neck, short circular foot, blue iridescence, sgn., 9.5" ht., 1905-30	450	680
Vase, conical, iridescent gold leaf and vine design, flared rim, 7" ht.	350	520
Vase, cylindrical, flaring rim, circular base, amber dec. w/ coalescent interlacing designs, 8.5" ht.	1000	1500
Vase, cylindrical, iridescent platinum King Tut pattern, narrow mouth, 5" ht.	300	500
Vase, cylindrical, scalloped rim, opalescent glass, w/ hearts and vines, 11" ht.	1000	1500
Vase, baluster, blue iridescent, amber iridescent foot, sgn., 14.5" ht.	450	680
Vase, cylindrical, swollen shoulders, silvery blue, sgn., 6.5" ht., 1905-20	450	680
Vase, elongated ovoid, waisted neck, flaring rim, blue iridescent, overlay clinging heart vine, 10.5" ht., 1905-1930	450	680
Vase, ovoid, flaring neck, iridescent blue, sgn., 10.5" ht., 1905-25	600	900

Le Verre Francais

Vase, cameo, trumpet form, mottled orange and yellow background, cut bouquets in bright orange to deep purple, sgn., 18.5" ht., c. 1920	400	600
Vase, compressed spherical tapering to trumpet-form neck, green background, overlaid in mottled orange, brown, and green, carved w/ flowers w/ honeycomb pattern around the base, 16.5" ht., c. 1920	800	1200
Vase, cylinder w/ tapering waisted neck, orange overlay shading to green and turquoise, cut w/ blossoms and leaves, honeycomb design on neck,		

	LOW	HIGH
26" ht., c. 1930	$ 1000	$ 1500

Vase, spherical, w/ cylinder neck, yellow background, cut in flowers
and tendrils in blue and orange, sgn., 12" ht., c. 1925 500   750

Loetz

Biscuit Jar, iridescent purple shaded to black, swing handle, silverplate
lid, 9" ht. 150   220

Bowl, bulbous w/ waisted base and neck, flaring rim, magenta background,
silvery blue designs of ripples, 10" dia., c. 1900 925   1400

Bowl, circular, green iridescent, fluted, 7.5" dia. 200   300

Bowl, ovoid, crimped lip and sides, oil-spotted yellow background w/ blue
striations, 10.5" len., c. 1900 900   1350

Bowl, ovoid, silvery amber iridescent background, amber iridescent wave
pattern, ruffled neck, unsgn., c. 1900 350   520

Lamp, iridescent cylinder, in bronze stand circling body, triangular base,
body in salmon w/ amber and silvery blue oil spots, 19.5" ht., c. 1900 .. 650   980

Lamp, melon-form base, silvery blue oil spots, helmet-shaped shade in
avocado green, both w/ 4 vertical hobnailed bands, 11" ht., c. 1900 1200   1800

Vase, baluster body, amber iridescent background, loops and trails in
orange, blue, and amber iridescent, 6.5" ht., c. 1900 800   1200

Vase, baluster, flaring lip, spreading base, iridescent orange, rose spotting
around foot, 8.5" ht., c. 1900 400   600

Vase, baluster, triangular mouth, orange oil spots, loops and swirls in silvery
blue and iridescent amber, 8.5" ht., c. 1900 400   600

Vase, bulbous, cylinder neck, everted rim, orange background, lavender
feathering, blue iridescent oil spots, silver overlay, 10.5" ht., c. 1900 900   1350

Vase, blue and green, iridescent pinched shoulder and ruffled collar, Loetz
Austria etched on bottom, 7" ht. 600   900

Vase, purple, wide lip on top, unsgn., 6.5" 400   600

Mary Gregory

Bowl, cranberry, 5" dia. 75   100

Box, emerald green, puffy shape, lift-off lid, white enamel dec. depicts
girl, 3" ht., 3.75" dia. 1250   1800

Box, lime green, hinged lid, white enamel dec. depicts boy, 1.5" ht.,
2.5" dia. 150   220

Box, patch, round, green, white enamel dec. girl, hinged, 1.5" ht., 2.5" dia. 150   220

Box, sapphire blue, round, hinged lid, white enamel dec. depicts girl,
2.75" ht., 3.5" dia. 160   240

Decanter, cranberry, white enamel dec. depicts girl w/ bouquet, clear
bubble stopper, 9" ht., 3.5" dia. 175   260

Handled Cup, cranberry, 3.25" ht. 75   100

Plate, cobalt, white enameled dec. depicts girl w/ butterfly net, ormolu
compote stand, 3 rings hang from holder, 6.5" dia. 150   220

Tumbler, cranberry, white enamel dec. depicts girl, 4.5" ht., 2.5" dia. 75   110

Vase, blue glass, fluted top, ht. 8" 60   90

Vase, covered, cobalt, white enamel dec. w/ girl and flower basket, 14" ht. ... 325   500

Vase, cranberry, ht. 5.5" 75   100

Vase, cranberry, white enamel dec. depicts boy w/ hat, 7.5" ht. 125   200

Vase, sapphire blue, scalloped top, white enamel dec. depicts boy w/
goblet, plated brass base w/ woman's-head handles, 14.5" ht., 3.5" dia. 250   380

	LOW	HIGH
Water Glass, cranberry, ht. 4.5"	$ 100	$ 150

Moser

	LOW	HIGH
Decanter, w/ stopper, clear to green, sgn., 8" ht.	175	260
Ewer, gold over crystal, enameled polychrome flowers and leaves, pedestal base, 5.5" ht., 2.5" dia.	150	220
Jug, enameled decorations, strap, twig handle, sgn., 9.5" ht.	75	110
Juice Glass, cranberry, polychrome and gilt enamel leaves and acorns, 4" ht.	150	220
Tumbler, cranberry glass w/ gold enameled flowers and colored bees, 3.75" ht.	175	260
Tumbler, crystal shades to blue, engraved w/ grouse and landscape, cut and gilt enamel dec., 5" ht., 3" dia., sgn.	350	520
Vase, dec. opaque pink to clear, applied scroll feet, gold filigree, enameled eagle, oak leaves, insect, applied acorns, 7" ht., 7" dia.	1500	2250
Vase, opalescent pink to clear, crimped glass handles burnished w/ gold, parrot and foliage in relief gilt polychrome enamel, 7.5" ht., Moser sgn ..	850	1280
Vase, multicolored enameled grape leaves and bee w/ applied yellow and red grape bunches, 4 applied feet of amber rosette, 5.5" ht., 2.5" dia.	350	520
Wine Glass, light ruby, elaborately dec., 5" ht.	300	450

Mother-of-Pearl Satin Glass

	LOW	HIGH
Decanter, diamond quilted pattern, ruffled edges, 6.75" ht.	200	300
Rose Bowl, blue color, herringbone pattern, pleated rim, 3.5"	175	260
Salt, raspberry color, teardrop pattern, pewter shaker top, 3.5"	275	410
Tumbler, deep rust shaded to pink, diamond quilted pattern, applied flowers, 4"	150	220
Tumbler, amber in coinspot pattern, 3.5"	120	180
Tumbler, blue in diamond quilted pattern, 4"	120	180
Vase, pink in coinspot pattern, ruffled edge, 9"	275	400
Vase, butterscotch drapery pattern over melon ribbed body, ruffled top, 8.25"	325	500

Muller Freres

	LOW	HIGH
Bowl, inverted cone, flaring rim, overlaid, carved, and enameled in fluro-gravure, harvest scene, sgn., 6.5" ht., c. 1900	2000	3000
Ewer, inverted cone, frosted green background, overlaid, carved, and enameled blossoms and leaves, sgn., 19" ht., c. 1900	2000	3000
Vase, baluster form, frosted blue background, carved overlay, enameled in flurogravure, winter scene w/ dogs and pheasant, sgn., 9" ht., c. 1900 ..	800	1200
Vase, double gourd form, purple background, cameo carved, sgn., 6.5" ht. ..	350	520
Vase, bulbous, waisted neck, lobed lip, orange background, overlaid in black, cut landscape, sgn., 4.5" ht., c. 1910	700	1050
Vase, cameo, storks w/ frosted yellow and gold, 7.5" ht.	1450	2200
Vase, cylinder, applied serpentine handle, green background, enameled berries and leaves, sgn., 10.5" ht., c. 1910	1000	1500
Vase, frosted pink background, w/ red roses, sgn., 7.5" ht., 3.5" dia.	1200	1800

Opalescent

Bowl, diamond quilted, light green shaded to pink, ruffled, pewter frame,

	LOW	HIGH
17.5" ht., 11.5" dia.	$ 350	$ 520
Bowl, flashed rainbow, fluted edge, dec. w/ enamel floras, 5" ht. 500		750
Ewer, striped white shaded to green, Vaseline applied leaf and handle, appliquéd flowers in pink, 8.5" ht., 3" dia. 250		380
Fairy Lamp, amber swirl, sgn. Clarke base, pyramid shade, 3.5" ht., 3.5" dia. . 200		300
Fairy Lamp, blue swirl satin finish, light blue glass cup and candle cup, matching sq. ruffled base, rare, 6.5" ht., 5.5" dia. 750		1120
Fairy Lamp, pink and white frosted swirl dec., dome shape, sgn. Clarke candle cup, sq. ruffled vase, 5.5" ht., 6" dia. 750		1120
Fairy Lamp, pressed glass, blue embossed rib design, sgn. Clarke base, 3.5" ht., 2" dia. 300		450
Vase, Jack-in-the-pulpit, fluted w/ purple edge, 7" ht., 4" dia. 150		220
Vase, white opalescent Monot Stumpf, pink shaded to white, fan shape, belltone, 7" ht., 6.5" dia. 450		680
Vase, white opalescent Monot Stumpf, pink shaded to striped white, pantin ruffled fan shape, belltone, 7.5" ht., 7.5" dia. 400		600
Water Tumbler, cranberry, 10-row hobnailed, 3.5" ht., 2.5" dia. 250		380
Water Tumbler, decorated peach, white flowers have gold leaves and centers, 4" ht., 2.5" dia. 150		220
Water Tumbler, lavender, 8-row hobnailed, 3.5" ht., 2.5" dia. 225		340

Orrefors

	LOW	HIGH
Bottle, elongated dome stopper, light green, clear, dec. internally w/ sea grass and starfish in maroon, sgn., 6.5" ht., c. 1938 800		1200
Bottle, thick-walled, clear, cartouche w/ dove, sgn. 6.5" dia., c. 1940 1500		2250
Bottle, thick-walled, stepped interior, green garlands and air bubbles in walls, sgn., 6.5" dia., c. 1940 400		600
Bottle, flaring, blue-tinted background, engraved scene of women and dolphin, scalloped border engraved around the rim, 8.5" long, c. 400		600
Bottle, octagon, light gray, cut w/ nudes and foliage, sgn., 11.5" c. 1928 ... 450		680
Bowl, aerial technique, teardrop-shaped bubbles radiating from center, 9" ... 700		800
Bowl, cylinder w/ expanding neck, cut w/ hunting scenes, sgn., 8.5" w., c. 1927 500		750
Bowl, lady in a hammock, engraved, egg shaped, c. 1960 450		550
Flask, flaring neck, 4 ball feet set on flattened dome base, clear, etched scene, sgn., 10.5" ht., c. 1930 600		900
Paperweight Vase, Fish and seaweed, 5", etched, Edw. Hald Graal No. 1680 on underside 375		450
Vase, oblong, young girl, stars and moon etched, F2769, ht. 4.25" 35		55
Vase, Graal glass, by Edward Hald, spiral-dec. baluster form, 9" 750		1000
Vase, Graal glass, fishbowl-dec. 500		650

Overlay

	LOW	HIGH
Bowl, shaded blue w/ embossed swirl rib design, 8-crimp top, white interior, 5" ht., 6" dia. 250		380
Fairy Lamp, candy striped in pink, matching candle cup, embossed, pink rib dome shade, clear applied fee,t ruffled base, 3 parts, 5.5" ht. 475		700
Fairy Lamp shade, dark green, sgn. Clarke base, 4.5" ht., 4" dia. 170		260
Finger Lamp and Chimney, blue, shaded, clear reeded applied handle, pink and white enameled flowers and gold color foliage, 5.5" ht., 4.5" dia. 175		260

	LOW	HIGH
Finger Lamp and Chimney, pink shaded, clear handle, red roses trimmed in green and dots of white, 6" ht., 5" dia.	$ 225	$ 340
Finger Lamp and Chimney, satin, lemon yellow, embossed shell and leaf, frosted reeded applied handle, 5" ht., 3.88" dia.	250	380
Finger Lamp, blue, shaded, clear reeded, applied handle, embossed design, 6" ht., 4.5" dia.	235	350
Goblet, white on crystal, dainty multicolor floral dec., white cut to clear and outlined in gold in places, Continental	240	360
Hand Lamp and Chimney, shaded chartreuse green, clear reeded applied handle, scroll decoration in beige, 5" ht., 3.5" dia.	190	280
Lamp, mushroom-shape shade has pink embossed flowers w/ ruffled top, white interior, silver-plated base, 17.5" ht., 6" dia.	400	600
Rose Bowl, diamond quilted, rose satin cut velvet, 8-crimp top, white interior, 3.5" ht., 3.5 dia.	280	420
Rose Bowl, fan shape w/ amber applied edging, hobnailed at top, 5.5" ht., 9" dia.	300	450
Tumbler, overlay shaded pink, w/ satin blue flowers and green leaves, gold trim, white interior, 4.5" ht., 3 dia.	220	330
Vase, Jack-in-the-pulpit, cranberry-edged, white background, 7.5" ht., 6" dia.	200	300
Vase, Jack-in-the-pulpit, dec. blue, w/ multi-colored, enameled flowers, branches and butterfly, dec. blue interior, 5.5" ht., 4.5" dia.	200	300
Vase, Jack-in-the-pulpit, green, white background, applied feet, 7" ht., 5" dia.	175	260
Vase, Jack-in-the-pulpit, purple, ruffled top, white background, 7.5" ht., 6" dia.	175	260
Vase, Jack-in-the-pulpit, purple shaded to lavender, ruffled, 7.5" ht., 6" dia.	175	260
Vase, Jack-in-the-pulpit, shaded green, clear applied feet, scalloped edges, 6.5" ht., 5.5" dia.	175	260
Vase, Jack-in-the-pulpit, shaded maroon, white background, ruffled edging, 7" ht., 6.5" dia.	200	300
Vase, pink, large applied crystal flower and branch, crystal around base, white interior, 8.5" ht., 4.5" dia.	200	300
Vase, silver floral leaves and swag etched over green, narrow, flaring neck, pear shape, 5" ht.	80	120
Vases, white w/ enameled blue flowers, clear applied edge, ruffled top, ormolu-handled holder, pink interior, 12.5" ht., 7" dia.	360	540

Overshot

Fairy Lamp, amber embossed swirl, sgn. Clarke base, 3.5" ht., 2.5" dia.	200	300
Fairy Lamp, cranberry, embossed hobnailed design, sgn. Clarke base, 4" ht., 3" dia.	225	340
Fairy Lamp, cranberry, embossed ribs, sgn. Clarke base, 3.5" ht., 3" dia.	235	350
Fairy Lamp, opaque yellow, w/ embossed swirl pattern, sgn. Clarke base, 3.5" ht., 2" dia.	250	380
Pitcher, ruffled, pink and white spatter glass, bulbous 3-way top, clear reeded applied handle, 7.5" ht., 5.5" dia.	250	380

Peachblow

Bowl, New England, flared scalloped rim, 2.5" ht., 5.5"	700	1100

LOW HIGH

Cruet, Wheeling, deep red shading to cream at base, clear amber faceted
    handle, reeded handle, 6.5" ht. .... $ 1100 $ 1650
Pitcher, Wheeling, 8" 400   500
Pitcher, Wheeling, shiny finish, exquisite color, applied amber handle,
    9.5" ht. 1000   1500
Pitcher, Wheeling, finest color, sq. top, amber handle, 10" ht. 1000   1500
Toothpick Holder, ruffled rim, cylindrical shape, 2.5" ht. 110   160
Toothpick Holder, wild rose color w/ ruffled top edge, paper label,
    "N. E.G.W./Wild Rose/PATd/MARCH 2, 1886," 2.5" ht. 525   800
Toothpick Holder, glossy finish, 2.75" ht. 200   300
Tumbler, Gunderson, w/ applied floral dec., 3.75" ht. 70   100
Tumbler, New England, shiny finish, wild rose upper half, 3.5" ht. 350   520
Vase, basket-weave, 5" 275   350
Vase, bulbous, gold and silver butterfly on gold and silver background, w/
    blue trim, 4.5" ht., 4.5" dia. 250   380
Vase, hummingbird on gold and silver background, narrow neck, 10.5" ht.,
    6" dia. 435   650
Vase, Mt. Washington, trumpet (lily), acid finish, pink shaded to blue,
    rare, 6.5" ht., 2.5" dia. 800   1200
Vase, New England, wild rose, satin finish, double gourd, red shading to
    white, 7" ht., 1880s 500   750
Vase, satin finish, ribbed pear design, narrow neck, 9" ht. 75   110
Vases, rose shaded to cream, Japanese-style blossoming branches, slender
    necks, pr., 7" ht. 200   300
Vase, Wheeling, bulbous, 2.5" 300   375

Pomona

Bowl, fluted, cornflower dec., 2" ht., 5.25" dia. 70   100
Juice Glass, first grind, delicate hobnailed interior, tapered, 3.5" ht. 120   180
Lemonade Pitcher, first grind, cylindrical, blue-tinted cornflowers, 12" ht. . 1200   1800
Pitcher, New England, first grind, miniature, sq. top 150   220

Loetz iridescent glass looks very much like that of Tiffany Studios. If it's unlabeled, it's more likely to be Loetz than Tiffany. — Photo courtesy of Phillips Auctioneers.

	LOW	HIGH
Spooner, second grind, inverted thumbprint w/ red stemmed blueberry dec. and crimped base, 5" ht.	$ 150	$ 220
Tumbler, first grind, spray of pansies and butterfly, 3.75" ht.	175	260
Tumbler, New England, second grind, cornflower staining	100	150
Water Carafe, New England, second grind, cornflower staining	225	340
Water Set, pitcher and 6 tumblers, first grind, pitcher is 6.5" ht.	900	1350
Water Tumbler, New England, blue cornflower pattern, 2nd grind, 3.5" ht.	250	380

Quetzal

	LOW	HIGH
Bowl, shallow, flaring lip, iridescent, sgn., 11.5" dia., 1901-25	600	900
Dish, circular shape, 2 ribbed handles, iridescent, 5.5" dia., 1901-25	250	380
Light Shade, flower form, scalloped, flared rim, iridescent yellow, sgn., 5.5" ht., c. 1900	300	450
Vase, elongated baluster, domed foot, yellow background, green feather designs, amber iridescence, 19.5" ht., c. 1901-25	2000	3000
Vase, Jack-in-the-pulpit, thin stem, flattened circular foot, opalescent, amber iridescent, striated green feathering, sgn., 10.5" ht., 1901-25	3000	4500
Vase, ovoid body, vertical lobbing, cylinder neck, flaring lip, opalescent background, green and amber iridescent draping, 6.5" ht., 1901-25	2500	3750
Vase, pear shape, amber iridescent. overlaid in silver, chased w/ flowers and leaves, strapwork, sgn., 8.5" ht., 1900-20	1200	1800

Satin

	LOW	HIGH
Bowl, embossed flowers of rose shaded to pink, white interior, 8-crimp top, 3.5" ht., 4" dia.	130	200
Bride's Bowl, overlay of pink, white on bottom, maroon flowers, green, yellow and lavender leaves, frosted, ruffled edging, gold trim, 4.5" ht.	270	400
Ewer, overlay of dec., shaded pink. applied frosted handle, enameled flowers, foliage of gold, white interior, 8.5" ht., 4.5" dia.	140	210
Ewer, overlay of dec., shaded pink, frosted, applied handle, enameled flowers, 9.5" ht., 3.5" dia.	120	180
Rose Bowl, overlay of blue diamond-quilted cut velvet, 4-crimp top, white interior, 3.5" ht., 3.5" dia.	175	260
Rose Bowl, overlay of dec. blue, flowers w/ butterfly, petal applied feet, 4-crimp top, white interior, 5.5" ht., 4.5" dia.	150	220
Rose Bowl, overlay of dec. light blue, applied frosted feet, enamel daisies w/ red jewel, 8-crimp top, white interior, 4.5" ht., 4.5" dia.	150	220
Tumbler, dec. shaded pink overlay, enameled flowers and leaves, white interior, 4.5" ht., 3" dia.	150	220
Vase, quilted, blue, 5.5"	85	
Vase, overlay of diamond-quilted rose cut velvet, white interior, ruffled, 7.25" ht., 3.5" dia.	200	300
Vases, pr., overlay of dec. rose shaded to pink, w/ white enameled flowers, gold foliage, white interior, 57" ht., 4.5" dia.	220	330
Vase, yellow web w/ prunus blossoms and butterfly in heavy gold, 3.5" ht., 4.5" dia.	350	520

Spatter

	LOW	HIGH
Box, cased glass, egg-shaped, dec. yellow, 3 applied feet in clear gold, branches and leaves of gold and white, floral dec., bluebell-shaped, 7.5" ht., 4.5" dia.	250	380

	LOW	HIGH
Finger Lamp and Chimney, peach w/ white and brown spatter, applied handle, 6.5" ht., 4.5" dia.	$ 130	$ 200
Jar, yellow, forget-me-nots in blue, applied final, 6.5" ht., 3.5" dia.	75	110
Tumbler, green and white embossed swirl, 3.5" ht., 2.5" dia.	60	90
Vase, Jack-in- the-pulpit, ruffled, diamond quilted, green, white and peach, 9.5" ht., 5.5" dia.	80	120
Vase, Jack-in- the-pulpit, diamond quilted, red and white 8" ht., 5" dia.	75	100

Stevens and Williams

	LOW	HIGH
Fairy Lamp, satin finish, striped green and white, sgn. Clarke, 5.5" ht., 4" dia.	200	300
Plate, Pastil, blue, fleur-de-lis, sgn., 7.5" dia.	40	60
Vase, Arbor, frosted cranberry w/ opaque white, frosted, reeded applied handles and pedestal foot, ruffled top, 6.5" ht., 3.5" dia.	140	200
Vase, green rib design, pinched floral form, 6" dia.	35	50

Webb

	LOW	HIGH
Fairy Lamp, acid fin., dome on sgn. Clarke candle cup	350	520
Rose Bowl, min., acid fin., crimped top, dec. w/ red berries, green and brown leaves, unsgn., 2.5" ht., 2.5" dia.	450	680
Vase, acid fin., flower petal top, salmon pink to yellow, polychrome dec. leaves and berries, 3.5" ht., 3.5" dia.	500	750
Vase, acid fin., fluted top, embossed striping, 3.5" ht., 3" dia.	400	600
Vase, acid fin., ruffled top and base, 4.5" ht., 2.5" dia.	300	450
Vase, acid fin., ruffled top, salmon pink to yellow, polychrome dec. flower and leaves, unsgn., 4.5" ht., 2.5" dia.	450	680
Vase, acid fin., ruffled top, widely flared, ball shape body, unsgn., 3.5" ht.	400	600
Vase, acid fin., salmon pink to yellow, dec. w/ foliage and red buds, unusual shape, 4.5" ht., 2.5" dia.	450	700
Vase, bulbous, acid red background w/ white floral dec., narrow neck, bulbous shoe, 5.5" ht.	675	1000

Two layer cameo vase, height 7.5", $3000-$5000. — Photo courtesy of Northeast Auctions.

	LOW	HIGH
Vase, bulbous, cylinder neck, peach shading, overlaid in white, cut w/ poppies and leaves, 7.5" ht., c. 1895	$ 4000	$ 6000
Vase, bulbous, long cylinder neck, greenish background, overlaid in white and pink, cut morning glories and leaves, stylized coils around neck, 8.5" ht., c. 1890	4000	6000
Vase, Peachblow, glossy, rose red and pink w/ raised gold prunus and bird dec., cream lining, 9" ht., 4" dia.	400	600
Vase, Peachblow, satin, rose and pink w/ floral and butterfly dec. in heavy gold, cream lining, 8" ht., 3" dia.	375	560
Vase, Peachblow, 2 applied handles, raised gold, green, and silver dec. w/squirrels, grapes and grape vines, 10" ht.	450	650
Vase, Queen's, acid fin., bottle, salmon pink to yellow, enamel ivy leaf dec., sgn. Thos. Webb Queen's Burmese Ware, 7.5" ht., 4.5" dia.	1200	1800
Vase, Queen's, acid fin., flower petal top, salmon pink to yellow, dec. w/ leaves and berries, sgn. Thos. Webb Queen's Burmese Ware, 2.5" ht., 3.5" dia.	600	900

Avon and Other Bottles

Many types of bottles found on the collectible market include: ale and gin, beer, cosmetic, bitters, crocks, cure, food, ink, medicine, mineral water, poison, pontil, soda and spirits. Because of their collector appeal, flasks and fruit jars, are listed in separate sections.

Avon

David Hall McConnell founded The California Perfume Company in New York City at the end of the 19th century. The firm changed its name to Avon in 1939. A pioneer in home sales, most people recognize the company's figural decanters produced in the late 1960s to the early 1980s. Prices are based on bottles in mint condition in original boxes of excellent to near mint condition. For further reading see *Avon Bottle Collector's Encyclopedia*, written and published by Bud Hastin, and *The Official Price Guide to Bottles, Old and New*, published by The House of Collectibles, Random House, NY.

*Top left to right: Super Cycle, 1972, $6-$8; '55 Chevy, 1975, $8-$12.
Below: Atlantic 4-4-2 Locomotive, 1973, $7-$9.*

	LOW	HIGH
American Eagle, 1971	$ 5	$ 7
American Schooner, 1972	8	10
Army Jeep, 1974	5	7
At Point Irish Setter, 1973	4	6
Atlantic 4-4-2 Locomotive, 1973	7	9
Avon Calling Candlestick Phone, 1969	10	15
Avon Calling Wall Phone, 1973	8	12
Betsy Ross, 1976	4	6
Betsy Ross, white on white glass, 1976	8	10
Big Mack Truck, 1973	7	9

	LOW	HIGH
Big Rig Tractor Trailer, 1975	$ 8	$ 12
Black Volkswagon, 1970	7	9
Bloodhound Pipe, 1976	4	6
Blue Volkswagon, 1973	6	8
Blunderbuss Pistol 1780, 1976	9	12
Bucking Bronco, 1971	6	8
Buffalo Nickel, 1971	5	7
Bugatti '27, 1974	8	12
Buick Skylark '53, 1979	10	12
Bulldog Pipe, 1972	6	7
Cable Car, 1974	8	10
Calabash Pipe, 1974	6	7
Canada Goose, 1973	7	9
Cannonball Express 4-6-0 Locomotive, 1976	6	8
Casey's Lantern, 1966	45	55
Catch-a-Fish, 1976	7	9
Cement Mixer, 1979	12	14
1876 Centennial Express Train, 1978	7	9
1926 Checker Cab, 1977	7	9
'55 Chevy, 1975	8	12
Chief Pontiac Car Mascot, 1976	8	10
Collector's Pipe, 1973	4	5
Colt Revolver 1851, 1975	8	10
'37 Cord, 1974	6	8
Corncob Pipe, 1974	4	6
Corvette Stingray '65, 1975	4	6
Country Kitchen (Rooster), 1973	4	6
Country Store Coffee Mill, 1972	4	6
Country Vendor, 1973	8	12
Covered Wagon, 1970	4	6
Cuper Cycle II, 1974	7	9
Dear Friends, 1974	8	10
Defender Cannon, 1966	8	12
Derringer, 1977	6	8
Dolphin (American), 1968	9	12
Dueling Pistol 1760, 1973	7	9
Dueling Pistol II, 1975	7	9
Dune Buggy, 1971	7	9
Dutch Pipe, 1973	6	7
Electric Charger, 1970	4	6
Electric Guitar, 1974	6	8
Extra Special Male (U.S. Mail Jeep), 1977	4	6
Faithful Laddie Collie, 1977	5	6
Ferrari '53, 1974	4	6
1910 Fire Fighter, 1975	6	8
First Volunteer Fire Pumper, 1971	8	12
Flower Maiden, 1973	5	7
Fly-a-Balloon, 1975	6	8
'36 Ford, 1976	6	8
1973 Ford Ranger Pickup Truck, 1978	5	7
Fragrance Hours (tall case clock), 1971	5	7

	LOW	HIGH
French Telephone, 1971	$ 15	$ 20
Garden Girl, 1975	7	9
Gas Pump, 1979	7	9
Gavel, 1967	8	10
General 4-4-0 Locomotive, 1971	7	9
Gold Cadillac, 1969	8	10
Golden Rocket Early Locomotive, 1974	7	10
Gone Fishing Boat, 1973	8	12
Greyhound Bus (1931), 1976	7	9
Harvester Tractor, 1973	8	12
Haynes Apperson 1902, 1973	6	8
Highway King, 1977	8	12
Homestead (Cabin), 1973	4	5
Indian Head Penny, 1970	5	7
Island Parakeet, 1977	4	6
Jaguar, 1973	6	8
Jeep Renegade, 1981	5	8
Kodiak Bear, 1977	6	8
Leisure Hours Clock, 1970	6	8
Leisure Hours Clock Miniature, 1974	4	5
Library Lamp, 1976	4	6
Longhorn Steer, 1975	6	8
Majestic Elephant, 1977	8	10
Mallard Duck, 1967	9	12
Maxwell '23, 1972	6	8
1936 MG, 1974	6	8
Mini-Bike, 1972	5	7
Model A, 1972	5	6
Mustang '64, 1976	4	6
Old Faithful St. Bernard, 1972	5	7
Open Golf Cart, 1972	7	9
Packard Roadster, 1970	6	8
Pepper Box Pistol (gold), 1982	7	9
Pheasant, 1972	8	10
Pheasant Reissue, 1977	7	9
Philadelphia Derringer, 1980	8	10
Pierce Arrow '33, 1975	6	8
Pipe Dream, 1967	6	8
Pipe Full (brown), 1971	4	5
Pipe Full (green), 1972	4	5
Pony Express, 1971	6	8
Pony Express Rider Pipe, 1975	5	7
Pony Post, 1972	5	7
Pony Post Miniature, 1973	3	5
Pony Post Tall, 1966	7	9
Quail, 1973	6	8
Rainbow Trout, 1973	7	9
Red Sentinel Firetruck, 1978	10	12
Revolutionary Cannon, 1975	4	5
Rio Depot Wagon, 1972	6	8
Road Runner, 1973	5	7

	LOW	HIGH
Rolls Royce, 1972	$ 7	$ 10
Royal Siamese Cat, 1978	5	7
Scottish Lass, 1975	5	7
Sea Maiden (Mermaid), 1971	6	8
Sea Trophy Swordfish, 1972	8	12
Short Pony, 1968	5	6
Side Wheeler, 1971	4	6
Silver Duesenberg, 1970	8	12
Skater's Waltz, 1979	7	9
Skip-a-Rope, 1977	6	8
Snoopy Surprise, 1969	8	10
Snow Mobile, 1974	8	10
Spanish Senorita, 1975	7	9
Spirit of St. Louis Airplane, 1970	9	12
Stage Coach, 1970	5	7
Stanley Steamer, 1971	6	8
Station Wagon, 1971	8	10
Sterling Six II, 1973	4	6
Sterling Six Silver, 1978	5	8
Stock Car Racer, 1974	5	7
Straight 8, 1969	5	7
Studebaker '51, 1975	5	7
Super Cycle, 1971	6	8
Sure Catch Fishing Lure, 1977	5	6
Sure Winner Race Car, 1972	6	8
Swinger Golf Bag, 1969	8	12
Ten Point Buck, 1973	6	8
The Camper, 1972	8	12
The Thomas Flyer 1908, 1974	7	9
Thomas Jefferson Hand Gun, 1978	8	10
Thunderbird '55, 1974	5	6
Touring T, 1969	6	8
Touring T Silver, 1978	5	8
Triumph TR-3, 1975	4	6
Twenty Paces Dueling Set, box, red lining, 1967	30	40
Twenty Paces Dueling Set, rare raised gun sight, 1967	70	90
Uncle Sam Pipe, 1975	5	6
Vantastic, 1979	6	8
Viking Discoverer Ship, 1977	12	15
Viking Horn, 1966	12	15
Volcanic Repeating Pistol, 1979	6	8
Volkswagon Love Bus, 1975	8	10
Volkswagon Rabbit, 1980	3	5
Western Boot, 1973	4	5
Wild Mustang Pipe, 1976	5	7
Wild Turkey, 1974	7	9

Left to right: West Bend, $25; Hollywood, $12; Pluto Water, $30.

Bitters

	LOW	AVG.	HIGH
Bitters Pharmacy, on label, clear, 4.5"	$ 5	$ 10	$ 15
Celery & Chamomile, on label, sq., amber, 10"	24	34	43
Compound Calisaya Bitters, tapered top, sq., amber, 9.5"	33	38	42
Dr. Boyce's Tonic, label, sample size, 12 panels, aqua, 4.5"	20	26	31
Dr. E. Chyder Stomach Bitters, N.C., amber, 10"	35	42	50
Fer-Kina Galeno, on shoulder, beer-type bottle, brown, 10.5"	21	27	33

Cure

24 Hour Cure Guaranteed, ring top, clear, 5"	18	22	26
Veno's Lightning Cough Cure, double ring top, aqua, 7.5"	15	20	25
While's Quick Healing Cure, amber, 6.25"	12	18	24
Wood's Great Peppermint for Coughs & Colds, clear, 6.5"	15	20	25

Food

Peppermint, marble in neck, aqua 7.5"	23	25	27
Planters, same in back, sq., glass top, peanut nobs, clear	65	75	85
Red Snapper Sauce Co., Memphis, 6 sides, clear, 9.5"	19	25	30
Warsaw Pickle Co., aqua, 8.5"	14	18	22

Ink

Angus & Co., cone, aqua, 3.5"	10	13	16
Arnold's, round, clear or amethyst,	15	19	23
Billing & Co., Banker's Writing Ink, aqua, 2"	35	45	55
S & B, pottery bottle, tan, 7.5"	16	18	22

Medicine

Brown Sarsaparilla, aqua, 9.5"	13	17	21
Brown's Instant Relief for Pain, aqua, embossed, 5.5"	7	9	11
Burnett, clear, 6.5"	16	21	25
Dr. Barkman's Never Failing Liniment, light green, 6.5"	11	14	17
F. Brown's, aqua, 5.5"	11	14	17
Medicine, T.B. Barton, clear or amethyst, 4.5"	7	10	13

Mineral

	LOW	AVG.	HIGH
Mineral, UTE Chief of Mineral Water, U.T. on base, purple, 8"	$ 10	$ 16	$ 20
San Francisco Glass Works, tapered neck, blob top, green, 7"	25	35	45
Saratoga Spring, honey amber, 9.5"	50	70	90
Shasta Water Co., Mineral Water Co., 10.5"	12	18	25
Veronica Mineral Water, on shoulder, sq., amber, clear, 10.25"	17	20	28
Weller Bottling Works, Saratoga, N.Y., blob top, aqua	17	23	30

Poison

	LOW	AVG.	HIGH
Baltimore, MD printed on bottom, amber, 3"	7	8	9
DPS, skull and cross, cross on 4 sides, ring top, cobalt	18	22	26
Eli Lilly & Co., Poison printed on panels, amber, 2"	12	18	24
F.S. & Co., on base, Poison vertically, ringtop, amber, 2.5"	15	25	35
R.C. Millings Bed Bug Poison, Charleston, clear, 6.5"	25	35	45
Rat Poison, printed on round bottle, clear or amethyst, 2.5"	35	45	55
Tincture Iodine, printed under skull and crossbones, sq., amber	13	18	23
Triloids printed on one panel, Poison on another, cobalt, 3.5"	14	20	25
Wyeth Poison, round ring base and top, cobalt, 2.5"	15	25	30

Pontil

	LOW	AVG.	HIGH
Bake's Dr., printed, tapered top, pale aqua, 5"	40	60	80
Balsam of Honey, printed, round bottle, ring top, aqua, 3"	40	50	60
Brown's, F., Ess. of Jamaica Ginger, Phila., oval, aqua, 5.5"	20	30	40
Cannington Shaw & Co., St. Helens, beading on shoulder	20	35	50
Cooke's Carmine Ink, printed, bell-shaped, ring top, aqua, 1.5"	30	35	40
Harrison's Columbia Ink, printed, round, ring top, cobalt, 4.5"	70	85	100
Hoover, Phila., 12 panels, ring top, light green	40	50	60
Pontil, Dolby's Criminate, printed, round, light ring top, 3.5"	40	50	60
Snuff, label, flare top, beveled corners, olive amber, 4.5"	25	35	45

Spirits

	LOW	AVG.	HIGH
Acker Merrall, label, A9 on bottom, amber, 11"	15	22	29
Belle of Nelson, label, whiskey, M.M. on bottom, clear, 12"	12	19	26

Cambridge Glass

The Cambridge Glass Co., located in Cambridge, OH, produced hand-finished glassware from 1904 till 1958. During the 1920s through the 1950s, Cambridge created "elegant" glassware that were veritable works of art. A triangle with a "C" inside was a mark used from the 1920s till 1936; thereafter a paper label was used for identification. Most Cambridge glassware is unmarked but is recognized by its etched patterns, of which "Rosepoint" is the most prevalent.

Rosepoint - Crystal

Ashtray, 2.5", sq.	$ 35
Ashtray, 4", oval	80
Basket, 3"	250
Basket, 6", 1 handled	225
Basket, 6", 2 handled	50
Bell, dinner	135
Bowl, 3", 4 ftd., nut	70
Bowl, 5", handled	40
Bowl, 5.5", nappy	45
Bowl, 5.5", 2 handled bonbon	35
Bowl, 6", bonbon, crimped	85
Bowl, 6", cereal	60
Bowl, 7", tab handled, ftd. bonbon	45
Bowl, 8", ram's head, sq.	300
Bowl, 8.5", rimmed soup	250
Bowl, 8.5", 3 part	150
Bowl, 9", 4 ftd.	200
Bowl, 9", ram's head	350
Bowl, 10", 4 tab ftd., flared	75
Bowl, 11", 4 ftd., oval	300
Butter, w/cover, round	175
Butter Dish, 1/4 lb	275
Candelabrum, 2 light w/bobeches/prisms	150
Candelabrum, 2 light	90
Candelabrum, 3 light	65
Candy Box, w/cover, 5", apple shape	800
Candy Box, w/cover, round	95
Celery Dish, 12"	50
Cheese and Cracker Set	110
Cigarette Box, w/cover	120
Coaster	50
Cocktail Shaker, metal top	150
Cocktail Shaker, 48 oz., glass stopper	180
Comport, 5"	40
Creamer/Sugar, ftd.	50
Cup/Saucer	45
Decanter, 32 oz., ball, w/stopper	350
Hat, 5"	110
Hurricane Lamp, w/prisms	300
Ice Bucket, chrome handle	150
Mayonnaise, 3 pieces	75
Oil, 2 oz., ball, w/stopper	75

Pickle Dish, 9" .... $ 60
Pitcher, 80 oz., Doulton 350
Pitcher, 60 oz., Martini 2000
Pitcher, 80 oz., ball (w/ or w/o ice lip) 200
Plate, 6", bread and butter 15
Plate, 6", 2 handled 25
Plate, 7.5"-8", salad 22
Plate, 9.5", crescent salad 225
Plate, 9.5", luncheon 50
Plate, 10.5", dinner 150
Plate, 11", 2 handled 60
Plate, 12", ftd. 100
Plate, 13", 4 ftd., torte 135
Plate, 13.5", rolled edge 85
Plate, 13.5", tab handled cake 75
Plate, 14", service 85
Plate, 14", torte 135
Punch Set, 15 pieces 4000
Relish, 5.5", 2 part, w/or w/o handle 35
Relish, 6.5", 3 part, w/or w/o handle 45
Relish, 7.5", 3 part, center handle 135
Relish, 8", 3 part, 3 handle 45
Relish, 10", 2 handled 70
Relish, 12", 5 part 75
Relish, 15", 4 part, handled 200
Salt and Pepper, pr. 80
Sandwich Tray, 11", center handle 145
Stem, 1 oz., brandy 100
Stem, 2 oz., sherry 50
Stem, 3 oz., cocktail 40
Stem, 3.5 oz., wine 60
Stem, 4.5 oz., claret 90
Stem, 6 oz., low or tall sherbet 25
Stem, 10 oz., water 40
Syrup, w/cover 400
Tray, 12", round 150
Tray for Sugar and Creamer 30
Tumbler, 2 oz., whiskey 100
Tumbler, 5 oz., straight side 50
Tumbler, 5 oz., ftd. juice 40
Tumbler, 10 oz., ftd. water 45
Tumbler, 12 oz., tall, ftd., ice tea 40
Urn, w/cover, 10"-12" 500
Vase, 5" 70
Vase, 7", ftd., Ivy Ball 250
Vase, 9", ftd., keyhole style 95
Vase, 10", cornucopia 185
Vase, 10", bud 95

Diane - Crystal

Bitters Bottle 150
Bowl, finger, w/liner 35

Bowl, 5", berry .... $ 25
Bowl, 6", 2 part relish 22
Bowl, 6", cereal 30
Bowl, 7", pickle 27
Bowl, 10", 4 ftd., flared 50
Bowl, 12", 3 part celery/relish 35
Bowl, 12", 4 ftd. flared 45
Butter Dish, round 135
Candlestick, 1 light, keyhole 25
Candlestick, 5" 20
Candlestick, 6", 2 light or 3 light 40
Candy Box, w/cover, round 85
Cocktail Shaker, metal or glass top 100
Comport, 5.5" 35
Creamer and Sugar 35
Cup and Saucer 30
Decanter, ftd. 175
Hurricane Lamp 185
Ice Bucket, w/chrome handle 190
Oil, 60 oz., w/stopper 125
Pitcher, ball shape 140
Pitcher, Doulton 300
Pitcher, Martini, rare 850
Plate, 6", bread and butter 8
Plate, 8", salad 15
Plate, 10.5", dinner 75
Plate, 14", torte 55
Platter, 13.5" 85
Salt and Pepper, pr. 35
Stem, 1 oz., cordial 65
Stem, 3 oz., cocktail 20
Stem, 3.5 oz., cocktail, 10", tall, rare 100
Stem, 4.5 oz., claret 30
Stem, 7 oz., low or tall sherbet 15
Stem, 11 oz., water 35
Tumbler, 5 oz., ftd. juice 30
Tumbler, 7 oz., Old Fashioned 45
Tumbler, 9 oz., water 20
Tumbler, 12 oz., ice tea 30
Vase, 9", keyhole 55
Vase, 10", bud 40
Vase, 13", flower 125

Wildflower - Crystal

Bowl, bonbon, 2 handled 25
Bowl, 3 part relish 20
Bowl, 4 ftd., 10" 45
Bowl, 2 handled, 11" 50
Bowl, 3 part, celery/relish, 12" 45
Bowl, 4 ftd., flared, 12" 50
Butter Dish, 5" 125
Candlestick, 5" 30

Candlestick, 2 light	$ 45
Candy Box, w/cover, round	65
Cocktail Shaker	80
Comport, 5.5"	50
Creamer and Sugar	35
Creamer and Sugar, individual	40
Cup/Saucer	30
Hat, 5"-6"	150
Hurricane Lamp	165
Ice Bucket, w/chrome handle	85
Oil, w/stopper, 6 oz.	85
Pitcher, ball, 80 oz.	145
Pitcher, Doulton	300
Plate, bread and butter, 6.5"	8
Plate, salad, 8"	20
Plate, dinner, 10.5"	80
Plate, cake, 2 handled, 13.5"	40
Plate, torte, 14"	45
Salt and Pepper, pr.	35
Stem, 1 oz., cordial	60
Stem, 3 oz., cocktail	25
Stem, 3.5 oz., wine	35
Stem, 6 oz., low or tall sherbet	20
Stem, 10 oz., water	30
Tray for Sugar and Creamer	20
Tumbler, 5 oz., juice	20
Tumbler, 10 oz., water	25
Tumbler, 12 oz., ice tea	30
Vase, 6"-8", ftd. flower	40
Vase, 9", keyhole	50
Vase, 10", bud	35
Vase, 13", ftd., flower	175

Carnival Glass

The turn-of-the-century craze for iridescent art glass spawned the birth of Taffeta (or Carnival) glass in 1905. Using mass production and new chemical techniques, Carnival glass was widely produced toward the end of the Art Nouveau period. Tastes changed, however, ushering in the streamlined Art Deco period. Though produced until 1930, by 1925 Carnival glass was sold by the trainload to fairs and carnivals and given out as prizes (hence, the name Carnival glass). Since the 1970s, Carnival glass has become a desired collectible. For further information see *The Official Price Guide to Glassware*, by Mark Pickvet, House of Collectibles, Random House, NY.

Patterns are given after each of the following entries.

	GREEN	MARIGOLD	BLUE	AMETHYST
Bowl, dia. 7" - 8.5", Acorn- Fenton	$ 30	$ 25	$ 30	$ 30
Bowl, 7" - 9", Apple Blossom-Dugan	42	37	42	42
Bowl, flat, dia. 10", Chrysanthemum-Fenton	50	35	50	—
Bowl, ftd, dia. 10", Chrysanthemum-Fenton	50	35	50	—
Bowl, Detroit, Elks-Fenton	330	—	330	330
Bowl, Parkersburg, Elks-Fenton	360	—	360	360
Candy Dish, Beaded Cable-Northwood	35	25	35	35
Plate, dia. 9", Acorn- Fenton	300	125	300	300
Plate, dia. 8.5", Apple Blossom-Dugan	70	48	70	70
Rose Bowl, Beaded Cable-Northwood	52	35	52	52
Tumbler, Banded Drape-Fenton	—	18	30	30
Water Pitcher, Banded Drape-Fenton	—	72	190	190

A selection of Carnival glass items including a molded grape pitcher (lower left). — Photo courtesy of George Kerrigan Photography.

Cut Glass

Cut glass features deep prismatic cutting in elaborate, often geometric designs. Developed during the 16th century in Bohemia, it remained popular until the invention of molded pressed glass in America about 1825. It enjoyed a revival during the Brilliant Period of cut glass in America from 1876-1916. The edges are sharp, refracting light clearly. It is thicker and heavier than most blown glass. Round shapes have a distinct bell tone when struck; however, if shaped like Massachusetts, it may sound like a diving helmet.

Making cut glass required patience and talent. Master craftsmen blew the finest 35-45% lead crystal or poured it into molds producing a shaped piece called a blank. These blanks measured from .25"-.5" thick, necessary for the deep cutting which distinguished this glass from later periods. The resulting product was exceedingly heavy. Cutting and polishing required four steps. First, the desired pattern was drawn on the blank with crayons or paint. Next, the deepest cuts were made by rough cutting, pressing the blank on an abrasive cutting wheel lubricated by a stream of water and sand. In the third step, the rough cuts were smoothed with a finer stone wheel and water. Finally, the craftsman polished or "colored" the piece on a wooden wheel with putty powder or pumice to produce the gleaming finish.

The prices here are for American cut glass made between 1880 and 1920. They represent an average range for the forms listed. Prices for some highly collected makers (e.g. Libbey and Hawkes) may go for much higher, depending on the piece. For further information see *The Official Price Guide to Glassware*, by Mark Pickvet, House of Collectibles, Random House, NY.

Left: Maple Glass Company brilliant period punch bowl on stand, diameter 15", $3500 at auction. —Photo courtesy of Northeast Auctions.

Above left to right: Two footed compotes; one quart pitcher.

	LOW	AVG.	HIGH
Basket, handled, 10"	$ 430	$ 455	$ 480
Bell	120	180	240
Bonbon, diamond shape, 6"	120	160	200
Bonbon, covered, 4.5"-5.5"	160	200	240
Bowl, 9"	110	185	260
Carafe, 10"	120	170	220
Celery Tray	80	145	210
Celery, upright	60	80	100
Champagne Glass	40	60	80
Claret Glass	50	75	100
Cologne Bottle, w/ stopper, 6"	60	150	240
Compote, 7"	80	120	160
Compote, 10"	140	200	260
Cordial Glass	50	55	60
Cream and Sugar	120	165	210
Cruet, 6"	60	95	130
Decanter, pt.	160	200	240
Decanter, pt., handled	200	240	280
Decanter, 1 qt.	400	600	800
Decanter, handled, 1 qt.	600	800	1000
Dish, cheese, covered	320	400	480
Dish, ice cream, 6"	220	270	320
Dish, shell form, 6"	160	200	240
Dish, sq., 8"	120	160	200
Dish, 4 section, 9"	160	200	240
Dish, 7"-8"	60	110	160
Finger Bowl	30	40	50
Fruit Bowl, 8"	80	120	160
Glass, water	40	50	60
Goblet	50	70	90
Inkwell, crystal	40	60	80
Jar, powder, covered, 4.5"-5.5"	120	160	200
Jar, tobacco, sterling top, 7"	160	200	240
Jug, whiskey, stoppered	280	340	400
Knife Rest, ball ends	40	50	60
Lemonade Mug	50	55	60
Lamp Base, 17"	480	600	720
Lamp, mushroom shade, 18"	600	800	1000
Mug	30	45	60
Nappy, 5"	50	65	80
Nappy, 8"	120	155	190
Nappy, handled, 5"	60	80	100
Pitcher, 1 pt.	120	155	190
Pitcher, 2 qt.	160	240	320
Pitcher, 1 qt. or 3 pt.	140	190	240
Platter, ice cream, oval, 13.5"	170	260	350
Powder Puff Box, covered, 4.5"-5.5"	80	100	120
Punch Bowl, on foot (2 part), 14"-15"	1200	1500	2000
Punch Bowl, single piece, 12"	290	505	720
Relish Dish, 7"	80	120	160
Salt, open, 2.5"	30	40	50
Shakers	80	120	160

Depression Glass

Colored glassware was machine-made during the late 1920s and early 1930s. The glass was available in ten-cent stores, given away at filling stations and theaters, and used for promotional purposes. There are over 80 Depression glass clubs that sponsor shows, with attendance in the thousands.

For more information on Depression glass see Mark Pickvet, *The Official Price Guide to Glassware* (House of Collectibles, Random House, NY), and Gene Florence, *Depression Glass*.

Adam

	PINK	GREEN
Bowl, 4.75"	$ 17	$ 16
Bowl, 5.75"	48	36
Bowl, 7.75"	25	26
Bowl, 9", w/ lid	60	100
Bowl, oval, 10"	25	32
Butter Dish, w/ lid	80	390
Cake Plate, 10" ftd.	20	28
Candlesticks, 4" pr.	87	117
Coaster, 3.25"	26	10
Creamer/Sugar	35	40
Cup/Saucer	32	30
Grill Plate, 9"	10	18
Jar, candy, w/ lid, 2.5"	86	100
Lamp	272	245
Pitcher, 8", 1 qt.	42	56
Plate, 6"	6	6
Plate, 7.75" sq.	13	15
Plate, 9" sq.	25	25
Platter, 11.75"	17	20
Relish Tray, 8"	15	20
Salt/Pepper, 4" ftd.	66	110
Sherbet, 3"	28	37
Tumbler, 4.5"	28	25
Tumbler, 5.25"	70	50
Vase, 7.5"	247	50

American Sweetheart

	PINK	WHITE	RED	BLUE	CREMEX
Bowl, 6"	$ 16	$ 15	—	—	—
Bowl, 6"	—	—	$ 250	$ 320	$ 15
Bowl, 9"	28	55	—	—	—
Bowl, 9"	—	—	300	355	58
Bowl, 18"	—	400	—	—	—
Bowl, 18"	—	—	1100	1270	—
Chop Plate, 11"	18	15	—	—	—
Creamer/Sugar	25	10	—	—	—
Creamer/Sugar	—	—	195	242	226
Cup/Saucer	17	15	—	—	—
Cup/Saucer	—	—	135	173	—
Pitcher, 2 qt.	700	—	—	—	—
Plate, 6"	—	—	—	25	—

	PINK	WHITE	RED	BLUE	CREMEX
Plate, 6"-7"	$ 3	$ 5	—	—	—
Plate, 8"	12	11	—	—	—
Plate, 8"	—	—	$ 70	$ 115	—
Plate, 9"-10"	20	10	—	—	—
Plate, 9"-10"	—	—	110	155	—
Platter, 12" round	15	15	—	—	—
Platter, 12" round	—	—	200	220	—
Platter, oval, 13"	30	50	—	—	—
Platter, oval, 13"	—	—	—	—	—
Salt/Pepper, ftd.	400	340	—	—	—
Server, 15.5"	—	250	—	—	—
Server, 15.5"	—	—	370	520	—
Server, 3 tier	—	260	—	—	—
Server, 3 tier	—	—	740	840	—
Sherbet, 4" ftd.	15	23	—	—	—
Sherbet, 4.25" ftd.	—	—	—	—	—
Soup Bowl, 4.5"	43	50	—	—	—
Soup Plate, 7.5"	65	—	—	—	—
Soup Plate, 9.5"	50	60	—	—	—
Tumbler, 3"-4", 5-9 oz.	61	—	—	—	—
Tumbler, 4.5", 10 oz.	90	—	—	—	—
Vegetable, oval, 11"	45	50	—	—	—

Anniversary

	CRYSTAL	PINK
Bowl, 5"	$ 2	$ 5
Bowl, 9"	12	10
Butter Dish, w/ lid	42	80
Cake Plate, w/ lid	17	23
Candlestick, 5" pr.	23	—
Creamer/Sugar, w/ lid	13	25
Cup/Saucer	5	11
Dish, 3 ftd.	5	12
Jar, candy, w/ lid	31	48
Pickle Dish, 9"	5	11
Plate, 6.25"	2	3
Plate, 9"	6	8
Relish Tray, 8"	8	11
Server, 12.5"	8	12
Sherbet, ftd.	5	8
Soup Plate, 7.5"	6	15
Vase, 6.5"	11	16
Wall Pocket	16	25
Wine Glass, 2.5 oz.	8	16

Aurora

	DARK BLUE	PINK
Bowl, 4.5"	$ 17	$ 15
Bowl, 5.5"	8	6
Creamer, 4.5"	15	10
Cup/Saucer	15	10

	DARK BLUE	PINK
Plate, 6.5"	$ 6	$ 5
Tumbler, 4.75", 10 oz.	16	12

Block Optic

	GREEN	YELLOW	PINK
Bowl, 4"-5"	$ 10	$ 20	$ 10
Bowl, 7"-9"	22	30	17
Butter Dish, w/ lid	66	75	—
Butter Tub, open	40	60	—
Candlesticks, low, pr.	60	70	—
Comport, 4" w.	20	40	—
Creamer/Sugar	31	32	27
Cup/Saucer	21	23	16
Goblet, 9 oz.	27	28	21
Grill Plate, 9"	10	23	17
Ice Bucket	40	50	—
Jar, candy, w/ lid	50	68	56
Mug	45	—	—
Pitcher, 7"-8", 2 qt.	70	80	—
Pitcher, 8.5", 3 qt.	45	47	—
Plate, 6"	2	3	2
Plate, 8"	5	7	5
Plate, 9"-10"	21	46	27
Salt/Pepper	43	95	85
Server, center handle	61	65	—
Sherbet, 3"-5"	11	15	10
Tumbler, 5-10 oz.	21	25	25
Wine Glass, 4.5"	27	21	—

Bubble, Bull's Eye, Provincial

	CRYSTAL	DK. GREEN	LT. BLUE	DK. RED
Bowl, 4"-5"	$ 5	$ 5	$ 12	$ 7
Bowl, 8"-9"	8	8	15	—
Creamer/Sugar	6	6	50	—
Cup/Saucer	3	3	6	10
Grill Plate, 9.5"	—	—	16	—
Pitcher, 2 qt., w/ lip	65	—	—	58
Plate, 6.75"	2	2	5	—
Plate, 9.5"	5	5	7	10
Platter, oval, 12"	8	8	16	—
Server, 2 tier	10	10	—	25
Soup Plate, 7.75"	6	6	13	—
Tumbler, 6-12 oz.	10	10	—	12
Tumbler, 16 oz.	12	12	—	25

Cameo, Dancing Girl, Ballerina

	GREEN	YELLOW	PINK	CRYSTAL
Bowl, cereal, 5.5"	$ 38	$ 36	—	$ 10
Bowl, cream soup, 4.75"	70	—	—	—
Bowl, sauce, 4.25"	—	—	—	7
Bowl, 7"-8"	45	—	$ 180	—

	GREEN	YELLOW	PINK	CRYSTAL
Bowl, 3 ftd., 11"	$ 65	$ 100	$ 35	—
Butter Dish, w/ lid	225	1000	—	—
Butter, open, 3" ht.	175	—	680	$ 280
Cake Plate, 10", 3 ftd.	22	—	—	—
Cake Plate, 10.5", flat	110	—	—	—
Candlesticks, pr., 4"	100	—	—	—
Comport, 5" w.	20	—	252	—
Cookie Jar, w/ lid	63	—	—	—
Creamer/Sugar, 3"-4"	46	31	167	—
Cup/Saucer	21	15	122	15
Decanter, w/ stopper, 10"	140	—	—	240
Goblet, 3.5"	300	—	—	—
Goblet, 4"-6"	50	—	222	—
Grill Plate, 10"-11"	12	11	—	57
Jam Jar, w/ lid, 2"	150	—	—	160
Jar, candy, w/ lid	100	82	600	—
Pitcher, 5.75", 1.5 pt.	223	293	—	—
Pitcher, 6", 1 qt.	65	—	—	—
Pitcher, 8.5", 56 oz.	56	—	1700	520
Plate, 6"	5	3	77	3
Plate, 7"-8"	13	5	30	6
Plate, 8.5" sq.	38	140	—	—
Plate, 9"-10"	18	11	53	50
Platter, closed handles, 12"	25	22	—	—
Relish Tray, 7.5" ftd., 3 part	36	93	—	—
Salt/Pepper, pr.	80	—	860	—
Server, center handle	3200	—	—	—
Sherbet, 3"	17	25	42	—
Sherbet, 5"	38	37	85	—
Soup Plate, 9"	45	—	—	—
Tumbler, 3 oz., ftd.	70	—	130	—
Tumbler, 5.25", 15 oz.	68	—	150	—
Tumbler, 6.38", 15 oz., ftd.	400	—	—	—
Tumbler, 9-11 oz., flat	41	45	125	13
Vase, 5.75"	200	—	—	—
Vase, 8"	25	—	—	—
Vegetable, oval, 10"	23	35	—	—

Charm (Square)

	JADE-ITE		AZUR-ITE	
	LOW	HIGH	LOW	HIGH
Bowl, 4.75"	$ 6	$ 9	$ 4	$ 6
Bowl, 6", Soup	10	15	8	12
Bowl, 8", Salad	10	15	8	12
Creamer/Sugar	15	20	10	15
Cup/Saucer	6	9	4	7
Plate, Salad, 6.25"	4	6	3	5
Plate, Dinner, 10"	15	20	12	16
Plate, Luncheon, 8.25"	10	12	8	10
Platter (Rectangular), 12"	15	20	12	15

Cherry Blossom

	PINK	GREEN	DELPHITE
Bowl, 4.75"	$ 12	$ 16	$ 15
Bowl, 5.75"	36	35	—
Bowl, 8.5"	22	25	55
Bowl, 2 handled, 9"	10	25	20
Bowl, 10.5", 3 ftd.	56	65	—
Butter Dish, w/ lid	88	115	—
Cake Plate, 3 ftd., 10.25"	23	20	—
Coaster	15	16	—
Creamer/Sugar	45	50	75
Cup/Saucer	22	25	25
Grill Plate, 10"	—	66	—
Grill Plate, 9"	30	30	—
Mug, 7 oz.	265	230	—
Pitcher, 7"-8", 1 qt.	52	75	100
Pitcher, 8", 42 oz.	52	67	—
Plate, 6"	7	7	15
Plate, 7"	20	25	—
Plate, 9"	18	10	17
Platter, 13"	51	55	—
Platter, oval, 11"	20	33	48
Platter, oval, 9"	1000	—	—
Salt/Pepper, scalloped	1700	1000	—
Server, 10.5"	18	22	23
Sherbet	16	20	20
Soup Plate, 7.75"	63	65	—
Tumbler, 3.75", 4 oz.	18	20	25
Tumbler, 4"-5", 8-9 oz.	26	35	—
Tumbler, 5", 12 oz.	58	70	—
Vegetable, oval, 9"	28	30	65

Cube, Cubist

	PINK	GREEN
Bowl, 4.5"	$ 7	$ 8
Bowl, 6.5"	12	18
Butter Dish, w/ lid	75	85
Coaster, 3.25"	6	8
Creamer/Sugar, w/ lid, 3"	28	30
Cup/Saucer	10	13
Jar, candy, w/ lid, 6.5"	35	45
Pitcher, 8.75", 3 pt.	215	245
Plate, 6"	3	3
Plate, 8"	5	7
Powder Jar, w/ lid, 3 ftd.	20	25
Salt/Pepper, pr.	42	45
Sherbet, ftd.	8	11
Tumbler, 4", 9 oz.	50	65

English Hobnail

	PINK	GREEN	CRYSTAL	AMBER
Ashtray	$ 30	$ 30	$ 5	$ 5

	PINK	GREEN	CRYSTAL	AMBER
Bowl, 2 handled, 8"	$ 62	$ 62	$ 35	$ 35
Bowl, 4"-5"	17	17	10	10
Bowl, 6"	17	17	10	10
Bowl, 8"	27	27	20	20
Candlesticks, 3.5" pr.	42	42	16	16
Candlesticks, 8.5" pr.	73	73	50	50
Candy, w/ lid, 3 ftd.	90	90	30	30
Celery Dish, 9"-12"	30	30	18	18
Cigarette Box	40	40	20	20
Cologne Bottle	45	45	20	20
Cordial Glass, 1 oz.	26	26	15	15
Creamer/Sugar	48	48	18	18
Cup/Saucer	20	20	15	15
Cup/Saucer, demitasse	47	47	25	25
Decanter, 20 oz., w/ stopper	92	92	55	55
Egg Cup	43	43	12	12
Goblet, 6.25", 8 oz.	30	30	10	10
Grapefruit, 6.5" flange	22	22	12	12
Lamp, 6.25"	82	82	35	35
Lamp, 9.25"	185	185	45	45
Marmalade, w/ lid	58	58	20	20
Nappies, 11"-12"	57	57	30	30
Pitcher, 1 qt.	215	215	50	50
Pitcher, 1.5 pt.	213	213	60	60
Pitcher, 2 qt., straight	300	300	80	80
Plate, 10"	35	35	14	14
Plate, 5"-7"	6	6	8	8
Plate, 8"	13	13	8	8
Relish Tray, 8"-12"	28	28	22	22
Salt/Pepper, pr.	125	125	25	25
Sherbet	20	20	15	15
Shot Glass	20	20	10	10
Soup Bowl	25	25	15	15
Tumbler, 5-13 oz.	25	25	12	12
Vase	120	120	35	35
Wine Glass, 2-5 oz.	22	22	10	10

Fire-King

RESTAURANT WARE

	JADE-ITE	
	LOW	HIGH
Bowl, 4"	$ 3	$ 5
Bowl, 5"	8	10
Cup/Saucer (3 Styles)	6	10
Egg Cup	5	10
Mug, 8oz	8	10
Plate, 10", dinner	8	12
Plate, 10", grill (3 part)	8	12
Plate, 4", bread and butter	3	5
Plate, 6", salad	4	6
Plate, divided, 5 part	15	25
Platter, 10"	15	25

	JADE-ITE	
	LOW	HIGH
Platter, 12"	$ 20	$ 30
Soup, flanged rim	25	45

JANE RAY

	JADE-ITE	
	LOW	HIGH
Bowl, 4.25"	$ 3	$ 5
Bowl, 5", oatmeal	5	8
Bowl, 7.5", flat soup	10	15
Bowl, 8", round vegetable	10	15
Creamer/Sugar, w/lid	15	20
Cup/Saucer	3	5
Cup/Saucer, demitasse	30	45
Plate, dinner, 9"	5	7
Plate, salad, 7.75"	3	5
Platter, oval, 12"	10	15

TURQUOISE BLUE

	JADE-ITE	
	LOW	HIGH
Ashtray, 3.5"	$ 3	$ 5
Ashtray, 4.5"	5	8
Ashtray, 5.75"	8	12
Batter Bowl	150	200
Bowl, 4.25", Berry	4	7
Bowl, 5", Cereal	5	8
Bowl, 6.5", Soup	10	15
Bowl, 8", Vegetable	10	15
Creamer/Sugar	8	12
Egg Plate	10	15
Mixing Bowl, round, 1 qt	8	12
Mixing Bowl, round, 2 qt	8	12
Mixing Bowl, round, 3 qt	10	15
Mixing Bowl, round, 4 qt	20	25
Mixing Bowl, teardrop, 1 pt	10	15
Mixing Bowl, teardrop, 1 qt	12	17
Mixing Bowl, teardrop, 2 qt	15	20
Mixing Bowl, teardrop, 3 qt	18	22
Mug	7	10
Plate, 10"	20	25
Plate, Bread and Butter, 6"	5	8
Plate, Dinner, 9"	5	7
Plate, Salad, 7"	7	10
Relish Tray, 3 part	8	12
Snack Set (plate w/cup)	6	10

Florintine (#1)

	GREEN	YELLOW	PINK	BLUE
Ashtray, 5.5"	$ 28	$ 45	$ 42	—
Bowl, 5"	12	10	15	$ 25
Bowl, 6"	15	20	22	—

	GREEN	YELLOW	PINK	BLUE
Bowl, 8.5"	$ 25	$ 37	$ 36	—
Butter Dish, w/ lid	180	225	170	—
Coaster/Ashtray, 3.75"	23	26	35	—
Creamer/Sugar, w/ lid	47	55	53	—
Creamer/Sugar, ruffled	65	—	77	$ 130
Cup/Saucer	13	10	17	100
Grill Plate, 10"	12	16	10	—
Pitcher, 6.5", 1 qt., ftd.	50	65	65	900
Pitcher, 7.5", 1.5 qt., flat	60	233	140	—
Plate, 6"	5	6	6	—
Plate, 8.5"	10	15	15	—
Plate, 10"	17	25	26	—
Platter, oval, 11.5"	16	21	25	—
Salt/Pepper, ftd.	55	60	76	—
Sherbet, 3 oz. ftd.	10	15	16	—
Tumbler, 3"-4", 5 oz. ftd.	10	25	23	—
Tumbler, 10-12 oz. ftd.	33	30	30	—
Tumbler, 5.25", 9 oz.	—	—	82	—
Vegetable, oval, 9.5", w/ lid	57	60	65	—

Florintine (#2)

	GREEN	YELLOW	PINK	BLUE
Bowl, 4.5"	$ 15	$ 16	$ 20	—
Bowl, 5.5"	33	25	43	—
Bowl, 6"	20	23	38	—
Bowl, 8"	26	31	31	—
Bowl, 9"	31	—	—	—
Butter Dish, w/ lid	150	—	210	—
Candlesticks, 2.75" pr.	52	—	83	—
Candy Dish, w/ lid	125	165	215	—
Coaster, 3.25"	15	22	27	—
Coaster, 3.75"	23	—	25	—
Coaster, 5.5"	25	—	47	—
Comport, 3.5" ruffled	20	10	28	$ 75
Creamer/Sugar, w/ lid	55	—	60	—
Cream Soup, 5"	15	15	23	55
Cup/Saucer	13	—	16	—
Custard Cup	73	—	115	—
Gravy Boat, w/ stand	—	—	115	—
Grill Plate, 10.25"	11	—	15	—
Parfait, 6"	35	—	70	—
Pitcher, 6.25", 1.5 pt., cone ft.	—	—	150	—
Pitcher, 7.5", 1.75 pt., cone ft.	32	—	32	—
Pitcher, 7.5", 1.5 qt.	75	160	245	—
Pitcher, 8", 4.75 pt.	125	320	280	—
Plate, 6", sherbet	5	—	7	—
Plate, 6.25", indented	22	—	30	—
Plate, 8.5"	10	10	12	—
Plate, 10"	18	22	18	—
Platter, oval, 11"	17	18	10	—
Relish Tray, 10"	22	26	28	—

	GREEN	YELLOW	PINK	BLUE
Salt/Pepper, pr.	$ 56	—	$ 65	—
Sherbet, ftd.	10	—	13	—
Soup Plate, 7.5"	—	—	86	—
Tumbler, 3"-4", 5-9 oz.	16	$ 11	26	$ 87
Tumbler, 5", 12 oz.	35	—	48	—
Vegetable, oval, 9" w/ lid	56	—	75	—

Flower Garden w/ Butterflies

	GREEN	YELLOW	PINK	BLUE
Candlesticks, 4" pr.	$ 83	$ 98	$ 150	$ 100
Candlesticks, 8" pr.	150	160	235	150
Candy, w/ lid, 6"-7.5"	167	180	265	175
Candy, w/ lid, heart-form	—	540	800	1300
Cologne Bottle, 7.5"	—	300	330	250
Comport, 3" ht.	28	35	45	30
Comport, 5"-7" ht.	90	116	135	95
Creamer/Sugar	—	210	—	135
Cup/Saucer	—	163	—	90
Plate, 7"-8"	26	30	43	30
Plate, 10"	55	52	73	50
Platter 10"-12"	70	100	135	—
Powder Jar, 6"-7.5", ftd.	111	137	200	185
Server, center handle	80	100	135	100
Tumbler, 7.5 oz.	155	—	—	—
Vase, 6.25"	126	150	180	130
Vase, 10.5"	—	172	246	200

Forest Green
GREEN

	LOW	HIGH
Ashtray	$ 4	$ 5
Bowl, 5"-7.5"	7	10
Creamer/Sugar	10	15
Cup/Saucer	5	8
Mixing Bowl	8	12
Pitcher, 1.5 pt.	18	22
Pitcher, 3 qt.	25	35
Plate, 6.5"	2	3
Plate, 8.5"	5	7
Plate, 10"	25	40
Platter, rect.	15	20
Punch Bowl, w/ stand	30	45
Punch Cup	2	3
Tumbler, 5-10 oz.	4	6
Vase, 4"-9"	5	7

Fortune

	PINK	CRYSTAL
Bowl, 4"-5"	$ 6	$ 7
Bowl, 8"	15	14
Candy Dish, w/ lid	25	22

	PINK	CRYSTAL
Cup/Saucer	$ 10	$ 8
Plate, 6"	5	4
Plate, 8"	10	8
Tumbler, 3.5"-4"	7	6

Georgian

	GREEN	CRYSTAL
Bowl, 4.5"	$ 5	$ 7
Bowl, 5.75"	20	25
Bowl, 6.5"	50	70
Bowl, 7.5"	50	65
Butter Dish, w/ lid	75	100
Creamer/Sugar, 3", w/ lid	40	50
Creamer/Sugar, 4", w/ lid	100	115
Cup/Saucer	12	17
Plate, 6"	4	5
Plate, 8"	7	10
Plate, 9"	20	25
Platter, 11.5"	60	75
Sherbet	10	12
Tumbler, 4", 9 oz.	45	55
Tumbler, 5.25", 12 oz.	80	120
Vegetable, oval, 9"	60	75

Hobnail

	PINK	CRYSTAL
Bowl, 5"-7"	$ 7	$ 5
Cup/Saucer	6	6
Creamer/Sugar	12	10
Decanter, w/ stopper, 1 qt.	25	—
Goblet, 10-13 oz.	10	—
Pitcher, 1 pt.	22	—
Pitcher, 1.5 qt.	40	33
Plate, 6"	2	2
Plate, 8.5"	5	3
Sherbet	5	5
Shot Glass	6	—
Tumbler, 3-15 oz.	8	—

Holiday

	PINK	CRYSTAL
Bowl, 5"	$ 10	$ 12
Bowl, 8.5"	25	30
Bowl, 11"	80	110
Butter Dish, w/ lid	50	60
Cake Plate, 10.5", 3 ftd.	75	100
Candlesticks, 3" pr.	75	100
Chop Plate, 13.75"	100	120
Creamer/Sugar, w/ lid, ftd.	30	40
Cup/Saucer	12	18
Pitcher, 4.75", 1 pt.	70	90

	PINK	CRYSTAL
Pitcher, 6.75", 3 pt.	$ 40	$ 50
Plate, 6"	5	7
Plate, 9"	15	20
Platter, 10.5"-11.5"	17	22
Sherbet	8	12
Soup Plate, 8"	35	45
Tumbler, 4", 10 oz.	35	40
Tumbler, 6", ftd.	100	120
Vegetable, oval, 9.5"	20	25

Jade-Ite

	LOW	HIGH
Batter Bowl	$ 10	$ 15
Chili Bowl	5	10
Milk Pitcher, plain	15	25
Milk Pitcher, raised hobs and spirals	50	75
Mixing Bowl, banded rim, 6"	6	10
Mixing Bowl, banded rim, 7.25"	8	12
Mixing Bowl, banded rim, 8.5"	10	15
Mixing Bowl, beaded rim, 4.5"	5	8
Mixing Bowl, beaded rim, 6"	8	10
Mixing Bowl, beaded rim, 7.25"	10	12
Mixing Bowl, round, 1 qt.	5	8
Mixing Bowl, round, 2 qt.	6	10
Mixing Bowl, round, 3 qt.	8	12
Mixing Bowl, round, 4 qt.	10	15
Mixing Bowl, swirl, 5" (rare)	25	30
Mixing Bowl, swirl, 6"	5	8
Mixing Bowl, swirl, 7"	8	12
Mixing Bowl, swirl, 8"	9	13
Mixing Bowl, swirl, 9"	10	15
Mixing Bowl, teardrop, 1 pt.	10	15
Mixing Bowl, teardrop, 1 qt.	12	18
Mixing Bowl, teardrop, 2 qt.	20	25
Mixing Bowl, teardrop, 3 qt.	25	30
Pitcher, 2 qt., ball-shaped	150	200

Lorain

	CRYSTAL	GREEN	YELLOW
Bowl, 6"	$ 37	$ 40	$ 75
Bowl, 7.25"	55	60	75
Bowl, 8"	100	115	185
Creamer/Sugar	37	40	48
Cup/Saucer	22	25	28
Plate, 5.5"	7	9	11
Plate, 8"	13	15	18
Plate, 10"	46	50	58
Platter, 11.5"	28	30	52
Relish Tray, 8", 4 part	25	27	30
Sherbet, ftd.	25	28	36
Tumbler, 4.75", 9 oz., ftd.	28	30	30
Vegetable, oval, 10"	47	55	70

Madrid

	AMBER	PINK	GREEN	BLUE
Ashtray, 6" sq.	$ 220	—	$ 130	—
Bowl, 8"-9.5"	22	$ 33	25	$40
Butter Dish, w/ lid	87	—	115	—
Cake Plate, 11.25"	16	16	27	—
Candlesticks, 2.25" pr.	28	23	—	—
Coaster, hot dish	45	—	50	—
Console, low, 11"	10	13	—	—
Cookie Jar, w/ lid	52	45	—	—
Creamer/Sugar, w/ lid	50	—	65	130
Cream Soup, 4.75"	16	—	—	—
Cup/Saucer	13	15	17	27
Gravy Boat, w/ stand	1600	—	—	—
Grill Plate, 10.5"	15	—	25	—
Jam Dish, 7"	20	—	23	35
Lazy Susan, w/ 7 dishes	800	—	—	—
Mold	15	—	—	—
Pitcher, 5.5", 1 qt.	40	—	—	—
Pitcher, 8", 2 qt.	55	60	175	175
Plate, 6"	5	6	5	11
Plate, 7.5"	15	15	13	23
Plate, 9"	10	11	12	23
Plate, 10.5"	45	—	47	80
Platter, oval, 11.5"	10	15	21	20
Relish Dish, 5"	10	10	10	13
Relish Tray, 10.25"	15	15	18	—
Salt/Pepper, pr.	65	—	90	168
Sherbet	11	—	13	16
Soup Plate, 7"	15	—	18	20
Tumbler, 4"-5.5", 5-12 oz.	27	10	42	33
Tumbler, 4", 5 oz., ftd.	36	—	50	—
Tumbler, 5.25", 10 oz. ftd.	33	—	40	—
Vegetable, oval, 10"	20	10	25	36

Miss American

	CRYSTAL	PINK	GREEN	RED
Bowl, 4"-6"	$ 11	$ 18	$ 13	—
Bowl, 8", curved in rim	57	83	—	$ 500
Bowl, 8.75", straight deep	37	62	—	—
Butter Dish, w/ lid	240	600	—	—
Cake Plate, 12"	26	40	—	—
Celery Dish, 10.5"	13	25	—	—
Coaster, 5.75"	17	27	—	—
Compote, 5"	18	30	—	—
Creamer/Sugar	25	46	—	450
Cup/Saucer	18	32	28	—
Goblet, 4"-6", 3-10 oz.	20	65	—	265
Grill Plate, 10.25"	12	22	—	—
Jar, candy, w/ lid, 11.5"	70	143	—	—
Pitcher, 8", 2 qt.	60	130	—	—
Plate, 5.75"	5	10	8	—

	CRYSTAL	PINK	GREEN	RED
Plate, 8.5"	$ 10	$ 21	$ 13	$ 100
Plate 10.25"	15	28	—	—
Platter, oval, 12.25"	18	27	—	—
Relish Tray, 8.75", 4 part	15	21	—	—
Relish Tray, 11.75", round divided	20	200	—	—
Salt/Pepper, pr.	42	71	430	—
Sherbet	11	17	—	—
Tumbler, 4", 5 oz.	21	57	—	—
Tumbler, 4.5", 10 oz.	21	30	22	—
Tumbler, 5.75", 14 oz.	37	72	—	—
Vegetable, oval, 10"	18	25	—	—

Modernstone

	COBALT	AMETHYST	FIRED COLORS
Ashtray, 7.75"	$ 140	—	—
Bowl, 5"	21	$ 11	$ 2
Bowl, 6.5"	62	43	$ 5
Bowl, 8.75"	38	32	10
Butter Dish, w/ lid	100	—	—
Cheese Dish, w/ lid	250	—	—
Creamer/Sugar	25	20	10
Cream Soup, 5"	10	17	—
Cup/Saucer	17	15	5
Custard Cup	18	15	—
Plate, 6"	6	5	1
Plate, 7"-8"	8	8	3
Plate, 9"	15	11	6
Plate, 10.5"	27	21	6
Platter, oval, 11"-12"	47	25	12
Salt/Pepper, pr.	48	46	23
Sherbet	13	12	6
Shot Glass	23	—	—
Soup Plate	60	57	7
Tumbler, 5-9 oz.	25	26	8
Tumbler, 12 oz.	85	60	—

Moonstone

	OPALESCENT
Bowl, 5"-7"	$ 12
Bowl, 9.5" crimped	22
Bowl, cloverleaf	15
Bud Vase, 5.5"	16
Candleholder, pr.	25
Creamer/Sugar	10
Cup/Saucer	15
Goblet, 10 oz.	25
Jar, candy, w/ lid, 6"	30
Plate, 6"	5
Plate, 8"	13
Plate, 10"	25
Powder Box, w/ lid, 4.75"	28

OPALESCENT

Relish Tray, 8"	$ 12
Soup Plate, 8"	13
Sherbet, ftd.	10

Oven Glass Fire-King

BLUE

	LOW	HIGH
Baker, 1 pt.	$ 6	$ 8
Baker, 1 qt.	8	12
Baker, 1.5 qt.	15	20
Baker, 2 qt.	18	25
Bowl, 4"-5.5"	15	25
Casserole, 1-4 pt., w/ knob lid	18	25
Casserole, 1 qt., pie plate lid	22	28
Casserole, 1.5" qt., pie plate lid	25	30
Casserole, 2 qt., pie plate lid	30	35
Casserole, 10 oz., tab handle lid	20	25
Custard Cup, 5-6 oz.	5	7
Hot Plate, tab handles	18	22
Leftover, w/ lid, 5"-9"	13	25
Loaf Pan, 9"	20	25
Measuring Cup, 8 oz., no spout	50	65
Measuring Cup, 8 oz., w/ spout	20	25
Measuring Cup, 16 oz.	20	25
Mug, 7 oz.	30	35
Nurser, 4-8 oz.	18	25
Pie Plate, 8"-9.5"	15	20
Pie Plate, 10.5" juice saver	60	75
Roaster, 8.75"	40	50
Roaster, 10.5"	60	75
Table Server, tab handles	18	22
Utility Bowl, 7"-10"	17	22
Utility Pan, 8" x 12.5"	10	15

Patrician

	AMBER	PINK	GREEN
Bowl, 5"	$ 12	$ 17	$ 13
Bowl, 6"	28	28	20
Bowl, 8.5"	47	28	20
Butter Dish, w/ lid	110	356	162
Cookie Jar, w/ lid	96	—	475
Creamer/Sugar, w/ lid	65	95	92
Cream Soup, 4.75"	16	25	28
Cup/Saucer	16	22	23
Grill Plate, 10.5"	15	15	16
Jam Dish	25	36	45
Pitcher, 8", 2.25 qt.	110	135	125
Plate, 6"	11	7	8
Plate, 7.5"	18	21	17
Plate, 9"	13	12	12
Plate, 10.5"	10	25	45

	AMBER	PINK	GREEN
Platter, oval, 11.5"	$ 10	$ 18	$ 21
Salt/Pepper, pr.	72	100	82
Sherbet	12	15	13
Tumbler, 4"-5.5", 5-14 oz.	35	37	35
Tumbler, 5.25", 8 oz., ftd.	47	—	66
Vegetable, oval, 10"	20	25	27

Patrick

	PINK	YELLOW
Bowl, 9", w/ handle	$ 35	$ 30
Bowl, 11"	35	32
Candlesticks, pr.	45	40
Candy Dish, 3 ftd.	50	45
Cheese Set	55	50
Creamer/Sugar	35	30
Cup/Saucer	18	15
Goblet, 4"-5"	25	20
Goblet, 6", 10 oz.	35	32
Plate, 7"-8"	10	8
Sherbet, 4.75"	22	20
Tray, 11"	37	35

Princess

	GREEN	PINK	YELLOW
Ashtray, 4.5"	$ 92	$ 95	$ 115
Bowl, 4.5"-5"	30	25	36
Bowl, 9" octagon	35	26	110
Butter Dish, w/ lid	92	120	700
Cake Stand, 10"	23	21	—
Candy Dish, w/ lid	62	70	—
Coaster	37	83	125
Cookie Jar, w/ lid	65	75	—
Creamer/Sugar, w/ lid	50	46	40
Cup/Saucer	18	17	16
Grill Plate, 9"	16	11	10
Pitcher, 6", 1 qt.	61	46	825
Pitcher, 7.5", 1.5 pt., ftd.	700	685	—
Pitcher, 8", 2 qt.	56	58	90
Plate, 6"	10	6	7
Plate, 8"	13	11	12
Plate, 9"	31	20	10
Plate, 11.5"	18	13	15
Platter, 12"	22	18	48
Relish Tray, 7.5", divided	31	21	81
Relish Tray, 7.5", plain	100	—	185
Salt/Pepper, pr.	70	53	73
Sherbet, ftd.	22	21	42
Tumbler, 3"-4", 5-9 oz.	35	28	32
Tumbler, 5.25", 10-13 oz.	40	26	30
Tumbler, 4.75", 9 oz. sq., ftd.	83	70	—
Tumbler, 6.5", 12.5 oz., ftd.	92	65	126

	GREEN	PINK	YELLOW
Vase, 8"	$ 36	$ 28	—
Vegetable, oval, 10"	28	25	$ 60

Royal Ruby

	LOW	HIGH
Ashtray, 4.5", sq.	$ 3	$ 5
Bowl, 10", deep	30	40
Bowl, 11.5", salad	25	30
Bowl, 4.25, berry	3	5
Bowl, 5.25"	8	12
Bowl, 7.5", soup	9	12
Bowl, 8.5", large berry	12	17
Card Holder	45	55
Creamer/Sugar, flat	10	15
Creamer/Sugar, ftd.	15	20
Creamer/Sugar, w/lid	15	20
Cup/Saucer, round or sq.	6	9
Goblet, ball stem	5	10
Pitcher, 3 qt., silted	30	45
Pitcher, 3 qt., upright	40	60
Pitcher, 42 oz., tilted or upright	30	45
Plate, 13.75"	20	30
Plate, 6.5", sherbet	2	4
Plate, 7", salad	3	5
Plate, 7.75", luncheon	4	7
Plate, 9-9.25", dinner	8	12
Punch Bowl, w/stand	65	85
Punch Cup	2	4
Sherbet, ftd.	5	8
Tumbler, 13 oz., ice tea	12	15
Tumbler, 2.5", ftd. wine	8	12
Tumbler, 3.5, cocktail	8	12
Tumbler, 5 oz., juice	5	8
Tumbler, 9 oz., water	5	8
Vase, 4", ball-shaped	3	5
Vase, 6.5"	4	8
Vase, 9"	12	15

Sandwich (Anchor Hocking)

	CRYSTAL	AMBER	RED	DK GREEN
Bowl, 5"	$ 5	$ 5	$ 16	$30
Bowl, 6.5"	11	10	35	45
Bowl, 7"-8"	12	12	45	60
Bowl, 9"	26	25	—	—
Butter Dish, w/ lid	50	—	—	—
Cookie Jar, w/ lid	40	30	—	—
Cookie Jar, no lid	—	—	—	20
Creamer/Sugar	28	20	—	45
Cup/Saucer	5	5	—	20
Custard Cup, w/ liner	16	5	—	5
Pitcher, 2 qt.	75	—	—	350
Plate, 7"	12	—	—	—

	CRYSTAL	AMBER	RED	DK GREEN
Plate, 9"	$ 17	$ 10	—	$ 90
Plate, 12"	13	15	—	—
Punch Bowl, w/ stand	40	—	—	—
Punch Cup	2	—	—	—
Sherbet	11	—	—	—
Tumbler, 3-5 oz.	10	—	—	5
Tumbler, 9 oz.	10	—	—	6
Tumbler, 9 oz., ftd.	27	125	—	—

Sandwich (Indiana Glass Co.)

	PINK & GREEN	BLUE	RED
Bowl, 4"-6"	$ 6	—	$ 2
Bowl, 6" hex.	—	$ 12	—
Bowl, 8"-10"	26	—	70
Butter Dish, w/ lid	280	267	—
Candlesticks, 3.5" pr.	25	—	—
Candlesticks, 7" pr.	66	—	—
Creamer/Sugar	26	—	130
Cruet, 6.5 oz., w/ stopper	—	212	—
Cup/Saucer	12	15	47
Decanter, w/ stopper	140	—	—
Goblet, 9 oz.	25	—	60
Pitcher, 2 qt.	145	—	—
Plate, 6"-7"	5	7	9
Plate, 8"	8	12	11
Plate, 10"-13"	21	—	—
Server, center handle	45	—	—
Sherbet, 3.25"	10	11	—
Tumbler, 3-8 oz., ftd.	22	—	—
Tumbler, 12 oz., ftd.	42	—	—
Wine Glass, 3", 4 oz.	28	—	—

Sharon

	AMBER	PINK	GREEN
Bowl, 5"	$ 10	$ 10	$ 13
Bowl, 6"	18	23	20
Bowl, 8.5"	7	28	35
Bowl, 10.5"	25	35	38
Butter Dish, w/ lid	75	60	115
Cake Plate, 11.5"	26	30	70
Candy Dish, w/ lid	61	50	186
Cheese Dish, w/ lid	275	900	—
Creamer/Sugar	28	31	43
Cream Soup	28	48	53
Cup/Saucer	20	21	25
Jam Dish, 7.5"	45	150	55
Pitcher, 2.5 qt.	160	160	533
Plate, 6"	6	6	8
Plate, 8"-10"	18	23	21
Platter, oval, 12.5"	10	23	25
Salt/Pepper, pr.	53	55	93

	AMBER	PINK	GREEN
Sherbet	$ 15	$ 16	$ 35
Soup Plate, 7.5"	38	42	40
Tumbler, 4"-7", 9-15 oz.	40	40	80
Vegetable, oval, 9.5	16	26	25

Ships

	BLUE	PINK
Cup/Saucer	$ 33	—
Cocktail w/ stir	30	—
Cocktail Shaker	33	—
Ice Tub	40	—
Pitcher, 2.5 qt.	55	—
Plate, 6"	17	—
Plate, 9"	26	—
Shot Glass	48	—
Tumbler, 5-12 oz.	13	$ 22

Spiral

	PINK
Bowl, 5"-8"	$ 8
Butter Tub	25
Creamer/Sugar	17
Cup/Saucer	8
Jam Jar, w/ lid	30
Pitcher, 7.5", 2 qt.	35
Plate, 6"-8"	3
Salt/Pepper, pr.	26
Server, center handle	26
Sherbet	5
Tumbler, 3"-5"	5

Twisted Optic

	PINK
Bowl, 5"	$ 3
Bowl, 7"	10
Candlesticks, 3" pr.	18
Creamer/Sugar	15
Cream Soup, 4.75"	10
Cup/Saucer	6
Jar, candy, w/ lid	25
Pitcher, 2 qt.	28
Plate, 6"-7"	3
Plate, 8"	5
Server, center handle	20
Server, 2 handle	10
Sherbet	7
Tumbler, 4.5", 9 oz.	8
Tumbler, 5.25", 12 oz.	11

Flasks

Glass flasks have a broad body and narrow neck, usually for alcoholic beverages, often fitted with a closure. Flask collectors search for examples from the early 1800s through the early 1900s. Before 1810, few glass containers were manufactured. Flasks with portraits of presidents or other politicians are highly sought. Many have been reproduced. Color is also an important consideration.

Some of the best flasks pass through Norman C. Heckler's auctions in Auburn, MA. The rarities cited in this list are auction prices seen at Heckler's auctions.

For an extensive listing and identification system of flasks, see *American Bottles and Flasks* by Helen McKearin and Kenneth Wilson.

	LOW	AVG.	HIGH
Anchor-Sheaf of Grain, 1860-70, Baltimore Glassworks, Prussian blue	$15,000	$30,000	$45,000
"Corn for the World," —Baltimore Glassworks, qt., 1860-80, purple,	38,500	67,500	100,000
"Corn for the World" —Baltimore Monument, qt., amber	1400	2500	4000
"Corn for the World" —Baltimore Monument, qt., prussian blue	8250	14440	22,500
General Taylor Never Surrenders, encircling a cannon "A Little More Grape, Capt. Bragg," pt., apricot color	3025	5300	8500
General Taylor Never Surrenders, encircling a cannon- "A Little More Grape, Capt. Bragg," pt., medium olive green	3575	6250	10,000
General Taylor Never Surrenders, encircling a cannon "A Little More Grape, Capt. Bragg," half pt., amber	1870	3250	5000
Horseman-Hound, pictoral pt. flask, Baltimore Glassworks, dark red	5000	8000	11,000
Soldier-Fanny Essler, Marilyn Glassworks of Baltimore, 1840-60, pt., pink glass	6000	10590	16,000
Soldier-Fanny Essler, Marilyn Glassworks of Baltimore, 1840-60, pt., lemon yellow	2100	3600	5750
Soldier-Fanny Essler, Marilyn Glassworks of Baltimore, 1840-60, pt., pale green	500	880	1400
Taylor-Cornstock, Baltimore Glassworks, 1830-50, pt., sapphire blue	40,000	70,000	110,000
Washington-Monument, Baltimore Glassworks, 1830-50, pt., cobalt blue	30,000	50,000	80,000
Washington-Taylor, portrait flask, Dyottville Glassworks, pt., cobalt blue	4400	7700	12,000

Left to right: modern reproduction; Masonic elements are prized.

Fostoria

Founded in Fostoria, OH, in 1887, Fostoria continues to produce at their Moundsville, WV, factory. Many of their glassware lines are considered as "elegant" Depression-era glass and are avidly sought by collectors.

Fairfax

	GREEN	CRYSTAL	BLUE	YELLOW	PINK
Ashtray	$ 33	—	$ 36	$ 25	$ 35
Bonbon Dish	27	—	34	20	30
Bowl, ftd., 11.5"	37	—	43	26	37
Bowl, oval, 10.5"	45	—	60	33	48
Bread and Butter Plate, 6"	7	—	8	5	7
Cake Plate, handles, 10"	25	—	33	25	30
Candy Dish, w/ lid, 3 section	70	—	87	60	66
Cereal Bowl, 6"	23	—	29	19	23
Cigarette Box	48	—	66	40	47
Claret Goblet, 4 oz.	43	—	50	37	40
Coaster, 3.5"	7	—	10	5	7
Cocktail Goblet, 3 oz.	38	—	40	33	38
Compote, 7"	35	—	40	30	38
Cordial Goblet, .5 oz.	56	—	57	43	58
Cream Soup	24	—	27	20	23
Creamer, ftd.	15	—	19	10	15
Cruet, ftd., handle	200	—	240	170	210
Cup, ftd.	11	—	16	9	10
Dinner Plate, 10.5"	50	—	50	40	47
Finger Bowl, 4.5" x 2"	23	—	26	20	25
Fruit Bowl, 5"	12	—	18	10	12
Grill Plate, 10.5"	25	—	33	19	24
Ice Bucket, metal handle	64	—	77	55	63
Luncheon Plate, 9.5"	15	—	18	14	14
Mayonnaise Dish	22	—	28	17	20
Mayonnaise Ladle	27	—	38	27	29
Oyster Cocktail, ftd., 5.5 oz.	26	—	30	18	25
Parfait, ftd., 6.5 oz.	26	—	36	25	28
Pitcher, ftd., 48 oz.	320	—	360	250	325
Platter, oval, 15"	83	—	90	66	83
Relish Tray, 2 section, 8.5"	25	—	27	17	23
Relish Tray, 3 section, 11.5"	34	—	44	25	33
Relish Tray, 3 section, round	27	—	30	20	27
Sauce Boat	55	—	66	48	57
Saucer	4	—	6	4	4
Sherbet, low, 6 oz.	27	—	23	23	26
Sherbet, tall, 6 oz.	25	—	30	26	27
Soup Bowl	29	—	30	24	26
Sugar, ftd.	12	—	22	9	13
Tray, handled 11"	40	—	55	34	44
Tumbler, ftd., 12 oz.	30	—	40	30	33
Tumbler, ftd., 9 oz.	25	—	33	24	25
Tumbler, ftd., 5 oz.	20	—	26	3	20
Tumbler, ftd., 2.5 oz.	20	—	29	20	20
Water Goblet, 10 oz.	33	—	40	30	34

June

	GREEN	CRYSTAL	BLUE	YELLOW	PINK
Ashtray	—	$ 47	$ 65	$ 67	$ 67
Baking Dish, egg shape, len. 9"	—	60	100	150	80
Bonbon, stemmed	—	23	19	43	36
Bouillon Bowl, pedestal foot w/ underplate	—	20	67	46	50
Bowl, dia. 10"	—	46	76	64	63
Bread and Butter Plate, dia. 6"	—	10	14	13	12
Cake Plate, handled, dia. 10"	—	46	93	68	78
Canapé Plate	—	18	30	25	26
Candlesticks, pr., ht. 2"	—	55	87	67	70
Candlesticks, pr., ht. 3"	—	67	87	78	76
Candlesticks, pr., ht. 5"	—	—	100	83	90
Candy Jar, w/ lid, capacity 2 cups	—	120	290	200	225
Candy Jar, w/ lid, capacity 6 cups	—	90	300	154	280
Celery Dish, len. 11"	—	40	76	65	70
Centerpiece Bowl, oval, len. 11"	—	40	85	63	90
Cereal Bowl, dia. 6"	—	30	50	56	45
Cheese and Cracker Set	—	45	80	60	85
Chop Plate, dia. 12"	—	40	83	70	70
Condiment Bottle, ftd., w/ stopper	—	280	600	450	600
Comport, dia. 5"	—	60	60	45	60
Comport, dia. 6"	—	75	135	110	115
Comport, dia. 7"	—	94	165	115	130
Comport, dia. 8"	—	114	180	125	150
Cordial Cup	—	40	100	63	83
Cordial Cup Saucer	—	14	24	17	19
Cordial Glass, stemmed	—	74	130	119	116
Creamer, collar base	—	44	66	45	60
Creamer, pedestal foot	—	34	43	35	30
Cup, pedestal foot	—	29	54	40	43
Decanter, w/ glass stopper	—	550	1000	840	845
Dessert Bowl, handled, dia. 8"	—	76	120	85	116
Dinner Plate, dia. 9"	—	20	36	44	28
Dinner Plate, dia. 10.5"	—	46	80	67	73
Fan Vase, pedestal foot	—	150	260	180	190
Finger Bowl	—	35	66	48	47
Fruit Bowl, dia. 5"	—	22	43	35	33
Mayonnaise Compote	—	58	97	60	70
Mint Dish	—	28	57	43	50
Nappy, flat, dia. 7"	—	20	40	33	30
Nappy, pedestal foot, dia. 6.5"	—	22	40	30	34
Oil Cruet, pedestal foot	—	317	900	550	730
Oyster Plate	—	40	58	40	43
Parfait Glass	—	37	66	84	50
Pitcher	—	—	900	657	650
Platter, dia. 11"	—	70	100	85	90
Platter, dia. 15"	—	110	245	165	200
Relish Dish, 2 comp., len. 8.5"	—	30	53	44	50
Sugar Bowl, small w/ lid	—	45	64	43	58
Tray, loop handle, dia. 11"	—	50	100	65	74
Tumbler, ht. 3.5"	—	43	74	63	67

	GREEN	CRYSTAL	BLUE	YELLOW	PINK
Tumbler, ht. 5"	—	$ 30	$ 50	$ 40	$ 40
Vase, ht. 7.5"	—	70	400	185	190
Water Glass, stemmed	—	38	55	43	60
Whipped Cream Bowl, large	—	140	280	210	250
Whipped Cream Bowl, small	—	35	50	40	43
Whiskey Tumbler, 2.5 oz.	—	40	88	67	60
Wine Glass, stemmed	—	40	100	80	77

Trojan

	GREEN	CRYSTAL	BLUE	YELLOW	PINK
Ashtray, large	—	—	—	54	53
Bonbon Bowl	—	—	—	25	25
Bouillon Bowl, ftd.	—	—	—	30	30
Cereal Bowl, dia. 6"	—	—	—	33	37
Compote, ht. 6"	—	—	—	40	45
Creamer, ftd.	—	—	—	30	35
Dinner Plate, dia. 10.5"	—	—	—	55	54
Finger Bowl, w/ liner	—	—	—	46	43
Grill Plate, dia. 10"	—	—	—	50	50
Luncheon Plate, dia. 8.5"	—	—	—	25	23
Mayonnaise Bowl, w/ liner	—	—	—	50	56
Parfait	—	—	—	50	50
Pitcher	—	—	—	475	450
Platter, dia. 12"	—	—	—	57	60
Platter, dia. 15"	—	—	—	83	90
Relish Dish, dia. 6.5"	—	—	—	25	23
Relish Dish, 3 section	—	—	—	47	45
Saucer	—	—	—	16	16
Sherbet, ht. 4.5"	—	—	—	38	36
Sugar Bowl, ftd.	—	—	—	33	33
Tray, dia. 11", center handle	—	—	—	53	55
Tumbler, ht. 4.5"	—	—	—	40	38
Tumbler, ht. 5.5"	—	—	—	29	30
Tumbler, ht. 6"	—	—	—	40	38
Vase, ht. 8"	—	—	—	115	110
Whipped Cream Tub	—	—	—	150	130

Versailles

	GREEN	CRYSTAL	BLUE	YELLOW	PINK
Ashtray	44	—	57	53	45
Bonbon Bowl	25	—	30	23	24
Bouillon Bowl	35	—	46	33	37
Bread and Butter Plate, dia. 6"	8	—	10	8	8
Cereal Bowl, dia. 6"	40	—	50	43	38
Chop Plate, dia. 13"	60	—	70	67	58
Compote, ht. 6"	44	—	60	55	46
Compote, ht. 7"	45	—	67	60	48
Creamer, ftd.	30	—	40	30	30
Decanter	270	—	380	290	280
Demitasse Cup and Saucer	40	—	93	64	44
Finger Bowl, w/ liner	38	—	56	48	23
Fruit Bowl, dia. 5"	28	—	34	26	29
Ice Bucket	166	—	158	150	123

	GREEN	CRYSTAL	BLUE	YELLOW	PINK
Lemon Bowl	$ 20	—	$ 27	$ 24	$ 19
Luncheon Plate, dia. 8.5"	15	—	20	20	15
Mayonnaise Bowl, w/ liner	66	—	90	85	75
Parfait	50	—	60	53	47
Pitcher	500	—	700	600	475
Platter, dia. 12"	63	—	80	65	60
Platter, dia. 15"	85	—	125	100	85
Relish, dia. 8.5"	67	—	80	70	60
Sauce Boat and Underplate	93	—	120	75	84
Saucer	8	—	10	7	8
Soup Bowl, dia. 7"	50	—	56	50	50
Sugar, ftd.	29	—	40	28	30
Tray, dia. 11", center handle	40	—	64	46	40
Tumbler, ht. 4.5", 5 oz.	43	—	45	46	40
Tumbler, ht. 5.25", 9 oz.	40	—	50	40	40

Fruit Jars

The Mason jar was produced by John Landis Mason in the early 1800s. One of Mason's innovations was a zinc lid which provided greater air tightness.

Nineteenth-century fruit jars for home canning are collected, especially those with the manufacturer's name or a decorative motif printed on the jar. Before 1810, few glass containers were manufactured.

	LOW	AVG.	HIGH
Acme, machine made, clear, sq., glass lid, wire bale .... $ 4	$ 5	$ 6
Advance, handmade, qt., aqua, glass lid, wire bale 70	75	80
Agnew, handmade, aqua, qt., wax seal 45	50	55
Air-tight, handmade, pt., amber, zinc lid 30	35	40
Alma, handmade, aqua, qt., threaded glass lid 70	75	80
American Fruit Jar, handmade, dark green, qt., glass lid, wire bale, eagle design 100	125	150
American Soda, machine made, clear, glass lid, wire bale 6	7	8
Anchor Hocking, machine made, clear, glass lid, wire bale 1	2	3
Anderson Preserving Co., machine made, clear, qt., metal lid 10	12	14
R. Arthur's Patent, handmade, aqua, qt., wax seal 250	275	300
Atlas Mason, handmade, aqua, qt., zinc lid 20	25	30
Atlas Good Luck, machine made, clear, aqua, glass lid, wire bale, embossed shamrock 3	4	5
Atlas Good Luck, machine made, clear, half pt. 4	5	6
Atlas Special Mason, machine made, clear, metal lid 3	4	5
Atlas Strong Shoulder Mason, machine made, aqua, clear, zinc lid 1	2	3
Atlas Strong Shoulder Mason, machine made, aqua, zinc lid 10	12	14
Atlas Whole Fruit Jar, machine made, clear, zinc lid 3	4	5
Atterbury, handmade, aqua, qt., tapered stopper 200	225	250
B & B, machine made, amber, qt., glass lid, metal band 20	25	30
Baker Bros., handmade, aqua, qt., wax seal 50	55	60
Ball Deluxe Jar, machine made, clear, glass lid, wire bale 3	4	5
Ball Eclipse Wide Mouth, machine made, clear, rounded sq., glass lid, wire bale 1	2	3
Ball Ideal, machine made, clear, glass lid, wire bale 1	2	3
Ball the Mason, machine made, aqua, zinc lid 3	4	5
Ball Mason's Patent Nov 30th 1858, handmade, aqua, qt., zinc lid, ground lip 3	4	5
Ball Sanitary Sure Seal, pat'd July 14 1908, machine made, clear, blue, glass lid 2	3	4
Ball Square Mason, machine made, clear, qt., rounded sq., zinc lid 1	2	3
Baltimore Glassworks, handmade, light green, qt., applied lid 100	125	150
Bamberger's Mason Jar, machine made, aqua, glass lid, wire bale 8	10	12
Beehive, machine made, light blue, glass lid, metal band 50	75	100
Bennett's #1, machine made, clear, aqua, qt., zinc lid 150	175	200
Best, machine made, light green, qt., glass lid, metal band 50	55	60
The Best, handmade, light green, qt., glass stopper, lid reads "Aug. 18th. 1868" 70	75	80
Boldt Mason, machine made, aqua, blue, zinc lid 25	30	35
Brighton, handmade, clear, qt., glass lid, toggle top 40	45	50
Buckeye, handmade, aqua, qt., glass lid, iron yoke 140	160	180
Cadiz Jar, handmade, aqua, qt., glass threaded lid 80	100	120

	LOW	AVG.	HIGH
Calcutt's, handmade, clear, aqua, qt., glass screw lid, ground lip, pat April 11 and November 7, 1893	$ 50	$ 60	$ 70
The Champion, pat Aug 31, 1869, handmade, aqua, qt., glass lid, iron screw yoke	80	90	100
Crown Mason, machine made, clear, zinc lid	1	2	3
Crystal Jar, handmade, clear, amethyst, qt., glass lid	25	38	50
Crystal Mason, handmade, clear, pt., qt., zinc lid	15	20	25
The Dandy, handmade, amber, glass lid, wire bale	50	55	60
The Dandy, handmade, clear, aqua, glass lid, wire bale	20	25	30
Diamond Fruit Jar, machine made, clear, glass lid, screw band	3	4	5
The Dictator, handmade, green, qt., wax seal	80	90	100
Double Safety, machine made, clear, glass lid, wire bale	4	6	8
Drey Mason, machine made, clear, green, zinc lid	1	2	3
Drey Square Mason, machine made, clear, zinc lid	2	3	4
Dunkley, machine made, clear, qt., hinged glass lid	25	30	35
Electric Fruit Jar, handmade, aqua, qt., glass lid	60	70	80
The Empire, handmade, aqua, qt., glass lid, cam lever	75	80	85
Empress, handmade, clear, qt., glass lid, zinc band	75	80	85
Everlasting Jar, machine made, clear, green, glass lid, toggle	15	20	25
Famous, machine made, aqua, glass lid, wire bale	12	15	18
Faxon, handmade, aqua, glass lid, zinc band	10	12	14
Flickinger, handmade, aqua, qt., glass lid, wire bale	18	20	22
Frank, handmade, aqua, qt., wax seal	40	45	50
The Gem, handmade, aqua, glass lid, screw band, embossed initials	15	18	21
Gem, Improved, handmade, green, qt., glass lid, screw band	3	4	5
1908 Gem, machine made, clear, glass lid, screw band	8	9	10
Glenshaw, machine made, clear, glass lid	3	4	5
Good House Keepers, machine made, clear, zinc lid	1	2	3
Halle, handmade, green, qt., wax seal	50	55	60
Hartells, handmade, aqua, qt., glass lid, metal clamp	60	70	80
Hawley, handmade, green, qt., zinc lid	18	20	22
Hazel Preserve Jar, machine made, clear, glass lid, wire bale	6	8	10
Hero, handmade, green, clear, pt., qt., glass lid, screw band	25	30	35
Hero Improved, handmade, green, pt., qt., glass lid, screw band	15	20	25
Hoosier Jar, handmade, aqua, qt., threaded glass lid	100	125	150
Jeannette Mason Home Packer, machine made, clear, pt., qt., glass lid, screw band	3	4	5
Kerr Glass Top, machine made, clear, glass top, screw band	1	2	3
Keystone, machine made, clear, pt., qt, zinc lid	8	10	12
Kline, handmade, blue, qt., glass stopper	35	40	45
Knox Mason, machine made, clear, metal lid	1	2	3
Lamb, machine made, aqua, clear, zinc lid	2	3	4
The Leader, handmade, amber, glass lid, wire bale	40	45	50
The Leader, handmade, clear, glass lid, wire bale	20	25	30
Lightning, machine made, clear, glass lid, wire bale, embossed anchor	1	2	3
Macomb, handmade pottery, gray, brown, pt., qt., threaded lid	8	10	12
The Marion Jar, handmade, green, zinc lid	8	10	12
Mason, handmade, clear, zinc lid	2	3	4
Mason, handmade, aqua, zinc lid, star and crescent moon embossing	30	35	40
Mason, machine made, clear, zinc lid, embossed anchor	1	2	3
Mason Jar, machine made, clear, metal lid, embossed star	1	2	3

	LOW	AVG.	HIGH
Mason Jar, Improved, handmade, clear, glass lid, screw band	$ 4	$5	$ 6
Mason's Union, handmade, aqua, zinc lid, embossed shield	10	12	14
Metro Easi-Pack, machine made, clear, zinc lid	1	2	3
Metro Easy-Pack, machine made, clear, zinc lid	1	2	3
Monarch, machine made, clear, glass lid, wire bale, embossed shield	4	5	6
Mountain Mason, machine made, clear, zinc lid	12	15	18
Newman's Patent, Dec. 20th 1959, handmade, aqua, qt.	100	125	150
The Nifty, handmade, clear, qt., glass lid, clip	25	30	35
The Penn, handmade, green qt., wax seal	60	70	80
Pine Mason, machine made, clear, zinc lid	3	4	5
Pine Deluxe Jar, machine made, clear, glass lid, wire bale	4	5	6
The Puritan, handmade, aqua, qt., glass lid, clamp	100	125	150
The Queen, handmade, aqua, pt., qt., glass lid, screw band	15	20	25
Rhodes, machine made, aqua, zinc lid	20	25	30
Root, handmade, aqua, green, yellow, pt., qt., zinc lid	5	6	7
The Rose, machine made, clear, qt., zinc lid	12	15	18
Samco, machine made, clear, zinc lid	2	3	4
Sealfast, machine made, clear, aqua, glass lid, wire bale	4	5	6
Security, handmade, clear, qt., glass lid, wire bale	8	10	12
Star, handmade, clear, glass lid, zinc band	50	55	60
The Star Glass Co., handmade, aqua, qt., wax seal	20	25	30
Temple, handmade, clear, pt., qt., zinc lid	40	45	50
Tillyer, handmade, aqua, qt., glass lid, wire bale	70	80	90
Veteran, machine made, clear, glass lid, wire bale	20	25	30
White Crown Mason, machine made, aqua, zinc lid	8	9	10
Woodbury, handmade, aqua, glass lid, metal clip	20	25	30

Heisey Glass

A partnership including George Duncan and Daniel C. Ripley established the A.H. Heisey Glass Co. in the 1860s in Newark, OH. It manufactured cut and pressed glasswares. Heisey glass is high quality. Many patterns are called "elegant Depression glass."

The Heisey Collectors of America, Inc. publishes *The Heisey News,* a newsletter with information on patterns, history of Heisey, and advertisements. Address: Box 27, Newark, OH 43055.

Ipswich Pattern

	GREEN	CRYSTAL	BLUE	YELLOW	PINK
Bowl, ftd., dia. 11", floral	—	$ 14	$ 250	—	—
Candlestick, h. 6"	$ 145	73	—	$ 130	$ 100
Candy Jar, w/ lid	240	39	—	190	140
Cocktail Goblet, 4 oz.	—	10	—	—	—
Cocktail Shaker, w/ strainer	440	140	—	340	240
Creamer	32	14	—	28	22
Cruet, w/ stopper, ftd., 2 oz.	85	48	—	75	65
Finger Bowl, w/ underplate	40	14	—	34	25
Goblet, champagne, 5 oz.	—	10	—	—	—
Goblet, 10 oz.	—	14	—	—	—
Pitcher, 2 qt.	400	95	300	190	140
Plate, sq., dia. 8"	25	15	—	26	22
Sherbet, 4 oz.	20	8	—	20	17
Sugar Bowl	30	15	—	36	27
Tumbler, curved rim, 10 oz.	28	8	—	27	24

Lariat Pattern

Ashtray, 4"	—	5	—	—	—
Basket, ftd., 10"	—	125	—	—	—
Bowl, 4"	—	14	—	—	—
Bowl, 12"	—	15	—	—	—
Bowl, 13"	—	18	—	—	—
Bowl, flat, 8"	—	13	—	—	—
Buffet Plate, 21"	—	33	—	—	—
Cake Plate, rolled edge, 12"	—	18	—	—	—
Candlestick, 2 candles	—	11	—	—	—
Goblet, 9 oz.	—	10	—	—	—
Goblet, blown, 10 oz.	—	12	—	—	—
Salad Plate, 7"	—	7	—	—	—
Salad Plate, 8"	—	8	—	—	—
Salt/Pepper, pr.	—	140	—	—	—
Server, 2 handles, 14"	—	28	—	—	—
Saucer	—	3	—	—	—
Sherbet, low, 6 oz.	—	4	—	—	—

Octagon Pattern

Basket, #500, 5"	78	48	—	83	68
Bonbon Dish, #1229, 8"	11	4	—	9	7
Bowl, 6.5"	14	10	—	15	13
Cheese Dish, 2 handles, #1229, 6"	11	4	—	9	7
Hors d'oeuvre Plate, #1229, 13"	29	14	—	24	19
Plate, 6"	9	3	—	7	5

Old Sandwich Pattern

	GREEN	CRYSTAL	BLUE	YELLOW	PINK
Ashtray	$ 35	$ 5	$ 40	$ 20	$ 30
Beer Mug, 12 oz.	240	24	270	195	185
Beer Mug, 18 oz.	290	28	320	245	220
Bowl, oval, ftd., 12"	68	25	—	58	46
Bowl, round, ftd., 11"	58	24	—	46	39
Compote, 6"	78	26	—	74	68
Cup	16	7	—	13	11
Decanter, w/ stopper	175	60	320	165	155
Finger Bowl	18	6	—	15	12
Goblet, 4 oz.	20	9	88	18	15
Goblet, 3 oz.	19	8	—	16	14
Oyster Cocktail Goblet, 4 oz.	12	3	—	10	9
Parfait	24	8	—	19	14
Pilsner Glass, 8 oz.	33	10	—	28	23
Pilsner Glass, 10 oz.	36	13	—	30	26
Pitcher, 2 qt.	125	55	—	120	115
Pitcher, ice lip, 2 qt.	130	63	—	125	120
Plate, sq., 6"	13	4	—	10	8
Plate, sq., 7"	15	4	—	14	10
Plate, sq., 8"	17	6	—	15	12
Salt/Pepper, pr.	58	28	—	48	38
Saucer	14	6	—	12	10
Tumbler, 12 oz.	26	9	—	21	16
Tumbler, ftd., 12 oz.	26	9	—	21	16
Tumbler, 5 oz.	19	3	—	14	11

Pleat and Panel Pattern

Bouillon Bowl, 2 handles, 5"	11	5	—	—	9
Bouillon Underplate, 6.5"	7	2	—	—	5
Bowl, 4"	9	4	—	—	7
Bowl, 6.5"	11	4	—	—	9
Cheese and Cracker Set, 10.5"	34	19	—	—	29
Compote, w/ lid, ftd., 5"	54	24	—	—	44
Creamer, institutional	14	4	—	—	9
Cruet, w/ stopper, 3 oz.	34	16	—	—	29
Cup	14	4	—	—	9
Goblet, champagne, 5 oz.	11	4	—	—	9
Jelly Bowl, 2 handles, 5"	11	5	—	—	9
Lemon Bowl, w/ lid, 5"	15	9	—	—	13
Marmalade Jar, 4.5"	16	6	—	—	11
Nappy, 4.5"	8	4	—	—	7
Nappy, 8"	16	9	—	—	14
Plate, 8"	11	4	—	—	9
Pitcher	65	30	—	—	50
Pitcher, ice lip	75	40	—	—	60
Plate, 8"	7	2	—	—	5
Platter, oval, 12"	34	18	—	—	29
Sandwich Plate, 14"	29	14	—	—	24
Saucer	5	2	—	—	4

Provincial Pattern

	GREEN	CRYSTAL	BLUE	YELLOW	PINK
Ashtray, sq., 3"	—	$ 11	—	—	—
Bonbon Dish, 2 handles, 7"	$ 29	9	—	—	—
Buffet Plate, 18"	—	24	—	—	—
Butter Dish, w /lid	—	55	—	—	—
Candleholder	—	14	—	—	—
Candelabra, 3 candles	—	34	—	—	—
Candy Box, w/ lid, tooled, 5.5"	220	60	—	—	—
Iced Tea Tumbler, ftd., 12 oz.	39	14	—	—	—
Plate, 7"	—	9	—	—	—

Insulators

Insulators are glass figures used to attach electrical wires to poles from 1844 (for telegraph lines) into the 20th century. Color, age, and design determine value. Threadless insulators are older, rarer, and usually more valuable than threaded ones. Clear glass is most common. Colors, including green, milk white, amber, amethyst, and cobalt blue are more valuable.

	LOW	AVG.	HIGH
A.T. & T. Co., aqua, 2-piece, 2.5" x 3.5"	$ 7	$ 10	$ 13
A.T. & T. Co., green, single skirt, 2.5" x 3.5"	8	13	18
Ages, clear amethyst, 3.25" x 2.5"	18	22	26
Armstrong, amber 4" x 3.5"	15	19	21
Armstrong, No. 5, clear, double petticoat, 3.5" x 3.5"	7	10	13
A.U. Patent, green, 4.5" x 2.5"	45	50	55
B. & O., aqua, 4" x 3.5"	45	50	55
B.F.G. Co., aqua, 4" x 3.5"	60	70	80
B.G.M. Co., clear amethyst, 3.5" x 2.5"	28	33	40
B.T. Co. of Canada, aqua, green, 3.5" x 2.5"	15	20	25
Barclay, aqua, double petticoat, 3" x 2.5"	27	33	40
Boston Bottle Works, aqua, 4.5" x 3"	60	70	80
Brookee, Homer, aqua, 3.5" x 2.5"	31	42	43
Brookfield, No. 45, aqua, green, 4.5" x 3.5"	10	13	16
Brookfield, No. 55, aqua, green, 4" x 2.5"	15	20	25
Brookfield, No. 83, aqua, green, 4" x 3.5"	25	35	45
Brookfield, dark olive green, double petticoat, 3.5" x 4"	11	14	17
C. & P. Tel. Co., aqua, green, 3.5" x 2.5"	14	18	21
C.E.L., amethyst, 4.5" x 2.5"	20	22	24
C.E.N., amethyst, 3.5" x 2.5"	55	60	65
C.G.I., clear, amethyst, 3.5" x 2.5"	30	35	40
Cable, aqua, green, 4.5" x 3.5"	30	38	46
California, aqua, green, 3.5" x 2.25"	34	38	42
California, CK-1 82, purple, double petticoat, 3.5" x 4"	11	13	15
Canadian Pacific, clear, amethyst, 3.5" x 2.5"	20	24	28
Castle, aqua, 4" x 2.5"	65	70	75
Chester, aqua, 4" x 2.25"	70	80	90
Columbia, aqua, green, 3.5" x 4"	57	47	67
Derflinger, T.N.I., aqua, green, 4" x 3.5"	25	30	35
Dominion No. 9, amber, aqua, and clear, 3.5" x 2.5"	4	7	10
Duquesne, aqua, green, 3.5" x 2.5"	45	50	55
Dwight, aqua, 4" x 3"	46	56	66
E.C. & M. Co., green, 4" x 2.5"	36	41	46
Electrical Supply Co., aqua, green, 3.5" x 2.25"	40	50	60
Folembray, No. 221, olive green, 2.25" x 3.5"	54	62	73
Gayner, 36-190, aqua, 3.5" x 3.5"	16	17	20
Gayner, green, double petticoat, 3.5" x 4"	35	37	42
H.G. Co., amber, double petticoat, 3.5" x 3.5"	19	22	25
H.G. Co. Petticoat, aqua, green, 3.5" x 3.5"	8	10	12
Hemingray, No. 8, aqua, green, 3.5" x 2.5"	20	23	26
Hemingray, No. 9, aqua, single skirt, 2.5" x 3.5"	25	30	35
Hemingray, No. 16, green, single skirt, 2" x 4"	5	7	9
Hemingray, No. 19, aqua, double petticoat, 3.5" x 3"	40	50	60
Hemingray, No. 25, aqua, green, 4" x 3.5"	21	24	30

	LOW	AVG.	HIGH
Hemingray, No. 95, aqua, green, 3.25" x 2.25"	$ 50	$ 55	$ 60
Hemingray Beehive, green, double petticoat, 3.5" x 4.5"	25	31	34
Hemingray Petticoat, cobalt blue, 4" x 3.5"	45	50	55
Hemingray Transportation, green, 4.5" x 3.5"	35	40	45
Isorex, clear, black, green, blue, 5.5" x 3.5"	7	9	13
Jeffery Mfg. Co., aqua, 3.25" x 2.5"	44	54	64
Jumbo, aqua, 7.5" x 5.5"	30	37	44
Knowles Cable, aqua, green, 4" x 3.25"	46	51	56
Fred M. Locke, No. 14, aqua, 4.25" x 3"	32	38	46
Fred M. Locke, No. 21, aqua, green, 4" x 4"	8	10	12
Lynchburg, No. 10, aqua, green, 3.5" x 2.5"	10	15	20
Lynchburg, No. 31, aqua, green, 3.5" x 2.5"	10	14	19
Lynchburg, No. 44, 4" x 3.25"	8	10	12
Maydwell, No. 9, clear, single skirt, 2.25" x 3.5"	7	9	11
Maydwell, No. 16, amber, 4" x 2.5"	7	10	13
Maydwell, No. 20, white milk glass, 3.25" x 3.5"	32	37	42
McLaughlin, No. 9, green, single skirt, 2.5" x 3.25"	17	19	26
McLaughlin, No. 18, amber, aqua, green, 3.25" x 2.25"	8	11	15
McLaughlin, No. 19, aqua, 3.5" x 3.5"	4	7	9
McLaughlin, No. 42, aqua, 4" x 3.25"	7	12	15
McLaughlin, No. 82, aqua, 3.25" x 3.25"	11	14	17
Mershon, aqua, 5" x 5.5"	45	50	55
Monogram H.I. Co., aqua, 4.5" x 3.5"	30	34	40
N.E.G.M. Co., aqua, green, 3.5" x 2.5"	22	23	26
N.E.G.M. Co., aqua, 3.5" x 3.5"	26	32	35
N.E.T. & T. Co., aqua, green, 3.25" x 2.5"	7	10	13
N.E.T. & T. Co., blue, 3.5" x 3"	17	23	26
Noleak, aqua, green, 4" x 4"	45	50	55
O.V.G. Co., aqua, 3.5" x 2.5"	10	15	20
O.V.G. Co., aqua, green, 3.5" x 2.5"	18	20	25
Peffingel Anderson Co., aqua, 4" x 2.5"	26	31	34
Pony, blue, 3.5" x 2.5"	33	37	38
Postal, aqua, green, 4.5" x 3.5"	21	25	29
Pyrex, Carnival glass, 3" x 3.5"	18	19	25
SIT. & T. Co., aqua, green, 3.5" x 2.5"	20	25	30
Santa Ana, aqua, green, 4.5" x 4.5"	43	47	55
Standard, clear, amethyst, 3.25" x 2.5"	18	23	26
Star, aqua, single skirt, pony, 2.5" x 3.5"	11	14	17
Sterling, aqua, 3.5" x 2.5"	22	26	27
T.C.R., aqua, 4" x 3.5"	17	23	29
T.H.E. Co., aqua, 4" x 3.5"	41	47	56
Thomas, brown pottery, 2.5" x 1.5"	8	12	15
Transportation, No. 2, aqua, 4.5" x 2.5"	30	34	38
U.S. Tel. Co., aqua, 3.5" x 2.25"	20	23	26
V.M.R. Napoll, aqua, green, 4" x 2.5"	19	22	27
W.F.G. Co., clear, amethyst, 3.5" x 2"	19	21	25
W.G.M. Co., clear, amethyst, 3.5" x 2.5"	35	36	46
W.V., No. 5, aqua, 4.5" x 2.5"	25	30	35
Westinghouse, aqua, green, 3.5" x 2.5"	35	40	45
Whitall Tatum, amber, 3.5" x 3.5"	20	25	30

Above left to right : Corning Carnival glass, $15-$22; Whitall Tatum, amethyst, $15-$22. Below left to right: threadless, $60-$80; beehive, straw color, $16-$22; Diamond Pony , deep amethyst, $14-$22.

Lalique

René Lalique (1860-1945) began his career as a jeweler in Paris and by 1900 had become one of the world's most celebrated Art Nouveau designers. He began to manufacture glass in 1910. Many regard him as the best glass designer of the 20th century. The company is still in business under the direction of René Lalique's granddaughter Marie-Claude Lalique. Most items produced before René Lalique's death in 1945 are marked *R. LALIQUE*, while later pieces are marked *LALIQUE*. Collectors focus on the earlier period, especially pieces in color and rare models. Many fakes and forgeries exist. They are often crude and easily recognizable. When examining Lalique never let a signature authenticate the object, let the object authenticate the signature.

Prices are for items in pristine condition, meaning no cracks, chips, stains, or restorations. We have shortened signatures of many of the following pieces; in addition to the *Lalique* or *R. Lalique* there may be a model number or the word *FRANCE*. The following terms refer to the signature of an item and are abbreviated: *en.*-engraved, *m.*-molded, *st.*- stamped, *stcl.*-stenciled, *whc.*-wheel cut.

Our consultant for this area is Nicholas Dawes, collector, dealer, and author of *Lalique Glass,* Crown, NY, 1986. He is listed in the back of this book. The Lalique Collector's Society can be reached at 400 Veterans Blvd., Carlstadt, NJ 07072, 1-800-CRISTAL. For information on fakes, see *A Guide to Fraudulent Lalique*, by Alice Bley and Carol Glaze.

	LOW	HIGH
Ashtray, Cygne, clear and frosted w/ swans, en. *Lalique*, ht. 9 cm., c. 1960	$ 200	$ 300
Ashtray, Jamaique, deep amber glass, whc. R. LALIQUE, dia. 14 cm., c. 1928	600	800
Ashtray, Deux Zephyrs, gray w/ 2 putti, stcl. R. LALIQUE, dia. 8 cm., c. 1913	300	500
Ashtray, Dindon, opalescent green w/ turkey, en. *R. Lalique*, dia. 12 cm., c. 1925	700	900
Ashtray, Moineau, green w/ sparrow, en. *R. Lalique*, dia. 12 cm., c. 1925	700	900
Ashtray, Simone, clear and frosted flowerhead, en. *R. Lalique*, dia. 9.8 cm., c. 1929	250	350
Auto Mascot, Coq Houdan, clear and frosted glass rooster, whc. R. LALIQUE, ht. 22.5 cm., c. 1929	4000	5000
Auto Mascot, Longchamp, clear and frosted horse's head, m. R. LALIQUE, ht. 15.5 cm., c. 1929	6000	8000
Auto Mascot, Tete, D'Aigle, clear and frosted eagle head, m. R. LALIQUE, ht. 10.7 cm., c. 1928	2000	3000
Bookends, Hirondelle, clear and frosted, w/ swallows, stcl. LALIQUE, ht. 16 cm., c. 1965	400	600
Bowl, Bulbes, opalescent, stcl. R. LALIQUE, dia. 20.5 cm., c. 1935	300	500
Bowl, Montigny, opalescent w/ stylized flowerheads, m. R. LALIQUE, dia. 30 cm., c. 1928	800	1200
Bowl, Perruches, opalescent mint green w/ parakeets, stcl. R. LALIQUE, dia. 24.5 cm., c. 1913	6000	8000
Bowl, Poissons, opalescent w/ fish, stcl. R. LALIQUE, dia. 23.9 cm., c. 1921	400	600
Box, aluminum, sepia patina, for Roger et Gallet, st. LALIQUE, c. 1922	150	200
Box, Chantilly, clear and frosted, sepia patina w/ deer, m. R. LALIQUE, dia. 8.5 cm., c. 1924	500	700
Box, Coquilles, clear w/ green patina, m. R. LALIQUE, dia. 7 cm., c. 1920	500	700

	LOW	HIGH
Box, Epines, clear and frosted, blue patina, en. *R. Lalique*, dia. 6 cm., c. 1920	$ 300	$ 500
Box, Quatre Papillons, clear and frosted glass, w/ 4 moths, m. LALIQUE DEPOSE, dia. 8 cm., c. 1911	1000	1500
Box, Vallauris, clear and frosted, en. *R. Lalique*, dia. 14 cm., c. 1928	500	700
Brooch, Deux Aigle, blue reflecting clear glass and gilt metal w/ eagles, st. LALIQUE, 9.6 cm.	700	900
Brooch, Dos a Dos, clear and frosted glass and gilt metal, w/ 2 crouching nudes, st. LALIQUE Poincon, ht. 3.5 cm., c. 1913	1000	1500
Brooch, Feuilles, amber reflecting glass and gilt metal, w/ leaves, st. LALIQUE Poincon, ht. 4.3 cm., c. 1919	800	1200
Brooch, Trois Marguerites, clear glass and gilt metal, gray patina, st. LALIQUE Poincon, dia. 3.3 cm., c. 1912	300	500
Candlesticks, Dahlia, clear and frosted, in 2 parts, stcl. R. LALIQUE, ht. 4.5 cm., c. 1934	700	900
Carafe, Cotes Plates, clear w/ vertical ribs, m. LALIQUE, ht. 24 cm., c. 1919	300	500
Champagne Glass, set of 6, w/ angels, en. *Lalique*, ht., c. 1970s	800	1200
Clock, clear and frosted, w/ naiades, en. *R. Lalique*, ht. 11.3 cm., c. 1926	1000	1500
Clock, deux Colombes, opalescent, w/ lovebirds, whc. R. LALIQUE, ht. 22.2 cm., c. 1926	4000	6000
Clock, Moineaux, clear and frosted, w/ sparrows, m. R. LALIQUE, ht. 15.5 cm., c. 1924	2000	2500
Frame, Bleutes, clear and frosted, stcl. R. LALIQUE, ht. 24 cm., c. 1926	3000	4000
Goblet, Marienthal pattern, amber glass, en. *R. Lalique*, ht. 10 cm., c. 1930	150	200
Letter Seal, Faune, clear and frosted glass, stcl. R. LALIQUE, ht. 7.4 cm., c. 1931	1200	1600
Letter Seal, Tete d'Aigle, black glass eagle head, en. *R. Lalique*, ht. 7.8 cm., c. 1911	800	1200
Pendant, Graines, blue glass, en. *R. Lalique*, ht. 5 cm., 1920	1000	1500
Perfume bottle, clear and frosted, w/ stars, for Worth, m. LALIQUE, ht. 13 cm., c. 1950	150	250
Perfume Bottle, Duncan, clear and frosted, w/ 3 nudes, stcl. LALIQUE, ht. 19 cm., c. 1950	300	500
Perfume Bottle, frosted, sepia patina, for La Belle Saison by Houbigant, m. R. LALIQUE, ht. 14 cm., c. 925	2000	3000
Perfume Bottle, green glass snuff bottle for Le Jade by Roger et Gallet, m. R. LALIQUE, ht. 8 cm., 1926	4000	5000
Perfume Bottle, Violette, clear w/ blue enamel, bushel of violets for Violette by Gabilla, m. R. LALIQUE, ht. 8 cm., c. 1925	3500	4500
Plate, annual, Hibou, en. *Lalique*, 1971	100	150
Plate, annual, Deux Oiseux, en. *Lalique*, 1965	1200	1600
Plate, Campanules, opalescent w/ tulips, stcl. R. LALIQUE, dia. 31.5 cm., c. 1932	600	800
Plate, Chiens, clear, sepia patina, w/ dogs, en. *R. Lalique*, dia. 21 cm., c. 1914	400	500
Plate, Fleurons, opalescent, stcl. R. LALIQUE, dia. 26.5 cm., c. 1933	400	600
Stautuette, Chrysis, clear and frosted glass, female nude, en. *Lalique*, ht. 14.5 cm., c. 1965	300	500
Statuette, Deux Danseuses, clear and frosted glass, 2 dancers, en. *Lalique*,		

	LOW	HIGH
ht. 25 cm., c. 1965	$ 1000	$ 1500
Statuette, Suzanne, opalescent glass, on illum. bronze base, m. R. LALIQUE, ht. 23 cm., c. 1925	15,000	20,000
Tray, Pissenlit, clear and frosted w/ dandelion leaves, m. VDA, dia. 19.5 cm., c. 1921	600	800
Vase, Archers, deep amber w/ male archers, en. *R. Lalique*, ht. 26 cm., c. 1921	5000	7000
Vase, Ceylan, opalescent, sepia patina, w/ parakeets, whc. R. LALIQUE, ht. 25 cm., c. 1924	4000	6000
Vase, Coupe Cabrera, clear and blue, tapering form, en. *Lalique*, ht. 9 cm., c. 1955	400	600
Vase, Ferrieres, cased green, florettes, en. *R. Lalique*, ht. 17 cm., c. 1929	3500	4500
Vase, Mimosa, clear and frosted, gray patina, m. R. LALIQUE, ht. 17 cm., c. 1921	1200	1600
Vase, Ondines, clear and frosted w/ sea nymphs, en. *Lalique*, ht. 23 cm., c. 1965	1000	1500
Wine Cooler, Riquewihr, clear and frosted, sepia patina, en. *Lalique*, ht. 12.5 cm., c. 1949	500	700

Left: Suzanne statuette on original base, c. 1925, figure ht. 25". This example is clear glass and worth $6000-$8000, opalescent examples are much rarer and are valued at $15,000-$20,000. Right: Box, Quatre Papillions, c. 1911, dia., $1000-$1500. —Photos courtesy Nicholas M. Dawes.

Pressed Glass

Small, crude objects and feet for footed bowls were first hand-pressed in England in the early 1800s, but pressing glass with machinery appears to have originated in America. Glass companies began producing pressed glass in matching tableware sets during the 1840s.

Although identification of pieces is mainly by pattern name, there is some confusion in this area. Most of the original names have been discarded by advanced collectors who have renamed the pattern in descriptive terms. Manufacturers' marks are exceedingly rare and there are few catalogs available from the period before 1850. By studying the old catalogs that do exist, along with shards found at old factory sites, some sketchy information has been provided. But because the competition quickly copied patterns, absolute verification of the manufacturer is impossible.

Earlier pieces contain many imperfections: bubbles, lumps, impurities, and sometimes cloudiness. Reproductions pose a problem to the beginning collector. Two popular patterns, Bellflower and Daisy and Button, have been reproduced extensively. With careful, informed scrutiny, collectors can detect the dullness and lack of sparkle characteristic of remakes. If the reproduction was made from a new mold (formed from an original object), the details will not possess the clarity and precision of the original article. For further information see *The Official Price Guide to Glassware*, by Mark Pickvet, House of Collectibles, Random House, NY.

Bakewell Block

	LOW	AVG.	HIGH
Celery	$ 105	$ 120	$ 135
Champagne Glass	100	115	130
Creamer/Sugar, w/ lid	285	300	315
Decanter	135	150	165
Spooner	60	75	90
Tumbler	85	100	115
Whiskey Tumbler, handle	135	150	165
Wine	65	80	95

Canadian

Butter Dish, w/ lid	75	90	105
Celery	50	65	80
Compote, high, w/ lid	75	90	105
Compote, low	65	80	95
Cordial Glass	45	60	75
Creamer/Sugar, w/ lid	145	160	175
Goblet	65	80	95
Jam Jar	60	75	90
Pitcher	115	130	145
Plate, 6.5"	45	60	75
Plate, 7.5"	85	100	115
Sauce, flat	15	25	35
Sauce, ftd.	20	35	50
Spooner	45	60	75
Wine Glass	65	80	95

Diamond Thumbprint

Butter Dish, w/ lid	210	225	240
Cake Stand	310	325	340
Celery	225	250	275

	LOW	AVG.	HIGH
Champagne Glass	$ 275	$ 300	$ 325
Compote, ftd., scalloped edge	45	60	75
Creamer/Sugar, w/ lid	375	425	475
Decanter, no stopper, 1 pt.	85	100	115
Decanter, w/ stopper, 1 qt.	185	200	215
Goblet	450	500	550
Honey Dish	10	25	40
Sauce Boat	10	15	30
Spooner	105	120	135
Tumbler	135	150	165
Waste Bowl	85	100	115
Water Pitcher	400	500	600
Whiskey Tumbler, handled	300	350	400
Wine Glass	275	300	325
Wine Jug, places for holding glasses	1000	1200	1400

Flute

	LOW	AVG.	HIGH
Ale Glass	20	35	50
Bottle, bitters	30	45	60
Bowl, scalloped edge	25	40	55
Candlesticks, pr.	45	60	75
Champagne Glass	15	30	45
Compote, open, dia. 8"	30	45	60
Creamer/Sugar	65	80	95
Decanter, 1 qt.	50	65	80
Egg Cup, single	15	25	35
Egg Cup, double	20	35	50
Goblet	15	30	45
Honey Dish	15	25	35
Lamp	85	100	115
Mug	25	40	55
Pitcher	65	80	95
Salt, ftd.	10	25	40
Sauce, flat	10	20	30
Tumbler, 8 oz.	15	30	45
Whiskey, handled	15	30	45
Wine	15	30	45

Lee

	LOW	AVG.	HIGH
Celery Dish	135	150	165
Champagne Glass	185	200	215
Creamer/Sugar, w/ lid	360	375	390
Decanter	85	100	115
Goblet	185	200	215
Tumbler	135	150	165

Minerva

	LOW	AVG.	HIGH
Butter, w/ lid	150	175	200
Cake Plate, dia. 12"	135	150	165
Compote, w/ lid	85	100	115
Creamer/Sugar, w/ lid	175	200	225
Goblet	90	110	130

	LOW	AVG.	HIGH
Jam Jar, w/ lid	$ 115	$ 140	$ 165
Pickle Dish, oval, "Love's Request Is Pickles"	50	65	80
Pitcher	150	175	200
Plate, tab handled	85	100	115
Platter, oval	65	80	95
Relish Dish, 3 part	40	55	70
Sauce, flat	25	40	55
Sauce, ftd.	30	45	60
Spooner	50	65	80

PICKET

Butter, w/ lid	100	120	140
Celery	65	80	95
Compote, high, w/ lid	75	90	105
Compete, low	55	70	85
Creamer/Sugar, w/ lid	145	160	175
Goblet	65	80	95
Jam Jar	50	65	80
Pickle Dish, w/ lid	45	60	75
Pitcher	85	100	115
Salt	15	30	45
Spooner	20	35	50
Toothpick	45	60	75
Tumbler	50	65	80
Wine Glass	30	45	60

SCROLL

Butter	30	45	60
Celery	35	50	65
Compote	20	30	40
Creamer/Sugar, w/ lid	50	65	80
Egg Cup	35	50	65
Goblet	10	20	30
Pitcher	45	60	75
Relish Bowl	15	30	45
Salt	10	25	40
Sauce, flat	10	15	20
Sauce, ftd.	15	30	45
Spooner	15	30	45
Wine Glass	20	30	40

Pressed glass footed pitcher,
$150-$200.

Steuben Glass

The Steuben Glass Company has concentrated on producing fine art glass since its founding in 1903. The Corning Glass Works purchased the company in 1918. Steuben pieces are marked with either the letter "S" or the entire name "Steuben" scratched neatly and in tiny letters on the underside of the base. The model number is usually scratched there as well.

Many famous designs are still in production. The prices listed include the current retail price when new (*new*), the price of a "second-hand" but perfect condition piece (*perf*), and the value if the piece has a small scratch (*sm scr*). Also, the size and model number are given after each entry.

	SM SCR	PERF	NEW
Apple, 4", 7874	$ 70	$ 140	$ 340
Archaic Vase, 9.75", 8585	350	700	1695
Archaic Vase, tall, 13", 8584	490	950	2375
Arctic Fisherman, 6.5", 1023	800	1500	3850
Athena Candlestick, 6", 8687	50	90	225
Balloon Rally, 10.25", 0361	2800	5520	13,800
Bear Hand Cooler, 2.5", 5521	30	60	150
Bull Hand Cooler, 2.5", 5524	30	60	150
Butterfly, 8", 0085	2600	5750	14,300
Calyx Bowl, 9.5", 8115	80	140	360
Candy Dish, Ram's Head, 5", 7936	130	260	640
Cat Hand Cooler, 2.5", 5520	30	60	150
Cat Nap, 3", 8704	50	90	225
Celestial Bowl, 8.25", 8563	90	170	425
Christmas Tree, 6.25", 8498	120	220	560
Chronos Bowl, 7.5", 8706	70	140	350
Close to the Wind, 8", 1068	850	1600	4200
Cut Vase, 6.5", 0098	820	1500	4000
Deep Flower Bowl, 10", 8091	170	320	800
Deep Pillar Bowl, 9", 8346	200	380	950
Eagle, 4.25", 8496	70	140	340
Eagle, 5.5", 8304	150	280	710
Eagle, 12", 8130	150	300	740
Eagle Hand Cooler, 2.75", 5519	30	60	150
Elephant, 7.5", 8128	170	330	825
Elusive Buck, 7.25", 0503	1500	3000	7500
Equinox Bowl, 9.5", 8517	180	350	875
Excalibur, 8", 1000	650	1240	3100
Fawn, Woodland, 4.75", 8640	60	120	300
Flower Vase, 8.5", 7913	110	210	525
Folded Bowl, 7.25", 8707	40	80	200
Folded Bowl, med., 9", 8708	60	120	300
Fox, 3.25", 8582	40	70	185
Framed Bowl, 16", 8631	3000	6400	16,000
Framed Vase, 8.5", 8632	2100	4400	11,000
Framed Vase, tall, 16.5", 8630	2500	5000	13000
Frog Hand Cooler, 2.5", 5510	30	60	150
Galaxy, 3.5", 8395	160	300	780
Gander, 5.25", 8358	70	140	350
Gazelle Bowl, 6.75", 0053	4750	9000	23,000
Glass House, 3.5", 8633	90	180	450

	SM SCR	PERF	NEW
Goose, 4", 8344	$ 70	$ 140	$ 350
Handkerchief Vase, 9.5", 8618	130	250	625
Handkerchief Vase, sm., 7", 8703	50	90	225
Heart, point down, 3.5", 8376	90	170	420
Heart, point up, 4", 8377	90	170	420
Heart Pendant, 1.75", 1105	580	1100	2800
Heart Throb, 3.25", 8566	80	160	405
Heart to Heart, 2.5", 8626	40	70	185
Hellenic Urn, 9.5", 8592	190	375	925
Heritage Flared Vase, 12", 7706	150	300	725
Highball, 6.5", 7923	60	110	275
Horse Head, 5", 7779	60	120	310
I Love Hope Cube, 2", 8713	60	120	300
Ice Bear, 6", 1022	790	1500	3800
Ice Hunter, 6.25", 1033	860	1600	4150
Juliet Vase, 5.25", 8629	40	80	195
Lighthouse, 8.5", 1159	450	860	2150
Lion, 9.5", 1126	500	960	2400
Low Teardrop Candlestick, 4.5", 7995	100	200	500
Lyre Vase, 7.75", 8113	90	160	410
Menorah, 9.5", 8682	750	1500	3650
Moby Dick, 11.25", 0055	4500	9400	23,500
Monkey Hand Cooler, 2.75", 5526	30	60	150
Monument Valley, 8.75", 0358	900	1750	4300
Moravian Star, 2.5", 8625	90	180	450
New York, New York, 17", 0353	5500	12,000	30,000
Nut Bowl, 6", 8345	50	100	245
Old Fashioned Glass, 3.5", 7933	50	100	240
Owl Hand Cooler, 2.5", 5516	30	60	150
Peach, 3", 8600	60	110	275
Penguin, 3.5", 8295	40	80	195
Peony Bowl, 12.75", 8101	230	450	1100
Pillar of Friendship, 6.5", 8581	160	300	760
Pisces, 2.75", 8620	40	70	185
Porpoise, 9.25", 8126	120	230	580
Prelude & Fugue, 6", 1160	610	1100	2950
Puppy Love, 2.75", 8524	40	70	185
Pyramid Block, 3.5", 8413	80	160	400
Quail, 5.5", 8533	90	170	435
Rabbit Hand Cooler, 2.75", 5523	30	60	150
Rising Star, 4.25", 8621	180	340	850
Rooster Hand Cooler, 3.25", 5527	30	60	150
Rose Vase, 11.5", 8090	150	300	740
Rosebud Necklace, 2", 1116	330	640	1600
Sailboat, 6.5", 8570	120	230	575
Saturn Paperweight, 5.5", 8609	100	190	475
Scallop, 3.5", 8572	40	80	195
Scroll Candlestick, 4.75", 8735	50	100	250
Seashell, 3.5", 8552	60	120	310
Seawave Vase, 8", 8550	110	220	540
Ship's Decanter, 10", 7912	270	520	1300

	SM SCR	PERF	NEW
Shore Bird, 8.25", 8303	$ 90	$ 180	$ 440
Snail, 3.25", 7982	40	80	210
Snow Pine, 4.25", 8611	110	210	525
Spiral Bowl, 7", 8060	80	150	375
Spiral Vase, 6.5", 8058	80	150	365
Star of David, 2.5", 8686	80	140	360
Star Stream, 5.25", 8567	120	220	560
Star-Spangled Banner, 6", 8623	330	640	1600
Stardust Bar Glass, 4.125", 8579	70	130	320
Stardust Decanter, 9.5", 8580	260	500	1250
Starfish, 4.75", 8622	40	80	195
Strawberry Pendant, 2", 1104	230	440	1100
Sunflower Bowl, 10", 8530	90	170	420
Sunflower Bowl, large, 15.5", 8531	200	380	950
Swan, curved neck, 7.5", 8484	110	210	515
Swan, straight neck, 6.5", 8483	110	210	515
Teardrop Candlestick, 8.75", 7792	140	270	675
Trout & Fly, 8", 1002	450	860	2150
Turtle Hand Cooler, 2.5", 5514	30	60	150
Twist Bowl, 8.75", 8501	90	170	420
Twist Bowl, large, 13.5", 8569	180	340	840
Twist Bud Vase, 8", 8499	60	120	295
Twist Candlestick, 6", 8502	130	240	600
Whirlpool Vase, 11", 8087	190	360	900

Waterford Crystal

The Waterford Glass House produced Waterford, the most famous Irish glass, from 1783 until 1850. Craftsmen cut blanks on a revolving iron wheel combined with sand and a water trickle, then polished them with a soft powder. Waterford items are marked "Penrose Waterford." The color of Waterford is whiter than other Irish glass, though it is often mistakenly thought to have a blue tinge.

Americans imported Waterford in the early 19th century. The characteristic Waterford items, most often associated with Ireland and Irish glass, include covered vases and jars for food, large serving bowls, oil and vinegar bottles, glasses, jugs, and salts.

In the late 1940s a new company started as Waterford. They make copies of original Waterford pieces, along with a variety of fine Cut glass items. This period produced the Waterford crystal listed here.

	LOW	AVG.	HIGH
Ashtray, notched sides, 5" dia.	$ 45	$ 60	$ 75
Bowl, fruit, spiked diamonds w/ panels and thumbprints, tapered sides, sgn., 4.5" ht., 12" dia.	250	285	320
Bowl, fruit, tapered sides, cut vesicas on sides and base, round, 3.5" ht., 8" len.	150	210	270
Bowl, notched diamonds, notched and paneled edge, star-cut design on base, oblong shape, sgn., 4.5" ht., 13.5" long	120	165	220
Bowl, salad, cut diamond design, notched edge. star-cut base on tapered base, sgn.. 4.5" ht., 10" dia.	160	230	300
Bowl, salad, marquise shape w/ daisy and button motif, flared rim, cylindrical, sgn., 3.5" ht., 9" dia.	150	205	260
Bowl, salad, slanted sides, cut zigzag vesicas, star-cut design on base, round, sgn., 4" ht., 8.5" dia.	120	170	220
Candlesticks, star-cut design on bases, 6" ht.	100	150	200
Compote, spiked diamond band, cut fans around scalloped rim, star-cut design on base, sgn., 5.5" ht., 5.5" dia.	120	165	210
Compote, spiked diamond band w/ thumbprint band, round, notched rim, notched base, sgn., 6" ht., 7.5" dia.	230	285	340
Compotes, pr., notched thumbprint, lid has spiral finials, base is 6-sided, 14.5" ht.	325	450	575
Decanter, Alana Pattern	150	200	250
Decanter, cut diamonds w/ sunburst design, thumbprints, notched neck, star-cut design stopper, sgn.	140	180	220
Decanter, paneled neck, base has cut sawtooth band, sgn., 11.5" ht.	150	200	250
Dish, round-shape spiked diamond bands, ball finial, star-cut design on base, sgn., 6" ht., 6" dia.	100	140	180
Dishes, pr., star design in center, 3.5" dia.	75	100	125
Jar, marmalade, pedestal base, 6" ht.	100	150	200
Jar, star-cut design on lid, cut crosses and panels, sgn., 5.5" ht.	150	200	250
Mug, notched sides, 4.5" ht.	45	60	75
Mugs, marquise shapes alternate w/ cane design in reserves, star-cut design on base, sgn., set of 4, 4.5" ht.	200	250	300
Napkin Ring, cut-diamond pattern	50	75	125
Vase, cut-diamond design, cylindrical shape, 6" ht.	75	100	130
Vase, cut-diamond panels w/ tapered sides, cylindrical shape, 10" ht.	120	165	210
Vase, fine panels of double-shield-form notching, cylindrical shape, sgn., 8" ht.	80	125	170

Holiday Decorations

Holidays are special events, times when we can get together with friends and family, exchange gifts, observe religious rites or dress in outrageous costumes. Collectors of holiday items can choose from a wealth of material. Many collectors focus on one holiday, such as Christmas or Halloween. Others prefer to specialize in a type of item, such as postcards. Whatever the method, displaying your finds is great fun and collecting can be enjoyed year round. For further information we recommend *The Official Price Guide to Holiday Collectibles*, Helaine Fendelman and Jeri Schwartz, House of Collectibles, Random House, NY, 1991; *Halloween in America: A Collector's Guide*, Stuart Schneider, Schiffer Publishing, Atglen, PA, 1995; and *Christmas Revisited*, Robert Brenner, Schiffer Publishing, Atglen, PA, 1986

Christmas decoration, snowman, plastic, ca. 1950, height 5", $10-$14.

Christmas

Figural Light Bulbs

	LOW	AVG.	HIGH
Andy Gump, milk glass	$ 70	$ 80	$ 90
Bear, w/ guitar, milk glass	26	30	34
Blue Bird, milk glass	26	30	34
Clock	26	30	34
Clown, milk glass	40	50	60
Elephant, milk glass	50	60	70
Fish, milk glass	20	25	30
Gingerbread Man	30	35	40
Grapes, milk glass	20	25	30
House, milk glass	20	25	30
Humpty Dumpty, milk glass	35	40	45
Lantern	12	15	18
Parrot, milk glass	32	42	52
Pinocchio	32	37	42
Puss N' Boots, milk glass	40	45	50
Santa, painted	60	70	80
Snowman, milk glass	25	30	35
Zeppelin, w/ flag	130	150	170

Greeting Cards

	LOW	AVG.	HIGH
A Merry Christmas and Happy New Year, children and Christmas tree, c. 1870s	$ 3	$ 5	$ 7
A Merry Christmas to You All, family in snowy woodland, c. 1880	3	4	5
Child, in 19th-century bonnet	3	4	5
Hail, Day of Joy, Prang, angel kneeling w/ dove on finger, c. 1870	16	19	22
Here, Open the Door, Kate Greenaway, messenger knocking on door, c. 1880	42	52	62
Here Comes the New Year w/ Lots of Good Cheer, child, tree and toys, c. 1870	4	6	8
Ice Pond, boy putting skates on a girl, fringed and embroidered, German	3	4	5
Merry Christmas and Happy New Year, children in snow, church, c. 1880	4	6	8
Merry Christmas to You All, L. Prang, brown-suited Santa, sq.	24	28	32
My Lips May Give a Message, Kate Greenaway, girl holding letter, c. 1880	42	52	62
Pop-Up Card, ice skating scene, England, c. 1890	18	22	26
Prang's American Third Prize Christmas Card, by C. Coleman, oriental scene	20	24	28
Season's Greetings, card shaped like fan	2	3	4
Season's Greetings, mechanical, boy w/ flowers, 19th century	16	20	24
Season's Greetings, river and small boat, 19th century	3	4	5
Victorian Card, paper lace border surrounds Season's Greeting, c. 1800s	10	13	16
Wishing You a Happy New Year, Prang, folded, girl on front, old man on back, fringed, w/ tasseled cord, c. 1884	15	18	21
Wishing You a Merry Christmas, Prang, fireplace, cat and kittens, sq., c. 1800s	15	18	21
W/ Best Christmas Wishes, Tuck, girl w/ spray of flowers, c. 1885	12	15	18

Ornaments

Angel, Dresden	210	260	310
Angel, paper, die-cut, trimmed w/ tinsel	50	60	70
Angel's Face, blown glass, ht. 2.5"	40	50	55
Baby in Basket, cardboard, Dresden	200	250	300
Baby in Bunting, blown glass, emb. lettering, len. 4"	70	80	90
Ball, amber	22	27	32
Basket, fruit-filled, blown glass	30	35	40
Bear w/ Muff, blown glass	60	70	80
Camel, cardboard, Dresden, flat	50	65	80
Camel, Dresden	55	65	75
Canary, blown glass	28	33	43
Carrot, blown glass, emb. detail, c. 1910, len. 4"	40	50	60
Child, milk glass	22	27	32
Church, blown glass	40	50	60
Clown Head, blown glass	40	50	60
Cuckoo Clock, blown glass, emb. and ptd.	50	60	70

	LOW	AVG.	HIGH
Doll's Head, blown glass, silver and flesh color, glass eyes ..... $ 85		$ 105	$ 125
Elephant, mercury glass w/ milk glass tusks, ht. 4" 70		80	90
Fish, blown glass 50		55	60
Football Player, milk glass 70		90	110
Foxy Grandpa, blown glass w/ applied legs, ht. 4.5" 150		175	200
Girl, blown glass... 40		60	80
Girl's Head, blown glass w/ blown glass eyes, ht. 2.5" 50		70	90
Happy Hooligan, blown glass w/ applied legs, ht. 4.5" 180		205	230
Heart, blown glass, large 40		50	60
Icicle, glass 20		30	40
Kugel, dark blue, grapes w/ metal cap 220		250	280
Lamp 50		70	90
Man in the Moon, blown glass, green, ht. 3" 70		80	90
Monkey Holding Stick, blown glass, ht. 2.5" 100		130	160
Moon, happy/sad full moon faces composition squeeze toy, c.			
1890 120		140	160
Ornament, pocket watch, blown glass w/ paper face 60		80	100
Peacock, blown glass, brush tail 40		60	80
Pear, pressed cotton 20		25	30
Penguin, blown glass, blue, silver, red, emb. feet 40		50	60
Pinecone, blown glass 15		18	21
Pipe, blown glass 20		25	30
Purse, blown glass, wire rapped 60		70	80
Santa carrying bag of toys, blown glass, ht. 2.5" 60		80	100
Santa Claus, celluloid, white and red, c. 1930s, ht. 4.5" 50		60	70
Santa, celluloid 50		70	90
Santa, w/ plaster face 40		50	60
Scottie Dog, blown glass, yellow and blue 80		90	100
Smiling Snowman, w/ broom, blown glass, c. 1910, ht. 3.5" 50		60	70
Stag, blown glass, blue w/ gold antlers, ht. 3" 40		50	60
Star, Dresden, 2-sided.. 40		50	60
Swan, blown glass w/ spun glass wings and tail, c. 1900 90		110	130
Teapot 30		35	40
Turkey, blown glass w/ spun glass wings and tail, c. 1900 90		110	130

Postcards

Postcard, hold-to-the-light, Santa Claus 125		138	150
Postcard, Santa in green, full figure 25		28	30
Postcard, Santa painting sled 10		13	15

Miscellaneous

Bank, Santa at chimney, plaster, c. 1950s, ht. 11" 60		80	100
Bank, Santa in armchair, plaster, c. 1950s, ht. 10" 70		90	110
Button, "Merry Christmas," Santa w/ pack in household, litho.			
tin 20		25	30
Button, "Santa Claus Gave This To Me," c. 1940s, dia. .5" 10		12	14
Button, Santa reading a book titled Good Boys-Good Girls,			
dia. 1" 10		12	14
Crèche, papier-mâché stable made of wood, set of 17 figures,			
c. 1930 110		140	170
Decoration, angel, wax, spun glass wings 45		55	65

	LOW	AVG.	HIGH
Decoration, snowman, w/ black stovepipe hat, pipe, red scarf, plastic, c. 1950s, ht. 5"	$ 10	$ 12	$ 14
Decoration, Snowman, w/ blue cap, red mittens and silver skates, c. 1950s, ht. 5"	12	15	18
Lamp, figural Santa, hard plastic, c. 1955, ht. 16"	25	35	45
Light, Santa glass globe on tin battery-box base, c. 1950	30	40	50
Lights, bells on a string	18	22	26
Plate, child's ABCs, features children and snowman	80	100	120
Snowdome, Figural, Santa and reindeer w/ dome center, plastic, c. 1950s, ht. 5"	18	21	24
Snowdome, figural, Santa w/ dome center, plastic, c. 1950s, ht. 5"	16	18	20
Tree, bottle brush, Japan, c. 1950, ht. 1950	4	5	6
Tree, feather, German, c. 1910, ht. 18"	220	270	320
Victorian Christmas Stocking	80	100	120

Easter

	LOW	AVG.	HIGH
Bunny Mobile, plastic, early style auto, c. 1950s	22	27	35
Candy Container, Easter egg, red, gold, and white litho. cardboard, c. 1940	20	25	30

Figural Santa Lamp, hard plastic, ca. 1955, height 16", $25-$45. —Photo courtesy of George Kerrigan.

	LOW	AVG.	HIGH
Candy Container, rabbit, pressed cardboard, removable head .. $ 90	$ 110	$ 120
Candy Container, rabbit, pressed cardboard, white, c. 1950s 35	45	55
Egg Cup, figural bunny and egg, plastic, c. 1950s, ht. 3" 4	6	8
Greeting Card, angels on front, by Whitney, New York, 19th		
century 4	5	6
Greeting Card, Bible verses, birds, late 19th century 2	3	4
Greeting Card, booklet, poem, cross w/ flowers, German 4	6	8
Greeting Card, child coming out of egg, gold-fringed 2	3	4
Greeting Card, cross on reef in sea, by Carter & Karrick, 19th		
century 3	4	5
Greeting Card, Cupid w/ ribbon holding flowers, 19th century 3	4	5
Greeting Card, floral cross on front, German, 19th century 2	3	4
Greeting Card, girl climbing out of an egg shell, fringed, German,		
19th century 5	7	9
Greeting Card, heads of children in flower pot, 19th century 2	3	4
Greeting Card, Shakespeare's, Heaven Give You Many Merry		
Days, 19th century 2	3	4
Toy, rabbit pulling cart, tinplate, Chein 75	85	95

Halloween

	LOW	AVG.	HIGH
Candlesticks, black cat and Jack-o-lantern, pr., plastic, c. 1950,		
ht. 2.5"15 19	22	25
Costume, gorilla, w/ gauze mask in original Collegetown		
Costumes box, c. 1940s 40	45	50
Decoration, black cat, cardboard fold-out, 1950s, ht. 20" 32	37	42
Decoration, Jack-o-lantern scarecrow on wheeled base,		
orange and black plastic, c. 1950s, ht. 5" 22	24	26
Decoration, Jack-o-lantern scarecrow, orange plastic w/		
black jacket, c. 1950s, ht. 5" 18	20	22
Decoration, Jack-O-Lantern scarecrow, orange plastic w/		
orange and black checked jacket, c. 1950s, ht. 5" 24	27	30
Decoration, snowman, orange and black plastic, ht. 5" 30	35	40
Decoration, witch and black cat dancers, accordion-fold		
crepe paper, 1960s, len. 28" 17	19	21
Decoration, witch, bats and black cat, orange, black and green		
pressed cardboard, c. 1940s, ht. 18" 50	55	60
Eyeglasses, figural hissing black cats, plastic 25	30	35
Game, Whirl-O-Halloween Fortune and Stunt Game, card w/		
spinner, 7" x 9" 30	40	50
Hat, orange and black crepe paper 8	10	12
Jack-O-Lantern, cardboard, accordion fold-out, 1950s, ht. 11" ... 30	35	40
Jack-O-Lantern, pressed cardboard w/ insert, ht. 8" 100	120	140
Jack-O-Lantern, pressed cardboard without insert, ht. 8" 70	77	85
Lantern, cardboard die-cut w/ various Halloween scenes over		
orange tissue paper, c. 1935, ht. 12" 45	55	65
Light, Jack-o-lantern glass globe on tinplate battery-box base,		
c. 1950 30	40	50
Light, pumpkin, orange plastic, battery operated, c. 1950s,		
dia. 2.5" 37	42	47
Mask, black cat, paper, round eyes, 11" x 8" 12	15	18
Mask, clown, paper, red, black and yellow, 8" x 9" 12	15	18

	LOW	AVG.	HIGH
Mask, devil, gauze	$ 15	$ 18	$ 21
Mask, owl, cardboard w/ cat and pumpkin band, 12" x 12" 30		35	40
Noisemaker, cylindrical shake type, litho. tin, Jack-o-lanterns and witches, c. 1950, dia. 4" 12		14	16
Noisemaker, paddle type, tinplate litho. w/ Jack-o-lantern, c. 1940s, len. 10" 26		30	34
Noisemaker, spin type, tinplate litho. w/ black cat motif, c. 1948, dia. 4" 10		12	14
Noisemaker, spin type, tinplate litho. w/ flapper witch and skyscrapers, c. 1940, dia. 4" 15		18	21
Noisemaker, tambourine type, tinplate litho. w/ Jack-o-lantern, c. 1940s, dia. 30		35	40
Party Favor, basket, black and orange plastic, c. 1950s, dia. 3.5" 10		12	14
Party Favor, black cat, holds lollipop, orange plastic w/ black-striped jersey, c. 1950s, ht. 5" 16		19	22
Party Favor, pumpkin, orange plastic, w/ metal bail, c. 1950s, dia. 3.5" 6		8	10
Postcard, Halloween, signed Clapsaddle 15		20	25
Postcard, Halloween, Tuck 12		14	16
Postcard, Halloween, Winsch 50		58	65

Thanksgiving

	LOW	AVG.	HIGH
Candlesticks, cornucopia shape, ceramic, pair, 3" 12		15	18
Candlesticks, pilgrims, ceramic, 2" pair 10		12	14
Candy Container, cornucopia, papier-mâché, c. 1910 50		60	70
Candy Container, turkey, composition, c. 1930s 20		30	35
Centerpiece, turkey, Hallmark, c. 1940 10		12	14
Cornucopia, wicker 12		15	20
Platter, decorated w/ Tom Turkey, Japan, c. 1935 18		18	21
Postcard, Thanksgiving, signed Brundage 15		23	28
Postcard, Thanksgiving, signed Clapsaddle 8		10	12

Thanksgiving Postcard, signed Clapsaddle, $8-$12.

Valentine's Day

	LOW	AVG.	HIGH
Easel Valentine, fold-back, free-standing, c. 1900 .... $ 15	$ 18	$ 21
German, large ship, mechanical pull-down 70	80	90
German, pulldown, children, c. 1915 6	8	10
German, pullout and stand-up cottage, c. 1910 12	15	18
German, pullout and stand-up steam boiler, c. 1910 12	15	18
German, stand-up, little girl holding opening parasol, c. 1920 15	20	25
Gibson Art, paper doll mechanical stand-up, little girl holding		
doll, German 20	25	30
Gibson Girl (from photo), Meek and Son, surrounded by lace,		
cherub heads, c. 1890 25	35	45
Hat Trimmer, Elton and Co., NY, glum looking woman sewing hat,		
w/ verse, c. 1880 22	26	30
Heart-Shaped, folder, Tuck, little girl on front 12	14	16
Heart-Shaped, lace c. 1905 9	12	15
Hearts Are Ripe, children picking heart-shaped apples from tree .. 3	5	7
Honeycomb, "Cupid's Temple of Love," c. 1928 6	8	10
Maggie and Jiggs, c. 1940 18	21	24
McLoughlin, three-layer, silver, white, lace, c. 1880 20	25	30
McLoughlin, three-layer, white, gold, lace, c. 1880 10	12	14
Mechanical, various animals, c. 1930 10	12	14
Popeye, c. 1940 18	21	24
Temple of Love, Tuck's Betsy Beauties series, young girl and		
butterfly 12	14	16
To My Valentine, from Tuck's Innocence Abroad series, 2		
children, verse 12	14	16
Victorian, fold-out, paper lace 20	22	24

Various Holidays

	LOW	AVG.	HIGH
Fourth of July, postcard 5	8	10
Happy Birthday, greeting card, blue-fringed, floral design, c.		
1880 3	4	5
Happy Birthday, greeting card, children, 19th century 2	3	4
Happy Birthday, greeting card, maroon floral, fringed, 19th		
century 3	4	5
Lincoln's Birthday, postcard 8	12	15
Memorial Day, postcard 5	8	10
Washington's Birthday, postcard 5	8	10

Irons

Irons were used in Asia for centuries before their 17th-century Western introduction. Nineteenth and 20th-century collectible irons include: the charcoal iron; the box iron which featured a heated metal slug placed inside the hollow iron; and the sadiron, a solid iron that was heated on the hearth or stove. In 1871 Mary Potts invented a detachable handle for the sadiron. The Potts iron led to self-heating irons fueled with gasoline or cooking gas. These were dangerous and unsatisfactory. The electric iron was patented in 1882.

Collectible irons are still reasonably priced. Collectors should seek odd-shaped irons.

Flat iron, $10-$14.

	LOW	AVG.	HIGH
Alcohol Iron, wooden handle, c. 1880	$ 90	$ 105	$ 120
Box Iron, English, heated slugs, c. 1800	110	150	190
Box Iron, heated slug, c. 1890	60	80	100
Box Iron, solid brass, punch decoration, ht. 5"	130	145	160
Charcoal Iron, brass fittings, chimney vent	90	110	130
Charcoal Iron, twisted handle, chimney vent	100	115	130
Charcoal Iron, wooden handle, c. 1890	60	70	80
Charcoal Iron, wooden iron, with trivet	80	100	120
Child's Iron, glass base, wooden handle	12	14	16
Flat Iron, all iron	10	12	14
Flat Iron, bail handle	10	15	20
Flat Iron, charcoal, chimney vent, c. 1860	40	50	60
Flat Iron, hollow handle	40	50	60
Flat Iron, metal handle, c. 1860	40	45	50
Flat Iron, no handle, Blass and Drake, Newark, NJ, ht. 6"	5	10	15
Flat Iron, removable handle, c. 1870	40	45	50
Flat Iron, rope handle	30	40	50
Flat Iron, stone body, metal handle, c. 1850	60	70	80
Flat Iron, wooden handle, child's, c. 1880	40	50	60
Flat Iron, wooden handle, large	50	55	60
Fluting Iron, brass rollers, enamel dec., 2 slugs, ht. 9"	110	130	150
Fluting Iron, double, with holder	90	100	110
Fluting Iron, Geneva, c. 1875	60	75	90
G.E. Electric Iron, c. 1905	60	65	70
G.E. Electric Iron, c. 1920	50	60	70
Gasoline Iron, Coleman	30	40	50
Gasoline Iron, wooden handle, c. 1910	80	90	100

	LOW	AVG.	HIGH
Laundry Stove, cast iron, double burner	$ 230	$ 285	$ 340
Laundry Stove, cast iron, single burner	170	205	240
Laundry Stove, fancy cast iron, c. 1895	620	750	880
Nickel-Plated Iron	30	45	60
Polishing Iron, oval shaped, c. 1845	70	80	90
Sadiron, alcohol iron, nickel plated, Foote Manufacturing Co. ...	70	80	90
Sadiron, for child, removable wooden handle, 2" x 4"	60	70	80
Sadiron, waffle pattern on bottom, "Genoa"	40	45	50
Tailor's iron	40	50	60

Stoneware iron stand, $40-$60.

Knives

	LOW	HIGH
A. J. Westersson, 1900	$ 10	$ 60
A. M. Leonard, Inc., 1885-present	10	95
A. R. Justice, 1897-1937	35	150
A. W. Flint & Co., 20th cent.	30	150
A. Wingen, 1875-present	5	90
B. Altman & Co., 1900s	10	40
B. B. Knife Co., 1880s	50	350
B. H Morse, 1857	25	125
B. H. Special, 1910	15	30
B. Svoboda, 1950-present	10	25
Banner Knife Co., pre-1915	15	45
Barrett-Hicks Co., 1920s	25	125
Battle Axe, 1980s	20	175
Battle Axe Cutlery Co., 1897-1937	35	150
Bauer, 1930	5	25
Bay State Mfg. Co., 1890s	45	250
Beaver Brook Knife Co., 1880	50	350
Bench Mark Knives, 1984-present	35	125
Berkshire Cutlery Co., 1890	20	45
Besteel Warranted, 1930s	10	25
Bingham Cutlery Co., 1841-1930	15	160
Blake & Lamb, 1930s	20	165
Brantford Cutlery Co., 1900s	20	150
Bridge Cutlery Co., 1915	65	375
Bridgeport Knife Co., 1904	40	150
Brighton Cutlery Works, 1900s	15	45
Bristol Line, 1950s	8	45
Bud Brand Cutlery Co., 1922	25	100
Buffalo Cutlery Co., 1915	35	160
Buster Brown Shoe Co., 1930s	15	125
Butler Bros., 1865-1952	25	120
Butler & Co., 1865-1952	15	75
Butterick Pattern Co., 1910s	10	25
C. Bertram, 1872-present	40	250
C. Platts Sons, 1900-1905	50	600
Cam, 1980s	10	65
Cameron Knife Co., 1920s	15	65
Canton Hardware Co., 1910	15	150
Capitol Knife Co., 1920s	15	125
Carl Schmidt Sohn, 1829-present	20	120
Carrier Cutlery Co., 1900-1921	45	225
Case Bros., 1912	75	1200
Case Cutlery Company, 1907-1911	50	700
Case Mfg. Co., 1898-1899	50	850
Catskill Knife Co., 1930s	15	150
Cattaraugus, 1984-present	15	50
Challenge Cut. Corp., 1891-1928	20	150
Chalmers & Murray, 1890s	35	95
Chicago Knife Works, 1911	25	125
Clauberg Cutlery Co., 1857-present	10	55

	LOW	HIGH
Clauss, 1887-present	$ 10	$ 75
Clay Cutlery Co., 1930s	30	300
Clements, 20th cent.	10	60
Clipper Cutlery Co., 1901	10	50
Commander, 1891-1928	65	100
Concord Cutlery Co., 1880s	25	150
Cook Brothers, 1890s	55	150
Corning Knife Co., 1930s	10	50
Cornwall Knife Co., 19th cent.	25	95
Cronk & Carrier Mfg. Co., 1900-1921	45	225
Cussins & Fearn, 1930s	25	75
Defender, 1912	200	600
Delmar Cutlery Co., 1910	25	95
Dictator, 1930s	10	25
Dixon Cutlery Co., 1920s	10	55
Dollar Knife Co., 1922	15	150
Dollar Knife Co., 1927	15	150
Domar Cutlery Co., 1916-1920	15	85
Duane Cutlery Co., 1910s	5	20
Dwight Divine & Sons, 1876-1941	35	175
E. Barnes & Sons, 1856-1865	25	200
E.K A., 1885-present	20	75
Eagle Brand, 1974-present	10	900
Eagle Cutlery Co., 1883-1945	10	150
Eagle Pencil Co., 1883-1945	5	25
Eagleton Knife Co., 1890s	20	125
Eagle/Phila, 1883-1945	20	70
Edge Mark, 1950-present	3	15
Edward Barnes, 1900s	50	750
Edward Barnes & Sons, 1856-1865	65	400
Edward Parker & Sons, 1900s	25	95
Edward Zin, 1920s	5	15
Enderses, 1918	30	125
Enterprise Cutlery Co., 1920s	25	85
Erber, 1890s	5	15
Erma, 1950s	5	50
Ernest G. Ahrens, 1930s	15	65
Esemco, 1921-1949	5	8
Essem Co., 1921-1949	10	20
Fabyan Knife Co., 1890s	25	110
Fairmont Cutlery Co., 1930s	20	65
Fall River Knife Co., 1900s	15	75
Fayetteville Knife Co., 1911	30	90
Federal Knife Co., 1920s	20	75
Frank Mills & Co., 1860s	8	85
Frost Cutlery Co., 1978-present	5	60
Fulton Cutlery Co., 1910s	35	125
G. Dunbab, 1901	5	25
Gellman Bros., 1920	15	60
George Dobson, 1880s	25	250
George Schrade Knife, 1925-1945	20	200

	LOW	HIGH
George Tritch Hdw. Co., 1910s	$ 25	$ 85
George W. Korn, 1880-1925	25	2000
Gilbert, 1900	60	150
Glenfall Cutlery Co., 1898	15	60
Globe Cutlery Co., 1922	20	55
Golden Gate Cutlery Co., 1890s	20	75
H. G. Long & Co., 1846-present	20	85
H. G. Long & Co., 1846-present	65	175
H. Keschner, 1920s	25	45
H. K. Co., 1916-1930	25	200
Hart Cutlery Co., 1920s	20	200
Hartford Cutlery Co., 1880s	150	410
Hen & Rooster, 1872-present	15	1000
Henckels International, 1970s	10	45
Henry Barge, 1850	25	200
Henry Hobson & Sons, 1860s	25	350
Herder & Co., 1872-present	10	125
High Carbon Steel, 1930s	20	150
Hillard & Chapman, 1850s	25	300
Holley, 18501930s	25	450
Holley Mfg. Co., 18501930s	25	450
Hollingsworth Knife Co., 1916-1930	25	200
Howard Cutlery Co., 1890s	45	200
Howes Cutlery Co., 1900s	25	135
Hudson Knife Co., 1927	20	65
Hudson Valley Cutlery Co., 1890s	25	200
I. Manson, 19th cent.	20	55
Indiana Cutlery Co., 1932	45	95
International Cutlery Co., 1920s	20	200
Iver John Sons. G. Co., 1912	25	150
J. A. Schmidt & Sohne, 1829-present	15	200
J. Curley & Bro., 1880-1925	25	175
J. D. Case, 1898-1899	40	400
J. H. Andrew & Co., Ltd., 1860s	25	300
J. H. Sutcliffe & Co., 1900s	20	125
J. Koester & Sons, 1930s	15	100
J. P. Snow Co., 1861	25	65
J. Russell & Co. Green, 1834-present	25	400
J. W. Billings, 1880s	25	200
Jackmaster, 1938-present	10	60
James Boden, 1860	15	200
James Rodgers, 1830s-1950s	25	300
John Kay, 1857	25	250
John Newton H., 1906	25	275
John W. Hobson, 19th cent.	25	300
Joseph Fenton & Sons, 1860s	25	300
Kamp Cutlery Co., 1910s	8	20
Kane Cutlery Co., 1910-1916	65	375
Ka-Bar Cutlery Co., 1923-1951	25	600
Ka-Bar/Union Cut. Co., 1923-1951	25	600
Keen Cutlery Co., 1910s	25	350

	LOW	HIGH
Keen Kutter, 1940-1960	$ 25	$ 200
Keener Edge, 1932	10	75
Keenwell Mfg. Co., 1910s	25	200
Kershaw, contemp.	5	125
Khyber, 1980s	3	15
Kipsi Kut, 1900	25	150
Kunde & Co., contemp.	20	95
Kutwell, 1930s	50	300
L.V. K. Assn., 1900-1905	75	250
Lakota Corp., contemp.	20	100
Layman Carey Co., 1920	25	175
Lenox Cutlery Co., 1910s	10	25
Liberty Knife Co., 1920s	25	60
Linden & Co., 1887-present	25	200
Long, 1880s	25	175
Lord Bros., 1880s	25	175
Luke Firth, 1850s	25	400
Lux, 1920s	5	55
M. W. H. Co., 1893-1963	25	150
Majestic Cutlery Co., 1910s	5	225
Manchester, 1920s	5	100
Marshall Wells Hdw. Co., 1893-1963	35	700
Martin Bros. & Naylor, 1860s	60	100
Marx & Co., 1800s	50	300
Mitchell & Co. Ltd., 1910s	10	150
Mount Vernon Cutlery Co., 1890s	10	50
New Cent. Cutlery Co., 1900s	20	55
New England Knife Co., 1910s	45	125
New Haven Cutlery Co., 1890s	15	90
North American Knife Co., 1920s	15	65
North West Cutlery Co., 1890	10	90
Norvell's Best, 1902-1917	25	300
Norvell-Shapleigh Hdw. Co., 1902-1917	15	300
O. N. B., 1910s	25	125
Oakman Bros., 1900s	25	500
Occident Cutlery Co., 1910s	25	200
Oklahoma City Hardware, 1911-1951	25	65
Old Cutlery, 1978-present	5	20
Osgood Bray & Co., 19th cent.	15	200
Pal Blade Co., 1929-1953	15	90
Pal Cutlery Co., 1929-1953	15	90
Paris Bead, 1920s	25	45
Parisian Novelty Co., 1915	5	20
Parker Bros, 1978-present	5	20
Pennsylvanla Knife Co., 1914-1921	45	200
Penn. Cutlery Co., 1914-1921	10	150
Phoenix Knife Co., 1892-1916	45	175
Platts, 1920s	25	175
Precise, contemp.	10	125
Presto George, 1925-1945	30	175
Q. C. C. C., 1922	12	300

	LOW	HIGH
Quick Point, 1930s	$ 25	$ 75
R. & W. Bradford, 1850s	15	150
Ranger, 1938-present	5	10
Red Stag, contemp.	20	125
Richard Abr. Herder, 1885-present	15	110
Richmond Cutlery Co., 19th cent.	25	100
Riverside Cutlery Co. N.Y., 1918	15	50
Robbins Clark & Biddle, 19th cent.	25	200
Robert Kerder, 1872-present	15	175
Robert Klaas, 1834-present	15	250
Robert Lingard, 19th cent.	25	1500
Robinson Bros. & Co., 1880-1925	45	300
Romo, contemp.	3	15
Runkel Bros., 1920s	15	35
S. B. Luttbell & Co., 1880	15	200
S. E. Oates & Sons, pre-1915	15	150
Sable, contemp.	4	12
Samuel Barlow Barlowz, 1780-1840	25	500
Samuel Bradfobd, 1850	15	150
Samuel Hague, 1830s-1950s	25	200
Samuel Robinson, 19th cent.	25	400
Sanders Manufacturing Co., contemp.	35	85
Schmidt & Ziegler, 1930s	20	95
Shapleigh Wade. Co., 1920-1960	15	400
Shapleigh, 1920-1960	15	150
Simmons Boss, 1940-1960	25	50
Singleton & Priessman, 1861	50	150
Smith & Clark, 1850	25	250
Smith & Hopkins, 1850	25	500
Smith & Wesson, 1974-present	20	1200
Spear Cutlery Co., pre-1915	10	25
Spring Cutlery Co., 1890	45	150
Standard Cutlery Co., 1901-1903	50	200
Standard Knife Co., 1901-1903	50	300
Summit Knife Co., 1906	10	35
Scanner, 1980s	5	50
Syracuse Knife Co., 1930s	15	75
T. C. Barnsley Mfg. Co., 1898	15	200
T. T. C. Diamond Brand, 1909	10	200
Tampa Hdw. Co., 1910	15	150
Taylor Cutlery Co., 1978-present	5	45
Terrier Cutlery Co., 1910-1916	45	110
Theo M. Green Co., 1916-1920	5	60
Thomas Mfg. Co., 1907-1911	40	150
Thornton, 1950s	5	15
Tombay Cutlery Co., 1910s	45	200
Twig Brand, 1911	15	75
Ulster Knife Co., 1876-1941	45	225
U. S. Knife Co., 1904	20	85
Union Cutlery Co., 1911-1951	45	2000
Valley Falls Cutlery Co., 1915	15	75

	LOW	HIGH
Valley Forge Cutlery Co., 1892-1916	$ 40	$ 300
Voyles Cutlery, 1970s	10	40
W. R. Humphreys & Co., 1875-present	10	25
W. Thornhill, 19th cent.	25	500
W. W. Bingham, 1841-1930	15	175
W. & T. Marsh, 1780-1840	25	500
Wadsworth, 1905-1917	5	40
Wadsworth & Sons, 1905-1917	10	45
Ward & Co., 1860s	10	400
Washington Cutlery Co., 1885-1927	25	175
Washington Cutlery Co., 1885-1927	15	150
Western Cutlery Co., 1978-present	5	65
Western States Cutlery Co., 1911-1951	10	500
Wilbert Cutlery Co., 1909	45	250
Wilheim Clauberg, 1857-present	10	150
Will Roll Bearing Co., 1920s	25	200
William Rodgers, 1830-present	25	500
Wilson, Hawksworth & Moss, 19th cent.	25	400
Woodbuby Cutlery Co., 19th cent.	25	250
X. C. D. W. & S., 1830-present	10	150
Yale Cutlery Co., 1800s	10	150

Metallic Collectibles
Aluminum

Although aluminum is a basic element on the periodic table, it was extremely difficult to purify. During the19th century it was a luxury metal. Not until after Charles Hill patented an inexpensive smelting method in 1886 did it become a "practical" metal. Nearly all aluminum wares on the market are 20th century.

For further information see *Collectible Aluminum*, by Everett Grist. Aluminum can be cleaned with soap and water or even paste silver polish. Be gentle in cleaning; aluminum dents and scratches easily. Salt will corrode aluminum.

"Good" pieces are not dented or heavily scratched. They are simple in form. "Best" pieces have a fine texture, such as a hammered finish, and have a striking visual appearance. This can be very subjective. One collector's treasure is another collector's junk.

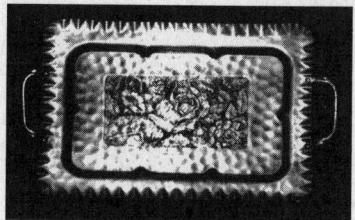 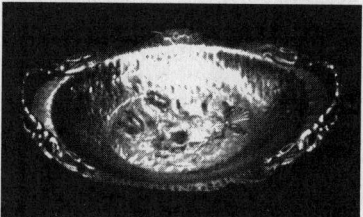

Above left to right: Hammered aluminum large serving tray by Cromwell, 11.5" x 18", $18-$22; hammered aluminum double-handled candy dish by Rodney Kent, len. 14", $10-$15.

	GOOD	BETTER	BEST
Ashtray	$ 10	$ 20	$ 50
Bar Tray	30	50	70
Basket	15	25	45
Bowl	10	15	45
Box, w/ lid	20	40	90
Bread Tray	15	30	50
Breakfast Set	30	50	75
Butter Dish	8	15	20
Cake Stand	12	20	25
Candelabra (pr.)	70	100	160
Candlesticks (pr.)	20	30	50
Candy Dish	10	15	25
Casserole	10	15	20
Cigarette Box	15	30	75
Coaster	2	5	8
Coaster Set	20	30	50
Coffee Urn	40	75	100
Compote	10	20	40

	GOOD	BETTER	BEST
Cream and Sugar	$ 10	$ 18	$ 35
Crumber and Tray	15	20	25
Cup, collapsible	1	3	8
Cup, hammered	1	5	10
Folding Server	30	50	80
Fondue Pot	15	20	30
Gravy Boat	10	15	20
Hurricane Lamp (pr.)	20	30	40
Ice Bucket	10	20	40
Lazy Susan	10	15	30
Magazine Rack	60	90	200
Matchbox Cover	10	25	50
Money Clip	5	10	15
Napkin Holder	10	15	30
Notebook Cover	50	100	200
Nut Bowl	15	20	30
Pitcher	20	30	50
Plate, fancy	15	30	50
Powder Box	10	15	20
Sandwich Tray	15	30	50
Serving Tray	20	50	80
Silent Butlers	20	30	50
Snack Tray	5	15	25
Teapot	15	20	40
Tidbit	15	30	45
Tray, whimsical shape	30	50	80
Tray Table	100	200	350
Tumblers	4	8	15
Vase, hammered	20	40	60
Well and Tree Platter	15	25	40

Brass

Brass is an alloy of copper and zinc. Early English and Continental pieces are the most valuable. Lighter-weight decorative brassware imported from Asia since the turn of the century often has intricate engraving and tooling, but is less valuable. Objects should be in excellent condition: no dents, no corrosion, even color. Brass may be polished without destroying its value (unlike bronze).

Richard A. Myers in Winston-Salem, North Carolina, sells superb reproductions of 17th-century brass candlesticks. They are sand cast with no silver sodder used. For those interested in such fine reproductions, contact Richard Myers at 2115 Bethabara Road, Winston-Salem, North Carolina 27106.

Left to right: Cribbage/Whist Board with five counters, $550; English Wax Jack with heart-form base, $700; English Snuffer and Stand, $350; English Standish with marble base, $1200 at auction. — Photos courtesy of Northeast Auctions.

	AUCTION	RETAIL Low	High
Andirons, pr., Amer. double-lemon top w/ spurred cabriole legs, ht. 23"	$ 1000	$ 1750	$ 2750
Andirons, pr., Amer. spire top w/ spurred cabriole legs, ht. 25"	1300	2280	3575
Andirons, pr., Amer. spire top w/ spurred cabriole legs, ht. 21"	900	1580	2475
Andirons, pr., Amer. spire top w/ matching shovel and tongs, ht. of first 22"	900	1580	2475
Andirons, pr., Amer. Chip.; w/ urn finial above turned column w/ plinth base on spurred cabriole legs w/ ball-and-claw feet, ht. 25"	1600	2800	4400
Andirons, pr., simple column form, ht. 18"	25	40	69
Argan Lamps, pr., simple column-form w/ plain chimneys, label of J. & I. Cox, NY, ht. 19"	800	1400	2200
Candlesticks, pr., Eng. fluted columnar; on square stepped bases w/ gadrooning, ht. 11"	400	700	1100
Candlesticks, pr., Eng. on stepped hexagonal base, ht. 7.5"	350	610	963
Candlesticks, pr., Eng. tapering fluted columnar; w/ sqare bobeches, capitals, and bases, w/ gadrooned edges, ht. 11.5"	900	1580	2475
Candlesticks, pr., Eng. mid-18th century; on petal bases w/			

	AUCTION	RETAIL Low	High
bobeches and detail on stem, the base w/ swirled line on alternating lobes, ht. 8.5"	$ 2600	$ 4550	$ 7150
Candlesticks, pr., Eng. mid-18th century; w/ candle cup w/ flaring notched rim; turned stem on circular base, square foot w/ notched corners, ht. 8.25"	1300	2280	3575
Candlesticks, pr., Eng. mid-18th century; w/ flaring mid-band candle cup on turned stem and sqare base w/ notched corners, ht. 7.25"	950	1660	2613
Candlesticks, pr., Eng. mid-18th century; w/ shaped petal-form bobeche and base, ht. 9.5"	1800	3150	4950
Candlesticks, pr., Eng. mid-18th century; w/ turned stem w/ crimped detail on slightly stepped base w/ notched corners, ht. 7"	850	1490	2338
Candlesticks, pr., Eng. mid-18th century hexagonal base; w/ shaped candle cups and trumpet-turned stems, ht. 6.25"	500	880	1375
Candlesticks, pr., Eng. mid-18th century petal base, each w/ candle cup w/ flaring rim and swelled petal-form detail on stem, ht. 9"	1850	3240	5088
Candlesticks, pr., French, ht. 9.5"	350	610	963
Candlesticks, pr., mid-18th century; w/ baluster-turned stems, sqare bases, fitted for electricity, ht. 9.5"	750	1310	2063
Chandelier, continental turned 6-scroll arm, dia. 24"	3000	5250	8250
Chandelier, Dutch Q.A.-style 6-arm, ht. 16"	1600	2800	4400
Chandelier, painted and decorated metal 3-arm; shaft w/ flat disks; curved candle-arms w/ candleholders, each w/ bo-beche, ht. 17", dia. 13"	600	1050	1650
Door Knocker, eagle-form cast, len. 10"	125	220	344

Above left: Continental eight-arm chandelier, $3000 at auction. Above right: Double arm student's lamp, $1000-$3000 retail. — Photos courtesy of Northeast Auctions.

Left: Nineteenth-century slide candlestick, $100-$200; Right: Dutch brass tobacco box with a harbor scene, $400 at auction. —Photo courtesy of Northeast Auctions.

	AUCTION	RETAIL Low	High
Fire Fender, Amer., w/ steel wire front, len. 27"	$ 120	$ 210	$ 330
Fire Fender, Amer., pierced, len. 35"	170	300	468
Fire Fender, Fed. serpentine-front w/ pierced anthemion motif, len. 41"	600	1000	1800
Fire Fender, N.E. wire and brass, w/ ball finials	400	750	1150
Fire Tools, pr., Amer. Empire	250	440	688
Fluid Lamp, marble base, w/ Cornelius label, electrified	250	440	688
Girandole Set, 3-piece, hung w/ crystal prisms, ht. of tallest 13"	150	260	413
Measure, Eng. copper and brass, engraved w/ crest	200	350	550
Planter, continental elliptical form, len. 18"	1200	2100	3300
Planter, Russian, oval, w/ simple repossé on paw feet, len. 14"	350	610	963
Spice Casters, set of 4, 18th century, ht. 5"	675	1180	1856
Spoon-Maker's Metal Tablespoon Template, len. 9"	50	90	135
Warming Pan, early Amer., engraved	150	260	413
Warming Pan, w/ engraved peacock, early 19th century, len. 42"	225	390	619

Seventeenth-century candlesticks are heavy and often unscrew at the base.

Bronze

Though bronze sculpture is of ancient origin, most specimens on the market are Victorian and 20th century. The name of the artist is the biggest factor in valuing bronzes. The name of the foundry is also important.

Don't clean a bronze sculpture with any highly abrasive cleaner. The color and condition of the "patina" is important. Vienna cole-painted bronzes should have their original paint in good condition.

Above, left to right: Animal figures; see prices below. —Photo courtesy of Northeast Auctions.

	LOW	AVG.	HIGH
American Art Foundry, Standing Goose, ht. 11"	$ 2000	$ 3440	$ 5440
Antoine Louis Barye, Hercules and the Erymanthean Boar, ht. 5"	2100	3612	5712
Antoine Louis Barye, Sleeping Jaguar, Barbedienne Foundry, len. 13"	2400	4128	6528
Antoine Louis Barye, Bronze Standing Ceremonial Bull, len. 7"	900	1548	2448
Antoine Louis Barye, Standing Pointer, len. 11"	900	1548	2448
E. Fremiet (French 1824-1910), Stretching Hound, len. 7"	700	1204	1904
Ruth Brooks Hoffman, The Staffordshire Terrier "War Spite," len. 8"	650	1118	1768
Anna V. Hyatt, Playful Bear, len. 4.5"	2400	4128	6528
Carl Kauba (Austrian 1865-1922), Seated Indian, Vienna cold-painted bronze, ht. 6"	1600	2752	4352
Monkey With Toasting Cup, Vienna cold-painted bronze, ht. 6"	1500	2580	4080
A.P. Proctor (American 1862-1950), Newborn Fawn, len. 9"	2200	3784	5984
A.P. Proctor (American 1862-1950), Prancing Doe, ht. 12"	2800	4816	7616
Frederick George Richard Roth (American, b. 1872,) Circus Elephant, ht. 6"	2200	3784	5984
Adolph Alexander Weinman (American 1870-1952), Indian Child, ht. 9"	2800	4816	7616

Copper

As the price of the metal itself has risen, so has the price for the well-crafted antiques and collectibles. "Good" examples must be in good condition, with only tiny dents. "Best" examples are undented and well proportioned, and show fine workmanship. All items are 20th century unless otherwise noted.

	GOOD	BETTER	BEST
Cup, w/ handle	$ 55	$ 80	$ 170
Dipper, 19th century	90	125	275
Dipper, 20th century	40	70	190
Funnel, ht. 23"	100	200	300
Funnel, tube-shaped, screen attachment, dia. 8"	55	80	170
Hot Water Bottle, egg-shaped, brass cap, ht. 12"	55	75	150
Hot Water Bottle, bail handle, brass lid, late 19th century	82	100	200
Hot Water Urn, early 19th century	480	770	1900
Kettle, apple butter, mid-1800s, dovetail bottom, dia. 25"	730	980	1900
Kettle, apple butter, century 1890	122	192	475
Kettle, bail handle, iron, swinging, molded lip iron stand	750	975	1800
Kettle, early 19th century	185	248	475
Kettle, iron bail handle, jelly kettle	98	135	300
Kettle, apple butter, used outdoors, dia. 25"	170	245	500
Kettle, 19th century, kitchen, brass knob, ht. 15"	145	200	400
Kettle, mid-19th century, ht. 9"	200	400	1000
Kettle, Early American, dia. 10", ht. 15"	212	300	665
Measure, flared spout, soldered handle, early 19th century, ht. 11"	100	180	400
Measure, pours, sloping edges, 1 pt.	40	55	115
Measure, pours, sloping edges, 1 qt.	40	65	133
Measure Set, 1 pt. to 2.5 qts.	275	370	720
Measure Set, 19th century, harvest measures	500	1200	3000
Measures, set of 3 for rum, 19th century	800	1300	2500
Measuring Cups, set of 7, wide-based, marked	2282	3350	7600
Milk Bucket, iron bail, handle, late 19th century	163	225	475
Milk Churn, 19th century, European, brass ring handles, ht. 32"	1385	2000	4500
Milk Jug	130	178	360
Miniature, pan, dia. 5", ht. 8"	15	25	60
Miniature, frying pan, dia. 5", brass handles	20	32	85
Miniature, kettle, pours, iron bail handle, dia. 3"	15	22	50
Miniature, wash tub, brass trim and handles, dia. 3"	15	20	50
Mixing Bowl, circular base, 1 handle, dia. 15", ht. 8"	73	108	245
Mixing Bowl, dia. 15", ht. 8"	82	125	300
Mold, bird, pt.	40	70	170
Mold, bundt, qt.	155	210	400
Mold, Easter egg, rabbit	90	125	245
Mold, jelly or pudding, qt.	40	70	170
Mold, jelly or pudding, pt.	40	65	150
Mold, circular base, fruit or floral motif, qt.	40	70	150
Mold, circular base, fruit or floral motif, pt.	20	30	90
Mold, fluted, scroll design at edge, 8"	15	25	45
Mold, pan, iron, handle, hanging eye	240	325	625
Mold, copper handles, dia. 20"	240	325	625
Mold, iron handle, dia. 13"	110	150	285

	GOOD	BETTER	BEST
Pitcher, 2 qt.	$ 65	$ 90	$ 200
Plate, dia. 9"	15	25	75
Pot, hand-crafted, handled, early 19th century, dia. 15"	155	210	418
Pots, set of 3, iron handles, tin interiors, lids, dia. 6", 7", and 8"	40	70	152
Reservoir, from kitchen stove, 19" x 8.75" x 11.5"	20	40	100
Salt Box, w. 7"	82	115	245
Saucepan, covered, brass handle, tin-lined, 1 qt.	82	115	245
Saucepan, covered, handle, tin-lined, 2 qt.	82	115	255
Saucepan, covered, brass handle, tin-lined, 3 qt.	90	135	310
Saucepan, covered, brass handle, tin-lined, 4 qt.	98	140	350
Saucepan, double boiler, 1 qt.	55	70	160

Above left: Turkish coffee pot, $10-$25; 1930s coffee pot, $25-$50; nineteenth century teapot, $500-$1000; 19th-century mug, $50-$100.

Graniteware and Enamelware

Graniteware is metalware with an enamel coating. It often has a mottled or marbleized appearance. Most graniteware is made for kitchen use. First featured in 1876 at the Centennial Exposition in Philadelphia, graniteware quickly gained popularity. It has been manufactured from the 1870s to the present.

"Good" pieces should have only traces of rust and no more than a few "dings" in the enamel. "Best" pieces should have no rust and no chipping of the enamel.

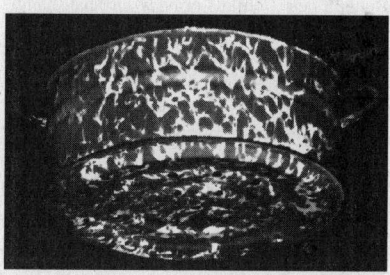

Right: Large blue and white colander, $60-$90.

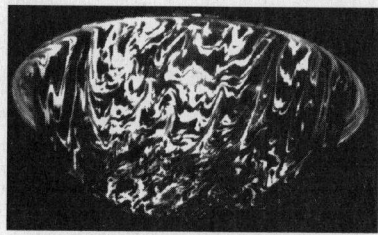

Left: Brown/maroon and white dish pan, $40-$60.

	GOOD	BETTER	BEST
Baby Food Cup, gray	$ 22	$ 33	$ 42
Baking Dish, blue and white mottled	20	30	38
Baking Dish, brown and white mottled	21	32	40
Baking Dish, dark green, shaded	24	36	46
Baking Dish, dark purple, shaded	25	38	48
Baking Dish, red, turquoise or yellow	12	18	23
Basting Spoon, blue and white mottled	12	18	23
Basting Spoon, brown and white mottled	14	21	27
Basting Spoon, dark purple, shaded	20	30	38
Basting Spoon, gray	10	15	20
Basting Spoon, white	2	3	4
Bedpan, gray, odorless tabbed lid	10	20	40
Bowl, blue swirl, dia. 9"	30	60	100
Bowl, cereal, pink w/ cobalt trim, rabbit decoration	10	20	45
Bowl, gray, 2 qt., shallow	10	25	45
Bread Box, white w/ blue swirls, circular, hinged lid	45	95	150
Bread Pan	10	25	40
Bread Raiser, gray mottled, tin lid w/ wood knob, dia. 15"	50	105	175

	GOOD	BETTER	BEST
Bread Tray, blue and white mottled	$ 14	$ 21	$ 27
Bread Tray, brown and white mottled	15	23	29
Bread Tray, dark green, shaded	16	24	30
Bread Tray, gray	12	18	23
Bread Tray, red, turquoise or yellow and white mottled (late)	10	15	19
Bread Tray, white	5	8	10
Bucket, berry, blue/white marbleized swirls, small	10	25	45
Bucket, berry, child's gray, w/ lid, bail handle	55	110	180
Bucket, berry, cobalt/white swirl	53	100	170
Bucket, berry, cobalt diffused	55	110	185
Candleholder, solid colors (late)	34	51	65
Candleholder, brown and white mottled	39	59	74
Candleholder, dark purple, shaded	42	63	80
Chamber, covered			
Chamber, covered, brown and white mottled	20	30	38
Chamber, covered, dark purple, shaded	24	36	46
Chamber, covered, white	9	14	17
Coffee Boiler, blue and white mottled	64	96	122
Coffee Boiler, brown and white mottled	70	105	133
Coffee Boiler, gray	66	99	125
Coffee Boiler, white	34	51	65
Coffee Boiler, brown/white marbleized, dome lid, 6 qt.	50	120	190
Coffee Boiler, gray mottled, half-moon shape, 5.5" handle, 9" x 5" x 4.5"	25	50	95
Coffee Boiler, gray, bail handles	35	70	125
Coffee Boiler, navy speckled w/ white, U.S. Navy, wire bail w/ wooden handle, large	20	40	80
Coffee Pot, dark green, shaded	60	90	115
Coffee Pot, dark purple, shaded	60	90	115
Coffee Pot, gray	46	70	85
Colander, blue and white mottled	22	33	42
Colander, brown and white mottled	30	45	57
Colander, dark green, shaded	34	50	65
Colander, dark purple, shaded	38	57	72
Cup/Saucer, solid colors (late)	18	27	34
Cup/Saucer, blue and white mottled	30	45	57
Cup/Saucer, dark green, shaded	38	57	72
Cup/Saucer, dark purple, shaded	38	57	72
Cup/Saucer, red, turquoise or yellow and white mottled (late)	16	24	30
Cup/Saucer, white	10	15	19
Dinner Pail, gray, tin lid, round, striped mottling, wood and bail handle, large	30	60	100
Dinner Plate, solid colors (late)	12	18	23
Dinner Plate, brown and white mottled	17	26	33
Dinner Plate, gray	12	18	23
Dinner Plate, white	5	8	10
Dipper, solid colors (late)	10	15	19
Dipper, dark purple, shaded	16	24	30
Dipper, red, turquoise or yellow and white mottled (late)	9	14	17
Double Boiler, red, turquoise or yellow and white mottled (late)	28	42	53
Double Boiler, white	18	27	34

	GOOD	BETTER	BEST
Funnel, solid colors	$ 8	$ 12	$ 15
Funnel, brown and white mottled	12	18	23
Funnel, gray	10	15	19
Funnel, white	4	6	8
Grater, cheese, steel handles	35	60	115
Invalid Feeder, gray, gooseneck spout	10	20	45
Iron, Coleman, turquoise, nickel over brass tank, nickel over steel base	25	50	85
Kerosene Stove, table top, gray, fancy, ornate nickel-coated trim, includes 1 qt. nickel-plated brass teakettle w/ ornate gooseneck spout and lid, bell-shaped bottom, wood and bail handle, tray w/ raised rim, by George Haller, dia. 11"	350	725	1150
Ladle, black/white mottled, 12"	10	20	30
Ladle, cobalt, 12"	10	20	35
Mixing Bowl, solid colors (late)	12	18	23
Mixing Bowl, brown and white mottled	18	27	34
Mixing Bowl, dark purple, shaded	21	32	40
Mixing Bowl, white	8	12	15
Mustard Pot, solid colors (late)	14	21	27
Mustard Pot, blue and white mottled	20	30	38
Mustard Pot, dark purple, shaded	34	51	65
Pan, blue, 9"	30	100	63
Pan, blue/white swirl, round, 8"	25	50	90
Pan, blue, round, 8"	25	50	80
Pan, blue, round, 11"	15	30	60
Pan, blue swirl, 11"	20	40	80
Pan, blue swirl, round, 8"	20	40	75
Pan, blue swirl, round, 9"	20	55	95
Pie Plate, solid colors (late)	12	18	23
Pie Plate, blue and white mottled	14	21	27
Pie Plate, brown and white mottled	17	26	33
Pie Plate, dark green, shaded	22	33	42
Pie Plate, dark purple, shaded	22	33	42
Pitcher and Bowl, dark green, shaded	121	181	230
Pitcher and Bowl, white	60	90	114
Pitcher, Cream, white	8	12	15
Skillet, gray	20	30	38
Soap Dish, brown and white mottled	30	45	57
Soap Dish, gray	16	24	30
Soap Dish, white	8	12	15
Soup Plate, solid colors (late)	12	18	23
Soup Plate, blue and white mottled	14	21	27
Soup Plate, brown and white mottled	17	26	33
Soup Plate, dark green, shaded	22	33	42
Soup Plate, red, turquoise or yellow and white mottled (late)	14	21	27
Soup Plate, white	5	8	10
Spittoon, blue and white mottled	50	75	95
Spittoon, brown and white mottled	56	84	106
Spittoon, gray	40	60	76
Sugar Bowl, dark green, shaded	38	57	72
Tea Kettle, gray	76	114	144

Above: The rust shown on this bundt pan lowers the value to $20-30.

	GOOD	BETTER	BEST
Teapot, 1 qt, blue and white mottled	$ 80	$ 120	$ 152
Teapot, 1 qt, dark purple, shaded	96	144	182
Teapot, 1 qt, gray	78	117	148
Teapot, 1 qt, red, turquoise or yellow and white mottled (late)....	78	117	148
Teapot, 1 qt, white	40	60	76
Teapot, 2 qt, white	30	45	57
Tumbler, dark green, shaded	38	57	72
Tumbler, gray	14	21	27

Ironware

Marked ironware pieces have greater value. Dates do not always indicate the year made: some dates stand for the year the patent was issued. Oiling or polishing old ironware decreases its value. Many reproductions are made in Indonesia. Careless welding is a sign of modern work or fakery. For further information see *Fabulous But Fake*, by Norman S. Young, Fake Publications, Inc.

"Cast" refers to cast iron, "wrought' to wrought iron. "Good" should have minimal rust and be 100% intact. "Best" pieces should have fine decorative motifs, superior craftsmanship, and no rust.

Fancy wrought-iron adjustable kettle tilter, ht. 30", $200 at auction. — Photo courtesy of Northeast Auctions.

	AUCTION	RETAIL Low	High
Andirons, pr., 18th century, on arched supports w/ penny feet, ht. 16"	$ 200	$ 250	$ 320
Andirons, pr., Amer. cast iron owl-form, w/ inset glass eyes, ht. 16"	550	960	1513
Andirons, pr., cast iron sunflower, attributed to Bradley and Hubbard, marked w/ patent number and date 1886, ht. 16"	550	960	1513
Andirons, pr., Geo. Washington figural cast iron, ht. 15"	600	1050	1650
Andirons, pr., gooseneck, wrought iron	50	90	138
Andirons, pr., Amer. penny-foot wrought iron knife blade w/ brass flame finials, ht. 24"	2200	3850	6050
Bullet Mold, Civil War era	50	65	80
Bullet Mold, late 18th century	70	85	110
Coal Tongs, len. 10"	50	60	80
Daybed, Empire painted iron swan and lyre-form, len. 94"	1400	2450	3850
Eagle Ornament on Sphere, cast iron, on stand, ht. 23"	550	960	1513
Ember Shovel, 18th century, turned wooden handle, len. 14"	320	400	500
Eyeglasses, late 18th century	200	250	320
Fireback, cast iron decorated w/ cherubs above swag and date 1687, ht. 30"	600	1050	1650
Fireplace Fork, w/ handle twist, len. 42.5"	90	115	140
Fireplace Log Lifter, 29.25"	70	90	110
Floor Lamps, wrought iron	100	175	275
Greyhound Garden Figure, MA cast iron, painted, Cephas Stetson Iron Foundry, Bridgewater, crouching posture,			

	AUCTION	RETAIL	
		Low	High
len. 52"	$ 1750	$ 3060	$ 4813
Hanging Wall Rack, wrought iron	150	260	413
Hearth Shovel, len. 24"	100	130	160
Hewing Axe, signed "William Beatly & Son," Chester N.H., 12.25" blade	140	175	220
Lantern Trammel, 18th century, extends to 32"	200	250	320
Leg Irons, early 19th century	190	235	300
Leg Irons, U.S. Navy/Civil War	190	240	300
Pot Lifter and Trivet Combination Tool, len. 14"	70	85	110
Scissors, 18th century, blacksmith-made	50	65	80
Shooting Gallery Pipe Target, w/ old blue paint	40	45	60
Spatula, blacksmith-made, len. 20"	60	75	90
Sugar Nippers, 18th century, len. 8"	240	300	380
Trade Axe, 18th century, stamped "T", 7.75"	120	145	180
Wall Mirror, French, wrought iron and ormolu, w/ elaborate leaf and scroll design, crest w/ mask, signed and dated lower left 'F. Marrou, 1884,' ht. 68", w. 43"	10,000	17,500	27,500

One of a pair of cast iron trig-form pattern benches, len. 51", $3500 at auction. — Photo courtesy of Northeast Auctions.

Above: Wrought-iron wick trimmer, len. 5", $20-$40 retail.

Pewter

Pewter is a tin alloy, often containing copper. It is usually dark gray and soft, but can be light and shiny, almost resembling silver. Early pewter should not be used for eating, drinking, or storing food, as it often contains lead, which can poison the food.

"Good" examples must be in reasonable condition, without any large dents. "Best" examples are undented and well proportioned, show exceptional workmanship, and usually contain a "touch" or hammered mark of the maker. These marks can be identified by various guides.

Left to right: Coffee pot, 18th-century, ht. 8", $600-$900; oil lamp, 19th-century, ht. 6", $300-$600; porringer, 19th-century, dia. 5", $80-$120. — Photo courtesy of Northeast Auctions.

	GOOD	BETTER	BEST
Basin, by Semper Eadam, Boston, dia. 9".	$ 1000	$ 1400	$ 1750
Brunnen Kessel, Swiss, 19th century	300	500	800
Candlestick, 19th century, ht. 12"	40	90	180
Chalice, Continental, 19th century, ht. 8"	75	100	125
Chamberpot, 19th century, dia. 14"	80	120	200
Charger, Eng., 18th century, dia. 18"	712	950	1188
Charger, European, 18th century, dia. 16"	200	250	500
Coffee Urn, Continental, 19th century, ht. 14"	75	100	125
Covered Pot, French, late 19th century	35	50	90
Flagon, covered, French, late 18th century, ht. 14"	600	800	1000
Flagon, octagonal, ram's head thumb-piece, 19th century, ht. 14".	75	150	225
Flagon, spouted, Continental	250	500	800
Flagon, spouted, French	450	600	750
Flask, octagonal, Continental, 18th century, ht. 13".	750	1000	1250
Fluid Lamp, German, 19th century	375	500	625
Funnel, 19th cent, len. 9"	35	60	90
Glocackenkann Spouted-Flask.	525	700	875
Jug, French, Louis XV style w/ engraved bust	375	500	625
Lamps, pr., Amer. acorn form, ht. 11".	525	700	875
Lavabo, Continental, 2-part	825	1100	1375
Measure, French, 19th century	25	30	50
Measures, set of 7, Eng. bulbous form, ht. to 5".	375	500	625

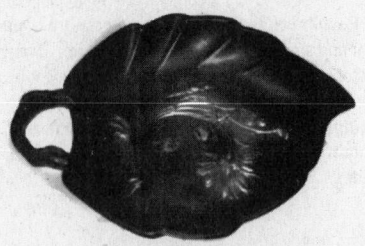

Left: Much late 19th-century pewter is "Britainia" metal. Right: Pewter ashtray in the Art Nouveau style, $25-$50.

	GOOD	BETTER	BEST
Measures, set of 7, French, ht. to 5"	$ 300	$ 400	$ 500
Mess Bowl, 19th century, dia. 8"	20	30	50
Pitcher, French Brocauvin	188	250	312
Plate, Amer., 18th century, dia. 8"	135	180	225
Plate, deep, 18th century, dia. 10"	225	300	375
Plate, European, dia. 10"	50	70	100
Plate, wavy-edge, French, 9"	25	35	60
Platter, wavy-edge, French, 12"	60	80	100
Porringer, Continental, 2-handled, dia. 5"	52	70	88
Porringer, Continental, 2-handled, dia. 6"	75	100	125
Porringer, dia. 6"	18	24	30
Soup Plate, 19th century, 8"	20	30	50
Spoon, 19th century	9	12	15
Spouted Flagon, Swiss, Stegkanne form, ht. 12".	450	600	750
Tankard, dated 1784, ht. 9".	600	800	1000
Tankard, dome top, crenalated lip, by John Will, NY, 1752-66, Jacob's Mark 280, ht.7".	20,000	34,000	42,500
Trophy Cup, armorial, Louis XV style, 19th century, ht. 12"	375	500	625

A different maker can mean a very different price. Below left: New York tankard by Frederick Bassett, $20,000 at auction. Below right: New York tankard by Francis Bassett failed to sell at $10,000.

Silver

Silver is alloyed with other metals for durability, as pure silver is too soft for most uses. The grade of silver is determined by the amount or percentage of alloy material contained. Sterling silver is 925 parts per 1000 pure (usually stated as .925).

The values listed are primarily for easily found items. However, some rare and valuable examples are included for comparison. "Good" examples are considered to be in excellent condition, but without any superlative features. "Best" examples are perfectly proportioned and show exceptional workmanship. Thicker, and therefore heavier, pieces are generally of better quality than light pieces. Although dents can be repaired by a skilled silversmith, it is not cheap. Also beware that a faker can add new marks, new decoration (such as chasing), or even new parts (such as a new base).

Coffee pot with farm motifs by E. Jones, New York, ca. 1820, height 9.5", $2000-$4000.

	GOOD	BETTER	BEST
Baby Mug, early 19th century, Amer., repoussé	$ 200	$ 270	$ 400
Baby Mug, late 19th century, Eng., engraved	100	180	300
Baby Rattle, mid-19th century, 3" foliate design	200	270	400
Baby Spoon, late 19th century, Amer.	30	40	60
Beaker, Amer., incised rings, by C. A. Burnett, ht. 3", 4 oz.	1800	2380	3500
Bodkin, early 20th century, Eng.	50	70	100
Book Cover, late 19th century	150	180	250
Bookmark, early 20th century, Eng.	50	90	150
Bookmark, late 19th century, Amer.	150	180	250
Boson's Whistle, late 19th century	300	360	500
Bottle Opener, early 20th century	30	50	80
Bottle Stopper, simple form, late 19th century	50	70	100
Bottle Stopper, whimsical form, late 19th century	200	220	300
Buckle, Art Deco, engine turned	100	110	150

	GOOD	BETTER	BEST
Buckle, Art Nouveau, late 19th century	$ 150	$ 220	$ 350
Button Hook, Art Nouveau, late 19th century	75	90	125
Button Hook, repoussé handle, late 19th century	50	70	100
Cake Basket, repoussé	500	760	1200
Calling Card Case, late 19th century, Eng.	200	320	500
Candle Snuffer, mid-20th century	40	50	80
Candlesticks, plain, low, weighted, 20th century	100	160	250
Cane Handle, late 19th century, cast and chased	300	360	500
Christmas Ornament, late 20th century	40	50	80
Cigar Cutter, whimsical shape, late 19th century, Eng.	100	160	250
Cigarette Case, enameled, mid-20th century	200	320	500
Cigarette Case, engraved, early 20th century	100	180	300
Compote, .950-silver, Ball, Black & Co., 30 oz.	1200	1350	1800
Compote, medallion pat., Ball, Black & Co., ht. 10", 22 oz.	1200	1800	2800
Creamer, Amer., by E. Moulton, oval engraved, ht. 5", 5 oz.	900	1080	1500
Creamer/Sugar, Amer., by E. Moulton, 13 oz.	1800	2840	4500
Darning Egg, silver mounts, early 20th century	40	50	80
Ewer, owned by Daniel Webster, by S. Kirk, marine motifs, ht. 11", 42 oz	10,000	15,750	25,000
Flask, Art Nouveau, repoussé, late 19th century	500	580	800
Flask, engine turned, late 19th century	300	360	500
Flask, engraved, early 20th century	100	180	300
Flask, Tiffany Japanese style, late 19th century	2000	2250	3000
Food Pusher, mid-19th century, Amer.	40	50	70
Frame, Art Nouveau, 7", early 20th century	200	270	400
Frame, repoussé, floral-decorated, late 19th century, 9"	600	720	1000
Frame, undecorated, mid-20th century, 6"	100	180	300
Frame, undecorated, mid-20th century, 9"	200	270	400
Funnel, early 19th century	500	680	1000
Funnel, early 20th century	100	180	300
Glove Stretcher, Amer., late 19th century	50	90	150
Inkstand, Art Nouveau, late 19th century	500	680	1000
Inkstand, Georgian style, late 19th century	400	540	800
Inkwell, late 19th century, Eng., engraved	150	220	350
Judaic Spice Tower, late 19th century, 10"	400	450	600
Letter Opener, engraved handle, mid-20th century	50	70	100
Letter Opener, repoussé handle, late 19th century	100	140	200
Luggage Tag, engraved, late 19th century	50	70	100
Luggage Tag, engraved, mid-20th century	25	40	75
Magnifying Glass, Art Nouveau, late 19th century	300	360	500
Magnifying Glass, engraved, mid-20th century	100	140	200
Matchsafe, enameled, early 20th century	200	270	400
Matchsafe, repoussé, late 19th century	150	220	350
Matchsafe, whimsical shape, late 19th century	400	540	800
Miniature Coffee Pot, 2", Dutch, late 19th century	100	180	300
Miniature Sofa, 3", Eng., early 20th century	100	140	200
Miniature Table, 2", Continental, early 20th century	100	140	200
Miniature Tray, 2.5", mid-19th century, Eng.	300	360	500
Mustache Comb, early 20th century	50	70	100
Napkin Ring, engraved, late 19th century	50	60	75
Napkin Ring, engraved, mid-20th century	10	30	50

Top row left to right: Tiffany & Co. Sterling Five-Pint Pitcher, height 10", $2000; Mappin & Webb English Soup Tureen, 1902, height 12", $3000; Georg Jensen Compote, height 11.5", $4250; middle row: Ball, Black & Co. three piece sterling tea set, height of teapot 11.25", $1400; bottom row left to right: Domininck & Haff, New York, set of four sterling candlesticks with floral decoration, height 11", $3400; George W. Sheibler & Co. Japanese style box, length 6", $550; Art Nouveau Sterling Compote with iris border, diameter 11", $1700; Tiffany & Co. Arts & Crafts hand hammered bowl, diameter 7.5", $700. —Photo courtesy of Northeast Auctions.

	GOOD	BETTER	BEST
Napkin Ring, hand-hammered, early 20th century	$ 20	$ 30	$ 50
Napkin Ring, repoussé, mid-19th century	50	70	100
Necessaire, 6 implements, early 20th century, French	200	270	400
Nutmeg Grater, engine turned, cylindrical, early 19th century	400	450	600
Nutmeg Grater, oval, early 19th century	300	360	500
Overlay Glass Cologne Bottle, clear glass, early 20th century	75	100	150
Overlay Glass Cologne Bottle, colored glass, early 20th century	150	220	350
Overlay Glass Decanter, clear glass, early 20th century	200	270	400
Overlay Glass Pitcher, clear glass, late 19th century	400	450	600
Paper Knife, late 19th century	200	270	400
Pencil, retractable, early 20th century	150	180	250
Pillbox, late 19th century, Eng.	200	270	400
Pin Cushion, animal shape, late 19th century	200	270	400
Pin Cushion, chatelaine type, late 19th century	100	140	200
Place Card Holders, animal shape, set of 4, early 20th century	300	360	500
Place Card Holders, engraved, late 19th century, set of 4	200	270	400
Playing Card Box, early 20th century, Eng.	150	220	350
Porringer, keyhole, coin-silver, K. Leverett, dia. 5.25", 6 oz.	2500	3380	5000
Posey Holder, embossed, late 19th century, Eng.	300	360	500
Posey Holder, filigree, late 19th century, Continental	400	400	500
Posey Holder, paneled, early 20th century	200	270	400
Powder Box, early 20th century, French, engraved	150	220	350
Riding Crop, silver handled, early 19th century	500	680	1000
Ring Box, early 20th century, Eng.	50	90	150
Scent Bottle, late 19th century	150	220	350
Seal, for sealing wax, late 19th century	200	270	400
Seal, for sealing wax, mid-20th century	50	90	150
Shoe Horn, engraved, early 20th century	75	100	150
Snuffbox, early 19th century, German	600	720	1000
Snuffbox, late 19th century, Eng.	300	360	500
Soap Case, embossed, late 19th century	100	110	150
Souvenir Spoon, early 20th century	30	40	70
Souvenir Spoon, late 19th century	50	70	100
Spurs (pr.), early 19th century, simple engraved	400	540	800
Spurs (pr.), early 20th century, simple engraved	200	270	400
Stamp Box, late 19th century	150	180	250
Stamp Box, whimsical form, late 19th century	300	360	500
String Holder, late 19th century	300	360	500
Table Bell, late 19th century, Eng.	150	270	450
Talc Shaker, late 19th century	100	140	200
Tankard, Amer., by R. Humphreys, ht. 7", 21 oz.	2500	3380	5000
Tatting Shuttle, late 19th century	50	90	150
Tea Infuser, ball form, late 19th century	75	90	125
Tea Infuser, whimsical form, late 19th century	300	360	500
Tea Infuser, whimsical form, mid-20th century	100	110	150
Tea Strainer, late 19th century	100	110	150
Tea Strainer, mid-20th century	50	70	100
Thimble, chased and engraved, early 19th century	300	360	500
Thimble, engraved, late 19th century	100	140	200
Thimble, engraved, mid-20th century	30	40	50

	GOOD	BETTER	BEST
Thread Holder, reticulated, late 19th century	$ 100	$ 140	$ 200
Toast Rack, early 20th century, Eng.	150	220	350
Tobacco Box, late 18th century, Eng.	500	630	900
Toothbrush Holder, early 20th century	50	70	100
Toothpick, early 20th century	20	30	50
Toothpick Holder, engraved, early 20th century	100	180	300
Torah Finials (pr.), early 20th century	500	580	800
Trophy Cup, 6", engraved, mid-20th century	300	400	600
Vinaigrette, mid-19th century, simple form	150	200	300
Vinaigrette, mid-19th century, whimsical form	500	680	1000
Walking Stick, silver handled, late 19th century	100	180	300
Whistle, penny whistle form, early 20th century	100	140	200
Wine Coaster, mid-19th century	300	360	500
Wine Label, crescent shape, late 19th century	50	90	150
Wine Label, engraved, late 18th century	150	200	300
Wine Taster, early 19th century, Continental	300	360	500
Wine Taster, mid-20th century	100	140	200

Above left: Boston pepper caster by Daniel Parker, 1768, with original bill of sale, $3500 at auction. Above right: Philadelphia soup ladle by Joseph Lownes, c. 1800, $800 at auction.
— Photos courtesy of Northeast Auctions.

Tiffany engraved silver letter opener, $30-$50

Silver Flatware

Silverware includes factory merchandise and products of individual craftsmen. Chief American manufacturers include Gorham, Reed and Barton, Towle, Wallace, Rogers, Oneida, Kirk, and International.

Values are given in two sections. In the first we list a large variety of tableware and serving pieces for a single pattern. Values are for visible worn pieces (W), excellent condition monogrammed pieces (M), and excellent condition pieces with no monogram (E).

In the second section, we list five key pieces for a variety of patterns listed under the name of their manufacturer: Dinner Fork (*DnF*), Dessert Fork (*DsF*), Serving Spoon (*SvSp*), Soup Spoon (*SpSp*), and Teaspoon (*Tsp*).

Buckingham Pattern
Gorham - 1910

	W	M	E
Berry Spoon, large	$ 127	$ 135	$ 125
Bouillon Spoon	27	34	27
Carving Fork	67	75	65
Cheese Scoop, large	145	155	145
Citrus Spoon	40	45	37
Cocktail Fork	28	32	25
Cold Meat (Buffet) Fork	112	125	110
Cream Soup Spoon	48	52	47
Cream Soup Spoon, small	37	42	35
Demitasse Spoon	22	27	22
Dessert Spoon	42	47	40
Dinner Fork	47	52	45
Dinner Knife	57	62	55
Fish Fork	40	45	40
Fish Knife	37	45	35
Five O'Clock Teaspoon	15	21	16
Flat Server	30	35	30
Fruit Knife	37	42	35
Gravy Ladle	100	110	95
Ice Cream Fork	40	45	40
Ice Cream Spoon	42	47	40
Iced Tea Spoon	52	57	50
Jelly Server, large	135	145	135
Lettuce Fork	95	100	95
Luncheon Fork	37	42	35
Luncheon Knife	45	50	43
Nut Picks	27	35	25
Olive or Pickle Fork	45	50	45
Pie Server	40	45	40
Salad Fork	47	53	45
Soup Ladle	250	260	250
Steak Knife	37	43	35
Sugar Shell	37	45	35
Sugar Tongs	45	50	45
Tablespoon/Serving Spoon	52	58	50
Teaspoon	21	27	19

Other Patterns

	YEAR	DnF	DsF	SvSp	SpSp	Tsp
ALVIN CO.						
Chateau Rose	1940	$ 53	$ 39	$ 111	$ 47	$ 37
Chippendale, new	1921	38	28	77	31	25
Delaware	1910	34	28	79	35	30
Duquesne	1921	27	24	68	29	26
Eternal Rose	1963	45	35	92	45	34
Evangeline	1907	34	28	71	33	29
Evangeline, No. 7	1908	35	28	78	32	30
Fleur de Lis	1907	70	60	170	70	45
Josephine	1910	35	31	83	33	33
Lorraine	1904	50	38	109	44	35
Modern Colonial	1927	38	30	75	33	30
Nuremburg	1903	61	46	118	50	36
Orange Blossom, new	1920	44	36	100	46	34
Orange Blossom, old	1905	78	61	161	72	34
Richmond	1921	38	30	86	32	32
Vivaldi	1966	69	51	130	61	42
BAKER-MANCHESTER MFG. CO.						
Roanoke	1916	32	28	72	30	31
Van Buren	1915	40	30	87	37	33
DOMINICK & HAFF						
Basket-of-Flowers	1920	35	29	78	31	26
Colonial Antique	1925	37	27	74	32	25
Contempora	1930	40	28	83	32	26
King	1890	70	56	154	66	42
La France	1916	37	32	98	38	39
La Salle	1928	30	26	76	33	32
Labors of Cupid	1900	206	156	398	180	81
Louis XVI, old style	1916	39	32	88	34	31
Mayflower	1911	33	24	68	32	26
New King	1898	78	63	158	65	49
Old English Antique	1880	35	28	75	34	24
DURGIN DIV. OF GORHAM						
Antique Sheaf	1893	55	40	109	50	33
Chrysanthemum	1893	75	62	169	68	47
Dolly Madison	1904	31	28	68	33	23

Left to right: Dominick & Haff mark; Durgin Division of Gorham mark.

Durgin Division of Gorham's Madame Royal pattern.

	YEAR	DnF	DsF	SvSp	SpSp	Tsp
English Antique	1887	$ 35	$ 29	$ 79	$ 32	$ 25
Fairfax	1910	47	37	93	43	37
French Antique	1875	41	30	84	34	32
Iris	1900	109	95	223	109	51
Marechal Niel	1896	105	82	207	100	48
Navarre	1909	38	35	96	40	34
New Standish	1905	49	39	107	47	39
New Vintage	1904	97	71	180	79	59
No. 19-C	1912	31	27	77	33	20
Sheaf of Wheat	1887	60	45	122	52	41
Shell	1892	38	34	94	40	27
Victorian (ex-Sheraton)	1918	38	30	80	38	27
Wellington	1908	44	39	105	47	30
Wentworth, engraved	1902	41	31	81	36	24
Wentworth, plain	1902	37	29	73	35	18

FESSENDEN & CO.

	YEAR	DnF	DsF	SvSp	SpSp	Tsp
Avon	1888	48	43	121	50	45
Langdon	1915	31	28	83	33	34
McKinley	1900	85	70	189	78	52
Narcissus	1915	87	78	207	85	66

FRANK M. WHITING & CO.

	YEAR	DnF	DsF	SvSp	SpSp	Tsp
Hagie	1885	41	33	96	43	31
Josephine	1890	66	54	139	63	43
Lily (ex-Floral)	1902	86	69	176	80	50
Marquis	1889	81	68	183	77	51
Narcissus	1886	60	52	137	61	44
Orleans	1892	58	43	122	48	47

FRANK SMITH SILVER CO.

	YEAR	DnF	DsF	SvSp	SpSp	Tsp
Bead	1917	36	28	84	34	26
Beverly	1917	36	29	82	32	29
Chippendale, old	1917	42	32	85	34	34

	YEAR	DnF	DsF	SvSp	SpSp	Tsp
Colbert	1921	$ 54	$ 45	$ 122	$ 48	$ 42
French Antique	1887	35	31	79	33	31
George VI	1912	53	46	119	53	42
Laurel	1919	35	26	74	29	25
Lincoln K	1915	47	34	97	36	33
Mayflower	1918	34	28	75	35	23
No. 9, engraved	1891	34	30	84	35	28
Priscilla	1918	37	31	96	37	35
Salem	1917	33	26	79	29	27
Tipt	1887	38	32	91	36	36
V. Kraft	1921	41	35	98	42	37
Winslow	1922	35	31	91	32	32

GORHAM

	YEAR	DnF	DsF	SvSp	SpSp	Tsp
Alencon Lace	1965	67	51	140	56	39
Buttercup	1899	67	57	157	67	47
Celeste	1956	36	32	95	36	31
Covington, hammered	1914	50	40	104	42	34
Decor	1953	77	63	179	72	53
Fanshawe	1922	40	29	91	35	30
Firelight	1959	35	28	84	35	30
Fleury	1909	56	43	117	56	41
Gossamer	1965	36	32	85	37	27
Hamilton	1908	27	22	63	26	23
King Edward	1936	60	49	136	57	39
Lancaster	1897	61	52	127	65	33
Lenox	1897	47	35	106	43	34
Lily of the Valley	1950	64	50	129	55	41
Lyric	1940	44	31	86	38	31
Melrose	1908	51	38	109	46	29
Mothers	1875	32	27	76	34	33
Newcastle	1895	41	33	87	42	28
Nocturne	1938	43	41	114	48	34
Norfolk	1903	36	32	92	31	36
Old Dominion	1912	42	32	81	36	26
Old English Tipt	1870	36	31	77	33	22
Old French	1905	58	42	110	43	40
Portsmouth	1918	39	30	82	34	32
Royal Oak	1904	67	49	129	57	33
Secret Garden	1959	55	43	112	44	33
Shamrock V	1931	37	36	88	40	27
St. Cloud	1885	125	76	178	51	38
St. Dunstan, chased	1917	66	55	132	54	35
Tuileries	1906	55	51	128	53	36
Versailles	1888	121	76	192	68	46
Vine	1909	66	49	139	58	40
Virginia	1905	61	51	139	54	40
Wreath	1911	43	37	101	43	38
Zodiac	1906	114	118	298	150	76

Gorham mark.

	YEAR	DnF	DsF	SvSp	SpSp	Tsp
INTERNATIONAL SILVER CO.						
Acanthus	1917	$ 41	$ 31	$ 95	$ 36	$ 31
Angelique	1959	57	45	113	51	39
Autocrat	1923	30	28	77	32	22
Berkeley (ex-Colonial)	1915	39	35	94	42	34
Brandon	1913	37	30	83	34	31
Cambridge	1899	44	35	95	43	32
Chesterfield	1914	51	39	107	42	43
Chimes	1938	36	29	74	32	24
Crown Princess	1949	67	45	124	42	39
Dawn Rose	1969	35	32	83	38	30
Dorchester	1910	35	29	82	35	31
Enchanted Rose	1954	52	46	121	54	41
Enchantress	1937	41	32	91	41	33
Florentine	1912	42	35	94	41	30
Fontaine	1924	48	43	105	44	37
Governor Bradford	1913	37	27	77	35	27
Grand Recollection	1956	48	39	101	42	39
Grand Trianon	1975	67	55	149	60	46
Irene	1902	38	32	88	40	32
Joan of Arc	1940	67	49	139	58	39
John Winthrop	1911	38	30	89	31	34
Kenilworth	1887	49	46	128	57	38
Litchfield	1898	47	43	112	53	32
Lorraine	1917	52	47	115	53	36
Moonbeam	1948	42	35	94	41	31
Nosegay	1938	46	38	108	47	33
Pansy	1909	56	48	123	60	41
Primrose	1936	80	77	180	95	43
Quincy	1917	40	34	87	36	30
Revere	1898	71	50	132	63	38
Riviera	1936	50	44	120	52	37
Serenity	1940	50	39	106	43	33
Shirley	1910	38	29	85	34	33
Silhouette	1957	49	37	108	41	32
Snowflake	1966	32	28	81	33	24
Southern Colonial	1945	68	54	144	61	39
Splendor	1939	44	34	97	36	32
Spring Bouquet	1940	43	34	94	39	32
Springtime	1935	89	71	187	95	50
Stratford	1902	94	74	187	87	46
Tranquility	1947	53	41	113	47	41
Trianon	1921	61	51	154	65	48
Trumbull	1908	42	32	95	39	30
Warwick	1898	53	45	127	50	38
Wedgwood	1924	55	42	117	47	38
LUNT SILVERSMITHS						
Belle Meade	1967	53	44	126	48	45
Charles II	1934	63	54	134	65	41
Chased Classic	1936	39	28	77	31	27

	YEAR	DnF	DsF	SvSp	SpSp	Tsp
Chateau	1919	$ 32	$ 28	$ 76	$ 32	$ 26
Colonial Manor	1940	32	28	83	32	28
Cortland	1921	34	28	78	34	30
Dorothy Q	1890	47	39	96	39	29
Elaine	1893	39	36	91	42	36
Eloquence	1953	85	63	175	74	52
Festival	1936	38	31	84	35	22
Floral Lace	1967	29	25	68	28	20
Georgian Manor	1958	43	36	99	39	32
Greenfield	1890	34	31	88	38	28
Knickerbocker	1913	47	37	101	45	29
Lasting Grace	1975	82	62	154	69	43
Madrigal	1961	35	31	86	32	28
Malvern	1970	65	54	133	61	41
Mignonette	1960	52	39	111	46	33
Modern Classic	1931	36	29	87	31	36
Navarre	1893	64	50	139	58	44
Nellie Custis	1915	39	29	76	32	23
Old Dominion	1898	40	35	101	41	31
Pynchon	1908	82	61	168	66	43
Rondelay	1963	71	57	144	58	43
Spring Serenade	1957	36	28	70	33	24
Warren	1883	31	26	64	30	26
Wentworth	1898	57	42	117	50	38
William and Mary	1921	43	35	103	40	29

MANCHESTER SILVER CO.

Amaryllis	1951	44	35	104	42	31
Colonnade	1936	44	41	106	50	38
Copenhagen	1936	43	36	92	43	28
Dixie	1920	40	29	85	37	29
Manchester	1928	37	25	65	28	20
Mary Warren	1920	32	29	80	31	26
Mayflower	1915	33	25	67	25	26
Park Avenue	1931	44	39	106	46	34
Plymouth	1933	25	22	59	26	19
Silverstream	1934	31	26	68	28	25
Valenciennes	1938	69	54	151	67	43

MOUNT VERNON CO.

Alamo	1905	40	35	91	42	36
Apollo	1892	50	41	118	50	36
George Washington	1910	48	41	118	50	39
Harvard	1915	49	42	116	48	35
Old South	1907	28	26	68	32	25
Ribbed Antique	1900	32	28	76	33	19
Rose	1910	74	58	156	63	46

ONEIDA, LTD.

Casa Grande	1967	43	39	103	45	34
Grandeur	1960	42	37	103	40	33

	YEAR	DnF	DsF	SvSp	SpSp	Tsp
Heiress	1942	$ 36	$ 30	$ 77	$ 33	$ 23
King Cedric	1949	52	45	124	53	41
Mediterranea	1967	61	49	123	50	42
Patrician	1914	32	27	77	32	30
Rubaiyat	1969	40	29	84	34	31
Silver Rose	1956	35	29	82	31	25
Twilight	1942	37	29	84	32	28
Venetian Scroll	1970	44	34	90	36	36

REED & BARTON

	YEAR	DnF	DsF	SvSp	SpSp	Tsp
18th Century	1971	49	41	113	46	36
Antique	1912	35	27	79	33	28
Athenian, engraved	1891	39	35	93	43	33
Cameo	1959	50	41	123	51	41
Classic Fashion	1941	39	37	101	42	33
Clovelly	1912	32	26	78	33	25
Dimension	1961	33	28	79	32	31
El Greco	1972	71	60	172	68	47
Hepplewhite, chased	1907	42	29	88	32	34
Jacobean, engraved	1911	52	41	106	49	37
Kings	1890	63	49	135	57	36
L'Elegante	1900	49	39	109	44	36
La Reine	1893	77	58	158	64	53
La Splendide	1902	78	57	164	72	51
Petite Fleur	1961	40	35	98	42	30
Romaine	1933	49	44	129	54	41
Savannah	1962	53	45	113	53	34
Trajan	1892	74	54	156	64	46
Tree of Life	1974	49	41	112	46	36
Vienna	1970	74	63	167	71	57

SAMUEL KIRK & SON, INC.

	YEAR	DnF	DsF	SvSp	SpSp	Tsp
Kingsley	1959	35	27	79	35	27
Primrose	1933	46	37	109	45	33
Repousse	1828	46	38	111	41	38

SCHOFIELD CO.

	YEAR	DnF	DsF	SvSp	SpSp	Tsp
Josephine	1912	41	34	87	36	31
Lady Caroline	1912	46	35	100	38	31
Old Baltimore	1920	55	40	104	42	31
Old English	1890	29	22	56	23	22
Persian	1915	33	28	73	34	23
Revere	1905	25	23	61	24	23
Scroll Engraved Edge	1905	34	26	74	32	24

STIEFF CO.

	YEAR	DnF	DsF	SvSp	SpSp	Tsp
Forget-me-not	1910	58	42	118	51	32
Rose Motif	1954	38	28	80	31	24

TOWLE MFG. CO.

	YEAR	DnF	DsF	SvSp	SpSp	Tsp
Aristocrat	1934	42	31	86	32	27

	YEAR	DnF	DsF	SvSp	SpSp	Tsp
Canterbury	1893	$ 53	$ 38	$ 98	$ 36	$ 34
Charlemagne	1963	63	53	135	66	46
Cordova	1902	35	31	85	37	32
D'Orleans	1923	45	37	95	42	28
Dorothy Bradford	1913	45	37	105	44	31
Dorothy Manners	1919	43	32	91	40	32
Fontana	1956	43	31	88	38	28
French Provincial	1948	51	40	107	46	36
Georgian	1889	88	69	186	87	46
La Fayette, engraved	1905	32	26	71	29	26
Meadow Song	1967	40	31	84	33	24
No. 38, engraved	1880	45	39	100	42	32
No. 43	1882	50	35	105	44	33
Novantique	1969	39	29	87	31	31
R.S.V.P.	1965	37	27	77	34	23
Rose Solitaire	1954	42	32	91	38	29
Rustic	1895	43	32	92	38	29
Silver Flutes	1941	40	30	77	32	26
Silver Spray	1955	32	29	83	31	26
Symphony, chased	1934	37	28	83	23	32

TUTTLE SILVER CO.

	YEAR	DnF	DsF	SvSp	SpSp	Tsp
Windsor Castle	1929	35	26	76	29	24
Beauvoir	1967	88	64	177	75	51
Charles II	1915	36	31	89	37	37
Crest of Arden	1954	71	57	153	66	45
Feather Edge	1938	37	29	82	34	31
Paul Lamerie	1925	72	54	135	58	41

WALLACE SILVERSMITHS

	YEAR	DnF	DsF	SvSp	SpSp	Tsp
Blenheim	1911	37	31	81	33	33
Campania	1914	38	35	100	43	34
Corinthian	1911	46	36	104	42	36
Custis	1911	34	29	82	35	28
Dawn Star	1958	39	30	84	31	32
Evening Mist	1963	44	34	88	40	34
Georgian Colonial	1932	32	28	75	31	32
Irian	1902	89	71	202	78	62
Juliet	1924	39	30	86	33	25
King Christian	1940	49	44	121	46	38
Kings	1903	65	51	139	63	44
La Reine	1921	69	54	147	63	46
La Viola	1912	48	41	114	47	45
Madison	1913	39	29	81	32	27
Michele	198	37	31	81	31	25
Mozart	1938	45	37	101	42	35
Orange Blossom	1923	40	32	93	40	35
Penrose	1962	36	31	82	35	33
Peony	1906	61	51	133	56	43
Pompeii	1916	35	28	80	34	32
Puritan	1910	33	29	82	35	29

Watson's Juliana pattern.

	YEAR	DnF	DsF	SvSp	SpSp	Tsp
Renaissance	1925	$ 40	$ 29	$ 83	$ 35	$ 36
Shenandoah	1966	42	32	87	35	35
Soliloquy	1963	49	36	105	39	36
Somerset	1913	42	31	83	31	32
Spanish Lace	1964	56	46	125	48	44
Versailles	1914	36	30	83	31	31
WATSON CO.						
Bunker Hill	1908	40	31	85	36	32
Carrollton	1914	57	43	117	47	35
Chippendale	1918	40	35	100	40	36
Commonwealth	1908	38	29	80	32	30
Dorian	1934	53	43	130	51	48
Foxhall	1942	50	43	126	51	41
George II	1936	47	43	122	47	43
John Adams	1911	34	28	88	35	30
Juliana	1937	57	45	132	52	42
Kenmore	1926	35	30	93	37	35
Liberty	1917	41	34	96	44	34
Martha Hilton	1914	51	40	115	47	40
Mayflower	1914	38	29	82	33	31
Old Colony	1921	46	34	102	42	33
WHITING DIV. OF GORHAM						
Antique Tip	1885	42	34	94	40	33
Bead	1885	40	33	90	35	29
French Thread	1850	39	36	91	41	32
Heraldic	1880	68	52	132	50	40
Hyperion	1888	68	56	155	62	47
Jenny Lind	1920	45	34	99	41	33

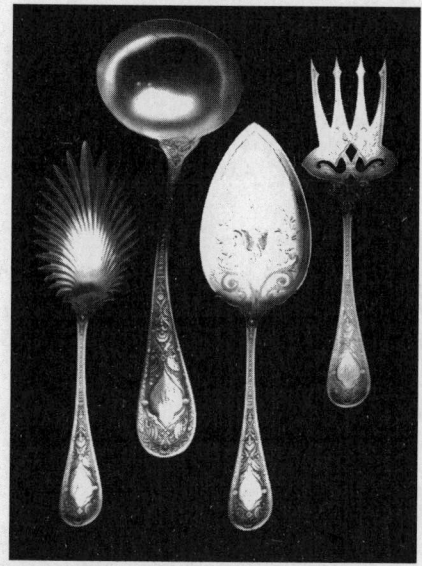

Whiting Division of Gorham's Persian pattern.

	YEAR	DnF	DsF	SvSp	SpSp	Tsp
King Edward	1901	$ 84	$ 67	$ 182	$ 81	$ 51
Madam Jumel	1908	39	37	92	40	37
Madam Morris	1909	39	31	92	36	32
Oval Thread	1850	35	31	80	33	28
Pompadour	1888	80	73	189	89	42
St. Martin's	1916	39	27	76	32	31
Stuart	1911	38	35	96	41	32

Whiting Division of Gorham mark.

Tin

Often overlooked, tin collectibles can still be found at many garage sales. "Good" examples must be in good condition, with only small unobtrusive bits of corrosion and only tiny dents. "Best" examples are undented and well proportioned, and show fine workmanship. All items are 20th century unless otherwise noted.

Left: Lithographed biscuit tin, $30-$60.

Right: Ninteenth-century tin lanterns, $150-$300.

	GOOD	BETTER	BEST
Mirror-Back Tin Sconce, circular form, c. 1850, ht. 12".	$ 500	$ 1500	$ 3500
Mixing Spoons, perforated bowls, wood handles, c. 1900	10	20	40
Mixing Spoons, set: .5 tsp-2 tbs, Rumford Co.	16	25	60
Mixing Spoons, slotted bowl, bottle opener on handle, advertising slogans	16	25	55
Mixing Spoons, slotted bowl, says "Rumford Cake Mix," c. 1900	16	25	68
Mold, bread or pudding, w. 11"	60	85	190
Mold, fluted edge handle, w. 3"	20	45	106
Mold, for cheese, grape pattern, w. 6"	40	75	190
Mold, ice-cream, c. 1880	40	80	200
Mold, jelly, c. 1890	40	80	200
Mold, lion, w/ base, w. 6"	52	85	213
Mold, pierced tin, heart form, for cheese, c. 1880	36	52	118
Mold, tubular, c. 1890	20	30	72
Muffin or Cupcake Pan, 12 cups, tin/sheet iron, c. 1890	28	30	80
Muffin or Cupcake Pan, 6 cups, tin/steel alloy, c. 1870	25	40	80
Muffin Pan, 8 cups, push-out function, c. 1910	16	30	50

	GOOD	BETTER	BEST
Muffin Rings, c. 1875	$ 5	$ 10	$ 25
Nurser, tin can, w/ lid, handle, spout	170	245	532
Nutmeg Grater, handmade drum type	35	50	125
Nutmeg Grater, wood handles, c. 1900, 4"	75	145	300
Oven, biscuit, self-powered w/ charcoal, legs	220	295	570
Oven, roasting, sits on hearth, w/ spit	260	353	700
Pail, lard, c. 1890, tin, bail handles	65	98	228
Pail, lunch, domed style, w/ dishes, cup	145	203	418
Pail, lunch, rd., handle, 6" dia.	36	55	133
Pail, lunch, w/ cups/dishes	82	115	245
Pail, milk, convex, c. 1890	65	95	200
Pail, milk, rd., late 1800s	55	85	190
Pastry Board, tinned sheet iron, w/ rolling pin	200	350	600
Pastry Board, w/ hanging loop, trough, 18"	100	200	400
Pastry Board, w/ rolling pin cradle, 22" x 18.5"	100	200	400
Pie Lifter, c. 1900	25	35	100
Pie Lifter, shovel type, wood handle, rd.	16	28	76
Pie Lifter, tin w/ wood handle	20	25	60
Pie Lifter, wire tines, heavy tin	16	25	60
Pie Pan, says "Balto. Pie Bakery"	25	38	95
Pie Plate, c. 1880	8	15	42
Pitcher, water, large globe form, 8-qt. size, w/ 6 tumblers	60	90	200
Pitcher, water, sloping sides, flared lip, qt.	40	60	150
Pitcher, water, sloping sides, hinged lid, qt.	40	75	170
Plate Warmer, bowl form, legs, handle	145	210	400
Plate Warmer, box form, legs, handle	120	300	600
Plate Warmer, cylindrical, handle, lid, plate	30	55	100
Popcorn Popper, plain, c. 1890, factory-made	2	38	100
Popcorn Popper, rect., wood handle, c. 1880	82	115	245
Pot, egg form, lid w/ hinge	40	63	150
Pot Chain, mesh circles for pot cleaning	8	15	38
Pot Chain, mesh circles for pot cleaning, w/ steel scraper	10	18	45

Tin roaster.

	GOOD	BETTER	BEST
Pot Chain, simple single ring style	$ 5	$ 12	$ 35
Press, food, c. 1930, zinc-plated iron	40	63	150
Press, meat loaf, tin w/ wood frame, top handle	65	95	200
Press, wine, perforated tin w/ wood frame, rd.	75	100	225
Pudding Mold, cylindrical, 2 qt., w/ lid	18	26	55
Pudding Mold, cylindrical, 2 qt., w/ lid, scalloped mold	26	38	85
Pudding Mold, oval, scalloped border, 1 qt.	16	25	60
Pudding Mold, oval, serrated rim, 1.5 qt.	23	35	76
Pudding Mold, oval w/ tulip, 2 qt.	28	30	85
Pudding Mold, pan form, w/ lid, c. 1890	16	25	60
Roaster, black tin, c. 1890	36	50	100
Roasting Oven, swing top, reflector type, w. 11"	163	225	450
Roiling Pin, wood handles	65	95	200
Salt Box, hanging	20	45	100
Salt Box, w/ raised letters, "SALT"	33	40	115
Sander, cylinder, dark finish, 2.5"	25	35	76
Sausage Gun, tapering tube w/ wood plunger	40	72	163
Sausage Gun, tavern size, 4"	100	130	285
Sausage Stuffer, w/ wood press	42	55	115
Scoops, curved handle, 5"	16	25	65
Scrapple Pan, tinned iron, Pennsylvania Dutch	700	1000	2500
Shaker, spice, Norton Brothers, 1890	20	30	65
Shoe Sole Templates, tin, 6 sizes, c. 1920	60	85	185
Sieves, perforated tin, c. 1900	16	28	76
Sifter, says "Kewpie," ht. 3"	40	60	133
Skillet, c. 1880	82	115	245
Skimmer, for candle wax, w/ perforated cover, wood handle	20	30	65
Skimmer, for milk, perforated/stamped, c. 1890s	13	10	45
Skimmer, shallow bowl, wood handle	16	28	76
Skimmer, stamped tin, 19th century	13	10	45
Spice Box, 7, enameled, tray w/ lid	115	160	345
Spice Box, tray, japanned, strap handle	40	70	160
Spice Boxes, 6 sq., w/ tray, nutmeg grater, wood handle	98	135	285
Spice Boxes, 6, w/ tray, wood handle	90	125	250
Steam Cooker, tall cylindrical, hinged lid, handle, dia. 12".	55	85	190
Stove Board, c. 1890	25	42	115
Strainer, cone form, handle loop	16	25	65
Strainer, hinged to fit various bowls, c. 1870	20	30	75
Strainer, meat pudding, tin, handmade, 2 pcs.	65	92	186
Strainer, perforated bowl w/ wood handle	40	63	150
Sugar Scoop, shovel head, handle strap	23	35	76

Toleware

Toleware is painted tinware. It ranges from the sophisticated forms produced in 18th-century France to the simple pieces from the backwoods of 19th-century America.

When buying toleware, pay attention to condition. Many pieces have flaked off much of their original paint and have been heavily restored or entirely repainted. Dents and rust also lower the value. Early American pieces are often reproduced and sometimes faked. Construction technique is often your best clue. Modern electrical welding is often smoothed out by grinding the surfaces near the weld. Look for modern grinding marks. For further information see *Fabulous But Fake*, by Norman S. Young, Fake Publications, Inc.

Planters are one of the most popular tole items, but beware of the formation of rust when they are used.

	AUCTION	RETAIL Low	RETAIL High
Birdcage, French, late 19th century, elaborate wirework dome top, ht. 31", len. 29"	$ 550	$ 960	$ 1500
Carrying Lantern, green-painted, late 19th century, ht. 13"	50	90	138
Document Box, painted and decorated dome top, len. 9"	350	610	963
Mirrored Sconces, pr., w/ twin arms, dia. 15"	900	1580	2475
Sconces, pr., late 19th century, painted and decorated, each V-form w/ circular smoke-plate, ht. 17"	850	1490	2338
Tea Canister Lamp, ht. 18"	250	440	688
Tea Canisters, pr. of Eng. w/ gilt chinoiserie decoration, fitted as lamps, ht. 32"	1700	2980	4675
Tea Canisters, pr. of Eng. w/ gilt decoration of oriental merchants, fitted as lamps, ht. 35"	1300	2280	3575
Tray, pierced-edge large circular, w/ original decoration, dia. 24"	350	610	963
Wall Clock, French, early 20th century, dia. 17"	75	130	206

Early 19th-century Neoclassical French painted mustard yellow toleware with gilt highlights:

Biscuit Box, oval, covered	750	1400	2500
Candlesticks, pr., w/ sq. bases.	1000	1800	3250
Chestnut Urns, pr., oval, covered	2800	5200	9000
Condiment Set, w/ glass bottles	475	880	1550
Dinner Bell, ht. 7"	100	200	330
Fruit Basket, oval, reticulated border	800	1500	2600
Peat Bucket	200	370	650
Rectangular Box, w. 10"	125	230	400
Round Box, dia. 7"	135	250	440
Sauce Boat, reticulated, on secured stand	275	500	900
Tea Kettle, large oval, on reticulated stand.	1300	2400	4000
Tea Urn, on burner stand	950	1700	3000
Tray, large oval, w. 26"	800	1500	2500
Tray, oval, w. 18"	1550	2750	5000
Trays, pr., oval, w. 15"	500	900	1600

Above: Set of French painted mustard yellow toleware with gilt highlights. All prices are auction results. Top row left to right: teakettle on stand, $1300; large oval tray, $800; oval fruit basket, $800. Middle row left to right: biscuit box, $750; covered chestnut urn (pr.), $2800; rectangular box, $150; oval tray, $1550; dinner bell, $125; round box, $150; sauce boat on stand, $275. Bottom row left to right: pair of candlesticks $1000; oval tray (pr.), $500; tea urn on stand, $950; condiment set, $475. — Photo courtesy of Northeast Auctions.
Below: The sophistication of the decoration makes a big difference in value. Left: Simply decorated tray, 12", $75 retail. Right: Ship decorated tray, 18", $2000 retail.

Military Memorabilia

Military memorabilia encompasses items pertaining to all branches of the military. Some hobbyists collect military memorabilia by type of item—for example, badges or swords—while others collect by military branch like the Navy, Army or Air Force. For more information consult *The Official Price Guide to Military Collectibles*, published by House of Collectibles, Random House, NY.

Warning! Federal law prohibits the sale of American military medals. Recently there has been a crackdown at military memorabilia shows.

Civil War Canteens, $300-$500 each.

Armor

	LOW	AVG.	HIGH
Breastplates, 16th century	$ 5000	$ 6500	$ 8000
Eighteenth-19th century	1500	2000	2500
Japanese Helmets (Kabuto)	2200	3100	4000
Jingasa	1500	2000	2500
Reproduction Armor (full suits)	5000	9500	14,000
Seventeenth century	2500	4000	5500

Badges and Other Insignia

	LOW	AVG.	HIGH
Aerial Gunner Badge, WWII	100	112	125
Airship Pilot Badge, c. 1921, authorized in 1921, dirigible took place of balloon	475	500	550
Bombardier Badge, WWII	100	115	125
British Pilot's Wings (WWI)	215	258	300
Combat (Aircraft) Observer Badge, WWII	140	158	175
Command Pilot Badge, WWII	140	155	170
Flight Surgeon's Badge, c. 1943	160	172	185
German Imperial	800	1250	1700
Third Reich badges (Note: many fakes)	270	555	840
U.S. (WWII Aviation)	150	225	300
Third Reich, armbands	150	275	400

	LOW	AVG.	HIGH
Third Reich, cuff titles (sleevebands)	$ 150	$ 425	$ 700
Japanese Pilot's Wings (WWII)	160	192	225
Third Reich, navy specialty patches	15	28	40
Third Reich, cuff title (landwacht)	25	40	55

Bayonets

	LOW	AVG.	HIGH
British Baker Bayonet	540	620	700
British Brown Bess Socket (19th century)	150	225	300
British Enfield Bayonet 1907	65	70	75
British Indian Bayonet	80	110	140
British Martini Henry	150	225	300
British Number 4 Mark II Spike	25	32	40
European Plug Bayonet (early 19th century)	270	555	840
French (late 19th century)	150	225	300
French Fusil Socket (early 18th century)	800	1100	1400
German Imperial	80	135	190
Italian (late 19th century)	55	85	115
Japanese Arisaka	80	110	140
Krag	150	160	170
Krag Bolo Blade	215	258	300
Krag Bowie Knife	1500	1600	1700
Mexican Remington Rolling Block 7 mm Rifle	150	170	190
Prussian Bayonet Model 1871	270	335	400
Ramrod	150	225	300
Ross Model 1905	190	208	225
Russian Imperial (late 19th century)	150	225	300
Siamese (late 19th century)	80	110	140
Socket (19th century)	100	135	170
Spanish Model 1941	60	72	85
Swiss Model 1931	80	98	115
U.S. (late 19th century)	100	200	300
U.S. Bannerman Cadet	160	192	225
U.S. Model 1860	270	335	400
U.S. Model 1942	160	192	225
Dahlgren Bowie Knife	1500	1600	1700
Dahlgren Saber Pattern	270	335	400

Epaulets

	LOW	AVG.	HIGH
British (early 1800s) Coldstream Guards	540	835	1130
French Officers (early 1900s)	800	900	1000
German (19th century)	350	525	700
U.S. (Civil War officers)	270	555	840
U.S. (late 19th century)	150	225	300

Gorgets

	LOW	AVG.	HIGH
Bavarian, late 19th century	270	335	400
British Officer's, 18th century	540	835	1130
British Officer's, 19th century	400	620	840

	LOW	AVG.	HIGH
Nazi political leader's	$ 1000	$ 1350	$ 1700
Nazi SA	1500	1750	2000
Prussian Flag Bearer's	670	830	990
Prussian Officer's, 18th century	2000	2250	2500

Guns

	LOW	AVG.	HIGH
Albion (Webley Patent) No. 2 MK I British Military Revolver, cal. 38 S&W	150	280	490
American Eagle Luger Semi-Auto Pistol, cal. 30 Luger, 1906	600	1100	1900
American Half Stocked Rifle, 38.5" octagonal barrel, cal. 32, ...	250	450	820
American Historical Foundation Uberti Lemat Gen. Jackson Commemorative, cal. 44 percussion	950	1750	3000
American Historical Foundation Uberti Commemorative Henry Rifle, cal. 44-40	2000	3750	6500
American, "Kentucky" Full Stock Long Rifle, 43.5" len., octagonal barrel, cal. 48	325	600	1000
Ansley H. Fox A-Grade Double Barrel Shotgun, cal. 12 ga	650	1200	2000
Ansley H. Fox A-Grade Three Barrel Set, cal. 12 ga	925	1700	3000
Ansley H. Fox Early A-Grade Double Barrel Shotgun, cal. 12 ga ...	500	900	16,000
Armscor AK47/22 Semi-Auto Rifle, cal. 22 LR	250	470	800
Auto-Ordnance M1927 Vietnam War Commemorative, cal. 45 ACP	900	1650	3000
Barrel Blank Pistol, cal. 22 blank	225	420	730
Belgian Browning Superposed Grade-I O/U Shotgun, cal. 12 ga	1000	1800	3260
Beretta Model 1934 Semi-Auto Military Pistol, cal. 32 ACP	250	470	820
Beretta Model 1934 Semi-Auto Military Pistol, cal. 9 mm Corto ...	400	740	1300
Browning A-5 F-Grade Semi-Auto Shotgun, cal. 12 ga	1400	2600	4500
Browning Bss Deluxe Sidelock Double Barrel Shotgun, cal.			

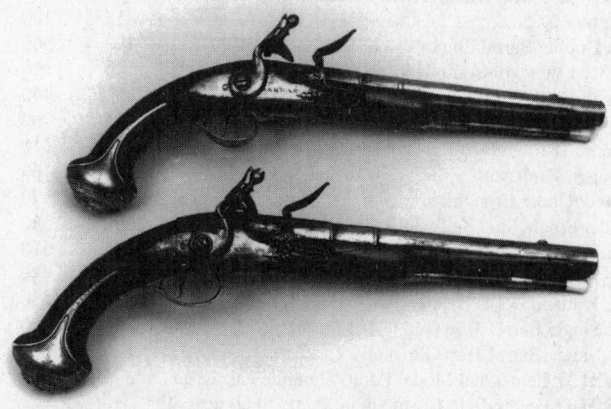

Matched pair of silver mounted English flintlock pistols, ca. 1770, by Barbar, $3500. —Photo courtesy of Northeast Auctions.

	LOW	AVG.	HIGH
12 ga	$ 1600	$ 3000	$ 5000
Browning Citori Superlight Over/Under Shotgun, cal. 28 ga	850	1500	2750
Browning Model 12 Grade-1 Pump Action Shotgun, cal. 20 ga ...	300	560	1000
Browning Superposed Exhibition Grade Over/Under Shotgun, cal. 12 ga	10,000	18,000	32,000
Colt 1911 WWI Commemorative 2nd Battle of the Marne, cal. 45 ACP	475	880	1550
Colt 2nd Generation 1851 Navy Robert E. Lee Commemorative, cal. 36 percussion	400	740	1300
Colt 2nd Generation 1851 Navy Ulysses S. Grant Commemorative, cal. 36 percussion	375	700	1220
Colt 2nd Generation 1862 Police, cal. 36 percussion	325	600	1000
Colt 2nd Generation U.S. Cavalry Commemorative Pair, cal. 44 percussion	950	1700	3100
Colt Frontier Scout Golden Spike Commemorative, cal. 22	325	600	1000
Colt Frontier Scout Lawman Series-Wyatt Earp, cal. 22 LR	350	650	1140
Colt Lightning Magazine Rifle, cal. 22	525	980	1700
Colt Lightning Pump Action Rifle, cal. 22	225	420	730
Colt Lightning Small Frame Pump Action Rifle, cal. 22 S	300	560	1000
Colt Model 1903 Large Frame Pocket Pistol, cal. 38 ACP	800	1500	2600
Colt Model 1911 John Browning Commemorative, cal. 45 ACP .	600	1100	1900
Colt Officers' Model Heavy Barrel Target Pistol, cal. 38 Special	250	470	820
Colt Officers' Model Match Target Revolver, cal. 38 Special	175	330	570
Colt Officers' Model Target Revolver, cal. 22 LR	350	650	1100
Colt Single Action Army Arizona Territorial Centennial Commemorative, cal. 45 Colt	700	1300	2200
Colt-Type AR15 Vietnam Commemorative, cal. 223	750	1400	2500
Colt Woodsman 3rd Model Sport Semi-Auto Pistol, cal. 22	275	510	900
Deluxe Flobert Action Fluted Barrel Single Shot Rifle, cal. 22	800	1490	2600
English Flintlock Pistol, made by Ketland & Co.	425	790	1400
European Single Barrel Half Stocked Percussion Fowler, mid-19th century	55	100	180
Exel Arms Double Barrel Smooth Bore Slug Gun, cal. 12 ga	300	560	980
Fed. Ord. M14 Vietnam Commemorative, cal. 7.62 mm (308) ..	1000	1860	3260
Frank Wesson Two-Trigger Rifle, cal. 38 Rf/Cf	250	470	820
French1777 Flintlock Pistol, cal. 69	425	790	1390
French Model 1886/93 Bolt Action Military Rifle, cal. 8 mm	220	410	720
German Luger Semi-Auto Military Pistol, cal. 9 mm	625	1160	2000
German Over/Under Combination Gun, cal. 9 mm	200	370	650
Hans Bradler Single Shot Stalking Rifle, cal. 6.5 x 57	3000	5580	9780
Harrington & Richardson Defender Revolver, cal. 38 S & W	275	510	900
Holland & Holland Double Rifle, cal. 360 Exp	8000	14,880	26,000
Holland & Holland Royal Ejector Two-Barrel Set, cal. 12 ga	6250	11,630	20,380
Ithaca 4-E Single Barrel Trap Gun, cal. 12 ga	450	840	1470
Ithaca 5-E Single Barrel Trap Gun, cal. 12 ga	1,650	3000	5380
Ithaca Model 37 Centennial Model Pump Shotgun, cal. 12 ga	375	700	1220
Ithaca Model 37 Featherlight Bicentennial Pump Shotgun, cal. 12 ga	400	740	1300
J.P. Sauer & Sohn Best Quality Double Barrel Shotgun, cal. 12 ga	800	1490	2610
J. & W. Tolley Sidelock Double Barrel Shotgun, cal. 12 ga	950	1770	3100

	LOW	AVG.	HIGH
James Beattie & Son Under Lever Hammer Double Rifle, cal. 577 .... $ 3000		$ 5580	$ 9780
Japanese Type 94 Semi-Auto Military Pistol, cal. 8 mm Nambu . 375		700	1220
K. Barthelmes Commercial Mauser Bolt Action Rifle, cal. 5.6 x 61 Vom Hofe 450		840	1470
Krieghoff Crown Grade Model 32 4-Barrel Set, cal. 12, 20 and 28 ga. and 410 16,000		27,000	52,000
Krieghoff Model 32 Over/Under Trap Gun, cal. 12 ga 1000		1950	3420
Luger Semi-Auto Military Pistol, cal. 9 mm, 1917 Erfurt 300		560	980
Luger Semi-Auto Military Pistol, cal. 9 mm, 1939/42 475		880	1550
Luicius W. Pond Single Action Pocket Revolver, cal. 32 rimfire . 225		420	730
Marlin Model 1881 Lightweight Lever Action Rifle, cal. 32-40 .. 400		740	1300
Marrone Over/Under Shotgun, cal. 12 ga 450		840	1470
Martini Action Rook Rifle, cal. 32-20 300		560	980
Massive Percussion Bench Rifle, cal. 40 percussion 1150		2140	3750
Mauser Commercial Obendorf Bolt Action Rifle, cal. 8 x 57 400		740	1300
Mauser Cone-Hammer Broomhandle Semi-Auto Pistol, cal. 30 Mauser 3250		6000	10,000
New England Firearms (H&R) Model R92 D.A. Revolver, cal. 22 LR 55		100	180
Otto Bock Commercial Mauser Bolt Action Rifle, cal. 8 x 57 200		370	650
Parker Double Barrel Hammer Shotgun, cal. 10 ga. 250		470	820
Parker Gh Double Barrel Shotgun, cal. 12 ga 350		650	1140
Parker N-Grade Damascus Double Barrel Shotgun, cal. 10 ga 700		1300	2280
Perugini-Visini Boxlock Double Rifle, cal. 9.3 x 74r 3250		6000	10600
Peter Longo Over/Under Deluxe Shotgun, cal. 12 ga 2750		5120	8970
Remington Model 1100 Semi-Auto Shotgun, cal. 12 ga 275		510	900
Remington Model 12-Cs Pump Action Rifle, cal. 22 Rem.			

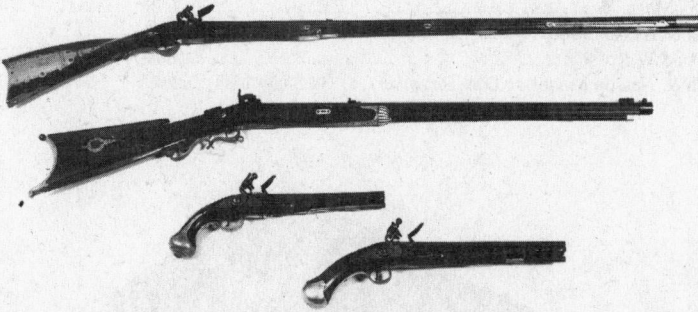

Top to bottom: Kentucky rifle of Pennsylvania manufacture, with curly maple stock and octagonal barrel, length 58", $14,000; Grudchos & Eggers rifle with silver mounts, gold inlay and elaborate engraving, length 50", $4500; English dragoon pistol, length 17", $1000; English dragoon pistol, length 19", $1400. —Photo courtesy of Northeast Auctions.

	LOW	AVG.	HIGH
Special	$ 450	$ 840	$ 1470
Remington Model 12a Pump Action Rifle, cal. 22 S, L, LR	200	370	650
Remington Model 12a Pump Action Rifle, cal. 22 S, L, LR	225	420	730
Remington Model 12a Pump Action Rifle, cal. 22 S, L, or LR	200	370	650
Remington Model 12c Pump Action Rifle, cal. 22 S, L, LR	300	560	980
Remington Model 12c Pump Action Rifle, cal. 22 S, L, or LR	275	510	900
Remington Model 16 Semi-Auto Rifle, cal. 22 Rem Auto	150	280	490
Remington Model 8 Takedown Semi-Auto Sporting Rifle, cal. 32 Rem	275	510	900
Remington Model 81 Semi-Auto Sporting Rifle, cal. 300 Sav	325	600	1000
Remington Rand Model 1911a1 Semi-Auto Military Pistol, cal. 45 ACP	550	1000	1750
Rizzini Model S780e Over/Under Shotgun, cal. 12 ga	575	1000	1850
Ruger Gp100 D.A. Stainless Steel Revolver, cal. 357 Mag	250	470	820
Ruger Model 77vbz Mkii Stainless Steel Varmint Rifle, cal. 220 Swift	400	740	1300
Ruger Red Label O/U Shotgun, cal. 12 ga	625	1160	2000
Ruger Security Six Stainless Steel Revolver, cal. 357 Mag	200	370	650
Ruger T-512 Mk-I Bumble Bee Special, cal. 22 LR	300	560	980
Savage Model 1899 Lever Action Takedown Rifle w/ 4 barrels, cal. 250	800	1500	2600
Savage Model 1905 Semi-Auto Pocket Pistol, cal. 32	200	370	650
Skb Model 505 Crown Field O/U Shotgun, cal. 20 ga	550	1000	1750
Smith Corona Model 03-A3 Bolt Action Rifle, cal. 30-06	325	600	1000
Smith & Wesson Hand Ejector 4th Change, cal. 32-20	150	280	500
Smith & Wesson K-22 Masterpiece, cal. 22.	325	600	1000
Smith & Wesson Model 14-4 K38 Masterpiece Revolver, cal. 38 Special	200	370	650
Smith & Wesson Model 17-6 Target Revolver, cal. 22 LR	250	470	820
Smith & Wesson Model 27-3 Fbi Commemorative Revolver, cal. 357 Mag	650	1200	2000
Smith & Wesson Model 3 Russian Second Model Revolver, cal. 44 S&W Russian	800	1490	2600
Smith & Wesson Model 31 D.A. Revolver, cal. 32 S&W long	200	370	650

Smith and Wesson Model K-14 target pistol, $700. —Photo courtesy of Northeast Auctions.

	LOW	AVG.	HIGH
Smith & Wesson Model 34-1 22/32 Kit Gun, cal. 22 LR	$ 220	$ 410	$ 720
Smith & Wesson Model 67-1 Stainless Steel Revolver, cal. 38			
Special	200	370	650
Smith & Wesson New Model No. 3 Single Action Revolver, cal.			
44 S&W	300	560	980
Smith-Corona 1903a3 National Match Rifle, cal. 30-06	800	1490	2600
Springfield 1903 National Match Type Rifle, cal. 30-06	650	1210	2000
Stevens Ideal Rifle No. 44.5, cal. 25 Rf	325	600	1000
Stevens Model 620 Pump Action Shotgun, cal. 16 ga	120	220	390
Steyr Model 1916 Military Pistol, cal. 9 mm Steyr.......................	175	330	570
Thompson Center High Plains Sporter, cal. 50 percussion	175	330	570
U.S. Model 1816 Musket, percussion Alteration. Type III	1200	2230	4000
U.S. Model 1847 Sappers Musketoon (Composite), cal. 69	700	1300	2250
U.S. Springfield 1903 Bolt Action Military Rifle, cal. 30-06	700	1300	2250
U.S. Springfield Armory M-1 Garand Possible Rifle, cal. 30-06 ..	2950	5500	9500
U.S. Springfield Model 1922 M-2 Bolt Action Training Rifle,			
cal. 22 LR	600	1120	1960
U.S. Springfield Model 1922 Mii Bolt Action Training Rifle,			
cal. 22 LR	550	1000	1750
Valmet Model 412 Over/Under Combination Gun 2 Bbl Set,			
cal. 12 x 12 and 12 x 308	750	1400	2450
Valmet Model 412 Over/Under Double Rifle, cal. 9.3 x 74r	750	1400	2450
W.W. Greener Best Quality Cape Gun, cal. 450 Exp. x 12 ga	1900	3530	6190
Weatherby Centurion-II 1980 Ducks Unlimited Semi-Auto			
Shotgun, cal. 12 ga.	600	1120	1900
Weatherby Mark V Premier Bolt Action Rifle, cal. 300 Wea/			
Mag	1750	3260	5700
Webley Mark-V British Military Revolver, cal. 455	325	600	1000
Whitney Howard Single Shot Patent Action Rifle, cal. 44 Rf	275	510	900
Winchester Buffalo Bill Comm. Lever Action Rifle, cal. 30-30 ...	400	740	1300
Winchester Cardboard Advertising Kit For Centennial '66	140	260	460
Winchester M-1 Carbine, cal. 30 Carb	850	1500	2750
Winchester Model '03 Semi-Auto Rifle, cal. 22 Win. Auto..........	225	400	730
Winchester Model '07 Semi-Auto Rifle, cal. 351 Sl......................	200	350	650
Winchester Model '12 Custom Engraved Pump Action Shotgun,			
cal. 12 ga...	400	750	1300
Winchester Model '12 Pump Action Trap Gun, cal. 12 ga............	450	800	1450
Winchester Model '12 Pump Action Trap Gun, cal. 12 ga............	550	1000	1750
Winchester Model 1886 Lever Action Rifle, cal. 40-82	1100	2000	3500
Winchester Model 1886 Standard Grade Lever Action Rifle,			
cal. 45-70	850	1500	2750
Winchester Model 1890 Pump Action Rifle, cal. 22 S	300	500	980
Winchester Model 1892 Lever Action Rifle, cal. 32 Wcf	275	500	900
Winchester Model 1892 Special Order Lever Action Rifle,			
cal. 44 Wcf...	1000	1950	3400
Winchester Model 1892 Special Order Saddle Ring Carbine,			
cal. 25-20	450	840	1400
Winchester Model 1894 Saddle Ring Carbine, cal. 30 Wcf	300	560	1000
Winchester Model 1894 Special Order Eastern Carbine, cal. 30			
Wcf	425	790	1400
Winchester Model 1894 Special Order Eastern Carbine, cal. 32			

	LOW	AVG.	HIGH
Special	$ 300	$ 560	$ 1000
Winchester Model 1894 Special Order Rifle, cal. 38-55	470	870	1530
Winchester Model 1894 Special Order Saddle Ring Carbine,			
cal. 30 Wcf..	375	700	1220
Winchester Model 1895 Takedown Rifle, cal. 30-06	550	1000	1790
Winchester Model 1897 Solid Frame Adams' Express Riot Gun,			
cal. 12 ga...	750	1400	2450
Winchester Model 61 Pump Action Rifle, cal. 22 S, L, LR	525	1000	1710
Winchester Model 62 Pump Action Rifle, cal. 22 S.L. or LR	425	790	1400
Winchester Model 62a Pump Action Gallery Rifle, cal. 22	250	470	820
Winchester Model 62a Pump Action Rifle, cal. 22 S, L, LR	300	560	1000
Winchester Model 70 Featherweight Bolt Action Rifle, cal. 308 .	525	980	1710
Winchester Model 71 Custom Engraved Deluxe Rifle, cal. 348 .	1200	2230	3800
Winchester Model 94 Illinois Sesquicentennial, cal. 30-30	300	560	1000
Winchester Model 97 Pump Action Shotgun, cal. 12 ga	350	650	1150

Helmet Plates

British (late 19th century)...	270	385	500
German Imperial	150	275	400
Poland	80	110	140
Russian Imperial	270	385	500
Swedish (late 19th century)	270	335	400
United States (19th century)	150	275	400

Halberds

British Artillery, 18th century	2200	2850	3500
British Ceremonial, 19th century	800	1000	1200
German Combat, 16th century	800	1100	1400
Swiss Combat, 16th century	1000	1350	1700
United States Colonial	2500	5250	8000

Headdress

Austrian Army Grenadier Cap, 18th century	15,000	20,000	25,000
Austrian Army Grenadier Cap, early 19th century	8000	11,000	14,000
Austrian Dragoon Cap, late 19th century	270	335	400
Austrian Field Artillery Officer's Cap, early 20th century	270	385	500
Austrian Hussar Officer's Shako, early 20th century	2150	2775	3400
Austrian Infantry Shako, 19th century	1500	2000	2500
Austrian Officer's Lancer's Cap (Czapka), late 19th century	2200	2850	3500
Bavarian Officer's Cap, 19th century	540	835	1130
Bavarian Officer's Lancer's Cap, 19th century	2500	3250	4000
Bavarian Other Ranks Lancer's Cap, 19th century	1500	2000	2500
Bavarian Shako, 19th century	1500	2000	2500
British Grenadier's Cap, 18th century	15,000	20,000	25,000
British Infantry Officer's Shako, 19th century	2200	2850	3500
British Mounted Police Officer's Pillbox Cap, late 19th century ...	370	412	455
British Officer's Fur Busby, late 19th century	800	1100	1400
British Officer's Patrol Cap, late 19th century	400	550	700

	LOW	AVG.	HIGH
British Other Ranks Fur Busby, late 19th century	$ 400	$ 550	$ 700
British Other Ranks Lancer's Cap, late 19th century	2200	2850	3500
British Royal Scots Bearskin Cap, early 20th century	800	1100	1400
British Staff Officer's Cocked Hat, early 19th century	1000	1350	1700
Canadian Militia Officer's Forage Cap, late 19th century	350	400	450
English Officer's Lancer's Cap, late 19th century	4000	4750	5500
French Foreign Legion Cap	55	62	70
French Officer's Lancer's Cap, 19th century	2500	4000	5500
French Officer's Shako, 19th century	1500	2000	2500
French Other Ranks Lancer's Cap, 19th century	1500	2000	2500
German Hussar's Officer's Cap	540	835	1130
German Imperial Officer's Busby, late 19th century	5000	6500	8000
German Imperial Other Ranks Busby, late 19th century	2500	3250	4000
German Officer's Grenadier's Cap, 18th century	20,000	22,500	25,000
Imperial German Grenadier's Cap, late 19th century	5000	9500	14,000
Imperial German Infantry Shako, late 19th century	1000	1500	2000
Imperial German Lancer's Cap, late 19th century	1000	1350	1700
Nazi Admiral's Visor Cap	4000	5500	7000
Nazi Airforce Officer's Visor Cap	270	385	500
Nazi Diplomatic Corps Visor Cap	5000	6000	7000
Nazi General Staff Officer's Cap	1500	1750	2000
Nazi Infantry Cap	270	385	500
Nazi Police Officer's Shako	540	690	840
Nazi SS Coffee Can Cap	2500	4000	5500
Prussian Officer's Black Beaver Hat, early 19th century	800	1100	1400
Prussian Other Ranks Black Felt Hat, late 18th/early 19th century	540	835	1130
Prussian Shako, 19th century	1000	1500	2000
Royal Fusiliers Officer's Racoon Skin Cap, late 19th century	1500	1750	2000
Royal Italian Cavalry Busby, early 20th century	1300	1650	2000
Russian Hussar's Shako, 19th century	2200	2850	3500
U.S. Enlisted Man's Artillery Hat, 19th century	800	1100	1400
U.S. Enlisted Man's Fatigue Cap, early 20th century	270	335	400
U.S. Enlisted Man's Forage Cap, early 19th century	400	450	500
U.S. Enlisted Man's Shako, 19th century	800	1250	1700
U.S. First Guard Other Ranks Grenadier Cap, 19th century	4000	5500	7000
U.S. Officer's Cocked Hat, early 19th century	1500	1750	2000
U.S. Officer's Grenadier's Cap, late 19th century	8000	11,000	14,000
U.S. Officer's Tricorn Hat, late 18th/early 19th century	1500	1750	2000

Knives

American Bowie Knife (19th century)	400	550	700
American Bowie Knife, w/ silver and ivory trim (19th century)	2500	3250	4000
British Bowie Knife (19th century)	400	550	700
British Trench Knife (WWI)	540	620	700
French Trench Knife (WWI)	270	335	400
German Trench Knife (WWI)	270	335	400
Italian Trench Knife (WWII)	150	180	210
U.S. Marine Corps KA-BAR Fighting/Utility Knife	150	225	300
U.S. Trench Knife (WWI)	200	278	355

Swords

	LOW	AVG.	HIGH
Army Foot Artillery Sword, Model 1833. Brass-scaled grip cast in 1-piece w/ short cross-guard w/ plain disk finials. Blade marked w/ American Eagle and "N.P. AMES SPRINGFIELD." American Eagle on pommel, hilt attached to tang of blade by 3 iron traverse rivets	$ 450	$ 488	$ 525
Army Officer's Sword, Model 1850. Based on French army model, half-basket hilt, gilt w/ gilt wire-wrapped leather-covered grips. Phrygian helmet pattern pommel, blade single edge and slightly curved, polished black leather scabbard w/ gilt/brass fittings	560	605	650
Army Officer's Sword, Model 1902. Generally similar to above, grips are notched on inside for fingers. Full back strap, simple rounded semicap pommel w/ small caspan top, D-shape knuckle guard divides into 3 parts. Turned down tear-shape finial, nickled scabbard	380	438	495

Uniforms

Army Air Force Officer's Blouse, U.S. buttons and cuff braid. Officer's U.S. and winged propeller collar insignia. Pilot's silver wings	140	155	170
Army Enlisted Man's Field Jacket, WWII, so-called "Eisenhower" jacket of stout OD material, 2 pleated pockets. Concealed button front. Embroidered 1st Division patch on left shoulder	60	70	80
Army Enlisted Man's Issue Blouse. WWI, 89th Division, patch on upper left sleeve. Bronze U.S. enlisted device on right collar and Signal Corps device on left side. Single overseas chevron	150	152	155
Marine Corps Enlisted Man's Coat, WWII period. Green coat w/ 4 bronze Marine Corps buttons down front and on 4 pockets. Marine 2nd Division patch on upper left shoulder. Corporal's stripes and one enlistment stripe on each sleeve. Red "Ruptured Duck" discharge device on right breast	60	68	75
Marine Sergeant OD Wool Blouse, WWI period. Four pockets w/ bronze Marine Corps buttons. Blouse has high collar w/ rare collar ornaments incl. disk bearing Marine Corps emblem. Sergeant's chevrons	245	260	275

Miniatures

Before the days of the wallet photo or the Polaroid, miniature paintings filled the need of a quick keepsake. Although some of these likenesses bear no more resemblance to the sitter than a cartoon character, they often capture a style and a mood of a bygone era. Most of the artists did not sign their work and many names have been lost to history. However, some artists (e.g., Rufus Porter) have a positive effect on the value of a piece.

Clockwise from top left: Pencil portrait of woman, height 3", $650; ink portrait of girl, age 12, height 4.5", dated 1827, $1300; pair of watercolor portraits attributed to Rufus Porter, height 4.5", $7500.
— Photo courtesy of Northeast Auctions.

	AUCTION	RETAIL Low	High
Ivory Miniature Portrait of Gentleman, in Empire coat, 4.5"....	$ 1000	$ 1860	$ 3260
Ivory Miniature Portrait of Gentleman, in white stock, 4"	500	930	1630
Ivory Miniature Portrait of Gentleman, w/ white stock and ruffle, 5"	1500	2790	4890
Ivory Miniature Portraits, pr., by Alvan Clark: Thomas and Mary Edge	2500	4650	8150
Ivory Miniature Portraits, pr., by Martha B. Willson Day (b. 1885): Cora and Charles Burlingham, c. 1929	100	190	330
Miniature on Ivory of David Copperfield's "Little Emily"	200	370	650
Miniature Portrait on Ivory of the Bruce Family, attrib. to Jacob B. Schoener (1805-1846)	750	1400	2450
Portrait Miniature of Hobart Cole, in white sailor suit, 1906, by Anne S.H. Foster	450	840	1470
Portrait Miniature on Ivory of Thomas Alva Edison	250	470	820
Silhouette of Gentleman, full-len., w/ beaver hat, in bird's-eye maple frame, ht. 13"	250	470	820
Silhouette of Gentleman, full-len., w/ interior scene in gilt frame, ht. 14.5"	400	740	1300
Silhouette of Woman, in manner of Miers	75	140	240
Silhouette Portrait of Miss Mary Taylor (1806-30), daughter of Revolutionary War hero Jonathan Taylor, attrib. to Ruth Bascom	750	1400	2450

Molds

Before ice cream producers could send the various shapes of ice cream now offered in the freezer of the corner market, local merchants made their own ice cream and sold it in shapes they pressed into molds themselves. Homemade ice cream also found its way into these molds. Because some pewter contains lead, it is not advisable to continue the practice.

All of the following figural molds are pewter unless otherwise indicated.

Flaming hearts ice cream mold, $25-$35.

Chocolate Molds

	LOW	HIGH
Cat, 8"	$ 100	$ 125
Dog Head, 4"	17	25
Filled Stocking	115	175
Jack O'Lantern	35	50
Rabbit Riding Rooster, 6"	46	70
Santa	23	35
Sitting Rabbit, 3.5"	23	35
Snowman, 4"	46	70
Teddy Bear, 11", #2644	175	260
Turkey, 3-part	52	80
Woven Basket	45	70

Ice Cream Molds

Asparagus Bunch	50	80
Bell, Krauss, #285	50	80
Chicken, E. & Co. N.Y., #652	50	80
Christmas Stocking, #596	100	150
Christmas Tree With Ornaments, #641K	50	80
Christmas Wreath, E. & Co. N.Y., #1146	100	160
Chrysanthemum, Krauss, #313	65	100
Conch Shell, S. & Co., #311	85	130
Corn on the Cob, S. & Co., #270	60	90
Cornucopia, #287	30	45
Cornucopia, E. & Co., #1004	85	130
Cupid, Krauss, #492	63	100
Daisy, E. & Co. N.Y., #317	50	80

	LOW	HIGH
Dove in Flight, E. & Co. N.Y., #677	$ 100	$ 150
Drum (3-part), Krauss, #511A	85	130
Duck, Krauss, #187	50	80
Flaming Hearts, Krauss, #300	60	90
George Washington, Krauss, #460	75	114
Grapes, Krauss, #159	50	80
Native American, Krauss, #458	85	130
Pumpkin, S. & Co.	40	60
Rabbitt, Krauss, #190	50	80
Rabbitt Standing, Krauss, #189	60	90
Roasting Turkey, Krauss, #364	45	70
Rocking Horse, E. & Co.	85	130
Rose, Krauss, #582	58	90
Rose With Bud and Leaves, S. & Co.	63	100
Santa at Chimney, E. & Co. N.Y., #1171	86	130
Santa, S. & Co., #427	52	80
Strawberry, Krauss, #503	75	115
Train Engine, #477	85	130
Triple Rose, Krauss, #391	52	80
Triple Strawberry, S. & Co.	63	100
Turkey, E. & Co. N.Y., #650	50	80
Witche's Cat, E. & Co. N.Y., #1175	86	130

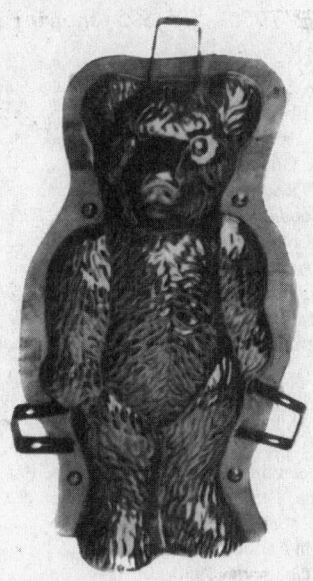

Teddy Bear chocolate mold.

Motion Lamps

Animated motion lamps draw the eye by presenting an illusion of a waterfall, a ship at sea, or a variety of action-packed images. The heat of the light bulb causes the cylinder to revolve inside a painted shade creating the illusion of a moving image. The light of the bulb shining through the shade casts a beautiful glow. The most prominent manufacturers were Scene in Action and National in the 1920s, and Econolite and L.A. Goodman in the 1950s through the 1960s. Prices are guided by condition, availability, and collector demand. Care must be taken to ensure that the original cylinder is inside the lamp because cylinders are not interchangeable. Values are given for lamps in mint condition.

Our consultants for this section are Jim and Kaye Whitaker, owners of Eclectic Antiques. They are listed in the back of this book.

Ship, L.A. Goodman, 1950s, $85-$95 (showing both sides).

	LOW	HIGH
Airplanes, plastic, Econolite, 1958, ht. 11"	$ 90	$ 100
Bar is Open, plastic, Visual Effects, 1970, ht. 13"	24	28
Bicycles, plastic, Econolite, 1950s, ht. 11"	85	95
Butterflies, cone shape, L.A. Goodman, ht. 9"	90	130
Ducks, plastic, Econolite, 1950s, ht. 12"	70	90
Firefighters, plastic, L.A. Goodman, 1950s, ht. 11"	90	110
Fireplace, plastic, Econolite, ht. 11"	70	80
Forest Fire, glass, Scene in Action, ht. 9"	100	130
Fountain of Youth, plastic, Econolite, 1950, ht. 11"	75	85
Hopalong Cassidy, cylinder style, Econolite (Roto -Vue Jr.), 1949, ht. 10"	250	400
Ko-Pak-Ta Nut Machine, chrome, Roy Stringer Co., 1930s, ht. 15"	250	350
Lighthouse/Ship, plastic, L.A. Goodman, 1950s, ht. 11"	85	95
Marine Scene, glass and white metal, Scene in Action, 1930s, ht. 9"	90	110
Merry Go Round, Disneyland, plastic, red and yellow, Econolite, 1950s, ht. 11"	250	350
Merry Go Round, yellow, Econolite (Roto-Vue Jr.), 1950s, 10"	85	95
Mill Scene, plastic, Econolite, 1950s, ht. 11"	75	85
Miss Liberty, plastic, Econolite, 1950s, ht. 11"	90	120
Niagara Falls, glass, Scene in Action, 1930s, ht. 9"	90	110
Niagara Falls, plastic, L.A. Goodman, 1950s, ht. 11"	65	75
Pot Bellied Stove, black or silver, Econolite, 1950s, ht. 12"	85	95
Santa and Reindeer, plastic, L.A. Goodman, 1950s, ht. 12"	100	140
Seattle World's Fair, plastic, Econolite, 1962, ht. 11"	90	120
Serenader, flat front, metal, SceneiIn Action, 1930s, ht. 13"	100	150
Snow Scene, church, plastic, Econolite, 1950s, ht. 11"	75	85

Music

CDs

Although they appeared in the market only 15 years ago, compact discs are already collector items. Music fans collect CDs for the sound they contain, often unique recordings that can't (or no longer can) be picked up by a quick visit to the local music emporium. Most of the more valuable CDs are promotional disks. Often companies only produced a relatively few such promos, but not always. Although most promos have a somewhat higher value, there are enough exceptions to trip up the unwary.

When we have listed only the recording artist, the price reflects the average range for this performer. Some noteworthy exceptions for individual albums are listed as such. All prices are for near mint examples. For further information refer to *The Official Guide to Compact Discs* by Jerry Osborne and Paul Bergquist, House of Collectibles, Random House, NY.

	LOW	HIGH
Abdul, Paula	$ 8	$ 12
AC/DC	8	12
Adams, Bryan	6	8
Adams, Bryan: The Bryan Adams Story, promo	20	25
Alpert, Herb	6	12
Alpert, Herb: Diamonds, promo	40	45
Armatrading, Joan	5	6
Arrowsmith	8	12
Arrowsmith: Pump, promo	30	35
B-52's	6	7
Bad Company	5	7
Bad Company: In the Studio, promo	25	30
Beastie Boys	7	15
Benatar, Pat	6	8
Benartar, Pat: One Love, promo	10	15
Black Crowes	6	10
Black Sabbath	7	8
Black Sabbath: Black Moon, promo	12	15
Blue Nile	5	7
Bolton, Michael	6	8
Bonjovi	6	12
Bonjovi: Wanted Dead or Alive, promo	25	30
Bowie, David	6	25
Brooks, Garth	8	10
Brooks, Garth: Friends in Low Places, promo	15	18
Brown, James	8	10
Campbell, Tevin	5	7
Carey, Mariah	6	10
Carey, Mariah: Profile Interview, promo	22	25
Cash, Johnny	6	7
Chapman, Tracy	5	10
Cher	6	8
Chicago	5	6
Chicago: Chicago II, promo	25	30
Clapton, Eric	6	8

	LOW	HIGH
Clapton, Eric: Crossroads Sampler, promo	$ 20	$ 25
Cocker, Joe	5	6
Cole, Natalie	5	8
Cole, Natalie: Pink Cadillac, promo	10	12
Costello, Elvis	4	8
Crowded House	5	12
Cure	5	8
Cure: Hot, Hot, Hot, promo	20	25
Dead Milkman	5	7
Denver, John	5	6
Depeche Mode	6	12
Depeche Mode: Strange Love, promo	15	17
Duran Duran	6	10
Earth, Wind, and Fire	4	8
Erasure	6	8
Estefan, Gloria	5	10
Eurythmics	6	8
Fine Young Cannibals	4	15
Flack, Roberta	4	6
Fleetwood Mac	4	8
Fleetwood Mac: Behind the Mask (oversized box)	25	30
Ford, Lita	6	8
Franklin, Aretha	5	8
Gabriel, Peter	5	10
Gabriel, Peter: Shaking the Tree, Geffen 4217, promo	4	6
Genesis	5	8
Gibson, Debbie	5	8
Grant, Amy	6	8
Great White	4	6
Great White: Live at the Ritz, promo	15	18
Guns 'n Roses	8	12
Hammer	4	6
Happy Mondays	4	7
Harrison, George: Cheer Down	6	8
Harrison, George: Cloud Nine, promo	50	60
Harrison, George: Got My Mind Set on You, Dark Horse 2846, promo, special envelope	100	120
Heart	8	12
Hitchcock, Robyn	4	12
Houston, Whitney	5	10
Hurricane	4	8
Ice-T	4	6
Indigo Girls	6	10
INXS	5	8
INXS: Masters of Rock, promo, 2 CDs	45	50
Jackson, Janet	8	12
Jackson, Michael	6	10
Jellyfish	4	6
Jethro Tull	6	12
Jett, Joan	6	7
John, Elton	5	8

	LOW	HIGH
Judd, Wynona	$ 5	$ 6
Khan, Chakha	4	6
Kiss	8	15
Kravitz, Lenny	4	7
LaBelle, Patti	5	8
Lang, k.d.	6	7
Lauper, Cyndi	5	7
Little Feat	4	5
Little Feat: Waiting for Columbus (radio show), promo	25	30
Lovett, Lyle	4	7
Madonna	5	8
Madonna: I'm Breathless, promo	25	28
Manilow, Barry	6	8
Marx, Richard	4	6
McCartney, Paul	6	8
McCartney, Paul: Rocks, promo	35	40
Mellencamp, John	5	7
Metallica	10	20
Midler, Bette	5	6
Mills, Stephanie	5	6
Money, Eddie	4	5
Money, Eddie: Can't Hold Back, promo	15	18
Morrison, Van	5	8
Motley Crue	6	8
Motley Crue: Angela, promo	6	7
Neville Brothers	4	5
Newton, Olivia	7	10
Nirvana	6	9
Orbison, Roy	6	8
Overkill	4	5
Palmer, Robert	4	8
Petshop Boys	6	10
Pixies	4	6
Pop, Iggy	4	6
Presley, Elvis: Elvis (RCA PCD11382)	500	600
Presley, Elvis: Elvis Gold Records Volume 2 (RCA PCD1-5197), only 50 copies made	3000	3500
Presley, Elvis: My Happiness (RCA 2645, promo)	40	45
Prince	6	10
Queen	7	12
Raitt, Bonnie	5	6
Red Hot Chili Peppers	6	8
REM	6	10
Rolling Stones	12	20
Rolling Stones: The Interview, promo	30	35
Ronstadt, Linda	5	6
Roth, David Lee	5	8
Shocked, Michelle	5	8
Simply Red	5	8
Smashing Pumpkins	5	6
Soul Asylum	5	8

	LOW	HIGH
Springsteen, Bruce	$ 8	$ 15
Stewart, Rod	4	7
Sting	5	8
Streisand, Barbra	6	8
Sweat, Keith	4	6
Tears For Fears	5	7
10,000 Maniacs	4	8
Thorogood, George	6	8
TLC	5	7
Turner, Tina	5	8
Turner, Tina: Foreign Affair, Capitol 93129 (limited)	15	20
U2	8	12
Van Halen	5	8
Vandross, Luther	4	6
White, Karyn	4	8
Williams, Hank Jr.	4	5
Winwood, Steve	5	6
Young, Neil	6	8
Young, Neil: Freedom, promo	20	22

Jukeboxes

A coin-operated phonograph that automatically plays records is a jukebox. Wurlitzer manufactured the most popular machines from 1938 to 1948. Collectors prize them for their imaginative cabinet work and see-through mechanisms. Favored models are the 850, 950, and 1015.

	LOW	AVG.	HIGH
AMI Model A, 40 tune selections, called "Mother of Plastic," lights up, "jewels" on front of case, c. 1948	$ 1000	$ 3250	$ 5500
AMI Model F, 20 tune selections, simple wood case in an Art Deco style, top glass panel is record mechanism and tune cards, c. 1932	700	1000	1300
AMI "Singing Tower," 10 tunes, looks like an Art Deco skyscraper, c. 1941	5500	7000	8500
AMI "Top Flight," 20 tune selections, straight rectangular case, metal trim, rounded speaker opening, lights up, c. 1936	1000	1600	2200
Capehart Jukebox, early example, simple rectangular oak case, glass panels to view mechanism, decorative grill, 1930s	1200	1600	2000
Filben "Maestro," 30 tune selections, very "Space Age" design, plastic top section, 1940s	2200	3250	4300
Gabel's Charme, 18 tune selections, all wood rectangular case, selection dial, some case decoration, tune cards inside clear glass window	600	1000	1400
Mills "Empress" Model 910, 20 tune selections, rounded wood case, large plastic panels, small window to view tune cards, lights up	3000	3950	4900
Mills Jukebox, 12 tune selections (78 rpm), arranged in a "Ferris Wheel" effect, wood case, some decoration, dial tune selector, volume control, doors open on front top of case, speaker grill in bottom, 1930s	1200	2300	3400
Mills "Throne of Music," 20 tune selections, plastic panels, very similar in appearance to "Empress"	1500	2650	3800
Packard Pla-Mor (Capehart), 24 tune selections, plastic and wood, large viewing window in top front, decorative grill in base, tune selection cards on wheel, coin mechanism in top center	1200	3100	5000
Rock-Ola "Luxury Light-Up," 20 tune selections, large rounded corners case, orange and green plastic panels, push-button tune selector in center, tune cards under plastic panel, grill panel and trim	1200	2850	4500
Rock-Ola "Multi-Selector," 12 tune selections, clear glass, top front panel to view mechanism, push-button tune selection, simple walnut case and front grill, c. 1935	1100	1600	2100
Rock-Ola "Rhythm King," 12 tune selections, wood base, plain case, viewing window to see mechanism, c. 1938	1800	2650	3500
Rock-Ola "Rocket" Model 1434, 50 tune selections, pushbutton, simple grill, colored panels, dome, top covers record mechanism, colored corner panels, 1950s	1200	2450	3700
Rock-Ola Style 1426, 20 tunes, "Classic" style, push-button, revolving lights, plastic, viewing window, c. 1947	3600	5150	6700
Seeburg Audiophone, 6 disc records, plain rectangular case,			

	LOW	AVG.	HIGH
oval glass on top front, "Ferris Wheel" mechanism with 8 turntables, speaker on door in front, c. 1928	$ 1200	$ 2100	$ 3000
Seeburg "Commander," 20 tune selections, "Space Age" 1930s look, plastic front, sides, top, decorative trim moldings, button next to each tune card, c. 1940	1800	3250	4700
Seeburg P147 (P148), 20 tune selections, "washing machine" case style, plastic panels, c. 1947	1800	2400	3000
Seeburg "Symphonoia," 12 tune selections, rectangular plain case style, window to view mechanism, selector dial, c. 1936	1300	2250	3200
Seeburg "Symphonoia Classic," 20 tune selections, push button, mainly wood and red plastic panels in front and top corners, decorative trim, lights up, c. 1938	1900	2650	3400
Seeburg "Symphonoia Regal," 20 tune selections, plastic panels, tune cards in top section (no viewing of mechanism), c. 1940	2400	3350	4300
Wurlitzer Counter Model 61, 12 tune selections, wood base and sides, some plastic (comes with floor stand), c. 1930	3000	3750	4500
Wurlitzer Counter Model 81, 12 tune selections, wood base and sides, curving plastic panels, graceful front grill, small viewing window with tune selection cards, push buttons, 1940s	3600	5550	7500
Wurlitzer Model P 10, 10 tune selections, rectangular wooden case, simple lines, glass window, tune selector dial, simple front grill on bottom, early version of "simplex," c. 1934	600	1100	1600
Wurlitzer Model 35, 12 tune selections, more elaborate walnut case, art deco style, clear glass front window to view mechanism, 1930s	900	1400	1900
Wurlitzer Model 416, 16 tune selections, simple wood case, tune selector dial, rounded front corner columns, decorative front grill over speaker, 1930s	800	1200	1600
Wurlitzer Model 616 Simplex, 16 tune selections, wood case, rounded rectangular style, simple lines, clear glass top front viewing panel, tune selector dial, decorative grill, 1930s ...	1800	3450	5100
Wurlitzer Model 700, 24 tune selections, wood case, plastic panels on front corners and top, push-button tune selections, decorative metal grill, c. 1940	2300	4500	6700
Wurlitzer Model 760, 24 tune selections, "Classic" style, plastic panels, viewing window, push buttons, c. 1938	3000	6250	9500
Wurlitzer Model 800, 24 tune selections, wood trim and base, large orange and red plastic corner side and top panels, decorative grill, clear glass panel to view mechanism and tune selections, lights up, c. 1940	3400	5950	8500
Wurlitzer Model 1016, 24 tune selections, "Classic" style, revolving lights in plastic bubble tubes, viewing window, c. 1946	4000	8000	12,000
Wurlitzer "Victory," 24 tune selections, distinctive design, wood case, multi-colored glass panels along front with musical instruments, harlequins, etc., small half circle viewing window, push buttons, decorative grill with colored panels behind, c. 1942	4300	7150	10,000

Music Boxes

The cylinder music box originated in 18th century Switzerland. They were popular from the mid-1800s until near the end of the century. The cylinder has an arrangement of tiny metal pins that pluck the teeth of a tuned metal comb as the cylinder revolves. This causes the tune to play. With the advent of the disc music box and other forms of home entertainment, cylinder music boxes lost popularity.

Cylinder music boxes: Check the condition of all cylinders. — Photo courtesy of Northeast Auctions.

Cylinder Music Boxes

	LOW	AVG.	HIGH
Conchon (Switzerland), 6 tune 11" cyl., mandolin zither attachment, operatic selections, veneered and decorated case, inlaid lid, base molding, tune sheet	$ 1900	$ 2600	$ 3300
Dawkins, 8 tune 13.5" cyl., interchangeable, burled walnut, gold painted decoration, inlay on cover, tune card, 1 cylinder	2500	3250	4000
Dawkins, 10 tune 8.5" cyl., with 5 bells, walnut with inlay decoration	2000	2850	3700
Dawkins, 12 tune 13" cyl., drum, bell, wood block, inlay on cover, tune card, large case	2900	4000	5100
Ducommon Girod, 4 tune 8" cyl., simple case, inlay on lid	1300	2250	3200
Ducommon Girod, 6 tune 6" cyl., simple case, tune sheet, stop/start and change levers, c. 1880	800	1300	1800
Ducommon Girod, 6 tune 11.5" cyl., c. 1840, walnut case, 3 control levers, simple case style	900	1300	1700
Ducommon Girod, 8 tune 16.5" cyl., 3 bells, castanets, inlaid case, full glass inner lid	2400	3250	4100
Ducommon Girod, 12 tune 19" cyl., rosewood veneered case with enamel and brass inlay decoration, operatic selections, tune sheet.........................	2500	3750	5000
Mermod Frs. (St. Croix, Switzerland), 4 tune 6" cyl.,			

	LOW	AVG.	HIGH
simple rosewood case, inner glass lid, ornate tune card, stop/start and change levers, late 19th century	$ 800	$ 1450	$ 2100
Mermod Frs., 6 tune 3.5" cyl., c. 1900, crank wind, simple wood case with decal decoration	300	550	800
Mermod Frs., 6 tune 7.5" cyl., simple case, inner glass lid, some decorations on case, tune card	750	1200	1800
Mermod Frs., 4 tune 8.5" cyl., key wind, early plain box, instant stop and change levers	1100	1600	2100
Mermod Frs., 4 tune 12" cyl., 3" dia. cyl., key wind, pianoforte, inlaid lid, tune card, len. 16"	5100	6450	7800
Mermod Frs., 6 tune 8" cyl., key wind, simple case	1000	1300	1800
Mermod Frs., 6 tune 11 cyl., simple case, some decoration, case len. 18", inner glass lid, lever wind	1600	2350	3100
Paillard, 2 tune 1.5" cyl., Musical Photograph Album, c. 1900, Art Nouveau case decoration, single comb, album sits on ornate corner feet	200	400	600
Rivene, 6 tune 13" cyl., interchangeable cyls. (5), tune card, zither attachment, double spring barrel, burled walnut panels on walnut case, inner glass lid, matching table with storage drawer for extra cylinders, turned legs, mother-of-pearl, ebony, and brass decoration	5000	7000	9500
Rivenc, 6 tune 13" cyl., interchangeable, w. 4" ("fat") cylinders, simple case style with some decoration	3500	5000	6250
Rivenc, 8 tune 6" cyl., duplex cylinder box (cylinders placed end to end), 2 combs, inlaid floral decorations on lid, marquetry borders on lid and sides	3200	4700	6200
Rivenc, 8 tune 11" cyl., interchangeable cyls., stop/start and change levers, mandolin attachment, tune indicator, brass figures of griffins, tune card, burled walnut case inlaid with satinwood swallows	2200	4250	6300
Unknown Maker, 3 tune 4.5" cyl., walnut, very simple, unadorned box	900	1200	1500
Unknown Maker, 4 tune 3.5" cyl., small box, mahogany (or walnut), decoration on lid, small inside glass lid, tune card, tune indicator	600	900	1200
Unknown Maker, 4 tune 5" cyl., simple case design, len. 11.5"	600	900	1200
Unknown Maker, 4 tune 6" cyl., simple case, tune card, len. 12"	1300	1700	2100
Unknown Maker, 4 tune 7.5" cyl., key wind, sectional comb, single comb, simple case style	1000	2000	3000

Other Music Boxes

	LOW	AVG.	HIGH
Birdcage Music Box, with mechanical singing bird, birdcage form, ht. 17"	300	500	700
Music Roll Player, with pin-studded wooden cylinder, c. 1890	700	900	1100
Criterion, studded 15.5" disk player, 1905	4000	5500	7000
Clarion Roll Organ, New York, hand-crank reed type, 1882	1000	1500	2000
Aeolian Organ and Music Co., Orchestral Cabinet, #0, c. 1885	1200	1600	1900

Records

Many people who discarded their record collections in the 1980s are buying them back in the 1990s. Collectors feel that the sound quality is richer and more subtle than CDs. People also love the photos and artwork of the covers. The nostalgic appeal of records is very strong; music is often a reminder of happy moments. Many collectors remember records as their first independent purchase as a teenager.

The following is a cross section of LPs; 45s are not covered. Each entry consists of the performer's name, the title of the LP, the company that produced it, the stock number, and the date. Condition is all important for records; collectors usually grade both the record and the album cover. Scratches on the record that interfere with sound quality can destroy the price of a record. Worn, torn, or stained covers also decrease the prices. The prices below are for records in excellent condition with excellent condition covers. That means that the record may have small scratches that can be seen but not heard. The covers should be crisp and clean with only slight wear. Near mint or mint examples will command higher prices than those listed below.

The world of records is filled with rare variations. Often these are subtle differences such as misspellings. Some people put more value on stereo or mono versions of the same record. In general, the prices below reflect the prices of the more common variations. For further reading see *The Official Price Guide to Records*, Jerry Osborne, House of Collectibles, Random House, NY, 1997 and *Goldmine's Price Guide to Collectible Records*, Neal Umphred, Krause Publications, Iola, IO, 1994.

Above left to right: Creedence Clearwater Revival, Chronicle, $8-$12; Bob Dylan, Blonde on Blonde, second pressing (seven interior photo not nine). Second pressings with 360 labels and stereo covers are common, $15-$30. Second pressings with 360 labels and mono covers are more difficult to find and are worth about ten times as much.

	LOW	HIGH
Acuff, Roy, The Voice of Country Music, Capitol, ST-2276, 1965	$ 18	24
Aerosmith, Toys in the Attic, Columbia, JCQ-33479, 1975	12	20
Andrews, Julie, My Fair Lady, Columbia, OL-5615, 1959	10	15
Animals, The Animals, MGM, E-4264, 1964	20	32
Ann-Margret, Bye Bye Birdie, RCA Vic., LOC-1081, 1963	12	18
Archies, The Archies, Calandar, KES-101, 1968	12	18
Arnold, Eddy, Let's Make Memories Tonight, RCA Vic., LPM-2337, 1961	12	15
Autry, Gene, Gene Autry and Champion, Columbia, CL-677, 1955	70	90

	LOW	HIGH
Avalon, Frankie, The Young Frankie Avalon, Chancellor, CHL-5007, 1960 ..	$ 20	$ 34
Bachelors, Presenting the Bachelors, London, LL-3353, 1964	10	15
Baez, Joan, In Concert, Vanguard, VRS-9112, 1962	15	25
Bailey, Pearl, Cultured Pearl, Coral, CRL-57162, 1957	20	30
Baxter, Les, Thinking of You, Capitol, T-474, 1954	20	32
Beach Boys, Little Deuce Coupe, Capitol, ST-1998, 1963	20	32
Beach Boys, Surfin' USA, Capitol, ST-1890, 1963	20	35
Bennett, Tony, Blue Velvet, Columbia, CL-1292, 1959	15	20
Berry, Chuck, Berry Is on Top, Chess, LP-1435, 1959	90	165
Berry, Chuck, Golden Hits, Mercury, MG-21103, 1967	12	15
Blues Magoos, Psychedelic Lollipop, Mercury, MG-21096, 1966	15	22
Boone, Pat, Star Dust, Dot, DLP-3118, 1958	15	20
Brewer, Teresa, Music, Music, Music, Coral, CRL-57027, 1956	15	22
Broonzy, Big Bill, Big Bill Broonzy, Folkways, FA-2315, 1957	25	54
Broonzy, Big Bill, Country Blues, Folkways, FA-2326, 1957	25	45
Brown, James, Live at the Apollo, King, KS-826, 1963	100	220
Brown, James, Night Train, King, 771, 1961	200	250
Brown, James, Papa's Got a Brand New Bag, King, 938, 1966	25	40
Browne, Jackson, For Everyman, Asylum, SD-5067, 1973	8	14
Bruce, Lenny, I Am Not a Nut, red vinyl, Fantasy, 7007, 1960	50	100
Byrds, Turn! Turn! Turn!, Columbia, CL-2454, 1965	15	22
Carpenters, Close to You, A & M, QU-54271, 1973	8	10
Cash, Johnny, The Fabulous Johnny Cash, Columbia, CS-8122, 1958	25	45
Chad & Jeremy, Distant Shores, Columbia, CL-2564, 1966	10	15
Charles, Ray, The Genius of Ray Charles, Atlantic, 1312, 1960	15	20
Checker, Chubby, Let's Twist Again, Parkway, P-7004, 1961	25	45
Chiffons, Sweet Talkin' Guy, Laurie, LLP-2036, 1966	40	75
Christy, June, Big Band Specials, Capitol, T-1845, 1962	10	18
Cline, Patsy, Patsy Cline Showcase, Decca, DL-74202, 1961	30	45
Clooney, Rosemary, Swing Around Rosie, Coral, CRL-57266, 1958	18	22
Coasters, Greatest Hits, Atco, 33-111, 1960	25	45
Como, Perry, A Sentimental Date, RCA Vic., LPC-1177, 1956	10	15
Cooke, Sam, My Kind of Blues, RCA Vic., LPM-2392, 1961	20	30
Cortez, Dave (Baby), In Orbit With ..., Roulette, R-25328, 1966	9	12
Creedence Clearwater Revival, Cosmo's Factory, Mobile Fid., MFSL-037	30	50
Crosby, Bing, In a Little Spanish Town, Decca, DL-8846, 1959	12	18
Darin, Bobby, Twist With Bobby Darrin, Atco, 33-138, 1961	20	30
Davis, Skeeter, The End of the World, RCA Victor, LSP-2699, 1962	20	30
Day, Doris, Day in Hollywood, Columbia, CL-749, 1955	10	16
Deep Purple, And the Royal Philharmonic, Tetragrammaton, T-131, 1968	150	260
Denny, Martin, Exotica, Liberty, LRP-3034, 1957	18	25
Diamond, Neil, Greatest Hits, Bang, BLPS-219, 1968	15	22
Drifters, Under the Boardwalk, white cover, Atlantic, 8099, 1964	35	65
Elliott, Ramblin' Jack, Country Style, Prestige, PRLP-13045, 1962	18	22
Everly Brothers, The Everly Brothers Best, Cadence, CLP-3025, 1969	40	80
Fabian, The Fabulous Fabian, Chanc., CHLX-5005, 1959	40	60
Fisher, Eddie, I'm In the Mood for Love, RCA Vic., LPM-1180, 1955	18	22
Flatt & Scruggs, Foggy Mountain Jamboree, Columbia, CL-1019, 1957	20	35
Flatt & Scruggs, When the Saints Go Marching In, Columbia, CL-2513, 1966	10	15
Fleetwoods, Mr. Blue, Dolton, BST-8001, 1959	50	86
Ford, Tennessee Ernie, Spirituals, Capitol, T-818, 1957	15	20

	LOW	HIGH
Four Seasons, Born to Wander, Philips, PHS-600-129, 1964	$ 12	$ 15
Four Seasons, Rag Doll, Philips, PHM-200-146, 1964	18	22
Four Tops, Four Tops, Motown, MS-622, 1964	20	30
Francis, Connie, Who's Sorry Now?, MGM, E-3686, 1959	20	30
Franklin, Aretha, The Electrifying ..., Columbia, CL-1761, 1962	25	35
Funicello, Annette, Annette's Pajama Party, Buena Vista, STER-3325, 1964 ...	50	90
Garland, Judy, The Wizard of Oz, Decca, DL-8387, 1957	30	40
Gaye, Marvin, Marvin Gay's Greatest Hits, Tamla, TS-252, 1964	18	26
Gibson, Don, No One Stands Alone, RCA Victor, LSP-1918, 1959	25	35
Gore, Lesley, Boys, Boys, Boys, Mercury, MG-20901, 1964	12	20
Gorme, Eydie, Love Is a Season, ABC-Para., ABCS-273, 1958	12	18
Grateful Dead, American Beauty, Mobile Fid., MFSL-014, 1980	30	60
Grateful Dead, The Grateful Dead, Warner Bros., WS-1689, 1967	30	45
Guy, Buddy, A Man and the Blues, Vanguard, VSD-79272, 1968	10	15
Haley, Bill & His Comets, Rock With Bill..., Essex, LP-202, 1955	250	400
Hendrix, Jimi, Band of Gypsys, red label, Capitol, STAO-472, 1970	18	22
Hendrix, Jimi, Pie, Live 'n' Dirty, Nutmeg, NUT-1001, 1978	18	22
Herman's Hermits, Introducing..., MGM, E-4282, 1965	12	19
Hollies, The Hollies-Beat Group, Imperial, LP-9312, 1966	20	30
Holly, Buddy, Buddy Holly, Coral, CRL-57210, 1958	200	320
Hooker, John Lee, Travelin', Vee Jay, LP-1023, 1960	45	65
Horne, Lena, At the Waldorf Astoria, RCA Vic., LSO-1028, 1957	30	40
Ian, Janis, Society's Child, Verve, V-5027, 1967	10	18
Impressions, Keep on Pushing, ABC-Para., ABCS-493, 1964	18	24
Ink Spots, The Ink Spots Greatest, Grand, LP-328, 1959	18	24
Ives, Burl, Down to the Sea in Ships, Decca, DL-8245, 1956	14	18
James, Tommy, I Think We're Alone Now, Roulettte, R-25353, 1967	12	20
Jan & Dean, Little Old Lady From Pasadena, Liberty, LRP-3377, 1964	18	26
Jerry & The Pacemakers, Greatest Hits, Laurie, SLLP-2031, 1965	18	26
King, B.B., My Kind of Blues, Crown, CLP-5188, 1961	15	22
King, B.B., Singin' the Blues, Crown, CLP-5020, 1957	40	80
King, Ben E., Greatest Hits, Atco, SD-33-165, 1964	20	32
Kingston Trio, String Along, Capitol, ST-1407, 1960	18	22
Knight, Gladys, Everybody Needs Love, Soul, SS-706, 1967	12	18
Lawrence, Steve & Eydie Gorme, Our Best to You, ABC-Para., ABCS-469, 1964	8	14
Leadbelly, Huddie Ledbetter's Best, Capitol, T-1821, 1962	35	60
Lee, Brenda, This Is Brenda, Decca, DL-74082, 1960	15	20
Lennon, John & Yoko Ono, Sometime in NYC, Apple, SVBB-3392, 1972	20	30
Lewis, Jerry Lee, The Return of Rock, Smash, SRS-67063, 1965	30	40
Liberace, Sincerely Yours, Columbia, CL-800, 1955	12	18
Little Richard, Little Richard, Camden, CAL-420, 1956	100	160
London, Julie, About the Blues, Liberty, LST-7012, 1958	20	30
Lovin' Spoonful, Do You Believe in Magic, Kama Sutra, KLPS-8050, 1965 ...	18	24
Lynn, Loretta, Hymns, Decca; DL-74695, 1965	15	20
Mancini, Henry, The Mancini Touch, RCA Vic., LSP-2101, 1960	12	15
Martin, Mary, South Pacific, Columbia, OL-4180, 1949	18	25
Mathis, Johnny, Warm, Columbia, CL-1078, 1957	20	30
Mayall, John, Blues Breakers With Eric Clapton, London, PS-492, 1966	18	22
McCartney, Paul, Band on the Run, with poster, Capitol, SO-3415, 1973	18	22
McGuire Sisters, While the Lights Are Low, Coral, CRL-57145, 1957	18	25

	LOW	HIGH
Monkees, Papa Jean's Blues, Colgems, COS-101, 1966	$ 25	$40
Monkees, Papa Jene's Blues, Colgems, COS-101, 1966	12	20
Monroe, Marilyn, Some Like It Hot, UA, UAL-4030, 1959	40	75
Muddy Waters, Muddy, Brass and Blues, Chess, LPS-1507, 1966	25	38
Nelson, Rick, Ricky, Imperial, LP-9048, 1964	15	24
Nelson, Rick, Ricky Sings Again, Imperial, LP-12090, 1962	75	135
Nelson, Tracy, Deep Are the Roots, Prestige, PRLP-7393, 1965	15	20
Nelson, Willie, And Then I Wrote, Liberty, LRP-3238, 1962	20	30
Orbison, Roy, At the Rock House, Sun, SLP-1260, 1961	300	550
Orbison, Roy, There Is Only One Roy Orbison, MGM, SE-4308, 1965	15	22
Owens, Buck, I've Got a Tiger By the Tail, Capitol, ST-2283, 1965	15	20
Page, Patti, This Is My Song, Mercury, MG-20102, 1955	15	20
Partridge Family, Partridge Family, with photo, Bell, 6050, 1970	15	20
Paul, Les & Mary Ford, Bye Bye Blues, Capitol, T-356, 1955	25	40
Peter, Paul & Mary, In the Wind, Warner Bros., W-1507, 1963	12	18
Pickett, Wilson, In the Midnight Hour, Atlantic, 8114, 1965	20	30
Pitney, Gene, Only Love Can Break a Heart, Musicor, MM-2003, 1962	15	22
Platters, Moonlight Memories, Mercury, MG-20759, 1963	15	20
Preston, Johnny, Running Bare, Mercury, MG-20592, 1960	60	90
Price, Ray, Talk to Your Heart, Columbia, CL-1148, 1958	15	20
Professor Longhair, New Orleans Piano, Atlantic, SD-7225, 1972	15	20
Ramones, Ramones, Sire, SASD-7520, 1976	15	20
Rascals, Once Upon a Dream, Atlantic, SD-8148, 1968	12	18
Redding, Otis, Soul Ballads, Volt, 411, 1965	40	60
Reed, Jimmy, Just Jimmy Reed, Vee Jay, LP-1050, 1962	18	28
Reese, Della, Della, RCA Victor, LSP-2157, 1960	15	20
Reeves, Jim, Jim Reeves Sings, Abbott, LP-5001, 1956	10	15
Reeves, Jim, The Intimate Jim Reeves, RCA Victor, LSP-2216, 1960	20	30
Reynolds, Debbie, Am I That Easy to Forget?, Dot, DLP-25295, 1960	18	22
Rich, Charlie, The Best Years, Smash, SRS-67078, 1966	18	24
Righteous Bros., You've Lost That Loving Feelin', Philles, PHLP-4007, 1965	15	20
Rodgers, Jimmie, Twilight on the Trail, Roulette, R-25081, 1959	15	20
Rogers, Roy, Song Wagon, Golden, GRC-6, 1958	60	80
Rolling Stones, 12 X 5, London, LL-3402, 1965	20	120
Rolling Stones, Flowers, London, LL-3509, 1967	20	35
Rolling Stones, Some Girls, Mobil Fid., MFSL-087	18	25

Left to right: Rolling Stones, Sticky Fingers, $15-$25,
Chubby Checker, All The Hits for your Dancin' Party, $20-$40.

	LOW	HIGH
Rolling Stones, Satanic Maj. Request, 3D, mono, London, NP-2, 1967	$ 100	$ 150
Rolling Stones, Satanic Maj. Request, 3D, stereo, London, NPS-2, 1967	25	35
Ruby & The Romantics, Our Day Will Come, Kapp, KL-1323, 1963	15	22
Rydell, Bobby, Bobby Sings, Cameo, C-1007, 1960	20	35
Sam the Sham & The Pharohs, Wooly Bully, MGM, SE-4297, 1965	18	28
Searchers, Meet the Searchers, Kapp, KL-1363, 1964	15	22
Seeger, Pete, Pete Seeger at Carnegie Hall, Folkways, FA-2351, 1958	15	20
Shannon, Del, The Best of Del Shannon, Dot, DLP-25824, 1967	20	30
Sharp, Dee Dee, It's Mash Potato Time, Cameo, D-1018, 1962	25	40
Shirelles, Golden Oldies, Scepter, SPS-516, 1964	25	40
Shore, Dinah, Dinah Down Home, Capitol, ST-1655, 1962	12	18
Simon & Garfunkel, Bridge Over Troubled Water, Columbia, CQ-30995, 1973	10	16
Sinatra, Frank, Come Dance With Me, Capitol, SW-1069, 1959	10	15
Sinatra, Frank, Days of Wine and Roses, Reprise, FS-1011, 1964	10	15
Sinatra, Frank, High Society, Capitol, SW-750, 1958	12	18
Snow, Hank, Railroad Man, RCA Victor, LPM-2705, 1963	18	22
Sonny & Cher, Look at Us, Atco, 33-177, 1965	12	15
Sons of the Pioneers, Favorite Cowboy Songs, RCA Victor, LPM-1130, 1955	30	45
Starr, Kay, The Hits of Kay Starr, Capitol, T-415, 1950s	14	18
Statler Brothers, Flowers on the Wall, Columbia, CL-2449, 1966	10	15
Stevens, Cat, Catch Bull at Four, A & M, QU-54365, 1974	10	16
Stone Poneys, The Stone Poneys, Capitol, ST-2666, 1967	20	30
Streisand, Barbra, I Can Get It For You..., Columbia, KOL-5780, 1962	50	80
Supremes, Supremes A' Go-Go, Motown, M-649, 1966	18	24
Taylor, James, James Taylor, Apple, SKAO-3352, 1969	18	25
Temptations, Meet the Temptations, Gordy, GS-911, 1964	20	30
The Band, Music From Big Pink, Capitol, SKAO-2995, 1968	10	15
The Fugs, The Fugs First Album, ESP-Disk, 1018, 1966	20	35
Tubb, Ernest, Ernest Tubb Favorites, Decca, DL-8291, 1956	35	65
Valens, Ritchie, The Original Ritchie Valens, Guest Star, GS-1469, 1963	20	30
Vanilla Fudge, Vanilla Fudge, Atco, 33-224, 1967	8	12
Vee, Bobby, Bobby Vee, Liberty, LST-7181, 1961	25	38
Ventures, Walk-Don't Run, Dolton, BST-8003, 1963	18	24
Wagoner, Porter, The Bluegrass Story, RCA Vic., LPM-2960, 1964	12	18
Wakeman, Rick, Journey to the Center..., A & M, QU-53621, 1975	9	16
Washington, Dinah, In the Land of Hi Fi, EmArcy, MG-36073, 1956	20	34
Watson, Doc, Doc Watson, Vanguard, VSD-79152, 1964	10	15
Weavers, The Best of the Weavers, Decca, DL-8893, 1959	20	35
Wells, Kitty, Kitty's Choice, Decca, DL-78979, 1960s	18	24
Whitman, Slim, Slim Whitman Sings, Imperial, LP-9026, 1958	15	22
Williams, Andy, Under Paris Skies, Cadence, CLP-3047, 1961	8	12
Williams, Hank, Honky Tonkin', MGM, E-3412, 1950	60	95
Winters, Jonathan, A Personal Appearance, Verve, MGV-15027, 1961	15	20
Wonder, Stevie, Stevie at the Beach, Tamla, T-255, 1964	35	45
Yardbirds, Greatest Hits, Epic, LN-24246, 1966	20	32
Young, Faron, Hello, Walls, Capitol, ST-1528, 1961	25	35
Zappa, Frank, We're Only In It For the Money, Verve, V-5045, 1968	50	90
Zappa, Frank, Weasels Ripped My Flesh, Bizarre, MS-2028, 1970	12	18
Zombies, The Zombies, Parrot, PAR-61001, 1965	25	40

Sheet Music

Sheet music is a musical composition. It was the first way of mass merchandising popular music. Tin Pan Alley originated off-Broadway on 28th Street in New York City. It was the center of American popular music in the late 19th and early 20th centuries. Publishers sought recognition for their songs. They backed shows and employed song pluggers to popularize their music. Waiters often supplemented their wages by belting out tunes.

Condition, rarity, and image establish the value of sheet music. Some collectors want the music, but many others are more interested in the graphics. Sheet music represents a great area for cross-over collecting. It includes themes such as movies, WWI and II, Disney, character, and illustration art. Winslow Homer and Norman Rockwell ("Over There") are a couple of artists that drew covers. Since sheet music was mass produced, most often in huge quantities, it is still relatively inexpensive. It can, however, be fragile, and mint examples are harder to find. Specimens are not always in top condition due to music store stamps, tape marks, staples, binder holes, and ownership signatures. Worn, incomplete copies sell for considerably less than those in mint condition described below.

Garage sales are a good source for sheet music, but be prepared to sort through stacks of material. Dealers that frame sheet music realize that they have a decorative item and reflect that in the price. Sheet music is best stored in unsealed plastic containers designed for paper conservation. If framing, use acid-free backing and make sure the process is reversible, i.e. don't use methods which can damage the sheet music.

Names following the titles listed below are descriptions of the cover; a celebrity's name denotes a photo of that person, "cast" features a group of actors. Sometimes there are different covers for the same composition or similar names for different works.

For further study we suggest *The Sheet Music Reference & Price Guide*, Marie-Reine and Anna Marie Guiheen, Collector Books, Paducah, KY, 1995, for composers' and cover artists' names and other information. For a history of the business try *American Sheet Music With Prices*, Daniel B. Priest, Wallace Homestead Book Co., Des Moines, IA, 1978.

Left to right: You'll Always Be The One I Love, 1946, $8-$10; Katy Darling, illustrated with an early Winslow Homer lithograph, $300-$500.

	LOW	HIGH
A-Tisket-A-Tasket, 1930	$ 7	$ 12
After Twelve O'Clock, 1932	4	7
Ain't Misbehavin', 1929	6	9
Ain't We Got Fun, 1921	9	12
America I Love You, 1915	38	46
Anchors Away, 1942	6	8
Are You from Dixie, 1915	18	22
Army Air Corps, 1942	8	12
As Time Goes By, Bogart and Bergman, 1941	22	32
Barney Google, 1923	50	85
Bess You Is My Woman, 1935	10	15
Bill Bailey, black couple, 1902	38	46
Blue Moon, 1934	9	15
Button Up Your Overcoat, 1928	4	7
By the Light of the Silvery Moon, 1932	9	12
Cascades, 1904	40	60
Casey Jones, Brave Engineer, 1909	22	32
Chattanooga Choo Choo, 1941	12	18
Chrysanthemum Rag, 1904	40	60
Climb Every Mountain, 1959	6	8
Country Club Ragtime, 1909	45	55
Custer's Last Charge, 1922	40	50
Daisy, 1904	12	14
Danny Boy, 1913	6	8
Dinah, E. Cantor, black face, 1925	20	30
Down by the Old Mill Stream, 1910	7	9
Dream River, 1928	4	6
Easter Parade, cast, 1947	9	12
Easy Winners, 1901	45	65
Edelweiss, Andrews and Plummer, 1959	8	12
Falling In Love Again, Dietrich, 1930	10	15
Forty Second Street, 1932	7	9
Girl from Ipanema, 1943	4	6
Gone With the Wind, 1937	20	30
Goodnight Sweetheart, E. Cantor, 1931	10	15
Great American, Theodore Roosevelt, 1919	40	60
Heartbreak Hotel, Elvis, 1956	40	60
Hello Ma Baby, 1899	40	50
Help, 1969	30	40
Here Comes Santa Claus, Gene Autry, 1947	20	30
Here Comes the Bride, 1912	15	20
Hey Jude, 1968	35	45
Honey Hula, 1921	4	6
How Much Is That Doggy in the Window?, P. Page, 1952	7	9
Hummingbird , 1955	4	6
I Got Rhythm, 1930	8	10
I'm Dreaming of the Girl I Love, 1912	6	8
If I Only Had a Brain, 1939	30	40
In My Merry Oldsmobile, 1905	25	35
It's a Long, Long Way to Tipperary, 1912	20	30
Jeepers Creepers, 1938	7	10
Lambeth Walk, 1937	8	12

Left to right: Wake Up America!, 1941, $8-$12; The Trolley Song, 1944, $12-$15.

	LOW	HIGH
Liberty Bell, 1917	$ 15	$ 25
Looking at the World, Rose Color Glasses, 1926	6	8
Love For Sale, Cole Porter, 1930	8	10
Meet Me in St. Louis, 1935	9	12
Memphis Blues, 1913	10	15
Moon River, A. Hepburn, 1961	6	8
Moxie Fox Trot, 1930	70	90
Now I Lay Me Down to Sleep, 1918	18	22
O Solo Mio, 1923	4	6
On the Street Where You Live, 1956	5	7
Over There, 1917	70	90
Penny Serenade, 1938	4	6
Ragtime Dance, 1906	50	75
Ramblin' Rose, Nat King Cole, 1962	8	10
She'll be Coming Around the Mountain, 1935	4	6
Shortnin' Bread, 1928	30	40
Shrine of St. Cecilia, 1940	3	4
Singing in the Rain, Gene Kelly, 1952	70	90
Someday, 1944	7	9
Someday My Prince Will Come, Snow White, 1937	50	85
Sousa's Grand March, 1895	20	30
Star Dust, 1929	3	5
Summer Place, 1959	4	6
Sunshine on My Shoulders, J. Denver, 1971	3	4
Swanee, Al Jolson, 1932	15	20
Tea For Two, 1940	4	6
Three Coins in a Fountain, cast, 1954	6	8
Time on My Hands, c. 1930, 1930	2	3
Toot-Toot Tootsie, Al Jolson, 1922	18	24
Wait 'Til the Sun Shines Nellie, Bing Crosby, 1942	5	7
White Christmas, cast, 1942	8	12
Who's Afraid of the Big Bad Wolf, 1934	50	80
Who's Sorry Now, Astaire, 1931	6	8
Yankee Doodle Boy, J. Jones on phone, 1931	30	50
You Are My Sunshine, 1940	5	7

Orientalia

Orientalia refers to objects originating in Asia. Although this could refer to an electronic calculator, the term is usually reserved for items that show the Asian aesthetic in decoration. This chapter is a representative overview; see other chapters in this section for specific areas.

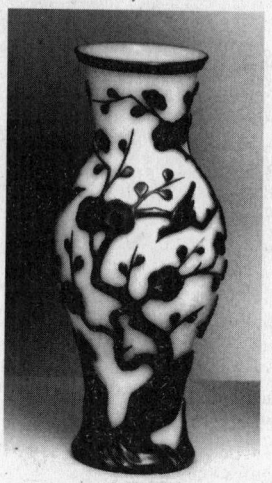

Red and white Peking glass vase, ht. 9", $300-$500, retail.

Assorted Items

	AUCTION	RETAIL Low	RETAIL High
Blue and White Vase, w/ oriental figures, ht. 25"	$ 500	$ 880	$ 1380
Bronze Lamps, pr., w/ dragon motif, ht. 36"	400	700	1100
Cabinet on Stand, China trade black and gold lacquer, small w/ ball and claw feet, ht. 55", w. 23"	650	1140	1800
Candlestand, China trade black and gold lacquer birdcage w/ paw feet, dia. 22"	700	1230	1930
Captain's Desk and Chest, China trade brass-bound camphor wood, w. 35"	3500	6130	9630
Cloisonné Baluster-Form Vases, pr., Japanese, w/ enamel over silver metal w/ dark-red ground and white and pink peonies, ht. 7.75"	200	350	550
Famille Rose Porcelain Figural Lamps, pr. ht. 15"	500	880	1380
Famille Verte Porcelain Leaf-Form Dish, len. 12"	100	180	280
Famille Rose Porcelain Soup Tureen and Underplate, circular covered, len. 14"	3750	6560	10,000
Han Dynasty Pottery Tomb Figures, pr., ht. 8"	300	530	830
Imari Umbrella Stand, blue and white w/ deer decoration	600	1050	1650
Jadeite Baluster-Form Vase, w/ rock and flower carved			

	AUCTION	RETAIL Low	High
base, bird and animal-form handles, lid w/ 2 free-carved rings, ht. 9"	$ 2500	$ 4380	$ 6880
K'ang H'si Plate, blue and white w/ lobed edge, dia. 10.5"	1100	1930	3030
Knife Box, Japanese lacquer and inlaid mother-of-pearl slope-top, ht. 14"	1100	1930	3030
Lacquer Picnic Box, Japanese, black and gold, fan decorated, 4 stacked compartments, ht. 15"	400	700	1100
Pagoda, soapstone 6-stage, ht. 28"	1400	2450	3850
Painting, Figures in Room and Garden Settings, China trade, circle of Spoilum, oil on canvas, 19.5" x 24.5"	3500	6130	9630
Painting, Macao Harbor, China trade oil on canvas, 23.5" x 36.25"	10,000	17,500	27,500
Painting, Portrait of Amer. Sea Captain, attributed to Foiequa, oil on canvas, 23.5" x 18"	3000	5250	8250
Painting, Shanghai Harbor, attributed to Yeuqua, China trade oil on canvas, 20.5" x 41"	11,000	18,000	28,000
"Paisley" Shawl, Indian, signed in center	1900	3330	5230
Pewter Figures of Chinese Merchants , pr., early 19th century, ht. 8"	2000	3500	5500
Pewter Figures of Dutch Merchants, w/ flower vases, pr., 17th century, rare, ht. 25"	10,000	18,000	28,000
Pigskin Boxes, len. of largest 16", 3 Chinese red and gold	300	530	830
Pith Paper Drawings of Flowers and Butterflies, set of 5, China trade, each 6" x 8"	850	1490	2340
Pith Paper Scenes by Yeuqua, depicting oriental figures, set of 6, China trade, each 13" x 8"	1500	2630	4000
Plant Stand, w/ marble top, carved Chinese hardwood, circular, ht. 37"	175	310	480
Pottery Figure of Ox, probably Wei, len. 8"	750	1310	2060
Pottery Figure of Sitting Came,l w/ pack, probably Wei, len. 11"	550	960	1510
Pottery Figure of Sitting Dog, probably Wei, len. 6"	900	1580	2480
Reverse Painting on Glass of Veiled Woman, China trade, ht. 12"	150	260	410
Reverse Paintings on Glass, pr., mirrored, China trade of courtesans seated at tables, ht. 22"	950	1660	2600
Sewing Stand, child's, China trade black and gold lacquer	700	1230	1930
Silk Embroidered Panel, blue and white, made for Swedish market	300	530	830
Silk Embroidered Panel, w/ dragons and peonies in landscape, within border, 63" x 45"	1600	2800	4400
Sung Dynasty Proto Celadon Figure, leaping hound, len. 9"	400	700	1100
Trade Signs, pr., red lacquer w/ Chinese characters, ht. 79"	350	610	960
Wallpaper, 5 panels of Chinese depicting figures, pavilions and gardens, ht. 60", len. 18'	1600	2800	4400
Woodblock, entitled "Tree Seller," Japanese, 10" x 14"	200	350	550
Woodblock, large black and white printed oriental panel of exotic birds, ht. 70"	150	260	400
Yuan/Ming Dynasty Glazed Pottery Figure, court official, ht. 17"	100	180	280

Chinese Export Porcelain

The word "china," as in "fine china," derives from the time when all porcelain came from China. Before Europeans learned the secrets of kaolin clay and the firing process, kings and princes spent fortunes (literally) on their porcelain collections. Even after Western entrepreneurs cracked these secrets, merchants imported shiploads of Chinese porcelain for an ever-growing number of dinner services. The Chinese fed this demand with pieces designed for the West. Chinese Export Porcelain (CEP) developed more or less standard designs that crossed the oceans throughout the 19th century. Canton, Nanking, and Fitzhugh are the well-known blue and white designs, while polychrome favorites are Rose Mandarin and Rose Medallion.

Pieces marked "Made in China" date after 1894. Some unscrupulous dealers have ground out this mark. Look for suspicious grinding marks or related flaws on the undersides of pieces. For further information see *Chinese Export Porcelain*, by Peter Herbert and Nancy Schiffer, Schiffer Publishing, Ltd.

Armorial pieces are among the most prized of Chinese export pieces. The more elaborate the crest, the more valuable the piece. — Photo courtesy of Northeast Auctions.

Armorial Pieces

	AUCTION	RETAIL Low	High
Cup and Saucer, crest decorated w/ armour	$ 250	$ 400	$ 600
Deep Plate, reticulated, crested, dia. 11"	900	1700	3000
Hot Water Plate, Arms of Snodgrass, len. 11"	425	800	1400
Mug, Clifford coat-of-arms and spearhead border, ht. 7"	3250	6000	10,000
Plate, Arms of Barrington, dia. 9"	750	1400	2400
Plate, Burrell impaling Raymond, dia. 9"	320	600	1000
Plate, Davis w/ Southerne in Pretence, dia. 9"	1250	2300	4000
Plates, pr., Arms of Parker, dia. 8.5"	700	1300	2300
Soup Tureen, covered, boar's head, matching platter, len. 14"	6250	12,000	20,000
Teapot, crest, ht. 9"	1400	2600	4600
Vegetable Dishes, pr., lidded, w/ strap handles, dec. w/ crest, liners and undertray, len. 15".	12,000	22,000	40,000

Canton

	AUCTION	RETAIL Low	High
Box, lidded, sq., ht. 7.25", len. 7"	$ 3250	$ 5360	$ 8610
Chop Platter, dia. 13.5"	650	1070	1720
Cider Pitcher, ht. 6.5"	400	660	1060
Creamer, paneled, ht. 5"	1100	1820	2920
Cut-Corner Bowl, len. 9"	800	1320	2120
Deep Dish, oblong, len. 11"	250	410	660
Dinner Plate, 9"	100	170	270
Egg Cup, ftd.	75	120	200
Fruit Bowl and Tray, oval reticulated, len. 11"	700	1160	1860
Ginger Jar, w/ cover, ht. 10"	150	250	400
Helmet-Form Creamer, ht. 4.5"	500	830	1330
Hot Water Plate, dia. 9"	200	330	530
Leaf-Form Dish, len. 8"	150	250	400
Lobed Salad Bowl, dia. 10.5"	700	1160	1860
Milk Pitcher, ht. 8.5"	1300	2150	3450
Monumental Pitcher, w/ bamboo form handle, ht. 15"	3000	4950	7950
Mug, strap-handle, ht. 4"	400	660	1060
Platter, oblong w/ cut corners, len. 16"	350	580	930
Sauce Boat, strap handle, len 7"	275	450	730
Scallop-Edge Circular Deep Dish, dia. 9.5"	450	740	1190
Scalloped Dish, w. 10"	550	910	1460
Serving Dish, sq., len. 8.5"	250	410	660
Shrimp Dish, len. 10"	450	740	1190
Vegetable Dish, sq., covered, len 8"	250	410	660
Vegetable Dishes, pr., sq., covered, w/ pod finials, len. 9"	500	830	1330
Water Bottle, ht. 10"	200	330	530
Well-and-Tree Platter, len. 17"	650	1070	1720

Canton blue and white has been exported from China almost continuously since before the American Revolution. Eighteenth century pieces are generally higher quality than late 19th-century ones. Left: A late 18th-century example. Right: An early 20th-century example.

Above left to right: Fitzhugh covered vegetable dish, platter, and plate.

Fitzhugh

	AUCTION	RETAIL Low	RETAIL High
Dinner Plates, 12 orange, dia. 10"	$ 5000	$ 8250	$ 13,250
Dinner Plates, 14 blue, dia. 10"	550	910	1460
Dinner Plates, 6 orange, dia. 10"	1400	2310	3710
Luncheon Plates, 16 orange, 8"	3500	5780	9280
Platter, green w/ Amer. eagle, len. 11.5"	3100	5120	8220
Platter, oval, orange, len. 13"	1200	1980	3180
Platter, oval, orange, len. 15"	1750	2890	4640
Platter, oval, orange, len. 16"	1800	2970	4770
Platter, oval, orange, len. 19"	2250	3710	5960
Platter w/ Mazarine Strainer, orange 17"	6000	10,000	15,000
Sauce Boats, pr., of orange strap-handle w/ undertrays, len. 7"	4000	6600	10,600
Sauce Dish, green	80	130	210
Soup Plates, 11", orange, dia. 10"	2000	3300	5300
Soup Plates, 13", orange, dia. 10"	3600	5940	9540
Soup Plates, 19", blue	600	990	1590
Soup Tureen, covered, blue and white w/ pod finial and strap handles	2100	3470	5570
Soup Tureen, orange w/ pod finial and strap handles, len. 15"	10,000	16,500	26,500
Vegetable Dishes, 4 orange, covered, w/ pod finials, len. 10"	8000	13,200	21,200

Garniture sets should be carefully checked to make sure all pieces are original to that set.

Nanking

	AUCTION	RETAIL Low	High
Boxed Sweetmeat Set	$ 650	$ 1200	$ 2100
Cider Jug	1000	1900	3300
Creamer	150	300	500
Dinner Service, owned by William Gray of Salem, MA, comprising covered tureen and stand, cut-corner salad bowl, sauce tureen, 2 sauce boats w/ stands, 6 platters, 18 soup plates, 18 dinner plates, and 2 deep plates	12,000	23,000	50,000
Hot Water Plate	200	400	700
Mug, "chicken skin" finish	400	750	1600
Platter, oval, len. 19"	500	900	1600
Platter and Strainer, len. 15.5"	1100	2400	4500
Sauce Boats, pr., strap handle, len. 7"	700	1200	2100
Serving Dishes, pr., shaped	2000	3700	6500
Silver-Form Coffee Pot	2200	4100	7200
Soup Tureen, lidded, len. 14"	100	1800	3000
Vases, pr., baluster form, "chicken skin" finish	900	1700	2900
Vases, pr., ovoid, "chicken skin" finish	900	1700	2900
Vegetable Dish, covered, shaped oval, len. 11"	350	700	1100
Water Bottle	550	1000	1800

Rose Mandarin

Charger, dia. 14"	650	1000	1750
Cups and Saucers, 6 sets	350	580	930
Cylindrical Vase, ht. 6"	300	500	800
Mug, w/ underglazed blue dec., ht. 5.5"	650	1000	1750
Platter, w/ pink and green border w/ bird-dec. reserves, len. 19"	2000	3300	5300
Punch Bowl, dia. 11.5"	2400	4000	6000
Punch Bowl, dia. 12"	900	1490	2390
Soup Plates, pr., dia. 10"	500	830	1330
Vase, dec. w/ court scene, ht. 24"	2500	4130	6630
Vase, w/ panel of court scene within pink lotus petal border, handles of winged dragon form, ht. 17"	1000	1650	2650
Water Bottle, ht. 12.5"	900	1490	2390

Nanking covered soup tureen, $1500 at auction. — Photo courtesy of Northeast Auctions.

Rose Medallion

	AUCTION	RETAIL Low	High
Bowl, w/ court scene, dia. 10".	$ 450	$ 800	$ 1500
Candlesticks, pr., ht. 6.5"	500	900	1600
Charger, dia. 16"	525	1000	1700
Chop Dish, ftd., len. 14.75"	600	1100	2000
Chop Dish, oval ftd., len. 16"	800	1500	2600
Coffee Pot, w/ side handle, ht. 9".	600	1100	2000
Dish, square open, len. 9"	350	700	1100
Dome-Top Teapot, ht. 8"	700	1300	2300
Double Gourd Vases, pr., ht. 8.5"	450	800	1500
Garden Barrel, pierced, vignettes of figures, gilt, ht. 19"	2200	4000	7200
Garden Barrels, pr., ht. 18"	5200	9000	17,000
Garden Seat, hexagonal, scenic vignettes and panels, gilt, ht. 18"	2300	4300	7500
Hot Water Plate, w/ knobbed lid, len. 11"	675	1300	2200
Octagonal Milk Jug, ht. 6.5"	475	900	1500
Punch Bowl, dia. 16 "	2900	5400	9500
Punch Bowl, ht. 6.5", dia. 14.5"	1200	2200	3900
Razor Box, len. 8"	550	1000	1800
Sauce Tureen and Undertray, rose medallion covered, len. 9"	650	1140	1788
Soup Tureen, w/ pod finial and strap handles, len. 14"	1400	2450	3850
Temple Jar, covered, ht. 18"	1800	3300	5900
Trefoil-Form Tray, len. 11"	450	800	1500
Vase, Ku-Form, dec. w/ figures and botanical motifs, ht. 15"	400	700	1300

Miscellaneous

	AUCTION	RETAIL Low	High
Bird and Butterfly Vases, pr., ht. 14"	500	880	1375
Blue and White Platter, octagonal, pagoda dec., len. 16"	500	900	1600
Bowl, Imari-style dec., dia. 10".	1200	2200	4000
Charger, Imari-style dec., dia. 15"	1200	2200	4000
Deep Plate, centering continental ship, dia. 8"	450	800	1500
Deep Plate, w/ Grisaille scene of European children, dia. 8"	175	300	600
Deep Saucer, Docai dec., deer on terrace, reign mark, dia. 6"	850	1600	3000
Dinner Service, sacred bird and butterfly, comprising covered tureen and stand w/ strap handles and pod finial, sauce tureen and stand, strap handle sauce boat and stand, sq. covered vegetable dish w/ pod finial, oval vegetable dish w/ pod finial, shrimp dish, 2 oval open vegetable dishes, sq. open vegtable dish, fish platter w/ mazarine, 6 grad. platters, 12 dinner plates, 18 soup plate and 15 luncheon plates	18,000	31,500	50,000
Dish, tobacco-leaf variant, dia. 9"	850	1600	2800
Garden Seats, pr., celadon ground octagonal, ht. 19".	2000	3700	6500
Garniture Set, 4-piece blue and white dec. w/ urn and flower motif, ht. 12"	750	1310	2063
Garniture Vase, blue urn dec., lidded, ht. 12"	425	800	1400
Ice Pail and Undertray, sepia landscapes, ht. 7.5".	3100	5800	10,000
Juno and the Peacock Tea Bowl and Saucer	350	700	1100
Masonic Mug, strap handle dec. w/ masonic devices, ht. 6"	1600	2800	4400
Mug, Blue & White, ht. 7"	1600	3000	5200
Platter, sepia dome-top, oval-lidded, len. 14".	800	1500	2600

	AUCTION	RETAIL Low	High
Razor Box, orange sacred bird and butterfly, len. 7".	$ 900	$ 1700	$ 2900
Reticulated Trays, pr., oval, monogram, len. 8"	2100	3900	6800
Rose Group Plate.	250	500	800
Sauce Tureen and Undertray, scenic medallion, len. 9"	600	1100	2000
Shrimp Dish, Famille Rose, orange-peel finish, len. 11"	450	800	1500
Strainer, Imari-style dec., fitted bamboo turned stand, dia. 14". ..	650	1200	2100
Teapot, floral, w/ domed lid, ht. 7"	1200	2100	3300
Thousand-Butterfly Service, 10 dinner plates, 12" platter, scalloped bowl, dia. 10"	2700	4730	7425
Tureen, w/ pod finial lid and strap handles, w/ undertray	6750	12,500	22,000

Above left: Batavia ware has a brown exterior and a blue and white interior. It generally sells for 20 -50% less than comparable Canton pieces. Right: High quality blue and white reproductions bring $10-$20 each for small pieces.

Left: Rose Manderin pattern. Right: Tobacco Leaf pattern.

Cinnabar

Cinnabar is the Chinese carved lacquer. Layers are built up over wood, porcelain, or metal thick enough to carve ornate designs. The color is usually deep red. Although Cinnabar has been made continuously for over 300 years, the majority of the collected pieces currently available date from the turn of the century, as do all pieces listed below.

"Good" pieces may show some wear with some minor flecks of lacquer chipped away. "Best" pieces must be in perfect condition with no chipping or cracks.

Best rectangular box with figures, 6", $400-$600.

	GOOD	BETTER	BEST
Bowl, 4 scenic views, 5.5" sq.	$ 170	$ 250	$ 600
Bowl, pedestal foot, w/ lid, 6" dia.	180	270	560
Bowl, red flower design, black background, w/ lid, 6" dia.	150	270	600
Bowl, scalloped rim, red, 6.5" dia.	150	250	550
Bowl, scenic design, black on red, very shallow, 8" dia.	130	200	450
Box, fan shape, floral and bird design, 15" w.	550	850	1850
Box, floral design, black on red, w/ lid, 6" dia.	200	350	700
Box, flower design, red on green, w/ lid, 6.5" dia.	400	620	1150
Box, melon shape, 6.5" dia.	150	300	700
Box, oblong, carved view, w/ lid, 6.5" w.	200	300	650
Box, scene of playing sports, black on red, w/ lid, 15" dia.	550	800	2000
Cup, flower design, flared rim, 4.5" dia.	270	420	950
Cup, footed, 5.5" dia.	170	270	600
Cup, w/ dragon handles, 4.5" dia.	230	350	800
Dish, overall floral design, 9.5" dia.	280	430	900
Ginger Jar, landscape scene, red on cream, 8.5" ht.	350	530	1130
Hand Mirror, rust-colored landscape, 10.5" w.	200	300	600
Incense Burner, pagoda style, Taoist mask design, 17" ht.	1700	2700	5500
Plate, double dragon design, 12.75" dia.	525	850	1850
Plate, floral scene, red on green, 13" dia.	600	960	2200
Plate, floral scene, w/ ftd. base, 8" dia.	250	380	800
Plate, flower and butterfly scene, 10.5" dia.	330	500	1150
Plate, geometric design, red on black, 8" dia.	150	250	500
Pot, Taoist markings, ftd., 7" dia.	400	600	1250
Screen, floral motif, 70" x 20" panels	6500	13,000	45,000

	GOOD	BETTER	BEST
Screen, floral scene w/ nightingale, ftd. base, 29" ht.	$ 3100	$ 8500	$ 22,000
Smoking Set, tray, ashtrays, and cigarette box, 11.5" dia.	220	350	750
Stool, Greek key border, floral medallion, 18" ht.	1600	2520	5750
Tray, bird and flower scene, reddish brown, 15" w.	850	1350	3000
Tray, floral and bird, red, yellow, and green, 15" w.	800	1250	2800
Tray, flowering tree, 12.5" w.	300	500	1100
Tray, gilded rim, 17" w.	280	450	950
Urn, red flower on black background, 6.5" ht.	100	170	370
Vase, dragon design, green, yellow, and red, 15" ht.	1400	2400	5500
Vase, fish shape, red, 7.5" ht.	250	400	950
Vase, floral scene, on porc. body, 6.5" ht.	200	350	800
Vase, Foo dog design, 15" ht.	950	1500	3500
Vase, landscape, on porc. body, 6.5" ht.	250	350	780
Vase, overall dragon design, 12" ht.	350	730	1500
Vase, phoenix bird shape, 8" ht.	600	950	2200
Vase, rect., animal handles, w/ lid, 10" ht.	300	450	1000
Vase, red flowers on black background, 8" ht.	130	200	450
Vase, scenic design, black on red, 8" ht.	150	250	600
Vase, swimming fish scene, 15" ht.	650	1600	3500

*Best rectangular vase, 8",
$800-$1000.*

Nippon Porcelain

Nippon porcelain resulted from the 1893 American tariff act requiring imports be marked (in English) with the country of origin. "Nippon" was an accepted name for Japan at that time. Nippon ware also represents Satsuma, Noritake, Imari, and other Japanese wares of that period.

The marks most frequently depict an M within a green wreath, and the word "Nippon" printed in curved letters underneath. There are many, many variations, however. By the late 1920s, "Japan" replaced "Nippon." Nippon ware has been faked and reproduced

	LOW	AVG.	HIGH
Bowl, 7" dia., blue, white background, pink, red floral medallions, handles, green M mark	$ 18	$ 22	$ 25
Bowl, 8" dia., enameled, raised chestnut motif, handles, green M mark	32	39	46
Bowl, 9" dia., bisque, walnut motif, green M mark	90	115	120
Bowl, 9" dia., mustard color, hand-painted, M wreath, blue mark, gold, jewels, rose motif	60	70	80
Bowl, 9" dia., red, black, figural, scenic, floral motif, unmarked	70	80	90
Bowl, strawberries, leaves and flowers, leaf-shaped handle	400	500	600
Box, 2" ht., blue, gold raised motif, green M mark	110	130	150
Candy Bowl, 6" sq., beaded, gold rim, blown-out sides, 2 gold handles, floral design	100	125	150
Candy Bowl, scene of palm trees, sailboat, in pastel colors, beaded gold trim, pierced handles	70	85	100
Candy Dish, 7" x 5", oval, hand-painted M wreath, green mark, scenic motif, open-work handles	60	68	76
Celery Dish, 9" x 4", satin finish, small houseboat w/ sail, w/ floral dec.	35	40	45
Cocoa Set, pot, 6 cups and saucers, lid top and bottom, in turquoise blue w/ sprays of roses	425	515	595
Coffee Set, 9" ht., pot, 5 cups and saucers, demitasse size, M mark	200	250	300
Compote, 3" ht., floral insects, medallion of Chicago Post Office, Oriental China Nippon mark	100	120	140
Compote, 5" x 12", bisque, Indian in canoe, surrounded w/ pictographs	190	230	270
Cookie Server, 10" dia., yellow background, floral motif, gold handle, M mark	30	40	50
Cream/Sugar, painted flowers, leaves, gold trim	60	80	100
Creamer, gold foliage motif, hand-painted Nippon mark	15	20	25
Cruets, 6" ht., Oriental garden motif, M mark, pr.	100	130	160
Cup, 3" ht., gold, grape vine motif, green M mark	21	25	28
Cup and Saucer, multi-colored floral motif, Art Nouveau, green M mark	11	13	15
Demitasse Set, pot, 5 cups, saucers, Art Deco, black outline, marked Nippon	175	225	275
Desk Set, 5 pieces, scenic cameos	325	425	525
Dish, 12" x 6", yellow, tan floral motif, green stems, black ribbons, lined in gold, green M mark	14	17	19
Dish, 6" dia., cream background, raised gold, multi-color, M mark	18	22	26
Dish, 7" w., fish shape, mythical bird motif, bordered; unmarked	80	100	120
Dish, 7" x 6", gold background, floral, foliage motif, M mark	35	44	53
Dish, 8" x 6", brown and tan panel, floral motif, gold handle, cover, rising sun mark	65	80	95
Dresser Set, 7" tray, stoppered bottle 3" ht., 2 covered patch boxes, rd., trimmed in gold, on white	75	95	115

	LOW	AVG.	HIGH
Egg Cup, white background, blue and amber butterflies	$ 30	$ 40	$ 50
Egg Warmer, 5" dia., green M in wreath	155	185	215
Ewer, 10" ht., bulbous body, band of violets, greens and violets, cabinet item unmarked	250	300	350
Ewer, 12" ht., 1900s, bulbous body, foliate center piece, red and violet	340	400	460
Fruit Bowl, 9" dia., handles, scalloped gold rim, geometric designs, flowers, signed w/ the blue leaf mark	115	135	155
Hat Pin Holder, gold, floral detail on dark blue background	55	66	78
Humidor, 4" ht., bisque finish, trimmed in gold, scene of playing cards	600	775	950
Jar, 4" ht., multi-colored floral, gold green M mark	30	37	44
Napkin Ring, satin finish, scene of windmill	90	110	130
Nut Set, bowl, 4 dishes on legs, flowers traced in gold line	50	60	70
Plate, 10" dia., multi-colored floral motif, green M mark	25	30	35
Plate, 10" dia., raised gold, red floral motif, pierced handles, marked	85	100	115
Plate, 5" dia., floral motif, Art Nouveau, green M mark	9	11	13
Plate, 6" dia., gold-outlined, oval floral medallions, blue mark	55	65	75
Plate, 7" dia., child holds bouquet, blue M mark	20	24	28
Plate, 7" dia., children playing, elephant motif, hand-painted Nippon	27	32	36
Plate, 8" dia., gold raised enamel leaves, vines, oval medallions, green M mark	35	40	45
Platter, 11" dia., autumn scene of lake, path into forest, applied handles	100	125	150
Salt Dip, polychrome floral motif, gold outline, green M mark	20	25	30
Shakers, pr., 2" ht., pink floral, foliage motif, gold handles, rising sun mark	30	38	46
Shakers, pr., designs filled w/ white enamel, salt is open-bowl type	37	46	55
Spoon Holder, floral motif, 2 handles, M mark	60	70	80

Left: Nippon was often sold in large sets.

Right: Gilt triangular planter $30-$60.

Occupied Japan Items

These are items Japan exported after World War II, when Japan was "occupied" by a foreign country for the first time in its history. The term "occupied" was essential to Japanese economic recovery. Hostile feelings ran high for many years after the war; Americans refused to buy anything with "Made in Japan" as its trademark. Since Japanese exports retained craftsmanship, beauty, and aesthetic symmetry, despite the scarcity of materials and manpower, the trademark "Occupied Japan" assured consumers that they were in no way contributing to the menacing powers of the pre-war era.

	LOW	AVG.	HIGH
Alpine Girl, 4.5" ht., black hat, green dress	$ 9	$ 13	$ 17
Bird, 2" ht., perched on 2 books, polychrome	8	11	14
Bird, 2" x 3", tan body, red head, multi-color wings, black tail	12	15	18
Bird, 3.5" ht., perched on branch, polychrome	12	15	18
Bird, 3.5" x 3", on floral branches, polychrome	11	14	17
Bird, 4.5" ht., perched on stump	15	20	25
Bird, 4.5" x 4.5", cocked head, raised tail, polychrome	22	28	34
Bird, 5" ht., perched on tree stump, leaves on base	14	18	22
Boxer, 3" ht., gray, standing	11	14	17
Boy, 4" ht., carrying bottles and a basket, polychrome	15	21	27
Boy, 4" ht., holding basket, duck at feet, polychrome	11	14	17
Boy, 4" ht., seated on bench w/ violin, polychrome	13	16	19
Boy, 4.5" ht., w/ toy boat, polychrome	10	13	16
Colonial Couple, 3" x 4", on pedestal, lady sitting w/ fan, man in long coat standing	13	17	20
Colonial Couple, 3.5" ht., lady seated w/ musical instrument, man standing	13	17	20
Colonial Couple, 3.5" ht., man holding hat, lady in long skirt	15	20	25
Colonial Couple, 3.5" ht., seated man w/ cape, standing lady w/ ruffled dress, polychrome	16	20	23
Colonial Couple, 4" ht., white, gold trim, lady w/ fan, man w/ book	20	25	30
Colonial Couple, 4.5" ht., dancing, polychrome	20	26	32
Colonial Couple, 4.5" ht., holding hands	20	26	32
Colonial Couple, 4.5" ht., man w/ striped breeches, lady w/ floral skirt, polychrome	20	25	30
Colonial Couple, 4.5" ht., seated lady, man holds hat, polychrome	18	23	28
Colonial Couple, 4.5" ht., seated, man holds rose, lady w/ flower basket, polychrome	20	25	30
Colonial Couple, 4.5" x 3", man stands w/ cape, lady seated	20	26	32
Colonial Couple, 4.5" x 5.5", each w/ musical instrument, polychrome	18	23	28
Crane, 4" ht., blue and yellow outstretched wings	10	13	16
Dog, 2", black spotted, long nose and ears, seated	8	11	13

Rugs, Oriental

Oriental rugs older than 50 years have long been collected and used in fine homes throughout the United States. They originated in Persia (modern Iran), Turkey, and the surrounding areas. The following representative examples show prices realized at auction (wholesale) and the corresponding retail range. "Karastan" rugs are machine-made and not collected by anyone we know. All the rugs listed here are hand-woven. European examples from the 19th century are particularly valuable. For further information see *The Official Price Guide to Oriental Rugs*, by Joyce C. Ware, House of Collectibles, Random House, NY.

Above left to right: Caucasian Cabistan prayer rug, 59" x 45", $3500; Antique Kazak prayer rug, 45" x 70", $4500 at auction. — Photos courtesy of Northeast Auctions.

	AUCTION	RETAIL Low	High
Afgan Bokhara Carpet, 8" x 14'	$ 2500	$ 3200	$ 6300
Afghar Rug, 30" x 42"	2200	2800	5500
Afshar Saddlebag, 22" x 19"	210	300	500
Afshar Saddlebag, 24" x 16.5"	1700	2200	4200
Antique Kuba Blossom Carpet, dark blue field w/ large-scale flowerheads and interconnecting vines, 6' 6" x 12' 8"	4400	5600	11,000
Ardebil Design Carpet, 9' 2" x 14', modern, Indian	3200	4000	8000
Baktiari Garden Carpet, signed and dated 1916, 10' x 16'	8600	10,000	21,000
Baktiari Long Scatter Rug, midnight-blue field filled w/ ascending design of cedar trees, birds, and palmettes, 3' 5" x 9'	2750	3400	6300
Baluch Bagface, 2'4" x 2'2"	7912	10,000	18,000
Baluch Flatweave Rug, 9'10" x 5'7"	5000	6500	12,600
Baluch Rug, 6' x 3'6"	1800	2300	4600

Kazak Cloudband rug, 45" x 70", $4500 at auction. — Photo courtesy of Northeast Auctions.

	AUCTION	RETAIL Low	High
Baluch Rug, 7' x 4'	$ 3300	$ 4200	$ 7700
Bidjar Oriental Carpet, medallion on red field, 11' x 19'	48,000	60,800	118,000
Bidjar Runner, blue field w/ overall Herati design within pale rust floral filled main border, 3' 11" x 15' 4"	3000	3800	7000
Bidjar Runner, midnight-blue field w/ diamond lattice and stylized flowers within green main border w/ flowers and woven inscription, 1337 AH/1918 AD.' 238" x 39"	7300	8800	17,500
Caucasian Karabagh Rug, 41" x 121"	1500	1900	3800
Caucasian Kazak Rug, medallion on blue field, 48" x 65"	7500	8800	18,000
Caucasian Kilim Pictorial Rug, horse and riders, 79" x 106"	7300	8800	17,500
Caucasian Scatter Rug, modern, 3' x 4' 5"	600	800	1700
Central Asian Yomut Turkoman Rug, 27" x 53"	3600	4600	8400
Chinese Carpet, antique, delicate yellow and brown rice motif field w/ large central soft blue Foo-dog medallion and complementary spandrels, 8' 6" x 12' 2"	37,000	47,200	92,400
Chinese Carpet, modern, w/ ivory field and blue border, 6' x 8'	430	500	1100
Chinese Scatter Rug, w/ tan field filled w/ coin motifs and a companion border, 3' 2" x 4' 6"	860	1100	2100
Chinese Wool Rug, 28" x 54"	250	300	600
Continental Room-Size Carpet, worked in style of 17th cent. Turkish carpet, tomato-red field w/ pale green central medallion and 3 partial blue medallions, 8' x 16' 9"	15,000	20,000	38,500
Dagastan Prayer Rug, ivory field w/ blue lattice filled w/ floral devices surrounded by red main border, 3' 6" x 4' 6"	1500	1900	3800
Daghestan Scatter Rug, 3' 6" x 4' 11"	2200	2400	5400
Ersari Turkoman Camel Bag, 15" x 53"	640	800	1500
Ersari Turkoman Camel-Bag Section, 15" x 53"	1720	2200	4200
Feraghan Carpet, antique, midnight-blue ground w/ Herati			

	AUCTION	RETAIL Low	High
field surrounded by pale green main border w/ geometric palmettes, 13' 8" x 24'	$ 9000	$ 11,200	$ 21,700
Feraghan Carpet, antique, pale blue-green field w/ repeating ivory floral clusters and connecting floral devices within wide soft red main border, 177" x 118"	11,000	13,600	27,300
Feraghan Rug, Herati design on blue field, 48.5" x 78"	3900	5000	9100
Feraghan Rug, medallion on ivory field, 49" x 72"	7740	9600	18,900
Feraghan Sarouk Rug, w/ floral design, 3' 10" x 6' 3"	2200	2800	5500
French Aubusson Carpet, w/ floral sprays, 13' 3" x 17' 4"	24,000	30,400	58,800
French Savonnerie Carpet, w/ floral ground, 14' 4" x 17' 5"	14,000	18,400	35,700
Hamadan Jojan Sarouk Design Rug, 6' 8" x 5'	2200	2800	5500
Hamadan Oriental Scatter Rug, 6' 11" x 5' 5"	170	200	400
Hamadan Rug, 6' 4" x 4' 10"	2200	2800	5500
Hamadan Runner, antique, light camel field w/ trellis design w/ ivory medallions within an ivory floral border and wide camel margin, 3' 1" x 12' 7"	1800	2300	4600
Hamadan Runner, blue and red field w/ small ivory medallion and stylized flowers within camel hair border, 3' 6" x 16' 8"	5000	6400	12,600
Hamadan Runner, field w/ small medallions and elliptical stylized floral motifs within camel hair border, 207" x 40.5"	4000	5200	9800
Hamadan Runner, midnight-blue field w/ overall floral design within an ivory floral border, 2' 8" x 6' 4"	860	1100	2100
Hamadan Runner, midnight-blue field w/ overall Herati design within red floral and vine border, 3' 3" x 16' 2"	6880	8000	16,800
Hamadan Runner, red predominant, 2' 6" x 13'	500	600	1300
Hamadan Scatter Rug, tomato-red field w/ red and blue boteh within multiple borders, 4' 4" x 7' 1"	1000	1400	2700

Double Diamond Kazak rug, 76" x 54", $3600 at auction. — Photo courtesy of Northeast Auctions.

	AUCTION	RETAIL Low	High
Heriz Carpet, w/ medallion and spandrels, 10' 11" x 8' 4" ...	$ 30,000	$ 38,400	$ 70,000
Heriz Carpet, w/ medallion on madder ground, 9' 6" x 6'	3000	3800	7000
Heriz Carpet w/ russet field and central dark blue medallion w/ attached pale green pendants and elongated pale blue spandrels, 8' x 12'	18,000	22,400	44,000
Heriz Rug, w/ stylized tree design, 49" x 59"	2200	2800	5500
Heriz Runner, tomato-red ground w/ 4 pulled medallions within camel hair border w/ geometric motifs, 101.5" x 31"	15,000	19,200	37,500
Indian Mugal Fragment, antique, soft-raspberry field w/ overall floral design within pale brown border, 6" x 3'	860	1100	2100
Isphahan Silk Rug, w/ central medallion, 8' 6" x 12' 2"	24,000	31,200	60,000
Joshagan Carpet, antique, ivory field w/ large-scale soft rose flowerheads and midnight-blue serrated leaves within soft red main border, 10' 10" x 18' 2"	43,000	54,400	100,000
Kajara Carpet, w/ brick red medallion, 9' 2" x 12' 7"	36,000	45,600	88,200
Karabach Runner, tomato-red field w/ 9 serrated-edge geometric motifs within green, white, and tomato-red borders, each w/ stylized flowers, 152" x 37"	8200	10,400	19,600
Karabagh Long Rug, field w/ alternating blue and white diagonal stripes filled w/ pinwheels w/ an ivory border w/ multi-colored 8-point stars, 8' 8" x 4' 4"	3200	4000	7700
Karachoff Kazak Long Rug, medium blue field w/ alternating ivory and red medallions within an ivory border w/ latchwork designs, 4' 7" x 9' 2"	7500	8800	18,200
Karagashli Kuba Scatter Rug, light blue field w/ geometric and stylized motifs in ivory, tomato, yellow and soft blue within 3 borders, 59.5" x 50"	7500	8800	18,200
Karaja Scatter Rug, red field w/ 3 medallions within light blue main border, 2' 11" x 4' 4"	1000	1300	2100
Karaja-Heriz Carpet, medallion on red field, 14' 6" x 25'	43,000	54,000	100,000
Kashan Carpet, blue medallion on floral field, 8' 8" x 11'.....	15,000	19,200	37,800
Kashan Carpet, on ivory field, 8' 6" x 11' 7", modern :.............	3000	3800	7000
Kashan Carpet, red flower-filled field w/ pulled dark blue medallions and companion spandrels within dark blue main border, 10' 4" x 21'	17,000	21,600	42,000
Kazak, Double-Eagle, abrashed red field w/ 2 large eagle medallions, 8' 3" x 5'	9000	11,200	21,000
Kazak Long Rug, field w/ 2 parallel rows of memling guls surrounded by an ivory border, 3' 8" x 8'	2200	2800	5500
Kazak Long Rug, pale rust field w/ 3 sewan Kazak medallions within dark-brown main border filled w/ geometric devices, 4' 3" x 12'	3200	4100	7700
Khorassan Rug, w/ military figures, 10' x 11' 7"	11,000	13,600	27,300
Kirman Carpet, antique, pale magenta field w/ overall latticework, flowerheads and buds within dark blue main border filled w/ flowerheads and leaves, 8' x 16' 4"	9000	11,200	21,700
Kirman Carpet, ivory field w/ cedar trees, flowering bushes and floral sprays, ivory main border w/ similar motifs, 8' 9" x 11' 9"	3440	4300	8400

	AUCTION	RETAIL Low	High
Kirman Mat, ivory floral field filled w/ dark blue medallion within an ivory floral border, 2' 3" x 3' 1"	$ 500	$ 600	$ 1300
Kirman Prayer Rug, w/ 3 cypress trees, 4' 1" x 6' 6"	6450	8000	15,400
Kirman Rug, medallion on ivory field, 48" x 72"	2200	2800	5500
Kirman Scatter Rug, antique, midnight-blue field filled w/ large raspberry medallions within 3 complementary borders, 3' 2" x 5' 2"	600	800	1500
Kirmanshaw Carpet, foliate medallion,11' 5" x 21' 2"	12,000	15,200	29,400
Konya Prayer Rug, 5' x 3'6"	13,000	16,800	33,600
Kuba Blossom Carpet, antique, medium blue field w/ overall large-scale shields and flowerheads within narrow red and blue reciprocal trefoil main border, 7' 6" x 18' 3"	7500	8800	18,200
Kuba Dragon Carpet Fragment, antique, With large octagonal medallion w/ geometric devices flanked by stylized dragons, 5' 3" x 7' 4"	8200	10,400	19,600
Kuba Prayer Rug, ivory field w/ diamond motifs and mirab w/ 2 stylized trees, 65" x 31.5"	1500	1900	3800
Kuba Rug, w/ bird motif, 54" x 84"	2580	3200	6300
Kuba Runner, w/ black field w/ trellis design, len. 6' 8"	860	1100	2100
Kuba Scatter Rug, antique, corroded black field w/ yellow latticework filled w/ floral devices surrounded by an ivory stepped medallion main border, 3' 1" x 4' 7"	1300	1700	3400
Kuba Scatter Rug, dark blue field w/ geometric devices within pale gold kufic border, 3' 10" x 5' 8"	1200	1500	2900
Kuba Soumak Rug, 48" x 58"	3000	3800	7000
Kula Prayer Rug, soft gold field filled w/ floral sprays within multiple borders w/ small flowerheads, 4' 4" x 6' 8"	1500	1900	3800
Lavar Kirman Rug, antique, ivory floral field w/ central blue medallion and raspberry spandrels within multiple floral borders, 6' x 9'	2700	3400	6700
Lori Runner, 59" x 114"	3440	4400	8400
Mahal Carpet, dark blue field w/ large-scale floral motifs within pale gold main border w/ palmettes and geometric leaves, 8' 7" x 11' 10"	7200	8800	17,500
Mahal Sultanabad Carpet, With russet field and overall design of clustered white flowers w/ connecting blue vines, 10' 9" x 13' 3"	12,000	16,000	31,500
Malayer Scatter Rug, midnight-blue field w/ small boteh, old main border w/ traversing flower and leaf design, 3' 11" x 6' 2"	5500	7000	13,300
Marasali Prayer Rug, 3'10" x 3'3"	29,000	36,800	70,000
Marasali Scatter Rug, blue field w/ overall small geometric motifs, ivory predominant, within 2 ivory and 1 blue borders, 81" x 40"	4400	5600	10,000
Marasali Shirvan Prayer Rug, 41.5" x 47"	5100	6500	12,600
Moteham Kashan Carpet, midnight-blue field w/ overall floral sprays within wide gold floral border, signed twice, 12' 10" x 14'	33,000	42,400	81,900
Moteham Kashan Carpet, palmette medallion, 55" x 79"	5100	6500	12,600
Mughal Millefleur Star Lattice Carpet (from the Vanderbilt estate) 12'8" x 13'6"	1,700,000	2,080,000	3,500,000

	AUCTION	RETAIL	
		Low	High
Northwest Persian Runner, blue field w/ geometric Caucasian influenced design within Heriz-style border, 182" x 39"	$ 3440	$ 4400	$ 8400
Northwest Persian Runner, Botek design, 3' 6" x 14'	2400	3000	5900
Northwest Persian Runner, field w/ diagonal rows of stylized flowers within an ivory primary border w/ large stylized flowers, 149" x 34.75"	3440	4400	8400
Northwest Persian Runner, midnight-blue field w/ geometric Caucasian-influenced devices within Heriz-style border, 192" x 40"	7900	9600	18,900
Northwest Persian Runner, red and brown field w/ 9 small medallions and an overall diamond pattern w/ stylized flowers within camel hair border, 277" x 53"	10,000	12,800	25,200
Northwest Persian Scatter Rug, medium blue field w/ oversized bidjov design within pale rust flowerhead and leaf border, 3' 2" x 6' 6"	1800	2300	4600
Oushak Carpet, red medallion, 12' 6" x 15' 11"	7740	9600	18,900
Persian Oriental Rug, antique, gold field w/ blue lobed medallion and rose spandrels, 3' 9" x 6' 4"	1400	1800	3600
Persian Oriental Rug, w/ ivory and blue repeating medallion field filled w/ vines and flowers, 4' 7" x 7' 8"	4400	5600	11,000
Persian Tabriz Carpet, field w/ concentric floral-filled medallions on cream ground w/ flower filled powder blue spandrels and border of floral cartouches, 9' x 12' 7"	49,000	62,400	122500
Pinwheel Kazak, 9' x 6'	15,000	19,200	37100
Salor Ensi, 6'5" x 4'5"	155,000	192,000	378,000
Sarouk Carpet, w/ ivory floral field w/ alternating taupe and pink medallions within a taupe main border w/ russet and blue flowerheads, 8" x 11'	8600	10,400	21000
Sarouk Ferahan, 11'11" x 8'	27,000	34,400	67900
Sarouk, late 19th century, 14' x 11'2"	23,000	29,600	58100
Seichor Scatter Rug, w/ black field filled w/ boteh, 3' 7" x 5' 6"	860	1100	2100
Senna Carpet, midnight-blue field w/ small-scale overall Herati design within wide rust border w/ bird and palmette motifs, 11' 8" x 19' 3"	13,000	16,800	33,600
Shirvan Long Rug, medium blue field w/ alternating red and blue medallions within an ivory main border w/ geometric motifs, 4' 4" x 9' 10"	11,000	13,600	26,600
Shirvan Long Rug, midnight-blue field w/ 3 medallions, figures and horse within an S-design border, 9' 2" x 4' 6"	2580	3300	6300
Shirvan Long Rug, midnight-blue field w/ alternating rows of pale green and red boteh within main border of red and white diagonal stripes, 37" x 11'	3000	3800	7000
Silk Suzani Carpet in soft palette w/ multiple circular medallions, 14' x 6' 7"	10,000	12,800	25,200
Silk Suzani Rug in soft palette w/ stylized lotus motif, 7' 2.5" x 4' 1"	860	1000	2100
Silk Tabriz Garden Carpet, red rondels, ivory grid serves as dividing waterway within garden, red cartouches w/			

	AUCTION	RETAIL Low	High
poetry, wide ivory border of cartouches w/ script, 8' x 10' 4"	$ 100,000	$ 128,000	$ 253,000
Sultanabad Carpet, soft gold field w/ overall floral design, 7' x 8' 11"	16,000	20,000	39,900
Tabriz Carpet, dark blue field w/ an overall Herati design within salmon main border, w/ bird medallion and flower-head motif overall, 9' x 12'	6450	8000	15,400
Tibetan Khotan Carpet, antique, soft aubergine field w/ 3 light blue circular medallions flanked by multiple gold geometric borders, 6' 4" x 13' 3"	10,000	13,600	25,900
Turkoman Yomud Ensi, tomato-red field divided into 4 panels w/ diamond motifs, 56" x 73"	1600	2000	4000

Satsuma

Satsuma is a cream-colored Japanese pottery, usually with a delicate crackled glaze and elaborately painted and gilt. Although it dates to the 17th century, most pieces seen today are from the 19th and 20th centuries. The following are 19th-century examples.

Above left to right: Charger, $2200 at auction. Large lobbed bowl with Thousand-Face interior, $2250 at auction.
— Photos courtesy of Northeast Auctions.

	AUCTION	RETAIL	
		Low	High
Bowl, w/ Thousand-Butterflies interior, 6"	$ 450	$ 810	$ 1220
Box, antique Satsuma, rect., children and swans dec., 3.5", c. 1790	600	650	700
Charger	450	810	1220
Koro, rect., len. 8.5"	850	1530	2300
Lobed Bowl, w/ Thousand-Face interior, dia. 16"	2250	3850	6000
Plate, w/ silver overlay	350	630	940
Ribbed Bowl	450	810	1220
Snuff Box, w/ blue ground	1000	1800	2700
Teapot	650	1170	1760
Vase, baluster form, ht. 9"	325	580	880
Vase, figural dec., ht. 7"	200	360	540
Vase, w/ flaring rim, ht. 15"	700	1260	1890

Snuff Bottles

Snuff bottles appeared with the growing popularity of snuff in China during the latter part of the 17th century. Originally a practical item, like a cigarette case, craftsmen of all sorts decorated these pieces with greater and greater sophistication. Eventually snuff bottles gained a life of their own. Collected and produced long after the fad of using snuff died out, they are still made today.

Judging snuff bottles is highly subjective. Craftmanship and beauty are the dominant factors, but rarity of materials also plays a part. Some jade examples are valued almost solely on the quality of the piece of jade, rather than age, craftsmanship, or design.

Agate

	LOW	AVG.	HIGH
Bamboo Shape, flat, c. 1900s	$1500	$1800	$2100
Flowering Mountain Motif, c. 1900s	1000	1250	1500
Hydra, bird motif, c. 1900s	600	800	1000
Shrimp, crab motif, c. 1900s	700	850	1000
Tree, boy, Foo dog motif, c. 1900s	670	800	970
White, duck and lilies motif, c. 1900s	1600	2000	2400

Amber

Brown, flat sides, rect., trees, rocks, and birds motif, c. 1800s	1200	1500	1800
Brown, pebble shape, c. 1800s	800	1000	1200
Dark yellow, cloud motif, c. 1800s	800	1000	1200
Yellow, streaked gold, knobby texture, c. 1800s	1000	1300	1600

Cinnabar

Floral Motif, c. 1900s	230	310	390
Landscape and Figurines, finely carved, c. 1900s	112	136	160

Cloisonné

Black background, dragon motif, c. 1900s	90	115	140
Blue, yellow, dragon motif, c. 1900s	100	130	160
Blue, yellow dragon, white cloud motifs, c. 1800s	400	500	600
Green Background, double-bottle shape, dragon motif, c. 1900s	600	700	800
Yellow, blue, cloudy, dragon motif, c. 1900s	600	700	800

Coral

Bamboo Shape, c. 1800s	900	1200	1500
Fish Shape, c. 1800s	600	775	950
Tree Shape, c. 1800s	630	780	930

Enamel

Blue and gray, dragon, wave motif, c. 1800s	1500	2100	2700
Blue, gourd shape, fruit and foliage motif, c. 1800s	687	838	990
Figural, landscape motif, c. 1800s	1800	2300	2800
White, plants and dragonfly motif, c. 1800s	750	1000	1250

Glass

Flattened sides, green, dragon motif, c. 1900s	160	190	220
Gold Fleck, flattened form, black metal w/ gold markings and stopper, c. 1900s	120	150	180

	LOW	AVG.	HIGH
Green and Red, bottle shape, c. 1800s	$1000	$1250	$1500
Turquoise, multi-colored enameled colors, figural mountain motif, c. 1800s	600	800	1000

Jade

	LOW	AVG.	HIGH
Streaked, brown and white, bat motif, mock handler, c. 1800s	700	800	900
Streaked, gray, lion and tree motif, mock handles, c. 1800s	659	839	1020
Streaked, green and gray, toad and landscape, c. 1800s	656	788	920
White, scenic motif, inscribed, c. 1900s	1000	1300	1600
Yellow, streaked beige, double-bottle shape, c. 1800s	1300	1600	1900

Lacquer

	LOW	AVG.	HIGH
Black, w/ ivory rim, purse-shaped, c. 1900s	700	850	1000
Brown, green, mother-of-pearl, shore line, water motif, c. 1900s	750	950	1150
Gold and Black, c. 1900s	225	300	375
Real Gourd, lacquered black, c. 1800s	584	727	870

Malachite

	LOW	AVG.	HIGH
Carved Gourds, on the front, banded, c. 1900s	220	300	380
Floral Motif, c. 1800s	300	375	45

Porcelain

	LOW	AVG.	HIGH
Blue and White, courtyard scene, 3", c. 1800s	550	700	950
Blue and White, motif of 2 figures under tree, c. 1800s	500	600	700
Blue and White, scenic motif, c. 1800s	300	400	500
Blue, motif of immortal, sea creature, plum branch, c. 1800s	500	600	700
Blue, red, white, courtyard motif, c. 1800s	440	545	650
Blue, white, dragon motif, c. 1800s	240	300	360
Cream, lions frolicking brocade balls, cream stopper, c. 1800s	1700	2100	2500
Fish Lotus, motif, paneled, c. 1800s	500	625	750
Green and White, dragon, cloud motif, c. 1800s	600	750	900
Green Enamel, yellow background, dragon motif, c. 1800s	550	700	850
Green, red figural motif, red seal on bottom, c. 1800s	400	500	600
Red, dragon motif, seal on base, c. 1800s	280	340	400
Red Foo Dog and Pup, c. 1900s	400	500	600
Red, warrior motif, c. 1800s	500	640	780
Robin's Egg Glaze, bird on branch, inscribed reverse, c. 1800s	650	775	900
White glaze, squirrel shape, c. 1800s	500	625	750

Quartz

	LOW	AVG.	HIGH
Pink, flat sides, spade shape, figural, cloud motif, c. 1800s	300	400	500

Rock Crystal

	LOW	AVG.	HIGH
Clear, sq. shape, basket-work motif, c. 1800s	1500	1900	2300
Clear, thin black lines, fish motif, c. 1800s	600	750	800
Clear, thin black lines, sq. shape, round edges, c. 1800s	800	1000	1200
Thin, brown hairlines, c. 1900s	1000	1200	1400
Thin gold lines, c. 1800s	900	1200	1500
Thin lines, reclining horse motif., c. 1800s	261	315	370

Paper Collectibles

Fruit Crate Labels

The decorative labels that adorned the sides of wooden fruit crates are popular collectibles. The oldest and rarest date to the 1880s. Rarity and design are the important variables with fruit crate labels. California labels are usually worth more than Florida labels, and orange labels usually have more ornate designs. Label designs changed over the years, and some collectors focus on labels that have undergone design changes.

	LOW	AVG.	HIGH
Airship, CA, citrus, pictures commercial airplane, royal blue, 10" x 11"	$ 12	$ 20	$ 28
Alpine Orchards, WA, pear, 3 pears, yellow, red, black background, pictorial	5	8	11
Blue Mountain, WA, apple, silhouette of trees and mountains, 2 apples in right corner, orange background, blue border	21	26	31
Blue Tip, CA, citrus, picture of a large feather, 9" x 9"	1	2	3
Blue Winner, WA, apple, cowboy on horseback picking up an apple in a rodeo, blue and white background	6	10	13
Boa Vista Ranch, CA, apple, mountains, orchard and farm house, one red and one golden apple, blue border	3	7	10
Bolero, CA, apple, Spanish dancer with 2 guitarists, black background	10	14	17
Bounty, CA, pear, bright yellow background, blue and red lettering, blue border	2	5	8
Briant, WA, apple, Washington State map, white and blue lettering, blue background	2	5	8
Briskey, WA, apple, snowy scene from Naches Pass, mountains and 2 red apples, black background, blue border	4	7	10
Broadway, CA, pear, red and black (old) graphic type, lettering, gold leaf, blue background, blue-green border	5	8	11
Bronco, CA, citrus, old stone litho of fully dressed cowboy riding a wild horse, very colorful	6	10	13
Brownie's, CA, citrus, pictures Brownies preparing orange juice against a yellow sun and blue background, 10" x 11"	2	5	8
Buckaroo, WA, apple, cowboy breaking a bucking horse, mountains and desert, yellow sky	12	17	21
Buddy, Michigan, broker label, smiling baby, blue background, green border, 1920	8	12	16
Bunting, WA, apple, one red apple, ribbon sash through the center, red lettering, blue background	7	10	13
Butler's Pride, WA, apple, branch with large red apple, white lettering, graphic, blue background	2	5	8
Cal-Flavor, CA, citrus, oranges, blossoms and leaves against a wood-grained and black background, 10" x 11"	2	5	8
Cambria, CA, citrus, brown border frames a brown eagle and 2 torches against a blue background, 10" x 11"	2	5	8
Chief Joseph, WA, apple, large white arrowhead with Chief Joseph's image in front of it, dressed in full headdress and beads, historic, red lettering, blue background	16	21	25
Cho Paks, WA, apple, trees, mountains, distant orchard scene, blue background	19	23	27

	LOW	AVG.	HIGH

Chore Best, WA, apple, aqua inset with block lettering, blue background . $ 2 $ 5 $ 8

Circle A&F, WA, apple, yellow and black lettering, circle in center with
  A & F in white loners, black background 7   11   14

Clasen, WA, apple, old litho of orchard homes and Mt, Adams in the
  background, 2 red apples on a limb, red lettering, 40 lbs. (old) 6   10   13

Cliff, WA, apple, rock cliffs with raging waterfall, span bridge over water
  with old sedan driving over it, orchard hills, blue sky and rod lettering,
  brown border 7   11   14

Clipper, FL, citrus, 3-mast schooner, 7" x 7", ... 2   4   6

Clipper Ship, WA, apple, large sailing ship on the ocean, blue background 40   45   50

Coed, CA, citrus, pictures smiling girl in graduate cap and gown against
  a purple background, 10" x 11" 2   5   8

Color Guard, WA, apple, blue bottom, yellow lettering, graphic, black
  background 5   8   11

Congden Refrigerated, WA, apple, first edition label, one red apple
  frozen in a block of ice, art deco lettering, black background 32   40   48

Congdon Refrigerated, WA, pear, pear frozen in a block of ice 9   13   17

Corona Uly, CA, citrus, white and gold speckled lily against a black
  background, 10" x 11" 3   6   9

Desert Bloom, CA, citrus, white, blooming yucca with desert greenery
  and mountains against a blue sky background, 10" x 11" 3   6   9

Dewy Fresh, WA, apple, modern green leaf, fairy in leafy skirt holding a
  wand, believed to be one of the last labels printed, white and red
  background, 1958 3   7   10

Diamond, OR, apple, red diamonds in center with white letters saying
  Hood River Apples (cartoon of apple head man), green background .. 12   17   21

Diamond, OR, pear, ML Hood scone, red diamond shipper is apple
  growers service 4   8   12

Diamond S, CA, pear, 2 horse heads, blue diamond 14   17   20

Dinner Gong, WA, apple, one red apple with leaves and stem, black
  bottom, blue background 2   5   8

Diving Girl, CA, apple, 1920s girl in swimming suit diving into the lake .. 13   19   24

Dixie Boy, FL, citrus, picture of a black boy, 9" x 9" 4   7   10

Don Juan, CA, pear, orchard scene in upper left corner, blue/black/red
  background 3   6   9

Don't Worry, WA, apple, blond boy holding apple with bite out of it,
  written white letters, shiny black background 10   14   17

Donnater, TX, citrus, pink grapefruit against a black background, 9" x 9" 1   2   3

Double A, CA, citrus, train supported by 2 capital letter As on a trestle,
  10" x 11" 2   4   5

Duckwall, OR, apple, stone wall with a very colorful duck in front, red
  background 32   40   49

Dunbar, OR, pear, cartoon pear skiing down snowy hill, yellow letter,
  blue sky 6   10   14

Eagle, CA, pear, eagle and 2 pears, red lettering, blue background,
  yellow border 8   12   16

Eatmor, WA, pear, 1920s boy in plaid knickers, holding a pear, red lettering,
  green background, rare 40   53   66

Eatum, WA, apple, one red and one golden apple, yellow letters, graphic
  type label, blue and black background 2   5   8

El Mejor, CA, citrus, pictures Sunkist orange, 10" x 11" 2   4   5

	LOW	AVG.	HIGH

Emerald Beauty, WA, pear, Spanish lady playing a guitar, rare .... $ 38 $ 45 $ 52

Emerald Green, WA, apple, suit of armor head with shield with a large
   emerald on it, green background 7 10 13

Empire, WA, apple, evaporated apples, old litho of mountains, orchards
   and trees 7 11 15

Empire Builder, WA, apple, mountains, large warehouse, trucks, train
   orchards, large apple covered wagon and four oxen 3 6 9

Endurance, CA, citrus, night scene pictures walking camels against a
   purple and black background, 10" x 11" 12 16 19

Esporanza, CA, citrus, pictures a senorita with a carnation in her hair,
   wearing a lace mantilla and holding a lace fan against a blue back-
   ground, 10" x 11" 2 4 5

Exeter, CA, citrus, Tulare Co., map against a multi-colored background,
   10" x 11" 2 4 5

Fide, CA, citrus, white puppy with black spot against a black background,
   12.5" x 8.5" 19 25 30

Fillmore Crest, CA, citrus, blue border frames 3 oranges and green
   leaves against a turquoise background, 10"x 11" 2 4 6

First Blue, WA, apple, photo of 3 apples, light blue and orange letters,
   on a yellow sash, blue background 3 6 9

Flavor Crest, treasure chest full of red and golden apples (apple label
   from New York), blue background 12 16 20

Florida Cowboy, FL, citrus, cowboy astride bucking bronco with
   diamond K brand palm trees in background, 9" x 9" 6 12 18

Florita, CA, citrus, dancing senorita and 2 guitarists against a black
   background, 10" x 11" 7 11 14

Flying V, WA, apple, photo of red apple, yellow written letters and a
   V with wings on it, blue background 7 15 22

Foothills, OR, pear, old stone litho of orchard, mountain, river and 2
   pears 10 14 17

Full O' Juice, CA, citrus, pictures half-peeled orange and a glass of
   orange juice, lavender background, 10" x 11" 2 5 8

Galleon, CA, citrus, galleon sailing on the open sea, sky background,
   12.5" x 8.5" 3 6 9

Gladiola, CA, citrus, 2 gladiola sprays on a gold and tan background,
   10" x 11" 3 6 9

Globes 0' Gold, CA, citrus, pictures 3 oranges, blossoms, leaves,
   10" x 11" 2 3 4

Gold Buckle, CA, citrus, outline of a belt with a gold buckle frames an
   orchard scene against a blue background, 10" x 11" 2 5 8

Gold Circle, CA, pear, gold circle, yellow circle, 2 pears, graphic,
   blue background 4 8 11

Kings Park, CA, citrus, pictures a waterfall and mountain stream,
   10" x 11" 3 6 9

La Relna, CA, citrus, hacienda scene with Spanish senorita holding a
   black fan against a blue background, 10" x 11 .... 2 3 4

Lake View, WA, apple, 2 goldens with a red apple between them,
   scene of the Pajaro Valley, old, blue background, green border 12 16 19

Lakecove, CA, pear, barefoot boy with straw hat on, loaning on a tree,
   lake and mountain 12 16 19

Lamb, WA, apple, Lamb's first printing, lamb standing on a hillside

LOW AVG. HIGH

with orchard mountain background, 2 red apples hanging over
its head, blue/black border, 19205 ar2rk, beautiful .... $ 125 $ 150 $ 175

Laurea, CA, citrus, pictures oranges, berries, laurel leaves, blue
background, 10" x 11" 2 3 4

Laurie, CA, apple, little girl with an apple in each hand, she has a pink
dress on, blue background, 1930s label, rare 22 27 31

Leavenworth, WA, pear, 2 green pears with white loners, blue
background 3 7 10

Legal Tender, CA, citrus, pictures U.S, currency in a $250 bundle
against a blue and black background, 10" x 11" 2 5 8

Lincoln, CA, citrus, portrait of Lincoln with oranges and leaves, 10" x 11" ... 3 6 9

Loch Lomond, CA, citrus, Scottish scene on blue and green plaid
background, 10" x 11" 2 3 4

Loop Loop, WA, apple, Indian chief on a palomino horse, he is picking
an apple from the horse's back 21 26 31

Loot of Ventura County, CA, citrus, multi-colored, 10"x11" 3 6 9

Lucky Lad, WA, apple, large red apple with image of the 1920s farm
boy in front of it, gold letters, black background, green border 110 130 150

Lure, WA, apple, image of a big, largemouth bass hooked on a fish plug,
bright red letters, blue border 60 70 80

Luxor, WA, apple, big red Maltese cross with the name Luxor in white
on it, blue background 23 27 31

Nimble, CL, citrus, pictures an orange and blossoms against an orchard
landscape, aqua background, 10"x11" 2 3 4

Nob Hill, CA, pear, Metropolitan skyscrapers, autos and street cars 11 15 19

Orchard King, CL, citrus, orange, with crown, royal blue background,
10" x 11" 2 3 4

Oriole, CA, citrus, oriole perched on a branch with orange, blossoms and
leaves, black background, 10" x 11" 6 10 13

Orland, CA, citrus, pictures old dam scene, 10" x 11" 9 14 18

Our Pride, WA, apple, parrot sitting on a twig, one red apple, black
background, blue border, copy 1923, 40 lbs. 11 15 19

Prinoeso, CA, citrus, princess in royal robes and crown jewels, with
grapefruits, leaves on a blue background, dated 1911 .... 3 5 7

Pyramid, Canada, apple, 3 pyramids with river, palm trees, camel
and rider, blue background 23 28 32

Queen Esther, CA, citrus, elegant queen dressed in turquoise gown,
golden crown, 10" x 11" 5 8 11

Queen Fruits, WA, pear, 2 pears, old queen in full dress, blue background 23 29 34

Quercus Ranch, CA, pear, orchard, sky, lake mountains and 2 pears 7 10 13

Rancheria, CA, pear, Indian Chief on horse by a maiden, teepees, black
background 5 9 13

Red Bird, CA, citrus, large red eagle, black background, 10" x 11" 2 3 4

Red Label, WA, apple, valley scene with town roads, river and mountains,
2 large red apples in the sky, red border 35 41 47

Red Peak, CA, citrus, landscape scene, 10" x 11" 2 3 4

Red Seal, WA, apple, red ribbon with old-time red wax seal, 2 red apples,
white letters, green background 4 7 10

Red Star, CA, apple, big red star in the center, red and white letters, black
background, red border 9 13 16

LOW AVG. HIGH

Red Streak, WA apple, 2 drawn apples, one red and one golden, red
    lightning streak shooting through the label, black background, red
    border .... $ 31 $ 38 $ 46

Red Wagon, WA, apple, cartoon boy pulling a red wagon full of red
    and golden apples, black background, yellow border 18   24   28

Redlands Best, CA, citrus, 4 blue arrows pointing to big orange in
    center, 10" x 11" 4   8   12

Reindeer, CA, citrus, reindeer and grove scene against a yellow back-
    ground, 10" x 11" 4   8   12

Repetition, WA, apple, 3 identical boys in front of 3 identical
    boxes of apples with the same label on them, black background 23   30   36

Rocky Hill, CA, citrus, Indian chief on horse standing on cliff against a
    blue background, 10" x11" 2   3   4

Rose, WA, apple, 2 large red roses with thorns and leaves, white letters,
    blue background 7   12   17

Round Robin, OR, pear, big red robin standing on a hill, old, blue
    background 18   24   30

Royal Feast, CA, citrus, pictures orange, blossoms, dark blue leaves
    with 2 lions in black framed by a black checkered border, 10" x 11" 2   3   4

Royal Knight, CA, citrus, knight on horseback against a yellow back-
    ground, 10" x 11" 2   3   4

Sails, WA, apple, large sailing ship in a rough choppy sea, yellow and
    red letters, blue background, red pen line border, 40 lbs. 12   16   20

Sam Birch, OR, apple, one red apple, yellow strip through the label with
    blue letters on it, blue background 19   23   26

Safe Hit, TX, vegetables, 1920s baseball player hitting a ball, grandstand
    in the background, 7" x 9" 5   9   12

Sun Smile, CA, pear, smiling face of the sun, blue letters, also a blue
    anchor, sunburst background 6   10   14

Sun Sugared, OR, pear, photo of an orange pear, black background 2   5   8

Super Crisp, WA, apple, 2 1/2 apples, one red and one golden,
    orchard, house, hill, writing in the sky, blue border, c. 1948 3   7   10

Super-Pak, WA, apple, blue ribbon in a triangle with the lettering on it,
    black background 2   5   8

Sure Mark, CA, pear, red stripes, blue background 6   10   13

Surety, WA, apple, stone litho of a steamship in a cove with pine trees,
    orchards, mountains, red sky with blue letters in the sky, in the corner
    it says "FROM TREE TO TRADE." a busy red-lace-type border 11   16   20

Swan, WA, apple, big white swan on the water, orange letters, black
    background 12   17   22

Sweet Sue, WA, apple, 3 red apples in the center of the label with an
    inset in front of them with 1920s lady's face, white letters, brown
    and green border 19   25   31

Maps

Maps have a long collecting history. Those listed here are some of the earliest still available on the market. You won't find these in the glove compartment of your car, but we've seen these treasures at estate sales and small auctions throughout the country.

Maps are more valuable with original hand coloring, but beware of old maps with new hand coloring. Tears, stains, poor printing, and trimmed margins all reduce value. Maps of the New World are more valuable than those of Europe, especially those of obscure central European areas. A map is almost always more valuable when sold in the area it depicts. The more important the mapmaker, the more valuable the map.

For further information, see *Mercator's World* magazine. An extensive listing of maps sold at auction appears in *American Book Prices Current*, edited by Katherine and Daniel Leab, at American Book Prices Current, Box 1236, Washington, CT 06793.

In the following entries, the maker is listed first, followed by the title of the map, the place of publication, the date, and the size. The following abbreviations are used: place of printing not identified-N.p.; London-L; New York-NY. Information given in brackets does not appear printed on the map itself.

Emanuel Bowen, A New Map of Georgia, w/ Part of Carolina....,London, 1742, $1250 at auction. — Photo courtesy of Northeast Auctions.

	AUCTION	RETAIL Low	High
Blaeu, Willem and Jan, Surria, vernacule Surrey., [Amst., 1667], 378 mm x 498 mm	$ 100	$ 125	$ 400
Blome, Richard, A Mapp or Generall Carte of the World...., L, [1670 or later], 427 mm x 533 mm	1200	2000	4000
Bowen, Emanuel, A New Map of Georgia, w/ Part of Carolina...., L, 1748, 363 mm x 475 mm	300	600	1200
Bradley, Abraham, Map of the United States...., [Phila., 1796], 4 sheets, totalling 880 mm x 955 mm	11,000	18,500	37,000
Brion De La Tour, Louis, Mappe monde geo-hydrographique, Paris 1786, 452 mm x 640 mm	170	200	600
Bry, Theodor De, America sive novus orbis respectu Europaeorum...., Frankfurt, 1596, 330 mm x 400 mm	2400	4060	8000

	AUCTION	RETAIL Low	High
Burr, David H., Map of New Jersey and Pennsylvania, Wash., 10 July 1839, 2 sheets, tog. 37.5" x 50.5"	$ 450	$ 750	$ 1500
Cantelli Da Vignola, G., Accuratis sima totius Regni Hispaniae...., Amst., [c.1680], 19.5" x 22.75".,	100	200	400
Cary, John, A New Map of Part of the United States...., L, 1811, 450 mm x 506 mm	130	200	400
Colton, J. H., Map of the United States of America...., NY, 1854, 32" x 50.5"	100	160	300
Colton, J. H., Map of the U.S....routes of ... Mail Steam Packets...., NY, 1849	750	1250	2500
Colton, J. H., Map of the U.S., the British Provinces, Mexico &c., NY, 1849, 483 mm x 635 mm	500	800	1800
Cook, James, A Draught of Port Royal Harbour...., L: E. Bowen, [1766], 547 mm x 761 mm	3000	5000	10,000
Cook, James, A Draught of West Forida...., L: E. Bowen, [1776], 540 mm x 1,326 mm	6000	10,000	20,000
De Lisle, Guillaume De, Carte d Afrique dressee pour l'usage du Roy., Paris, 1722, 482 mm x 622 mm	100	125	400
De Wit, Frederick, Regnum Hungaria...., Amst., [c. 1680], 19" x 23".	150	250	500
Eddy, William M., Official Map of San Francisco...., Wash., 1849, 25" x 19"	360	500	1200
Ellicott, Andrew, Plan of the City of Washington...., Phila., 1792, 338 mm x 420 mm	3750	6250	12,500
Ellicott, Andrew, Territory of Columbia., [Phila., 1793-94], 588 mm x 590 mm	5250	8750	17,500
Endasian, Elia, Amerika, [Venice: Monastery of St. Lazar,1787], 553 mm x 724 mm	2600	4300	8800
Evans, Lewis, ... Middle British Colonies in America...., Phila., 1755, 549 mm x 745 mm	800	1300	2800
Evans, Lewis, A Map of Pensilvania, New-Jersey, New-York..., Phila., 1749, 635 mm x 495 mm	21,000	35,000	70,000
Evans, Lewis, A Map of the Middle British Colonies in America...., L, 1776, 595 mm x 978 mm	2800	4600	9400
Faden, William, A Plan of the Town...of Charlestown..., L, 1780, 548 mm x 719 mm	600	1000	2200
Faden, William, Plan of the City and Environs of Quebec, with its Siege and Blockade by the Americans...., L, 1776, 445 mm x 617 mm	750	1250	2500
Faden, William, The Province of New Jersey., [L, 1777], 810 mm x 614 mm	1400	2500	5000
Flemming, C., Texas, Glogau, [c.1840-45] 16" x 12.75"	250	400	800
Gascoigne, John, A Plan of Port Royal in South Carolina, [L: Jeffreys & Faden, 1776], 841 mm x 661 mm	15,000	20,000	47,500
Goos, Pieter, Pascaerte van Nieu Yederlandt and Virginies., [N.p., c. 1660], 434 mm x 535 mm	1800	3000	6000
Harenberg, I.C., Palaestina seu Terra olim Sancta...., Nuremberg: Heredes Homaniani, 1744, 500 mm x 585 mm	100	200	400
Harrison, John, Map of the City of New-York...., NY, 1852, 24 sections, 2305 mm x 1225 mm	600	1000	2000

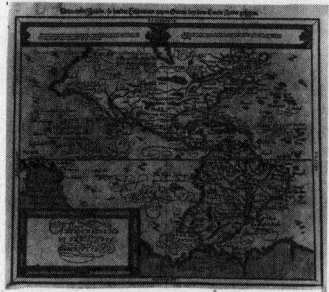
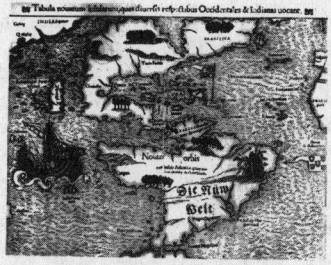

Above: When detail is lacking because the area was unexplored, the value is increased. — Photos courtesy of Phillips Auctioneers. Below: When detail is lacking because the map maker was trying to save time and space, the value is decreased.

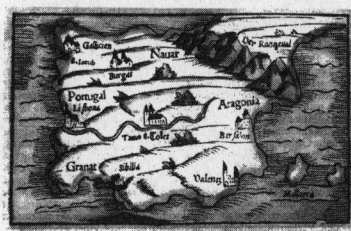

	AUCTION	RETAIL	
		Low	High
Hills, John, Sketch of the Position of the British Force at Elizabeth..., L, 1784, 666 mm x 551 mm	$ 2400	$ 4000	$ 8000
Holme, Thomas, A Mapp of Ye Improved Part of Pensilvania..., L, [1715], 444 mm x 578 mm	5000	8000	17,500
Homann, Johann B., Judaea seu Palaestina...., Nuremberg, [1720], 498 mm x 585 mm	100	125	400
Homann, Johann B., Nova Anglia septentrionali Americae..., Nuremberg, 1716, 485 mm x 578 mm	300	500	1000
Hondius, Jodocus, Tartaria., [Amst., 1613], 340 mm x 490 mm, hand-colored	100	150	300
Hutawa, Julius, Map of Mexico and California., St. Louis, 1863	400	800	1600
Hutchins, Thomas, A New Map of the Western Parts of Virginia, Penn...., L, 1778, 28 sections, tog. 900 mm x 1002 mm	6750	11,000	22,500
Janssonius, Joannes, America noviter delineata, Amst., [c.1650], 14.6" x 19.5".	860	1400	2900
Jefferson, T. H., Map of the Emigrant Road From Independence, Mo. to St. Francisco, Calif...., NY, 1849, 4 sec., tog. 396 mm x 555 mm	20,000	40,000	95,000
Jefferys, Thomas, A Map of the Most Inhabited Part of New England...., L, 1755, 4 sheets joined as 2.	5600	9300	18,000

	AUCTION	RETAIL Low	High
Keeler, William J., National Map of the...United States...., Wash., J.F. Gedney, [1867], 50" x 60"	$ 500	$ 800	$ 1800
Keulen, Gerard Van, Pas Kaart van de Zee Kusten van Virginia, Amst., [1684], 530 mm x 605 mm	600	1000	2000
Keulen, Gerard Van, Pas-Kaart vande Zee kusten van, Nieuw Nederland anders genaamt Niew York, Amst., [1684 or later], 528 mm x 608 mm	1600	2500	5000
Lawson, J. T., Lawson's Map From Actual Survey of the Gold..., Regions of Upper California...., NY: Dewitt & Davenport. [c.1849], 14.8" x 20.75"	1000	1800	3800
Lotter, Conrad, A Map of the Most Inhabited Part of New England, Augsburg 1776, 674 mm x 552 mm	1200	2000	4200
Lotter, T. C., Pensylvania, Nova Jersey et Nova York...., Augsburg, [c.1748], 570 mm x 500 mm	250	400	800
Lotter, Tobias C., America Septentrionalis, Concinnata..., 452 mm x 580 mm	300	660	1300
Madison, James, A Map of Virginia, formed from surveys, 9 sheets, ea. 585 mm x 875 mm	17,250	30,000	57,000
Mather, W.W., Geological Map of Long & Staten Islands..., NY, 1842, 22.5" x 50.7"	300	500	1000
Melish, John, United States of America, Phila., 1820, 16.75" x 21"	200	470	900
Mercator, Gerard, Guiana, sive Amazonum regio. Amst., [1636, or later], 375 mm x 485 mm	100	300	600
Moll, Hermann, A General Map of New France...., L, 1703. 8.75" x 13.25"	100	125	400
Moll, Hermann, Map of South America, L, [1720], 22.75" x 37.5"	250	400	800
Montanus, Arnoldus, Guiana sive Amazonum Regio., [N.p., 1671], 11" x 14".	100	160	300
Montresor, Capt. J., A Map of the Province of New York...., L, 1777, 4 sheets, 757 mm x 967 mm	1800	3000	6000
Montresor, John, A Plan of the City of New-York & Its Environs...., L, [1775], 2d issue, 678 mm x 554 mm	3000	5000	10,000
Mouzon, Henry, An Accurate Map of North and South Carolina, L, 1794, 4 sheets joined as 2, ea. 534 mm x 1448 mm	1500	2500	5000
Muenster, Sebastian, Altera generalis tabula secundum Ptolemaeum., [Basel?, c.1545, or later], 251 mm x 345 mm	300	600	1200
Munster, Sebastian, Novus Orbis, [Basel, 1540], 312 mm x 391 mm	2060	3400	7000
Ortelius, Abraham, Aevi veteris typus. ..[the Ancient World], Antwerp, 1590 [i.e. 1612], 12.25" x 17.25"	200	300	800
Ortelius, Abraham, Americae sive novi orbis..., [Antwerp, 1570 or later], 420 mm x 554 mm	2250	3750	7500
Ortelius, Abraham, Culiacanae, Americae... Hispaniolae, Cubae...., [Antwerp, 1603], 2 maps on 1 sheet, 14" x 19.5"	450	750	1500
Ortelius, Abraham, Tusciae antiquae typus., [Amst., 1601], 12.75" x 18.75"	100	160	300
Ortelius, Asraham, Hiberniae Britanicas Insulae.., [Antwerp, 1595 or later], 349 mm x 476 mm	360	500	1200
Park, Moses, Plan of the Colony of Connecticut..., 24 Nov 1776,			

Above: Historical associations, like this 1852 map of California's gold regions, add to the value of a map. Below: An early map of a current popular vacation destination is far more valuable than an unvisited wasteland. — Photos courtesy of Phillips Auctioneers.

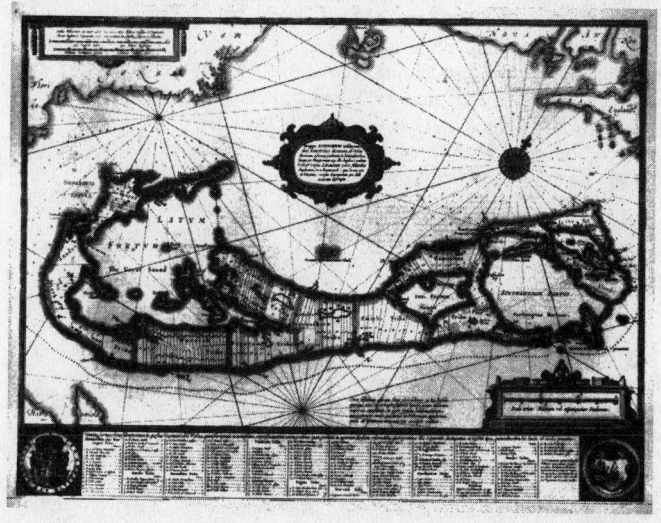

	AUCTION	RETAIL Low	High
546 mm x 788 mm	$ 9000	$ 15,000	$ 30,000
Randel, John, The City of New York, NY, 1821, 16 parts, 655 mm x 950 mm	1200	2000	4000
Ratzer, Bernard, Plan of the City of New York...., [L, c. 1767], 1st State, 624 mm x 940 mm	6000	10,000	20,000
Ratzer, Bernard, Plan of the City of New York..., Surveyed in the Years 1766 & 1767, L, 1776, 2 sheets, ea. 634 mm x 922 mm	10,000	17,500	35,000
Sanson, Guillaume, Atlantis insula, Paris, 1669, 397 mm x 556 mm	600	1000	2000
Santini, Francois, Carte des Nouvelles Decouvertes..., Venice, [c.1776], 445 mm x 620 mm	100	125	400
Sauthier, Claude J., A Plan of the Operations of the King's Army, under the Command of General Sr. William Howe...., L, 1777, 2d, issue, with 3 British ships off "Terry Town," 758 mm x 552 mm	1600	2800	5600
Schenk, Pieter, America Septentrionalis, Amst, [early 18th c.], 19" x 22.5"	100	150	300
Scull, N. & Heap, G., A Plan of the City and Environs of Phila...., L: Faden, 12 Mar 1777, 625 mm x 460 mm	100	200	400
Seutter, Matthaeus, Africa juxta navigationes et observationes...., Augsburg, [1735], 497 mm x 579 mm	100	125	400
Seutter, Matthaeus, Pensylvania, Nova Jersey et Nova York...., Augsburg, [c. 1735], 580 mm x 500 mm	650	1000	2000
Smith, John Calvin, Colton's Map of the United States, NY, 1852, 36 sections totalling 1,643 mm x 2,071 mm	750	1250	2500
Smith, John Calvin, Map of North America...., NY, 1850, 527 mm x 482 mm plus margins.	450	750	1500
Speed, John, A New and Accurat Map of the World, L, [1626?], 395 mm x 520 mm	2400	4000	8000
Speed, John, Europ, and the Chief Cities...., L: G. Humble, 1626, 395 mm x 510 mm	400	600	1400
Taylor, Benjamin, A New & Accurate Plan of the City of New York...., NY, 1797, 625 mm x 978 mm	12,000	20,000	40,000
Tirion, Isaac, Nieuwe Kaart van het Westelykste Deel der Weerald...., Amst., 1754, 350 mm x 365 mm	100	150	300
Tirion, Isaak, Kaart van het Nieuw Mexico en van California, Amst., 1765, 12.25" x 13.5"	100	125	400
Visscher, Nikolaus, Insulae Americanae in Oceano..., [N.p., c. 1690], 18.25" x 22"	360	500	1200
Vrients, J. B., Serenissimae Reipublicae Genuensis..., Antwerp, 1608, 391 mm x 538 mm	100	200	400
Wells, Edward, A New Map of the Terraqueous Globe., Oxford, [c.1700], 14" x 20"	250	400	800
Whitman & Searl, Map of Eastern Kansas, Bost.: J.P. Jewett, 1856, 695 mm x 535 mm	400	600	1400
Williams, W., A New Map of the United States, Phila., 1853, 25" x 29.5"	150	250	500
Young, J. H., The Tourist's Pocket Map of the State of Indiana, Phila., 1833, 15.75" x 13.25"	100	150	300

Movie-Related Memorabilia

In 1909, the Motion Picture Patents Company standardized the size and purpose of posters. Currently, there are seven poster sizes. "Half sheets" (or display cards) are posters 28" x 22"; "one sheets" are 41" x 21"; "three sheets" are 81" x 41". Lobby cards are a set of 8 photos, each 14" x 11" depicting 8 different scenes from the movie. Sets that have four one quarter inch triangular cuts on the photos from mounting are worth 30% to 50% less. Heralds or flyers usually have similar artwork to larger posters, but are most often in two colors printed on 12" x 9" paper. Window cards measure 22" x 14" and inserts are 36" x 14".

Movie titles and dates followed by "R" refer to a re-release of the film, not the first first release.

Movie Posters

HALF SHEETS

	LOW	HIGH
Appointment With Shadow, 1958, B Keith	$ 10	$ 15
Arson For Hire, 1957, S Brodie	12	18
Buckskin Lady, 1957, P Medina	15	20
Cop Hater, 1958, R Loggia	10	18
Dangerous Passage, 1951, R Lowery	15	25
Date With Death, 1959, G Mohr	12	18
Hell Bound, 1957, M Woode	12	18
Hell Drivers, 1958, S Baker	15	20
High Hell, 1958, J Derek	10	18
Jet Attack, 1958, J Agar	10	15
Naked and the Dead, 1956, C Robertson	20	25
Natchez Trace, 1959, Z Scott	10	18
OSS 117, 1958, M Noel	10	15
Outlaw's Son, 1957, D Clark	12	18
Pier 5 Havanna, 1959, C Mitchell	15	20
San Quentin, R, 1950, J Cagney	140	194
Ten Thousand Bedrooms, 1957, D Martin	25	35
Under Fire, 1957, H Morgan	10	18
Verdict, 1946, P Lorre	60	86
Violent Road, 1958, B Keith	10	18

ONE SHEETS

Alexander the Great, 1955, R Burton	10	15
Barefoot Mailman, 1951, R Cummings	10	15
Bat, R, Vincent Price	40	53
Bittersweet, 1940, J MacDonald	550	750
Bribe, R-1965, A Gardner	10	15
Brother Rat and A Baby, 1940, R Reagan	150	200
Buck Rogers 1977, B Crabbe	30	47
Call of the Rockies, C Starrett	100	150
Camille, 1936, G Garbo	3500	5000
Captains Courageous, 1962, S Tracy	10	15
Casanova's Big Night, 1954, B Hope	30	50
Charlie Chan at the Olympics, W Oland	1500	2000
Chocolate Soldier, R-1962, N Eddy	10	15
City Lights, R-1972, C Chaplin	10	15

	LOW	HIGH
Damsel in Distress, 1937, F Astaire	$ 1300	$ 1900
Darby O'Gill and Little People, R, S Connery	10	15
David Copperfield, R-1962, WC Fields	10	15
Disraeli, R-1930, G Arliss	120	175
Dr Cadman's Secret/Silent Death, R, B Karloff	10	15
Fantasia, R-1989	50	70
Featurettes, 1949	10	15
Firefly, 1937, J MacDonald	230	320
Fishermans's Wharf, 1938, B Breen	900	1300
Flesh and Flame, R-1961, R Danton	10	15
For the First Time, 1959, M Lanza	10	15
Forbidden Planet, R-1975	10	15
Four Sons, 1940, D Ameche	80	114
Four Wives, 1939, P Lane	110	154
Four's A Crowd, 1938, E Flynn	700	1000
Forty-five Fathoms, 1937, J Withers	90	125
Good Earth, R-1962, P Muni	10	15
Grand Hotel, R-1970, G Garbo	10	15
Great Dan Patch, R-1960, D O'Keefe	10	15
Great Dictator, R-1972, Chaplin	10	15
Great Guns, 1941, L/H	1000	1500
Great Lie, 1941, B Davis	900	1250
Green Dolphin Street, R-1955, L Turner	20	28
Green Light, R, duotone	10	15
Harrigan's Kid, 1943, B Readick	50	65
He Married His Wife, 1939, J McCrae	80	115
House of Wax, R-1981, V Price	10	15
In Old Kentucky, 1935, W Rogers	550	765
In the Meantime Darling, 1944, J Crain	60	84
Irish Eyes Are Smiling, 1944, J Haver	80	115
Janie, 1944, J Leslie	70	96
Janie Gets Married, 1946, J Leslie	50	65
Julius Caesar, 1953, M Brando	10	15
Keeper of the Flame, 1943, Tracy/Hepburn	600	900
King in New York, R-1960, Chaplin	10	15
King of the Lumberjacks, 1940, J Payne	60	86
Lady Let's Dance, 1944, Belita	40	56
Lili, 1953, L Caron	10	15
Little Men, 1935, R Morgan	20	32
Little Women, R-1962, E Taylor	10	15
Love Finds Andy Hardy, 1938, J Garland	900	1200
Magnificent Obsession, R-1947, I Dunne	40	60
Make Your Own Bed, 1943, J Wyman	60	86
Man Who Knew Too Much, R-1983, J Stewart	10	15
Major Bowes Amateur Theatre, 1935	90	125
Miss Susie Slagles, 1946, V Lake	150	200
Mr.Skeffington, 1943, B Davis	640	900
Mrs Miniver, R-1971, G Garson	10	15
Monsieur Verdoux, R-1972, Chaplin	10	15
Moon Is Blue, R-1960, W Holden	10	15
Mother Carey's Chickens, 1938, R Keeler	250	350

	LOW	HIGH
Mother Wore Tights, 1947, B Grable	$ 360	$ 500
Mutiny in the County, R-1950, E Kennedy	10	15
Mutiny on Bounty, R-1971, C Gable	10	15
National Velvet, R-1971, E Taylor	10	15
Old Maid, 1939, B Davis	1500	2000
Old Yeller, R-1965, T Kirk	10	15
Out of This World, 1945, V Lake	80	115
Pardners, R-1965, Lewis/Martin	10	15
Park Avenue Logger, 1937, G O'Brien	80	115
Perilous Holiday, 1946, P O'Brien	60	86
Philadelphia Story, R, C Grant	10	15
Pillow Talk/Operation Petticoat, R	10	15
Pin Up Girl, 1940, B Grable	1000	1500
Prairie Thunder, R, D Foran	40	60
Pride and Prejudice, R-1962, L Olivier	10	15
Rainbow on River, 1937, B Breen	90	125
Romance and Rhythm, R-1953, P Silvers	10	15
Rose Marie, R-1962, H Keele	10	15
Royal Scandal, 1945, T Bankhead	160	230
Samson and Delilah, R-1968, V Mature	10	15
San Francisco, R-1971, C Gable	10	15
Say It in French, 1938, R Milland	70	95
Sayonara, 1957, M Brando	10	15
Sgt York, 1941, G Cooper	1300	1900
Shaggy Dog, R-1967, T Kirk	10	15
Skipper Surprised His Wife, 1950, R Walker	10	15
Stablemates, R-1975, M Rooney	10	15
Statlon West, R-1954, D Powell	10	15
Stranger at My Door, 1956, M Carey	10	15
Strawberry Blonde, 1941, J Cagney	550	750
Sweet Rosie O'Grady, 1943, B Grable	460	637
Sweethearts, R-1962, J MacDonald	10	15
Tale of Two Cities, R-1962, R Colman	10	15
Test Pilot, 1938, C Gable	10	15
Thief of Damascus, 1952, P Henreid	10	15
This is Cinerama, R-1973	10	15
This is the Life, J Withers	90	125
Three Secrets, 1950, E Parker	10	15
Three Sons O Guns, 1941, W Morris	10	15
Thunderhoof, 1948, P Foster	10	15
Treasure Island, R-1975, R Newton	10	15
Trouble With Harry, R-1983, S MacLaine	10	15
Twinkle in God's Eye, 1955, M Rooney	10	15
Ulysses, R-1960, K Douglas	10	15
Uncle Tom's Cabin, R-1954, R Massey	10	15
Vanquished, 1953, J Payne	10	15
Virginia, 1941, M Carrol	400	550
Virginia Judge, 1935, W Kelly	10	15
Viva Cisco Kid, 1940, C Romero	160	230
Wallflower, 1948, J Reynolds	10	15
War of Worlds/When Worlds Collide, R-1977	40	53

	LOW	HIGH
Way to the Gold, 1957, J Hunter	$ 10	$ 15
When's Your Birthday, J E Brown	150	200
Wild and Wolfy, R, T Avery	40	53
Windjammer, 1937, G O'Brien	90	125
Women of Paris, R-1953, G Sanders	10	15
Wrong Room, R-1952, L Errol	10	15
Yes My Darling Daughter, 1939, P Lane	90	125
You Can't Ration Love, 1944, B Rhodes	70	100
You Can't Run Away From It, 1956, J Allyson	10	15
Young As You Feel, 1940, Jones Family	80	115

THREE SHEETS

Charlie McCarthy Detective, 1939, E Bergen	10	14
Cleopatra, 1934, C Colbert	20	26
Dust Be My Destiny, 1939, J Garfield	10	14
Half Angel, 1936, F Dee	9	13
His Girl Friday, 1940, C Grant	12	16
I'll Tell the World, 1934, L Tracy	10	14
Mr Smith Goes to Washington, 1939, J Stewart	12	16
My Love Came Back, 1940, O DeHavilland	10	14
Petticoat Fever, 1936, W Powell	10	14
Phantom of Rue Morgue, 1954, K Maldon	90	128
Private Lives of Elizabeth and Essex, 1939, Davis/Flynn	10	14
Professional Soldier, 1935, V McLaughlin	9	13
Scarlet Empress, 1934, M Dietrich	20	26
She Loves Me Not, 1934, B Crosby	10	14
Shipmates Forever, 1935, R Keeler	9	13
Spring Parade, 1940, D Durbin	9	13
Wings in the Dark, 1934, C Grant	10	15

Pressbooks

Animal Crackers, R, 1974, Marx Bros	12	16
Buckaneer, 1958, Y Brynner	8	10
Dancing Pirate, 1936, C Collins	12	16
Gold Rush, R, 1973, Chaplin	8	10
Imitation of Life, R, 1965, L Turner	8	10
Jamboree, 1957, F Domino	6	8
Limelight, R, 1972, Chaplin	8	10
Man Who Knew Too Much, R, 1963, J Stewart	12	16
North by Northwest, R, 1966	8	10
Pack Train, 1953, G Autry	12	16
Streetcar Named Desire, R, 1970, M Brando	10	12
Ten Seconds to Hell, 1959, J Chandler	9	11
Thunder Over Arizona, 1956, S Homeier	8	10
White Christmas, R, 1961, B Crosby	8	10
Words and Music, R, 1962, J Garland	8	10

Lobby Cards

	LOW	HIGH
Affair With a Stranger, 1953, V Mature	$ 20	$ 25
Affairs of Dobie Gillis, 1950, D Reynolds	20	25
All Ashore, 1953, M Rooney	20	25
All This and Heaven Too, 1940, B Davis	1090	1530
Angry Hills, 1957, R Mitchum	25	30
Anything Can Happen, 1952, J Ferrer	20	25
Arena, 1953, G Young	20	25
Around the World in 80 Days, 1958, D Niven	35	50
Arsenic and Old Lace, 1940, C Grant	730	1020
Ask Any Girl, 1959, D Niven	20	25
Auntie Mame, 1958, R Russell	25	30
Autumn Leaves, 1955, J Crawford	20	25
Bachelor of Hearts, 1958, H Kruger	20	25
Bachelor Party, 1957, D Murray	15	20
Bandit of Zhobe, 1959, V Mature	15	20
Battle Stations, 1956, J Lund	15	20
Beau Brummel, 1957, E Taylor	20	25
Bedeviled, 1955, A Baxter	20	25
Beyond the Time Barrier, 1959, R Clarke	15	20
Black Dakotas, 1954, G Merrill	15	20
Black Knight, 1954, A Ladd	20	25
Black Orchid, 1959, S Loren	20	25
Blackjack Ketchum, Desperado, 1956, H Duff	20	25
Blood and Steel, 1959, J Lupton	20	25
Blue Grass of Kentucky, 1950, B Williams	20	25
Bobbikins, 1959, M Bygraves	15	20
Bomba and the Jungle Girl, 1952, J Sheffield	20	25
Bonjour Tristesse, 1958, D Kerr	20	25
Boots Malone, 1950, W Holden	20	25
Brigand, 1952, A Dexter	15	20
Bring Your Smile Along, 1950, F Laine	15	20
Broken Arrow, 1950, J Stewart	20	25
Brothers Karamazov, 1958, Y Brenner	20	25
Brothers Rico, 1957, R Conte	15	20
But Not For Me, 1959, C Gable	25	30
Caddy, 1953, J Lewis	25	30
Calypso Heat Wave, 1957, J Desmond	20	25
Calypso Joe, 1957, H Jeffries	20	25
Camille, 1936, G Garbo	4500	6500
Captain Lightfoot, 1955, R Hudson	20	25
Captain's Table, 1959, J Gregson	20	25
Case Against Brooklyn, 1958, D McGavin	15	20
Cave of Outlaws, 1951, M Carey	15	20
Cell 2455, Death Row, 1955, W Campbell	20	25
Challenge the Wind, 1954, Graham	15	20
City of Fear, 1959, V Edwards	20	25
Cobweb, 1955, R Widmark	20	25
Dalton Girls, 1957, M Anders	25	30
Damsel in Distress, 1937, F Astair	1800	2500
Dangerous Crossings, 1953, J Crain	20	25

	LOW	HIGH
Dangerous Exile, 1958, L Jordan	$ 20	$ 25
Dawn at Socorro, 1954, R Calhoun	20	25
Detective, 1954, A Guiness	20	25
Devil's Canyon, 1953, D Robertson	20	25
Devil's Disciple, 1959, B Lancaster	20	25
Diamond Horseshoe, 1945, B Grable	460	637
Disc Jockey, 1951, G Simms	20	25
Disraeli, R, 1930, G Arliss	180	254
Don't Give Up the Ship, 1959, J Lewis	30	45
Dr's Dilemma, 1959, L Caron	10	15
Drums of Tahiti, 1953, D O'Keefe	15	20
Fake, 1953, D O'Keefe	15	20
Family Secret, 1951, J Derek	15	20
Fiend Without a Face, 1958, M Thompson	20	25
Fighter, 1952, R Conte	15	20
Fighting Lawmen, 1954, W Morris	20	25
Finders Keepers, 1951, T Ewell	15	20
Finger of Guilt, 1956, R Basehart	20	25
Flood Tide, 1958, G Nader	15	20
Floods of Fear, 1959, H Keel	20	25
Flying Fontaines, 1959	20	25
Footsteps in the Fog, 1955, S Granger	20	25
Francis Goes to West Point, 1952, D O'Conner	20	25
Frontier Marshall, 1939, R Scott	150	212
Fugitive Lady, 1951	20	25
Full of Life, 1957, J Holliday	20	25
Fury at Gunsight Pass, 1956, D Brian	15	20
Goddess, 1958, K Stanley	15	20
Going Steady, 1958, H Bee	10	15
Good Morning Judge, 1928, R Denny	150	207
Great Diamond Robbery, 1954, R Skelton	20	25
Gun Belt, 1953, G Montgomery	20	25
Gun for a Coward, 1956, F MacMurray	10	15
Gun Glory, 1957, S Granger	15	20
Handle With Care, 1958, D Jones	15	20
I Accuse, 1957, J Ferrer	20	25
I've Lived Before, 1956, J Mahoney	20	25
Illegal, 1955, E Robinson	25	30
Imitation General, 1958, G Ford	25	30
Indian Fighter, 1955, K Douglas	20	25
It Happened in Rome, 1959, J Laverick	15	20
Jayhawkers, 1959, J Chandler	20	25
Julie, 1956, D Day	20	25
Kind Lady, 1951, E Barrymore	20	25
Last Train From Gun Hill, 1959, K Douglas	30	45
Living It Up, 1954, J Lewis	30	45
Long Gray Line, 1954, T Power	20	25
Look Back in Anger, 1959, R Burton	25	35
Love Me or Leave Me, 1955, D Day	20	25
Mambo, 1954, M Rennie	15	20
Man From Bitter Ridge, 1955	15	20

	LOW	HIGH
Man Who Never Was, 1956, C Webb	$ 20	$ 25
Massacre Canyon, 1954, P Carey	15	20
Miss Sadie Thompson, 1953, R Hayworth	40	60
Mrs Mike, 1949, D Powell	20	25
Miller's Beautiful Wife, 1957, S Loren	30	45
Mr Drake's Duck, 1951, D Fairbanks Jr	20	25
My Teenage Daughter, 1958, S Syrns	15	20
Navy Air Patrol, 1955, J Derek	20	25
Never Steal Anything Small, 1959, J Cagney	20	25
Night Holds Terror, 1955, J Kelly	20	25
Odongo, 1956, R Fleming	15	20
Outlaw Stallion, 1954, P Carey	15	20
Paratroop Command, 1959, R Bakalyan	10	15
Paula, 1952, L Young	20	25
Pharoah's Curse, 1957, M Dana	20	25
Port Sinister, 1953, J Warren	15	20
Prisoner, 1955, A Guinness	25	30
Quo Vadis, 1950, D Kerr	15	20
Rabbit Trap, 1959, E Borgnine	20	25
Redhead and the Cowboy, 1952, G Ford	20	25
Reluctant Debutante, 1958, R Harrison	20	25
Ride the High Iron, 1956, R Burr	20	25
Robbery Under Arms, 1957, P Finch	10	15
Rock-A-Bye Baby, 1958, J Lewis	20	25
Savage Horde, 1949, W Elliott	20	25
Scandal Inc, 1956, R Hutton	20	25
Secret of Treasure Mountain, 1956, R Burr	20	25
Serpent of the Nile, 1953, R Fleming	20	25
Shall We Dance, 1937, Astaire/Rogers	3540	5000
Shanghai Story, 1954, R Roman	20	25
She Played With Fire, 1958, J Hawkins	20	25
Silk Stockings, 1957, F Astaire	30	50
Silken Affair, 1957, D Niven	25	35
Slight Case of Larceny, 1953, M Rooney	20	25
South Paclfic, 1959, M Gaynor	20	25
Stopover Tokyo, 1957, R Wagner	15	20
Strange One, 1957, G Peppard	20	25
Subway in the Sky, 1959, V Johnson	10	15
Summer Place, 1959, S Dee	15	20
Svengali, 1955, H Neff	15	20
Take the High Ground, 1953, R Windmark	20	25
Teahouse of the August Moon, 1956, M Brando	20	25
Tennessee Champ, 1954, S Winters	20	25
Tension at Table Rock, 1956, R Egan	15	20
Teresa, 1951, J Ericson	10	15
That Man FromTangier, 1953, N Asther	15	20
Timbuktu, 1959, V Mature	15	20
Tip on a Dead Jockey, 1957, R Taylor	20	25
To Have and Have Not, 1940, H Bogart	900	1275
Tokyo After Dark, 1959, M Kobi	20	25
Toward the Unknown, 1956, W Holden	20	25

	LOW	HIGH
Trail Blazers, 1953, A Hale Jr	$ 20	$ 25
Trap, 1959, R Widmark	20	25
True Story of Lynn Stuart, 1958, B Palmer	10	15
Until They Sail, 1957, P Newman	25	55
Uranium Boom, 1956, D Morgan	20	25
Valerie, 1957, A Ekberg	15	20
Value for Money, 1955, J Gregson	10	15
War and Peace, 1955, H Fonda	20	25
Warrior and the Slave Girl, 1959, E Manni	20	25
Watch on Rhine, 1943, B Davis	900	1275
Werewolf, 1956, S Ritch	20	25
Where's Charlie?, 1952, R Bolger	10	15
Whistle at Eaton Falls, 1951, L Bridges	20	25
Wicked as They Come, 1956, P Carey	15	20
Wonderful Country, 1959, R Mitchum	20	25
Yankee Doodle Dandy, 1942, J Cagney	900	1275
Yesterday's Enemy, 1959, S Baker	10	15
You're Never Too Young, 1954, Lewis/Martin	30	50

Other

Big Hangover, 1950, V Johnson, insert, 36" x 14"	24	35
Bombs Over China, R, 1961, R Reagan, 60" x 40"	37	50
Chatterbox, 1943, J Canova, insert, 36" x 14"	33	43
Evening With Batman and Robin, R, 1966, insert, 36" x 14"	27	35
Gone With theWind, R, 1954, 81" x 81"	350	600
Henry and Dizzy, 1942, J Lyden, insert, 36" x 14"	18	30
I Was a Teenage Caveman, 1958, R Vaughn, insert, 36" x 14"	90	120
Jailhouse Rock, R, Elvis, 40" x 30"	30	40
Masquerade in Mexico, 1945, D Lamour, insert, 36" x 14"	33	45
She Devil, 1957, M Blanchad, 60" x 40"	36	45
Vertigo/To Catch a Thief, R, 1963, window card, 22" x 14"	30	40
What Price Glory, 1952, J Cagney, insert, 36" x 14"	35	45
Wild One, R, M Brando, 40" x 30"	30	40

Postcards

Picture postcards in the United States started in 1893 at the Columbian Exposition. By 1910, they were a national craze with nearly a billion cards being sent through the mail. In 1914, the introduction of the folding greeting card began the rapid decline of this "Golden Age" of postcards. While collectors are mainly looking for postcards from this early period, there are many wonderful cards from the 1920s through the present day that are also prized by collectors.

Postcards are roughly divided into three categories: greeting cards, view cards, and real photo cards. A greeting card is any card designed by an artist. This includes all the holidays (including the popular Halloween and Santa cards), children, animals, advertising, romance, Art Nouveau, etc. Many of the better greeting cards are embossed, highly colorful and beautifully designed. Some of the best-known publishers include Tuck, Winsch, and PFB . Many of these cards are "artist signed," meaning that the artist's name is on the front of the card. Some of the rarer types of greetings include hold-to-the-lights and mechanicals.

View cards are pictures of specific places, typically prints made from a photograph. They may be black and white or colored and were usually mass produced. Views are the most widely collected postcards since nearly every city, town, or hamlet in the United States can be found on a postcard. Many collectors are interested in how their hometown looked at the beginning of the century. Expositions, transportation (trains, planes, autos, ships), commercial enterprises, and main streets are among the views prized by collectors. Things that have changed little, such as monuments and waterfalls, as well as frequently visited tourist areas (Niagara Falls, Washington, D.C., National Parks, etc.) are common and not very desirable.

The real photo card, our third category, has skyrocketed in value over the past decade. A real photo card is simply a photograph printed directly onto a postcard. Usually black and white, they are occasionally colored. The reason for the interest in these cards is their subject matter and scarcity. While the bigger cities had millions of published views, many small towns and villages are represented only on photo postcards. Unidentified views and family portraits have little value, but Main Streets, train stations, commercial enterprises, occupational photos, political and social themes (e.g. suffragettes, labor unions, presidential campaign stops, criminals), postal and photographic history, and any other unique subject matter is of great interest to collectors.

Condition is a major factor in determining value. Prices listed are for mint condition. Even a slight flaw will reduce the value considerably while a serious flaw may render the card uncollectible. For further information see *Postcard Collector* magazine.

Our consultant for this section is Adam G. Perl, owner of Pastimes Antiques in Ithaca, NY (he is listed in the back of this book).

	LOW	AVG.	HIGH
Advertising, Campbell Kids, horizontal	$ 50	$ 62	$ 75
Advertising, Campbell Kids, vertical	75	88	100
Advertising, Red Star Line, poster style	25	35	45
Antelope Hunting, 2-tone, undivided back, Wild West Series,			
Ridley, artwork by Charles M. Russell	22	25	28
April Fool, signed Hutaf	15	18	20
Austrian Cavalry Patrol Crossing River, Underwood & Underwood, color	7	9	10
Beef Herd on Water, black and white, undivided back, Morris & Kirby	6	7	8
Branding Calves, 2-tone, undivided back, Holmes & Warren	5	6	7
Buster Brown and Tige, Resolved: "That Nothing Can Stop Us,"			
signed Outcault	15	18	22
Children, signed Clapsaddle	12	15	18
Christmas, children with toys	5	6	7

Clockwise from right:
Thinking Of You, signed
Philip Boileau, $45-$65;
Gossip, metamorphic
face made of women,
$45-$65; Christmas,
look-through transparent
panel, $35-$45.
— Items courtesy of
Pastimes.

	LOW	AVG.	HIGH
Christmas, Santa in green, full figure	$ 25	$ 28	$ 30
Christmas, Santa painting sled	10	13	15
Columbian Exposition, 1893, pub. Goldsmith	25	28	30
Fur Canoe, color, undivided back, Wild West Series, MacFarlane	10	12	14
Halloween, signed Clapsaddle	25	28	30
Halloween, Tuck	15	20	25
Halloween, Winsch	65	75	85
Hold-to-the-Light, 1904 St. Louis Expo.	25	30	35
Hold-to-the-Light, Santa Claus	125	150	175
Home Sweet Home, color, undivided back, Tammen	12	14	15
Horse-Drawn Double Decker Buses in London's Ludgate Circus, color, Louis Levy, divided back	6	7	8
Hudson-Fulton Expo, Redfield Floats	5	6	7
Indian Encampment on River Bank, color, undivided back, Illinois Postcard Co.	5	6	7
Indians, Chief Spotted Tail, color, undivided back, Leighton	5	6	7
Iron Ore Docks of Toledo, color, undivided back, Clinton & Close	7	9	11
Kewpies, signed Rose O'Neill	25	32	40
Levee Scene, color, undivided back, Erker #221	5	6	7
Lewis and Clark Exposition, pub. B.B. Rich	10	13	15
Missouri State Building, color, undivided back, Sun. Post Dispatch (St. Louis), 1900	7	9	11
Oklahoma Building, color, undivided back, Samuel Cupples	7	9	11
Pan-American Expo, 1901, pub. Niagara Env.	15	20	25
Patriotic, Fourth of July	5	8	10

	LOW	AVG.	HIGH
Patriotic, Lincoln	8	12	15
Patriotic, Memorial Day	$ 5	$ 8	$ 10
Patriotic, Washington	5	8	10
Political, Bryan, campaign	15	25	35
Political, Prohibition	15	25	45
Political, Taft, campaign	10	13	15
Political, Teddy Roosevelt, campaign	10	15	20
Political, Teddy Roosevelt, family	5	7	8
Real Photo, dry goods store interior	25	30	35
Real Photo, girl with doll	15	18	20
Real Photo, horse-drawn milk wagon with adv.	65	70	75
Real Photo, Spencer, NY, parade on Main St.	20	23	25
Real Photo, train in station, good detail	45	48	50
Red River Carts, color, divided back, Wild West Series, MacFarlane	10	12	14
Red Roof Tower at Left of Mountains, German Tyrolean Alps Series, Samuel Cupples	15	18	20
Residence House at Roof Square, German Tyrolean Alps Series, Samuel Cupples	15	18	20
Roper, 2-tone, undivided back, Wild West Series, Ridley, artwork by Charles M. Russell	20	23	26
Soulard Market, color, undivided back, Erker #246	5	6	7
Thanksgiving, signed Brundage	15	20	25
Two Crow Papooses, black and white, undivided back, Miller	5	6	7
Valentine, The Westmount Club of Montreal, color, divided back	6	7	8
Village Square, German Tyrolean Alps Series, Samuel Cupples	16	18	20

Above left to right: Fish playing the accordion, fantasy card, $60-$80; Railroad Crossing Warning, poster style card, $40-$50. Below left to right: Indian Baking Soda, mechanical advertising card, $60-$70; mechanical Valentine card, with turning wheel, $70-$80. — Items courtesy of Pastimes.

Pens and Pencils

Pens can be either dip pens (the earliest type), fountain pens or ballpoint pens. Dip pens are the style of modern calligraphy pens: a pointed nib is dipped in ink and used quickly. Fountain pens (FP) contain their own ink supply, as do ballpoints (BP) and roller balls (RB). Pencils are either traditional or mechanical.

The fountain pen, invented in the 1880s by Lewis Waterman, is the most collectible type. It experienced its heyday in the 1920s and 1930s. The important makers from that time are Waterman, Parker, Conklin, Sheaffer, and Wahl. Rarity and condition are very important. Historical importance may also play a part, though only in isolated instances, such as a presidential pen used to sign important legislation into law.

We have seen some pens listed on the Internet. For further information see *Collecting Pen World* magazine.

	LOW	AVG.	HIGH
Autopoint, gold filled, 1930s	$ 30	$ 45	$ 60
Century, Durapoint, rod woodgrain, marbled, 1928	300	450	600
Chilton, cream and gold, marbled, gold plated trim, golf pencil, 1930	60	75	90
Conklin, 2P, black chased hard rubber, crescent filler, 1918	70	100	130
Conklin, Endura, orange, lever filler, gold plated trim, 1920s	80	100	120
Conklin, Nozak, gray and rod pearl, gold plated trim, 1931	70	100	130
Cross, Townsend, Medalist gold filled, FP and RB set	80	100	120
Cross, Townsend, black lacquer, FP and pencil set	80	100	120
Doric, pearly lined nickel plated trim, pencil, 1935	50	85	120
Dunn, sterling silver, fine point, 1922	300	400	500
Eversharp, green, chrome gold banded cap, 1951	60	80	100
Eversharp, Skyline, black, 1945	40	50	60
Lincoln, red, marbled, 1926	60	85	110
Majestic, black and cream, 1930s	70	85	100
Mont Blanc, 146 FP and pencil set, black	150	175	200
Parker, 51, Blue Diamond, black, gold plated trim, Lustraloy cap, 1940	90	120	150
Parker, 51, demi size black barrel gold filled cap	30	40	50
Parker, 51s, Lustraloy cap	30	35	40
Parker, 75, burgundy set, FP and BP	60	75	90
Parker, 75, tortoise lacquer, FP, pencil, RB set	80	100	120
Parker, 75, GF stripe pattern, FP and BP set	100	150	200
Parker, burgundy and black streamline pencil	25	30	35
Parker, Deluxe Challenger, gold plated trim, 1930s	80	100	120
Parker, Duofold Centennial size, orange, FP and pencil set	250	300	350
Parker, Duofold International, burgundy, flat band	90	125	160
Parker, Duofold, gold pearl and black, gold plated trim, 1939	150	175	200
Parker, Duofold Jr., black, gold plated trim, 1927	100	110	120
Parker, Duofold Sr., Big Red, gold plated trim, 1924	250	350	450
Parker, gold filled metal, button filler, 1926	130	170	210
Parker, Lady Duofold, red, gold plated trim	90	130	170
Parker, Premier. sterling grid pattern	90	125	160
Parker, Premier, GF with black stripes	90	125	160
Parker, Premier, gold barleycorn patter	90	125	160
Parker, Premier, lacquer, FP and pencil set	90	125	160
Parker, Pastel, blue, gold plated trim, 1926	90	120	150
Parker, silver plate, pencil, 1921	150	180	210

	LOW	AVG.	HIGH
Parker, Sonnet, Sterling Silver Cisele	$ 80	$ 100	$ 120
Parker, Sonnet, 23 GP Laque, FP and pencil set	150	200	250
Parker, Sonnet Sterling Fougere	80	100	120
Parker, T-1 set, FP and BP	500	600	700
Parker, Vacumatic, black, 1947	60	85	110
Peerless, black and cream, gold plated trim, lever filler, 1930	50	70	90
Peerless, lever filler, gold plated trim, black veined cream, 1920s	50	70	90
Pilot, black lacquer and hand-painted design, gold fittings, Japanese	140	180	220
Recife, brown, flat top model	60	75	90
Royal, Parker Duofold imitation, yellow, gold plated trim, 1928	100	115	130
Saltz, black hard rubber, with cream ends, nickel trim	25	30	35
Sanford and Bennett, black, eye dropper filler, 1904	90	125	160
Sheaffer, 30, black, lever filler, gold plated trim, ladies', 1930s	40	55	70
Sheaffer, Balance, pearl and black marbled, pencil, 1931	120	155	190
Sheaffer, black, gold plated trim, pencil, 1925	80	115	150
Sheaffer, Crest, colored	60	75	90
Sheaffer, Crest silver plate set, FP and RB	100	150	200
Sheaffer, Lifetime, black and pearl, lever filler, gold plated trim, 1932	230	270	310
Sheaffer, sterling silver, early feed, ladies', lever filler, 1916	110	130	150
Sheaffer, Targas, colored	75	100	125
Sheaffer, Triumph, striped, plunger filled, 1946	80	110	140
Swann, solid gold 14K, fine point, 1920s	160	210	260
Wahl, # 4, gold filled metal, 1924	210	250	290
Wahl, lever filler, gold filled, 1926	100	125	150
Wahl-Eversharp, gold filled metal, pen and pencil set, 1924	270	335	400
Waterman, #412, orange with silver overlay, eye dropper filler, 1905	930	1075	1220
Waterman, #452, gothic sterling silver, 1925	320	350	380
Waterman, #5116, Ink View, gray pearl, gold plated trim, 1939	110	140	170
Waterman, # 52, black chased hard rubber, nickel plated trim, 1923	60	80	100
Waterman, #554, lower end covered, solid 14K gold, gothic, 1926	1200	1350	1500
Waterman, black, chased hard rubber, pencil, 1920	40	55	70
Waterman, Gentleman, sterling, FP and pencil set	150	200	250
Waterman, LeMan 100, black	100	150	200
Waterman, LeMan 200s (smaller size)	80	100	120
Waterman, Olive Wood LeMan 100 (large size)	150	200	250
Waterman, Opera	70	90	110
Waterman, Patrician (modern version), blue	150	175	200
Waterman, Rhapsody (first of the modern version editions), gray	80	100	120
Waterman, Rhapsody (same as 6), blue	80	100	120
Waterman, Rhapsody (same as 6 and 7), red	80	100	120
Waterman, Taperite, gold filled cap, 1946	60	75	90

Photographs

Assorted Subjects

In the following entries, photographs are listed by subject matter. The values quoted are the average retail price for various types of prints. Daguerreotypes (D) generally average 4" x 3" on silver plates; Tintypes (T) generally average 3" x 2" (these values are not for the thumbnail-size variety); Carte-de-Visites (CdV) average 4" x 2.5" on cardboard; Studio Photos (SP) are about 6" x 4" on cardboard; and Stereopticon Cards (Str) have a double image for observing in one of a variety of viewers.

The value of photographs is determined by age and subject matter. Prints made in the studios of important photographers such as Edward Curtis, Matthew Brady, Alfred Stieglitz, and Carleton Watkins command high prices. Tintypes were invented in 1858 and declined by the 1870s. Stereographs with a revenue stamp on the back date between 1864-66. In 1868, many publishers listed the views in a particular stereographic series by underlining or outlining a card number or title. After 1880, curved stereographs appeared, believed to have a more 3-D quality.

The fagility of paper should be heeded. *An Ounce of Prevention: A Guide to the Care of Papers and Photographs*, by Craig Tuttle, is worth consulting.

Above left: Daguerreotypes are cased to protect the image. Although they can be cleaned, many amateur attempts have destroyed such photos. Above right: Tiny thumbnail-sized tintypes are generally valued only for the album that contains them. Below: Early sporting photos have greatly increased in value.

Historical Events

	D	T	CdV	SP	Str
Chicago Fire of 1871	$ 900	$ 250	$ 40	$ 65	$ 15
Mill Creek Flood of 1874	500	150	—	45	10
San Francisco Earthquake, 1906	—	300	150	250	30
Spanish American War	—	75	25	35	20
World War I	—	—	—	10	6

Landscapes

Death Valley	550	200	—	45	7
France	75	25	10	15	5
House	35	15	5	10	10
Landscape	100	50	—	30	7
Mining Scene	400	200	—	50	10
New York City, landmark	250	75	40	50	10
Niagara Falls	750	175	—	50	10
Street Scene	100	45	—	15	12
Western USA landscape, w/ mountains	200	100	—	50	8
Yosemite Falls	400	200	50	75	30

People and Portraits

Actor/Actress	45	15	7	12	12
African American	200	120	40	55	25
Booth, Edwin	300	75	35	45	20
Booth, John Wilkes	750	500	300	350	200
Bryan, William Jennings	300	80	40	55	20

Left: Stereoscope. Below: Comic scenes are a common subject matter for stereopticon photos.

	D	T	CdV	SP	Str
Circus Performer	$ 150	$ 55	$ 25	$ 45	$ 30
Civil War Officer	200	125	35	50	15
Civil War Soldier	175	75	30	50	40
Cowboy	75	25	10	15	10
Edison, Thomas Alva	—	225	75	100	60
Ford, Henry	—	150	50	75	50
Lindbergh, Charles	—	—	75	120	35
Native American	260	150	50	85	25
Nude, woman	260	75	35	50	25
Opera Star	65	25	15	20	15
Portrait of a Beautiful Woman	50	7	7	12	—
Portrait of a Cat (or other pet)	100	25	10	15	7
Portrait of a Child	50	1	1	1	—
Portrait of a Man	15	1	1	1	—
Portrait of a Woman	15	1	1	1	—
Professional (portrait holding tools, etc.)	100	50	20	30	15
Rockefeller, John D.	—	—	50	75	25
Sporting Figure	350	200	35	50	35
Tom Thumb	300	200	75	100	40

Presidents

	D	T	CdV	SP	Str
Arthur, Chester A.	—	75	20	35	35
Buchanan, James	300	100	50	50	20
Cleveland, Grover	—	125	25	50	40
Garfield, James	—	75	20	35	35
Grant, U.S.	750	175	45	90	45
Harrison, Benjamin	—	65	20	40	35
Hayes, R.B.	—	75	20	35	35
Johnson, Andrew	400	100	50	65	12
Lincoln, Abraham	rare	rare	2000	4000	50
McKinley, William	—	100	25	50	40

Left : Typical carte-de-visite. Right: Civil War posed camp scenes are not as valuable as battle scenes, but more valuable than simple portraits of unknown soldiers. — Photo courtesy of Phillips Auctioneers.

Wallace Nutting

At the same time he was reproducing American antique furniture, Wallace Nutting funded his many projects with money earned from selling photographs of quaint scenes. Often signed, these photographs have been collected since their first appearance.

	LOW	AVG.	HIGH
Abbott House, 13" x 16"	$ 250	$ 300	$ 360
Above the Bridge, 12" x 15"	80	90	110
Above the Orchard, 11" x 14"	90	120	140
Above the Orchard, 10" x 16"	140	180	210
Above the Road, 11" x 14"	90	120	140
Across Dunmore, 14" x 17"	110	140	160
Across the Charles, 10" x 16"	140	170	200
Admiration, 13" x 16"	200	250	300
Adorable Maids, 13" x 16"	300	370	440
Afternoon Tea, 12" x 15"	210	260	310
Afternoon Tea, 15" x 18"	260	330	390
All in a Garden Fair, 14" x 17"	300	370	440
Ambush for a Redcoat, 13" x 16"	680	840	1000
Among October Birches, 13" x 16"	110	140	160
Among the Ferns, 13" x 16"	110	140	160
Ancestral Chamber, 14" x 17"	260	330	390
Apple Pool, 14" x 17"	200	240	290
Apple Tree Bend, 14" x 17"	110	140	160
April in the South, 14" x 17"	270	340	400
Artist's River, 11" x 14"	60	70	90
August in the Meadow, 10" x 12"	110	140	160
Autumn Grotto, 14" x 17"	210	260	310
Awaiting a Visitor, 11" x 14"	140	180	210
Barnard Pool, 13" x 16"	130	160	190
Barre Brook, 14" x 17"	140	180	210
Berkshire Village, 11" x 14"	120	150	180
Between Hill and Tree, 13" x 16"	130	160	190
Between the Streams, 11" x 14"	60	70	90
Billows of Blossoms, 14" x 17"	130	160	190
Birch Cove, 11" x 14"	70	80	100
Birch Grove, 12" x 15"	90	120	140
Birch Hilltop, 13" x 19"	130	160	190
Birch Stand, 8" x 10"	50	60	80
Birch Windings, 11" x 14"	80	90	110
Birch Wood, 11" x 14"	90	120	140
Birches in June, 11" x 14"	90	120	140
Birthday Flowers, 11" x 14"	170	210	250
Bit of Gossip, 13" x 16"	300	370	440
Block House Through Blossoms, 11" x 14"	140	180	210
Blooms by the Lake, 11" x 14"	80	90	110
Blossom Bordered, 11" x 14"	90	120	140
Blossom Cottage, 11" x 14"	90	110	130
Blossom Landing, 13" x 16"	100	130	150
Blossom Point, 13" x 16"	170	210	250
Blossom Pond, 11" x 17"	130	160	190
Blossoms of Lake Bomaseen, 13" x 17"	190	230	280

	LOW	AVG.	HIGH
Blossoms on Lake Bomaseen, 11" x 14"	$ 110	$ 140	$ 160
Blow Me Down Bridge, 11" x 14"	90	120	140
Blue Pool, 13" x 16"	280	350	410
Bonnie May, 13" x 16"	130	160	190
Braiding a Rag Rug, 12" x 16"	180	220	260
Braiding a Straw Hat, 12" x 15"	180	220	260
Bridesmaids' Procession, 12" x 16"	130	160	190
Bridesmaids' Procession, 14" x 17"	190	230	280
Bridge Bows, 12" x 16"	90	120	140
Bridge Path, 13" x 16"	130	160	190
Bridgewater Road, 13" x 16"	130	160	190
Broken Lights, 13" x 16"	140	180	210
Brook and Blossom, 11" x 14"	80	90	110
Brookside Blooms, 13" x 16"	110	140	160
By the Old Arch, 13" x 16"	110	140	160
By the Wayside, 11" x 14"	140	170	200
Caherlough, 12" x 18"	780	970	1150
Call of the Country, 11" x 14"	140	180	210
Call of the Road, 13" x 16"	130	160	190
Canal in Sunshine, 13" x 16"	400	490	590
Caroline's Garden, 13" x 16"	300	370	440
Colonial Corner, 14" x 17"	330	410	490
Colonial Dames at Tea, 13" x 16"	380	470	560
Connecticut Blossoms, 11" x 17"	190	230	280
Corner Cupboard, 15" x 18"	330	410	490
Corner Cupboard, 10" x 16"	180	220	260
Counting the Spoons, 13" x 16"	230	280	340
Country Silence, 14" x 17"	130	160	190
Cove Landing, 14" x 17"	140	180	210
Cup That Cheers, 11" x 14"	190	230	280
d'Este Garden, 11" x 14"	210	260	310
Daguerreotype, 13" x 16"	300	370	440
Dear Old Connecticut, 13" x 16"	210	260	310
Dell Blossoms, 11" x 14"	150	190	230
Dixville Notch, 11" x 14"	190	230	280
Dixville Shadows, 11" x 14"	210	260	310
Double Drawing Room, 13" x 17"	450	560	660
Dream Lights, 11" x 14"	90	110	130
Dutch Maids, 15" x 18"	600	740	880
Dutch Sails, 14" x 17"	470	580	690
Dykeside Blossoms, 11" x 17"	140	180	210
Dykeside Blossoms, 12" x 16"	140	180	210
Early June Brides, 11" x 14"	90	120	140
Early May, 11" x 17"	70	80	100
Elm and Bridge, 11" x 14"	160	200	240
Elm Drapery, 12" x 15"	130	160	190
Embroidering, 18" x 22"	380	470	560
English Door, 13" x 16"	260	330	390
Fairhaven Blossoms, 12" x 18"	140	170	200
Fairway, 12" x 15"	110	140	160
Favorite Corner, 14" x 17"	300	370	440

	LOW	AVG.	HIGH
Favorite Corner, 13" x 16"	$ 280	$ 350	$ 410
Fine Effect, 13" x 16"	250	300	360
Fire Room Accessories, 11" x 14"	140	180	210
Fragrant Highway, 11" x 14"	130	160	190
Franconia Brook, 11" x 14"	130	160	190
Gable of Roses, 13" x 16"	210	260	310
Garden in the Forest, 13" x 16"	190	230	280
Garden Steps, 11" x 14"	130	160	190
Going Forth to Conquer, 13" x 16"	160	200	240
Good Night, 14" x 17"	300	370	440
Gorge of the Penobscot, 11" x 14"	150	190	230
Gothic Arch, Lenox, 11" x 14"	90	110	130
Gothic Stream, 11" x 14"	110	140	160
Grafton Windings, 13" x 22"	170	210	250
Grandfather's Clock, 12" x 16"	260	320	380
Grandius Parlor Corner, 13" x 16"	300	370	440
Green Hills, 13" x 16"	190	230	280
Green Hills, 11" x 14"	80	90	110
Harmony, 13" x 16"	250	300	360
Hawthorne Bridge, 11" x 14"	110	140	160
Heart of New England, 13" x 16"	140	180	210
Hearty Welcome, 13" x 16"	370	450	540
Her Father's Wall, 13" x 16"	220	270	330
Hesitancy, 13" x 16"	700	860	1030
Hidden Road, 11" x 14"	140	180	210
Hidden View of Samoset Garden, 13" x 16"	210	260	310
Highland Blossoms, 12" x 16"	140	180	210
Highland Brae, 11" x 14"	90	110	130
Highlands, 12" x 15"	90	120	140
Hill Road Oak, 7" x 9"	80	90	110
Home Room, 10" x 16"	230	280	340
Honeymoon Drive, 16" x 20"	210	260	310
Honeymoon Drive, 13" x 16"	130	160	190
In Days of Old, 13" x 16"	300	370	440
In Dedham Vale, 12" x 16"	130	160	190
In Tender Leaf, 11" x 17"	140	170	200
In the Brave Days of Old, 13" x 16"	300	370	440
In the Midst of Her China, 14" x 17"	560	690	830
Informal Call, 18" x 22"	600	740	880
Inside the Gate, 14" x 17"	300	370	440
Interrupted Letter, 18" x 22"	550	680	810
Into the Birchwood, 22" x 26"	130	160	190
Irish Brook, 13" x 16"	140	180	210
Italian Spring, 14" x 17"	230	280	340
Ivy and Rose Cloister, 14" x 17"	310	390	460
Jersey Banks, 14" x 17"	130	160	190
Jersey Blossoms, 14" x 17"	210	260	310
Joyous Anniversary, 11" x 14"	110	140	160
June Joys, 14" x 17"	90	110	130
Justifiable Vanity, 12" x 16"	300	370	440
Killarney Castle and Cove, 16" x 20"	300	370	440

	LOW	AVG.	HIGH
Laneside, 10" x 12"	$ 60	$ 70	$ 90
Life of the Golden Age, 14" x 17"	470	580	690
Life of the Golden Age, 16" x 20"	510	630	750
Liffrey Crags, 11" x 14"	130	160	190
Lined With Petals, 13" x 15"	110	140	160
Litchfield Minster, 14" x 17"	280	350	410
Little Killarney Lake, 16" x 20"	280	350	410
Little River With Mt. Washington, 20" x 40"	640	790	940
Maine Cove, 15" x 18"	280	350	410
Many Happy Returns, 11" x 14"	80	90	110
Maple in May, 11" x 14"	90	120	140
May Lane, 11" x 14"	80	90	110
Meadow Beauty, 16" x 20"	130	160	190
Meadow Beauty, 11" x 14"	110	140	160
Meadow Blossoms, 14" x 17"	190	230	280
Meadow Blossoms, 11" x 14"	120	150	180
Meadow Pasture, 11" x 17"	490	610	730
Meeting of the Ways, 13" x 16"	210	260	310
Meeting of the Ways, 11" x 14"	50	60	80
Mills at the Turn, 13" x 16"	220	270	330
Minnewaska Road, 13" x 16"	190	230	280
Misty Morning, 10" x 12"	80	90	110
Morning Among the Birches, 13" x 16"	130	160	190
Morning Errand, 11" x 14"	300	370	440
Morning Mail, 13" x 15"	200	240	290
Morning Side, 11" x 14"	210	260	310
Mother of the Revolution, 13" x 16"	230	280	340
Mount Washington Road, 11" x 14"	90	120	140
Mountain Orchard, 13" x 16"	110	140	160
Mystery Lights, 11" x 14"	90	120	140
Nearing the Crest, 11" x 17"	130	160	190
Nest, 14" x 17"	280	350	410
Nethercote, 13" x 16"	190	230	280
New England Elms, 10" x 12"	60	70	90
New England Road in May, 13" x 16"	130	160	190
New Hampshire in June, 10" x 12"	90	120	140
New Hampshire Roadside, 12" x 15"	80	90	110
New Life, 11" x 14"	320	400	480
New Life, 11" x 14"	280	350	410
New Parasol, 12" x 15"	230	280	340
News in Brief, 11" x 14"	210	260	310
Not One of the 400, 13" x 16"	330	410	490
Nurringham Pool, 12" x 15"	300	370	440
Obstructed Brook, 14" x 17"	130	160	190
October Array, 16" x 20"	160	200	240
October Splendors, 16" x 20"	20	30	30
October Splendors, 14" x 17"	130	160	190
Old Back Door, 11" x 14"	180	220	260
Old Colonial House Room, 11" x 14"	230	280	340
Old England in New England, 13" x 16"	190	230	280
Old Fashioned Paradise, 13" x 16"	380	470	560

	LOW	AVG.	HIGH
Old Hudson, 13" x 16"	$ 270	$ 340	$ 400
Old Wentworth Days, 14" x 17"	380	470	560
On the Avon, 14" x 17"	370	460	550
On the Quinnebaug, 11" x 14"	130	160	190
Orta in Blossom Time, 12" x 16"	140	180	210
Orta in Blossom Time, 11" x 14"	230	280	340
Over the Picket Fence, 13" x 16"	140	180	210
Over the Valley, 13" x 16"	140	180	210
Parlor at Brandon, 13" x 16"	190	230	280
Pasture Dell, 13" x 16"	2000	2480	2950
Pasture Lane, 11" x 14"	90	120	140
Path of Roses, 13" x 16"	130	160	190
Peace, 11" x 14"	130	160	190
Pebbles and Grasses, 13" x 16"	140	180	210
Pennsylvania Hillside, 13" x 16"	300	370	440
Petal Shower, 11" x 14"	140	180	210
Petals on the Path, 10" x 12"	60	70	90
Pinning the Lace, 11" x 17"	250	300	360
Plymouth Curves, 14" x 17"	130	160	190
Plymouth Glimpse, 10" x 12"	100	130	150
Pool in Winter, 10" x 12"	370	460	550
Precise Adjustment, 11" x 14"	280	350	410
Preparing an "At Home," 12" x 15"	330	410	490
Preparing an "At Home," 10" x 13"	190	230	280
Primrose Cottage, 13" x 16"	110	140	160
Proud as Peacocks, 16" x 20"	360	440	530
Prudence Drawing Tea, 14" x 17"	270	340	400
Purity and Grace, 14" x 17"	90	120	140
Rag Rug Weaving, 13" x 16"	300	370	440
Ready for Callers, 15" x 18"	300	370	440
Red, White, and Blue, 13" x 16"	100	130	150
Red, White, and Blue, 10" x 12"	70	80	100
Restless Deep, 13" x 16"	380	470	560
Rheinstein (Germany), 12" x 16"	480	600	710
River Archway, 10" x 12"	70	80	100
Rock Creek, in April, 11" x 14"	210	260	310
Rock Creeks Banks, 10" x 12"	140	170	200
Romance of the Revolution, 13" x 15"	190	230	280
Russet and Gold, 13" x 16"	190	230	280
Salem Beautiful, 13" x 16"	560	690	830
Samoset Fleur De Lis, 13" x 16"	250	300	360
Saturday Baking, 11" x 14"	250	300	360
Scotland Beautiful, 12" x 15"	170	210	250
Scotland Forever, 11" x 14"	280	350	410
Sea Barriers, 13" x 17"	380	470	560
Sea Captain's Daughter, 10" x 16"	360	440	530
Sea Ledges, 11" x 14"	360	440	530
Shadows Athwart, 14" x 17"	140	180	210
Shadowy Orchard Curves, 11" x 14"	110	140	160
Sheltered Road, 13" x 16"	90	120	140
Silent Shore, 11" x 17"	140	180	210

	LOW	AVG.	HIGH
Slack Water, 20" x 40"	$ 200	$ 240	$ 290
Sleeping Canal, 13" x 16"	260	320	380
Smoke of Evening Fire, 13" x 17"	250	300	360
Softening Lights, 11" x 14"	90	120	140
Spanish Moss, 14" x 17"	320	400	480
Sparkling Place, 12" x 15"	300	370	440
Spinet Corner, 14" x 17"	300	370	440
Spring in the Dell, 11" x 14"	130	160	190
Springfield Blossoms, 13" x 16"	100	130	150
State Chamber Tea, 11" x 14"	280	350	410
Stepping Stones at Bolton Abbey, 13" x 15"	210	260	310
Still Waters, 11" x 14"	80	90	110
Stitch in Time, 10" x 16"	370	460	550
Summer Clouds, 13" x 16"	130	160	190
Swimming Pool, 26" x 30"	310	380	450
Swimming Pool, 11" x 14"	80	90	110
Swimming Pool, 14" x 17"	110	140	160
Swirling Seas, 14" x 17"	430	530	630
Sylvan Dell, 13" x 16"	140	180	210
Treasure Bag, 11" x 14"	210	260	310
Trimming the Pie, 12" x 15"	160	200	240
Turn Homeward, 11" x 14"	70	80	100
Unbroken Flow, 12" x 20"	210	260	310
Unbroken Flow, 13" x 22"	140	180	210
Under the Blossoms, 14" x 17"	190	230	280
Under the Drooping Bough, 14" x 17"	340	420	500
Upper Thames, 11" x 14"	130	160	190
Vermont Road, 18" x 22"	180	220	260
Vermont Spring, 14" x 16"	140	180	210
Vico Equesne, 12" x 15"	600	740	880
Village Dale, 10" x 12"	160	200	240
Vines and Thatch, 11" x 14"	190	230	280
Virginia Reel, 10" x 12"	110	140	160
Waiting for Jacob, 13" x 16"	260	320	380
Wallace Nutting Letter, 11" x 15"	170	210	250
Walpole Road, 10" x 16"	140	180	210
Warm Spring Day, 11" x 17"	330	410	490
Water Maples, 13" x 16"	150	190	230
Wayside Inn Approach, 11" x 14"	110	140	160
Wayside Inn Old Dining Room, 12" x 16"	210	260	310
Wayside Inn Parlor, 14" x 17"	260	320	380
Well at Sorento, 13" x 16"	380	470	560
Wells, from the Palace Pool, 12" x 15"	210	260	310
West Chester Byway, 13" x 16"	210	260	310
Westfield Water, 12" x 15"	90	110	130
Westmore Drive, 12" x 18"	120	150	180
Where the Road Turns, 11" x 14"	140	180	210
Whitehall Blossoms, 12" x 16"	620	770	910
Whitsunday, 11" x 14"	140	180	210
Wilburton Slope, 11" x 14"	90	120	140
Willow Pastoral, 14" x 17"	350	430	510

Plates, Collector

Collector plates began in 1895 with the Bing and Grondahl Christmas plate. Despite much publicity about increasing values, selling a collection of plates may realize only pennies on the dollar. As with all collectibles, buy what you love because you love it, not as an investment.

The following entries are listed by company name, with collection titles indented under each entry.

Above: Reco International. The high limitation number (25,000) will considerably diminish chances of an increase in value.

	LOW	AVG.	HIGH
Accent on Art			
Mother Goose, 1978	$ 77	$ 80	$ 83
Nobility of the Plains, 1978-79	77	80	83
Count Agazzi			
Children's Hour Series (animals), 1970-73	11	12	13
Easter Series, 1971-73	11	12	13
Famous Personalities Series, 1968-73	8	11	15
Father's Day, 1972-73	20	27	35
Mother's Day, 1972-73	20	27	35
Allison and Company			
Late to Party, 1982-83	30	35	40
Nature's Beauty, 1981-82	70	72	74
American Artists			
Family Treasures, 1981-83	40	40	40
Famous Fillies, 1987-92	63	65	68
Horses of Fred Stone Series, 1982-85	65	87	110
Zoe's Cat Series, 1985	25	27	30
American Commemorative			
Southern Landmark Series, 1973-80	45	67	90
American Crystal			
Christmas Series and Mother's Day Series, 1970-73	15	20	25
American Express			
American Trees of Christmas, 1976-77	60	62	64
Birds of North America Series, 1978	38	39	40
Four Freedoms Series, 1976	35	36	38
Roger Tory Peterson (bird series), 1981-82	55	57	60
American Heritage			
Africa's Beauties, 1983-84	60	65	70
American Sail, 1983	38	40	42

	LOW	AVG.	HIGH
Celebrity Clown Series, 1982	$ 50	$ 52	$ 55
Craftsman Heritage, 1983	40	41	42
Vanishing West, 1982-83	55	60	65
American Legacy Co.			
Special Heart, 1982-83	33	35	37
American Rose Society			
American Rose Series, 1975-85	50	95	140
Anheuser Busch			
Civil War, 1992-93	42	45	48
1992 Olympic Team, 1991-92	33	35	37
Anna-Perenna			
American Silhouettes Collection, 1981-84	75	77	80
Bashful Bunnies, 1981-83	62		
Children of Mother Earth Series (seasons), 1983	240	245	250
Flowers of Count Bernadotte, 1982-84	75	85	95
Happy Village, 1983	55		
Rhythm and Dance Series, 1983	30	31	32
Romantic Love Series, 1979-82	90	95	100
Anri			
Christmas Series, 1971-84	100	150	200
Christmas Series, (Alpine horn), 1973	375	400	425
Father's Day Series, 1974-77	35	60	
Ferrandiz Wooden Birthday Series, 1973-74	10	15	20
Mother's Day Series, 1972-76	50	57	65
Antique Trader			
All series	9	11	13
Arabia of Finland			
Christmas Series, 1978-82	50	72	95
Kalevala Series, 1977-85	40	65	90
Kalevala Series, 1976	230	235	240
Arizona Artisan			
All series	15	17	20
Armstrong's/Crown Parian			
American Folk Heroes, 1983-85	35	37	40
Beautiful Cats Series of the World, 1979-82	60	70	80
Butterflies of the World Series, 1978	60	61	62
Oriental Bird Series, 1975-76	400	400	400
All other bird series	50	65	80
Sporting Dog Series, 1980-82	56	56	56
Artists of the World			
Children of Aberdeen, 1979-84	50	55	60
Holiday Mini-Plates, 1980-85	15	18	20
Western Series, 1986-89	60	65	70
Avendale			
Cameo's of Childhood, 1978-81	65	60	75
Barewther			
Christmas, 1967	75	85	95
Christmas, 1968-72	20	22	25
Christmas, 1990-94	50	55	60
Barthmann			
Christmas, 1977-80	300	325	350

	LOW	AVG.	HIGH
Belleek Pottery			
Irish Wildlife, 1978-1983	$ 65	$ 75	$ 85
Berlin Design			
Historical, 1975-79	30	40	50
Bing and Gondahl			
Cat Portraits, 1987	40	40	40
Christmas, 1895	4000	5000	6000
Christmas, 1896	2000	2200	2400
Christmas, 1897-1900	800	1000	1200
Christmas, 1901-02	300	375	450
Christmas, 1903	225	250	275
Christmas, 1904-07	100	125	150
Christmas, 1908-20	80	100	120
Christmas, 1921-37	60	80	100
Christmas, 1991-96	70	75	
Gentle Love, 1985	40	45	50
Moments of Truth, 1984-86	30	30	30
Santa Claus Collection, 1989-93	65	70	75
Boehm Studios, Edward Marshall			
Boehm Owl Collection, 1980	50	55	60
Seashells, 1975-76	450		
Waterbirds, 1981	60	62	64
Bradford Exchange			
Dog Days, 1993-94	30	32	34
Family Circles, 1993-94	30	32	34
Little Bandits, 1993-94	30	32	34
Sovereigns of the Wild, 1993-94	30	32	34
Brantwood Collection			
All series	30	40	50
Braymer Hall			
All series	25	37	50
Briant, Paul and Sons			
All series	80	100	120
Brindle Fine Arts			
Lenore Beran Special Series, 1980	125	127	130
All other series	60	67	75
Bydgo			
Christmas Series, 1969-72	10	10	10
Byliny Porcelain			
Russian Fairy Tale Princesses, 1992	35	36	37
Russian Seasons, 1992-93	30	33	35
California Porcelain Incorporated			
All series	30	50	70
Canadian Collector Plates			
Children of the Classics, 1982-83	78	78	78
Discover Canada Series (sawmill), 1979	300	350	400
Discover Canada Series, 1980-84	125	137	150
Capo di Monte			
Christmas Series, 1972-76	60	75	90
Mother's Day Series, 1973-76	68	68	68
Carmel Collection			
All series	30	37	45

	LOW	AVG.	HIGH
Carson Mint			
American Has Heart Series, 1980	$ 130	$ 135	$ 140
American Has Heart Series, 1981-83	30	35	40
Old-Fashioned Mother's Day Series, 1979-82	40	60	80
All other series	30	40	50
Castleton China			
All series	35	50	65
Chilmark			
All series	70	80	90
Christian Bell Porcelain			
Age of Steam Series, 1981	250	260	270
Age of Steam Series, 1982-83	90	95	100
Last Spike Centennial, 1986	140	145	150
All other series	45	55	65
Christian Fantasy Collectibles			
All series	50	50	50
Christian Seltmann			
Velvet Paws, 1991-93	30	33	36
Continental Mint			
All series	62	62	62
Crown Delft			
All series	15	22	30
Curator Collection			
Gift Edition, 1982-87	37	37	38
Magical Moments Series, 1981-83	30	45	60
Masterpieces of Impressionism Series, 1980-82	35	42	50
Masterpieces of the West Series, 1980-82	35	50	65
Portraits of American Brides Series, 1987	29	29	30
Sailing Through History, 1986	42	45	47
D'Arceau Limoges			
Cambier Four Seasons Series, 1978-80	100	110	120
Christmas Series, 1975-82	30	37	45
Les Femmes Du Siecle, 1976-79	25	35	45
Lafayette Legacy Series, 1973-75	15	20	25
Les Sites Parisiens de Louis Dali Series, 1979-83	25	27	30
Daum			
Art Nouveau Series, 1979-81	125	150	175
Famous Musicians Series, 1971-72	75	75	75
Four Seasons Series, 1970	150	150	150
David Kaplan Studios			
Fiddler's People Series, 1978-81	60	60	60
Delphi			
Commemorating the King, 1993-94	30	31	32
Fabulous Cars of the Fifties, 1993-94	25	27	29
Legends of Baseball	25	26	27
Dominion China Co.			
Portraits of the Wild, 1991-92	30	32	35
Treasures of the Arctic, 1990-91	30	32	35
Dresden			
Christmas Series, 1971-77	30	40	50
Duncan Royale			
History of Santa Claus, 1985-86	40	40	40

	LOW	AVG.	HIGH
Enesco			
Christmas Collection, 1981-84	$ 40	$ 50	$ 60
Precious Moments Collections, 1980-82	30	30	30
All other series	50	70	90
R.J. Ernst Enterprises			
Busy Bears, 1986	20	21	22
Classy Cars, 1982	25	26	27
Liebschen, 1983	20	21	22
Star Trek,1984-85	50	65	90
Star Trek Commemorative, 1986-88	30	32	34
Escalera Production Art			
Olympiad Triumphs Collection, 1984	60	60	60
Evergreen Press			
Catalina Island Series, 1986-87	39	39	40
Fairmont China			
Famous Clown Series, 1976	500	500	500
Famous Clown Series, 1977-79	75	75	75
Israeli Commemorative Series, 1978	80	85	90
Memory Annual Series, 1977-80	80	85	90
The Fleetwood Collection			
All series	40	55	70
Franklin Mint			
American Revolution Series, 1976-77	75	77	80
Arabian Nights Series, 1981-82	30	30	30
Audubon Society Series, 1972-73	100	110	120
Bernard Buffet Series, 1973-77	250	262	275
Bicentennial Series, 1973-76	200	205	210
Birds and Flowers of Beautiful Cafe Series, 1981-83	40	40	40
Birds and Flowers of the Orient Series, 1979-80	60	60	60
Butterflies of the World Series, 1977-79	250	262	275
Clipper Ships Series, 1982-83	55	57	60
Country Year Series, 1980-82	55	57	60
Currier and Ives Series, 1977-79	40	45	50
Days of the Week Series, 1979-80	40	42	45
Fairy Tales in Miniature Series, 1979-84	15	17	20
Flowers of the American Wilderness Series, 1978-80	40	42	45
Flowers of the Year Series, 1976-78	50	50	50
Game Birds of the World Series, 1978-80	55	55	55
Grimm's Fairy Tale Series, 1978-79	42	43	45
Hans Christian Andersen Series, 1976-77	50	60	70
International Gallery of Flowers Series, 1980-81	55	57	60
James Wyeth Series, 1972-76	130	155	180
Mark Twain Series, 1977-78	40	45	50
Poor Richard's Series, 1979-81	14	16	18
Robert's Zodiac Series, 1973-80	150	160	170
Norman Rockwell Series, 1970-79	150	175	200
Seven Seas Series, 1976-82	120	120	120
Songbirds of the World Series, 1977-81	55	55	55
Songbirds of the World Miniatures, 1980-83	15	16	18
Woodland Birds of the World, 1980-82	65	67	70
World's Great Porcelain Houses Series, 1981-83	20	22	25

	LOW	AVG.	HIGH
Frankoma Pottery			
Christmas Series, 1965-67	$ 100	$ 150	$ 200
Christmas Series, 1968-87	20	30	40
Teenagers of the Bible, 1973-82	20	25	30
Furstenberg			
Deluxe Christmas Series, 1971-73	45	55	65
All other series	20	30	40
W.S. George			
America's Pride, 1992-93	30	33	35
America the Beautiful, 1988-90	30	35	40
Classic Waterfowl. 1988-90	35	40	45
Elegant Bird, 1988-90	32	35	37
Garden of the Lord, 1992-93	30	33	36
Heart of the Wild, 1991-92	30	31	32
On Golden Wings, 1993-94	30	31	32
Poetic Cottages, 1992-93	30	31	32
Romantic Gardens, 1989-90	30	31	32
Treasury of Songbirds, 1992-93	30	32	34
Ghent Collection			
American Bicentennial Wildlife Series, 1976	200	250	300
Christmas Wildlife Series, 1974-78	30	40	50
Mother's Day Series (animals),1975-79	35	37	40
Goebel Collection			
American Heritage Series, 1979-81	100	115	130
Hummel Annual Series, 1971	500	600	700
Hummel Annual Series, 1972-88	80	100	120
Mother's Series (animals), 1975-80	40	57	75
Winged Fantasies Series, 1982-84	50	50	50
Gorham Collection			
Boy Scout Plates Series (Norman Rockwell),1975-80	40	50	60
Christmas Series (Norman Rockwell), 1974-87	30	40	50
Cowboy Series, 1980	35	37	40
Moppets (all series), 1973-83	15	17	20
Remington Western Series, 1973-76	30	35	40
Charles Russell Series (western), 1981-83	40	45	50
Grande Copenhagen			
Christmas Series, 1975-82	30	45	60
Christmas Series, 1983 (Little Mermaid)	100	125	150
Greentree Potteries			
All series	10	17	25
Dave Grossman Designs			
Norman Rockwell (all series)	40	60	80
All other series	30	40	50
Hackett American			
All series	30	45	60
Hamilton Collection			
America at Work (Normal Rockwell), 1984	30	30	30
Children of the American Frontier, 1986-87	25	25	25
Chinese Symbols of the Universe, 1984	90	90	90
Country Garden Calendar (Bing and Grondahl), 1984	55	57	60
Fairy Tales of Old Japan, 1984	40	40	40

	LOW	AVG.	HIGH
Flower Festivals of Japan Series, 1985	$ 50	$ 52	$ 55
Gardens of the Orient Series, 1983	20	20	20
Greatest Show on Earth Series, 1981-82	30	40	50
The Little Rascals, 1985	25	25	25
Majestic Birds of Prey, 1983-84	60	62	65
Noble Owls of America, 1986-87	45	45	45
The Story of Heidi Series, 1981-82	45	47	50
Summer Days of Childhood, 1983	30	30	30
Tale of Genji Series, 1985	45	45	45

Haviland

Bicentennial Series, 1972-76	40	45	50
Christmas Series, 1970	80	100	120
Christmas Series, 1971-81	40	50	60
French Collection Mother's Day Series, 1973-80	30	40	50
Historical Series (great Americans), 1968-71	70	75	80
1001 Arabian Nights Series, 1979-82	27	50	60
Visit from Saint Nicholas Series, 1980-85	55	60	65

Haviland and Parlon

Christmas Madonnas Series, 1972-79	50	75	100
Tapestry Series, 1971-82	50	75	100

Heinrich Porzellan

Flower Fairies Series, 1979-85	30	40	50
Russian Fairy Tale Series, 1980-83	70	95	120

Heirloom Traditions

All series	35	45	55

Hibel Studios

Production Series of 500 or less	1000	2000	3000
Production Series of 2000-5000	200	300	400
Production Series 15,000 and over	50	75	100

Historic Providence Mint

Alice in Wonderland Series, 1986	28	30	32
America the Beautiful Series, 1981	37	38	39
Lil' Peddlers Series, 1986	30	30	30
Vanishing Barn Series, 1983	40	40	40

Hornsea

Christmas Series, 1979-81	40	45	50

House of Global Art

American Heritage Series, 1979-81	100	112	125
Dolly Dingle Series, 1982-83	30	30	30

Hoyle Products

All series	30	45	60

Hudson Pewter

All series	35	40	45

Hutschenreuther

Country Birds of the Year, 1983-86	30	30	30
Nibelungen Series, 1986	125	125	125
Enchantment Series (princesses), 1979-82	60	75	90
Glory of Christmas Series, 1982-85	80	90	100
Gunther Granget Series, 1972-78	80	100	120
Gunther Granget Series (Freedom in Flight-Gold), 1976	200	200	200
Hans Achtziger Series, 1979-85	150	200	250

	LOW	AVG.	HIGH
Legend of St. George, 1985	$ 100	$ 100	$ 100
Love for All Seasons Series, 1981-83	125	125	125
Songbirds of North America Series, 1981	60	60	60
Waterbabies Series, 1983-84	45	45	45
Zodiac Series, 1978	125	130	135

Imperial

America the Beautiful Series, 1969-75	20	21	22
Christmas Series, 1970-81	20	27	35

Incolay Studios

Great Romances of History Series, 1979-82	65	67	70
Romantic Poets Series, 1977-85	70	80	90
Voyage of Ulysses Series, 1984-86	50	55	60
Christmas Series, 1974-79	75	87	100

International Museum

Letter Writer's Series, 1982-84	38	39	40
Stamp Art Series, 1979-83	40	60	80

Georg Jensen

Christmas Series, 1972-76	25	37	50

Svend Jensen

Christmas/Andersen Fairy Tales Series, 1970-84	40	50	60
Mother's Day Series, 1970-84	30	45	60

Josair

Bicentennial Series, 1972-76	250	250	250

Kaiser

Anniversary Series, 1972-83	25	32	40
Christmas Series, 1970-82	20	30	40
Fairy Tale Series, 1982-84	40	45	50
Famous Lullabies, 1985-88	40	45	50
Feathered Friends Series, 1978-81	80	90	100
Happy Days Series, 1981-83	75	75	75
Mother's Day Series, 1971-83	30	45	60
People of the Midnight Sun Series, 1978-83	70	80	90
Traditional Fairy Tales Series, 1983-85	40	40	40
Woodland Creatures, 1985	37	38	40
Yesteday's World Series, 1978-84	70	75	80

Kera

Christmas Series, 1967-71	15	20	25

Kern Collectibles

Adventures of the Old West Series, 1981-85	65	70	75
Children's World Series, 1983-84	45	45	45
Companions Series, 1978-81	60	70	80
Leaders of Tomorrow Series, 1980-83	50	50	50
Mother's Day Series, 1976-80	40	45	50
Sugar and Spice Series, 1976-80	80	100	120
This Little Pig Went to Market, 1982-85	40	42	45

King's

Christmas Series, 1973-76	150	200	250
Flower Series, 1973-77	120	150	180

Edwin Knowles

American Holidays Series, 1976-84	25	30	35
Annie Series, 1983-86	25	30	35

	LOW	AVG.	HIGH
Biblical Mothers Series, 1983-86	$ 50	$ 65	$ 80
Birds of Your Garden Series, 1985-87	20	25	30
Gone With the Wind Series, 1978-79	150	200	250
Gone With the Wind Series, 1980-85	50	65	80
Frances Hook Legacy Series, 1985-87	20	22	25
Oklahoma Series, 1985-87	20	20	20
Sound of Music Series, 1986-87	20	21	23
Wizard of Oz Series, 1977-80	30	45	60
Konigszelt			
Grimm's Fairy Tales, 1981-87	25	30	35
Hedi Keller Christmas Series, 1979-86	35	40	45
Koscherak Brothers			
All series	50	55	60
KPM			
Christmas Series, 1969-73	200	300	400
Christmas Series, 1974-77	100	150	200
Christmas Series, 1978-80	50	62	75
Lalique			
Annual Series, 1965-76	80	100	120
Lenox			
American Wildlife Series, 1983	65	65	65
Boehm Bird Series, 1970	100	150	200
Boehm Bird Series, 1971-81	50	70	90
Boehm Woodland Wildlife Series, 1973-82	60	80	100
Butterflies and Flowers Series, 1982-85	60	67	75
Christmas Tree Series, 1976-82	50	65	80
Nature's Nursery Series, 1982-86	65	72	80
Lihs Linder			
America the Beautiful, 1975	42	43	45
Christmas Series, 1972-78	30	40	50
Easter Series, 1973-75	30	37	45
Limoges-Turgot			
Durand's Children's Series, 1978-80	35	37	40
Morals of Perrault Series, 1983-85	30	32	35
Lladro			
Christmas Series, 1971-79	40	60	80
Mother's Day Series, 1971-79	40	60	80
Longton Crown Pottery			
Canterbury Tales Series, 1981-82	30	32	35
Jean-Paul Loup			
Christmas Series, 1971-76	500	650	800
Lund and Clausen			
All series	12	15	18
Lynell			
All series	40	50	60
Marmot			
Christmas Series, 1970-76	20	30	40
Mother's Day Series (polar bear), 1973	100	125	150
Mother's Day Series, 1972-76	25	32	40
President's Series, 1972-73	25	27	30

	LOW	AVG.	HIGH
Mason			
Christmas Series, 1975-80	$ 75	$ 75	$ 75
Meissen			
Annual Series, 1973-80	80	100	120
Metal Arts Company			
All series	25	37	50
Mettlach			
Christmas Series, 1978-80	150	175	200
Michelon			
All series	75	75	75
Mingolla			
Christmas Series (enamel and copper), 1973-77	120	150	180
Four Seasons Series, 1978	150	150	150
Modern Concepts Limited			
All series	25	37	50
Modern Masters			
All series	30	42	55
Moser			
Christmas Series, 1970-83	80	100	120
Moussalli			
Birds of Four Seasons, 1977-79	375	412	450
Newell Pottery Company			
Calendar Series, 1984-86	20	25	30
Noritake			
Annual Series, 1977-80	400	500	600
Christmas Series, 1975-80	50	87	125
Nostalgia Collectibles			
James Dean Collection, 1985	15	15	15
Elvis Presley Collection, 1985	15	15	15
Shirley Temple Collection, 1983-86	35	35	35
Shirley Temple Collectibles (autographed), 1982-83	100	125	150
O.K. Collectibles			
All series	40	55	70
Opa's Haus			
Annual German Christmas, 1978-84	55	57	60
Pacific Art Limited			
All series	30	45	60
Palisander			
All series	50	57	65
Parkhurt Enterprises			
International Wildlife Foundation Series, 1984	60	60	60
Pemberton and Oakes			
Childhood Friendship Series, 1987-88	20	22	25
Children at Christmas Series, 1981-86	60	70	80
Moments Alone Series, 1980-83	30	37	45
Wonder of Childhood Series, 1982-87	20	35	50
Pickard			
Annual Christmas Plate Series, 1976-81	60	75	90
Beautiful Women Series, 1981-84	75	75	75
Children of Mary Cassatt Series, 1983-84	60	60	60
Children of Renoir Series, 1978-80	70	90	110

	LOW	AVG.	HIGH
Legends of Camelot Series, 1982	$ 60	$ 62	$ 65
Let's Pretend Series, 1984-85	79	80	81
Lockhart Wildlife Series, 1970-80	150	200	250
Lockhart Wildlife Series (American bald eagle), 1974	600	750	900
Symphony of Roses Series, 1982-85	90	95	100
Pollerat			
Calendar Series, 1972-73	100	125	150
Christmas Series, 1972-73	350	375	400
Poole Pottery			
Medieval Calendar Series, 1972-77	100	112	125
Porcelaine Ariel			
Greatest Show on Earth Series, 1981-82	30	45	60
The Rubaiyat of Omar Khayyam, 1980-82	45	47	50
Waltzes of Johann Strauss Series, 1981-82	25	27	30
Porcelana Granada			
Christmas Series, 1971-82	15	20	25
Porsgrund			
Christmas Series, 1968	80	100	120
Christmas Series, 1969-83	20	30	40
Easter Series, 1972-77	15	20	25
Father's Day Series, 1971-80	15	20	25
Mother's Day Series, 1970-84	15	20	25
Traditional Norwegian Christmas Series, 1978-82	30	37	45
Ram			
Boston 500 Series (holidays), 1973	30	35	40
Rare Bird			
All series	45	47	50
Raynaud (Limoges)			
All series	40	45	50
Reco International			
Becky's Day Series, 1985-86	25	30	35
Childhood Almanac Series, 1985	30	35	40
Dresden Christmas Series, 1971-77	30	40	50
Dresden Mother's Day, 1972-77	20	25	30
Games Children Play Series, 1979-82	45	50	55
Great Bible Stories Series, 1987	30	30	30
Little Professional Series, 1982-85	40	47	55
Mother Goose Series (Mary, Mary), 1979	200	300	400
Mother Goose Series, 1980-86	30	40	50
Sophisticated Ladies Series, 1985-86	30	32	35
Springtime of Life Series, 1986-86	30	30	30
Vanishing Animal Kingdom Series, 1986-87	30	35	40
Reed and Barton			
American Christmas Series, 1976-78	65	70	75
Annual Series, 1972-75	65	65	65
Audubon Series (Pine Siskin), 1970	150	175	200
Audubon Series, 1971-77	65	70	75
Christmas Series, 1973-76	65	65	65
Currier and Ives Series, 1972-74	80	85	90
Founding Fathers Series, 1974-76	60	65	70
Kentucky Derby Series, 1972-74	80	85	90
Missions of California Series, 1971-76	60	70	80

	LOW	AVG.	HIGH
Old Fashioned Christmas Series, 1977-81	$ 55	$ 60	$ 65

Rhea Silva Porcelain Collection

	LOW	AVG.	HIGH
All series	40	50	60

Ridgewood

Christmas Series, 1975-76	30	35	40
Tom Sawyer Series, 1974	10	12	15
Wild West Series, 1975	15	17	20

River Shore

American Songbirds Series, 1985	20	22	25
Baby Animal Collection, 1979-82	60	80	100
Lovable Teddies Series, 1985	20	22	25
Rockwell Four Freedoms Series, 1981-82	60	65	70
Rockwell Good Old Days Series, 1982	22	25	28
Signs of Love Series, 1981-83	20	22	25
Vignette Series, 1981-82	20	22	25

Rockwell Museum

American Families Series (Baby's First Step), 1979	100	125	150
American Families Series, 1979-81	30	45	60
Christmas Collectibles Series, 1979-84	60	75	90
Classic Plates Series, 1981-82	25	27	30
A Touch of Rockwell Series, 1984	15	20	25
World of Children Bas Relief Series, 1982	40	45	50

Rockwell Society

American Dream Series, 1985-87	20	22	25
Christmas Series, 1974-84	30	45	60
Heritage Series, 1977-78	100	125	150
Heritage Series, 1979-85	30	45	60
Mother's Day Series, 1976-78	80	100	120
Mother's Day Series, 1979-87	30	35	40
Rockwell Tour Series, 1983-84	20	30	40
Rockwell's Rediscovered Women Series, 1982-84	25	35	45

Roman, Inc.

Cat Series, 1984-85	25	30	35
Frances Hook Collection, 1982-83	50	62	75
Lord's Prayer Series, 1986	20	25	30
Magic of Childhood Series, 1984-85	20	25	30
Masterpiece Collection, 1979-82	60	80	100
Sweetest Songs Series, 1986	40	42	45

Rorstrand,

Christmas Series (Bringing Home the Tree), 1968	350	400	450
Christmas Series, 1969-86	20	35	50
Father's Day Series, 1971-84	20	30	40
Mother's Day Series, 1971-84	25	35	45

Rosenthal

Christmas Series (Winter Peace), 1910	400	500	600
Christmas Series, 1911-45	200	300	400
Christmas Series, 1946-47	700	850	1000
Christmas Series, 1948-70	200	225	250
Christmas Series, 1971-74	80	100	120
Classic Rose Christmas Series, 1974-85	100	150	200
Famous Women and Children Series, 1980-82	300	400	500

	LOW	AVG.	HIGH
Fantasies and Fables Series, 1976-77 .... $ 50		$ 65	$ 80
Lorraine Trester Series, 1975-77 100		110	120
Nobility of Children Series, 1976-79 120		135	150
Oriental Gold Series, 1973-79 400		600	800
Wiinblad Christmas Series (Maria and Child), 1971 800		1000	1200
Wiinblad Christmas Series, 1972-82 200		300	400

Royal Bayreuth

	LOW	AVG.	HIGH
Christmas Series, 1972-79 40		50	60
Mother's Day Series, 1973-82 60		80	100
Sunbonnet Babies Playtime Series, 1981-82 50		60	70

Royal Copenhagen

	LOW	AVG.	HIGH
Christmas Series (Madonna and Child), 1908 1500		1750	2000
Christmas Series, 1909-15 120		135	150
Christmas Series, 1916-31 80		100	120
Christmas Series, 1932-39 100		125	150
Christmas Series, 1940-45 300		400	500
Christmas Series, 1946-56 150		200	250
Christmas Series, 1957-70 100		125	150
Christmas Series, 1971-84 70		85	100
Historical Series, 1975-80 30		45	60
Motherhood Collection, 1982-85 30		40	50
Mother's Day Series (American Mother), 1971 100		125	150
Mother's Day Series, 1972-82 30		45	60
National Parks of America Series, 1978-81 70		75	80

Royal Cornwall

	LOW	AVG.	HIGH
Alice in Wonderland Series, 1979-80 40		50	60
Beauty of Bouguereau Series, 1979-80 35		50	65
Classic Christmas Collection, 1978 65		75	85
Courageous Few Series, 1982-83 60		62	65
Creation Series, 1977-80 80		115	150
Crystal Maidens Series, 1979 70		75	80
Charles Dickens Series, 1980-82 60		62	65
Dorothy's Day Plates Series, 1980-81 50		55	60
Exotic Bird of Tropique Series, 1981-82 45		50	55
Four Seasons, 1978 50		60	70
Golden Age of Cinema, 1978-79 40		45	50
Golden Plates of the Noble Flower Maidens Series, 1982 .. 60		65	70
Grandma Moses Memories of America, 1980-81 100		110	120
Impressions of Yesteryear Series, 1982-83 55		60	65
Kitten's World Series, 1979-80 50		60	70
Legend of the Peacock Maidens Series, 1982 70		72	75
Legendary Ships of the Sea Series, 1980-81 50		60	70
Leyendecker Classic Collection, 1980 55		60	65
Little People Series, 1980-81 30		35	40
Love's Precious Moments Series, 1981 50		55	60
Memories of the Western Prairies Series, 1983-84 45		50	55
Most Precious Gifts of Shen Lung Series, 1981 45		50	55
Promised Land Series, 1979-80 45		47	50
Puppy's World Series, 1982 45		50	55
Treasures of Childhood Series, 1979-80 45		47	50

	LOW	AVG.	HIGH
Two Thousand of Ships Series, 1982-84	$ 40	$ 42	$ 45
Windows on the World Series, 1980-82	40	45	50

Royal Delft

	LOW	AVG.	HIGH
Christmas Series (large), 1915 (Christmas Bells)	5000	6000	7000
Christmas Series (large), 1916 (star floral design)	600	700	800
Christmas Series (large), 1916-86	250	350	450
Christmas Series (9"), 1955-58	150	200	250
Christmas Series (small), 1915 (Christmas Star)	2000	3000	4000
Christmas Series (small), 1926-32	250	300	350
Christmas Series (small), 1959-86	120	150	180
Easter Series, 1973-76	150	175	200
Father's Day Series, 1972-76	80	100	120
Mother's Day Series, 1971-76	80	100	120
Space Series, 1957-72	50	75	100
Halley's Comet, 1910	600	700	800

Royal Devon

	LOW	AVG.	HIGH
All series	40	60	80

Royal Doulton

	LOW	AVG.	HIGH
All God's Children Series, 1979-84	70	85	100
American Tapestries Series, 1978-81	70	85	100
Annual Christmas Series, 1983-87	35	40	45
Behind the Painted Mask Series, 1982-83	95	97	100
Beswick Christmas Series, 1972-78	40	55	70
Children of the Pueblo Series, 1983	55	60	65
Commedia Dell'Arte Series, 1974-78	70	75	80
Festival Children of the World Series, 1983	60	65	70
Flower Garden Series, 1975-79	70	80	90
I Remember America Series, 1977-80	70	80	90
Jungle Fantasy Series, 1980-83	80	90	100
Leroy Nieman Special Series, 1980	80	85	90
Log of the Dashing Wave Series, 1976-84	80	100	120
Portraits of Innocence Series, 1980-83	100	150	200
Ports of Call Series, 1975-78	65	77	90
Reflections on China Series, 1976-79	70	80	90
Victorian Christmas Series, 1977-82	40	47	55
Victorian Valentine Series, 1976-84	40	50	60

Royal Grafton

	LOW	AVG.	HIGH
Twelve Days of Christmas Series, 1976-80	20	25	30

Royal Oaks Limited

	LOW	AVG.	HIGH
Love's Labor Series, 1983	50	50	50

Royal Orleans

	LOW	AVG.	HIGH
Coca Cola/Santa Claus Series, 1983-85	55	60	65
Elvis in Concert Series, 1984-85	30	35	40
Famous Movies Series, 1985		15	30
Marilyn Monroe, 1983-85	30	35	40
Nostalgic Magazine Covers Series, 1983	30	35	40
Pink Panther Christmas Series, 1982-85	15	17	20
TV Series, 1983	25	30	35

Royal Tettau

	LOW	AVG.	HIGH
Papal Series, 1971-73	100	150	200

Royal Doulton, Kristina and Child, designed by Edna Hibel, 1975, one of 15,000, $30.

	LOW	AVG.	HIGH
Royal Worcester			
Audubon Bird Series, 1977-78	$ 125	$ 150	$ 175
Bicentennial Series, 1972-76	50	65	80
Birth of a Nation Series, 1972-76	80	100	120
Currier and Ives Series (American produced), 1974-76	60	65	70
Currier and Ives Series (British produced), 1974-77	100	125	150
Doughty Birds Series, 1972-83	100	150	200
English Christmas Series, 1979-80	60	65	70
Famous Bird Series, 1976-78	60	65	70
Kitten Classics Series, 1985	25	30	35
Water Birds of North America Series, 1985	50	55	60
Royale			
Christmas Series, 1969-77	30	45	60
Father's Day Series, 1970-77	30	45	60
Game Plates Series, 1972-75	200	235	270
Mother's Day Series (animals), 1970-77	30	45	60
Royale Germania			
Annual Flower Series, 1970-76	300	450	600
Royalwood			
Leyendecker Series, 1978	20	25	30
John A. Ruthven			
Moments of Nature Series, 1977-80	35	40	45
Sango			
Christmas Series, 1974-77	30	40	50
Santa Clara			
Christmas Series, 1970-79	30	35	40
Mother's Day Series, 1971-72	30	35	40
Schmid			
Beatrix Potter Series, 1978-80	45	50	55
Berta Hummel Christmas Series, 1971-87	50	65	80
Berta Hummel Christmas Series (Nativity), 1973	400	450	500
Berta Hummel Mother's Day Series, 1972-87	25	37	50
Cat Tales Series, 1982-83	40	50	60
Country Christmas Annual Series, 1983-87	45	50	55
Disney Annual Series, 1983-86	20	22	25
Disney Christmas Series, 1973-74	200	300	400

	LOW	AVG.	HIGH
Disney Christmas Series, 1975-82	$ 20	$ 25	$ 30
Disney's Mother's Day Series, 1974-82	20	30	40
Ferrandiz Beautiful Bounty Porcelain Series, 1982	40	45	50
Ferrandiz Mother and Child Series, 1977-79	60	80	100
Golden Moments Series, 1978-81	200	250	300
Music Makers Series, 1981-82	25	27	30
Nature's Treasures Series, 1974	40	45	50
Paddington Bear Series, 1979-81	15	20	25
Peanuts (all series)	20	30	40
Prairie Woman Series, 1982	30	35	40
Prime Time (television) Series, 1984	25	30	35
Raggedy Ann (all series), 1980-84	15	25	35
Reflections of Life Series, 1980-81	80	85	90
Schmid Design Series, 1971-80	20	30	40
Zemsky Star Series, 1981-82	25	30	35
Schonfield Gallery			
Clowns Series, 1986	45	50	55
Schumann			
Christmas Series, 1971-75	12	15	18
Imperial Christmas Series 1979-82	80	90	100
Sebastian			
America's Favorite Scenes, 1978-79	70	75	80
Seven Seas			
Christmas Carols Series, 1970-80	15	20	25
Mother's Day Series, 1970-73	20	25	30
New World Series (Christmas), 1970-72	20	25	30
Signature Collection			
Angler's Dream Series (fish), 1983	50	55	60
Baker Street Series, 1983	50	55	60
All other series	30	40	50
Southern Living Gallery			
Game Bird of the South Series, 1983	40	42	45
All other series	35	40	45
Spode			
Christmas Series, 1970-81	30	45	60
Maritime Series, 1980	140	150	160
Sports Impressions			
Baseball Series, 1987	60	92	125

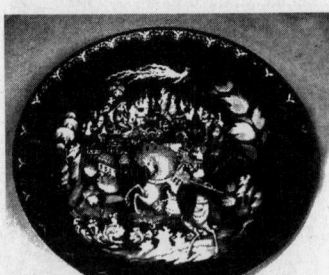

Left: Russian examples are appearing, but their prices are rarely appreciating.

	LOW	AVG.	HIGH
All other series	$ 60	$ 92	$ 125

Sterling America

Christmas Customs Series, 1970-74	20	25	30
Mother's Day Series (animals), 1971-75	15	20	25
Twelve Days of Christmas Series, 1970-77	20	22	25

Stieff

Bicentennial Series, 1972-76	45	50	55

Stratford Collection

All series	35	40	45

Stuart International

Childhood Secrets Series, 1983	30	35	40

Studio Dante Di Volteradici

All series	40	50	60

Stumar

Christmas Series, 1970-78	20	25	30
Egyptian Series, 1977-78	45	50	55
Mother's Day Series, 1971-78	15	20	25

Tirschenreuth

Christmas Series, 1969-73	15	20	25
Songbirds of Europe Series, 1985-87	20	22	25

Topsy Turvy

Storybook Series, 1982	15	20	25

U.S. Historical Society

Annual Historical Series, 1977-78	60	70	80
Annual Spring Flowers Series, 1983-84	125	137	150
Buffalo Bill's Wild West Series, 1984	50	55	60
Christmas Carol Series, 1982-87	55	60	65
Great American Sailing Ships, 1983-85	130	140	150
Stained Glass Cathedral Christmas Series, 1978-83	100	125	150
Two Hundred Years of Flight, 1984	45	50	55

Vague Shadows

Chieftain Series (Sitting Bull), 1979	400	500	600
Chieftain Series, 1979-81	100	125	150
Chieftain II Series, 1983-84	60	70	80
Indian Nations Series, 1983	45	50	55
Legends of the West Series, 1982-84	60	65	70
Masterworks of Impressionism Series, 1980-81	30	35	40
Masterworks of the West Series, 1980-81	35	37	40
Nature's Harmony Series, 1982	50	75	100
Pride of America's Indians Series, 1986-87	20	25	30
The Princesses Series, 1981-82	80	90	100
The Professionals Series, 1979	100	110	120
The Professionals Series, 1980-83	30	45	60
The Storybook Collection, 1980-82	40	45	50
The Thoroughbreds Series, 1984	50	65	80
War Ponies Series, 1983-84	80	100	120

Val St. Lambert

American Heritage Series, 1969-71	200	300	400
Annual Old Masters Series, 1969-72	70	80	90

Veneto Flair

American Landscape Series, 1979-80	70	75	80

	LOW	AVG.	HIGH
Cat Series, 1974-76	$ 45	$ 50	$ 55
Children's Christmas Series, 1979-82	65	80	95
Christmas Card Series, 1975-78	40	45	50
Dog Series, 1972-76	40	55	70
Four Seasons Series, 1972-74	80	100	120
La Belle Femme Series, 1978-80	70	75	80
Mother and Child Series, 1981	90	92	95
Valentine's Day Series, 1977-80	60	65	70

Vernonware

Christmas Series, 1971-79	30	45	60
Corvette Collector Series, 1986-87	25	27	30

Viletta China

Alice in Wonderland Series, 1980-81	20	25	30
Carefree Days Series, 1982	20	22	25
Christmas Annual Series, 1978-80	45	50	55
Coppelia Ballet Series, 1980-82	25	27	30
Disneyland Series, 1976	80	90	100
Israel's 30th Anniversary Series, 1979	55	60	65
Making Friends Series, 1978-80	40	45	50
Nutcracker Ballet, 1978-80	30	45	60
Portraits of Childhood Series, 1981-83	20	22	25
Rufus and Roxanne, 1980	10	12	15
Seasons of the Oak Series, 1979-80	50	55	60
Unicorn Fantasies Series, 1979-82	50	55	60
Women of the West Series, 1979-80	40	42	45

Waldenburg Porcelain

All series	30	35	40

Enoch Wedgwood

Avon Christmas Series, 1973-79	25	30	35
Bicentennial Series, 1972-76	40	60	80
Blossoming of Suzanne Series, 1977-80	40	50	60
Calendar Series, 1971-88	20	30	40
Children's Story Series, 1971-85	10	15	20
Christmas Series (Windsor Castle), 1969	150	200	250
Christmas Series, 1970-87	40	60	80
Eyes of the Child Series	60	65	70
Mother's Day Series, 1971-88	30	40	50
Peter Rabbit Christmas Series, 1981-87	25	27	30

Western Authentics

All series	30	40	50

Westminster Collectibles

Holidays Series, 1976-77	35	37	40

Wildlife International

All series	60	75	90

Zanobia

All series	30	35	40

Political Memorabilia

Every political campaign from dog catcher to president produces memorabilia. In addition to the familiar campaign buttons, there is literature of all types, including posters, pictures, brochures and newspaper ads. Such variety and the number of candidates over the years creates a rich and broad collecting field. Political memorabilia offers a history lesson, a chance to discover the movers and shakers of other eras. Most collectors concentrate on national elections and well-known politicians. There are others that focus on third party and more obscure candidates.

Buttons are a favorite area of specialization for many collectors. There are several types of buttons. Celluloid buttons are produced by placing a thin piece of paper over a metal disc and then sealing it with a coating of celluloid. Tin lithograph buttons are produced by printing directly onto the tin. A curious term to novices is "jugates," which are buttons picturing both presidential and vice presidential candidates.

Although some items are worth thousands of dollars, this collecting field offers items for every budget. Our consultant for this area is long-time collector Karen Gagliardi (she is listed in the back of this book).

Assorted

	LOW	HIGH
"America's Pride," colored and embossed cigar box label, pictures George Washington, 7" x 9"	$ 10	$ 25
Blaine, James and John Logan, campaign bandanna, sq. 18"	180	220
Bryan, "Back to the Farm-Three Strikes and Out," Anti-Bryan cartoon postcard	14	20
Bryan, "Bottom Is Out of the Full Dinner Pail," postcard, 1908	10	20
Bryan, "Next Occupant of the White House," campaign postcard for William J. Bryan	8	14
Carter, "The Interview, Carter Talks in Playboy," Playboy magazine folder with 2.5" button, 1976 campaign	8	12
Cleveland, Grover and Thomas Hendricks, campaign bandanna, sq. 18"	200	300
Eisenhower, "I Like Ike," sticker, 1952 or 1956, 3" x 3.5"	6	9
Garfield, clear glass bust cologne bottle, ht. 9"	800	1200
Kennedy, musical doll in rocking chair	200	300
"Lincoln Bouquet," colored and embossed cigar box label, c. 1910, 6" x 10"	10	25
McCarthy Scarf	6	8
McGovern, lithograph "McGovern for McGovernment," by Alexander Calder	375	400
McKinley, pottery tile, glazed, sq. 3"	40	50
Nixon, "Let's Back Nixon," paper sticker showing Nixon pointing his finger at Khrushchev, 1960 campaign, 4" x 6"	15	20
Roosevelt, FDR poster	15	25
Roosevelt, FDR mug "Happy Days Are Here Again"	30	50
Roosevelt, "Dee Lighted," a postcard picturing Teddy Roosevelt, 1905	12	20
Roosevelt, Teddy, *Puck* magazine, issue contains 2 large political cartoons, one of Teddy Roosevelt, 1906	15	25
Taft, "Nation's Choice," embossed postcard picturing Taft and Sherman	10	15
Taft, "Our Next President William H. Taft: Glory and Prosperity For Our Country," colored postcard picturing Taft	8	12
Taft, "Our Next President and Vice President," postcard picturing Taft and Sherman	8	12

	LOW	HIGH

"Vote Democratic," paper window sticker, c. 1948, 4" x 4" .... $ 7 $ 12

Wilson, "I Think We've Got Another Washington and Wilson Is His Name,"
song sheet, 1915 15   20

Wilson, "Never Swap Horses When You're Crossing a Stream," song sheet
with portrait of Woodrow Wilson, 1916 15   20

Political Buttons

Carter, "The Grin Will Win Jimmy in '76, Carter for President" 6   10

Chafin, "Eugene Chafin for President," 1908 Prohibition Party candidate,
black and white, .875" 36   40

Coolidge, lithographed tin, blue and white 14   18

Coolidge/Davis, jugate, celluloid, black and white, 7/8" 35   45

Eisenhower, "I Like Ike," lithographed tin, red lettering on white background,
no illustration, used in 1952 2   3

Hoover, black and white, 1.25" 45   50

Hoover, lithographed red, white and blue, .875" 4   8

Johnson/ Humphrey, jugate, photos in outline of the U.S., "Vote Democratic,"
red, white and blue, 3.5" 10   15

Kennedy, "For President John F. Kennedy," red, white, blue and black 10   14

McKinley/Hobart, jugate, mechanical gold bug, 1896 200   250

McKinley/Theodore Roosevelt, Jugate, "Employment for Labor, A Full
Dinner Bucket," sepia, 1.25" 100   145

Nixon/Lodge, jugate, lithographed tin, from campaign of 1960 which
Richard Nixon lost to John Kennedy 2   3

Reagan, "Ronald Reagan for Governor," lithographed tin, white border 2   3

Roosevelt, "Carry On," lithographed tin, 1" 4   8

Roosevelt, "Rally Round Roosevelt, The People's Choice for President, RRR,"
red, white and blue 25   35

Roosevelt, FDR/Wallace, jugate, sepia with red, white and blue border 42   52

Roosevelt,Teddy, portrait button 20   30

Smith/Robinson, jugate, lithographed tin, from 1926 campaign 20   30

Stevenson, "Our Next President Adlai Stevenson," red, white, and blue,
1.75" 10   14

Taft, celluloid, multicolor 35   40

Taft/Sherman, jugate, gray and white 100   140

Truman, Inauguration, January 20, 1949, red, white and blue with gray photo,
1.75" 18   22

Wilkie, "If I Were 21 I'd Vote for Wilkie," green and white, 1.25" 6   9

Willkie, white and black with shoulder-length portrait, wording "For President"
at top 18   22

Wilson/Marshall, jugate, celluloid, black and white, "Win With Wilson and
Marshall," .875" 32   40

*Franklin Roosevelt and
Garner jugate, $140-
$160. — Item courtesy
of Pastimes Antiques.*

Pottery & Porcelain: By Manufacturer

J.A. Bauer Pottery

The J.A. Bauer Company started with clay flowerpots in 1909. After the introduction of stoneware and art pottery, his company added colored dinnerware in 1930, which it produced until 1962.

Marks: an impressed mark with *Bauer* or a combination of the words *Bauer*, *Los Angeles*, *Pottery*, and *USA*. Many items are unmarked or stamped *Made in USA*.

BAUER   *J.A. Bauer backstamp.*

La Linda (1939-59)

	LOW	AVG.	HIGH
La Linda appears in at least 14 colors, some matte, some glossy.			
Butter Dish	$ 45	$ 56	$ 67
Chop plate, 13"	26	29	32
Cookie Jar, plain	50	63	76
Cream/Sugar	20	25	30
Cup	10	13	16
Cup/Saucer, jumbo	25	30	35
Custard	6	8	10
Dish, 5"-6"	9	12	15
Gravy Boat	15	20	25
Pitcher, ball form	35	46	57
Plate, 6"	4	5	6
Plate, 7.5"	7	9	12
Plate, 9"	11	14	16
Platter, 10"-12"	14	17	20
Salt/Pepper	9	11	13
Saucer	3	4	5
Soup Plate, 7"	16	19	21
Teapot, 6 cup	33	38	42
Tumbler, 8 oz.	13	16	19
Vegetable, 8"-10"	20	27	34

Monterey (1936-1945)

	LOW	AVG.	HIGH
Orange Red and Burgundy are the most desirable of the 10 colors.			
Beverage Server, w/ cover	100	120	140
Butter Dish	60	73	86
Cake Plate, pedestal	80	90	100
Candleholder	25	30	35
Chop Plate, 13"	30	40	50
Coffee Server	32	37	42
Console set, 3 piece	200	240	280
Dish, 6"	11	14	17
Fruit, ftd., 12"	45	54	63
Fruit, ftd., 8"-9"	27	36	44
Gravy Boat	33	38	43

	LOW	AVG.	HIGH
Pitcher, 2 qt.	$ 33	$ 38	$ 42
Plate, 10.5"	26	29	31
Plate, 6"-7.5"	8	10	12
Plate, 9"	13	15	17
Platter, oval, 12"-17"	30	37	45
Relish Tray, 3-piece, 11.5"	42	50	58
Salad, 11.5"	31	36	42
Salt/Pepper	12	16	19
Sauce Boat	38	42	46
Soup Plate, 7"	16	19	21
Teapot, new, 6 cup	45	55	65
Tumbler, 8 oz.	15	18	21
Vegetable, oval, 10.5"	30	38	45
Vegetable, round, 9.5"	25	28	30

Pastel Kitchenware

Batter Bowl, qt.	25	30	35
Batter Bowl, 2 qt.	45	65	85
Casserole, metal holder, 1.5 pt.	25	35	45
Casserole, metal holder, 1 qt.	35	45	55
Mixing Bowl, pt.	10	12	14
Mixing Bowl, qt.	15	20	25
Mixing Bowl, .5 gal.	25	30	35
Pitcher, 1.5 pt.	18	24	30
Pitcher, 1 qt.	25	30	35
Pitcher, ice lip, 2 qt.	30	40	50
Teapot, Aladdin, 4 cup	35	45	55
Teapot, Aladdin, 8 cup	100	150	200

Ring (c. 1931)

Ring is the most popular pattern. It is reputedly the line that influenced Homer Laughlin to create Fiesta. The pattern appears in many colors. Black pieces are worth more than the values quoted below.

Baker, Pie, no holder, 9"	20	25	30
Barrel Mug, 12 oz	45	60	75
Barrel Pitcher	100	125	150
Batter Bowl, 1-2 qt.	60	80	100
Beating Bowl, 1 qt.	32	38	44
Beating Bowl Pitcher, 1 qt.	40	50	60
Beer Pitcher	160	180	200
Beer Stein	50	60	70
Bowl, nesting, 6"-7"	22	27	32
Bowl, nesting, 8"-9"	31	43	55
Butter Dish	110	130	150
Candlestick, spool	30	35	40
Canister, 4"-6"	60	80	100
Canister, 6.75"	100	130	150
Carafe, metal handle	35	40	45
Casserole, ind., 5.5"	65	70	75
Casserole, metal holder, 6.5"-7.5"	45	60	75
Casserole, metal holder, 8.5"-9.5"	60	85	110

	LOW	AVG.	HIGH
Chop plate, 12"-14"	$ 42	$ 55	$ 68
Chop plate, 17"	75	90	106
Cigarette Jar	150	180	210
Coffee Pot, 8 cup	120	160	180
Coffee Server, wood handle, 6-8 cup	50	65	80
Custard	8	10	12
Dish, baking, w/ lid, 4"	20	23	26
Dish, fruit, 5"	13	15	17
Egg Cup	65	74	82
Goblet	61	74	86
Gravy Bowl	38	44	50
Jar, Storage, open	15	18	21
Mixing Bowl, 1 gal.	42	48	55
Mixing Bowl, 1 pt.	13	16	19
Mixing Bowl, 1 qt.	20	23	25
Mixing Bowl, 1.5 pt.	16	19	22
Mixing Bowl, 1.5 qt.	22	25	27
Mustard	100	125	150
Pedestal Bowl, 14"	160	180	200
Pickle Dish	16	19	22
Pitcher, 1 qt.	26	30	33
Pitcher, 1.5 pt.	21	25	28
Pitcher, 2 qt.	33	38	43
Pitcher, 3 qt.	42	52	62
Pitcher, ball form	65	75	85
Pitcher, cream, 1 pt.	35	45	45
Pitcher, ice lip, w/ metal handle, 2 qt.	68	80	93
Plate, 10.5"	31	36	40
Plate, 5-9"	12	16	20
Platter, oval, 12"	27	30	33
Platter, oval, 9"	22	24	26
Punch Bowl, 14"	160	180	200
Punch Cup	16	19	22
Relish Tray, 5 pc.	36	43	50
Salad, low, 12"-14"	60	75	90
Salad, low, 9"	31	36	41
Salad/Punch, 11"	160	190	220
Salad/Punch, 9"	100	130	160
Saucer, coffee/tea	5	7	9
Shaker, barrel shape	5	7	9
Shaker, low	5	7	9
Shaker, sugar bowl	50	60	70
Sherbet	32	38	44
Soufflé Dish	138	150	163
Soup Plate	27	30	32
Teapot, 2-6 cup	50	60	70
Teapot, wood handle, 6 cup	65	75	85
Tumbler, 3-12 oz	11	19	27
Tumbler, barrel shape, w/ metal handle	32	37	42
Vegetable, oval, 8"-10"	26	28	30
Vegetable, oval, divided	45	55	65

Jim Beam Bottles

Jim Beam bottle figural liquor containers were first issued in the 1950s. The company produces a variety of themes including the Executive Series, Regal China Series, and Political Figures Series. Early Beam bottles made before the figural series are also collectible. In 1953, the company produced its first figural decanter. When the decanters sold well, Beam began producing decorative bottles on a large scale.

Jim Beam bottle,
New Hampshire,
$10-$15.

	LOW	AVG.	HIGH
AC Spark Plug, 1977, ht. 11.5"	$ 8	$ 10	$ 12
Antique Globe, 1980, ht. 8"	30	35	40
Barney's Slot Machine, 1978, ht. 9"	30	35	40
Big Apple, 1979, ht. 8.5"	12	10	20
Blue Gill Fish, 1974, ht. 9.75"	8	10	12
Bobby Unser Olsonite Eagle, 1975, len. 19.25"	40	45	50
Bull Dog, 1979, ht. 9.5"	20	20	30
Caboose, 1980, len. 11.25"	35	40	50
Canteen, 1979, ht. 9"	18	20	22
Cathedral Radio, 1979, ht. 8.5"	15	20	20
Chain Saw, 1979, len. 15.5"	20	25	30
Charlie McCarthy, 1976, ht. 12.5"	30	35	40
Figaro, w/ music box, 1977, ht. 15"	350	370	470
Florida ABC, 1973, ht. 9"	8	10	12
Giant Panda, 1980, ht. 12.5"	23	20	30
Jewel T. Delivery Wagon, 1974, ht. 7.75"	100	110	140
Kangaroo, 1977, ht. 11.75"	20	20	30
King Kong, 1976, ht. 9.75"	12	10	20
Large Mouth Bass, 1973, ht. 13"	8	10	12
Milwaukee Stein, 1972, ht. 11"	75	87	100
Mississippi Fire Engine, 1978, len. 14"	50	60	70
Model A Ford, 1980, len. 15"	40	45	50
Mortimer Snerd, 1976, ht. 12"	30	35	40
Mt. St. Helen's, 1980, ht. 9.25"	15	23	20
New Mexico, 1972, ht. 9.5"	8	10	12
Rainbow Trout, 1975, ht. 7.5"	8	10	12
Shriner's, 1970, ht. 8.75"	5	10	15
St. Bernard, 1979, ht. 6.5"	65	78	90
Stutz Bearcat 1914, 1977, len. 16.25"	42	40	60
Telephone, wall model, 1975, ht. 9.5"	30	35	40

Edwin Bennett Pottery

For 90 years, the Edwin Bennett Pottery Company manufactured a variety of products from stoneware and parianware to majolica and semiporcelain. It is most famous for its Cameo line of dinnerware. The firm opened in 1846 and closed in 1936.

Marks: backstamps include: *Bennett Bakeware* and *Bennett, S-V, Baltimore*, and *Il Duce*.

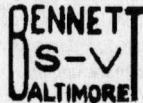 *Edwin Bennett backstamp.*

	LOW	AVG.	HIGH
Baker, Pie	$ 12	$ 14	$ 16
Bean Pot	16	18	20
Butter Dish	20	23	25
Cake Plate	12	14	16
Cake Server	20	25	30
Canister	39	46	52
Casserole	24	28	32
Casserole	30	35	40
Cream/Sugar	12	14	16
Cup/Saucer	8	10	12
Custard Cup	4	5	6
Dish, 5.5"	2	3	4
Drip Jar	25	28	30
Gravy Boat	12	15	18
Mixing Bowl	20	30	40
Mug, barrel	15	18	21
Pitcher	20	25	30
Pitcher, syrup	38	44	51
Pitcher, w /lid	38	43	48
Plate, 6"-8"	2	4	6
Plate, 9"	8	9	10
Platter, rect.	10	11	12
Salad Bowl	17	19	21
Salt Box	40	45	50
Salt/Pepper	25	35	45
Soup Plate, 7.5"	8	10	12
Tray	20	26	32
Vegetable	10	11	12

Bennington Pottery

The period of true Bennington was brief, from 1842 to 1858, but this is deceiving since the output during those 16 years was heavy. In 1842 Julius Norton (a grandson of the founder) went into partnership with Christopher Fenton. Norton and Fenton set out to duplicate the surface of Rockingham wares. From the original name of "Norton and Fenton," it became "Fenton's Works," then "Lyman, Fenton and Co." Finally, the company used the name "United States Pottery" from 1850 until its collapse in 1858.

The earliest mark of Norton and Fenton, in 1842, was a circular wording of *NORTON & FENTON, BENNINGTON, Vt.* Block lettering was used without any symbol. When the company name changed, after Norton left in 1847, the mark became *FENTON'S WORKS, BENNINGTON, VERMONT* enclosed in a rectangular decorative border. This distinctive mark was set in two styles of lettering with *FENTON'S WORKS* in slanting characters resembling italics. The address was set in standard vertical lettering. The next mark, that of Lyman, Fenton and Co., sat within a plain oval frame and read *LYMAN FENTON & CO., FENTON'S ENAMEL, PATENTED 1849, BENNINGTON, Vt.* This ushered in the era of colored glazes. Within this mark, the year (1849) is very prominently displayed. The United States Pottery Co. era introduced two different marks, both reading *UNITED STATES POTTERY Co., BENNINGTON, VT.* One carries the wording in an oval frame with two small ornamental flourishes; the other is a modified diamond shape composed of decorative printer's type, but without further ornamentation.

Left to right: Diamond pattern rockingham pitcher, height 9", $350; octagonal pitcher with tulip and heart motif, marked, height 11", $900; flint enamel eight panel pitcher with tulip and heart motif, height 7.5", $450. — Photo courtesy of Northeast Auctions.

Flint Enamel "Rockingham"
Glazed Pieces

	AUCTION	RETAIL Low	High
Baking Dish, 1849 mark, dia. 7"	$ 175	$ 400	$ 660
Book Flask, "Bennington Battle," ht. 7.5"	700	1650	2650
Book Flask, "Departed Spirits," ht. 5"	425	1000	1600
Book Flask, "Departed Spirits," ht. 8"	700	1650	2650
Book Flask, extended spout, rare small 1849 mark, ht. 6"	900	2120	3400
Book Flask, 4 qt., largest size	1600	3500	6000
Book Flask, "Lexington Battle," ht. 7"	600	1420	2250
Candlesticks, pr., ht. 9.25"	725	1700	2750
Candlesticks, pr., ht. 8"	500	1180	1900
Chamber Pitcher, scalloped rib pattern, 1849 mark, ht. 12.75"	750	1750	2700
Chamber Pot, diamond pattern w/ lid, dia. 10"	350	830	1330
Coffee Pot, 1849 mark	250	600	950
Coffee Pot, scalloped rib pattern, ht. 12"	650	1500	2500
Cow Creamer, complete, lid, len. 7"	350	830	1330
Creamer, seated Toby, w/ 1849 mark	550	1300	2000
Creamer, tulip and heart pattern, 1849 mark, ht. 6"	300	700	1140
Curtain Tieback, len. 4.5", dia. 4.5"	30	70	100
Cuspidor, scalloped rib pattern, 1849 mark, dia. 8.25"	100	240	380
Doorknob	25	60	90
Foot Warmer, ht. 9"	100	240	380
Goblet, ht. 4.75"	200	470	760
Goblet, ftd., w/ handle, ht. 4.5"	250	590	950
Honey-Colored Coachman Toby, w/ 1849 mark, ht. 10.5"	475	1200	1800
"Hoo Doo King" Book Flask, ht. 5.5"	1300	3000	5000
Mold, Turk's head, dia. 6.5"	150	350	570
Mug, ht. 3.25"	60	140	230
Nameplate, len. 8"	125	300	470
Oval Picture Frame, 8" x 7"	400	850	1400
Picture Frame, Rococo, 10" x 9"	1600	3500	6000
Picture Frame, scalloped or serpentine, 5.75" x 6.75"	150	350	570
Pint Book Flask, "Departed Spirits," w/ exceptional color	700	1650	2650
Pipkin, w/ lid, ht. 7.5"	450	1000	1700
Pitcher, 8 panel, molded tulips and hearts, ht. 7"	450	1000	1700
Pitcher, alternate rib, 1849 mark, ht. 10"	900	2000	3400
Pitcher, alternate rib pattern, ht. 6.75"	150	350	570
Pitcher and Bowl Set, 1849 mark	375	900	1420
Pitcher, diamond pattern, ht. 9"	350	800	1350
Pitcher, early, "Norton & Fenton East Bennington VT," ht. 8"	800	2000	3000
Pitcher, w/ mask under spout, ht. 8.75"	200	450	750
Relish Dish, len. 10"	350	800	1350
Slop Jar Base, 1849 mark	450	1000	1700
Tile, 1849 impressed mark, 7" sq.	400	940	1500
Tobacco Jar, w/ lid, alternate rib pattern, ht. 6.75"	300	700	1100
Toby Pitcher, vintage handle, ht. 6"	350	830	1300
Toby Snuff Jar, lidded, dark greenish-brown glaze	600	1400	2200
Toby Snuff Jar, w/ 1849 mark	1450	3400	5500
Toothbrush Holder, lidded, alternate rib pattern	500	1200	1900
Tulip Vase, fine and colorful glaze, ht. 10"	600	1400	2250
Wash Bowl, paneled, 1849 mark, dia. 13.5"	475	1100	1800

Parian Pieces

	AUCTION	RETAIL	
		Low	High
Bust of Girl, w/ bird, ht. 5"	$ 50	$ 120	$ 190
Creamer, Bennington-type handle, ht. 4.25"	55	120	190
Doorknob, in rosette pattern	25	50	80
Miniature Vase, hand holding flower, ht. 3"	15	20	40
Pitcher, pond lily pattern, U.S. Pottery ribbon mark, ht. 10"	175	410	660
Pitcher, wild rose pattern, ht. 10"	200	470	760
Porcelain Figural Vase, ht. 7"	100	240	380
Trinket Box, blue and white, len. 5"	30	70	110
Trinket Box, molded flower lid, len. 5.5"	15	25	40
Trinket Box, sleeping child on lid, len. 4.25"	15	25	40
Vase, molded grapevine pattern, scalloped top, ht. 4.5"	50	120	200
Vase, songbird pattern, blue and white, ht. 4"	25	60	90

*Top row left to right: Toby pitcher, $350; "Departed Spirits" book, 9",
$800; figural covered jar, $250, humidor, $600; toothbrush holder,
$100; alternate rib pitcher, $1200; "Departed Spirits" book, 6", $300;
flask, $900. Bottom row left to right: Creamer, $300; pilgrim flask,
$1500; spittoon, $250; candlestick, $ 925; spittoon, $250, cow creamer,
$450, night stick, $500. — Photo courtesy of Northeast Auctions.*

Boehm Figures

Edward Marshall Boehm founded a pottery studio in Trenton, New Jersey, in 1949. Following Boehm's death, his wife Helen took over the company. In addition to the Trenton studio, Boehm studios started in England in 1971.

Boehm birds are some of the most fragile porcelain ever made. Chipped and broken foliage can be easy to overlook, but the value is considerably less. Current items range all the way from a $20 cup and saucer to a $400 Prince Rudolph's Blue Bird of Paradise.

Boehm Ptarmigans, $5000-$7000.

	LOW	AVG.	HIGH
Blue Grosbeak	$ 1300	$ 1650	$ 2000
Bobolink	1600	1900	2200
Boxer, large size	1500	1800	2100
Carolina Wrens	7000	9000	11,000
Catbird	2550	2955	3360
Crested Flycatcher	3400	3800	4200
Downy Woodpecker	2100	2300	2500
Fledgling Blue Jay	240	260	280
Fledgling Canada Warbler	2000	2500	3000
Fledgling Goldfinch	300	350	400
Fledgling Magpie	1000	1250	1500
Fledgling Red Poll	260	300	340
Green Jays	7000	8000	9000
Lazuli Bunting Paperweight	180	205	230
Mourning Doves	7000	8000	9000
Nuthatch	360	430	500
Oven-Bird	2000	2400	2800
Parula Warbler	3800	4200	4600
Polo Player	6200	6800	7400
Prothonotary Warblers	600	750	900
Read Runner	6000	7000	8000
Rufous Hummingbirds	3000	3400	3800
Scottish Terrier	600	800	1000
Standing Poodle, apricot-colored	2300	2650	3000
Thoroughbred and Exercise Boy, decorated	10,000	11,500	13,000
Towhee	2970	3300	3630
Tufted Titmice	1500	1900	2300
Varied Buntings	7000	9000	11,000
Whippets	5000	6000	7000

Ezra Brooks Bottles

Ezra Brooks produces figural bottles with themes from sports and transportation to antiques. The antique series includes an Edison phonograph and a Spanish cannon. Ezra Brooks rivals Jim Beam as one of the chief whiskey companies manufacturing figural bottles.

	LOW	AVG.	HIGH
American Legion, 1971, distinguished embossed star emblem, of WWI, blue and gold, on blue base	$ 38	$ 44	$ 50
American Legion, 1972, City of Chicago, host of the Legion's 54th National Convention	85	100	115
American Legion, 1973, Hawaii, hosted the American Legion's 1973 Annual Convention	15	17	19
American Legion, 1977, Denver	30	34	38
American Legion, 1973, Miami Beach	12	14	16
Amvets, 1974, Dolphin	24	28	32
Amvet, 1973, Polish Legion	22	27	32
Antique Cannon, 1969	8	9	10
Antique Phonograph, 1970, white, black, "Morning Glory" horn, red, detailed in gold	12	14	15
Arizona, 1969, man w/ burro in search of "Lost Dutchman Mine," gold base, "ARIZONA" imprinted	7	9	10
Auburn, 1932, 1978, Classic Car	45	50	55
Badger No. 1, 1973, Boxer	20	24	28
Badger No. 2, 1974, Football	24	28	30
Badger No. 3, 1974, Hockey	24	28	30
Baltimore Oriole Wild Life, 1979	53	60	70
Bare Knuckle Fighter, 1971	9	11	12
Baseball Hall of Fame, 1973, Heritage China	22	26	30
Basketball Player, 1974	12	14	15
Bear, 1968	7	8	9
Bengal Tiger Wild Life, 1979	50	55	60
Betsy Ross, 1975	17	20	22
Big Daddy Lounge, 1969, white, green, red	7	8	9
Bighorn Ram, 1973	11	13	15
Bird Dog, 1971	14	17	20
Bordertown, Borderline Club, brown, red, white, club building w/ vulture on roof stopper	7	8	9
Bowler, 1973	8	9	10
Brahma Bull, 1972	17	20	23
Clown, 1978, Imperial Shrine	28	32	38
Club Bottle, 1973, 3rd commemorative, shape of America, each gold star represents the location of an Ezra Brooks Collectors Club	30	35	40
Clydesdale Horse, 1973	15	18	21
Colt Peacemaker, 1969, gun-form flask	6	7	8
Conquistador's Drum and Bugle, 1972	15	18	20
Corvette Indy Pace Car, 1978	62	68	73
M & M Brown Jug, 1975	28	31	34
Maine Lobster, 1970, lobster shape	28	32	36
Maine Lighthouse, 1971	25	29	32
Man O'War, 1969, race horse in brown and green, gold base, embossed "MAN-O-'WAR"	14	17	19

	LOW	AVG.	HIGH
Map, 1972, U.S.A. Club Bottle	$ 12	$ 14	$ 16
Masonic Fez, 1976	14	17	20
Max, 1976, the hat, Zimmerman	35	41	47
Milady Tank, 1971	22	26	30
Minnesota Hockey Player, 1975	27	30	33
Minuteman, 1975	19	21	23
Missouri Mule, 1972, brown	17	20	22
Moose, 1973	33	36	40
Motorcycle, motorcycle rider and machine, Stars 'n' Stripes helmet, on silver base	12	14	15
Mountaineer, 1971, figure dressed in buckskin, holding rifle, *"MOUNTAINEERS ARE ALWAYS FREE"* trimmed in platinum, one of the most valuable	60	70	80
Mr. Foremost, 1969, bottle-shaped symbol of Foremost Liquor stores,"Mr. Foremost," red, white, and black	13	15	17
Mr. Maine Potato, 1973	9	10	11
Mr. Merchant, 1970, *JUMPING MAN,* whimsical, caricature of shopkeeper, leaping, arms outstretched, yellow, black	12	14	16
Mustang Indy Pace Car, 1979	19	21	22
Nebraska-"Go Big Red," 1972, Heritage China game ball and fan, trimmed in gold	15	17	19
New Hampshire State House, 1970, 150-year-old State House, eagle stopper, gray building w/ gold	15	17	19
North Carolina Bicentennial, 1975	15	18	21
Nugget Classic, golf pin presented to golf tournament participants, gilt finish	12	14	15
Oil Gusher, oil drilling rig, all silver, black stopper as gushing oil	7	9	11
Old Capitol, 1971, shape of Iowa's seat of government as frontier territory, *"OLD CAPITOL, IOWA 1840-1857,"* old dome stopper	23	26	29
Old Ez, 1977, No. 1, barn owl	67	76	86
Old Ez, 1978, No. 2, eagle owl	90	105	120
Old Ez, 1979, No. 3, snow owl	60	70	80
Panda Giant, 1972, Giant Panda ceramic bottle	20	23	26
Penguin, 1972, Heritage China ceramic figural bottle	12	14	16
Reno Arch, 1968, arch shape w/ *"RENO"* embossed, decal of dice, rabbit's foot, roulette wheel, slot machine, etc.	8	9	10
Sailfish, 1971, blue-green, on green "waves" base	11	14	17
Salmon, 1971, Washington King	18	21	24
San Francisco Cable Car, 1968	15	17	19
Sea Captain, 1971, holding pipe, on "wooden" stanchion base	15	17	19
Senator , 1971, cigar-chomping state senator, stumping on a platform, swallow-tail coat, string tie, gold, black, red, white	17	20	23
Senators of the U.S., 1972, Heritage ceramic "Old Time" senator	17	20	22
Setter, 1974	17	21	24
Shrine King Tut Guard, 1979	42	50	58
Silver Saddle, 1973	37	40	44
Silver Spur Boot, 1971, cowboy-boot-shaped bottle w/ silver spur buckled on, *"SILVER SPUR CARSON CITY NEVADA,"* platinum trim	12	14	15

Canonsburg Pottery

The Canonsburg Pottery manufactured dinnerware for the first three quarters of this century. It is often marked by backstamps with a cannon.

Priscilla (1932)

	LOW	AVG.	HIGH
Casserole	$ 25	$ 30	$ 35
Cream/Sugar	12	16	18
Cup/Saucer	4	6	8
Plate, 6-7"	2	3	4
Plate, 9"	4	5	6
Teapot	15	20	25

Westchester (1935)

Casserole	15	20	25
Coffee Pot	20	25	30
Cream/Sugar	9	16	23
Cup/Saucer	4	6	8
Plate, 6-7"	2	4	6
Plate, 9"	4	5	6
Platter, oval, 11-12"	5	6	7
Teapot	15	20	25

Ceramic Arts Studio

Ceramic Arts Studio is famous for its novelties manufactured between 1941 an 1955. They are usually stamped with the words "Ceramic Arts Studio" underlined or with a half circlular "Madison, Wisconsin." Sometimes the piece is named.

Snuggles or Lap-Sitters are pairs of figures that fit together.

Snuggles

	LOW	AVG.	HIGH
Baby Chick in Nest	$ 20	$ 25	$ 30
Bear, mother w/ baby	18	25	32
Boy w/ Chair	16	22	28
Clown and Clown Dog	16	22	28
Cow, mother w/ baby	18	24	30
Dog w/ Doghouse	18	25	32
Elephant and Native Boy	30	35	40
Girl w/ Chair	16	22	28
Kangaroo, mother w/ baby	18	25	30
Kitten and Pitcher	20	25	30
Monkey, mother w/ baby	18	25	30
Mouse and Cheese	18	25	30
Native Boy on Alligator	35	40	45
Oak Sprite, sitting on leaf	16	22	28
Oak Sprite, straddling leaf	16	22	28
Seahorse and Coral	15	20	25
Skunks mother w/ baby	20	25	30
Suzette on Pillow	15	20	25

Crooksville China

The Crooksville China Company manufactured semiporcelain dinnerware and kitchenware from 1902 until 1959. Several backstamps exist.

 *Crooksville backstamp.*

Euclid (1935)

	LOW	AVG.	HIGH
Baker, pie, 9"-10"	$ 10	$ 15	$ 20
Casserole, 8"	20	25	30
Coaster, 4"	8	12	16
Coffee Pot	40	45	50
Cream/Sugar	12	16	18
Cup/Saucer	4	6	8
Custard Cup	2	3	4
Mixing Bowl, 6-11"	10	20	30
Pitcher, batter	20	25	30
Pitcher, syrup	15	20	25
Plate, 6"	1	2	3
Plate, 9-10"	4	5	6
Platter, rect., 11-15"	5	10	15
Pudding Dish	4	5	6
Tea Tile	17	20	23
Vegetable, rect., 9.25"	8	10	12

Pantry Bak-in Ware (1931)

Baker, pie, 10"	5	7	9
Bean Pot	14	17	20
Cake Plate	4	5	6
Canister	21	23	24
Casserole, 4"-8"	14	17	20
Coffee Pot, w/ drip	25	30	35
Cookie Jar	16	18	20
Custard Cup	2	3	4
Leftover, 4"-8"	4	7	10
Leftover, oval w/ lid	20	23	25
Mixing Bowl, 6"-12"	5	15	25
Pitcher	19	22	25
Reamer	38	44	48
Teapot	15	18	20
Tray, sq., 9"	4	5	6
Tumbler	8	9	10

Frankoma Pottery

In 1933, while working at the University of Oklahoma Ceramics Department, John Frank started Frank Potteries. By 1938, he had left the university, moved to Sapulpa, OK, and renamed his company Frankoma Pottery. John Frank designed all of Frankoma's dinnerware lines such as Mayan-Aztec (1945), Lazybones, Plainsman (1948), Wagon Wheels (1941), and Westwind. Most are still in production.

Marks: impressed *Frankoma* on the bottom of the piece; some early pieces have *Frankoma* stamped in black. An impressed panther in front of a vase appeared from 1936 to 1938.

Frankoma impressed mark.

	LOW	AVG.	HIGH
Baker, 2qt.-3qt.	$ 18	$ 22	$ 25
Baker, ind.	40	50	60
Bowl, 4.5 qt.	28	34	40
Bowl, 8-20 oz.	5	7	8
Bowl, rd. 1-2 qt.	11	13	15
Butter Dish	10	13	16
Candleholder	28	36	43
Chop Plate, ftd., 15"	13	17	20
Corn Dish	4	5	6
Cream/Sugar	10	13	16
Cup/Saucer	10	15	20
Custard Cup	4	6	7
Gravy, 2-spout	11	13	15
Gravy Boat	15	20	25
Horseshoe	13	17	20
Lazy Susan	39	50	60
Mug, 8 oz.-14 oz.	8	10	12
Pitcher, 1-3 qt.	16	20	24
Plate, 7"	6	7	8
Plate, 9"-10"	8	10	12
Platter, oval, deep, 13"	16	21	25
Platter, oval, deep, 17"	23	30	36
Platter, oval, deep, lug, 13"	13	16	19
Platter, oval, shallow, 17"	20	25	29
Platter, rect., deep, 13"-17"	14	20	26
Platter, rect., shallow, 9"-13"	6	9	12
Salad, crescent	4	5	6
Salt/Pepper	7	9	11
Teapot, 12 cup	21	27	32
Teapot, rd., 2-6 cup	12	20	28
Teapot, tall, 2 cup	25	31	37
Teapot, tall, 6 cup	40	50	61
Tray, rect., 9"	6	8	9
Tumbler, 6 oz.-12 oz.	5	6	7
Vegetable, 1 qt.	8	10	12
Warmer	11	15	18

French-Saxon China

The Sebring family of Sebring, OH, owned both the French China Company and the Saxon China Company. The bankruptcy of the American Chinaware Company pulled both under in 1932. W.V. Oliver bought the Saxon plant and named his company French-Saxon. It made semiporcelain kitchenware and dinnerware. Royal China bought the company in 1964. The Zephyr pattern (1938) listed below appeared in solid colors decorated with decals. The two solid-color lines are called Romany (red, yellow, dark blue, and green) and Rancho (maroon, gray, chartreuse, and dark green).

Marks: backstamps included a knight and shield graphic backstamp and a circular Union mark. Romany and Rancho have only their names stamped.

UNION MADE
U. S. A.

French-Saxon backstamp.

	LOW	AVG.	HIGH
Bowl, 36s	$ 7	$ 8	$ 9
Chop Plate, 13"	9	12	15
Coffee Pot	36	40	45
Cream/Sugar	22	26	30
Cup/Saucer	7	9	11
Dish, 5"-6"	2	3	4
Gravy Boat	15	17	19
Plate, 6"-7"	4	5	6
Plate, 9"-11"	7	8	9
Salt/Pepper	11	15	18
Soup Plate, 7.75"	7	8	9
Vegetable, 8.5"	16	17	18

Garnier Bottles

The Garnier Company began producing figural bottles in 1899. Those produced prior to World War II are scarce. Some of the better known include the Cat, 1930; Clown, 1910; Country Jug, 1937; and Greyhound, 1930.

	LOW	AVG.	HIGH
Antique Cars, Transportation Series, 1969	$ 7	$ 11	$ 14
Apollo, Commemorative Series, #235, 1969	13	20	26
Barrel w/ Stand, Figural Specialties, #75, 1935	12	18	24
Bellows, Figural Specialties, #232, 1969	12	18	24
Bouquet, Figural Specialties, #222, 1966	13	20	26
Broc, #88, 1936	15	23	30
Broc Decor Cerises, #42, 1935	24	36	48
Broc Godron, #77, 1936	19	29	38
Broc Lijay, #60, 1936	24	36	48
Broc Six Sides, #65, 1935	24	36	48
Bull, Wildlife Figurals, #202, 1963	15	23	30
Candlestick, Figural Specialties, #134, 1955	24	36	48
Clown, Figurines, #137, 1955	18	27	36
Coffee Pot, Figural Specialties, #192, 1962	21	32	42
Country Jug, #101, 1937	21	32	42
Country Jug, #103, 1937	21	32	42
Diamond Bottle, Glass Specialties, #234, 1969	9	14	18
Drunkard, Figurines, #145, 1956	15	23	30
Duckling, Wildlife Figurals, #148, 1956	24	36	48
Duo, Multi-Compartment Glass, #168, 1959	9	14	18
Falcon Trocadero, Glass Specialties, #113, 1949	15	23	30
Five-Handle Jug, #170, 1959	13	20	26
Glass Decanter, Glass Specialties, #94, 1935	15	23	30
Goddess, Figurines, #196, 1963	27	41	54
Goose, Wildlife Figurals, #141, 1955	15	23	30
Grenadier, Figurines, #109, 1949	45	68	90
Hoola Hoop, Glass Specialties, #173, 1959	18	27	36
Horse Pistol, Figural Specialties, #205, 1964	12	18	24
Inca, Figurines, #236, 1969	15	23	30
Lafayette, Figurines, #107, 1949	48	72	96
Liquer D'Or, Glass Specialties, #101, 1938	12	18	24
Locomotive, Transportation Series, #237, 1969	7	10	13
Marquise, Figurines, #55, 1931	48	72	96
Musical Lamp, Glass Specialties, #209, 1964	27	41	54
Partridge, Wildlife Figurals, #177, 1961	27	41	54
Penguin, Wildlife Figurals, #50, 1932	45	68	90
Petanque, Figural Specialties, #217, 1966	21	32	42
Rainbow, Multi-Compartment Glass, #143, 1955	12	18	24
Rocket, Figural Specialties, #167, 1958	9	14	18
Rooster, Wildlife Figurals, #132 (black), 1952	15	23	30
Round Log, Figural Specialties, #156, 1958	27	41	54
Sheriff, Figurines, #164, 1953	15	23	30
Sommelier, Glass Specialties, #159, 1958	24	36	48
St. Tropez Jug, #182, 1961	15	23	30
State Bird Series, 1969	9	14	18
Three Decanter Oak Tantalus, Glass Specialties, #93, 1938	24	36	48
Three Decanter Tantalus, Glass Specialties, #140, 1955	24	36	48

W.S. George Pottery

In 1903 William S. George bought the East Palestine Pottery Company from the Sebring brothers from whom he had leased the plant. The plant produced his semiporcelain dinnerware for the next half century. The company used many different backstamps; some were unique to their shape.

W. S. GEORGE
MADE IN U.S.A.

Backstamp marks.

Bolero (mid-1933)

	LOW	AVG.	HIGH
Casserole	$ 18	$ 20	$ 22
Compote	14	16	18
Cream/Sugar	17	19	21
Cup/Saucer	5	6	7
Custard Cup	3	4	5
Dish, lug, 6.5"	2	3	3
Gravy Boat	12	13	14
Pickle Dish	3	5	6
Plate, 6"-8"	2	3	4
Plate, 9"-10"	4	5	6
Platter, 11"-12"	7	8	9
Relish, shell-form	7	8	9
Salt/Pepper	12	16	19
Soup Bowl, w/ lid	11	13	14
Soup Plate	5	6	7
Teapot	29	31	33
Vegetable	10	12	13

Elmhurst (1938)

Bowl, 36s	4	5	6
Casserole	15	20	25
Cream/Sugar	12	16	18
Cup/Saucer	4	6	8
Dish, 5-6"	1	2	3
Gravy Boat	8	12	16
Pickle Dish	3	4	5
Plate, 6-8"	2	4	6
Plate, 9-10"	4	5	6
Platter, 11-16"	5	10	15
Soup Bowl	4	5	6
Teapot	15	20	25
Vegetable	8	10	12
Vegetable, w/lid	15	20	25

W.S.George
Georgette

Backstamp mark.

Georgette (1933)

	LOW	AVG.	HIGH
Georgette is often called "Petal"			
Bowl, 36s	$ 5	$ 6	$ 7
Cream/Sugar	16	19	22
Cup/Saucer	5	7	9
Dish, 5"-7"	1	2	3
Gravy Boat	11	12	13
Plate, 6"-8"	4	5	5
Plate, 9"-10"	6	7	8
Vegetable, oval, 9"	11	12	13

Lido (1932)

	LOW	AVG.	HIGH
Bowl, 36s	5	6	7
Butter Dish	19	22	24
Candlestick	18	20	22
Casserole	18	22	25
Cream/Sugar	15	18	21
Cup/Saucer	5	7	9
Dish, 5"-6"	1	2	3
Egg Cup	6	8	10
Gravy Boat	10	12	13
Pickle Dish, 7.5"	4	5	5
Plate, 6"-8"	2	3	4
Plate, 9"-10"	5	6	7
Platter, 11"-13"	6	8	10
Salt/Pepper	12	15	17
Soup Plate, 7.75"	5	6	7
Teapot	33	35	37
Vegetable, 9"	10	12	14

Ranchero

	LOW	AVG.	HIGH
Simon Slobodkin designed this line.			
Butter Dish	15	20	25
Casserole	23	27	30
Coffee Pot	30	35	40
Cream/Sugar	19	22	25
Cup/Saucer	6	8	10
Dish, 5"-6"	2	3	4
Egg Cup	8	9	10
Gravy Boat	15	17	18
Plate, 6"-7"	2	3	4
Plate, 9"	6	7	8
Platter	8	10	12
Salt/Pepper	15	17	19
Teapot	20	25	30
Vegetable	12	15	18

Gladding, McBean

The Gladding, McBean & Company started as a sewer pipe manufacturer in 1875. It introduced its famous earthenware Franciscan line of art and dinnerware in 1934. In 1963 the company changed its name to the Interpace Corporation. Wedgwood (England) purchased it in 1979 and continued production until 1986. Franciscanware is now produced in England.

Franciscan Classics was Gladding-McBean's name for the three most popular patterns of embossed, hand-painted underglaze dinnerware. These were Apple (1940), Desert Rose (1941), and Ivy (1948). Both Apple and Desert Rose have seen continuous production since the early 1940s.

Marks: various backstamps and decals, including *GMB* in an oval, *F* in a box for Franciscan. Current pieces are backstamped *England*.

Gladding, McBean
and Franciscan
Classics backstamps.

Coronado

	LOW	AVG.	HIGH
Butter Dish	$ 27	$ 29	$ 31
Casserole, 10.5"	31	34	36
Casserole, ind., 5.5"	12	16	19
Chop Plate, 12"-14"	18	23	27
Cigarette Box	29	34	38
Coffee Pot	37	40	44
Cream/Sugar	18	21	23
Cream/Sugar, ftd.	27	30	33
Cup/Saucer	6	8	10
Cup/Saucer, 10 oz.	11	15	18
Custard Cup	6	8	9
Dish, 5"-6"	4	7	9
Dish, crescent	9	11	12
Gravy Boat	15	18	20
Nut Dish, ftd.	12	16	19
Party Plate	16	17	17
Pitcher	26	31	36
Plate, 6"-8"	4	6	7
Plate, 9"-11"	9	13	16
Platter, oval, 10"-13"	12	16	19
Platter, oval, 15.5"	27	31	35
Relish Tray, handled	12	14	16
Salad Bowl, 10"	31	32	33
Salt/Pepper	12	16	20
Soup Bowl/Saucer	21	24	27
Soup Plate, 8"	12	14	16
Teapot	70	80	90
Vegetable, 9"-10"	15	19	22

	LOW	AVG.	HIGH
Desert Rose (1941)			
Buffet Plate, rd., div.	$ 25	$ 35	$ 45
Butter Dish	43	52	62
Candleholder	23	30	36
Casserole, 1.5 qt.	100	115	130
Casserole, 2.5 qt.	130	150	170
Cheese Server	90	103	116
Chop Plate, 12"-14"	60	80	100
Coffee Pot	80	90	100
Compote	60	90	120
Cookie Jar	175	200	225
Cream/Sugar	60	75	90
Crescent Dish	23	29	35
Cup/Saucer	18	24	30
Cup/Saucer, 12 oz.	35	40	45
Dish, 5"-6"	15	25	35
Egg Cup	25	31	36
Goblet	55	65	75
Gravy Boat	40	50	60
Ladle, 10"	80	90	100
Mixing Bowl	75	110	145
Mug, 7-12 oz.	31	42	52
Party Plate, rd	37	41	45
Pitcher, 1 pt-2.5 qt	30	72	115
Plate, 6"-8"	15	22	29
Plate, 9"-10"	23	32	41
Platter, 12"-14"	58	84	110
Platter, 17"	200	240	280
Porringer	31	38	45
Relish Tray	31	44	58
Salad	100	120	140
Salt/Pepper	47	60	72
Salt/Pepper Mill	175	200	225
Server, 2 tier	72	90	109
Sherbet	32	33	34
Soup Plate	28	36	43
Teapot	75	100	125
Tray, heart form	24	31	38
Trivet	15	22	29
Tumbler, 6-10 oz.	24	34	43
Tureen	215	288	360
Vegetable	44	61	78
Ivy (1948)			
Butter Dish	21	24	27
Casserole, 1.5 qt.	46	52	59
Cheese Server	43	49	55
Chop Plate, 12"-14"	27	37	47
Cigarette Box	47	50	54
Coffee Pot	40	48	55
Compote	27	42	56
Cookie Jar	79	88	97

	LOW	AVG.	HIGH
Cream/Sugar	$ 28	$ 34	$ 39
Crescent Dish	10	13	16
Cup/Saucer	8	11	14
Cup/Saucer, 12 oz.	16	18	20
Dish, 5"-6"	7	11	14
Gravy Boat	21	24	27
Ladle	40	44	48
Mixing Bowl	35	50	64
Mug, 7-12 oz.	14	20	26
Party Plate, rd.	16	18	20
Pitcher, 1 pt.-2.5 qt.	13	34	55
Plate, 6"-8"	7	10	13
Plate, 9"-10"	10	15	20
Platter, 12"-14"	26	38	50
Platter, 17"	90	115	140
Relish Tray	13	21	28
Salad	47	54	62
Salt/Pepper	22	28	34
Server, 2-tier	34	40	45
Sherbet	13	15	17
Soup Plate	13	16	19
Teapot	42	48	54
Trivet	7	11	14
Tumbler, 6 oz.-10 oz.	11	16	20
Tureen	100	134	168
Vegetable	20	28	35

Metropolitan (1940)

Morris Sanders designed Metropolitan for its namesake, the Metropolitan Museum of Art. All shapes are square or rectangular.

	LOW	AVG.	HIGH
Butter Dish	24	26	28
Casserole, ind.	20	22	24
Chop Plate, sq., 13"	20	22	23
Coffee Pot	41	46	52
Cream/Sugar	27	32	36
Cup/Saucer	9	12	14
Dish, 5"-6"	4	7	9
Gravy Boat	17	19	20
Pitcher, 1.5 qt	42	45	48
Plate, 10"	10	11	12
Plate, 6"-8"	5	7	9
Platter, rect., 14"	14	15	16
Relish Tray	14	16	17
Salad, 10"	23	25	27
Salt/Pepper	17	20	22
Soup Plate	11	12	13
Teapot	35	41	47
Tumbler	14	16	17
Vegetable, div.	23	31	38

Grueby Potteries

Grueby Potteries operated from 1891 to 1907. After 1907 all Grueby pottery was manufactured and sold under the name of Tiffany. Grueby produced expensive, high quality vases, ornamental wares including statuettes, and decorative tiles. These usually have a factory stamp and an artist's mark, either straight-line or circular.

Grueby incised mark.

	LOW	AVG.	HIGH
Bowl, 4.5", mottled green brown glaze, pressed bulbous form. ...	$ 235	$ 300	$ 345
Bowl, 6.5" x 5" matte blue, thick glaze	435	500	875
Paperweight, 4.5", matte green glaze	180	200	250
Tile, 4", plain, solid color	15	35	65
Tile, 4", windmill design	150	185	220
Tile, 6", grape motif...	75	100	125
Tile, 8.5" sq., blue, painted w/ flowers, artist's init.	400	500	600
Tile, horse, 6.5" sq., blue, painted w/ horse, artist's init.	380	470	560
Tile, landscape, 4" sq., green and beige, artist's init.	180	225	275
Vase, 10", green, decorated by Erickson, artist's init.	1000	2000	2600
Vase, 11", green, molded w/ leaves.	300	445	500
Vase, 11", matte green glaze, molded bud and leaf, signed...........	725	824	925
Vase, 12.5", green, cylindrical shape, leaf and bud motif	1000	1200	1400
Vase, 3.5", green, flared neck, rounded lip, thick glaze	195	240	290
Vase, 4.5", green, molded leaf design, bulbous body, artist's init. ...	400	484	564
Vase, 5.5", brown glaze (speckled), flattened spherical form.	400	500	600
Vase, 6.5", green glaze, squared cylindrical neck, artist's init.	590	720	850
Vase, 7", green, ovoid form w/ molded panels, artist's init..	653	780	900
Vase, 7.5", ovoid flask form, pinched neck, dec. by L. Newman..	735	860	1000
Vase, 8", matte green glaze, molded/ buds above leaves, sgn.	350	400	450
Vase, 8", bulbous body, 3 handles, matte glaze, loaf design	950	1275	1500

Hall China

Robert Hall named his 1903 acquisition the Hall China Company and continued making the semiporcelain dinnerware and toiletware the old company had produced. After his death, his son experimented with firing the body and the glaze at the same time. He introduced the process in 1911. Hall still makes this vitrified hotel and restaurant ware. In 1920, the famed gold-decorated teapots appeared. In 1931, decal-decorated kitchenware and dinnerware was introduced. Hall reissues many classic designs. All are decorated in solid colors (no decal or gold decoration pieces). Many pieces are in new colors or color combinations.

Early marks read *HALL'S CHINA* in a circular frame, containing a mold or pattern number. *MADE IN U.S.A.* sometimes sat beneath the stamp. Later, a rectangular frame surrounded *HALL'S SUPERIOR QUALITY KITCHENWARE* or *HALL*, with a trademark *R*.

Hall backstamp.

Autumn Leaf (1933)

Autumn Leaf was produced in 1933 for the Jewel Tea Co.

	LOW	AVG.	HIGH
Baker, 9.5"	$ 35	$ 44	$ 53
Bowl, 3.5"	10	13	15
Bowl, 5"	12	15	17
Bowl, 6.5"	19	24	28
Bowl, 8"	24	30	35
Casserole Set, w/ lid, 3 pieces	140	170	200
Casserole, w/ lid, rd.	58	72	87
Coffee Pot, w/ lid, metal insert	85	110	135
Cream/Sugar, ruffled	31	40	48
Cup/Saucer	9	12	15
Custard Cups, set of 6	71	91	111
Dish, 7.5", swirl design	17	21	24
Gravy	18	24	30
Mixing Bowl Set, 6"-9.5"	60	80	100
Pickle Dish	20	24	28
Pitcher, 6"	34	44	54
Pitcher, ice lip	45	60	75
Plate, 10"	12	15	18
Plate, 13", oval	30	40	50
Plate, 6"-7"	5	6	7
Plate, 8"-9"	10	12	14
Salad Bowl, c. 1937	30	35	40
Salt/Pepper, stove	20	24	28
Sauce, 5.5"	12	15	18
Teapot, Newport	150	180	210
Vegetable Dish, 10.5", oval, open	16	21	26
Vegetable Dish, w/ lid	37	46	54

Cameo Rose (1950s)

	LOW	AVG.	HIGH

Cameo Rose was produced for the Jewel Tea Company.

	LOW	AVG.	HIGH
Butter Dish, w/ lid	$ 60	$ 75	$ 90
Casserole, w/ lid, 2 tab handles	50	60	70
Cereal Bowl, 6"	7	9	11
Cream/Sugar	15	18	21
Cup	12	15	18
Fruit Bowl, 5.5"	5	6	7
Gravy Boat	24	30	36
Plate, 10"	9	12	15
Plate, 6.5"	5	6	7
Plate, 8"	5	6	7
Plate, 9.5"	7	9	11
Platter, 11"	20	25	30
Platter, 13"	24	29	34
Relish Dish, 9"	17	21	24
Salt/Pepper Shakers, pr.	23	31	38
Saucer	2	3	4
Soup Plate	12	15	18
Sugar Bowl, w/ lid	20	25	30
Teapot	60	80	100
Vegetable Bowl, oval	20	25	30
Vegetable Bowl, rd., 9"	15	19	23

Crocus (1930s)

	LOW	AVG.	HIGH
Baker	28	36	44
Bean Pot, w/ lid	100	130	160
Bowl, 5.5"	7	9	11
Bowl, 6"	12	16	20
Cream/Sugar	59	76	94
Cup/Saucer	14	18	22
Custard Cup	7	9	11
Drip Jar	48	58	69
Drip-o-later, china	47	60	72
Gravy Boat	36	44	52
Mixing Bowl, 6"	16	21	26
Mixing Bowl, 7.5"	22	27	32
Mixing Bowl, 9"	28	36	45
Mug	50	60	71
Pie Plate	24	30	35
Pitcher, ball form #3	115	135	155
Plate, 10"	36	46	56
Plate, 6"	7	9	11
Plate, 8.5"	9	12	15
Platter, 11.5"-13.5"	26	34	42
Refrigerator Jar, sq.	50	60	70
Salad Bowl, 9"	25	31	36
Server, 3 tier	60	80	100
Soup Plate, 8.5"	20	25	30
Teapot, New York	115	145	175
Tureen, w/ lid	150	185	220
Vegetable Bowl, oval	24	30	36

Mums

	LOW	AVG.	HIGH
Bowl, 9"	$ 30	$ 36	$ 42
Casserole	68	82	96
Cereal Bowl, 6"	10	13	15
Cream/Sugar	50	60	70
Cup/Saucer	12	15	17
Custard Cup	5	6	7
Fruit Bowl, 5.5"	8	10	11
Plate, 10"	20	24	28
Plate, 6"	5	6	7
Plate, 8.5"	12	15	18
Platter, 11"-13"	34	42	49
Salt/Pepper	25	31	37
Saucer	2	3	3
Soup Plate, 8.5"	15	19	23
Sugar Bowl, w/ lid	21	28	34
Teapot	116	144	172

Pastel Morning Glory (1930s)

Bean Pot, w/ lid,1 handle	99	120	142
Bowl, 5.5"	10	12	14
Bowl, 6"	12	15	18
Bowl, 9"	24	31	37
Bowl, oval	30	38	46
Casserole, w/ lid, closed tab handles	57	71	85
Cream/Sugar	39	50	60
Cup/Saucer	12	15	18
Drip Jar	34	41	48
Gravy Boat	43	54	65
Pitcher, ball form #3	46	58	70
Plate, 6"	5	6	7
Plate, 8.5"	7	9	10
Plate, 9"	20	25	30
Platter, 11"-13"	36	45	54
Salt/Pepper	36	44	52
Soup Plate, 8.5"	21	28	34

Range Poppy (1933)

Range Poppy was produced for the Great American Tea Company.

Baker	24	30	36
Bean Pot, w/ lid, 1 handle	88	106	123
Bowl, 6"-7.5"	20	25	30
Bowl, 9"-10"	36	45	54
Bread Box, metal	92	118	144
Cake Plate	25	31	36
Canisters, set of 4, metal	71	88	106
Casserole, 11", w/ lid, oval	130	165	200
Casserole, w/ lid, 2 handles, rd.	35	46	57
Casserole, w/ lid, oval, 8"	44	55	66
Coffee Pot	73	92	110
Cream/Sugar	41	54	67

	LOW	AVG.	HIGH
Cup/Saucer	$ 12	$ 16	$ 19
Custard Cup	31	39	47
Drip Jar	32	40	47
Pitcher, ball form #3	33	42	52
Plate 7"	7	9	11
Plate, 7.5"	9	12	14
Plate, 9"	14	18	22
Platter, 11.5"-13.5"	34	45	56
Pretzel Jar, w/ lid	85	108	132
Refrigerator Jar, oval, loop handle	46	59	72
Salad Bowl, 9"	22	28	33
Salt/Pepper	13	16	19
Sifter, metal	36	46	56
Soup Plate, 6.5"	19	24	28
Spoon	70	88	105
Vegetable Bowl, 9.5"	44	54	63

Red Poppy (early 1950s)

Red Poppy was produced for Grand Union Tea Company.

Baker	32	40	48
Bowl, 6"	19	24	29
Bowl, 7.5"	24	29	34
Bowl, 9"	38	44	51
Cake Plate	25	30	35
Cereal Bowl, 6"	10	12	14
Coffee Pot	36	44	51
Cream/Sugar	40	45	50
Cup/Saucer	15	20	25
Custard Cup	7	9	11
Fruit Bowl, 5.5"	7	9	11
Gravy Boat	42	53	64
Pitcher, ball form #3	49	60	70
Plate, 10"	14	18	21
Plate, 7"	7	9	10
Plate, 9.5"	12	16	19
Plato, 6"	2	3	4
Platter, 11"	29	36	43
Platter, 13"	35	45	55
Salad Bowl, 9"	21	27	32
Salt/Pepper Shakers, set	14	18	21
Soup Plate	21	27	32
Teapot, Aladdin shape	72	88	103
Teapot, New York shape	69	90	111
Vegetable Bowl, oval 10"	35	44	53

Rose Parade (1940s)

Baker	24	31	37
Bean Pot, w/ lid, tab handles	72	91	110
Bowl, 6"	19	25	30
Bowl, 7.5"	25	31	36
Bowl, 9"	28	36	44

	LOW	AVG.	HIGH
Casserole, w/ lid, tab handles	$ 37	$ 44	$ 52
Cream/Sugar	30	38	45
Custard Cup	10	12	14
Drip Jar	34	42	49
Pitcher, 5"-7.5"	49	62	76
Salad Bowl, 9"	24	29	34
Salt/Pepper	25	30	34
Teapot, 4-6 cup	41	52	63

Rose White (1940s)

Baker	19	24	29
Bean Pot, w/ lid, tab handles	60	76	92
Casserole, w/ lid, tab handles	44	54	64
Cream/Sugar	27	33	39
Custard Cup	10	12	14
Drip Jar, w/ lid, tab handles	25	30	35
Pitcher, 5"-7.5"	34	43	52
Salad Bowl, 9"	20	25	30
Salt/Pepper	24	30	36
Teapot, 4-6 cup	41	52	64

Royal Rose (1940s)

Casserole, w/ lid	43	56	68
Drip Jar, w/ lid	32	42	52
Mixing Bowl, 6"-8.5"	28	34	41
Pitcher, ball form #3	47	60	72
Salt/Pepper	28	36	43
Teapot	58	72	86

Serenade (1930s)

Serenade dinnerware was produced for the Eureka Tea Co.

Bowl, 5.5"	7	9	10
Bowl, 6"	12	15	18
Bowl, 7.5"	19	25	30
Bowl, 9"	26	33	40
Casserole, w/ lid	48	60	73
Cereal Bowl, 6"	10	12	14
Coffee Pot	37	46	56
Cup/Saucer	10	13	15
Gravy Boat	25	30	35
Plate, 6"	2	3	4
Plate, 8.5"	7	9	11
Plate, 9"	8	10	11
Platter, 11"-13"	31	38	45
Pretzel Jar, w/ lid, tab handles	93	118	143
Salt/Pepper	36	44	53
Soup Plate, 8.5"	18	23	28

Silhouette (1930s)

Baker	25	31	36
Bowl, 6"	15	19	22

	LOW	AVG.	HIGH
Casserole, w/ lid	$ 48	$ 60	$ 73
Coffee Pot, drip.	252	310	368
Cup/Saucer	12	15	18
Drip Jar, w/ lid	25	31	37
Fruit Bowl, 5.5"	7	9	10
Mug	49	60	72
Pitcher	35	45	55
Pitcher, ball form #3	60	75	90
Plate, 6"	14	18	21
Plate, 8.5"	10	13	15
Plate, 9.5"	11	15	18
Platter, 11"-13"	37	44	52
Pretzel Jar, w/ lid, closed tab handles	93	122	150
Refrigerator Jar, w/ lid, rect.	38	46	54
Refrigerator Jar, w/ lid, sq.	50	60	70
Salad Bowl, 9"	20	24	28
Salt/Pepper	19	24	29
Soup Plate, 8.5"	21	28	34
Teapot, New York shape	100	135	170

Springtime

	LOW	AVG.	HIGH
Bowl, 5.5"	7	9	11
Bowl, 6"	160	210	260
Casserole, w/ lid, 2 tab handles	47	60	74
Coffee Pot, drip, china	10	12	14
Cream/Sugar	24	31	37
Cup	12	15	18
Drip Jar, thick	24	30	36
Gravy Boat	37	44	52
Pie Plate	23	31	38
Pitcher, ball form #3	47	58	70
Plate, 6"	2	3	4
Plate, 8.5"	7	9	11
Plate, 9.5"	23	30	37
Platter, 11"	28	34	39
Platter, 13"	30	39	48
Salad Bowl, 9"	21	27	33
Salt/Pepper	35	46	56
Saucer	2	3	4
Soup Plate, 8.5"	17	22	26

Taverne

	LOW	AVG.	HIGH
Baker, Flute French	30	35	40
Baker, Pie	50	60	70
Bean Pot, #4	200	250	300
Bowl, Colonial, #3-5	30	35	40
Bowl, Sunshine, #3-5	40	45	50
Casserole, Colonial	70	80	90
Casserole, Sunshine	90	110	130
Coffee Pot, Banded	90	110	130
Coffee Pot, Colonial	90	110	130

	LOW	AVG.	HIGH
Coffee Pot, Kadota	$ 275	$ 325	$ 375
Colonial Covered Drip	40	45	50
Colonial Drip Coffee	275	325	375
Cream/Sugar, Colonial	60	70	80
Cream/Sugar, MaryLou	50	60	70
Cup/Saucer	30	35	40
Dish, 5-6"	10	15	20
Mug	70	80	90
Pitcher, Ball, #3	100	125	150
Pitcher, Classic	150	175	200
Pitcher, Colonial, #2-3	40	45	50
Plate, 6-8"	10	15	20
Plate, 9-10"	20	25	30
Platter, 11-13"	30	35	40
Pretzel Jar	150	175	200
Salad Bowl	30	35	40
Salt/Pepper	30	35	40
Shaker, Banded	30	35	40
Shaker, Colonial	30	35	40
Shaker, Egg drop	50	60	70
Shaker, Handled	50	60	70
Soup Plate, 8.5"	30	35	40
Tea Tile, rd., 6"	200	250	300
Teapot, Banded	90	110	130
Teapot, Colonial	80	95	110
Teapot, New York	200	235	270
Teapot, Streamline	225	275	325
Vegetable, oval, 10.5"	40	45	50

Tulip

Tulip was produced for the Cook Coffee Company.

Baker	23	30	37
Cereal Bowl, 6"	9	12	14
Coffee Pot, drip, china	156	192	227
Cream/Sugar	34	42	49
Cup	7	9	11
Custard Cup	7	9	11
Drip Jar	31	40	48
Fruit Bowl, 5.5"	7	9	10
Gravy Boat	35	43	51
Mixing Bowls, set of 3	96	116	137
Plate, 10"	12	15	17
Plate, 6"	2	3	4
Plate, 7"	5	6	7
Plate, 9"	7	9	11
Platter, 11"-13"	32	40	47
Salad Bowl, 9"	18	23	28
Salt/Pepper	19	25	30
Saucer	2	3	4
Soup Plate, 8.5"	20	25	29

Wild Poppy (1930s)

	LOW	AVG.	HIGH
Baker	$ 33	$ 40	$ 48
Bean Pot, w/ lid	75	90	105
Canister	110	140	170
Casserole, oval	24	30	36
Cream/Sugar	14	18	22
Custard Cup	7	9	11
Mixing Bowls, set of 3	50	60	70
Salt/Pepper	23	29	35
Teapot, 4-6 cup	70	85	100

Wildfire (1950s)

Wildfire was produced for the Great American Tea Company.

Baker	19	24	29
Bowl, 9"	19	24	28
Casserole, w/ lid, tab handles	47	60	72
Cereal Bowl, 6"	9	12	14
Coffee Pot	49	59	69
Cream/Sugar	23	31	38
Cup/Saucer	15	18	21
Custard Cup	10	12	14
Drip Jar	23	29	34
Egg Cup	47	61	75
Fruit Bowl, 5.5"	7	9	11
Gravy Boat	24	31	37
Mixing Bowl, large	42	54	66
Mixing Bowl, medium	19	24	28
Mixing Bowl, small	14	18	22
Pie Plate	19	24	29
Plate, 10"	17	21	25
Plate, 6"	5	6	7
Plate, 7"	7	9	10
Platter, 11"	20	25	29
Platter, 13"	24	30	36
Salt/Pepper	37	46	55
Soup Plate, 8.5"	20	24	27
Teapot, Aladdin shape	70	88	105
Tidbit Tray, 3 tier	50	61	72

Yellow Rose

Baker	22	27	32
Bowl, 5.5"	7	9	11
Bowl, 6"	10	12	14
Casserole, w/ lid	36	45	54
Coffee Pot, drip, Norse shape	76	96	116
Cream/Sugar	29	37	45
Cup/Saucer	10	13	15
Custard Cup	5	6	7
Gravy Boat	25	30	35
Plate, 6"	2	3	3
Plate, 8.5"	7	9	10

	LOW	AVG.	HIGH
Plate, 9"	$ 17	$ 21	$ 25
Platter, 11"-13"	24	30	36
Salad Bowl, 9"	20	24	28
Salt/Pepper Shakers, pr.	35	46	56
Soup Plate, 8.5"	17	22	26
Teapot, New York shape	58	74	89

Hall Teapots

	LOW	HIGH
Airflow	$ 50	$ 70
Aladdin	50	70
Albany	50	70
Automobile	600	750
Baltimore	40	60
Basket	125	175
Basketball	600	700
Birdcage	400	500
Boston	30	50
Cleveland	60	90
Doughnut	300	400
Football	500	700
French	25	35
Globe	70	90
Hollywood	40	60
Hook Cover	30	50
Illinois	200	250
Indiana	225	250
Kansas	250	300
Los Angeles	40	60
Melody	175	225
Moderne	30	50
Nautilus	200	250
New York	20	40
Ohio	175	225
Parade	30	50
Philadelphia	30	50
Rhythm	150	175
Saf-handle	100	150
Sani-grid	40	60
Star	70	90
Streamline	50	70
Surfside	100	150
Windshield	40	80

Harker Pottery

The Harker Pottery Company began in 1890. In 1931, it bought the E.M. Knowles plant in Chester, WV, and closed its own East Liverpool, WV operations. The Chester plant operated until 1972. The Cameoware line and the Hotoven Kitchenware are the favorites. An arrow backstamp is common.

Harker and Hotoven backstamps.

Hotoven Kitchenware (1926)

Hotoven Kitchenware claimed to be the first decal-decorated line of ovenware ever made.

	LOW	AVG.	HIGH
Bean Pot, ind.	$ 4	$ 5	$ 6
Cake Server	14	16	18
Casserole, 7"-9"	17	20	23
Cup/Saucer, 10 oz.	9	10	11
Custard Cup	2	4	6
Drip Jar, Skyscraper	14	16	18
Fork and Spoon	30	50	70
Leftover, paneled	14	16	18
Mixing Bowl, 9"-10"	11	14	17
Pie Plate, 9"-10"	6	8	10
Pitcher	17	20	22
Rolling pin	40	45	50
Scoop	23	26	28
Stack set, 3-4 piece	30	38	47
Tea tile, octagonal	20	22	23
Teapot	29	32	35

Modernage

Modernage pieces have narrow, oval bodys and "lifesaver" finials.

Cake Server	25	28	30
Cake Tray, lug, 11.5"	8	9	10
Casserole, 6"-9"	30	35	40
Cookie Jar	31	34	38
Cream/Sugar	24	28	32
Custard Cup	4	5	6
Drip Jar	13	15	17
Fork and Spoon	30	40	50
Mixing Bowl, 11"	30	33	36
Pitcher	29	40	50
Platter, rd., 11.5"	10	12	14
Teapot	31	36	41

Royal Gadroon backstamp.

Royal Gadroon

Royal Gadroon pieces have a gadrooned (or lobed) edge.

	LOW	AVG.	HIGH
Chop Plate	$ 12	$ 14	$ 16
Cream/Sugar	23	28	33
Cup/Saucer	10	15	20
Dish, 5"-6"	4	5	6
Dish, w/ lid	12	14	16
Gravy Boat	16	18	20
Pickle Dish	8	10	12
Plate, 6"-8"	4	6	8
Plate, 9"-10"	8	9	10
Plate, sq., 8-9"	6	9	12
Platter, 11"-15"	10	15	19
Salad Bowl	16	18	20
Salt/Pepper	10	13	16
Server, 3-tier	17	20	23
Soup Bowl	8	9	10
Soup Plate, 8.5"	8	9	10
Teapot	30	36	42
Vegetable, 9"	18	20	21

Virginia

Virginia pieces are square.

	LOW	AVG.	HIGH
Bowl, 36s	8	9	10
Casserole	21	26	30
Cream/Sugar	25	29	33
Cup/Saucer	10	14	17
Dish, 5"-6"	2	3	4
Plate, 6"-8"	4	6	8
Plate, 9"-10"	8	9	10
Platter, 11"-14"	10	13	16
Soup, 7.75"	8	9	10
Vegetable, 8.25"	14	15	16

White Clover (1951)

Russell Wright designed White Clover. Some pieces have a cloverleaf decoration, others are a solid color.

	LOW	AVG.	HIGH
Casserole, w/ lid, 2 qt./C	$ 45	$ 49	$ 53
Chop Plate, 9"-11"/C	12	15	17
Clock	90	100	110
Cream/Sugar /C	34	38	42
Cup/Saucer/C	14	16	18
Dish, 5-7"/C	4	7	10
Gravy Boat/C	23	25	26
Pitcher, w/ lid, 2 qt./C	50	55	60
Plate, 11"	20	23	26
Plate, 6"-8"	6	8	10
Plate, 9"-10"/C	9	12	15
Platter, 13.25"/C	24	26	28
Salt/Pepper	26	29	32
Vegetable, 7"-9"	23	35	47

Zephyr

Lidded Zephyr pieces are known with two different finials, a ball knob or a stylized wing finial.

Box, w/ lid	34	38	42
Casserole, 7"-9"	25	31	37
Casserole Tray, 8"-10"	7	8	9
Cookie Jar	25	29	33
Custard Cup	4	5	6
Leftover, rd., 4"-6"	7	12	17
Mixing Bowl, 10"	26	28	30
Salt/Pepper	18	19	20
Serving Bowl, 6"-9"	10	17	24
Stack Set, 3 piece	43	46	50
Teapot, 5 cup	35	40	45
Tray, rd., 10"	11	13	15

A.E. Hull Pottery

Begun as a stoneware company, the A.E. Hull Pottery Company moved on to semi-porcelain dinnerware in 1907 with the purchase of the Acme Pottery Co. It slowly added various lines until the late 1930s, when Hull introduced its famous matte-finished pastel art pottery. Production continued through the 1950s when manufacturing operations ceased.

Prices for gilt pieces are higher, glossy pieces somewhat less. The listings include pattern numbers. Early marks include an impressed *H* in a circle or diamond. Later marks include *Hull*, *Hull Art*, or *Hull Ware* written in block letters or script.

For further information contact the Hull Pottery Association at 15475 Hilltop Road, Council Bluffs, IA 51503. Membership is $10 for individuals $15 for couples. Also consult The Hull Pottery News, a monthly newsletter published by Dan and Kimberly Pfaff, 466 Foreston Place, Webster Groves, MO 63119, e mail at <hullnews@aol.com>.

Blossom Flite

Blossom Flite features multi-colored flowers over a basketweave background of high gloss pink with blue lattice decor and green interior, or black decor with pink interior.

	LOW	AVG.	HIGH
Basket, low, T8, 8" x 9"	$85	$100	$115
Basket, T2, 6"	44	50	55
Basket, T4, 8.5"	67	84	100
Bowl, low, handled, T9, 10"	84	100	115
Candleholder, pr., T11	49	60	72
Console Bowl, T10	70	80	90
Cornucopia, T6, 10.5"	75	80	85
Cream/Sugar, T15/16	80	90	100
Ewer, T13, 13.5"	140	170	200
Flower Bowl, T12	60	75	90
Hanging Basket, T9, 10"	60	100	140
Pitcher, T1	30	35	40
Pitcher, T3, 8.5"	70	80	90
Pitcher Vase, T13, ht. 12.5"	90	120	150
Teapot, T14	75	90	105

Bow-Knot (1949)

Bow-Knot is decorated with high-relief multi-colored flowers and bows in matte finish on a background of pink with blue, or blue with blue or turquoise.

	LOW	AVG.	HIGH
Basket, B12, 10.5"	600	700	800
Basket, B25, 6.5"	160	175	190
Basket, blue, B29, 12"	3000	3800	4600
Candleholders, pr., B17	120	140	160
Console Bowl, B16, 13.5"	196	220	245
Cornucopia, B5, 7.5"	70	85	100
Cornucopia, double, B13, 13"	163	169	175
Creamer, B21	80	90	100
Ewer, B1, 5.5"	80	100	120
Ewer, B15, 13.5"	1100	1300	1500
Jardiniere, B19, 9.75"	1500	1900	2300
Sugar Bowl, B22	80	90	100
Teapot, B20	300	350	400
Vase, B14, 12.5"	1650	2150	2650
Wall Plaqu,e pink, B28, 10"	2000	2500	3000

Butterfly

Butterfly has pink and blue flowers and butterflies with black that decorate either cream-colored matte with turquoise interiors or glossy all-white pieces.

	LOW	AVG.	HIGH
Basket, B13, 8"	$ 100	$ 110	$ 120
Basket, B17, 10.5"	170	200	230
Bonbon Dish, B4, 6.5"	130	170	210
Bowl, fruit, B16	90	100	110
Bud Vase, pitcher shape, B1	56	63	70
Candleholders, pr., B22	70	82	94
Candy Dish, bonbon, B4	33	36	40
Candy Dish, urn shape, open, B6	40	45	50
Console Bowl, 3 feet, B21	110	135	160
Cornucopia, B12	60	70	80
Cornucopia, B2, 6.5"	27	35	43
Cream/Sugar, B19/20	80	103	126
Ewer, B15, 13.5"	125	143	161
Lavabo Set, B24/B25, 16"	160	190	220
Pitcher/Vase, Handled, B11	81	94	108
Serving Tray, B23, 11.5"	150	200	250
Teapot, B18	150	175	200
Window Box, B8	56	68	81

Calla Lily

Calla Lily is also called Jack-in-the-Pulpit. It has embossed flowers in matte-color combinations with green leaves.

Bowl, 500-32, 10"	140	170	200
Candleholders, pr., 508-39	135	150	165
Console bowl, 500-32, 10"	330	430	530
Cornucopias, 570-33, 8"	84	94	104
Ewer, pink and blue, 506, 10"	450	590	730
Vase, brown and tan, 530-33, 9"	510	665	820
Vase, 520-33, 10"	350	455	560
Vase, cream and blue, 560-33, 13"	310	405	500

Continental (1959-60)

Vase, dark green, C57, 14.5"	190	245	300
Basket, orange, C55, 12.75"	120	160	200
Base, C54, 12.5"	70	95	120

Dogwood

This line has raised dogwood flowers.

Basket, 501, 7.5"	200	250	300
Bowl, low, 521, 7"	90	110	130
Candleholders, pr., 512, 4"	140	170	200
Console Bowl, 511, 11.5"	180	220	260
Cornucopia, 522, 4"	50	62	75
Ewer, 505, 8.5" (marked 6.5")	133	168	202
Ewer, 505, 5.5"	370	485	600
Ewer, pink and blue, 519, 13.5"	1000	1400	1800
Ewer, 519, 13.5"	500	620	740
Ewer, 520, 4.75"	85	100	115
Teapot, 507, 6.5"	200	250	300
Window Box, 508, 10.5"	100	125	150

Ebbtide

Ebbtide shows glossy fish and seashell designs on various backgrounds.

	LOW	AVG.	HIGH
Basket, E11, 16.5"	$ 180	$ 200	$ 220
Candleholder, pr., E13, 2.5"	38	44	51
Console Bowl, E12, 15.75"	128	142	156
Cornucopia, E3/E9, 7"-12"	91	104	116
Cream/Sugar, E15/E16	100	122	143
Ewer, E10, 13"	210	330	
Pitcher Vase, E10, 14"	200	250	300
Pitcher Vase, EA, 8.25"	90	100	110
Teapot, E14	180	200	220

Iris (1940)

Iris has embossed iris flowers on matte-finished bodies.

Basket, 408, 7"	200	240	280
Candleholders, pr., 411, 5"	125	135	145
Console Bowl, 409, 12"	200	220	240
Ewer, 401, 5"	70	80	90
Ewer, 401, 8"	145	160	175
Ewer, 401, 13.5"	450	590	730
Rose Bowl, 412, 4"	80	100	120
Rose Bowl, 413, 7"	100	115	130
Console Bowl, 409, 12"	320	420	520
Vase, 403, 10.5"	370	485	600
Vase, 404, 10.5"	450	590	730
Vase, 413, 9"	370	485	600
Vase, pink and blue, 414, 16"	700	900	1100

Little Red Riding Hood

This was a popular figural line with Little Red Riding Hood and the Wolf.

Butter Dish	500	550	600
Canister, snack	1000	1250	1500
Canister, staples	800	900	1000
Casserole Dish, red handle	1400	1600	1800
Covered Jar, basket in front, 8.5"	400	450	500
Covered Jar, basket on side, 9"	350	400	450
Cream/Sugar, ruffled skirt	510	580	650
Cream/Sugar, side open	257	285	313
Creamer, spout on top of head	180	200	220
Grease Jar, Wolf	800	950	1100
Jar, spice	600	750	900
Mustard Jar, 4.5"	500	550	600
Mustard Jar, w/spoon, 5.5"	400	440	480
Pitcher, batter, 5.5"	200	260	320
Pitcher, milk, 8"	323	332	341
Salt/Pepper, 3.5"	60	66	72
Salt/Pepper, 5.5"	120	135	150
Shaker, sugar bowl (4 holes on top)	60	78	95
String Holder, 9"	1600	1800	2000
Sugar Bowl, "creeping," hands on table	180	200	220
Teapot	300	350	400

Magnolia [matte] (1946)

Matte Magnolia has embossed magnolia flowers on colored backgrounds.

	LOW	AVG.	HIGH
Basket, 10, 10.5"	$ 190	$ 250	$ 310
Candleholders, pr., 27, 4.5"	80	90	100
Console Bowl, 26, 12.5"	123	129	135
Cornucopias 19, 8.5"	60	65	70
Cream/Sugar, 24/25	80	90	100
Ewer, 14, 4.75"	44	49	54
Ewer, 18, 13.5"	202	230	258
Teapot, 23	122	136	150

Magnolia, glossy

Glossy Magnolia has embossed magnolia flowers on colored backgrounds.

Basket, H14, 10.5"	200	230	260
Cornucopia, double, H15, 12"	100	110	120
Cornucopia, H10, 8.5"	80	90	100
Cream/Sugar, H21/22	83	98	112
Ewer, H11, 8.5"	88	92	96
Ewer, H19, 13.5"	325	375	425
Teapot, H20	125	135	145

Open Rose

Also called Camellia, this pattern has polychrome roses on pastel matte backgrounds.

Basket, 107, 8"	200	275	350
Basket, 140, 10.5"	550	700	850
Basket, hanging, 132, 7"	180	230	280
Candleholders, dove-shape, pr., 117, 6.5"	160	200	260
Console Bowl, 116, 12"	200	250	300
Cornucopia, 101, 8.5"	97	120	144
Cornucopia, 141, 8.5"	113	137	161
Cream/Sugar, 111/112, 5"	108	140	171
Ewer, 115, 8.5"	145	185	225
Teapot, 110, 8.5"	230	290	351

Parchment and Pine

Parchment and Pine has pine cones on glossy backgrounds.

Basket, S3, 6"	60	75	90
Basket, S8, 16"	100	125	150
Candleholder, pr., S10, 2.75"	40	50	60
Console Bowl, S9, 16"	58	73	88
Cornucopia, S2, 8"	42	54	66
Cornucopia, S6, 12"	70	90	110
Cream/Sugar, S12/13	49	62	74
Ewer, S7, 13.5"	120	150	180
Teapot, S11	70	90	110
Teapot, tall, S15, 8"	117	150	184

Serenade

Serenade has birds on branches.

	LOW	AVG.	HIGH
Basket, bonbon, S5, 6.75"	$ 60	$ 70	$ 80
Basket, S14, 12"	250	320	380
Bowl, ftd. fruit, S15, 11.5"	75	100	125
Candleholder, pr., S16, 6.5"	60	70	80
Casserole, S20, 9"	80	100	120
Cornucopia, S10, 11"	50	60	70
Cream/Sugar, S18/S19	60	70	80
Ewer, S13, 13.25"	250	330	410
Ewer, S8, 8.5"	75	86	96
Pitcher, beverage, S21	100	110	120
Pitcher, vase, S2, 6.5"	55	60	66
Teapot, S17	106	119	132
Window Box, S9, 12.5"	50	58	65

Sunglow

Sunglow has flowers, and butterflies and bows (not on all pieces).

Basket, 84, 6.5"	54	60	67
Bowl, 50, 5-10"	22	34	47
Casserole, 51, 7.5"	42	48	54
Cornucopia, 96, 8.5"	63	72	81
Drip Jar, 53	32	38	43
Ewer, 90, 5.5"	35	38	41
Pitcher, 52, 24 oz.	45	48	52
Pitcher, 55, 7.5"	90	100	110
Salt/Pepper, 54	18	21	23

Tokay (1958)

Also called Tuscany, Tokay has embossed grapes and leaves on high-gloss backgrounds.

Basket, 11, 10.5"	70	78	86
Basket, 15, 12"	87	111	135
Bowl, fruit, 7, 9.5"	110	130	150
Candy Dish, w/ lid, 9C, 8.5"	60	70	80
Consolette, 14, 15.75"	110	127	144
Cornucopia, 6-11"	30	45	60
Cream/Sugar, 17/18	80	90	100
Ewer, 13, 12"	200	250	300
Ewer, 21, 16"	300	340	380
Ewer, 3, 8"	60	65	70
Teapot, 16	97	120	143
Urn, 5 , 5.5"	30	35	40

Tropicana (1959)

Ashtray, T52, 10"	500	650	800
Basket, T55, 12.75"	1000	1350	1700
Planter, T57, 14.5"	1000	1350	1700
Ewer, T56, 12.5"	700	900	1100
Vase, T54, 12.5"	750	950	1150
Vase, flat-sided, T53, 8.5"	600	800	1000

Tulip (1938-41)

	LOW	AVG.	HIGH
Basket, 102-33, 6"	$ 260	$ 340	$ 420
Ewer, 109-33, 13"	540	700	860
Jardiniere, 115-33, 7"	400	525	650
Vase, 100-33, 10"	370	485	600
Vase, 101-33, 9"	300	390	480
Vase, 107-33, 8"	290	375	460
Vase, 105-33, 8"	270	355	440
Ewer, 109-33, 8"	270	355	440

Water Lily

This line has water lilies on pastel backgrounds.

Basket, L14, 10.5"	280	310	330
Candleholder, pr., L22, 4.5"	110	118	125
Console Bowl, L21, 13.5"	171	184	198
Cornucopia, double, L27, 12"	148	162	175
Cornucopia, L7, 6.5"	74	86	99
Cream/Sugar, L19/L20	113	124	136
Ewer, L17, 13.5"	350	400	450
Ewer, L3, 5.5"	67	72	76
Jardiniere, pink and green, L24, 8.5"	270	355	440
Teapot, L18	160	180	200
Vase, pink and green, L15, 12.5"	600	800	1000
Vase, L13, 10.5"	330	430	530
Vase, pink and green, L16, 12.5"	370	485	600

Wild Flower, numbered series (1942-43)

Basket, pink and blue, 79, 10.25"	2600	3300	4000
Basket, pink and blue, 66, 10.25"	3000	4000	5000
Ewer, beige or tan, 55, 13.5"	1400	1900	2400
Basket, low, pink, 65, 7"	1000	1300	1600
Vase, dusty pink, 71, 12"	800	1000	1200
Vase, tan, 53, 8.5"	500	650	800

Wild Flower "W" series (1946-47)

Basket, pink and blue, W16, 10.5"	300	390	480
Candle Holders, W22, 8"	100	150	200
Console Bowl, W21, 12"	170	205	240
Vase, pink and blue, W18, 12.5"	400	500	600
Vase, W17, 12.5"	300	390	480
Vase, fan, W15, 10.5"	210	270	330
Vase, floor, W20, 15"	360	470	580

Woodland, matte (1949-50)

Basket, pink and green, W22, 10.5"	1200	1500	1800
Candle Holders, W30, 9"	350	475	600
Console Bowl, W29, 14"	250	325	400
Cornucopia, double, pink base, W23, 14"	800	1000	1200
Ewer, cream and pink, W24, 13.5"	1000	1350	1700
Jardiniere, beige, W21, 9.5"	800	1000	1200

Hummel Figurines

Hummels are ceramic figurines, usually of children. Berta Hummel, an artist and nun, created the concept and the original designs in 1935. For more information, consult *The Official Price Guide to Hummel Figurines and Plates,* published by The House of Collectibles, Random House, NY.

Each design has a title and a number. We have listed the designs by number, followed by the title. Through 1990, all marks fall into six basic categories (although variations exist): Crown Mark (CM), 1935-49; Full Bee (FB), 1950-56; Stylized Bee (SB), 1956-63; 3-line mark (3-L), 1963-72; Goebel/V (V-G), 1972-79; and Goebel (G), 1979-90. (Since 1991 a "New Crown Mark" is used.)

Above left to right: Crown Mark, Full Bee, Stylized Bee.
Below left to right: 3-line mark, Goebel, Goebel/V.

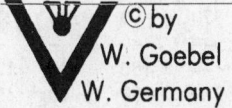 

Below left to right: The Builder #305, SB, $3000, 3-L, $150, V-G, $120, G, $100; Doll Bath #319, SB, $340, 3-L, $180, V-G, $120, G, $100.
—Photos courtesy of Jim Glaab's Collector's Showcase.

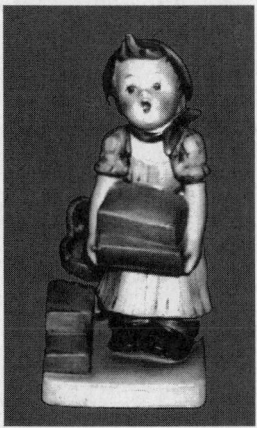 

	CM	FB	SB	3-L	V-G	G
151/W, Madonna Holding Child	$ 2340	$ 1910	$ 1990	—	$ 190	$ 190
151, Madonna Holding Child	2980	2390	1970	—	—	—
151/II, Madonna Holding Child	—	—	—	—	520	440
152A/0, Umbrella Boy	—	800	380	$ 390	320	260
152B/0, Umbrella Girl	—	790	400	370	290	270
152A/II, Umbrella Boy	—	1560	990	860	840	820
152B/II, Umbrella Girl	—	1540	1040	890	840	770
153/0, Auf Wiedersehen	—	290	200	140	100	100
153/1, Auf Wiedersehen	1030	560	470	350	160	130
153, Auf Wiedersehen	1060	590	490	—	—	—
154/0, Waiter	410	260	180	130	110	90
154/1, Waiter	760	380	230	140	130	120
154, Waiter	950	—	—	—	—	—
163, Whitsuntide	1340	1040	820	—	160	150
164, Worship	250	170	60	50	40	30
165, Swaying Lullaby	1080	880	510	—	90	80
166, Boy w/ Bird	410	250	140	140	90	90
167, Angel Bird	220	150	60	50	30	30
168, Standing Boy	1080	860	600	—	90	90
169, Bird Duet	260	190	130	90	90	60
170/I, School Boys	—	—	710	580	560	550
170/III, School Boys	2560	2130	1490	1360	1360	1440
171, Little Sweeper	240	140	120	90	70	70
172/0, Festival Harmony w/ Mandolin	—	—	—	150	150	110
172/II, Festival Harmony w/ Mandolin	—	1050	370	300	230	210
172, Festival Harmony w/ Mandolin	2570	2990	—	—	—	—
173/0, Festival Harmony w/ Flute	—	—	—	150	130	120
173/II, Festival Harmony w/ Flute	700	1130	360	280	210	190
173, Festival Harmony w/ Flute	2650	2750	—	—	—	—
174, She Loves Me, She Loves Me Not	370	270	150	120	80	70
175, Mother's Darling	400	220	150	130	100	80
176/0, Happy Birthday	300	290	180	130	110	100
176/1, Happy Birthday	690	530	340	280	170	150
176, Happy Birthday	810	510	—	—	—	—
177/I, School Girls	—	—	790	610	570	510
177/III, School Girls	2660	2150	1540	1370	1460	1360
177, School Girls	2350	2090	1640	—	—	—
178, The Photographer	480	280	180	130	110	120
179, Coquettes	440	270	170	110	120	100
180, Tuneful Goodnight	720	520	430	290	170	90
182, Good Friends	420	250	140	120	90	80
183, Forest Shrine	1680	1070	620	280	280	—
184, Latest News (sq. base)	390	300	220	170	150	110
185, Accordion Boy	690	230	160	90	90	80
186, Sweet Music	730	250	150	120	100	90
187, Store Plaque in English	1490	870	540	370	—	—
187/A, Store Plaque in English	—	—	—	—	50	40
188, Celestial Musician	740	340	190	150	140	90
192, Candlelight	670	690	330	120	90	80
193, Angel Duet	460	230	140	110	100	90
194, Watchful Angel	670	370	260	180	150	140

	CM	FB	SB	3-L	V-G	G
195/2/0, Barnyard Hero	$ 220	$ 210	$ 140	$ 100	$ 100	$ 70
195/1, Barnyard Hero	370	280	230	160	140	120
195, Barnyard Hero	600	550	—	—	—	—
196/0, Telling Her Secret	430	320	220	150	160	140
196/1, Telling Her Secret	840	780	480	270	240	230
197/2/0, Be Patient	—	220	130	120	90	80
197/1, Be Patient	300	240	170	130	110	100
197, Be Patient	560	500	—	—	—	—
198/2/0, Home From Market	150	150	100	70	70	60
198/1, Home From Market	310	230	170	120	100	90
198, Home From Market	490	370	—	—	—	—
199/0, Feeding Time	310	250	170	130	100	90
199/1, Feeding Time	360	290	240	160	110	100
199, Feeding Time	470	420	—	—	—	—
200/0, Little Goat Herder	250	200	180	90	90	90
200/1, Little Goat Herder	270	220	180	220	110	90
200, Little Goat Herder	450	420	360	—	—	—
201/2/0, Retreat to Safety	180	190	140	100	80	80
201/1, Retreat to Safety	350	380	190	170	100	100
201, Retreat to Safety	530	340	—	—	—	—
203/II/0, Signs of Spring	400	180	130	100	90	70
203/I, Signs of Spring	260	230	200	120	110	90
203, Signs of Spring	460	300	—	—	—	—
204, Weary Wanderer	460	320	220	150	100	100
205, Store Plaque in German	1070	850	—	—	—	—
206, Angel Cloud	560	440	290	90	40	30
207, Heavenly Angel	260	110	40	40	30	30
208, Store Plaque in French	—	2730	—	—	—	—
209, Store Plaque in Swedish	—	4170	—	—	—	—
210, Schmid Brothers Store Plaque	—	5000	—	—	—	—
211, Store Plaque in English	—	4420	—	—	—	—
213, Store Plaque in Spanish	—	2880	—	—	—	—
214, Nativity Set	—	2840	1220	1090	1040	880
217, Boy w/ Toothache	—	170	140	100	80	80
218/2/0, Birthday Serenade	—	460	470	400	100	80
218/0, Birthday Serenade	—	720	690	580	130	120
218, Birthday Serenade	—	770	590	—	—	—
220, We Congratulate	—	200	170	100	90	80
220, We Congratulate	—	360	—	—	—	—
222, Madonna	—	1400	1080	—	—	—
223, To Market	—	580	320	290	230	250
224/I, Wayside Harmony	—	320	240	220	200	180
224/II, Wayside Harmony	—	540	380	300	240	230
224, Wayside Harmony	—	540	470	—	—	—
225/I, Just Resting	—	340	250	230	190	190
225/II, Just Resting	—	500	430	290	280	220
226, Mail Is Here	—	810	510	430	300	250
227, She Loves Me, She Loves Me Not	—	580	310	190	200	180
228, Good Friends	—	540	310	200	180	180
229, Apple Tree Girl	—	710	280	210	180	170
230, Apple Tree Boy	—	760	240	210	200	170

	CM	FB	SB	3-L	V-G	G
231, Birthday Serenade	—	$ 1980	—	—	$ 290	$ 230
232, Happy Days	—	1560	—	—	270	260
234, Birthday Serenade	—	1940	$ 1450	$ 1050	$ 220	220
235, Happy Days	—	1200	810	560	270	220
238A, Angel w/ Lute	—	—	—	50	40	30
238B, Angel w/ Accordion	—	—	—	50	30	30
238C, Angel w/ Trumpet	—	—	—	50	40	30
239A, Girl w/ Nosegay	—	—	—	60	40	30
239B, Girl w/ Doll	—	—	—	50	30	30
239C, Boy w/ Horse	—	—	—	50	40	30
240, Little Drummer	—	150	90	80	60	60
241B, Angel Lights	—	—	—	—	160	150
243, Madonna and Child	—	150	60	40	40	30
246, Holy Family	—	150	100	60	40	30
248, Guardian Angel	—	—	140	60	40	30
250A & B, Little Goat Herder/Feeding Time	—	280	210	160	180	170
251A & B, Good Friends/She Loves Me	—	300	270	210	200	160
252A & B, Apple Tree Girl and Boy	—	280	240	190	190	170
255, Stitch in Time	—	—	260	140	110	90
256, Knitting Lesson	—	—	320	290	230	210
257, For Mother	—	—	230	90	80	70
258, Which Hand?	—	—	230	100	70	60
260, Nativity Set (16 pieces)	—	—	—	3570	3450	2700
261, Angel Duet	—	—	—	310	100	90
262, Heavenly Lullaby	—	—	—	350	100	90

Left: Wayside Harmony, #111, CM, $440, FB, $280, SB, $200, 3-L, $140. Right: Weary Wanderer, #204 (see listing). —Photos courtesy of Jim Glaab's Collector's Showcase.

Iroquois China

The Iroquois China Company produced hotel ware from 1905 until 1969. The company is best known to collectors today for its Russell Wright and Ben Seibel lines.

Casual China (1946)

Russell Wright designed Casual China. Of the many colors produced, aqua, brick, red, and cantaloupe are the most sought. Add a premium for these pieces.

	LOW	AVG.	HIGH
Bowl	$ 30	$ 33	$ 36
Carafe	80	100	120
Casserole, 2-4 qt.	40	55	70
Casserole, 3 qt.-6 qt.	70	85	100
Chop Plate, 14"	32	36	40
Coffee Pot	55	60	65
Cream/Sugar	28	34	41
Cup/Saucer	9	13	16
Cup/Saucer, Art Deco	60	64	68
Dish, 5"-7"	8	9	10
Dutch Oven	85	100	115
Frying Pan, w/ lid	60	70	80
Gravy, w/ lid, old	29	37	45
Mug	60	70	80
Party Plate	30	35	40
Pitcher	78	77	76
Plate, 6"-8"	6	8	10
Plate, 9"-10"	9	11	13
Platter, 12"-14"	18	24	30
Salad Bowl, 10"	26	30	34
Sauce Pan, w/ lid	60	65	75
Shaker, stacking	11	13	15
Soup Plate, 8.5"	21	23	25
Teapot	45	58	72
Vegetable, 8"-10"	22	29	36
Vegetable, div., w/ lid	50	54	58

Casual backstamp.

Impromptu

Impromptu was designed by Ben Seibel.

	LOW	AVG.	HIGH
Butter Dish	$ 17	$ 20	$ 23
Casserole, w/ lid	22	25	28
Coffee Pot	29	31	33
Compote	18	20	22
Cream/Sugar	14	16	18
Cup/Saucer	6	9	12
Gravy Boat	14	16	18
Plate, 6"-8"	2	4	6
Plate, 9"-10"	4	5	6
Platter, 12"-15"	6	9	11
Relish Tray	6	7	8
Salt/Pepper	14	16	18
Soup Plate	7	8	9
Vegetable	9	12	15

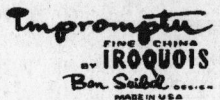 

Left: Impromptu backstamp. Right Informal backstamp.

Informal

Informal was designed by Ben Seibel.

Butter Dish	18	21	24
Casserole, 2 qt.	23	26	29
Coffee Pot, 9 cup	48	54	60
Cream/Sugar	13	16	19
Cup/Saucer	5	6	7
Dish, 5"-6"	1	2	3
Dutch Oven, w/ lid	23	26	29
Frying Pan, w/ lid	23	26	29
Gravy Boat	14	16	18
Plate, 6"-8"	2	4	6
Plate, 9"-10"	4	5	6
Platter, 12"-15"	7	9	11
Salt/Pepper	14	16	18
Samovar, w/ stand	36	42	48
Sauce Pan, w/ lid	22	26	30
Soup Plate	7	8	9
Soup, w/ lid	13	15	17
Vegetable	9	12	15

Josef Originals

Muriel Joseph George of Arcadia, CA, designed Josef Originals Figurines from 1946-82. (The spelling was a printing error on the labels that time did not allow them to correct.) In 1982 she sold the company to her long-time partner and representative George Good, but she continued designing figures through 1985. These pieces were produced in California through 1960, when production was moved to Japan. Examples below are from the 1940s through the 1980s. In this time period the girls were all made with black eyes and a glossy finish, the animals with a semigloss finish. Figures are now produced by Applause who purchased the firm in 1985.

Prices are for figurines in perfect condition with no damage. All original figurines are marked on the bottom, either incised or ink-stamped "Josef Originals c" and have a Josef oval sticker with either the California or Japan designation. Beware of copies, which have only a Josef label. Our consultants for this area are Jim and Kaye Whitaker, co-authors of *Josef Originals* and owners of Eclectic Antiques (they are listed in the back of this book).

Left to right: September, "Doll of the Month" series, green dress, ht. 3.5"; elephant, flower on head, ht. 4.5". —Photos courtesy of Eclectic Antiques.

Animals

	LOW	HIGH
Bees, various poses, each	$ 14	$ 18
Elephant, flower on head, ht. 4.5"	35	45
Frogs, various poses, each	10	14
German Shepherd Dog, ht. 3"	18	22
Hippo, ht. 2.5"	20	25
Mice, various poses and costumes, each	14	18
Monkeys, various poses and costumes, each	14	18
Ostrich Babies, each, ht. .5"	20	25
Ostrich Mama, ht. 5"	40	50
Rabbits, various poses, each	10	14
Siamese Cat, ht. 2"	14	18

Josef Originals of California 1946-52

	LOW	HIGH
Autumn Leaf, Asian girl, white dress, black fan up, ht. 4.5"	$ 40	$ 50
Cherry Blossom, Asian girl, white dress, black fan down, ht. 4.5"	40	50
Cho Cho, tall Asian girl, white w/ pink fan up, ht. 10.75"	85	95
Hedy, girl in pink dress w/ hat holding gift, ht. 4.25"	40	50
Little TV Cowboy, large hat, rope in hands, ht. 5.25"	60	70
Mama, blue dress sitting w/ book, ht. 7.25"	70	80
May, "Dolls of the Month," green w/ green jewels, ht. 3.25"	25	35
Pitty Sing (the first Chinese boy), large hat	42	48
Sakura, tall Oriental girl, white dress, w/ pink fan down, ht. 10.75"	85	95
Saturday, "Days of the Week" series, yellow w/ pie, ht. 4"	30	40
Teddy, boy in gray suit holding flowers, ht. 4.25"	40	50
The Prince, boy sitting w/ thumb in mouth, ht. 3.75"	45	55
Wee Ching, Chinese boy w/ dog	35	45
Wee Ling, Chinese girl w/ kitten	35	45

Josef Originals of Japan, 1960-85

Adeline, "Gibson Girl" series, green dress w/ guitar, ht. 6.5"	80	100
Africa, "Little Internationals," white dress, pink feather, ht. 3.5"	27	35
America, Indian girl, "Little Internationals," brown dress, feather, ht. 3.5"	27	35
Antonio, barefoot man in brown pants w/ flower basket, ht. 6"	65	75
August, "Birthstone Dolls" series, green dress, green jewel, ht. 3"	16	22
Baby w/ Kitten, blue, pink or yellow, ht. 3", each	28	32
Birthday Girls #1, angel w/ wings, blue dress	22	28
Birthday Girls #14, angel w/ wings, pink dress	25	35
Blue Bird, girl in yellow dress w/ bird on hand, ht. 9"	80	100
Christmas Girl, red dress w/ green front, cape, ht. 6"	25	35
Christmas Girl, white dress w/ pink trim, basket, ht. 6"	25	35
Debby, "First Love" series, pink dress w/ hat, ht. 5"	22	28
"Gigi" Series, pink dress, w/ hat, and puppy, ht. 6"	80	100
Happiness Is, boy in bed, puppy	22	28
High Heels, "Sweet 16" series, green dress, ht. 7.5"	80	100
"Housekeepers" Series, green dress w/ teapot, ht. 3"	22	28
January, "Doll of the Month" series, rose dress w/ hat, ht. 3.5"	22	28
Jeanne, "Colonial Days" series, lavender dress, ht. 9.5"	80	100
Jill, "Nursery Rhymes," green dress, w/ bucket, ht. 4"	22	28
Lara's Theme Music Box, couple, green suit and rose dress	65	75
Love Rendezvous, girl w/ light blue dress and hat, ht. 9"	80	100
Mary Holding Jesus, white gown, ht. 5"	25	35
Mighty Like a Rose, girl in white dress, pink flower hat, ht. 4"	22	28
New Hat, "A Mother's World" series, blue and yellow dress, hat, ht. 7.5"	80	100
October, "Birthstone Dolls" series, blue dress w/ pink jewel, ht. 3"	16	22
Robin, "Musicale" series, in blue dress w/ harp, ht. 6"	55	65
Russia, "Little Internationals" series, rose dress, white hat, ht. 3.5"	27	35
School Belle, yellow dress w/ apple, ht. 3"	22	28
September, "Doll of the Month" series, green dress, hat, ht. 3.5"	22	28
Shepherd, ht. 3"	22	28
Sweden, "Little Internationals," gray and white dress w/ flowers, ht. 3.5"	27	35
Tammy, "Musicale" series, in pink dress w/ piano, ht. 6"	55	65
The Bridal March Music Box, couple in tuxedo and bridal gown	65	75
The Engagement, "Romance" series, in blue dress w/ ring, ht. 8"	80	100

Edwin M. Knowles China

Edwin M. Knowles, son of the founder of Knowles, Taylor, Knowles, manufactured his own semiporcelain from 1901 until 1963. There are many different backstamps.

EDWIN M. KNOWLES
CHINA CO.

Knowles backstamp.

Beverly (1941)

	LOW	AVG.	HIGH
Bowl, 36s	$ 8	$ 9	$ 10
Bowl, coupe, 8"	10	12	14
Butter, open	21	23	25
Candleholder, pr.	24	27	29
Casserole	20	25	30
Chop Plate	12	14	16
Coaster	10	13	16
Cream/Sugar	18	22	26
Cup/Saucer	10	15	20
Custard Cup	4	5	6
Dish, 6"	2	3	4
Gravy Boat	12	14	16
Pickle Dish	6	7	8
Plate, 6"-8"	4	6	8
Plate, 9"-10"	8	9	10
Platter, 8"-12"	12	16	20
Salt/Pepper	24	28	32
Soup Plate	8	9	10
Teapot	25	30	35

Deanna (1938)

	LOW	AVG.	HIGH
Bowl, 36s	7	8	9
Butter, open	15	20	25
Casserole	27	31	34
Chop Dish	14	16	18
Coaster	14	16	18
Cream/Sugar	21	24	27
Cup/Saucer	9	13	16
Dish, 4"-5"	2	3	4
Egg Cup, double	9	11	13
Gravy Boat	14	16	18
Pickle Dish	5	7	9
Plate, 6"-8"	4	6	7
Plate, 9"-10"	7	8	9
Platter, 8"-12"	8	13	18
Salt/Pepper	21	24	27
Soup, coupe	7	8	9
Teapot	27	31	34
Vegetable, 7"-10"	13	15	17

Esquire (1956)

Esquire was designed by Russel Wright.

	LOW	AVG.	HIGH
Compote	$ 58	$ 61	$ 64
Cream/Sugar	42	44	46
Cup/Saucer	15	19	22
Dish, 5"-7"	12	14	16
Gravy Boat	36	39	42
Pitcher, 2 qt.	84	94	104
Plate, 6"-7"	9	12	14
Plate, 9"-10"	15	16	17
Platter, 9"-14"	26	31	36
Salt/Pepper	25	32	39
Server, 22"	45	50	55
Teapot	100	110	120
Vegetable	46	58	69

Yorktown (1936)

Yorktown has an Art Deco appearance.

	LOW	AVG.	HIGH
Bowl, 36s		9	10
Bowl, coupe, 6"	4	5	6
Butter, open	21	23	25
Candleholder, pr.	24	27	29
Casserole	30	36	41
Chop Plate	12	15	17
Coaster	10	13	16
Cream/Sugar	24	28	32
Cup/Saucer	10	15	20
Custard Cup	4	5	6
Dish, 6"	2	3	4
Gravy Boat	14	16	18
Pickle Dish	6	7	8
Plate, 6"-8"	4	6	8
Plate, 9"-10"	8	9	10
Platter, 8"-12"	11	18	25
Salt/Pepper	24	28	32
Soup Plate	8	9	10
Teapot	40	45	50

Homer Laughlin China

Founded in 1874 as the Laughlin Brothers Pottery, it became the Homer Laughlin China Co. in 1896. Homer's brother, Shakespeare, withdrew in 1877. Homer Laughlin mainly produced semiporcelain. In 1959, vitreous dinnerware and institutional ware lines were introduced. The company is one of the largest still manufacturing today.

Homer Laughlin is most famous for its Fiesta dinnerware (listed separately under Fiesta). The company is also well known because of its dinnerware designed by Frederick Rhead, head designer from 1928 to 1942, and Don Schreckengost, head designer from 1945 to 1960. Laughlin used a variety of backstamps.

Early Homer Laughlin backstamps.

Brittany

	LOW	AVG.	HIGH
Bowl, 6"	$ 6	$ 8	$ 10
Cream/Sugar	25	30	35
Cup/Saucer	10	15	20
Dish, 5"	5	6	7
Egg Cup	15	20	25
Gravy Boat	18	22	26
Pickle Dish	10	12	14
Plate, 6"-7"	4	7	10
Plate, 9"-10"	7	10	13
Plate, sq., 8"	9	14	19
Platter, 11"-13"	25	30	35
Platter, 15"	25	28	31
Soup Plate, 9"	20	22	24
Teapot	35	45	55
Vegetable, 8"-9"	20	30	40

Century (1931)

Century is an early square shape in dinnerware.

Butter Dish	75	85	95
Casserole	34	40	46
Cream/Sugar	18	22	26
Cup/Saucer	12	14	16
Dish, 5"	6	7	8
Dish, 6"	12	14	16
Gravy Boat	15	20	25
Pickle Dish	16	17	18
Pitcher, Batter	80	100	120
Pitcher, Syrup	80	88	96
Plate, 6"-7"	6	8	10
Plate, 9"-10"	15	20	25
Platter, 11"-15"	16	23	29

	LOW	AVG.	HIGH
Soup Bowl/Saucer	$ 50	$ 60	$ 70
Soup Plate, 8"	12	14	16
Teapot	75	85	95
Vegetable, 9"	20	22	24

Epicure backstamp.

Epicure

Epicure was designed by Don Schreckengost and glazed in solid colors.

Casserole	42	46	50
Coffee Pot	95	110	125
Cream/Sugar	25	30	34
Cup/Saucer	15	17	19
Dish	12	15	18
Gravy Boat	21	23	24
Plate, 6"-8"	8	10	12
Plate, 9"-10"	12	15	18
Salt/Pepper	20	23	26
Soup Plate	11	14	16

Fiesta Ware

The Homer Laughlin China Company introduced this brightly colored pottery tableware in 1935. Frederick H. Rhead's graduated ring design was one of the most widely manufactured tablewares of the 20th century.

Colors include red, rose, dark green, medium green, light green, chartreuse, yellow, old ivory, gray, turquoise, and dark blue. Pieces are trademarked in the mold or with an ink hand-stamped mark. Reissued and restyled from the originals in 1986, Fiesta pieces are still available. Prices are for old, not reissued pieces. Medium green is the most valued, followed by rose, gray, and forest green.

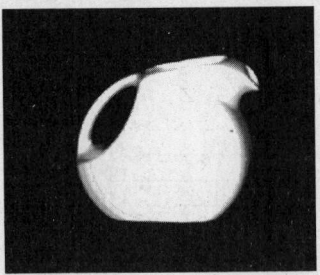 

Left to right: Small yellow disk pitcher; Fiesta backstamp.
— Item courtesy of Cerise Foster.

	AUCTION	RETAIL	
		Low	High
Bud Vase, red	$ 88	$ 140	$ 220
Carafe, ivory	231	370	570
Carafe, red	209	330	510
Casserole, French, yellow	165	260	400
Coffee Pot, light green	193	310	470
Creamer, ind., red	209	330	510
Creamer, stick handle, light green	30	50	70
Creamer, stick handle, red	66	110	160
Cup and Saucer, chartreuse	25	40	60
Cup and Saucer, cobalt	20	30	50
Cup and Saucer, forest green	33	50	80
Cup and Saucer, light green	17	30	40
Cup and Saucer, rose	30	50	70
Cup and Saucer, yellow	18	30	40
Deep Plate, cobalt	35	60	90
Deep Plate, ivory	27	40	70
Deep Plate, light green	33	50	80
Deep Plate, medium green	105	170	260
Deep Plate, red	35	60	90
Deep Plate, turquoise	33	50	80
Deep Plate, yellow	25	40	60
Demitasse Cup and Saucer, turquoise	69	110	170
Dinner Plate, chartreuse, 9"	14	20	30
Dinner Plate, cobalt, 9"	13	20	30
Dinner Plate, medium green, 9"	39	60	100
Dinner Plate, rose, 9"	22	40	50
Disk Pitcher, cobalt	100	160	250
Disk Pitcher, ivory	70	110	170
Disk Pitcher, light green	60	100	150
Disk Pitcher, medium green	800	1280	1960
Disk Pitcher, red	150	240	370
Disk Pitcher, rose	110	180	270
Disk Pitcher, turquoise	90	140	220
Disk Water Pitcher, cobalt	99	160	240
Fork, light green	83	130	200
Marmalade, large, cobalt	308	490	750
Mug, medium green	22	40	50
Nappy, chartreuse, 8.5"	30	50	70
Nappy, medium green, 8.5"	94	150	230
Nappy, rose, 8.5"	39	60	100
Nappy, rose, 8.5"	30	50	70
Nappy, turquoise, 8.5"	19	30	50
Nappy, yellow, 8.5"	28	40	70
Plate, chartreuse, 9"	14	20	30
Plate, cobalt, 9"	13	20	30
Plate, ivory, 9"	7	10	20
Plate, light green, 9"	7	10	20
Plate, medium green, 9"	37	60	90
Plate, red, 9"	12	20	30
Plate, rose, 9"	22	40	50

	AUCTION	RETAIL	
		Low	High
Plate, turquoise, 9"	$ 8	$ 10	$ 20
Plate, yellow, 9"	8	10	20
Plate, Four Seasons, from 1939 World's Fair	60	100	150
Platter, gray	36	60	90
Salad Bowl, ind., medium green	77	120	190
Salad Bowl, ind., turquoise	72	120	180
Sauce Boat, gray	50	80	120
Soup, covered onion, ivory	358	570	880
Soup, covered onion, yellow	413	660	1010
Stick-Handle Creamer, light green	30	50	70
Syrup Pitcher, red	385	620	940
Teapot, medium green	770	1230	1890
Teapot, rose	154	250	380
Teapot, yellow	88	140	220
Teapot, ball, large, medium green	770	1230	1890
Tray, figure 8, cobalt	99	160	240
Tray, utility, cobalt	25	40	60
Tray, utility, red	55	90	130
Vase, cobalt, 8"	605	970	1480
Vase, ivory, 12"	800	1280	1960
Vase, ivory, 11"	770	1230	1890

Harlequin (1938)

Similar to Fiesta, it has bright colors, simple shapes and a series of rings, but not on the rim. Pieces were unmarked.

	LOW	AVG.	HIGH
Bowl, 36s	17	20	23
Butter, .5 lb	50	75	100
Candlestick, pr.	80	110	140
Casserole	51	63	75
Cream/Sugar	18	25	31
Cup/Saucer	7	10	13
Cup/Saucer, jumbo	49	58	67
Dish, 5.5"	4	7	10
Dish, 6.5"	16	19	22
Egg Cup	9	12	14
Gravy Boat	11	14	17
Jug, 22 oz.	18	22	26
Jug, ball form	32	38	44
Marmalade	90	105	120
Plate, 10"	17	21	25
Plate, 6"-7"	3	6	9
Plate, 9"	7	9	11
Platter, 10"-13"	17	22	26
Relish Tray, 4 part	160	190	220
Shaker	6	8	10
Soup Plate	11	13	15
Syrup Pitcher	160	190	220
Teapot	52	64	75
Tumbler	24	28	32
Vegetable, 9"	13	18	23

Rhythm

Rhythm was designed by Don Schreckengost.

	LOW	AVG.	HIGH
Cream/Sugar	$ 25	$ 29	$ 33
Cup/Saucer	10	14	18
Dish, 5"-6"	4	5	6
Gravy Boat	16	18	20
Pickle Dish, 9"	8	9	10
Pitcher, 2 qt.	50	60	70
Plate, 6"-8"	4	6	8
Plate, 9"-10"	8	9	10
Platter, oval, 11"-15"	15	20	24
Salt/Pepper	12	15	18
Soup Plate, 8"	8	9	10
Spoon rest	130	165	200
Teapot	43	48	53
Vegetable, 9"	17	19	20
Vegetable, w/ lid	30	34	38

Riviera

Riviera was based on the Century design.

Butter Dish	150	165	180
Casserole	135	145	155
Cream/Sugar	34	42	50
Cup/Saucer	25	28	31
Dish, 5"	12	14	16
Dish, 6"	37	44	52
Gravy Boat	31	40	48
Pickle Dish	30	34	38
Pitcher, batter	145	182	220
Pitcher, syrup	130	155	180
Plate, 6"-7"	12	16	20
Plate, 9"-10"	30	40	50
Platter, 11"-15"	31	46	62
Soup Plate, 8"	24	28	31
Teapot	150	175	200
Vegetable, 9"	40	45	50

Serenade (1939)

Serenade used an embossed wheat sheaf decoration.

Casserole	15	20	25
Cream/Sugar	12	16	20
Cup/Saucer	5	9	13
Dish, 6"	2	3	4
Gravy Boat	8	10	12
Pickle Dish, 9"	4	5	6
Plate, 6-7"	3	4	5
Plate 9-10"	4	5	6
Chop Plate, 13"	8	10	12
Platter, oval, 12.5"	6	7	8
Salt/Pepper	12	15	18
Soup Plate, 8"	5	6	7
Teapot	15	20	25
Vegetable, 9"	8	10	12

Swing (1938)

Swing has delicate round handles and finials.

	LOW	AVG.	HIGH
Butter Dish	$ 19	$ 22	$ 25
Casserole	31	34	38
Coffee Pot	30	34	38
Cream/Sugar	28	32	36
Cup/Saucer	8	10	12
Egg Cup	10	13	15
Muffin Cover	29	36	42
Plate, 6"-8"	4	5	6
Plate, 9"-10"	8	9	10
Platter, 11"-13"	10	11	12
Salt/Pepper	14	16	18

Tango

Tango is rare and widely sought.

Casserole	35	45	55
Cream/Sugar	35	45	55
Cup/Saucer	10	13	15
Dish, 6"	6	8	10
Egg Cup	35	45	55
Plate, 6"-7"	6	8	10
Plate, 9"-10"	10	13	15
Platter, 11.5"	16	18	20
Salt/Pepper	17	22	27
Soup Plate	17	19	21
Vegetable, 8"-9"	19	21	23

Wells backstamp.

Wells (1930)

Wells was designed by Frederick Rhead. It has a thin rim and open handles.

Bowl, 36s	11	13	15
Casserole	44	52	60
Coffee Pot	45	53	61
Covered Toast	44	52	60
Cream/Sugar	35	40	46
Cup/Saucer	12	15	18
Dish, 5"	3	5	6
Egg Cup	14	18	22
Gravy Boat	22	25	28
Pickle Dish	9	12	14
Pitcher	58	64	70
Plate, 6"-8"	6	9	11

	LOW	AVG.	HIGH
Plate, 9"-10"	$ 12	$ 14	$ 15
Plate, sq.	11	13	14
Platter, 11"-15"	14	22	30
Soup Bowl/Saucer	39	44	50
Soup Plate	22	26	30
Teapot	52	57	62
Vegetable, rd., 8"-9"	14	16	18

World's Fair/Expositions

Four Seasons Plate	55	60	65
George Washington Pitcher, 2"	31	38	44
George Washington Pitcher, 5"	52	54	57
Golden Gate Plate	80	86	92
Martha Washington Pitcher, 2"	45	51	57
Martha Washington Pitcher, 5"	65	70	75
New York World's Fair Plate	120	135	150
Potter's Plate	28	36	44
Vase, 6"-10"	85	90	95
Zodiac Cup/Saucer	85	90	95

Yellowstone

Yellowstone is octagonal.

Bowl, 36s	8	9	10
Butter Dish	20	22	24
Casserole	29	32	34
Cream/Sugar	25	29	33
Cup/Saucer	10	15	20
Dish, 5"-6"	2	3	4
Gravy Boat	17	19	21
Pitcher 1 pt.	12	14	15
Plate, 6"-7"	4	5	6
Plate, 9"-10"	8	9	10
Platter, 9"-12"	11	12	13
Soup Plate, 8.5"	10	12	14
Teapot	30	36	42
Vegetable, 9"-10"	17	19	21

Limoges China

The Sterling China Company changed its name to Limoges early in this century. After WWII, legal action brought by Limoges of France forced the name change to American Limoges. Production halted in 1955. Viktor Schreckengost designed some American Limoges. Limoges is not the same quality dinnerware as the French company of the same name. Don't pay French Limoges prices for American Limoges pieces.

Limoges backstamps.

Casino (c. 1954)

Casino has the shape of playing card suits, with matching decal decoration.

	LOW	AVG.	HIGH
Cream/Sugar, diamond	$ 20	$ 30	$ 40
Cup, club	10	14	18
Dish, diamond	6	7	8
Plate, spade	9	13	16
Platter, diamond	18	22	24
Saucer, heart	4	5	6

Thin Swirl

Square has rounded corners and an arrow-head finial.

Butter Dish	20	22	24
Casserole	20	23	26
Cream/Sugar	12	14	16
Cup/Saucer	4	5	6
Gravy Boat	12	14	16
Plate, 6"-7"	2	3	4
Plate, 9"	7	8	9
Teapot	30	35	40

Triumph (1937)

Viktor Schreckengost designed Triumph with horizontal fluting.

Casserole	20	23	26
Chop Plate, 11"-13"	12	16	20
Coffee Pot	40	45	50
Cream/Sugar	13	15	17
Cup/Saucer	4	5	6
Dish, 5"-6"	1	2	3
Gravy Boat	8	9	10
Plate, 10"-11"	4	5	6
Plate, 6"-7"	1	2	3
Platter, oval, 11"-15"	10	14	18
Salt/Pepper	8	10	12
Soup Plate, 8.25"	10	11	12
Vegetable, rd.,8.75"	15	17	20

Luxardo Bottles

The Luxardo Company has produced wines in the Padua region of Italy since the early 19th century. In 1952, the Hulse Company became their sole American distributor. Under the Hulse influence, the Italian company produced various elaborate decanters for their products. Produced in both glass and ceramics, these bottles are still widely collected.

Majolica Figurals

	LOW	AVG.	HIGH
Bantu, 1962, #B5, ht. 12"	$ 27	$ 45	$ 36
Blue and Gold Amphora, 1968, ht. 22"	17	27	21
Buddha Goddess, 1961, #B135, ht. 8"	22	36	28
Classical Fragment, 1961, #S130, ht. 10"	27	45	36
Coffee Carafe, 1962, #E2, 10.25"	17	27	21
Congo, 1960, #B99, ht. 9"	27	45	36
Deruta Pitcher, 1953, #59, ht. 9"	49	80	64
Diana, 1956, #117, ht. 8"	31	53	43
Dragon Amphora, 1953, #30, ht. 8.75"	39	63	50
Duck Surrealist, 1955, #132, ht. 7"	46	73	57
Egyptian, 1959, #91, ht. 14.25"	18	31	26
Etrusca B, 1959, #86B, ht. 10.5"	24	41	34
Euganean Bronzy, 1952-55, #70, ht. 7.5"	37	58	45
Euganean Coppered, #71, ht. 7.5"	37	58	45
Faenza Majolica, 1956, #120, ht.8"	43	71	57
Fakir, 1960, #B95, ht. 10.75"	46	73	57
Fiori, 1956, #122, ht. 7.5"	34	55	43
Jogan Buddha Brown, 1961, #B136, ht. 12.5"	27	45	36
Jogan Buddha Gray, 1962, #B136, ht. 12.5"	22	36	28
Marabou Surrealist, 1957, #134, ht. 10"	46	73	57
Mayan, 1960, #B98, ht. 11"	31	53	43
Opal Majolica, 1957, #76, ht. 10"	46	73	57
Paestum, 1959, #89, ht. 9"	31	49	38
Pear, 1960, #106, ht. 3.75"	18	31	26
Purple and Gold Urn, 1958, #66, ht. 7.5"	22	36	28
Ruby and Gold Amphora, 1958, #79, ht. 10.5"	29	46	36
Spugnata, 1956, #123, ht. 8"	32	51	40
Tower of Fruit, 1968, ht. 22.25"	16	26	20
Warrior, 1956, #119, ht. 7.5"	34	55	43
Zebra Surrealist, 1957, #130, ht. 7.25"	46	73	57

Venetian Glass

	LOW	AVG.	HIGH
Alabaster Candlestick, 1961, #L15, ht. 12.5	39	61	47
Alabaster Goose, 1960, #L3, ht. 15.5"	41	65	50
Blue Fiammetta, 1957, #149, ht. 11"	22	36	28
Cellini, 1952, ht. 11.25"	34	55	43
Cellini, 1957, ht. 11.25"	34	55	43
Curva Vaso, 1961, #L13, ht. 11.25"	31	48	37
Dogal Silver Ruby A, 1952-55, #138A, ht. 9.5"	27	45	36
Dolphin, 1959, ht. 16.5"	110	179	142
Green and Gold Fish, 1960, #L5, ht. 10"	37	58	45
Murano Ruby and Gold, 1952, #75, ht. 15"	110	179	142
Ruby Fish, 1961, #L12, ht. 11.5"	40	64	50
Venetian Merletto, 1957, #146, ht. 10.5	34	55	43
Venetian Silver Violet, 1952-55, #143, ht. 11"	24	43	36

Marblehead Pottery

Marblehead Pottery started as a therapeutic resource for invalids. In 1916, it was bought by artist Arthur Baggs. It ceased production in 1936. The wares were heavy and dark. Later, Baggs introduced a cream-colored ware with multi-colored decoration and a line of children's pieces.

Prices have become very strong in recent years. As with much Arts and Crafts pottery, valuation is highly subjective, depending on the subtleties of shape, color and design. Small defects will severely devalue a piece. Backstamps include a sailing ship with a *M* and *P* on opposite sides and a monogram of Arthur E. Baggs.

Marblehead impressed mark.

	LOW	AVG.	HIGH
Bookends, sailing ship in relief, blue glaze, 6" x 5"	$ 300	$ 400	$ 500
Bowl, dark blue glaze, 6"	100	160	220
Candlesticks, pr., blue glaze, 3"	120	180	240
Pitcher, dark blue glaze, 4.5"	150	200	250
Planter, turquoise glaze, artist signed, 1934	300	350	400
Tile, brown and yellow glaze, floral motif, 6.5" x 6.5"	200	250	300
Vase, bulbous shape, gray matte w/ blue flecks, 3.5"	100	120	140
Vase, black glaze, 6"	550	700	850
Vase, cylindrical, stylized trees on a mustard ground, 5.5"	3000	4000	5000
Vase, cylindrical, tree motif, gray and green glaze, signed, 7"	500	650	750
Vase, dark blue glaze, 7"	250	280	310
Vase, green glaze, 6.5"	200	240	280
Vase, monochrome, 6"	700	800	900

Metlox Pottery

Metlox Potteries makes art ware, novelties, and Poppytrail dinnerware. Although solid color wares may date to 1927, decorated wares date from the 1940s through the present.

California Ivy

	LOW	AVG.	HIGH
Butter Dish	$ 50	$ 55	$ 60
Chop Plate, 13"	30	35	40
Coaster	12	15	18
Coffee Pot	100	120	140
Cream/Sugar	30	35	40
Cup/Saucer	14	18	21
Dish, 5"-7"	11	17	22
Gravy Boat	35	38	41
Mug	22	25	28
Pitcher, 2.5 qt.	50	60	70
Plate, 10"	21	25	28
Plate, 6"-8"	14	17	20
Platter, oval, 9"-13"	33	46	58
Salad Bowl, 11"	34	38	42
Salt/Pepper	14	21	28
Soup Bowl, 5"	8	10	12
Soup Plate, 7"	17	19	21
Teapot	100	125	150
Tumbler, 13 oz.	40	45	50
Vegetable, 9"-11"	40	45	50

Homestead Provincial

Homestead Provincial has American folk art themes using the same shapes as Rooster.

Bread Server, rect., 9.5"	50	60	70
Butter Dish, rect.	50	55	60
Canister Set, 4 piece	225	250	275
Casserole, hen lid, 1 qt.	57	64	71
Chop Plate, 12.25"	30	35	40
Coaster, 3.75"	11	14	17
Coffee Pot, 7 cup	100	112	125
Cookie Jar	70	85	100
Cream/Sugar	30	35	40
Cruet	50	55	60
Cruet set, 2-5 piece	100	125	150
Cup/Saucer	16	22	28
Dish, 5"-6"	8	10	12
Egg Cup	23	25	27
Gravy Boat	32	38	43
Lazy Susan, 7 piece	90	115	140
Mug, 8 oz.	16	19	21
Pitcher, 1 qt.-2 qt.	50	60	70
Plate, 10"	23	26	28
Plate, 6"-8"	12	16	20

	LOW	AVG.	HIGH
Platter, oval, 11"-16"	$ 40	$ 55	$ 70
Salad, 11"	34	38	42
Salt/Pepper	14	22	30
Shakers, hen/rooster	45	48	52
Soup Plate, 8"	16	20	23
Tankard, 1 pt.	45	50	55
Teapot	110	125	140
Tumbler, ftd, 11 oz.	110	125	140
Vegetable, 7"-12"	29	39	49
Vegetable, w/lid, 1 qt.	57	62	67

Red Rooster

Red Rooster is a toleware-influenced design; note the "rivets" on the hollowware pieces.

	LOW	AVG.	HIGH
Bread Server, rect., 9.5"	70	80	90
Butter, rect.	60	65	70
Canister Set, 4-piece	200	250	300
Casserole, hen lid, 1.25 qt.	65	75	85
Casserole, ind., hen lid	110	120	130
Chop Plate, 12"	29	32	36
Coaster, 3.75"	14	17	20
Coffee Pot	110	130	150
Cookie Jar	150	170	180
Cream/Sugar	36	43	50
Cruet set, 2-5 piece	100	150	200
Cup/Saucer	21	27	32
Dish, 6"	18	22	25
Egg Cup	29	32	36
Gravy Boat	42	47	52
Jewelry Box	130	145	160
Lazy Susan set, 7-piece	450	500	550
Marmalade	130	150	170
Mug, 8 oz.	28	31	34
Pitcher, 1.5 pt.-2.25 qt.	50	70	90
Plate, 6"-8"	11	18	25
Platter, oval, 9"-16"	40	60	80
Salad, 11.5"	40	47	54
Salt Box	170	185	200
Salt/Pepper	17	26	35
Salt/Pepper Mill	150	160	170
Shakers, hen and rooster	50	60	70
Soup, ind., 5"	11	13	15
Soup Plate, 8"	22	26	30
Tankard, 1 pt.	50	60	70
Teapot	135	155	175
Tumbler, ftd., 11 oz.	140	160	180
Tureen	500	750	1000
Vegetable	40	60	80
Watering Can	70	80	90

Morton Pottery

Morton Pottery expanded into novelties in the late 1930s and continued producing until 1971. Its best-known marks are *Morton* and *USA* incised.

The following entries are from the Woodland pattern, which has a brown and green splatter on yelloware.

	LOW	AVG.	HIGH
Baker, pie, 9"	$ 80	$ 100	$ 120
Casserole	60	75	90
Coffee Server, 8-cup	70	85	100
Custard Cup	16	21	25
Grease Jar, 3"-4"	30	40	50
Mixing Bowl, 4"-8"	45	60	75
Pitcher	50	70	90
Salt/Pepper	75	100	125
Teapot, 3-9 cup	60	75	90
Vase, bulbous, 11"	100	125	150

Mt. Clemens Pottery

The Mt. Clemens Pottery Co. manufactured semiporcelain dinnerware from 1915 until 1987.

Petal

Medium green is most common.

	LOW	AVG.	HIGH
Bowl, 36s	4	5	6
Butter Dish	10	12	14
Cream/Sugar	12	16	20
Cup/Saucer	4	6	8
Dish, 5-6"	2	3	4
Gravy Boat	8	10	12
Plate, 6-8"	2	3	4
Plate, 9-10"	4	5	6
Platter, 11-13"	6	8	10
Platter, lug, 15"	8	10	12
Soup Bowl	5	6	7
Soup Plate, 8"	4	5	6
Vegetable, rd., 7-9"	7	9	11

Vogue

Vogue rim is embossed with stylized birds and flowers.

Butter Dish	10	12	14
Cream/Sugar	12	16	20
Cup/Saucer	4	6	8
Plate, 6-7"	2	3	4
Plate, 9-10"	4	5	6
Platter, 11"-12"	6	7	8

Newcomb Pottery

The Newcomb College Art Department in New Orleans began producing pottery for sale in 1896. Newcomb wares carry underglaze designs, picturing subjects from nature.

There are usually five marks on each piece: the mark of Newcomb (a white-on-black vase with the initials *N.C.*, or merely the *N* within the *C*, or *NEWCOMB COLLEGE* spelled out), a potter's mark, an artist's or decorator's mark, a recipe mark, and a registration mark.

     Newcomb impressed mark.

	LOW	AVG.	HIGH
Bowl, 5", painted flowers, applied roses and leaves	$ 130	$ 160	$ 190
Candlesticks, 7.5", pr., trumpet form, matte glaze, c. 1925	450	525	600
Lemonade Set, Maria de Hoa LeBlanc, pitcher and 6 cups and saucers, pitcher 10"	—	—	13,750
Trivet, floral motif, signed	260	310	360
Vase, 4", green, lavender, and rose, high-gloss finish	300	350	400
Vase, 5", polychrome flowers and leaves, blue ground, signed	700	800	900
Vase, 5", floral motif, bulbous body, matte glaze, signed, 1910 ...	550	600	650
Vase, 5", ovoid, foliate motif, matte glaze, signed, c. 1910	800	900	1000
Vase, 6", moon shining in trees motif, blue ground, signed	1900	2100	2300
Vase, 6", white floral motif, blue background, signed	1000	1100	1200
Vase, 6.5", blue background, 3-color floral design, artist signed GK31AM, incised N,B, mold mark 252	1,800		
Vase, 8", floral motif, signed	600	700	800
Vase, 8", beige glaze, dogwood motif, signed, c. 1910	800	1000	1200

Niloak Pottery

Niloak Pottery is old classic redware, influenced by Greek, Roman, and Native American design, but with a striking marbleized texture. Potters threw Niloak ware on a wheel. Many pieces have only an inside glaze. The word "niloak" is kaolin (the chief ingredient in porcelain) spelled backwards. Niloak pottery is completely unlike porcelain. Most successful during the 1920s, the firm survived until 1946.

The pottery had an impressed mark or a circular paper label, reading simply *NILOAK POTTERY*. Paper labels became standard in later years.

ℕ𝕀𝕃𝕆𝔸𝕂   *Niloak incised or impressed mark.*

Hywood (1930s)

	LOW	AVG.	HIGH
Ewer, 10", semimatte glaze, molded eagle on side	$ 40	$ 70	$ 90
Pitcher, miniature	15	25	40
Vase, matte white glaze, 12"	150	200	230
Vase, 6", applied handles, matte glaze	40	70	95
Vase, 7.5", matte rose glaze	50	80	100
Vase, 8", 2 handled, scalloped rim, rose to blue glaze	60	90	130

Mission Ware (early 1900s)

	LOW	AVG.	HIGH
Bowl, 10", earthtone swirls	75	100	130
Matchholder, swirls	40	65	85
Vase, 3.5", swirls	35	60	80
Vase, 4", dark blue, cream and blue swirls	40	68	90
Vase, 4.5", tan and blue swirls	50	75	100
Vase, 5", brown, blue and cream swirls	40	55	80
Vase, 5.5", blue and brown swirls	42	65	85
Vase, 6.5", blue and white swirls	50	80	110
Vase, 6", bulbous body, flared rim, swirls	63	85	110
Vase, 6", swirls	42	65	85
Vase, 6.5", tan, ivory and blue swirls	70	95	115
Vase, 9", swirls	115	145	175
Vase, 10", swirls	165	200	235

George Ohr Pottery

George Ohr, of Biloxi, MS, designed and manufactured all pieces himself. Ohr pottery is free-hand work, like doodles in clay, all produced between the early 1880s and 1906. Ohr's markings have no set pattern. Most are marked G.E. OHR, BILOXI.

	LOW	AVG.	HIGH
Ashtray, 2.5", brown, w/ shaped rim.	$ 300	$ 375	$ 450
Ashtray, 2.5", brown-green, caved-in sides, high gloss glaze.	800	1000	1200
Bowl, 3.5", beige, squat form w/ cylindrical sides flaring into wide base, crimped lip, ornaments along base rim.	180	220	260
Bowl, 3.5", green and mud-brown, squat design.	320	400	485
Bowl, 4", green, flecked w/ dark brown, circular.	400	500	600
Bowl, 7", shades of brown, V-form, severely crimped sides.	430	525	650
Ink Stand, 6.5", artist's palette form, thumbhole and brush.	445	520	650
Pitcher, 5", green mottling, fish form, w/ tail handle.	800	1000	1200
Teapot, 4", brown and green splatter glaze, ovoid bulbous form w/ thumbprint designing, braided handle, disc-type lid.	1000	1200	1400
Vase, 10", blue, cylindrical form widening slightly at bottom.	700	800	900
Vase, 3.5", brown, bulbous form w/ pinched and dented sides.	250	325	400
Vase, 3.5", brown smear glaze, bulbous form, crimped neck.	550	700	850
Vase, 5.5", burnt orange and green glaze, cologne bottle-form, dome-shaped bowl, pinched, funnel-type neck and mouth.	250	325	400
Vase, 5.5", burnt orange and olive glaze, hurricane lamp-form w/ bulbous body, wide mouth, applied caterpillar.	700	850	1000

Paden City Pottery

The Paden City Company manufactured semiporcelain dinnerware from 1914 through 1963. It exhibited at the 1938-39 World's Fair. The Caliente line is the favorite of collectors.

Blue Willow (1937)

Paden City etched its version of the Blue Willow design into the body of seven different items. They glazed it in blue, allowing the design to remain visible.

	LOW	AVG.	HIGH
Bowl, salad	$ 15	$ 17	$ 19
Cup/Saucer	9	13	16
Dish, 5"-6"	3	4	5
Plate, 7"	3	4	5
Plate, 9"	8	9	10
Platter	13	14	15

Caliente backstamp.

Caliente

The Caliente line, identified by bright colors on the Elite/Shellcrest shape, was introduced in 1936.

Casserole	22	27	31
Cream/Sugar	19	21	23
Cup/Saucer	6	8	10
Dish, 5"-6"	2	3	4
Gravy Boat	11	13	15
Plate, 6"-7"	3	4	5
Plate, 9"-11"	6	7	8
Platter, oval, 12"-16"	9	12	15
Salt/Pepper	18	21	23
Soup Plate	6	7	8
Teapot	44	48	52
Vegetable, 9"-10"	12	14	16

Highlight (1951-1953)

Designed by Russet Wright.

Cream/Sugar	50	60	70
Cup/Saucer	25	30	35
Dish, 5-6"	10	15	20
Gravy Boat	32	35	37
Plate, 6-7"	8	10	12
Plate, 8"	18	20	22
Plate, 9-10"	32	35	44
Platter, oval, 12-15"	25	35	45
Salt/Pepper	40	50	60
Vegetable, oval	35	45	50

Shellcrest (1937)

	LOW	AVG.	HIGH
Casserole	$ 15	$ 20	$ 25
Cream/Sugar	12	16	20
Cup/Saucer	4	6	8
Dish, 5-6"	2	3	4
Gravy Boat	8	10	12
Plate, 6-7"	2	3	4
Plate, 9-11"	4	5	6
Platter, oval, 12-16"	6	10	14
Salt/Pepper	12	15	18
Soup Plate	4	5	6
Teapot	30	35	40
Vegetable, 9-10"	8	10	12

Shenandoah

Shenandoah was decorated with hand-painted-style decals.

	LOW	AVG.	HIGH
Casserole	15	20	25
Cream/Sugar	12	16	20
Cup/Saucer	5	9	13
Pickle Dish, 9"	3	4	5
Plate, 6-7"	2	3	4
Plate, 9-10"	4	5	6
Platter, oval, 13-16"	5	10	15
Salt/Pepper	12	15	18

Pfaltzgraff Pottery

The Pfaltzgraff Pottery Company is the oldest family-owned pottery in continuous operation in America, dating to the early 19th century. The company has operated under the Pfaltzgraff name since 1896. It produced art pottery during the 1930s when it began manufacturing the kitchenware still made today.

An embossed or stamped Keystone or Castle mark are most common.

The following entries are from the Country-Time pattern. Ben Seibel designed this pattern to be made in white or solid colors. Sunburst and a fruit-and-leaf motif appeared on lighter pieces.

    *Pfaltzgraff backstamps.*

	LOW	AVG.	HIGH
Butter Warmer	$ 35	$ 45	$ 55
Casserole, 2 qt.	40	45	50
Casserole, ind., 12 oz.	20	25	30
Casserole, w/ 2-3 lids	100	120	140
Coffee Pot, 10-cup	45	50	65
Cream/Sugar	26	31	35
Cruet	20	25	30
Cup/Saucer	10	13	16
Gravy Boat	30	35	40
Pitcher, 2 qt	30	35	40
Plate, 8"-11"	10	14	18
Platter, 11"-13"	18	24	30
Relish Tray, 16"	30	35	40
Salad Bowl, 10.5"	20	25	30
Salad Bowl, ind., 6"	12	14	15
Salt/Pepper	23	26	29
Samovar, 28-cup	80	90	100
Tureen, 6 qt	65	75	85

Purinton Pottery

Bernard Purinton moved the company from its 1936 home of Wellsville, OH, to Shippenville, PA, in 1941. It remained there until its close in 1959. It is best known for its hand-painted slip decoration under the glaze on dinnerware, kitchenware, and novelties.

Marks: script *Purinton* backstamps; *Slip Ware* in block letters sometimes appears. Many pieces are unmarked.

Apple

	LOW	AVG.	HIGH
Bean Pot	$ 30	$ 40	$ 45
Bowl, 14.5" rect.	70	85	100
Butter Dish	60	90	120
Casserole, 9"	50	70	90
Chop Plate, 12"	45	60	75
Coffee Pot, 8 cup	55	70	85
Cream/Sugar	30	40	50
Cup/Saucer	12	16	20
Dish, 5"-7"	10	12	14
Fruit, 12"	30	40	50
Party Plate, 8.5"	20	25	30
Pickle Dish, 6"	9	12	15
Plate, 6"-8"	10	13	15
Plate, 9"-10"	15	20	25
Platter, 11"-12"	20	30	40
Relish Tray, 3 piece	30	40	50
Salad, 11"	41	50	60
Teapot, 2 cup	19	24	28
Teapot, 6 cup	40	49	58
Tray, 11"	35	45	55
Vegetable, 8"	25	30	35
Vegetable, div.	40	50	60

Intaglio

Butter Dish	72	84	96
Casserole, 9"	48	56	64
Chop Plate, 12"	24	28	32
Coffee Pot, 8 cup	60	70	80
Cookie Jar	60	70	80
Cookie Jar, w/ wooden lid	96	112	128
Cream/Sugar	36	42	48
Cup/Saucer	14	17	19
Dish, 5"-7"	11	13	14
Fruit, 12"	37	43	50
Marmalade	48	56	64
Pickle Dish, 6"	11	13	14
Plate, 6"-8"	11	13	14
Plate, 9"-10"	20	24	27
Platter, 11"-12"	30	35	40
Relish Tray, 3-pc.	42	49	56
Salad, 11"	48	56	64
Teapot, 2 cup	24	28	32
Tray, 11"	30	35	40
Vegetable, 8.5"	23	27	30

Pennsylvania Dutch

	LOW	AVG.	HIGH
Bean Pot	$ 45	$ 55	$ 65
Butter Dish	90	108	126
Casserole, 9"	60	72	84
Chop Plate, 12"	30	36	42
Coffee Pot, 8 cup	80	95	110
Cookie Jar	75	90	105
Cookie Jar, w/ wooden lid	120	144	168
Cream/Sugar	45	54	63
Cup/Saucer	18	22	25
Dish, 5"-7"	14	16	19
Fruit, 12"	47	56	65
Marmalade	60	72	84
Pickle Dish, 6"	14	16	19
Plate, 6"-8"	14	16	19
Plate, 9"-10"	26	31	36
Platter, 11"-12"	38	45	53
Relish Tray, 3-pc.	53	63	74
Salad, 11"	60	72	84
Teapot, 2 cup	30	36	42
Tray, 11"	38	45	53
Vegetable, 8.5"	30	35	40

Tea Rose

	LOW	AVG.	HIGH
Butter Dish	80	95	110
Casserole, 9"	60	72	84
Chop Plate, 12"	30	36	42
Coffee Pot, 8 cup	75	90	100
Cookie Jar	75	90	100
Cream/Sugar	45	54	63
Cup/Saucer	18	22	25
Dish, 5"-7"	14	16	18
Fruit, 12"	47	56	65
Marmalade	60	72	84
Pickle Dish, 6"	12	16	20
Plate, 6"-8"	14	16	18
Plate, 9"-10"	26	31	36
Platter, 11"-12"	38	45	53
Relish Tray, 3-pc.	53	63	74
Salad, 11"	60	72	84
Teapot, 2 cup	30	36	42
Tray, 11"	38	45	53
Vegetable, 8.5"	28	34	46

Red Wing Pottery

The Red Wing Potteries, Inc., traces its roots to 1878, although it operated under that name only from 1936 until its close in 1967. The early Red Wing stoneware and the dinnerware produced from the thirties onward are collected.

Backstamps often use a wing motif.

Red Wing backstamp.

Bob White (1955)

Charles Murphy designed the Bob White pattern.

	LOW	AVG.	HIGH
Beverage Server, w/ lid	$ 80	$ 90	$ 100
Bread Tray, 24"	60	75	90
Butter Dish	70	80	90
Butter warmer, w/ lid	45	60	75
Casserole, 1-4 qt.	50	75	100
Cocktail Tray	30	45	60
Coffee Cup	20	28	36
Cookie Jar	40	60	80
Cream/Sugar	60	75	90
Cruet, w/ stopper	140	160	180
Dish, 5"-6"	20	30	40
Gravy Boat, w/ lid	45	57	70
Lazy Susan	90	95	100
Mug	58	64	70
Pepper Mill, tall	450	475	500
Pitcher, 1.5 qt.	60	72	85
Pitcher, 3.5 qt.	140	170	200
Plate, 10"	23	26	29
Plate, 6"-8"	11	17	22
Platter, 13"	30	37	44
Platter, 20"	60	80	100
Relish Tray, 3 piece	40	50	60
Salad Bowl, 12"	58	66	74
Shaker, tall	28	36	43
Soup Plate	28	36	44
Teapot	60	80	100
Trivet	100	105	110
Tumbler	175	200	225
Vegetable	29	44	60
Water Jar, w/ base, 2 gal.	454	532	610

Fondoso (1939)

Belle Kogan designed Fondoso as one of four shapes for Gypsy Trail Hostessware (also Chevron, Reed, and Plain). It appeared in many pastel colors.

Butter Dish, large	35	38	40
Casserole, 8.5"	60	75	90
Chop Plate, 14"	28	34	40
Coffee Pot	40	50	60

	LOW	AVG.	HIGH
Coffee Server	$ 36	$ 44	$ 52
Console Bowl	30	38	46
Cookie Jar	30	50	70
Cream/Sugar, large	60	64	67
Cream/Sugar, small	36	41	46
Cup/Saucer	25	32	39
Custard Cup	23	27	30
Dessert cup, ftd., 4"	11	15	19
Dish, 5"-6"	18	24	30
Mixing Bowl, 5"-7"	14	21	28
Mixing Bowl, 8"-9"	33	44	55
Pitcher, Batter	60	65	70
Pitcher, straight, 1-5 pt.	40	60	80
Pitcher, syrup	42	50	57
Pitcher, tilt, 2 qt.	57	66	74
Plate, 6"-8"	11	16	21
Plate, 9"-12"	19	27	34
Platter, oval, 12"	30	32	34
Relish Tray	24	32	40
Salad Bowl, 12"	35	40	45
Salt/Pepper	30	37	44
Soup Plate, 7.5"	18	21	24
Teapot	40	50	60
Tray, batter set	45	50	55
Tumbler, 7 oz.-10 oz.	25	35	45
Vegetable, rd., 8"	25	30	35

Town and Country (1947)

Eva Zeisel designed Town and Country as an irregular, off-beat pattern. For example, the plates are slightly higher on one side than the other.

	LOW	AVG.	HIGH
Bean Pot	140	160	180
Casserole	50	65	80
Casserole, ind.	28	33	38
Cream/Sugar	31	36	42
Cruet, w/ lid	37	40	42
Cup/Saucer	22	26	30
Dish, 5"-6"	11	14	17
Mixing Bowl, 9"	70	90	110
Mug	40	50	60
Mustard Jar	41	52	64
Pitcher, milk	50	65	90
Pitcher, syrup	50	60	70
Plate, 10"-11"	10	14	18
Plate, 6"-8"	6	9	12
Platter, 9"-15"	26	38	50
Relish Tray, 7"	20	25	30
Salad Bowl, 13"	35	55	75
Salt/Pepper, large	30	45	60
Salt/Pepper, small	20	25	30
Teapot	100	112	125
Vegetable, oval, 8"	30	35	40

Rookwood Pottery

Rookwood manufactured pottery from 1879 to 1967. Its heyday was from 1890-1930. It featured large, bold underglaze painting.

Products bore a factory and artist mark. They sometimes bore a clay mark, size mark, and process mark (add 10-30%).

Right: Typical Rookwood impressed marks. The number of "flames" surrounding the logo varies with the date.

	LOW	AVG.	HIGH
Ashtray, #7111, 1957, sq. 9"	$ 66	$ 110	$ 160
Bookends, 2564, 1953, wine madder	270	430	660
Bookends, panther, wine madder	297	480	730
Bowl, turquoise and mirror black, #2256, 1922, dia. 9.5"	99	160	240
Clock, ivory, 1950, ht. 7.5"	231	370	570
Creamer, 1949, Egyptian turquoise	100	160	250
Creamer, 1949, yellow gloss	110	180	270
Creamer and Sugar, 547, 1943, light blue matte	70	110	170
Creamer and Sugar, 547, 1949, pink gloss	70	110	170
Dish, embossed w/ Rookwood Pottery gates, 1958, dia. 6"	231	370	570
Donkey, ivory matte	264	420	650
Figure, 6972, 1952, emerald green	160	260	390
Figure, 6972, 1953, mirror black, clair de lune	180	290	440
Paperweight, 2777, 1925, blue crystalline, tan	240	380	590
Paperweight, 2777, 1928, ivory matte	220	350	540
Paperweight, 2777, 1934, ivory matte	210	340	510
Paperweight, 2777, 1934, Nubian black	240	380	590
Paperweight, bunny, turquoise gloss	176	280	430

Above: Size and elegance of shape are important factors. The vase on the right is the most valuable of these three. — Photo courtesy of Northeast Auctions.

	LOW	AVG.	HIGH
Paperweight, pup, ivory matte	$ 242	$ 390	$ 590
Paperweight, pup, Nubian black	264	420	650
Pheasant, rose gloss	165	260	400
Plaque, depicting snowy landscape, Katherine Van Horne, 1915, 5" x 7"	4300	6880	10,540
Potpourri, 1321E, 1928, green pink matte	200	320	490
Potpourri, 1321E, 1938, Chinese turquoise	260	420	640
Rooster, blue crystalline glaze over tan matte	264	420	650
Sleeping Nude Pin Tray, ivory matte	154	250	380
Sleeping Nude Pin Tray, wine madder	154	250	380
Swan Dish, ivory matte,	176	280	430
Tea Tile, Vellum, polychrome, #3077, 1929, 6" sq.	242	390	590
Vase, 1681, 1914, green, pink matte	140	220	340
Vase, 1681, 1916, purple gloss	100	160	250
Vase, 1681, 1921, yellow matte	300	480	740
Vase, 2095, 1913, tan matte	160	260	390
Vase, 2095, 1921, cocoa matte	210	340	510
Vase, 778, 1960, pumpkin	150	240	370
Vase, 778, 1961, violet gray	280	450	690
Vase, aerial blue, Bruce Horsfall, depicting St. Francis, 1894, 6.75"	13,200	21,000	32,340
Vase, baluster form, Kataro Shirayamadani, prunus blossoms, 1897	16,000	25,600	39,200
Vase, baluster form, Kataro Shirayamadani, silver overlay by Gorham, 15.5"	26,400	42,240	64,680
Vase, black iris, iris dec., Carl Schmidt, 1911, 13"	62,700	100,320	153,620
Vase, black iris, Japanese irises, Carl Schmidt, 1909, 9.5"	15,400	24,640	37,730
Vase, blue matte glaze, 1927, 6.5"	110	180	270
Vase, French red, peacock dec., Sara Sax, 1921, 16.25"	34,000	54,400	83,300
Vase, gray/green matte, #2782, 1925, ht. 10"	231	370	570
Vase, handled blue high gloss glaze, 1946, 11"	150	240	370
Vase, high glaze, bird dec., Arthur Conant, 1921, 16"	28,600	45,760	70,000
Vase, incised w/ wysteria blossom dec., 14"	35,000	56,000	85,750

Above: Unpainted pieces like this bowl are worth $50-$150.

	LOW	AVG.	HIGH
Vase, Iris, chrysanthemums, John Wareham, 1902, 14.25" ...	$ 9000	$ 14,400	$ 22,050
Vase, Iris, dec. w/ hydrangea, Albert Valentien, 1904, 12.5"	10,700	17,120	26,220
Vase, Iris, depicting snow geese, Albert Valentien, 1905, 13.25"	16,500	26,400	40,430
Vase, Iris, depicting swimming fish, Lenore Asbury, 1898, 5.75"	5800	9280	14,210
Vase, Iris glaze, blue and yellow crocuses on black to green to white ground, Carl Schmidt, 1908, 10.5"	18,700	29,920	45,820
Vase, Iris glaze, wisteria decorated, Carl Schmidt, 1909, 10.75"	11,500	18,400	28,180
Vase, pink/green matte, #2324, 1931, ht. 8"	198	320	490
Vase, sea green, carved chrysanthemum dec., Matt Daly, 1900, 10.5"	12,000	19,200	29,400
Vase, standard glaze, dec. w/ poppies, Kataro Shira-yamadani, 1899, 15"	12,650	20,240	30,990
Vase, vellum, floral dec., Elizabeth McDermott, 1919, 13"	1750	2800	4290
Vase, vellum, fuschia dec., E.T. Hurley, 1942, 5"	930	1490	2280
Vase, vellum, pink tulip dec., Ed Diers, 1908, 10"	1100	1760	2700
Vase, vellum, wild rose dec., Ed Diers, 1924, 5.5"	1200	1920	2940
Vase, wine madder, #6865, 1944, ht. 4.5"	176	280	430
Vase, yellow matte, #1712, 1929, ht. 9"	440	700	1080
Vase, yellow matte, #6108, 1937, ht. 4.5"	154	250	380

Roseville Pottery

The Roseville factory opened in 1885 in Roseville, OH. In 1902, the factory bought a stoneware plant in Zanesville and made art pottery there until 1954. In 1910, the Roseville arm of the company closed. Roseville called its art ware Rozane (from ROseville and ZANEsville). Various lines included: Egypto, Mongol, Woodland, Mara, and Royal. The main line was vases, although water pitchers, jugs, lamp bases and ashtrays were made.

Most of the art pottery is marked Rozane or Rozane Ware, with an artist's mark. Often, a figure of a rose appears within a circle.

For further information see the *Collectors' Compendium of Roseville Pottery and Price Guide: Volume I,* by Randall Monsen. And yes, Volume I is the only one available as we write.

Roseville
U.S.A.   *Incised mark.*

	LOW	AVG.	HIGH
Bowl, Carnelian II, 3" x 8", pink w/ green, purple and yellow	40	63	86
Bowl, Imperial I, 9", w/ handle	30	50	70
Candlesticks, Luffa, 4.5", brown w/ original seal, pr.	170	210	250
Compote, Carnelian I, 9.5" x 7", pink and blue drip, mkd. RV	53	73	93
Conch, Magnolia, shape #453, 6", brown	42	62	82
Console, Montacello, oval, 13" x 3", blue	165	220	265
Console Set, Florentine, 10" bowl, 2" candleholders, blond, set	100	130	160
Cornucopia, Apple Blossom, shape #321, 6", green	25	44	64
Ewer, fuchsia, shape #902, 10.5", green and brown	100	125	150
Hanging Basket, Bushberry, green, berries and leaves	75	100	125
Humidor, Old Ivory, 6", blue tint, w/ lid, spherical, no mark	200	250	300
Jardiniere, Bleeding Heart, shape #651, 10", pink	315	375	435
Jardiniere and Pedestal, Donatello, w/ molded classical scenes, ht. 28"	650	700	750
Jardiniere and Pedestal, Imperial I, polychrome dec., dia. 10"	700	750	800
Jardiniere, Jonquil, 9.5" x 7" x 4.5"	360	435	510
Mug, Holland, 4", embossed figure, simple shape, no mark	45	65	85
Mug, Peony, shape #2, 3/2", green	30	50	70
Pitcher, Autumn, 8.5", orange, bulbous, no mark	825	1050	1275
Planter, Bittersweet, shape #828, 10"	30	50	70
Planter, Poppy, shape #336-5, 8.5" x 2.5", pink	40	60	80
Pot, Morning Glory, 5", aqua, 2 handles, bell form, no mark	150	200	250
Soap Dish, Colonial, 4", lid, mottled green, spherical, no mark	120	150	180
Sugar Bowl, Persian, 4", lid and 2 handles, 4 sided, no mark	50	70	90
Teapot, Peony, modern design, ht. 8"	225	250	275
Vase, Azurean, 9", landscape, egg form, narrow neck, no mark	2400	2600	2800
Vase, Cherry Blossom, 8"	425	525	625
Vase, Dogwood, 10", green, marked RV	90	115	140
Vase, Freesia, shape #117, 6", green	30	50	70
Vase, Fujiyama, flowers, lighthouse shape, marked in ink	1000	1250	1500
Vase, Futura, 7"	375	450	525
Vase, Imperial II, 5.5", yellow, beehive shape, no mark	100	150	200
Vase, Lustre, 10", pink, cylindrical, no trim, paper label, black	60	80	100
Vase, Matt Green, 4" x 5", marked H 1/170/bot 2/2	30	50	70

Royal China

The Royal China Company's semiporcelain dinnerware, cookware, and premiums date to 1933. After a series of owners in the 1970s, the plant closed in 1986.

Royal backstamp.

Regal (1937)

Thin fluting charaterizes the Regal pattern.

	LOW	AVG.	HIGH
Cream/Sugar	$ 12	$ 14	$ 15
Cup/Saucer	5	6	7
Plate, 11"	7	8	9
Plate, 6"-8"	5	7	9
Salt/Pepper	10	12	14
Teapot	21	23	25
Vegetable, 9"	7	8	9

Royalty (1936)

Royalty consists of spider-web embossing with decal decorations.

Casserole	20	22	24
Cream/Sugar	12	14	16
Cup/Saucer	5	6	7
Dish, 5"	1	2	3
Gravy Boat	8	9	10
Pickle Dish, 8"	6	7	8
Plate, 6"-8"	4	5	6
Plate, 9"-10"	6	8	10
Salt/Pepper	10	12	14
Teapot	21	23	25

Royal Doulton

Royal Doulton figures are ceramic works of art. Although the English company produces other items, its HN series is the best known. The company was begun in the early 1800s by John Doulton. The HN series was introduced in 1913 and named after Harry Nixon, head colorist at the time.

Besides their figurines, there are many different Royal Doulton collectibles, including Toby jugs, plates, limited editions, and bird and animal figures. Royal Doulton figures are identified by the HN prefix followed by numbers in a chronological sequence. Subjects in this series are highly diverse representing the works of many different artists at different time periods.

The earliest Royal Doulton figures (with the lower HN numbers) are usually the most desirable to collectors. For more information, consult *The Official Price Guide to Royal Doulton*, published by The House of Collectibles, Random House, NY.

Royal Doulton backstamps.

HN#	TITLE	LOW	AVG.	HIGH
HN 1	Darling (1st version)	$ 1730	$ 2100	$ 2480
HN 10A	Madonna of the Square	1550	1720	1880
HN 27	Madonna of the Square	1900	2070	2240
HN 28	Motherhood	2560	2820	3090
HN 31	Return of Persephone	4700	5400	6110
HN 33	An Arab	2080	2580	3090
HN 36	Sentimental Pierrot	2320	2610	2900
HN 44	Lilac Shawl	1840	2070	2300
HN 57A	Flounced Skirt	1900	2070	2240
HN 77	Flounced Skirt	1900	2070	2240
HN 92	Welsh Girl	2920	3160	3390
HN 307	Sentimental Pierrot	2320	2610	2900
HN 311	Dancing Figure	4110	4500	4900
HN 316	Mandarin (1st version)	3510	3900	4300
HN 318	Mandarin (1st version)	3510	3900	4300
HN 324	Scribe	1130	1380	1630
HN 335	Lady of the Fan	1960	2160	2360
HN 348	Carpet Vendor (1st version)	4110	4810	5510
HN 364	Moorish Minstrel	3750	4060	4360
HN 369	Cavalier (1st version)	4700	5400	6110
HN 370	Henry VIII (1st version)	4110	4500	4900
HN 373	Boy on a Crocodile	5890	6300	6720
HN 376	Geisha (1st version)	2920	3360	3810

HN#	TITLE	LOW	AVG.	HIGH
HN 384	Pretty Lady	$ 1010	$ 1200	$ 1390
HN 385	St. George (1st version)	5300	5700	6110
HN 391	Princess	3210	3450	3690
HN 400	Puff and Powder	2320	2520	2720
HN 414	Bouquet	2560	2820	3090
HN 421	Contentment	1730	1920	2120
HN 422	Bouquet	2560	2820	3090
HN 432	Puff and Powder	2320	2520	2720
HN 442	In Grandma's Days	1900	2070	2240
HN 444	Lady of the Georgian Period	2320	2700	3090
HN 482	One of the Forty (12th version)	1430	1660	1880
HN 489	Polly Peachum (2nd version)	300	420	540
HN 495	One of the Forty (1st version)	1430	1660	1880
HN 496	One of the Forty (13th version	1430	1660	1880
HN 498	One of the Forty (2nd version)	1430	1660	1880
HN 523	Sentinel	6490	7210	7930
HN 524	Lucy Lockett	650	780	910
HN 542	Cobbler (1st version)	1370	1500	1630
HN 548	Balloon Seller	1370	1620	1880
HN 553	Pecksniff (2nd version)	360	450	540
HN 556	Mr. Pickwick (2nd version)	390	500	600
HN 559	Goosegirl	3210	3450	3690
HN 562	Fruit Gathering	2920	3300	3690
HN 566	Crinoline	1430	1590	1750
HN 567	Bouquet	2920	3300	3690
HN 589	Polly Peachum (1st version)	420	540	670
HN 609	Falstaff (1st version)	1370	1680	2000
HN 619	Falstaff (1st version)	1370	1680	2000
HN 624	Lady With Rose	1960	2160	2360
HN 647	One of the Forty (2nd version)	1430	1660	1880
HN 652	Crinoline Lady (miniature)	890	1080	1270
HN 655	Crinoline Lady (miniature)	890	1080	1270
HN 667	One of the Forty (11th version)	1610	1840	2060
HN 673	Henry VIII (1st version)	4110	4500	4900
HN 693	Polly Peachum (1st version)	540	660	790
HN 720	Butterfly	1370	1560	1750
HN 725	Proposal (male)	1670	1900	2120
HN 730	Butterfly	1550	1740	1940
HN 734	Polly Peachum (2nd version)	480	580	670
HN 745	Victorian Lady	650	820	1000
HN 756	Modern Piper	2920	3300	3690
HN 760	Polly Peachum (3rd version miniature)	480	600	730
HN 772	London Cry, Strawberries	1490	1620	1750
HN 773	Bather (2nd version)	2080	2580	3090
HN 789	Flower Seller	770	930	1090
HN 793	Katharine	1900	2070	2240
HN 795	Pierrette (2nd version, miniature)	890	1140	1390
HN 1202	Bo-Peep (1st version)	1610	1920	2240
HN 1209	Proposal (male)	2200	2430	2660
HN 1210	Boy With Turban	1010	1200	1390
HN 1216	Falstaff (1st version)	1370	1680	2000

HN#	TITLE	LOW	AVG.	HIGH
HN 1231	Cassim (1st version)	$ 950	$ 1140	$ 1330
HN 1234	Geisha (2nd version)	1100	1350	1600
HN 1247	Baba	980	1120	1270
HN 1249	Circe	2320	2520	2720
HN 1253	Kathleen	770	900	1030
HN 1254	Circe	2320	2520	2720
HN 1256	Captain MacHeath	770	930	1090
HN 1262	Spanish Lady	1130	1350	1570
HN 1264	Judge and Jury	9460	10510	11560
HN 1266	Ko-Ko	890	1050	1210
HN 1268	Yum-Yum	770	930	1090
HN 1273	Negligee	2200	2490	2780
HN 1277	Victorian Lady	770	960	1150
HN 1288	Susanna	1250	1380	1510
HN 1302	Gypsy Girl With Flowers	2920	3160	3390
HN 1309	Spanish Lady	1130	1350	1570
HN 1313	Sonny	1250	1380	1510
HN 1324	Fairy	1730	1960	2180
HN 1326	Swimmer	1960	2160	2360
HN 1331	Sweet Anne	270	380	480
HN 1349	Scotties	2920	3300	3690
HN 1353	One of the Forty (2nd version)	1430	1660	1880
HN 1391	Pierrette (3rd version)	1370	1680	2000
HN 1393	Fairy	1070	1230	1390
HN 1419	Dulcinea	1370	1620	1880
HN 1425	Moor	1730	1960	2180
HN 1442	Child Study	950	1080	1210
HN 1452	Victorian Lady	300	420	540
HN 1470	Chloe	240	330	420
HN 1475	In the Stocks (1st version)	2320	2700	3090
HN 1481	Dreamland	3510	3750	3990
HN 1486	Phyllis	710	840	970
HN 1488	Gloria	1730	1920	2120
HN 1491	Dorcas	950	1080	1210
HN 1494	Gwendolen	890	1080	1270
HN 1497	Rosamund (2nd version)	2560	2820	3090
HN 1503	Gwendolen	890	1080	1270
HN 1520	Eugene	980	1110	1240
HN 1535	Fairy	890	1080	1270
HN 1538	Janet (1st version)	710	840	970
HN 1564	Pamela	1070	1260	1450
HN 1567	Patricia	1070	1260	1450
HN 1570	Gwendolen	890	1050	1210
HN 1577	Suzette	710	840	970
HN 1579	Hinged Parasol	600	760	910
HN 1582	Marion	1610	1800	2000
HN 1584	Willy-Won't He	360	480	600
HN 1585	Suzette	710	840	970
HN 1587	Fleurette	540	700	850
HN 1615	Bookend, Micawber	2320	2700	3090
HN 1631	Sweet Anne	300	420	540

HN#	TITLE	LOW	AVG.	HIGH
HN 1639	Dainty May	$ 420	$ 510	$ 600
HN 1640	Ladybird	1730	2100	2480
HN 1647	Granny's Shawl	450	540	640
HN 1648	Camille	860	1000	1150
HN 1657	Moor	1730	1960	2180
HN 1669	Anthea	1130	1350	1570
HN 1707	Paisley Shawl (1st version)	770	930	1090
HN 1736	Camille	1070	1260	1450
HN 1746	Rustic Swain	2620	2860	3090
HN 1754	Eleanore	1550	1720	1880
HN 1759	Orange Lady	240	330	420
HN 1760	Four O'clock	1010	1200	1390
HN 1762	Bride (1st version)	830	1050	1270
HN 1770	Maureen	270	360	450
HN 1777	Spirit of the Wind (ltd. ed., miscellaneous)	7680	8710	9740
HN 1801	An Old King	1840	2040	2240
HN 1802	Estelle	890	1020	1150
HN 1805	To Bed	120	210	300
HN 1819	Miranda	1490	1680	1880
HN 1835	Verena	1370	1620	1880
HN 1838	Vanessa	860	1000	1150
HN 1840	Christine (1st version)	770	930	1090
HN 1846	Modena	1730	1980	2240
HN 1854	Verena	1370	1620	1880
HN 1860	Millicent	2140	2370	2600
HN 1862	Jasmine	890	1050	1210
HN 1865	Sweet and Fair	1010	1260	1510
HN 1869	Dryad of the Pines	5300	6010	6720
HN 1872	Annabella	600	780	970
HN 1881	Lambeth Walk	2920	3300	3690
HN 1923	Spring Morning	710	840	970
HN 1939	Windflower (2nd version)	2320	2700	3090
HN 1958	Lady April	300	420	540
HN 1963	Honey	1430	1620	1820
HN 1968	Madonna of the Square	950	1080	1210
HN 1969	Madonna of the Square	950	1080	1210
HN 1974	Forty Winks	210	300	390
HN 1992	Christmas Morn	170	240	300
HN 2004	A'Courting	600	720	850
HN 2006	Lady Anne Nevill	770	900	1030
HN 2010	Young Miss Nightingale	480	600	730
HN 2015	Sir Walter Raleigh	770	900	1030
HN 2019	Minuet	240	360	480
HN 2020	Deidre	390	500	600
HN 2026	Suzette	240	360	480
HN 2028	Kate Hardcastle	540	660	790
HN 2035	Pearly Boy (2nd version)	150	240	330
HN 2037	Goody Two Shoes	110	170	230
HN 2044	Mary Mary	90	160	240
HN 2057	Milkmaid	120	210	300
HN 2058	Hermione	1370	1620	1880

HN#	TITLE	LOW	AVG.	HIGH
HN 2063	Little Jack Horner	$ 420	$ 510	$ 600
HN 2079	Damaris	1610	1780	1940
HN 2080	Jack Point (Prestige Series)	2560	2640	2720
HN 2087	Autumn (2nd version)	510	620	730
HN 2091	Rosemary	420	540	670
HN 2108	Baby Bunting	180	300	420
HN 2109	Wendy	70	130	190
HN 2113	Maytime	210	330	450
HN 2118	Good King Wenceslas	300	440	570
HN 2128	River Boy	120	210	300
HN 2132	Suitor	390	500	600
HN 2137	Lilac Time	270	380	480
HN 2138	La Sylphide	420	540	670
HN 2145	Wardrobe Mistress	450	560	670
HN 2156	Polka	240	340	450
HN 2181	Summer's Day	390	500	600
HN 2183	Boy from Williamsburg	90	180	270
HN 2208	Silversmith of Williamsburg	120	220	330
HN 2214	Bunny	120	210	300
HN 2226	Cellist	390	500	600
HN 2234	Michelle	170	240	300
HN 2248	Tall Story	160	240	330
HN 2251	Masquerade (2nd version)	330	400	480
HN 2254	Shore Leave	150	240	330
HN 2256	Twilight	90	180	270
HN 2264	Elegance	120	200	270
HN 2266	Ballad Seller	240	360	480
HN 2271	Melanie	90	160	240
HN 2275	Sandra	170	240	300
HN 2284	Craftsman	420	540	670
HN 2318	Grace	90	180	270
HN 2335	Hilary	80	160	250
HN 2339	My Love	240	300	360
HN 2345	Clarissa (2nd version)	120	200	270
HN 2376	Indian Brave (ltd. ed., figurines)	7000	8400	9800
HN 2379	Ninette	240	330	420
HN 2421	Charlotte	120	210	300
HN 2423	Charlotte	210	320	420
HN 2429	Elyse	240	330	420
HN 2441	Pauline	270	340	420
HN 2446	Thanksgiving	210	300	390
HN 2481	Maureen	140	220	300
HN 2483	Flute (ltd. ed., lady musicians)	1100	1230	1360
HN 2554	Masque	180	280	390
HN 2679	Drummer Boy	300	400	510
HN 2702	Shirley	130	220	300
HN 2725	Santa Claus	290	360	420
HN 2726	Centurion	150	260	360
HN 2735	Young Love	1070	1140	1210
HN 2748	Wedding Day	110	180	240
HN 2754	Private, 3rd North Carolina Reg., 1778	1070	1320	1570

HN#	TITLE	LOW	AVG.	HIGH
HN 2783	Good Friends	$ 160	$ 230	$ 300
HN 2826	Leda and the Swan	2920	3060	3210
HN 2834	Emma (Kate Greenaway)	90	140	190
HN 2840	Chinese Dancer	830	960	1090
HN 2846	Private, Pennsylvania Rifle Battalion, 1776	830	990	1150
HN 2867	Kurdish Dancer	890	1020	1150
HN 2868	Cleopatra and Slave	1250	1440	1630
HN 2878	Her Majesty Queen Elizabeth II	530	600	660
HN 2896	Good Day Sir	170	240	300
HN 2908	Ajax (ltd. ed., ships figurehead)	830	920	1020
HN 2912	Frado (J.R.R. Tolkien Series)	50	80	110
HN 2914	Bilbo (J.R.R. Tolkien Series)	50	80	110
HN 2919	Rachel	120	210	300
HN 2928	Nelson (ltd. ed., ships figureheads)	1000	1200	1400
HN 2935	Balloon Lady	140	220	300
HN 2944	Rag Doll Seller	170	240	300
HN 2977	Magic Dragon	80	100	120
HN 2994	Helen	80	100	120
HN 3004	Emily in Autumn	300	420	540
HN 3005	Sarah in Winter	300	420	540
HN 3019	Sisters, Black	50	130	210
HN 3024	April Showers	80	100	120
HN 3025	Rumplestiltskin	90	160	230
HN 3033	Springtime (Collectors Club figurine)	300	420	540
HN 3037	Miranda	200	270	340
HN 3052	Winter's Walk	160	230	300
HN 3058	Andrea	40	110	180
HN 3070	Cocktails	140	220	300
HN 3073	Strolling	170	240	300
HN 3074	Pafadise	130	220	300
HN 3076	Bolero	160	230	300
HN 3090	Charisma	110	180	240
HN 3097	Happy Anniversary	200	280	360
HN 3107	Daybreak ((Jefferson Quartet)	110	180	250
HN 3109	Pensive	100	180	250
HN 3137	Summertime (Collector Club figure)	110	180	240
OM 5	Sweet Anne	240	330	420
OM 6	Sweet Anne	330	450	570
OM 19	Shepherd	1500	1800	2100
OM 21	Polly Peachum	300	400	500
OM 34	Denise	540	660	790
OM 38	Robin	540	700	850
OM 55	Artful Dodger	50	75	100
OM 67	Dainty May	360	480	600
OM 90	Dick Swiveller	50	75	100

Royal Haeger

	LOW	AVG.	HIGH
Apple Candleholder, 2.5"	$ 10	$ 11	$ 12
Banana Leaf Bowl, 13"	10	11	12
Banana Leaf Bowl, 18"	10	11	12
Butterfly Candleholder, 6.5"	14	16	18
Calla Lily Dish, 7.5"	18	20	22
Chinese Figures Candleholder, 5"	12	13	14
Cornucopia	6	8	10
Dolphin Dish, 7.5"	24	27	30
Elephant Ear Leaf Bowl, 11"	10	11	12
Elephant Ear Leaf Bowl, 13"	10	11	12
Fish Candleholders, pr.	24	27	30
Fish Pitcher, 9"	24	27	30
Horse Head Dish, 7"	24	27	30
Leaf Candleholder, 5"	6	8	10
Leopard Dish, 7"	24	27	30
Lily Leaf Bowl, 11"	10	11	12
Oyster Shell Bowl, 15"	12	15	18
Plume	6	8	10
Polar Bear Dish, 7.5"	24	27	30
Sailfish Planter, 11"	36	39	42
Starfish Bowl, 14"	18	20	22
Starfish Candleholder, 6"	10	11	12
Swan Candleholder, 5.25"	14	16	18
Tropical Leaf Bowl, 10"	10	11	12
Tropical Leaf Bowl, 14"	10	11	12
Turtle Dish, 9.25"	30	33	36
Violin Dish, 17"	24	27	30
Wine Leaf Bowl, 10"	10	11	12
Wine Leaf Bowl, 15"	10	11	12

Salem China

The Salem China Company reached its 100th year in 1968 solely as a distributor. Its semiporcelain dinnerware, famous in the 1930s and 1940s, ceased production in 1967.

Bonjour

	LOW	AVG.	HIGH
Bowl, oval, 9"	$ 10	$ 12	$ 14
Cake Plate, 10"	5	6	7
Casserole	22	28	34
Cream/Sugar	12	15	17
Cup/Saucer	6	9	12
Dish, 5.5"	2	3	4
Gravy Boat	12	15	18
Plate, 6"-7"	4	6	8
Plate, 9-10"	8	12	16
Platter, oval, 11"-13"	7	8	9
Salt/Pepper	13	16	19
Soup Bowl	10	12	14
Soup Plate, 8.25"	5	6	7
Vegetable, rd., 8"	10	12	14

Briar Rose
By Salem
Made In
America

Salem Briar Rose backstamp.

Briar Rose (c. 1930)

J. Palin Thorley designed Briar Rose for the American China Corporation. Salem purchased the pattern when ACC went bankrupt.

Butter Dish, open	14	16	18
Cake Plate, 10"	5	6	7
Casserole	20	23	26
Cream/Sugar	13	16	18
Cup/Saucer	7	9	11
Dish, 5"-6"	3	4	5
Gravy Boat	11	13	15
Pickle Dish	4	5	6
Plate, 6"-7"	4	6	8
Plate, 9"-10"	9	11	13
Platter, 11"-13"	7	9	10
Platter, 22"	40	50	60
Soup, coupe, 7"	5	6	7
Vegetable, 8"-9"	11	13	15

TRICORNE
By
Salem
U. S. PATENT

Salem Tricorne backstamp.

Tricorne (1934)

Tricorne was an avant garde shape using many angles. Originally produced only in bright red (Mandarin), it later appeared with tamer decals: Polo (pony and rider), Sailing (sailboats), Dutch Petitpoint (boy and girl), and Bridge (card suits).

	LOW	AVG.	HIGH
Casserole	$ 31	$ 34	$ 37
Compote	18	20	22
Cream/Sugar	25	30	35
Cup/Saucer	13	16	19
Dish, 5"-6"	3	4	5
Nut Dish, 4"	6	7	8
Plate, 5"-6"	3	4	5
Plate, 9"-12"	8	12	14

Salem Victory backstamp.

Victory (1938)

Viktor Schreckengost designed Victory. It appears with many decal motifs: Godey Ladies, Indian Tree, Basket Petitpoint, and Parkway.

Bowl, 6"-7"	6	8	10
Cake Plate, 10"	5	6	7
Candleholder	15	17	19
Casserole	22	28	34
Coffee Pot	30	40	50
Cream/Sugar	12	15	17
Cup/Saucer	6	9	12
Dish, 5"-7"	2	3	4
Gravy Boat	10	12	13
Mustache Cup	16	18	19
Plate, 10"	8	11	13
Plate, 6"-7"	1	3	5
Platter, oval, 11"-13"	7	8	9
Salt/Pepper	13	16	19
Soup Bowl/Saucer	8	10	12
Soup Plate, 8.25"	5	6	7
Vegetable, rd., 8"	10	12	14

Sebring Pottery

The Sebring family established the town of Sebring, OH, in 1899. There they consolidated their various business ventures and built the Sebring Pottery to produce semiporcelain dinnerware, etc. Some art ware and kitchenware was made in the 1930s. The name Sebring vanished in the 1943 takeover by National Unit Distributors, although some patterns continued manufacture.

Aristocrat (1932)

	LOW	AVG.	HIGH
Casserole	$ 18	$ 22	$ 25
Coffee Pot	24	29	34
Cream/Sugar	13	15	16
Cup/Saucer	6	7	8
Plate, 6"-7"	3	4	4
Plate, 9"	5	6	6
Platter, 13"	9	10	10
Salt/Pepper	10	11	12
Soup Plate, 7.5"	5	6	6
Teapot	25	29	32

Doric (1930)

Doric is a square form with ribs, scalloped edges, and shell finials.

Cream/Sugar	13	16	20
Cup/Saucer	4	5	6
Dish, 5-6"	1	2	3
Gravy Boat	8	10	12
Pitcher, batter	20	22	25
Plate, 6-7"	2	3	4
Plate, 9"	4	5	6
Platter, rect., 11-13"	5	6	7
Soup Plate, 8"	4	5	6
Soup, coupe, 7.5"	4	5	6
Vegetable, 8"	7	9	11

Backstamp mark.

Trojan

Trojan is a round version of Doric.

Casserole	21	25	28
Coffee Pot	22	26	30
Cream/Sugar	15	18	21
Cup/Saucer	8	10	12
Dish, 5"-6"	2	3	4
Egg Cup	7	9	11
Gravy Boat	12	14	15
Plate, 6"-7"	2	3	4
Plate, 9"-11"	6	8	10
Vegetable, oval, 9"	12	13	14

Shawnee Pottery

The Shawnee Pottery Company produced earthenware art pottery and brightly colored dinnerware and kitchenware from 1937 through 1961.

Marks include an embossed *USA,* and/or *Shawnee*, and/or a shape number. Some pieces are unmarked. Gilt trim is worth more.

The following entries are from the Corn King pattern

	LOW	AVG.	HIGH
Casserole	$ 50	$ 75	$ 100
Cereal Bowl	40	50	60
Cookie Jar	140	160	190
Dish, 6"	10	12	14
Mixing Bowl, 5"-8"	20	30	40
Mug	40	50	60
Pitcher, 1 qt.	80	90	100
Plate, 10"	35	50	65
Platter, 12"	50	60	70
Relish Tray	40	45	50
Salt/Pepper	20	30	40
Teapot, 30 oz.	60	80	100
Tumbler	30	35	40
Utility Jar	40	50	60

Southern Pottery

Southern Potteries, Inc. produced decal-decorated hotel ware and dinnerware from 1920 to 1957. It is famed for its earthenware pieces.

Colonial (1939)

	LOW	AVG.	HIGH
Butter Pat, 4"	$ 18	$ 21	$ 25
Butter Dish	18	28	38
Cake Plate, rd., 10.5"	18	25	31
Cake Plate, sq., 12"	26	35	44
Cake Server	18	25	31
Casserole, French, 5-7"	18	28	38
Celery Tray	12	18	25
Chop Plate, 11"-12"	18	25	31
Coffee Pot	78	92	106
Coffee Pot, art deco	54	74	94
Covered Toast	84	98	113
Cream/Sugar	19	22	25
Cream/Sugar, art deco	24	37	50
Cup/Saucer	6	10	15
Cup/Saucer, 12 oz.	18	21	25
Dish, 5-6"	5	7	9
Egg Cup	18	25	31
Fork and Spoon	54	64	75
Gravy Boat	10	16	23
Grill Plate	22	29	38
Party Plate, 8.5"	14	20	25
Pickle Dish	12	15	19
Plate, 6-8"	5	7	10
Plate, 9-10"	7	13	19
Plate, sq.	6	12	19
Platter, oval, 9-15"	12	21	31
Salad Bowl, large	30	43	56
Server, 1-3 tier	18	25	31
Shaker, all shapes, pr.	10	17	25
Sherbet	12	18	25
Soup Plate, 8"	10	12	15
Teapot, Ball	54	64	75
Teapot, Colonial	54	80	106
Teapot, Piecrust	60	77	94
Teapot, rope handle	48	64	81
Teapot, Skyline	48	61	75
Tray, art deco (rect. or oval)	48	67	88
Vegetable	12	17	23
Vegetable, w/lid	42	58	75

Trellis

Butter Pat, 4"	34	39	45
Butter Dish	34	51	68
Cake Plate, rd., 10.5"	34	45	56
Cake Plate, sq., 12"	50	64	79
Cake Server	34	45	56

	LOW	AVG.	HIGH
Casserole, French, 5-7"	$ 34	$ 51	$ 68
Celery Tray	23	34	45
Chop Plate, 11"-12"	34	45	56
Coffee Pot	146	169	191
Coffee Pot, art deco	101	135	169
Covered Toast	158	180	203
Cream/Sugar	36	41	45
Cream/Sugar, art deco	45	68	90
Cup/Saucer	11	19	27
Cup/Saucer, 12 oz.	34	39	45
Dish, 5-6"	9	12	16
Egg Cup	34	45	56
Fork and Spoon	101	118	135
Gravy Boat	18	29	41
Grill Plate	41	54	68
Party Plate, 8.5"	27	36	45
Pickle Dish	23	28	34
Plate, 6-8"	9	14	18
Plate, 9-10"	14	24	34
Plate, sq.	11	23	34
Platter, oval, 9-15"	23	39	56
Salad Bowl, large	56	79	101
Server, 1-3 tier	34	45	56
Shaker, all shapes, pr.	18	32	45
Sherbet	23	34	45
Soup Plate, 8"	18	23	27
Teapot, Ball	101	118	135
Teapot, Colonial	101	146	191
Teapot, Piecrust	113	141	169
Teapot, rope handle	90	118	146
Teapot, Skyline	90	113	135
Tray, art deco (rect. or oval)	90	124	158
Vegetable	23	32	41
Vegetable, w/lid	79	107	135

Woodcrest

	LOW	AVG.	HIGH
Butter Pat, 4"	23	27	31
Butter Dish	23	34	47
Cake Plate, rd., 10.5"	23	31	39
Cake Plate, sq., 12"	33	43	54
Cake Server	23	31	39
Celery Tray	15	23	31
Chop Plate, 11"-12"	23	31	39
Coffee Pot	98	114	132
Coffee Pot, art deco	68	92	116
Covered Toast	105	122	140
Cream/Sugar	24	27	31
Cream/Sugar, art deco	30	46	62
Cup/Saucer	8	13	19
Cup/Saucer, 12 oz.	23	27	31
Dish, 5-6"	6	8	11

	LOW	AVG.	HIGH
Egg Cup	$ 23	$ 31	$ 39
Fork and Spoon	68	80	93
Casserole, French, 5-7"	23	34	47
Gravy Boat	12	20	28
Grill Plate	27	37	47
Party Plate, 8.5"	18	24	31
Pickle Dish	15	19	23
Plate, 6-8"	6	9	12
Plate, 9-10"	9	16	23
Plate, sq.	8	15	23
Platter, oval, 9-15"	15	27	39
Salad Bowl, large	38	53	70
Server, 1-3 tier	23	31	39
Shaker, all shapes, pr.	12	21	31
Sherbet	15	23	31
Soup Plate, 8"	12	15	19
Teapot, Ball	68	80	93
Teapot, Colonial	68	99	132
Teapot, Piecrust	75	95	116
Teapot, rope handle	60	80	101
Teapot, Skyline	60	76	93
Tray, art deco (rect. or oval)	60	84	109
Vegetable	15	21	28
Vegetable, w/lid	53	72	93

Staffordshire

Staffordshire Pottery refers to pottery produced in and around Staffordshire, England, from the mid-18th century through the end of the 19th century. Originally conceived as an affordable alternative to Chinese porcelain, Staffordshire wares are now recognized in their own right. Important makers include Enoch Wood, Ridgway, and Clews. With the development of the transfer decoration process, manufacturers covered dinnerware with scenes of popular landmarks and historical vignettes. "Historical Blue" had its heyday in the second half of the 19th century. Many popular designs are still produced.

Dinnerware

	AUCTION	RETAIL Low	High
Albany, dark blue soup plate, dia. 10" .... $ 600		$ 960	$ 1470
Alms House in the City of New York, dark blue plate by Stevenson, dia. 10" 700		1120	1720
Arms of New York, dark blue plate by T. Mayer, dia. 10" 750		1200	1840
Battery, New York, dark blue plate by Stevenson, dia. 7" 450		720	1100
Brooklyn Ferry, dark blue platter by Stevenson, dia. 10.5" 3800		6080	9310
Castle Garden, Battery, New York, dark blue cup plate by Enoch Wood, dia. 3.5" 250		400	610
Castle Garden, Battery, New York, dark blue platter by Enoch Wood, len. 19" 2400		3840	5880
Castle Garden, Battery, New York, dark blue platter by Enoch Wood, len. 20.5" 3400		5440	8330
Catholic Cathedral, New York, dark blue plate by A. Stevenson, dia. 6.25" 700		1120	1720
Catskill House, Hudson, dark blue plate by Enoch Wood, dia. 6.5" 650		1040	1590
Catskill Mountains, Hudson River, dark blue rect. bowl by Enoch Wood, len. 9.75" 800		1280	1960
Catskill Mountains, Hudson River, dark blue sauce boat by Enoch Wood, len. 7" 350		560	860
Church in the City of New York, dark blue plate by Stubbs, dia. 6.25" 600		960	1470
City Hall, New York, dark blue cup and saucer by Stubbs 375		600	920
City Hall, New York, dark blue plate by Stubbs, dia. 6.75" 225		360	550
City Hall, New York, dark blue plate marked "Ridgway's Beauties of America," dia. 9.75" 275		440	670
City Hall, New York (mis-marked Staughton's Church), dark blue platter marked "Ridgway's Beauties of America," len. 16.75" 800		1280	1960
City Hotel, New York, dark blue plate by Stevenson, dia. 8.5" . 350		560	860
City of Albany, State of New York, dark blue plate by Enoch Wood, dia. 10" 600		960	1470
Columbia College, New York, dark blue plate by Stevenson, dia. 6.5" 300		480	740
Commodore MacDonough's Victory, dark blue dome-top coffee pot by Enoch Wood, ht. 10.5" 2400		3840	5880
Commodore MacDonough's Victory, dark blue plate by Enoch Wood, dia. 6.5" 300		480	740
Entrance of the Canal Into the Hudson at Albany, dark blue plate by Enoch Wood, dia. 10" 700		1120	1720

Top row: New York City Hotel, 8", $150; Nahant Hotel near Boston, 8", $475. Middle row: Union Line, 10", $600; Table Rock Niagara, 9.5", $375. Bottom row: Park Theater, New York, 9", $325; Mitchel & Freeman's China and Glass Warehouse, Boston, 9", $150. —Photo courtesy of Northeast Auctions.

	AUCTION	RETAIL Low	High
Fort Gansevoort, New York, dark blue plate by Stevenson, dia. 6.75"	$ 800	$ 1280	$ 1960
Highlands at West Point, Hudson River dark blue plate by Enoch Wood, dia. 6.5"	950	1520	2330
Highlands, Hudson River, Near Newburg, dark blue plate by Enoch Wood, dia. 6.5"	1050	1680	2570
Hoboken in New Jersey, dark blue plate by Stubbs, dia. 7.75"	200	320	490
Hudson River View, dark blue plate by Enoch Wood, dia. 5.5"	500	800	1230
Lake George, State of New York, dark blue platter by Enoch Wood, len. 16.5"	2000	3200	4900
Landing of Lafayette at Castle Garden, New York, 16 August 1824, dark blue rectangular bowl by Clews, len. 11.25"	1700	2720	4170
Landing of Lafayette at Castle Garden, New York, 16 August 1824, dark blue tray w/ handles, by Clews, len. 9.75"	900	1440	2210
New York from Brooklyn (Heights), dark blue plate by A. Stevenson, dia. 10.25"	950	1520	2330
New York from Heights of Brooklyn, dark blue platter by A. Stevenson, len. 16.25"	2500	4000	6130
New York from Weehawk, dark blue platter by A. Stevenson, len. 18.5"	3500	5600	8580
Niagara from the American Side, dark blue undertray for soup tureen, by Enoch Wood, len. 14"	800	1280	1960
Park Theatre, New York, dark blue plate by Stevenson, dia. 10"	400	640	980
Pass in the Catskill Mountains, dark blue plate by Enoch Wood, dia. 7.75"	500	800	1230
Passaic Falls and Pass in the Catskill Mountains, dark blue covered gravy tureen, stand, and ladle by Enoch Wood, len. of tureen 8"	2750	4400	6740
Pine Orchard House, Catskill Mountains, dark blue plate by Enoch Wood, dia. 10"	550	880	1350
Scudder's American Museum, dark blue plate by Stevenson, dia. 7.5"	950	1520	2330
Scudder's American Museum (mismarked Staughton's Church), dark blue plate by Stevenson. dia. 5"	650	1040	1590
St. Paul's Church, New York, dark blue plate by Stevenson. dia. 6.25"	950	1520	2330
States Plate, dark blue soup plate by Clews, dia. 10.25"	350	560	860
Table Rock, Niagara, dark blue plate by Enoch Wood, dia. 10"	400	640	980
Table Rock, Niagara, dark blue soup plate by Enoch Wood, dia. 10.25"	400	640	980
Tappan Zee from Greensburgh, dark blue platter by Enoch Wood, len. 9.75"	1200	1920	2940
Tappan Zee from Greensburgh, dark blue vegetable dish by Enoch Wood, dia. 8.75"	1500	2400	3680
Troy, View from Mt. Ida, dark blue platter by A. Stevenson, len. 10"	200	320	490
Union Line, dark blue plate by Enoch Wood, dia. 10"	500	800	1230
View Near Catskill on the River Hudson, dark blue platter by A. Stevenson, len. 12.5"	1600	2560	3920

	AUCTION	RETAIL	
		Low	High
View of New York Bay, dark blue plate by Stubbs, dia. 8.5" ..	$ 2800	$ 4480	$ 6860
View of Trenton Falls, New York, dark blue plate by Enoch Wood, dia. 7.5"	400	640	980
View on the Road to Lake George, dark blue plate by A. Stevenson, dia. 8.75"	850	1360	2080
West Point Military Academy, dark blue tray w/ openwork border by Enoch Wood, len. 10"	1500	2400	3680
Windsor Castle, platter, Clews Staffordshire, scroll borders, 13" x 17"	525	840	1290

Above left to right: Shakespeare, ht. 15", $300-$350; boy on zebra, ht.7.5", $200-$250. — Items courtesy of Valerie Hoyt.

Figures

	Low	High
Figural Group, The New Marriage Act 350	602	952
Figural Pair, Uncle Tom and Little Eva 500	860	1360
Inkwells, pr., in form of estate hounds, on cobalt bases, ht. 5" .. 550	946	1496
Poodles, pr., on scrolled bases, mother w/ 3 pups, ht. 5" 450	774	1224
Recumbent Dogs, on mottled bases, early 19th c., len. 6.5" 1100	1892	2992
Recumbent Dogs, pr., w/ black markings, len. 6" 550	946	1496
Recumbent Dogs, pr., w/ red and black markings, len. 4.5" 100	172	272
Recumbent Dogs, pr., w/ red markings, len. 4.5" 100	172	272
Standing Dogs, pr., w/ russet markings, len. 7" 700	1204	1904
Standing King Charles Spaniels, pr., rare, len. 13" 1800	3096	4896

Top row left to right: Pair of recumbent dogs with black markings, length 6", $550; figural group of Uncle Tom and Eva, height 7", $200; figural group of Uncle Tom and Eva, height 8", $300; pair of early recumbent dogs on mottled bases, length 6.5", $1100. Middle row: rare pair of standing King Charles Spaniels, length 13", $1800. Bottom row left to right: pair of recumbent dogs with red and black markings, length 4.5", $100; pair of recumbent dogs with red markings, length 4.5", $100. —Photo courtesy of Northeast Auctions.

Stangl Pottery

In 1926, John M. Stangl, acting as president of Fulper, bought the Anchor Pottery Company of Trenton and began manufacturing there as the Stangl Pottery Company. After his death in 1972, the Wheaton Glass Co. purchased and ran the company until 1978.

The following entries are from the Colonial Dinnerware line. This line has a fluted shape and carries the shape number 1388 inscribed on the bottom. Ranger (cowboy) pieces are a favorite and worth somewhat more.

	LOW	AVG.	HIGH
Baker, pie	$ 25	$ 35	$ 45
Baking Shell	14	19	24
Bean Pot	45	55	65
Bean Pot, ind.	20	30	40
Bowl, soup w/ lid	21	27	33
Butter Chip	7	9	11
Candelabra	35	45	55
Candlestick	14	18	22
Carafe, w/ lid, wood handle	40	55	70
Casserole, 5"-8"	30	40	50
Chop Plate, 12"-14"	30	38	46
Cigarette Box, 8.5"	28	35	42
Coaster	10	13	16
Coffee Pot	46	60	75
Compote, 7"	21	26	31
Console Bowl, 12"	38	46	54
Cream/Sugar	26	32	38
Cup/Saucer	16	20	24
Custard Cup	9	12	15
Dish, 6"	12	15	18
Egg Cup	11	14	17
Gravy Boat	22	28	33
Hors d'Oeuvre, 9"-12"	27	36	44
Jar, storage, w/ lid	45	60	75
Mixing Bowl, 5"-14"	30	38	45
Mug	12	15	17
Pitcher, 3"-6"	21	28	34
Pitcher, ball form	46	58	69
Pitcher, syrup	27	34	41
Plate, 6"-8"	6	7	8
Plate, 9"-10"	13	17	20
Plate, grill, 10"	17	22	26
Platter, oval, 12"-14"	17	21	24
Relish Tray Dish, 2 piece, 7"	15	19	23
Salad Bowl, lug, 8"-10"	24	32	40
Salt/Pepper	18	23	27
Teapot, 6 cup	50	60	70
Teapot, ind.	28	36	43
Vegetables, oval, 10"	18	23	28

Steubenville Pottery

Steubenville made the most popular dinnerware in America. From 1879 to 1959 when Canonsburg Pottery bought the molds it sold over 125 million pieces. American Modern is the best known Steubenville line.

Adam (Antique) (1932)

	LOW	AVG.	HIGH
Coffee Pot	$ 15	$ 17	$ 20
Covered Muffin	15	17	20
Cream/Sugar	12	14	16
Cup/Saucer	5	6	7
Dish, 5-6"	2	3	4
Egg Cup	5	6	7
Gravy Boat	8	10	12
Hot Water Pitcher	15	17	20
Pitcher, 1-2 qt	10	12	15
Pickle Dish	3	4	5
Plate, 6-8"	2	3	4
Plate, 9-11"	4	5	6
Platter, 11"	5	6	7
Salt/Pepper	10	12	15
Soup Bowl/Saucer	6	8	10
Teapot	34	37	40

American Modern (1939-1959)

Designed by Russell Wright.

	LOW	AVG.	HIGH
Bowl, rect.	18	20	22
Bowl, sq.	45	50	55
Butter	140	150	160
Carafe	80	90	100
Casserole	45	50	55
Celery	22	25	28
Coffee Cup Cover	75	100	125
Coffee Pot	60	80	100
Cream/Sugar	23	26	29
Cup/Saucer	10	12	14
Cup/Saucer (art deco)	20	28	36
Dish	8	10	12
Fork and Spoon	45	50	55
Gravy Boat	15	18	21
Hors d'Oeuvre Tray	140	150	160
Pitcher, w/lid	90	100	110
Pickle Dish	12	15	18
Plate, 6"	4	5	6
Plate, 8"	10	12	14
Plate, 10"	9	11	13
Plate, party	30	35	40
Platter, div.	50	60	70
Platter, sq. or rect.	22	26	30
Relish Tray, w/handle	110	120	130
Salt/Pepper	5	7	10
Storage Dish, w/lid	140	150	160

Taylor, Smith and Taylor China

In 1901 the Taylor, Smith and Lee Co. changed it name to Taylor, Smith and Taylor. It produced semiporcelain toilet ware, dinnerware, kitchenware, and specialties. However, it is most famous for its Lu-Ray line, a pastel solid-colored dinnerware. Anchor Hocking bought the company in 1972.

Lu-Ray (mid-1938)
Lu-Ray was named after the Luray Caverns.

	LOW	AVG.	HIGH
Bowl, 36s	$ 28	$ 30	$ 32
Bud Vase	100	125	150
Butter Dish	30	35	40
Cake Plate, lug, 11"	25	30	35
Casserole, 8"	70	75	80
Chop Plate, 14-15"	20	25	30
Coaster	25	30	35
Cream/Sugar	9	11	13
Cream/Sugar (art deco)	38	46	55
Coffee Pot (art deco)	75	80	85
Cup/Saucer	5	7	9
Cup/Saucer (art deco)	13	15	17
Dish, 5"	2	3	4
Egg Cup	12	15	18
Epergne	60	70	80
Gravy Boat	15	20	25
Grill Plate, 10"	15	18	21
Pitcher, 1 qt.	60	68	75
Pitcher, 2 qt.	35	42	50
Mixing Bowl, 5"-7"	45	52	60
Mixing Bowl, 8"-10"	50	62	75
Muffin Cover	65	60	75
Nut Dish, 4.5"	20	25	30
Pickle Dish, 9.5"	15	18	21
Plate, 6"-8"	3	5	7
Plate, 9"-10"	7	9	11
Platter, 11"-14"	10	12	14
Relish Tray, 4 piece	75	80	85
Salad Bowl, 10"	30	35	40
Salt/Pepper	8	11	14
Soup Bowl/Saucer	35	40	45
Soup Plate, 8"	8	10	12
Teapot	45	55	65
Tumbler, 5 oz	20	25	30
Tumbler, 9 oz	40	45	50
Vegetable, 9"-11"	8	10	12

Vzstosa (1938)

Chop Plate, 11"-14"	15	20	25
Cream/Sugar	25	30	35
Cup/Saucer	15	20	25
Dish, 5"	8	10	12
Egg Cup	25	30	35

Van Briggle Pottery

Artus and Anne Van Briggle founded this arts and crafts pottery in 1901. It dominated the western market with pots and vases of stylized tree limbs, cactus, and other plants. Colors included Mountain Craig (green to brown), Midnight (black), Moonglo (off-white), Persian Rose, Turquoise Ming, and Russet.

The first and most famous mark consisted of the letters AA, the initials of Van Briggle and his wife, Anne. The mark often included the date of production until 1920. These are the most desireable pieces. A stock number often appeared, especially on later pieces. The words "HAND CARVED" are often on pieces with raised decoration.

Van Briggle marks.

	LOW	AVG.	HIGH
Ashtray, 5.25", Indian Girl, rose color, matte, signed	$ 280	$ 335	$ 390
Ashtray, 5.5", rose, spiral interior	30	35	40
Ashtray, 6.5", trapezoid, Turquoise Ming	30	35	40
Ashtray, female nude w/ shell, 7", blue, matte, signed	340	370	400
Bookends, pr., rams, red and blue glaze	220	250	280
Bowl, 12" #762, pine cone	90	100	110
Bowl, 12.5", rose glaze, leaf motif	280	350	420
Bowl, 10.5", #283, Moonglo, flower and stem motif, c. 1908	240	280	320
Bowl, 3", acorn form, brown, c. 1915	230	265	300
Bowl, 3", rose, butterfly decor	90	100	110
Bowl, 3.5", rose glaze, cherry, leaf and vine motif	130	140	150
Bowl, 4", fiat, small base, brown, leaf motif, c. 1917	130	145	160
Bowl, 4", red, leaf motif across top, c. 1914	50	55	60
Bowl, 5", plain dec., maroon, signed, c. 1918	180	220	260
Bowl, 5", rose, scalloped rim, flared ends	30	35	40
Bowl, 5.25", green, floral and leaf motif	180	200	220
Bowl, 6", acorn and leaf motif across top	40	50	60
Bowl, 6", flat, yellow, leaf motif, c. 1903	740	845	950
Bowl, 6", rose, swirled ivy motif	50	55	60
Bowl, 8", #22, styled leaves, bronzed, c. 1905	1300	1600	1900
Bowl, 8", #22, styled leaves, yellow w/green on leaves, c. 1917	1800	2000	2200
Bowl, 8", #762, pine cone and branches	50	60	70
Bowl, 8", #22, styled leaves, Turquoise Ming, c. 1902	1000	1200	1400
Bowl, #878, 2", bulbous shape, band of berries and leaves, pink and green, c. 1908	230	260	290
Bowl, 8.5", #903D, frog and dragonfly motif, Turquoise Ming	90	110	130
Candlesticks, 6", pr., rose, double tulip motif	50	55	60
Conch, 9", Turquoise Ming	50	55	60
Creamer, 2", hexagon, Turquoise Ming	20	20	20
Cup, 3.25", 6 incised panel lines, Turquoise Ming, c. 1917	50	55	60
Figurine, 3", elephant, on base, yellow and brown	50	55	60
Figurine, 4", donkey, Turquoise Ming	40	50	60

	LOW	AVG.	HIGH
Figurine, 4" elephant, rose, triangular ears	$ 110	$ 125	$ 140
Figurine, 4.5", elephant, Turquoise Ming, trunk raised	40	50	60
Figurine, 8", cat, sits on base, long neck	70	90	110
Figurine, 8", detailed girl grinding corn, Turquoise Ming	40	50	60
Figurine, 8.5", rearing horse, on stand, brown	70	80	90
Figurine, 9.5", owl on stump, brown	390	485	580
Jug, 7", "Firewater," #12, yellow, c. 1905	10,000	12,500	15,000
Lamp, 18", flat base, narrow neck, horse motif, red	100	110	120
Lamp, 20", bulbous, Moonglo	70	80	90
Mug, 5.5", #28B, plain, blue, c. 1912	700	800	900
Ornament, 3", oval, angel w/ trumpet, natural glaze, c. 1980	30	35	40
Ornament, 4", "Noel," natural glaze, c. 1978	40	45	50
Paperweight, 3.5", rabbit, green and brown	90	105	120
Paperweight, rabbit, 2.5", Turquoise Ming, c. 1914	110	125	140
Pitcher, 11", bulbous, Turquoise Ming	70	85	100
Pitcher, 3", Moonglo	30	35	40
Pitcher, 3.5", bulbous, handled, collared neck, Turquoise Ming, c. 1908	200	240	280
Planter, 12.5", rose shell form	70	85	100
Planter, 9", blue, floral motif	50	60	70
Plaque, 4.5", oval, rose glaze, Indian head design	70	85	100
Plate, 8", #20, stylized poppy, blue, c. 1917	450	475	500
Plate, 8", #20, stylized poppy, green, white, c. 1904	2200	2600	3000
Tile, 6", water lilies, green leaves, Turquoise Ming, c. 1910	950	1120	1290
Vase, 2", bulbous body, red, leaf and stem motif, c. 1919	80	90	100
Vase, 2", rose, c. 1918	120	135	150
Vase, 3", bulbous body, blue butterfly motif, c. 1921	110	120	130
Vase, 3", flared rim, feather motif, Turquoise Ming	30	35	40
Vase, 4", rose, c. 1917	210	245	280
Vase, 4", rose, ivy and floral motif	50	55	60
Vase, 4" rose, tulip-shaped, scalloped rim	20	25	30
Vase, 4.5", #645, violet floral, white w/green buds, c. 1911	600	700	800
Vase, 4.5", #645, violets and leaves, blue, c. 1908	50	60	70
Vase, 4.5", #645, violets and leaves, green, c. 1918	250	270	290
Vase, 4.5", ivy and floral motif, Turquoise Ming	30	35	40
Vase, 4.5", rose, butterfly motif	110	140	170
Vase, 5", bulbous body, collared neck, green, leaf motif, c. 1908	110	125	140
Vase, 5", rose and green, floral motif, c. 1905	630	700	770
Vase, 5", rose, floral motif	40	50	60
Vase, 5.25", rose, heart-shaped, ivy motif	40	50	60
Vase, 5.5", #833, flowers, green, c. 1923	620	670	720
Vase, 5.5", #833, flowers, Turquoise Ming, c. 1930	30	35	40
Vase, 6", #132, flowers, black, c. 1909	2100	2500	2900
Vase, 6", #132, flowers, green, c. 1919	1500	1750	2000
Vase, 6", #132, flowers, rose, c. 1905	1200	1500	1800
Vase, 6", #132, flowers, white flowers, c. 1910	3500	4000	4500
Vase, 6", flowers, bronzed, c. 1915	2250	2500	2750
Vase, 4.5", #645, violets and leaves, brown w/ green, c. 1930	50	60	70
Vase, 7", cylinder shape, collared neck, Turquoise Ming, c. 1916	400	430	460
Vase, 8", bulbous body, narrow neck, handled, red and blue, leaf motif, c. 1920	60	75	90

	LOW	AVG.	HIGH
Vase, 8", floral dec., blue, c. 1986	$ 40	$ 45	$ 50
Vase, 8", floral dec., brown, c. 1970	60	65	70
Vase, 8", floral dec., brown w/ green drip	30	35	40
Vase, 8", floral dec., Moonglo matte white, c. 1965	40	45	50
Vase, 8", floral dec., Turquoise Ming matte, c. 1960	40	45	50
Vase, 8", floral dec., yellow, c. 1989	30	35	40
Vase, 8.5", Moonglo, bird of paradise motif	30	35	40
Vase, 9", open handles, rose color, matte, signed, c. 1920	400	470	540
Vase, 9", rose, flower and leaf motif	100	115	130
Vase, 10", #17, white, c. 1916 11,000		13,000	15,000
Vase, 10", #17, lorelei, maroon, c. 1911	1000	1200	1400
Vase, 10.5", #240, ribbed, handles, green, c. 1910	1080	1195	1310
Vase, 10.5", #240, ribbed, handles, maroon, c. 1915	290	320	350
Vase, 12", 3-head Indian, 12", maroon, c. 1912	350	405	460
Vase, 12", 3-head Indian, brown, c. 1915	2400	2800	3200
Vase, 12.25", urn form, ribs, handles, Turquoise Ming, matte, signed, c. 1920	350	425	500
Vase, 14", #139, Yucca, floral dec., c. 1910	4000	4500	5000
Vase, 14", #139, Yucca, maroon, c. 1904	2000	2200	2400
Vase, 14", #139, Yucca, red flowers, c. 1903	6000	7000	8000

Pottery and Porcelain: Miscellaneous

Bookends

Dating back to before either television or the Internet, bookends were considered far more a necessity than today. But for those of us who can find no end to our books, these pottery shelf stoppers are well worth their collectors' dollars. Look for bold forms and, as always, beware of cracks and chips.

	LOW	AVG.	HIGH
Buddha, Fulper	$ 325	$ 365	$ 405
Cactus, Abingdon, 6"	67	86	104
Calla Lily, Royal Haeger, 5.5"	25	29	35
Clydesdale, Frankoma, 5"	320	420	520
Dolphin, Abingdon, 5.5"	22	27	32
Dreamer Girl, Frankoma, 6"	130	155	180
Duck Head, Frankoma, 5.5"	155	180	205
Eagles, Morton, 6"	42	52	62
Elephants, Cliftwood	130	155	180
Fern Leaf, Abingdon, 5.5"	52	62	72
Flying Geese, Shawnee, 6"	32	42	52
Foxglove, Roseville, pattern #10, pink and blue, pr.	85	100	115
Horse, Royal Haeger, 8.5"	36	43	50
Horse Head, Abingdon, 7"	45	60	75
Horse Head, Royal Haeger, 7.5"	27	35	43
Irish Setter, Frankoma, 6"	115	145	175
Leopard, Frankoma, 7"	100	125	150
Leopard, Royal Haeger, 15"	58	73	88
Lion Head, Royal Haeger, 7.5"	28	35	42
Monk, Catalina, 7"	400	500	600
Mountain Girl, Frankoma, 7"	75	100	125
Owl, Van Briggle, 6"	275	344	413
Owls, Rookwood, blue/green matte	410	460	510
Owls, Rookwood, wine madder	240	280	320
Panthers, Rookwood, wine madder	300	350	400
Parrots, Morton, 6"	34	43	52
Quill, Abingdon, 8.25"	80	95	110
Ram, Royal Haeger, 9"	35	43	50
Ramses, Fulper	650	700	750
Ram's Head, Royal Haeger, 5.5"	26	32	38
Rook, Rookwood, black matte	400	450	500
Rookwood, pattern #2564, 1940, brown gloss	350	400	450
Rookwood, pattern #2564, 1953, wine madder	350	400	450
Rookwood, pattern #2564, 1924 green matte	300	350	400
Rookwood, pattern #2564, 1925, brown matte	210	250	290
Russian, Abingdon, 6.5"	60	80	100
Scotty, Abingdon, 7.5"	70	90	110
Sea Gull, Abingdon, 6"	50	60	70
Seahorse, Frankoma, 6"	300	400	500
Temple Gate, Fulper	4000	4500	5000
Water Lily, Royal Haeger, 5"	21	27	33
Woodpeckers, Cliftwood, 6.5"	130	160	185

Cookie Jars

These beloved containers of the kitchen hold the comforting treat we have pursued for years. Cookie jar collecting gained momentum in the early eighties. Sotheby's 1988 auction of the estate of pop artist Andy Warhol catapulted figural cookie jars to national prominence. Hearing a cookie jar brought over $20,000 (it was actually for a lot of several jars), people scrambled to their kitchen and attics in hopes of striking gold. As the head of the collectibles department at Christie's, I had to deliver the sobering news to scores of people that their cookie jars were worth considerably less than those of the artist. Following the sale, cookie jar collecting flourished and today many jars command thousands of dollars rather than hundreds.

Collectors can specialize in manufacturers, themes or characters. Many times jars by one firm are referred to by the same name as similar jars by another producer. Make sure you know which jar you are purchasing. Recently, crossover interest from character memorabilia collectors fueled a rapid rise in prices of jars such as the Flintstones series (which has been reproduced), Casper the Ghost, Popeye, and others. Collectors of black memorabilia seek the Mammy cookie jars.

The prices below are for jars in excellent condition, with a minimal amount of paint loss, and no chips or cracks. The amount these faults affect value depends on severity, how it alters the jar's visible appeal, and personal tolerance. Cookie jar collectors are generally more tolerant of paint loss than other collectors, but top condition still brings a premium price. For more information we recommend *The Official Price Guide to Pottery and Porcelain*, Harvey Duke, House of Collectibles, Random House, NY, 1995, and *The Complete Cookie Jar Book*, Mike Schneider, Schiffer, West Chester, PA, 1991.

Left to right: Little Red Riding Hood (no gold), Hull, $220-$350; Happy Face, McCoy, $25-$45. —Photos courtesy of Nancy Heller.

	LOW	HIGH
Animal Crackers, McCoy	$ 60	$ 80
Apple, yellow, McCoy	40	50
Astronauts, McCoy	500	850
Baby Huey, ABC	2000	3200
Baby Pig, Regal China	400	500
Ball of Yarn w/ Kittens, ABC	90	140
Bananas, McCoy	80	100
Barnum's Animals, McCoy	300	400
Barrel, ABC	25	35
Baseball Boy, McCoy	200	300
Basket of Eggs, McCoy	40	60
Basket of Fruit, McCoy	45	65
Basket of Strawberries, McCoy	40	60

	LOW	HIGH
Basket w/ Dog Lid, McCoy	$ 50	$ 70
Basket w/ Duck Lid, McCoy	50	70
Basket w/ Kitten Lid, McCoy	45	65
Basket w/ Lamb Lid, McCoy	50	60
Bear and Beehive, McCoy	30	40
Bear, Ballerina, Metlox	90	130
Bear, cookies in pocket, cold painted, McCoy	50	70
Bear, Honey, flasher, ABC	350	750
Bear, w/ open eyes, ABC	70	90
Beehive w/ Cat, ABC	45	65
Bell, Liberty, ABC	90	110
Betsy Baker, McCoy	200	350
Big Bird, Calif. Org.	60	80
Bird Feed Sack, McCoy	25	45
Black Cat, McCoy	300	400
Boots, Cowboy, ABC	180	230
Bugs Bunny, McCoy	200	250
Casper, ABC	1000	1500
Chef w/ Spoon, ABC	90	140
Chef's Head, McCoy	80	120
Chick, wearing a beret, ABC	60	80
Chiffonnier, McCoy	50	70
Chipmunk, McCoy	80	120
Christmas Tree, Calif. Org.	200	300
Christmas Tree, McCoy	450	650
Churn, McCoy	180	240
Circus Horse, McCoy	180	220
Circus Tent, Brayton	320	450
Clock, 653, Abingdon	70	100
Clock, Cookie Time, 203, ABC	60	80
Clown, in barrel, tan and white, McCoy	80	120
Clown, on stage, 805, ABC	200	425
Clown Head, Metlox	100	570
Coalby Cat, McCoy	380	450
Coffee Grinder, McCoy	25	40
Coffee Mug, McCoy	30	40
Coffee Pot, ABC	30	40
Coffee Pot, metal handle, ABC	30	40
Cookie, Girl's Face, glasses, pigtails, Abingdon	80	100
Cookie Box, McCoy	100	150
Cookie Boy, McCoy	200	300
Cookie Jug, dark brown top, white bottom, McCoy	20	25
Cookie Monster, Calif. Org.	40	60
Cookie Truck 2 sizes, ABC	80	100
Covered Wagon, Brush	500	700
Covered Wagon, w/ lid, McCoy	55	85
Cow, ABC	70	90
Cow Jumped Over the Moon, 806, ABC	800	1000
Cow, brown, Brush	100	150
Cow, cat on back, blue, purple or black, Brush	900	1300
Cowboy, Lane	400	700
Dalmatians on Rocking Chair, McCoy	350	450

	LOW	HIGH
Davy Crockett, bust, McCoy	$ 450	$ 650
Davy Crockett, bust, Regal China	500	700
Davy Crockett, w/ gold, Brush	500	800
Davy Crockett, boy, ABC	300	500
Davy Crockett, man, ABC	800	1100
Davy Crockett, without gold, Brush	250	350
Dino, Flintstones, ABC	900	1300
Dog and Basket, Brush	250	300
Dog in Doghouse, McCoy	180	220
Donald Duck on Pumpkin, Calif. Org.	150	200
Donkey and Cart, Brush	350	450
Drum, McCoy	60	80
Drum, Metlox	100	150
Drum Majorette, ABC	300	450
Duck, McCoy	200	300
Dutch Boy, McCoy	45	55
Dutch Boy, cold painted, ABC	35	45
Dutch Boy, cold painted, Shawnee	80	120
Dutch Girl, Regal China	600	900
Dutch Girl, cold painted, ABC	35	45
Dutch Girl and Boy, McCoy	100	150
Eagle Basket, McCoy	30	40
Ear of Corn, McCoy	100	150
Elephant w/ Beanie, ABC	90	130
Elephant, whole trunk, McCoy	300	400
Elephant, w/ ice cream cone, Brush	400	500
Elsie the Cow, barrel, Pottery Guild	250	350
Fat Boy, 495, Abingdon	300	400
Fish, Brush	400	500
Football Boy, McCoy	200	250
Formal Pig, black coat, Brush	180	220
Fred Flinstone, ABC	900	1500
Friar Tuck, blue, Red Wing	90	110
Frog, Holiday	25	35
Frontier Family, McCoy	30	50
Frosty the Snow Man, Robinson-Ransbottom	450	650
Goldilocks, Regal China	300	400
Grandma, Brayton	400	500
Granny, ABC	140	180
Granny, Brush	300	400
Granny, McCoy	80	120
Hamm's Bear, McCoy	200	250
Helen Hetula, 11.5"	1000	1300
Hen on Nest, McCoy	70	90
Hippo, Happy, bar jar, 549, Abingdon	300	400
Hippo, monkey handle, Brush	500	700
Hobby Horse, McCoy	100	150
Hocus Rabbit, McCoy	40	50
Honey Bear, yellow, McCoy	80	120
Honeycomb Jar, McCoy	55	75
Horse, Circus, Brush	700	1400
Horse, sitting, ABC	900	1200

	LOW	HIGH
Howdy Doody, Purinton	$ 700	$ 900
Humpty Dumpty w/ Beanie, Brush	200	250
Humpty Dumpty, in cowboy attire, Brush	200	300
Indian Head, McCoy	250	350
Jack-in-the-Box, ABC	100	150
Jack-O-Lantern, McCoy	400	600
Jack-O-Lantern, 674, Abingdon	300	400
Kangaroo, blue, McCoy	250	300
Kangaroo, tan, McCoy	360	420
Katrina, Dutch girl, green, Red Wing	150	200
Katrina, Dutch girl, brown, Red Wing	90	120
King of Hearts, Red Wing	650	800
Kitten, on basket, McCoy	90	110
Kitten, on beehive, ABC	50	75
Koala Bear, McCoy	75	95
Lady Pig, ABC	90	120
Lamb in Hat, ABC	100	150
Lamb on Basket, McCoy	50	70
Lemon, McCoy	40	60
Leprechaun, McCoy	1000	1300
Lion, Hubert, Regal China	800	1000
Little Boy Blue, w/ gold, Brush	600	800
Little Girl, 693, Abingdon	90	100
Little Miss Muffet, 662, Abingdon	200	250
Little Red Riding Hood, McCoy	300	450
Little Red Riding Hood, Pottery Guild	125	175
Little Red Riding Hood, w/ gold, large or small, Brush	800	1600
Little Red Riding Hood, without gold, large or small, Brush	400	800
Log Cabin, McCoy	70	90
Lollipops, McCoy	60	80
Ludwig Von Drake, ABC	900	1200
Ma and Pa Owls, McCoy	85	105
Mammy, Brayton	900	1200
Mammy, aqua or yellow, McCoy	600	900
Mammy, cold painted, McCoy	180	220
Mammy, red, Metlox	700	800
Mammy w/ Cauliflowers, McCoy	900	1200
Mickey and Minnie, turnabouts, Leeds	300	400
Milk Can, McCoy	35	45
Monk, McCoy	35	45
Mother Goose, McCoy	100	150
Mouse, McCoy	35	45
Mugsey the Dog, Shawnee	400	600
Oaken Bucket, McCoy	30	40
Olive Oyl, ABC	2400	2900
Orange, McCoy	45	55
Oscar the Grouch, Calif. Org.	60	80
Owl, white and brown, one eye closed, Shawnee Co.	100	150
Owl, Collegiate, ABC	65	85
Owl, glossy brown, McCoy	30	40
Peek-A-Boo Bear, Regal China	900	1300
Penguins, kissing, white, McCoy	60	80

	LOW	HIGH
Peter Pan, w/ gold, Brush	$ 550	$ 850
Phone, antique wall, Cardinal Pottery	45	55
Picnic Basket, McCoy	55	65
Pig, Farmer, ABC	100	150
Pig, Sheriff, Robinson-Ransbottom	120	160
Pig, sitting, Brush	400	500
Pig, Smiley, red bandanna, flowers, Shawnee Co.	300	400
Pineapple, McCoy	70	110
Pineappple, Metlox	90	110
Pirate Chest, McCoy	80	100
Popeye, ABC	750	1000
Pot Belly Stove, black, McCoy	30	40
Pumpkin Coach, Brush	250	300
Puppy Holding Sign, McCoy	80	100
Puppy, in blue pot, ABC	45	65
Quaker Oats, Regal China	90	130
Rabbit in Hat, ABC	55	75
Raggedy Ann, McCoy	90	110
Red Riding Hood, Hull	300	400
Rooster, McCoy	75	85
Rubble House, Flintstones, ABC	900	1300
Rudolph the Red Nose Reindeer, ABC	700	950
Saddle, ABC	200	300
Sailor Boy, white, Shawnee Co.	90	110
Sandman, flasher, ABC	250	350
Santa, winking, ABC	350	550
Schoolhouse Bell, ABC	35	55
Spaceship, ABC	250	350
Spaceship w/ Spaceman, ABC	800	1100
Squirrel on Log, Brush	200	250
Strawberry, '50s, McCoy	50	70
Strawberry, '70s, McCoy	30	40
Swee 'Pea, ABC	2800	4000
Teapot, black, McCoy	45	55
Thinking Dog	35	55
Toby, Regal China	900	1200
Tortoise and Hare, flasher, ABC	675	875
Toy Soldier, ABC	40	50
Train, 651, Abingdon	120	160
Train, Cookie RR, ABC	80	100
Tug Boat, ABC	150	250
Whale, Robinson-Ransbottom	600	800
Windmill, McCoy	100	150
Windmill, 678, Abingdon	200	250
Wise Bird, Robinson-Ransbottom	60	90
Wishing Well, McCoy	30	50
Woodsy Owl, McCoy	100	150
Wren House, McCoy	120	160
Yogi Bear, ABC	400	600

Earthenware Pottery

Using less sophisticated kilns and whatever clays were found locally, country potters produced a diverse array of beautiful and imaginative kitchenwares and tablewares. Design and coloration are key in determining values. But a crack or chip puts a major dent in the price.

Dedham Pottery was handmade in molds and free-hand decorated in cobalt blue from the end of the 19th century until 1943. Mochaware was decorated in various methods that included finger-painting (to create "earthworm" designs) and spitting a tobacco juice concoction (to create "seaweed" designs). Redware gets its name from the red clay used. Spongeware was decorated with sponges, usually in blue. Yellowware gets its name from the yellow glaze in which it was dipped.

Below left to right, rare mochaware pieces: "earthworm" caster, $950; simple polychrome caster, $700; "seaweed" milk jug, $1500; cream pitcher, $800; marbleized caster, $900; marbleized creamer, $950. — Photos courtesy of Northeast Auctions.

Above left to right: Mochaware marbleized bowl, diameter 6", $300-$500, mochaware mug with "earthworm" decoration, height 5", $400-$600.

Dedham Plates

	AUCTION	RETAIL Low	High
(See low end for 6" plates and high end for 10" plates.)			
Azalea	$ 75	$ 250	$ 300
Birds in Orange Tree	200	600	800
Butterny	100	300	600
Crab	250	600	900
Duck	125	300	500
Elephant	300	700	900
Grape	125	250	350
Horse Chestnut	100	300	350
Iris	100	300	350
Lobster	250	700	900
Magnolia	125	250	300
Mushroom	300	300	500
Polar Bear	400	800	1200
Pond Lily	125	300	400
Rabbit	75	175	250
Turkey	175	400	800

Mochaware

Bowl, pearlware, earthworm dec., dia. 9"	825	1490	2230
Jug, qt., black mocha trees on seafoam green	176	320	480
Jug, qt., blue	210	380	570
Jug, qt., pear form, C.T. Maling & Co., Newcastle-Upon-Tyne, c. 1900	193	350	520
Measure, half gal., 7.5", early 20th cent.	193	350	520
Measure, pt., Newcastle-Upon-Tyne, c. 1900	110	200	300
Measure, qt., 7.5", early 20th century	200	360	540
Mug, half pt., earthworm dec.	187	340	500
Mug, pt., black and blue banded w/ sprigged verification mark, c. 1870	182	330	490
Mug, pt., Hanley, Staffordshire	220	400	590
Mug, qt., Hanley, Staffordshire	220	400	590
Mug, qt., T.G. Green	220	400	590
Porter Mug, pt., yellow bodied, banded in white and brown	182	330	490

Redware

Deep Dish, brown glazed oblong, w/ alternating serpentine and wavy line motif, the rim plain, 12" x 14"	1800	3000	5000
Deep Dish, circular, w/ crimped rim and yellow slip triple-serpentine motif, dia. 13"	2400	4000	6500
Deep Dish, large brown-glazed oblong, w/ 2 yellow slip stylized evergreens, rim plain, 14" x 16"	2300	3910	6000
Deep Dish, rect., w/ coggled rim and brown slip pinstripe motif on yellow ground, 13" x 11"	1700	2890	4420
Deep Dish, dark-brown glazed oblong, w/ plain rim and yellow slip wavy line dec., 13" x 14"	1000	1700	2600
Deep Dish, glazed and slip-dec., brown slip feather combed, 12" x 15"	1000	1700	2600
Deep Dish, dark-brown glazed circular, w/ yellow slip spiraling and scalloped line, rim plain, dia. 14"	450	700	1200

	AUCTION	RETAIL	
		Low	High

Deep Dish, brown glazed, w/ alternating serpentine and wavy line
motifs in yellow slip, dia. 15" .... $ 2500 $ 4250 $ 6500
Deep Dish, brown-glazed oblong w/ alternating serpentine and wavy
lines, w/ plain rim, 12" x 14" 1800 3000 5000
Jug, slip-glazed handled w/ leaf dec. and owner's name, ht. 12". .... 350 600 , 900
Mariner's Jug, English, slip-dec., ht. 11" 850 1400 2200
Mug, ht. 4" 350 600 910
Ovoid Jar, ht. 9" 275 470 720
Plate, w/ slip dec., dia. 11" 225 380 580
Shaving Mug, ht. 4" 375 640 970

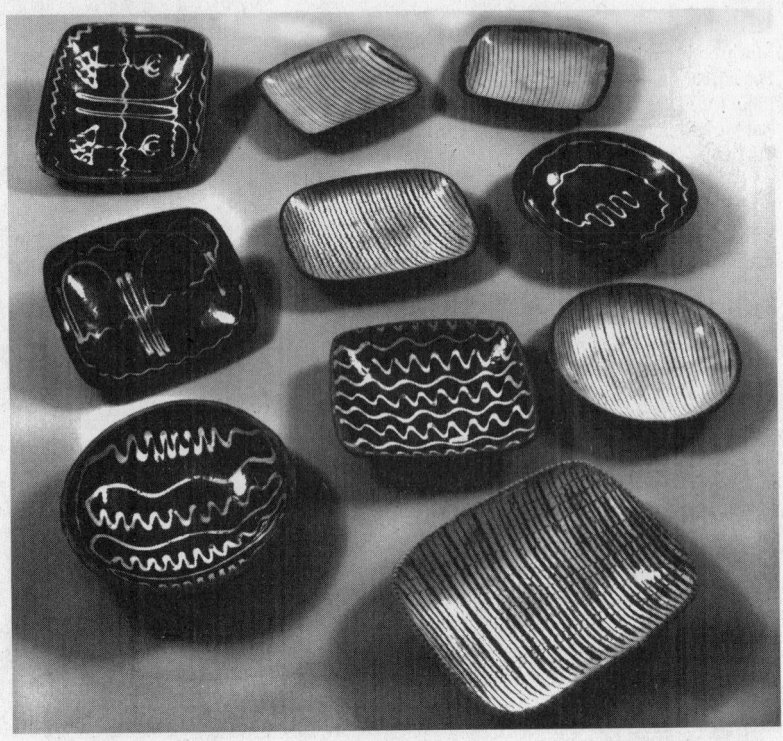

Top row left to right: Brown-glazed deep dish, 16.75", $2300; deep dish with brown pinstripes, 11.5", $1700; deep dish with brown pinstripes, 13.5", $1300. Second row left to right: Stylized ram's head deep dish, 14.5", $1000; feather combed deep dish, 15", $1000; spiral decorated charger, 15", $450. Third row left to right: Wavy line decorated charger, 15.25", $2500; wavy line decorated platter, 14", $1800; yellow-ware deep dish, 13.5", $1000. Bottom right: yellow ware platter, 17.25", $1500. — Photo courtesy of Northeast Auctions.

	AUCTION	RETAIL Low	High
Spongeware			
Bowl, 1 qt.	$ 100	$ 170	$ 260
Bowl, 2 qt.	200	340	520
Bowl and Pitcher Set	275	470	720
Cookie Jar, 4 qt.	200	340	520
Crock, 2 qt.	100	170	260
Pie Plate	50	80	130
Pitcher, 1 qt.	125	210	320
Pitcher, 2 qt.	150	260	390

Yellowware

	AUCTION	RETAIL Low	High
Deep Dish, feather combed slip motif and notched rim, 13" x 17"....	1200	2040	3120
Deep-Dish, notched rim and brown slip striped design, dia. 13.5"	1100	1870	2860
Deep Platter, brown, feather-combing motif, 16" x 20.5"	2100	3570	5460
Deep Dish, crimped rim and brown-slip stripes, 11" x 13"	1300	2210	3380
Deep Dish, notched rim and combed brown slip design, dia. 13.5" ..	1000	1700	2600
Deep Dish, notched rim and brown slip feather combed, 13" x 17.5" .	1500	2550	3900
Miniature Pot, w/ knopped lid, overall w/ brown polka-dots, ht. 3.5"	1200	2040	3120

Above: Dedham potttery with rabbit pattern, — Photo courtesy of Northeast Auctions.

Right: Spongeware pitcher, one quart, $125 at auction.

English and Continental Pottery and China

With few potteries of its own, the early Americans imported from Europe many tablewares. Delftware is the generic name for the tin-glazed earthenwares made in great numbers in Holland and England during the 17th and 18th centuries. The name comes from the Dutch city of Holland where many of these pieces originated. Do not confuse these pieces with those made by the modern corporation "Delft," whose wares pay tribute to the fine early pieces. The pitchers made in Liverpool, England, often called "Liverpool Jugs," sported many patriotic American themes. Lustreware is decorated in a bright metallic finish, usually having a pink or silvery appearance. Majolica was the tradename used by the Minton Company in England to describe wares that imitated Majolica pieces from the Italian Renaissance. Collectors now use the term to refer to similar pieces made by many English potters of the mid-19th century.

Beware of English 18th-century-style earthenware pieces of various glazes, especially tortoiseshell glaze. The Dewitt Wallace Decorative Arts Gallery at Colonial Williamsburg in Virginia has documented many modern fakes including candlesticks and teapots. Some brilliant examples potted by Guy Timothy Davies have fooled many knowledgeable dealers and collectors.

Continental pottery with a similar look to Delft polychrome wares will sell for similar prices. The continental barber bowl on the right sold for $300 at auction, about what a Delft example should bring.

	AUCTION	RETAIL Low	High
Delft			
Charger, Dutch, blue and white floral dec., dia. 14"	$ 550	$ 940	$ 1430
Charger, Dutch, w/ polychrome parrot dec., dia. 13"	850	1440	2210
Charger, Dutch, w/ polychrome parrot dec., dia. 14"	950	1620	2470
Charger, Dutch, w/ polychrome bird and vase dec., dia. 13"	1000	1700	2600
Charger, Dutch, w/ polychrome bird and flower pot motif, dia. 13"	900	1530	2340
Charger, Dutch, manganese and chrome-yellow, dia. 17"	1700	2890	4420
Charger, Dutch, manganese and yellow dec. putti, dia. 14"	950	1620	2470
Charger, Dutch, polychrome	400	680	1000
Charger, Eng., blue and white, dia. 12"	400	680	1000
Cows, pr., w/ milkers, ht. 7"	200	340	520
Cows, pr., w. 8"	150	260	400
Flower Brick, Eng., blue and white, w. 5"	350	600	910
Flower Brick, Eng., blue and white, w. 7"	500	850	1300
Garniture Vase, Dutch, blue and white, fitted as a lamp	310	530	810

Above left: Chinese-style blue and white hexagonal Delft plate,
$80 at auction. Above right: Modern Delft, $10-$20 retail.

	AUCTION	RETAIL Low	High
Garniture Vases, set of 5, blue and white, w/ biblical scenes, ht. 10"	550	940	1430
Garniture Vases, pr., Dutch, blue and white, covered, ht. 15"	1200	2000	3100
Plaques, pr., Dutch manganese dec. w/ figures and animals, ht. 11"	1300	2210	3380
Punch Bowl, polychrome	450	760	1150
Recumbent Horse, blue and white, w. 6"	1500	2550	3900
Tankard, Dutch, pewter-mounted, ht. 10"	500	850	1300
Tazza, English, blue and white, dia. 7"	450	760	1170
Tobacco Jar, Dutch, blue and white, marked Rappee, ht. 13"	800	1360	2080

Gaudy Dutch

	AUCTION	RETAIL Low	High
Bowl, Carnation pattern, dia. 5.5"	150	250	400
Bowl, Dove pattern, dia. 5.5", ht. 2.5"	600	990	1500
Bowl, Dove pattern, dia. 6.5", ht. 3"	1350	2230	3580
Bowl, Oyster pattern, dia. 5.5"	135	220	360
Cup and Bowl, Single Rose pattern, bowl dia. 5.5"	325	540	860

Gaudy Dutch Carnation pattern plate, diameter 8".

	AUCTION	RETAIL	
		Low	High

Liverpool

Pitcher, Amer. market w/ Amer. ship in polychrome, Amer. eagle, seal, "SW" in wreath; reverse w/ "The Parting Lovers" and verse "my love is fix'd...," ht. 9.5"	$5000	$8750	$13,750
Pitcher, Amer. market transfer-printed depicting Salem ship yards, ht. 8"	3200	4500	7500
Pitcher, Amer. market transfer-printed: "Washington in Glory" Memorial, "Peace, Plenty & Independence," w/ traces of original gilt, ht. 11"	4800	8000	12,000
Red Ale Mug, Amer. market transfer-printed w/ portrait medallion, "James Lawrence, Esq., Late of The United States Navy," ht. 6"	5250	9000	14,500

Lustre

Copper Lustre Pitcher, w/ yellow band, ht. 8"	200	350	550
Canary Lustre Cup and Saucer	100	175	275
Pink Lustre House Pattern Tea Set w/ tea plates, 30 pieces	400	700	1100

Majolica

Cheese Dish, Wedgwood	275	470	720
Cheese Dish, w/ fern motif	1000	1700	2600
Ewer, w/ gargoyle handle, Minton	1500	2550	3900
Figural Pitchers, pr., Minton	1400	2380	3640
Game Dish, w/ bird cover.	900	1530	2340
Palissy-Type Oval Dish, w/ fish, snake, and other animals, w. 16"	850	1440	2210
Palissy-Type Circular Dish, w/ fish and other animals, dia. 11"	1000	1700	2600
Pineapple Pitcher, Minton	650	1100	1690
Planter, w/ Masques, Minton	600	1020	1560
Strawberry Dish and 12 Berry Dishes, Wedgwood	950	1620	2470
Syrup Pitcher, w/ motto, Wedgwood	400	680	1040

Above left to right: Lustre pitcher from William Henry Harrison presidential campaign, $4500 at auction; Liverpool pitcher "The Betsy," ht. 10", $3700 at auction; 15-star Liverpool pitcher, ht. 9", $1200 at auction. — Photos courtesy of Northeast Auctions.

Head Vases

Head vases are figural vases most often depicting women and young girls. They were popular in the 1950s and '60s. Ladies with thick eyelashes, long gloves, dangle earrings and elaborate hats capture an exaggerated 1950s' look. Although the U.S. manufactured some vases, Japan produced the majority. Identification is difficult because many were unmarked or had only paper labels.

When handling a head vase be careful not to harm the label, the finish or delicate details such as jewelry. Beware of cracks and chips that decrease value. Watch out for reproductions or new head vases. Interest in head vases has intensified in the last five years and prices have risen accordingly. For further reading see *Head Vases*, Kathleen Cole, Collector Books, Paducah, KY, 1989 and *The Official Price Guide to Pottery and Porcelain*, Harvey Duke, House of Collectibles, Random House, New York, 1995.

Left to right: Woman, black glove and lashes, mkd. "C3282B" Napco, $50-$70; woman, brown gloves and eyelashes, mkd. "4228" Lefton, $75-$95; woman in black lace, dangle pearl earrings, Enesco Imports, $50-$70. — Photo courtesy of George Kerrigan Photography. Items courtesy of Pauline Alberta.

	LOW	HIGH
Becky, Ceramic Arts Studio, mkd. H306, ht. 5.5"	$ 60	$ 90
Blackamoor in Turban, Royal Copley, ht. 8.5"	60	90
Bonnie, Ceramic Arts Studio, ht. 7"	90	110
Clown, w/ patched hat, bow tie, Relpo, ht. 5.5"	40	60
Dutch Girl, w/ white hat, hand below chin, Inarco, ht. 5.5"	40	50
Girl, in bonnet, holding bouquet, w/ plaid side bow, Relpo, ht. 5.5"	50	70
Girl, in wide-brimmed hat, wall pocket, Royal Copley, ht. 8"	25	35
Girl, w/ closed eyes, applied eyelashes, hat and cutout bangs, Napco, ht. 6"	35	45
Girl, applied flowers in hair, w/ umbrella, mkd. CN, ht. 5"	28	32
Lotus, large Chinese woman, Ceramic Arts Studio, ht. 8"	100	130
Madonna, in blue and white, praying, Royal Windsor, ht. 8"	25	35
Manchu, Chinese man, Ceramic Arts Studio, ht. 7.5"	100	120
Mei Ling, Chinese woman, Ceramic Arts Studio, ht. 5"	80	100
Svea, girl w/ pigtail, Ceramic Arts Studio, ht. 6"	70	90
Sven, boy in hat, Ceramic Arts Studio, ht. 6.5"	70	90
Woman, in black lace, black eyelashes, dangle pearl earrings, Enesco Imports, ht. 5.5"	50	70

Woman, in green hat, pearl necklace, dangle earrings, hand raised, mkd. Napco
   C3343C, 1958, ht. 4.5" .... $ 35 $ 45
Woman, in yellow, wall pocket, roses at bodice and sun bonnet, high lustre finish,
   ht. 6" 30   40
Woman, w/ closed eyes, painted lashes, honey blond hair, turquoise blouse,
   molded flower, ht. 6" 25   35
Woman, in green, w/ gold accents, hat, and lashes, ht. 4" 15   20
Woman, w/ turban and pearl necklace, Napco, ht. 5" 30   35
Woman, black glove and lashes, pearl necklace, mkd. C3282B Napco, 1956,
   ht. 5" 50   70
Woman, black hair, applied black lashes, molded hood, Inarco, ht. 6" 40   60
Woman, brown gloves and eyelashes, mkd. 4228 Lefton, ht. 6" 75   95
Woman, brown hair, pearl earrings, necklace and brooch, ht. 7.5" 45   55
Woman, closed eyes, green and gold, applied bow and flowers in hat, ht. 4.5" 20   25
Woman, in blue, molded flower in hair, ht. 6" 20   30
Woman, small, closed eyes, painted lashes, blond hair, blue blouse, flower in
   hair, ht. 4" 20   25
Woman, wall pocket, lashes, black hair, high lustre, wide-brim green hat, ht. 7" ... 20   30

Hotel and Restaurant China

China and silver patterns, with unique and prominently displayed names and logos, have been in frequent use since the late 19th century by restaurant, lodging and entertainment businesses to help distinguish their operations by creating favorable customer impressions. China items are often styled in a way nostalgically evoking a particular era or region, and range from simply designed and effective advertising, to multi-colored and highly sophisticated decorative pieces. Often, these pieces are among the only surviving artifacts of once legendary places, such as the Astor Hotel, Chicago's Blackstone Hotel (home of the original "smoke filled room" of political image fame), or of earlier eras of modern operations, like the Pennsylvania Hotel. Some of the most sought-after designs include figures of people, animals, buildings and monuments. Some people collect all china and silver pieces from a particular establishment, city or region; some, the same type of piece from many businesses (e.g. teapots, celery trays), by manufacturer (e.g. Buffalo), or by pictorial subject (Indians). While sturdily made for constant use, condition is important to the value of an object, especially if it is damaged by chips, cracks, deeper dents or heavy wear. Our consultants for this area are Christopher Wolfe and Scott Townsend of Townsend, Wolfe & Company, they are listed in the back of this book.

	LOW	AVG.	HIGH
Ashtray, Horn & Hardart Automat, top and back marked, thistle border, c. 1935	$ 60	$ 75	$ 85
Ashtray, "Luchows Restaurant-Since 1882," 6" beer stein design, pottery	45	65	75
Ashtray and Match Holder, Hotel Dennis, Atlantic City	25	35	40
Ashtray and Match Holder, Copley Plaza Hotel, Boston, silver plate, c. 1920	20	28	35
Bouillon Cup, The William Foor Hotels, double handled, china, 1920s-30s	12	17	20
Bread Plate, Desert Inn, Las Vegas, 5.5", c. 1960	10	15	18
Bud Vase, Bellevue Stratford Hotel, Philadelphia, ht. 4.5", china, gold crest	20	25	28
Butter Pat, LaSalle Hotel, Chicago, silver plate, sq., c. 1925	5	10	18
Carafe, water, Palmer House, Chicago, glass w/ silver plate frame, ht. 9.5"	85	100	125
Celery Tray, Hotel Astor, New York, china, thistle border, c. 1925	25	35	40
Celery Tray, Oriental Cafe, Detroit, china, Chinese room scene, c. 1920	60	70	85
Child's Dinner Plate, Holiday Inn, back marked only, c. 1962	20	28	35
Coffee Mug, Dunkin Donuts, pink side logo, 1970s	8	12	15
Coffee Pot, Hotel Sherman, Chicago, silver plate, c. 1910	60	70	85
Coffee Pot, Hotels Statler, silver plate, Gorham, side and bottom marked, 1917	40	45	60
Compote, ftd., Hotel Lennox, New York, dia. 4.5", c. 1925	35	40	45
Cordial, stemmed, Plaza Hotel, New York, 5.5", etched crest, 1910-20	25	30	35
Creamer, Gimbel Bros Tea Room, New York, 6 oz., silver plate	30	38	45
Creamer, Holiday Inn, ind. size, older sign logo, china, c. 1965	12	18	25
Creamer, Lindy Bros, Coney Island, silver plate, 1910s-20s	45	55	60
Creamer, Queen Hotel, Halifax, N.S., ind. size, c. 1930	12	18	25
Cup and Saucer, The Biltmore, Los Angeles, c. 1940	15	22	27
Cup and Saucer, Toddle House, side and top marked, 1964	15	20	28
Demitasse Cup and Saucer, Astor Hotel, New York, c. 1925	20	25	30
Demitasse Cup and Saucer, Fairmont Hotel, Shenango, c. 1970	15	20	25

	LOW	AVG.	HIGH
Desert Dish, John Ringling Hotel, silver plate, double handled, c. 1930	$ 35	$ 40	$ 50
Dinner Plate, Battle Creek Sanitarium, green, red and gold border, 9.75", c. 1925	45	50	60
Dinner Plate, Columbia Hotel, Kalamazoo, Michigan, 10", c. 1940	20	30	40
Dinner Plate, Everglades Hotel, Miami, 9", c. 1945	15	20	25
Dinner Plate, Harrison Orange Drink distinctive logo, 10" 1920s-30s	70	85	110
Dinner Plate, Hotel Traymore, Atlantic City, 9", c. 1940	25	30	35
Dinner Plate, Liggetts Drug Store, "Indian Tree" pattern, 9", 1940s-50s	15	18	22
Dinner Plate, St. Francis Hotel, San Francisco, 9.5", c. 1945	25	30	40
Dinner Plate, divided, Howard Johnson's, orange Pie Man logo, 1960s-70s	17	28	35
Dresser Plate, Statler Hotel, 1935-40	35	40	50
Fork, dinner, Pennsylvania Hotel, New York, top and bottom marked	10	13	16
Ice Cream Shell, La Concha Hotel, Key West, wave and palm tree border, 1920s	35	45	60
Luncheon Plate, The Blackstone Hotel, Chicago, Buffalo, 1925	40	45	55
Mustard Pot, w/ lid, Horn & Hardart Automat, ht. 3.25", back marked, 1940s	40	50	60
Mustard Pot, w/ lid, same border design as above but without H&H back mark	8	15	20
Mustard Pot, w/ lid, Stevens Hotel, Chicago, 1940s-50s	10	13	18
Nut Dish, Hotel Peabody, Memphis, china, c. 1950	10	14	20
Oval Platter, Howard Johnson's traveling scenes and compass full border, 1950s	14	18	25
Pedestal Grape Holder, Hotel Pennsylvania, silver plate w/ pierced sides, 1920s	25	30	35
Salad Bowl, double, United Hotels Co., c. 1940	20	25	30
Salad Plate, Mayflower Hotel, Washington D.C., Buffalo, c. 1925	15	20	25
Sauce Boat, Hilton Hotels, china, c. 1945	12	15	20
Service Plate, "Sarah Siddons," Ambassador East Hotel, Chicago, Syracuse	80	95	110
Shot Glass, double, Hotel Stuyvesant, Buffalo, N.Y.	12	18	25
Soup Plate, Astor Hotel, New York, c. 1925	35	45	55
Souvenir Plate, John Wanamaker, 50 year (Philadelphia) Jubilee, 4.375", 1911	45	55	70
Spoon, Soup, Howard Johnson's, Pie Man logo, top marked	9	12	18
Sugar Bowl, without lid, Howard Johnson's, 1960s	20	28	35
Teapot, Hotel St. Francis, San Francisco, silver plate, c. 1920	40	45	55
Teaspoon, "Ellis Island Commissary," silver plate, 1910s-20s	13	20	25

Left to right: Dresser plate, Statler Hotel, 9", 35-$50; soup plate, Astor Hotel, 9", $35-$55. —Photo courtesy of Townsend, Wolfe & Company.

Planters

Are planters the final frontier in figural ceramic collecting? Planter collectors think so, but something new is always being discovered. Collectors boast that planters are the perfect size; they demand less shelf space than cookie jars and display better than the smaller salt and pepper shakers. Shawnee, McCoy, and other firms that produced cookie jars and salt and pepper shakers made many planters. So far, planters don't enjoy the widespread collecting base of cookie jars and salt and pepper shakers. Perhaps people are deterred by the clumps of dirt and flora that cling to many planters. Beneath all that is often a sparkling gem. Be cautious, however; cracks, chips, and dull finishes are also found under the grime.

We listed style numbers of the various pieces and the manufacturer when known, and "Japan" under company name for items so identified. Shawnee often marked pieces with "USA," sometimes with a style number.

This attribution is not foolproof because other firms also used the "USA" mark. Many planters had a paper label or are unmarked, so do your homework. We recommend *The Official Price Guide to Pottery and Porcelain*, Harvey Duke, House of Collectibles, Random House, NY, 1995; *Shawnee Pottery*, Jim and Bev Mangus, Collector Books, Paducah, KY, 1995; *McCoy Pottery*, Sharon and Bob Huxford, Collector Books, Paducah, KY, 1991; and *Royal Haeger*, Lee Garmon and Doris Frizzell, Collector Books, Paducah, KY, 1989.

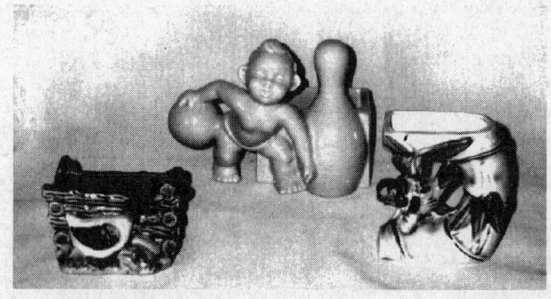

Above: Bowling boy, blue, Royal Haeger, $25-$35; bird on C-shaped bamboo, $7-$9; duck and logs, Occupied Japan, $15-$18

Right: Turtle planter, green, McCoy, $30-$40; turtle sprinkler, green, McCoy, $35-$45.

	LOW	HIGH
Bambi, ht. 5.5"	45	65
Basket, green leaf, red berry, ht. 9", McCoy	30	40
Basket, w/ bird on handle, Camark	30	35
Bed, canopy style, 734, len. 8", Shawnee	75	95
Bird and Flower, raised base, ht. 4"	15	20
Bird in Flight, w/ flowers, ht. 5"	10	15
Bird on Basket, w/ flowers, ht. 6", Shawnee	10	15
Bird on C-shaped Bamboo, ht. 5.25"	7	9
Bird on Log, on metal stand, ht. 7"	22	28
Birds on Double Branches, ht. 5.25"	8	10
Boot, "tooled" design, ht. 6.5", Shawnee	10	15
Bow, w/ gold highlights, wall pocket, 534, ht. 3.5", Shawnee	20	25
Bowling Boy, blue, ht. 6", Royal Haeger	25	35
Boy at Stump, 533, Shawnee	9	14
Bug, w/ metal feet, ht. 3"	15	20
Burro, 673, ht. 4.5", Abingdon	30	35
Burro, sleeping man in sombrero , ht. 5.75"	30	40
Caboose, 553, Shawnee	30	40
Calypso Band, 3 piece, ht. 7.5", Napco	70	100
Cat Playing Sax, 729, Shawnee	32	52
Cat, black, painted eyes, len. 15"	30	40
Chick, w/ cart, 720, Shawnee	15	20
Chick, w/ egg, 730, ht. 3.5", Shawnee	15	20
Chinese Figures Carrying Basket, 537, Shawnee	12	18
Chinese Girl, ht. 7", Royal Copley	25	35
Chinese Man, w/ basket and umbrella, 617, ht. 4.5", Shawnee	15	20
Circus Wagon, Shawnee	30	35
Coach, ht. 4.5", Germany	8	10
Covered Wagon, small, 617, ht. 3.5", Shawnee	20	26
Doe and Fawn, ht. 7", McCoy	32	38
Dog Cart, ht. 5", McCoy	25	30
Dog in Cup, wall pocket, ht. 5"	12	15
Donkey, w/ basket, 722, ht. 5.5", Shawnee	12	15
Donkey, 669, ht. 7.5", Abingdon	37	47
Double Dog Profile, ht. 5"	15	20
Drum and Dog, ht. 3"	18	24
Duck and Logs, ht. 3", Occupied Japan	15	18
Dutch Boy and Girl, ht. 6.5"	20	30
Dutch Boy at Wall, ht. 5.5"	12	14
Dutch Girl and Oxcart, ht. 3.5", Japan	12	18
Dutch Shoe, len. 5", Abingdon	30	50
Elephant, Shawnee, ht 6"	22	27
Elephant, small, 759, Shawnee	8	10
Elephant and Leaf, 501, Shawnee	50	70
Fawn, 645, ht. 6.5", Morton	10	15
Fawn, 672, ht. 5", Abingdon	20	30
Fish, black bass, ht. 4.5"	20	30
Fish, green and yellow, wall pocket, ht. 8"	30	50
Fish in Swirling Waves, green, ht. 7.5"	18	24
Flamenco Dancers, ht. 9"	30	40
Flamingo and Foliage, ht. 9.5"	30	40

	LOW	HIGH
Frog and Lilly Pad, ht. 3.75"	$ 9	$ 12
Gazelle, large, len. 17", Royal Haeger	90	130
Girl and Basket, 534, Shawnee	10	15
Gondolier, 657, len. 19.5", Royal Haeger	30	50
Horse, large, rearing, ht. 9.5"	25	35
Horses, racing, 883, len. 11", Royal Haeger	30	50
Jalopy, len. 7", Relpro	7	9
Jardiniere, diamond design, len. 7", McCoy	10	12
Jardiniere, green rocky rect., ht. 5.75", McCoy	7	9
Jardiniere, oblong, molded berry and leaf, len. 8", McCoy	12	18
Jardiniere, rect., pine cone feet, len. 8", McCoy	18	22
Lady, w/ donkey cart, ht. 5.5", Japan	15	20
Leopard, 760, Royal Haeger	25	35
Lovebirds on Pine Cone, ht. 4"	20	30
Madonna, blue, ht. 4.5", Royal Windsor	15	20
Madonna, white, large, 650, ht. 9", Royal Haeger	25	35
Mexican Boy, ht. 5.5", Royal Copley	30	40
Panther, maroon, rocky base, len. 9"	20	25
Pelican on Bamboo Log, len. 9", Japan	65	90
Penguin and Igloo, yellow, ht. 3.25"	9	12
Pheasant, black, gold highlights, len. 17"	20	30
Piano, 528, Shawnee	20	30
Pirate, ht. 3.5", Brush	25	35
Pixie, winged, 536, ht. 4", Shawnee	7	10
Plaid Cat, ht. 5.25", Japan	6	8
Poodle, w/ green square, ht. 7"	15	20
Poodle, yellow, whimsical, ht. 5"	12	16
Pot and Saucer, button-tufted design, ht. 3.5", McCoy	9	14
Rickshaw and Driver, len. 5", Shawnee	7	9
Rabbit, ht. 7"	10	14
Rooster, 501, Camark	18	22
Santa and Chimney, ht. 7", Morton	20	25
Shoe and Pup, Shawnee	9	12
Swan, black, ht. 5.5"	8	12
Swan, blue w/ gold floral dec., ht. 6"	15	20
Three Pigs, Shawnee	8	10
Top Hat, star spangled, ht. 3", Shawnee	7	9
Tragedy and Comedy Mask, on rect., ht. 3.5", McCullogh	10	12
Train Box Car, 552, Shawnee	20	30
Train Engine, 550, Shawnee	50	60
Train Set, 550, 551, 552 , 553, Shawnee	130	190
Train Tender, 551 , Shawnee	25	35
Turkey, ht. 5", Morton	10	15
Turtle, green, len. 7", McCoy	30	40
Turtle, green sprinkler, len. 9", McCoy	35	45
Violin, len. 17", Royal Haeger	25	35
Wagon Wheel and Cow Skull, ht. 8", McCoy	30	40
Wheelbarrow and Watering Can, ht. 3"	14	18
Wishing Well, ht. 6.5", McCoy	25	35
Wishing Well, Dutch Kids, ht. 5.5", Shawnee	25	35

Shakers

Salt and pepper shakers are on most dinner tables (very few of us use salt cellars). Although people obtain S & Ps to match table settings, we listed shakers that are considered novelty or figural shakers; some even advertise products. Collectors are drawn to the strange forms and bright colors. Many shakers match a more expensive cookie jar by the same firm such as Shawnee or Regal. Shakers draw collectors not only from the cookie jar field but from the fields of Black Americana, comic character, and advertising memorabilia. With so many shapes and themes, crossover collecting is nearly endless. Collectors talk about sets such as one piece (one container), nodders (which sit in a base and rock back and forth), nesters (which sit inside one another), or huggers (which fit together). (The Huggies in the listing refers specifically to the work of Ruth Van Telligen Bendel.) Sometimes a pair of salt and peppers aren't really a pair but two different forms that share a theme such as a cow jumping over the moon or a bowling ball and pin. Many times there are other pieces, such as a condiments jar, a tray, or bench, that are required for a complete set. Be alert to reproductions or copies of expensive shakers and missing pieces. Prices listed are for excellent condition examples-no chips, cracks, or flaking finish.

The shakers below usually range from 1" to 5" in height, so nearly everyone has room for two or three....hundred. Many more common shakers can be purchased for less than $10. For further reading we recommend *The Official Price Guide to Pottery and Porcelain*, by Harvey Duke, House of Collectibles, Random House, New York, 1995; *The Complete Salt and Pepper Shaker Book,* by Mike Schneider, Schiffer, Atglen, PA 1993; and *Salt and Pepper II*, by Helene Guarnaccia, Collector Books, Paducah, KY, 1989.

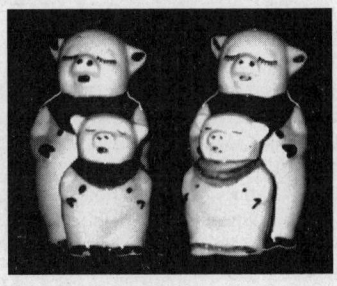

Above left: Goose that laid the golden egg, $15-$20; Shawnee pigs, 5.5", $70-$90; Shawnee pigs, 3.5", $35-$65. Below: One piece giraffe, $10-$15. — Items courtesy Cerise Foster.

	LOW	HIGH
Alice in Wonderland, Regal	$ 420	$ 620
Aunt Jemima, Uncle Moses, plastic, '50s, ht. 5.5"	24	32
Bert and Harry Piel, '50s, ht. 3.5"	37	47
Black Boy w/ Watermelon	65	85
Bo Peep and Sailor Boy, ht. 3.25", Shawnee	25	35
Bowling Ball, pin and tray, wooden	10	12
Campbell Kids, plastic, '50s, ht. 4.5"	32	42
Cats, black, wooden, leather ears	6	9
Chanticleers, no gold, small, ht. 3", Shawnee	25	35
Chef and Jemima, Brayton	160	210
Colonel and Mrs. Sanders, plastic, '60s, ht. 4"	65	85
Cow Jumps Over the Moon, len. 5"	28	36
Dachshund, long body, one piece, len. 10", Japan	10	15
Ducks, ht. 3", Shawnee	20	30
Dutch Kids, no gold, ht. 5", Shawnee	40	50
Dutch Shoes, Frankoma	20	30
Elephant, Frankoma	60	70
Elsie and Elmer, ceramic, '50s, ht. 4"	65	85
Fifi and Fido, Ken-L Ration Dogs, plastic, '60s, h. 3.5"	25	35
Fish, in base, 3 piece nodder	50	70
Flamingos, one head up, one down	12	18
Flower Pots, no gold, ht. 3.25", Shawnee	18	22
Gingham Dog and Calico Cat, Brayton	35	55
Giraffe, long body, one piece, len. 10", Japan	10	15
Handy Flame, ceramic, '50s, ht. 4"	18	25
Hedge Hog Chefs	12	18
Huggies, Bunny, brown and black, Van Tellingen, Regal	25	35
Huggies, Love Bug, small, Van Tellingen, Regal	70	110
Huggies, Mermaid/Sailor, unpntd., Van Tellingen, Regal	90	140
Huggies, Bear, mkd. Van Tellingen, Regal	20	30
Huggies, Boy/Dog, Van Tellingen, Regal	70	90
Huggies, Duck, Van Tellingen, Regal	30	50
Huggies, Dutch Boy/Girl, Van Tellingen, Regal	35	45
Huggies, Love Bug, large, Van Tellingen, Regal	200	300
Huggies, Mary/Lamb, Van Tellingen, Regal	40	60
Humpty Dumpty, Regal	150	200
Humpty Dumpty Before the Fall, plastic	10	15
Ice Cream Cones, glass and tin, h. 4", Enesco Imports	20	30
Jack and Jill, ht. 5", Shawnee	40	60
Jug, Frankoma	14	18
Magic Chef, ceramic, '50s, ht. 5"	55	75
Magic Chef, plastic, '50s, ht. 5"	35	45
Milk Bottles, Sealtest	25	35
Milk Cans, ht. 3.25", Shawnee	18	24
Monkeys in Tree, ht. 4.5", Dee Bee Imports	6	8
Mount Rushmore	6	9
Mr. and Mrs. Mushroomhead, ht. 6"	8	12
Mr. and Mrs. Snowman, formal attire	10	12
Mr. Peanut, single color, plastic, '50s, ht. 4"	18	22
Mr. Peanut, yellow w/ black top hat	30	40
Mugsey, small no gold, ht. 3", Shawnee	35	55

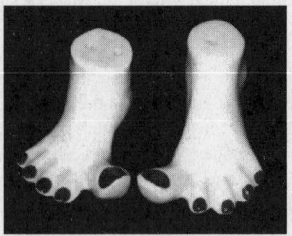

Left to right: Monks by Goebel, $10-$12; feet, $6-$9.
— Items courtesy Cerise Foster.

Left: Plastic croquet
mallet S & P with steak
markers, with original
box, $18-$22; without
box, $12-$15 . — Item
courtesy Jim Glaab's
Collector's Showcase.

Right: Plastic soda fountain
sodas, $9-$12. — Item
courtesy of Cerise Foster.

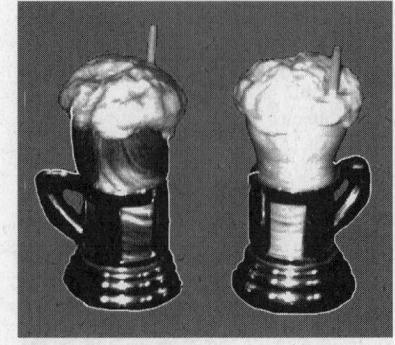

Left to right: Nesting chickens, $12-$16; swinging monkeys, Dee Bee Imports, Japan, $6-$8.

	LOW	HIGH
Native Children on Carrots	$ 80	$ 120
Niagra Falls, *Maid of the Mist* boat, 3 piece nester	100	150
Nipper and Phonograph, plastic, '50s, ht. 3"	25	35
Old Woman Who Lives in a Shoe, ht. 4"	15	20
Old Salt and Pepper, his wife, Purinton	100	150
Owls, no gold, ht. 3.25", Shawnee	20	30
Peek-a-Boo, small, Regal	200	300
Peek-a-Boo, large, Regal	400	500
Pigs, Brayton	35	45
President Kennedy in Rocking Chair	45	55
Puss-n-Boots, no gold, ht. 3.25", Shawnee	15	25
"S" and "P" letters, Camark	10	15
7-Up Bottles, glass, '50s	10	12
Skunks, w/ hats	9	12
Smiley Pigs, blue or red scarves, ht. 5.5", Shawnee	70	90
Smiley Pigs, ht. 3.5", Shawnee	35	65
Smoky the Bear, ceramic, '60s, ht. 4"	22	302
Spot, tall tan and white dogs	8	12
Statue of Liberty, Empire State Building on tray	20	30
Steam Irons, plastic	8	12
Sword Fish, ht. 4.5", Japan	6	8
Tappan Chefs, ceramic, '60s, ht. 4"	22	32
Teepee, Frankoma	25	35
Toaster, w/ removable toast, plastic, ht. 2.5"	10	15
Trylon and Perisphere, plastic	70	90
TV Set, plastic	15	20
Tweedle Dee and Tweedle Dum, Regal	600	800
Willie and Millie Penguin, plastic, '50s, ht. 3"	10	15

Steins

Europeans have produced steins since the 13th century. Collections of early steins can be extremely valuable. Steins from the 19th and 20th centuries, however, are widely available. Collectors of modern steins prize those produced by the Villeroy & Bock Company of Mettlach, Germany. They also seek those manufactured by Merkelbach & Wick, and Simon Peter Gerz. For further information see *The Mettlach Book*, by Gary Kirsner, Glentiques, Ltd., Coral Springs, FL.

Mettlach steins, left to right, #1154, $600-$900, #2373, $500-$700, #2027, $600-$900. — Photo courtesy of Northeast Auctions.

	LOW	AVG.	HIGH
Lithophane, clown, .5 liter	$ 460	$ 520	$ 570
Lithophane, German scene, 6.5"	130	140	150
Mettlach, #1675, half liter stein depicting Heidelberg	400	500	600
Mettlach, #1772, pitcher Wedgwood style	800	900	1000
Mettlach, #1786, half liter w/ dragon	430	550	670
Mettlach, # 1934, soldiers, inlaid lid	750	875	1000
Mettlach, # 2002, Munich, .5 liter	460	500	540
Mettlach, #2036, half liter owl stein	460	500	540
Mettlach, #2040, pitcher stein, drinking German soldiers	2000	2200	2400
Mettlach, # 2136, Brewmaster, .5 liter	400	450	500
Mettlach, # 2181, Pug, .5 liter	400	450	500
Mettlach, # 2277. inlaid top, castle and clock tower	490	550	610
Mettlach, # 2333, dancing gnomes, pewter top	160	170	180
Mettlach, #2718, one liter, David and Goliath	1600	1800	2000
Mettlach, #2765, turret top stein	900	1000	1100
Mettlach, #2893, pitcher w/ German coats of arms	230	300	370
Mettlach, #3092, one liter, barrel man stein w/ inlaid lid	750	850	950
Monk, Gesetzlicht, .5 liter	230	250	270
Musterschutz Crying Radish, .5 liter	520	580	640
Musterschutz Happy Turnip, .5 liter	560	600	650
Musterschutz Singing Pig, .5 liter	390	440	480
Muskau Stoneware Stein, baluster shape marked H.D.H. 1671	1800	2000	2200
Pottery, Marzi Remi, tavern scene	40	50	60
Puss in Boots, 6.5"	60	70	80
Regimental, 18th Infantry, 1 liter	390	430	470
Regimental Stein, Strassburg, c. 1912	200	250	300

Stoneware Crocks

Although specimens date back to 1641, most thick earthenware crocks were made in the 19th century; those with an interior glaze appeared after 1900. With the introduction of the automatic glassblowing machine in 1903, the use of pottery crocks declined.

Although most crocks sell for under $1000, fine examples of 19th-entury potting with superior blue painted designs bring high prices, as those listed below.

Above: Animal and figure decorated crocks are generally more valuable than those with abstract designs.

Left: reproduction Early American crock, 7", $10-$20.

	AUCTION	RETAIL Low	High
Cowden & Wilcox, Harrisburg, PA, 3 gallon crock, flower design ...	$ 300	$ 530	$ 830
Hamilton & Jones, Greensboro, PA, 2 gallon crock, "prime butter" ..	1025	1790	2820
James Hamilton & Co., Greensboro, PA, 10 gallon crock, stencil dec.	600	1050	1650
Mason & Russel, Cortland, 4 gallon crock, ovoid shape, blue flower design	350	610	960
W. Roberts, Binghamton, NY, 3 gallon crock, spotted bird design	1050	1840	2900
E. & L.P. Norton, Bennington, VT, 4 gallon jug, feather design	325	570	900
N.A. White & Son, Utica, NY, 3 gallon crock, blue floral design	225	390	620
R.T. Williams, New Geneva, PA, 10 gallon crock, whimsical dec.	800	1400	2200
West Troy New York Pottery, 2 gallon jug, abstract design	225	390	620

Tiles

	LOW	AVG.	HIGH
American and Caustic Tiling Co., child w/ dog, molded, 6" sq.	$ 275	$ 440	$ 650
American and Caustic Tiling Co., winter scene, molded, 12" x 18"	1950	3000	4750
Isaac Broome (artist), molded classical female profile, signed, 13" x 10"	1250	2000	3000
William H. Grueby, stylized floral design, 4" sq.	35	60	100
Minton and Company/Patent/Stoke Upon Trent, stylized flower, 6" sq.	55	90	130
Minton and Co./Patent/Stoke Upon Trent, encaustic tile dec. w/ birds, 6" sq.	55	90	130
John B. Owens, Zanesville, dec. in cuerda seca depicting elf, 6" sq.	1650	2600	4000
C. Pardee Works/M.C.M., polychrome fountain, 4.25" sq.	575	920	1400
Rookwood Faience, classical figures, molded, 12" sq.	875	1400	2000
Rookwood Faience, cuenca dec. depicting a woman in garden, 12" sq.	2600	4160	6000
Rookwood Faience, polychrome ship, dec., from the Fort Pitt Hotel in Pittsburgh, 16.5" dia.	2900	4500	7000
JosiahWedgwood and Sons/Etruria, Shakespeare topics, transfer dec., 6" sq.	125	200	310

Polychrome tile labeled "Minton & Co., patent, Stoke upon Trent," 8" x 8", $30-$50.

TV Lamps

TV lamps have been described as outrageous forms for subtle lighting. We define TV lamps as those lamps and lamp/planter or lamp/clock combinations that produce an indirect light either shaded by its position within its figural structure or by a screen shade or an inset shade. These lamps serve in many capacities but are now categorized as TV lamps. The need for TV lamps arose from the fear that flickering TV images could harm eyesight if not offset by another source of light. The lamps also allowed 1950s homemakers a means to lessen the intrusiveness of the electronic box. In the early 1950s manufacturers such as Royal Haeger often revamped vases and figural pieces based on pre-war designs. It is not uncommon to see a vase produced in the late 1930s fitted as a lamp in the 1950s (collectors avoid home conversions). As the fifties progressed makers integrated bold and sometimes bizarre themes of fashion and design into TV lamps. They produced lights in the shape of pink poodles, Siamese cats, and flying ducks.

Avoid chipped or cracked examples, especially when these defects detract from the lamp's visual appeal. When using a lamp make sure it is wired properly. One common mistake is using a higher wattage bulb than the lamp's specification. This causes the singe marks sometimes seen on shade screens and cracks around the lighting fixtures of many lamps. Low-wattage low-heat bulbs are recommended. For further reading we recommend *Turned On*, Leyland and Crystal Payton, Abbeville Press, NY, 1989.

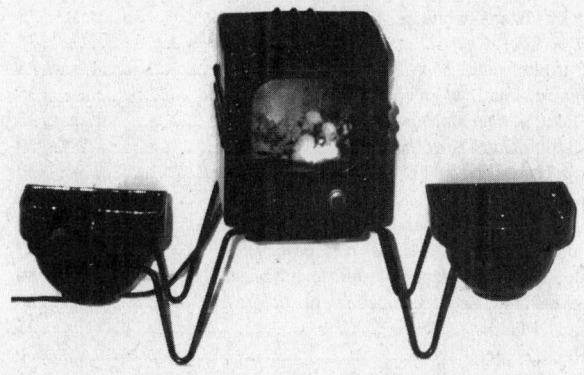

Unusual Television form lamp with inset floral screen flanked by planters, $100-$150.

	LOW	HIGH
Antelope and Leaf, brown, green highlights, Royal Haeger, 11" x 17"	$ 30	$ 40
Black King, in maroon and gold (head vase style)	80	100
Blacksmith at Forge, plaster	25	35
Blue Birds, double, plaster tray, Lane, 11" x 13"	50	75
Cabin Cruiser, metal sails, light-up portholes, 14" x 17"	60	80
Carp, pink, gold accents, 6.5" x 13"	25	35
Cats, Siamese, cutout eyes, mkd. Kron, Texans Inc., ht. 13"	50	70
Chinese Figures, pr. of lamps w/ pierced gold fixtures, ht. 11"	90	130
Chinoiserie Double Planter, green, brass surround, 7.5" x 11"	18	24

	LOW	HIGH
Comedy and Tragedy Mask "Tri-Wonder Lamp," Royal Haeger, ht. 8"	$ 80	$ 100
Cougars, double, brown and cream, 8" x 11"	30	40
Cowboy Horse, w/ red fiberglass conical shade, 11" x 11"	25	35
Criss-Cross Sides, w/ green shade insert, 7" x 12.5"	60	90
Dancer, leaping, gold and black plaster, 13" x 15"	40	60
Deer, porcelain, w/ plaster tray, 13" x 13.5"	50	70
Deer, small running, green, w/ leaf and vine, 5" x 10"	15	20
Doves, white and gold, Royal Fleet Company	20	30
Farm Scene, vinyl, cylindrical, pierced gold metal base, ht. 11.5"	15	20
Fawn, white, pink planter, Electrolite, ht. 8"	25	35
Fish, double, gray and maroon	50	70
Flower in Basket, green, ht. 9"	25	35
Galleon Clock/Lamp, wooden, Gilbrator Precision, 18" x 13"	30	45
Galleon, multi-color, 9.5" x 12"	45	55
Gazelle, leaping, black, green and cream, Royal Haeger, 10" x 12"	45	65
Gazelle, leaping, black, swirling base, 11" x 16"	45	65
Gazelles, leaping twin, planter, swirl plume base, 11" x 14"	35	65
Horse, porcelain, on plaster rocky bluff base, Lane, 11" x 13.5"	30	40
Horse, small, black, 5.5" x 10.5"	20	30
Horse Head Bust, brown, ht. 14.5"	25	35
Horse Head, knight style, gray, cutout eyes, ht. 14"	45	55
Horse on Rocky Plateau, white, ht. 13"	35	45
Leaf Form, 7" x 12"	25	35
Leaf, green, "triple frond," 5" x 13.5"	25	35
Leopard in Forest, small, w/ green screen, ht. 9"	35	45
Mallard in Flight, planter surround, 11.5" x 14.5"	35	50
Mallard in Flight, planter surround, small, 11" x 10"	30	45
Mare and Colt, brown, 8.5" x 11"	30	40
Mare and Colt, gray, 9.5" x 10"	35	45
Mermaid, w/ deep sea background, 7.5" x 9.5"	100	150
Mountain Lion, crouching, "chiseled" rock base, 7.5" x 18"	45	65
Nude, reclining accordion player, plaster, screen back, 9" x 14"	80	100
Owl, cutout eyes, mkd. Kron, Texans Inc., ht. 12"	80	100
Owl, whimsical, Maddux	25	35
Panther on Rock, beige, 9" x 9"	30	40
Panther on Rock, brown and cream, 8.5" x 9"	35	45
Panther, black planter, len. 22"	25	45
Panther, black w/ rhinestone eyes, len. 22"	25	45
Panther, brown planter, len. 22"	25	45
Panther, cut outeyes, lime green, Royal Haeger, len. 20"	35	50
Panther, leaf and log base, gray base, 9" x 15"	30	50
Panther, leaf and log base, pink and gray base, 9" x 15"	45	55
Panther, plaster w/ green screen background, 8.5" x 17"	45	65
Panther, small, black w/ gold accents, len. 15"	25	30
Panther, small, green, 5" x 11"	20	30
Panther, small, pink, 6" x 9"	25	35
Panther, white screen, oval base, Royal Haeger	40	60
Pierced Metal, black, inner shade & wire legs, ht. 13"	12	18
Plastic Surround Landscape, ht. 10"	12	18
Poodles, double pink, 10" x 13	100	150
Rooster, crowing, maroon, ht. 10"	24	32

Above left to right: Galleon, $40-$50; ship on green wave base, $30-$40. Below left to right: Mermaid, deep sea screen background $90-$140; nude with accordion, plaster, $70-$90.

 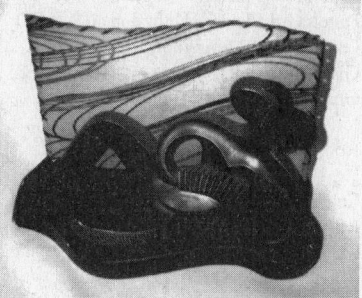

	LOW	HIGH
Sailboat Planter, small, green, ht. 8.5"	$ 15	$ 25
Sailing Ship, gray waves base, ht. 11"	30	40
Sampan, w/ Asian couple, green, gold highlights, 6" x 16"	35	45
Shell, conch, pink w/ white & gold, Premco, ht. 11"	35	55
Ship, green stylized wave base, 10" x 11"	30	40
Stag, leaping, green, 11.5" x 10.5	20	30
Stallion, running, black, yellow, & white highlights, 11" x 15"	40	60
Swan, small, pink w/ plastic rose, ht. 10"	10	15
Swan, white, blue water base, Maddux, ht. 11"	20	30
Tree Trunk, stylized, brown, green, & white, ht. 10"	18	22
Tropical Leaves, Lane, 13.5" x 10.5"	50	70
TV, stylized, metal, porthole w/ scene, 7" x 11"	30	40
Vase, gold & green vine & leaves, signed Cell	25	35
Wolfhounds, Dashing, green, 11.5" x 10.5"	35	45

Wall Pockets

	LOW	AVG.	HIGH
Acanthus Bracket, Abingdon, 7", #589	$ 49	$ 61	$ 73
Acanthus Bracket, Abingdon, 8.75", #649	41	53	64
Acanthus Wall Vase, Abingdon, 8.75", #648	46	55	64
Basketweave, Catalina, 9.5"	214	226	238
Birdhouse, Shawnee, #830	15	18	20
Book, Abingdon, 6.5", #676	55	68	80
Bow, Shawnee	8	10	12
Butterfly, Abingdon, 8.5", #601	32	40	47
Calla Lily, Abingdon, 9", #586	32	37	41
Camellia, Hull #125, 8.5"	245	270	295
Carriage Lamp, Abingdon, 10", #711	53	62	70
Cherub, Abingdon, 7.5", #587	60	69	78
Cook Book, Abingdon, #676	56	62	68
Cup and Saucer, Hull, Bow-Knot, #B24	98	112	125
Cup and Saucer, Hull, Sunglow, #80	38	41	43
Daisy, Abingdon, 7.75", #379	50	61	71
Dutch Boy Planter, Abingdon, 10", #489	113	112	110
Dutch Girl Planter, Abingdon, 10", #490	97	112	127
Female Mask, Abingdon, 7.5", #376F	114	121	128
Girl, w/rag doll, Shawnee, #810	20	22	24
Grape Vine, Royal Haeger, #745	20	22	23
Ionic, Abingdon, 9", #457	56	64	71
Iron, Hull, Sunglow	39	48	56
Ivy Basket, Abingdon, 7", #590	99	98	97
Leaf, Abingdon, #724	49	63	76
Little Jack Horner, Shawnee, #585	20	22	24
Male Mask, Abingdon, 7.5", #376M	130	130	130
Mantel Clock, Shawnee, #530	18	20	22
Match Box, Abingdon, 5.5", #675	35	45	54
Metlox Potteries	43	48	53
Morning Glory, Abingdon, 7.5", #377	18	23	28
Morning Glory, Abingdon, double, 6.5", #375	28	34	40
Pitcher, Hull, Bow-Knot #B26	92	101	110
Pitcher, Hull, Sunglow #81	29	35	40
Poppy, Hull, #609, 9"	246	260	273
Purinton Pottery	31	33	35
Rocking Horse, Royal Haeger, #724	18	20	22
Rosecraft Vintage, brown w/ fruit and grapevines, Roseville	90	120	150
Rosella, Hull, #R10	58	65	71
Scoop, w/embossed flowers, Camark, #N45	17	21	24
Shell, Abingdon, 7", #508	40	48	55
Telephone, Shawnee, #529	22	25	28
Whisk Broom, Hull, Bow-Knot #B27	91	103	115
Whisk Broom, Hull, Sunglow, #82	33	38	42
Woodland Glossy, Hull, 7.5"	47	53	58
Woodland Matte, Hull, 7.5"	96	108	120

Printed Media

Bibles

Johann Gutenberg printed the first typeset Bible in 1455. Since then, the Bible has been reprinted more than any other book. Some collectors buy only rare Bibles of the 15th and 16th centuries. Others specialize in miniature Bibles (12mo, 24mo, or 32mo), or Bibles translated into exotic languages.

Almost everyone has an old family Bible, but most 19th-century examples are worth about $50; most 18th-century examples are worth around $100. However, there are many valuable Bibles. For an extensive listing of Bibles sold at auction consult *American Book Prices Current*, edited by Katherine and Daniel Leab, at American Book Prices Current, Box 1236, Washington, CT 06793.

	AUCTION	RETAIL Low	High
1540: Antwerp, A. Goinus, (Latin)	$ 230	$ 410	$ 500
1541: [Great Bible] London, E. Whitchurch, 6th ed., (Eng.) ..	2800	5000	6600
1549: London, T. Raynalde & W. Hyll, (Eng.)	1500	2700	3500
1550: [Great Bible ver.] London, E. Whytchurche, (Eng.)	1400	2500	3300
1553: Newe Test. of Our Lord Jesus, London, R. Jugge, (Eng.)	2800	5000	6600
1555: [Paris] R. Estienne, (Latin)	200	355	470
1558: Lyons, Guillaume Rouille, 16mo, (Latin)	175	300	400
1564: Catholische Bibell, Koln, Heirs of Quentel, (German)	750	1335	1800
1567: Antwerp, Plantin, (Latin)	400	710	950
1583: [Geneva ver.] London, C. Barker, (Eng.)	750	1300	1770
1585: [New Test.] London, Henricus Middletonus, (Latin)	110	200	250
1587: Venice, Hieronymus Polus, (Latin)	160	300	370
1592: London, Christopher Barker, (Eng.)	120	200	280
1595: [Bishops' Bible] London, Deputies of C. Barker, (Eng.) .	450	800	1000
1597: [Geneva ver.] London, Deputies of C. Barker, (Eng.)	450	800	1000
1600: [2d Ed. in Eng. of Douai New Test.] Antwerp, (Eng.)	275	500	650
1600: [Bishops' Bible] London, R. Barker, (Eng.)	500	900	1200
1600: [Geneva ver.] London, R. Barker, (Eng.)	375	650	900
1600: London, R. Barker, (Eng.)	300	535	700
1649: London, Companie of Stationers, (Eng.)	175	300	400
1650-51: The Holy Bible, London, (Eng.)	400	710	945
1653: [New Test.] London, John Field, 2 vols., 24mo, (Eng.) ...	625	1000	1475
1657: Cambr., John Field, 16mo, (Eng.)	100	170	230
1660: London, Henry Hills and John Field, (Eng.)	2000	3560	4700
1669: Sainte Bible, Amst., Elzevir., 4 pts. in 2 vols., (French) ..	200	350	470
1674: Cambr., J. Hayes, (Eng.)	120	200	280
1692: [Luther's ver.] Nuremberg, (German)	700	1200	1650
1696: New Test. of Our Lord Oxford Univ., 12mo, (Eng.)	130	230	3000
1700: Leipzig, (German)	80	140	200
1715: Oxford, John Baskett, (Eng.)	100	170	250
1716-17: ["Vinegar" Bible] Oxford, J. Baskett, 2 vols., (Eng.) ...	2000	3500	4700
1716: Edin., James Watson, 12mo, (Eng.)	100	170	250
1719: Edin., 12mo, (Eng.)	75	150	177
1736: Nuremberg, Endters, (German)	170	300	400
1748: Venice, 2 vols., (Latin)	150	267	355

	AUCTION	RETAIL	
		Low	High
1750-51: Oxford, (Eng.)	$ 200	$ 355	$ 470
1791: Dublin, 2 vols., (Eng.)	600	1000	1400
1791: The Holy Bible, Phila., W. Young, 2 vols., 12mo, (Eng.)	3400	6000	8000
1791: Trenton, Isaac Collins, (Eng.)	150	260	350
1792: NY, T. Allen, (Eng.)	275	500	640
1792: Self-Interpreting Bible, NY, Hodge and Campbell, (Eng.)	120	200	300
1794: New Hieroglyphical Bible for Children, Bost., W. Norman, 1st Amer. Ed., 18mo, (Eng.)	350	600	820
1795: Holy Bible Abridged, Bost., S. Hall, 32mo, (Eng.)	300	500	900
1796: Curious Hieroglyphick Bible for the Amusement of Youth, London, R. Bassam, 12mo, (Eng.)	160	280	375
1800: London, T. Macklin, 6 vols., (Eng.)	500	890	1100
1836: [New Test.] London, S. Bagster, (Eng.)	200	350	475
1837: Cambr., Pitt Press, 2 vols., (Eng.)	6000	10,000	14,000
1837: [New Test.] London, S. Bagster, (Eng.)	750	1335	1770
1846: The Illuminated Bible, NY, (Eng.)	200	355	475
1848: London, W. Pickering, trans. by J. Wycliffe, (Eng.)	400	710	900
1856: Genesi, Park Hill, OK, Mission Press, (Cherokee)	200	350	470
1856: Iu Otoshki, New Test., trans. into Ojibwa, NY, 8vo	120	200	280
1858: London, illus. by D. Roberts, (Eng.)	700	1200	1600
1866: Tours, illus. by G. Dore, 2 vols., (French)	130	200	300
1876: Hartford, trans. by J. E. Smith, (Eng.)	50	80	100
[1900]: London, Grolier Soc., 1 of 1000, 14 vols., (Eng.)	80	140	180
1910-11: London, Ballantyne Press, 1 of 750, 3 vols., (Eng.)	225	400	530
[1934-36]: New Test., London, illus. by E. Gill, 4 vols., (Eng.)	350	600	825
[1934]: Bost, R. H. Hinkley, 1 of 488, 14 vols., (Eng.)	200	350	470
1941: [New Test.], NJ, St. Anthony Guild, 1 of 1000, (Eng.)	120	210	280
1949: Cleveland, 1 of 975, designed by B. Rogers, (Eng.)	400	710	950
1956: Paris, Teriade, 1 of 275, illus. by Marc Chagall, 2 vols., (French)	30,000	55,000	75,000
1959: NY, Abradale Press, (Eng.)	70	125	165
1961: Paterson and NY, Pageant Books, 1 of 1000, 2 vols., facsimile of Gutenberg Bible, (Latin)	1500	2670	3500
1965: Cleveland, World Publishing Co., facsimile of 1st Ed. of King James ver., 1611, (Eng.)	340	600	800
1970: Jerusalem Bible, Garden City, illus. by S. Dali, (Eng.)	65	115	150
1974: Leaf from 1st Ed. of Coverdale Bible, 1535, San Francisco, Book Club of Calif., 1 of 425, 4to	200	355	470
1977-78: Munich, Idion Verlag, 1 of 895, 2 vols. plus Kommentar band, Facsimile of Gutenberg Bible, (Latin)	6000	11,000	14,750
1985: Paris, Les Editions des Incunables, 4 vols., w/ commentary, facsimile of Gutenberg Bible, (Latin)	1700	3000	4000

Books

Classic Books

Books were first printed around 1450, although handwritten books date back thousands of years. Many book collectors limit themselves to one or two favorite writers or a favorite subject, since the field of book collecting is vast. A collection is judged on quality rather than quantity. Books with water damage, broken bindings, or missing pages are usually worth almost nothing.

For an extensive listing of books sold at auction consult *American Book Prices Current*, edited by Katherine and Daniel Leab, at American Book Prices Current, Box 1236, Washington, CT 06793. For information on books traded at many flea markets, consult *The Official Price Guide to Old Books*, by Marie Tedford and Pat Goudey, House of Collectibles, Random House, NY.

Values quoted are for First Editions (F), Leather-bound copies (L), Limited Edition Club copies (LEC), Heritage Press copies (HP), and Cloth-bound copies (C).

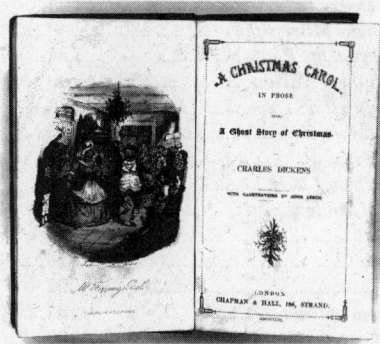

Charles Dickens, A Christmas Carol, *has appeared in many editions. Only the first edition in pristine condition with its original binding is worth $2500. — Photo courtesy of Northeast Auctions.*

	F	L	LEC	HP	C
Adams, H., *Education of Henry Adams*	$ 3800	$ 27	$ 75	$ 13	$ 11
Aeschylus, *Oresteia*	—	18	45	9	8
Aesop, *Fables*	—	45	100	16	14
Allen, Hervey, *Anthony Adverse*	550	25	55	10	8
Aristotle, *Politics and Poetics*	—	29	75	13	11
Bacon, Francis, *Essays or Counsels...*	5500	25	55	10	8
Balzac, Honore de, *Droll Stories*	—	35	90	13	10
Baudelaire, Charles, *Flowers of Evil*	—	27	70	12	10
Bellamy, Edward, *Looking Backward*	330	25	65	10	7
Benet, Stephen V., *John Brown's Body*	340	40	100	14	12
Bierce, Ambrose, *Devil's Dictionary*	—	23	70	11	8
Blake, William, *Poems*	—	29	75	13	10
Boccaccio, Giovanni, *Decameron*	—	25	65	11	8
Boswell, James, *Life of Samuel Johnson*	4000	40	100	14	12
Bradbury, Ray, *Fahrenheit 451*	300	40	100	14	11

	F	L	LEC	HP	C
Bradbury, Ray, *Martian Chronicles*	$ 750	$ 50	$ 120	$ 17	$ 13
Brecht, Bertolt, *Threepenny Opera*	—	25	65	11	8
Browning, E., *Sonnets from the Portuguese*	—	35	80	15	12
Browning, Robert, *Ring and the Book*	200	25	50	8	6
Bryant, William Cullen, *Poems*	6500	25	65	10	7
Bunyan, John, *Pilgrim's Progress*	—	30	80	15	12
Burns, Robert, *Poems*	5000	22	50	8	6
Butler, Samuel, *Erewhon*	—	32	80	15	12
Caesar, Julius, *Gallic Wars*	—	35	80	14	11
Camus, Albert, *The Stranger*	—	37	90	13	10
Casanova, Giacomo, *Memoirs*	—	30	70	12	10
Cellini, Benvenuto, *Life of Benvenuto Cellini*	—	36	90	13	10
Cervantes, Miguel de, *Don Quixote*	—	32	80	14	11
Chaucer, Geoffrey, *Canterbury Tales*	—	35	85	15	12
Cicero, Marcus Tullius, *Orations and Essays*	—	16	50	8	6
Clemens, Samuel, *Huckleberry Finn*	1350	45	100	14	12
Clemens, Samuel, *Life on the Mississippi*	480	50	170	18	14
Clemens, Samuel, *Prince and the Pauper*	—	35	90	12	10
Clemens, Samuel, *Puddin-head Wilson*	550	30	70	12	10
Clemens, Samuel, *Roughing It*	450	30	75	13	10
Clemens, Samuel, *Tom Sawyer*	4500	55	170	18	14
Colette, Sidonie, *Break of Day*	—	25	70	11	8
Collier, John Payne, *Punch and Judy*	1500	35	90	13	10
Collins, Wilkie, *Woman in White*	3850	20	50	8	6
Confucius, *Sayings*	—	32	75	13	10
Conrad, Joseph, *Nostromo*	350	29	65	11	8
Crane, Hart, *The Bridge*	2600	22	55	9	7
Crane, Stephen, *Red Badge of Courage*	3400	34	80	14	11
Dante Alighieri, *Divine Comedy*	—	25	70	12	10
Darwin, Charles, *Descent of Man*	—	30	80	15	12
Darwin, Charles, *...Voyage of the HMS Beagle*	9,500	35	90	12	10
Darwin, Charles, *On the Origin of Species*	16,000	50	130	17	13
De Quincey, T., *Confessions of an... Opium-Eater*	—	25	70	11	8
Defoe, Daniel, *Moll Flanders*	—	18	55	9	7
Defoe, Daniel, *Robinson Crusoe*	9000	35	70	12	10
Diaz, Bernal, *...Conquest of Mexico*	—	30	80	15	12
Dickens, Charles, *Chimes*	—	50	230	18	15
Dickens, Charles, *A Christmas Carol*	2600	20	50	9	7
Dickens, Charles, *Cricket on the Hearth*	350	37	90	13	10
Dickens, Charles, *Pickwick Papers* (book)	1600	35	85	15	12
Dickinson, Emily, *Poems*	3500	27	60	10	8
Dodgson, Charles, *Alice... in Wonderland*	4000	55	400	22	18
Dodgson, Charles, *Through the Looking Glass*	700	55	450	22	18
Donne, John, *Poems*	13,500	22	45	8	6
Dostoevsky, Fyodor, *Brothers Karamazov*	—	30	75	13	10
Dostoevsky, Fyodor, *Crime and Punishment*	—	25	55	10	7
Dostoevsky, Fyodor, *House of the Dead*	—	22	50	9	7
Dostoevsky, Fyodor, *Idiot*	—	25	60	10	7
Dostoevsky, Fyodor, *Possessed*	—	40	100	16	13
Doyle, A.C., *Adven. of Sherlock Holmes*	2600	35	85	15	12
Doyle, A.C., *Later Adven. of Sherlock Holmes*	—	25	55	10	7

	F	L	LEC	HP	C
Dreiser, Theodore, *An American Tragedy*	$ 400	$ 25	$ 65	$ 10	$ 7
Dreiser, Theodore, *Sister Carrie*	—	35	90	13	10
Dumas, Alexandre, *Camille*	—	55	450		
Dumas, Alexandre, *Count of Monte Cristo*	—	35	85	15	12
Emerson, Ralph Waldo, *Essays, 1st & 2nd Series*	2600	22	50	8	6
Erasmus, Desiderius, *In Praise of Folly*	—	25	65	11	8
Fielding, Henry, *History of Tom Jones*	3500	22	55	9	7
Fitzgerald, F. Scott, *Great Gatsby*	650	22	50	9	7
Flaubert, Gustave, *Madame Bovary*	—	22	50	9	7
Francis of Assisi, *Little Flowers*	—	25	65	11	8
Franklin, Benjamin, *Autobiography*	550	22	45	8	6
Frazer, James George, *Golden Bough*	300	25	60	10	7
Frost, Robert, *Complete Poems*	—	50	350	20	16
Garcia Marquez, Gabriel, *100 Years of Solitude*	—	25	65	11	8
Gibbon, E., *...Fall of the Roman Empire*, 7 vols	2700	100	220	30	30
Gilbert and Sullivan, *1st Night...*	—	40	100	14	11
Grahame, Kenneth, *Wind in the Willows*	2600	60	600	23	18
Grass, Gunter, *Flounder*	—	45	220	19	16
Graves, Robert, *Poems*		22	50	9	7
Grimm Brothers, *Fairy Tales*, (English 1823-26)	4000	28	85	14	11
Hardy, Thomas, *Far from the Madding Crowd*	1500	20	60	10	7
Hardy, Thomas, *Jude the Obscure*	625	26	80	13	10
Hardy, Thomas, *Tess of the D'Urbervilles*	—	30	80	15	12
Hawthorne, N., *House of the Seven Gables*	900	22	50	9	7
Hawthorne, N., *Scarlet Letter*	800	30	80	13	10

Left: Modern first editions should have their original dust jackets. — Photo courtesy of Phillips Auctioneers. Right: The "First Edition Library" makes excellent reproductions including dust jackets. Make sure that the dust jacket on a first edition is original to that book.

	F	L	LEC	HP	C
Hawthorne, N., *Twice-Told Tales*	—	$ 23	$ 70	$ 11	$ 8
Hemingway, E., *For Whom the Bell Tolls*	$ 400	50	250	20	16
Hemingway, E., *Old Man and the Sea*	400	50	250	19	16
Hesse, Hermann, *Steppenwolf*	—	25	50	10	7
Homer, *Iliad*	—	45	100	16	13
Homer, *Odyssey*	—	50	200	19	16
Hugo, Victor, *Battle of Waterloo*	—	20	45	8	6
Hugo, Victor, *Notre-Dame de Paris*	—	55	150	18	14
Hugo, Victor, *Toilers of the Sea*	—	25	55	10	7
Irving, Washington, *Alhambra*	200	22	50	9	7
Irving, Washington, *Rip Van Winkle*	300	27	60	10	8
James, Henry, *Portrait of a Lady*	1200	22	50	10	9
Joyce, James, *Dubliners*	2200	50	150	18	14
Joyce, James, *Ulysses*	7800	140	4000	50	40
Kafka, Franz, *Metamorphoses*	—	50	160	18	14
Keats, John, *Poems*	4000	22	50	9	7
Kingsley, Charles, *Westward Ho!*	400	22	45	8	7
Kipling, Rudyard, *Jungle Book*	1200	27	60	10	8
la Fontaine, Jean de, Fables	—	25	60	10	7
le Sage, Alain-Rene, *Adven. of Gil Blas*	—	30	70	12	10
Lewis and Clark, *Journals...*	8500	60	125	17	15
Lewis, Sinclair, *Main Street*	200	45	220	19	16
Livius, Titus, *History of Early Rome*	—	30	70	12	10
London, Jack, *Call of the Wild*	800	36	90	12	10
London, Jack, *White Fang*	350	22	45	8	6
Lytton, Edward, *Last Days of Pompeii*	385	25	55	10	7
Machiavelli, Niccolo, *The Prince*	—	25	55	10	8
Malory, Thomas, *Le Morte D'Arthur*	—	40	100	16	13
Mann, Thomas, *Magic Mountain*	—	30	75	13	10
Marlowe, Christopher, *Four Plays*	—	27	65	11	8
Marquez, Gabriel (see Garcia Marquez, Gabriel)					
Maugham, W.S., *Of Human Bondage*	200	55	410	21	17
Melville, Herman, *Moby Dick*	16,000	45	100	15	14
Melville, Herman, *Typee*	1350	32	80	14	11
Merimee, Prosper, *Carmen*	—	26	60	10	7
Miller, Arthur, *Death of a Salesman*	270	50	350	20	16
Milosz, Czeslaw, *Captive Mind*	—	22	50	9	7
Milton, John, *Masque of Comus*	—	28	80	14	11
Mitchell, M., *Gone With the Wind*	2200	30	80	15	12
Moliere, Jean, *Tartuffe*	—	16	50	8	6
Montaigne, Michel, *Essays*	—	30	65	11	8
More, Sir Thomas, *Utopia*	—	26	65	10	7
Nietzsche, F., *Thus Spake Zarathustra*	—	23	70	11	8
Nordhoff and Hall, *Mutiny on the Bounty*	450	30	80	15	12
Omar Khayyam, *Rubaiyat*	—	30	80	15	12
O'Neill, Eugene, *Ah, Wilderness!*	270	30	70	13	10
Ovid, *Metamorphoses*	—	40	100	14	11
Paine, Thomas, *Rights of Man*	—	27	65	11	8
Parkman, Francis, *Oregon Trail*	200	44	130	17	13
Paz, Octavio, *Three Poems*	—	51	3500	20	16
Pepys, Samuel, *Diary*	—	30	85	15	12

	F	L	LEC	HP	C
Plato, *Republic*	—	$ 30	$ 70	$ 12	$ 10
Plato, *Trial... of Socrates*	—	33	100	13	10
Poe, Edgar A., *Fall of the House of Usher*	—	50	260	19	16
Poe, Edgar A., *...Arthur Gordon Pym*	$ 660	22	45	8	6
Poe, Edgar A., *Tales of Mystery...*	250	21	60	10	7
Polo, Marco, *Travels*	—	25	70	12	10
Porter, William, *Voice of the City...*	—	46	200	18	14
Prescott, William, *...Conquest of Peru*	350	25	70	12	10
Proust, Marcel, *Swann's Way*	—	50	180	19	16
Pushkin, Aleksandr, *Golden Cockerel*	—	47	110	17	13
Rabelais, F., *Gargantua and Pantagruel*	—	35	85	15	12
Raspe, Rudolph, *...Baron Munchausen*	—	30	70	13	10
Rimbaud, Arthur, *A Season in Hell*	—	76	1800	30	24
Rostand, Edmond, *Cyrano de Bergerac*	—	22	45	8	7
Scott, Sir Walter, *Ivanhoe*	570	16	50	8	7
Shakespeare, William, *Hamlet*	—	50	180	18	14
Shakespeare, William, *Poems and Sonnets*	—	55	170	18	14
Shelley, Mary, *Frankenstein*	—	30	75	13	10
Sheridan, Richard, *Rivals*	400	27	60	10	7
Sheridan, Richard, *School for Scandal*	—	21	65	10	7
Sienkiewicz, Henryk, *Quo Vadis?*	—	25	65	11	8
Sinclair, Upton, *The Jungle*	—	25	60	10	8
Singer, Isaac, *Gentleman from Cracow*	—	38	90	13	10
Singer, Isaac, *Magician of Lublin*	—	45	210	19	16
Spenser, Edmund, *Faerie Queene*	22,000	35	75	13	10
Steinbeck, John, *Grapes of Wrath*	1350	53	470	21	17
Steinbeck, John, *Of Mice and Men*	1000	25	50	9	8
Stephens, James, *Crock of Gold*	200	25	60	12	10
Sterne, Laurence, *Tristram Shandy*	6750	35	80	14	11
Sterne, Laurence, *A Sentimental Journey*	1100	30	85	15	12
Stevenson, R. L., *Child's Garden of Verses*	750	23	65	11	8
Stevenson, R.L., *Dr. Jekyll and Mr. Hyde*	1100	26	60	10	7
Stoker, Bram, *Dracula*	1850	25	60	10	7
Stowe, Harriet B., *Uncle Tom's Cabin*	2200	55	200	18	14

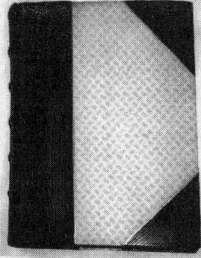

Right to left: Three-quarter leather bindings often used on bound sets; a full leather binding with a gilt-embossed crest will usually add several hundred dollars to the value of a 17th-century volume.

	F	L	LEC	HP	C
Swift, Jonathan, *Gulliver's Travels*	$ 11,000	$ 40	$ 90	$ 13	$ 11
Tennyson, Alfred, *Idylls of the King*	—	30	70	12	10
Thackeray, William M., *Henry Esmond, Esq*	650	22	45	8	6
Thackeray, William M., *The Newcomes*	200	25	55	10	7
Thackeray, William M., *Vanity Fair*	2800	35	50	15	12
Thoreau, Henry David, *Cape Cod*	550	24	65	10	7
Thoreau, Henry David, *Walden*	2600	50	375	18	16
Thucydides, *Peloponnesian War*	—	27	60	10	7
Tolstoy, Leo, *War and Peace*	—	50	110	16	13
Virgil, *Aeneid*	—	30	65	11	8
Virgil, *Georgics*	—	32	80	14	11
Verne, Jules, *From the Earth...*	—	24	60	10	8
Verne, Jules, *Mysterious Island*	—	47	110	17	13
Voltaire, Francois, *Candide*	—	22	45	8	6
Wallace, Lew, *Ben-Hur*	—	22	45	8	6
Walton, I. & Cotton, C., *Compleat Angler*	—	55	150	18	16
Warren, Robert P., *All the King's Men*	—	45	110	16	13
Whitman, Walt, *Leaves of Grass*	16,000	60	600	22	18
Wilde, Oscar, *Lady Windemere's Fan*	400	23	50	9	8
Wilde, Oscar, *Picture of Dorian Gray*	—	33	80	14	11
Wilde, Oscar, *Salome*	1600	50	110	16	13
Wilder, Thornton, *Bridge of San Luis Rey*	525	30	75	13	10
Wilder, Thornton, *Our Town*	275	25	70	12	10
Williams, T., *A Streetcar Named Desire*	—	50	140	17	14
Wister, Owen, *The Virginian*	—	22	50	9	7
Yeats, W.B., *Poems of W.B. Yeats,* 1949	2600	25	50	9	8

*Full leather bindings popular during the late 19th and early 20th
centuries are often not affected by the value of the work they cover.
— Photo courtesy of William Doyle Galleries.*

Comic Books

Comic book collecting enjoys a huge following. Collectors have actively pursued this area for years but it gained prominence in the early 1990s. There is an endless number of characters and new, exciting books appear each day. The selection below covers a tiny area of the comic book world and concentrates on early, well-known characters. Because comic books (especially early ones) are fragile, condition is crucial to determining value. Grading a comic book is both an art and a science. We suggest you consult the *Overstreet* guide cited below. We list two ranges of prices. The first is loosely described as average condition (what collectors generally refer to as very good). This means the book is intact but shows wear, the color of the paper may be brownish and there may be minor inside creases or a small tear or two. Our second range is superior, although not near-mint; it is what collectors consider fine condition. Near mint and, where available, mint-condition books bring considerably more than the values listed below. There are reissues of many books, and some bear a striking resemblance to the original but command only a fraction of the original's price. As in any collecting area, do your homework.

The following listings are organized by publisher with the subhead being the name and date of the series. Each entry includes the issue number, name of the issue, main characters and descriptive information. For more information and extensive listings, refer to *The Overstreet Comic Book Price Guide*, Robert M. Overstreet, Confident Collector, New York, 1995.

D-C/NATIONAL PERIODICAL PUBLICATIONS
ACTION, 1938

	VERY GOOD	FINE
7, Superman (Pep Morgan, Scoop Scanlon), Adventures of Marco Polo, Superman on cover	$ 500-700	$ 1000-2000
14, Superman vs. Ultra (Pep Morgan, Chuck Dawson, Clip Carson), Adventures of Marco Polo, Zatara on cover	300-500	800-1000
17, Superman vs. Ultra, last installment of Adventures of Marco Polo, Superman on cover	400-500	800-1200
18, Three Aces, begins.	300-500	700-1000
19, Superman vs. Ultra (Chuck Dawson, Clip Carson, Three Aces) Superman on cover	300-500	700-1000
20, Superman vs. Ultra	300-500	700-1000
22, Last Chuck Dawson, had appeared continuously from #1	200-300	400-500
23, Superman vs. Luthor, Luthor shown w/ red hair initially, first appearance of The Black Pirate. Created by Sheldon Moldoff, this short-lived series ran for only 19 issues and was never regarded as a major feature, but it was superbly illustrated	500-600	700-1000
33, Mr. America, origin, created by artist Bernard Bailey	150-250	300-400
37, Superman Charged With Violation of Law, first appearance of Congo Bill, created by Whitney Ellsworth, first appeared as a minor feature in D-C's More Fun Comics for 11 issues, then was dropped. One month later, Action Comics introduced a new series of Congo Bill in which he suddenly became a movie star. The movie serial turned out to be one of the better ones of the 1940s	120-180	200-300
42, Origin of The Vigilante, last Black Pirate, Mr. America uses his cape as a flying carpet for the first time. Vigilante soon became one of D-C's star attractions and he headlined their new entry, Leading Comics, which began as a quarterly publication in January 1942	100-175	200-300

	VERY GOOD	FINE
43, The Vigilante vs. The Shade (Billy Gunn)	$ 100-175	$ 200-300
45, The Vigilante, first appearance of Stuff, the Chinatown Kid. ..	100-175	200-300
46, The Vigilante vs. Rainbow Man	100-175	200-300
51, Superman vs. The Prankster (first appearance)	100-150	200-300
52, Origin of Americommando, cover features montage w/		
Superman, Zatara, Congo Bill and The Vigilante	100-150	200-300
56, Americommando vs. Dr. Ito	90-110	150-200
60, Lois Lane, Superwoman	90-110	150-200
64, Superman vs. The Toyman (first appearance)	90-120	150-200
68, Lois Lane, niece Susie is introduced	90-120	220-280

BATMAN *(1940)*

2, The Crime Master (Adam Lamb), The Case of the Missing		
Link (Hackett and Snead, Professor Drake).	1800-2200	3000-4000
3, The Ugliest Man in the World (Carlson, Ugly Horde,		
Detective McGonicle), The Crime School for Boys (Big		
Boy Daniels), Batman vs. the Cat Woman, first appearance		
of Cat Woman in costume, cover: Batman and Robin running		
toward reader w/ capes flying	1000-1400	2000-3000
4, More Whirlwind Adventures of Batman and Robin, Black-		
beard's Crew and the Yacht Society (Thatch), cover: Batman		
climbing rope ladder	900-1100	1500-2000
5, The Case of the Honest Crook (Smiley Sikes), The Riddle of		
the Missing Card (Queenie), Diamond Jack Deegan (Clumbsy),		
cover: Batman weighs fugitives on "scales of justice." Last		
issue published quarterly, switches to 6 issues per year w/ #6	750-850	1500-2000
6, Suicide Beat (Jimmy Kelly, Fancy Dan, Alderman Skigg)	500-600	800-1000
7, The Trouble Trap (Linda Page, Commissioner Gordon), The		
People vs. the Batman (Horatio Delmar, Weasel Venner,		
Freddie Hill)	550-650	800-1000
8, The Strange Case of Professor Radium (Professor Rose),		
Stone Walls Do Not a Prison Make, The Superstition		
Murders (Johnny Glim),The Cross-Country Crimes		
(Namtab /Batman)	500-600	800-1000
9, The Case of the Lucky Law Breaker, The White Whale		
(Capt. Burly), (Bob Cratchit, Timmy Cratchit)	500-600	800-1000
10, Sheriff of Ghost Town (Five Aces Frogel), Report Card		
Blues (Tommy Trent)	550-600	800-1000
11, Four Birds of a Feather (Buzzard Benny, Joe Crow, Canary,		
The Penguin), Payment in Full (Joe Dolan)	500-600	900-1200
12, The Wizard of Words (The Joker), They Thrill to Conquer		
(Joe Kirk)	400-500	600-800
13, The Story of the 17 Stones (Rocky Grimes), Comedy of Tears		
(The Joker)	400-450	600-800
14, Prescription for Happiness (Pills Mattson), Swastika Over		
the White House (Count Felix, Fritz Hoffner), The Case Batman		
Failed to Solve	475-525	700-1000
15, Your Face Is Your Fortune (Elva Barr), The Loneliest Man		
in the World (Dirk Dagner, Tom Wick), The Boy Who Wanted		
to be Robin (Knuckles Conger, Bobby Deen)	$ 350-550	$ 700-900
16, Grade-A Crime (Winthrop, character without first name),		

	VERY GOOD	FINE

Here Comes Alfred, Adventures of the Branded Tree
(Squidge, character without first name), The Joker Reforms
(Joe Kerswag) .... $ 500-700 $ 1000-2000

17, Adventure of the Vitamin Vandals (Archie Gibbons), The
Penguin Goes a-Hunting, Rogues Pageant (Alfred the Butler) . 150-250   400-600

18, The Secret of the Hunter's Inn (Alfred the Butler, Tweed
Cousins), first appearance of Police Stories 150-250   400-600

19, Collector of Millionaires (Ali, Ali's Health Resort), The Case
of the Timid Lion (The Joker), Atlantis Goes to War (Emperor
Taro, Empress Lanya) 150-250   400-600

20, The Centuries of Crime (Ecla Tate, Swami Meera Kell, The
Joker), Bruce Wayne Loses the Guardianship of Dick Grayson
(Alfred the Butler, Fatso Foley), The Trial of Titus Keyes
(Slick Fingers/George Collins) 150-250   400-600

21, Batman and Robin Whoop It Up in Four Whirlwind Action
Stories, The Streamlined Rustlers (Brule, character without
first name), His Lordship's Double (Lord Hurley Burleighm
C.L.J. Carruthers), The Three Eccentrics (The Penguin),
Blitzkrieg Bandits (Chopper Gant, Hannibal B. Brown) 150-250   350-450

47, Special! The Peril-Packed Inside Story of the Origin of
Batman (retold), The Chain Gang Crimes (Warden Beltt,
Whiskers Mob), cover: Batman as a boy reading *Gotham
Gazette* w/ headline "Socialite Thomas Wayne Slain by
Mystery Killer!" Thomas Wayne was Batman's father.
The *Gotham Gazette* neglected to mention that Batman's
mother was killed at the same time 250-350   700-900

48, The Thousand Secrets of the Batcave (Wolf Brando), Fowls
of Fate (The Penguin), Crime from Tomorrow (Morton,
character without first name) 120-160   200-300

49, Scoop of the Century (Jervis Tetch, Vicki Vale), Batman's
Arabian Nights (The Crier, Professor Carter Nichols, The
Joker) 180-220   300-400

50, The Second Boy Wonder (Waxey Wilson), Lights-Camera-
Crime (Vicki Vale, Stilts Tyler, Tom Macon) 100-150   200-300

51, The Stars of Yesterday (Rufus Lane), Pee-Wee the Talking
Penguin, The Wonderful Mr. Wimble (Warts) 90-120   150-200

52, Batman and the Vikings (Olaf Erickson, Professor Carter
Nichols), The Man With the Automatic Brain (Alfred the
Butler), The Happy Victims (The Joker, Mrs. Carlin) 100-150   200-300

57, The Walking Mummy (Andrews, character without a first name,
he was a museum curator), The Funny Man Crimes (The Joker) 90-120   150-250

58, The Brand of a Hero (Joaquin Murieta), The State Bird
Crimes (The Penguin), The Black Diamond (Bulls-Eye Kendall,
Barracuda Brothers, Nitro Nelson). Joaquin Murieta was a
real-life desperado of the Old West, here worked into a time-
travel piece 90-120   150-250

59, Batman in the Future (Erkham, character without first name),
The Man Who Replaced Batman (Deadshot/Floyd Lawton,
Commissioner Gordon), The Forbidden Cellar (Professor Vincent) .90-120   150-250

60, The Auto Circus Mystery (Lucky Hooton) 90-120   150-250

61, The Birth of Batplane II (Boley Brothers), Wheelchair Crime
Fighter (Vicki Vale), Mystery of the Winged People (The Penguin) . 75-100   175-275

	VERY GOOD	FINE

Superman *(1939)*

	VERY GOOD	FINE
2, Superman vs. Luthor (first appearance)	$ 1000-1500	$ 2000-3000
4, Superman vs. Luthor	500-700	1000-2000
10, Superman vs. Luthor	400-450	600-800
12, Superman vs. Luthor	275-325	700-800
19, Superman Movie Cartoons, redone into book format	220-260	600-700
30, Superman vs. Mr. Mxyztplk, 1st appearance of Mr. Mxyztplk; in later issues the name was spelled Mxyzptlk	220-260	600-700
45, Lois Lane, Superwoman (Hocus, Pocus)	90-130	250-300
53, Anniversary Issue, origin retold	375-425	800-1200
54, Superman vs. The Wrecker (first appearance)	90-110	200-250
61, Superman Returns to Krypton, first Kryptonite story	190-210	450-500
76, Guest Appearances by Batman and Robin	200-250	550-650
78, Lois Lane's Meeting With Lana Lang	80-90	180-220
81, Superman's Secret Workshop, discovered by arch-foe Luthor	80-90	180-220
100, Origin Retold, for the second time	200-250	700-800
113, The Superman of the Past, part I	35-45	90-110
114, The Superman of the Past, part II	35-45	70-90
115, The Superman of the Past, part III	25-35	70-90
123, Girl of Steel	25-35	70-90
125, Clark Kent in College	25-35	70-90
127, Return of Titano	25-35	70-90
128, Kryptonite Story	25-35	70-90
130, Krypton Grows Up	25-35	70-90
133, How Parry White Hired Clark Kent	20-25	50-70
135, Lori Lemaris	20-25	50-70
138, Lori Lemaris	20-25	50-70
139, Story of Red Kryptonite	20-25	50-70
140, Superman and the Son of Bizarro	20-25	50-70
141, Superman Returns to Krypton and Meets Lyla Lorry	15-20	40-50
142, Guest Appearances by Batman and Robin	15-20	40-50
143, Return of Bizarro	15-20	40-50
144, Superboy's First Public Appearance	15-20	40-50
145, Great Boo-Boo	15-20	40-50
146, Superman's Life Story	20-25	50-70
147, Superman vs. The Legion of Super Villains (first appearance)	18-22	45-60
148, Guest Appearance by Aquaman	18-22	45-55
149, Death of Superman (fantasy)	18-22	45-55
156, Last Days of Superman, w/ appearances by Batman and Robin	8-10	20-25
158, Nightwing and Flamebird	8-10	20-25

FAWCETT
Captain Marvel *(1941)*

	VERY GOOD	FINE
19, Cover: Santa Claus riding on Captain Marvel's back, w/ Mary Marvel wording (at upper right): "On sale every third Friday"	70-90	180-220
26, Cover: Captain Marvel soaring skyward against huge American flag, wording "War, Stamps for Victory"	60-70	150-175
27, Captain Marvel Joins the Navy, cover: Captain Marvel rearing back to hurl bomb as if it were a football, wording: "This is the insignia recently adopted by a naval air squadron" (referring to the lightning bolt on Captain Marvel's shirtfront)	60-70	150-175

	VERY GOOD	FINE

28, Cover: Captain Marvel standing at attention w/ hands at sides, receiving medal from Uncle Sam while column of soldiers watch .... $ 60-70 $ 150-175

31, Captain Marvel in Buffalo, City Saved From Doom; Captain Marvel Fights His Own Conscience, cover: Captain Marvel in close-up w/ angel on one shoulder and devil on the other 55-65   140-160

42, Cover: close-up portrait of Captain Marvel in Christmas wreath, "Season's Greetings" 40-50   90-110

47, Cover: Captain Marvel stands facing old man w/ long beard who holds scroll. On wall are names Solomon, Hercules, Atlas, Zeus, Achilles, Mercury, and "Seventh War Loan, buy stamps and bonds" 30-40   90-110

60, Captain Marvel Battles the Dread Atomic War, cover: Captain Marvel in nuclear devastated city, poised to catch falling atomic bomb 30-40   60-70

70, Captain Marvel and the Horror in the Box, cover: Captain Marvel peering into box that has a question mark on the lid 28-32   50-60

73, Cover: Captain Marvel speeds past the Woolworth Building in New York City 28-32   50-60

97, Captain Marvel Is Wiped Out, cover: Captain Marvel standing full-length, a hand w/ an eraser is "wiping out" the drawing. He exclaims, "Holy moley! What goes on?" 25-30   75-85

104, Mr. Tawny's Masquerade, cover: Mr. Tawny (w/ cape) delivering knockout punch, Captain Marvel exclaims, "Attaboy, Mr. Tawny" 20-25   50-60

112, Captain Marvel and the Strange Worrybird, cover: Worrybird pacing ground w/ dark cloud of gloom over its head, as Captain Marvel stands by mystified 20-25   50-60

MARVEL COMICS
THE AMAZING SPIDERMAN, *(1963)*

1, Origin Retold, Spiderman vs. Chameleon (John Jameson), Fabulous Four, Ditko artwork, Lee stories, inking unknown 1000-1500   5000-7000

2, Duel to the Death With the Vulture, Uncanny Threat of the Terrible Tinkerer, Ditko artwork, Lee stories, Duffy lettering 250-350   400-800

4, Nothing Can Stop the Sandman (Betty Brant), Ditko artwork, Lee stories 100-200   300-600

5 , Marked for Destruction by Dr. Doom (Fabulous Four), Ditko artwork, Lee stories, Rosen lettering 100-200   300-600

6, Face to Face With the Lizard, Ditko artwork, Lee stories, Simek lettering 100-200   300-600

7, Return of the Vulture, Ditko artwork, Lee stories, Simek lettering 80-160   300-500

8, Living Brain, Spiderman Tackles the Human Torch (Fabulous Four), Kirby and Ditko artwork, Lee stories, Simek lettering, Ditko inking 100-150   300-400

9, A Man Called Electro, Ditko artwork, Lee stories, Simek lettering 120-160   300-600

10, Enforcers (Fredrick Foswell, The Ox, Montana, Fancy Dan), Ditko artwork, Lee stories, Rosen lettering 100-150   380-420

11, Turning Point (Spiderman, Tracer, Dr. Octopus), Ditko artwork, Lee stories, Rosen lettering 60-80   180-200

	VERY GOOD	FINE
12, Unmasked by Dr. Octopus, Ditko artwork, Lee stories, Simek lettering	$ 60-80	$ 180-200
13, Menace of Mysterio, Ditko artwork, Lee stories, Simek lettering	80-100	250-300
14, Green Goblin (Hulk, Enforcers, Ox, Montana, Fancy Dan), Ditko artwork, Lee stories, Simek lettering (premium value because of Hulk appearance)	450-550	800-900
15, Kraven the Hunter (Chameleon), Ditko artwork, Lee stories, Simek lettering	80-100	200-250

Little Golden Books

The first 12 Little Golden Books® titles produced in 1942 sold for the bargain price of 25¢ apiece. Early books have a dust jacket and blue binding. Many titles are reprinted for years. The prices below are for first printings, usually called "As." Some books give the date and printing up front. More often the book has a code on the lower portion of the last page squeezed next to the back cover. "A" refers to a first printing, "B" to a second, etc. Prime condition "A" printings command the highest prices. Collectors are a little more willing to accept a later printing on rare or early titles. *A Poky Little Puppy* ® from the 1970s will command a fraction of the price of a first printing. This method of dating a book is a good rule of thumb but the system breaks down on later books. The original price found on the cover is also a way to date a book. Currently titles based on television series are very popular. Books with dolls, puzzles, and games are difficult to find intact; complete examples are worth several times incomplete ones. The prices quoted are for books in excellent condition showing minimal amounts of wear on the covers and pages.

Our consultant for this area is Rebecca Greason, owner of Rebecca of Sunny Book Farm and author of *Tomart's Price Guide to Little Golden Books*, Tomart Publications 1991 (she is listed at the back of this book).

Clockwise from above left: Rootie Kazootie Baseball Star, *1954, #190, $25-$30;* Brave Cowboy Bill, *1950, #93, with puzzle $70-$90, puzzle missing, $12-$18;* Dale Evans and the Lost Goldmine, *1954, #213, $20-$30;* Lassie Shows the Way, *1956, #255, $16-$20. —Items courtesy of Bill Alberta.*

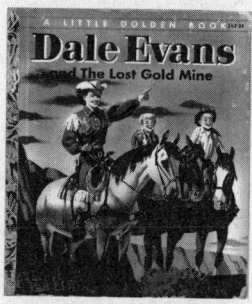 

	Year	NO.	LOW	HIGH
About the Seashore	1957	284	$ 10	$ 12
Albert's Stencil Zoo, punched	1951	112	20	30
Albert's Stencil Zoo, unpunched	1951	112	50	60
Ali Baba	1958	323	10	15
All Aboard	1952	152	18	22
Animal Stories	1957	5006	8	12
Animals Merry Christmas	1958	329	14	18
Animals of Farmer Jones, w/ dust jacket	1942	11	75	125
Animals of Farmer Jones, without dust jacket	1942	11	12	18
Annie Oakley and the Rustlers	1955	221	20	30
Baby Looks	1960	404	24	30
Benji, Fastest Dog in the West	1978	165	8	12
Bible Stories for Boys and Girls	1953	174	7	10
Birds	1958	5011	18	22
Bobby the Dog	1961	440	12	16
Bow Wow! Meow!	1963	523	15	20
Bozo the Clown	1961	446	12	16
Brave Cowboy Bill, w/ puzzle	1950	93	70	90
Brave Cowboy Bill, puzzle missing	1950	93	12	18
Buffalo Bill, Jr.	1956	254	18	22
Bugs Bunny Gets a Job	1952	136	15	20
Bullwinkle	1962	462	18	22
Busy Timmy	1948	50	18	24
Captain Kangaroo	1956	261	16	22
Cars and Trucks	1959	366	10	15
Cave Kids	1963	532	15	18
Charmin' Chatty	1964	554	18	24
Chitty Chitty Bang Bang	1968	581	15	20
Christmas ABC	1962	478	20	25
Christmas Carols	1946	26	12	15
Christmas in the Country	1950	95	12	15
Christopher and the Columbus	1951	103	9	14
Cinderella	1950	D13	18	24
Cinderella's Friends	1950	D17	18	24
Circus Time, dial intact	1955	A2	18	22
Color Kittens	1949	86	18	25
Count to Ten	1957	A6	12	14
Counting Rhymes	1960	361	12	15
Cowboys and Indians	1958	5019	20	30
Dale Evans and the Coyote	1956	253	20	30
Davy Crockett's Keelboat Race	1955	D47	25	30
Day at the Beach	1951	110	30	35
Day at the Zoo	1950	88	18	22
Dick Tracy	1962	497	25	30
Doctor Dan at the Circus, w/ Band-Aids	1960	399	90	120
Doctor Dan at the Circus	1960	399	14	18
Dogs	1957	5008	14	18
Donald Duck and the Mouseketeers	1956	D55	20	30
Donald Duck in Disneyland	1955	D44	15	20
Donald Duck Prize Driver	1956	D49	15	20
Dumbo	1942	D3	30	40

	Year	NO.	LOW	HIGH
Dumbo, w/ dust jacket	1942	D3	$ 90	$ 140
Fish	1959	5023	10	12
Five Little Firemen	1949	301	14	18
Flintstones	1961	450	20	25
Fly High	1971	597	7	10
Four Little Kittens	1957	322	9	12
Four Puppies	1960	405	9	12
Gaston and Josephine	1948	65	18	24
Gene Autry	1955	230	20	30
Giant With Three Golden Hairs	1955	219	15	20
Ginger Paper Doll, uncut	1957	132	75	90
Gingerbread Shop	1952	126	14	18
Golden Book of Birds	1943	13	18	20
Grandpa Bunny	1951	D21	20	30
Gunsmoke	1958	320	25	35
Hansel and Gretel	1954	217	8	12
Happy Birthday, uncut	1949	384	30	45
Hey There, It's Yogi Bear	1964	542	18	24
Hi Ho! Three in a Row	1954	188	25	30
How to Tell Time	1957	285	16	20
Howdy Doody's Animal Friends	1956	252	25	30
J. Fred Muggs	1955	234	12	18
Jamie Looks	1963	522	28	32
Jetsons	1962	500	20	30
Katie Kitten	1949	75	12	18
Lassie and Her Day in the Sun	1958	307	15	20
Leave It to Beaver	1959	347	20	25
Lion's Paw	1959	367	15	20
Little Black Sambo	1948	57	85	125
Little Boy With a Big Horn	1950	100	10	15
Little Eskimo	1952	155	12	15
Little Fat Policeman	1950	91	14	18
Little Golden Book of Uncle Wiggly	1954	148	15	18
Little Golden Holiday Book	1951	109	18	22
Little Indian	1954	202	10	15
Little Man of Disneyland	1955	D46	10	14
Little Yip Yip	1950	75	15	20
Lively Little Rabbit	1943	15	20	30
Lone Ranger and the Talking Pony	1958	310	30	40
Lucky Mrs. Ticklefeather	1951	122	18	22
Lucky Puppy	1960	D89	15	20
Lucky Rabbit	1955	Din7	10	14
Mad Hatter's Tea Party	1951	D23	20	25
Madeline	1954	186	20	30
Make Way for the Thruway	1961	439	12	18
Marvelous Merry Go Round	1950	87	8	12
Maverick	1959	354	18	24
Mickey Mouse and His Space Ship	1952	D29	20	30
Mickey Mouse Christmas Shopping	1953	D33	20	25
More Mother Goose Rhymes	1958	317	10	12
Mr. Ed the Talking Horse	1962	483	20	25

	YEAR	NO.	LOW	HIGH
My Baby Sister	1958	340	$ 12	$ 15
My Christmas Treasury	1957	5003	9	12
My Little Golden Book of God	1956	268	9	12
My Magic Slate Book, intact, w/ pencil	1959	5025	35	40
New Baby	1948	412	15	20
New Brother, New Sister	1966	564	14	18
New Kittens	1957	302	9	14
Noah's Ark	1952	D28	15	20
Noises and Mr. Flibberty Jib	1947	290	20	25
Nursery Rhymes	1948	59	14	18
Off to School	1958	5015	18	22
Once Upon a Wintertime	1948	D12	18	22
Ookpik, the Arctic Owl	1968	579	12	15
Our World	1955	242	8	12
Out of My Window	1955	245	15	20
Pantaloon	1951	114	18	24
Party in Sheriland	1959	360	18	22
Peter Pan and the Pirates	1952	D25	18	22
Pinocchio	1948	D8	20	30
Play Street	1962	484	18	22
Poky Little Puppy w/ dust jacket	1942	8	70	90
Poky Little Puppy, without dust jacket	1942	8	90	120
Prayers for Children	1952	205	8	10
Puss in Boots	1953	137	12	15
Quick Draw McGraw	1960	398	14	18
Raggedy Ann and Andy Help Santa	1979	156	8	10
Rin Tin Tin and Rusty	1955	246	18	22
Ronald McDonald and the Talking Plant	1984		18	24
Rootie Kazootie Detective	1953	150	25	35
Rootie Kazootie Joins the Circus	1955	226	28	36
Roy Rogers and the Mountain Lion	1955	231	28	32
Roy Rogers and the New Cowboy	1953	177	18	25
Saggy Baggy Elephant	1947	385	15	20
Santa's Toy Shop	1950	D16	10	14

Left to right: The Night Before Christmas, *second version, 1949, #20, $18-$24;* How To Tell Time, *1957, #285, $16-$20.* —*Items courtesy of Bill Alberta.*

Left to right: The Taxi That Hurried, *1946, # 25, $20-$30,
earlier blue spine with dustjacket, $75-$125;* The Seven
Sneezes, *1948, #51, $22-$28. —Items courtesy of Bill Alberta.*

	YEAR	NO.	LOW	HIGH
Scuffy the Tugboat	1946	30	$ 20	$ 30
Sleeping Beauty Paper Doll, uncut	1959	133	90	110
Smokey and His Animal Friends	1960	387	14	18
Smokey the Bear and the Campers	1961	423	14	18
Snow White and Rose Red	1955	228	15	18
Steve Canyon	1959	356	18	24
Supercar	1962	492	25	35
Taxi That Hurried	1946	25	20	30
Tin Woodman of Oz	1952	159	20	30
Tom and Jerry	1951	117	12	18
Tootle	1945	21	15	20
Touche Turtle	1962	474	20	30
Twelve Days of Christmas	1963	526	8	12
Two Little Gardeners	1951	108	10	15
Ugly Duckling	1952	D22	15	20
Ukelele and Her New Doll	1951	102	18	25
Ukelele and Her New Doll, w/ puzzle	1951	102	80	110
Uncle Mistletoe	1953	175	18	22
Up in the Attic	1948	53	15	20
Wagon Train	1958	236	25	30
Waltons, Birthday Present	1975	134	7	10
We Help Daddy	1962	468	10	15
We Help Mommy	1959	352	10	12
When I Grow Up	1950	96	15	20
Where is the Bear?	1967	586	8	10
Winky Dink	1956	266	18	22
Wonders of Nature	1957	293	12	16
Zorro	1958	D68	20	25

Whitman TV Books

Whitman has published books and produced puzzles and games for over 50 years. Their product line includes Little Golden Books and various juvenile series. In the 1950s they started producing books based on TV shows. There are four series of these books under the names of *Authorized TV Adventure, Authorized Edition, Authorized TV Edition*, and *Walt Disney's Authorized Edition*. These designations usually appear on the spine. Unlike earlier Whitman books there are no dust jackets. Instead, they feature action-packed illustrated covers bonded to the boards, covered with a shiny thin plastic finish. Covers feature heroes of classic television shows. Other series appeared in the same style but the TV themes drew the most interest. These books appeal to series collectors and TV memorabilia enthusiasts. When shelved with their covers showing, they form a chronicle of early TV shows. Later covers lacked the protective coating, giving a more muted effect. The same book might appear under different series.

Prices quoted below are for near mint to mint examples. That means no peeling or lifting of the transparent coating, no broken binders, no torn or crayon scrawled pages. For further reading see the *Yellowback Library*, Yellowback Press, P.O. Box 36172, Des Moines, IA, 50315.

Clockwise from above left: The Munsters and the Great Camera Caper, *1965, #1510, $20-$30;* Roy Rogers and the Rimrock Renegades, *1954, #2305:49, $25-$35;* Man From U.N.C.L.E., Goldrunners' Gold, *1967, #1543, $12-15.*

	LOW	HIGH
Annette, Mystery at Moonstone Bay, 1962, 1537	$ 8	$ 12
Annette, Mystery at Smugglers Cove, 1963, 1574	12	14
Annie Oakley, Danger at Diabolo, 1955, 1549	18	22
Annie Oakley, Double Trouble, 1958, 1538	18	22
Bat Masterson, 1960, 1550	12	15
Beverly Hillbillies, 1963, 1572	12	15
Circus Boy, Under the Big Top, 1957, 1549	14	18
Dale Evans, Danger in Crooked Canyon, 1959, 1506	18	24
Dr. Kildare, Assigned to Trouble, 1963, 1547	5	7
Dr. Kildare, The Magic Key, 1964, 1519	5	7
Dragnet, 1957, 1527	18	22
F Troop, The Great Indian Uprising, 1966, 1544	8	10
Family Affair, Buffy Finds a Star, 1970, 1567	18	22
Flipper, Mystery of the Black Schooner, 1966, 2324	12	14
Fury, Mystery at Trapper's Hole, 1959, 1557	10	15
Garrison's Gorillas, Fear Formula, 1968, 1548	10	15
Gene Autry, Arapaho War Drums, 1957, 1512	18	24
Green Hornet, Disappearing Dr., 1966, 1570	22	32
Gunsmoke, 1958, 1587	18	22
Gunsmoke, Showdown on Front Street, 1969, 1520	6	8
Have Gun Will Travel, 1959, 1568	18	22
Hawaii Five-O, Top Secret, 1969, 1511	6	8
I Spy, Message From Moscow, 1966, 1542	10	14
Invaders, Dam of Death, 1967, 1545	10	15
Land of the Giants, Flight of Fear, 1969, 1516	9	11
Lassie, Forbidden Valley, 1959, 1508	10	14
Lassie, Lost in the Snow, 1969, 1504	6	8
Lassie, Treasure Hunter, 1960, 1552	12	15
Leave It to Beaver, 1962, 1526	18	24
Lucy, The Madcap Mystery, 1963, 1505	20	25
Man From U.N.C.L.E., Gentle Saboteur, 1966, 1541	9	12
Maverick, 1959, 1566	14	18
Mission Impossible, Money Explosion, 1970, 1512	7	10
Mod Squad, The Hideout, 1970, 1517	8	12
Monkees, Who's Got the Button?, 1968, 1539	18	22
Munsters, The Last Resort, 1966, 1567	20	30
Munsters, The Great Camera Caper, 1965, 1510	20	30
Patty Duke, Mystery Mansion, 1964, 1514	10	15
Rat Patrol, Iron Monster Raid, 1968, 1547	10	15
Restless Gun, 1959, 1559	14	18
Rin Tin Tin, Ghost Wagon Train, 1958, 1579	16	19
Ripcord, 1962, 1522	15	20
Roy Rogers, King of the Cowboys, 1956, 1503	15	20
Roy Rogers, Enchanted Canyon, 1954, 1502	18	22
Sea Hunt, 1960, 1541	14	18
Spin and Marty, Trouble at the Triple R, 1958, 1577	10	15
Voyage to the Bottom of the Sea, 1965, 1517	10	12
Wagon Train, 1959, 1567	18	24
Wells Fargo, Danger Station, 1958, 1588	10	15
Wyatt Earp, 1956, 1548	18	24
Zorro, 1958, 1586	18	22

Catalogs

Trade catalogs are issued by manufacturers, wholesalers and retail merchants. Watch for specialized catalogs which pertain to one subject rather than general merchandise catalogs. Sears Roebuck catalogs are some of the most popular. Not all reprints are clearly marked; don't mistake them for valuable originals.

Usually trade catalogs received a great deal of use. It is often difficult to find them in excellent condition. "Good" catalogs must be intact, but may show wear and use. "Best" catalogs should not be marked or torn. The covers should not be faded and the spines should be solid.

Miscellaneous

	GOOD	BETTER	BEST
Bicycles, Keating, 1896 Catalogue, Keating Wheel Co., Holyoke, 32 pp	$ 30	$ 37	$ 45
Bicycles, Tires, Motorcycle and Bicycle Accessories, Edwards & Crist Co., Chicago and Phila., 122 pp., 1923	25	35	50
Bottling Supplies and Household Utensils, Consumers Products Co., Brooklyn, N.Y., 20 pp., 1927	12	17	22
Busiest House in America, illus., general merchandise, 640 pp., 1908	80	115	150
Civil Engineers' and Surveyors' Instruments, W. & L.E. Gurley, Troy, NY, 34 pp., 1878	50	75	100
Columbia Bicycles, Pope Manufacturing Co., Hartford, CT, 31 pp., 1897	40	50	65
Counting Machines, W.N. Durant, Milwaukee, 20 pp., c. 1905 ..	25	35	50
Florence Home Needle-Work, Nonotuck Silk Co., 96 pp., 1891 .	15	20	25
Galvanized Patent Stock Trough, Foltz Manufacturing & Supply Co., Hagerstown, MD, 8 pp., c. 1902, price list of livestock troughs	7	10	13
Great Western Gun Works, Catalogue #40, J.H. Johnston Co., Pittsburgh, 64 pp., 1888	60	80	100
Hand-Book and Illustrated Catalogue of the Engineer's and Surveyor's Instruments of Precision, C.L. Berger & Sons, Bost., 212 pp., 1902	45	65	85
Hersey Water Meters, price list, Hersey Manufacturing Co., South Bost., 7 pp., 1908	5	7	9
Hibbard Baskets, Hibbard Basket Works, Lyons, NY, 12 pp., 1900	17	24	31
High Grade Bicycles, Special Catalogue, Cash Buyers' Union, Chicago, 40 pp., 1895	43	55	70
Illustrated Catalogue of Metal Broom Locks and Braces, M. Gould's Son & Co., Newark, NJ, 16 pp., 1908	20	25	30
Jaros Hygienic Wear, I. Jaros, NY, 79 pp., 1890	30	35	40
Masonic Ledge Supplies, Catalogue #2, Henderson Ames Co., Kalamazoo, MI, 110 pp., 1905	30	40	50
Patent Medicines, Proprietary Articles, Plasters, Antiseptic Dressings, Etc., Fuller & Fuller Co., Chicago, 189 pp., c. 1906	20	25	35
Photographic Card Stock, A.M. Collins Manufacturing Co., price list, Phila., 47 pp., 1898	30	40	50
Powell Brothers Shoe Co., Spring Catalogue, NY, 49 pp., 1902 .	14	18	25

	GOOD	BETTER	BEST
Saddlery and Horse Furnishings, Carriage and Sleigh Trimmings, James Bailey Co., Portland, ME, 1913, 7" x 10"	$ 35	$ 50	$ 65
Schoenhut's Marvelous Toys, A. Schoenhut Co., Phila., 36 pp., 1904	120	150	180
Soda Fountain Supplies, Fuller & Fuller Co., Chicago, 189 pp., c. 1906	30	40	50
Vertical Gas, Gasoline, Kerosene and Distillate Engines for All Power Purposes, Fairbanks, Morse & Co., Chicago, 32 pp., 1904	12	18	25
Washington Stoves and Ranges, Grey & Dudley Hardware Co., Nashville, TN, 110 pp., c. 1918	25	30	40

Sears Roebuck

	GOOD	BETTER	BEST
1897, general catalog, Chicago, IL	250	310	370
1899, general catalog	200	265	330
1900-10, most editions, food, groceries, tobacco	50	70	120
1902, general catalog #111, 50¢ cover price	145	165	200
1902, general catalog, 1969 reprint (Crown Pub., NY)	10	15	20
1905, general catalog	147	180	225
1906, general catalog	164	200	250
1907, general catalog, 1240 pp.	170	230	265
1908, general catalog, 1232 pp.	200	250	300
1910, general catalog, spring and summer, 1182 pp.	200	260	320
1911-20, most editions, food, groceries, tobacco	55	65	85
1922, general catalog, spring and summer	145	185	210
1926, general catalog, autumn and winter	125	150	180
1931, general catalog, spring and summer	125	160	200
1944, general catalog, autumn and winter	90	122	150
1947, Christmas catalog	50	70	90
1949, general catalog, autumn and winter	45	60	75
1951, business equipment	10	14	20
1951, Christmas catalog	45	55	65
1955, general catalog, spring and summer	30	40	55
1960, Christmas catalog	20	30	45
1963, general catalog, autumn and winter	15	20	40
1965-75, general catalogs, most editions	10	15	20

Magazines

Magazines are history in the first person. Few things capture the moods of the American nation as the magazines we read. Few things are as American as *Life Magazine*. But magazines, unlike books, were meant to be read and discarded. Although publishers printed large numbers, readers saved only a small percentage. These saved copies may turn up anywhere, from a church bazaar to the bottom of an auction box lot.

Collectors of magazines want clean, crisp copies. They should not be marked, torn or frayed. The best copy is an unread copy.

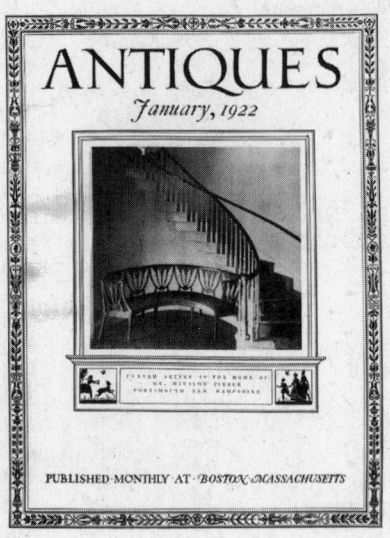

Left: The Magazine Antiques *is valued by antique collectors when sold as a complete, or near complete, run. Bound or unbound, a complete set from January 1922 through December 1996 is worth $6000-$8000 at auction.*

	LOW	AVG.	HIGH
American Mag., 1950-54	$ 5.00	$ 6.00	$ 7.00
American Mag., 1955, Aug. (Amazing Secret of Walt Disney)	10.00	11.00	12.00
American Mag., 1955-56	3.00	4.00	5.00
American Monthly Review of Reviews, 1900-06	9.00	10.50	13.00
American Monthly Review of Reviews, 1906, July (Olympics)	17.00	18.50	20.00
American Monthly Review of Reviews, 1906, May (Earthquake)	20.00	22.50	25.00
American Neptune, 1941-50	4.00	4.75	6.00
Argosy, 1882-90	4.00	4.75	6.00
Argosy, 1891-1900	3.25	4.00	4.75
Argosy, 1901-10	2.75	3.38	4.00
Argosy, 1911-20	2.25	2.75	3.25
Arizona Highways, 1955-60	4.00	4.75	5.50
Arizona Highways, 1961-65	3.25	4.13	5.00
ArtNews, 1942, 10/14 (Charles Dana Gibson)	20.00	23.50	27.00
Asia, 1929, Jan.	26.00	29.50	32.00
Association Men (YMCA Publication), 1917	5.00	6.00	7.00
Atlantic Monthly, 1887, June	14.00	15.00	16.50
Atlantic Monthly, 1950-59	2.75	3.00	3.25
Atlantic Monthly, 1960-69	2.00	2.38	2.75

	LOW	AVG.	HIGH
Atlantic Monthly, 1970	$ 1.25	$ 1.63	$ 2.00
Audubon Mag., 1950-55	4.50	5.75	7.00
Audubon Mag., 1956-60	4.00	5.00	6.00
Bandleaders, 1946, June	11.50	12.50	13.50
Baseball Mag., 1923	12.00	14.00	16.00
Baseball Mag., 1955	3.25	3.88	4.50
Beatles Monthly Book, 1965, Mar.	20.00	23.50	27.00
Better Homes and Gardens, 1920-30	6.75	8.00	9.50
Better Homes and Gardens, 1950-60	3.25	4.00	5.00
Better Homes and Gardens, 1961-70	2.25	2.75	3.25
Black Mask, 1921, Nov.	200.00	225.00	255.00
Black Mask, 1925, Mar.	70.00	75.00	80.00
Black Mask, 1926, Feb.	70.00	75.00	80.00
Black Mask, 1927, Apr.	130.00	143.50	165.00
Black Mask, 1927, Feb.	70.00	75.00	80.00
Black Mask, 1928, Aug.	130.00	142.50	155.00
Black Mask, 1930, Jan. (Maltese Falcon)	130.00	142.50	155.00
Black Mask, 1930, Mar.	35.00	37.50	40.00
Black Mask, 1935, Jan.	60.00	65.00	70.00
Black Mask, 1936, May	70.00	75.00	80.00
Boy's Life, 1946-65	3.25	3.88	4.50
Boys' Life, 1948, Feb. (Norman Rockwell)	18.00	19.00	20.00
Boys' Life, 1959, Feb. (Norman Rockwell)	12.00	13.00	14.00
Brigitte Bardot, 1958, one issue only	40.00	45.00	50.00
Brown Book of Boston, 1903-05	7.00	9.00	11.00
Brown Book of Boston, 1905, Apr.	17.50	18.50	19.50
Captain Future, 1940-42	15.00	22.50	30.00
Carnival, 1953-54	1.75	2.00	2.25
Cartoon Comedy Parade, 1963	1.00	1.25	1.50
Cartoon Parade, 1962, 1/1	5.00	6.00	7.00
Cartoon Parade, 1962-68	1.00	1.50	2.00
Century Mag., 1887, Oct.	14.50	15.50	16.50
Century Mag., 1892, Feb.	8.00	9.00	10.00
Child Life, 1936	4.00	4.75	5.50
Clic, 1938-40	4.00	5.50	7.00
Collier's, 1902-10	8.00	9.00	10.00
Collier's, 1910-20	5.00	6.00	7.00
Collier's, 1920-60	3.00	4.00	5.00
Collier's, 1937, 11/6 (Mickey Mouse)	42.00	47.00	52.00
Collier's, 1951, 2/17 (Herbert Hoover's Memoirs)	11.00	12.00	13.00
Comedy, 1956-60	1.00	1.25	1.50
Complete Detective, 1938, May, first issue	45.00	50.00	55.00
Complete Photographer, 1941	6.00	7.00	8.00
Cosmic Science Fiction, 1941	40.00	42.50	45.00
Cosmopolitan, 1890-99	16.75	20.88	25.00
Cosmopolitan, 1900-10	13.50	16.75	20.00
Cosmopolitan, 1911-20	12.00	14.38	16.75
Cosmopolitan, 1921-30	2.75	6.38	10.00
Country Gentleman, 1853-60	7.75	11.00	14.00
Country Gentleman, 1861-70	6.75	9.00	12.00
Country Gentleman, 1871-80	4.00	5.38	6.75

	LOW	AVG.	HIGH
Dileneator, 1873-80	$ 5.50	$ 7.00	$ 8.00
Dileneator, 1881-90	4.50	6.00	7.50
Doc Savage, 1933, Sept.	200.00	220.00	240.00
Doc Savage, 1935, Jan.	65.00	70.00	75.00
Doc Savage, 1939, Jan.	50.00	55.00	60.00
Doc Savage, 1939-48	20.00	30.00	40.00
Doc Savage, 1944, Dec.	70.00	75.00	80.00
Double Detective, 1937-40	50.00	55.00	60.00
Esquire, 1944-55	14.00	15.00	16.00
Esquire, 1951, Sept. (Monroe)	47.00	52.00	57.00
Esquire, 1956-66	2.00	3.00	4.00
Esquire, 1967-72	1.50	2.50	3.50
Etude, 1900-10	1.35	2.05	2.75
Family Circle, 1950-59	1.00	1.18	1.35
Family Circle, 1960-69	.75	.88	1.00
Farmer's Wife, 1928-31	2.00	3.50	5.00
Fawcett Figure Photography, 1954, one issue only	8.00	9.00	10.00
Field and Stream, 1896-1900	2.75	3.38	4.00
Field and Stream, 1901-10	2.25	2.75	3.25
Field and Stream, 1911-20	2.00	2.38	2.75
Field and Stream, 1921-30	1.00	1.88	2.75
Film Stars, Winter, 1953 (Monroe)	47.00	52.00	57.00
Film Weekly, 1931-37	25.00	32.50	40.00
Filmland, 1951-57	10.00	15.00	20.00
Focus, 1951-53	1.75	2.00	2.25
Focus, 1938, Apr.	5.00	6.00	7.00
Focus, 1953, May (Monroe)	20.00	22.50	25.00
Fotorama, 1955-61	1.75	2.00	2.25
Fotorama, July, 1959 (Elvis)	3.50	4.00	4.50
Front Page Detective, 1936-45	8.00	10.00	12.00
Front Page Detective, 1946-56	4.00	6.00	8.00

World War II aviation magazines, left to right: Flying, $5-$8; Flying Age, $5-$8.

	LOW	AVG.	HIGH
Front Page Detective, 1957-60	$ 2.00	$ 4.00	$ 6.00
Front Page Detective, 1960-69	1.00	1.50	2.00
Fun House Comedy, 1964	1.00	1.25	1.50
Godey's Lady's Book, 1844-53	5.50	7.00	8.50
Godey's Lady's Book, late 1860s	2.75	3.50	4.25
Good Housekeeping, 1902-20	7.00	8.00	9.00
Good Housekeeping, 1921-28	5.00	6.00	7.00
Good Housekeeping, 1929-39	3.25	3.88	4.50
Good Housekeeping, 1940-49	2.25	2.75	3.25
Good Housekeeping, 1950-61	1.50	1.75	2.00
Good Housekeeping, 1961, Aug. (Caroline Kennedy)	4.00	5.00	6.00
Good Literature, 1907	2.00	3.00	4.00
Groove, 1947-49	10.00	11.00	12.00
Harper's Bazaar, 1893	4.00	4.75	5.50
Harper's Monthly, 1850	7.00	8.00	9.00
Harper's Monthly, 1851-55	11.00	15.50	20.00
Harper's Weekly, 1850-59	5.50	6.63	7.75
Harper's Weekly, 1860, 4/21 (Stephen Douglas)	27.50	30.00	32.50
Harper's Weekly, 1860-65	10.00	25.00	40.00
Harper's Weekly, 1865, 11/18 (woodcut, baseball)	50.00	60.00	70.00
Harper's Weekly, 1865, 11/25 (woodcut, Brooklyn Baseball)	50.00	60.00	70.00
Harper's Weekly, 1866-80	2.75	11.38	20.00
Harper's Weekly, 1904, 4/30 (St. Louis Fair)	9.00	11.25	13.50
Harper's Weekly, after 1880	2.00	4.38	6.75
High Society, 1978, Apr. (Monroe)	17.00	18.00	19.00
High Society, 1981, July (Nastassja Kinski)	14.00	15.00	16.00
High Times, No. 1, 1974	82.00	92.00	102.00
Holiday, 1950-55	3.00	4.00	5.00
Hollywood, 1934-43	15.00	20.00	25.00
Hollywood Life Stories, 1952-58	10.00	17.50	25.00
Hollywood Pinups, 1953, No. 1, w/ 3-D glasses	70.00	80.00	90.00
House Beautiful, 1919-29	7.00	8.50	10.00
House Beautiful, 1930-45	4.00	5.00	6.00
House Beautiful, 1946-60	2.00	3.00	4.00
Illustrated Blue Book, 1926-29	25.00	30.00	35.00
Inside Detective, 1936-58	9.00	11.00	13.00
Inside Detective, 1959-70	6.00	7.00	8.00
Inside Detective, 1970, Mar. (Charles Manson)	9.00	10.00	11.00
James Bond 007, 1964, one issue only	50.00	60.00	70.00
Jest, 1951-59	2.50	3.50	4.50
Jet, 1954	3.00	4.00	5.00
Ladies' Home Journal, 1890-10	10.00	13.50	17.00
Ladies' Home Journal, 1911-29	7.00	8.50	10.00
Ladies' Home Journal, 1930-40	3.00	5.00	7.00
Leslie's Weekly, Frank, 1890-99	5.00	7.13	9.25
Leslie's Weekly, Frank, 1900-10	4.75	6.25	7.75
Leslie's Weekly, Frank, 1911-20	4.00	5.00	6.00
Liberty, 1924-30	1.35	1.68	2.00
Liberty, 1931-40	1.00	1.88	2.75
Liberty, 1936-44	4.00	8.00	12.00
Life, 11/9 (Monroe)	19.00	20.00	21.00

Below left to right: Life, *Joe DiMaggio cover, May 1, 1939;* Life, *Jackie Robinson cover, May 8, 1950; Sports figures on the cover are issues popular with collectors. — Items courtesy of Pastimes.*

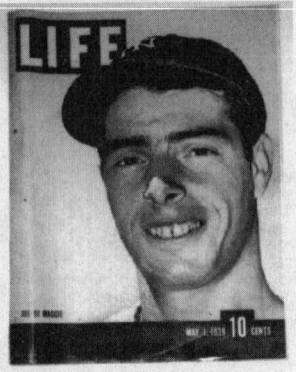

	LOW	AVG.	HIGH
Life, 1936	$ 20.00	$ 22.50	$ 25.00
Life, 1936, 11/23	90.00	100.00	110.00
Life, 1936, 11/30	40.00	42.50	45.00
Life, 1937	8.00	12.00	16.00
Life, 1937, 1/4 (FDR)	22.00	24.50	27.00
Life, 1937, 11/8 (Garbo)	32.00	34.50	37.00
Life, 1937, 5/17 (Quintuplets)	40.00	42.50	45.00
Life, 1937, 5/3 (Jean Harlow)	27.00	29.50	32.00
Life, 1938	7.00	10.50	14.00
Life, 1938, 2/7 (Cooper)	20.00	22.50	25.00
Life, 1938, 5/23 (Errol Flynn)	20.00	22.50	25.00
Life, 1938, 6/20 (Valentino)	25.00	27.50	30.00
Life, 1938, 7/11 (Shirley Temple)	32.00	34.50	37.00
Life, 1939	6.00	9.00	12.00
Life, 1939, 3/13 (World's Fair)	25.00	27.50	30.00
Life, 1939, 9/11 (Mussolini)	19.00	20.00	21.00
Life, 1940	5.00	7.50	10.00
Life, 1940, 12/9 (Ginger Rogers)	13.00	14.00	15.00
Life, 1940, 7/15 (Rita Hayworth)	13.00	14.00	15.00
Life, 1941	4.00	6.00	8.00
Life, 1941, 1/27 (Churchill)	10.00	11.00	12.00
Life, 1941, 12/8 (MacArthur)	22.00	24.50	27.00
Life, 1942	4.00	5.00	6.00
Life, 1942, 3/30 (Shirley Temple)	12.00	13.00	14.00
Life, 1942, 4/27 (Nelson Rockefeller)	8.00	9.00	10.00
Life, 1943, 7/12 (Roy Rogers)	37.00	39.50	42.00
Life, 1943-45	4.00	5.00	6.00
Life, 1944, 12/11 (Judy Garland)	13.00	14.00	15.00
Life, 1945, 4/16 (Eisenhower)	17.00	18.00	19.00
Life, 1945, 4/23 (Truman)	22.00	24.50	27.00
Life, 1945, 9/3 (MacArthur)	22.00	24.50	27.00

	LOW	AVG.	HIGH
Life, 1946, 2/4 (Hope and Crosby)	$ 11.00	$ 12.00	$ 13.00
Life, 1946, 4/8 (Circus)	13.00	14.00	15.00
Life, 1946-57	3.00	4.50	6.00
Life, 1947, 7/14 (Elizabeth Taylor)	11.00	12.00	13.00
Life, 1948, 11/22 (Truman)	9.00	10.00	11.00
Life, 1948, 9/27 (football player Doak Walker)	8.00	10.00	12.00
Life, 1949, 8/1 (DiMaggio)	11.00	12.00	13.00
Life, 1950, 1/2 (special issue)	11.00	12.00	13.00
Life, 1950, 6/12 (Bill Boyd)	18.00	19.00	20.00
Life, 1952, 4/7 (Monroe)	27.00	29.50	32.00
Life, 1953, 5/25 (Monroe and Jane Russell)	25.00	27.50	30.00
Life, 1953, 6/8 (Roy Campanella)	19.00	20.00	21.00
Life, 1953, 7/20 (JFK and Jackie)	22.00	24.50	27.00
Life, 1954, 4/26 (Grace Kelly)	9.00	10.00	11.00
Life, 1954, 9/15 (Judy Garland)	9.00	10.00	11.00
Life, 1955, 8/22 (Sophia Loren)	5.00	8.00	11.00
Life, 1955, 9/12 (Joan Collins)	8.00	9.00	10.00
Life, 1956, 6/25 (Mickey Mantle)	14.00	15.00	16.00
Life, 1957, 3/11 (JFK)	14.00	15.00	16.00
Life, 1958, 1/6 (Astronaut)	8.00	9.00	10.00
Life, 1958, 12/1 (Ricky Nelson)	11.00	12.00	13.00
Life, 1958, 4/28 (Willie Mays)	11.00	12.00	13.00
Life, 1958-60	2.00	3.00	4.00
Life, 1959, 10/3, 1955 (Rock Hudson)	10.00	11.00	12.00
Life, 1959, 4/20 (Monroe)	19.00	20.00	21.00
Life, 1959, 8/24 (Jackie Kennedy)	11.00	12.00	13.00
Life, 1960, 12/26 (double issue)	19.00	20.00	21.00
Life, 1960-65	2.00	3.00	4.00
Life, 1961, 1/13 (Gable)	4.00	5.00	6.00
Life, 1962, 11/2 (Cuban missile crisis)	4.00	5.00	6.00
Life, 1962, 6/22 (Monroe)	13.00	14.00	15.00
Life, 1963, 11/29 (JFK assassination)	19.00	20.00	21.00
Life, 1963, 12/13 (Johnson)	6.00	7.00	8.00
Life, 1963, 12/13 (Kennedy Memorial)	9.00	10.00	11.00
Life, 1963, 8/2 (Koufax)	6.00	7.00	8.00
Life, 1964, 11/6 (Goldfinger)	5.00	6.00	7.00
Life, 1964, 2/21 (Oswald)	6.00	7.00	8.00
Life, 1964, 8/28 (The Beatles)	20.00	22.50	25.00
Literary Digest, 1910-29	.75	1.00	1.25
Literary Digest, 1920's, w/ Norman Rockwell covers	4.50	5.25	6.00
Literary Digest, 1924	3.00	4.00	5.00
Literary Digest, 1924, 6/25 (Lindberg)	9.00	10.00	11.00
Literary Digest, 1930-38	.75	.88	1.00
Look, 1930-38	6.75	8.18	9.60
Look, 1939, 1/3 (Duke of Windsor)	11.00	12.00	13.00
Look, 1939-43	6.00	8.00	10.00
Look, 1940, 9/24 (Charlie Chaplin)	18.00	20.00	22.00
Look, 1944-53	5.00	6.50	8.00
Look, 1954, 12/28 (Lucille Ball)	9.00	10.00	11.00
Look, 1954-56	3.00	5.00	7.00
Look, 1957, 1/8 (20th Anniversary)	8.00	9.00	10.00

	LOW	AVG.	HIGH
Look, 1957-59	$ 2.00	$ 2.50	$ 3.00
Look, 1960-64	1.00	1.75	2.50
Mademoiselle, 1941, Dec. (Christmas issue)	5.00	6.00	7.00
Master Detective, 1929-40	10.00	12.50	15.00
McCall's 1873-1910	6.00	8.50	11.00
McCall's, 1911-20	4.00	6.00	8.00
McCall's, 1921-30	3.75	5.18	6.60
McCall's, 1931-45	3.25	4.63	6.00
McCall's, 1945-55	2.00	3.50	5.00
McCall's, 1956-75	1.00	2.50	4.00
McClure's Mag., 1899-1904	8.00	10.00	12.00
Modern Movies, 1937-38	20.00	23.50	27.00
Modern Priscilla, 1887-99	2.00	2.63	3.25
Modern Priscilla, 1913-25	3.00	4.50	6.00
Modern Priscilla, 1921-30	4.50	5.25	6.00
Modern Romances, 1937-39	7.00	8.50	10.00
Modern Screen, 1931-39	25.00	35.00	45.00
Modern Screen, 1940-45	22.00	26.00	30.00
Modern Screen, 1943, Jan. (Ronald Reagan and Jane Wyman)	70.00	80.00	90.00
Modern Screen, 1946-53	15.00	17.50	20.00
Modern Screen, 1948, Aug. (Shirley Temple)	27.00	29.50	32.00
Modern Screen, 1953, Oct. (Monroe)	45.00	50.00	55.00
Modern Screen, 1954-59	8.00	10.00	12.00
Modern Screen, 1955, Oct. (Monroe)	38.00	41.00	43.00
Modern Screen, 1959, June (Rock Hudson)	20.00	22.50	25.00
Modern Screen, 1960-64	5.00	6.50	8.00
Modern Screen, 1962, Nov. (Monroe)	25.00	27.50	30.00
Modern Screen, 1964, Dec. (JFK and Jackie)	25.00	27.50	30.00
Modern Screen, 1965-68	2.00	3.50	5.00
Modern Screen, 1969-79	1.00	1.50	2.00
Modern Screen, 1979, June (Elvis)	8.00	9.00	10.00
Motion Picture, pre-1920	14.50	17.50	21.00
Motion Picture, 1921, Sept.	60.00	65.00	70.00
Motion Picture, 1921-30	20.00	22.50	25.00
Motion Picture, 1931-40	15.00	17.50	20.00
Motion Picture, 1941-50	10.00	12.50	15.00
Motion Picture, 1951-55	7.00	9.50	12.00
Motion Picture, 1955-64	5.00	7.50	10.00
Motion Picture, 1965-70	2.00	3.00	4.00
Motion Picture, 1965-75	1.00	1.50	2.00
Motion Picture, 1971-75	1.00	1.50	2.00
Motion Picture News, pre-1930	5.50	6.50	7.50
Movie Classic, 1933-42	27.00	37.00	47.00
Movie Classic, 1940-45	20.00	27.50	35.00
Movie Life, 1939-44	25.00	27.50	30.00
Movie Life, 1945-48	20.00	22.50	25.00
Movie Life, 1949-58	15.00	17.50	20.00
Movie Life, 1952, Nov. (Monroe)	47.00	52.00	57.00
Movie Life, 1955, Apr. (Monroe)	42.00	44.50	47.00
Movie Life, 1958, July (Natalie Wood)	25.00	27.50	30.00
Movie Life Yearbook, 1946-66	10.00	17.50	25.00

	LOW	AVG.	HIGH
Movie Mirror, 1934-39	$ 25.00	$ 37.50	$ 50.00
Movie People, 1954, May (w/ 3-D glasses)	60.00	65.00	70.00
Movie Show, 1946-48	20.00	22.50	25.00
Movie Stars Parade, 1944-60	15.00	20.00	25.00
Movie Stars Parade, 1953, Oct. (Monroe)	45.00	50.00	55.00
Movie Story, 1937-49	20.00	27.50	35.00
Movie Story, 1950-onwards	15.00	17.50	20.00
Movie World, 1952-54	14.00	16.00	18.00
Movieland, 1947-60	20.00	35.00	50.00
Movies, 1935-48	20.00	32.50	45.00
Munsey, 1895-1896	7.00	9.00	11.00
National Geographic, 1880, Vol. 1, No. 1	550.00	613.00	676.00
National Geographic, 1880, Vol. 1, No. 2	200.00	262.50	325.00
National Geographic, 1888	320.00	420.00	520.00
National Geographic, 1890-94	80.00	115.00	150.00
National Geographic, 1898, Mar.	45.00	52.50	60.00
National Geographic, 1899	25.00	37.50	50.00
National Geographic, 1900-04	20.00	30.00	40.00
National Geographic, 1905-13	13.50	16.75	20.00
National Geographic, 1914-19	5.00	6.50	8.00
National Geographic, 1920-29	2.00	3.00	4.00
National Geographic, 1930-49	1.00	2.00	3.00
National Geographic, 1950-95	1.00	1.50	2.00
National Monthly, 1913-16	4.00	5.00	6.00
Nature, 1920-29	.75	1.05	1.35
Nature, 1945-46	1.50	1.75	2.00
Nature, pre-1920	1.00	1.50	2.00
Needlecraft, 1909	1.35	2.93	4.50
Needlecraft, 1910-	1.36	2.68	4.00
Needlecraft, 1920-29	.75	.88	1.00
New Movie, 1930-33	30.00	35.00	40.00
Newsweek, 1950-55	2.00	2.63	3.25
Newsweek, 1956-60	1.76	2.26	2.75
Newsweek, 1961-65	1.36	1.68	2.00

Right: Chess Review, *featuring Bogart and Friends, 1943, $25-$35.*

	LOW	AVG.	HIGH
Newsweek, 1966-70	$ 1.00	$ 1.18	$ 1.35
Official Detective (13" x 10.5"), 1937-56	6.00	8.00	10.00
Oui, 1972, Oct. (first issue)	20.00	22.50	25.00
Oui, 1973-74	2.50	3.00	3.50
Outdoor Life, 1915-16	7.00	8.00	9.00
Penthouse, 1972-74	4.00	6.00	8.00
People Today, 1954	1.50	2.00	2.50
People's Home Journal, 1902	3.00	4.00	5.00
Peterson's Mag., 1844-59	4.50	5.25	6.00
Peterson's Mag., 1860-65	6.00	7.25	8.50
Photo, 1952, June (first issue)	3.50	4.00	4.50
Photo, 1952-55	2.00	2.25	2.50
Photo Life, 1958-61	2.00	3.00	4.00
Photo Play, 1919-29	40.00	52.50	65.00
Photo Play, 1930-37	27.00	33.50	40.00
Photo Play, 1938-43	22.00	27.50	33.00
Photo Play, 1944-45	18.00	21.50	25.00
Photo Play, 1946-50	15.00	17.50	20.00
Pic, 1940-45	3.00	5.50	8.00
Pictorial Review, World War I era	2.75	4.50	5.75
Picture Digest, 1956-57	1.00	1.25	1.50
Picture Life, 1954	1.50	2.00	2.50
Picture Play, 1930-38	20.00	30.00	40.00
Picture Show, 1945-49	15.00	17.50	20.00
Playboy, 1954-55	30.00	45.00	60.00
Playboy, 1956	18.00	20.00	22.00
Playboy, 1957-66	10.00	12.50	15.00
Playboy, 1967-75	7.00	8.50	10.00
Playboy, 1976-79	3.00	5.00	7.00
Playboy, Dec., 1953	90.00	100.00	110.00
Playboy, Jan., 1954	90.00	100.00	110.00
Popular Mechanics, 1900-10	10.00	15.00	20.00
Popular Mechanics, 1951-53	2.00	2.50	3.00
Popular Mechanics, 1960-69	.75	1.13	1.50
Popular Science, pre-1900	20.00	27.50	35.00
Popular Science, 1901-10	20.00	22.50	25.00
Popular Science, 1911-30	15.00	17.50	20.00
Prairie Farmer, 1920-29	1.00	1.50	2.00
Puck, early 1900s	4.00	5.38	6.75
Puck, late 1800s	7.00	11.38	15.75
Pulse, 1954-55	1.50	2.00	2.50
Radio Broadcast, 1929	5.00	6.00	7.00
Radio Craft, 1929, Oct. (first issue)	10.00	11.00	12.00
Radio Craft, 1929-40	3.00	4.50	6.00
Radio Electronics, 1949-52	2.50	3.00	3.50
Reader's Digest, 1930s	.75	1.05	1.35
Reader's Digest, 1940-60	.50	.75	1.00
Redbook, 1950-60	2.00	3.50	5.00
Saturday Evening Post, 1900-07	10.00	13.38	16.75
Saturday Evening Post, 1908-10	8.00	9.00	10.00
Saturday Evening Post, 1911-20	5.00	7.50	10.00

	LOW	AVG.	HIGH
Saturday Evening Post, 1921-30	$ 4.00	$ 5.00	$ 6.00
Saturday Evening Post, 1931-40	2.75	3.38	4.00
Saturday Evening Post, 1933-37 (Norman Rockwell covers)	20.00	25.00	30.00
Science and Mechanics, 1942-56	3.00	5.00	7.00
Scientific American, 1950-60	1.25	1.50	1.75
Screen Album (quarterly), 1951-54	15.00	17.50	20.00
Screen Book, 1929-39	25.00	37.50	50.00
Screen Guide, 1939-45	15.00	22.50	30.00
Screen Guide, 1946-51	8.00	11.50	15.00
Screen Hits Annual, 1949-52	10.00	15.00	20.00
Screen Life, 1941-49	10.00	12.50	15.00
Screen Life, 1950-60	5.00	7.50	10.00
Screen Life, 1961-68	3.00	5.00	7.00
Screen Play, 1936-37	30.00	35.00	40.00
Screen Romances, 1934-38	22.00	31.00	40.00
Screen Stars, 1946-49	12.00	14.00	16.00
Screen Stars, 1950-57	5.00	7.50	10.00
Screen Stories, 1948-55	8.00	11.00	14.00
Screen Stories, 1956-60	5.00	6.50	8.00
Screen Stories, 1961-72	2.00	4.00	6.00
Screenland, 1924-32	22.00	27.00	32.00
Screenland, 1933-39	17.00	20.00	23.00
Screenland, 1940-48	12.00	15.00	18.00
Screenland, 1949-55	7.00	9.50	12.00
Screenland, 1956-65	2.00	4.00	6.00
Scribner's Mag., 1881-1894	8.00	10.00	12.00
Scribner's Monthly, World War I era	.50	.63	.75
Sexology, 1952-67	1.00	1.50	2.00
Silver Screen, 1939-64	10.00	15.00	20.00
Snappy, 1956-60	2.00	2.50	3.00
Sports Afield, 1890-1940	3.25	5.00	6.75
Stage, 1935-37	20.00	25.00	30.00
Startling Detective, 1931-39	9.00	11.00	13.00
Startling Detective, 1940-57	4.00	6.00	8.00
Tab, 1952-66	2.00	2.25	2.50
Tab, 1966, Aug. (Sophia Loren)	4.00	5.00	6.00
Theatre, 1910-14	25.00	27.50	30.00
Theatre Mag., 1925-26	20.00	27.50	35.00
Time, 1932-39	6.00	7.00	8.00
Time, 1939, 12/25 (Gone With the Wind)	25.00	27.50	30.00
Time, 1940-59	1.50	2.00	2.50
Time, 1960-66	1.00	1.50	2.00
True Detective, 1924-39	11.00	16.00	21.00
True Detective, 1940-61	8.00	10.00	12.00
TV Guide, see separate listing			
Woman's Home Companion, 1900-10	4.00	5.38	6.75

TV Guides

TV Guide is a weekly magazine that includes local television listings and articles about Hollywood stars. The nationally distributed editions began in 1953. Before 1953, there were local forerunners. Issues which have popular Hollywood stars on the cover are usually more valuable than other editions. Editions with Lucille Ball, Ronald Reagan and Elvis Presley on the cover are highly valued by collectors.

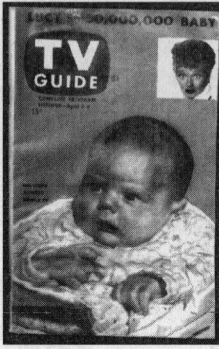 

Left to right: TV Guide, *Volume 1, No. 1 Lucy's Baby, $600-$1200;* TV Guide, *Fred and Ethel Mertz, March 1953, $70-$95. — Items courtesy of Pastimes.*

	LOW	AVG.	HIGH
April 3-9, 1953, #1, photo of Lucille Ball's baby	$ 600	$ 900	$ 1200
April 10-16, 1953, #2, Jack Webb	40	50	60
April 17-23, 1953, #3, caricatures of Lucille Ball, Arthur Godfrey, Milton Berle, Sid Caesar and Imogene Coca	60	70	80
April 24-30, 1953, #4, Ralph Edwards	10	15	20
May 1-7, 1953, #5, Eve Arden	12	16	20
May 8-14, 1953, #6, Arthur Godfrey	25	28	31
May 22-28, 1953, #8, Red Buttons	15	18	21
June 12-18, 1953, #11, Eddie Fisher	15	18	21
June 19-25, 1953, #12, Ed Sullivan	30	40	50
July 3-9, 1953, #14, Perry Como	20	25	30
July 17-23, 1953, #16, Lucille Ball and Desi Arnez	80	120	160
July 24-30, 1953, #17, caricature of Groucho Marx	30	40	50
August 14-20, 1953, #20, Patti Page	25	35	45
August 21-27, 1953, #21, Mary Hartline and Claude Kirchner	15	18	22
August 28-September 3, 1953, #22, Jane and Audrey Meadows	40	60	80
October 28, 1953, #27, Red Skelton	25	35	45
October 19-22, 1953, #29, TV beauty contestants	20	25	30
October 23-29, 1953, #30, Arthur Godfrey	25	28	31
October 30-November 5, 1953, #31, Beulah Witch, Kukla and Ollie	20	30	40
June 27-July 3, 1959, #326, Lloyd Bridges, w/ article on death of George Reeves ("Superman" on TV)	30	35	40
November 7-13, 1959, #345, Jack Benny	25	30	35

	LOW	AVG.	HIGH
December 12-18, 1959, #350, Danny Thomas	$ 15	$ 18	$21
January 9-15, 1960, #354, Jane Wyatt	10	12	14
February 27-March 4, 1960, #361, Robert Stack	10	14	18
May 7-13, 1960, #371, Elvis Presley	120	140	160
June 11-17, 1960, #376, cast of Bachelor Father	10	12	14
August 13-19, 1960, #385, Nick Adams	14	18	22
October 15-21, 1960, #394, Carol Burnett	20	30	40
January 29-February 3, 1961, #409, Ron Howard (pre-"Happy Days")	40	50	60
May 27-June 3, 1961, #426, Ronald Reagan	40	50	60
July 1-7, 1961, #431, The Flintstones	20	30	40
December 19-22, 1961, #455, Richard Chamberlain	18	22	26
January 9-12, 1962, #458, Vince Edwards	10	12	14
March 10-16, 1962, #467, Jack Paar	20	25	30
April 21-27, 1962, #473, Connie Stevens	14	16	18
November 10-16, 1962, #502, Beverly Hillbillies	30	40	50
December 12-16, 1964, #611, Julie Newmar	40	50	60
January 28, 1965, #614, The Munsters	50	65	80
March 9-12, 1965, #623, David Janssen	14	16	18
September 11-17, 1965, #650, Fall Preview Issue	35	40	45
October 19-22, 1965, #655, Red Skelton	8	10	12
November 13-19, 1965, #659, Joey Heatherton	9	11	13
December 11-17, 1965, #663, F Troop	20	25	30
January 1-7, 1966, #666, Carol Channing	10	15	20

Above left to right: TV Guide, *Lassie and John Provost, July, 1959 $75-$100;* TV Guide, *David and Ricky Nelson, May, 1953 $100-$125. — Items courtesy of Pastimes.*

Newspapers

Valuable newspapers are those with major events in the headlines. One of the most valuable 20th-century papers carries the premature "Dewey Defeats Truman" headline. For more information, consult *The Official Price Guide to Paper Collectibles*, published by The House of Collectibles, Random House, NY.

Prices are for whole issues, not just front pages. Front pages alone are worth less than the prices shown. The major papers of the major American cities are the most valuable. Values are given for New York (NY), Chicago (CH), and Washington, D.C. (W). It should be understood that this is for the main city newspapers, such as *The New York Times, The Chicago Tribune* and *The Washington Post*.

	NY	CH	W
Assassinations			
Archduke Francis Ferdinand	$ 32	$ 27	$ 32
Mahatma Gandhi	12	8	10
James Garfield Shot (still alive)	34	24	29
James Garfield Dies of Wound	25	22	25
John F. Kennedy	51	41	52
Robert Kennedy Shot (still alive)	14	12	13
Robert Kennedy Dies of Wound	12	8	9
Martin Luther King, Jr.	13	9	11
Abraham Lincoln	600	550	650
Huey Long	16	14	15
William McKinley Shot (still alive)	50	40	50
William McKinley Dies of Wound	45	40	45
Benito Mussolini	30	20	28
Anwar Sadat	2	1	2
Leon Trotsky	25	18	21
Attempted Assassinations			
Charles de Gaulle	4	3	3
Gerald Ford	2	1	2
Hitler	22	17	19
Franklin D. Roosevelt	11	8	10
Harry S. Truman	8	6	7
George Wallace	7	4	5
Pope John Paul II	3	2	2
Deaths of Celebrities			
Jack Benny	6	4	4
Charlie Chaplin	10	6	8
Winston Churchill	14	9	11
Calvin Coolidge	9	6	7
Edward VII	9	6	7
Adolph Eichmann (executed)	19	11	15
Dwight D. Eisenhower	7	5	6
Judy Garland	42	28	35
Charles de Gaulle	6	4	5
Warren Harding	10	6	8
Adolph Hitler (unconfirmed)	51	41	42
Herbert Hoover	7	4	6

	NY	CH	W
Lyndon Johnson	$ 6	$ 3	$ 4
Nikita Khrushchev	7	4	6
John Lennon	3	2	3
Ethel Merman, *New York Times*	3	2	3
Marilyn Monroe	50	35	42
Elvis Presley	42	36	36
Queen Victoria	42	35	35
Franklin D. Roosevelt	40	28	36
Theodore Roosevelt	19	11	15
William H. Taft	8	6	7
Harry Truman	7	4	6
John Wayne	2	1	2
Woodrow Wilson	14	10	11

News Events

	NY	CH	W
Astronauts Killed in Fire	8	7	7
Atomic Bomb Dropped on Hiroshima	90	70	80
Battle of Little Big Horn	375	290	330
Billy the Kid Slain by Pat Garrett (Note: This was not treated as "front page" news by most newspapers. The lengthier and more prominent the coverage, the more valuable.)	120	150	130
Bonnie and Clyde Shot	90	80	85
John Wilkes Booth Slain	100	75	90
Aaron Burr Slays Alexander Hamilton in Duel	260	—	235
Chicago Fire	200	900	200
Coolidge Sworn in After Harding's Death	40	35	40
Coronation of Elizabeth II	13	9	11
D-Day	52	40	46
John Dillinger Shot	60	60	60
Germany Surrenders (World War II)	40	35	35
John Glenn Orbits Earth	20	15	20
Bruno Hauptmann Executed	130	100	100
Hindenberg Explodes	130	100	100
Jesse James Killed	200	175	175
Japan Surrenders	35	30	35
John F. Kennedy Inaugurated	21	20	25
Charles Lindbergh Baby Kidnapped	35	35	35
Charles Lindbergh Crosses Atlantic	150	100	100
Marilyn Monroe Marries Joe Di Maggio	40	30	35
Moon Landing (first, 1969)	25	25	25
Richard Nixon Resigns	21	15	18
Lee Harvey Oswald Slain by Jack Ruby	30	20	23
Pearl Harbor Attacked	50	40	45
Prince Charles/Princess Diana's Marriage	3	2	3
Russian Sputnik Launched	40	31	40
1929 Stock Market Crash	130	100	110
Titanic Sinks	200	150	180
Triangle Shirtwaist Factory Fire	10	6	8
Truman Relieves Gen. MacArthur of Command	30	20	27

	NY	CH	W
Presidential Elections			
1860, Lincoln/Douglas	$ 210	$ 180	$ 220
1864, Lincoln/McClellan	155	140	160
1868, Grant/Seymour	45	30	40
1872, Grant/Greeley	40	25	35
1876, Hayes/Tilden	22	14	20
1880, Garfield/Hancock	22	14	18
1884, Cleveland/Blaine	22	14	20
1888, Harrison/Cleveland	22	14	20
1892, Cleveland/Harrison	22	14	20
1896, McKinley/Bryan	25	12	20
1900, McKinley/Bryan	25	12	20
1904, Roosevelt/Parker	22	14	18
1906, Taft/Bryan	19	11	15
1912, Wilson/Roosevelt/Taft	25	12	20
1916, Wilson/Hughes	19	11	15
1920, Harding/Cox	14	8	11
1924, Coolidge/Davis	10	6	8
1926, Hoover/Smith	10	6	8
1932, Roosevelt/Hoover	25	22	25
1936, Roosevelt/Landon	14	10	11
1940, Roosevelt/Wilkie	14	10	11
1944, Roosevelt/Dewey	14	10	11
1946, Truman/Dewey	14	10	11
1946, "Dewey Defeats Truman"	—	500	—
1952, Eisenhower/Stevenson	10	6	8
1956, Eisenhower/Stevenson	7	4	6
1960, Kennedy/Nixon	25	16	20
1964, Johnson/Goldwater	7	4	6
1968, Nixon/Humphrey	7	4	6
1972, Nixon/McGovern	7	4	6
1976, Carter/Ford	6	3	4
1980, Reagan/Carter	3	2	3
1984, Reagan/Mondale	2	2	2
1988, Bush/Dukakias	1	1	1
1992, Clinton/Bush	1	1	1

Prints and Lithographs
Audubon

John James Audubon is a name synonymous with bird pictures. His "Birds of America" series is recognized worldwide. Between 1826 and 1842, Audubon traveled throughout the United States and Canada gathering material to paint this famous work.

Today, experts believe there are less than 200 sets of "Birds of America" actually bound in volumes. The work was engraved by R. Havell and Son in London. There are 435 plates in a complete set. In 1971 an exact facsimile edition of 250 copies was printed in Amsterdam.

We list the original Havel prints, first with a typical auction range; next, a retail price is given (R), followed by retail prices for the later Bien edition (B) and the Amsterdam printing (A). Entries are listed sequentially by plate number, followed by subject. For further information refer to *The Official Price Guide to Collector Prints,* published by The House of Collectibles, Random House, NY.

Above: Plate 297, Harlequin Duck.
Below: Plate 287, Yellow Shank.

PLATE NO.	SUBJECT	AUCTION RANGE		R	B	A
1	Turkey Cock	$13,000	$20,000	$40,000	$3200	$2400
2	Yellow-billed Cuckoo	2600	3500	7500	620	500
3	Prothonotary Warbler	825	1100	2300	200	160
4	Purple Finch	600	1100	2150	150	120
5	Bonaparte's Flycatcher	825	1200	2500	200	160
6	Hen Turkey	11,000	16,000	33,000	2500	2150
7	Purple Grackle	3200	4500	8800	750	600
8	White-throated Sparrow	1100	1500	3100	250	200
9	Selby's Flycatcher	825	1100	2200	200	160
10	Brown Titlark	5500	700	7100	1250	1100
11	Bird of Washington	3200	4500	8800	750	600
12	Baltimore Oriole	3200	5500	11,000	750	600
13	Snow Bird	825	1100	2200	200	160
14	Prairie Warbler	1500	2500	5500	380	300
15	Blue Yellow-backed Warbler	1500	2150	4400	380	300
16	Great-footed Hawk	3200	4500	8800	750	600
17	Carolina Turtle Dove	10,000	13,000	27,000	2150	1600
18	Bewick's Wren	825	1100	2200	200	160
19	Louisiana Water Thrush	825	1100	2200	200	160
20	Blue-winged Yellow Warbler	2150	3200	6200	500	400
21	Mockingbird	4500	5500	11,200	1100	825
22	Purple Martin	2150	3200	6200	500	400
23	Maryland Yellow Throat	1200	1800	3800	300	240
24	Roscoe's Yellow Throat	825	1100	2200	200	160
25	Song Sparrow	825	1100	2200	200	160
26	Carolina Parrot	7750	12,500	25,000	1750	1400
27	Red-headed Woodpecker	2150	3200	6200	500	400
28	Solitary Flycatcher	600	925	1900	150	120
29	Towhe Bunting	825	1200	2500	200	160
30	Vigor's Warbler	1100	1100	2500	250	200
31	White-headed Eagle	3200	5500	11,000	750	600
32	Black-billed Cuckoo	4500	5500	12,500	1100	825
33	American Goldfinch	2500	3540	7600	620	500
34	Worm-eating Warbler	1100	1500	3100	250	200
35	Children's Warbler	600	1100	2150	150	120
36	Stanley Hawk	2150	2500	5600	500	400
37	Golden-winged Woodpecker	3200	4500	8800	750	600
38	Kentucky Warbler	825	1200	2500	200	160
39	Crested Titmouse	1200	1800	3800	300	240
40	American Redstart	2150	3200	6200	500	400
41	Ruffed Grouse	4500	6500	12500	1100	825
42	Orchard's Oriole	825	1200	2500	200	160
43	Cedar Bird	2150	3200	6200	500	400
44	Summer Red Bird	2150	3200	6200	500	400
45	Traill's Flycatcher	600	925	1900	150	120
46	Barred Owl	3200	5500	11,000	750	600
47	Ruby-throated Hummingbird	11,000	16,000	31,200	2500	2150
48	Azure Warbler	825	1200	2500	200	160
49	Blue-green Warbler	825	1200	2500	200	160
50	Black and Yellow Warbler	600	925	1900	150	120
51	Red-tailed Hawk	3200	4500	8800	750	600

*Right: Plate 68,
Cliff Swallow.*

*Left: Plate 107,
Canada Jay.*

PLATE NO.	SUBJECT	AUCTION RANGE		R	B	A
52	Chuck Will's Widow	$2150	$4500	$8500	$500	$400
53	Painted Finch	2150	3200	6200	500	400
54	Rice Bird	825	1200	2500	200	160
55	Cuvier's Regulus	825	1200	2500	200	160
56	Red-shouldered Hawk	6500	10,000	19,000	1500	1200
57	Loggerhead Shrike	1100	1500	3100	250	200
58	Hermit Thrush	825	1200	2500	200	160
59	Chestnut-sided Warbler	1200	1800	3800	300	240
60	Carbonated Warbler	1200	1800	3800	300	240
61	Great Horned Owl	6500	10,000	17,500	1500	1200
62	Passenger Pigeon	5500	10,000	18,000	1250	1100
63	White-eyed Flycatcher or Vireo	825	1200	2500	200	160
64	Swamp Sparrow	825	1200	2500	200	160
65	Rathbon's Warbler	825	1200	2500	200	160
66	Ivory-billed Woodpecker	4500	7750	13,800	1100	825
67	Redwinged Starling	2150	3200	6200	500	400
68	Cliff Swallow	825	1200	2500	200	160
69	Bay-breasted Warbler	1100	1800	3500	250	200
70	Henslow's Bunting	1200	1800	3800	300	240
71	Winter Hawk	2150	3200	6200	500	400
72	Swallow-tailed Hawk	3200	5500	11,000	750	600
73	Wood Thrush	1100	1500	3100	250	200
74	Indigo Bunting	1200	1800	4000	300	240
75	Le Petit Caporal	1100	1500	3100	250	200
76	Virginia Partridge	3200	5500	11,000	750	600
77	Belted Kingfisher	2150	4500	7500	500	400
78	Great Carolina Wren	2150	2500	6200	500	400
79	Tyrant Flycatcher	1100	1500	3100	250	200
80	Prairie Titlark	1100	1500	3100	250	200
81	Fish Hawk or Osprey	15,000	25,000	50,000	3950	3200
82	Whip-Poor-Will	1700	7000	11,000	380	310
83	House Wren	2150	3200	6200	500	400
84	Blue-gray Flycatcher	825	1200	2500	200	160
85	Yellow-throated Warbler	825	1200	2500	200	160
86	Black Warrior	2150	3200	6200	500	400
87	Florida Jay	2150	4500	7500	500	400
88	Autumnal Warbler	825	1200	2500	200	160
89	Nashville Warbler	825	1200	2500	200	160
90	Black and White Creeper	700	925	2150	180	140
91	Broad-winged Hawk	4500	6500	13,500	1100	825
92	Pigeon Hawk	1100	1500	3100	250	200
93	Sea Side Finch	2150	4500	7500	500	400
94	Bay-winged Bunting	600	925	1900	150	120
95	Blue-eyed Yellow Warbler	825	1200	2500	200	160
96	Columbia Jay	2150	3200	6200	500	400
97	Little Screech Owl	2150	4500	7500	500	400
98	White-bellied Swallow	600	925	1900	150	120
99	Cow Pen Bird	825	1200	2500	200	160
100	Marsh Wren	600	925	1900	150	120
101	Raven	2150	4500	7500	500	400
102	Blue Jay	825	1200	2500	200	160

Left: Plate 324,
Bonaparte's Gull.

Below: Plate 210, Least Bittern.

PLATE NO.	SUBJECT	AUCTION RANGE		R	B	A
103	Canada Warbler	$850	$1250	$2700	$200	$160
104	Chipping Sparrow	700	1100	2100	180	140
105	Red-breasted Nuthatch	600	925	1900	150	120
106	Black Vulture	1100	2150	3800	250	200
107	Canada Jay	1100	1500	3100	250	200
108	Fox-colored Sparrow	825	1200	2500	200	160
109	Savannah Finch	825	1200	2500	200	160
110	Hooded Warbler	500	700	1500	120	100
111	Pileated Woodpecker	11,000	16,000	33,000	2500	2150
112	Downy Woodpecker	1500	2500	5500	380	300
113	Blue Bird	1200	1800	3800	300	240
114	White-crowned Sparrow	600	925	1900	150	120
115	Wood Pewee	600	925	1900	150	120
116	Ferruginous Thrush	1500	2500	5500	380	300
117	Mississippi Kite	1500	2500	5500	400	300
118	Warbling Flycatcher	1500	2500	5500	380	300
119	Yellow-throated Vireo	825	1200	2500	200	160
120	Pewee Flycatcher	500	700	1500	120	100
121	Snowy Owl	27,000	37,000	80,000	6250	5500
122	Blue Grosbeak	825	1200	2500	200	160
123	Black and Yellow Warbler	2150	3200	6200	500	400
124	Green-black Capped Flycatcher	825	1200	2500	200	160
125	Brown-headed Nuthatch	600	825	1800	150	120
126	White-headed Eagle (young)	2150	4500	7500	500	400
127	Rose-breasted Grosbeak	2150	4500	7500	500	400
128	Cat Bird	825	1200	2500	200	160
129	Great Crested Flycatcher	600	925	1900	150	120
130	Yellow-winged Sparrow	700	1100	2100	180	140
131	American Robin	4500	6500	13,500	1100	825
132	Three-toed Woodpecker	2150	4500	7500	500	400
133	Black Poll Warbler	825	1200	2500	200	160
134	Hemlock Warbler	825	1200	2500	200	160
135	Blackburnian Warbler	1100	1500	3100	250	200
136	Meadow Lark	10,000	13,000	26,000	2150	1600
137	Yellow-Breasted Chat	3200	5500	11,000	750	600
138	Connecticut Warbler	1200	1800	3800	300	240
139	Fed Sparrow	825	1200	2500	200	160
140	Pine-creeping Warbler	1100	1500	3100	250	200
141	Goshawk	2150	3200	6200	500	400
142	American Sparrow Hawk	2150	3200	6200	500	400
143	Golden Crowned Thrush	700	1100	2100	180	140
144	Small Green-crested Flycatcher	1100	1500	3100	250	200
145	Yellow Red Poll Warbler	700	925	2150	180	140
146	Fish Crow	2150	3200	6200	500	400
147	Night Hawk	3200	5500	10,000	750	600
148	Pine Swamp Warbler	600	925	1900	150	120
149	Sharp-tailed Finch	825	1200	2500	200	160
150	Red-eyed Vireo	600	925	1900	150	120
151	Turkey Buzzard	1500	2500	5500	380	300
152	White-breasted Nuthatch	2150	4500	7500	500	400
153	Yellow-rump Warbler	1500	2500	5500	380	300

PLATE NO.	SUBJECT	AUCTION RANGE		R	B	A
154	Tennessee Warbler	$800	$1200	$2500	$200	$160
155	Black-throated Blue Warbler	1100	1500	3300	250	200
156	American Crow	2150	4500	7500	500	400
157	Rusty Grackle	600	925	1900	150	120
158	American Swift	500	700	1500	120	100
159	Cardinal Grosbeak	5500	8200	16,000	1250	1100
160	Black-capped Titmouse	825	1200	2500	200	160
161	Caracara Eagle	4500	6500	12,500	1100	825
162	Zenaida Dove	825	1200	2500	200	160
163	Palm Warbler	825	1200	2500	200	160
164	Tawny Thrush	1100	1500	3100	250	200
165	Bachman's Finch	1200	1800	3800	300	240
166	Rough-legged Falcon	3200	5500	11,000	750	600
167	Key West Quail Dove	3200	5500	11,000	750	600
168	Fork-tailed Flycatcher	3200	5500	11,000	750	600
169	Mangrove Cuckoo	1500	2500	5500	380	300
170	Gray Tyrant	825	1200	2500	200	160
171	Barn Owl	7750	11,000	23,000	1750	1400
172	Blue-headed Pigeon	1200	1800	3800	300	240
173	Barn Swallow	2150	3200	6200	500	400
174	Olive-sided Flycatcher	825	1200	2500	200	160
175	Marsh Wren	600	925	1900	150	120
176	Spotted Grouse	3200	5500	11,000	750	600
177	White-crowned Pigeon	3200	5500	11,000	750	600
178	Orange-crowned Warbler	500	700	1500	120	100
179	Wood Wren	825	1200	2600	200	160
180	Black-capped Titmouse	825	1200	2600	200	160
181	Golden Eagle	4500	6500	12,500	1100	825
182	Ground Dove	2600	3600	7500	620	500
183	Golden-crested Wren	600	925	2100	150	120
184	Mangrove Hummingbird	2150	3200	6700	500	400
185	Bachman's Warbler	1100	1500	3300	250	200
186	Pinnated Grouse	6500	10,000	19,000	1500	1200
187	Boat-tailed Grackle	2150	3200	6200	500	400
188	Tree Sparrow	700	1100	2100	180	140
189	Snow Bunting	825	1200	2500	200	160
190	Yellow-bellied Woodpecker	1200	1800	3800	300	240
191	Willow Grouse	3200	5500	11,000	750	600
192	Great American Shrike	825	1200	2600	200	160
193	Lincoln Finch	1200	1800	3800	300	240
194	Canadian Titmouse	500	700	1500	120	100
195	Ruby-crowned Wren	825	1200	2500	200	160
196	Labrador Falcon	2600	3600	8000	620	500
197	American Crossbill	1200	1800	3800	300	240
198	Worm-eating Warbler	825	1200	2500	200	160
199	Little Owl	825	1200	2500	200	160
200	Shore Lark	600	925	1900	150	120
201	Canada Goose	4500	6500	12,500	1100	825
202	Red-throated Diver	2150	4500	7500	500	400
203	Fresh Water Marsh Wren	1100	1500	3100	250	200
204	Salt Water Marsh Wren	600	825	1800	150	120

PLATE NO.	SUBJECT	AUCTION RANGE		R	B	A
205	Virginia Rail	$700	$1100	$2100	$180	$140
206	Summer or Wood Duck	10,000	13,000	27,000	2150	1800
207	Booby Gannet	1200	1900	3800	300	240
208	Esquimaux Curfew	825	1200	2500	200	160
209	Wilson's Plover	500	700	1500	120	100
210	Least Bittern	1500	2600	5500	380	300
211	Great Blue Heron	27,000	37,000	80,000	6250	5500
212	Common Gull	1200	1800	3800	300	240
213	Puffin	2150	3200	6200	500	400
214	Razor Sill	825	1200	2500	200	160
215	Phalarope	600	925	1900	150	120
216	Wood Ibis	11,000	16,000	33,000	2500	2150
217	Louisiana Heron	16,000	27,000	55,000	4000	3400
218	Foolish Guillemar	825	1200	2500	200	160
219	Black Guillemar	1500	2500	5500	380	300
220	Piping Plover	600	925	1900	150	120
221	Mallard Duck	20,000	30,000	62,500	5500	4500
222	White Ibis	3200	5500	10,000	750	600
223	Pied Oyster Catcher	1100	1500	3300	250	200
224	Kittiwake Gull	600	925	1900	150	120
225	Kildeer Plover	500	700	1500	120	100
226	Whooping Crane	11,000	16,000	31,200	2500	2150
227	Pin-tailed Duck	5500	7750	16,000	1250	1100
228	Green-wing Teal	3200	5500	11,000	750	600
229	Scaup Duck	2150	4500	7500	500	400
230	Ruddy Plover	600	825	1800	150	120
231	Long-billed Curlew	11,000	22,000	37,500	2500	2150
232	Hooded Merganser	3200	5500	11,000	750	600
233	Sora or Rail	500	700	1500	120	100
234	Tufted Duck	1500	2500	5500	380	300
235	Sooty Tern	600	950	1900	150	120
236	Night Heron	4500	6500	12,500	1100	825
237	Great Esquimaux Curlew	1100	1500	3100	250	200
238	Great Marbled Codwit	1100	1500	3100	250	200
239	American Coot	1250	1900	4200	300	240
240	Roseate Tern	2150	3200	6200	500	400
241	Black-backed Gull	1100	1500	3100	250	200
242	Snowy Heron	16,000	27,000	55,000	3750	3200
243	American Snipe	2150	3200	6200	500	400
244	Common Gallinule	825	1200	2500	200	160
245	Thick-billed Murre	600	825	1800	150	120
246	Eider Duck	11,000	16,000	33,000	2600	2150
247	Velvet Duck	2150	3200	6200	500	400
248	American Pied-bill Dobchick	1500	2500	5500	380	300
249	Tufted Auk	1100	1500	3100	250	200
250	Arctic Tern	2150	3200	6200	500	400
251	Brown Pelican	13,000	19,000	40,000	3600	2400
252	Florida Cormorant	1500	2500	5500	380	300
253	Pomarine Jager	1100	1500	3100	250	200
254	Wilson's Phalarope	700	925	2150	180	140
255	Red Phalarope	825	1200	2500	200	160

PLATE NO.	SUBJECT	AUCTION RANGE		R	B	A
256	Purple Egret	$5500	$7750	$16,000	$1300	$1150
256	Purple Heron	4500	6500	12,500	1100	825
257	Double-crested Cormorant	1500	2500	5500	380	300
258	Hudsonian Godwit	825	1200	2500	200	160
259	Horned Grebe	1200	1900	3800	300	240
260	Fork-tail Petrel	825	1200	2500	200	160
261	Whooping Crane	13,000	19,000	40,000	3600	2500
262	Tropic Bind	2150	4500	8000	500	400
263	Curlew Sandpiper	825	1200	2500	200	160
264	Fulmar Petrel	825	1200	2500	200	160
265	Buff-breasted Sandpiper	825	1200	2600	200	160
266	Common Cormorant	1100	1500	3400	250	200
267	Arctic Jager	1100	1500	3100	250	200
268	American Woodcock	2150	3200	6900	500	400
269	Greenshank	1200	1800	3800	300	240
270	Stormy Petrel	500	700	1500	120	100
271	Frigate Pelican	2150	4500	8000	500	400
272	Richardson's Jager	600	925	2100	150	120
273	Cayenne Tern	1100	1600	3300	250	200
274	Semipalmated Snipe	825	1200	2500	200	160
275	Noddy Tern	500	700	1500	120	100
276	King Duck	2150	3600	6900	500	400
277	Hutchins' Goose	1500	2600	5500	400	300
278	Schinz's Sandpiper	600	925	1900	150	120
279	Sandwich Tern	1200	1800	3800	300	240
280	Black Tern	600	825	1800	150	120
281	Great White Heron	16,000	27,000	55,000	3750	3200
282	White-winged Silvery Gull	825	1200	2500	200	160
283	Wandering Shearwater	600	825	1800	150	120
284	Purple Sandpiper	600	925	1900	150	120
285	Fork-tailed Gull	825	1200	2500	200	160
286	White-fronted Goose	3200	5500	11,000	750	600
287	Ivory Gull	1200	1800	4200	300	240
288	Yellow Shank	3200	5500	11,000	750	600
289	Solitary Sandpiper	1200	1800	3800	300	240
290	Red-backed Sandpiper	825	1200	2500	200	160
291	Herring Gull	3200	5500	11,000	750	600
292	Crested Grebe	2150	3200	6200	500	400
293	Large-billed Puffin	1500	2500	5500	380	300
294	Pectoral Sandpiper	825	1200	2500	200	160
295	Manx Shearwater	500	700	1500	120	100
296	Barnacle Goose	3200	4500	9500	750	600
297	Harlequin Duck	1200	1800	4200	300	240
298	Red-nicked Grebe	825	1200	2500	200	160
299	Dusky Petrel	600	925	1900	150	120
300	Golden Plover	400	600	1200	100	80
301	Canvasback Duck	600	925	1900	150	120
302	Black Duck	2150	3200	6200	500	400
303	Upland Sandpiper	1500	2500	5500	380	300
304	Turnstone	600	825	1800	150	120
305	Purple Gallinule	2150	3200	6200	500	400

Above: Plate 328, Long Legged Avocet.

Above: Plate 325, Bufflehead.

PLATE NO.	SUBJECT	AUCTION RANGE		R	B	A
306	Common Loon	$1500	$2600	$5500	$380	$300
307	Little Blue Hen	11,000	16,000	33,000	2500	2150
308	Greater Yellow Legs	825	1200	2500	200	160
309	Common Tern	2150	3200	6200	500	400
310	Spotted Sandpiper	825	1200	2500	200	160
311	American White Pelican	16,000	27,000	55,000	3750	3200
312	Long-tailed Duck	1200	1800	3800	300	240
313	Blue-winged Teal	3200	5500	11,000	825	600
314	Laughing Gull	825	1200	2500	200	160
315	Sandpiper	600	925	1900	150	120
316	Black-bellied Darter	3200	4500	8800	750	600
317	Surf Duck	1100	1500	3100	250	200
318	Avocet	1200	1800	3800	300	240
319	Lesser Tern	1500	2500	5500	380	300
320	Little Sandpiper	825	1200	2500	200	160
321	Roseate Spoonbill	10,000	13,000	27,000	2150	1600
322	Red-head Duck	2150	4500	7500	500	400
323	Black Skimmer	2150	3200	6200	500	400
324	Bonaparte's Gull	825	1200	2500	200	160
325	Bufflehead	2150	3200	6200	500	400
326	Gannet	3200	5500	11,000	750	600
327	Shoveller Duck	7750	11,000	23,000	1750	1400
328	Long-legged Avocet	1500	2500	5500	380	300
329	Yellow Rail	600	925	1900	150	120
330	Plover	500	700	1500	120	100
331	American Merganser	4500	6500	12,500	1100	825
332	Labrador Duck	1500	2500	5500	380	300
333	Green Heron	3200	5500	11,000	750	600
334	Black-bellied Plover	400	600	1200	100	80
335	Red-bellied Sandpiper	825	1200	2500	200	160
336	Yellow-crowned Night Heron	3200	5500	11,000	750	600
337	American Bittern	1500	2500	5500	380	300
338	Bemaculated Duck	3200	5500	11,000	750	600
339	Little Auk	600	925	1900	150	120
340	Stormy Petrel	600	925	1900	150	120
341	Great Auk	2150	3200	6200	500	400
342	Golden-eyed Duck	2150	3200	6200	500	400
343	Ruddy Duck	1500	2500	5500	380	300
344	Long-legged Sandpiper	600	925	1900	150	120
345	American Widgeon	1500	2500	5500	380	300
346	Black-throated Diver	4500	6500	13,500	1100	825
347	American Bittern	1500	2500	5500	380	300
348	Gadwall Duck	2150	3200	6200	500	400
349	Least Water Hen	825	1200	2500	200	160
350	Rocky Mountain Plover	500	700	1500	120	100
351	Great Cinereous Owl	3200	5500	11,000	750	600
352	Black-winged Hawk	825	1200	2500	200	160
353	Chestnut-Backed Titmouse	2150	3200	6200	500	400
354	Louisiana Tanager	2150	4500	7500	500	400
355	MacGillivray's Finch	825	1200	2500	200	160
356	Marsh Hawk	3200	5500	11,000	750	600

PLATE NO.	SUBJECT	AUCTION RANGE		R	B	A
357	American Magpie	$1200	$1900	$4200	$300	$240
358	Pine Grosbeak	500	700	1500	120	100
359	Arkansas Flycatcher	825	1200	2500	200	160
360	Winter and Rock Wren	700	1100	2100	180	140
361	Long-tailed Grouse	1500	2500	5500	380	300
362	Yellow-billed Magpie	1500	2500	5500	380	300
363	Bohemian Chatterer	825	1200	2500	200	160
364	White-winged Grossbill	1100	1500	3100	250	200
365	Lapland Longspur	500	700	1500	120	100
366	Iceland Falcon	13,000	19,000	40,000	3200	2400
367	Band-tailed Pigeon	3200	5500	11,000	750	600
368	Rock Grouse	1200	1800	3800	300	240
369	Mountain Mockingbird	1200	1800	3800	300	240
370	American Water Ouzel	600	925	1900	150	120
371	Cock of the Plains	3200	5500	11,000	750	600
372	Common Buzzard	1100	1500	3100	250	200
373	Evening Grosbeak	825	1200	2500	200	160
374	Sharp-shinned Hawk	825	1200	2500	200	160
375	Lesser Red Poll	825	1200	2500	200	160
376	Trumpeter Swan	3200	5500	10,000	750	600
377	Scolopaceys Courlan	1800	2200	5500	450	360
378	Hawk Owl	1100	1500	3100	250	200
379	Ruff-necked Hummingbird	3200	5500	11,000	750	600
380	Tengmalm's Owl	600	925	1900	150	120
381	Snow Goose	2150	4500	7500	500	400
382	Sharp-tailed Grouse	1200	1800	3800	300	240
383	Long-eared Owl	1200	1800	3800	300	240
384	Black-throated Bunting	700	1100	2100	180	140
385	Bank Swallow	200	1200	1800	50	40
386	Great American Egret	13,000	19,000	37,500	3200	2400
387	Glossy Ibis	3200	5500	11,000	750	600
388	Troopial (Orioles)	500	700	1500	120	100
389	Red-cocked Woodpecker	700	1100	2100	180	140
390	Prairie Finch	600	925	1900	150	120
391	Brant Goose	2150	3200	6200	500	400
392	Louisiana Hawk	1200	1800	3800	300	240
393	Blue-winged Teal	600	925	1900	150	120
394	Buntings and Finches	1100	1500	3300	250	200
395	Audubon's Warbler	825	1200	2500	200	160
396	Burgomaster Gull	1500	2500	5500	380	300
397	Scarlet Ibis	3200	5500	11,000	750	600
398	Lazuli Finch	600	925	1900	150	120
399	Black-throated Warbler	825	1200	2500	200	160
400	Townsend's Finch	600	925	1900	150	120
401	Red-breasted Merganser	2150	4500	8000	500	400
402	Auks and Guillemots	1100	1500	3100	250	200
403	Golden-eyed Duck	1200	1800	3800	300	240
404	Eared Grebe	825	1200	2500	200	160
405	Semipalmated Sandpiper	600	925	1900	150	120
406	Trumpeter Swan	3200	5500	11,000	750	600
407	Dusky Albatross	825	1200	2500	200	160

PLATE NO.	SUBJECT	AUCTION RANGE		R	B	A
408 .... American Scoter Duck		$1200	$1800	$3800	$300	$240
409 .... Havell's Tern		1200	1800	3800	300	240
410 .... Marsh Tern		1500	2500	5500	380	300
411 .... Common American Swan		13,000	19,000	40,000	3200	2500
412 .... Violet Green Cormorant		1100	1500	3100	250	200
413 .... California Partridge		1100	1500	3100	250	200
414 .... Golden-winged Warbler		600	925	1900	150	120
415 .... Brown Creeper		1100	1500	3100	250	200
416 .... Hairy Woodpecker		3200	5500	11,000	750	600
417 .... Maria's Woodpecker		2150	3200	6200	500	400
418 .... American Ptarmigan		825	1200	2500	200	160
419 .... Little Tawny Thrush		500	700	1500	120	100
420 .... Prairie Starling		825	1200	2500	200	160
421 .... Brown Pelican, young		10,000	13,000	27,000	2150	1600
422 .... Rough-legged Falcon		1200	1800	3800	300	240
423 .... Plumed Partridge		1200	1800	3800	300	240
424 .... Lazuli Finch		500	700	1500	120	100
425 .... Columbian Hummingbird		1500	2500	5500	380	300
426 .... California Condor		2150	4500	7500	500	400
427 . White-legged Oyster Catcher		1200	1800	3800	300	240
428 .... Townsend's Sandpiper		500	700	1500	120	100
429 .... Western Duck		825	1200	2500	200	160
430 .... Slender-billed Guillemot		600	925	1900	150	120
431 .... American Flamingo		22,000	34,000	70,000	5500	4500
432 .... Burrowing Owl		825	1200	2500	200	160
433 .... Bullock's Oriole		400	600	1200	100	80
434 .... Little Tyrant Pewee, 1		400	600	1200	100	80
435 .... Columbian Water Ouzel		400	600	1200	100	80

Plate 313, Blue Winged Teal.

Currier & Ives

In 1835, Nathaniel Currier started a lithography company in New York. James Ives joined in 1852 as a bookkeeper. Currier and Ives was unique in its ability to combine artistic talent, skilled craftsmanship, appropriate technology, and merchandising acumen into a successful business enterprise. It employed well-known artists of the day, including Maurer, Palmer, Tait, and Worth. The finest materials were used: stones from Bavaria (where lithography was invented), lithographic crayons from France, and colors from Austria. The firm invented a lithographic crayon, reputed to be superior to all others, and produced a lithographic ink of beef suet, goose grease, white wax, castile soap, gum mastic, shellac, and gas black. Mass distribution and low cost were the keys to success. Uncolored prints sold for as little as six cents each and even large-colored folios sold for no more than three dollars. Prints were sold door-to-door by peddlers and in the streets by pushcart vendors, and even overseas through agents. The firm of Currier and Ives was dissolved in 1907. Although an estimated ten million prints sold, only a small percentage survive today.

Published in various sizes, the prints are commonly grouped into folio sizes shown below:

Very Small: up to approximately 7" x 9"

Small: approximately 8.8" x 12.8"

Medium: approximately 9" x 14" to 14" x 20"

Large: anything over 14" x 20"

The sizes pertain to the image only, not the margin. Often, print owners trimmed the margins of the pictures, so an uncut print is more valuable than a pared one.

Most prints were struck in black and white and then hand colored. Because of this method, different colorings of the same print are found. Folio sizes Very Small, Small, and Medium were completed in this manner. However, the Large folios were sometimes partially printed in color and then finished by hand, usually by only one artist. Many of these prints have been reprinted often. Beware buying a modern calendar print. For further information see *Currier's Price Guide to Currier and Ives Prints*, Kaminski Auctioneers, (800) 344-0760.

Each print is given with its Conningham number (C#), a reference to the checklist by Frederic Conningham, *Currier and Ives Prints*. Over 50 years ago, Mr. Conningham referred to the "Best Fifty" in both the Large Folio size and the Small Folio size. Many of these are still the top valued prints of Currier and Ives, though some have fallen from grace. We've listed these 100 prints with their current retail ranges. C#'s followed by an asterisk are known to appear on more than one composition

THE GREAT WEST.

The Great West, small folio, C# 2658, $1000-$1500.
—Photo courtesy of Northeast Auctions.

	C#	LOW	HIGH
The Best Fifty (small folio)			
1. The Express Train	1790*	$ 2200	$ 4500
2. American Railroad Scene-Snowbound	187*	2100	4400
3. Beach Snipe Shooting	445	2600	3400
4. Ice-boat Race on the Hudson	3021	2100	4500
5. Central Park in Winter	953	2100	2600
6. The Star of the Road	5701	600	800
7. The High Bridge at Harlem, NY	2810*	300	500
8. Maple Sugaring, Early Spring in the Northern Woods	3975	1000	1600
9. Shakers Near Lebanon	5475	1600	2600
10. Winter Sports-Pickerel Fishing	6747	1250	1850
11. The American Clipper Ship *Witch of the Wave*	115	800	1200
12. Gold Mining in California	2412	1250	1850
13. The Great International Boat Race	2623	1250	1850
14. Wild Turkey Shooting	6677	600	800
15. Perry's Victory on Lake Erie	4754	500	700
16. Washington at Mount Vernon, 1797	6515	400	600
17. The Whale Fishery, "Laying On"	6626	1000	1600
18. Chatham Square, New York.	1020	500	700
19. Water Rail Shooting	6567	600	900
20. The Sleigh Race	5554	1600	2600
21. Franklin's Experiment	2128	600	900
22. Washington Crossing the Delaware	6523*	300	500
23. American Homestead Winter	172	600	900
24. Washington Taking Leave of the Officers of His Army	6547	300	500
25. Steamboat Knickerbocker	5727	500	700
28. Kiss Me Quick!	3349*	400	600
27. On the Mississippi Loading Cotton	4607	1000	1600
28. Bound Down the River	627	800	1200
29. American Whalers Crushed in the Ice	205	1600	2600
30. Dartmouth College	1446*	2100	4500
31. Terrific Combat Between the *Monitor*, 2 Guns, and the *Merrimac*, 10 Guns	5996*	400	600
32. General Francis Marion	2250	400	600
33. Art of Making Money Plenty	275	500	700
34. Hon. Abraham Lincoln	2895	200	400
35. Gen. George Washington (w/ cape)	2261	150	250
36. Black Bass Spearing	543	2200	2600
37. Early Winter	1652	3400	5500
38. Woodcock Shooting	6773*	500	700
39. "Dutchman" and "Hiram Woodruff"	1640	600	800
40. Great Conflagration at Pittsburg. Pa.	2581	600	800
41. Bear Hunting, Close Quarters	446*	1600	2100
42. The Destruction of Tea at Boston Harbor	1571	800	1250
43. Cornwallis Is Taken	1258	400	600
44. Landing of the Pilgrims at Plymouth, 11th Dec., 1620	3435*	300	500
45. The Great Fight for the Championship	2613	300	500
46. Benjamin Franklin	499*	400	600
47. Noah's Ark	4494*	200	400
48. Black-eyed Susan	551	200	400
49. The Bloomer Costume	573*	300	500
50. The Clipper Yacht *America*	1173*	1000	1600

Winter Morning in the Country, small folio, C# 6742, $1200-$1800.
— Photo courtesy of Northeast Auctions.

Trotting Mare Goldsmith Maid, large folio, C# 6189, $1200-$1800.
— Photo courtesy of Northeast Auctions.

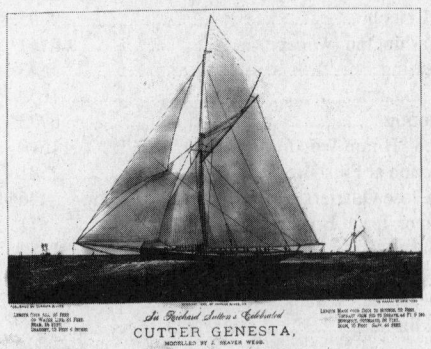

Sir Richard Sutton's Celebrated Cutter Genesta, small folio, C# 5536,
$300-$500. — Photo courtesy of Northeast Auctions.

The Best Fifty (large folio)	C#	LOW	HIGH
1. Husking	3008	$ 8500	$ 12,500
2. American Forest Scene-Maple Sugaring	157	11,000	16,000
3. Central Park Winter-The Skating Pond	954	15,000	20,000
4. Home to Thanksgiving	2882	13,000	19,000
5. Life of a Hunter-A Tight Fix	3522	43,000	65,000
6. Life on the Prairie-The Buffalo Hunt	3527	5000	7000
7. The Lightning Express Trains Leaving the Junction	3535*	11,000	16,000
8. Peytona and Fashion	4763	10,000	15,000
9. The Rocky Mountains- Emigrants Crossing the Plains	5196	13,000	18,000
10. Trolling for Blue Fish	6158	9000	12,000
11. Whale Fishery-The Sperm Whale in a Flurry	6627	5000	10,000
12. Winter in the Country-The Old Grist Mill	6738	9000	13,000
13. American Farm Scenes No. 4 (Winter)	136	7000	9000
14. American National Game of Baseball	180	27,000	37,000
15. American Winter Sports-Trout Fishing on Chateaugay Lake	210*	7000	9000
16. Mink Trapping-Prime	4139	9000	13,000
17. Preparing for Market	4870*	3400	5000
18. Winter in the Country-Getting Ice	6737	11,000	16,000
19. Across the Continent-Westward the Course of Empire Takes Its Way	33	12,000	18,000
20. Life on the Prairie-The Trappers Defense	3528	5000	7000
21. The Midnight Race on the Mississippi	4116	5000	8000
22. The Road Winter	5171	15,000	25,000
23. Summer Scenes in New York Harbor	5876	4000	6000
24. Trotting Cracks at the Forge	6169	7000	10,000
25. View of San Francisco	6409	8000	12,000
26. Wreck of the Steamship *San Francisco* (also known as "Ships Antarctic of N.Y." and "3 Bells")	5492	4000	6000
27. Taking the Back Track "A Dangerous Neighborhood"	5961	5000	7000
28. American Field Sports-Flushed	149	3000	5000
29. American Hunting Scenes-A Good Chance	174	5500	8000
30. American Winter Scenes-Morning	208	5500	7500
31. Autumn in New England-Cider Making	322	11,000	16,000
32. Catching a Trout-"We Hab You Now, Sar"	845	4000	6000
33. Clipper Ship *Nightingale*	1159	4000	6000
34. The Life of a Fireman-The Race	3518	2000	3000
35. Mac and Zachary Taylor-Horse Race	3848	1500	2500
36. New England Winter Scene	4420	7000	9500
37. Rail Shooting on the Delaware	5054	4000	6000
38. Snowed Up-Ruffed Grouse-Winter	5581	5500	7500
39. Surrender of General Burgoyne at Saratoga	5907	2000	3000
40. Surrender of Cornwallis at Yorktown	5906	2000	3000
41. Clipper Ship *Red Jacket*	1165*	5500	7500
42. American Winter Sports-Deer Shooting on the Shettagee	209	7500	9500
43. The Bark "Theoxana"	371	7500	9500
44. The Cares of a Family	814*	2500	3500
45. The Celebrated Horse Lexington	887*	2000	3000
46. Grand Drive-Central Park	2481	3000	4000
47. The Great Fire at Chicago	2615	6000	8500
48. Landscape, Fruit and Flowers	3440	5500	7500
49. The Life of a Fireman-The Metropolitan System	3516	3000	5500
50. The Splendid Naval Triumph on the Mississippi	5659	2000	2500

Louis Icart Prints

Louis Icart's works demonstrate a mastery of dry point, line etching, aquatint, and their variations. Icart produced up to 500 prints each of over 1,000 subjects. However, his works are scarce, because many have been lost or destroyed.

Most prints bear his hallmark near the edge of the print. His signature is also easily identifiable, although subject to forgery and sometimes found on lithographic reproductions of his prints. Earlier works will have his signature but may not bear the hallmark. Most will, however, bear the stamp of his gallery, an oval shape with the letters EM for "estampe moderne." It is possible to have an original Icart with no hallmark at all, but this is rare. Icart often pulled two editions, one for Europe and one for American distribution. Sometimes the number is preceded by the letter "A" for an American edition, for example "A 75/120." Not all prints were numbered.

Clockwise from above: Before the Raid, $2000; Illusion, $14,000; Melody Hour, $2000; Zest, $3000. — Photos courtesy of Phillips Auctioneers.

	LOW	AVG.	HIGH
Angry Steed	$ 2200	$ 3200	$ 4200
Apache Dancer	2000	4000	6500
Arrival	850	1425	2000
Attic Room	2100	4150	6200
Autumn Leaves	700	900	1100
Backstage	880	1440	2000
Bathing Beauties	1550	2275	3000
Before the Raid	2250	3125	4000
Bird of Prey (w/ eagle)	1900	2950	4000
Bird Seller	925	1462	2000
Black Fan	750	1125	1500
Blue Buddha	1100	1700	2500
Bubbles	2100	4200	6300
Carmen	900	1450	2000
Cassanova	1500	2800	4000
Charm of Montmarte	900	1500	2100
Cinderella	825	1200	1575
Coach, The	825	1300	1775
Conchita	1350	1875	2400
Coursing II	2000	4000	6000
Coursing III	1700	3400	5000
D'Artagnan	1175	2088	3000
Dame Rose	1000	1600	2400
Dancer (Finale)	1000	1600	2400
Date Tree	1000	1600	2400
Dear Friends	2000	4000	6000
December	1000	2000	3000
Defense of the Homeland	2500	4250	6000
Descending Coach	1050	1925	2800
Dollar	700	1250	1800
Don Juan	1600	3000	4400
Dream Waltz	1250	1925	2600
Ecstacy	2300	4150	6000
Embrace	900	1500	2100
Eve (Large Oval)	1300	1850	2400
Fair Dancer	1000	1600	2400
Fashion Early	1200	2200	3200
Faust	1100	1850	2600
Favorite	1500	3000	4500
Feeding Time	1000	1900	2800
Finlandia	1275	2338	3400
Flower Vendor	1000	1800	2600
Follies	1500	2750	4000
Forbidden Fruit	1150	2075	3000
Fountain, The	1400	2500	3600
Four Dears	1475	2738	4000
France de Foyer	1950	3475	5000
French Bus	1375	2488	3600
French Doll	800	1300	1800
Frou Frou	1500	3000	4500
Gay Senorita	1100	1900	2700

	LOW	AVG.	HIGH
Gay Trio	$ 1000	$ 1500	$ 2000
German Eagle	1600	2800	4000
Girl in Crinoline	1650	3325	5000
Golden Veil	1600	2800	4000
Goosed	950	1675	2400
Green Broken Jug	1000	1500	2000
Green Robe	1400	2100	2800
Guardian	1300	2350	3400
Gust of Wind	1400	2300	3200
Happy Birthday	2600	5300	8000
Hop-la	1000	1500	2000
Hydrangas	2500	3750	5000
Illusion	9,000	14,500	20,000
Imprudence	1000	1500	2000
In the Trenches	2200	3300	4400
Intimacy	2800	4200	5600
Japanese Garden	1200	1800	2400
Joan of Arc	900	1350	1800
Joy of Life	6000	9000	12,000
Kiss of the Motherland	600	900	1200
Kittens	3000	4500	6000
Lady of the Camelias	1500	2250	3000
Lassitude	900	1350	1800
Laughing	1800	2700	3600
Leda and the Swan	4600	6900	9200
Lilies	3000	4400	5800
Little Bo Peep	1300	2050.	2800
Little Kittens	800	1200	1600
Louise	1200	1800	2400
Love's Awakening	1200	1800	2400
Love's Blossom	2400	3600	4800
Madame Bovary	1100	1550	2000
Meditation	1700	2550	3400
Memories	2300	3300	4300
Mimi	800	1200	1600
Minuet	1200	1800	2400
Modern Eve	1800	2700	3600
My Model	3000	4400	5800
New Friends	1200	1800	2400
Nineteen Thirty	1500	2250	3000
On the Branches	900	1350	1800
Orchids	3000	4400	5800
Papillons	1800	2700	3600
Parasol	900	1350	1800
Parfum de Fluers	2400	3600	4800
Recollections (woman at desk)	600	900	1200
Red Alcove	1000	1900	2800
Red Riding Hood	1200	2200	3200
Reflections Pool	2250	4125	6000
Salomé	1200	2100	3000
Sappho	1200	2200	3200

	LOW	AVG.	HIGH
Scherazade	$ 1100	$ 1950	$ 2800
Seashell	1700	3200	4700
Secrets or Blue Book	1100	2000	2900
Singing Lesson	1000	1800	2600
Sleeping Beauty	1275	2238	3200
Smoke	1600	2800	4000
Spanish Dancer	1300	2400	3500
Speed (w/ greyhound)	1800	3300	4800
Spilled Apples	980	1690	2400
Springtime	1250	2225	3200
Summer Music	800	1400	2000
Swans	1500	2450	3400
Sweet Mystery	1400	2600	3800
Symphony in Blue	1200	2000	2800
Symphony in White	1500	2550	3600
Tennis	1100	1850	2600
Thoroughbreds	2400	4000	5600
Tosca	1200	2100	3000
Treasure Chest	900	1650	2400
Trenches	2500	3800	5000
Unmasked	1250	2025	2800
Venetian Nights	1150	1975	2800
Venus (companion to Eve)	1500	2450	3400
Victory in the Skies	1575	2688	3800
View of Montmartre	1000	1900	2800

Maxfield Parrish Prints

Maxfield Parrish illustrated magazines and advertisements for various national companies during the early 1900s. He also created many limited edition prints. There are many reproductions on the market.

Left: Advertising posters and cards should contain all their original text.

Below: Calenders should be as originally issued, including ribbon and tear-away months. Figures are generally preferred over landscapes or seascapes. —Photos courtesy of Phillips Auctioneers.

	LOW	AVG.	HIGH
Above the Balcony, knaves and maidens in garden	$ 90	$ 120	$ 150
Air Castles, nude in bubbles	300	350	400
Aladdin and the Lamp, 10" x 12"	180	220	260
Aladdin in Cave of 40 Thieves, 12" x 16.5", on quality paper	210	250	290
Ancient Trees, large oak tree by lake	220	270	320
Argonauts, In Quest of the Golden Fleece	120	150	180
Arizona, landscape of mountain, rich blues, 11" x 13"	120	150	180
Atlas, giant holding up sky	180	220	260
Aucassin Seeks Nicolotte, knight on horse, bookplate SM	60	80	90
Autumn, maiden standing on hilltop	175	225	275
Below the Balcony, knaves and maidens in garden	90	112	135
Bookplate, John Cox-His Book	60	75	90
Brazen, The Boatman, 10" x 12"	160	200	240
Brown and Bigelow Landscape, the village church, 24" x 27"	400	500	600
Cadmus Showing the Dragon's Teeth, 10" x 12"	120	150	180
Canyon, maiden in canyon, 12" x 5"	300	375	450
Circles Palace, maiden standing on porch	120	150	180
Cleopatra, rare, large	900	1200	1500
Community Plate, 11" x 13", 1918	70	85	100
Contentment, large Edison Mazda Calendar	750	950	1150
Dawn, maiden sitting on rock, Mazda print	120	150	180
Daybreak, large size	475	575	675
Daybreak, nude and maiden on porch, small size	250	350	450
Dinkey Bird, nude on swing, 13.5" x 18", 1904	250	350	450
Djer-Kiss Ad, maiden on swing in forest, 10.5" x 14"	120	150	180
Dream Castle in the Sky, 9" x 12"	90	112	135
Dreaming, large size	700	850	1000
Dreaming, nude sitting under oak, medium size	400	500	600
Dreamlight, maid on swing, Edison Mazda Calendar, 9.5" x 20.5", 1925	500	650	800
Duchess at Prayer, illustration for L'Allegro, 10" x 15", 1901	60	75	90
Ecstasy, large Edison Mazda Calendar	1200	1450	1700
Ecstasy, maiden standing on rock, small size	225	300	375
Enchantment, maiden standing on stars at night, 9.5" x 20.5", large	850	1100	1350
Errant Pan, Pan sitting by stream, 6" x 8", small	70	85	100
Evening, nude sitting in lake, 13" x 17"	180	225	270
Evening, nude sitting on rock in lake	250	300	350
Fisherman and the Genie, The, 10" x 12"	150	188	225
Florentine Fete, maidens in garden, 10" x 16"	80	100	120
Garden of Allah, 3 maidens sitting in garden, medium size	200	300	400
Garden of Allah, large Edison Mazda Calendar	550	750	950
Garden of Opportunity, prince and princess	650	850	1050
Garden of Opportunity Triptych, 10" x 13"	120	150	180
Golden Hours, maidens in forest, large Edison Mazda Calendar	800	1000	1200
Harper's Weekly, poster	2600	3200	3800
Hilltop, large size, House of Art	920	1150	1380
Hilltop, small size	175	200	225
Hilltop, youths sitting on mountain, medium size, House of Art	420	525	630
His Christmas Dinner, tramp eating dinner	120	150	180
Interlude, maidens in garden playing lutes	240	300	360
Isola Bella Scene, 9" x 10"	52	65	78
Jason and His Teacher Chiron the Centaur, 1910	90	112	135

	LOW	AVG.	HIGH
King of the Black Isles, king on throne, on quality paper, 9" x 11" ..	$ 180	$ 230	$ 280
King's Son, Arab in garden by fountain	120	150	180
Knave of Hearts Book, mint	650	850	1050
Knaves and Maidens, conversing in garden	120	150	180
Lamplighters, Mazda Calendar, 9" x 13", 1924	200	250	300
Lampseller of Baghdad, The, maiden on steps, Mazda Calendar	650	850	1050
Land of Make-Believe, The, maiden in garden	65	80	95
Little Princess, princess sitting by fountain	60	75	90
Lute Players, large size, House of Art	800	1100	1400
Lute Players, small size, House of Art	150	175	200
Milkmaid, maiden walking on mountain	60	75	90
Morning, maiden sitting on rock, 13" x 16"	260	325	390
Night Call, bare-breasted girl in surf, 6" x 8"	60	80	100
October-1900, woman w/ fruit draped in her gown, orange moon, 18" x 23"	60	80	100
Old King Cole	800	1000	1200
Old Romance, nude sitting in pool, 8" x 8"	130	170	210
Pandora's Box, maiden sitting by large box	160	200	240
Pierrot, clown w/ lute, sky glittering, 1912	240	300	360
Pipe Night, comical men w/ pipes and coffee urns sitting facing each other at table, 9" x 12.5"	70	88	105
Pool of the Villa D'Este, nude lying besides luminous pool, 7.5" x 10.5"	56	70	84
Post Standing, by river in forest	70	88	105
Potpourri, nude in garden picking flowers	120	150	180
Prince, from Knave of Hearts, 10" x 12.5", rare	270	338	405
Prince Goodad, pirates on boat	160	200	240
Prosperina, maiden in the sea, 10" x 12"	160	200	240
Providing It By the Book, 2 gents at table	56	70	84
Queen Guinare, maiden on porch, 10" x 12"	160	200	240
Reveries, large Edison Mazda Calendar	450	550	650
Reveries, 2 maidens sitting by fountain	90	112	135
Sandman, w/ full moon, 6" x 7.5"	80	100	120
Sea Nymphs, 12" x 14", 1914	120	150	180
Search for the Singing Tree	90	120	150
Seven Green Polls at Cintra, 6" x 8"	70	90	110
Shepherd w/ Sheep, 8.5" x 13.5"	56	70	84
Ship in Ocean, 11" x 13.5"	90	112	135
Sinbad and the Cyclops, 10" x 12"	90	112	135
Sing a Song of Sixpence, 9" x 21"	650	950	1150
Singing Tree, The, 10" x 12"	100	125	150
Stars, House of Art, large size, nude sitting on rock	1100	1300	1500
Stars, House of Art, medium size, nude sitting on rock	500	700	900
Story From Phoebus, 8" x 10", 1901	50	65	80
Sunlit Valley, scenic of river and mountains	270	338	405
Sunrise, Edison Mazda Calendar, rare, large	1000	1250	1500
Sunrise, Edison Mazda Calendar, small	270	338	405
Swifts Ham Ad, Jack Sprat and wife	100	125	150
Turquoise Cup, man sitting in villa	50	65	80
Twilight Had Fallen, 2 figures on beach	60	80	100
Valley of Diamonds, Arab in valley	90	112	135

	LOW	AVG.	HIGH
Venetian Lamplighter, Edison Mazda Calendar, 1924	$ 160	$ 210	$ 260
Villa D'Este, nude sitting by pool	90	110	130
Wails of Jasper, youth and castle, 12" x 14"	150	200	250
Waterfall, large Edison Mazda Calendar	1200	1400	1600
Waterfall, small Edison Mazda Calendar	230	330	430
White Birch, farmer under large birch	90	120	150
Wild Geese, girl on rock, 13" x 16"	280	340	400

Above: A Mazda lamp advertising display may have replaced lightbulbs, but they must be Mazda bulbs identical to the originals. Below: A complete advertising display is worth more than twice the value of either half. —Photos courtesy of Phillips Auctioneers.

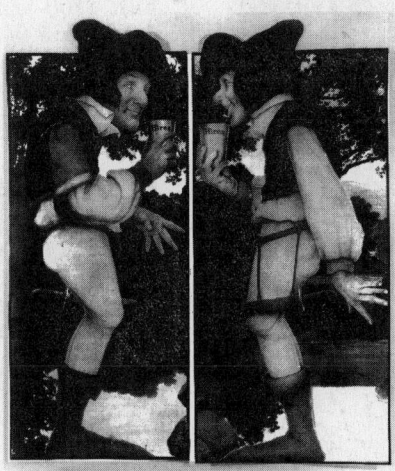

Radios

The following section encompasses several areas of radio collecting. Included are early examples from the 1920s, Catalin plastic case radios from the 1930s and 1940s, later Cold War-era radios from the 1950s and 1960s, early transistor radios from the same era, and novelty radios and advertising radios.

Catalin are the beautiful marbleized or mottled-look radios. They are often mistakenly called Bakelite. Catalin refers to a clear plastic that can be colored, first developed by the Catalin Corporation. The prices of Catalin radios shot up dramatically in the late 1980s to early 1990s. Interest has cooled but they still draw great interest. In the case of Catalin radios many collectors suggest "don't touch that dial" because heat can crack the cases. Catalins have also been known to shrink, crack, and fade.

There are those who prefer the early wooden case models. Many new collectors, however, or those frustrated by Catalin's prices, have turned to what we call the dashboard-type radios, due to their ultrasleek "techno" designs. Others pursue newer advertising radios.

In the following entries, each radio is first listed by make, followed by the type of radio it is in parentheses. (T)-table top [includes wooden cases, Catalin radios, plastic and others], (N)-novelty [includes character and interestingly shaped radios], (P)-portable, (TR)-transistor, (C)-crystal (A)-advertising, (F)-floor models. Next follows a brief description, along with the approximate date of manufacture. All prices are for radios in complete and excellent condition. Radios should also be in working order with the possible exception of some of the plastics (since heat can crack the case).

We suggest these books: *Guide to Old Radios*, David and Betty Johnson, Wallace-Homestead, Radnor, PA, 1989; *The Collector's Guide to Antique Radios*, Marty and Sue Bunis, Collector Books, Paducah, KY, 1995; *Radios, the Golden Age*, Philip Collins, Chronicle Books, San Francisco, CA, 1978; *Radios Redeux*, Philip Collins, Chronicle Books, San Francisco, CA, 1991; *Collector's Guide to Novelty Radios*, Marty Bunis and Robert F. Breed, Collector Books, Paducah KY, 1995.

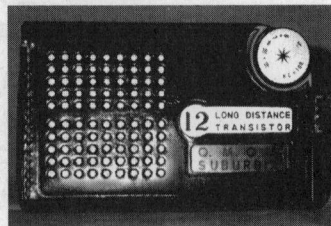

Left: This Baseball form radio appeals to novelty radio collectors as well as sports fans, $800-$1200. —Photo courtesy of Phillips Auctioneers. Below: OMS Suburbia with leather case, $25-$35.

MAKE	TYPE	DESCRIPTION	DATE	VALUE
Admiral	(T)	brown plastic, gold dial	1950	$ 40-50
Admiral #5Z22	(T)	brown plastic, metal dial	1952	35-45
Admiral #7C65W	(F)	4 knobs	1950	50-80
Admiral #7L12	(TR)	solar powered	1956	150-250
Air Castle #106B	(T)	plastic	1947	70-90
Baseball	(N)	Trophy	1941	800-1200
Bendix #55X4	(P)	plastic, hinged front	1949	50-80
Bowling Ball	(N)	Trophy	1941	550-750
Bulova #670 Bantam	(TR)	jewel decoration	1960	200-300
California Raisin	(A)	California Raisins	1988	30-40
Channel Master #6506	(TR)	pocket	1958	30-40
Charlie McCarthy	(N)	Majestic	1938	900-1200
Charlie the Tuna	(A)	Star Kist Tuna	1970	60-80
Coca-Cola Cooler	(A)	Coca-Cola	1950	600-800
Crosley #538	(T)	wooden slant front	1926	80-100
Crosley X	(T)	wooden	1922	150-200
Crosley VI #VR78	(T)	wooden	1922	100-150
Dahlberg Pillow Speaker	(N)	coin operated	1955	250-350
DeForest #D10	(T)	wooden, loop antenna	1923	400-600
DeForest D6	(T)	wooden, rectangular	1923	900-1100
DeForest #DT600	(T)	wooden, crystal "Everyman"	1923	250-350
Detrola #219 Pee Wee	(T)	plastic (rare colors more)	1940	300-500
Emerson #888 Vanguard	(TR)	pink or blue	1960	80-120
Emerson Patriot #400	(T)	Catalin,	1940	1000-1500
Emerson Tombstone	(T)	Catalin (rare colors more)	1940	1000-1500
Fada #252 Temple	(T)	Catalin (rare colors more)	1940	300-500
Fada #115 Bullet/Streamliner	(T)	Catalin (rare colors more)	1940	600-800
Fada #1000 Bullet/Streamliner	(T)	Catalin (rare colors more)	1946	600-800
Federal #57	(T)	wooden, 1 dial	1922	400-500
Federal #61	(T)	metal, 3 dials	1923	700-900
Federal #58DX	(T)	metal, "Orthosonic"	1922	400-500
Freshman #SF2	(T)	wooden, 3 dials, "Masterpiece"	1924	90-120
G.E. Clock Radio	(T)	pink plastic	1960	18-22
General Electric #675	(TR)		1956	80-100
Goulden's Mustard Jar	(A)	Goulden's Mustard	1982	30-40
Grand Old Granddad Bottle	(A)	Whiskey	1965	45-65
Grebe #CR5	(T)	wooden, 3 dials	1921	400-500
Grebe #MU1	(T)	wooden, "Synchrophase"	1925	150-200
Helping Hand	(A)	Hamburger Helper	1980	30-40
Hitachi #666	(TR)	pocket, red or gray	1958	80-120
Hopalong Cassidy	(N)	Arvin	1950	300-400
Kadette Jewel	(T)	plastic, various models	1935	200-300
Knight's Helmet w/ Crest	(N)		1970	30-40
Lafayette #D140	(T)	ivory plastic deco	1939	90-110
Little Sprout	(A)	Green Giant	1980	30-40
Lone Ranger	(N)	Airline	1951	500-800
Magnavox #TRF5	(T)	wooden, doors	1925	80-120
Manola	(TR)	table red plastic	1958	20-30
Mercedes Auto Grill	(N)		1965	30-40
Mickey Mouse	(N)	brown case	1940	1200-1800
Mork Egg Radio	(N)		1978	30-50

MAKE	TYPE	DESCRIPTION	DATE	VALUE
Motorola	(P)	"V" shield, handle turns	1958	$ 40-60
Motorola	(T)	aqua plastic clock radio	1958	20-30
New World (globe and stand)	(N)	Colonial	1933	800-1200
Philco	(T)	brown plastic, "services" dial	1954	25-40
Philco #525			1929	90-120
Philco #49501	(T)	boomerang Transitone	1949	200-300
Philco #T7	(TR)	black and white	1956	80-120
Philco Cathedral	(T)	wooden	1931	150-200
Polaroid 600 Plus	(A)	Polaroid Film	1980	25-35
Punchy	(A)	Hawaiian Punch	1972	40-60
Raid Bug Clock Radio	(A)	Raid Insecticide	1980	100-150
RCA Radiola X	(T)	wooden	1925	300-400
RCA Aeriola Jr.	(C)		1922	120-180
RCA Radiola 26	(P)	wooden	1925	300-400
RCA #7QBK	(F)		1940	80-100
Regency #TR1	(TR)	white or black, pocket	1954	250-350
Snow White (tan case)	(N)	Emerson	1938	1000-1500
Sony #TR63	(TR)	pocket	1957	300-500
Spartan #558	(T)	blue mirror, deco	1937	200-3000
Stromberg Carlson Clock Radio	(T)	gray and salmon plastic	1957	20-30
Tide Box	(A)	Tide Detergent	1980	40-50
Tony the Tiger	(A)	Sugar Frosted Flakes	1980	35-45
Toshiba #5TR	(TR)	lacey face plate	1958	150-200
Westinghouse	(A)	aqua plastic, tapering shield	1960	18-25
Westinghouse #H685	(TR)	table top with clock	1959	20-30
Zenith #64	(F)	ornate chest on stand	1919	350-450
Zenith #L515 Clock Radio	(T)	brown, dashboard look	1954	80-120
Zenith Royal #500	(TR)	pocket, black	1956	80-100

 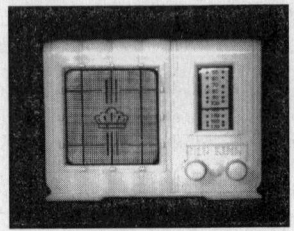

Above left to right: Motorola with rotating handle, 1950s, $40-$60; Air King, $70-$90. Below left to right: Admiral tabletop, 1950s, $25-$35; Zenith dashboard style, $75-$100.

Scrimshaw

Scrimshaw is artwork done on bone. It can be carved or painted. Carved scrimshaw, which seldom has any painted decoration, is mostly in the nature of little trinkets, boxes, pins, or forks, for example. Painted scrimshaw is done directly on the tooth or bone. It is accomplished by scratching the design into the surface with needles, then working India ink into the scratches. Whalebone is the most commonly found material, followed by walrus tusk. Occasionally a low-grade ivory such as whale tooth is used.

The age, size, artistic quality, subject matter, and state of preservation all go into determining the value of scrimshaw. Beware of fakes made from polymers. See *Fakeshaw* by Stuart Frank, Kendall Whaling Museum, 1993. Also beware of various endangered species laws. Differences in federal and state regulations make this a tricky topic. Check with local authorities before buying or selling scrimshaw.

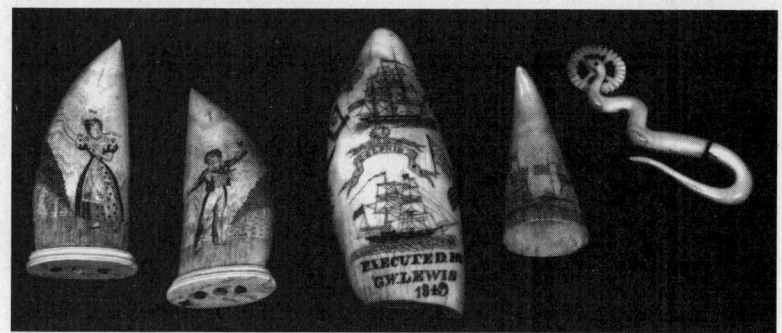

Left to right: Pair of teeth depicting sailor and sweetheart, height 6", $2750; tooth depicting the brig "Dolphin", 1849, height 7.5", $3750; tooth depicting fort and ship, height 4.5", $650, serpent-form whalebone jagging wheel, ca. 1849, length 6", $2100.
— Photo courtesy of Northeast Auctions.

	AUCTION	RETAIL Low	High
Busk, decorated w/ pinwheels, hearts, and basket of flowers, bearing date 1872, ht. 12"	$ 650	$ 1210	$ 2120
Busk engraved w/ lighthouse below public buildings, len. 13"	550	1020	1790
Cane w/ turned ivory and baleen details, len. 34"	500	930	1630
Coconut-Shell Dipper, w/ vine motifs, scrimshaw end, 15"	600	1120	1960
Double-Block, w/ rope fitting, 2.5"	325	600	1060
Eskimo Walrus Tusk Cribbage Board, tip in form of an open-mouth fish, len. 13.5"	550	1020	1790
Eskimo Walrus Tusk Cribbage Board, tip in form of fish, mounted on carved seals, len. 17"	500	930	1630
Eskimo Walrus Tusk Cribbage Board, w/ designs of hawk and sea animals, signed "Herman Toolie, Alaska.," len. 24.25"	450	840	1470
Eskimo Walrus Tusk Cribbage Board, w/ designs of whale, walrus, and foxes, len. 24.25"	450	840	1470
Eskimo Walrus Tusk Cribbage Board, w/ sea animals and hunters, len. 18.5"	500	930	1630

	AUCTION	RETAIL Low	High
Fid, pierced, carved, w/ open-work heart motifs, 6.5"	$ 700	$ 1300	$ 2280
Jagging Wheel, inlaid w/ abalone diamond, len. 6.5"	700	1300	2280
Jagging Wheel, w/ finely shaped and pierced handle, len. 6" ..	1100	2050	3590
Jagging Wheel, w/ fluted wheel, len. 6"	350	650	1140
Knife Sharpener, bone handle carved in form of gloved hand, len. 16"	400	740	1300
Nantucket Pocketbook, w/ scrimshaw whale by Jose Formosc Reyes, oval, len. 10"	800	1490	2610
Net Mender, len. 14"	100	190	330
Pie Crimper, tapering fluted form, inlaid w/ abalone heart, len. 7"	500	930	1630
Pie Crimper w/ hand-form handle and sawtooth decorated wheel, len. 6"	2300	4280	7500
Rolling Pin, mah., acorn-form handles, 18"	950	1770	3100
Rope Seamer, sailor-made, 5.5"	400	740	1300
Teeth, pr., engraved w/ floral panels, ht. 4"	500	930	1630
Walrus Tusks, pr., w/ vignettes of women, ships, walrus, and penguin, each marked "Susan," len. 13"	550	1020	1790
Watch-Hutch Mantel Ornament, on mah. stand w/ facing engraved teeth and panbone watch holder, teeth w/ fanciful dolphin motifs, ht. 7.5", len. 12"	3000	5580	9780
Whale's Teeth, pr., w/ anchor, sailor, whale and Oriental figure, the second w/ ship, Scotsman, palm tree and pelican, ht. of teeth 5"	1700	3160	5540
Whale's Tooth, decorated w/ scene of sailor at cannon holding flag	450	840	1470
Whale's Tooth, w/ allegorical representation of Neptune on shell pulled by sea horses and mermaid, len. 7.5"	1600	2980	5220
Whale's Tooth, w/ barque flying American flag, len. 7"	650	1210	2120
Whale's Tooth, w/ portrait of John Paul Jones and American 3-masted whale ship	550	1020	1790
Whale's Tooth, w/ vignettes of sailor's life, dockside scene, "The Last Minstrel," len. 6.25"	550	1020	1790

Shaker Collectibles

The Shakers formed a socioreligious organization in England in 1747. Their doctrines advocated simplicity and celibacy. They were nicknamed "Shakers" because of their devotional dancing in religious services. Ann Lee led a group to America in 1776 and attracted many converts. Known for their fine quality, Shakers made products that symbolized beliefs of purity and utility from the early 19th century to the 20th century. Although the Shakers made furniture for their own use, much was made for commercial sale.

Pieces are worth more if the collector can identify the Shaker community of origin. For the sampling of pieces listed below, the following abbreviations are used: Alfred, Maine = *ALF,* Canterbury, New Hampshire = *CANT,* Enfield, Connecticut = *ENF,* Harvard, Massachusetts = *HAR,* Hancock, Massachusetts = *HAN,* Mt. Lebanon, New York = *MtL,* New Lebanon, New York = *NL,* Pleasant Hill, Kentucky = *PLH,* Sabbathday Lake, Maine = *SDL,* Watervliet, New York = *WVLT.*

Identifying Shaker pieces can be difficult. There are large numbers of fakes and countless reproductions. Note that the famed Shaker oval box with long "fingers" fastening the sides are probably not true Shaker unless the fingers of the lid and the body are pointing the same direction. For further information see *By Shaker Hands,* by June Sprigg. Auctioneers who specialize in Shaker pieces include Willis Henry.

Above: Pair of maple tilting side chairs with orginal tape seats, $1600; oval maple carrier, $3000; rectangular pine carrier, $800; oval maple carrier, $3000; oval maple box, $1700. — Photo courtesy of Northeast Auctions.

	LOW	HIGH
Armchair, maple, rush seat, MtL, c.1870, #7	$ 5500	$ 8500
Armchair, maple, tape seat, MtL, c.1870, #3	1250	1850
Basket, ash, hickory, rect., hoop handle, PLH, c. 1850, w., 20"	1800	2700
Basket, ash, orig. green stain, hinged lid, sq. 12.5"	3000	4500
Basket, ash, rect., hoop handle, open-weave bottom, signed, w. 14.5"	1000	1460
Basket, maple, 2-handle, double-wrapped rim, ENF, c. 1850, dia. 7.5"	1650	2500
Basket, splint, hoop handle, attached lid, signed, HAR, c. 1850, w. 9"	1800	2700
Basket, maple, ash, flared top, ENF, c. 1850, ht. 29", sq. 17"	4200	6300
Basket, ash, swing handle and side handle, w. 18"	3600	5400
Basket, oak, swing handle, wrapped rim, SDL, c. 1840, dia. 14"	1500	2250
Bench, maple, bootjack ends, ENF, c. 1870, w. 45"	7,000	10,000
Blanket Chest, pine, red paint, cutout base, ENF, c. 1850, w. 41"	2400	3600
Bonnet, linen trimmed, paper label, #5	600	900
Box, oval, 1 finger on lid and base, len. 3.5" , w. 2"	100	200
Box, oval, c. 1840, 3 fingers, 11 copper brads, len. 6,25, w. 4.5"	435	650
Box, pine, orig. red stain, molded lid, NL, c. 1830, w. 14.5"	1500	2250
Box, poplar, satin-lined, orig. "Canterbury Shakers" box, sq. 4.5"	900	1350
Box, poplar, rect., SDL, blue satin, w. 5.5"	150	220
Bucket, pine, orig. red paint, ENF, c. 1840, dia. 10"	1350	2000
Bucket, w/ lid, pine, blue paint, MtL, c. 1850, dia. 9.75"	2400	3600
Candle Chest, bootjack ends, SDL, c. 1840, ht. 36", w. 33"	3000	4500
Candlestand, snake leg, orig. finish, NL, c. 1840, ht. 23.5", dia. 16"	8000	12,000
Cape, wool, mother-of-pearl buttons, initialed, len. 32"	680	1000
Chatelaine, w/ plastic rings forming chain, bows on top and bottom, len. 11"	165	250
Chair Table, orig. red, CANT, c. 1840, w. 73"	14,000	20,000
Cheese Basket, black ash, ALF, c. 1840, dia. 21"	2400	3600
Cheese Box, orig. green paint, copper nails, pegged, HAN, dia. 16.5"	2550	3820
Child's Chair, maple, orig. yellow stain, spindle back, CANT, c. 1880, ht. 29"	900	1350
Child's Rocking Chair, maple, taped seat, #0, MtL decal, ht. 23"	6500	9500
Child's Side Chair, dark varn., orig. tape, #1, MtL decal, ht. 28"	4500	7000
Child's Side Chair, refinished	570	900
Child's Tilt Chair, birch, orig. varn., taped seat, ENF, c. 1830, ht. 32"	6000	9000
Cloak, blue wool, satin, labeled "Enfield, N.H.," len. 56"	900	1350
Clothes Brush, horsehair, 8.75"	450	680
Covered Bucket, pine, orig. red paint, signed "Enfield," dia. 9.75"	3000	4500
Cream Tub, orig. blue paint, wire handles, ENF, c. 1840, dia. 10"	2550	3820
Cutlery Basket, ash, carved medial handle, w. 17"	3300	5000
Desk Box, CANT, c. 1840, w. 18"	3300	5000
Desk Box, chestnut, cherry and pine, orig. red stain, c. 1850, w. 16"	2100	3150
Dipper Ash, orig. cream yellow paint, len. 6.5"	1650	2480
Document Box, pine, orig. blue paint, SDL, c. 1850, w. 6.5"	1650	2480
Dough Box, orig. red paint, cutout handles, WVLT, c. 1840, w. 32"	3300	5000
Dressing Chair, birch, rush seat, double dowel back, MtL, c. 1880	3000	4500
Dry Sink, pine, refinished, NL, c. 1830, ht. 35", w. 31"	2700	4000
Drying Basket, ash, natural brown, 20" dia.	1800	2700
Drying Basket, black ash, open work, cheese basket design, 2 wrapped handles, 2 runners, c. 1850, ht. 20", dia. 23"	2700	4000
Drying Rack, dark varn., arched foot, NL, c. 1840, ht. 38", w. 24"	1200	1800
Drying Rack, orig. red paint, arched base, WVLT, c. 1850, ht. 55"	3000	4500

	LOW	HIGH
Elder's Rocking Chair, serpentine arms, NL, c. 1850	$ 4500	$ 6750
Flax Wheel, oak, maple, signed, complete w/ distaff	900	1350
Folding Drying Rack, orig. salmon paint, 4 part, ENF, c.1840, ht. 60"	3300	5000
Footstool, maple, orig. dark varn., rush seat, #0, decal, MtL, w. 13"	1500	2250
Hanger, clothes, pine, initialed, NL, c. 1850, w. 17"	200	320
Hanger, clothes, pine and hickory, CANT, c. 1850	220	340
Hanger, clothes, walnut, ENF, c. 1840, w. 12.5"	600	900
Knife Box, canted sides, finger holes, c. 1850, ht. 5", w. 13.25"	900	1350
Land Grant, w. 12"	1350	2000
Medicine Bottle, green, orig. stopper, "New Leb., NY," ht. 9.25'"	1720	2500
Milk Tub, pine, orig. blue exterior, c. 1840, dia. 9.5"	1350	2000
Mirror, oval wooden frame w/ 2 mother-of-pearl aecents on handle, len. 10.5"	500	700
Neckerchief Silk, hand-woven, initialed, 1846, sq. 35"	1350	2000
Oval Box, maple, pine, orig. red paint, 3 fingers, PLH, c. 1840, len. 6"	1950	2900
Oval Box, pine, birch, orig. white paint, 5 fingers, c. 1840, len. 12.5"	4500	6750
Oval Box, pine, maple, orig. varn., 3 fingers, SDL, c. 1850, len. 3.25"	1800	2700
Oval Carrier, orig. yellow varn., 2 fingers, CANT, c. 1830, dia. 10"	2700	4000
Oval Gift Box, pine, cedar, natural finish, 3 fingers, dia. 3.5"	2400	3600
Oval Sewing Carrier, maple, clear varn., 4 fingers, satin-lined, fitted, "SDL" trademark, w. 11"	1200	1800
Oval Sewing Carrier, maple, clear varn., satin-lined, fitted, "SDL" trademark, dia. 7"	1350	2000
Oval Spit Box, maple, pine, yellow stain, 2 fingers, CANT, c. 1840, w. 11"	2700	4000
Pail, pine, orig. paint, wire bail, NL, c. 1820, dia. 6.25"	1000	1500
Peg Rail, pine w/ birch pegs, len. 60"	600	900
Pie Lifter, wood, w/ spring action and locking ring, len. 17"	145	250
Revolving Chair, 8 spindles, NL, c. 1840, ht. 27"	17,000	25,000
Rocking Chair, cherry, shawl bar, tape seat, MtL, c. 1870, #7	2700	4000
Rocking Chair, shawl bar, ebony finish, tape seat, MtL, c. 1870, #3	1500	2250
Rocking Chair, maple, black walnut finish, old tape seat, MtL, #5	3900	5850
Rocking Chair, maple, shawl bar, tape seat, MtL, c. 1870, #7	4200	6300
Rocking Chair, maple, stained finish, shawl bar, MtL, c . 1870, #4	1950	2920
Rocking Chair, maple, tape seat, MTL, decal, c. 1900, #7	2700	4000
Round Carrier, pine, maple, HAR, c. 1830, dia. 10.75"	2250	3400
Round Carrier, poplar, maple, orig. green paint, swing handle, dia. 9"	1500	2250
Rug, silk, cotton backing, black border, polychrome field, 24" x 40"	450	680
Sampler, 3 alphabets and numerals, ENF, 10" x 12"	12,000	18,000
Shawl, wool, stripe border, fringe, SDL, 64" sq.	900	1350
Seed Box, pine, label "Fresh Garden Seeds Raised," ht. 5.5", w. 14"	2000	3000
Seed Box, orig. red paint, "Shakers Seeds, Mt. Leb.," ht. 3.5", w. 23.5"	3900	5800
Seed Carrier, pine, orig. red stain, CANT, c. 1830, ht. 9.5", sq. 10.5"	3000	4500
Sewing Basket, maple, side handles, 15.5" sq.	1350	2000
Sewing Basket, splint, sq. base, fitted lid, MtL, ht. 3.5", sq. 5.75"	2400	3600
Sewing Chest, walnut, c.1860, ht. 31", w. 40"	14,000	22,000
Sewing Desk, butternut, pine, birch, orig. paint, signed, SDL, w. 30"	120,000	180,000
Sewing Desk, pine, old varn., 5 drawers, c. 1830, w. 22.5"	9750	14,000
Sewing Stand, orig. red stain, 1 drawer, HAN, c. 1850, w. 22"	3000	4500
Sewing Stand, maple, chestnut, birch top, dark varn., tapered leg, CANT, c. 1840, w. 15.5"	10,000	15,750

	LOW	HIGH
Shovel, ash, dark varn., NL, c. 1870, len. 34"	$ 2000	$ 4000
Side Chair, bird's-eye maple, fitted w/ tilters	2450	3850
Side Chair, cherry, orig. varn., tilters, split reed seat, #3	1650	2500
Side Chair, maple, mustard yellow paint, taped seat, ALF, c. 1830, ht. 41"	2700	4000
Side Chair, maple, orig. varn., cane seat, tilters, CANT, c. 1840, ht. 41"	19,000	29,000
Side Chair, tiger maple, orig. finish and tape, tilters, NL, c. 1830, ht. 41"	6300	9500
Sorting Table, oak, tray top, NL, c. 1860, w. 76"	6600	10,000
Sorting Table, poplar, oak, brown stain, sawbuck base, flat stretchers, HAR, c. 1860, ht. 29", w.17.5"	1850	2750
Spice Chest, 4 drawers, walnut, w. 13", ht. 7.25"	550	750
Spice Chest, 13-drawer, walnut, WVLT, c. 1850, ht. 17", w. 17"	2400	3500
Spool Rack and 6 Spools, cherry, orig. varn., horn spindles, thimble holder ht. 5", dia. 5"	5250	7500
Spoolholder, orig. varn., tomato pincushion, thimble holder, dia. 5.5"	1500	2250
Stand-up Desk, lift lid, dovetailed drawer, shelf, ht. 51", w. 28"	3900	5850
Storage Box, w/ yellow paint, CANT, ht. 11" w. 25"	1400	2200

Above: Shaker boxes with finger joints should have the finger on the lid point the same direction as those on the body, as in the examples on the left. Boxes whose finger joints point in opposite directions are rarely Shaker made, as in the examples on the right. Left: Print, "Shakers Near Lebanon", 11.5" x 14" $1000 at auction. — Photos courtesy of Northeast Auctions.

	LOW	HIGH
Storage Box, maple burl, HAN, c. 1850, ht. 8.25", w. 16"	$ 3600	$ 5400
Storage Box, orig. brown paint, WVLT, c. 1840, ht. 7.5", w. 15.5"	2700	4000
Stove, iron, canted sides, straight legs, NL, c. 1840, ht. 19", len. 29"	1800	2700
Straw Press, cherry, varn. finish, mortise and pegged, threaded knobs, ALF, c. 1830, ht. 18", w. 13"	2400	3600
Swift, maple, orig. mustard paint, ht. 21"	1350	2000
Tailoring Stick, cherry, MtL, c. 1840, len. 36"	3600	5400
Tall Clock, wooden works, paper dial, dated "1835," ht. 80", w. 17"	60,000	125,000
Triple Hanger, butternut, pine, MtL, c. 1840, ht. 19.5"	1000	1500
Triple Hanger, walnut stain, init., PLH, c. 1850, ht. 6.25", w. 14"	1350	2000
Trustee's Desk, fall-front lid, inner compartments, 2 drawers, ALF, c. 1840, ht. 46.5", w. 37.5"	6500	9500
Wash Table, pine, orig. blue-gray paint, tapered leg, arched ends, separate drying rack, SDL, c. 1840, ht. 32.5", w. 28.5"	8000	12,000
Washstand, pine, refinished, 1 drawer, dovetailed, gallery w/ cup holders, CANT, c. 1850, ht. 39.5", w. 19"	2850	4000
Washstand, traces of orig. paint, 2 paneled doors, orig. threaded knobs, ENF, c. 1840, ht. 35", w. 32.5"	11,000	15,000
Wool Basket, carved double handles, ht. 13", w. 27.5"	1650	2400
Wool Wheel, weathered finish, initialed, SDL, c. 1830	1000	1580
Work Stand, 1 drawer, cherry, CANT, c. 1840, ht. 27", w. 17"	5100	7500
Work Stand, 1 drawer, cherry, pine, MtL, ht. 27.5", w. 20"	2800	4000
Work Stand, 1 drawer, cherry, poplar, ENF, c. 1840, ht. 27.5", w. 18"	9000	14,000
Work Table, pine, birch, red base, scrub top, tapered round legs, CANT, c. 1820, ht. 28", w. 63"	5500	7700
Work Table, pine, maple, orig. red finish, turned leg, ALF, c. 1820, ht. 28", w. 34"	4250	6500
Work Table, pine, oak, red stain finish, 1 drawer, chamfered legs, SDL, c. 1860, ht. 27.5", w. 20.5"	1000	1500
Yarn Winder, maple, clock reel, CANT, c. 1839, ht. 37"	1750	2500

Right: Sabbathday Lake, Maine mark on oval carrier.

Ship Models

There are four main types of ship models. *Wright's models* (*W*) were made by a shipwright (a ship builder) as a working model for an actual ship. *Sailor's models* (*S*) were made while the sailor served on a ship. *Collector's models* (*C*) made after the ship was constructed, often after it ceased to exist, using photographs or drawings in books. *Kit models* (*K*) are built from components and directions furnished in a commercially sold kit.

Wright's models are the most desired and expensive. Sailor's models may be crude, but they are often highly regarded. The value of a collector's model is determined by age, size, intricacy of detail, and state of preservation. Models of steamships are generally not as valuable as sailing vessels.

	AUCTION	RETAIL Low	High
American Hermaphrodite Brig, w/ white painted hull and detailed rigging, sternboard w/ "Frank Bacon," len. of case 52", *S*	$ 4500	$ 8370	$ 14,670
American Schooner, outfitted as privateer w/ cannon, deck covered w/ finely detailed ropes, sails, and accessories, len. of case 45", *S*	5000	9300	16300
Bone Ship, Amer. Barkentine, c. 1830, rigged, case 27.5", *S*	15,000	30,000	45,000
Builder's Half-Hull of Amer. Steamship, w. 96", *W*	650	1300	2000
Cutty Sark, w/ rigging and lifeboats mounted on stand, len. 54", *C*	1000	1860	3260
Four-Masted Vessel w/ rigging and lifeboats, len. of case 33", *C*	1750	3260	5710
McCalla, by Alan Raven, scratch-built cased waterline destroyer depicted in 1942, len. 31", *C*	700	1300	2280
Sailing Ship, planked, w. 40", *C*	1700	3400	5000
Shadowbox Half-Hull of 7-Mast Schooner, w. 44", *W*	2600	5000	8000
Shadowbox Half-Hull of Amer. Ship, w. 33", *W*	1300	2500	4000
Ship in a Bottle, *Old Ironsides*, len. 4", *K*	100	150	250
Whale Boat, Amer., fitted w/ whaling equip. and sail, w. 24", *S*	4500	9000	13,000

Half Hull of the American steamship Raven, 48", *$800-$1200 retail value.*

Silhouettes

Silhouettes are profiles cut out of one color paper and attached to a background of contrasting color. Sometimes detail is added in chalk, pen or watercolor. Most collected silhouettes date to the first half of the 19th century. Modern and semimodern silhouettes have little or no value. The value depends on the age, quality and size of the specimen. The fame of the subject is also very important.

Silhouette family group by William Henry Brown. —Photo courtesy of Northeast Auctions

	AUCTION	RETAIL Low	High
Aitken Family by Todd, hollow-cut, pr., depicting young man and woman, w/ stamped mark, inscription on reverse, 5.5" x 10.5" ..	$ 200	$ 350	$ 550
Children, pr., full-length, inscribed Frith, 1841, highlighted w/ gilt	450	790	1240
Couple, mirrored pr., in carved frames, ht. 7"	450	790	1240
Couple, pr., hollow-cut, in eglomisé mat	300	530	830
Couple, pr., hollow-cut, man w/ striped vest, young woman, stamped "Williams," (Henry Williams, Amer. 1787-1830)	125	220	340
Eng. Silhouette, signed Miers, ht 4"	110	190	300
Family Group, 1849, William Henry Brown (1808-83), full-length, w/ chalk details, signed and dated l9th cent.	1000	1750	2750
Father and Child, full-length, w/ gilt highlights, attributed to William James Hubard (1807-62), ht. 13"	450	790	1240
Gentleman by William M.S. Doyle, hollow-cut, w/ pencil details, signed, ht. 5.75"	400	700	1100
Gentleman, w/ monocle and Edwardian background, full-length, ht. 14.25"	700	1230	1930
Gentleman, w/ umbrella, full-length, w/ stamp of Master Hankes on reverse, embellished w/ gilding, ht. 13.5"	200	350	550
Gentleman, mechanical silhouette, stamped (William) King, hollow-cut, ht. 5"	275	480	760
Henry Hubbard, Charlestown, NH, by Augustin Edouart, Feb. 21, 1841, full-length, w/ inscription on front and reverse, ht. 12"	550	960	1510
Seated Couple, by Samuel Metford, pr., w/ chalk and gilt details, each signed, in carved frames, ht. 11.5"	300	530	830
Seated Matron, signed (Samuel) Metford, full-length, ht. 12.25"	150	260	410
Triple Silhouettes of Gentlemen of the Leighton Family of Yarmouthport, Maine, watercolor and ink decorated, depicting 2 generations, rare, 3.75" x 8.25"	900	1580	2480
Woman, in manner of Miers	75	130	210
Woman, hollow-cut, in blue watercolor dress w/ floral sprig and parasol, attrib. to William Chamberlain, Dunbarton, NH., c. 1830, ht. 3.5"	3250	5690	8940
Young Couple by Augustus Day, pr., hollow-cut, w/ pencil details, signed, ht. 8"	800	1400	2200

Telephones

Alexander Graham Bell's new company first installed telephones for public use in the United States in 1877. That company, AT&T, otherwise known as "Ma Bell," dominated the telephone industry for the next century. Many small independent companies produced telephones which are highly collectible today. These companies include Stromberg Carlson Telephone Manufacturing Company, Manhattan Electrical Supply Company and Strowger Automatic Telephone Exchange.

Bell telephone, c. 1950, $50-$100.

	LOW	AVG.	HIGH
Adapter Plug, modular receiver for 4 prongs, WW I era	$ 7	$ 9	$ 10
Back Cup, for transmitter, brass, patented Nov. 1910, 3"	8	13	17
Bell, from wall phone, single, solid brass, dome shape, c. 1895	4	8	12
Candlestick Phone, Western Electric, brass with black paint, c. 1928	50	80	110
Clapper Cover, brass, c. 1915	6	9	11
Directory, 1881 Boston Telephone Directory, 56 pages	500	650	800
Magneto Wall Phone, box style, cabinet of walnut, c. 1910, ht. 21", w. 9"	350	450	550
Magneto Wall Phone, box style, oak, c. 1910, ht. 21", w. 9"	400	525	650
Mouthpiece from Candlestick Phone, black, c. 1925	4	6	8
Mouthpiece from Candlestick Phone, brass, c. 1930	40	50	60
Mouthpiece from Wood Magneto Phone, black, c. 1910	5	7	9
Pay Phone, wall model, wood and brass, bells and crank at top, receiver hangs at side, mouthpiece stationary, c. 1900 ...	1000	1500	2000
Receiver Cap, Stromberg Carlson, 1.5"	20	30	40
Receiver, outside terminal, 1882, 7.5"	100	150	200
Shelf for Wall-mounted Phone, oak, late 1800s	60	90	120
Swivel Bracket, Kellog, early 1900s, 4.5"	10	15	20
Transmitter, Kellog type, brass, 1910 patent date, 7"	32	44	55
Transmitter, Western Electric, brass back cup, brass front plate, 1910 patent, 8.5"	30	45	60

<u>*Textiles*</u>

Coverlets

Coverlets are bedspreads woven on a loom. They fall into two categories: geometrics and Jacquards. The geometrics are generally earlier and have small simple designs such as the star, diamond, or snowball. The Jacquards, produced using a loom device made by Frenchman Joseph Jacquard, have curving, ornate designs such as flowers, birds, and trees.

The early geometric coverlets were woven at home usually by women. The Jacquards were more often made by professional male weavers. The Jacquard device enabled the weaver to put his name on his work, the simple loom didn't. Two threads are used in weaving. The warp threads (vertical) are usually cotton, and the weft threads (horizontal) are usually wool. Red and blue dye was primarily used until the middle of the 19th century when synthetic dyes brought a greater color variety. The development of the power loom brought an end to most manual loom weaving.

Most collected coverlets date to the middle of the 19th century. Jacquards are more popular with collectors than the geometrics. Expect higher prices for the rare all-cotton or all-wool coverlets. The listings are identified as geometric or Jacquard. Following the identification are color, description, and dates, when available.

For further information see *American Woven Coverlets* by Carol Strickler.

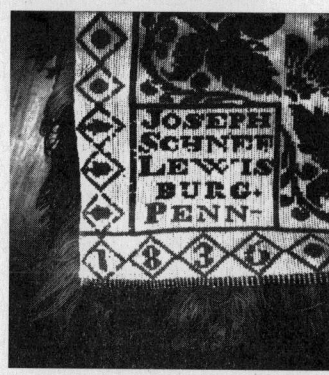

*Coverlets are often labeled
and dated at the corner.*

Geometric

	LOW	AVG.	HIGH
Blue and White, double weave	$ 280	$ 325	$ 370
Blue and White, c. 1840	430	535	640
Blue and White, design, c. 1830	560	620	680
Indigo and Cream, double weave	480	580	680
Log Cabin design	480	560	640
Red, White, Blue, center seam	440	500	560

Jacquard

Black and White, birds and flowers	600	675	750
Blue and White, crossed rose sprays and stars center, w/ eagle corners, double weave, c. 1850	1200	1300	1400
Blue and White, floral and geometric motifs, house, horse and tree border, double weave, center seam, c. 1835	800	900	1000
Blue and White, floral medallions and Amer. eagles and star border, double weave, c. 1830	900	1200	1500
Blue and White, garlands and flowers, spread-winged eagle, double weave, center seam, c. 1855	800	900	1000
Blue and White, patriotic motif, signed, c. 1860	1600	2000	2400
Blue and White, rosettes, leaves, snowflakes, double weave	800	890	980
Red and White, floral motif	560	665	770
Red and White, lilies and floral sprays, signed	600	660	720
Red, Blue, Green, White, double house border, single weave, center seam	1200	1300	1400
Red, eagle motif, unsigned	600	700	800
Red, eagle motif, signed	650	750	850
Red, Green, White, oak leaf and flower design	600	700	800
Red, Gold, Blue, stars and leaves w/ grapes on border, center seam, c. 1850	1000	1200	1400
Red, Tan, Ivory, eagle motif, "Independence, Virtue, Liberty"	1350	1475	1600
Red, White, Blue, exotic birds	1200	1350	1500
Red, White, Blue, star and flower motif	560	665	770
Red, White, Gold, bird medallions, double weave	540	630	720
Red, White, Gold, Green, central medallions and floral borders, double weave	560	665	770
Red, White, Green, flowers, stars, spread-winged eagle	640	745	850
Tree of Life, signed, c. 1848	830	880	930

Reproduction

"Old Colony," white and blue rosettes, double weave 48" x 68"	40	45	50
"Victorianna," white and blue w/ house border, double weave, 48" x 68"	40	45	50
24-Panel "Everlasting," 3 color, triple weave, 48" x 68"	60	65	70
6-Panel "Starburst," 3 color, triple weave, 48" x 68"	60	65	70
24-Panel "Bear Paw," 3 color, triple weave, 48" x 68"	60	65	70

Hooked Rugs

Hooked rugs made from discarded rags or scraps from the cutting room show a wealth of American imagination. The best are 19th century examples with scenes and/or figures. But those are difficult to find in good condition. Collectors can find fine examples from the early 20th century more easily.

Watch out for rotted and unraveled examples. They may look good from the back of the auction hall, but restoring them can cost more than the value of the rug itself.

Floral rug, approximately 3' by 5', $600.

	AUCTION	RETAIL	
		Low	High
Angel Treading on Devil, late 19th cent., 40" x 29"	$ 495	$ 700	$ 1300
Farm, w/ animals, late 19th cent., signed, 40" x 50"	1000	2000	3500
Flowers, late 19th cent., 60" x 100"	460	700	1500
Hearts and Geometric Motifs, early 20th cent., 84" x 96"	500	900	1600
Horse, surrounded w/ leafy boughs, 15" x 35"	650	1200	2100
House, early 20th cent., 24" x 37"	275	425	725
Rooster, circular, w/ braided borderl, late 19th cent., dia. 29"	675	1200	2000
Ship w/ American Flag, late 19th cent., 40" x 59"	1155	1800	2500
Sleigh Ride in Town, early 20th cent., 31" x 41"	350	700	1100
Stars, 6-point, brown, black, red, and white, 30" x 36"	315	600	1000

Quilts

Amish quilts are the leaders in hobbyist appeal and in value, though they are not invariably the most valuable.

Pieced and appliqued cotton quilt, 81" x 79", $1400 at auction.

	AUCTION	RETAIL Low	RETAIL High
Amish Quilt, geometric pieced, 69" x 86".	$ 250	$ 440	$ 700
Appliqué Floral Wreath Quilt, w/ drapery swag border and elaborate stitching overall, 100" x 100".	150	250	400
Appliqué North Carolina Lily Quilt, w/ saw-tooth border, 77" x 75"	900	1500	2500
Appliqué Quilt, 19th century, floral pattern	100	180	280
Appliqué Quilt, floral and vine, green and red print, 4-flower devices w/ 8 pt. star in center of each, vine and floral border, 97" x 97"	400	700	1100
Appliqué Quilt, w/ stylized tulips.	125	220	340
Bedcover, Amer. quilted sateen, in pink and beige striped fabric, 75" x 77".	150	260	400
Bedcover, Continental floral chintz quilted, in wide goldenrod border, 82" x 106".	300	530	830
Bedcover, floral chintz quilted, European, in wide goldenrod border, 82" x 106"	300	530	800
Lone Star Quilt, reds and greens, minor stains, 73" x 81"	350	610	1000
Patchwork Quilt, 19th century, ring-pattern	150	260	400
Pieced Pinwheel Pattern Quilt, in brown and blue, w/ cut corners, 61" x 81"	325	570	900
Pieced Quilt, w/ repeated triangles and cut corners, in print fabrics. 84 X 84".	375	650	1000
Whitework Stuffed and Quilted Cotton Coverlet, w/ central medallion and floral motifs, 81" x 92"	150	250	400

Tools

Hand tools of the 18th, 19th, and 20th centuries often represent fine craftsmanship and engineering. Values vary with quality, rarity, and also usability. Many craftsmen prefer the high quality of some antique tools over those now available. Watch out for missing parts.

"Good" pieces show wear but no damage and are still capable of use. "Best" pieces are in perfect condition with superior quality manufacture. For further information see *The Antique Tool Collector's Guide to Value*, by Ronald S. Barlow.

Right: Moulding plane, $20.

Left: Draw knife, $15.

Right: Folding rule, $90.

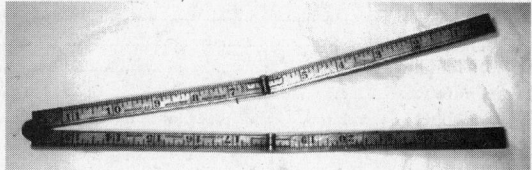

	GOOD	BETTER	BEST
Adz	$ 16	$ 42	$ 105
Anvil, Jeweler's	12	30	75
Anvil, Bench	15	45	100
Auger, Handled	20	50	100
Axe, Mortising	30	45	75
Axe, Ice	11	22	43
Axe, Hewing	30	60	100
Axe, Kent	15	30	50
Axe, Cooper's	20	35	75
Boring Machines	70	100	170
Brace	10	30	100
Brace (18th century)	80	160	320
Brace (Sheffield)	60	100	310
C-Clamp, 4"	5	8	15
C-Clamp, 8"	8	12	25
Calipers	6	18	50
Chisel (wood carving)	9	16	35

	GOOD	BETTER	BEST
Chisels (set of 14)	$ 110	$ 220	$ 450
Clamp, Violin	10	18	30
Clamp, Floor	25	40	80
Clamp, Mitre Jack	15	25	45
Cobbler's Bench	100	200	500
Compass, Woodworker's, 8"	5	10	25
Compass, Drafting	5	10	30
Draw Knife	10	15	30
Drill, Bow	150	275	650
Drill, Breast	20	42	85
Drill, Hand	10	20	40
Hacksaw	20	30	50
Hammer, Ball Pien	10	20	40
Hammer, Claw	5	15	35
Hand Screw (all wood)	10	20	35
Lathe, w/ Treadle	150	330	600
Level, 6"	8	15	30
Level, 15"	15	40	75
Marking Gauge	8	20	75
Plane, Badger	12	34	80
Plane, Block	12	40	120
Plane, Compass	18	45	160
Plane, Horn	30	85	225
Plane, Jack	20	35	80
Plane, Jointer	25	45	125
Plane, Moulding	10	20	40
Plane, Plow	25	90	300
Plane, Rabbet	12	35	100
Plane, Smoothing	30	60	175
Pliers	5	15	30
Plumb, 5"	10	18	40
Plumb Bob	10	30	50
Router (hand)	15	40	80
Saw, Bow	50	100	200
Saw Set (sharpener)	20	40	60
Screwbox	30	50	150
Screwdriver	6	12	25
Sextant	100	250	500
Sextant (boxed)	150	300	750
Sharpening Stone (hard Arkansas)	10	20	50
Shears	8	15	25
Spokeshave	10	20	50
Square (all steel)	10	15	35
Square (rosewood)	15	20	50
Surveying Compass	50	100	275
Tool Chest (machinist's)	80	130	275
Trammel	30	60	120
Vise, Bench	50	90	180
Vise, Swivel	40	70	100
Whetstone, Turning Wheel	30	60	140
Wrench (wooden handle)	10	20	45

Toys and Playthings

Baby Toys

Baby rattles are a universal toy. Almost every culture in the world has its own traditions and superstitions surrounding them. Available examples range from Georgian coral and bells to the plastic ones of today. Rattles can be of gold, silver, ivory, tin, celluloid, paper, and plastic. Collectors must compete with silver collectors and toy collectors for the prime examples, but flea markets, antique shows, and some auctions are still good resources.

Prices give a typical retail range. Our consultant for this section is Marcia Hersey.

Three English silver "coral and bells", late 18th/early 19th century, left to right: 3", $275; 5", 400; 4.5", $350.

Rattles

	LOW	AVG.	HIGH
American, c. 1900, wood "tramp art"	$ 210	$ 260	$ 310
American, c. 1910, tin, painted w/ pony cart	200	250	300
American, c. 1920, celluloid Kewpie doll w/ tennis racquet	125	155	185
American, Gorham, silver rabbit in ring, silver handle	80	95	110
American, silver, man-in-the-moon w/ mother-of-pearl	625	775	925
American, Tiffany, c. 1920, silver and mother-of-pearl	460	560	660
American, c. 1991, wood ice cream sandwich, hand carved	20	25	30
Austrian, c. 1750, adapted silver coin w/ bells	360	460	560
Birmingham, 1807, silver-gilt and coral	575	700	825
Birmingham, 1869, silver w/ mother-of-pearl	300	375	450
Dutch, c. 1850, silver-gilt, carnelian handle	450	550	650
English, 1745, silver w/ stained ivory handle	1700	2200	2600
English George II, 1735, silver w/ coral handle	1600	1900	2200
English, silver dog head, ivory handle	550	650	750
French, Art Deco, c.1930, silver w/ ivory ring.	120	150	180
French, c. 1800, gold w/ mother-of-pearl handle	3000	3500	4500
German, c. 1902, silver house, ivory handle	300	400	500
Indian, stuffed cloth, 1980	20	25	30
Italian, tin, painted w/ saint's picture	200	250	300
Japanese, c. 1900, leather and woods	210	260	310
Portuguese, silver fish w/ ivory handle, c. 1940	80	100	120
Russian, c.1900, silver w/ niello (bracelet attached)	900	1150	1400
Spanish, c.1850, silver mermaid	400	500	600

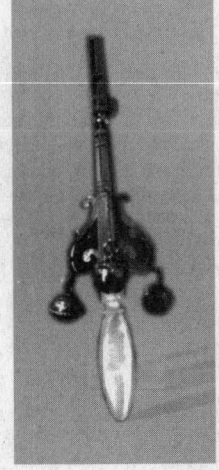

Left: French gold rattle. Above:
Russian rattle. — Photos courtesy of
Marcia Hersey.

Other Baby Items	LOW	AVG.	HIGH
Baby Teether, English, 1799, silver and coral, Bateman mark ..	$ 750	$ 950	$ 1150
Doll's Rattle, English, c.1910, silver acorn, ivory ring	60	75	90
Doll's Rattle, French, c. 1880, silver gilt w/ ivory handle.	600	700	800

Spanish mermaid rattle. — Photo courtesy of Marcia Hersey.

Banks

Mechanical Banks

The values indicated for mechanical banks in this section reflect prices realized at private sales and recent public auctions. When evaluating a bank, one must consider market trends, subject matter, personal taste, and, most importantly, the subtleties of condition. Prices are given for each bank in three condition categories. We define fair as working, with 60% original paint, minor repairs, and some professional restoration. Average is working with 80% original paint, and perhaps a minor repair. Our highest category is not mint but superb, with 98% original paint, no repairs, and working. Superb condition banks are rare and collectors pay a premium price for them. Many banks have been reproduced and most of these are poor quality and easy to detect. Beware of banks that are badly rusted and look like they have been buried in somone's backyard, since that may have been done in order to simulate age. Banks that bear the mark "The Book of Knowledge" are 1930's reproductions that are handsome but worth only a fraction of the originals. Repairs and some reproductions are harder to detect but, with practice, these skills can be developed. As in all areas of collecting, do your homework.

Our consultant for this area is Sy Schreckinger, collector, dealer, appraiser, and contributing author to *Antique Toy World Magazine*. Mr. Schreckinger is also a member of the Mechanical Bank Collectors of America, the Still Bank Collectors Club of America, and the Toy Collectors of America. He is listed in the back of this book. For further reading we recommend *The Bank Book*, Bill Norman, Accent Studios, San Diego, CA, 1984, and *Penny Lane*, Al Davidson, Longs Americana, Mokelumne Hill, CA, 1987.

Cat and Mouse, Cat Balancing. —Photo courtesy of Phillips Auctioneers.

	FAIR	AVG.	SUPERB
Acrobat	$ 2000	$ 5500	$ 11,000
Artillery	375	1100	4500
Bad Accident	1200	3200	8500
Bank Teller	20,000	45,000	75,000
Bear and Tree Stump	200	550	2000
Bird on Roof	750	1600	6500
Boy on Trapeze	1300	2900	9800
Boy Robbing Birds Nest	1850	6800	20,000
Boy Scout Camp	2000	7500	17,000
Boys Stealing Watermelons	1200	3000	8500
Bucking Mule	400	1200	2500
Bull Dog, coin on nose	650	1400	5200
Bull Dog Savings	1800	3500	12,000
Butting Buffalo	1800	5500	15,000
Butting Goat	250	550	1600
Cabin	350	650	2500
Calamity	3000	12,000	35,000
Cat and Mouse, balance	700	3000	8500
Chief Big Moon	550	2500	5500
Chimpanzee	1800	4200	15,000
Circus	5500	16,500	45,000
Circus Ticket Collector	850	2200	6800
Clown on Globe	750	2750	11,000
Confectionery	4500	9500	28,000
Creedmoor	200	450	2000
Darktown Battery	900	2300	8800
Dentist	3000	9200	25,000
Dinah	350	900	3200
Dog on Turntable	200	400	1800
Dog Tray Bank	1700	4500	9500
Eagle and Eaglets	275	650	2500
Elephant 3 Clowns	750	2000	6000
Elephant Howdah, man pops out	250	550	3000
Elephant Pull Tail	150	450	1200
Frog on Rock	200	500	1500
Frog on Round Base	350	700	2500
Frogs Two	650	2000	8500
Gem	200	400	1200
Girl in Victorian Chair	2500	6500	17,000
Girl Skipping Rope	5500	18,000	65,000
Goat, Frog, Old Man	2000	3500	12,000
Halls Excelsior	100	250	1800
Halls Liliput, w/ tray	200	500	2500
Hen and Chick, white hen	2500	5500	20,000
Hen and Chick, brown hen	2000	4500	16,000
Hindu	800	2500	10,000
Hold the Fort	2000	5000	11,000
Home Bank	550	1000	5800
Horse Race, flanged base	3500	10,000	30,000
Humpty Dumpty	500	900	10,000
Indian Shooting Bear	650	2000	7500

*Above top row left to right: Clown on Globe; William Tell, Frogs Two.
Above bottom row left to right: Speaking Dog, Organ Bank, Cat and
Dog, Trick Pony. — Photos courtesy of Phillips Auctioneers.*

	FAIR	AVG.	SUPERB
Initiating, First Degree	$ 3500	$ 8500	$ 23,000
Jolly N Bank	100	350	1500
Jonah and the Whale, Johah tosses coin into whale's mouth	1200	2500	8500
Leap Frog	1300	2500	9500
Lion and Two Monkeys	600	2500	7500
Lion Hunter	2500	6500	12,000
Little Joe	100	350	750
Magic Bank	550	1500	3500
Magician	1700	4500	14,000
Mammy and Child	1850	6500	21,000
Mason	1700	6500	15,000
Milking Cow	4000	10,000	35,000
Monkey Bank (Hubley)	200	550	1500
Monkey and Coconut	800	3000	6000
Mosque	500	1550	3500
Mule Entering Barn	400	750	4500
New Creedmoor	200	550	2000
Novelty Bank	450	1400	4100
Organ Bank, Boy and Girl	500	1450	3500
Organ Bank, Cat and Dog	200	750	2500
Organ Bank, medium	300	550	1600

	FAIR	AVG.	SUPERB
Organ Bank, miniature	$ 350	$ 750	$ 2500
Organ Grinder and Performing Bear	2500	3500	12,000
Owl, slot in head	350	750	1500
Owl, turns head	200	500	1600
Paddy and the Pig	1500	3800	9500
Panorama	2000	8000	18,000
Patronize the Blind Man and His Dog	2000	6000	14,000
Peg-Leg Beggar	800	2500	5000
Pelican	1000	2000	4500
Picture Gallery	5500	16,000	32,000
Pig in a High Chair	300	700	2700
Presto Bank, trick drawer	100	250	1200
Professor Pug Frogs	3200	9500	25,000
Pump and Bucket	750	1500	3500
Punch and Judy	750	2000	5500
Rabbit in Cabbage	250	400	1600
Reclining Chinaman	2500	6500	15,000
Rooster	200	450	2000
Santa Claus at Chimney	1000	2500	6500
Speaking Dog	550	1800	5000
'Spise A Mule, bench	600	1800	4300
'Spise A Mule, jockey	400	1800	5000
Springing Cat, lead	5000	12,000	22,000
Squirrel on Tree Stump	750	2000	4500
Stump Speaker	1500	3500	8500
Tabby	450	1200	2500
Tammany	200	800	2000
Teddy and the Bear	750	1800	4500
Toad on Stump	350	600	2500
Trick Dog, 6-part base	400	1200	3500
Trick Pony	550	1800	3700
Uncle Remus	2000	5000	12,000
Uncle Sam	1500	3500	8500
Uncle Tom	200	650	2500
U.S. and Spain	2000	3500	12,000
Watchdog Safe	200	400	2000
Weedens Plantation, tin	800	2000	5500
William Tell	250	750	2500
Wireless	200	400	1200
World's Fair, Columbus	350	850	3000
Zoo Bank	600	1200	3500

Still Banks

Still banks are aptly named since there are no mechanical actions required to make the deposit. When collecting still banks, beware of rust, reproductions, and repaints.

The M numbers in the following listing refer to *The Penny Bank Book*, Andy and Susan Moore, Schiffer Publishing, Exton, PA, 1984. The book includes photographs and names of manufacturers of most of the banks listed below. Unless specified, the following banks are made of cast iron. When bronze or copper is noted this refers to the type of finish, just as gold and silver refer to paint colors. Banks featuring several colors are described as "multi." In some cases we have listed paint variations under the description as *var.* (They may have another Moore number that we have not listed.) All measurements are approximate.

Prices are for examples in excellent condition (at least 90% paint intact). These pieces should have no major paint loss, no cracks, repairs, or repaints. Such faults decrease the value of a bank. Mint or near mint condition examples will command a premium price, 20%-50% more than the prices listed below.

Our consultants for this area are Leon and Steven Weiss, owners of Gemini Antiques in New York City, who specialize in antique toy, and still and mechanical banks (they are listed in the back of this book).

Left to right, Horse on tub, with brown saddle, M509, $225-$300; lion, M757, green, red or blue, $175-$225, gold, $70-$90; lamb, gold, M601, $400-$600. Beware of reproduction lambs, M600, which are painted white. —Photo courtesy of Gemini Antiques.

	LOW	HIGH
Air Mail on Stand, red, blue, and white accents, ht. 6.38", M848	$ 200	$ 300
Bank of Columbia, nickel, ht. 4.88", M906	100	200
Baseball Player, gold, red, and flesh-tone /var., ht. 5.75", M18	350	450
Basket, woven, bronze finish, ht. 2.88", M917	75	125
Basset Hound, gold, ht. 3.13", M380	800	1000
Bean Pot Nickel Register, red, nickel-finish top, dia. 3.5", M951	150	200
Billiken, gold, ht. 4.13", M74	50	100
Billiken, on throne, gold, red and black accents, ht. 6.38", M73	100	200
Blackpool Tower, unpainted, ht. 7.38", M984	250	350
Bucket Penny Register, nickel, ht. 2.75", M912	100	150
Buffalo Amherst Stoves, black, ht. 4.38", M556	150	200
Buffalo, small, gold, len. 4.38", M560	100	150
Bungalow, ht. 3.75", M999	200	300

	LOW	HIGH
Buster Brown and Tige, gold, red, and multi /var., ht. 5.5", M241	$ 150	$ 200
Captain Kidd, multi, ht. 5.75", M38	300	500
Castle, bronze, ht. 4", M1088	600	800
Cat on Tub, gold, ht. 4.13", M358	150	200
Cat, w/ ball, gray, ht. 2.5", M352	200	250
Church Towers, ht. 6.75", M956	1200	1500
Clown, gold, red accents, ht. 6.25", M211	75	100
Colonial House, w/ porch, gold, ht. 3", M993	150	200
Cupola Bank, red, len. 5.5", M1145	350	600
Dog on Tub, gold, ht. 4", M359	150	200
Dog Seated, "Cutie," black, red accents, ht. 3.88", M414	100	150
Double-Door Bank Build., dark, gold accents, ht. 5.5", M1125	150	225
Eiffel Tower Bank, ht. 10.38", M1075	700	1000
1884 Bank, small rabbit, oval base, green and white, ht. 2.25", M569	1200	1500
Elephant on Tub, gold, ht. 5.5", M483	75	100
Elephant on Wheels, ht. 4", M446	250	300
Elephant w/ Chariot, gray, red and yellow, len. 7.25", M467	300	400
Elephant w/ Howdah, gray, silver and gold, ht. 3.5", M477	75	100
Elephant w/ Howdah, large, gold, ht. 4.88", M474	125	175
Empire State Building, lead, ht. 5.63", M1046	100	150
Fidelity Safe, large, black or green, gold trim, ht. 3.5", M863	200	300
Fido, black and gold, red, white trim, ht. 5", M417	50	75
Flat Iron Building, silver, gold trim, small trap, ht. 5.75", M1160	300	500
Frowning Face, ht. 5.75", M12	1000	1200
General Butler, multi, ht. 6.5", M54	2000	3000
Give Billy a Penny, silver, or red, black and flesh-tone, ht. 4.75", M15	300	400
Globe Savings Fund 1888, multi, ht. 7", M1199	1200	2000
Golliwog, multi, ht. 6.25", M85	400	600
High Rise, silver, gold accents, ht. 5.5", M1217	300	400
Home Bank, bronze w/ green wash, ht. 4", M1019	400	500
Horse on Tub, silver paint, ht. 5.5", M510	200	250
Independence Hall, len. 9.38", M1242	1000	1200
Independence Hall, gold, len. 15.5", M1243	2000	3500
Independence Hall, bronze, ht. 9.38", M1244	700	900
Independence Hall Tower, ht. 9.5", M1202	400	600
Indian, w/ tomahawk, multi, ht. 6", M228	200	250
Labrador, black, gold collar, ht. 4.63", M412	300	400
Liberty Bell, Harper, bronze, ht. 3.75", M780	500	700
Lighthouse, ht. 10", M1115	1500	2700
Lion, gold, red accents, ht. 5", M754	50	75
Lion, gold, red accents, ht. 4", M755	50	75
Lion on Tub, decorated, gold, red, and blue, ht. 5.5", M746	100	150
Lion on Tub, small, gold, ht. 4.13", M747	100	150
Lion on Wheels, gold, ht. 4.63", M760	250	300
Litchfield Cathedral, ht. 6.5", M968	200	250
Main Street Trolley, no passengers, gold paint, len. 6.75", M1469	250	350
Middy Bank, metallic finish, ht. 5.13", M36	100	200
Mosque Bank, w/ combination door, gold, ht. 5.13", M1176	300	400
Old Doc Yak, multi, ht. 4.5", M30	600	800
Old Doc Yak, silver, ht. 4.5", M30	500	600
Old South Church, ht. 5.63", M990	2000	2500

	LOW	HIGH
Old South Church, ht. 13", M991	$ 5000	$ 6500
One-Car Garage, gold paint, ht. 2.5", M1009	200	300
Palace, black, gold accents, ht. 7.5", M1116	1500	2200
Pershing, copper, ht. 7.75", M150	100	150
Policeman, ht. 5.5", M182	300	400
Polish Rooster, ht. 5.5", M541	1200	1800
Prancing Horse, large, gold, ht. 7.25", M520	100	150
Prancing Horse, oval base, black, ht. 5.13", M513	100	150
Presto Trick Bank, black and red, ht. 4.5", M1171	400	500
Pupo on Pillow, black and white, ht. 5.5", M442	150	200
Rabbit, Begging, gold, red accents, ht. 5.13", M566	150	200
Roof Bank, dark, gold accents, ht. 5.25", M1122	150	225
Rooster, ht. 4.75", M548	100	150
Safe, Arabian, desert scenes, ht. 4.5", M882	100	150
Safe, Time, nickel, ht. 7.13", M895	350	450
Save and Smile Money Bank, black w/ red lips, ht. 4.25", M24	350	450
Scottie (white metal), red, white or black, ht. 4.75", M433	50	75
Security Safe, black, gold accents, ht. 6", M889	150	200
Six-Sided Building, ht. 2.5", M1007	150	200
Skyscraper Bank, silver, gold accents, ht. 5.5", M1240	75	125
Soldier, gold, ht. 6", M44	300	400
Spitz, gold, ht. 4.25", M409	300	400
St. Bernard, w/ pack, dark, gold and silver, ht. 5.38", M437	100	150
State Bank, brown, gold accents, ht. 5.75", M1080	75	150
Statue of Liberty, silver, ht. 6.38", M1165	100	150
Tally-Ho, brown, gold and silver, ht. 4.5", M535	125	175
Teddy Roosevelt, gold, silver, and red, ht. 5", M120	200	250
Three "No Evils" Monkeys, gold, len. 3.5", M743	200	300
Tower Bank, comb. lock, red and black, gilt, ht. 7", M1198	1000	1200
Turkey, large, bronze w/ red, ht. 4.25", M585	300	400
Two-Car Garage, silver and blue, ht. 2.5", M1010	200	300
Two Kids, black, green and silver, ht. 4.38", M594	600	800
Two-Faced Black Boy, large, black and gold, ht. 4.13", M83	150	225
Two-Faced Black Boy, small, gold and black, ht. 3", M84	75	125
Two-Faced Devil, red, black, and white, ht. 4.25", M31	600	800
U.S. Mail, silver, red trim, comb. trap, ht. 4.75", M835	100	150
Westminster Abbey, ht. 6.38", M974	200	250
Woolworth Building, gold, no base, ht. 7.88", M1041	150	200

Tower bank, M1208, $450-$650. —Photo courtesy of Gemini Antiques.

Board Games

Board games are a part of practically everyone's lives. Beginning in the 1840s mass-produced games have offered hours of fun and provided glimpses of their eras. A large number of those listed below are based on television shows, a theme that dominates post-war collecting. There are also examples of card, skill, and target games included. The majority are by American companies.

The following prices are for games ranging from the 1880s to the 1980s. There are differences between post-WWII and pre-war collecting but condition and quality are sought by all collectors. Prices for post-war games are for *near mint complete*. These examples must have no tears, stains, broken corners, or missing pieces. Prices of the pre-war games, particularly before 1920, are a bit more lenient on condition due to age. They reflect examples that are complete with no stains or tears on the box or board image, but may have minor flaws: repaired inner corner or small skirt tears, and some dirt but nothing that affects the illustration.

All dates are approximate. Abbreviations: *AF*-Alderman Fairchild, *AG*-Adventure Games, *AL*-All Fair, *BB-B & B* American Novelties, *G*-Gems, *GB*-Gabriel, *GR*-Gardners, *HB*-Hasbro, *ID*-Ideal, *JS*-J. Spears, *KN*-Knapp, *KR*-Kenner, *L*-Lowell, *M*-Mattel, *MB*-Milton Bradley, *Mc*-McLoughlin, *MX*-Marx, *NG*-National Games, *PB*-Parker Brothers (after 1888), *GP*-George S. Parker (pre-1888), *PR*-Pressman, *RM*-Remco, *SB*-Sudbury, *SP*-Schaper, *SR*-Selchow & Righter, *ST*-Standard Toykraft, *T*-Topper, *TR*-Transogram, *UG*-United Game, *US*-United States Soldier Company, *UT*-Utopia Enterprises, *W*-Whitman.

For further reading see *American Board Games and Their Makers*, Bruce Whitehill, Wallace-Homestead, Radnor, PA, 1992; *Warman's Antique American Games*, Lee Dennis, Warman Publishing Co., Elkins Park, PA, 1986; *Spin Again*, Rick Polizzi and Fred Schaefer, Chronicle Books, San Francisco, 1991; *Toys of the Sixties*, Bill Bruegman, Cap'n Penny Productions, Akron, OH, 1992. The American Game Collector's Association is an active group that can be contacted at AGCA, PO Box 44, Dresher, PA, 19025.

Mickey Mouse Tidleywinks, 1935, $400-$700.
—Photo courtesy of Phillips Auctioneers.

	COMPANY	DATE	LOW	HIGH
Across the Continent	PB	1922	$ 180	$ 220
Addams Family	ID	1965	120	160
Addams Family Target	ID	1965	200	300
Agent Zero-M Spy Detector	M	1964	70	90
Air Mail	MB	1927	120	180
Alley Oop	MB	1937	35	45
Amusing Game of Corner Grocer	GP	1887	70	90
Annie Oakley	MB	1950	90	130
Archie Bunker Card	MB	1972	12	18
Archie's	W	1969	20	30
Atom Ant Saves the Day	TR	1966	80	120
Auction Letters	PB	1900	50	70
Auto Fahrt Fur Alles	(German)	1950	60	80
Babe Ruth's Baseball Game	MB	1926	700	1500
Barbie's Little Sister Skipper	M	1964	60	80
Barney Google	MB	1923	100	150
Bash!	ID	1967	18	24
Batman	MB	1966	70	95
Batman Target	HB	1966	100	150
Bats in the Belfrey	M	1964	40	60
Battleship	MB	1965	18	22
Beatles Flip Your Wig	MB	1964	150	250
Bewitched Samantha and Endora	G	1965	60	80
Bing Crosby's Call Me Lucky	PB	1954	60	90
Blackout	MB	1939	50	80
Booby Trap	PB	1965	20	30
Bop the Beetle	ID	1963	50	70
Boris Karloff's Monster Game	G	1965	150	200
Branded	MB	1966	40	70
Bulls and Bears	Mc	1883	12,000	18,000
Bulls and Bears	PB	1936	80	120
Bullwinkle Hide 'N' Seek	MB	1961	60	90
Camelot	PB	1930	25	50
Camp Granada	MB	1968	30	50
Candid Camera	L	1963	55	85
Captain America	MB	1966	90	120
Captain Gallant	TR	1956	50	70
Cimarron Strip	ID	1967	90	110
Cities Card Game	AL	1932	30	40
Clue, Sherlock Holmes ed.	PB	1949	50	70
Combat	ID	1963	50	70
Cootie	SP	1949	25	40
Crazy Clock	ID	1964	65	85
Creature of the Black Lagoon Mystery Game	HB	1963	200	300
Dark Shadows	W	1968	90	130
Dark Shadows Barnabas Collins	MB	1969	180	220
Davy Crockett Frontierland	PB	1955	90	130
Dial-a-Quiz	TR	1961	20	30
Dick Tracy Master Detective	SR	1961	55	75
Dick Van Dyke	ST	1965	85	105
Dim Those Lights	AL	1932	200	300

Above left to right: Peter Coddle's Trip to New York, 1890, $40-$60. First made in 1858, there are many variations by numerous makers of this fun-filled reading game; Skunk Dice Game, 1955, $20-$30.

Above: Bionic Woman, 1976, $7-$13. —Photo courtesy of Jim Glaab's Collector's Showcase. Below: Dim Those Lights (playing board shown), 1932, $200-$300.

	COMPANY	DATE	LOW	HIGH
Dino the Dinosaur	TR	1961	$ 60	$ 100
Disney Fantasyland	PB	1956	70	90
Dr. Kildare	ID	1962	35	45
Dracula Mystery	HB	1963	140	180
Dragnet	TR	1955	80	100
Dynamite Shack	MB	1968	40	50
Electric Questioner	KN	1920	40	55
F-Troop	ID	1965	70	90
Fascination	RM	1962	25	35
Felix the Cat	MB	1960	45	55
Fess Parker/Daniel Boone Trail Blazers	MB	1964	75	95
Finance and Fortune	PB	1936	30	40
Fireball XL-5	MB	1963	120	160
Flintstones Hoppy the Hopparoo	TR	1965	90	130
Flintstones Stone Age	TR	1961	60	90
Flipper Flips	M	1965	60	90
Formula 1 Car Racing	PB	1968	45	65
Frankenstein Mystery	HB	1963	150	200
Game of Man in the Moon	Mc	1901	3000	5000
Game of Venetian Fortune Teller	PB	1898	100	150
Garrison's Gorillas	ID	1967	75	95
Geography Up to Date	PB	1898	45	55
George of the Jungle	PB	1968	80	120
Get Smart, Exploding Time Bomb	ID	1965	90	130
Gidget Fortune Telling	MB	1965	30	40
Gilligan's Island	G	1965	250	350
Godzilla	ID	1963	200	400
Gomer Pyle	TR	1965	50	75
Green Acres	ST	1965	70	90
Green Ghost	TR	1965	70	90
Green Hornet Quick Switch	MB	1966	300	400
Gunsmoke	L	1958	90	140
Hashimoto-San	TR	1963	40	70
Haunted House	ID	1963	150	200
Hector Heathcote, Minute & A Half Man	TR	1963	90	120
Hickety Pickety	PB	1924	30	40
Hogan's Heroes Bluff Out	TR	1966	90	130
Hold the Fort	PB	1895	150	200
Honey West	ID	1965	100	150
Hopalong Cassidy	MB	1950	150	200
Howdy Doody's Own Game	PB	1950	120	160
Huckleberry Hound, Western	MB	1959	60	90
I Dream of Jeannie	MB	1965	90	130
I Spy	ID	1966	80	100
It's About Time	ID	1967	120	180
Jackie Gleason and Away We Go	TR	1956	150	200
Jackie Gleason Story Stage	UT	1955	200	300
James Bond 007 Goldfinger	MB	1966	120	160
James Bond Message for M	ID	1966	300	400
Jetsons Fun Pad	MB	1963	120	160
Jetsons Out of This World	TR	1963	180	220

Top to bottom: Nellie Bly (playing board shown), 1900, $50-$150, complete game $200-$400; Magic Robot, 1955, $90-$130.

	COMPANY	DATE	LOW	HIGH
Jonny Quest	TR	1964	$ 200	$ 500
Ka-Bala	TR	1965	70	90
Kentucky Derby	W	1938	18	22
La Mare aux Grenouilles	(French)	1900	80	120
Land of the Giants	ID	1968	120	200
Land of the Giants Target Game	HB	1968	250	300
Leave It to Beaver, Money Maker	HB	1959	80	100
Leave It to Beaver, Rocket to the Moon	HB	1959	100	150
Let 'Em Have it	AG	1942	40	50
Lie Detector	M	1961	45	65
Little Orphan Annie	MB	1927	200	300
Lost in Space	MB	1965	120	220
Magilla Gorilla	ID	1964	80	100
Man From U.N.C.L.E.	ID	1965	90	130
Mary Poppins	PB	1964	20	30
Melvin the Moon Man	RM	1962	70	110
Mission Impossible	ID	1968	90	120
Mod Squad	RM	1968	65	85
Monkees	TR	1967	80	120
Mouse Trap	ID	1963	45	65
Munsters Card Game	MB	1964	50	60
Munsters Drag Race	HB	1964	200	300
Mystery Date	MB	1966	70	90
Mystic Skull Voodoo	ID	1964	50	75
New Pretty Village Church	Mc	1898	120	160
New Pretty Village Boat House	Mc	1898	120	160
Operation	MB	1965	12	18
Outer Limits	MB	1964	200	300
Palmistry and Psychology of the Hand	BB	1919	80	120
Perry Mason	TR	1959	60	90
Peter Coddles Trip (old man, cars)	MB	1925	25	35
Peter Coddles Visit to NY	MB	1888	40	60
Peter Coddles Visit to NY	UG	1910	20	40
Phil Silvers, Sgt. Bilko	GR	1955	70	120
Pigs in the Clover	MB	1930	35	45
Pike's Peak or Bust	PB	1895	100	140
Pirate and Traveler	MB	1936	50	70
Pooch	HB	1956	60	80
Prisoners Base	PB	1896	300	350
Raiders of the Lost Ark	KR	1981	8	12
Rat Patrol Desert Combat	TR	1967	80	100
Rin Tin Tin	TR	1955	80	100
Ring My Nose (clown)	MB	1925	35	45
Risk	PB	1959	40	60
Sea Hunt	L	1960	80	100
Secret Agent Man	MB	1966	50	80
Silly Safari Jungle Game	T	1966	80	100
Six Million Dollar Man	PB	1975	8	12
Skunk	SP	1955	20	30
Snap (swan on cover)	MB	1920	18	25
Space, 1999	MB	1975	15	20

	COMPANY	DATE	LOW	HIGH
Span-It	SB	1948	$ 18	$ 25
Spin 'Em	PB	1938	30	45
Spot a Car Bingo	HB	1950	25	35
Star Trek	ID	1967	80	120
Star Wars	KR	1977	30	40
Stop, Look and Listen	MB	1926	75	95
Stratego	MB	1961	35	45
Teddy Bear Panda ABC	PB	1950	30	40
Tell It to the Judge (Eddie Cantor)	PB	1936	60	90
Tennessee Tuxedo	TR	1963	150	200
The Game of Life	MB	1960	15	20
The Game of India	NG	1950	18	22
The Kennedys	TR	1962	100	150
The Merry Milkman	HB	1954	70	90
The Muppet Show	PB	1977	10	15
The Rifleman	MB	1959	90	130
This Is Your Life (R. Edwards)	L	1954	45	65
Through the Locks to the Golden Gate	MB	1918	180	220
Time Bomb	MB	1965	45	65
Time Tunnel	ID	1966	180	260
Time Tunnel Spin to Win	PR	1967	120	200
Tiny Tim	PB	1970	60	80
Tiny Town Post Office (English)	JS	1910	150	230
Touche Turtle	ID	1964	120	180
Touring Card Game	PB	1926	18	22
Twenty-One	L	1956	90	140
Twiggy	MB	1967	60	90
Twilight Zone	ID	1964	150	220
Twister	MB	1966	30	50
Underdog	MB	1964	170	200
Untouchables	TR	1961	80	100
Voodoo Doll	SP	1967	40	60
Wally Gator	TR	1962	90	140
What's the Time?	PB	1898	60	80
When My Ship Comes In (card)	GP	1888	45	65
Wipe-out Hot Wheels Race	M	1968	80	100
Wolfman Mystery	HB	1963	200	300
Wonderful Game of Oz (metal pieces)	MC	1921	1500	2500
World War Game	US	1914	500	700
You Bet Your Life, Groucho	L	1955	80	120
Zorro	PB	1966	70	90

Cootie, 1949, $25-$40.

Character Toys

Character toys and memorabilia charm children and adults alike. They are based on familiar faces seen in the comics, heard on the radio or seen on a movie screen or TV. The following items range from the Yellow Kid (turn of the century) to Pee-Wee Herman (1980s). Since there is such a diversity of materials, collecting criteria varies a bit. Most of the keywind tinplate character toys have a lithographed or printed finish while cast-iron toys are usually painted. Overall the condition reported below is for excellent and better. Prices are given for the item and in many cases a separate range is listed for the item in its original box or package. We do not give a range for toys that are unlikely to be found with their original box nor do we give a price for items that have little value without their packaging such as records.

For further information about character and other toys we suggest *Toys of the Sixties*, Bill Bruegman, Cap'n Penny Productions, Akron, OH, 1992; *Toys and Prices,* edited by Roger Case and Tom Hammel, Krause Publications, Iola, WI; *The Official Identification and Price Guide to Antique Toys,* Richard Friz, House of Collectibles, Random House, NY; *Tomart's Price Guide to Action Figure Collectibles*, Carol Markowski, Bill Sikoria, and T.N. Tumbusch, and *A Celebration of Comic Art and Memorabilia*, Robert Lesser, Hawthorn Books, New York, 1975. There are also character items in the following sections of this book: Little Golden Books, Comic Character Watches, Dolls, Whitman Books, Radios, Premiums, Advertising, Robots and Space Toys.

I Love Lucy toys and dolls from the 1950s are quite rare, these items which were in near mint condition sold extremely well at auction in 1996. From left to right Lucy Doll, $1840; Ricky Jr. Puppet Doll by Zany Toys, with original box $1092; Ricky Jr. playset by American Doll, $920; Ricky Jr. Doll by American doll with original box, $1495. —Photos courtesy of Phillips Auctioneers.

	UNBOXED	BOXED
A Team, Amy A. Allen Figure, plastic, Galoob, c. 1984, ht. 6.5"	$ 12-14	$ 20-30
A Team, B. A. Barcus Figure, plastic, Galoob, c. 1984, ht. 6.5"	8-10	18-22
A Team, Hannibal Figure, plastic, Galoob, c. 1984, ht. 6 .5"	5-7	15-20
Addams Family, Gomez Hand Puppet (box), Ideal, c. 1965, ht. 11" ..	90-120	200-300

	UNBOXED	BOXED
All in the Family Mug, 1970s	$9-12	—
Alvin the Chipmunk, Soakie, c. 1960s	25-32	—
Amos 'N' Andy Fresh Air Taxi Cab, keywind tinplate, Marx, len. 8"	600-900	$1000-1500
Amos 'N' Andy Taxicab, cast iron, len. 6"	800-1000	1200-1800
Amos Walker, keywind tinplate, Marx, c. 1930, ht. 12"	700-1000	—
Andy Gump Car, cast iron, Arcade, c. 1924, len. 5.75"	1200-1800	—
Andy Walker, keywind tinplate, Marx, c. 1930, ht. 12"	700-1000	—
Aquaman Figure, plastic, Comic Action Heroes, Mego, c. 1975, ht. 3.75"	20-25	50-70
Archies, Archie Doll, Marx, c. 1975, ht. 10"	12-18	35-65
Archies, Betty Doll, Marx, c. 1975, ht. 10"	12-18	35-65
Archies, Jalopy, Marx, c. 1975, ht. 10"	25-30	50-70
Archies, Jughead Doll, Marx, c. 1975, ht. 10"	12-18	35-65
Archies, Sabrina Paper Doll	9-12	18-22
Archies, Veronica Doll, Marx, c. 1975, ht. 10"	12-18	35-65
Babar, Arthur Figure, Bikin, c. 1989	2-3	8-10
Babar, King Babar Figure, plastic, Bikin, c. 1989	2-3	8-10
Babar, Queen Celeste, Bikin, 1989	3-4	10-12
Bambi Soakie, c. 1960s	20-30	—
Banana Splits, Bingo the Bear Doll, Sutton, c. 1970	40-60	90-120
Banana Splits, Drooper the Lion Doll, Sutton, c. 1970	40-60	90-120
Banana Splits, Fleagle Beagle the Dog Doll, Sutton, c. 1970	40-60	90-120
Banana Splits, Snorky the Elephant Doll, Sutton, c. 1970	40-60	90-120
Barnacle Bill the Sailor and Punching Bag, keywind tinplate, Chein, ht. 7.5"	500-800	—
Barney Google Wooden Jointed Figure, Schoenhut, c. 1922, ht. 8.5"	400-650	—
Bat Masterson Holster Set, w/ cane and vest, Carnell, c. 1960s	100-150	250-350
Batbike, Corgi, len. 4.25"	40-60	80-100
Batman and Robin Book: *From Alfred to Zowie!*, Golden Press, 1966	15-20	—
Batman and Robin Bookends, 1966, 4" x 7"	70-90	100-150
Batman and Robin Ceramic Figural Bank, 1966	60-80	90-150
Batman and Robin Society Member Button, full color, 1960s	30-40	—
Batman, 45 record, die-cut sleeve in the form of Batman's head, c. 1966	—	50-70
Batman, Batcave, Toy Biz, c. 1989	8-12	20-30
Batman, Batcycle, Toy Biz, c. 1989	4-6	10-15
Batman, Batman, magnetic w/ fly-away action, Mego, c. 1979, ht. 12.5"	60-90	120-180
Batman, Batmobile, w/ remote control, Toy Biz, c. 1989	15-20	30-40
Batman, Batphone, Marx, c. 1966, len. 8"	90-110	140-180
Batman, Batwing, Toy Biz, c. 1989	9-14	20-30
Batman, Ceramic Figural Bank, c. 1966, ht. 7"	60-70	80-100
Batman, Charm Bracelet, w/ 5 on original store card, 1966	30-40	80-100
Batman, Coloring Book, Western Publishing Co.	8-10	40-60
Batman, Figural Ceramic Music Box, Price/National, c. 1970s, ht. 7"	50-70	100-150
Batman, Flashlight, 1976	10-12	20-30
Batman, Flying Copter, Remco, c. 1966	50-70	90-130
Batman, Fork, metal, Imperial, 1966, len. 6"	8-10	15-20
Batman, Hair Brush, plastic figural handle, Avon, 1976 len., 8.5"	8-12	20-25

	UNBOXED	BOXED
Batman, Halloween Costume, w/ mask, Ben Cooper, 1960s	$ 20-25	$ 40-60
Batman, Joker van, Toy Biz, c. 1989	7-9	18-22
Batman, Joker, Figural Ceramic Music Box, ht. 7, Price/National, c. 1970s	50-70	100-150
Batman, License Plate, 1966, 4" x 7 .5"	10-15	20-30
Batman, Meets Blockbuster Coloring Book, Whitman, 1966	8-12	40-60
Batman, Mug, white plastic w/ illustrations of Batman and Robin	70-90	—
Batman, Paint By Numbers Set, Hasbro, c. 1966	60-80	100-160
Batman, Penguin Figural Ceramic Music Box, Price/National, c. 1970s, ht. 7"	50-70	100-150
Batman, Riddler, Figural Ceramic Music Box, Price/National, c. 1970s, ht. 7"	50-70	100-150
Batman, Robin, Flashlight, 1976	8-10	20-25
Batman, Soundtrack LP Record, 20th Century Fox, 1966	—	120-160
Batman, Utility Belt, Ideal, c. 1966	500-700	800-1200
Batman, Wallet, 1966	20-30	—
Batmobile, Bubble Bath, plastic, Avon	10-15	20-30
Batmobile, Gold Hubs, Corgi, 1966, len. 5"	200-250	350-500
Beatles, Paul Doll, Remco, c. 1964, ht. 5"	70-90	150-200
Beatles, George Doll, Remco, c. 1964, ht. 5"	70-90	150-200
Beatles, John Doll, Remco, c. 1964, ht. 5"	70-90	150-200
Beatles, Ringo Doll, Remco, c. 1964, ht. 5"	70-90	150-200
Betty Boop Composition Figure, c. 1940, ht. 14".	500-800	—
Betty Boop Composition Head Doll, Cameo, ht. 12"	400-700	—
Betty Boop the Acrobat, keywind celluloid and tinplate, ht. 8.5"	500-750	—
Beverly Hillbillies Car, plastic, Ideal, 1963, len. 22"	200-250	400-600
Bewitched, Broom, Amsco, c. 1965, len. 36"	30-50	80-120
Bewitched, Samantha Doll, Ideal, c. 1965, ht. 12"	200-250	400-600
Big Bad Wolf Stuffed Doll, c. 1930s, ht. 21"	700-900	—
Bionic Woman, Bionic Beauty Salon, Kenner, c. 1976	15-20	30-40
Bionic Woman, Jamie Sommers Figure, Kenner, c. 1976	18-22	40-60
Bionic Woman, Sports Car, Kenner, c. 1976	20-30	50-70
Blondie's Jalopy, keywind tinplate, Marx, len. 15"	1500-2000	2200-2800
Bluto Dippy Dumper Truck, tinplate and celluloid, Marx, len. 8.75"	400-600	700-900
Bonanza Holster Set, c. 1960, Halpern Nichols	90-120	150-220
Bonanza, 4-in-1 wagon, plastic, American Character, c. 1966	90-140	250-350
Bonanza, Album, *Party Time*	—	25-35
Bonanza, Ben and Palomino, plastic, American Character, c. 1966	65-85	180-220
Bonanza, Hoss and Stallion, plastic, American Character, c. 1966	75-95	200-250
Bonanza, Jigsaw Puzzle, Ponderosa Ranch	—	25-35
Bonanza, Little Joe and Pinto, plastic, American Character, c. 1966	75-95	200-250
Bonanza, movie viewer, National Broadcasting Co.	10-15	20-30
Bonanza, *One Man With Courage*, paperback, Media Books, 1966	7-9	
Bonanza, *The Living Legend of Bonanza*, paperback	8-10	—
Bonzo Scooter, tinplate, Chein, ht. 7"	500-750	—
Boob McNutt, Wooden Jointed Figure, Schoenhut, ht. 9"	1000-1500	—
Bozo the Clown Soakie, c. 1960s	20-30	—
Brady Bunch, Coloring Book, Whitman , c. 1970s	8-10	25-35
Brutus Soakie, c. 1960s	25-30	—
Buck Rogers Police Patrol Spaceship, keywind tinplate, Marx, c. 1939 , len. 12"	800-1200	1800-2200

	UNBOXED	BOXED
Buck Rogers, Ardella Figure, plastic, Mego, c. 1979, ht. 3.75"	$ 4-6	$ 10-15
Buck Rogers, Atomic Pistol, chrome plating, Daisy, c. 1930s	100-150	200-300
Buck Rogers, Battlecruiser, Tootsie Toy, c. 1937	100-150	200-300
Buck Rogers, Buck Figure, plastic, Mego, c. 1979, ht. 3.75"	4-6	10-15
Buck Rogers, Buck Figure, plastic, Mego, c. 1979, ht. 12"	15-20	40-60
Buck Rogers, Combat Holster Set, Daisy, c. 1934	180-220	300-400
Buck Rogers, Copper Disintegrator Cap Gun, cast iron, c. 1930s	100-150	300-400
Buck Rogers, Draco Figure, plastic, Mego, c. 1979, ht. 3.75"	10-12	20-30
Buck Rogers, Laserscope Fighter, plastic, Mego, c. 1979	12-15	25-40
Buck Rogers, Pencil Case, cardboard, top pictures Buck, c. 1938	35-55	—
Buck Rogers, Pocket Pistol, Daisy, c. 1930s	120-180	250-350
Buck Rogers, Printing Set	60-80	150-200
Buck Rogers, Rubber Band Gun, large litho. cardboard punch-out, c. 1930s, Onward.	30-40	60-80
Buck Rogers, Sonic Ray Gun, plastic, battery powered, Norton Engineering, 1950s	60-90	120-180
Buck Rogers, Star Fighter Command Center, Mego, 1979, c. 1979, 3.75" figs.	25-35	50-70
Buck Rogers, Strato-Kite, Aero Kite, c. 1946	45-65	—
Buck Rogers, Tiger Man Figure, plastic, Mego, c. 1979, ht. 12"	15-20	30-50
Buck Rogers, Walking Twiki, plastic, Mego, c. 1979, ht. 12"	20-30	45-65
Buffalo Bill Jr., Western Outfit, c. 1950s	70-90	100-150
Bugs Bunny, Pull-String Talking Doll, Mattel, c. 1970s	30-40	80-120
Bullwinkle Soakie, c. 1960s	25-35	—
Buster Brown Dog Cart, cast iron, len. 7.5"	400-600	—
Buttercup and Spare Ribs, Pull Toy, tinplate, Nifty, c. 1925, ht. 7.5"	900-1600	—
Captain America Figure, plastic, Comic Action Heroes, Mego, c. 1975, ht. 3.75"	15-20	40-50
Casper, Talking Ghost Doll, Mattel, c. 1960s, ht. 15"	50-80	150-200
Charlie Chaplin Jointed Doll, Boucher, ht. 7.5"	1800-2200	—
Charlie Chaplin Walker, keywind, Boucher, ht. 8"	1000-2000	—
Charlie McCarthy Benzine Buggy, keywind tinplate, Marx, len. 8"	600-900	1000-1500
Charlie McCarthy Composition Ventriloquist Doll, Effanbee, ht. 20"	500-800	1000-1500
Charlie McCarthy Drummer, keywind tinplate, Marx, ht. 8"	500-700	800-1200
Charlie McCarthy Walker, keywind tinplate Marx , ht. 8"	250-350	400-600
Charlie's Angels, Gift Set, Sabrina, Kelly, and Kris Dolls, Hasbro, c. 1977, ht. 8.5"	30-40	60-90
Charlie's Angels, Jill (Farah Fawcett) Doll, Hasbro, c. 1977, ht. 8.5"	25-35	50-70
Charlie's Angels, Kelly (Jacyln Smith) Doll, Hasbro, c. 1977, ht. 8.5"	20-30	35-45
Charlie's Angels, Kris (Cheryl Ladd) Doll, Hasbro, c. 1977, ht. 8.5"	20-30	35-45
Charlie's Angels, Sabrina (Kate Jackson) Doll, Hasbro, c. 1977, ht. 8.5"	20-30	35-45
Cinderella, Drinking Glass, #8, fitted for shoe, c. 1950, ht. 4.63"	9-12	
Clarabelle Cow, Drinking Glass, red, seated w/ mirror, c. 1936, ht. 4.75"	20-30	—
Cowpuncher Porky, keywind tinplate, Marx, ht. 8"	200-400	500-800
Creature From the Black Lagoon Soakie, Colgate Palmolive, c. 1963, ht. 10"	80-120	—
Dagwood the Driver Car, keywind tinplate, Marx, c. 1935, len. 8"	400-600	900-1400

	UNBOXED	BOXED
Dagwood's Solo Flight Airplane, keywind tinplate, Marx, len. 9" ..	$ 500-700	$ 900-1200
Daniel Boone Flintlock Pistol, Marx, 1960s	60-80	150-200
Dick Tracy Police Station, w/ car, keywind tinplate, Marx, len. 7.5" ..	250-350	400-600
Dick Tracy Siren Squad Car, tinplate, friction and battery, Marx, len. 11"...	250-350	400-600
Dick Tracy Squad Car #1, keywind tinplate, Marx, c. 1939, len. 11" .	300-400	500-700
Dick Tracy Tinplate Police Squad Car, friction, Marx, len. 6.75" ...	120-160	200-300
Donald Duck Composition and Cloth Doll, in Russian costume, ht. 9"	1000-1500	—
Donald Duck Duet, keywind Donald and Goofy dancing, c. 1946, ht. 10.5"	700-900	1000-1500
Donald Duck on a Tricycle, tinplate, Linemar, ht. 4"	300-400	600-800
Donald Duck Rowboat, wood and paper, Chad Valley	700-900	—
Donald Duck and Pluto car, hard rubber, Sun Rubber, c. 1950, len. 6.5"	100-150	—
Donald Duck, Ceramic Figural Cowboy Bank, c. 1940, ht. 6.5"	80-130	—
Donald Duck, Ceramic Figural Milk Pitcher, c. 1940, ht. 6.5"	80-120	—
Donald Duck, Figural Toothbrush Holder, bisque double Donald, c. 1940, ht. 4.5"	200-250	—
Donald Duck, Paint Box, litho. tinplate c. 1930s	80-120	—
Donald Duck, Sunshine Straws, c. 1950s	—	20-30
Donald Duck, The Bubble Duck, plastic, Morris Plastics, c. 1955	90-130	—
Donald Duck, Watering Can, tin, Ohio Art, c. 1930s, ht. 6"	120-190	—
Dopey Soakie, c. 1960s	20-30	—
Dopey Figurine, plaster, c. 1930s, ht. 14"	70-100	—
Dr. Doolittle Doll, Mattel, c. 1967, ht. 6"	30-50	100-150
Dr. Seuss, Cat in the Hat Jack-in-the-Box, c. 1960s	50-60	90-130
Dumbo, Composition Figure, swiveling trunk, googlie eyes, Cameo Doll, c. 1941, ht. 9"	300-600	—
Dumbo, Timothy Mouse Cloth Doll, ht. 14"	300-400	—
Ed Sullivan, Topo Gigio Nodding Head Doll, c. 1960	20-30	50-70
Family Affair, Buffy and Mrs. Beasley Doll Set, Mattel, c. 1967	30-40	80-120
Farfel, Hand Puppet, vinyl and flannel, Juro, c. 1950s	60-80	90-140
Felix the cat, Cloth Doll, ht. 14.5"	500-700	—
Felix the cat, Doll, Schuco, ht. 10.5"	200-300	—
Felix the cat, Speedy Felix Car, wooden, Nifty, c. 1935, len. 12" ...	700-900	—
Felix the cat, Standing Figure, composition, ht. 13"	500-700	—
Flash Gordon, Arresting Ray Gun, Marx, 1930s	180-230	300-400
Flash Gordon, Easter Egg Decals, features The Phantom and others, c. 1940	20-30	80-100
Flash Gordon, Figure, standing at attention, wood, ht. 5"	250-350	—
Flash Gordon, Flash Dueling Ming Button, 1970s	6-9	—
Flash Gordon, Radio Repeater Gun, litho. tinplate, Marx, 1930s	200-250	300-500
Flash Gordon, Rocket Fighter, litho. tinplate, Marx, c. 1930s, len. 13"	500-700	800-1200
Flash Gordon, Rocketfighter Spaceship, keywind tinplate, Marx, c. 1939, len. 12"...	500-700	800-1200
Flash Gordon, Solar Commando Figures, litho. card w/ three 3" plastic figures, Premier, 1952	50-70	120-160
Flash Gordon, Space Compass, flexible plastic band, 1950s	30-40	60-80
Flintstones, Bamm-Bamm Doll, Ideal, c. 1963, ht. 16"	60-80	150-200

	UNBOXED	BOXED
Foghorn Leghorn Figure, Dakin, c. 1970, ht. 6"	$ 20-30	$ 50-75
Foxy Grandpa Bell Ringer Toy, cast iron, ht. 6.75"	800-1200	—
Foxy Grandpa Doll, composition, ht. 17"	900-1400	—
Frankenstein Soakie, c. 1960s	90-120	—
Gabby Hayes, Foldout Book, Bonnie Book, c. 1954	80-100	—
Gene Autry Cowboy Spurs, c. 1950	40-60	70-90
Get Smart Agent 86 Pen/Radio, c. 1966	20-30	40-60
Goofy and Wilbur, Drinking Glass, Disney All Star Parade, c. 1939, ht. 4.88"	25-35	—
Green Goblin Figure, plastic, Comic Action Heroes, Mego, c. 1975, ht. 3.75"	20-25	45-52
Green Hornet, Billfold, c. 1966	20-30	40-60
Green Hornet, Black Beauty Car, Corgi, c. 1966, len. 5"	150-240	350-500
Grumpy, Christmas Light Bulb, c. 1940	25-35	—
Gumby, Electronic Drawing Set, Lakeside, c. 1966	20-25	50-70
Gunsmoke, Handcuffs, c. 1950s	15-20	30-40
Happy Hooligan and Rabbit Candy Container, ht. 7.5"	1200-1800	—
Happy Hooligan Donkey Cart, tinplate, Ingap, 7.5"	1200-1800	—
Happy Hooligan Goat Cart, cast iron, 7.5"	1800-2200	—
Happy Hooligan Nodder Donkey Cart, cast iron, len. 6.5"	500-700	—
Happy Hooligan Nodder Horse Cart, cast iron, Kenton, 10.5"	1000-1500	—
Happy Hooligan Walker, keywind tinplate, Chein, ht. 6"	300-600	—
Harold Lloyd Donkey Cart, litho. tinplate, c. 1929, Spain, len. 9"	3000-5000	—
Harold Lloyd Walker, keywind tinplate, Marx, ht. 10.75".	600-900	—
Henry on Elephant, keywind celluloid toy, c. 1934, Ck, ht. 8"	1200-1800	2000-3000
Henry on Trapeze, keywind celluloid, Ck, ht. 7.75"	300-500	700-900
Hogan's Heroes, Peri-peeper Periscope, ID card, badge	30-40	60-80
Honey West Doll, plastic, Gilbert, c. 1965, ht. 12"	90-130	200-250
Hopalong Cassidy, Holster Light, Aladdin, c. 1950s	250-350	—
Hopalong Cassidy, Record Album	60-80	—
Hopalong Cassidy, Belt, leather	20-30	40-60
Hopalong Cassidy, Milk Container, c. 1955, pt.	80-100	—
Hopalong Cassidy, Pocket Knife, black w/ image of Hoppy and Topper	25-35	—
Hopalong Cassidy, Wallet	20-30	30-40
Horace Horsecollar, Drinking Glass, full figure in red, c. 1936 ht. 4.75"	25-35	—
Howdy Doody, Piano Band, keywind tinplate, Unique Art, c. 1940, ht. 8.5"	700-900	1200-1500
Howdy Doody, Wooden Jointed Figure, c. 1950, ht. 12.5"	400-700	—
Howdy Doody, Figural Ear Muffs	20-30	70-90
Howdy Doody, Jack-in-the-Box, plastic, c. 1970s, ht. 5"	18-22	30-50
Howdy Dowdy, Figural Howdy Piggy Bank, porcelain, c. 1950s	180-220	—
Huckleberry Hound Figural Bank, hard plastic, similar to a Soakie, c. 1960s, ht. 10"	25-35	—
Huckleberry Hound Soakie, c. 1960s	25-35	—
Humphrey Mobile, keywind tinplate, Wyandotte, len. 9"	300-500	800-1000
I Dream of Jeannie, Jeanie Doll, Ideal, c. 1966, ht. 18"	200-300	400-600
Ignatz Mouse Car, tinplate litho., Ingap, c. 1930, len. 6"	2500-3500	—
Indiana Jones, Adv. of, Cairo Swordsman Figure, Kenner, c. 1982, ht. 3.75"	8-12	20-30

Above left to right : Donnie and Marie Puppet Demonstrator. A point of purchase display that appeals to character fans and advertising collectors, $200-$300. —Photo courtesy of Phillips Auctioneers. An intriguing aspect of collecting character toys and memorabilia is that there are always new items coming on the market such as this Legends of Batman figure.

Left to right: Charlie McCarthy and Mortimer Snerd Private Car, c. 1938, $1000-$1800; Joe Penner and his Duck Goo-Goo, $500-$800. —Photo courtesy of Phillips Auctioneers.

	UNBOXED	BOXED
Indiana Jones, Adv. of, Indy Figure in German Uniform, Kenner, c. 1982, ht. 3.75"	$ 28-32	$ 12-16
Indiana Jones, Adv. of, Marion Ravenwood Figure, on card, Kenner, c. 1982, ht. 3.75"	30-40	180-220
Indiana Jones, Adventures of, Desert Convoy Truck, Kenner, c. 1982	35-45	18-22
Indiana Jones, Adventures of, Indy Figure, plastic, Kenner, c. 1982, ht. 3.75"	15-20	60-90
It Takes a Thief, Book #1, paperback	12-18	—
Jackie Coogan Walker, keywind tinplate, German, c. 1920, ht. 7"	600-900	—
James Bond Doll, w/ suit, plastic (original issue), Gilbert, c. 1964, ht. 12"	120-180	300-400
James Bond, Aston Martin Car, battery operated, Gilbert, c. 1965, len. 12"	200-250	400-500
James Bond, Attaché Case, MPC, c. 1965, 18" x 12"	200-250	400-600
Jeff Felt Stuffed Doll, c. 1930, ht. 12"	100-150	—
Jetsons, Rosy the Robot, keywind tinplate, Marx, c. 1965	180-220	350-450
Jiggs Cloth Doll, c. 1925, ht. 18"	1200-1800	—
Jiggs Composition and Cloth Doll, ht. 7.5"	200-300	—
Jiggs in His Jazzcar, keywind tinplate, Nifty, c. 1924 , 6.5"	2000-3000	—
Jiminy Cricket, Christmas light bulb, c. 1950	25-35	—
Jiminy Cricket, Drinking Glass, w/ poem on reverse side, ht. 4.75", c. 1940	10-15	—
Jiminy Cricket, Hand Puppet, vinyl and cloth, Gund, c. 1960	25-35	50-80
Joe Penner and Goo Goo Walker, keywind, Marx, c. 1939, ht. 8"	500-800	900-1200
Katzenjammer Spanking Toy, cast-iron donkey wagon, Kenton, c. 1906, len. 11.75"	2500-3500	—
Komical Kat Walker, Keywind Tinplate, Gama, c. 1929, ht. 7"	400-600	
Krazy Kat Chasing Mice, on a tinplate wheeled platform, Nifty, c. 1932, 7.5"	600-900	—
Krazy Kat Cloth Doll, c. 1916, len. 3"	600-800	—
Krazy Kat 3-wheel Scooter, keywind, c. 1925, 7.75"	500-700	—
Land of the Giants, Signal Ray Space Gun, Remco, c. 1968	50-70	100-150
Land of the Giants, Target Rifle, Remco, c. 1968, len. 28"	90-140	200-300
Lassie, Stuffed Lassie Doll, c. 1950s	70-120	—
Little Lulu Cloth Doll, Georgene Novelties, c. 1944, ht. 13.5"	400-600	—
Little Nemo, Dr. Pimm Roly Poly, Schoenhut, ht. 11.5"	3000-4000	—
Li'l Abner Dog Patch Band, keywind tinplate, Unique Art, c. 1950, ht. 9"	500-700	800-1200
Lone Ranger and Silver, keywind tinplate base, Marx	200-250	350-600
Lone Ranger Composition and Cloth Doll, Dollcraft, ht. 20"	600-900	1200-1700
Lone Ranger, Holsters, fiberboard, set of 2, c. 1945, len. 11"	20-30	50-70
Lost in Space, Robot, plastic, AHI, c. 1977, ht. 12"	50-75	100-150
Lost in Space, Robot, plastic, Remco, c. 1966, ht. 12"	250-350	500-700
Lost in Space, Roto Jet Gun, Mattel, c. 1966	700-900	1500-2000
Maggie and Jiggs tinplate squeeze toy, c. 1925, len. 8"	1000-1500	—
Maggie Cloth Doll, c. 1925, ht. 18"	1200-1800	—
Mama Katzenjammer Ball-Jointed Figure, Boucher, ht. 7"	400-600	—
Mama Katzenjammer Cloth Doll Tea Cozy, Steiff, c. 1908, ht. 15"	2000-3000	—
Mama Katzenjammer, Celluloid Figure, ht. 5"	300-400	—
Man From U.N.C.L.E. Illya Kuryakin Doll, plastic, Gilbert,		

	UNBOXED	BOXED
c. 1965, ht. 12"	$ 120-180	$ 300-350
Man From U.N.C.L.E. Illya Kuryakin Gun Set, Ideal, c. 1965, len. 8"	200-250	400-600
Man From U.N.C.L.E. Napoleon Solo Doll, plastic, Gilbert, c. 1965, ht. 12"	60-80	180-230
Man From U.N.C.L.E. Napoleon Solo Gun Set, Ideal, c. 1965	250-320	600-800
Man From U.N.C.L.E. Passport Set, Ideal, c. 1965	45-60	90-130
Man From U.N.C.L.E. Thrush Rifle, Ideal, c. 1966, len. 36"	800-1300	1700-2200
Man From U.N.C.L.E. *ABC's of Espionage*, paperback	8-12	—
Man From U.N.C.L.E. Car, blue, fires missiles, Corgi, 1966	50-80	120-160
Man From U.N.C.L.E. LP Album, RCA, 1966	45-75	—
Man From U.N.C.L.E., MGM Promotional Still	30-40	—
Merrymakers Mouse Band, keywind tinplate, Marx, 1930s ht. 9" ...	700-900	1200-1500
Mickey and Donald Sand Pail, w/ Daisy and Nephews, Chein, 1930s, ht. 4.5"	100-150	—
Mickey and Minnie Car, wooden, Gong Bell, c. 1933, 10.75"	1200-1900	—
Mickey and Minnie Mouse Playland, keywind, Japan, ht. 10.5" ...	2500-3500	—
Mickey and Minnie Mouse, Bisque Toothbrush Holder, c. 1930, ht. 4.5"	250-350	—
Mickey Mouse and Cat Wooden Pull Toy, len. 13.5"	500-700	—
Mickey Mouse and Donald Duck Fire Truck, hard rubber, Sun Rubber, c. 1950	90-140	—
Mickey Mouse and Minnie Mouse, Drinking Glass, black on pink, c. 1950, ht. 5.88"	15-20	—
Mickey Mouse Cloth Doll, c. 1930, Knickerbocker, ht. 15"	900-1200	—
Mickey Mouse Cowboy Cloth Doll, Knickerbocker, c. 1935, ht. 19.5"	2500-3500	—
Mickey Mouse Drummer, battery operated, Linemar, c. 1955, ht. 11"	600-800	1000-1500
Mickey Mouse in Rowboat, wooden, Fun-E-Flex, len. 10.75"	2000-3000	—
Mickey Mouse Large Cloth Doll, Knickerbocker, c. 1930s, 15.5"	800-1200	—
Mickey Mouse Piano, litho. wood, c. 1935, Marks Brothers, ht. 10"	1500-2000	—
Mickey Mouse the Magician, tinplate, battery operated, Linemar, ht. 10"	900-1400	1800-2400
Mickey Mouse Tumbling Toy, keywind, Schuco, ht. 4"	200-250	300-400
Mickey Mouse, Donald Duck and Pluto Cup, tug of war, Patriot China, c. 1930s	20-30	—
Mickey Mouse, Recipe Scrap Book, Peter Pan Bread, premium, c. 1930	50-80	—
Mickey Mouse, Seed Packets, Colorforms, c. 1977	—	5-7
Mickey Mouse, Spoon, Mickey on handle, Bransford, c. 1935, len. 5.5"	32-42	—
Milton Berle, Crazy Car, keywind tinplate, Marx, c. 1950s	180-220	300-350
Minnie Mouse Cloth Doll, c. 1930, Knickerbocker, ht. 15"	900-1200	—
Minnie Mouse Knitting, keywind tinplate, Linemar, c. 1950, ht. 6.5"	500-700	900-1200
Monkee Mobile Battery Operated Car, ASC, c. 1967, len. 12"	200-300	500-600
Moon Mullins and Kayo Handcar, Marx, c. 1940, ht. 6"	500-700	800-1000
Mortimer Snerd Walker, keywind tinplate, Marx, len. 8.5"	200-300	400-600
Mr. Ed, Pull-String Talking Hand Puppet, Mattel, c. 1962, ht. 12"......	20-30	60-90

	UNBOXED	BOXED
Mr. Magoo Soakie, c. 1960s	$ 28-36	—
Mr. Magoo, Automobile, tinplate and plastic, battery operated	90-150	$ 300-400
Mummy Soakie, Colgate Palmolive, c. 1963, ht. 10"	80-120	—
Munsters, Herman Doll, Remco, c. 1964, ht. 6"	160-220	350-550
Munsters, Herman Pull-String Talking Hand Puppet, Mattel, c. 1964, ht. 12"	150-200	300-400
Munsters, Hypodermic Needle Squirt Gun, Hasbro, c. 1964, len. 8"	60-80	150-200
Munsters, Koach Toy, AMT, c. 1964, len. 12"	200-300	500-700
Mutt and Jeff, Jeff Jointed Metal Figure, Boucher, c. 1922, ht. 6.5"	300-500	—
Mutt and Jeff, Mutt Jointed Metal Figure, Boucher, c. 1922, 6.5"	300-500	—
Mutt, Felt Stuffed Doll, c. 1930, ht. 14"	100-150	—
My Favorite Martian, Beanie w/ Antenna, c. 1960s, dia. 7"	50-80	—
Olive Oyl Ballet Dancer Top Toy, tinplate, Linemar, c. 1950	200-250	400-500
Oliver Hardy Cloth Doll, Lenci, ht. 10"	700-1000	—
Orphan Annie Skipping Rope, keywind tinplate, Marx, c. 1937, ht. 5"	300-400	700-900
Orphan Annie's Sandy w/ Suitcase, keywind tinplate, Marx, c. 1937, ht. 4.5"	250-350	600-800
Orphan Annie, Sandy the dog playing w/ a ball, Marx, len. 8"	350-450	500-600
Osmonds, Pictorial Activity Book, c. 1970s	7-9	12-18
Peanuts, Snoopy Figural Soap Dish, soft plastic	10-14	18-22
Peanuts, Snoopy, See and Say, Mattel, c. 1960s	25-35	60-80
Pee-Wee's Playhouse, Playset, Matchbox, 1988	18-22	30-50
Pee-Wee's Playhouse, Talking Pee-Wee Doll, c. 1988, ht. 18"	20-30	60-80
Pinocchio the Acrobat, keywind tinplate, Marx, c. 1939, 14.75"	300-400	700-900
Planet of the Apes, Cornelius Doll, box, Mego, c. 1973, ht. 8"	35-45	100-150
Planet of the Apes, Zira Doll, box, Mego, c. 1973, ht. 8"	35-45	100-150
Popeye and Olive Oyl Ball Toss, keywind tinplate, Linemar, c. 1950, len. 19"	700-900	1200-1900
Popeye and Olive Oyl Handcar, tinplate, Linemar, len. 9.5"	700-900	1000-1300
Popeye and Olive Oyl Roof Band, Marx, c. 1935, ht. 9.5"	700-900	1200-1800
Popeye and Upright Punching Bag, keywind tinplate, Chein, c. 1935, ht. 8"	1000-1600	—
Popeye Dippy Dumper Truck, tinplate and celluloid, Marx, len. 8.75"	500-700	800-1400
Popeye Express, baggage, wheelbarrow and parrot, Marx, ht. 8"	250-450	800-1200
Popeye Handcar, tinplate and rubber, Marx, c. 1935, ht. 6.5"	700-900	1200-1500
Popeye Heavy Hitter Hammer and Bell Toy, keywind, Chein, c. 1932, ht. 11.5"	1800-2800	3500-5000
Popeye Lamp, cast-iron, w/ litho. paper shade, c. 1935, ht. 17"	700-1000	—
Popeye on a Motorcycle, cast iron, Hubley, c. 1938, len. 9"	2000-3000	—
Popeye Overhead Punching Bag, keywind tinplate, Chein, c. 1932, 9.75"	2000-3000	3500-5500
Popeye Rooftop Jigger, keywind tinplate, Marx, c. 1936, ht. 9.75"	700-900	1000-1300
Popeye Rowing a Rowboat, keywind tinplate, Hoge, c. 1935, 15.5"	6000-8000	—
Popeye Soakie, c. 1960s	25-35	—
Popeye Somersaulter, keywind tinplate, Linemar, ht. 5"	700-1000	—
Popeye Spinach Delivery Motorcycle, cast iron, Hubley	600-900	—
Popeye the Champ Boxing Toy, keywind tinplate and celluloid, Marx, c. 1936, 7" X 7"	2000-2500	3000-5500

	UNBOXED	BOXED
Popeye Tinplate Sparkler, Chein, c. 1959, ht. 5", 120-180	$ 200-300	$ 400-600
Popeye Tricycle, keywind tinplate, Linemar, ht. 4"	300-500	600-800
Popeye Wooden Jointed Figure, c. 1932, ht. 10"	300-400	—
Popeye Wooden Jointed Figure, c. 1935, ht. 11"	450-650	—
Popeye Wooden Jointed Figure, w/ cap and pipe, c. 1935, ht. 14" ..	400-600	—
Popeye, Bubble Blowing, battery tinplate, Linemar, c. 1950s, ht. 8.5"	900-1100	1800-2200
Popeye, Eugene the Jeep, painted wood jointed figure, ht. 7"	700-1000	—
Popeye, Smoking, tinplate, Linemar, ht. 8.5"	800-1000	1500-2000
Popeye, Thimble Theatre Mystery Playhouse, w/ 3 walkers, c. 1939, 9.5 x 12"	1800-2500	—
Porky Pig Soakie, c. 1960s	20-30	—
Porky Pig w/ Umbrella, keywind tinplate, c. 1939, Marx, ht. 8.5"	300-400	500-600
Powerful Katrinka Lifting Jimmy, keywind tinplate, c. 1925, ht. 6.75"	3000-4000	—
Rin Tin Tin Stuffed Doll, Smile Novelty, c. 1959	80-120	—
Roy Rogers Bedspread, c. 1950s	125-175	—
Roy Rogers Guitar, litho. cardboard, c. 1950s	80-100	120-160
Roy Rogers, Fix-It Stage Coach, plastic, Ideal, c. 1956	90-130	220-280
Roy Rogers, Lantern, battery-operated tinplate, c. 1956	70-90	100-150
Seven Dwarfs Doll, Bashful, Ideal, ht. 7"	200-300	400-600
Seven Dwarfs Doll, Doc, Ideal, ht. 7"	200-300	400-600
Seven Dwarfs Doll, Dopey, Ideal, ht. 7"	200-300	400-600
Seven Dwarfs Doll, Grumpy, Ideal, ht. 7"	200-300	400-600
Seven Dwarfs Doll, Happy, Ideal, ht. 7"	200-300	400-600
Seven Dwarfs Doll, Sleepy, Ideal, ht. 7"	200-300	400-600
Seven Dwarfs Doll, Sneezy, Ideal, ht. 7"	200-300	400-600
Shazam Figure, plastic, Comic Action Heroes, Mego, c. 1975, ht. 3.75"	15-20	40-50
Sightseeing Auto, cast iron, w/ comic character passengers, Kenton, c. 1910, len. 10.5"	5000-7000	—
Six Million Dollar Man, Steve Austin Doll, bionic grip, Kenner, c. 1976	12-18	30-60
Snow White Doll, Ideal, ht. 15.5"	300-400	500-700
Snowflakes and Swipes Pull Toy, litho. tinplate, c. 1929, len. 7.5" ...	900-1200	—
Sparkplug Wooden Jointed Figure, ht. 9", ...	400-600	—
Sparkplug, Racing Platform Toy, litho. keywind tinplate, c. 1924, ht. 9"	5000-7000	—
Stan Laurel Cloth Doll, Lenci, ht. 10"	700-1000	—
Superman, Figural Ceramic Music Box, Price/National, c. 1970s, ht. 7"	50-70	100-150
Superman, Rollover Airplane, keywind tinplate, Marx, c. 1940, len. 6"	800-1000	—
Superman, Turnover Tank, keywind tinplate, c. 1940, Marx, len. 4" ..	400-600	700-1000
Superman, Badge, movie promotional, emblem shape (for *Superman I*)	18-22	—
Superman, Belt Buckle, tin, blue and red, chains portrait, 1940s	120-160	—
Superman, Button, Kellogg's Pep Cereal premium, multicolor litho. tin, 1950s	25-35	—
Superman, Candy Coated Peanuts, box only, illustrated lid, 1966, len. 5"	30-40	—

	UNBOXED	BOXED
Superman, Dime Register Bank, litho. tinplate, 1940s	—	$ 260-320
Superman, Doll, composition and wood, painted, jointed w/ cape, Ideal, ht. 13"	$ 1200-1800	—
Superman, Doll, stuffed fabric, full length w/ cape, Toy Works, 1970s, ht. 25"	10-15	22-28
Superman, Pencil Case, Mattel, 1960s	18-22	—
Superman, Standing Figure, Syrocco, 1940s, ht. 5"	3000-4000	—
Superman, *The Magic Ring*, two 78 records and booklet, Musette, c. 1947	100-150	—
Superman, Toothbrush, battery operated	20-30	50-70
Sylvester and Tweety, Sylvester Soakie, c. 1960s	25-35	—
Sylvester and Tweety, Tweety Bird Figure, Dakin, c. 1960s, ht. 6"	8-12	18-22
Tarzan, Thingmaker Mold, Mattel, c. 1966	20-25	40-50
Three Little Pigs Figure, keywind, Schuco, ht. 4.75"	100-150	200-250
Thumper the Rabbit Soakie, c. 1960s	20-30	—
Tom and Jerry, Jerry Mouse Stuffed Toy, Merry Thought, c. 1950s, ht. 6"	45-60	—
Tonto Composition and Cloth and Doll, Dollcraft, ht. 20"	500-700	1000-1500
Toonerville Trolley, tinplate, c. 1925, ht. 7"	400-600	700-900
Uncle Wiggily Crazy Car, len. 7"	300-500	600-800
W.C. Fields Doll, Effanbee, ht. 19"	400-600	1000-1500
Wagon Train, 45 Rpm Record, w/ picture sleeve, Mitch Miller and Orchestra, 1957	—	20-30
Wagon Train, Tray Puzzle, Whitman, c. 1960, 14" x 11"	10-15	20-30
Waltons, paper doll	6-8	15-20
Wild, Wild West, Writing Tablet	12-15	—
Winky Dink and You, Magic TV Kit, Standard Toy, 1960s	50-70	—
Wolfman Soakie, Colgate Palmolive, c. 1960s, ht. 10"	80-120	—
Woody Woodpecker Soakie, c. 1960s	25-35	—
Woody Woodpecker, Tray Puzzle	18-22	—
Yellow Kid Figure, cast iron in burlap dress, ht. 6.5"	700-1000	—
Yellow Kid Goat Cart, cast iron, len. 7.5"	400-600	—
Yogi Bear, Magic Slate, c. 1960s	20-30	—

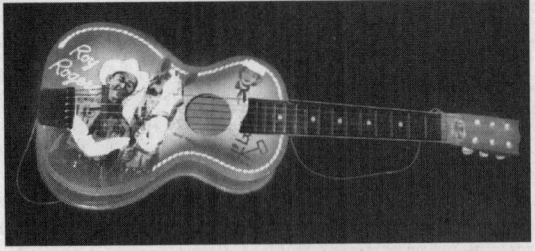

Above: Roy Rogers Guitar, $80-$100.

Children's Dishes

This chapter includes both toy dishes and children's tableware. Produced extensively throughout America, Europe and the Orient from the 1880s through the 1950s, they are found in every material common to full-size dishes and tablewares. As miniatures of "Mother's" dishes, many are accurate down to the smallest detail. Reproductions and new items made in the style of an earlier period are not worth as much as period pieces.

For further information on children's dishes refer to *The Official Price Guide to Depression Glass* published by The House of Collectibles, Random House, NY, and *Collector's Encyclopedia of Children's Dishes*, Margret and Kenn Whitmyer, Collector Books, Paducah, KY, 1993.

Left to right: Pitcher, Shirley Temple, blue glass, dia. 6.5", $35-$50; Hopalong Cassidy mug , white milk glass, ht. 3", $25-$35. — Items courtesy of Jim Glaab's Collector's Showcase.

	LOW	HIGH
Bowl, Blue Marble, England, oval, 4.5"	$ 28	$ 33
Bowl, Blue Willow, Made in Japan, 3.5"	28	34
Bowl, Hopalong Cassidy, white milk glass, 5"	25	40
Bowl, Shirley Temple, blue glass, 6.5"	40	60
Butter Dish, pattern glass, Bead and Scroll, clear, w/ dome lid, 4"	135	155
Casserole, Blue Willow, Made in Japan, 4.75"	32	36
Casserole, Blue Willow, Made in Japan, 5"	35	40
Casserole, Blue Willow, Occupied Japan	38	42
Casserole, graniteware, blue and white, w/ lid, 2.88"	80	100
Casserole, Noritake, Bluebird, 6"	30	40
Casserole, Pagodas, England, w/ lid, 5.5"	40	50
Coffee Pot, aluminum., tapered w/ wooden handle lid, embossed "Drink Thomson Malted Milk," 1930s, 5"	28	32
Creamer, Blue Willow, Made in Japan, 1.5" -	7	9
Creamer, Blue Willow, Made in Japan, 2"	8	10
Creamer, Blue Willow, Occupied Japan	12	18
Creamer, depression glass, Cherry Blossom, pink, 2.75"	25	30
Creamer, depression glass, Doric and Pansy, pink, 2.75"	25	30
Creamer, glass, Akro Agate, Chiquita, green opaque, 1.5"	3	5
Creamer, Noritake, Bluebird, 1.88"	12	15
Creamer, pattern glass, Acorn, clear, 3.38"	80	100
Creamer, Sunset, Made in Japan, 1.88"	3	5
Creamer, Water Hen, England, 3.13"	20	25

	LOW	HIGH
Crock, lid, brown and gray, 1920s, 4"	$ 9	$ 15
Cup and Saucer, Blue Willow, Made in Japan, cup 1.13"	7	9
Cup and Saucer, Blue Willow, Made in Japan, cup 3.5"	7	9
Cup and Saucer, Blue Willow, Occupied Japan	10	12
Cup and Saucer, depression glass, Cherry Blossom, pink, cup 1.5"	25	30
Cup and Saucer, depression glass, Doric and Pansy, cup 1.5"	25	30
Cup and Saucer, Noritake, Bluebird	7	12
Cup and Saucer, Noritake, Silhouette, pale lavender w/ girl pushing doll buggy, cup 1.25"	9	12
Cup and Saucer, Silhouette, Made in Japan, man and woman, cup 1.5"	6	8
Cup and Saucer, Sunset, Made in Japan, cup 1.25"	6	8
Cup and Saucer, Water Hen, England, cup 2"	15	18
Dishpan, aluminum, flat sides, rolled edge, loop handles, 4"	6	8
Frying Pan, graniteware, blue and white, 4.5"	75	100
Grater, graniteware, blue and white, 4"	70	85
Gravy Boat, Blue Marble, England, 1.5"	30	40
Gravy Boat, Blue Willow, Made in Japan	24	28
Grill Plate, Blue Willow, Made in Japan, 5"	30	40
Mold, graniteware, blue and white, fluted, 2.75"	75	100
Mug, glass, Hopalong Cassidy, white milk glass, 3"	25	35
Pitcher and Wash Bowl, ironstone, white w/ green shading, 24-kt gold bands, roses, scalloped edges, scroll handle, 4"	30	50
Pitcher, graniteware, blue and white, 2.5"	75	100
Plate, Blue Marble, England, 4"	10	12
Plate, Blue Willow, Made in Japan, 3.75"	6	8
Plate, Blue Willow, Made in Japan, 5"	13	15
Plate, Blue Willow, Occupied Japan	8	10
Plate, depression glass, Cherry Blossom, pink, 5.88"	7	9
Plate, depression glass, Doric and Pansy, pink, 5.88"	6	8
Plate, glass, Akro Agate, Concentric Rib, green opaque, 3.25"	2	3
Plate, Hopalong Cassidy, white milk glass, 7"	30	40
Plate, Noritake, Bluebird, 4.25"	5	7
Plate, Pagodas, England, 4.5"	10	12
Plate, Sunset, Made in Japan, 4.25"	3	5
Platter, Blue Marble, England, 4.5"	30	40
Platter, Blue Willow, Made in Japan, 4.63"	20	30
Platter, Blue Willow, Made in Japan, 6"	30	35
Platter, Blue Willow, Occupied Japan	30	35
Platter, Noritake, Bluebird, 7.13"	18	22
Platter, Pagodas, England, 7.13"	25	32
Presentation Cup, porcelain, "To My Sister," pink roses, 24-kt scrolling, closed loop handle, 1890, 2.38"	20	35
Sugar Bowl, Blue Willow, Made in Japan, w/ lid, 2"	10	15
Sugar Bowl, Blue Willow, Made in Japan, w/ lid, 2.75"	10	14
Sugar Bowl, Blue Willow, Occupied Japan, w/ lid	14	18
Sugar Bowl, depression glass, Cherry Blossom, pink, 2.63"	22	26
Sugar Bowl, depression glass, Doric and Pansy, pink, 2.5"	20	30
Sugar Bowl, Noritake, Bluebird, w/ lid, 2.75"	14	20
Sugar Bowl, pattern glass, Block, blue, w/ lid, 4.5"	90	110
Sugar Bowl, Sunset, Made in Japan, w/ lid, 3.13"	8	12
Sugar Bowl, Water Hen, England, w/ lid, 4.5"	25	30

	LOW	HIGH
Table Utensils, tin, 5 knives w/ 2-piece riveted bone handles, 5 forks, 1910, 3.5"	$ 25	$ 35
Teapot, Blue Willow, Made in Japan, w/ lid, 2.63"	35	45
Teapot, Blue Willow, Made in Japan, w/ lid, 3.75"	40	55
Teapot, Blue Willow, Occupied Japan, w/ lid	20	25
Teapot, glass, Akro agate, J.P., transparent green, w/ lid, 1.5"	30	40
Teapot, Noritake, Bluebird, w/ lid, 3.5"	40	50
Teapot, Noritake, Silhouette, pale lavender w/ black silhouette of little girl pushing a doll buggy, 3.5"	40	50
Teapot, Silhouette, Made in Japan, man and woman, w/ lid, 4"	12	18
Teapot, Sunset, Made in Japan, w/ lid, 3.75"	18	22
Teapot, Water Hen, England. w/ lid, 5.25"	40	50
Tea Set, china, 9, covered teapot, creamer, covered sugar, 2 cups, 2 saucers, white w/ blue shading, 24-kt gold decoration, scalloped edges, German, 1910, tallest 5.5"	100	150
Tea Set, depression glass, Homespun, pink, 14 pc's, original box	200	300
Tea Set, glass, Akro Agate, Chiquita, green opaque, 22 pc's, original box	100	150
Tea Set, glass, Akro Agate, Concentric Ring, 21 pc's, marbleized blue, original box	400	475
Tea Set, glass, Akro Agate, Interior Panel, transparent topaz, 8 pc's, original box	75	100
Tea Set, Palissy china, 23 pc's., covered teapot, creamer, covered sugar, 6 cups and saucers, 6 plates, white w/ brown flower, berry and leaf decoration, gold trim, elaborate shape, Palissy blue mark, early 1800s, teapot 4.5"	200	300
Tea Set, porcelain, 16 pieces, covered teapot, creamer, sugar, 6 cups and saucers, teddy bear decoration	300	500
Tea Set, porcelain, 7 pc's., covered teapot, sugar, creamer, 2 cups and saucers, Dolly Dingle decoration	80	100
Tea Set, porcelain, 7 pc's., covered teapot, sugar, creamer, 2cups, 2 saucers, Peter Rabbit decoration	120	180
Toleware, tin, pitcher, cup, saucer, painted blue and cream w/ still-life scenes, 1920, pitcher 2"	30	50
Tumbler, Hopalong Cassidy, white milk glass, 10 oz., 3"	35	45
Tureen, Blue Willow, Made in Japan, w/ lid, 4"	35	45
Tureen, Blue Willow, Occupied Japan, w/ lid	40	50
Tureen, ironstone, lid, moss rose decoration, rococo styling, 24-kt trim on handles, 1890	40	50
Tureen, semiporcelain, Johnson Brothers, lid, white w/ gold trim and sprays of tiny roses, 1800s, 7" x 4.5"	60	70
Turkey Roasting Pan, aluminum, oval, lid, riveted iron handles on ends of pan and top of lid, 1920s, 5.5" x 3.5"	18	22

Comic Character Watches

Mention "comic character watches" and you will invariably hear the reply, "You mean like a Mickey Mouse watch?" It was Mickey who ushered in the first comic watch in 1933 and the market has been thriving ever since. Prices for watches in their original, colorful boxes have skyrocketed due to scarcity and increasing demand. Promotional watches requiring boxtops or proof of purchase and acquired by mail have gained in popularity.

The prices listed in the MNP column are for mint condition working watches, without their packaging or original boxes; the second price range (MIP) is for working, mint in the package examples. MIP for promo watches means that they come with their original mailing material. We have abbreviated some titles, removed 19 from the date, and substituted PW for pocket watch and WW for wristwatch.

The following are our codes for manufacturers: *BR* -Bradley, *BY* -Bayard, *CT* -Columbia Time, *EX* -Exacta Time, *FW* -Fawcett, *GC* -Glen Clock, *GT* -Gilbert, *HD* -Haddon, *HL* - Helbros, *IG* -Ingraham, *IN* -Ingersol, *L* -Lorus, *PWC* -Patent Watch Company, *RT* -Ralston, *SF* -Starkist Foods, *Sk* -Seiko, *SM* -Smith, *SW* -Swiss (maker unknown), *UK* -Unknown, *UST* -U.S. Time, *W* -Wilane, *WB* -Warner Brothers,

Our consultant for this section is Howard S. Brenner, collector and author of *Comic Character Clocks and Watches,* Books Americana, 1987 (he is listed in the back of this book).

Left to right: Woody Woodpecker wall clock in original box, $400-700; Woody Woodpecker clock and watch store display 700-1200; Woody Woodpecker alarm clock, in original box, $750-$850. —Photo courtesy of Phillips Auctioneers.

COMPANY	CIRCA	MNP	MIP
Alice in Wonderland WW, plastic teacup pack. ... UST	1950	$ 100-140	$ 425-475
Babe Ruth WW, plastic baseball package .... EX	1949	300-400	1500-1800
Bambi Alarm Clock .... BY	1964	150-200	200-300
Batman WW .... TX	1978	60-80	140-160
Betty Boop PW .... IG	1934	900-1100	2200-2500
Buck Rogers PW, light. bolt hands, monster bk. ...... IG	1935	800-900	1400-1600
Bugs Bunny Alarm Clock .... IG	1951	400-450	700-800
Bugs Bunny WW .... WB	1951	450-500	700-800
Captain Marvel WW (deluxe), 1 jewel .... FW	1948	300-350	550-600
Captain Marvel WW (larger than deluxe) .... FW	1948	400-450	700-750
Charlie McCarthy Alarm Clock, animated .... GT	1938	1500-2000	3000-3500
Charlie the Tuna WW, promo .... SF	1971	60-80	90-120
Cinderella WW, slipper box .... UST	1950	150-170	450-525
Cinderella WW, porcelain statue pack. .... TX	1958	130-160	400-475
Dale Evans WW, pop-up display box .... IG	1951	200-300	400-600
Dan Dare PW, double animation .... IN	1953	700-750	900-1000
Davy Crockett Clock, electric, animated .... HD	1954	400-475	500-600
Davy Crockett Clock .... UK	1955	200-300	400-450
Davy Crockett WW, powder horn box .... UST	1954	140-200	400-500
Davy Crockett WW, 3-D pop-up display box .... BR	1956	140-200	425-525
Dick Tracy WW .... NH	1948	180-220	450-550
Donald Duck Clock, animated .... GC	1950	380-420	600-700
Donald Duck Clock, animated .... BY	1964	180-220	280-320
Gene Autry WW .... W	1948	250-300	500-600
Gene Autry WW, Six Shooter, animated .... NH	1951	500-550	750-850
Goofy WW, runs backwards .... H	1972	650-750	1000-1300
Hopalong Cassidy WW, in saddle stand box .... UST	1950	140-180	400-450
Hopalong Cassidy Alarm Clock .... UST	1950	350-450	600-700
Hopalong Cassidy PW .... UST	1950	500-600	900-1100
Howdy Doody WW, moving eye, window box ... PWC	1954	250-300	500-650
Lone Ranger PW, w/ pistol and holster .... NH	1939	400-450	750-850
Lone Ranger WW .... NH	1939	320-380	650-750
Little Pig (Disney Fiddler pig)WW .... UST	1947	350-400	650-750
Mickey Mouse Alarm Clock, animated wind-up ..... IN	1933	850-950	1900-2100
Mickey Mouse Alarm Clock, animated, round case ... IN	1934	850-950	1900-2100
Mickey Mouse Alarm Clock, elec., revolving MM .. IN	1933	1000-1200	2200-2600
Mickey Mouse Alarm Clock, pocket watch form .. BR	1979	60-80	100-150
Mickey Mouse Alarm Clock, moving feet .... BR	1983	60-80	100-150
Mickey Mouse Clock, Magic Castle, animated ..... BR	1979	300-350	450-550
Mickey Mouse Clock, square case .... IN	1933	850-950	1900-2100
Mickey Mouse Deluxe WW, Mickey on second hand . IN	1938	500-600	1000-1300
Mickey Mouse PW, shield fob .... IN	1933	600-650	1000-1200
MM PW, debossed back, round fob .... IN	1933	600-650	1000-1200
Mickey Mouse PW, Bicentennial .... BR	1976	100-125	200-300
Mickey WW, "Ambassador to the World" .... SK	1986	350-400	450-500
Mickey WW Digital .... BR	1973	180-200	250-300
Mickey/Donald WW (1st time tog.) L	1986	175-200	220-260
Mickey WW, Electric .... TX	1968	475-525	650-750
Mickey WW, 50th Birthday .... BR	1978	250-300	350-400
Mickey WW, Pluto Wag. Head (200 made) .... BR	1978	750-850	900-1100
MM WW, "Mickey #1," leather band .... IN	1933	600-650	800-900

Three Little Pigs
Pocket watch in
original box with
fob, $2200-$2600.
— Photo courtesy of
Howard S. Brenner.

Cinderella wristwatch,
slipper box, $450-$525
— Photo courtesy of
Howard S. Brenner.

Left to right: Captain Marvel wristwatch (larger than deluxe), in
original box, $700-$750; Superman wristwatch, large pre-war, in
original box, $1600-$1800; Bugs Bunny wristwatch, in original box,
$700-$800. — Photos courtesy of Howard S. Brenner

	COMPANY	CIRCA	MNP	MIP
Mickey Mouse WW, "Mickey #1" steel band	IN	1933	$ 500-600	$ 750-850
Mickey Mouse WW, 1973, 1st issue	BR	1973	160-180	200-230
Mickey Mouse WW wagging head, animated	BR	1978	200-250	320-380
Mickey and Minnie WW, promo	SW	1976	60-80	90-110
Minne Mouse WW, animated wagging head	BR	1978	375-425	500-600
Minnie Mouse WW, 1973, 1st issue	BR	1973	170-200	220-260
Mister Peanut WW, promo	SW	1975	60-80	90-110
Orphan Annie WW	NH	1948	250-300	450-500
Popeye Alarm Clock, animated	SM	1968	300-350	450-550
Popeye PW, animated, Thimble Theatre char. face	NH	1934	650-700	850-950
Popeye PW	NH	1935	450-500	700-800
Popeye WW	NH	1935	400-450	850-950
Porky Pig WW, round case	IG	1949	350-400	550-650
Raid WW, promo	SW	1975	60-80	90-110
Roy Rogers Alarm Clock, animated	IG	1951	350-400	550-700
Roy Rogers PW, w/ charm	BR	1959	350-400	700-800
Roy Rogers WW, Roy and Trigger posing on face	IG	1951	350-400	500-600
Roy Rogers WW, posing, round case, pop-up box	IG	1951	300-350	500-600
Snow White WW, large size, pre-war	IN	1939	350-400	550-600
Snow White WW, magic mirror box	UST	1959	160-180	500-550
Star Trek WW, Spock	BR	1979	25-35	40-50
Star Wars WW, Darth Vader	BR	1977	35-45	50-85
Star Wars WW, R2D2 and C3PO	BR	1977	35-45	50-75
Superman PW	BR	1959	500-550	1000-1200
Superman WW, large pre-war	NH	1939	500-550	1600-1800
Superman WW	NH	1948	350-400	1400-1600
Superman WW, large	TX	1976	90-110	160-180
Superman WW, small	TX	1976	60-80	140-160
Three Little Pigs Alarm Clock, animated Wolf	I	1934	400-450	2200-2600
Three Little Pigs PW, animated, debossed back	IN	1934	800-900	2200-2600
Three Little Pigs WW, figural steel band	IN	1934	1000-1200	2800-3200
Tom Mix WW, promo	RT	1983	300-350	450-550
Woody Woodpecker Alarm Clock , animated	CT	1950	400-450	750-850
Zorro WW, sombrero package	UST	1957	90-130	450-500

Babe Ruth wristwatch, plastic baseball package, $1500-$1800. — Photo courtesy of Howard S. Brenner.

Cracker Jack

F.W. Ruckenheim and his brother developed this famous mixture of popcorn, peanuts, and molasses. In 1893 they sold it at the Columbian Exposition in Chicago where it was an overnight sensation. In 1896 it was named Cracker Jack and soon after prizes were introduced. At first coupons were used which the customer could trade for various prizes. The company began putting the actual prize in each box by 1912. Cracker Jack prizes have been made of lead, paper, porcelain, plastic, tin, and wood. The little sailor, Jack, is based on the founder's grandson Robert (for trivia fans, the dog's name is Bingo).

The following prices are for items in excellent to mint condition; dates are approximate. For more information see *Cracker Jack Prizes*, Alex Jarmillo, Abbeville Press, NY, 1989.

	LOW	HIGH
Air Corps Wings, metal, emb.	$ 50	$ 75
Badge, junior detective, metal, emb., ht. 1.25"	50	60
Charm for Bracelet, blue celluloid, comical head of man	20	30
Clicker, metal, black and silver, instructions on front, ht. 2.13"	20	30
Clicker, Whistle, metal, emb. CJ, w. 2"	20	30
Coconut Corn Crisp, full-color round tin, ht. 3.5"	70	90
Corkscrew, Angelus, metal, w. 3.75"	55	75
Flip Book, Charlie Chaplin, pre-1922	90	130
Game #1, red, white, and blue, w. 2.5"	40	50
Horse and Wagon, die-cast metal, len. 2"	200	300
Hummer Band, metal, emb., dia. 1"	35	45
Iron-Ons, paper, 4 attached on a sheet, 1945	8	12
Jumper, tin, frog, green and silver, 1935, len. 1.88"	25	35
Magazine Adv., *Sat. Even. Post*, June, 1919, red, white and blue	20	30
Magic Puzzle, donkey, paper and plastic, w. 1.5"	12	18
Magic Puzzle, fish	12	18
Magic Puzzle, man w/ cigar, marked CJ Co. on reverse	15	20
Paper Booklet, #12, Bess and Bill, ht. 2.5"	70	90
Paper Frog, outside is green, black, and white, opens to red and tan inside	45	65
Paper Golf Top, red, white and blue, rules back, intact	40	60
Paper, Jack at blackboard, turn dial, he writes and erases name, sq. 2"	145	195
Pin, Lady	30	40
Pin, Lady, celluloid, paper insert in back for "CJ 5 Cents"	30	40
Pocket Watch, tin, gold, black, and white, dia. 1.5"	50	70
Postcard, bears, #13	30	40
Postcard, bears, #15	30	40
Puzzle Book, #1, copyright 1917, ht. 4"	30	40
Puzzles, #1-15, complete set	200	350
Rainbow Spinner, cardboard,1920s, len. 2.5"	15	25
Sign, cardboard, red, white and blue box on blue background, 11" x 15"	400	700
Spinner, tin, red, white, and blue illust. of CJ package, w. 1.5"	25	45
Tin Top	25	35
Tin Top, fortune teller	40	60
Tin, standup Harold Teen	50	90
Tin, standup Orphan Annie	70	130
Tin, standup Perry	50	90
Truck, plastic, emb. on 4 sides, gold, 1940s, len. 1.63"	30	40
Truck, tin, red, white and black, "Cracker Jack," other "Angelus," len. 1.63"	75	95
Whistle, metal, emb. CJ	40	60
Whistle, paper, red and white, rvrs. mkd. CJ Whistle, ht. 2"	25	35
Whistle, tin, silver and blue, 1940s, 2.5"	15	25

Dollhouses

Dollhouses and dollhouse furniture are difficult areas to evaluate because of their diversity. Quality craftsmanship and attention to detail are important considerations for wooden items. Because most earlier dollhouses are hand crafted, price is often determined by collector's individual taste. Collectors of paper on wood examples rely on manufacturer, style and condition. Later, tinplate dollhouses made by Marx and other firms are worth more money if unassembled in the original box with all accessories intact. Dollhouse furniture and accessories have similar criteria; elaborate, well-crafted early items in excellent condition command the highest prices. Many items have been reproduced or created in the style of earlier periods; these items are not worth as much as similar period pieces. Color variations can occasionally affect the prices of plastic dollhouse accessories; prices listed are for more common colors. Our consultants for this area are Joan and Gaston Majeune of Toys in the Attic, they are listed in the back of this book.

Marx Colonial tinplate house, c. 1950 (unboxed), $85-$148.
—Photo courtesy of Toys in the Attic.

	LOW	HIGH
Arcade Toy Company, cast-iron living rm. sofa and chair, c. 1927, painted pink, cast-iron pillows are removable	$1000	$1400
Bliss "Alphabet House," paper litho. on wood, full front porch, 2nd floor balcony, 2 side balconies, unusual litho. interior, w/ alphabet border on 1st floor missing letter Z, ht. 24", w. 19", d. 12"	3000	3800
Bliss Doll Furniture, 1890s, wood w/ paper litho. in soft blues and reds, paper shows children at play, 7 pieces	600	950
Bliss "Seaside Residence," American paper litho. on wood, marked Bliss on front door, 3 rms., front and side openings, ht. 24", w. 18", d. 10"	2500	3600
Bliss "Semi-detached" House, paper litho. on wood, marked Bliss on front door, 4 rms., opens on both ends, ht. 24", w. 18", d. 10"	2200	3200
T. Cohn Tinplate House, c. 1941, red and white, "red tile" roof, tin windows do not open, 5 rms., (unboxed)	40	90
German "Blue Roof," by Maurice Gottschalk, paper litho. on wood, no marking, 2 rms., front opening, ht. 20", w. 14", d. 11.5"	1950	3400
German Grocery Store, 1910, dark wood frame, counter and shelves, green patterned paper walls, porcelain drawer tags, "parquet" paper floor, dolls and many accessories	2800	3600

	LOW	HIGH
German "Red Roof," painted wood, 2 floors and hinged dormer to attic rms., ht. 21.5", w. 17", d. 9.5"	$ 1700	$ 2700
German Wooden Kitchen, 1900, blue and white paper on floors and walls, blue and white painted wood furnishings, many accessories, ht. 14", w. 30", d. 15"	2750	3800
German Wooden Stable by Maurice Gottschalk, paper litho. and painted, 4 horse and carriage stalls, metal feed racks, 2nd floor doors open, w/ horses and wagons, ht. 15"	1100	1650
Marklin "Bentwood Metal Furniture," painted black, 6-piece "solarium"	550	850
Marx Colonial Tinplate House, c. 1950, red upper story, white below, tinplate awnings, chimney, garage w/ deck above, 5 rms., ht. 18.75", w. 33.5", d. 12", (unboxed)	85	148
McLoughlin 1894 Folding Doll House, 4 rms., lithographed on hinged cardboard which folds flat to fit in box	550	850
Playsteel "Buck's County," Tinplate House, c. 1948, 5 rms., ht. 19", w. 22", d. 12", (unboxed)	65	125
Rare 2-Part House, paper litho. on wood, smaller rm. and roof fit into larger rm. for packing, unusual interior lithography, larger rm. ht. 17", w. 11", d. 8"	2800	4200
Rich Colonial House, gypsum and hardboard, steel reinforced edges, steel interior stairs, 6 rms., 1930s, ht. 25", w. 35", d. 14"	275	450
Schoenhut 1928 Model, wood and fiberboard painted yellow, red "tile" roof, 8 rms., interior stairs, window boxes, metal Schoenhut tag attached to side base, ht. 24", w. 23", d. 24"	1000	1600
Unmarked Wooden House, w/ paper litho., 2 rms., front opening, ht. 14", w. 11", d. 8"	1050	1750

German "Red Roof" painted wood , c. 1900, 21.5" x 17" x 9.5", $1700-$2700. —Photo courtesy of Toys in the Attic.

Dolls

Doll collecting has grown remarkably in the last twenty-five years to become one of the top hobbies in the United States. It rivals stamps and coins. Individual appeal seems to be the magic ingredient which drives the marketplace. The prices of dolls cover such a wide range that any collector can find a category to fit his budget. Interesting and varied collections can be assembled by specializing in dolls of a certain era, a specific material, or all the various dolls produced by a single manufacturer.

In doll collecting, condition is all important. Prices given here are for dolls in excellent condition. Dolls with original or true period clothes will carry an incrementally higher value depending on quality. Deductions must be made for any missing or replaced parts; worn-out or faded clothes and wigs, and most importantly broken, chipped or cracked heads.

For further reading see *The Collector's Encyclopedia of Dolls*, Dorothy S., Elizabeth A., and Evelyn J. Coleman, Crown, New York, NY, 1968. *The Collector's Encyclopedia of Dolls Volume II*, Coleman, Dorothy S., Elizabeth A., and Evelyn J., Crown, NY, 1986, *The Official Identification and Price Guide to Antique and Modern Dolls*, Julie Collier, House of Collectibles, Random House, NY, 1989. *Patricia Smith's Doll Values, Antique to Modern*, Collector Books, Paducah, KY, 1992. Our consultant for the bisque doll portion of this section is Matrix Quality Antique Dolls.

Antique

Left: SFBJ Paris, early version of the SFBJ 301, no mold number, bisque head, sleep eyes, French jointed body, ht. 24", $1800-$2200. Middle: China head of glazed porcelain, with painted features, molded hair, cloth body and period clothes, ht. 16", $275-$325. Right: Bebe Jumeau'Déposé, bisque head, paperweight eyes, and closed mouth, on Jumeau jointed composition body, ht. 20", $5000-$6000. This doll is earlier than and commands a higher price than a Tete Jumeau. — Photos courtesy of Matrix Quality Antique Dolls.

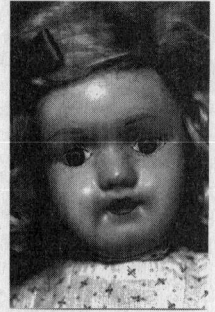 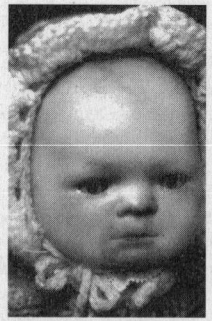 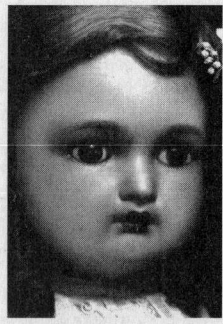

*Left: Schoenhut Dolly, mint and all original, ht. 17", $700-$800.
Middle: Bye-lo Baby, bisque head, sleep eyes, cloth body, and period
clothes, ht. 12", $500-$550. Brown eyes command a bit more. Right:
Kämmer and Reinhardt Child, bisque socket head, glass sleep eyes,
jointed composition body, period clothes and wig, ht. 24", $900-
$1200. — Photos courtesy of Matrix Quality Antique Dolls.*

	LOW	HIGH
Armand Marseille, '370,' German bisque shoulder head child with wig, glass sleep eyes, open mouth with four teeth, kid leather body with bisque arms, ht. 12"	$ 140	$ 160
Armand Marseille, '370,' ht. 15"	180	220
Armand Marseille, '370,' ht. 20"	360	380
Armand Marseille, '1894,' German bisque shoulder head child with wig, glass sleep eyes, open mouth with four teeth, kid leather body with bisque arms, ht. 12"	180	220
Armand Marseille, '1894,' ht. 15"	240	260
Armand Marseille, '1894,' ht. 20"	380	420
Armand Marseille, '390,' German bisque socket head child with wig, glass sleep eyes, open mouth with four teeth, ball-jointed composition body, ht. 12"	180	220
Armand Marseille, '390,' ht. 20"	380	420
Armand Marseille, '390,' ht. 24"	480	520
Armand Marseille, '390,' ht. 30"	750	850
Armand Marseille, 'Florodora,' German bisque shoulder head child with wig, glass sleep eyes, open mouth with four teeth, kid leather body with bisque arms, ht. 12"	140	180
Armand Marseille, 'Florodora,' ht. 15"	180	240
Armand Marseille, 'Florodora,' ht. 20"	360	400
Armand Marseille, '990,' German bisque socket head baby with wig, glass sleep eyes, open mouth with two teeth, five-piece composition baby body, ht. 10"	280	340
Armand Marseille, '990,' ht. 20"	460	500
Armand Marseille, '990,' ht. 24"	675	750
Armand Marseille, '971,' German bisque socket head baby with wig, glass sleep eyes, open mouth with two teeth, five-piece composition baby body, ht. 10"	300	350

	LOW	HIGH
Armand Marseille, '971,' ht. 20"	$ 475	$ 600
Armand Marseille, '971,' ht. 24"	700	850
Armand Marseille, '326,' German bisque socket head baby with solid crown, glass sleep eyes, open mouth with two teeth, five-piece composition baby body, ht. 10"	340	360
Armand Marseille, '326,' ht. 15"	525	575
Armand Marseille, '326,' ht. 20"	675	750
Armand Marseille, '341,' known as Dream Baby, German bisque head with flange neck, solid crown, glass sleep eyes, closed mouth, cloth body with celluloid hands, ht. 9"	180	220
Armand Marseille, '341,' ht. 13"	360	380
Armand Marseille, '341,' ht. 20"	625	675
Armand Marseille, '351,' known as Dream Baby, German bisque head with flange neck, solid crown, glass sleep eyes, open mouth with two teeth, cloth body with celluloid hands, ht. 9"	180	220
Armand Marseille, '351,' ht. 13"	360	380
Armand Marseille, '351,' ht. 20"	625	750
Bye-Lo Baby, 'Grace S. Putnam,' German bisque head with flange neck, solid crown, glass sleep eyes, closed mouth, cloth body with celluloid hands, ht. 12"	500	550
Bye-Lo Baby, ht. 15"	650	750
Bye-Lo Baby, ht. 20"	1200	1500
Bye-Lo Baby, 'Grace S. Putnam,' German bisque socket head, solid crown, glass sleep eyes, closed mouth, five-piece composition baby body, ht. 13"	1100	1300
Bye-Lo Baby, ht. 15"	1300	1400
Bye-Lo Baby, 'Grace S. Putnam,' composition head with flange neck, solid crown, painted eyes, closed mouth, cloth body with composition hands, ht. 13"	340	360
Bye-Lo Baby, 'Grace S. Putnam,' German bisque socket head, solid crown with wig, glass sleep eyes, closed mouth, all bisque baby body with jointed limbs, ht. 4"	700	750
Bye-Lo Baby, ht. 8"	1100	1300
China Head, molded hairdo with curly waves, sometimes showing ears, black or blonde hair, painted blue eyes, closed lips, cloth or leather body, with cloth, leather, china or bisque arms, ht. 8"	90	125
China Head, ht. 12"	200	250
China Head, ht. 16"	275	325
China Head, ht. 24"	500	600
Heinrich Handwerck, '99,' German bisque socket head child with wig, glass sleep eyes, open mouth with four teeth, pierced ears, ball-jointed composition body, ht. 16"	600	650
Heinrich Handwerck, '99,' ht. 24"	750	850
Heinrich Handwerck, '99,' ht. 30"	1100	1300
Heinrich Handwerck, '109,' German bisque socket head child with wig, glass sleep eyes, open mouth with four teeth, pierced ears, ball-jointed composition body, ht. 16"	600	650
Heinrich Handwerck, '109,' ht. 24"	750	850
Heinrich Handwerck, '109,' ht. 30"	1100	1300
Heinrich Handwerck, '69,' German bisque socket head child with wig, glass sleep eyes, open mouth with four teeth, pierced ears, ball-jointed		

	LOW	HIGH
composition body, ht. 16"	$ 625	$ 675
Heinrich Handwerck, '69,' ht. 24"	750	850
Heinrich Handwerck, '69,' ht. 30"	1200	1400
Heinrich Handwerck, '79,' German bisque socket head child with wig, glass sleep eyes, open mouth with four teeth, pierced ears, ball-jointed composition body, ht. 16"	625	675
Heinrich Handwerck, '79,' ht. 24"	750	850
Heinrich Handwerck, '79,' ht. 30"	1200	1400
Heinrich Handwerck, '119,' German bisque socket head child with wig, glass sleep eyes, open mouth with four teeth, pierced ears, ball-jointed composition body, ht. 16"	625	675
Heinrich Handwerck, '119,' ht. 24"	750	850
Heinrich Handwerck, '119,' ht. 30"	1200	1400
Heinrich Handwerck, '89,' German bisque socket head child with wig, glass sleep eyes, open mouth with four teeth, pierced ears, ball-jointed composition body, ht. 16"	725	775
Heinrich Handwerck, '89,' ht. 24"	850	950
Heinrich Handwerck, '89,' ht. 30"	1400	1600
Heinrich Handwerck, '420,' German bisque socket head character doll with wig, glass sleep eyes, open mouth with two teeth, ball-jointed, toddler or baby body, ht. 20"	750	850
Bebe Jumeau 'Déposé, Tete Jumeau, Bte SGDG' in red ink, French bisque socket head child with cork pate and wig, glass paperweight eyes, open mouth with six teeth, pierced ears, ball-jointed composition body, ht. 16" .	1800	2200
Bebe Jumeau 'Déposé, Tete Jumeau, Bte SGDG,' ht. 20"	2400	2600
Bebe Jumeau 'Déposé, Tete Jumeau, Bte SGDG,' ht. 24"	2800	3200
Bebe Jumeau 'Déposé, Tete Jumeau, Bte SGDG' in red ink, French bisque socket head child with cork pate and wig, glass paperweight eyes, closed mouth, pierced ears, ball-jointed composition body, ht. 16" .	3500	3800
Bebe Jumeau 'Déposé, Tete Jumeau, Bte SGDG,' ht. 20"	3800	4200
Bebe Jumeau 'Déposé, Tete Jumeau, Bte SGDG,' ht. 24"	4000	4500
Kämmer and Reinhardt '403,' German bisque socket head child with wig, glass sleep eyes, open mouth with four teeth, pierced ears, ball-jointed composition body, ht.12"	725	775
Kämmer and Reinhardt, '403,' ht. 16"	725	775
Kämmer and Reinhardt, '403,' ht. 24"	900	1200
Kämmer and Reinhardt, '403,' ht. 30"	1300	1500
Kämmer and Reinhardt, '100,' known as Kaiser baby, German bisque socket baby head with solid crown, painted eyes, open/closed mouth, five-piece composition baby body, ht. 12"	550	600
Kämmer and Reinhardt, '100,' ht. 15"	700	750
Kämmer and Reinhardt, '100,' ht. 20"	900	1100
Kämmer and Reinhardt, '126,' German bisque socket head baby with wig, glass sleep eyes, open mouth with two teeth, five-piece composition baby body, ht. 12"	475	525
Kämmer and Reinhardt, '126,' ht. 15"	625	675
Kämmer and Reinhardt, '126,' ht. 20"	800	900
Kämmer and Reinhardt, '121,' German bisque socket head baby with wig, glass sleep eyes, open mouth with two teeth, five-piece composition baby body, ht. 12"	600	650
Kämmer and Reinhardt, '121,' ht. 15"	750	800

	LOW	HIGH
Kämmer and Reinhardt, '121,' ht. 20"	$ 900	$ 1100
Kämmer and Reinhardt, '122,' German bisque socket head baby with wig, glass sleep eyes, open mouth with two teeth, five-piece composition baby body, ht. 12"	600	700
Kämmer and Reinhardt, '122,' ht. 15"	750	850
Kämmer and Reinhardt, '122,' ht. 20"	900	1200
J.D. Kestner, '154,' German bisque shoulder head child with plaster pate and wig, glass sleep eyes, open mouth with four teeth, kid body with bisque arms, ht. 12"	375	425
J.D. Kestner, '154,' ht. 16"	450	500
J.D. Kestner, '154,' ht. 20"	575	625
J.D. Kestner, '148,' German bisque shoulder head child with plaster pate and wig, glass sleep eyes, open mouth with four teeth, kid body with bisque arms, ht. 12"	425	475
J.D. Kestner, '148,' ht. 16"	500	550
J.D. Kestner, '148,' ht. 20"	650	750
J.D. Kestner, '195,' German bisque shoulder head child with plaster pate and wig, glass sleep eyes, inset fur eyebrows, open mouth with four teeth, kid body with bisque arms, ht. 15"	425	475
J.D. Kestner, '195,' ht. 20"	525	575
J.D. Kestner, '171,' German bisque socket head child with plaster pate and wig, glass sleep eyes, open mouth with four teeth, composition ball-jointed body, ht. 16"	675	725
J.D. Kestner, '171,' ht. 24"	850	900
J.D. Kestner, '171,' ht. 30"	1100	1300
J.D. Kestner, '161,' German bisque socket head child with plaster pate and wig, glass sleep eyes, open mouth with four teeth, composition ball-jointed body, ht. 16"	750	850
J.D. Kestner, '161,' ht. 24"	900	1100
J.D. Kestner, '161,' ht. 30"	1300	1500
J.D. Kestner, '167,' German bisque socket head child with plaster pate and wig, glass sleep eyes, open mouth with four teeth, composition ball-jointed body, ht. 16"	700	800
J.D. Kestner, '167,' ht. 24"	900	1000
J.D. Kestner, '167,' ht. 30"	1100	1300
J.D. Kestner, '214,' German bisque socket head child with plaster pate and wig, glass sleep eyes, open mouth with four teeth, composition ball-jointed body, ht. 16"	725	775
J.D. Kestner, '214,' ht. 24"	900	1000
J.D. Kestner, '214,' ht. 30"	1100	1300
J.D. Kestner, '129,' German bisque socket head child with plaster pate and wig, glass sleep eyes, open mouth with four teeth, composition ball-jointed body, ht. 16"	750	850
J.D. Kestner, '129,' ht. 24"	900	1100
J.D. Kestner, 129, ht. 30"	1300	1500
J.D. Kestner, '152,' German bisque socket head child with plaster pate and wig, glass sleep eyes, open mouth with four teeth, composition ball-jointed body, ht. 16"	750	850
J.D. Kestner, '152,' ht. 24"	900	1100
J.D. Kestner, '152,' ht. 30"	1300	1400
J.D. Kestner, '174,' German bisque socket head child with plaster pate		

	LOW	HIGH
and wig, glass sleep eyes, open mouth with four teeth, composition ball-jointed body, ht. 16"	$ 800	$ 900
J.D. Kestner, '174,' ht. 24"	1000	1200
J.D. Kestner, '174,' ht. 30"	1400	1600
J.D. Kestner, '211,' German bisque socket head baby with plaster pate and wig, glass sleep eyes, open mouth with two teeth, five-piece composition baby body, ht.12"	650	750
J.D. Kestner, '211,' ht. 16"	800	900
J.D. Kestner, '211,' ht. 20"	1000	1200
J.D. Kestner, '226,' German bisque socket head baby with plaster pate and wig, glass sleep eyes, open mouth with two teeth, five-piece composition baby body, ht.12"	650	750
J.D. Kestner, '226,' ht. 16"	850	950
J.D. Kestner, '226,' ht. 20"	1100	1300
J.D. Kestner, 'JDK,' German bisque socket head baby with solid crown, glass sleep eyes, open mouth with two teeth, five-piece composition baby body, ht.12"	550	650
J.D. Kestner, 'JDK,' ht. 16"	700	800
J.D. Kestner, 'JDK,' ht. 24"	1300	1500
J.D. Kestner, 'Hilda,' German bisque socket head baby with solid crown or plaster pate with wig, glass sleep eyes, open mouth with two teeth, five-piece composition baby body, ht. 15"	3400	3600
J.D. Kestner, 'Hilda,' ht. 20"	4200	4800
J.D. Kestner, 'Hilda,' ht. 24"	5500	6500
Kewpie, Rose O'Neil, all bisque standing figure, with side glancing eyes, stiff neck with little blue wings, feet joined in standing position, jointed arms with starfish hands, ht. 2"	60	80
Kewpie, Rose O'Neil, all bisque standing figure, ht. 4"	100	125
Kewpie, Rose O'Neil, all bisque standing figure, ht. 6"	150	200
Kewpie, Rose O'Neil, all bisque standing figure, ht. 8"	400	500
Kewpie, Rose O'Neil, all bisque standing figure, ht. 10"	900	1000
Kewpie, Rose O'Neil, all bisque standing figure, ht. 12"	1200	1500
Kewpie, Rose O'Neil, Composition standing figure, with side glancing eyes, stiff neck with little blue wings, feet joined in standing position, jointed arms with starfish hands, ht. 12"	250	350
Schoenhut Baby, wooden socket head with or without wig, painted eyes, open or closed mouth, five-piece body, original paint, normal wear, ht. 12"	500	600
Schoenhut Baby, ht. 15"	650	800
Schoenhut Walker, wooden socket baby head with or without wig, painted eyes, open or closed mouth, bent arms and straight hinged legs, original paint, normal wear, ht. 12"	700	850
Schoenhut Walker, ht. 16"	800	950
Schoenhut Dolly, wooden socket head child with wig, decal eyes, open mouth showing teeth, spring-jointed body, original paint, normal wear, ht. 14"	400	550
Schoenhut Dolly, ht. 17"	550	750
Schoenhut Dolly, ht. 21"	800	950
Schoenhut Carved Hair, wooden socket head child with hair carved in various hairdos, sometimes with carved ribbon, carved eyes, closed mouth, spring-jointed body, original paint, normal wear, ht. 14"	1200	1600

	LOW	HIGH
Schoenhut Carved Hair, ht. 17"	$ 1500	$ 1800
Schoenhut Carved Hair, ht. 21"	1800	2500
Schoenhut Character, wooden socket head child with wig, carved eyes, closed mouth, or showing teeth, spring-jointed wooden body, original paint, normal wear, ht. 14"	700	900
Schoenhut Character, ht. 17"	900	1200
Schoenhut Character, ht. 21"	1200	1500
SFBJ '301,' French bisque socket head child with wig, glass sleep eyes, open mouth with four teeth, pierced ears, ball-jointed composition body, ht.15	750	850
SFBJ '301,' ht. 20	900	1000
SFBJ '301,' ht. 24"	1100	1300
Shirley Temple, made by Ideal, all composition head and body (in good condition) marked 'Shirley Temple' with size number, socket head, sleep eyes, jointed body, original wig, original dress with label, ht. 11"	550	650
Shirley Temple, ht. 13"	525	575
Shirley Temple, ht. 15"	550	650
Shirley Temple, ht. 18"	650	750
Shirley Temple, ht. 20"	800	900
Shirley Temple, ht. 25"	900	1100
Shirley Temple, ht. 27"	1100	1300
Shirley Temple, made by Ideal, all composition head and body (in good condition) marked 'Shirley Temple' with size number, socket head, sleep eyes, jointed body, original wig, original Captain January blue sailor suit with label and white cap, ht. 11"	550	650
Shirley Temple, ht. 13"	850	950
Shirley Temple, ht. 15"	800	900
Shirley Temple, ht. 18"	900	1100
Shirley Temple, ht. 20"	1000	1200
Shirley Temple, ht. 25"	1200	1400
Shirley Temple, ht. 27"	1400	1600
Shirley Temple, made by Ideal, all composition head and body (in good condition) marked 'Shirley Temple' with size number, socket head, sleep eyes, jointed body, original wig, original Texas Ranger cowgirl outfit with label, gun, holster and hat, ht. 11"	900	1100
Shirley Temple, ht. 13"	900	1000
Shirley Temple, ht. 15"	1000	1200
Shirley Temple, ht. 18"	1100	1300
Shirley Temple, ht. 20"	1200	1400
Shirley Temple, ht. 25"	1400	1600
Shirley Temple, ht. 27"	1600	1800
Shirley Temple, made by Ideal, all composition head and body (in good condition) marked 'Shirley Temple' with size number, socket head, sleep eyes, jointed body, original wig, original Little Colonel southern belle outfit with label and large bonnet, ht. 11"	900	1100
Shirley Temple, ht. 13"	900	1000
Shirley Temple, ht. 15"	1000	1200
Shirley Temple, ht. 18"	1100	1300
Shirley Temple, ht. 20"	1200	1400
Shirley Temple, ht. 25"	1400	1600
Shirley Temple, ht. 27"	1600	1800

	LOW	HIGH
Shirley Temple, made by Ideal, all composition head and body (in good condition) marked 'Shirley Temple,' brown color tone, black wig, original Hawaiian grass skirt and lei, ht. 18"	$ 900	$ 1100
Baby Shirley, made by Ideal, composition head with flirty eyes, open mouth, socket head on shoulder plate with cloth torso and composition limbs, original wig and baby dress with label, ht.12"	900	1100
Baby Shirley, ht. 18"	1400	1600
Simon & Halbig, '1079,' German bisque socket head child with wig, glass sleep eyes, open mouth with four teeth, ball-jointed composition body, ht. 16"	525	575
Simon & Halbig, '1079,' ht. 24"	725	775
Simon & Halbig, '1079,' ht. 30"	1000	1200
Simon & Halbig, '1078,' German bisque socket head child with wig, glass sleep eyes, open mouth with four teeth, ball-jointed composition body, ht. 16"	525	575
Simon & Halbig, '1078,' ht. 24"	725	775
Simon & Halbig, '1078,' ht. 30"	1000	1200
Simon & Halbig, '550,' German bisque socket head child with wig, glass sleep eyes, open mouth with four teeth, ball-jointed composition body, ht. 16"	475	525
Simon & Halbig, '550,' ht. 24"	650	750
Simon & Halbig, '550,' ht. 30"	1400	1600
Simon & Halbig, 'Santa,' German bisque socket head child with wig, glass sleep eyes, open mouth with four teeth, red 'V' mark on lower lip, ball-jointed composition body, ht. 16"	800	900
Simon & Halbig, 'Santa,' ht. 24"	1100	1300
Simon & Halbig, 'Santa,' ht. 30"	1600	1800

Left: Kämmer and Reinhardt '100,' Kaiser Baby, solid crown head, painted eyes, composition body, ht. 15", $700-$750 Middle: A trio of Rose O'Neil Kewpies, The Thinker, ht. 5", $375-$425, flanked by two standers, ht. 3", each $80-$120. Right: Kestner Child, bisque head, open mouth, glass sleep eyes, jointed Kestner body with original clothes, ht. 23", $1100-$1300. — Photos courtesy of Matrix Quality Antique Dolls.

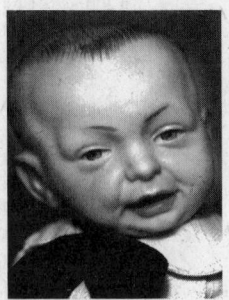  

Barbie

Barbie was born in 1959, arriving as a svelte, young woman. Mattel founders Elliot and Ruth Handler had already bought out their partner Harold Matson when they introduced the doll named after their daughter. She was modern and little girls could role play with her, dressing her in countless costumes. Barbie had elegant gowns, mirroring many of the best designers of the day, as well as work togs and casual clothes. They advertised on "The Mickey Mouse Club." Barbie rapidly became the "must have" doll of the baby-boomer area. Ken (named after the Handler's son) and a group of friends soon joined Barbie. The doll is still going strong after 36 years. Many adults who adored her as a child now collect her today. Her 30th birthday in 1989 was a gala event covered by news services around the world

Collectors look for condition. The most desirable Barbies are pristine examples from the 1950s and '60s. Collectors shy away from much '70s material because there is a perception of inferior quality.

The prices below are based on items in near mint to mint condition. Since the same item can be bought at a variety of locations and prices and many dolls are no longer in their original boxes, we have devised a double range system. The low range (MNP) includes items that are near mint to mint without packaging. The higher-end range (MIP) reflects the prices of near mint to mint items in near mint to mint original boxes. Therefore, prices below are for the best items available; scratched, chipped, or altered are not included. Cut hair, missing clothes, and cracked or stained plastic greatly reduce the price of Barbie. Each entry lists the approximate year of introduction and the item number.

See *The Collectors Encyclopedia of Barbie Dolls and Collectibles*, Sybil DeWein and Joan Ashabraner, and *Doll Fashion Anthology & Price Guide,* A. Glenn Mandeville, Hobby House Press, Grantsville, MD, 1994.

BARBIE AND FRIENDS

	INTRO. YEAR	NO.	MNP	MIP
Barbie #1, blond	1959	850	$ 1900-2600	$ 3500-5500
Barbie #1, brunette	1959	850	2400-3000	4000-6000
Barbie #2, blond	1959	850	1600-2000	2600-3500
Barbie #2, brunette	1959	850	1900-2600	3500-4500
Barbie #3, blond	1960	850	400-500	700-800
Barbie #3, brunette	1960	850	450-550	800-1000
Barbie #4, blond	1960	850	200-250	400-600
Barbie #4, brunette	1960	850	250-300	500-700
Barbie, bendable legs, rare side flip hairdo	1965	1070	1800-2400	3200-3600
Barbie, bendable legs, American girl hairdo	1965	1070	300-400	700-900
Barbie, bendable legs, American girl hairdo	1966	1070	300-400	900-1200
Benefit Performance Porcelain Barbie	1988	5475	100-140	340-420
Bubble Cut Barbie	1961	850	140-160	250-350
Bubble Cut Barbie	1962	850	140-160	250-300
Color Magic Barbie	1966	1150	650-750	1200-2000
Fashion Queen Barbie	1963	870	100-150	400-500
Francie Twist 'N' Turn, bendable legs	1967	1170	70-90	260-320
Francie, bendable legs, black	1967	1100	300-350	700-900
Francie, bendable legs, white	1966	1130	60-90	200-300
Free Moving Barbie	1975	7270	12-18	50-70
Free Moving Ken	1975	7280	10-15	30-40

	INTRO. YEAR	NO.	MNP	MIP
Gold Medal Olympic Skater Barbie	1975	7262	$ 12-16	$ 80-100
Happy Holidays Barbie, red velvet gown	1988	1703	120-180	380-420
Happy Holidays Barbie, white satin gown	1989	3253	50-80	120-160
Hawaiian Barbie	1977	7470	25-35	70-90
Hawaiian Ken	1978	2960	15-20	30-40
Hispanic Barbie	1979	1292	12-16	50-60
International Barbie, Canadian	1988	4928	8-12	25-32
International Barbie, Eskimo	1982	3898	60-80	120-160
Julia,1 piece nurse outfit	1970	1127	40-60	100-150
Julia, 2 piece nurse outfit	1969	1127	50-80	120-180
Julia, talking	1969	1128	50-80	120-180
Ken, bendable legs	1970	1124	25-35	80-120
Ken, bendable legs	1965	1020	90-130	200-300
Ken, flocked, crew cut hair	1961	750	50-70	130-180
Ken, painted crew cut hair	1962	750	40-50	100-150
Live Action Barbie, blond	1971	1155	30-50	90-130
Malibu Barbie	1971	1067	12-18	40-50
Midge, bendable legs	1965	1080	200-250	400-500
Midge, straight legs	1964	860	40-60	140-180
Miss Barbie (sleep-eye)	1964	1060	250-350	700-900
Mod Hair Ken	1973	4224	40-50	90-120
Pink Jubilee Barbie (1200 made)	1989	—	700-900	1400-1800
Quick Curl Barbie	1973	4220	12-18	60-90
Ricky, straight legs	1965	1090	50-60	90-120
Skipper, bendable legs	1965	1030	40-60	90-110
Skipper, straight legs	1964	950	40-60	100-150
Skipper, straight legs, reissues, pinker skin	1970	950	50-70	120-180
Skooter, bendable legs	1966	1120	60-80	220-280
Standard Barbie	1967	1190	80-100	280-320
Swirl Pony Tail Barbie	1964	850	200-250	400-700
Talking Barbie	1969	1115	60-80	200-250
Talking Ken	1969	1111	40-60	110-130
Talking P.J.	1969	—	50-70	120-160
Talking Truly Scrumptious	1969	1107	120-160	320-360
Truly Scrumptious, straight legs	1969	1108	100-150	350-450
Twiggy	1967	1185	70-90	220-320
Twist and Turn Barbie	1967	1160	80-100	280-340
Walk Lively Barbie	1972	1182	50-70	120-180
Walk Lively Ken	1972	1184	25-35	60-80
CLOTHING				
Aboard Ship	1965	1631	90-140	200-250
American Airlines Stewardess	1961	984	50-75	150-200
Arabian Knights	1964	874	90-120	200-250
Ballerina	1961	989	40-60	130-160
Barbie in Japan	1964	821	190-220	360-420
Barbi-Q Outfit	1959	962	55-75	140-180
Beautiful Bride	1967	1698	300-500	800-1000

	INTRO. YEAR	NO.	MNP	MIP
Benefit Performance	1966	1667	$ 300-350	$ 600-800
Campus Sweetheart	1964	1616	200-300	400-600
Career Girl	1963	954	60-80	180-220
Cheerleader	1964	876	60-80	150-200
Commuter Set	1959	916	300-400	600-800
Debutante Ball	1966	1666	200-300	400-700
Doctor Ken	1963	793	50-70	90-120
Easter Parade	1959	971	750-1000	1500-2000
Gay Parisienne	1959	964	400-600	1200-1800
Gold 'N Glamour	1965	1647	300-400	700-800
Here Comes the Bride	1966	1665	350-400	700-900
Ken Campus Hero	1961	770	20-30	50-70
Ken Country Clubbin'	1964	1400	40-60	90-110
Ken Fraternity Meeting	1964	1408	25-35	60-70
Ken Here Comes the Groom	1966	1426	250-350	600-900
Ken Mr. Astronaut	1965	1415	180-240	400-500
Ken Tuxedo	1961	787	40-60	100-140
Little Red Riding Hood & the Wolf	1964	880	180-220	380-420
Miss Astronaut	1965	1641	300-350	600-700
Modern Art	1965	1625	150-200	280-320
Nighty-Negligee	1959	965	40-50	90-130
Pajama Party	1964	1601	12-18	50-80
Pan American Stewardess	1966	1678	500-800	1500-2000
Poodle Parade	1965	1643	200-250	400-500
Roman Holiday	1959	968	1200-1800	2200-2800
Saturday Matinee	1965	1615	320-380	600-800
Shimmering Magic	1966	1664	450-500	900-1300

GIFT SETS AND ACCESSORIES

Barbie and Ken Tennis Gift Set	1962	892	250-350	800-1200
Barbie Beautiful Blues Gift Set	1967	3303	300-350	700-900
Barbie's Sparkling Pink Gift Set	1964	1011	250-350	600-800
Barbie's Sport Plane (Irwin)	1964	—	300-400	600-900
Barbie's Wedding Party Gift Set	1964	1017	400-600	1000-1800
Casey Goes Casual Gift Set	1967	3304	300-400	700-1000
Fashion Queen Barbie and Ken Trousseau Gift Set	1964	864	250-350	800-1000
Midge's Ensemble Gift Set	1964	1012	300-400	800-1000

G.I. Joe

Joe recently turned 30 and is still going strong. Hasbro introduced him in 1964. The Irwin Company produced some of Hasbro's early vehicles for Joe. Plastic and 11.5" tall, Joe was marketed as a fighting or action figure and not as a doll. Thus the action-figure toy was created. A huge success with boys, girls often substituted him for Ken, to act as Barbie's date. Joe has changed with the times. In 1977 Hasbro reduced his height to 8.5". Following the enormous success of the *Star Wars* action-figure line, Joe was reintroduced in the 3.75" size in 1982 and is still being produced. Collectors are beginning to seek these figures. The following list, however, focuses on the earlier 11.5" figures.

The prices below are based on items in excellent or mint condition. Since the same item can be bought at a variety of locations at different prices we devised a range system. The low range covers complete, near mint to mint items without the original box or package (*MNP*). The higher range reflects the prices of complete, near mint to mint items in near mint to mint boxes (*MIP*). Prices below are for complete "like new" items. Completeness is an important factor for G.I Joes.

The Encyclopedia of G.I. Joe, by Vincent Santelmo, Krause Publications, Iola, WI, 1993, describes in great detail what each set contained.

The year listed is the year of introduction, unless it's a reissue or update. Following the date is the series: Action Marine-(*AM*), Action Girl-(*AG*), Action Sailor-(*ALS*), Action Soldiers of the World-(*ASW*), Action Soldier-(*ASD*), Action Pilot-(*AP*), Adventure Team-(*ADT*), and Adventure Pack-(*ADP*), a designation not a series. Words are abbreviated to conserve space. Following the series is the product number. We have put in *Fig.* (figure), *Unf.* (uniform), or *Equip.* (equipment) to avoid confusion between similarly named sets. Each term encompasses everything that originally came with the set.

	YEAR	SERIES	NO.	MNP	MIP
Action Black Soldier Fig.	1965	ASD	7900	$ 700-900	$ 1000-1600
Action Marine Fig.	1964	AM	7700	120-180	320-380
Action Nurse Fig.	1967	AG	8060	1300-1600	2000-3200
Action Sailor Fig.	1964	ASL	7600	150-200	300-400
Action Soldier Fig.	1964	ASD	7500	120-180	260-320
Air Acad. Cadet Unf. Set	1967	AP	7822	400-500	800-1000
Air Sea Rescue Unf. Set	1967	AP	7825	400-600	1500-2000
Annapolis Cadet Unf. Set	1967	ASL	7624	400-500	800-1200
Astronaut Unf. Set	1967	AP	7824	300-400	1200-1500
Austr. Jungle Ftr. Stnd. Set, w/ fig.	1966	ASW	8205	400-600	1200-1400
Austr. Jungle Ftr. Equip.	1966	ASW	8305	150-200	300-400
Austr. Jungle Ftr. Dlx. Set, fig. and equip.	1966	ASW	8105	500-700	2000-2600
Basic Foot Locker	1965	AS	8000	40-50	90-140
Beachhead Flamethrower Set	1964	AM	7718	50-60	80-100
Bivouac Sleeping Bag	1964	ASD	7515	25-35	60-80
British Commando Stnd. Set, w/ fig.	1966	ASW	8204	400-500	1000-1600
British Commando Equip.	1966	ASW	8304	160-200	300-350
British Com. Dlx. Set, fig. and equip.	1966	ASW	8104	500-600	2000-2500
Combat Fatigue Pants	1964	ASD	7504	40-50	80-100
Combat Fatigue Shirt	1964	ASD	7503	30-40	90-120
Combat Field Jacket	1964	ASD	7505	60-90	180-240
Comma. Post Field Radio Tel. Set	1964	ASD	7520	40-50	80-100
Comma. Post Poncho	1964	ASD	7519	30-50	90-120
Commu. Flag Set	1964	AM	7704	200-250	400-500

	YEAR	SERIES	NO.	MNP	MIP
Crash Crew Fire Truck Set	1967	AP	8040	$1800-2200	$3000-3500
Deep Freeze Unf. Set	1967	ASL	7623	300-400	900-1400
Deep Sea Diver Unf. Set, reissue	1968	ASL	7620	300-500	900-1300
Desert Patrol Jeep Set, w/ fig.	1967	ASD	8030	800-1000	1500-2200
Dress Unf.	1964	AP	7803	300-500	1400-2000
Fighter Pilot Unf. Set	1967	AP	7823	500-700	1500-2000
Forward Base Set, w/ fig. (Sears)	1966	ASD	5969	300-400	600-900
Fr. Res. Fighter Stnd. Set, w/ fig.	1966	ASW	8203	400-500	1000-1300
Fr. Res. Fighter Equip.	1966	ASW	8303	120-180	250-300
Fr. Res. Ftr. Dlx. Set, fig. and equip. ...	1966	ASW	8103	300-500	1800-2200
German Soldier Stnd. Set, w/ fig.	1966	ASW	8200	300-500	1200-1400
German Soldier Equip.	1966	ASW	8300	160-200	300-350
German Soldier Dlx. Set, fig. and equip.	1966	ASW	8100	400-500	1800-2200
Green Beret Equip.	1966	ASD	7533	70-90	200-300
Green Beret fig.	1966	ASD	7536	400-500	1800-2200
Green Beret Mach. Gun Opst, 2 figs. ...	1966	ASD	5978	600-800	1200-1500
Japanese Imp. Sold. Stnd. Set, w/ fig. .	1966	ASW	8201	550-650	1300-1600
Japanese Imp. Sold. Dlx. Set, fig. and equip.	1966	ASW	8101	600-700	2200-2600
Japanese Imp. Sold. Equip.	1966	ASW	8301	200-250	350-500
Jet Fighter Airplane	1967	ASD	5396	400-500	800-1000
Jungle Fighter Unf. Set	1967	AM	7732	600-900	1800-2200
M.P. Duffel Bag	1964	ASD	7523	25-35	50-70
M.P. "Ike" Jacket	1964	ASD	7524	50-70	90-120
Mach. Gun Set, w/ fig. (Sears)	1965	ASD	7531	350-450	700-1100
Marine Demo. Set (Reissue)	1968	AM	7730	100-150	350-450
Marine Weapons Rack	1967	AM	7727	120-160	350-500
Military Staff Car	1967	ASD	5652	300-350	500-700
Official Jeep Set, w/ eng. sound	1965	ASD	7000	250-350	500-600
Russian Soldier Equip.	1966	ASW	8302	170-200	300-350
Russian Soldier Stnd. Set, w/ fig.	1966	ASW	8202	400-500	1200-1400
Russian Soldier Dlx. Set, fig. and equip.	1966	ASW	8102	500-600	1800-2200
Sea Sled and Frogman Fig. Set	1966	ASL	8050	180-220	350-500
Ski Patrol Equip. Set	1965	ASD	7531	300-350	600-900
Space Capsule Set (Sears)	1966	AP	5979	300-350	600-800
Special Forces Unf. Set, w/ bazooka ...	1966	ASD	7532	300-400	700-900
Talking Action Marine Fig.	1967	AM	7790	200-300	600-800
Talking Action Pilot Fig.	1967	AP	7890	450-650	1200-2000
Talking Action Sailor Fig.	1967	ASL	7690	300-400	600-900
Talking Action Soldier Fig.	1967	ASD	7590	190-230	350-450
Talking Adv. Tm. Black Com. Fig.	1974	ADT	7291	250-350	600-800
Talking Fig., w/ command post items .	1968	ADP	90517	500-600	1600-2200
Talking Fig., w/ LSO equip.	1968	ADP	90621	600-800	2000-2500
Talking Fig., w/ Sp. Forces items	1968	ADP	90532	600-800	2000-2500
Talking Mar. Fig., w/ field pack equip.	1968	ADP	90712	400-600	1600-2000
Tank Com. Unf. Set	1967	AM	7731	350-450	900-1400
West Point Cadet Unf.	1967	ASD	7537	400-500	800-1000

Paper

Paper dolls date to the 1400s and appeared as children's toys in the late 1700s. Collectors usually specialize either in antique examples or in specific types such as celebrity, advertising, works of favorite artists, or companies. Dolls based on movie and TV stars attract collectors from other areas.

A paper doll's collectibility depends upon artist, subject, age, construction, condition, and size. Prices below are for uncut near mint condition examples. Near mint, cut dolls may command prices 20%-50% of uncut dolls. Abbreviations have been used throughout the listings; for example, lg.-large, astd.-assorted, num.-numerous, bk.-book, cstms.-costumes, and clr.-color.

For further information see *The Official Price Guide to Paper Collectibles*, published by The House of Collectibles, Random House, NY; *A Collector's Guide to Paper Dolls*, Second Series, Mary Young, Collector Books, Paducah, KY, 1984; and *Paper Dolls of Famous Faces*, Jean Woodcock, Hobby House Press, Cumberland, MD, 1980.

	LOW	HIGH
Bride and Groom, 1970, Whitman bk. #1989, punch-outs, pink cover	$ 10	$ 15
Bride and Groom, England, 1971, coloring bk. and paper dolls, 2 dolls, astd. outfits	7	9
Candy Stripers, 1973, Saalfield	7	9
Captain Big Bill, 1956, Samuel Lowe	9	13
Career Girls, 1942, Samuel Lowe	25	45
Career Girls, 1950, Samuel Lowe	20	35
Career Girls, by Doris Lane Butler, 1944, Whitman bk. #973, 3 dolls: Ann, Marty, and Dottie, clothlike outfits	35	50
Carmen Miranda, 1942, Whitman #995	90	125
Carmen Miranda, 1952, Saalfield #1558, 2 dolls, astd. outfits	80	110
Carmen Miranda Paper Dolls, by Tom Tierney, 1 doll, astd. cstms.	8	15
Carmen, Rita Hayworth, 1948, 2 dolls, astd. outfits, thin cover	60	80
Dolls Across the Sea, by Queen Holden, 1969, Platt and Munk, Hans, Ingrid, Yvonne, and Juliane, foreign cstms., boxed	8	12
Dolls for All Seasons-Rosy Ruth, by Raphael Tuck, 1 doll w/ 3 dresses and 1 hat	100	150
Dolls of All Nations-Russia, *Boston Sunday Globe*	12	18
Dolls of Other Lands, 1968, Watkins, 6 dolls, 42 cstms.	8	12
Dolly Dingle's World Flight in Italy, December 1932, boy doll, 3 cstms.	30	40
Dolly Dingle's World Flight in Russia, March 1933, 1 doll, pets	30	40
Dolly Dingle's World Flight in Sweden, February 1933, boy, cstms.	30	40
Dolly Dingle's World Flight in Switzerland, September 1931	30	40
Dolly Dingle's World Flight, June 1932, 4 dresses	30	40
Donna Reed, 1959, Saalfield #4412, 2 dolls, astd. clothes, folder	50	75
Doris Day, 1952, Whitman bk. #210325, statuette dolls, astd. outfits, folder	50	75
Doris Day, 1954, Whitman bk. #1179:15, 2 dolls, 8 pages of outfits	60	80
Doris Day, 1955, Whitman bk. #1952, statuette dolls, astd. clothes, folder	60	80
Doris Day, 1956, Whitman bk. #1952, astd. outfits	50	75
Dorothy Provine, 1962, Whitman bk. #1964, 1 doll, astd. outfits, folder w/ handle	35	45
Dr. Kildare and Nurse Susan, #2740, punch-outs, 3 dolls, astd. outfits	25	35
Dr. Kildare Play Book, Samuel Lowe	25	35
Dress-up Doll Book, by Sally de Frehn Ogg, 1953, Treasure bk. # T- 167, 5 dolls, astd. outfits to be colored	20	25
Hansel and Gretel Push-Out Book, 1954, Whitman	12	18

	LOW	HIGH
Happiest Millionaire, 1967, Saalfield	$ 10	$ 14
Happy Birthday, 1939, Merrill	30	40
Happy Bride, 1967, Whitman bk. #1958, 4 dolls, 1960s-style clothes	18	22
Happy Days Playset Characters, various scenes, characters, incl. Arnold's Drive-in and Fonzie's motorcycle	18	22
Happy Family, 1973, Samuel Lowe	6	8
Happy Holiday, reprint of Carmen Miranda, Saalfield bk. #2722, 2 dolls, astd. outfits	20	35
Hayley Mills in *Summer Magic*, 1963, Whitman bk. #1966, 1 doll, astd. cstms., folder	50	70
Hayley Mills in *The Moon Spinners*, 1964, Whitman bk. #1960, 1 doll, astd. clothes	50	70
Hedy Lamarr, 1942, Merrill #3482, 2 dolls, 22 outfits, 29 access.	50	60
Hedy Lamarr, 1951, Saalfield	50	60
Hee-Haw, punch-out, by George and Nan Pollard, 1971, C.B.S. Artcraft bk. #5139, Gunilla, Lulu, Kathy, and Jeannie	15	20
In Old New York, 1957, Saalfield bk. #4411, clr. and paper dolls, bk., 2 dolls, astd. cstms.	25	35
In Old New York, Saalfield bk. #1772, 2 dolls, 2 pages of cstms., thin cover	25	35
In Our Background, 1941, Samuel Lowe	25	35
Jack and Jill, bk. #1561, 4 dolls, animals, astd. storyland cstms.	15	20
Jack With Magic Eyes, Queen Holden, 1963, James and Jonathan #9301-P, lg. doll, disc eyes	50	70
Jackie and Caroline, #107	60	80
Journey Friends, toy from Germany, by Ann Eshner, Jack and Jill set, Dec. 1952	10	12
Judy, 1951, Merrill	10	15
Judy and Jim, by Hilda Miloche and Wilma Kane, Simon and Shuster, astd. outfits	40	50
Judy Garland, Queen Holden, 1940, Whitman #996	100	150
Judy Garland, Queen Holden, 1945, Whitman #999, 2 dolls, large assortment of outfits	100	150
Judy Holiday, 1954, Saalfield bk. #159110, 3 dolls, 4 pages of clothes, thin cover	45	55
Julia, 1968, Saalfield	35	50
Julie Andrews, 1958, Saalfield	35	50
June Allyson, 1950, Whitman bk. #970, 2 dolls, astd. outfits	50	70
June Allyson, 1950/1952, Whitman bk. #119015, 8 pages of clothes	50	75
June Allyson, 1953, Whitman bk. #1173:15, 2 dolls, 8 pages of dresses and cstms.	50	75
June Allyson, 1957, Whitman bk. #2089, 2 dolls, 6 pages of clothes	50	75
June Allyson, 1960s, Watkins/Strathemore bk. #1820, 2 statuette dolls, 1 green, 1 pink and gray, astd. clothes	50	75
June Bride, by Art Tanchon, 1946, Stephens Company bk. #136	25	35
June and Stu Erwin, w/ Jackie and Joyce (*Trouble With Father*), 1954, #159210	50	70
Jungletown Jamboree, Samuel Lowe	6	8
Junior Miss, 1942, Saalfield bk. #250, large dolls	35	45
Junior Prom, 1942, Saalfield	35	45
Karen Goes to College, 1955, Merrill	35	45
Keepsake Folio-Mini Doll, 1964, Samuel Lowe	15	20
Keepsake Folio-Trudy Doll, 1964, Samuel Lowe	20	30
Kewpie Kin, by Joseph Kallus, 1967, Saalfield bk. #4413, punch-out, wrap-around dresses, blue cover	22	34

Kewpies, 1963, large Skootles on cover, 2 smaller Kewpies on back, astd.
  clothes .... $ 25 $ 38
Kewpies in Kewpieville, 1966, Saalfield, Rose O'Neill's dolls 22   34
Kiddie Circus, Saalfield 10   12
Little Ballerina, 1969, Whitman bk. #1963, 4 dolls, astd. outfits, folder 10   15
Little Brothers and Sisters, 1953, Whitman, 4 dolls, astd. outfits 15   20
Little Cousins, 1940, Samuel Lowe 15   20
Little Dolls, 1972, Samuel Lowe 6   8
Little Fairy, 1951, Merrill bk. #154715, 4 children w/ astd. cstms. 30   40
Little Folks Dolls Set, 1900s, Milton Bradley #4727, 3 True-Life dolls, 3 sheets
  of colored clothing, 25 sheets of clothes to color 70   100
Little Girls, 1969, Samuel Lowe 6   8
Little Joy San, McCalls, October 1919, 1 doll, Japanese girl, dress, toy, lantern .. 12   18
Little Kitten to Dress, 1942, Samuel Lowe 20   30
Party Time, 1952, Whitman 10   15
Pat Boone, 1959, Whitman #1985 50   70
Pat Boone, 1959, Whitman bk. #1968, 2 statuette dolls in folder, astd. clothes 50   70
Pat Crowley, 1955, Whitman bk. #2050, 2 dolls, 8 pages of clothes 50   70
Pat the Stand-Up Doll, front and back dresses, 1946, Lowe bk. #1042, astd.
  clothes 35   45
Patches and Petunia, by Betty Bell Rea, 1937, Saalfield bk. #2160, lg. doll,
  astd. clothes 35   45
Patchwork, 1971, Saalfield 8   12
Patchy Annie, 1962, Saalfield 7   10
Patience and Prudence, 1959, Abbott bk. #1807, 2 dolls, astd. outfits, thin cover ... 35   45
Patti Page, 1958, Abbott bk. #1804, 2 dolls, astd. outfits, thin cover 40   60
Patty Duke, 1965, Whitman bk. #1991:59, 2 dolls, 6 pages of punch-out clothes ... 50   75
Polly Pal, 1976, Samuel Lowe 4   6
Preschool, 1958, Saalfield 10   15
Pretty As a Rose, 1963, Saalfield 15   20
Prince and Princess, Saalfield bk. #4464, coloring bk. and paper dolls, punch-
  outs, horse and rider, medieval cstms. 40   50
Princess Diana Paper Doll Bk. of Fashion, by Clarissa Harlow and Mary Anna
  Bedford, num. outfits, 40-page bk. 6   8
Prom Home Permanent, 1952, Samuel Lowe 20   30
Puppy and Kitty Cut-outs, 1938, Florence Salter, 21 pieces of clothing 20   30
Quiz Kids, 1942, Saalfield 35   45
Raggedy Ann, 1970, Whitman 6   9
Raggedy Ann, by Ethel Hays Simms, Saalfield bk. #369, thin cover 40   50
Raggedy Ann and Raggedy Andy, 1961, bk. #1728, 2 dolls, yellow cover 20   30
Raggedy Ann and Andy, by Ethel H. Simms, coloring and paper doll bk., 1944,
  Saalfield bk. #4409, Marcella and the Raggedies 40   50
Raggedy Ann and Raggedy Andy, by Ethel Hays Simms, 1961, Saalfield bk.
  #2715, Raggedies on front, Marcella on back 30   40
Raggedy Ann and Raggedy Andy Sticker Kit Circus, 1941, #546, sticker
  pictures 25   35
Ranch Family, 1957, Merrill 25   35
Rave Doll Dressing Bk., England, possibly based on "The Avengers" 50   60
Ricky Nelson, 1959, Whitman bk. #2081, 2 dolls, 6 pages of clothes 70   90
Ride a Pony-Judy and Jill, 1944, Merrill 12   18
Rita Hayworth, 1942, Merrill bk. #3478, 2 dolls, astd. outfits 60   80

LOW HIGH

Robin Hood, 1973, Walt Disney, press-out finger puppets, scenery and castle .. $ 12 $ 17
Robin Hood and Maid Marian, Saalfield bk. #2784, astd. cstms., die-cut
 covers 50 60
School Friends, 1955, Merrill bk. #1556, Linda, Bobbie, and Diane, dresses
 and cowgirl suits 20 30
School Girl, 1942, Saalfield bk. #2400, large dolls, astd. clothes 35 45
Schoolmates, 1947, Saalfield 12 18
Sesame Street Characters, 1976, Whitman, Big Bird, Oscar, Cookie Monster, etc. 6 8
Seven and Seventeen, 1954, Merrill bk. #3441, 4 dolls, astd. clothes 35 45
Seven Children, by Queen Holden, large assortment of clothes 50 70
Shari Lewis, 1958, Saalfield 40 60
Shari Lewis and Her Puppets, 1960, Saalfield 35 45
Sheree North, 1957, Saalfield bk. #1728, front and back dolls, 4 pages of dresses,
 thin cover 40 60
Sherlock Bones, 1955, Samuel Lowe, ... 8 12
Sherry and Terry, Lowe bk. #1847, Kewpie-style dolls 12 18
Shirley Temple, 1930s, adv., front and back doll, blue plaid dress, white collar,
 black tie 50 70
Shirley Temple, 1934, Saalfield bk. #2112, 4 dolls, astd. clothes, num. access. . 100 150
Shirley Temple, 1937, Saalfield bk. #1761, 2 toddler dolls, 2 dresses 70 90
Shirley Temple, 1942, die-cut teenage set, 2 dolls, yellow formal, astd. outfits,
 thin cover 150 200
Shirley Temple, 1950s, Gabriel #300, statuette doll, snap-on clothes, real picture
 faces, num. outfits 40 65
Shirley Temple, 1958, Saalfield bk. #5110, statuette doll, astd. dresses, folder 80 100
Shirley Temple, 1976, Whitman bk. #1986, 1 doll, astd. clothes, pink tote bag 8 12
Shirley Temple-Her Movie Wardrobe, 1938, 1 doll in pink slip, astd. outfits 80 120
Sparkle Plenty, baby from the Dick Tracy comic strip, 1948 .... 30 50
Sports Time, 1952, Whitman bk. #2090, blonde doll in white slip 18 24
Square Dance, 1950, Saalfield #2717, 5 dolls, 6 pages of cstms. 20 30
Stand-Up Dolls, 1960s, Artcraft, 6 dolls 8 10
Star Babies, 1945, Merrill 20 25
Star Trek, 1975, Saalfield bk. #C2272, activity bk., punch-out, stand-up dolls,
 Kirk, Spock, McCoy, Uhura, and Sulu 50 75

Hess Trucks

Every year around Thanksgiving signs go up at Hess gas stations around the country announcing the arrival of the Hess toy. These vehicles have been parked under Christmas trees since 1964. They are sold for a limited time only during the Christmas Season. This tradition continues today with many collectors looking forward to the event as much as kids. Collectors pay top prices for earlier toys or rare variations. We have listed price ranges for mint in box (MIB) examples. Boxes and packing materials are crucial in determining value. The MIB prices listed below are for items that are practically in the same condition as they were when picked up at the Hess Station. Valuations are tricky because sometimes the same truck is used two different years with only small changes to the truck but with different boxes. The box therefore becomes the determining factor in dating an item. There may be a few rare variations not listed below so do your homework. For further information see *Toy Truck Collectors Official Price Guide*, Toy Truck Collector, Englewood, NJ, 1995, and *Collecting Toys, No. 7, Richard O'Brien,* Books Americana, Florence, AL, 1996. Our Consultant for this section is Jim Glaab, owner of Jim Glaab's Collectors Showcase in Greene, NY (he is listed in the back of this book).

	LOW	HIGH
1964, Model B Mack Tanker Truck, w/ funnel	$ 2000	$ 2500
1965, Model B Mack Tanker Truck, w/ funnel	2000	2500
1966, Voyager Tanker Ship w/ stand	2000	3000
1967, Split Window Tanker Truck, w/ red velvet base box	2400	2800
1968, Split Window Tanker Truck, without red velvet base, Perth Amboy, NJ	650	750
1969, Split Window Tanker Truck, Woodbridge, NJ on box	700	800
1969, Amerada Hess Split Window Tanker Truck (not issued to the public)	2000	3000
1970, Red Pumper Fire Truck	700	800
1971, Red Pumper Fire Truck in Season's Greeting's box	2500	3000
1972, Split Window Tanker Truck	300	400
1974, Split Window Tanker Truck	300	400
1975, Box Truck w/ 3 unlabeled oil drums, one-piece cab, made in Hong Kong	300	400
1976, Box Truck w/ 3 Hess labeled oil drums, 2-piece cab, made in Hong Kong	300	400
1977, Tanker Truck w/ large rear label	180	220
1978, Tanker Truck w/ slightly smaller label than 1977	180	220
1980, GMC Training Van	350	450
1982, '33 Chevy, "The First Hess Truck", red switch	80	120
1983, '33 Chevy, "The First Hess Truck, bank	80	120
1984, Hess Tanker Truck Bank, similar to 1977 truck	80	120
1985, '33 Chevy, "The First Hess Truck" Bank, reissue of 1983	90	120
1985, Hess Tanker Truck Bank, reissue of 1984	90	120
1986, Red Aerial Ladder Fire Truck	100	150
1987, White Box Truck w/ 3 labeled oil drums,	60	90
1988, Slant Bed Truck w/ race car	75	95
1989, White Ladder Fire Truck	45	65
1990, White Tanker Truck	40	50
1991, Slant Bed Truck w/ race car, similar to 1988	30	40
1992, Race Car Hauler, car inside	30	50
1993, Patrol Car w/ 2 sirens and flashing lights	25	30
1993, Premium Diesel Tanker Truck (not issued to the public)	900	1200
1994, Rescue Truck	20	25
1995, Truck and Helicopter	25	35

Hot Wheels

Hot Wheels burst onto the toy scene in 1968 as Mattel's answer to Matchbox Toys. Their popularity soared because the product lived up to its name:
- The design of the axles and wheels produced a smooth fast ride
- They emulated the souped-up drag racing cars popular at the time
- The metallic paint was attractive

The amazing aspect of collecting Hot Wheels is the number of variations possible for what seems to be the same model. Most differences in value are due to the different paint jobs or details such as wheels, applied logos, and decoration. Many times a model is introduced in a more desirable paint color. Early vehicles finished in metallic pink seem to command higher prices, as the color was discontinued after a short production run. Conversely, common colors produced in huge quantities or for several years often deflate the price of a vehicle. The same model (with slight changes such as color) was introduced over the years but age doesn't necessarily constitute value. Nineteen seventy-three was a disastrous year for Mattel. Trying to cut costs, they removed the button from the package and changed the paint from the metallic Spectra Flame finish to less costly enamels. Sales plummeted. Although terrible for the company, it was a boon for collectors. The 1973 line is more difficult to find than other years, thus prices are consistently higher. Collectors can be fickle; what is thought rare and sought after one year may be displaced by something else the next.

Since the same item can be bought at a variety of locations and because condition and color variations further complicates pricing, we have devised a range system. The low range includes items that are excellent to mint without packing (MNP). The higher-end price reflects the prices of excellent to mint items in excellent to mint boxes (MIP). Therefore prices below are for the best items available; scratched, chipped or altered are not included. We have seen poor-condition Hot Wheels ranging from $1 to the prices listed below and beyond. In our opinion, bad-condition models are worth little unless extremely rare. On the other hand, some special colors (frequently metallic pink) are rare and worth considerably more than the general prices listed here. Because of the many variations, exact identification can be tricky. We have also used the following abbreviations within the descriptions: *rl* .-redline tires, *bwl* .-blackwall tires, *var.*-various paint finishes, *met.*-stands for metallic paint (other colors may also be abbreviated). For each entry, date of manufacture and model number are also listed.

We suggest *Tomart's Price Guide to Hot Wheels* by Michael Strauss, Tomart Publications, Dayton, OH, 1993. This guide has an excellent wheel dating chart and many photos. You may also want to consult *Hot Wheels Newsletter*, 26 Maderas Ave., San Carlos, CA 94070, and *Crusin' Connection*, 2648 E. Workman Ave., West Covina, CA 91791.

	DATE	NO.	MNP	MIP
Alive '55, var.	1973	6968	$ 90-140	$ 300-450
Alive '55, blue	1974	6968	70-90	300-400
Alive '55, chrome rl. or bwl.	1977	9210	15-20	30-40
Alive '55, dk. grn., op. hood	1983	6968	50-70	90-110
Ambulance, var.	1970	6451	40-60	45-75
Ambulance, white	1970	6451	80-100	100-150
American Tipper, red	1976	9089	16-22	26-36
American Victory, lt. blue	1975	7662	15-20	30-40
AMX/2, var.	1971	6460	35-45	60-80
AMX/2, met. pink	1971	6460	60-70	80-100
Backwoods Bomb, lt. blue	1975	7670	30-40	60-80
Backwoods Bomb, grn. rl. or bwl.	1977	7670	30-40	70-90
Beatnik Bandit, var.	1968	6217	15-25	30-50

	DATE	NO.	MNP	MIP
Boss Hoss, var.	1971	6406	$ 50-70	$ 100-150
Bragham Repco F1, var.	1969	6264	10-15	25-35
Bugeye, var.	1971	6178	35-45	70-90
Buzz Off, var.	1973	6976	90-120	250-350
Buzz Off, blue	1974	6976	35-45	70-90
Bye-Focal, var.	1971	6187	70-90	200-250
Carabo, var.	1970	6420	25-35	45-55
Carabo, pink	1970	6420	60-70	90-110
Carabo, lt. grn.	1974	7617	30-40	50-60
Carabo, yellow	1974	7617	250-350	400-600
Cement Mixer, var.	1970	6452	25-35	35-45
Chapparal 2G, var.	1969	6256	15-20	30-40
Chapparal 2G, pink	1969	6256	50-70	90-140
Chevy Monza 2+2, green	1975	7671	180-220	250-300
Chevy Monza 2+2, orange	1975	7671	40-50	70-90
Chief's Special, red	1975	7665	30-40	40-60
Classic '31 Ford Woody, var.	1969	6251	12-18	40-60
Classic '36 Ford Coupe, var.	1969	6253	12-18	30-50
Classic '32 Ford Vicky, var.	1969	6250	18-22	45-55
Classic '36 Ford Coupe, lt. blue	1969	6253	35-45	50-70
Classic '36 Ford Coupe, pink	1969	6253	70-90	100-150
Classic '57 T-Bird, var.	1969	6252	20-30	50-70
Classic '57 T-Bird, pink	1969	6252	70-90	100-150
Classic Cord, var.	1971	6472	125-175	300-400
Classic Nomad, var.	1970	6404	40-60	70-90
Cockney Cab, var.	1971	6466	40-50	70-90
Corvette Stingray, red	1976	9241	30-40	55-70
Custom AMX, var.	1969	6267	40-60	80-100
Custom Barracuda, var.	1968	6211	50-60	200-300
Custom Camaro, var.	1968	6208	40-70	200-300
Custom Charger, var.	1969	6268	50-80	120-160
Custom Con. Mk III, var.	1969	6266	20-30	40-60
Custom Corvette, var.	1968	6215	50-80	200-250
Custom Cougar, var.	1968	6205	60-80	300-400
Custom Eldorado, var.	1968	6218	30-50	100-150
Custom Firebird, var.	1968	6212	40-60	200-250
Custom Fleetside, var.	1968	6213	40-60	150-200
Custom Mustang, var.	1968	6206	60-80	300-400
Custom Police Cruiser, wht.	1969	6269	50-60	100-150
Custom T-Bird, var.	1968	6207	60-80	200-300
Custom VW Bug, var.	1968	6220	12-20	40-60
Demon, var.	1970	6401	15-20	30-40
Deora, var.	1968	6210	40-60	300-350
Double Header, var.	1973	5880	80-100	250-350
Double Vision, var.	1973	6975	80-100	200-300
Drag Race Act. Set (add val. 2 cars in set)	1968	6202	20-30	50-70
Dump Truck, var.	1970	6453	18-22	30-40
Dune Daddy, var.	1973	6967	80-100	250-350
El Rey Special, var. grn.	1974	8273	40-60	70-90
Emergency Squad, red	1975	7650	12-16	40-50
Evil Weevil, var.	1971	6471	35-45	60-80

	DATE	NO.	MNP	MIP
Ferrari 312P, var.	1970	6417	$ 15-20	$ 30-40
Ferrari 312P, met. red, wht. int.	1970	6417	100-150	180-220
Ferrari 312P, var.	1973	6973	200-250	600-800
Ferrari 512S, var.	1972	6021	80-100	180-240
Fire Chief Cruiser, red	1970	6469	10-14	18-22
Fire Engine, var.	1970	6454	30-50	50-70
Ford J-Car, var.	1968	6214	10-15	30-50
Ford Mark IV, var.	1969	6257	8-12	25-35
Fuel Tanker, white enamel	1971	6018	50-70	100-150
Full Curve Pak	1968	6225	8-10	18-22
Funny Money, gray	1972	6005	50-60	180-220
Funny Money, magenta	1974	7621	30-40	40-60
Grass Hopper, var.	1971	6461	30-40	50-75
Grass Hopper, eng. on hd., green	1974	7622	35-45	50-70
Gremlin Grinder, green.	1975	7652	25-35	40-50
Gun Slinger Jeep, olive	1975	7664	25-35	40-50
Hairy Hauler, var.	1971	6458	30-40	35-45
Heavy Chevy, var.	1970	6408	35-45	50-70
Heavy Chevy Silv. Sp., chr.	1970	6189	40-50	90-110
Heavy Chevy, var.	1974	7619	45-55	80-90
Hiway Robber, var.	1973	6979	80-100	200-250
Hood, var.	1971	6175	30-40	40-60
Hood, met. pink	1971	6175	60-80	60-80
Hot Heap, var.	1968	6219	12-18	30-50
Ice "T," yellow	1971	6184	40-50	120-180
Ice "T," var.	1973	6980	90-140	300-500
Indy Eagle, var.	1969	6263	10-15	30-40
Indy Eagle, gold chrome	1969	6263	50-70	160-200
Jack Rabbit Jack-in-the-Box promo	1970	6421	100-150	200-250
Jack Rabbit Special, white	1970	6421	10-15	35-45
Jet Threat, var.	1971	6179	50-70	100-150
King 'Kuda, var.	1970	6411	30-40	60-80
King 'Kuda, chrome club kit	1970	6190	50-60	80-120
Light My Firebird, var.	1970	6412	18-22	50-60
Lola GT 70, var.	1969	6254	8-12	20-30
Lotus Turbine, var.	1969	6262	10-15	25-35
McLaren M6A, var.	1969	6255	8-12	30-40
Mercedes 280SL, var.	1969	6275	18-22	35-45
Mercedes 280SL, var.	1973	6962	90-120	300-400
Mercedes C-111, var.	1972	6169	80-100	200-250
Mercedes C-111, var.	1974	6978	180-220	300-400
Mighty Maverick, var.	1970	6414	35-45	60-80
Mod Quad, var.	1970	6456	18-22	30-40
Mongoose Rail Drag. (2 pk), blue	1971	5952	70-90	500-600
Mongoose Funny Car, red	1970	6410	50-60	120-160
Mongoose II, met. blue	1971	5954	70-90	200-300
Moving Van, var.	1970	6455	35-45	70-90
Mutt Mobile, var.	1971	5185	50-80	90-120
Nitty Gritty Kitty, var.	1970	6405	35-55	100-150
Noodle Head, var.	1971	6000	50-80	90-140
Olds 442, var.	1971	6467	200-250	500-600

	DATE	NO.	MNP	MIP
Open Fire, var.	1972	5881	$ 80-100	$ 200-300
Paddy Wagon, dk. blue.	1970	6402	9-12	25-35
Peepin Bomb, var.	1970	6419	10-15	25-35
Pit Crew, white	1971	6183	60-80	300-500
Porsche 917, var.	1970	6416	12-18	30-40
Porsche 917, var.	1973	6972	180-220	400-700
Power Pad, var.	1970	6459	30-40	60-90
Python, var.	1968	6216	15-20	35-50
Racer Rig, white or red	1971	6194	70-90	250-350
Rear Eng. Mongoose, blue	1972	5699	140-180	300-500
Rear Engine Snake, yellow	1972	5856	140-180	300-500
Red Baron, red, black interior	1970	6400	20-30	30-40
Rocket Bye Baby, var.	1971	6186	50-70	120-180
Rolls R. Sil. Sh., var.	1969	6276	25-45	50-70
S'Cool Bus, yellow	1971	6468	100-150	600-700
Sand Crab, var.	1970	6403	12-18	30-40
Scooper Dump Truck, var.	1971	6193	80-100	200-300
Seasider, var.	1970	6413	50-70	100-150
Shelby Turbine, var.	1969	6265	12-18	30-50
Short Order, var.	1971	6176	40-50	80-120
Side Kick, var.	1972	6022	80-100	175-225
Silhouette, var.	1968	6209	12-18	35-50
Six Shooter, var.	1971	6003	60-80	125-175
Sky Show Fleetside, var.	1970	6436	350-500	600-700
Snake Funny Car, yellow	1970	6409	50-80	200-250
Snake II, white	1971	5953	50-60	200-250
Snake Rail Dragster, white	1971	5951	70-90	500-600
Snorkel, var. (2 pak)	1971	6020	60-80	120-160
Special Delivery, blue	1971	6006	40-60	150-200
Splittin' Image, var.	1969	6261	10-15	30-40
Staff Car	1976	9521	500-700	—
Street Eater, yellow	1975	7669	30-50	80-100
Street Snorter, var.	1973	6971	90-110	250-350
Strip Teaser, var.	1971	6188	50-80	150-200
Sugar Caddy, var.	1971	6418	40-60	60-80
Super Van, Toys R Us	1975	7649	125-175	200-250
Super Van, black	1975	7649	30-40	40-60
Super Van, King Radio	1975	7649	80-100	120-180
Superfine Turbine, var.	1973	6004	200-300	500-900
Sweet -16, var.	1973	6007	80-100	200-300
Swingin' Wing, var.	1970	6422	20-30	40-50
T-4-2, var.	1971	6177	40-50	90-140
Talking Serv. Center	1969	5159	40-70	80-120
Team Trailer, white or red	1971	6019	60-80	150-200
TNT Bird, var.	1970	6407	30-40	60-80
Torero, var.	1969	6260	12-15	30-50
Torero, pink	1969	6260	60-70	80-100
Torino Stocker, red	1975	7647	30-40	40-60
Tough Customer, olive	1975	7655	14-20	40-60
Tow Truck, var.	1970	6450	25-35	45-55
Tri Baby, var.	1970	6424	20-30	40-50

	DATE	NO.	MNP	MIP
Turbofire, var.	1969	6259	$ 10-15	$ 40-60
Twin Mill, var.	1969	6258	12-22	40-50
Twin Mill II, orange	1976	8240	18-22	25-30
Vega Bomb, orange	1975	7658	35-45	70-90
VW Beach Bomb, surf bds./rear, var.	1969	6274	2200-3500	—
VW Beach Bomb, surf bds./side, var.	1969	6274	40-50	80-100
Volkswagen Bug, orange, bug on roof	1974	7620	30-40	50-60
Volkswagen Bug, orange w/ stripes	1974	7620	140-180	300-400
Waste Wagon, var.	1971	6192	70-90	200-300
What 4, gold	1971	6001	80-100	180-220
What 4, var.	1971	6001	60-80	100-150
Whip Creamer, var.	1970	6457	20-40	40-60
Winnipeg, yellow	1974	7618	60-90	95-135
Xploder, var.	1973	6977	90-120	300-350

Japanese Automotive Tinplate Toys

Two decades before Japan threatened Detroit for the auto market they dominated the post-war tinplate toy industry. Ford, GM, and American Motors refined the art of the automobile in the 1950s and Japan replicated their efforts in toys. A score of Japanese toy companies produced these toys. Even four decades later, very little is known about these firms.

Collectors of post-war Japanese automotive toys favor those models in the 10"-16" category, followed by the 8" category. Many oversized models are less popular because of the amount of shelf space they require. The *creme de la creme* of this area is the 16" 1962 Chrysler Imperial, a car any collector will find space for.

When collecting these vehicles examine them carefully and make sure there are no missing parts, including mirrors and trim. Make sure there is no restoration; battery boxes should be checked closely. Never leave a battery in a toy; it can leak and cause damage. The prices below are for mint without box (MNB) and mint in the box (MIB) examples. Rust, scratches, and restoration will lower these prices. All dates refer to the year the vehicle most closely resembles; production is usually around the same time. These are toys and not exact models, so there are differences between them and their real life counterparts. In the cases where a model looks the same for several years, we used *c.* Abbreviated company names are unidentified firms, as is *UK* (unknown). Regarding power, *BT* stands for battery operated, *BR* battery operated with remote control, *BL* battery operated with lights, and *F* friction powered.

An excellent source of information on this subject is *Collecting the Tin Toy Car 1950-1970*, Dale Kelly, Schiffer Publishing, Exton, PA, 1984. Our consultant for this area is Jack Herbert, collector and contributing author to *Antique Toy World Magazine*, a must-have publication for toy collectors (see our list of publications). Mr. Herbert's address is listed in the back of this book.

Above: 1956 Messerschmitt by Bandai, 8.5", $700-$1000.
— Photo courtesy of Jack Herbert.

Model	YEAR	CO.	SIZE	POWER	MNB	MIB
Aston-Martin (James Bond car)	'65	Gilbert	11"	BT	$ 350-400	$ 600-800
Austin Healy Sports Car	'54	Bandai	8"	F	300-400	400-500
BMW 600 Isetta, 4 whls.	c. '50	Bandai	9"	F	500-700	600-800
Buick	'53	Marusan	7"	F	600-800	700-1000
Buick	'59	Nomura	11"	F	600-700	800-1000
Buick	'60	Ichiko	17.5"	F	700-800	900-1100
Buick	'61	Nomura	16"	F	700-900	900-1200
Buick Convertible	'49	UK	8.5"	F	250-350	400-500
Buick Emerg.Car	'61	Nomura	14"	F	500-600	800-900
Buick Future Car Convertible	'51	Yonezawa	7.5"	F	800-900	1000-1200
Buick LeSabre	'66	Asahi	19"	F	700-900	800-1000
Buick Sportswagon	'68	Asakusa	15"	F	700-900	800-1000
Buick Station Wagon	'54	UK	8"	BT	400-600	500-700
Cadillac	'51	Marusan	11"	BT	1200-1500	1800-2000
Cadillac	'60	Yonezawa	18"	F	1600-1900	2000-2500
Cadillac	'62	Yonezawa	22"	F	1000-1200	1400-1600
Cadillac	'67	Ichiko	28"	F	1600-2200	2000-2500
Cadillac Convertible	'52	Alps	11.5"	F	1800-2200	2200-2500
Cadillac Convertible	'52	Nomura	13"	BL	400-600	500-800
Cadillac Convertible	'59	Bandai	11"	F	300-400	500-700
Cadillac Convertible	'60	Bandai	11"	F	400-600	500-700
Cadillac Eldorado Convertible	'67	UK	10.75"	F	300-500	400-600
Cadillac Eldorado	'68	Ichiko	29"	F	500-700	800-1000
Cadillac Eldorado	'67	Kosuge	10.5"	F	600-700	900-1100
Cadillac Fleetwood	'61	S.S.S.	17.5"	F	300-400	500-700
Cadillac, 4 Door	'59	Bandai	11"	F	300-400	500-700
Cadillac, 4 Door	'65	Ichiko	22"	F	700-900	1200-1400
Champion's Racer	c. '54	Yonezawa	18"	F	1200-1500	1400-1800
Chevrolet	'55	Marusan	11"	BL	500-700	700-900
Chevrolet	'62	Asahi	11"	F	400-500	600-700
Chevrolet Camaro	'71	Taiyo	9.5"	BT	150-200	250-300
Chevrolet Convertible	'59	S.Y.	11.5"	F	600-800	800-900
Chevrolet Corvette	'62	Bandai	8"	BT	500-600	600-800
Chevrolet Corvette	'63	Bandai	8"	F	300-350	400-500
Chevrolet Corvette	'68	Taiyo	9.5"	BT	150-200	250-300
Chevrolet Impala Convert.	'61	Bandai	11"	F	700-800	900-1000
Chevrolet Impala Sedan	'61	Bandai	11"	F	600-800	700-900
Chevrolet Pick-Up	'63	UK	8"	F	100-125	150-175
Chevrolet Wagon	'60	UK	12"	F	400-500	500-600
Chrysler Imperial	'62	Asahi	16"	F	10 -15,000	15 -18,000
Chrysler Sedan	'67	Nomura	12"	F	300-350	400-600
Citroen	'55	Bandai	12"	F	400-600	500-700
Datson 280Z	'76	Alps	19"	F	300-350	450-550
Dodge	'58	Nomura	11"	F	600-800	700-900
Dodge Pick-Up	'59	M.	18.5"	F	1000-1200	1200-1500
Edsel	'58	Asahi	10.75"	F	700-800	900-1200
Edsel Convertible	'58	Haji	10.25"	F	1200-1500	1500-2000
Edsel Station Wagon	'58	Haji	10.5"	F	800-900	1000-1200
Ferrari 250G Convertible	'57	Asahi	9.5"	F	500-600	600-800
Fiat Hardtop Sedan	'55	Nomura	15"	F	200-300	300-400
Ford	'56	Yonezawa	12"	F	800-1000	1000-1200

Model	YEAR	CO.	SIZE	POWER	MNB	MIB
Ford	'57	Ichiko	12"	F	$ 800-1200	$ 1000-1400
Ford Country Sedan Station						
Wagon	'61	Bandai	10.5"	F	400-600	500-700
Ford Convertible	'56	Haji	11.5"	F	4000-5000	5000-7500
Ford Convertible, trunk opens	'55	Bandai	12"	F	800-900	900-1200
Ford Country Sedan Station						
Wagon	'62	Asahi	12"	F	800-900	900-1200
Ford Fairlane Convertible	'57	Ichiko	10"	F	400-600	500-700
Ford Flower Del. Wagon	'55	Bandai	12"	F	1000-1200	1200-1500
Ford Galaxie	'65	Mod. Toys	11"	F	400-600	500-700
Ford GT	c. '68	Bandai	10"	BT	400-600	500-700
Ford Gyron	'60	Ichida	11"	BT	400-600	500-700
Ford Mustang	'65	Bandai	11"	BT	300-500	400-600
Ford Mustang	'67	Bandai	13"	BT	400-600	500-700
Ford Ranchero	'55	Bandai	12"	F	400-600	500-800
Ford Ranchero	'57	Bandai	12"	F	500-600	600-700
Ford Sedan	'52	H	7.5"	F	200-250	300-400
Ford Station Wagon	'55	Bandai	12"	F	400-600	500-800
Ford Station Wagon	'57	Bandai	12"	F	400-600	500-700
Ford T-Bird Convertible,						
retract. roof	'62	Yonezawa	11"	BT	400-500	500-700
Ford Thunderbird	'56	Nomura	11"	BL	600-700	700-800
Ford, 2 door	'56	Marusan	13"	F	1800-2200	2500-2800
Good Humor Truck	'50	K.T.S.	10.75"	F	700-900	1000-1500
International Cement Truck	c. '55	S.S.S.	19"	F	1200-1500	1500-2000
Isetta 3 Wheeler	c. '50	Bandai	6.5"	F	500-700	600-800
Jaguar XK-120	'65	Alps	6.5"	F	300-500	400-600
Jaguar XKE	c. '65	T.T.	10.5"	F	400-600	500-700
Jeepster Station Wagon	'66	Daiya	10.5"	F	150-175	200-250
Land Rover	'60	Bandai	7.5"	F	500-700	700-800
Lincoln	'55	Yonezawa	12"	F	900-1200	1000-1400
Lincoln	'60	Yonezawa	11"	BT	600-800	800-1000
Lincoln Futura	'56	Alps	11"	BT	800-1200	1200-1500
Lincoln Mark II	'56	Line Mar	12"	B	2500-3000	3000-3500
Lincoln Mark II	'56	Line Mar	12"	F	2500-3000	3000-3500
Lincoln Mark III	'58	Bandai	11"	F	500-700	600-800
Lincoln Sedan	'63	Nomura	10.5"	BT	300-350	400-500
Lotus Elite	c. '58	Bandai	8.5"	F	150-200	200-250
Mercedes Benz 220S	'62	S.S.S.	12"	BT	600-800	700-1000
Mercedes Benz 250 SE	'65	Ichiko	13"	BT	200-300	300-400
Mercedes Benz 300 SL	c. '58	Cragstan	9"	BT	600-800	700-900
Mercedes Benz Racer	'55	Line Mar	9.5"	F	700-900	800-1000
Mercedes Benz Racer W196	'55	Marusan	10"	BT	400-600	500-700
Mercedes Benz (reissued)	'70	Ichiko	24"	F	80-100	90-120
Mercury	'58	Yonezawa	11.5"	F	900-1000	1000-1200
Mercury Cougar	'67	Taiyo	10"	BT	400-600	500-700
Messerschmitt	'56	Bandai	8.5"	F	500-600	700-1000
MG 1600 Mark II	c. '58	Bandai	8.5"	F	175-225	200-300
MG A	'57	Asahi	10"	F	400-600	500-700
MG TD	'55	S.S.S.	6.5"	F	125-175	150-200
MG TF	'52	UK	8.5"	F	300-500	400-600

MODEL	YEAR	CO.	SIZE	POWER	MNB	MIB
MG TF	'55	Bandai	8"	F	$ 300-400	$ 400-600
Olds Toronado	'66	Bandai	11"	BT	400-600	500-700
Oldsmobile	'56	UK	10.5"	F	600-800	700-900
Oldsmobile	'58	Yonezawa	16"	F	1200-1800	1800-2000
Opel	c. '55	Yonezawa	11.5"	BL	500-600	600-700
Packard Convertible	'53	Alps	16"	F	5000-7000	7000-8000
Packard Sedan	'53	Alps	16"	F	4000-6000	5000-7000
Plymouth	'56	Alps	12"	BT	500-700	700-800
Plymouth	'61	Ichiko	12"	F	600-900	800-1000
Plymouth Ambulance	'61	Bandai	12"	F	600-700	700-800
Plymouth Convertible	'59	Asahi	10.5"	F	600-700	700-900
Plymouth Hard Top Convertible	'59	Asahi	10.5"	F	600-900	800-1000
Plymouth Station Wagon	'58	Bandai	8.5"	F	150-200	200-300
Pontiac Firebird	'67	Bandai	9.5"	BT	500-600	600-700
Porsche Rally 911	c. '65	Alps	9.5"	BT	300-500	400-600
Rambler (Nash) Sedan	'53	K	8"	F	250-300	400-500
Rambler Station Wagon	'59	Bandai	11"		400-500	500-600
Renault 750	'58	Masudaya	7"	F	400-600	500-700
Renault 750	'58	Yonezawa	7.5"	F	400-600	500-700
Rolls Royce	'60	UK	10.5"	F	1000-1200	1200-1500
Rolls Royce	c. '58	Bandai	12"	BT	400-600	500-700
Rolls Royce Convertible	c. '55	Bandai	12"	F	400-600	500-700
Studebaker	'53	UK	9"	F	500-600	600-700
Studebaker Avante	c. '55	Bandai	8"	F	500-600	600-700
Toyota 2000 GT	'67	Asahi	15"	F	200-250	250-300
Volkswagon Bug	c. '60	Bandai	15"	BT	450-500	550-600
Volkswagon Bus	c. '65	Bandai	9.5"	BT	400-600	500-700
VW Convertible Bug	c. '60	Masudaya	9.5"	F	500-700	700-800
VW Convertible Bug	c. '60	Taiyo	10.5"	BT	400-600	500-700
VW Karman-Ghia Conv.	c. '60	Bandai	7.5	F	300-350	400-450
VW Pick-Up Truck	c. '65	Bandai	8"	BR	250-350	400-500

Left to right: 1959 Plymouth Hardtop by Ashai, 10.5", $600-900; 1961 Plymouth by Ichiko, 12", $600-900. —Photo courtesy of Jack Herbert.

Lionel Trains

Joshua Lionel Cohen founded America's best-known toy train producer, Lionel, in 1901. In the following descriptions we give the numbers and titles of various locomotives and cars. Descriptions of locomotives contain the wheel configuration, such as 4-4-4; four forward wheels, four wheels in the middle and four in the back. Locomotive descriptions contain engine type, steam or electric (elec.). This describes the style of the locomotive, not the power that runs the toy. Unless otherwise noted, electricity is the power source. The number of some locomotives is followed by *E*, which refers to an E-Unit reverse system. *Sp* following a number stands for Special. Gauge for cars and locomotives is listed, such as *Std*. (Standard), and *O*. Gauge refers to the track width. Although specific years are not listed, *post* and *pre* indicate if an item was produced before WWII (pre) or after WWII (post).

The following prices are given in a double-range format. The first range is for items in good condition, having scrapes and some light corrosion. The second range is for items in excellent or like-new condition.

There are many variations of Lionel trains. Color and stylistic differences can dramatically influence prices. The prices below, unless specified, are for the more common variations.

For further information we recommend *Lionel Trains Standard of the World*, Donald S. Fraley, M.D., Ed., Train Collectors Association, 1976; *Greenberg's Pocket Price Guide to Lionel Trains*, Allen W. Miller, Kalmbach Publishing, Waukesha, WI, 1994; *Greenberg's Guide to Trains*, 1901-42, volumes I-III; and *Greenberg's Guide to Trains 1945-69*, volumes I-VI. The Train Collector's Association can be reached at TCA, P.O. Box 248, 300 Paradise Lane, Strasberg, PA 17579, 717-687-8623.

Our consultant for this area is Stuart Waldman, collector and owner of Toy Treasures specializing in trains and antique toys (he is listed in the back of this book).

Lionel 400E Blue Comet standard gauge set, c. 1931, with brass and copper trim, $2500-$4500. —Photo courtesy of Phillips Auctioneers.

	GOOD	EXCELLENT
5, Loco 0-4-0, No Tender, steam, Std., pre	$ 450-550	$ 650-750
6, Loco 4-4-0, steam, Std., pre	450-550	650-750
6, Sp., Loco 0-4-0, steam, Std., pre	1400-1600	2800-3200
7, Loco 4-4-0, steam, Std., pre	1800-2200	2800-3000
9E, Loco 0-4-0, elec., Std., pre	550-650	900-1100
10, Loco 0-4-0, elec., Std., pre	90-110	180-220
16, Ballast, Std., pre	90-110	140-160

	GOOD	EXCELLENT
17, Caboose, Std., pre	$ 65-80	$ 90-110
31, Combine, Std., pre	60-80	90-100
32, Mail, Std., pre	60-80	90-100
33, Loco 0-4-0, elec., Std., pre	60-80	90-110
33, Loco 0-6-0, elec., Std., pre	400-600	800-1000
34, Loco 0-6-0, elec., Std., pre	400-600	900-1100
38, Loco 0-4-0, elec., Std., pre	90-110	180-200
42, Loco 0-4-4-0, square, elec., Std., pre	200-300	450-550
50, Loco 0-4-0, elec., Std., pre	90-110	180-220
53, Loco 0-4-4-0, elec., Std., pre	1800-2200	3500-4000
53, Loco 0-4-0, elec., Std., pre	900-1100	1400-1600
54, Loco 0-4-4-0, elec., Std., pre	2800-3000	3800-4000
61 Sp., Loco 0-4-4-0, Schwartz, elec., Std., pre	900-1100	1800-2200
117, Caboose, Std., pre	45-55	60-80
150, Loco 0-4-0, elec., O, pre	60-80	90-110
152, Loco 0-4-0, elec., O, pre	90-100	110-130
153, Loco 0-4-0, elec., O, pre	90-100	110-130
154, Loco 0-4-0, elec., O, pre	140-160	180-220
156, Loco 0-4-0, elec., O, pre	280-320	450-500
158, Loco 0-4-0, elec., O, pre	90-110	140-160
201, Loco 0-6-0, steam, O, pre	280-320	380-420
203, Loco 0-6-0, steam, O, pre	280-320	380-420
203, Loco 0-4-0, armored, elec., O, pre	650-750	900-1100
204, Loco 2-4-2, steam, O, pre	90-110	140-160
214R, Refrigerator, Std., pre	280-320	575-600
224E, Loco 2-6-2, steam, O, pre	140-160	180-200
225E, Loco 2-6-2, steam, O, pre	160-180	220-260
226E, Loco 2-6-4, steam, O, pre	240-260	340-380
227, Loco 0-6-0, steam, O, pre	450-550	650-760
228, Loco 0-6-0, steam, O, pre	650-750	900-1100
229, Loco 2-4-2, steam, O, pre	60-80	90-110
233, Loco 0-6-0, steam, O, pre	900-1100	1400-1600
238, Loco 4-4-2, steam, O, pre	140-160	180-220
248, Loco 0-4-0, elec., O, pre	40-60	80-100
249, Loco, steam, O, pre	140-160	180-220
250, Loco 0-4-0, elec., O, pre	40-60	90-110
250E, Loco 0-4-0, Hiawatha, steam, O, pre	450-550	700-800
251, Loco 0-4-0, elec., O, pre	180-220	380-420
252, Loco 0-4-0, elec., O, pre	60-80	90-110
253E, Loco 0-4-0, elec., O, pre	90-110	180-220
254, Loco 0-4-0, elec., O, pre	180-220	380-420
255E, Loco 2-4-2, steam, O, pre	180-220	280-320
256, Loco 0-4-4-0, elec., O, pre	450-550	650-750
258, Loco 2-4-2, steam, O, pre	40-60	90-110
259, Loco 2-4-2, steam, O, pre	40-60	90-110
260E, Loco 2-4-2, steam, O, pre	180-220	280-320
261, Loco 2-4-2, steam, O, pre	60-80	110-130
262, Loco 2-4-2, steam, O, pre	90-110	130-160
263E, Loco 2-4-2, steam, O, pre	180-220	280-320
263E, Loco 2-4-2, blue, steam, O, pre	450-550	650-750
264E, Loco 2-4-2, steam, O, pre	180-220	380-420

	GOOD	EXCELLENT
289E, Loco 2-4-2, steam, O, pre	$ 90-110	$ 140-160
309, Pullman, Std., pre	50-70	90-110
310, Baggage, Std., pre	50-70	90-110
318E, Loco 0-4-0, elec., Std., pre	90-110	180-220
322, Observation, Std., pre	50-70	90-110
380E, Loco 0-4-0, elec., Std., pre	180-220	280-320
381E, Loco 4-4-4, elec., Std., pre	1800-2200	2800-3200
384, Loco 2-4-0, steam, Std., pre	180-220	350-400
385E, Loco 2-4-2, steam, Std., pre	450-550	650-750
390, Loco 2-4-2, black, steam, Std., pre	450-550	650-750
390E, Loco 2-4-2, blue, steam, Std., pre	900-1100	1800-2200
392, Loco 4-4-2, steam, Std., pre	450-550	900-1100
400E, Loco 4-4-4, steam, Std., pre	900-1100	1800-2200
400E, Loco 4-4-4, blue, steam, Std., pre	1800-2200	2800-3200
402E, Loco 0-4-4-0, elec., Std., pre	450-550	650-750
408E, Loco 0-4-4-0, elec., Std., pre	900-1100	1800-2000
431, Diner, Std., pre	375-400	575-625
450, Loco 0-4-0, Macy's Sp., elec., O, pre	180-220	380-420
600, Pullman, O, pre	60-75	90-100
601, Observation, O, pre	60-75	90-100
652, Gondola, O, pre	20-25	30-40
653, Hopper, O, pre	35-45	50-60
671, Loco 6-8-6, steam, O, post	140-160	180-220
681, Loco 6-8-6, steam, O, post	90-110	140-160
700, Loco 0-4-0, elec., O, pre	180-220	280-320
700E, Loco 4-6-4, Sc. Hud. 5344, steam, O, pre	900-1100	1400-1600
701, Loco 0-4-0, elec., O, pre	180-220	280-320
703, Loco 0-4-0, elec., O, pre	900-1100	1400-1600
708, Loco 0-6-0, steam, O, pre	900-1100	1400-1600
726, Loco 2-8-4, steam, O, post	180-220	380-420
736, Loco 2-8-4, steam, O, post	140-160	180-220
746, Loco 4-8-4, N & W, steam, O, post	550-650	900-1100
752E, Loco Streamliner, Diesel, O, pre	240-260	380-420
763E, Loco 4-6-4, Scale Hudson, steam, O, pre	650-750	850-950
773, Loco 4-6-4, Hudson, steam, O, post	750-850	1100-1300
804, Tank, Shell, O, pre	30-40	50-60
805, Box Car, O, pre	30-40	50-60
806, Cattle, O, pre	35-45	50-60
807, Caboose, O, pre	25-35	40-50
820, Floodlight, O, pre	90-110	140-160
831, Lumber, O, pre	18-22	28-32
831, Flat, O, pre	18-22	28-32
1100, Handcar Mickey and Minnie, pre	300-400	600-900
1103, Handcar Bunny and Basket, pre	500-600	700-900
1105, Handcar Santa, pre	500-600	700-900
1107, Handcar Donald Duck, pre	300-400	600-800
1651E, Loco 0-4-0, elec., O, pre	40-60	65-80
1661E, Loco 2-4-0, steam, O, pre	40-60	65-80
1662, Loco 0-4-0, steam, O, pre	60-80	90-110
1663, Loco 0-4-0, steam, O, pre	90-110	140-160
1664, Loco 2-4-2, steam, O, pre	60-80	90-110

	GOOD	EXCELLENT
1666, Loco 2-6-2, steam, O, post	$ 40-60	$ 70-90
1674, Pullman, steam, O, pre	60-80	90-110
1689E, Loco 2-4-2, steam, O, pre	90-110	140-160
1835E, Loco 2-4-2, steam, Std., pre	450-550	650-750
1910, Pullman Car, Std., pre	1800-2200	900-1100
1911, Loco 0-4-0 early, elec., Std., pre	900-1000	1800-2200
1911 Sp., Loco 0-4-4-0, elec., Std., pre	2400-2600	3800-4200
1912, Loco 0-4-4-0, elec., Std., pre	1800-2200	3800-4200
1912 Sp., Loco 0-4-4-0, elec., Std., pre	3800-4200	5500-6000
2037, Loco 2-6-4, steam, O, post	90-110	140-160
2055, Loco 4-6-4, steam, O, post	90-130	160-180
2056, Loco 4-6-4, steam, O, post	90-130	160-180
2810, Derrick, O, pre	140-160	180-220
2816, Hopper, O, pre	140-160	180-220
3357, Hydraulic Maint. Car, O, post	90-110	180-220
3409, Helicopter Car, O, post	90-110	180-220
3413, Mercury Capsule Car, O, post	140-160	240-260
3470, Target Launcher, O, post	65-80	140-160
3472, Automatic Milk Car, O, post	65-80	140-160
3510, Satellite Car, O, post	90-110	180-220
3859, Dump, O, pre	60-75	90-100

Original boxes, like the one pictured above, add value to the set. —Photo courtesy of Phillips Auctioneers.

Lunch Boxes

Steel lunch boxes produced from the 1950s to the 1980s were one of the last holdouts of the lithographed metal process once prevalent in the production of toys. In order to deter sandlot warriors from injuring each other, steel boxes were discontinued in the 1980s. Soon after, they burst onto the collecting scene. Buying back a box from their youth, collectors relived grade school memories and the late summer ritual of shopping for school supplies. Collectors also love the diversity of topics represented. Many of the boxes are based on classic TV shows, and they frame their topics like small screens. The steel boxes are not the only ones sought by collectors; some of the vinyl examples are among the costliest. After a meteoric rise, the market cooled in the early '90s. However, today's growing interest in TV memorabilia is bringing in a new group of collectors.

We devised a range system for pricing. Since bottles often become separated from the box, we have given estimates for boxes and bottles separately. The prices below reflect items that are in excellent to mint condition. Rust and dents decrease the value of boxes and bottles. The "NB" designation in the bottle column means that a bottle was not produced for that particular box.

See *The Fifties and Sixties Lunch Box*, by Scott Bruce, Chronicle Books, San Francisco, CA, 1988, and *The Illustrated Encyclopedia of Metal Lunch Boxes*, by Allen Woodall and Sean Brickell, Schiffer Publishing, West Chester, PA, 1992.

Abbreviations: we removed "The" from titles such as "The Munsters," shortened words so that vinyl, with blue steel glass bottle becomes V, bl stl gl bot. Under Features we have listed distinguishing features such as V for Vinyl; if it isn't vinyl assume it is steel; D stands for dome, Em for embossed. Company name abbreviations are as follows: King Seeley Thermos (KST), Aladdin (A), Adco Liberty (AL), Universal (Un), Air Flite (AF), Ohio Art (OA), Ardee (AR), Okay Industries (OK), and Standard Plastic Products (Stnd). Dates reflect our best approximation.

Left: Rough Rider, 1973, $25-$35. Below left to right: Auto Race, 1967, with spin game, $40-$60, without spin game, $25-$35; Walt Disney's Wonderful World, 1980, $15-$25.

	BOX	BOTTLE
Action Jackson, OK, 1973	$ 450-550	$ 160-190
Adam-12, EM, A, 1973	60-80	18-22
Addams Family, KST, 1974	80-120	30-50
All American, map, met. hndl., Un, 1954	300-350	50-70
All Star, V, A, 1960	350-450	50-60
Alvin, V, KST, 1963	220-280	60-80
Annie Oakley, A, 1956	200-250	50-80
Archies, EM, A, 1970	55-75	18-22
Astronaut, D, KST, 1960	120-180	40-50
Atom Ant, KST, 1966	150-200	45-55
Batman, EM, A, 1966	140-180	50-60
Beatles, EM, A, 1966	300-350	90-110
Beatles Air Flite, V, AF, 1965	400-500	NB
Beatles Kaboodle, V, Stnd, 1965	500-700	NB
Beverly Hillbillies, EM, A, 1963	120-160	40-60
Bionic Woman, car/bk., A, 1977	25-30	8-10
Black Hole, EM, A, 1980	35-45	8-12
Bonanza, Blk. rim, A, 1968	110-140	50-70
Bond XX, OA, 1966	130-170	NB
Bozo the Clown, A, 1964	200-250	60-80
Brady Bunch, KST, 1970	200-250	50-75
Brave Eagle, KST, 1955	220-260	50-80
Buccaneer, D, A, 1957	180-220	60-90
Bullwinkle, V, bl stl. gl bot., KST, 1962	400-500	90-130
Bullwinkle and Rocky, Steel, Un, 1962	500-700	190-230
Captain Kangaroo, V, KST, 1964	200-250	40-50
Carnival, Un, 1959	400-500	180-230
Casey Jones, D, Un, 1960	500-700	80-120
Charlie's Angels, EM, A, 1978	40-50	10-15
Chitty Chitty Bang Bang, KST, 1969	70-90	30-40
Chuck Wagon, D, A, 1958	120-180	60-80
Close Encounters, KST, 1978	60-80	10-12
Daniel Boone, A, 1965	90-130	40-50
Davy Crockett/Kit Carson, AL, 1955	190-210	80-100
Disney Fire Fighters, D, A, 1969	70-90	15-20
Disney School Bus, A, 1961	30-40	12-16
Doctor Doolittle, EM, A, 1968	75-95	30-40
Dr. Seuss, EM, A, 1970	70-95	20-30
Dr. Seuss, V, A, 1970	250-400	20-30
Dudley Do-Right, Steel, Un, 1962	500-800	180-240
E.T., EM, A, 1983	25-35	7-9
Eats 'n Treats, V, KST, 1959	180-220	30-40
Emergency, D, A, 1977	70-90	8-12
Empire Strikes Back, KST, 1980	35-45	8-12
Family Affair, KST, 1969	60-80	25-30
Fat Albert and The Cosby Kids, KST, 1973	25-35	5-7
Fess Parker/Daniel Boone, KST, 1965	120-160	40-60
Fireball XL-5, KST, 1964	120-180	40-60
Flag-O-Rama, UN flags, Un, 1954	320-420	70-90
Flintstones, 2nd dsgn., A, 1964	80-100	30-40
Flintstones and Dino, EM, A, 1962	80-120	35-45

Above left to right: Johnny Lightning, 1971, $60-$80; Scooby Doo, 1973, $30-$40; Space Orbiter Enterprise, 1979, $35-$45. Below left to right: Roy Rogers and Dale Evans, showing obvious rim ware, 1953, $30-$40 (when mint $100-$130); Johnny Lightning Bottle, 1971, $20-$30. —Items courtesy of Jim Glaab's Collector's Showcase.

	BOX	BOTTLE
Flipper, KST, 1966	$ 90-140	$ 40-50
Flying Nun, EM, A, 1968	80-130	30-40
Fraggle Rock, KST, 1984	12-15	4-6
Gene Autry, Un, 1954	250-300	90-110
Gentle Ben, A, 1968	60-80	15-20
Get Smart, KST, 1966	140-180	35-45
Girl and Poodle, V, AR, 1960	80-100	8-12
Gomer Pyle, EM, A, 1966	90-140	30-40
Green Hornet, KST, 1967	260-320	60-90
Gremlins, EM, A, 1984	12-15	4-6
Grizzly Adams, D, A, 1978	55-75	20-30
Gunsmoke, red rim, Em, A, 1962	140-180	45-55
Gunsmoke, Splash /bk., A, 1972	50-70	18-25
Gunsmoke, Stage/bk., A, 1973	90-110	18-25
H.R. Pufnstuf, EM, A, 1970	90-110	18-22
Hair Bear Bunch, KST, 1972	30-40	12-20
Happy Days, KST, 1977	45-55	15-20

	BOX	BOTTLE
Hogan's Heroes, D, A, 1966	$ 200-250	$ 60-80
Hopalong Cassidy, curve decal, A, 1950	100-150	40-60
Hopalong Cassidy, full pict., A, 1954	200-250	60-80
Hot Wheels, KST, 1970	50-70	18-24
Indiana Jones, KST, 1984	15-20	5-8
It's About Time, D, A, 1967	190-210	50-70
James Bond-Agent 007, EM, A, 1966	180-220	50-70
Jet Patrol, A, 1957	250-300	55-75
Jetsons, D, A, 1963	750-950	180-240
Johnny Lightning, EM, A, 1971	60-80	20-30
Kiss, KST, 1979	50-70	12-20
Lance Link, KST, 1971	80-120	35-45
Land of the Giants, EM, A, 1969	120-160	35-45
Laugh-In, A, 1969	90-110	20-30
Little House on the Prairie, KST, 1979	35-45	7-9
Lone Ranger, AL, 1954	380-420	NB
Lost in Space, D, KST, 1967	500-600	50-70
Man From U.N.C.L.E., KST, 1966	120-180	50-70
Masters of the Universe, EM, A, 1983	9-14	2-3
Mickey Mouse/Donald Duck, AL, 1954	200-250	80-100
Monkees, V, KST, 1967	250-300	50-70
Mork and Mindy, KST, 1980	28-34	8-10
Munsters, KST, 1965	150-200	50-80
Partridge Family, KST, 1971	40-50	20-30
Pigs in Space, KST, 1979	18-22	4-6
Planet of the Apes, EM, A, 1975	80-100	20-30
Porky's Lunch Wagon, D, KST, 1959	300-350	50-80
Red Barn, clsd. drs., KST, 1957	50-60	18-22
Red Barn, D, op. drs., KST, 1958	40-50	18-22
Return of the Jedi, KST, 1983	30-40	7-9
Roy Rogers Chow Wagon, D, KST, 1958	180-240	40-60
Roy Rogers and Dale Evans, wood bk., bd., KST, 1953	100-130	30-40
Roy Rogers and Dale Evans, hide/8 scns, KST, 1955	80-100	30-40
Scooby Doo, KST, 1973	30-40	6-8
Sesame Street, EM, A, 1980	8-12	4-5
Space: 1999, KST, 1976	30-40	7-9
Space Explorer, A, 1960	300-350	60-80
Star Trek, D, A, 1968	550-650	140-180
Star Wars, KST, 1978	35-45	7-9
Stewardess, V, A, 1962	300-500	40-60
Supercar, steel, Un, 1962	200-250	90-120
Superman, met. hdl., Un, 1954	600-800	150-200
Tom Corbett Space Cadet, curve decal, A, 1952	190-230	60-70
Tom Corbett Space Cadet, full pic., A, 1954	450-500	70-90
Under Dog, Steel, OK, 1973	700-900	200-250
Waltons, EM, A, 1974	25-35	4-6
Welcome Back Kotter, EM, A, 1977	28-36	4-6
Wild, Wild West, EM, A, 1969	150-200	45-55
Winnie the Pooh, V, A, 1967	400-450	40-50
Yellow Submarine, KST, 1969	350-450	90-130
Zorro, blue sky, A, 1958	120-160	40-60

Matchbox Toys

Leslie Smith and Rodney Smith (no relation) started Lesney Toys in England in 1947. They produced their first toys in 1948 and had a huge success with a coach produced in 1952 for the Queen's coronation in 1953. In 1953 they started producing small die-cast vehicles packed in what appeared to be matchboxes. These toys are known as the 1-75 Series. They range from approximately 1.5" to 3". Lesney has produced other series over the years but the list below refers mainly to the 1-75 Series. Exceptions are the early toys which have no product number, and the Yesteryear Series, denoted by Y as the first letter in the product code. Both these series are larger than the 1-75 Series. Matchbox toys are still produced, but the Lesney name was removed in 1982.

Since the same item can be bought at a variety of locations at different prices, we devised a range system. The low range covers complete, near mint to mint items without the package. The higher range reflects the prices of complete, near mint (*MNB*) to mint items in the original near mint to mint boxes (*MIB*). Prices below are for complete like-new items. Prices of scratched, chipped or altered examples are not included. Beware of high prices for poor quality. We have seen many poor condition Matchbox vehicles ranging from $1 to the prices listed below. In our opinion these bad condition models are worth very little unless extremely rare.

In the listing *sf* stands for super fast wheels and axles, a system Lesney developed to battle Hot Wheels. For the most part, collectors prefer the regular wheels (*rw.*). The numbering system is not foolproof; sometimes a model produced for this country has a different number than the same vehicle originally sold exclusively in England. The letters that precede a number is a system designed by collectors to distinguish different models with the same number; the earlier the letter the earlier the model. Because there are so many variations, exact identification can be tricky. We suggest *Matchbox Toys 1948-1993*, by Dana Johnson, Collector Books, Paducah, KY, 1994.

	YEAR	NO.	MNB	MIB
Airport Crash Tender	1964	63-B	$ 18-24	$ 28-34
Army Half-track Mk III Person Carr.	1958	49-A	20-30	30-40
Aston Martin DB2 Saloon	1959	53-A	28-35	38-45
Austin A50 Sedan	1957	36-A	20-30	35-40
Aveling Barford Diesel Road Roller	1948	—	300-400	430-520
Bedford Compressor Truck	1956	28-A	32-38	40-50
Bedford Duplé Long Dist. Coach	1956	21-A	38-46	50-60
Bedford Milk Delivery Van	1956	29-A	25-30	35-40
Bedford Tipper Truck	1957	40-A	25-35	40-50
Bedford Ton Tipper	1961	3-B	18-22	28-32
Berkeley Cavalier Travel Trailer	1956	23-A	28-32	35-45
Boat and Trailer, rw.	1966	9-C	8-12	18-22
Cadillac Ambulance, rw.	1965	54-B	18-24	28-32
Cadillac Ambulance, sf.	1970	54-C	6-8	10-12
Cadillac Sedan	1960	27-C	30-35	40-50
Caterpillar Crawler	1964	18-D	22-28	32-42
Caterpillar D8, w/ red blade	1956	18-A	28-32	40-50
Caterpillar Tractor	1955	8-A	40-50	60-80
Cement Mixer	1953	3-A	32-38	45-55
Chevrolet Impala	1961	57-B	25-30	32-38
Citroen DS19	1959	66-A	30-35	42-48
Claas Combine Harvester	1967	65-C	7-9	12-18
Commer 30 CWT Van "Nestle's"	1959	69-A	30-35	40-50
Commer Milk Truck	1961	21-C	28-32	34-38

	YEAR	NO.	MNB	MIB
Conestoga Wagon, no barrels	1955	—	$ 90-120	$ 150-200
Conestoga Wagon, w/ barrels	1955	—	140-180	200-250
Daimler Ambulance	1956	14-A	30-35	40-50
Dennis Fire Escape engine, metal whls.	1955	9-A	30-40	50-60
Dodge Cattle Truck, sf.	1970	37-E	5-7	9-12
Dodge Charger	1970	52-C	5-7	9-12
Dodge Crane Truck, rw.	1968	63-C	10-14	16-22
Dodge Dump Truck, rw.	1966	48-C	12-15	18-22
Dodge StakeTruck, rw.	1967	4-D	8-10	12-16
Dodge Wreck Truck, "BP," rw.	1965	13-D	14-16	20-25
Dumper	1953	2-A	45-50	55-70
ERF 686 Truck	1959	20-B	35-45	50-60
Euclid Quarry Truck	1957	6-B	28-38	44-54
Ferrari F1 Racing Car	1962	73-B	30-36	40-46
Ford Customline Station Wagon	1957	31-A	28-34	40-50
Ford Fairlane Station Wagon	1960	31-B	25-35	35-40
Ford Galaxie Fire Chief Car, rw.	1966	59-C	10-14	18-22
Ford Galaxie Police Car	1966	55-C	15-20	25-30
Ford Mustang Fastback, rw.	1966	8-E	8-10	12-16
Ford Pickup, rw.	1968	6-D	10-14	15-20
Ford Thunderbird	1960	75-A	32-38	45-52
Ford Zodiac Convertible	1957	39-A	40-50	60-80
GMC Tipper Truck, small sf.	1970	26-D	8-10	12-16
Harley Davidson Motorcycle Sidecar	1962	66-B	40-45	55-65
Honda Motorcycle and Trailer, rw.	1967	38-C	12-15	20-25
Honda Motorcycle and Trailer, sf.	1970	38-D	6-8	10-15
Horse-Drawn Milk Cart	1949	—	120-160	200-300
Horse-Drawn Milk Float, gray metal whls.	1954	7-A	50-65	80-100
Hot Rocker Mercury Capri	1973	67-D	5-7	9-12
Hoveringham Tipper	1963	17-C	12-18	24-32
Jaguar, 3.4 Litre	1959	65-A	18-22	28-34
Jaguar, D-Type	1957	41-A	35-40	45-55
Jeep Gladiator Pickup Truck	1964	71-B	18-25	28-32
Land Rover, w/ driver	1955	12-A	30-40	45-55
Leyland Royal Tiger Coach	1961	40-B	15-18	22-28
Lincoln Continental, rw.	1964	31-C	15-18	22-28
Lincoln Continental, sf.	1969	31-D	6-8	10-15
London Bus	1954	5-A	38-44	50-60
Mack Dump Truck, rw.	1968	28-D	8-12	18-22
Massey Harris Tractor, w/ fenders	1954	4-A	35-45	60-70
MG Sports Car	1956	19-A	42-48	55-65
Mobile Canteen Refresh. Bar	1959	74-A	40-45	55-65
Pontiac Convertible	1962	39-B	40-45	55-65
Quarry Truck	1954	6-A	38-42	50-60
Rolls Royce Silver Cloud	1958	44-A	25-35	45-65
Saracen Person. Carr.	1959	54-A	28-32	35-55
Scammell Breakdown Truck	1959	64-A	20-25	32-38
VW 1200 Sedan	1960	25-B	30-35	40-50
1862 Am. General Loco.	1959	Y-13-A	35-45	50-70
1909 Thomas Flyabout	1967	Y-12-B	18-22	25-35
1924 Fowler "Big Lion" Showman's Eng.	1958	Y-9-A	55-65	75-85

Pez Dispensers

Pez is so American, a part of growing up from the 1950s to present day. Like most of us, Pez has its roots in a different country. Eduard Haas introduced it in 1927 in Austria. It takes its name from the German word for peppermint, *pfefferminz*. Originally sold as a breath mint/candy, it came with a handy dispenser with grip (called regulars). Pez redesigned its product for the American market in 1952. They added character heads and introduced fruit flavors. Pez became a kids' candy.

In recent years, Pez collecting has been a very active area. Christie's auction house even included a section of Pez in one of its sales. Collectors tend to concentrate on the head of a Pez dispenser; most do not collect based on stem or container differences. That is because heads can be switched from stem to stem. There is a feet vs. no-feet controversy. Most containers have a rounded base. Some people call them shoes but they are more often referred to as no feet (nf). Feet (f) are the bases that appeared on figures beginning around 1987. They are thin, flat, and have a stylized "V" indentation. Many collectors go back to the "only the head matters" theorem, while others place a higher value on no-feet examples. Packaging is also an area of some controversy. Collectors contend that packaging for the most part does not matter since early Pez containers came in unattractive bags or boxes. The matter is harder to determine when evaluating Pez sold on blisterpacks or blistercards. We feel that original packaging will increase the value of an item, especially the more elaborate and interesting packaging. Most notable is the Stand-By-Me Pez, which must have the orginal packaging, including the movie poster, or it is just a Pez Pal Boy.

The prices below are for mint nonpackaged examples except where noted differently. Pez dispensers are hard to date, so the decades we suggest are our best guess. For further reading we reccommend *Pez Collectibles*, by Richard Geary, Schiffer, Atglen, PA, 1994.

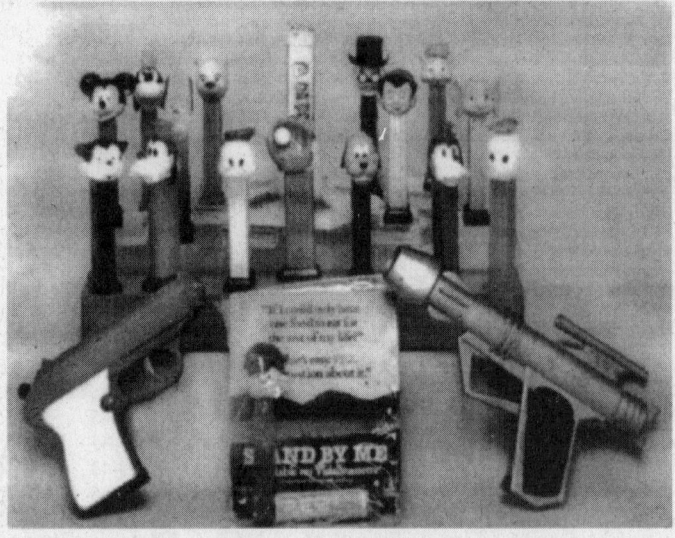

A selection of Pez dispensers. —Photo courtesy of Christie's East.

	LOW	HIGH
Alpine Man, mustache, Olympics, nf, 1972	$ 275	$ 500
Angel A, sm. light blue eyes, nf, 1980s	14	18
Annie, nf, 1980s	30	40
Arithmetic, nf, 1960s	200	300
Arlene, f, 1980s	2	3
Astronaut A, sm. helmet, nf, 1955	150	250
Astronaut B, pointed helmet, nf, 1970s	70	90
Baloo, blue head, f, 1980s	15	20
Bambi, f, 1980s	5	9
Barney Bear, f, 1980s	10	16
Baseball Glove, ball, nf, 1960s	130	220
Baseball Glove, ball, bat, plate base, 1960s	220	340
Batgirl, soft head, nf, 1970s	60	80
Batman, w/cape, nf, 1960s	100	150
Batman, soft head, nf, 1970s	70	100
Betsy Ross, nf, 1970s	40	75
Big Top Elephant, w/ pointed hat, nf, 1960s	50	60
Big Top Elephant, flat hat, nf, 1960s	35	55
Big Top Elephant, hair, nf, 1960s	150	300
Bouncer Beagle, f, 1990s	3	5
Bozo, cutout side, nf, 1960s	80	140
Bride, nf, 1960s	400	500
Brutus, nf, 1950s	90	150
Bullwinkle, nf, 1960s	150	200
Candy Shooter Gun, Pez on grip, 1970s	90	140
Captain, nf, 1970s	50	70
Captain America, nf, 1980s	45	65
Captain Hook, nf, 1970s	25	38
Casper, nf, 1960s	60	80
Casper, w/ "Casper" on side, nf, 1960s	80	120
Clown, collar, nf, 1960s	25	35
Cockatoo, nf, 1970s	30	50
Cocoa Marsh Astronaut, nf, 1950s	90	170
Cowboy, nf, 1960s	220	350
Creature from the Black Lagoon, grn. head, nf, 1960s	200	250
Crocodile, nf, 1960s	55	85
Daffy Duck, f, 1980s	2	3
Dalmatian Pup, f, 1980s	22	32
Daniel Boone, nf, 1970s	100	150
Dino, f, 1990s	2	3
Doctor, nf, 1960s	45	65
Donald Duck, die-cut face, nf, 1960s	90	120
Donkey Kong Jr., prem. w/card, nf, 1980s	250	370
Dopey, nf, 1960s	100	150
Droopy Dog, attached ears, f, 1980s	8	10
Easter Bunny, w/rabbit & eggs, cut-out sides, nf, 1950s	300	525
Eerie Spectres Air Spirit, fish head, nf, 1980s	35	50
Eerie Spectres Diabolic, nf, 1980s	35	50
Eerie Spectres Scarewolf, nf, 1980s	35	50
Eerie Spectres Spook, nf, 1980s	35	50
Eerie Spectres Vamp, nf, 1980s	50	75

	LOW	HIGH
Eerie Spectres Zombie, nf, 1980s	$ 50	$ 75
Engineer, nf, 1960s	25	38
Fireman, nf, 1960s	12	18
Fishman, looks like Black Lagoon Creature, nf, 1970s	100	150
Foghorn Leghorn, nf, 1980s	32	45
Fozzie Bear, f, 1980s	2	3
Frankenstein, nf, 1960s	170	250
Garfield, w /smile, hat, f, 1980s	2	3
Giraffe, nf, 1960s	38	48
Girl, f, 1980s	1	2
Girl, Pez Pal, nf, 1960s	15	20
Green Hornet, nf, 1960s	200	300
Groom, nf, 1960s	150	250
Henry Hawk, f, 1980s	25	38
Hippo, nf, 1970s	400	500
Hulk, f, 1990s	2	3
Hulk, nf, 1970s	20	30
Indian Brave, nf, 1970s	120	180
Indian Chief, nf, 1970s	50	75
Indian Maiden, nf, 1970s	50	80
Jerry, nf, 1990s	2	3
Jerry, inside of ears pink, nf, 1990s	15	20
Jerry (Tom and Jerry), nf, 1980s	10	18
Jiminy Cricket, nf, 1970s	30	45
Joker, soft head, nf, 1970s	70	90
Make-a-Face, nf, 1970s	1000	1800
Mary Poppins, nf, 1960s	325	525
Mickey Mouse, f, 1980s	2	3
Mickey Mouse D, removable nose, nf, 1970s	10	15
Muselix, nf, 1970s	950	1600
Olympic Snowman, 1976, 1976	200	350
One-Eye Monster, nf, 1960s	50	75
Orange, nf, 1970s	70	90
Pear, nf, 1970s	500	750
Penguin, soft head (Batman), nf, 1970s	60	90
Petunia Pig, nf, 1980s	12	16
Pilgrim, nf, 1970s	70	90
Pineapple, nf, 1970s	700	1100
Psychedelic Eye, hand holding eye, nf, 1960s	300	400
Regular, w/ advertising, 1950s	275	450
Santa, full body, 1950s	150	200
Santa, w/ small head, painted face, nf, 1950s	100	150
Snoopy, f, 1980s	1	3
Snowman, nf, 1990s	1	2
Space Trooper, full body, 1950s	300	400
Spaceman, nf, 1950s	90	130
Stand By Me, must be mint in the package, 1980s	170	250
Tinkerbell, nf, 1980s	75	125
Tom, C (Tom and Jerry), f, 1990s	1	2
Uncle Scrooge McDuck, nf, 1980s	8	12
Vucko Wolf, Olympics, 3 variations, ea., f, 1980s	300	500

Playing Cards

Playing cards most likely appeared in the Far East around the 1100s. Europeans probably developed printed playing cards in Switzerland around 1430. Standard playing cards feature kings, queens and jacks as the court subjects on a face card. The subjects differ on a nonstandard decks. Tarot cards are also very collectible; they are used in fortune-telling.

Age usually determines value, although the quality of the artwork has some influence.

	LOW	AVG.	HIGH
Advertising, Lorrilard Splendid Cut Plug Tobacco, 52 cards plus joker, American Playing Card Co., backs in red/white/blue, c. 1880, believed to be the earliest American advertising deck w/ pictorial backs	$ 300	$ 400	$ 500
Advertising, souvenir of the 11th Annual Convention of the United Drug Co., 52 cards, each w/ photographs of Rexall club officers, 1913	300	375	450
American Indian Souvenir Playing Cards, 52 cards plus joker and title card, Lazarus and Melzer, 1900	150	200	250
At Sea, 52 cards, Congress, gold borders	40	50	60
Barking Dog, pinochle deck, Standard Playing Card Co., gold edges, c. 1910	40	50	60
Bezique, Samuel Hart, square corners, one way courts, believed to be pre-Civil War	250	300	350
Bicycle Bridge, 52 cards plus joker, United States Playing Card Co., c. 1945	17	21	24
Brown Derby, 52 cards plus 2 jokers, each card has caricature of a show business personality (including Ronald Reagan), 1951	56	68	81
Canary Playing Cards, 52 cards plus joker, backs have black and white picture of lady w/ long curls and large hat, c. 1910	27	32	37
Chicago World's Fair, deck, c. 1934	31	42	53
Chinese Art Treasures, double deck	30	38	45
Circus World Museum Souvenir Deck, 52 cards, backs picture Buffalo Bill's Wild West Show, c. 1975	13	16	18
Civil War Pack, Union Playing Cards, American Card Co., NY, 2-color, eagles, stars, flags, shields, suits	1000	1500	2000
Coca-Cola, double deck	12	20	27
Culbertson's Own, 52 cards, Russell, each card has bridge tips printed on it, 1932	54	63	72
Cupid's Secret, 52 cards, gold edges, 1907	43	53	63
Deck, 36 cards, 2 information cards, The Game of Kings, Adams, NY, portraits of British monarchs, 1845	500	600	700
Deck, 52 cards, Andrew Dougherty, tiny picture of card in 2 corners, c. 1870	250	360	470
Deck, Andrew Dougherty, NY, Owen Jones designs, c. 1860	100	200	300
Double Action, 52 cards, 1935	60	80	100
Fish Up, 52 cards plus 2 jokers, Creative Playing Card Co., all have cartoon backs w/ fishing themes, 1963	13	18	23
Fleet Wing Gasoline, advertising deck, c. 1910	36	42	47
Flinch Cards, c. 1910	50	58	66
France Royale, double deck, by Platnik	18	22	26
French Suited Pack, L.I. Cohen, large size, gold trim, mint	450	600	750
Grover Cleveland, campaign deck, reprint of 1868 issue	7	12	17
Gypsy Witch, fortune telling deck	20	30	40

	LOW	AVG.	HIGH
Hard-A-Port-Cut Plug, tobacco premium, 52 cards plus joker, c. 1880s	$ 450	$ 600	$ 750
Hollyhocks, 52 cards, Dougherty, 1921	25	33	41
Huntress, 52 cards, Andrew Dougherty, gold edges, ace of spades is neutral	27	32	37
Illuminated Deck, 52 cards, A. Dougherty, all pips gold-outlined in style of medieval cards, Civil War era, considered one of the classic American packs	400	500	600
Indian Wars, 52 cards, Humphrey, w/ black spades, red hearts, yellow diamonds, blue clubs, rare	3000	3500	4000
Jack Daniels, 1972 edition	8	13	17
Jaws, double deck, Stancraft, motion picture inspired w/ shark reverses, c. 1978	14	19	24
Mardi Gras, deck, reprint of 1925 issue	7	12	17
Nixon, politicards, 1971 edition	18	24	30
Panama Souvenir Cards, 53 plus information cards, USPC, photos, c. 1908	90	135	180
Picturesque Canada, 52 cards plus Joker, backs picture Chateau Frontenac	44	50	56
Picturesque Nova Scotia, 52 cards plus joker, Canadian Playing Card Co., Montreal, illustrated on both sides, c. 1920	48	65	82
Rita, double deck in double box, total of 4 jokers	50	62	75
Sebago, pinochle deck, Dougherty, gold edges, World War I era	27	32	38
Serenader, 52 cards, Russell, gold edges	19	23	27
Shooting the Rapids, 52 cards, 1910	135	190	245
Souvenir of the Canary Islands, 52 cards, Fournier, 1973	20	30	40
Steamboats, 52 cards plus joker, U.S. Printing Co., pre-1900	100	125	150
Texas Souvenir Deck, 52 cards plus joker, gold edges, c. 1905	160	200	240
Uncle Sam's Cabinet, 1901	60	75	90
Vanity Fair Transformation Deck, United States Playing Card Co., America's first true transformation deck, 1895	1000	1300	1600
Verkehrvelt Tarock, reproduction of 1810 edition, "Topsy Turvy Animal Tarot"	100	125	150
W.C. Fields, 52 cards plus 2 jokers, J.L. Brown, scenes from his movies on courts and aces plus booklet w/ hints on cheating, 1971	30	35	40
Washable Plastic Deck, 52 cards plus joker, Dale, c. 1950	15	21	27

Premiums

The excitement of getting a prize or an extra gift is a temptation for consumers. Combining this with a child's favorite radio, comic book, or television hero creates a powerful inducement to purchase. Premiums gained momentum in the radio days of the Great Depression. Cereal, soap and other companies hosted programs; in turn radio Orphan Annie, Captain Midnight, The Lone Ranger, and others promoted the host's product. When television replaced radio many programs made the switch as well. These personalities induced young viewers with mail-in offers for membership packages, decoder rings, books, badges and toys. Other premiums were included with the package and occasionally offered at the store.

Collectors actively seek these items. They collect a range of items basing their collection on characters or types of items like decoders or rings. In recent years astounding prices have been paid for rare premium rings. Collectors are also seeking newer premiums from the 1960s and '70s. Quisp and Quake items are currently very popular. Packaging and instructional materials increase the prices of premiums, so don't touch that dial and don't throw that material away. Premiums are still used as sales inducements, mainly by the cereal industry. Prices below are for items in excellent to near mint condition. Each entry contains the character who promoted the product, a brief description of the premium, the date, and the company who made the product.

For further reading see *Radio Premium and Cereal Box Collectibles*, Tom Tumbusch, Wallace Homestead Book Company, Radnor, PA, 1991 and *Overstreet Premium Ring Price Guide*, Robert M. Overstreet, Gemstone Publishing, Inc., Timonium, MD, 1994.

	LOW	HIGH
Amos 'N Andy, Amos Driving Cab, cardboard, 1931, Pepsodent	$ 150	$ 200
Bobby Benson, Code Rule, cardboard, 1935, Hecker-H-O	100	150
Buck Rogers, Birthstone Initial Ring, 1939, Popsicle Pete	300	400
Buck Rogers, Repeller Ray Ring, 1930s, Cream of Wheat	2500	3000
Buck Rogers, Ring of Saturn Ring, 1930s, Post	525	825
Buck Rogers, Wilma Pendant, 1930s, Cream of Wheat	80	120
Cap'N Crunch, Button, 1965, Quaker	20	30
Cap'N Crunch, Figural Bank, 1966, Quaker	80	100
Cap'N Crunch, Figural Ring, 1963, Quaker	225	325
Cap'N Crunch, Jean Lefoot Figural Bank, 1966, Quaker	70	90
Cap'N Crunch, Oath of Allegiance, 1964, Quaker	35	45
Cap'N Crunch, Sea Cycle, 1965, Quaker	25	45
Cap'N Crunch, Ship Shake, 1968, Quaker	25	45
Captain Marvel, Pinback, 1940s, Comic	45	65
Captain Marvel, Rocket Raider Compass Ring, 1946, Comic	2000	3000
Captain Midnight, Decoder, 1957	300	350
Captain Midnight, Membership Card, 1939	60	80
Captain Midnight, Mirro-Flash Code-O-Graph, 1946, Ovaltine	180	220
Captain Midnight, Mug, 1940s, Ovaltine	50	70
Captain Midnight, Mystic Sun God Ring, 1947, Ovaltine	1600	3000
Captain Midnight, Secret Squadron Decoder Badge, 1955	180	240
Captain Midnight, Secret Squadron Mem. Manual, 1941, Ovaltine	100	170
Captain Midnight, Shake-Up Mug, 1947, Ovaltine	100	170
Captain Tim, Ivory Stamp Club Album, 72-pg., 1934, Ivory Soap	30	50
Captain Video, Flying Saucer Ring, w/ 2 saucers, 1950s, Powerhouse	800	1200
Captain Video, Mystocoder Instruction Folder, 1950s, TV	100	150
Captain Video, Photo Ring, 1950s, Powerhouse	200	300

	LOW	HIGH
Charlie McCarthy, Die-cut-Cardboard Figure, 1938, Chase and Sanborn	$ 80	$ 120
Charlie McCarthy, Spoon, 1938, Chase and Sanborn	30	40
Crackle, Rubber Head Ring, 1950s, Rice Crispies	300	400
Death Valley Days, Story of Death Valley, 24-pg. bk., 1931, Borax	35	45
Dick Tracy, Pocket Flashlight, 1939, Quaker Oats	100	150
Dizzy Dean, Winners Club Member Pin, 1930s, Post Cereal	60	90
Don Winslow, Squadron of Peace Ring, 1939, Kellogs	3000	4000
Droopy Dog, Popping Head Figure, 1960, General Mills	30	40
Eddie Cantor, Trick Cards and Instructions, 1935, Pobeco Toothpaste	30	40
Fibber McGee and Molly, Cast Photo, 1940s, Johnson Wax	25	35
Flash, Flash Pinback Button, 1943, Comic	1000	2000
Flash Gordon, Movie Serial Button, 1930s, Theater	400	600
Frank Buck, Black Leopard Ring, rare Jungleland vers., 1939	4000	6000
Frank Buck, Ivory Initial Ring, 1939, Ivory Soap	300	400
Funny Face, Chug-a-Lug Mug, 1960s, Funny Face	15	20
Funny Face, Walkers, 1960s, Funny Face	80	100
Green Hornet, Seal Ring, 1966, General Mills	18	22
Green Hornet, Secret Compart, Glow-in-Dark Ring, 1947, General Mills	900	1200
Hopalong Cassidy, Savings Club Folder, 1950s, Savings and Loan	40	60
Howdy Doody, Jack-in-the Box Ring, 1950s, Poll Parrot	3000	5000
Howdy Doody, Pinback, 1950s, TV	40	70
Junior Detective, Junior Det. Corps Captain Badge, 1933, Post Toasties	40	60
Linus the Lionhearted, Stuffed Doll, 1965, Post	40	60
Lone Ranger, Blackout Kit, 1943	150	200
Lone Ranger, Membership Badge, 1935, Silver-Cup Bread	60	90
Lone Ranger, Movie Film Ring, w/ film, 1948, Cheerios	150	200
Lone Ranger, Secret Comp. Ring, 2 photos, 1945, Kix	600	900
Lone Ranger, Secret Compartment Ring, 1 photo, 1945, Kix	350	450
Lone Ranger, Silver Bullet/Compass, 1947, Cheerios	50	70
Lone Ranger, Six Shooter Gun Ring, 1947, Kix	100	150
Lone Wolf, Manual, 32 pg., 1932, Wrigley Gum	100	150
Mandrake the Magician, Figural Membership Button, 1934, Taystee Bread ...	100	150
Mary Poppins, Chimney Toy, 1964, Kellogs	80	100
Melvin Purvis, Badge, 1936, Post Toasties	60	90
Melvin Purvis, Sacred Scarab Ring, 1937, Post	1000	1500
Orphan Annie, 6 Die-cut Cardboard Shadowettes, 1938	90	140
Orphan Annie, Altascope, 1940s, sold at auction in 1994	12,650	
Orphan Annie, Pin, 1934, Ovaltine	50	70
Orphan Annie, Pin, 1935, Ovaltine	50	70
Orphan Annie, Puzzle, 1933, Ovaltine	60	80
Orphan Annie, Secret Guard Magnifying Ring, 1940s	2200	3200
Orphan Annie, Secret Society Manual, 1940, Ovaltine	200	300
Orphan Annie, Shake-Up Mug, 1, full fig., 1931	50	70
Orphan Annie, Shake-Up Mug, 2, bust fig., 1935, Ovaltine	50	70
Orphan Annie, Shake-Up Mug, 3, Annie dancing, 1938, Ovaltine	80	120
Orphan Annie, Shake-Up Mug, 4, jumping rope, 1939, Ovaltine	80	120
Orphan Annie, Sunburst Decoder Pin, 1937, Ovaltine	80	100
Pop, Rubber Head Ring, 1950s, Rice Crispies	300	500
Quake, Earth Digger Car, 1965, Quaker	150	200
Quake, Figural Ring, 1966, Quaker	400	600
Quisp, Friendship Ring, 1966, Quaker	1000	1500

	LOW	HIGH
Quisp, Meteorite Ring, 1960s, Quaker	$ 300	$ 400
Quisp, Unicycler, 1969, Quaker	80	100
Rootie Kazootie, Club Button, 1950s	30	40
Rootie Kazootie, Lucky Spot Seal Ring, 1950s	350	650
Roy Rogers, Badge/Whistle, 1950, Quaker	80	100
Roy Rogers, Branding Iron Ring, black cap, 1948, Quaker	180	220
Roy Rogers, Figural Mug, plastic, 1950, Quaker	35	55
Roy Rogers, Postcard, 1949, Quaker	20	30
Roy Rogers, Two 45-Record Set, 1950s	80	100
Sekatary Hawkins, Membership Card oath on back, 1932, Ralston	30	50
Sgt. Preston, Celluloid Membership Button, 1950s, Quaker	800	1600
Sgt. Preston, Totem Pole Set, 1950s, Quaker	70	90
Shadow, Black Stone Crocodile Ring, 1947, Carey Salt	700	1000
Shadow, Blue Coal Glow-in-the-Dark Ring, 1941, Blue Coal	400	600
Shadow, Matchbook, 1930s, Blue Coal	80	100
Sky King, Detectowriter, 1950, Peter Pan	90	130
Sky King, Microscope, 1947, Peter Pan	100	150
Sky King, Navaho Treasure Ring, 1950, Peter Pan	180	220
Sky King, Secret Signal Scope, 1947, Peter Pan	100	150
Sky King, Teleblinker Ring, 1950s, TV	150	200
Snap, Rubber Head Ring, 1950s, Rice Crispies	200	250
Superman, Secret Compartment Ring, 1940 Superman Gum sold at auction in 1994	16,100	
Superman Tim, Membership Button, 1950	45	65
Ted Williams, Figural Ring w/ Ball on Wire, 1948, Nabisco	800	1000
Tom Mix, Badge, 1945, Ralston	70	90
Tom Mix, Bandanna, 1933, Ralston	80	100
Tom Mix, Book, " Trail of the Terrible Six," 1935, Ralston	25	35
Tom Mix, Brass Compass Magnifier, 1940, Ralston	90	130
Tom Mix, ID Bracelet, 1947, Ralston	90	110
Tom Mix, Illust. Manual, 24 pg., 1933, Ralston	50	70
Tom Mix, Illustr. Booklet, 8 pg., 1934, Nat. Chicle Gum	40	60
Tom Mix, Paper Face Mask of Tom, 1930s	200	400
Tom Mix, Six Gun Decoder, 1941, Ralston	90	110
Tom Mix, Straight Shooter Bangle Bracelet, 1930s, Ralston	80	100
Tom Mix, Telephone Set, 1938, Ralston	100	150
Trix, Rabbit Mug and Bowl, 1963, Mills	30	40
Valric the Viking, Ring, 1940s, All Rye Flakes	3000	5500
Winnie the Pooh, Plastic Spoon Hanger, 1965, Nabisco	15	20
Wizard of Oz, *Ozma, The Little Wizard* Book, 1933, Jell-O	60	90
Wonder Woman, Litho. Pinback Button, 1942, Comic	1000	1800
Wyatt Earp, Marshall's Badge Ring, 1958, Cheerios	45	65

Robots and Space Toys

The word robot is derived from "robata" for forced labor. Robot first appeared in the 1921 play *R.U.R.* by Czechoslovakian playwright Karl Capek. It was not until the futuristic 1950s that robots really hit their stride, when toy robots and spacecraft started to appear. Although some were made in the United States (by firms such as Marx, Remco and Ideal) and Germany, the majority were produced in Japan. Friction drives and keywind mechanisms were employed but battery power increased the complexity of the toy. With batteries, metal monsters and spaceships could twirl, spin, light up, roll backwards, change directions, and perform a multitude of other tricks. Collectors call this "action" and it attracts them to these toys.

Most of the toys listed below are Japanese lithographed tinplate with battery power produced in the 1950s and '60s We have noted when the predominant material is something other than tinplate and when a toy is friction or keywind, otherwise assume that it is battery operated. The term *rc* refers to remote control, *UK* stands for manufacturer unknown.

When collecting these toys beware of condition; make sure there are no missing parts, including remote controls, battery boxes, or antennas. Make sure there is no restoration; battery boxes should be checked closely. Never leave a battery in a toy; it can leak and cause damage. The prices below are for mint without box (MNB) and mint in the box (MIB) examples. Rust, scratches, and restoration will lower these prices. In recent years astronomical prices of rare items (over $25,000 at auction for a Robby Space Patrol car) have encouraged people to create new robots such as the Robby Space Patrol, Mr. Atomic and the Rosko Astronauts. Some of these toys are incredible reproductions of the original toy, right down to the box. Other robots are old style new products. Be sure of what you are buying. Robots are listed either by the name that appears on the original box or the name coined by collectors. Different robots often have the same or similar names. To clarify things, we have listed reference numbers after the name. The B# refers to *Robot-Robots et autres Fusees d'vant la lune*, Pierre Boogaerts, Futuropolis, Paris, 1978. The K# refers to *Robots, Tin Toy Dreams*, Teruhisa Kitahara, Chronicle Books, CA, 1985.

Left to right: Gama zooming satellite, Germany, c. 1958, $200-$400; C-3PO collector's case, mint and sealed, $45-$55; attacking Martian by Horikawa, $300-$350. —Photo courtesy of Phillips Auctioneers.

	MNB	MIB
Acrobat (K #119), blue, yellow and red plastic, ht. 10"	$ 100-150	$ 250-350
Action Planet Robot (B #292), keywind Robby style, black and red, w/ sparking mech., Yoshiya, ht. 9"	180-220	300-500
Answer Game Machine (K #105), multi-color w/ buttons for calculations, Ichida, ht. 14"	600-800	900-1500
Apollo 11 Moon Rocket, friction powered, Asahi, ht. 14"	40-60	90-130
Apollo 11 Eagle Lunar Module (B #68), w/ 7 automatic actions, Daishin, for Mego, ht. 8"	80-140	220-320
Astro Captain (B #210), keywind, Mego, ht. 6"	70-90	150-220
Astronaut w/ Child's Head (K #65), blue, similar to the red Cragstan Astronaut, Daiya, ht. 12"	700-900	1000-1500
Atom Boat (B #124), friction drive, Chinese, len. 10"	80-120	200-250
Atomic Robot Man (K #81), keywind, boiler plate style, litho. w/ die-cast hands, UK, ht.	400-600	700-1300
Atomic Rocket (B #92), push lever action, w/ side fins displaying Saturn and star motif, Masudaya, len. 6"	150-200	300-400
Attacking Martian (B #191), rotomatic, w/ guns in hinged door chest, ht. 12"	150-200	300-350
Battery Operated Tractor (similar to K #112), red and black w/ 1200 plaque on battery case, Nomura, len. 7"	400-600	700-900
Big Loo Moon Robot, Marx, ht. 38"	600-800	1000-1500
Blink-a-Gear Robot (B #7), black w/ transparent chest panel housing rotating gears, Taiyo, ht. 14"	500-700	900-1300
Blue Rosko Astronaut (B #230), Rosko toys, ht. 13"	900-1300	1500-2200
Bulldozer w/ Robot Operator (similar to B #144), silver robot on blue and red dozer, UK, len. 9"	200-300	500-700
Busy Cart Robot (B #269), black and yellow w/ hardhat and wheel-barrow, Horikawa, ht. 12"	700-900	1000-1500
Capsule 7 (B #188), w/ rotating astronaut, Masudaya, len. 10"	60-90	120-180
Chime Trooper (K #137), keywind, boy astronaut plays music, Aoshin, ht. 9.5"	1200-1500	2000-3000
Circus 8 Car (B #154), friction, clown robot driving a Circus 8 Mercedes, Ashai, len. 8"	600-900	1200-1600
Colonel Hap Hazard (B #61), astronaut in white NASA spacesuit w/ whirling copter blade, Marx, ht. 11"	800-1000	1200-1800
Cragstan X-07 Space Surveillant (B #108), the oval shaped flying sauce w/ astronaut pilot under bubble dome, Masudaya, len. 9"	70-90	150-200
Cragstan's Mr. Robot (K #25), red body, litho. chest panel, swiveling domed-head, Yonezawa, ht. 11"	450-650	800-900
Cragstan's Talking Robot (K #134), red, similar to the Mercury robot, Yonezawa, ht. 10"	400-700	800-1000
Dino Robot (K #97), robot head folds down to reveal a roaring dinosaur, Horikawa, ht. 11"	500-700	900-1400
Driving Robot (K #74), keywind, robot driven auto swing, ht. 6" ...	300-500	600-900
Dux Astroman, Western Germany, green plastic astroman w/ radar antenna over clear dome, white head w/ red features, rock crushing action, rc, ht. 14"	1200-1500	2000-3000
Earth Man (K #144), tan astronaut, silver helmet w/ sounding and blinking gun, rc, Nomura, ht. 9"	700-900	1200-1800
Engine Robot (B #2), keywind, w/ sparks and gears in chest window panel, ht. 9"	180-220	300-400

	MNB	MIB
Engine Robot (B #213), gray w/ whirling gears in see-through chest panel, Horikawa, ht. 9"	$ 100-150	$ 200-300
Fighting Space Man (B #159), chest panel w/ swiveling gun and litho. circuitry, Horikawa, ht. 12"	100-150	200-300
Fighting Space Man (B #159), yellow w/ domed astronaut's head, Horikawa, ht. 12"	200-250	300-400
Firebird Space Patrol (K #57), similar to Sonicon Rocket, finished in green and red, Masudaya, len. 14"	300-400	500-700
Flying Jeep, circular vehicle on wheels, KKS, ht. 3"	70-90	120-180
Forbidden Planet Robby the Robot Talking Figure, hard plastic, Masudaya, c. 1980s, ht. 15"	90-140	180-230
Forklift Robot (B #270), yellow and w/ red cap, plastic forklift, and crate, Horikawa, ht. 11.5"	1000-1500	1800-2400
Friendship 7-Space Capsule (B #95), friction drive w/ interior floating astronaut, Horikawa, len. 9"	50-70	100-140
Gear Robot (K #50), chest window gear display and speed control switch on head, ht. 11"	120-180	250-350
Great Garloo, green plastic, Marx, c. 1961, ht. 18"	250-350	500-700
Great Garloo, Son of, keywind, green plastic, Marx, c. 1962, ht. 6" ...	120-160	250-350
Hi-Bouncer Moon Scout (K #63), silver astronaut w/ copter blade, shoots balls from chest, rc, Marx Toys, ht. 12"	1000-1500	2000-3000
High Wheel Robot (K #32), blue w/ red feet, see-through chest panel, moving gears, rc, Yoshiya, ht. 9"	400-500	700-1100
Hysterical Robot (K #128), plastic, laughs and grins, UK, ht. 13" ..	100-150	250-350
Interplanetary Space Fighter, tinplate vehicle w/ retractable side fins, Nomura, len. 12"	200-300	400-500
Jumping Rocket (B #251), keywind, robot rocket w/ feet, len. 6" ...	100-150	250-350
King Jet 8 Futuristic Racer (B #119), light blue, friction drive, bubble dome w/ driver, len. 12"	200-300	500-700
Krome Dome (K #131), multi-color plastic w/ clam-shaped head and accordion torso, Yonezawa, ht. 10"	60-80	120-180
Laughing Robot, plastic, clown head, ht. 14"	150-180	200-300
Lavender Robot (K #28), a.k.a. Nonstop Robot, lavender w/ litho-graphed machinery panels and gauges, Masudaya, ht. 14"	3000-4500	5000-8000
Lighted Space Vehicle (B #226), blue car w/ domed cockpit, astronaut, and floating ball action, Masudaya, len. 9"	90-140	200-300
Man in Space, tinplate celluloid astronaut, w/ remote control, Alps ..	100-200	600-900
Man Made Satellite (B #109), litho. base w/ signal missile, Mars, and Earth w/ satellite, Hoku, len. 7"	200-250	400-600
Mars King or Tank Robot (K #133), w/ side-mounted tracks and TV screen in chest, Horikawa, ht. 9"	150-200	300-400
Martian Supersensitive Radar Patrol, friction-drive Jeep, UK len. 9" ..	700-900	1400-2000
Marvelous Mike Tractor, yellow w/ silver robot operator, Saunders, len. 12.5"	120-160	200-300
Mechanical Sparking Robot (K #77), keywind, red plastic spark panel centered on chest, Yonezawa	70-90	120-170
Mechanical Walking Space Man (K #90), keywind, gray w/ red feet, Sy Toys, ht. 9"	200-250	300-500
Mighty Robot (K #129), keywind, red body w/ gray plastic head and jointed arms, Yonezawa, ht. 9.5"	400-600	900-1500
Mirror Man (K #198), gray and red w/ vinyl arms and head, yellow		

	MNB	MIB
eyes, Bull Mark, ht. 16"	$ 400-600	$ 800-1200

Missile Man (B #260), gray and red, w/ disc antenna and 5
missiles in hinged chest panel, ht. 16.5" 900-1200   1800-2500

Moon Capsule (B #21), friction, 2 pilots, Horikawa, len. 6" 50-70   80-120

Moon Detector (B #66), cylindrical-shape space vehicle w/ bubble
dome front end and astronaut, Yonezawa, len. 10" 400-600   700-900

Moon Explorer (K #116), dark gray, featuring clock and seesaw
mechanical display window, Bandai, ht. 17" 1400-1800   2500-3800

Moon Explorer (K #136), keywind Robby-style body w/ domed
astronaut head, Yoshiya, ht. 7" 300-400   500-800

Moon Patrol Space Division #3 (B #202), similar to the Robby
Space Patrol blue w/ star and satellite motif, astronaut driver
and bubble-covered astro globe, Nomura, len. 12" 2000-3000   4000-6000

Moon Rocket Vehicle (K #169), astronaut in bubble front cockpit
and astronaut on roof, Masudaya, len. 10" 80-120   200-300

Moon Space Ship (B #201), light blue, similar to the Robby
Space Patrol, but w/ bubble-encased radar mechanism,
Nomura, len. 13" 1200-1800   2500-3500

Mr. Hustler (B #128), astronaut-headed robot w/ flexing
shoulders, ht. 11" 180-220   350-450

Mr. Machine, keywind, plastic, later version, mkd. 1977, Ideal,
ht. 16" 60-80   100-150

Mr. Machine, plastic, keywind, whistling, c. 1960s, ht. 16" 180-240   400-600

Mr. Mercury (K #120), gold w/ gray arms and red dome, green pilot-
form eyes, rc, Yonezawa, ht. 13" 600-800   900-1500

Mr. Robot the Mechanical Brain (K #9), keywind and battery, boiler-
plate style, (rc), Alps, ht. 8.5" 900-1300   1800-2200

Mr. Xerox (B #35), having guns in open chest, ht. 9" 100-150   200-300

New Fighting Robot (K #42), light-up dome on head and guns in
chest, Horikawa, ht. 12" 100-130   200-300

New Space Station (K #157), circular, tinplate w/ plastic bottom,
stop-and-go action, Horikawa, dia. 10 .5" 400-600   700-1000

Outer Space Patrol (B #253), friction drive w/ astronaut camera-
man, len. 8" 150-200   300-500

Planet Explorer (B #122), tinplate vehicle w/ bubble front and
astronaut, Masudaya, len. 9.5" 80-120   200-250

Planet Y Space Station (B #91), Nomura, dia. 8" 100-150   200-300

R-35 Robot (K #15), bucket-shaped head, remote control box litho.
w/ robots, Masudaya, ht. 7" 700-900   1000-1400

R-7 Flashy Jim (B #51), silver boilerplate-style robot, red head-
phones, rc, Ace/S. N. K., ht. 6.5 " 900-1300   1800-2200

R-8 Sparking Robot (B #49), small keywind sparky-style robot,
blue w/ "R" and "8" on shoulders, ht. 7" 700-900   2000-3000

Radar Scope Space Scout Robot (B #36), TV image on chest,
ht. 9.5" 90-145   200-250

Radicon (K #29), gray textured finish, gauge and light inset in
chest, rc, Masudaya 3500-4500   8000-15,000

Ranger Robot (K #113), ribbed clear plastic, smoking action,
Daiya, ht. 13" 600-900   1000-1500

Red Cragstan Astronaut (B #98), w/ gun, Daiya, ht. 14" 1200-1600   2000-3000

Red Rosko Astronaut (B #230), conical-shaped dome, walkie-

	MNB	MIB
talkie and dual oxygen tanks, ht. 13"	$ 900-1300	$ 1500-2200
Remote Control Piston Action Robot (K #2), Robby-style, gold w/ deep blue legs, Nomura, ht. 9"	1200-1800	2500-3500
Robby the Robot (mechanized robot) (K #1), tinplate, black w/ red accents, 6-battery box, Nomura, ht. 13.5"	900-1600	2000-4000
Robert the Robot (K #99), crankwind, gray plastic, red arms, w/ voicebox, and rc, Ideal, ht.	100-150	200-300
Robot Commando, plastic w/ ball-throwing action, Ideal, ht. 22"	200-300	400-600
Robot in Mercedes, friction drive, w/ sparking gun on hood, len. 8"	200-300	400-600
Robot Space Auto (B #70), Robby-style robot driving a light blue roadster, len. 8"	900-1300	1600-2000
Robot St-1, by Strenco, Germany, boilerplate style, w/ coil and diamond-shaped antennas, ht. 6.5"	500-700	800-1200
Rocket Express, keywind, race to the moon toy, Technofix, ht. 14"	150-200	300-400
Rocket Man in Space Armor (B #136), plastic, robot head opens to reveal an astronaut head, w/ 2 rockets on back, Alps, Rosko, ht. 12"	1200-1800	2000-3000
Rocket No. 3 (K #156), early, green, red and yellow w/ friction power, Masudaya, len. 7"	90-140	200-300
Roto Robot (K #132), w/ shooting guns in chest, hinged head battery compartment, Horikawa, ht. 9"	80-120	180-220
Rt-Z Robotank Z (K #70), gray w/ red and white rockets embossed on the sides, Nomura, ht. 8"	400-500	600-800
Satellite X-107 (B #162), flying saucer w/ floating astronaut, dia. 8"	50-70	90-140
Sky Patrol (B #239), space boat w/ pilot and swivel gun turret, len. 13.5"	100-150	250-350
Sonicon Rocket (K #54), vehicle which responds to sound, w/ robot driver, Masudaya, len. 13.5"	400-600	900-1200
Space Car (B #40), w/ robot driver and floating ball, Yonezawa, len. 8"	1000-1500	2200-3200
Space Chick (B #271), keywind, Yone, ht. 3"	80-120	150-200
Space Dog (K #106), keywind, silver w/ spark window, Yoshiya, len. 6.5"	500-600	800-1000
Space Dog (K #106), red w/ friction drive and spark window, Yoshiya, len. 6.5"	500-600	800-1000
Space Explorer (K #104), gray, initially square, raises to reveal head, arms and 3-D TV screen, Yonezawa, ht. open 12"	500-700	800-1400
Space Fighter Rocket Car (B #183), friction, blue, red and yellow w/ 2 pilots and sparking mechanism, len. 18.5"	700-1000	2000-3000
Space Giant (B #13), saucer, gray and red w/ domed cockpit (largest flying saucer toy), dia. 12"	700-900	1200-1500
Space Giant Robot (K #l 18), charcoal, w/ red accents, pop-out guns, Horikawa, ht. 16"	100-150	200-300
Space Guard MS-61 (B #257), space tank w/ dual spring-loaded rockets, rc, Masudaya, len. 9.5"	180-220	300-400
Spaceman (B #175), astronaut in silver suit w/ red leggings, white helmet w/ head lamp, flashlight and gun, rc, ht. 8.5"	700-1000	1200-1600
Space Patrol (B #239), helmeted driver w/ firing gun, ht. 9"	100-150	200-350
Space Patrol Car (B #82), astronaut driver w/ lighting gun, Nomura, ht. 9.5"	200-300	400-600

	MNB	MIB

Space Patrol X-11 (B #206), green w/ hinged door cockpit, Yonezawa, len. 8.5" .... $ 40-60 $ 70-90

Spaceship X-11 (B #161), saucer w/ 2 tinplate pilots and a floating spaceman, Masudaya, dia. 8" 50-65   80-120

Space Sight Seeing Bus (B #285), V-shaped astro bus, domed cockpit w/ litho. pilots and passengers, len. 13.5" 150-200   500-700

Space Tank (B #227), bubble dome w/ radar shield and astronaut pilot, Masudaya, len. 8" 70-90   180-220

Space Trip (B #121), a racing game similar to Terre a la Lune, Masudaya, len. 19" 200-250   400-600

Space Whale (K, Yesterday of Toys, #85), keywind, space blue w/ Saturn motif, Yoshiya, len. 8" 500-700   1000-1500

Sparky Robot (K #84), keywind, silver and red, ht. 6" 180-240   350-500

Star Strider Robot, red and gray, guns in hinged chest, Horikawa, ht. 11" 100-150   200-250

Strolling Space Station, keywind, Yone, dia. 3.5" 50-80   120-180

Swinging Baby Robot (K #72), mechanical tot in keywind swing, Yonezawa, ht. 6" 200-300   400-600

Television Robot (K #52), robot head, double loop antenna and TV in chest, Horikawa, ht. 12" 100-150   200-250

Television Spaceman (B #196), keywind, TV screen chest, Alps, ht. 6" 80-100   150-220

Television Spaceman (B #217), gray, plastic legs, TV screen chest, Alps, ht. 10" 300-500   600-900

Terra Lune (B #120), keywind race to the moon toy, Technofix, German, c. 1947, len. 18" 500-700   800-1200

Tetsujin 28-GO (K #218), keywind, in purple Armor, moveable arms, Nomura, ht. 10" 400-600   700-900

Thor Delta 54 (B #141), friction w/ connected capsule, Daiya, ht. 12" 80-100   150-200

Train Robot (K Yesterday of Toys #28), a.k.a. Sonic Robot, large red and black w/ siren, Masudaya, ht. 14" 2500-4000   6000-9000

Traveling Sam the Peace Corps Man, keywind, stars and stripes litho. body w/ global wheels and flapping jaw, Sy Toy, ht. 7" 120-160   250-400

Tremendous Mike (K #36), keywind, gray w/ red arms and bolt-headed shoulders, Aoshin, ht. 10" 700-900   1200-1800

Twirly Whirly Rocket Ride (K #165), 2 rockets orbiting a tripod base, Alps, ht. 12" 200-300   500-800

Two-Stage Earth Satellite (B #54), tinplate rocket w/ crankwind base, Linemar, len. 9" 180-220   300-500

Two-Stage Rocket Launching Pad (B #102), technician at control panel screen, w/ silo and 2 rockets, Nomura, ht. 7.5" 300-400   500-800

U.N. Planet Cruiser 751 (B #106), w/ light-up rotary engine, len. 10" .. 180-220   300-400

UFO X-5 Flying Saucer, Masudaya, dia. 7" 50-70   80-120

Ultra Man (K #197), gray and green, removable mask, Bullmark, ht. 13" 300-400   500-750

Ultra Man Leo (K #200), keywind, red body and green vinyl head, Bull Mark, ht. 9" 400-600   700-900

Unit 5 Area Radiation Tester Vehicle (B #107), manufacturer unknown (Sears Exclusive), len. 19.5" 200-300   400-600

Universe Car (B #189), blue w/ plastic fins and light-up bubble

	MNB	MIB
dome, Chinese, len. 10"	$ 80-120	$ 150-200
Uran (K #188), keywind, tinplate body w/ vinyl head (Uran is the younger sister of Tetsuwan Atom), Nomura/Bandai, ht. 8.5"	500-700	800-1100
V-2 Space Tank (B #-28), w/ Robby-style robot driver, Yoshiya, len. 6.5"	60-80	100-150
Voyage a la Lune, friction drive, w/ rocket ship on perforated steel band, Gunthermann, len. 7"	180-220	300-400
Wheel-a-Gear Robot (K #31), similar to Blink-a-Gear Robot, gears are belt driven, retractable antenna on back, Taiyo, ht. 14"	1000-1500	1800-2200
Wind-Up Moon Astronaut (B #179), red w/ blue helmet, gun in right hand, Daiya, ht. 9"	700-900	1800-2200
Winkie, keywind, gray tinplate w/ red feet, 3-D winking eyes, meter on chest, Yonezawa, ht. 9"	450-550	700-900
Winner-23 (B #185), jet-style vehicle, domed cockpit, len. 6"	80-120	200-300
Wizard of Oz Tin Man Robot, silver and blue plastic, Remco, ht. 21"	80-140	180-220
X-25 Robot, keywind, round human head and oversized glasses, Daiya, ht. 7"	80-120	180-220
X-70 Space Robot (K #121), petals open to TV camera and screen, UK, ht. 12"	800-1200	1500-2300
X-80 Planet Explorer (B #96), saucer w/ light-up central dome, dia. 8"	40-60	70-90
X-9 Space Robot Car (K #58), robot-driven green car w/ bubble dome w/ pop-up balls, Masudaya, len. 7"	1200-1800	2000-3000
Z Man Missile (B #250), wheeled, friction-powered rocket w/ robot pilot, len. 7"	180-220	300-400

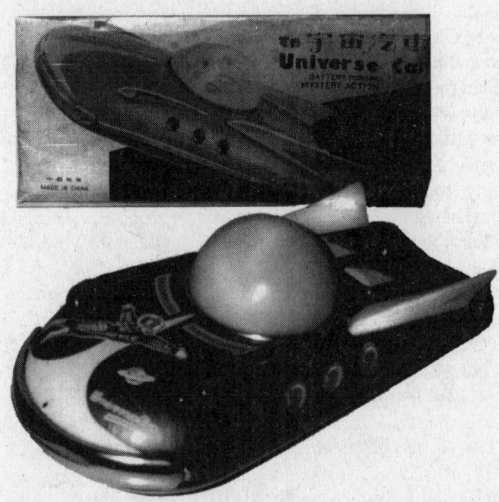

A Chinese Universe Car, c. 1970, in original box $150-$200.

Schoenhut Animals

Albert Schoenhut began production of the Humpty Dumpty Circus at his Philadelphia toy company in 1903. Advertised as "The World's Most Popular Toy," the animals and personnel are valued today for their lively representations and charm.

For further information we reccommend *Schoenhut's Humpty Dumpty Circus from A to Z,* by Evelyn Ackerman and Fredrick E. Keller, Era Industries, Inc., Los Angeles, California, 1975. Our consultant for this area is Judith Lile (she is listed at the back of this book).

In the following chart the designation *NA* means that the animal was not produced in that style. Collectors look for pieces that are as close to the original as possible; some paint or fabric wear and missing ears or tails are considered minor flaws, but repaints, touch-ups or replaced clothing affect the prices more significantly.

Above left to right: Painted eye sea lion, glass-eyed sea lion. Below left to right: Glass-eyed zebra, reduced-size giraffe, bisque head gent acrobat. —Photos courtesy of Judith Lile.

Animals

	PAINTED EYE			GLASS EYED			REDUCED SIZE		
	Fair	Good	Exc.	Fair	Good	Exc.	Fair	Good	Exc.
Alligator	$ 200	$ 300	$ 375	$ 350	$ 500	$ 650	—	NA	—
Brown Bear	275	375	450	425	550	650	$ 300	$ 375	$ 450
Buffalo, cloth mane	—	NA	—	450	575	650	—	NA	—
Buffalo, carved mane	200	300	400	600	900	1400	250	325	400
Bulldog	600	750	900	900	1350	1800	—	NA	—
Burro	200	300	350	300	375	450	—	NA	—
Camel, 1 hump	275	325	400	350	475	600	—	NA	—
Camel, 2 humps	200	300	375	900	1300	1600	225	325	400
Cat	800	1100	1500	2000	3000	3500	—	NA	—
Cow	300	400	500	400	650	850	—	NA	—
Deer	300	500	700	600	900	1200	—	NA	—
Donkey	75	100	125	100	150	200	60	80	100
Elephant	95	150	175	125	200	275	75	100	125
Gazelle	600	750	1000	1200	1800	2400	—	NA	—
Giraffe	275	350	500	400	500	600	275	350	425
Goose	275	375	500	—	NA	—	—	NA	—
Gorilla	1600	2000	2400	—	NA	—	—	NA	—
Hippopotamus	275	350	450	350	500	600	300	375	450
Horse, brown	125	200	250	225	325	400	75	125	150
Horse, white	150	200	275	225	325	400	75	125	150
Hyena	1100	1500	1800	1800	2800	3800	—	NA	—
Kangaroo	600	750	900	800	1100	1300	—	NA	—
Leopard	275	375	450	400	550	700	250	300	350
Lion, cloth mane	—	NA	—	400	550	650	—	NA	—
Lion, carved mane	225	300	400	600	1000	1400	250	300	350
Monkey	300	400	500	—	NA	—	—	NA	—
Ostrich	275	375	500	400	550	750	300	450	550
Pig	250	325	375	325	425	500	300	450	550
Polar Bear	550	700	900	800	1200	1600	—	NA	—
Poodle, cloth mane	—	NA	—	200	275	350	—	NA	—
Poodle, carved mane	150	200	250	600	900	1200	300	400	500
Rabbit	500	650	800	2000	3000	3500	—	NA	—
Rhinocerous	250	350	450	325	500	650	250	350	425
Sea Lion	400	550	750	600	900	1300	—	NA	—
Sheep	300	400	600	450	600	750	—	NA	—
Tiger	275	375	450	400	550	700	200	275	325
Wolf	1000	1500	1800	1800	2500	3500	—	NA	—
Zebra	225	300	400	400	550	700	225	325	425
Zebu	1000	1500	1600	2000	2500	3500	—	NA	—

Personnel

	1-PART HEAD			BISQUE HEAD			REDUCED SIZE		
	Fair	Good	Exc.	Fair	Good	Exc.	Fair	Good	Exc.
Chinaman	$ 300	$ 450	$ 600	—	NA	—	—	NA	—
Clown	75	100	150	—	NA	—	$ 75	$ 110	$ 135
Gent Acrobat	—	NA	—	$ 300	$ 450	$ 600	—	NA	—
Hobo	200	300	400	—	NA	—	325	400	450
Lady Acrobat	300	400	450	300	450	550	—	NA	—
Lady Circus Rider	225	300	350	275	375	450	175	225	275
Lion Tamer	300	450	600	300	450	600	—	NA	—
Negro Dude	325	400	500	—	NA	—	375	450	500
Ring Master	300	375	450	350	425	550	175	225	275

*Right: Early monkey.
— Photo courtesy of
Judith Lile.*

Above: Glass-eyed hippo. — Photo courtesy of Judith Lile.

Star Trek Memorabilia

Star Trek first appeared on N.B.C. on September 8, 1966 but lasted only three seasons. When N.B.C. canceled it, enraged fans bombarded the network with over one million letters of protest. Ironically, the show became even more popular in syndication. Reruns spurred the production of books, pins, fanzines, and toys. "Trekkie" fan clubs and conventions evolved. Speculation regarding the series' return was surpassed only by rumors of a Beatles reunion.

Star Trek: The Motion Picture spawned a lot of material, but the 1979 film was a disappointment. Less material was produced for *Star Trek II: The Wrath of Khan*. That film re-established *Star Trek* and has been followed by five movies and several new TV shows. The films and programs have created a new generation of fans and collectors.

The prices below are based on items in excellent or mint condition. Since the same item can be bought at a variety of locations at different prices, we devised a range system. The low range covers complete, near mint to mint items without the package. The higher range reflects the prices of complete, near mint to mint items in near mint to mint boxes. Prices below are for complete like-new items. Prices of scratched, chipped, or altered examples are not included.

Abbreviations: Regarding manufacturers, *M*-Mego, *G*-Galoob, *E*-Ertl, *R*-Remco, *Ry*-Rayline, *ID*-Ideal, and *B*-Bradley. To conserve space we have shortened some words. After the manufacturer we also list the production the item was based on: *TVS*-the original TV series, *NGTV-The Next Generation* TV show, *STMP-Star Trek: The Motion Picture* (Star Trek I), *ST III-Star Trek III: The Search for Spock*, and *FF-The Final Frontier Movie*. Most items in this section are action figures and toys followed by a small group of books. Years listed are approximate.

For more information see *House of Collectibles Price Guide to Star Trek*, Sue Cornwell and Mike Kott; *Tomart's Price Guide to Action Figure Collectibles*, Carol Markowski, Bill Sikoria, and T.N. Tumbusch; *Greenberg's Guide to Star Trek Collectibles*, Chris Gentry and Sally Gibson-Downs, and *Toy Shop* listed in the front of this book.

Above: Star Trek, The Motion Picture *Board Game, $10-$15. Right:* Star Trek, The Next Generation *Phaser, mint in package, $18-$22.*

Action Figures and Toys

	MAKER	PROD.	YEAR	MNP	MIP
Andorian, 8"	M	TVS	1974	$ 180-220	$ 400-500
Antican, 3.75"	G	NGTV	1988	20-30	45-65
Arcturian, 3.75"	M	STMP	1979	60-90	120-180
Arcturian, 12"	M	STMP	1979	40-50	70-100
Astro Wlke Tlkes	R	TVS	1968	70-90	110-140
Betelgeusian, 3.75"	M	STMP	1979	70-100	180-220
Cheron, 8"	M	TVS	1974	60-90	120-180
Com. Bridge, 3.75"	M	STMP	1979	50-80	100-150
Data, dark face, 3.75"	G	NGTV	1988	22-28	45-55
Data, flesh face, 3.75"	G	NGTV	1988	10-12	20-30
Data, blue/green face, 3.75"	G	NGTV	1988	50-70	90-150
Data, spot face, 3.75"	G	NGTV	1988	12-14	20-30
Decker, 3.75"	M	STMP	1979	8-12	18-24
Decker, 12"	M	STMP	1979	50-70	90-140
Dr. McCoy, 8"	M	TVS	1974	25-40	60-75
Dr. McCoy, 3.75"	M	STMP	1979	10-14	20-30
Enterprise Bridge, 8" fig.	M	TVS	1974	80-120	200-250
Ferengi, 3.75"	G	NGTV	1988	20-30	50-60
Ferengi Ftr Veh, 3.75"	G	NGTV	1988	15-25	35-60
Gorn, 8"	M	TVS	1974	80-100	180-220
Ilia, 3.75"	M	STMP	1979	5-8	14-18
Ilia, 12"	M	STMP	1979	25-35	50-75
Kirk, 8"	M	TVS	1974	18-22	40-50
Kirk, 3.75"	M	STMP	1979	8-12	20-30
Kirk, 12"	M	STMP	1979	40-50	80-100
Kirk, 3.75"	E	ST III	1984	6-9	18-24
Kirk, 7"	G	FF	1989	15-18	30-40
Klaa, 7"	G	FF	1989	15-20	30-40
Klingon, 8"	M	TVS	1974	20-25	40-50
Klingon, 12"	M	STMP	1979	50-60	120-160
Klingon, 3.75"	M	STMP	1979	70-90	150-200

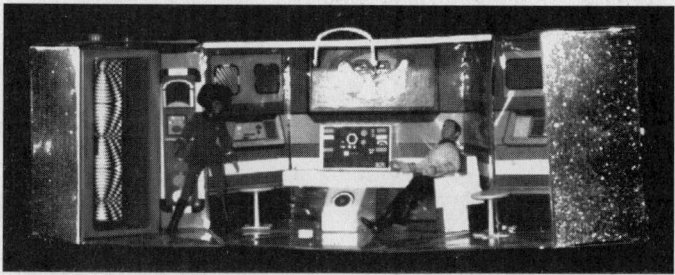

U.S.S. Enterprise Playset, mint in box, $200-$250; Captain Kirk, ht. 8", by Mego, mint, no package, $18-$22; Lt. Uhura, ht. 8", by Mego, mint, no package, $30-$40. — Items courtesy Jim Glaab's Collector's Showcase

	MAKER	PROD.	YEAR	MNP	MIP
Kruge and dog, 3.75"	E	ST III	1984	$ 8-10	$ 30-40
La Forge, 3.75"	G	NGTV	1988	3-5	9-12
Lt. Uhura, 8"	M	TVS	1974	30-40	90-120
McCoy, 7"	G	FF	1989	15-20	35-40
Megarite, 3.75"	M	STMP	1979	90-120	150-200
Mis. Gam. VI, 8" fig.	M	TVS	1976	250-350	500-700
Mugato, 8"	M	TVS	1974	125-175	250-350
Neptunian, 8"	M	TVS	1974	80-100	140-220
Phaser	R	TVS	1975	30-40	50-80
Phaser Battle Game	M	TVS	—	200-250	350-450
Picard, 3.75"	G	NGTV	1988	5-7	12-15
Q, 3.75"	G	NGTV	1988	25-35	60-80
Rigellian, 3.75"	M	STMP	1979	70-190	140-180
Riker, 3.75"	G	NGTV	1988	3-4	10-12
Romulan, 8"	M	TVS	1974	250-350	500-700
Scotty, 8"	M	TVS	1974	30-40	60-80
Scotty, 3.75"	M	STMP	1979	9-12	18-24
Scotty, 3.75"	E	ST III	1984	7-9	18-22
Selay, 3.75"	G	NGTV	1988	20-30	50-75
Galileo Craft, 3.75"	G	NGTV	1988	18-22	35-55
Spock, 8"	M	TVS	1974	20-25	45-60
Spock, 3.75"	M	STMP	1979	10-15	25-30
Spock, 12"	M	STMP	1979	30-40	60-90
Spock, 3.75"	E	ST III	1984	9-12	20-30
Spock, 7"	G	FF	1989	10-15	25-35
S.T. Bd. Game	ID	TVS	1966	—	80-120
Sybok, 7"	G	FF	1989	10-15	25-35
Talosian, 8"	M	TVS	1974	120-160	250-350
The Keeper, 8"	M	TVS	1974	80-100	170-220
Tracer Pistol	RY	TVS	1966	50-70	90-120
Tricorder	M	TVS	1976	70-90	120-160
Worf, 3.75"	G	NGTV	1988	3-5	8-12
Watch, Spock	B	STMP	1979	25-35	40-50
Yar, 3.75"	G	NGTV	1988	8-12	15-25
Zaranite, 3.75"	M	STMP	1979	70-100	120-160

Super Phaser II Target Game, mint in box, $45-$65.

Star Trek Books

Abode of Life, Corey, 1982, pbk. .... $ 4-6
Best of Trek, 1974 -1991, based on mag., 16 dif., #1-16 pbks., ea. 3-5
Chekov's Enterprise, W. Koenig, 1980, pbk. 15-20
Come and Be With Me, L. Nimoy, 1978, pbk. 18-22
Covenant of the Crown, Weinstein, 1981, hrdcov. 8-12
Death's Angel, K. Sky, 1981, pbk. 12-18
Making of Star Trek II, Asherman, 1982, pbk. 14-18
Star Trek Maps, an intro. to navigation, Jeff Maynard, 1980 70-90
Starfleet Medical Manual, Palestine, Ballantine, 1977 15-20
Coloring Book, 1968 20-30

Left to right: Trek Times, $6-$8; Ilia Action Figure, by Mego,
Star Trek: The Motion Picture, *3.75", if mint on mint card $14-*
$18, small damage to this card reduces it to $10-$12.

Star Wars Memorabilia

Star Wars burst onto movie screens in 1977. Stunning special effects made it an instant success. Two equally successful sequels followed, *The Empire Strikes Back* (ESB) in 1980 and *Return of the Jedi* (ROTJ) in 1983. *Star Wars* not only revolutionized special effects, it also introduced a smaller sized action figure. Although sizes vary they are generally 3.75" or smaller figures. Most of the following toys are the 3.75" figures and the vehicles made for them. Kenner made the figures and most of the toys listed below.

Dating carded *Star Wars* figures is relatively easy. The back of each card pictures each figure in the product line; as the line grows so do the number of illustrations. The original 12 figures are referred to as 12 backs. Packaging is more important in *Star Wars* items than any other area. The same figure on a *Star Wars* card is worth more than on an ESB or ROTJ card and an ESB carded figure is worth more than an ROTJ card. Power of The Force (POTF), produced in 1985, is a series of figures that usually includes a collector coin. These figures are generally more valuable than ROTJ or ESB. The other factor affecting price is condition. The first prices quoted are for mint items on mint cards. The other range is for mint complete figures. Many times figures came with weapons or clothing. Loose figures are devalued if they are lacking this original equipment. Because Kenner marketed *Star Wars* toys worldwide, there is an incredible range of packaging variation.

The demand for toys and *Star Wars* products continues. With anticipation of a new *Star Wars* movie in the late 1990s prices have soared. The sharpest increases are for early small figures, produced for the first movie, in mint condition on mint cards. Another area that has seen significant increases are the large figures. For more information see *House of Collectibles Official Price Guide to Star Wars Collectibles*, Sue Cornwell and Mike Kott; *Tomart's Price Guide to Action Figure Collectibles*, Carol Markowski, Bill Skier, and T.N. Tumbusch; and *1995 Toys and Prices,* Krause Publications, 1995.

Above left to right: Talking alarm clock, $50-70; Princess Leia bubble bath, $12-18.

	SERIES	FIGURE	IN PACK.
A Wing Pilot	POTF	$ 10-15	$ 60-80
Admiral Ackbar	ROTJ	4-6	18-24
Amanaman	POTF	20-25	90-130
Anakin Skywalker	POTF	20-30	80-100
AT-AT	—	50-70	160-220
AT-AT Commander	ESB	6-8	35-45
AT-AT Driver	ESB	6-8	35-45
AT-ST Driver	ROTJ	4-5	15-20
B-Wing Fighter	ROTJ	25-35	70-90
B-Wing Pilot	ROTJ	5-7	15-20
Barada	POTF	8-12	80-100
Ben Kenobi, large figure		90-110	220-300
Ben (Obi-Wan) Kenobi	SW 20/21 back	8-10	90-110
Ben (Obi-Wan) Kenobi	SW 12 back	8-10	150-200
Ben (Obi-Wan) Kenobi	ESB	8-10	50-70
Ben (Obi-Wan) Kenobi	ROTJ	8-10	30-35
Ben (Obi-Wan) Kenobi	POTF	8-10	70-80
Bespin Security Guard, black	ESB	5-7	35-45
Bespin Security Guard, white	ESB	6-8	40-50
Bib Fortuna	ROTJ	5-7	18-24
Biker Scout	ROTJ	4-6	18-22
Blue Snaggletooth, Sears	SW 20/21 back	90-120	—
Boba Fett, large figure	—	100-150	300-400
Boba Fett	SW 20/21 back	20-30	200-250
Boba Fett, working Rocket Launcher	SW (mail in)	30-50	350-550
Bossk (Bounty Hunter)	ESB	8-10	50-65
C-3PO, large figure	Star Wars	50-75	120-180
C-3PO	SW 12 back	8-10	100-135
C-3PO	SW 20/21 back	8-10	70-90
C-3PO	ESB	8-10	40-55
C-3PO, removable limbs	ESB	8-10	45-65
C-3PO	ROTJ	8-10	25-30
C-3PO	POTF	8-10	50-70
C-3PO bust case, gold chrome	—	18-22	45-55
Cantina Adventure Set, Sears	Star Wars	90-130	350-500
Chewbacca, large figure		50-65	120-150
Chewbacca	SW 12 back	8-10	100-170
Chewbacca	SW 20/21 back	8-10	60-90
Chewbacca	ESB	8-10	50-70
Chewbacca	ROTJ	8-10	25-35
Chewbacca	POTF	8-10	70-90
Chewbacca Bandoiler Strap	ROTJ	3-4	12-18
Chief Chirpa	ROTJ	5-7	18-24
Cloud Car Pilot	ESB	5-7	35-45
Creature Cantina	Star Wars	30-50	90-110
Darth Vader, large figure	—	60-80	150-200
Darth Vader	SW 12 back	8-10	150-200
Darth Vader	SW 20/21 back	8-10	70-90
Darth Vader	ESB	8-10	50-70
Darth Vader	ROTJ	8-10	30-40
Darth Vader	POTF	8-10	70-90

Above left to right: B-Wing Pilot, Power of the Force, mint on card, $16-$20; The Emperor, Power of the Force, mint on card, $30-$50.

Above left to right: With speculation of a new Star Wars movie coming out in the late 1990s, new toys, such as this diecast Luke Skywalker figure, are appearing at toy stores; R2-D2 with Sensorscope, Return of the Jedi, *mint on card, $40-$50.*

Right: Speeder Bike in original box, Return of the Jedi, *$20-$30.*

	SERIES	FIGURE	IN PACK.
Darth Vader 2-Part Mask	—	$ 50-60	$ 60-70
Darth Vader Bust Case (plastic)	—	18-22	40-50
Darth Vader TIE Fighter	Star Wars	25-35	80-110
Death Squad Commander	SW 12 back	8-10	120-180
Death Squad Commander	SW 20/21 back	8-10	90-120
Death Squad Commander	ESB	8-10	70-80
Death Squad Commander	ROTJ	8-10	50-60
Death Star Droid	SW 20/21 back	8-10	100-130
Death Star Playset	Star Wars	60-70	150-190
Dengar	ESB	6-8	40-50
Desert Sail Skiff	ESB	5-7	22-26
Droid Factory	Star Wars	25-35	80-120
Early Bird, 4 figures in mailing box	Star Wars	80-100	400-500
Early Bird Kit	Star Wars	80-100	400-500
8D8	ROTJ	5-7	18-24
Emperor's Royal Guard	ROTJ	4-5	22-26
Endor Forest Ranger vehicle	ESB	7-9	20-30
EV-9D9	POTF	12-18	90-110
Ewok Assault Catapult	ROTJ	7-9	20-30
Ewok Combat Glider 8	ESB	7-9	20-30
Ewok Village	ROTJ	30-40	70-90
4-Lom	ESB	6-8	70-90
FX-7 Medical Droid	ESB	6-8	50-60
Gamorrean Guard	ROTJ	4-6	18-22
General Madine	ROTJ	4-6	18-22
Greedo	SW 20/21 back	8-10	90-110
Hammerhead	SW 20/21 back	8-10	90-120
Han Solo, large figure	—	120-180	350-500
Han Solo	SW 12 back	10-14	300-500
Han Solo	SW 20/21 back	10-14	200-300
Han Solo	ESB	10-14	150-200
Han Solo (Bespin outfit)	ESB	8-10	60-70
Han Solo (Hoth outfit)	ESB	10-12	45-65
Han Solo	ROTJ	10-14	20-30
Han Solo, trench coat	ROTJ	8-10	30-40
Han Solo	POTF	10-14	90-120
Han Solo in Carbonite Chamber	POTF	50-70	180-220
Ice Planet Hoth Playset	ESB	35-45	80-120
IG-88, large figure	—	200-250	400-500
IG-88 (Bounty Hunter)	ESB	6-8	45-55
Imperial Commander	ESB	5-7	30-40
Imperial Dignitary	POTF	18-22	50-80
Imperial Gunner	POTF	18-22	80-100
Imperial Shuttle	ROTJ	40-60	150-200
Imperial Stormtrooper (Hoth battle gear)	ESB	7-9	18-22
Imperial TIE Fighter vehicle	Star Wars	25-35	80-110
Imperial Tie Fighter Pilot	ESB	5-7	55-75
Imperial Troop Transporter	Star Wars	25-30	90-120
Jabba the Hutt Throne	ROTJ	10-12	35-45
Jawa, large figure	—	60-80	175-225
Jawa, cloth cape	SW 12 back	10-12	100-150

Above: Millennium Falcon, unboxed, $60-$80.

Below left to right: Yoda handpuppet, unboxed, $18-$22; Sy Snootles and the Rebo Band, Return of the Jedi, mint on card, $50-$80.

	SERIES	FIGURE	IN PACK.
Jawa, plastic cape	SW 12 back	$ 150-250	$ 600-900
Jawa, cloth cape	SW 20/21 back	10-12	80-90
Jawa, cloth cape	ESB	10-12	70-90
Jawa, cloth cape	ROTJ	10-12	30-40
Jawa, cloth cape	POTF	10-12	50-60
Klaatu	ROTJ	5-7	15-20
Klaatu (Skiff Guard outfit)	ROTJ	4-6	18-22
Lando Calrissian	ESB	8-10	35-45
Lando Calrissian (Skiff guard disguise)	ROTJ	6-8	18-24
Lando Calrissian, General Pilot	POTF	18-22	70-90
Landspeeder	Star Wars	20-30	70-90
Laser Rifle Case	ROTJ	15-20	35-45
Lobot	ESB	6-8	35-45
Logray	ROTJ	4-6	15-20
Luke Skywalker	ROTJ	10-14	25-35
Luke Skywalker	ESB	10-14	50-70
Luke Skywalker	SW 20/21 back	10-14	150-200
Luke Skywalker	SW 12 back	10-14	200-300
Luke Skywalker, battle poncho	POTF	18-22	80-100
Luke Skywalker (Bespin fatigues)	ESB	8-10	90-110
Luke Skywalker (Hoth battle gear)	ESB	8-10	60-80
Luke Skywalker (Jedi knight outfit)	ROTJ	10-15	60-80
Luke Skywalker, large figure	—	90-120	200-300
Luke Skywalker (Stormtrooper outfit)	POTF	50-70	200-300
Luke Skywalker X-Wing Pilot	SW 20/21 back	10-14	100-130
Lumat	POTF	8-12	30-40
Millennium Falcon Spaceship	Star Wars	60-80	150-220
Nien Nunb	ROTJ	4-6	18-24
Nikto	ROTJ	4-6	18-22
Paploo	POTF	8-12	30-40
Patrol Dewback Playset	SW	15-20	50-70
Power Droid	SW 20/21 back	8-10	90-110
Princess Leia, large figure	—	90-120	200-300
Princess Leia	SW 12 back	10-14	200-300
Princess Leia	SW 20/21 back	8-10	220-260
Princess Leia (Bespin gown)	ESB	15-20	60-80
Princess Leia (Hoth outfit)	ESB	10-12	45-60
Princess Leia, combat poncho	ROTJ	10-12	30-40
Princess Leia	ESB	10-14	180-220
Princess Leia (Boushh disguise)	ROTJ	10-15	40-50
Prune Face	ROTJ	5-7	15-20
R2-D2, large figure	—	50-60	120-160
R2-D2	SW 12 back	10-14	90-120
R2-D2	SW 20/21 back	10-14	70-90
R2-D2	ESB	8-10	40-60
R2-D2, sensorscope	ESB	8-10	40-50
R2-D2	ROTJ	8-10	25-30
R2-D2, pop-up lightsaber	POTF	25-35	120-160
R5-D4	SW 20/21 back	8-10	80-100
Rancor Keeper	ROTJ	5-7	15-20
Rancor Monster	ROTJ	10-15	35-45

	SERIES	FIGURE	IN PACK.
Rebel Armored Snowspeeder, vehicle	ESB	$ 30-40	$ 80-100
Rebel Commander	ESB	5-7	30-40
Rebel Commando	ROTJ	5-7	18-22
Rebel Soldier (Hoth battle gear)	ESB	6-8	40-50
Rebel Transport	ESB	25-35	80-100
Ree-Yees	ROTJ	5-7	15-20
Romba	POTF	8-12	30-40
Sand People (Tusken Raider)	SW 12 back	9-12	140-200
Sand People (Tusken Raider)	SW 20/21 back	9-12	90-130
Sand People (Tusken Raider)	ESB	9-12	70-80
Sand People (Tusken Raider)	ROTJ	9-12	45-60
Scout Walker	ESB	20-25	60-90
Slave 1	ESB	30-40	80-120
Snaggletooth	SW 20/21 back	8-10	90-110
Speeder Bike	ROTJ	7-9	20-30
Squid Head	ROTJ	7-9	18-22
Stormtrooper, large figure	—	60-80	200-250
Stormtrooper	SW 12 back	7-9	150-190
Stormtrooper	SW 20-21 back	7-9	60-80
Stormtrooper	ESB	7-9	50-60
Stormtrooper	ROTJ	7-9	100-125
Stormtrooper	POTF	7-9	50-60
Sy Snootles and the Rebo Band, boxed	ROTJ	20-30	50-80
Tauntaun, solid belly	ESB	10-15	25-35
Tauntaun, split belly	ESB	12-18	40-50
Teebo	ROTJ	4-6	18-22
The Emperor	ROTJ	8-10	25-30
Twin-Pod Cloud Car	ESB	20-25	60-90
2-1B	ESB	6-8	50-70
Ugnaught	ESB	6-8	50-60
Walrus Man	SW 20/21 back	8-10	90-110
Warok	POTF	8-12	30-40
Weequay	ROTJ	4-6	18-22
Wicket W. Warrick	ROTJ	5-7	18-22
X-Wing Fighter, battle damage	SW	25-35	90-110
X-Wing Fighter Vehicle	SW	25-35	90-110
Y-Wing Fighter	ROTJ	30-40	80-100
Yak Face	POTF	90-130	300-400
Yoda	ESB	6-8	45-55
Yoda Handpuppet	—	18-22	30-40
Zuckuss	ESB	6-8	40-55

Return of the Jedi lunchbox, 1983, $30-$40. —Item courtesy of Jim Glaab's Collector's Showcase.

Tonka Toys

Tonka toys became the post-war symbol of the well-crafted American toy. In an industry turning increasingly to plastic and smaller sizes, Tonka's large, light, pressed steel vehicles ruled sandbox construction sites. The firm began as Mound Metal Works in 1946. The Tonka name came with the move to Minnetonka, MN.

Since children used the vehicles for heavy duty projects and often left them outside (moms often banished the heavy toys from the house), the condition of Tonka toys is often poor. In the following listing we give two price ranges: *excellent* for toys with some light wear but no significant rust or major paint loss, *near mint* for toys with only traces of wear and come with excellent original boxes. Keep in mind that collectors often pay a hefty premium for mint in mint box examples. Such toys may bring more than prices quoted below. Rusty, damaged pieces will bring significantly less than those in excellent or better condition.

For further information see *Collector's Guide to Tonka Trucks*, 1947-1963, Don and Barb DeSalle, L-W Book Sales, Gas City, IN, and *Collecting Toys*, #7, Richard O'Brien, Books Americana, Florence, Alabama, 1995.

	EXC.	NEAR MINT
Allied Van Lines #400, 1953	$ 90-110	$ 200-300
Big Mike State Hi-Way Dept. Dump Truck #45, orange w/ V-shape plow, 1958	250-350	500-750
Big Mike State Hi-Way Dept. Dump Truck #45, orange, 1957	200-320	400-630
Car Carrier #840, yellow w/ 3 cars, 1963	200-300	400-500
Carnation Milk Delivery Van #750, 1955	150-200	320-380
Carry-All Tractor Trailer w/ Crane and Clam #170 and #150, yellow and green, 1949	200-250	300-400
Carry-All Tractor Trailer #120, red cab, blue trailer, 1949	100-120	180-220
Carry-All Tractor Trailer #120, blue cab, blue trailer w/ #50 Steam Shovel, 1949	200-250	320-440
Cement Truck #120, red and white, 1960	200-250	300-400
Clipper Boat and Trailer # AC360, 1960	80-120	200-250
Crane and Clam #150, yellow and black, 1947	90-140	200-300
Crane and Clam w/ Tracks #150, yellow and black, 1949	80-120	200-250
Dump Truck #180, red and green, 1949	100-150	200-250
Dump Truck, red cab, green box, 1955	70-90	160-210
Fire Truck, Hydraulic Aerial Ladder, red w/ # 5 and TFD decals, 1957	200-230	300-400
Gasoline Truck #33, red, 1958	250-400	600-800
Grain Hauler #550, semi, red cab w/ aluminum box, 1952	90-150	200-250
Green Giant Tractor Trailer Transport #650, white w/ Green Giant decals, 1953	120-180	250-350
Green Giant Utility Truck #175, white w/ Green Giant decals and solid rubber tires, 1953	120-160	280-320
Hydraulic Dump Truck, brown, 1957	70-90	180-220
Jeep Wrecker #375, white, w/ winch and plow, 1964	200-300	400-600
Livestock Semi #500, red, 1952	80-140	190-240
Log Hauler #575, red cab, 1953	90-130	200-250
Minute Maid Box Van #750, w/ dual rear wheels, 1955	250-350	400-600
Pickup Truck #02, bronze, 1960	60-90	120-180
Pickup Truck #02, dark blue, 1956	100-150	200-300
Pickup Truck #02, dark blue, 1958	60-90	120-180
Pickup Truck, w/ camper #530, 1963	100-150	220-280
Pickup Truck Sportsman #05, dark blue w/ cap, 1958	90-130	180-220

	EXC.	NEAR MINT
Power Lift Truck and Trailer #200, 1948	$ 120-160	$ 200-250
Rescue Van #105, 1960-61	100-150	300-400
Road Grader #600, 1953	50-70	90-110
Sanitary System Truck #140, rounded back, 1960	250-300	400-500
Sanitary System Truck #B203, square back, w/ bins and scoop, 1959	300-400	500-700
Ser-vi-Car # 201, 3 wheel cart, white	60-80	100-130
Star-Kist Tuna Box Van #725, 1954	250-350	420-620
State Hi-Way Dept. Dump Truck, orange, 1956	90-1120	200-250
State Hi-Way Dept. Dump Truck, orange w/ side dump, 1957	90-130	200-300
Steam Shovel #100, red and black w/ tracks, 1949	80-130	200-250
Steam Shovel #100, red and black, wheels, 1947	80-130	200-250
Steam Shovel #50, red and blue, 1949	80-120	180-220
Steel Carrier Tractor Trailer #145, cab orange or yellow w/ green box, 1950	100-130	200-250
Suburban Pumper #46 Fire Truck, red w/ # 5 decal and fire hydrant, 1956	200-250	300-400
Tonka Air Express Box Van and "Piggyback" Trailer, 1959	180-220	350-450
Tonka Farms Stock Rack Truck, 1957	200-250	350-400
Tonka Marine Service #41, blue semi w/ 4 boats, 1959	250-350	450-550
Tonka Service Van #103, 1961	80-130	200-250
Tonka Tanker, 1960	150-200	350-450
Tonka Toy Transport Tractor Trailer #140, red, box features opening doors, 1949	200-250	300-400
Utility Truck #175, green cab w/ yellow body, 1950	80-130	180-220
Wrecker Truck #250, 1953	100-150	220-280

Fire Engine Suburban Pumper #46, 1956, $200-$250 (unboxed with fire hydrant). — Photo courtesy of George Kerrigan Photography.

Toy and Miniature Soldiers

The soldiers in the following section are lead. Of the various producers of toys and miniature soldiers, we chose Britains, Mignot, and Courtenay.

In 1893 William Britain, founder of a London toy firm, and his sons developed hollow-cast lead toy soldiers. They were cheaper to produce and ship than earlier solid figures. They were packaged in distinctive red boxes with elaborate labels. They established 54mm (2 1/8") as a standard size, and by the early 1900s were outproducing their German and French competitors. Britains production reached a peak between the two world wars and in the 1950s. Pre-World War II sets usually command a premium price and are listed as pre-war in the descriptions below. Production of hollow cast lead figures ceased in 1966. The company now produces a new line of metal toy soldiers and plastic figures. Because Britains improved designs and updated uniforms over the years, there can be many variations of the same set. For further information see *The Art of the Toy Soldier,* Henry I. Kurtz and Burtt R. Ehrlich, Abbeville Press, NY, 1987; and *Britains Toy Soldiers 1893-1932,* James Opie, Harper and Row, NY, 1985.

Three French toy makers founded C.B.G. Mignot in the 1820s. The firm is known for fine quality 55mm toy soldiers representing the French army, with special emphasis on the Napoleonic Wars and World War I. Although still in existence, production is limited, and figures are made for collectors rather than children. The sets listed below were made in the 1970s and '80s. Dates following descriptions refer to the period of the unit represented rather than the year of production. For further information see *The Art of the Toy Soldier,* Henry I. Kurtz and Burtt R. Ehrlich, Abbeville Press, NY, 1987.

Although Richard Courtenay began by producing a line of toy figures in the 1920s, he is best known for his line of high quality, miniature medieval knights, produced from 1938 to 1963. These spectacular figures are now highly sought by connoisseur collectors. The figures represent knights of the 100 Years War, specifically, the Battle of Poitiers (1356). Courtenay assigned numerical designations according to the position of the knight, e.g. a knight lunging with battle ax is position 7. We have listed position numbers in the descriptions below. Courtenay signed many of his figures but not all. An unsigned figure will bring approximately 20% less than the prices listed. For further information see *Heraldic Miniature Knights*, Peter Greenhill, Guild of Master Craftsmen, East Sussex, 1991.

We list two price ranges for Britains and Mignot sets: one for excellent unboxed sets, the second for excellent to near mint condition sets in their original boxes. Courtenay figures are listed with one range for excellent to near mint condition, no box. Set numbers and the number of figures are included for Britains. Prices are based primarily on recent auction results.

Our consultant for this section is Henry Kurtz, co-author of *The Art of the Toy Soldier* and president of Henry Kurtz Limited, an auction house specializing in toy and miniature soldiers. He is a member of the Appraisers Association of America and is listed in the back of this book.

Britains

NO. FIG.	SET NO.	UNBOXED	BOXED
11th Hussars, pre-war 5	12	$ 200-250	$ 300-400
16th/5th Lancers, pre-war 5	33	125-150	225-275
1st King George V's Own Gurkha Rifles 8	197	100-125	150-200
3rd Hussars 5	13	300-350	500-600
4.5" Anti-Aircraft Gun .... —	1522	200-250	300-400
4th/7th Dragoon Guards, pre-war 5	127	300-350	500-600
6th Dragoon Guards, pre-war 15	106	300-350	500-600
7th Bengal Infantry, pre-war 8	1342	250-350	600-700
9th Queen's Royal Lancers, pre-war 5	24	150-175	250-300

*Top: Britains, the Black Watch, standing firing in tropical dress,
$250-350. Middle: A selection of Courtenay Knights in various
positions, prices range from $250-$450. Bottom left to right:
Mignot, British Life Guards, $200-$250; Mignot, Austrian
Cuirassiers, $250-300. —Photo courtesy of Phillips Auctioneers.*

	NO. FIG.	SET NO.	UNBOXED	BOXED
Arabs of the Desert on Foot, Camels, Horses . 11		224	$ 200-250	$ 300-400
Argyll and Sutherland Highlanders, pre-war 8		15	125-150	200-250
Armoured Car .... —		1321	250-350	400-500
Band of the Life Guards in State Dress 12		101	300-400	400-500
Band of the Royal Air Force 12		2116	400-500	700-900
Band of the Royal Berkshire Regiment 25		2093	800-1000	1000-1500
Band of the Royal Marines 12		1291	200-300	400-500
Bikanir Camel Corps, pre-war 3		123	250-350	450-550
Black Watch 6		11	80-100	150-175
Black Watch, pre-war 8		11	125-150	200-250
British Infantry 8		195	80-100	150-175
British Infantry in Tropical Dress 8		1924	200-250	400-500
British Territorial Infantry 8		1537	300-350	400-500
Cameronians 7		1913	700-900	1000-1500
Changing of the Guard 83		1555	600-800	1000-1500
Chinese Infantry 8		241	200-250	350-450
Coldstream Guards 8		2082	90-120	150-200
Coldstream Guards, three positions 24		90	450-550	600-800
Colour Party of the Black Watch 6		2111	350-450	500-700
Danish Life Guard 7		2019	200-250	350-450
Drum and Fife Band of the Line 17		321	500-700	1000-1500
Drums and Fifes of the Welch Guards 12		2108	500-700	900-1200
Duke of Connaught's Own Lancers 5		66	100-125	150-200
Egyptian Camel Corps 3		48	150-175	200-300
Egyptian Cavalry 5		115	125-150	175-225
Fire Fighters of the Royal Air Force 8		1758	400-500	700-900
French Foreign Legion in Action 8		2095	200-250	350-450
French Infantry of the Line, pre-war 8		141	200-250	300-400
Gentlemen at Arms 9		2149	500-700	1000-1200
Gordon Highlanders 6		77	80-100	150-175
Gov. General's Horse Guards of Canada 5		1631	125-150	175-225
Greek Evzones 8		196	90-120	150-175
Grenadier Guards 8		312	90-120	150-200
Her Majesty's State Coach 10		1470	200-300	350-450
Indian Army Service Corps 8		1893	120-140	175-225
Italian Cavalry 5		165	400-500	800-1000
Italian Infantry 8		166	250-300	400-500
Japanese Infantry, pre-war 8		134	400-500	700-900
Knight w/ Mace, mounted, Agincourt 1		1569	90-120	150-175
Knight w/ Sword, mounted, Agincourt 1		1660	110-130	150-175
Knights of Agincourt on Foot 4		1664	125-150	200-250
Life Guards 5		400	100-125	150-200
Mexican Infantry (Rurales), pre-war 8		186	300-350	500-700
Mounted Band of the Life Guards 12		101	300-350	400-500
Mounted Band of the Royal Scots Greys 7		1720	250-350	500-600
Mountain Gun of the Royal Artillery 12		28	200-250	300-400
New Zealand Infantry 8		1542	100-125	175-225
Papal Swiss Guards 9		2022	150-175	250-300
Pipe Band of the Black Watch 20		2109	600-800	1000-1200
Prussian Hussars 5		153	200-300	350-450
Regiment Louw Wepener 8		1900	500-600	900-1200

	NO. FIG.	SET NO.	UNBOXED	BOXED
Rodeo Set	12	2043	$ 200-300	$ 400-500
Royal Company of Archers	13	2079	200-300	400-500
Royal Engineers Pontoon Sect., Rev. Order	7	203	500-600	800-1000
Royal Horse Artillery at the Gallop	13	39	300-400	400-600
Royal Marine Light Infantry	8	97	500-600	900-1200
Royal Marines	7	2071	90-120	150-200
Royal Marines in Tropical Dress	8	1619	500-700	900-1200
Royal Navy Landing Party	11	79	200-250	300-400
Royal Scots Greys, pre-war	5	32	125-150	200-250
Royal Welch Fusiliers	8	74	80-100	150-200
Russian Infantry	8	133	175-225	300-400
Seaforth Highlanders	17	2062	300-350	500-600
Somersetshire Light Infantry	8	17	125-150	200-250
South Australian Lancers	5	49	350-450	700-900
Standard Bearer, mounted, Agincourt	1	1662	100-125	150-175
State Open Road Landau	10	9402	300-350	400-450
U.S. Cavalry	8	228	90-120	150-175
U.S. Marine Corps	8	228	90-120	150-200
U.S. Marine Corps Band in Summer Dress	25	2112	1000-1500	2000-2500
U.S. Marine Corps Color Guard	4	2101	150-200	200-300
U.S. Military Band "The Snowdrops"	12	1301	300-400	500-700
U.S. Navy Blue Jackets, pre-war	8	230	125-150	200-250
U.S. Navy White Jackets	8	1253	100-125	150-200
Uruguayan Cavalry	4	220	100-125	200-250
Venezuelan Infantry	15	2105	175-225	300-350
Waterloo Period Line Infantry, 1815	9	1518	150-200	200-300
West India Regiment	9	19	200-300	400-500
West Point Cadets	8	299	90-120	150-175
Yeomen of the Guard	9	1257	125-150	200-250
Zulu Warriors of Africa	8	147	100-125	150-200

Mignot

	NO. FIG.	UNBOXED	BOXED
Departmental Guard of Paris (1810)	12	$ 175-225	$ 200-300
English First Life Guards (1815)	6	125-150	200-250
Fr. Napoleonic Marines of the Guard	12	150-175	250-300
Israeli Infantry in Action	12	200-250	250-350
Legion of the North (1806)	12	175-225	250-300
Monaco Royal Guards	12	175-225	200-300
Mounted Band of the Polish Lancers (1810)	11	400-500	700-900
Vistula Legion (1808)	12	150-175	250-300

Courtenay

	SINGLE FIG.
Boy Prince Philip "Le Hardi," position 21	$ 300-350
Erle of Armagnac, position Z-5	350-450
Erle of Rochechouaret, position 12	350-450
Fallen Knight, Sieur de la Rosay, position 13	350-450
French Knight Matthew de Rouvray, position 7	350-450
King John of France, position 3	350-450
Lord de Chargny, position 6	600-800

SINGLE FIG.

Lord de la Warr, position 15 .... $ 300-350
Pierre, Sieur de Loigny, position 15 600-800
Sieur de Basentian, position 14 300-400
Sieur John de Landis, position Z-2 300-400
Sir Bartholomew Burghursh, position H-1 500-700
Sir John de Clinton, position H-2 600-800
Sir John Treffrey, position X-2 350-450
Sir Nele Loring, K.G., position H-6 700-900
Sir Thomas Warenhale, position H-3 600-800
Sir William Thorne, position 16 300-400

Trolls

Do you have trolls? You may have them or remember them from the mid-1960s to the early 1970s. Although trolls have existed in folklore for hundreds of years, the trolls we are addressing trace their roots to the late 1950s in Denmark, when Thomas Dam made a troll for his daughter. By the mid-1960s Dam produced and exported the dolls with crazy hair and scrunched up faces. They were a sensation which, in turn, created a troll-collecting frenzy and competition for Dam from Scandia House (they later joined forces) and Uneeda Doll Company, who called their trolls "Wishniks." There were also lower-quality imitators. The following listing focuses on Dam and Wishniks. In the 1990s another wave of troll mania hit, introducing trolls to a younger generation. After their burst of success, the Dam toys were not available in the United States for many years. They are now marketed here as Norfins. Wishniks never really left the scene, with its company repackaging and releasing trolls over the years. Dam Trolls were the standard of the troll world, just as their successors, Norfins, are today. The troll market also boasts Russ Trolls, Magic Trolls, and Treasure Trolls, and again a host of lower-quality imitators.

The following are just a few of the thousands of trolls produced. Since trolls are still manufactured and identification is an art rather than a science, do some research. Compare new and old, high quality and cheap imitators. The Dam Animals, some of the most widely sought trolls, were recast from the original molds by Norfin in 1990. They were limited to a run of 500, sold for $50 and comprise the large horse, the large cow, the large elephant, and the lion. Since the edition was so limited, it probably will have little or no effect on the price of the originals. Dam trolls may bear a variety of "Dam" markings, and Wishniks may bear the double horseshoe mark or "Uneeda Wishnik" or "Uneeda Dolls."

The prices below are based on items in excellent to mint condition with original clothing, accessories, and tags. Packaging is not as important as in other areas but it always adds value and desirability. Permanent marks and stains on the trolls themselves, as well as damaged hair and clothes, adversely affect value. Clothing and accessories are an important factor in determining value. Some trolls were sold without clothes, therefore clothes aren't really an issue. Many times trolls are redressed or missing part of their original ensemble. Replacement clothes may add some value, but crisp original clothes with original accessories are the trolls most sought after by collectors. The following descriptions list what is currently known as outfits and accessories for the specific troll.

For further information see *Troll Identification and Price Guide* by Debra Clark, Hobby House, Inc., Cumberland, MD, 1993, and *Collector's Guide to Trolls*, by Pat Petersen, Collector Books, Paducah, KY, 1994. See also troll monthly, *Trolling Along*, 585 Washington St., Whitman, MA 02382

	LOW	HIGH
Astronaut, w/ helmet/spacesuit, Dam, ht. 7"	$ 60	$ 90
Black Girl, Dam, ht. 12"	300	425
Boy in Raincoat Bank, w/ pants and cap, Dam, ht. 7"	40	70
Boy Bank, purple and white outfit, Dam, ht. 7"	35	45
Car, log-shaped, Irwin	70	100
Cow, limited edition, Dam, ht. 7"	60	80
Cow, small, Dam, ht. 3"	30	50
Cow, w/ bell, Dam, ht. 6"	120	200
Cowboy, w/ guns and hat, Wishnik, ht. 5.5"	12	18
Cowboy Bank, w/ hat, six shooters, kerchief, shirt, and pants, Dam, ht. 7"	50	70
Doctor, in 2-piece uniform, w/ hat and stethoscope, Dam, ht. 3"	15	25
Donkey, Dam, ht. 3"	30	40
Donkey, w/ jointed head, Dam, ht. 9"	120	200
Double-Nik, 2-headed troll, Wishnik, ht. 4"	50	70

	LOW	HIGH
Elephant, blue, w/ cap, bow tie and saddle blanket, Japan, ht. 4"	$ 22	$ 32
Elephant, Dam, ht. 3"	34	42
Elephant, Dam, ht. 6"	140	220
Giraffe, Dam, ht. 11.5"	90	140
Girl in Raincoat Bank, w/ pants and cap, Dam, ht. 7"	40	70
Girl Bank, purple and white outfit, Dam, ht. 7"	35	45
Here Comes the Judge "Laugh In" Troll, in printed black smock, Wishnik, ht. 6"	40	50
Horse, Dam, ht. 3"	30	55
Hula-Nik, w/ skirt, Wishnik, ht. 5"	25	35
Hunt-Nik, w/ rifle, pants and checked flannel shirt, Wishnik, ht. 3"	25	35
Iggy-Normous, in cave man outfit w/ tag, Dam, ht. 12"	100	160
Iggy-Normous, in sailor costume, tag, Dam, ht. 12"	120	190
Indian (Girl) Bank, w/ headband, feather, belt, and wrap, Dam, ht. 7"	50	70
It's a Dam Dam World book, by Hal Goodman and Larry Klein	10	15
Lamp, featuring a 5.5" troll on wooden base, Wishnik, ht. 18"	80	100
Lion, Dam, ht. 5"	80	120
Monkey, R. Shekter, ht. 3.5"	25	35
Mouse, Dam, ht. 5"	60	85
Nurse, uniform, hat, and shoes, Scandia House, ht. 3"	15	25
Outa Sight, groovies series, w/ rhinestone eyes and outfits printed w/ various sayings, Wishnik, ht. 3"	18	25
Pirate (Boy) Bank, w/ striped shirt, 1 earring, pants, belt, and eye patch, Dam, ht. 7"	50	75
Pirate (Girl) Bank, striped shirt, 2 earrings, pants, belt, vest and hat, Dam, ht. 7"	50	75
Playboy Bunny, including tail, tie, ears, and cuffs, Dam, ht. 5.5"	40	50
Playboy Bunny, including tail, tie, ears, and cuffs, Scandia House, ht. 3"	20	30
Rock-Nik, black and red outfit w/ attached guitar, Hong Kong, ht. 6"	20	30
Santa, Dam, ht. 12"	175	225
Sock-It-to-Me, troll w/ large white eyes, dressed in smock w/ "Laugh-In" expressions, Wishnik, ht. 6"	50	60
Superman, in man of steel costume w/ cape, Wishnik, ht. 5.5"	50	70
Tartan Girl, Dam, ht. 12"	125	175
Troll Cave Carrying Case, Standard Plastics, ht. 9.5"	30	40
Troll w/ Tail and Jointed Head, Dam, ht. 6.5"	150	220
Turtle, molded green shell, Dam, ht. 3"	175	225
Viking, w/ molded plastic hat, 1-piece outfit w/ belt and red wrist tag, Dam, ht. 6.5"	120	160

Viewmaster

Visitors to the 1939 World's Fair were treated to many spectacular new inventions, including the Viewmaster, which was introduced there by Sawyer. The invention of Harry Gruber, Viewmaster produced reels for the war effort. Pre-1945 single reels were either dark blue with a gold sticker or blue and tan. These early reels command a premium price among collectors. After the war, Sawyer did numerous travel sites and National Parks reels. In 1952 they purchased their competitor, Tru-Vue, thereby acquiring the licensing rights to Disney productions. Some of the most sought after reel packs are those depicting classic TV shows and cartoons from the 1950s and 1960s. There is a lot of cross-over collecting from the television memorabilia field. The firm stopped selling three-packs in 1980 but are still in business. Having been owned by five different companies, including Sawyer and GAF, they are now owned by Tyco. Collectors love the frozen-time aspect of Viewmaster, this century's stereoscope.

The prices below are based on items in near mint to mint condition, which means no damage to the reels or package, including all flaps (4). If the package states that instructions are enclosed they should be there. Blister packs should display virtually no signs of wear. We removed "The" in several titles for ease of use. All those listed are three-packs except those that specify *1R* (one reel), or *BP* (Blister pack). Dates are approximate and the number of each pack is listed after the date.

Above, left to right: Bugs Bunny, Big Top Bunny, Talking Viewmaster, $5-$7; Wizard of Oz, Talking Viewmaster, $8-$10. Right: World's Fair (B760), $20-$25. — Item courtesy of Stephen Kiss.

	LOW	HIGH
Addams Family, 1965	$ 80	$ 100
Batman-Catwoman, 1966, B492	20	45
Beverly Hillbillies, 1963, B570	20	40
Bonanza, 1965, B471	25	35
Brave Eagle, 1956, B466	25	35
Bryce Canyon, 1955, A346	8	10
Bugs Bunny and Elmer Fudd, 1R, 1951, 800	6	8
California State Tour, 1950, A170	18	22
Daniel Boone, 1965, B479	25	35
Dark Shadows, 1968, B503	70	90
Death Valley, 1950, A203	8	12
Deputy Dawg, 1962, B519	28	36
Desert Wildflowers, 1956, 985-A	4	6
Dr. Who, BP, 1975, Bd214	60	90
Flipper, 1966, B485	20	25
Flying Nun, 1966, B495	25	35
Gene Autry 1R, 1950, 950	12	15
Goldilocks and the Three Bears, 1R, 1946, FT6	7	9
Grand Canyon, 1950, A361	7	9
Green Hornet, 1966, B	90	130
Jack and the Beanstalk, 1R, 1951, FT3	6	9
Land of the Giants, 1975, B494	40	65
Laugh-In, 1969, B497	25	35
Little Black Sambo, 1R, 1948, FT8	18	26
Lone Ranger, 1956, B465	25	35
Long Island, 1957, 57-A	3	5
Lost in Space, 1965, B482	80	100
Man From U.N.C.L.E., 1966, B484	45	60
Mission Impossible, 1967, B505	20	30
Mod Squad, 1969, B478	20	30
Monkees, 1967, B493	45	55
Munsters, 1964, B481	80	120
New York World's Fair, 1964, A671	25	35
Planet of the Apes, B507	30	40
Popeye, 1962, B516	12	18
Queen Elizabeth Visits Canada/USA, 1957, B925	15	20
Roy Rogers 1R, 1955, 945	10	15
Secret Squirrel and Atom Ant, 1966, B535	25	35
Sequoia National Park, 1954, 117	6	8
Six Million Dollar Man, 1974, B559	10	15
Star Trek TV Series, 1968, B499	40	60
Tarzan Rescues Cheetah, 1R, 1950, 975	5	7
Thunderbirds, 1965, B453	50	70
Time Tunnel, 1966, B491	50	70
Tom and Jerry Cat Trapper, 1R, 1951, 810	6	9
Voyage to the Bottom of the Sea, 1966, B483	40	50
Welcome Back Kotter, 1977, J19	15	20
Wild Bill Hickok, 1959, B473	30	40
Wizard of Oz, 1957, FT45abc	30	40
Woody Woodpecker, 1955, B522	20	25
Yellowstone National Park, 1948, A361	5	7
Zorro, 1958, B469	40	50

Tramp Art

This section was written by Helaine Fendelman and Jonathan Taylor. It is excerpted from their forthcoming book on Tramp Art, to be published in cooperation with the Museum of American Folk Art, New York City.

Tramp Art combined thin pieces of found wood that were shaped, edge-carved and layered most often in geometric patterns to create three-dimensional objects which were usually utilitarian in nature. While cigar box wood was by far the most popular material, wooden packing crates for soap, fruit, starch and others were also used. While most Tramp Art was produced between the 1870s and the 1940s and was once thought to be strictly a product of tramps and itinerant wanderers, it has been shown to have been most popular as a home craft. Evidence indicates that tramps and hobos did indeed make some Tramp Art but the bulk of what is found today is from the hands of home craftsmen whiling away evening hours. Boxes and frames are the most common because they were the easiest to make and the most useful. Small jewelry and dresser-top boxes and sewing boxes are also prevalent. Not as common, but still plentiful, are wall pockets, wall boxes, comb cases and pieces of doll-sized furniture. Rarer are religious artifacts such as altars, crosses and crèches. Full sized pieces of furniture are even more unusual. But the rarest are the fanciful wooden creations, such as the "Statue of Liberty" lamp, and other whimsical work.

Dimensions are given as height by width by depth.

Left to right: Church, footed box, "Statue of Liberty Lamp," pedestal box; see descriptions in listings. —Photo courtesy of Fendelman/Taylor.

	LOW	HIGH
Bedroom Set, made by black man, queen size bed, 2 dressers similar but of different pattern w/ mirrors, vanity, picture frame w/picture of maker	$ 25,000	$ 35,000
Candlesticks, pr., simple straight shafts w/ layers on bottom and top, ea. 10" x 4"	300	350
Church, w/ 6 drawers, steeple-faced on all sides and arrow weathervanes, 32" x 16.5" x 7.5"	1500	2000
Doll's Bed, minimal layering and simple unfinished design, 16" x 33" x 17"	200	300
Double Pedestal Box, unfinished simple pyramidal design a classic Tramp Art form, 8.5" x 12" x 8"	175	250
Double Star Mirror Frame, looks like 2 stars overlapping, an exceptional frame w/great depth and 3 dimensionality, 20" x 25.5" x 5"	1500	2000
Eiffel Tower, a wonderfully whimsical construction w/ tons of detail work in 3 sections, 96" x 40" x 40"	15,000	18,000
Floor Lamp, octagon shade w/clear glass on top of a column w/3 step-downs covered in light and dark layers to accentuate the pattern, 70" x 18.5" x 18.5"	2500	3500
Footed Box, in gold paint, simple yet interesting example of a lift-top box, 6.5" x 10" x 6"	100	200
Jewelry Box, mirror, polychrome in dark colors w/ lift top and 3 drawers, 10" x 13" x 8.5"	250	350
Lift-Top Desk, ornately carved inside and out w/ many carved cubbyholes, 46" x 42" x 25"	4500	5500
Mirrored Comb Case, w/ 4 elk, 2 kissing wings, clover, flowers, mirror hearts, 3 drawers and 3 pockets, dated 1931, 27" x 15" x 15"	850	1000
Pedestal Box, 3 tiered, w/ 2 outriggers, 25" x 24" x 13"	1500	2500
Picture Frame, large, w/ 38 layers on the interior and 10 layers on the exterior, 57" x 47" x 8.5"	2500	3500
Pier Mirror Frame, characterized by a formal quality rarely seen in Tramp Art, long dark lines w/ fine carving and bevelled mirror, 84" x 36" x 10"	2500	3500
Polychrome Box (Germany), w/ polychrome interior, 6.5" x 12" x 6.25"	250	350
Polychrome Planter, w/bold carving and packing crate wood painted in deep greens to red and yellow, 28.5" x 16" x 16"	1000	1200
Polychrome Sewing Box, bright colors and an over-stuffed sense of construction, 12.5" x 10" x 10"	850	1000
Small Dresser, w/ mirror, nice geometric carving, 8 drawers, inlaid tile top and 2 boxes built into top, 36" x 23" x 11"	1500	1800
"Statue of Liberty Lamp," delicate yet simple carving and Liberty's crown's spikes make this a wonderfully whimsical lamp, 36" x 19.5" x 4"	1000	1200
Table Lamp, nicely proportioned geometric patterning, 23" x 8.5" x 8.5"	350	550
Tall Clock Case, heavily carved and layered, 71" x 19" x 12"	5000	6000

Transportation Collectibles
Automobiles

The antique car market is coming back. Cars from the sixties and early seventies show increased prices even for ordinary models. Flashy cars from the late fifties are extremely popular, especially those with big fins. However the cars of the eighties, even the high end models, have yet to see a return on investment for their buyers.

The cars listed in this selection are given in six categories: A) salvageable only for parts, B) restorable, C) working order, but deteriorated, D) very good, drivable original or good amateur restoration, E) fine, well-restored or well-maintained original with minimal wear, F) excellent, professional quality restoration or perfect original.

For further information, see *Special Interest Autos* and *Hemmings Motor News*. Another good guide is *The Standard Guide to Cars and Prices*, edited by James T. Lenzke and Ken Buttolph, published by Krause Publications.

American Motors Corporation

	A	B	C	D	E	F
1958						
American Super	$ 200	$ 600	$ 900	$ 2200	$ 3900	$ 5500
1962						
Ambassador	150	350	800	1500	3000	4500
1965						
Classic	150	300	750	1400	3000	4000
1967						
Rebel	150	250	750	1250	2500	3700
1969						
Rambler	150	300	750	1250	2700	4000
1972						
Hornet SST	150	400	750	1350	2700	4000
1974						
Matador	150	300	750	1350	2700	4000
1977						
Gremlin	150	359	750	1250	2500	3500
1980						
Concord	150	350	750	1250	2500	3500
1983						
Alliance	150	350	750	1250	2500	3500

Buick

	A	B	C	D	E	F
1919						
Sedan	650	2000	3200	6500	10,000	14,500
1921						
Sedan	450	1300	2200	4200	8000	10,000
1923						
Sedan	450	850	1600	2600	6200	7900
1924						
Sedan	550	1300	2200	4300	7400	9500
1926						
Sedan	550	1300	2300	4300	6500	11,000
1928						
Sedan	550	1500	2700	4400	8000	11,500

	A	B	C	D	E	F
1930						
Sedan .... $ 550	$ 1600	$ 2700	$ 5400	$ 9500	$ 12,500
1932						
Sedan 800	2100	3200	6300	11,500	16,500
1934						
Sedan 750	1850	3100	4600	9300	12,500
1936						
Limited Series Sedan 725	2250	3750	7500	12,400	18,500
1938						
Limited Series Sedan 850	2600	4200	8300	14,500	21,000
1940						
Limited Sedan 1100	2700	4750	10,500	16,750	25,000
1942						
Century 550	1550	2750	5400	9500	13,500
1946						
Roadmaster Convertible 1000	3500	6000	12,000	20,000	30,000
1950						
Roadmaster Convertible 1000	3000	5000	10,000	18,000	25,000
1953						
Roadmaster Convertible 1000	3000	5000	10,000	18,000	25,000
1955						
Roadmaster Sedan 450	1250	2200	4400	7500	11,000
1957						
Convertible 1000	3200	5000	10,000	18,000	25,000
1959						
Sedan 450	750	1250	2600	4200	6600
1961						
Sedan 225	650	1100	2200	4200	6600
1963						
Sedan 200	600	1000	2200	4000	6300
1965						
Sedan 200	500	900	2000	3500	5200
1967						
Sedan 150	350	750	1500	3000	4200
1969						
Sedan 150	300	700	1200	2500	4000
1971						
Skylark 125	250	700	1200	2300	3500
1973						
Electra 150	400	750	1400	3100	4700
1974						
Electra 150	400	750	1500	3000	4200
1975						
Regal 125	200	650	1100	2400	3400
1976						
Skylark 125	250	700	1200	2500	3500
1977						
Century 125	250	700	1200	2500	3600
1978						
Riviera 200	600	1000	2000	4000	6000
1979						
LeSabre 150	300	750	1400	3000	4000

1980	A	B	C	D	E	F
Riviera .... $ 250	$ 700	$ 1100	$ 2300	$ 4500	$ 6500
1983						
Skylark 200	350	750	1500	3000	4200
1985						
LeSabre 225	650	1000	2200	4200	5700
1986						
Somerset 235	525	850	200	3500	5300

Cadillac

1903						
Model "A" 1400	4200	7500	15,000	25,000	35,000
1907						
Model "G" 1250	3700	6200	12,000	20,000	30,000
1912						
Model 30 1500	4500	8000	16,000	26,000	38,000
1918						
Type 57 1300	4200	7500	13,000	23,000	38,000
1927						
Fleetwood 1700	5500	9500	18,000	33,000	45,000
1930						
Series 353, sedan 1700	5500	9000	18,000	32,000	46,000
1931						
Series 370, sedan 7000	20,000	32,000	65,000	110,000	150,000
1935						
Fisher body 2200	6300	10,500	19,000	33,000	48,000
1940						
Series 62, convertible 2100	7250	11,400	22,500	38,500	55,000
1948						
Sedan 900	2700	4300	8750	15,500	22,000
1954						
Series 75 1100	3600	5750	11,500	21,000	29,000
1960						
DeVille, sedan 625	1850	3100	6200	10,500	16,000
1963						
El Dorado 1000	3000	5000	10,000	17,500	25,000
1968						
Calais 400	1000	1500	3000	6000	9500
1973						
DeVille 325	750	1100	2300	4400	6500
1977						
Fleetwood 350	700	1200	2300	4700	6700
1980						
Seville 350	700	1100	2400	4700	6500
1985						
DeVille 225	750	1100	2500	4750	7000

Chevrolet

1913						
Classic 1200	3500	6000	12,000	20,000	30,000
1918						
Series "D" 850	2600	4300	8500	15,000	22,000

	A	B	C	D	E	F
1923						
Sedan	$ 350	$ 750	$ 1250	$ 2400	$ 5000	$ 7000
1927						
Model "AA," sedan	350	750	1250	2400	5000	7000
1931						
Model "AE," sedan	500	1500	2500	5000	9000	13,000
1934						
Master Coupe	400	1200	2000	4000	7000	10,000
1937						
Master Sedan	450	1000	1600	3300	6300	9000
1939						
Master 85, station wagon	900	2700	4500	9000	16,000	23,000
1942						
Fleetwood	500	1000	1700	3600	6500	9500
1946						
Stylemaster	350	850	1500	3100	6000	8500
1951						
Styleline Special	350	800	1300	2600	5500	7700
1955						
Bel Air, sedan	400	1300	2300	4500	8000	11,000
1958						
Biscayne	225	600	1000	2300	4200	6300
1961						
Impala, sedan	250	700	1250	2500	4500	6500
1966						
Chevelle	175	400	750	1600	3200	4500
1969						
Impala, station wagon	175	350	750	1500	3000	4000
1970						
Camaro	500	1500	3000	5000	8500	12,000
1974						
Nova	175	300	750	1400	2800	4000
1977						
Monza	150	250	700	1200	2500	3500
1981						
Citation	150	250	700	1200	2500	3500
1985						
Celebrity	175	450	750	1500	3000	4000

Chrysler

	A	B	C	D	E	F
1925						
Town Car	500	1600	2750	5100	9250	13,500
1928						
Series 62, sedan	350	800	1450	2750	5600	8300
1931						
Series 77, coupe	550	1750	2800	5750	10,000	15,000
1933						
Royal Sedan	550	1600	2750	5600	9500	14,000
1939						
New Yorker	550	1700	3000	5800	10,000	14,500
1942						
Saratoga, coupe	400	1300	2200	4500	8000	12,500

	A	B	C	D	E	F
1949						
Crown Imperial	$ 500	$ 1600	$ 2700	$ 5500	$ 10,000	$ 14,000
1953						
New Yorker	400	1000	1700	3000	6000	10,000
1957						
LeBaron	500	1600	2700	5500	10,000	14,000
1960						
Saratoga, sedan	200	600	1000	2500	4000	6000
1964						
Newport, sedan	150	275	750	1200	2750	4000
1968						
New Yorker	250	600	1000	2000	4000	5500
1972						
Imperial	250	600	1000	2200	4200	6200
1977						
LeBaron	175	300	700	1300	2800	4300
1981						
Newport	175	400	750	1600	3000	4700
1985						
Laser	175	400	750	1600	3000	4600

Corvette

	A	B	C	D	E	F
1955						
Convertible	1200	4500	7500	15,000	25,000	37,000
1963						
Sport Coupe	1000	3000	5000	10,000	20,000	26,000
1972						
Convertible	700	2000	3000	7500	13,000	18,000
1986						
Corvette	500	1600	2600	5500	9000	14,000

Desoto

	A	B	C	D	E	F
1930						
Model "CK" Coupe	450	1000	1750	3700	6750	9700
1934						
Airflow	450	1250	2000	4500	7500	11,000
1940						
S7 Deluxe	350	800	1250	2500	5000	7500
1946						
S11, sedan	200	700	1200	2400	4500	6500
1953						
Powermaster 6	300	700	1200	2400	4700	7000
1958						
Firesweep, sedan	200	600	1000	2300	4000	5700
1960						
Adventurer, sedan	200	600	1000	2000	3700	5500

Dodge

	A	B	C	D	E	F
1917						
Coupe	400	950	1750	3250	6500	9500
1923						
Sedan	250	550	950	2100	3600	5200

1930	A	B	C	D	E	F
Series "DD," sedan	$ 350	$ 800	$ 1500	$ 3000	$ 6000	$ 8000
1934						
Convertible	1200	3500	6000	12,500	22,000	31,000
1939						
Coupe	450	1000	1600	3500	6500	9000
1946						
Coupe	350	800	1300	2500	5500	8300
1953						
Coronet	350	750	1200	2500	5000	7500
1957						
Royal Sedan	250	600	1000	2500	4000	6000
1960						
Seneca	250	550	1000	2200	3750	5750
1963						
Polara Sedan	200	500	900	2000	3500	5000
1966						
Monoco	250	600	1000	2200	4000	5500
1969						
Monoco	175	400	800	1800	3500	4750
1973						
Colt	150	250	600	1000	2200	3500
1976						
Crestwood	150	300	700	1200	2500	4000
1980						
Diplomat	175	300	700	1200	2600	4000
1984						
Aries	175	350	750	1500	3100	4200
1986						
Lancer	225	500	1000	2000	3500	5200

Ford

1909						
Model "T"	750	2200	4000	8000	13,500	21,000
1914						
Model "T"	500	1500	2700	5250	9500	15,5000
1926						
Model "T," coupe	400	800	1400	2750	6500	8000
1930						
Model "A," station wagon	600	1800	3000	6000	10,000	14,500
1935						
Model 48, sedan	500	1100	1700	3500	6500	10,000
1939						
Model 922, coupe	400	1300	2300	4500	8000	11,000
1942						
Model 21A, sedan	400	800	1200	2750	5300	7500
1952						
Sedan	225	500	850	2000	4000	5500
1956						
Mainline	250	600	1000	2200	4000	6000
1958						
Thunderbird, convertible	1000	3000	5500	12,000	20,000	30,000

1962	A	B	C	D	E	F
Galaxy 500, sedan	$ 200	$ 500	$ 900	$ 2000	$ 3500	$ 5000
1964						
Sprint	400	1300	2300	4600	8000	11,000
1967						
Futura....................................	200	500	800	2000	3500	5000
1970						
Cobra	600	2200	3500	7000	12,000	18,000
1972						
Maverick	150	300	700	1200	2500	4500
1974						
LTD.......................................	150	350	750	1300	2700	4500
1978						
Thunderbird	250	650	1000	2000	4000	6000
1982						
Escort....................................	150	300	700	1200	2600	3800
1985						
Tempo	125	250	700	1200	2500	3500

Hudson

1911						
Model 33	1000	3000	5000	10,000	18,000	25,000
1915						
Sedan	700	2000	3500	7000	12,000	17,500
1920						
Coupe....................................	450	1100	1700	3700	7000	10,000
1924						
Sedan	350	800	1500	2850	6100	8200
1928						
Coupe....................................	450	1500	2500	5000	9200	12,500
1931						
Sedan	500	1000	1700	3500	6500	10,000
1934						
Challenger, coupe	350	750	1300	2500	5500	8000
1937						
Custom 6, sedan	350	750	1200	2400	5000	7000
1939						
Big Boy..................................	600	1750	3000	6000	10,000	15,000
1942						
Traveller	400	1000	1700	3500	6500	9000
1950						
Pacemaker, sedan	500	1250	2100	4000	7000	10,000
1953						
Hornet, sedan	400	1250	2100	4000	7000	10,000
1957						
Sedan	450	1250	2100	4000	7000	10,000

Lincoln

1920						
Sedan	1300	4500	7500	15,000	25,000	35,000
1923						
Towncar	2000	5000	9000	17,500	31,000	46,000

	A	B	C	D	E	F
1926						
Convertible .... $ 2000	$ 7000	$ 11,000	$ 22,500	$ 40,000	$ 55,000
1929						
Town, sedan 1250	4000	6200	12,500	24,000	35,000
1932						
Model "KB," sedan 1500	4700	7500	15,000	25,000	37,500
1936						
Zephyr 900	3000	5000	10,000	18,000	25,000
1939						
Series "K," sedan 1500	5000	8000	15,000	27,000	38,000
1942						
Zephyr, sedan 500	1600	2700	5500	9500	14,000
1950						
Cosmopolitan, sedan 425	1350	2250	4500	8000	11,000
1956						
Capri, sedan 500	1500	2500	5000	9000	13,000
1960						
Premier, sedan 500	1000	1700	3500	6500	10,000
1965						
Lincoln Continental, sedan ... 400	800	1500	3000	6000	8500
1967						
Lincoln Continental, sedan ... 400	800	1500	3000	6000	8500
1970						
Continental Mark III 500	1500	2500	5000	8500	12,500
1975						
Mark IV 500	1000	1700	3500	6500	9000
1980						
Versailles 200	600	900	2000	4000	6000
1983						
Towncar 350	700	1200	2400	5000	7000

Mercury

	A	B	C	D	E	F
1940						
Sedan 500	1000	1700	3500	6500	9500
1942						
Coupe 400	1300	2200	4500	8000	11,000
1946						
Sedan 350	800	1500	3000	6000	8500
1951						
Mercury, convertible 750	2500	4000	8000	14,000	20,000
1955						
Montclaire, sedan 350	900	1500	3000	6000	8500
1957						
Monterey, sedan 300	700	1200	2400	4500	6500
1959						
Parklane, convertible 900	2500	4000	8500	14,000	22,000
1961						
Meteor 600 200	500	900	2000	3700	5500
1962						
Comet 200	600	1000	2200	4000	5500
1964						
Comet, sedan 200	500	900	2000	3500	5000

	A	B	C	D	E	F
1967						
Capri	$ 200	$ 600	$ 1000	$ 2200	$ 4000	$ 5500
1970						
Marquis	150	400	750	1500	3000	4500
1974						
Cougar	200	600	1000	2300	4000	5700
1975						
Bobcat	125	250	700	1200	2600	3700
1977						
Marquis	150	300	750	1400	3000	4200
1979						
Zephyr	150	300	700	1200	2500	3700
1981						
Grand Marquis	200	500	900	2000	3400	5000

Nash

	A	B	C	D	E	F
1918						
Sedan	500	1000	1700	3500	6750	10,000
1920						
Coupe.....................................	400	900	1750	3200	6500	9500
1922						
Sedan	350	750	1250	2600	5250	7500
1925						
Light 6, sedan	225	500	1000	2400	4500	6000
1928						
Standard, sedan	350	750	1200	2400	5000	7500
1930						
Single, coupe	350	700	1300	2750	5000	8000
1933						
Ambassador, coupe	500	1500	2500	5000	9000	12,500
1935						
Lafayette	350	750	1300	2500	5000	7000
1937						
Ambassador, sedan	350	750	1200	2300	5000	6500
1940						
Ambassador, coupe	350	750	1400	2700	5500	8500
1942						
Ambassador 600, sedan	350	700	1200	2400	5000	7000
1946						
600	200	500	900	2000	3500	5000
1949						
600 Custom............................	200	600	1000	2200	4000	6000
1952						
Statesman, sedan	200	600	1000	2300	4000	6000
1955						
Rambler	200	600	1000	2200	4000	6000
1957						
Rambler	200	600	1000	2000	3700	6000

Oldsmobile

	A	B	C	D	E	F
1905						
Touring Car..........................	1200	4000	6500	13,000	23,000	35,000

	A	B	C	D	E	F
1909						
Model "Z" .... $ 1500	$ 5000	$ 8000	$ 17,000	$ 30,000	$ 40,000
1912						
Defender 1350	4200	7500	14,500	25,000	35,000
1915						
Model 42 1100	3250	5000	11,000	18,000	26,000
1917						
Model 45 1100	3250	5000	11,000	20,000	27,000
1920						
Model 37-B 400	1300	2300	4500	8250	12,500
1923						
Model 43-A, sedan 500	1200	1800	4000	7250	10,000
1926						
Coupe 350	900	1500	3000	6000	9000
1929						
Sedan 400	800	1500	3000	6000	8500
1931						
Model F-31 500	1500	2500	5000	8000	12,000
1934						
Model F-34 400	1000	1700	3500	6500	9500
1938						
Model F-38 450	1000	1600	3400	6000	9000
1940						
Series 70 400	1000	1600	3500	6500	9000
1942						
Station wagon 1000	3000	5500	12,000	20,000	30,000
1946						
Special Series, convertible ... 800	2500	4000	8500	15,000	21,000
1949						
Futuramic 76, sedan 200	600	1000	2000	4000	6000
1953						
Classic, convertible 1000	3500	6000	12,000	20,000	30,000
1956						
Series 98, sedan 400	1300	2200	4500	7500	10,000
1959						
Series 88, sedan 400	750	1300	2500	5000	8000
1961						
Dynamic 88 300	700	1000	2200	4200	6000
1963						
Jetfire 350	1000	1600	3300	6000	9000
1965						
Cutlass 350	800	1200	2500	5000	8000
1967						
Vista Cruiser 200	600	1000	2000	3700	5500
1969						
Delta 88 350	750	1200	2500	5000	7000
1971						
Delta 98 200	500	900	1800	3600	5000
1973						
Cutlass 175	300	700	1200	2700	4000
1976						
Omega 150	200	650	1200	2400	3500

	A	B	C	D	E	F
1979						
Delta 88 .... $ 175	$ 300	$ 750	$ 1300	$ 2700	$ 4000
1981						
Delta 98 200	500	900	2000	3500	5000
1983						
Cutlass 150	450	750	1700	3300	5000

Packard

	A	B	C	D	E	F
1904						
Model "L" 2500	7500	13,500	26,000	46,000	66,000
1912						
Model "NE" 1500	4500	7000	15,000	25,000	37,500
1915						
Model 5-48 2000	6000	10,500	19,000	32,000	45,000
1921						
Single 6 1200	4000	7000	12,000	21,000	35,000
1924						
Single 8, sedan 1100	3300	6000	11,000	20,000	30,000
1928						
Standard, coupe 1100	3000	5000	10,000	17,000	25,000
1931						
Model 833, coupe 2000	7000	11,000	23,000	40,000	57,000
1932						
Model 900, sedan 1000	3500	6000	11,000	20,000	30,000
1933						
Model 10005, sedan 2000	6000	10,000	20,000	40,000	55,000
1935						
Series 1204, coupe 2000	7000	11,000	23,000	40,000	57,000
1937						
Model 120-C, sedan 1000	3500	6000	12,000	20,000	30,000
1939						
Model 1801, convertible 2000	5000	10,000	18,000	31,000	45,000
1942						
Series 2001 700	2200	3600	7500	13,000	20,000
1946						
Clipper 500	1500	2500	5000	9000	14,000
1949						
Super Eight, sedan 1000	2000	4000	7000	13,000	20,000
1953						
Patrician 700	2000	3500	7000	12,000	18,000
1956						
Caribbean 1200	4000	6000	11,000	18,000	27,000

Pierce-Arrow

	A	B	C	D	E	F
1903						
One cylinder 1250	4100	6750	12,500	25,000	36,000
1906						
Great Arrow 3000	8000	13,000	30,000	50,000	70,000
1909						
Model 40 2000	6000	10,000	20,000	34,000	50,000
1913						
Model 66A 3000	10,000	16,000	30,000	50,000	75,000

	A	B	C	D	E	F
1915						
Model 66A .... $ 3000	$ 10,000	$ 17,000	$ 35,000	$ 60,000	$ 80,000
1919						
Model 48-B-5 2500	8000	13,000	27,000	44,000	62,000
1923						
Model 38, sedan 1200	4000	6500	13,000	24,000	35,000
1926						
Model 33, touring car 2000	7000	12,000	23,000	39,000	54,000
1929						
Model 126 3000	9000	15,000	30,000	47,000	67,000
1933						
Model 1236 1700	5000	9000	18,000	30,000	45,000
1936						
Salon 12 2000	5000	9000	18,000	30,000	42,000
1938						
Pierce-Arrow 8 1500	4000	7000	15,000	25,000	40,000

Plymouth

	A	B	C	D	E	F
1928						
Model "Q," sedan 350	800	1500	3000	6000	8500
1933						
PC, coupe 400	1000	1600	3300	6000	9000
1937						
Roadking 300	700	1200	2500	4500	6500
1940						
P9 Roadking 300	700	1200	2300	4500	7000
1946						
P15 Deluxe, sedan 225	600	1000	2200	4000	5700
1949						
Deluxe 300	800	1200	2500	5000	8000
1952						
Cambridge 300	700	1300	2500	5000	7500
1955						
Plaza 200	700	1200	2500	4500	6200
1959						
Suburban 225	500	900	2000	3700	5500
1962						
Belvedere 225	500	900	2000	3500	5000
1966						
Valiant 225	400	800	1500	3000	4500
1969						
GTX 700	2300	3500	7300	11,000	17,000
1971						
Regent Wagon 175	300	700	1300	2700	4000
1974						
Fury 175	250	700	1200	3000	4000
1976						
Volare 175	300	750	1500	3000	4000
1978						
Arrow 175	300	700	1200	2500	3750
1981						
Reliant 175	300	700	1300	2600	3800

ANTIQUES AND COLLECTIBLES

	A	B	C	D	E	F
1984						
Tourismo	$ 175	$ 400	$ 750	$ 1700	$ 3000	$ 4500

Pontiac

	A	B	C	D	E	F
1926						
Model 6-27	400	1000	1550	3100	6250	9500
1929						
Model 6-29A, sedan	400	800	1200	2400	5000	7500
1932						
Model 302, sedan	400	1300	2200	4300	7500	11,000
1936						
Silver Streak, sedan	400	750	1250	2500	5000	7000
1939						
Special Series, coupe	400	1000	1600	3200	6000	9000
1941						
Torpedo	350	800	1400	2600	5500	8000
1946						
Torpedo, coupe	300	700	1200	2400	5000	7000
1949						
Chieftain	300	700	1200	2400	4800	7000
1953						
Chieftain	400	900	1500	2500	5000	8000
1957						
Chieftain	300	700	1200	2500	5000	7000
1960						
Safari	200	700	1100	2300	4500	6500
1963						
Catalina	300	700	1000	2300	4000	6500
1966						
GTO	500	1500	3000	5000	10,000	15,000
1968						
Tempest	300	700	1000	2000	3700	6000
1970						
GTO	800	2300	4000	8000	14,000	20,000
1972						
Bonneville	200	500	800	1700	3200	4800
1975						
LeMans	100	200	700	1200	2400	3500
1978						
Sunbird	100	200	600	1100	2200	3000
1980						
Phoenix	150	300	700	1200	2700	4000
1984						
Parisienne	150	450	800	1800	3300	5000

Studebaker

	A	B	C	D	E	F
1905						
Model 9502	1000	3000	5000	10,000	18,500	27,500
1909						
Model "B"	1200	4000	7500	14,500	25,000	35,000
1914						
Model 1 SC	900	2700	4500	9000	16,000	23,000

	A	B	C	D	E	F
1918						
Series 19, sedan	$ 350	$ 900	$ 1500	$ 3000	$ 6000	$ 8500
1923						
Model EK, coupe	525	1200	2100	4250	7500	11,000
1927						
Commander, coupe	525	1150	1850	3500	7500	11,000
1930						
Dictator, sedan	500	1000	1700	3500	6500	11,000
1933						
Commander, coupe	600	2000	3000	6000	11,000	16,000
1936						
President 8, sedan	400	1300	2200	4300	7500	12,000
1939						
Model "G," sedan	350	750	1200	2400	5000	7300
1942						
Commander Skyway	500	1500	2500	5000	9000	13,000
1947						
Champion, sedan	200	600	1000	2300	4400	6500
1951						
Champion Deluxe	300	650	1200	2500	4500	6500
1956						
Champion	150	400	750	1750	3350	4750
1959						
Lark Regal	200	600	900	2000	3500	5500
1965						
Daytona	200	500	900	2000	3750	5600

Aviation

Aviation memorabilia ranges from the era of early flight—in balloons, bi-planes, and airships—through the period of early scheduled commercial transcontinental Clipper flight and World War II combat flight, to the present day of commercial jets and space exploration. As with other commercial enterprises, those offering service to the public distinguished their particular operations by the type and design of objects used in passenger service, such as dining china and silver, in-flight giveaways, and flight badges and uniforms. These items, together with passenger time tables, promotional photographs of aircraft, early calendars, airport related objects (e.g. ashstands with metal aircraft figures, restaurant and earlier souvenir china), and crash fragments are highly collectible. Our consultants for this area are Christopher Wolfe and Scott Townsend of Townsend, Wolfe & Company, they are listed in the back of this book.

	LOW	AVG.	HIGH
Beverage Glass, National Airlines, Sun King side logo .... $ 10		$ 14	$ 18
Blanket, TWA passenger service, 1960s 25		30	40
Calendar, TWA, 1943, monthly photos, w/ wartime route suspensions .. 30		40	50
Cap, junior flight captain, TWA, ca. 1965 15		20	25
Casserole Dish, Piedmont Airlines, back-marked in china mold, white/ ivory 4		7	10
Coaster, Delta Airlines, multi-color printed metal, ca. 1960 4		5	6
Coffee Cup and Saucer, Newark Airport profile w/ DC-3, 1944 45		55	65
Coffee Cup and Saucer, United Airlines, silver logo on white china, ca. 1970 25		35	45
Coffee Mug, Northeast Airlines "Yellowbird" 15		20	25
Coffee Pot, Pan Am, silver plate, side winged logo, large size, 1940 . 175		200	225
Coffee Pot, TWA silver plate, large size, side marked logo, ca 1960 ... 55		75	100
Cordial Glass, United Airlines, stemmed, side logo, ca. 1960 10		15	20
Creamer, Western Airlines, individual size 8		10	15
Cup and Saucer, TWA "Royal Ambassador," solid red stripe w/ gold crest 10		15	20
Demitasse Cup and Saucer, Pan Am, PAA/wing side logo 100		125	150
Dinner Plate, President Eisenhower, on front: "DDE" w/ colored flowers, gold; reverse includes: "The Presidential Plane / Colum- bine / May 1956," Syracuse 450		530	615
Food Warmer, American Airlines, silver plate w/ wood handle, ca. 1950 40		55	65.
Juice Cup, United Airlines, side logo, light blue plastic, 1935-1960s 4		8	12
Knife, dinner, American Airlines "Flagship," ca. 1935 20		25	35
Letter Opener, souvenir of airship "Akron," Duralum, late 1920s 70		85	100
Miniature Liquor Bottle, North Central Airlines, full and w/ tax stamp, ca. 1968 20		25	30
Miniature Liquor Bottle Series, KLM, Dutch buildings, Delft, w/ blue detailing, 1970s, unopened and w/ tax stamp, each 30		40	50
Model, "Graf Zeppelin," cloth around frame, w/ stand, 1928 175		195	225
Model, travel agent, TWA Constellation, metal, ca. 1953 1200		1500	2000
Plate, oval, Eastern Airlines, white w/ silver pinstripe, 9.375" x 6.5" .. 10		14	16
Playing Cards, Piedmont Airlines, 1984 4		6	10
Playing Cards, TWA Collector Series, 1966 6		10	14
Playing Cards, TWA Stratoliner, ca. 1940 100		150	175
Postcard, "Graf Zeppelin," 1936, unused 20		30	45
Salad Dish, Delta Airlines, white w/ red and blue side logo, ABCO, maker 3		5	7

Graf Zeppelin Model, 1928, length 24", height 13", $175-$225. —Photo courtesy of Townsend, Wolfe & Company.

	LOW	AVG.	HIGH
Service Plate, Air America (C.I.A.), 10.525", platinum logo, Noritaki, ca 1970s	$ 150	$ 175	$ 200
Service Plate, National Aviation Club, 10.525", top logo, legend on reverse	25	35	45
Shot Glass, Southern Airways, 10th-year anniversary	40	50	60
Souvenir Mug, Lufthansa, side-marked	10	15	18
Tea or Breakfast Plate, Airship "Hindenburg," dia. 7.5", on board service, 1936	1200	1400	1700
Tea or Breakfast Plate, Airship "Graf Zeppelin," on-board service, 1928	1200	1400	1600
Teapot, Northwest Airlines, silver plate	55	70	90
Timetable, American Airlines, ca. 1950	12	16	20
Timetable, Continental Airlines, ca. 1935	35	40	50
Timetable, Eastern Airlines, 1948	10	15	20
Timetable, Pan American Airways, 1937	25	35	45
Timetable, TWA, ca. 1946	12	17	20

Below left to right: Broadside advertising mail rates on the Graf Zeppelin, 13.75" x 10.25", $165-$240; TWA calender, 1942, 24" x 16.5" (open), $30-$50. —Photos courtesy of Townsend, Wolfe & Company.

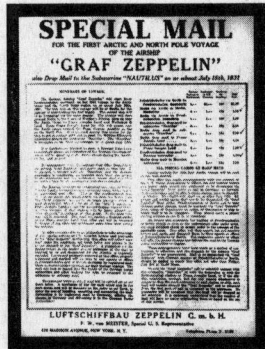

Bicycles

Bicycles fall into four categories. Running machines, known as hobby-horses, the precursor to the bicycle, were introduced in 1817 and do not have pedals. The addition of cranks and pedals to the front driving wheel in the early 1860s created the first bicycle, generally known as the velocipede or boneshaker. Enlarging the front driving wheel for greater speed created the high wheel bicycle (c. 1870-1892). The rear wheel size was reduced to save weight and facilitate mounting the machine. As these bicycles were quite dangerous to ride, safer versions called high wheel safeties were developed. High wheel tricycles fall into this category and became quite popular in the 1880s. Finally, the bicycle with chain drive to the rear wheel was introduced in 1885, and began entering the market around 1888. These were called, quite simply, safeties. The addition of pneumatic tires in the early 1890s lead to the "golden age" of the bicycle. In the 1920s, bicycles began assuming a motorized look, with tanks and balloon tires. In the 1930s they became streamlined. Balloon-tire bicycles are known as Classic bicycles.

As with automobiles, prices for bicycles vary widely depending on model, year, and condition. This is particularly true with balloon-tire bicycles. Therefore, the prices below only represent a general average, though in each case values represent machines that are complete with original parts. Girls' models usually fetch a lower price than boys' bicycles, being that men are usually doing the buying! Also note that the following listing is in chronological order, according to the year each type of bicycle was introduced.

Velocipede (boneshaker), c. 1869.

	LOW	AVG.	HIGH
Running Machine (Hobby-Horse) 1818 & later	$ 7000	$ 15,000	$ 25,000
Velocipede (Boneshaker), c. 1869	2500	5000	6500
Velocipede Tricycle, c. 1869	6000	9000	12,000
Child's Velocipede Tricycle, c. 1869-1875	1000	1500	1800
Child's Velocipede Horse Tricycle, c. 1869	1500	2000	3000
High Wheel Bicycle, c. 1879	3500	5500	6500
High Wheel Bicycle, c. 1883-1891	2500	4000	5000
High Wheel Safety, c. 1880-1890: Star	6000	7500	9000
Eagle, Facile, Kangaroo, 'Xtraordinary, etc.	8500	12,000	14,000
Child's High Wheeler, c. 1885	1800	2500	3500
High Wheel Tricycle, c. 1885	8000	14,000	16,000
Child's High Wheel tricycle, c. 1885	4500	5500	6500
Tandem/Sociable Adult Tricycle, c. 1885	15,000	17,000	20,000

	LOW	AVG.	HIGH
Solid Tire Safety, often w/ spring forks, c. 1888-1892 (a spring-fork Victor sold at auction in 1996 for $14,750) .... $ 4000		$ 5500	$ 8500
Pneumatic Safety, standard model, c. 1896 250		550	750
Pneumatic Safety, tandem, c. 1896 1,200		1800	2400
Chainless bicycle, c. 1900 800		1200	1600
Safety, c. 1910 150		300	450
Balloon-Tire Bicycles (Classic), after 1920			
Schwinn Aerocycle, Elgin Bluebird, Roadmaster, (a Western Flyer Shelby Speedline Airflow sold at auction in 1996 for $5000) 6000		8000	10,000
Schwinn Black Phantom 800		2000	3500
Silver King 500		1500	3000
Character Bikes: Donald Duck, Hopalong Cassidy, etc. 1500		2500	4000
Bowden Spacelander 4000		6000	8000
Schwinn Sting Ray 100		350	850

Above: Victor Safety Bicycle (solid tires, spring forks, c. 1889), a spring-fork Victor sold at auction in 1996 for $14,750. Right: High wheel tricycle, c. 1885.

Carriages

	LOW	AVG.	HIGH
Buckboard, with box frame wooden wheels	$ 600	$ 1050	$ 1650
Dog Cart	2300	4030	6300
Farm Wagon, painted	600	1050	1650
Four Wheel Runabout, Rattermann & Luth, late 19th century	750	1300	2000
Freight Wagon, w/ sideboards, spring body, and 2 seats	1250	2000	3500
Full Horse Runabout, late 19th century	9250	16,000	25,000
Hearse, black painted	3500	6000	9500
Kimball Bros. Co. Carriage	1200	2100	3300
Phaeton Ladies Carriage, Italian, mid-19th century	2350	4000	6500
Pony Cart, Wilform Viceroy, for 2 ponies, early 20th century	250	440	700
Pony Runabout	675	1200	1850
Portland Cutter	875	1500	2406
Railroad Wagon	275	480	750
Runabout, single horse, restored	6300	11,000	17325
Sleigh	400	700	1100
Stagecoach, three-quarter size	11,000	19,000	30,000
Sulky, Houghton Sulky Co., light wood	600	1050	1650
Sulky, light wood and upholstered spring seat	500	880	1375
Surrey, 3 seats, fringe on top	15,250	26,000	42,000
Surrey, Means and Hopkins, restored	2100	3600	5775
Surrey, undercut, black painted	1700	3000	4750
Victoria, restored	4500	8000	12,000
Vis a Vis, new	5500	9500	15,000
Wagon, Weber, original paint	2700	4750	7500

Railroad Memorabilia

Before airplanes and the interstate highway system, railroads crisscrossed the United States. The building of the transcontinental railroad in the post-Civil War era ignited the growth of heavy industry; with the establishment of regular shipping routes for agricultural and industrial products, mail and passenger service, and uniform time zones, the United States was on its way toward becoming the nation as we know it today.

Collectors of railroad memorabilia may concentrate on lines that once ran through their hometowns or region. This fosters regional differences of what people collect and how much they pay for items. Other collectors concentrate on a topic, or type of item, regardless of region. The following prices are for items in excellent condition.

Beware of items with no identifying marks or provenance. Some railroads used stock china patterns, with or without custom top or back marks. If special markings are documented to a railroad, authentic pieces are most often required to have these markings. Some railroad china patterns have been reproduced, but not all are clearly and permanently labeled as such. "Fantasy pieces" are china patterns never made for any railroad but are produced with actual railroad logos and colors. These are often produced in smaller, less common shapes, such as butter pats, teapots, and mustard pots. Be particularly wary of over-glaze decoration, as the manufacturers of originals ordinarily applied all but metallic coloring under the glaze. If a part of the glaze over an important part of a piece is more yellowed than the glaze overall, it could indicate applied fraudulent additions.

Fake glass signs purportedly used in railroad stations recently appeared on the market, as well as expertly manufactured, fraudulent badges. Very small rubber stamps with a railroad logo, which may or may not be authentic, have been offered for sale, and could of course have been illegitimately used. Finally, beware of items with interchangeable parts. Lanterns, in particular, have appeared as marriages of fraudulent intent.

Our consultants for this area are Christopher Wolfe and Scott Townsend of Townsend, Wolfe & Company, they are listed in the back of this book.

Platter, Pullman, "Indian Tree" pattern; Service plate, Missouri Pacific, 1949-1961. —Photo courtesy of Townsend, Wolfe & Company.

	LOW	AVG.	HIGH
Ashtray, Atchison, Topeka & Santa Fe, "Turquoise Room," 3.875" x 4.75" .... $ 20	$ 20	$ 25	$ 30
Ashtray, Chesapeake & Ohio, "Chessie" (cat) logo, Syracuse 65	65	75	90
Ashtray, w/ match safe and stylized striking surface, Plant System, 1920s 200	200	235	280
Badge, conductor's hat badge, New York Central 30	30	40	50
Badge, Philadelphia & Reading RR Railway Police, round w/ cut out star, 1910 50	50	65	80
Badge, Penn Central RR Police. 40	40	45	50
Badge, porter's hat badge, Illinois Central 105	105	125	135

	LOW	AVG.	HIGH
Badge, Missouri Pacific RR, Conductor's cap badge, copper color ..	$ 125	$ 150	$ 160
Bowl, grapefruit, Alaska RR, logo Mt. McKinley, dia. 6.5", Shenango ..	210	260	300
Bread tray, Pere Marquette, silver plate, oval 8.5", Wallace, side, back marked	135	160	180
Brochure, Colorado Midland Ry, 12 panels w/ map, 1897	90	100	110
Bud Vase, Great Northern, ht. 6.75", silver plate, IS, 1948, side and back marked	160	200	225
Butter Pat, Atlantic Coast Line, "Flora of the South," 3.5", back marked, Buffalo	85	100	110
Butter Pat, Boston & Albany, dia. 3.875", silver plate, R&B, back marked	45	55	65
Calendar, Chicago & Illinois Midland RR, "Goin' Fishin," 26" x 30", 1949	40	50	60
Calendar, Great Northern, Glacier National Park, 1932	25	35	45
Calendar, Pennsylvania RR, "Dynamic Progress," 1955, complete pad ...	65	80	90
Celery Tray, Erie RR, "Susquehana" pattern, top and back marked, 10"	160	175	200
Champagne Goblet, Chicago, Milwaukee, St. Paul & Pacific, 3.525" ht., side logo	55	65	80
Chocolate Pot, Atchison, Topeka & Santa Fe, "California Poppy," no back mark	100	130	150
Chocolate Pot, as above w/ Santa Fe back mark	250	325	375
Coffee Cup and Saucer, Canadian National, side and back marked, Syracuse	25	40	50
Coffee Cup and Saucer, Union Pacific RR, "Challenger" pattern, Syracuse	70	85	95
Coffee pot, Chicago, Minneapolis & St. Paul, 1 pt., silver plate, back marked, IS, c. 1910	175	210	230
Demitasse cup and saucer, Baltimore & Ohio, "Centenary" (blue), Lamberton	70	90	115
Dinner Plate, Pullman "Calumet," name in black w/ pinstripes, 9.75", OP Co	150	175	210
Divided Plate, Fred Harvey's orange "FH" monogram in circle at top, "Southwest" pattern, 10.5", 3 sections, Liberty, maker	90	110	125
Egg Cup, double, Missouri Pacific "Eagle," side logo only, Syracuse ...	75	85	100
Finger Bowl, Pennsylvania RR, silver plate, pierced sides, side and back marked, IS	125	150	165
Fork, Gulf, Mobile & Ohio, "Broadway" pattern, top marked	20	25	29
Fork, dinner, Grand Trunk, "Westfield" pattern, top marked	24	30	36
High Ball Glass, Long Island Railroad, "Dashing Commuter" side mark, 14 oz.	20	25	35
Ladle, cream, New York Central, "Century" pattern, back marked	20	23	27
Lantern, Chicago, Cleveland, Cincinnati & St. Louis, Handlan clear cast globe	80	90	100
Menu, Great Northern, dinner, 1932	15	20	25
Oiler, long spout, New York Central, embossed mark	20	30	40
Pass, Canadian Northern, 1904	30	35	40
Pass, Central RR of New Jersey, 1892	45	50	55
Pass, Lehigh Valley RR, 1889, ornate	50	55	60
Pass, Kansas City, Ft. Scott & Memphis RR, 1900	30	35	40
Pass, New York, Chicago & St. Louis, 1927	7	10	15

Tip tray, Canadian Intercolonial Railway; Chocolate pot, Atchison, Topeka & Santa Fe, "California Poppy". —Photo courtesy of Townsend, Wolfe & Company.

	LOW	AVG.	HIGH
Pass, Rio Grande Southern RR, 1944	$ 10	$ 12	$ 15
Pass, Wabash RR, 1894	20	25	30
Plate, Hotel Pennsylvania, 8", top logo, blue and gold, OP Co	15	20	25
Plate, Union Pacific "Winged Streamliner," 6.5", top and back marked, Syracuse	25	35	40
Platter, "Liberty Bell" logo, Lehigh Valley Traction Co, 13.5" oval, American	700	800	925
Platter, Pullman, "Indian Tree" pattern, w/ center design, 8.25", Buffalo	75	85	100
Playing Cards, Florida East Coast, diesel through orange grove, boxed	25	30	35
Service Plate, Missouri Pacific, center diesel w/ state capitols on border, 1949-1961, always back marked, Syracuse	275	315	350
Soup Plate, New York Central, "Vanderbilt" pattern (gold pinstripe, green and orange geometric border), 9.25", back marked, Buffalo	95	105	120
Spoon, bouillon, Union Pacific, "Westfield" pattern, IS	20	24	27
Spoon, grapefruit, Southern RR, "Century" pattern, IS	21	24	29
Spoon, iced tea, Erie RR, "Grecian" pattern, top marked, IS	23	28	33
Stock Certificate, Colorado Midland, preferred stock, 1898	55	65	75
Stock Certificate, Western Maryland RR, 1917	16	23	28
Sugar Bowl and Lid, Chicago & Eastern Illinois, 8 oz., silver plate, R&B, 1946	150	185	215
Sugar Tongs, Atlantic Coast Line, "Cromwell" pattern, side marked, IS	85	95	110
Teapot, Amtrak "National" pattern, Hall china	10	15	20
Teapot, Michigan Central, silver plate, 7 oz., Reed & Barton, back marked, c. 1917	195	225	265
Thermos, Pullman, ht. 9", silver-colored, side marked	50	75	85
Timetable, Ann Arbor RR and SS lines, w/ fold-out map, 1923	60	65	70
Timetable, Central New England Ry, broadside, 16" x 23", 1915	50	55	60
Timetable, Nashville, Chattanooga & St. Louis, ornate, 34 pages, 1914	35	40	50
Timetable, Reading RR, Philadelphia-Atlantic City, 1913, broadside 22" x 14"	40	60	75
Timetable, Southern Pacific, Sunset Route, 1891, 20 pages w/ map	60	65	70
Timetable, Wabash RR, Winter 1905	20	25	30
Tip Tray, Canadian Intercolonial Railway, litho w/ moose logo, dia. 5.5"	225	260	275
Tureen, w/ lid and attached liner, Chicago, Cincinnati, Chicago & St. Louis, silver plate, 1 pt., R&B, back marked, c. 1910	235	265	285
Water Glass, Union Pacific, ht. 4.25", white frosted band	12	15	19

Watches

Fine watches contain a varying number of jewels, usually synthetic ruby which is second in hardness only to diamond, within the movement mechanism to reduce friction and wear. They improve the accuracy of the watch and generally, the more valuable the watch.

We abbreviate "jewel" as "j" (e.g., 17j means 17 jewels). American pocket watch movements are described in standard sizes (abbreviated as "s" in this book), ranging from 20s to 0s, 00s, 000s, etc. The most common pocket watch size is 18s, or 1.766". Other popular sizes include 16s (1.7"), 12s (1.566"), 10s (1.5"), 0s (1.166"), and 000s (1.1").

For purposes of simplicity we have given three value levels: Low—rough, serviceable but needs repair or restoration. These watches are priced as needing a minimum of $100 in parts or repair. You must decide whether the cost to repair outweighs any possible profit. Average—normal to extended wear depending on age. Minor cost for parts or repair. High— in fine condition with minimum wear, needing only possible cosmetic touch-ups.

Numerous fakes are circulating on the open market including 24j examples of Illinois and Rockford watches as well as original Rolex and Piaget movements in bogus cases. As always, it pays to do your homework prior to any purchase. If it looks too good to be true, it probably is.

Our consultant for this section is Brett O'Connor, G.G., of Christie's Jewelry Dept. For further information, see *The Official Price Guide to Watches*, by Cooksey Shugart and Tom Engle, House of Collectibles, Random House, NY.

Pocket Watches and Wrist Watches

Pocket Watches

	LOW	AVG.	HIGH
American, 18s, Appleton, Tracy and Co., M#1877-1892	$ 50	$ 100	$ 150
American, 18s, P.S. Barlette, M#1857	200	300	400
American, 18s, Broadway, 7-11j	50	100	150
American, 18s, Crescent Street, 15j, M#1883	100	150	200
American, 18s, Samuel Curtis, 11-15j	2000	3000	4000
American, 18s, Wm. Ellory, M#1857	50	100	150
American, 18s, Export, 7-11j	50	100	150
American, 18s, Paragon, 15j	100	150	200
American, 18s, R.E. Robbins, 13j	100	150	200
American, 18s, Sol, 7-17j	50	100	150
American, 18s, Tourist, 7-11j	50	75	100
American, 16s, Premier, 9-17j	50	75	100
American, 16s, Repeater, 16j	2000	3000	4000
American, 16s, Riverside, 15-19j	50	100	150
American, 16s, 16j, Riverside Maximus	400	500	600
American, 16s, Royal, 15-17j	50	100	150
American, 0s, Royal, 16j	75	100	125
American, 0s, Seaside, 7-15j	100	150	200
Ansonia Clock Co.	40	55	70
Ansonia Sesqui-Centennial	250	300	350
Aurora Watch Co., 18s, 7-11j	100	150	200
Aurora Watch Co., 18s, 15j	200	300	400
California Watch Co., 18s, 11-15j	1000	1500	2000
Cornell Watch Co., 18s	300	450	600
Dudley Watch Co., Masons, 14s	3000	4000	5000
Dudley Watch Co., Masons, 12s	1500	2000	2500

	LOW	AVG.	HIGH
Elgin, 18s, Father Time, 17j	$ 50	$ 100	$ 150
Elgin, 18s, Father Time, 21j	150	175	200
Elgin, 18s, Overland, 17j	100	150	200
E.H. Flint, 18s, 4-7j, 18k	4000	5000	6000
Fredonia, 18s, 7-16j	150	250	350
Jonas G. Hall, 18s, 15j	1500	2000	2500
Hamilton, 18s, 15-21j	150	250	350
Hamilton, 16s, 16-17j	200	300	400
Hamilton, 12s, 17-19j	50	100	150
Hampden Watch Co., 18s, 15-18j	100	150	200
Hampden Watch Co., 16s, 7-15j	50	100	150
Hampden Watch Co., 12s, 7-15j	50	75	100
Hampden Watch Co., 000s, 7-15j	100	150	200
E. Howard and Co., N size (18), I-VIII, 15j	1000	2000	3000
E. Howard and Co., L size (18), V, 15j	1000	1250	1500
E. Howard Watch Co. , 12s, series 6-8	200	300	400
Illinois Watch Co., 18s, Allegheny 11j	50	100	150
Illinois Watch Co., 18s, Baltimore and Ohio RR Special	500	750	1000
Illinois Watch Co., 18s, Bunn, 15j	500	750	1000
Illinois Watch Co., 18s, Bunn Special, 21j	150	200	250
Illinois Watch Co., 18s, Columbia, 11j	75	125	175
Illinois Watch Co., 18s, Currier, 11j	75	125	175
Illinois Watch Co., 18s, Montgomery Ward, 17j	150	175	200
Illinois Watch Co., 18s, The National, 11j	75	100	125
Illinois Watch Co., 18s, Time King, 17-21j	150	225	300
Illinois Watch Co., 16s, Ariston, 11-15j	50	88	125
Illinois Watch Co., 16s, Ariston, 17-19j	150	225	300
Illinois Watch Co., 16s, Ariston, 23j	500	750	1000
Illinois Watch Co., 16s, Ben Franklin, 17-21j	300	450	600
Illinois Watch Co., 16s, Burlington, 15-17j	75	125	175
Illinois Watch Co., 16s, Dispatcher, 19j	50	100	150
Illinois Watch Co., 16s, Getty model, 17-21j	100	150	200
Illinois Watch Co., 16s, Great Northern Special, 17-21j	250	300	350
Illinois Watch Co., 16s, Lakeshore, 17j	100	150	200
Illinois Watch Co., 16s, Railroad King, 17j	200	250	300
Illinois Watch Co., 16s, Sangamo, 21j	150	200	250
Illinois Watch Co., 16s, Santa Fe Special, 17j	150	200	250
Illinois Watch Co., 14s, 7-21j	50	100	150
Illinois Watch Co., 4s, 7-15j	50	88	125
Illinois Watch Co., 0s, 201-204, 11-17j	75	112	150
Ingersoll, Dollar type, Buck	50	88	125
Ingersoll, Dollar type, Climax	40	58	75
Ingersoll, Dollar type, Colby	20	30	40
Ingersoll, Dollar type, Crown	20	30	40
Ingersoll, Dollar type, Defiance	30	45	60
Ingersoll, Dollar type, Ensign	30	40	50
Ingersoll, Dollar type, Escort	20	30	40
Ingersoll, Dollar type, Gotham	15	25	35
Ingersoll, Dollar type, Kelton	15	20	25
Ingersoll, Dollar type, Major	10	15	20
Ingersoll, Dollar type, Patrol	40	50	60

	LOW	AVG.	HIGH
Ingersoll, Dollar type, Pilgrim	$ 40	$ 50	$ 60
Ingersoll, Dollar type, Radiolite	30	40	50
Ingersoll, Dollar type, Saturday Post	150	200	250
Ingersoll, Dollar type, Solar	25	38	50
Ingersoll, Dollar type, Trump	40	50	60
Ingersoll, Dollar type, Uncle Sam	40	50	60
Ingersoll, Dollar type, G. Washington	150	200	250
Ingersoll, Dollar type, Winner	20	30	40
E. Ingraham Co., Autocrat	15	20	25
E. Ingraham Co., Baltimore	10	15	20
E. Ingraham Co., Clipper	20	30	40
E. Ingraham Co., Cub	15	20	25
E. Ingraham Co., Dot	15	20	25
E. Ingraham Co., Laddie	20	30	40
E. Ingraham Co., Overland	30	40	50
E. Ingraham Co., Pilot	30	45	60
E. Ingraham Co., Rex	15	20	25
E. Ingraham Co., St. Regis	15	20	25
E. Ingraham Co., Century	25	30	35
E. Ingraham Co., Sturdy	10	15	20
E. Ingraham Co., Top Notch	40	50	60
E. Ingraham Co., Trail Blazer	150	200	250
E. Ingraham Co., Viceroy	20	30	40
E. Ingraham Co., Zep	150	200	250
Kelly Watch Co., 16s, aluminum	50	100	150
Keystone Standard Watch Co., 18s, 7-15j	75	125	175
Knickerbocker Watch Co., 6-18s	50	75	100
Lancaster, 18s, Comet	150	175	200
Lancaster, Ben Franklin	250	300	350
Lancaster, Malvern	50	75	100
Lancaster, Radnor	100	150	200
Lancaster, Sidney	100	125	150
McIntyre Watch Co., 16s, 21-25j	5000	6000	7000
Melrose Watch Co., 18s, 7-15j	250	350	450
New England Watch Co., Alden	40	50	60
New England Watch Co., Columbian	20	25	30
New England Watch Co., Putnam	70	85	100
New England Watch Co., Tuxedo	20	30	40
Otay Watch Co., 15j	1200	1600	2000
Peoria Watch Co., 18s, 15j	200	300	400
Philadelphia Watch Co., 18s, 11j	150	200	250
Rockford, 18s, Belmont USA	200	250	300
Rockford, 18s, Dome model	150	200	250
Rockford, 18s, Ramsey, 11-15j	100	125	150
Rockford, 18s, 7j	50	100	150
Rockford, 18s, 13j	100	150	200
Rockford, 18s, #825	150	175	200
Rockford, 18s, #835	100	150	200
Rockford, 18s, #870	50	100	150
Rockford, 18s, #910	150	200	250
Rockford, 18s, #950	2000	3000	4000

	LOW	AVG.	HIGH
Rockford, 18s, #170	$ 50	$ 75	$ 100
Rockford, 16s, Peerless	75	100	125
Rockford, 16s, Prince of Wales	300	450	600
Rockford, 16s, 7j	100	150	200
Rockford, 16s, Winnebago	150	225	300
Rockford, 16s, #102	150	175	200
Rockford, 16s, #104	50	60	70
Rockford, 16s, #445	800	1000	1200
Rockford, 16s, #535	200	300	400
Rockford, 16s, #566	150	175	200
San Jose Watch Co., 16s	1500	2000	2500
South Bend, 18s, 15j	100	150	200
South Bend, 18s, Studebaker	200	300	400
South Bend, 18s, #309	75	100	125
South Bend, 18s, #333	100	125	150
South Bend, 18s, #344	300	400	500
South Bend, 18s, #355	1000	1250	1500
South Bend, 16s, 7-9j	50	100	150
South Bend, 16s, #207	50	100	150
South Bend, 16s, #211	50	100	150
South Bend, 16s, #280	100	125	150
South Bend, 16s, #290	200	250	300
South Bend, 16s, #294	300	400	500
South Bend, 12s, Chesterfield	50	100	150
South Bend, 12s, #407	30	45	60
South Bend, 12s, #419	150	175	200
Seth Thomas, 18s, Century	50	100	150
Seth Thomas, 18s, Eagle Series	50	100	150
Seth Thomas, 18s, Edgemere	50	100	150
Seth Thomas, 18s, Keywind	200	300	400
Seth Thomas, 18s, Maidenlane, 17-24j	1000	1500	2000
Seth Thomas, 18s, Henry Molineux	500	1000	1500
Seth Thomas, 18s, #33-#201	50	100	150
Seth Thomas, 18s, #245	1000	1250	1500
Seth Thomas, 18s, #281-382	150	200	250
Seth Thomas, 16s, Centennial	50	75	100
Seth Thomas, 16s, Locust	50	100	150
Seth Thomas, 16s, Republic	50	62	75
Seth Thomas, 16s, #25-336	50	100	150
Seth Thomas, 12s, Republic	50	60	70
Seth Thomas, 12s, #25-328	50	75	100
Seth Thomas, 0s, 7-17j	50	100	150
Trenton Watch Co., 18s, "M" #3-5	50	100	150
Trenton Watch Co., 16s, "M" #1-3	50	88	125
Trenton Watch Co., 12s, Fortuna	50	60	70
Trenton Watch Co., 6s, 7-15j	40	50	60
Trenton Watch Co., 0s, 7-15j	50	60	70
U.S. Watch Co., 18s, Wm. Alexander	200	300	400
U.S. Watch Co., 18s, F. Atherton, 15-17j	250	350	450
U.S. Watch Co., 18s, F. Atherton, 19j	600	900	1200
U.S. Watch Co., 18s, S. M. Beard	250	350	450

	LOW	AVG.	HIGH
U.S. Watch Co., 18s, Centennial Phila.	$ 2000	$ 2250	$ 2500
U.S. Watch Co., 18s, G. Channing	250	350	450
U.S. Watch Co., 18s, J.W. Deacon	200	300	400
U.S. Watch Co., 18s, Fellows	400	500	600
U.S. Watch Co., 18s, Asa Fuller	200	300	400
U.S. Watch Co., 18s, North Star	300	400	500
U.S. Watch Co., 18s, Penna. RR	2500	3000	3500
U.S. Watch Co., 18s, H. Randel	250	350	450
U.S. Watch Co., 18s, Edwin Rollo	200	300	400
U.S. Watch Co., 18s, Rural NY	200	300	400
U.S. Watch Co., 18s, F. Stratton	250	350	450
U.S. Watch Co., 18s, I. H. Wright	200	300	400
U.S. Watch Co., 16s, 15-19j	500	750	1000
U.S. Watch Co., 14s, 7-15j	250	350	450
U.S. Watch Co., 10s, 11-15j	100	200	300
Waterbury Watch Co., Series B-E	200	250	300
Waterbury Watch Co., Series G-H	200	275	350
Waterbury Watch Co., Series I-Z	75	112	150
Waterbury Watch Co., Oxford	50	75	100
Westclox, Boy Proof	40	50	60
Westclox, Bulls eye	15	20	25
Westclox, Country Gentleman	40	50	60
Westclox, Dax	10	15	20
Westclox, Everbrite	20	25	30
Westclox, Explorer	200	250	300
Westclox, Ideal	30	40	50
Westclox, Mark IV	40	50	60
Westclox, Maxim	30	40	50
Westclox, Mustang	40	50	60
Westclox, Smile	25	38	50
Westclox, Vote	25	38	50
Westclox, Zep	200	250	300

Left to right: Cartier "copy watch," a pirated design that looks deceptively like the real thing; genuine Longines, S.J. Brozèn, $200-$300.

Wrist Watches

	LOW	AVG.	HIGH
American Waltham, 17j, barrel-shaped dial, c. 1920, 14k	510	580	650
American Waltham, 17j, Cromwell	80	105	130
American Waltham, 17j, Oberlin	80	105	130
American Waltham, 17j	110	330	550
American Waltham, wandering minute, jumping hour, 2 windows, c. 1933	700	1000	1300
American Waltham, 17j, Stanhope	75	100	125

	LOW	AVG.	HIGH
American Waltham, Winfield	$ 75	$ 100	$ 125
American Waltham, Albright, 21j	100	125	150
American Waltham, 21j, Sheraton	125	150	175
American Waltham, 15j, protective grill, c. 1907	1300	1450	1600
American Waltham, 17j, w/ hackset stainless steel	50	62	75
American Waltham, 17j, curvex	200	450	700
American Waltham, 17j, triangular, Masonic symbols, c. 1950	1800	2250	2700
Angelus, 17j, c. 1943, 18k	750	950	1150
Angelus, same, 14k	400	500	600
Angelus, same, gold-filled	150	200	250
Angelus, 27j, quarter repeater, stainless steel	2700	2950	3200
Aramis, 15j, self-winding, c. 1933, stainless steel	600	750	900
Arbu, 17j, triple date, moon phase, 18k	800	1000	1200
Arbu, 17j, double cronog., stainless steel	200	300	400
Aristo, 17j, cronog., stainless steel	100	162	225
ARSA, 15-17j, moon phase, 18k	900	1050	1200
ARSA, same, stainless steel	300	350	400
Asprey, 16-17j, 9k	200	350	500
Asprey- 15j, duo-dial, 18k	1500	1850	2200
Audemars Piguet, 19j, tourbillon, sundial design, 18k	15,000	16,500	18,000
Audemars Piguet, 29j, repeater, c. 1907, 18k	110,000	120,000	130,000
Audemars Piguet, 36j, octaganal case, triple date, moon phase, 18k	5,000	18,500	22,000
Audemars Piguet, 18j, "Le Brassus," skeletonized, 18k	20,000	22,500	25,000
Audemars Piguet, 17-18j, other skeletonized models, 18k	5000	6750	8500
Audemars Piguet, 17-36j, modern	1200	2600	4000
Autorist, 15j, lug action	400	900	1400
Ball W. Co., 25j	375	438	500
Baume and Mercier, 17-18j, 14k or stainless steel	400	550	700
Baume and Mercier, 17-18j, 18k, triple chronog.	1200	1900	2600
Benrus, 15-18j, mystery diamond dial, 18k	500	600	700
Benrus, 15j, date, c.1948, stainless steel	50	60	70
Benrus, 15j, c.1950, 14k or gold-filled	100	175	250
Breguet, 21j, skeletonized, 18k, c&b	7000	7500	8000
Breguet, 17j, chronog., triple date, moon phase, stainless steel	8000	9000	10,000
Breguet, 17j, silver dial, Finn model, 18k	1200	1400	1600
Breitling, 17j, chronog., Chronomat, 18k	1500	1600	1700
Breitling, 17j, chronog., Chronomat, 18k, gold-filled	300	400	500
Breitling, 17j, chronog., Chronomat, 18k, stainless steel	250	350	450
Breitling, 17j, chronog., Navitimer, 18k	3000	3300	3600
Breitling, 17j, chronog., Navitimer, 18k, stainless steel	500	600	700
Bueche-Girod, 17j	600	700	800
Bulova, Accutron "spaceview," 14k	400	550	700
Bulova, Accutron "spaceview," 18k	600	700	800
Bulova, Accutron "spaceview," stainless steel	100	175	250
Bulova, diamond dial, rectangular, late '30s-early '40s	200	275	350
Bulova, 17j, duo-dial, c. 1935, stainless steel	300	350	400
Bulova, 17j, fancy bezel, 14k or gold-filled	100	200	300
Cartier American Tank, mechanical, large, 18k	1700	2800	4200
Cartier Cougar, ss, 32mm	350	650	1200
Cartier Diablo, quartz, large, 18k	900	1800	3000

	LOW	AVG.	HIGH
Cartier Pasha, ss, automatic diver	$ 700	$ 1100	$ 1700
Cartier Tank, quartz, large, 18k	750	1100	1800
Cartier Tank, gold plated, large	100	250	450
Cartier 21, gold plated, large, quartz	175	500	800
Chevrolet, 6j, in form of car radiator, c. 1927, silver	400	500	600
Cheopard, 18j, skeletonized, diamond dial and hands, 18k	4000	4500	5000
Clebar, 17j, chronog., stainless steel	75	88	100
Concord -17j, 14k	125	150	175
Cortebort, 15-17j, gold-filled or stainless steel	50	75	100
Cortebort, 17j, "sport," triple date, moon phase, 18k	1000	1200	1400
Corum, 17j, in form of Rolls Royce car radiator, 18k	1800	2000	2200
Corum, 17-21j, 18k	400	650	900
Croton, 17j, diamond bezel, 14k	700	800	900
Croton, 17j, chronog., stainless steel	100	125	150
Cyma, 17j, 18k	200	250	300
Cyma, 17j, 14k	175	212	250
Cyma, 17j, stainless steel	65	75	85
Daynite, 7j, 8-day movement, stainless steel	250	325	400
P. Ditisheim, 17j, "Solvil," diamond dial, platinum	700	1150	1600
Dome, 25j, triple dates, 18k	500	600	700
Doxa, 17j, chronog., triple dates, moon phase	1200	1400	1600
Doxa, 17j, center sec., w/ or without chronog., 14k or stainless steel	100	200	300
Ebel, 21j, chronog., perpetual calendar, 18k	7000	8000	9000
Ebel, 17-18j, chronog.	400	525	650
Ebel, 17j, slide open to wind, silver	200	250	300
Eberhard, 18j, split sec., chronog., 3 reg., 18k	7000	9000	11,000
Eberhard, 17j, tele-tachymeter, c1930, 18k	2600	3100	3600
Eberhard, 17j, chronog., stainless steel	400	500	600
Electra W. Co., 17j, chronog., silver	500	600	700
Elgin, 17j, rectangular, 14k	200	275	350
Elgin, 15-17j, rectangular, gold-filled	100	120	140
Elgin, 7j, gold-filled	60	130	200
Elgin, 7j, stainless steel	50	65	80
Elgin, 15j, "Official Boy Scout Model," stainless steel	100	138	175
Elgin, same, 7j, stainless steel	50	68	85
Elgin, 15j, round dial, aux. sec., silver	150	188	225
Lord Elgin, 17-21j, stepped case, fancy bezel, gold-filled	100	120	140
Enicar -17j, stainless steel	30	40	50
Eska, 17j, enamel dial, 18k	3100	3600	4100
Evans, 17j, chronog., 2 reg., c. 1940, 18k	300	400	500
Gallet, 15j, autowind, stainless	50	75	100
Gallet, 17j	200	300	400
Geneve, 15j, dual dial	300	350	400
Girard-Perragaux, 39j	300	350	400
Glycine- 17-18j	100	150	200
Grouen, 17j, curvex	200	300	400
Grouen, 17j, double dial	500	600	700
Grouen, 17j, autowind	300	400	500
E. Gubelin, 19j, 18k	400	500	600
E. Gubelin, 25j, triple date	3500	4500	5500
Hamilton, Altair	500	600	700

	LOW	AVG.	HIGH
Hamilton, Clearview	$ 100	$ 150	$ 200
Hamilton, Meteor	200	250	300
Hamilton, Pacer	150	200	250
Hamilton, Skip Jack	70	80	90
Hamilton, Vantage	150	200	250
Hamilton, Victor II	150	200	250
Hamilton, Ventura	1000	1500	2000
Hamilton, Otis, reversible	1200	1500	1800
Hamilton, Bolton	100	150	200
Hamilton, Brock	100	150	200
Hamilton, Dunkirk	300	400	500
Hamilton, Essex	100	150	200
Hamilton, Lee	100	150	200
Hamilton, Midas	300	350	400
Hamilton, Perry	100	125	150
Hamilton, Winthrop	200	250	300
Hamilton, Yorktown	150	175	200
Hampton, 15j	75	125	175
Harvard, 17j	50	100	150
Helbros, 17j	200	250	300
Hydepark, 17j, flip top	450	550	650
Illinois, 17j, Aviator	150	200	250
Illinois, Chieftain	300	400	500
Illinois, Console	300	400	500
Illinois, Jolly Roger	200	250	300
Illinois, Major	200	250	300
Illinois, Picadilly	500	600	700
Illinois, Pilot	150	200	250
Illinois, Speedway	200	250	300
Ingersoll, Radiolite dial	10	20	30
Ingersoll, Grill cover	50	60	70
Ingraham, 7j, Wristfit	5	10	15
International, 17j, 14k	500	750	1000
International, 17j, 18k	850	1050	1250
International, 36j, Da Vinci	6500	8000	9500
Jewel, 15j, dual dial	200	250	300
Kurth, 17j, Certina	30	40	50
Le Coultre, 17j	400	500	600
Le Coultre, 17j, Astronomic	1800	2300	2800
Le Coultre, 17j, Futurematic	700	1000	1200
Le Coultre, 17j, Reverso, 18k	6500	8000	9500
Le Coultre, 17j, Reverso, stainless	2000	2500	3000
Lemania, 17j, stainless	50	60	70
Lemania, 17j, chronog., 18k	600	750	900
Lip, stainless	200	300	400
Longines, 17j, Lindberg, 18k	40,000	45,000	50,000
Longines, 17j, Lindberg, silver	9000	10,000	11,000
Longines, 17j, Lindberg, nickel	6000	7500	9000
Longines, 17j, chronog.	500	1000	1500
Longines, 17j, diamond dial, 14k	400	500	600
Longines, 17j, flared	400	600	800

	LOW	AVG.	HIGH
Mappin, 15j, dual dial	$ 1000	$ 1250	$ 1500
Meylan, 27j, chronog.	800	1000	1200
Mido, 15j, car radiator	2000	2500	3000
Mido, 17j, multifort	150	200	250
Mido, 17j, chronog.	500	600	700
Minerva, 29j, repeater	45,000	55,000	65,000
Minerva, 17j, chronog., stainless	200	300	400
Minerva, 17j, autowind	70	85	100
Monarch, 7j	50	75	100
Movado, 15j	400	500	600
Movado, 17j, polypan, elongated	1500	2000	2500
Movado, Calendarmeto (center opening)	600	750	900
Movado, Ermeto Purse Watch, 17j, manual wind, c. 1940, 14KYG	700	1200	1700
Movado, Jump Hour, 15j, manual wind, 1930s, 14KYG	3200	3800	4200
Movado, Reverso Duo Dial, 17j, c. 1939, 18KYGW gold	24,000	27,000	30,000
U. Nardin, 17j, chronog.	2500	3500	4500
U. Nardin, 29j, Astrolabium	6500	8000	9500
National, 17j	50	100	150
New Haven, 7j	10	15	20
Omega, 17j, Seamaster, 14k	1500	2000	2500
Omega, 17j, Seamaster, stainless	800	1000	1200
Omega, 17j, Flightmaster	6000	7000	8000
Omega, 17j	300	400	500
Orvin, 17j	70	80	90
Patek Philippe, rectangle flared "hourglass," manual wind, c. 1955, 18KYG, bevelled crystal	6000	7000	8000
Patek Philippe, Asymetrical, 18j, c. 1958, 18KYG	20,000	23,000	25,000
Patek Philippe, Rectangular Platinum, 18j, c. 1920	2400	2700	3000
Patek Philippe, Ellipse, 18j, c. 1969, 18KYG	1500	1700	1900
Patek Philippe, Round, fancy lugs, 18j, c. 1954	6500	7200	8000
Piaget, 18j, $20 gold piece	2000	2250	2500
Piaget, 18j	400	550	700
Piaget Minute Repeater, 30j, c. 1950, 18 KYG	28,000	32,000	35,000
Piaget Polo, onyx dial, quartz, c. 1982, 18 KWGYG w/ bracelet	8000	10,000	13,000
Piaget, round stepped bezel automatic, c. 1960's, 18 KYG	350	500	750
Record, 17j, 4-dial chronog.	5000	6000	7000
Roamer, 17-23j	30	45	60
Rolex Air King, oyster, perp. ss	600	1100	1400
Rolex, 26j, Milgauss, stainless	400	500	600
Rolex, 17j, Daytona, 18k	10,000	12,500	15,000
Rolex, 17j, Daytona, stainless	2000	2250	2500
Rolex, 17j, Prince, dual dial, 18k	6000	7500	9000
Rolex, 17j, Prince, dual dial, silver	3000	4000	5000
Rolex, 17j, Prince, dual dial, stainless	2000	3000	4000
Rolex, 26j, Presidential, diamond dial	5000	7000	9000
Rolex, 26j, GMT-Master	4000	5000	6000
Rolex, 26j, Submariner, 18k	6000	7500	9000
Rolex, 26j, Submariner, stainless	600	800	1000
Rolex Yachtmaster, 18k	8300	10,500	13,000

	LOW	AVG.	HIGH
Rolex, 17j, Benvenuto Cellini	$ 1500	$ 2000	$ 2500
Rolex Thunderbird, oyster, perp., date juste, 18K	8000	8500	9000
Tiffany, 26j, repeater, automaton	8000	10,000	12,000
Tiffany, 15-21j	1000	1250	1500
Universal, 17j, chronog., 18k	2000	3000	4000
Universal, 17j, chronog., stainless	400	600	800
Vacheron, 17j, triple date	5000	7000	9000
Vacheron, 18j, 18k	2000	3000	4000
Vacheron & Constantin-Le Coutre, galaxy diamonds, c. 1950's, mysterious hands, 14KYG	1000	1200	1400
Vacheron & Constantin, round w/cloisonne enamel, map dial, 17j, c.1950, 18 KYG	16,000	18,000	30,000
Vacheron & Constantin Bombe, 14 KYG, 16j	2200	2600	3000
Zenith, 19j	100	125	150
Zenith, 17j, chronog., 18k	1000	1250	1500
Zenith, 36j, stainless	500	600	700

Swatch Watches

Swatch™ watches appeared out of nowhere (Switzerland) to become an instant hot collectible. Their brightly colored flashy plastic dials are seen on chic and trendy (and other) wrists around the world. Original bands are a must! Although occasionally showing up at auction, they're more often found on the Internet.

	LOW	AVG.	HIGH
100 Chrono-Olympics 1994 (special box)	$ 60	$ 85	$ 110
11 PM	80	100	130
Aritists Special (1995)—6 watches in lucite box	380	500	630
Beach Virgin	50	60	80
Boggie Mood	50	60	80
Bonaparte without special box	110	150	190
Cancun	20	30	40
Chicchirichi (special packaging)	40	50	60
Color Wheel	30	40	50
Coloured Love	110	150	190
Cool Fred	20	30	40
Crash!!	50	65	80
Crystal Suprise (special packaging)	110	140	180
Despiste	60	85	110
En Vauge	40	55	70
Engineer	70	90	110
Europe in Concert	90	120	150
First	60	85	110
Fitz N'Zip, signed by Kenny Scharf	50	60	80
For Your Heart Only (boxed)	60	85	110
Golden Jelly	190	250	310
Gulp!!	60	80	100
Hocus Pocus (special packaging)	320	420	530
Lady Limelight	190	250	310
Limelight II	210	275	340
Lots of Dots	110	140	180
Meooow	60	80	100
Monster Time Maxi	60	75	90
Monster Time, signed by Kenny Scharf	50	60	80
Photoshooting	60	80	100
Point of View (boxed)	70	90	110
Putti (boxed)	90	120	150
Putti (special packaging)	80	110	140
Ravenna	70	95	120
Sex-Teaze	70	95	120
Sir Limelight	230	300	380
Spark Vessel	50	60	80
Swatch pins	10	15	20
Top Class	20	30	40
Twelve Apostles	40	50	60
Veruschka (special packaging)	70	90	110
Yuri (special packaging)	40	50	60
Zapping (special packaging)	80	100	130

Weathervanes

The most valued weathervanes are those handmade of sheet copper before 1850. These are quite rare. In the 19th and early 20th centuries factory workers made weathervanes of copper hammered in iron molds. Important makers include Cushing and White of Waltham, MA, and the J. Howard Company of East Bridgewater, MA. Many reproductions have been made from original molds.

Values listed below are for fine examples for auction (A), semiantique reproduction (S-R), and retail (R).

Left to right: American large full-bodied copper Marino ram, length 36", $7000 at auction; A.L. Jewell & Co. full-bodied copper stag, height 25", $19,000 at auction.

	A	S-R	R
Arabian Charger, sheet-copper, 19th century, h. 20"	$ 800	$ 400	$ 2500
Automobile, copper, E.G. Washburn, c. 1912, w. 28"	12,000	2500	32,000
Bird, w/ raised leg, full-bodied copper, h. 38"	5500	1700	14,000
Cow, cast iron and copper, full bodied, w. 27"	3000	1000	8000
"Hambeltonian," full-bodied copper, A.L. Jewell, w. 29"	2100	1100	5600
"Hambeltonian" Horse, copper, W.A. Snow and Co., w. 26"	1000	550	2900
Horse, copper, gilt, J. Howard, mid-19th century, w. 20"	6000	1500	16,000
Horse, copper, full-bodied, late-19th century, w. 26"	1000	550	2700
Horse, Rochester Ironworks, cast iron, mid-19th century, w. 36"	9000	1500	24,000
Horse and Rider, red ptd. sheet iron, 19th century, w. 52"	1000	450	2700
Indian Archer, Berks Co., PA, ptd. sheet iron, c. 1880, h. 25"	850	450	2300
Jockey and Running Horse, copper, J.W. Fiske, #515, w. 30"	3600	1700	9000
Locomotive and tender, ptd. copper, gilt, c. 1890, w. 62"	22,000	3500	60,000
Mountain Boy, copper and gilt, on stand, w. 38"	1000	550	2700
Peafowl, full-bodied copper, old patina, h. 29"	4250	1000	11,400
Peafowl, gilt, copper, full-bodied, h. 18"	1250	650	3300
Pig, copper, gilt, full-bodied, L.W. Cushing, c. 1883, w. 36"	16,500	1500	44,000
Quill-form, copper, w. 36"	1700	935	4500
Rooster, full-bodied molded, ptd. highlights, h. 23"	1500	800	4000
Rooster, carved wood, gray paint, h. 12"	750	400	2000
Rooster, cast iron, h. 23"	1500	825	4050

	A	S-R	R
Rooster, full-bodied molded copper, h. 19"	$ 1700	$ 900	$ 4500
Rooster, full-bodied molded copper, h. 22"	1500	800	4000
Running Horse, gilt copper, green patina, w. 31"	2900	1600	7500
Running Horse and Jockey, full-bodied copper, w. 29"	3250	1750	8000
Running Horse, J. Harris and Son, full-bodied copper, w. 28" ..	850	468	2200
Schooner, w/ metal sails and rigging, ptd. , c. 1910, w. 35"	400	220	1000
Steeplechase Horse, copper, A.L. Jewell, c. 1860, w. 30"	13,000	2500	35,000
Steer, molded copper and cast iron, w. 29"	1300	715	3500
"The Smuggler," full-bodied copper, w. 29"	350	192	900
Uncle Sam w/ Donkey Cart, silhouette, sheet-metal, w. 33" ...	1900	1000	5000

*American monumental full-bodied copper cow,
length 46", $8250 at auction.*

Wood

While many types of wood items are highly sought-after collectibles, this section lists wooden kitchen utensils. Wooden utensils are most commonly made of maple. Other woods used include cedar, pine, hickory, ash and oak. Prices vary depending on item and type of wood.

Left to right: Swedish burl-walnut tankard, 18th century, $2000 at auction; American barrel-form pitcher, 19th century, $150 at auction.

	LOW	AVG.	HIGH
Apple Butter Paddle, paddle stirrer, perforated spatula, len. 60" ...	$ 110	$ 140	$ 170
Apple Drying Rack, open slats, 3 sided, legged, c. 1870	250	300	350
Apple Peelers, hardwood gears, c. 1700s	400	500	600
Apple Peelers, wooden w/ iron gears, 7" x 14"	400	450	500
Bandbox, egg shaped, plain, len. 5"	140	170	200
Barrel, for pickles, staved, 2 concentric wood bands, 12" x 20"	80	115	150
Bread Raiser, lid, tin, len. 12"	100	125	150
Broom, oak splint	150	200	250
Bucket, mincemeat, lid, concave, dia. 11"	200	215	230
Bucket, oak, for well	100	140	180
Bucket, sap, dia. 9.5"	310	345	380
Bucket, sugar, floor standing, red	580	635	690
Bucket, sugar, loop handles, lid, flat handle, c. 1890, dia. 5"	380	405	430
Bucket, sugar, stave constructed, enameled, dia. 13"	290	310	330
Bucket, tin top, walnut, "S" shaped legs, dia. 17"	350	370	390
Bucket, water, one piece wood, side handles, rope bail	240	280	320
Butcher's Block, sycamore, decoratively carved	1400	1600	1700
Butter Churn, cylinder type, white cedar, one gallon	160	175	190
Candlestick, adjustable stem, English, c. 1790, ht. 8"	2800	3100	3400
Candlestick, walnut, c. 1760, dia. 6"	680	750	820
Churn, staved, dasher, 4 gallon capacity	480	565	650
Churn, windmill paddles, side turn handle, ht. 15"	470	520	570
Clothes Wringer, crank, handle and roller	40	50	60
Coaster, 18th cent., treen, octagonal	500	550	600
Coaster, oak, English, c. 1810, dia. 12"	2500	2750	3000
Coffee and Spice Mill, c. 1760, ht. 9"	2500	3000	3500

	LOW	AVG.	HIGH
Coffee Grinder, 19th cent., wooden, French maker	$ 160	$ 200	$ 240
Coffee Grinder, box type	170	210	250
Coffee Grinder, lap, cherry box, brass fittings, crank	200	245	290
Coffee Grinder, lap type, handled, cherry	220	240	260
Coffee Grinder, wood, carved handle	130	170	210
Coffee Mill, hand crank, iron blade, storage box	130	150	170
Colander, wooden, circular, c. 1700s	600	700	800
Cookie Board, carved pattern, walnut, len. 8"	140	165	190
Cookie Board, 4 different molded designs, len. 6"	50	70	90
Cookie Board, walnut construction, grape relief design, len. 9"	40	60	80
Lemon Squeezer, short handle, ridged press, len. 10"	50	60	70
Lemon Squeezer, hinged, wood and ceramic, hinged, len. 9"	60	80	100
Lemon Squeezer, wood and nickel, juicer is perforated	70	90	110
Lemon Squeezer, wooden, on stand, 14" x 9"	240	270	300
Mortar and Pestle, bird's-eye maple, early	150	185	220
Muffineer, Tunbridge ware, c. 1790	380	435	490
Noodle Board, wooden circle w/ paddle handle, len. 24"	180	205	230
Noodle Roller, maple, perforated crank, c. 1840, len. 21"	10	115	220
Noodle Rolling Pin	30	45	60
Nutcracker, 18th cent.	450	530	610
Nutcracker, bear's head, c. 1880, len. 9"	140	175	210
Nutcracker, large size, c. 1750, len. 10"	400	460	520
Nutcracker, wood w/ iron presses, c. 1650, len. 5.5"	730	805	880
Toddy Stick, early 19th cent.	40	70	100
Toddy Stick, pestle style, hand carved, turned wood	20	30	40
Washtub, oak slats, natural varnish, len. 23"	160	190	220
Whisk Broom, Fuller Brush Company, len. 8"	90	115	140
Wooden Box, Shaker	440	485	530
Wooden Shovel, grain	570	640	710
Wooden Wash Bowl, chestnut, c. 1790	280	350	420
Wool Comb, carved handle, len. 13"	30	50	70
Yarn Winder, box-type, spindle suspended on spike over box,18"	70	90	110
Yarn Winder, duck feet	210	265	320
Yarn Winder, floor model, spindled legs, yard counter	170	220	270
Yarn Winder, maple	220	265	310

Burlwood examples are usually worth triple the value (or more!) of plainer grained woods. The greater the burl, the greater the value.

Board of Collectors

Jeanne Bertoia
Bill Bertoia Auctions
2413 Madison Avenue
Vineland, NJ 08360
609 692 1881
Doorstops, Identification & Values is
available from the author for $9.95 plus
$2.00 for shipping and handling.

Howard Brenner
106 Woodgate Terrace
Rochester, NY 14625
Copies of *Comic Character Clocks and
Watches* can be ordered directly from the
author at the address above for $16.00
postpaid.

Nicholas Dawes
67 East 11th Street #724
New York, NY 10003
212 473 5111

Grover Van Dexter
Second Childhood
283 Bleeker Street
New York, NY 10014
212 989 6140

Helaine Fendelman
PO Box 271
Hartsdale, NY 10530

Karen Gagliardi
Eshelman Mill Rd.
Lancaster, PA 17602

David Galt
Games and Names
302 West 78th Street
New York, NY 10024
212 769 2514

Jim Glaab's Collector's Showcase
78 Genesee Street
Greene, NY 13778
607 656 8805

Rebecca Greason
Rebecca of Sunny Book Farm
PO Box 209
Hershey, PA 17033
717 533 3039

Nancy Heller
440 East 79th Street #15C
New York, NY 10021

Jack Herbert
267 1/2 West 11th Street
New York, NY 10014
212 989 5175

Henry Kurtz
163 Amsterdam Avenue
Suite 136
New York, NY 10023
212 642 5904

Judith Lile Antiques
346 Valleybrook Drive
Lancaster, Pa 17601
717 569 8175

Matrix Quality Antique Dolls
PO Box 1410
New York, NY 10023
212 787 7279

Bill Mugrage
3819 190th Place S.W.
Lynnwood, WA 98036
206 774 9849 (7 PM to 12 midnight
Pacific time or weekends)

Brett O'Connor
Christie's Los Angeles
Jewelry Department
360 North Camden Drive
Beverly Hills, CA 90210

Adam G. Perl
Pastimes Antiques
Dewitt Bldg.
Ithaca , NY 14850
607 277 3457
aperl@lightlink.com

Michael F. Robinson
Middleburg, VA 22117

Sy Schreckinger
PO Box 104
East Rockaway, NY 11518
516 536 4154

Stu Waldman
Toy Treasures
718 447 0512

Toys in the Attic
Gaston and Joan Majeune
167 Phelps Ave.
Englewood, NJ 07631
201 568 6745

Steven and Leon Weiss
Gemini Antiques
12 East 76th St. Apt 3
New York, NY 10021
212 734 3681

Jim and Kaye Whitaker
Eclectic Antiques
PO Box 475
Lynnwood, WA 98046
Copies of *Josef Originals* can be ordered
directly from the authors at the address
above for $28.95 postpaid.

Christopher Wolfe and Scott Townsend
Townsend, Wolfe & Company
PO Box 158
Coopersburg, PA 18036
610 282 4831

Photography and Other Contributions

Bill Bertoia Auctions
2413 Madison Avenue
Vineland, NJ 08360
609 692 1881

Christie's East
219 East 67th Street
New York, NY 10021
212 606 0430

Eclectic Antiques
PO Box #475
Lynnwood, WA 98046

Douglas-Chew Ho

James D. Julia Inc.
PO Box 830
Fairfield, ME 04937
207 453 7125

George Kerrigan Photography
56 West 22nd Street
New York, NY 10010
212 645 7979

Kessie & Co. Antiques and Gifts
163 East 87th Street
New York, NY 10128
212 987 1732

Stephen Kiss

Northeast Auctions
PO Box 363
Hampton, NH 03842

Phillips Fine Art Auctioneers
406 East 79th Street
New York, NY 10021
212 570 4830

Sotheby's
1334 York Avenue
New York, NY 10021
212 606 7000

Thelma Shaffer

Dorothy Shelton

Jonathan Taylor
5 West 20th Street
New York, NY 10011

INDEX

ABOUT THE AUTHORS

ERIC ALBERTA has headed the Collectibles Department at both Christie's and Phillips auction houses. With over twenty-five years' experience, he now runs an appraisal and consulting firm.

ART MAIER teaches appraising at New York University. He is a consultant for international auction houses and their clients.

HOUSE OF COLLECTIBLES

THE OFFICIAL® IDENTIFICATION AND PRICE GUIDES TO

AMERICAN INDIAN
ARROWHEADS
1st edition
John L. Stivers
876-37913-7 $17.50

ANTIQUE
AND MODERN
FIREARMS
8th edition
Robert H. Balderson
876-37907-2 $17.00

ANTIQUE AND
MODERN TEDDY
BEARS
1st edition
Kim Brewer and Carol-
Lynn Rossel Waugh
876-37792-4 $12.00

ANTIQUE CLOCKS
3rd edition
876-37513-1 $12.00

ANTIQUE JEWELRY
(ID) 6th edition
Arthur Guy Kaplan
876-37759-2 $21.00

ARTS AND CRAFTS
*The Early Modernist
Movement in
American Decorative
Arts, 1894–
1923* (ID)
2nd edition
Bruce Johnson
876-37879-3 $12.95

AUTOMOBILIA
1st edition
David K. Bausch
676-60030-1 $19.95

THE BEATLES
*Records and
Memorabilia*
1st edition
Perry Cox and Joe
Lindsay, with an
introduction by Jerry
Osborne
876-37940-4 $15.00

BEER CANS
5th Edition
Bill Mugrage
876-37873-4 $12.50

BOTTLES
11th edition
Jim Megura
876-37843-2 $14.00

CIVIL WAR
COLLECTIBLES
1st edition
Richard Friz
876-37951-X $17.00

COLLECTIBLE TOYS
(ID), 5th edition
Richard Friz
876-37803-3 $15.00

COLLECTOR CARS
8th edition
Robert H. Balderson
676-60024-7 $17.00

COLLECTOR
HANDGUNS
5th edition
Robert H. Balderson
676-60038-7 $17.00

COLLECTOR KNIVES
11th edition
C. Houston Price
876-37973-0 $17.00

COLLECTOR PLATES
6th edition
Rinker Enterprises
876-37968-4 $17.00

COMPACT DISCS
1st edition
Jerry Osborne
876-37923-4 $15.00

COUNTRY MUSIC
RECORDS
1st edition
Jerry Osborne
676-60004-2 $15.00

ELVIS PRESLEY
RECORDS AND
MEMORABILIA
1st edition
Jerry Osborne
876-37939-0 $14.00

FINE ART
2nd edition
Rosemary and
Michael McKittrick
876-37909-9 $20.00

FRANK SINATRA
RECORDS AND CDs
1st edition
Vito R. Marino and
Anthony C. Furfero
876-37903-X $12.00

GLASSWARE
1st edition
Mark Pickvet
876-37953-6 $15.00

OLD BOOKS
1st edition
Marie Tedford and
Pat Goudey
876-37915-3 $15.00

ORIENTAL RUGS
2nd edition
Joyce C. Ware
676-60023-9 $15.00

POSTCARDS (ID)
1st edition
Diane Allmen
876-37802-5 $9.95

POTTERY
AND PORCELAIN
8th edition
Harvey Duke
876-37893-9 $15.00

ROCK AND ROLL—
MAGAZINES,
POSTERS, AND MEM-
ORABILIA (ID), 1st
edition
David K. Henkel
876-37851-3 $12.50

STAR TREK
COLLECTIBLES
4th edition
Sue Cornwell
and Mike Kott
876-37994-3 $19.95

WATCHES
10th edition
Cooksey Shugart &
Tom Engle
876-37808-4 $18.00

BECKETT GREAT SPORTS HEROES

TROY AIKMAN
676-60035-2 $15.00

WAYNE GRETZKY
676-60032-8 $15.00

ANFERNEE
HARDAWAY
676-60033-6 $15.00

MICHAEL JORDAN
876-37979-X $15.00

DAN MARINO
676-60034-4 $15.00

JOE MONTANA
876-37981-1 $15.00

SHAQUILLE O'NEAL
876-37980-3 $15.00

FRANK THOMAS
676-60029-8 $15.00

More listings and order form on following page